D1136861

The **Good Pub Guide** 2012

Edited by

Alisdair Aird and Fiona Stapley

Managing Editor: Karen Fick
Associate Editor: Patrick Stapley
Editorial Assistance: Fiona Wright

EBURY PRESS
LONDON

Please send reports on pubs to

The Good Pub Guide
FREEPOST TN1569
Wadhurst
East Sussex
TN5 7BR

or **feedback@goodguides.com**

or visit our website:
www.thegoodpubguide.co.uk

If you would like to advertise in the next edition of *The Good Pub Guide*,
please email **goodpubguide@tbs-ltd.co.uk**

Published in 2011 by Ebury Press, an imprint of Ebury Publishing

A Random House Group Company

Text © 2011 Random House Group Ltd
Maps © 2011 Perrott Cartographics

Cover design by Two Associates
Cover photographs reproduced by kind permission of the pubs:
Front: The Kings Head Inn, Bledington, Glos. *Spine:* The Royal Oak Inn, Meavy, Devon.
Back: The Holly Bush Inn, Salt, Staffs

The Random House Group Limited Reg. No. 954009

Addresses for companies within the Random House Group can be found at
www.randomhouse.co.uk

A CIP catalogue record for this book is available from the British Library

The Random House Group Limited supports The Forest Stewardship
Council (FSC®), the leading international forest certification organisation.
Our books carrying the FSC label are printed on FSC® certified paper.
FSC is the only forest certification scheme endorsed by the leading
environmental organisations, including Greenpeace. Our paper
procurement policy can be found at www.randomhouse.co.uk/environment.

Typeset from authors' files by Clive Dorman
Edited by Nicky Thompson and Jacqueline Krendel
Project managed by Nicky Thompson

Printed in the UK CPI Group (UK) Ltd, Croydon, CR0 4YY

ISBN 9780091930271

To buy books by your favourite authors and register for offers visit
www.randomhouse.co.uk

Contents

Introduction	7
What is a Good Pub?	25
Using the *Guide*	33
Editors' Acknowledgements	37

THE SOUTH WEST 39
Cornwall ● Devon ● Dorset ● Scilly Isles ●
Somerset ● Wiltshire

THE SOUTH EAST & LONDON 209
Berkshire ● Buckinghamshire ● Hampshire ●
Isle of Wight ● Kent ● Oxfordshire ● Surrey ●
Sussex ● London

THE EAST OF ENGLAND 469
Bedfordshire ● Cambridgeshire ● Essex ●
Hertfordshire ● Norfolk ● Suffolk

THE EAST MIDLANDS 587
Derbyshire ● Leicestershire ● Lincolnshire ●
Northamptonshire ● Nottinghamshire ● Rutland

THE HEART OF ENGLAND 683
Gloucestershire ● Herefordshire ●
Shropshire ● Staffordshire ● Warwickshire ●
West Midlands ● Worcestershire

THE NORTH WEST 813
Cheshire ● Cumbria ● Greater Manchester ●
Lancashire ● Merseyside

THE NORTH EAST & YORKSHIRE 907
Cleveland ● County Durham ● Northumberland ●
Tyne & Wear ● Yorkshire

SCOTLAND 1007

WALES 1037

A Little Further Afield	1077
Pubs Serving Food All Day	1079
Pubs Near Motorway Junctions	1082
Maps	1083
Report Forms	1113
Index of Advertisers	1136

Introduction

It's no secret that pub drinks' prices are lowest in the North of England – the North West, North East and Yorkshire. What may come as a surprise is how big the price gap between North and South has grown. In the North, beer on average now costs nearly 30p a pint less than in the most expensive area – the South East & London.

Against the national average price of beer in good pubs, now £3 a pint, pubs brewing their own score brilliantly, keeping their price down to an average of just under £2.50 a pint – scarcely any increase since last year, while in other pubs beer prices have jumped by a little over 7%.

GOOD BEER & GOOD BEER PUBS
Here are our Top Ten own-brew pubs:
in the East Midlands – Tobie Norris in Stamford (Lincolnshire), Malt Shovel in Northampton (Northamptonshire), Black Horse at Caythorpe (Nottinghamshire) and Grainstore in Oakham (Rutland)
in the Heart of England – Victory in Hereford (Herefordshire) and Talbot at Knightwick (Worcestershire)
in the North West – Watermill at Ings (Cumbria) and Church Inn at Uppermill (Lancashire)
in the North East & Yorkshire – New Inn at Cropton
in Scotland – Fox & Hounds in Houston.

The Church Inn at Uppermill is good fun, and the beers it brews are amazing value – especially their bargain offer. It is **Own-Brew Pub of the Year 2012**.

A select band of breweries score for value, too, with beers that you can find quite widely available as the cheapest stocked by a pub, and at a price that's comfortably below the national average. Even one national brand, John Smiths, scores on price, but most of these price champions are regional or even local. Some of the most readily available we found were, starting with the cheapest, Donnington, Nethergate, Moorhouses, Weetwood, Exmoor, Branscombe Vale, Timothy Taylors, Hydes, Hobsons, Bowman and Robinsons. Nethergate, now based in Essex, avoided any price increase in our pubs this year. It produces a splendid range of interesting beers, many available in bottles as well as on draught. Nethergate is our **Brewery of the Year 2012**.

Nowadays it's fairly easy to find a pub with a wide choice of beers. Add in a really convivial atmosphere, and a landlady or landlord who really knows their ales, and you've reached the gold standard. Our Top Ten beer pubs are:
in the South West – Crown at Churchill (Somerset)
in the East of England – Fat Cat in Norwich (Norfolk)
in the East Midlands – Malt Shovel in Northampton (Northamptonshire) and Grainstore in Oakham (Rutland)
in the Heart of England – Old Spot in Dursley (Gloucestershire) and Nags Head in Malvern (Worcestershire)
in the North West – Bhurtpore at Aston (Cheshire), Watermill at Ings (Cumbria) and Philharmonic Dining Rooms in Liverpool
in Scotland – Bon Accord in Glasgow.

An absolute charmer, with a lovely buoyant atmosphere, the Nags Head in Malvern has up to 14 interesting beers, all on top form. It is **Beer Pub of the Year 2012**.

OTHER DRINKS IN GOOD PUBS

Good pubs in Britain today are likely to have nicer wine by the glass, and a wider choice, than a typical bar in France. In some, the quality and choice is exceptional, with enthusiastic licensees arranging tastings, doubling as wine merchants or wine shops, even in one case (Woods of Dulverton, Somerset) letting you pay for just a glass from any of their 400 listed wines.

Britain's Top Ten wine pubs, more than a match for France's most serious bars, are:
in the South West – Harris Arms at Portgate (Devon), Woods in Dulverton (Somerset) and Vine Tree at Norton (Wiltshire)
in the South East – Inn at West End (Surrey)
in the East of England – Old Bridge Hotel in Huntingdon (Cambridgeshire), Bell in Horndon-on-the-Hill (Essex) and Crown at Stoke-by-Nayland (Suffolk)
in the Heart of England – Yew Tree at Clifford's Mesne and Wheatsheaf in Northleach (Gloucestershire)
in the North West – Old Harkers Arms in Chester (Cheshire).

Woods in Dulverton stands out even in this distinguished group, for the range and quality of its wines, and the enthusiasm of its helpful, extremely knowledgeable landlord. A previous winner, Woods in Dulverton is **Wine Pub of the Year 2012**.

Good pubs should keep at least a reasonable choice of interesting whiskies. After all, there is very little risk of the spoilage which can plague real ales or an over-ambitious range of wines by the glass. So we would like to see more pubs stocking more than just the standard few brands. Pubs which set a splendid example are:
in the South West – Nobody Inn at Doddiscombsleigh (Devon)
in the South East – Old Orchard at Harefield near Uxbridge (Outer London)
in the North West – Bhurtpore at Aston, Combermere Arms at Burleydam,

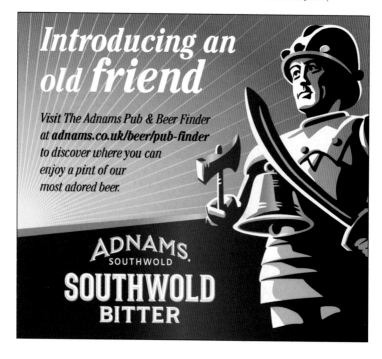

Pheasant at Burwardsley and Old Harkers Arms in Chester (Cheshire – where there's no doubt that they certainly do like their whisky!)
in the North East – Sandpiper in Leyburn (Yorkshire)
in Scotland, undeniably the home of good whisky – Bow Bar in Edinburgh, Fox & Hounds in Houston and Stein Inn at Stein on Skye
in Wales – Pant-yr-Ochain in Gresford.
The Old Orchard and Pant-yr-Ochain are both Brunning & Price pubs; this group has a notable choice of whiskies in each of its pubs.

The Bow Bar in Edinburgh, just a few steps down the Royal Mile from the Castle, couldn't be a nicer place for a wee dram or two – and if you tried a different one each week, it would take you four years to get through their collection. The Bow Bar is **Whisky Pub of the Year 2012**.

Good coffee is now available in almost all good pubs, occasionally in a cafetière, more often from an espresso machine dispensing all your cappuccinos, lattes and so forth, or one of the new breed of capsule coffee machines. What a shame, though, that our national survey of opening times shows that this year nearly half of all pubs (42%, to be exact) don't open until noon – long after most of us would have enjoyed dropping in for a mid-morning cup.

TOWN PUBS
Why is it that so very few town and city pubs have the character and charm that we find in so many hundreds of country pubs? So often, they are just like countless others – pleasant enough, but with service that's OK instead of being genuinely friendly and interested, and with drinks, food (if they do it), furnishings and décor all apparently from the same vast warehouse hidden away in some anonymous off-motorway wasteland.

The Cricketers
CLAVERING

The Cricketers at Clavering – a delightful 16th century English Country Inn with award winning food and accommodation, roaring log fires, beamed ceilings, well-kept cask ales and a friendly, relaxed atmosphere.

The Cricketers is situated in the charming, rural village of Clavering, North Essex, near to the borders of both Hertfordshire and Cambridgeshire and boasts lovely country walks and thatched cottages.

Near to Stansted Airport and close to the historic market town of Saffron Walden and Audley End House, The Cricketers is also convenient for Cambridge, The Newmarket Race Courses and the Imperial War Museum in Duxford.

Superb restaurant with fresh local produce where possible, we make fresh bread for our guests every day and our son, Jamie Oliver, supplies the wonderful seasonal vegetables, herbs and leaves from his certified organic garden nearby. Meals are served noon to 2pm and 6.30pm to 9.30pm every day.

The Cricketers, Clavering, Nr Saffron Walden, Essex, CB11 4QT
Tel: 01799 550442   Fax: 01799 550882
Email: info@thecricketers.co.uk   www.thecricketers.co.uk

Thank goodness there are plenty of exceptions to this rule of mediocrity, if you know where to look. We are delighted to have found some shining examples this year:
in the South West – Highbury Vaults in Bristol (Somerset)
in the South East – Olde Mitre in London, Black Boy in Headington, Little Angel in Henley and Turf Tavern in Oxford (all Oxfordshire)
in the East of England – Tobie Norris in Stamford (Lincolnshire)
in the Heart of England – Old Joint Stock in Birmingham and Nags Head in Malvern (Worcestershire)
in the North West – Old Harkers Arms in Chester (Cheshire)
in Scotland – Café Royal in Edinburgh.

Town Pub of the Year 2012 is the Olde Mitre in Central London. Here, as so often, it's the long-serving hands-on landlord and landlady, who make this so special.

UNSPOILT PUBS
When we started the *Guide* 30 years ago, people worried that the genuinely unspoilt traditional pub was rapidly disappearing and would soon die out. That's actually been a theme of pub chat for decades. Yes, of course lots of pubs have closed, but even in these last few difficult years the actual rate of closure seems to have been lower than the rate at which high-street shops have closed. And the truly unspoilt pub, particularly in the hands of a really caring landlord or landlady, has been remarkably resilient. This edition has plenty of fine examples – including hundreds well worth a visit among the smaller entries. Here are ten of the very best:
in the South West – Rugglestone near Widecombe (Devon), Digby Tap in Sherborne and Square & Compass at Worth Matravers (both Dorset) and Rose & Crown at Huish Episcopi (Somerset)
in the South East – Harrow at Steep (Hampshire)
in the East of England – Viper at Mill Green (Essex)

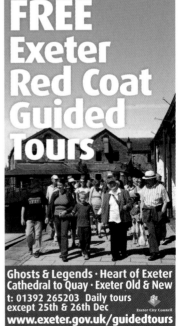

in the East Midlands – New Inn at Peggs Green (Leicestershire)
in the Heart of England – Boat at Ashleworth Quay (Gloucestershire) and Fleece at Bretforton and Three Kings at Hanley Castle (both Worcestershire).

The beautifully placed Square & Compass at Worth Matravers, complete with its rows of cider casks, and chickens wandering outside, seems hardly changed since the family took it on over a century ago. It is **Unspoilt Pub of the Year 2012**.

STAYING IN PUBS
More than half of the top pubs with full entries in this edition have bedrooms. Forget the days of dreary uncomfortable garrets and traipsing down a cold corridor to queue with the publican's family for the bathroom. By introducing our Place to Stay Awards in 1987, we pointed the way forward and helped towards raising standards. Today, pub accommodation spans virtually the whole range of hotel quality, from simple, clean and reasonably comfortable at an attractive price to luxurious, stylish and very fully equipped.
It is a treat to stay at any of our top recommendations:
in the South West – Rock at Haytor Vale and Sea Trout at Staverton (Devon), Hunters Moon at Middlemarsh (Dorset) and Royal Oak at Luxborough (Somerset)
in the East of England – Crown in Stoke-by-Nayland (Suffolk)
in the East Midlands – Devonshire Arms at Pilsley (Derbyshire), Wheatsheaf in Woodhouse Eaves (Leicestershire) and Olive Branch at Clipsham (Rutland)
in the North West – Inn at Whitewell (Lancashire)
in the North East – Black Swan at Oldsteads (Yorkshire)
in Wales – Olde Bulls Head in Beaumaris.

The atmosphere of the Royal Oak at Luxborough makes this Exmoor-edge inn a real favourite with everyone who stays there. It is **Inn of the Year 2012**.

JENNINGS
EXPLORE MORE

WIN A SIP OF A LIFETIME ON A WEEKEND FOR TWO AT THE LODORE FALLS HOTEL

Jennings is giving you the chance to enjoy a Sip of a Lifetime with a weekend escape for two at the stunning Lodore Falls Hotel in the Lake District. With a whole world of adventures and experiences to uncover as you explore the Lakes (not to mention the rather superb Jennings' Ales) you could be in for a weekend you won't forget.

Explore more and win a fantastic weekend enjoying and exploring your Sip of a Lifetime in the Lake District. Visit www.jenningsbrewery.co.uk/goodpubguide and enter the code 'GOODPUBGUIDE' for your chance to win.

EATING OUT IN PUBS

This year 647 top pubs featured in the *Guide* told us what their customers' favourite main course is.

Forget lasagne – this scored a zero in our list of the current top choices. Curry or balti? Hardly – not even 1%. And in the few pubs where this was still popular, there was a good reason – imaginative variations such as thai fish with watermelon, goat, or nile perch in a red thai curry with coconut rice. Even those old staples, sausage and mash or ham and egg, have slipped in the popularity stakes, with just 2% of pubs now finding each of these their favourite.

Today's number 1 choice is steak in ale pie, in all its glorious variations, including quite a few steak and kidney puddings. This topped the list in 18% of pubs.
Fish and chips, often 'beer-battered' is a close runner-up, at 15%.
All sorts of non-beef pies – most often fish, also chicken and ham, venison, rabbit, even wild boar, goose or duck – were the star offering in 8% of pubs.
Lamb was the favourite in 7% of pubs, most often slow-cooked with redcurrant featuring in some way.
The fashionable pork belly was close on its heels, at 6%. Many pubs are coming up with really rewarding ways of cooking this cheap meat. We found it chilli-glazed, with white bean cassoulet, with bramley boulangère, with plum and star anise, or with haggis or black pudding mash.
Steaks are decidedly the thing in 5% of pubs – it's more of a favourite in the moneyed South East.
A few years ago when this *Guide* first started championing local produce in pub cooking, it rarely featured on pub menus. It's now the norm, and has made a real difference throughout the full spectrum of pub meals, from simple light lunches to the special meals out offered by these top dining pubs:

in the South West – Lord Poulett Arms at Hinton St George (Somerset) and Potting Shed at Crudwell (Wiltshire)
in the South East – Hinds Head in Bray (Berkshire) and Jolly Sportsman at East Chiltington (Sussex)
in the East of England – Cock at Hemingford Grey (Cambridgeshire), Bell in Horndon-on-the-Hill (Essex) and White Horse at Sibton (Suffolk)
in the Heart of England – Stagg at Titley (Herefordshire) and Fox at Chetwynd Aston (Shropshire)
in the North East – Crown at Roecliffe (Yorkshire).

The Stagg at Titley, drawing on its large kitchen garden for its creative food, remains very much a proper pub under the couple who have run it so lovingly for the last 15 years. It is **Dining Pub of the Year 2012**.

OUR NEW VALUE AWARD
In the present grim economic climate, the hunt for value is vital. Nearly 1,000 of the reports which readers have sent us this year are specifically about value. So this year we have launched a new award, the Value Award. This is different from our previous Bargain Award. The Value Award recognises pub cooking that gives impressive value for money rather than simply rock-bottom prices (you can find a really good choice under £10).

Over one in six pubs in this edition have qualified for the new Value Award. These are pubs whose chefs succeed in creating tasty and interesting dishes at a sensible price – even in some of the UK's richest areas. Pubs giving outstanding value considering the quality of their tempting food are:
in the South East – Yew Tree at Lower Wield (Hampshire), Turf Tavern in Oxford and, for lunch, Kings Arms in Woodstock (Oxfordshire) and Cock at Ringmer (Sussex)

You may not figure Sue Barker for a regular pubgoer. But then the King's Arms is not exactly a regular pub

Located at the heart of the pretty town of Askrigg, itself nestled in the bosom of the Yorkshire Dales, the pub – like Sue – is no stranger to television cameras, having featured in the long-running TV series *All Creatures Great & Small* (though both town and pub had to endure a name-change; the King's Arms was dubbed "The Drovers", while Askrigg itself became, famously, "Darrowby").

With all the charm and conviviality you would expect of a traditional hostelry, plus 11 beautifully appointed en-suite rooms, the King's Arms truly offers the best of both worlds.

Try it once and you, too, might become a regular.

Just ask Sue.

www.hpb.co.uk/kingsarms

in the **East of England** – Carpenters Arms at Great Wilbraham for lunch (Cambridgeshire) and Bell at Middleton and Lord Nelson in Southwold (both in Suffolk)
in the **East Midlands** – Church Inn at Chelmorton and Red Lion at Litton (both in Derbyshire)
in the **North West** – Rising Sun in Tarporley (Cheshire).

The thatched Bell at Middleton, with its wide and very sensibly priced choice of good interesting country cooking, wins the title of **Value Pub of the Year 2012**.

LANDLORD OF THE YEAR
You cannot have a Good Pub without a good landlord or landlady (or both). All too often we have seen pubs nose-dive out of the *Guide* after a change of licensee. And it works the other way, too: the flow of reports on a particular pub can suddenly become much warmer and more enthusiastic under a new publican. Here are the ten pubs with individuals or couples who are right at the top of their profession:
in the **South West** – Peter & Angela Gatling of the Merry Harriers at Clayhidon (Devon) and Jeremy Lee at the New Inn in Cerne Abbas and Dean & Emma Mortimer of the Hunters Moon at Middlemarsh (both in Dorset)
in the **South East** – Tim Gray of the Yew Tree at Lower Wield and Hassan Matini of the Trooper near Petersfield (Hampshire)
in the **East of England** – Aubrey Sinclair Ball of the Blue Bell in Helpston (Cambridgeshire)
in the **East Midlands** – Julie & Justin Satur of the Church Inn at Chelmorton and Suzi Turner of the Red Lion at Litton (Derbyshire)
in the **Heart of England** – Norman & Janet Whittall of the Three Horseshoes at Little Cowarne (Herefordshire)
in the **North West** – Alan & Grace Smith of the Egerton Arms at Astbury (Cheshire).

Jeremy Lee, who took over as tenant of the New Inn at Cerne Abbas in 2010, has made a great impression at this attractive pub, with his enthusiastic attention to detail and his friendly warmth. He is **Landlord of the Year 2012**.

OUTSTANDING PUBS OF THE YEAR
Four of this edition's new entries are outstanding – so much so that they come straight into the *Guide* with a star. They are the Tobie Norris in Stamford (Lincolnshire), Yew Tree at Spurstow (Cheshire), Waddington Arms in Waddington and – more of a dining pub – Freemasons Arms at Wiswell (both in Lancashire). The Tobie Norris, a captivating refurbishment of a medieval building, with good food and drink and a great atmosphere, is **Newcomer of the Year 2012**.

Also outstanding are ten magnificent pubs which have featured in the *Guide* before. All have the knack of giving customers who have extremely varied tastes a memorably enjoyable time. A tour of all ten – plus the four mentioned above – would give you an almost encyclopedic experience of all that's best about the British Pub. They are:
in the **South West** – Blue Peter in Polperro (Cornwall) and Potting Shed at Crudwell (Wiltshire)
in the **South East** – Yew Tree at Lower Wield (Hampshire)
in the **East of England** – White Horse at Sibton (Suffolk)
in the **Heart of England** – Fossebridge Inn (Gloucestershire), Red Lion at Hunningham (Warwickshire) and Bell & Cross at Holy Cross (Worcestershire)
in the **North West** – Masons Arms at Cartmel Fell (Cumbria) and Eagle & Child at Bispham Green (Lancashire)
in the **North East** – Tempest Arms at Elslack (Yorkshire).

The Potting Shed at Crudwell has plenty of individuality, and scores all round, on food, drinks, service and above all atmosphere. It is our **Pub of the Year 2012**.

Great days out in Rural Warwickshire

Enjoy charming, historic market towns, scenic walks, real ales and lots of luscious local food.

Indulge

Savour the flavours of true beer-lovers' country on a tour of **Church End Brewery** or **North Cotswold Brewery**, Stretton on Fosse. **Purity Brewing Company**, Great Alne, is famed for environmentally friendly beer-making, and **The Griffin Inn** at Shustoke brews in the barn – lunch and a light pint of Gorgeous George, anyone?

Time your visit for March 2012 and catch **The Edible Garden Show**, Stoneleigh Park. Indulge in artisan goodies at **Alcester & Forest of Arden Food Festival** in May. Share a late summer toast or two at **Harbury Beer Festival.**

Escape

Also make the perfect getaway to pretty market towns and villages – amble the quaint Tudor-meets-Victorian streetscape of **Alcester** and lunch at the 17th-century **Holly Bush**. Then discover the Gunpowder Plot secrets of nearby **Coughton Court** and quirky sculpture trail at **Ragley Hall**.

Or explore **Henley-in-Arden** with its alluring mile-long High Street of 12th–18th century buildings and irresistible 16th-century **ice cream parlour**. There's divine drinking at **The Bluebell**, where they've researched the 'perfect serve' of more than 130 tipples.

Refresh

Refresh the parts that even beer can't reach, walking in quintessential English countryside. Ramble **Ilmington Down** on the Cotswold fringe for lofty panoramic views, then stay in the 400-year-old **Howard Arms** beside

Ilmington's village green, or **The Bell** gastropub at Alderminster.

Another day, combine canals and culture on a seven-mile circular route from picturesque Lapworth, past National Trust **Packwood House** and **Baddesley Clinton**. Relax at **The Navigation Inn** or **The Boot Inn**. Good food, great ales, superb days out.

Find out more

Rural Warwickshire, right in the heart of England, is easily accessible by road or rail. Find more ideas for great days out, excellent pubs and places to stay at **www.withinwarwickshire.co.uk.**

Images

1. National Trust Baddesley Clinton. 2. Lapworth Flight, Stratford-upon-Avon Canal. 3. Alcester Food and Drink Festival.

defra
Department for Environment
Food and Rural Affairs

The European Agricultural Fund
for Rural Development: Europe
investing in rural areas

WEST MIDLANDS
RURAL
DEVELOPMENT
PROGRAMME

Warwickshire
County Council

cottages4you

And just round the corner...
a country pub, real ale and great food

Discovering the best of Britain's pubs is a real pleasure when you have your own country cottage as a base.

We've got more than 10,000 lovely holiday cottages to choose from in stunning coast and countryside settings…many within easy reach of real ale inns, gastropubs and microbreweries. Perfect for a getaway with friends or a romantic break with a loved one. Families too will love the freedom of a cottage holiday… especially when there's no need to leave the pet at home.

Stay for a few days, a week or more. No-one offers more choice.

Property Ref: GRL

To book visit: **www.cottages4you.com**
or call: **0845 268 6193**

The Good Pub Guide Awards 2012

Own-Brew Pub of the Year	Church Inn, Uppermill (Lancashire)
Brewery of the Year	Nethergate
Beer Pub of the Year	Nags Head, Malvern (Worcesterhire)
Wine Pub of the Year	Woods, Dulverton (Somerset)
Whisky Pub of the Year	Bow Bar, Edinburgh
Town Pub of the Year	Olde Mitre, Central London
Unspoilt Pub of the Year	Square & Compass, Worth Matravers (Dorset)
Inn of the Year	Royal Oak, Luxborough (Somerset)
Dining Pub of the Year	Stagg, Titley (Herefordshire)
Value Pub of the Year	Bell, Middleton (Cheshire)
Landlord of the Year	Jeremy Lee of the New Inn, Cerne Abbas (Dorset)
Newcomer of the Year	Tobie Norris, Stamford (Lincolnshire)
Pub of the Year	Potting Shed, Crudwell (Wiltshire)

What is a Good Pub?

The entries for top pubs featured in this *Guide* have been through a two-stage sifting process. First of all, some 2,000 regular correspondents keep in touch with us about the pubs they visit, and double that number report occasionally. We also get a flow of reports sent to us at **feedback@goodguides.com**. This keeps us up-to-date about pubs included in previous editions – it's their alarm signals that warn us when a pub's standards have dropped (after a change of management, say), and it's their continuing approval that reassures us about keeping a featured top pub for another year. Very important, though, are the reports they send us on pubs we don't know at all. It's from these new discoveries that we make up a shortlist, to be considered for possible inclusion as new top pubs. The more people who report favourably on a new pub, the more likely it is to win a place on this shortlist – especially if some of the reporters belong to our hard core of about 600 trusted correspondents on whose judgement we have learned to rely. These are people who have each given us detailed comments on dozens of pubs, and shown that (when we ourselves know some of those pubs, too) their judgement is closely in line with our own.

This brings us to the acid test. Each pub, before inclusion as a featured top pub, is inspected anonymously by one of the editorial team. They have to find some special quality that would make strangers enjoy visiting it. What often marks the pub out for special attention is good value food (and that might mean anything from a well made sandwich, with good fresh ingredients at a low price, to imaginative cooking outclassing most restaurants in the area). The drinks may be out of the ordinary – maybe several hundred whiskies, remarkable wine lists, interesting ciders, or a wide range of well kept real ales possibly with some home-brewed or bottled beers from

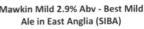

all over the world. Perhaps there's a special appeal about it as a place to stay, with good bedrooms and obliging service. Maybe it's the building itself (from centuries-old parts of monasteries to extravagant Victorian gin-palaces), or its surroundings (lovely countryside, attractive waterside, extensive well kept garden), or what's in it (charming furnishings, extraordinary collections of bric-a-brac).

Above all, though, what makes the good pub is its atmosphere – you should be able to feel at home there, and feel not just that *you're* glad you've come but that *they're* glad you've come. A good landlord or landlady makes a huge difference here – they can make or break a pub.

It follows from this that a great many ordinary locals, perfectly good in their own right, don't earn a place in the *Guide*. What makes them attractive to their regular customers (an almost clubby chumminess) may even make strangers feel rather out-of-place.

Another important point is that there's not necessarily any link between charm and luxury. A basic unspoilt village tavern, with hard seats and a flagstoned floor, may be worth travelling miles to find, while a deluxe pub-restaurant may not be worth crossing the street for.

This year, for the first time, we have asked the top pubs featured with full entries to pay a fee. This is a necessary change without which we could not cover our research and production costs, because of the way people are now using the *Guide* – with fewer buying the printed version, and more using the Internet version or the iPhone app. However, selection of the pubs for inclusion remains exactly as before. No pub can gain an entry simply by paying a fee. Only pubs which have been inspected anonymously, approved and then invited to join are included.

With a new wave of Great Country Pubs comes great accommodation

If you're planning an escape to the country for a few days, choosing the best country pub in which to revive or rest your head can make all the difference.

Maybe you want a pint beside the river after a relaxing stroll on a sunny day? Or perhaps an evening meal beside a crackling fire before you retire at the end of a hard day exploring? Whatever your heart desires, you'll find it at www.greatcountrypubs.com

- Pubs offering warm hospitality and comfortable accommodation throughout the South East
- Search by location or facilities
- Profile pages packed with handy information to help make your stay as perfect as possible

From the bar to the bedrooms, each of the pubs is infused with its own unique charm to ensure a memorable visit and a restful night's sleep. But one thing they all guarantee is the warm Great Country Pub welcome.

www.greatcountrypubs.com

Image: The Royal Oak, East Lavant, West Sussex

The Royal Borough of Windsor & Maidenhead

With over 900 years of history and a thousand sights to see, make the most of this beautiful and historic part of England. Combine contemporary shopping and dining, with beautiful countryside and pretty riverside villages and you have the formula for one of Britain's 'must do' visitor destinations.

The Royal Borough is bursting at the seams with top visitor attractions. Windsor Castle, Eton College, The Savill Garden and Windsor Great Park, open top bus tours, horse drawn carriage rides, River

Thames cruises, guided walking tours, Stanley Spencer Gallery, the Theatre Royal and more.

All this deserves more than a

day visit especially when you add in excellent quality shopping not only in Windsor but along the length of Eton High Street too. What's more with Bray just a stone's throw away you'd be crazy to miss the opportunity of experiencing some of the best food in the world.

Within this guide you'll find 21 great pubs located within the Royal Borough so whether you prefer a traditional, historic or modern setting you're sure to find some fine ales, great food and a lively atmosphere in the Borough's towns and villages.

Seventy-nine years after the closure of Windsor's last brewery, Windsor & Eton

brewery are delighted to have brought craft brewing back to the heart of Windsor and have recently celebrated their first birthday. In their first year they have built a new brewery from scratch and launched four ales – Guardsman Best, Knight of The Garter Golden Ale, Conqueror Black IPA and the topical Windsor Knot Royal Wedding Ale. Look out for these popular ales during your visit.

For help with where to stay and what to do contact the Royal Windsor Information Centre.

Please call +44 (0)1753 743900, email windsor.tic@rbwm.gov.uk or visit www.windsor.gov.uk

THE PHEASANT

Country Pub with Rooms

Real ales including our own pheasant bitter made with smoked hops

Freshly prepared seasonal food, salad leaves, fruit and vegetables grown in our 1 acre garden

Smoked fish a specialty with our own smokery on site and selection of smoked produce to purchase at the bar.

5 luxurious rooms with views of the surrounding countryside

CONTACT US:

Phone: 01787 461196

Email: info@thepheasant.net

Website: thepheasant.net

The Pheasant, Church Street, Gestingthorpe, Essex, CO9 3AU

Using the *Guide*

THE REGIONS

We have divided England into seven main regions (see Contents page). Within each region, the featured top pubs are listed in alphabetical order of their town or village. Other pubs worth knowing in the region are then listed county by county.

The county boundaries we use are those for the administrative counties (not the old traditional counties, which were changed back in 1976). London is included in the South East chapter. Scotland and Wales each have their own chapters.

We list pubs in their true county, not their postal county. Occasionally, when the village itself is in one county but the pub is just over the border in the next-door county, we have used the village county, not the pub one.

STARS ★

Really outstanding pubs are awarded a star, and in a few cases two stars: these are the aristocrats among pubs. The stars do NOT signify extra luxury or specially good food – in fact, some of the pubs which appeal most distinctively and strongly of all are decidedly basic in terms of food and surroundings. The detailed description of each pub reveals its particular appeal, and this is what the stars refer to.

FOOD AWARD ⑪

Pubs where food is quite outstanding.

STAY AWARD ⇔

Pubs that are good as places to stay at (obviously you can't expect the same level of luxury at £60 a head as you'd get for £100 a head). Pubs with bedrooms are marked on the maps at the back of the book as a dot within a square.

WINE AWARD ♀

Pubs with particularly enjoyable wines by the glass – often a good choice.

BEER AWARD ◀

Pubs where the quality of the beer is quite exceptional, or pubs which keep a particularly interesting range of beers in good condition.

VALUE AWARD £

This distinguishes pubs that offer really good value food. In all the award-winning pubs, you will find an interesting choice at under £10.

RECOMMENDERS

At the end of each featured pub, we include the names of readers who have recently recommended that pub (unless they've asked us not to).

Important note: the description of the pub and the comments on it are our own and not the recommenders'; they are based on our own personal inspections and on later verification of facts with each pub.

OTHER GOOD PUBS

The second part of each regional chapter is a county-by-county descriptive listing of the other pubs that we know are worth a visit – many of them, indeed, are as good as the featured top pubs (these are identified with a star). We have inspected and approved nearly half of these ourselves. All the others are recommended by our trusted reader-reporters. The descriptions of these other pubs, written by us, usually reflect the experience of several different people, and sometimes dozens.

It is these other good pubs which may become featured top pub entries in future editions. So do please help us know which are hot prospects for our inspection programme (and which are not!) by reporting on them. There are report forms at the back of the *Guide*, or you can email us at **feedback@goodguides.com**, or write to us at The Good Pub Guide, FREEPOST TN1569, Wadhurst, East Sussex TN5 7BR.

LOCATING PUBS

To help readers who use digital mapping systems we include a **postcode** for every pub (at the end of the directions for the top pubs and on the right for other pubs).

Pubs outside London are given a British Grid four-figure **map reference**. Where a pub is exceptionally difficult to find, we include a six-figure reference in the directions. The map number (featured top entries only) refers to the map at the back of the *Guide*.

PRICES AND OTHER FACTUAL DETAILS

The *Guide* went to press during the summer of 2011, after each pub was sent a checking sheet to confirm up-to-date food, drink and bedroom prices, and other factual information. By the summer of 2012, prices are bound to have increased, but if you find a significantly different price please let us know.

Breweries or independent chains to which pubs are 'tied' are named at the beginning of the rubric of useful information at the end of each featured top pub. That generally means the pub has to get most, if not all, of its drinks from that brewery or chain. If the brewery is not an independent one but just part of a combine, we name the combine in brackets. When the pub is tied, we have spelled out whether the landlord is a tenant, has the pub on a lease, or is a manager. Tenants and leaseholders of breweries generally have considerably greater freedom to do things their own way, and in particular are allowed to buy drinks including a beer from sources other than their tied brewery.

Free houses are pubs not tied to a brewery. In theory they can shop around but in practice many free houses have loans from the big brewers, on terms that bind them to sell those breweries' beers. So don't be too surprised to find that so-called free houses may be stocking a range of beers restricted to those from a single brewery.

Real ale is used by us to mean beer that has been maturing naturally in its cask. We do not count as real ale beer which has been pasteurised or filtered to remove its natural yeasts. If it is kept under a blanket of carbon dioxide to preserve it, we still generally mention it – as long as the pressure is too light for you to notice any extra fizz, it's hard to tell the difference. (For brevity, we use the expression 'under light blanket pressure' to cover such pubs; we do not include among them pubs where the blanket pressure is high enough to force the beer up from the cellar, as this does make it unnaturally fizzy.)

Other drinks We've also looked out particularly for pubs doing enterprising non-alcoholic drinks (including good tea or coffee), interesting spirits (especially malt whiskies), country wines, freshly squeezed juices, and good farm ciders.

Bar food usually refers to what is sold in the bar; we do not describe menus that are restricted to a separate restaurant. If we know that a pub serves sandwiches, we say so – if you don't see them mentioned, assume you can't get them. Food listed is an example of the sort of thing you'd find served in the bar on a normal day, and we try to indicate any difference we know of between lunchtime and evening.

Children If we don't mention children at all, assume that they are not welcome. All but one or two pubs allow children in their garden if they have one. 'Children welcome' means the pub has told us that it lets them in with no special restrictions. In other cases, we report exactly what arrangements pubs say they make for children. However, we have to note that in readers' experience some pubs make restrictions that they haven't told us about (children only if eating, for example). If you come across this, please let us know, so that we can clarify with the pub concerned for the next edition. The absence of any reference to children in the shorter entries for pubs also worth a visit means we don't know either way. Children's Certificates exist, but in practice children are allowed into some part of most pubs in this *Guide* (there is no legal restriction on the movement of children over 14 in any pub). Children under 16 cannot have alcoholic drinks. Children aged 16 and 17 can drink beer, wine or cider with a meal if it is bought by an adult and they are accompanied by an adult.

Dogs If the licensees of featured top pubs have told us they allow dogs in their pub or bedrooms we say so; absence of reference to dogs means dogs are not welcome. If you take a dog into a pub, you should have it on a lead. We also mention in the text any pub dogs or cats (or indeed other animals) that we've come across ourselves, or heard about from readers.

Parking If we know there is a problem with parking, we say so; otherwise assume there is a car park.

Credit cards We say if a pub does **not** accept them; some which do may put a surcharge on credit card bills, to cover charges made by the card company. We also say if we know that a pub tries to retain customers' credit cards while they are eating. This is a reprehensible practice, and if a pub tries it on you, please tell them that all banks and card companies frown on it – and please let us know the pub's name, so that we can warn readers in future editions.

Telephone numbers are given for all featured top pubs that are not ex-directory.

Opening hours are for summer; we say if we know of differences in winter, or on particular days of the week. In the country, many pubs may open rather later and close earlier than their details show (if you come across this, please let us know – with details). Pubs are allowed to stay open all day if licensed to do so. However, outside cities many pubs in England and Wales close during the afternoon. We'd be grateful to hear of any differences from the hours we quote.

Bedroom prices normally include full english breakfasts (if available), VAT and any automatic service charge. If we give just one price, it is the total price for two people sharing a double or twin-bedded room for one night. Otherwise, prices before the '/' are for single occupancy, prices after it for double. A capital B against the price means that it includes a private bathroom, a capital S a private shower. As all this coding packs in quite a lot of information, some examples may help to explain it:

£60	on its own means that's the total bill for two people sharing a twin or double room without a private bath or shower; the pub has no rooms with a private bath or shower, and a single person might have to pay that full price
£60B	means the same – but all the rooms have a private bath
£60S	means the rooms have a private shower
£60(£90B)	means rooms with private baths cost £30 extra
£35/£60(£90B)	means the same as the last example, but also shows that there are single rooms for £35, none of which has a private bathroom

If there's a choice of rooms at different prices, we normally give the cheapest. If there are seasonal price variations, we give the summer price (the highest), but during the winter you may find all sorts of cheaper rates and bargain breaks.

Meal times Bar food is commonly served from 12-2 and 7-9, at least from Monday to Saturday. If we don't give a time, assume you can get bar food at those times. However, we do spell out the times if they are significantly different. To be sure of a table, it's best to book before you go. Sunday hours vary considerably from pub to pub, so it makes sense to ring to check they are open.

Disabled access Deliberately, we do not ask pubs about this, as their answers would not give a reliable picture of how easy access is. Instead, we depend on readers' direct experience. If you are able to give us help about this, we would be particularly grateful for your reports.

SAT NAV AND ELECTRONIC ROUTE PLANNING
In conjunction with Garmin *The Good Pub Guide* is now available for your Sat Nav. Available as an SD card or download, it integrates quickly and easily into your Garmin Sat Nav and gives you access to all recommended pubs in the *Guide*. The Sat Nav guide will tell you the nearest pubs to your current location, or you can get it to track down a particular pub. Microsoft® AutoRoute™, a route-finding software package, shows the location of *Good Pub Guide* pubs on detailed maps and shows our text entries for those pubs on screen.

iPHONE AND iPAD
You can download an iPhone or iPad version of this edition from Apple's App Store. The iPhone is brilliant for us as it means users can report on a pub even while they are in it – perhaps adding a photo.

OUR WEBSITE: www.thegoodpubguide.co.uk
Our website includes every pub in this *Guide* plus many more. It has sophisticated search tools and shows the location of every pub on detailed maps.

CHANGES DURING THE YEAR – PLEASE TELL US
Changes are inevitable during the course of the year. Landlords change, and so do their policies. We hope that you will find everything just as we say but if not please let us know. You can find out how by referring to the Report Forms section at the end of the *Guide*.

Editors' Acknowledgements

We could not produce the *Guide* without the huge help we have from the many thousands of readers who report to us on the pubs they visit, often in great detail. Particular thanks to these greatly valued correspondents: Paul Humphreys, Phil and Jane Hodson, Chris and Angela Buckell, George Atkinson, Jeremy King, the Didler, Michael and Jenny Back, Tony and Wendy Hobden, Guy Vowles, N R White, LM, Phil Bryant, Alan and Eve Harding, Michael Doswell, Dennis Jenkin, Brian and Anna Marsden, Martin and Karen Wake, Michael Dandy, Gordon and Margaret Ormondroyd, John Wooll, Tracey and Stephen Groves, Ian Phillips, Ann and Colin Hunt, Joan and Michel Hooper-Immins, Roger and Donna Huggins, Phyl and Jack Street, Clive and Fran Dutson, Gerry and Rosemary Dobson, Simon and Mandy King, Martin and Pauline Jennings, Val and Alan Green, Michael Butler, Dennis Jones, Andy and Claire Barker, Pat and Tony Martin, Terry Buckland, Susan and John Douglas, David Jackman, Tony Hobden, Edward Mirzoeff, Reg Fowle, Helen Rickwood, Peter Meister, Ed and Anna Fraser, Steve Whalley, Barbarrick, Brian and Janet Ainscough, Ian Herdman, Sara Fulton and Roger Baker, Brian Glozier, John Beeken, Richard Tilbrook, David and Sue Smith, J F M and M West, Dave Braisted, Sue and Mike Todd, GSB, B and M Kendall, John Prescott, JJW, CMW, Chris Flynn, Wendy Jones, Mike Gorton, Mike and Eleanor Anderson, Mike and Mary Carter, Richard and Jean Green, John and Eleanor Holdsworth, Roy Hoing, Sheila Topham, Mrs Margo Finlay and Jörg Kasprowski, M G Hart, R K Phillips, Derek and Sylvia Stephenson, Dr and Mrs C W Thomas, Peter F Marshall, Comus and Sarah Elliott, Ian Malone, Andy and Jill Kassube, Rob and Catherine Dunster, John Pritchard, Mrs Susan Brooke, MLR, Barry and Anne, Dr and Mrs A K Clarke, Ryta Lyndley, Tony and Maggie Harwood, Dr Kevan Tucker, Tony and Jill Radnor, Christian Mole, Simon Collett-Jones, Les and Sandra Brown, Dr J Barrie Jones, Martin and Judith Tomlinson, Neil and Anita Christopher, Canon Michael Bourdeaux, Terry and Nickie Williams, Ross Balaam, Pete Flower, Hunter and Christine Wright, John and Helen Rushton, Bob and Margaret Holder, R T and J C Moggridge, Mr and Mrs P R Thomas, Giles and Annie Francis, David M Smith, Anthony Longden, Peter Crozier, Phil and Sally Gorton, Paul Rampton, Julie Harding, Chris Johnson, Tony and Gill Powell, Roger and Lesley Everett, Colin and Louise English, John and Gloria Isaacs, MP, R C Vincent, Mike Proctor, R L Borthwick, Martin Smith, Jim and Frances Gowers, Roger and Marion Brown, Margaret Dickinson, Theocsbrian, Conor McGaughey, Taff Thomas, Tim Maddison, Chris and Jeanne Downing, JCW, John Saville, Di and Mike Gillam, Nick Lawless, C and R Bromage, Charles and Pauline Stride, Ewan Shearer, Ian Barker, D and M T Ayres-Regan, Richard Fendick, Roger and Kathy Elkin, KC, MDN, Tim and Sue Halstead, Denys Gueroult, John and Joan Nash, Sue Rowland, David Lamb, Neil Kellett, Tim and Ann Newell, Bill Adie, Bruce and Sharon Eden, Stanley and Annie Matthews, Robert Lester, Andrew and Ruth Triggs, Mark, Amanda, Luke and Jake Sheard, Steven King and Barbara Cameron, Chris Evans, Ian and Helen Stafford, Robert Watt, Meg and Colin Hamilton, John and Sylvia Harrop, David Crook, Ann and Tony Bennett-Hughes, Lucien Perring and David and Gill Carrington.

Warm thanks, too, to John Holliday of Trade Wind Technology, who built and looks after our database.

Alisdair Aird and Fiona Stapley

The South West

Cornwall

Devon

Dorset

Scilly Isles

Somerset

Wiltshire

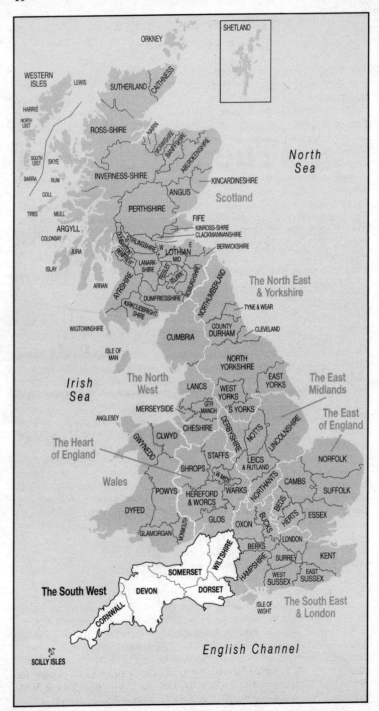

EDITORS' FAVOURITES
THE SOUTH WEST

The region's top pub is the Potting Shed at Crudwell (lovely atmosphere, excellent food and interesting drinks). Other great **Wiltshire** pubs include the Castle at Bradford-on-Avon (a super all-rounder), Compasses in Chicksgrove (lots of character), Red Lion at Cricklade (**Wiltshire Dining Pub of the Year**, imaginative local-based cooking), Fox & Hounds at East Knoyle (charming, with consistently good food), Malet Arms in Newton Tony (enthusiastic landlord) and the new Seven Stars at Winsley (they even home-smoke their fish and meat). Other Good Pubs are the Red Lion in Axford, Horseshoe at Ebbesbourne Wake, Red Lion in Kilmington, King John in Tollard Royal, and Bridge Inn at West Lavington.

Top **Cornwall** picks are the Finnygook in Crafthole (modern take on an old smugglers' inn), Gurnards Head Hotel (lovely modern food – **Cornwall Dining Pub of the Year**), Victoria at Perranuthnoe (another thriving dining pub), friendly and chatty harbourside Blue Peter in Polperro, character Driftwood Spars just by Trevaunance Cove (good beers brewed here); and among other Good Pubs the Miners Arms at Mithian, beautifully placed Ship in Porthleven and the St Kew Inn.

The best **Devon** pubs include the Fountain Head at Branscombe (this lovely old place brews its own beers), Merry Harriers at Clayhidon (**Devon Dining Pub of the Year**, with a charming landlord), Rock in, Haytor Vale (highly enjoyable, very well run), Elephants Nest at Horndon (a character place to stay), Sea Trout in Staverton (also a smashing stay, interesting ales and food) and Rugglestone at Widecombe (delightful unspoilt retreat). Other Good Pubs include the Cherub in Dartmouth, Wheelwright at Colyford, Turf at Exminster, Ship at Kingswear, Ship at Noss Mayo, Fox & Goose in Parracombe, Peter Tavy Inn at Peter Tavy, London in Molland and Bridge at Topsham.

In **Dorset** this year, we've particularly enjoyed the New Inn at Cerne Abbas (**Dorset Dining Pub of the Year**), Museum at Farnham (stylish, smart, with beautiful food), Digby Tap in Sherborne (quite unchanging, very cheap food), Langton Arms at Tarrant Monkton (super food, comfortable bedrooms) and Square & Compass at Worth Matravers (totally unspoilt, a treasure). Other Good Pubs include the Stapleton Arms at Buckhorn West, Anchor in Chideock, Chetnole Inn at Chetnole, Scott Arms at Kingston, New Inn at Stoke Abbott and West Bay in West Bay.

First-class **Somerset** pubs include the Highbury Vaults in Bristol (cheerfully traditional), Kings Arms at Charlton Horethorne (super food and bedrooms), Crown at Churchill (friendly, homely, great beer), Lord Poulett Arms in Hinton St George (**Somerset Dining Pub of the Year**, antiques-filled rooms and fine bedrooms), Rose & Crown at Huish Episcopi (utterly unspoilt) and the Royal Oak in Luxborough (good stay, plenty of character, interesting food). Other Good Pubs include the Square & Compass at Ashill, Coeur de Lion and Old Green Tree in Bath, Luttrell Arms at Dunster and Devonshire Arms in Long Sutton.

ALDBOURNE Wiltshire   SU2675 Map 2

Blue Boar £
The Green (off B4192 in centre); SN8 2EN

Bags of character in chatty, low-beamed, traditional pub

Right at the heart of the village and opposite the green, this is an unspoilt and thoroughly enjoyable pub with an easy-going atmosphere and a friendly welcome for all. The left-hand bar is homely, with pubby seats around heavily rustic tables on the bare boards or flagstones, lots of low black beams in the ochre ceiling, a boar's head above the bigger of the two fireplaces, a stuffed pine marten over one table; darts, board games and a corner cupboard of village trophies. Lots of unusual bottled beers line the rail above the dark pine dado. Wadworths IPA and 6X and a couple of guest beers from maybe Hook Norton and Vale on handpump and 20 malt whiskies. A separate bare-boards dining bar on the right, stretching back further, has more table space and is rather more modern in style (though with the same pubby atmosphere). There are picnic-sets and a couple of tall hogshead tables under big green canvas parasols in front of the pub.

As well as lunchtime sandwiches, the well liked pubby food includes ham and egg, chilli and rice, and daily specials such as garlic mushrooms, vegetable lasagne, beer-battered haddock, and chicken with bacon and brie. *Benchmark main dish: steak and kidney pie £9.10. Two-course evening meal £14.00.*

Wadworths ~ Tenants Jez and Mandy Hill ~ Real ale ~ Bar food (12-2(2.30 weekends), 6.30-9.30(9 Sun)) ~ Restaurant ~ (01672) 540237 ~ Children welcome ~ Dogs allowed in bar ~ Open 11.30-3, 5.30-11.30; 11.30am-midnight Fri and Sat; 12-11.30 Sun

Recommended by Richard Tilbrook, Suzy Miller, Mary Rayner

APPLEY Somerset   ST0721 Map 1

Globe
Hamlet signposted from the network of back roads between A361 and A38, W of B3187 and W of Milverton and Wellington; OS Sheet 181 map reference 072215; TA21 0HJ

Unspoilt, small-roomed country pub, tasty food, real ales, and seats in the garden

Surrounded by graceful hilly pastures, this 15th-c pub is friendly and unspoilt and has plenty of honest character. The simple beamed front room has a built-in settle and bare wood tables on the brick floor and another room has a GWR bench and 1930s railway posters; there's a further room with easy chairs and other more traditional ones, open fires, a growing collection of musical posters and instruments, art deco items and *Titanic* pictures; skittle alley. A brick entry corridor leads to a serving hatch with Cotleigh Harriers and O'Hanlons Yellowhammer on handpump. There are seats outside in the garden; the path opposite leads eventually to the River Tone.

Well liked bar food includes lunchtime filled baguettes, popular home-made burgers (moroccan lamb, pork and apple, vegetarian and so forth), venison pie, teriyaki salmon with pak choi and noodles, and lamb tagine. *Benchmark main dish: smoked haddock with bacon £13.95. Two-course evening meal £15.25.*

Free house ~ Licensee LeBurn Maddox ~ Real ale ~ Bar food (not Mon) ~ Restaurant ~ (01823) 672327 ~ Children welcome ~ Open 11-3, 6.30-11.30; 12-3, 7-10.30 Sun; closed Mon; Sun evening Jan-April

Recommended by Bob and Margaret Holder, Kay Wheat, S G N Bennett, John Prescott, the Didler, Stephen Bennett, Barry Collett, Derek Goldrei

ASHCOTT Somerset   ST4337   Map 1

Ring o' Bells 🍺

High Street; pub well signed off A39 W of Street; TA7 9PZ

Friendly village pub with traditional décor in several bars, separate restaurant, tasty bar food, and local ales

---

Handy for Ham Wall Nature Reserve, this is a traditional village pub run for some years by the same friendly family. The three main bars are on different levels but all are comfortable with maroon plush-topped stools, cushioned mate's chairs and dark wooden pubby tables on the patterned carpet, horsebrasses along the bressumer beam above the big stone fireplace and a growing collection of hand bells. Flowerpots Perridge Pale, RCH Pitchfork and Teignworthy Amy's Ale on handpump, eight wines by the glass and farm and local bottled cider. There's also a separate restaurant and a skittle alley/function room. The terrace and garden have plenty of picnic-sets.

Tasty bar food includes sandwiches, fresh grilled sardines, vegetable lancashire hotpot and gammon and egg, with specials like yorkshire puddings filled with beef and mushrooms in ale, whole plaice with lemon and parsley butter, and barnsley chop with a redcurrant, cranberry and port sauce. *Benchmark main dish: smoked chicken with bacon and mushrooms au gratin £10.45. Two-course evening meal £15.50.*

Free house ~ Licensees John and Elaine Foreman and John Sharman ~ Real ale ~ Bar food (12-2, 7-10) ~ Restaurant ~ (01458) 210232 ~ Children welcome ~ Dogs welcome ~ Live folk music first Sat and third Weds of month ~ Open 12-3, 7-11(10.30 Sun)

Recommended by Frank Willy, Ian and Nita Cooper

AVONWICK Devon   SX6958   Map 1

Turtley Corn Mill ♀

0.5 miles off A38 roundabout at SW end of South Brent bypass; TQ10 9ES

Careful conversion of tall mill house with interestingly furnished areas, local beers, modern bar food, and huge garden; bedrooms

Surrounding this carefully converted mill house is an extensive garden with interesting ducks on a small lake, plenty of well spaced picnic-sets and a giant chess set; it's all rather delightful on a sunny day. Inside, there's a spreading series of linked areas with big windows looking over the grounds, a pleasant array of prints, a history of the mill and framed 78rpm discs on pastel-painted walls, elderly wireless sets and house plants dotted about and a mix of comfortable dining chairs around heavy baluster-leg tables. Also, bookcases, fat church candles and oriental rugs in one area, dark flagstones by the bar, a strategic woodburning stove dividing one part, a side enclave with a modern pew built in around a really big table, and so on. Dartmoor Legend, St Austell Tribute, Sharps Doom Bar and Summerskills Tamar on handpump, several wines by the glass and around 30 malt whiskies. They will keep your credit card if you eat outside. This is under the same ownership as the Finnygook at Crafthole in Cornwall.

🍴 Modern bar food includes sandwiches, crayfish, crab and prawn vol-au-vent, aubergine, lentil and sweet potato moussaka, local mackerel fillet with harissa and coriander couscous, steak burger topped with gruyère and bacon, and chicken breast with vermouth, tarragon and lemon. *Benchmark main dish: battered local haddock and chips £13.25. Two-course evening meal £18.50.*

Free house ~ Licensees Lesley and Bruce Brunning ~ Real ale ~ Bar food (12-9) ~ Restaurant ~ (01364) 646100 ~ Children welcome ~ Dogs allowed in bar ~ Open 11-11; 12-10.30 Sun ~ Bedrooms: /£89S

Recommended by Bruce and Sharon Eden, Ian Malone, P and M Spencer

BABCARY Somerset   ST5628   Map 2

Red Lion 🍴 ♀

Off A37 S of Shepton Mallett; 2 miles or so N of roundabout where A37 meets A303 and A372; TA11 7ED

Thatched pub with informal atmosphere in comfortable rambling rooms, interesting daily-changing food, and local beers

There's usually a good mix of customers (and maybe their dogs, too) in this stone-built thatched pub where several distinct areas work their way around the carefully refurbished bar. To the left of the entrance is a longish room with dark pink walls, a squashy leather sofa and two housekeeper's chairs around a low table by the woodburning stove, and a few well spaced tables and captain's chairs. There are elegant rustic wall lights, some clay pipes in a cabinet, local papers or magazines to read and board games. Leading off here, with lovely dark flagstones, is a more dimly lit public bar area with a panelled dado, a high-backed old settle and other more straightforward chairs; table skittles and piped music. The good-sized smart dining room has a large stone lion's head on a plinth above the open fire (with a huge stack of logs to one side), a big rug on polished boards and formally set tables. Otter Bright, Teignworthy Reel Ale and a guest from Glastonbury on handpump and around ten wines by the glass. The long informal garden has picnic-sets and a play area for children. The pub is handy for the A303 and for shopping at Clarks Village in Street.

🍴 Often interesting and from a daily changing menu, the food might include sandwiches, pressed pork, fennel and spinach terrine with drunken figs, moules frites, honey-roast ham and eggs, pasta with melting goats cheese and pesto, battered haddock and chips, and crunchy chilli chicken with parmentier potatoes. *Benchmark main dish: fish pie £11.75. Two-course evening meal £18.75.*

Free house ~ Licensee Charles Garrard ~ Real ale ~ Bar food (12-2.30, 7-9.30) ~ Restaurant ~ (01458) 223230 ~ Children welcome ~ Dogs allowed in bar ~ Open 12-3, 6-midnight

Recommended by Guy Consterdine, Bob and Margaret Holder, Rod and Chris Pring, Bob and Angela Brooks, Jan and Alan Summers, Ian Herdman, Peter and Giff Bennett, Steve Collett

---

If a service charge is mentioned prominently on a menu or accommodation terms, you must pay it if service was satisfactory. If service is really bad, you are legally entitled to refuse to pay some or all of the service charge as compensation for not getting the service you might reasonably have expected.

BAMPTON Devon   SS9622 Map 1

Quarrymans Rest
Briton Street; EX16 9LN

**Bustling village pub with friendly staff, several real ales, comfortable
bars and enjoyable bar food cooked by the landlord; bedrooms**

Whether you are a visitor or a local, you can be sure of a genuinely
friendly welcome from the licensees and their staff in this well run
village pub. The beamed and carpeted main bar has leather sofas in front
of the inglenook woodburning stove, dining chairs and some
housekeeper's chairs around a mix of wooden tables set with church
candles. Greene King Old Speckled Hen, Otter Ale, Sharps Doom Bar and
a guest from Exmoor on handpump, any wine by the glass from their list
of around 40 and 15 malt whiskies. A couple of steps lead up to the
comfortable stripped-stone dining room with high-backed leather chairs
and heavy pine tables. There are daily papers, a shelf of paperback books,
pool and a games machine. The prettily planted back garden has some
picnic-sets and there are a few more in front of the building. The
bedrooms are well liked and the breakfasts are good.

Using local produce and cooked by the landlord, the enjoyable bar food
includes lunchtime sandwiches, devon blue, spinach and mushroom tart,
smoked haddock and pea risotto with a poached egg, steak and kidney in ale suet
pudding, and bass fillet on crushed potato and chorizo with fish bisque. *Benchmark
main dish: slow-cooked pork belly £12.50. Two-course evening meal £19.45.*

Free house ~ Licensees Donna and Paul Berry ~ Real ale ~ Bar food (12-2, 6-9.30;
12-4 Sun; not Sun evening) ~ Restaurant ~ (01398) 331480 ~ Children welcome but
must leave bar area by 7pm ~ Dogs allowed in bar ~ Open 11.45am-11pm(midnight Sat);
12-10.30 Sun ~ Bedrooms: £55S(£60B)/£75S(£85B)
Recommended by M G Hart, Mike and Linda Hudson

BATCOMBE Somerset   ST6839 Map 2

Three Horseshoes 🛏
Village signposted off A359 Bruton—Frome; BA4 6HE

**Handsome old inn with smart bar rooms, enjoyable food, local ales and
friendly owners; comfortable bedrooms**

The licensees of this 400-year-old honey-coloured stone inn work very
hard to create an atmosphere where all customers feel comfortable –
drinkers, diners, walkers (with their dogs) and families. The long, rather
narrow main room is smartly traditional: beams, local pictures, built-in
cushioned window seats, solid chairs around a nice mix of old tables and
a woodburning stove at one end with a big open fire at the other. There's
also a pretty stripped-stone dining room; best to book to be sure of a
table, especially at weekends. Butcombe Bitter, Cheddar Ales Potholer
and a guest like Moor Revival on handpump, a dozen wines by the glass
and several malt whiskies. The pub is on a quiet village lane by the
church, which has a striking tower. This is a nice place to stay and the
bedrooms are delightful.

Using seasonal local produce, the enjoyable food includes sandwiches,
smoked mackerel pâté, tagliatelle with parmesan, wild mushrooms and wilted
wild garlic, beer-battered fish, honey-roasted pork chop with cider sauce, and
bass fillets with creamed leeks and fennel potatoes. *Benchmark main dish:*

sausage and mash £8.70. Two-course evening meal £18.60.

Free house ~ Licensee Kav Javvi ~ Real ale ~ Bar food (12-2.30, 6-9.30(9 Sun)) ~ Restaurant ~ (01749) 850359 ~ Children welcome ~ Dogs allowed in bar ~ Open 11-3, 6-11; 11-11 Sat; 12-10.30 Sun ~ Bedrooms: £60B/£85B

Recommended by Neil and Karen Dignan, Mr and Mrs A H Young, Richard Oake, Claire Denyer

 BEESANDS Devon   SX8140   Map 1

 Cricket

About 3 miles S of A379, from Chillington; in village turn right along foreshore road; TQ7 2EN

Welcoming small pub by beach with enjoyable food (especially fish) and real ales; bedrooms

Many of our readers enjoy staying at this busy little pub (most of the bedrooms have sea views) and the food, cooked by the landlord's son, is very good indeed. It's neatly kept and open-plan with dark traditional pubby furniture (carpeted in the dining areas and with a stripped wooden floor by the bar), and some nice, well captioned photographs of local fisherpeople, knots and fishing gear on the walls. Otter Ale and Bitter and St Austell Tribute on handpump, several wines by the glass and local cider. The extended restaurant is airy and attractive; piped music. The cheerful black labrador is called Brewster. There are picnic-sets beside the seawall and Start Bay beach is just over the other side. The pub is popular with South Devon Coastal Path walkers; good wheelchair access.

With most emphasis on fresh local fish and shellfish, the well liked bar food includes lunchtime sandwiches, crab soup, diver-caught scallops with shi-itake mushrooms and cauliflower purée, a vegetarian dish of the day, their famous seafood pancake, and line-caught bass with chorizo and smoked pancetta ragu. *Benchmark main dish: seafood pancake £11.00. Two-course evening meal £21.50.*

Heavitree ~ Tenant Nigel Heath ~ Real ale ~ Bar food (12-2.30, 6-8.30) ~ Restaurant ~ (01548) 580215 ~ Children welcome ~ Dogs allowed in bar ~ Open 11-11; 11-3, 6-10.30 weekdays in winter ~ Bedrooms: £55S/£75S

Recommended by John and Gina Ollier, Alan Sutton, Richard Tilbrook, Roy Hoing, Adrian and Dawn Collinge, Sally and John Quinlan

 BLISLAND Cornwall   SX1073   Map 1

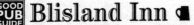 Blisland Inn

Village signposted off A30 and B3266 NE of Bodmin; PL30 4JF

Village local by the green with fine choice of real ales, beer-related memorabilia, pubby food, and seats outside

There's a fine choice of up to eight real ales in this much-enjoyed small pub and some interesting beer-related memorabilia, too. Every inch of the beams and ceiling is covered with beer badges (or their particularly wide-ranging collection of mugs), and the walls are similarly filled with beer-related posters and such like. Tapped from the cask or on handpump, the ales might include two brewed for the pub by Sharps – Blisland Special and Bulldog – as well as Bass, Coastal Hop Monster, Oakham Bishops Farewell and Sharps Doom Bar. They also have a changing farm cider, fruit wines and real apple juice; good service. The carpeted lounge has a number of barometers on the walls, toby jugs on the beams and a few standing timbers, and the family room has pool, table skittles, euchre, cribbage and dominoes; piped music. Plenty of picnic-sets outside. The popular Camel Trail cycle path is close by – though the hill up to Blisland is pretty steep. As with many pubs in this area, it's hard to approach without negotiating several single-track roads.

Straightforward pubby food includes filled lunchtime baps, popular sausage or ham with egg and chips, burgers, scampi, and daily specials. *Benchmark main dish: sausage, egg and chips £7.25. Two-course evening meal £11.75.*

Free house ~ Licensees Gary and Margaret Marshall ~ Real ale ~ Bar food ~ (01208) 850739 ~ Children in family room only ~ Dogs welcome ~ Open 11.30-11.30 (midnight Sat); 12-10.30 Sun

Recommended by R K Phillips, Henry Fryer, Dr and Mrs M W A Haward, the Didler, Comus and Sarah Elliott, Peter Salmon

BODINNICK Cornwall   SX1352 Map 1

Old Ferry

Across the water from Fowey; coming by road, to avoid the ferry queue turn left as you go down the hill – car park on left before pub; PL23 1LX

Bustling local across the water from Fowey, simple little rooms with nautical bits and pieces, and lots of summer customers

Perhaps the best way to reach this old-fashioned family-run inn is to use the public car park in Fowey and take the small ferry across the water; the pretty river views can be enjoyed from seats on the front terrace, from the homely restaurant and from most bedrooms. Three simply furnished small rooms have quite a few bits of nautical memorabilia, a couple of half model ships mounted on the wall and several old photographs, as well as wheelback chairs, built-in plush pink wall seats and an old high-backed settle. The family room at the back is actually hewn into the rock; background music and TV. Sharps Own and, in summer, Sharps Coaster on handpump, several wines by the glass and a farm cider. Mobile phones are banned and a 50p fine goes to the RNLI. The lane beside the pub, in front of the ferry slipway, is extremely steep and parking is limited. There are lovely circular walks from here.

Bar food includes sandwiches, pasties, burgers, vegetable lasagne, and fresh scallop, monkfish and king prawn curry. *Benchmark main dish: fish pie £9.75. Two-course evening meal £19.00.*

Free house ~ Licensees Royce and Patricia Smith ~ Real ale ~ Bar food (12-3, 6-9; 12-2.30, 6.30-8.30 in winter) ~ (01726) 870237 ~ Children welcome ~ Dogs allowed in bar and bedrooms ~ Open 11-11; 12-10 Sat in winter ~ Bedrooms: £90S(£95B)/£105B
Recommended by Dave Webster, Sue Holland, Christopher Turner

BOSCASTLE Cornwall   SX0991 Map 1

Cobweb

B3263, just E of harbour; PL35 0HE

Heavy beams, flagstones, lots of old jugs and bottles, a cheerful atmosphere, several real ales, and friendly staff

This old village pub takes its name from pre-Food & Safety Act cobwebs belonging to spiders that were once used to kill off the wine flies. They have obviously long gone but it remains an interesting place and the two bars have heavy beams hung with hundreds of bottles and jugs, lots of pictures of bygone years, quite a mix of seats (from settles and carved chairs to more pubby furniture) and cosy log fires. They keep four real ales such as St Austell Tribute, Sharps Doom Bar, Tintagel Harbour Special and a guest on handpump and a local cider and, especially at peak times, there's a cheerful, bustling atmosphere; games machine, darts and pool. The restaurant is upstairs. There are picnic-sets and benches outside – some under cover. They rent out self-catering apartments.

Bar food includes sandwiches, ham and egg, lamb curry, shank of lamb in wine and rosemary, and several fish dishes. *Benchmark main dish: lamb curry £8.95. Two-course evening meal £17.25.*

Free house ~ Licensees Ivor and Adrian Bright ~ Real ale ~ Bar food (11.30-2.30, 6-9.30) ~ Restaurant ~ (01840) 250278 ~ Children welcome ~ Dogs welcome ~ Live music Sat evenings and some Sun afternoons ~ Open 10.30am-11pm (12.30 Sat); 11-11 Sun in winter

Recommended by the Didler, Steve and Liz Tilley, Peter and Judy Frost

BRADFORD-ON-AVON Wiltshire ST8261 Map 2

Castle ★ ◖

Mount Pleasant, by junction with A363, N edge of town; extremely limited pub parking, spaces in nearby streets; BA15 1SJ

Handsome building well reworked in relaxed contemporary style, with enjoyable food all day, good drinks and charming service; comfortable bedrooms

Particularly well run by a friendly young landlady and her cheerful staff, this is an imposing square-cut 18th-c stone building and a former toll house. There's a splendid and highly individual atmosphere and the bar, dominated by its long panelled mahogany serving counter, has a good log fire, restful lighting including church candles, anything from armchairs and chapel chairs to a heavy green leather settle on its polished dark flagstones, plenty of daily papers, and unobtrusive piped music; board games. Lightly ragged ochre walls have *Vanity Fair* cartoons above a high brown dado, and a couple of boarded-floor rooms on the right, with a rather darker décor, are similarly comfortable and relaxed. Glastonbury Lady of the Lake, Plain Ales Sheep Dip, Stonehenge Spire Ale and Three Castles Barbury Castle and their own-label Flatcappers beers (also from Three Castles) on handpump, proper farm cider, a fine blackboard range of wines by the glass and proper coffee (hot milk if you want). Beside a lawn, the front terrace has unusual long tables and benches – and sweeping views over the town. Our readers like staying here very much.

As well as serving breakfast from 9am, the rewarding bar food includes sandwiches, various tapas, proper burgers with bacon or cheese toppings, sweet potato, butternut squash and spinach curry, crab linguine with lime and chilli, and chicken and gammon pie with tarragon sauce. *Benchmark main dish: beer-battered cod £10.95. Two-course evening meal £14.50.*

Free house ~ Licensee Victoria Hill ~ Real ale ~ Bar food (9am(10am Sun)-10pm (9.30pm Sun)) ~ (01225) 865657 ~ Children welcome ~ Open 9am-11pm; 10-10.30 Sun ~ Bedrooms: /£100S(£130B)

Recommended by David Eberlin, Ian Phillips, Howard and Elaine Lee, Mike Gorton, Taff Thomas, Susan and Nigel Wilson

 BRANSCOMBE Devon   SY1888   Map 1

Fountain Head 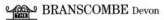 £

Upper village, above the robust old church; village signposted off A3052 Sidmouth—Seaton, then from Branscombe Square follow road up hill towards Sidmouth, and after about a mile turn left after the church; OS Sheet 192 map reference SY188889; EX12 3BG

Old-fashioned pub with own-brewed beers and reasonably priced food

Our readers love this unspoilt and friendly 500-year-old stone pub as there's always a good mix of visitors and chatty locals and the helpful staff make everybody feel welcome. The atmosphere is old-fashioned and unchanging – no games machines, piped music or TV – and the room on the left (formerly a smithy) has forge tools and horseshoes on the high oak beams; also, a log fire in the original raised firebed with its tall central chimney, cushioned pews and mate's chairs, and their own-brewed Branscombe Vale Branoc, Summa That and changing guest beer on handpump. Their annual beer festival is held in June and they have several wines by the glass and local cider. On the right, an irregularly shaped, more orthodox snug room has another log fire, a white-painted plank ceiling with an unusual carved ceiling-rose, brown-varnished panelled walls and rugs on its flagstone-and-lime-ash floor. Local artists' paintings and greeting cards are for sale; darts and board games. You can sit outside on the front loggia and terrace listening to the little stream gurgling under the flagstoned path and the surrounding walks are very pleasant.

Using own-grown fruit and vegetables, the fair-priced bar food includes lunchtime sandwiches, fresh local crab salad with mango salsa, roasted pepper filled with ratatouille topped with blue cheese, beef in ale pie, beer-battered cod and chips and chicken and gammon with ginger and honey. *Benchmark main dish: beef in ale pie £9.00. Two-course evening meal £14.50.*

Free house ~ Licensees Jon Woodley and Teresa Hoare ~ Real ale ~ Bar food ~ Restaurant ~ (01297) 680359 ~ Children welcome away from main bar area ~ Dogs allowed in bar ~ Live music on summer Sun evenings ~ Open 11-3, 6-11; 12-3, 6-10.30 Sun

Recommended by Phil and Sally Gorton, Warren Marsh, the Didler, Mrs Sheena and Emily Killick, R and S Bentley, Peter and Giff Bennett, C Cooper, Revd R P Tickle

 BRANSCOMBE Devon   SY2088   Map 1

Masons Arms ♀  🛏

Main Street; signed off A3052 Sidmouth—Seaton, then bear left into village; EX12 3DJ

Rambling low-beamed rooms, woodburning stoves, a fair choice of real ales and wines, quite a choice of food and seats in quiet terrace and garden; cottagey bedrooms

Since it's in an especially pretty village and just a stroll from the sea, this picturesque 14th-c longhouse does get busy at peak times and it's best to arrive early for a parking space – as well as a table during those times. The rambling main bar is at the heart of the place and with a good mix of both locals and visitors you can be sure of a cheerful, bustling atmosphere. There are comfortable seats and chairs on slate floors, ancient ships' beams and a log fire (where spit roasts are held) with a massive hearth. The Old Worthies bar also has a slate floor, a fireplace with a two-sided woodburning stove and woodwork that has been stripped back to the original pine. As well as a restaurant warmed by one side of the woodburning stove, there's another beamed one above the main bar. Branscombe Vale Summa That and St Austell Proper Job and Tribute on handpump and several wines by the glass. Outside, the quiet flower-filled front terrace, with its thatched-roof tables, extends into a side garden. This is a nice place to stay with bedrooms in converted cottages.

Bar food includes sandwiches (all day until 6pm), crispy fried squid with a sweet and sour dip, mussels in a thai broth, wild mushroom and spinach pasta, popular beer-battered haddock, pork loin steak with leek mash and blue cheese rarebit, and slow-roasted lamb shank with basil pesto. *Benchmark main dish: beer-battered haddock £11.25. Two-course evening meal £18.50.*

St Austell ~ Manager Paul Couldwell ~ Real ale ~ Bar food ~ Restaurant ~ (01297) 680300 ~ Children allowed in bar but not in restaurant ~ Dogs allowed in bar and bedrooms ~ Open 11-11; 12-10.30 Sun ~ Bedrooms: /£80S(£85B)

Recommended by Dr Phil Putwain, David Randall, David and Sue Smith, Nick Wallis, Steve Whalley, David West, Tim and Joan Wright, David and Stella Martin, Malcolm and Sue Scott, the Didler, Mike Gorton, Mrs C Roe, Alan Clark, Chris Clark, Barry Steele-Perkins, Tim Gray

BRISTOL Somerset   ST5773   Map 2

Albion ♟

Boyce's Avenue, Clifton; BS8 4AA

Dining pub close to boutiquey shops, with modern food and a good choice of drinks

Just ten minutes from the famous suspension bridge, this is a bustling and friendly little 18th-c pub down a cobbled alley in the heart of Clifton village. By the main door there's a flagstone area with a big old pine table and a couple of candlesticks, a dresser filled with jars of pickles and an open kitchen. Further in, the L-shaped bar has high chairs by the counter, chapel chairs around good oak tables on the stripped wooden floor, brown leather armchairs in front of the woodburning stove with its neat log stacks on either side of the brick fireplace, and some cushioned wall seats; up a step is an end room with a rather fine and very long high-backed new settle right the way across one wall, similar tables and chairs and unusual silvery peony-type wallpaper (elsewhere, the sage green half-panelled walls are hung with portraits). Bath Ales Gem Bitter, Otter Bitter and Sharps Cornish Coaster and Doom Bar on handpump, good wines by the glass, 30 malt whiskies and winter hot cider; piped music, board games. The covered and heated front terrace, with church candles in hurricane lanterns, has plenty of picnic-sets and other seats under fairy lights.

As well as interesting tapas (served all day though from 3pm Sat), the sensibly short choice of imaginative – if not especially cheap – dishes might include sandwiches, prosciutto, pear, walnut and rocket, spaghetti with broad beans, mint, ricotta and wild garlic, cod with tomato and chickpeas, and dry-aged rump steak with horseradish and shallot salad. *Benchmark main dish: pork belly with romesco sauce £16.50. Two-course evening meal £22.00.*

Enterprise ~ Lease James Phillips ~ Real ale ~ Bar food (12(11 weekends)-3, 7-10; not Mon) ~ Restaurant ~ (0117) 973 3522 ~ Children welcome until 9pm ~ Dogs allowed in bar ~ Open 12(11 weekends)-12; closed Mon until 5pm

Recommended by Steve and Liz Tilley, Comus and Sarah Elliott, Pamela Rogers

BRISTOL Somerset   ST5873   Map 2

Highbury Vaults 🍺 £
St Michael's Hill, Cotham; BS2 8DE

Cheerful town pub with up to eight real ales, good value tasty bar food, and friendly atmosphere

This is a well run and extremely popular unpretentious pub with a fine range of real ales and proper home cooking. The little front bar, with the corridor beside it, leads through to a long series of small rooms – wooden floors, green and cream paintwork and old-fashioned furniture and prints, including lots of period royal family engravings and lithographs in the front room. There's a model railway running on a shelf the full length of the pub, including tunnels through the walls. Bath Ales Gem Bitter, Brains SA, St Austell Tribute, Wells & Youngs Bitter and London Gold, and guests such as Box Steam Derail Ale and Teignworthy Reel Ale on handpump and several malt whiskies. The attractive back terrace has tables built into a partly covered flowery arbour. In early Georgian days, this was used as the gaol where condemned men ate their last meal – the bars can still be seen on some windows.

Good value and well liked bar food includes filled rolls, burgers such as beef and stilton, sausages or a pie and mash, various curries, and winter casseroles. *Benchmark main dish: chilli con carne £5.50. Two-course evening meal £11.00.*

Youngs ~ Manager Bradd Francis ~ Real ale ~ Bar food (12-2(2.30 Fri and Sat, 4 Sun), 5.30-8.30; not Sat or Sun evening) ~ No credit cards ~ (0117) 973 3203 ~ Children welcome ~ Dogs allowed in bar ~ Open 12-12(11 Sun); closed evening 25 Dec, 26 Dec and 1 Jan

Recommended by Roger and Donna Huggins, the Didler, Jenny and Peter Lowater, Chris and Angela Buckell

BROUGHTON GIFFORD Wiltshire   ST8763   Map 2

Fox 🍴 🍷
Village signposted off A365 to B3107 W of Melksham; The Street; SN12 8PN

Comfortably stylish pub with good, interesting food, real ales and several wines by the glass, and a nice garden

There's a chatty, relaxed atmosphere in each of the interconnected areas in this civilised pub and the big bird and plant prints, attractive table lamps and even the white-painted beams contrast nicely with its broad dark flagstones. You can sink into sofas or armchairs by a table of daily papers and another with magazines and board games, take one of the padded stools by the pink-painted bar counter, or go for the mix of gently old-fashioned dining chairs around the unmatched stripped dining tables, which have candles in brass sticks. Bath Ales Gem Bitter, Butcombe Bitter and Purity Pure UBU on handpump, a log fire in the stone fireplace and friendly service. The terrace behind has picnic-sets, and leads out on to a good-sized sheltered lawn.

They rear their own pigs and chickens and grow much of their own vegetables and fruit at this pub where the interesting food might include sandwiches, chicken liver and mushrooms on toast, beetroot and goats cheese risotto, their own sausages with braised lentils, spinach and red wine sauce, fish and chips with truffled pea purée, and rib-eye steak with café de paris butter; also, two- and three-course set menus. *Benchmark main dish: home-reared pork with garden greens £15.95. Two-course evening meal £19.75.*

Free house ~ Licensee Derek Geneen ~ Real ale ~ Bar food (12-2.30, 6.30-9.30; 11.30-3.30, 6.30-9.30 Sat; 12-4 Sun; not Sun evening or Mon) ~ Restaurant ~ (01225) 782949 ~ Children welcome ~ Dogs welcome ~ Open 12(11.30 Sat)-midnight; closed Mon; 25 Dec, 1 Jan

Recommended by Philip and Jan Medcalf, David and Stella Martin, Mrs J P Cleall

 BUCKLAND BREWER Devon   SS4220   Map 1

Coach & Horses

Village signposted off A388 S of Monkleigh; OS Sheet 190 map reference 423206; EX39 5LU

Friendly old village pub with a mix of customers, open fires, changing bar food and real ales; good nearby walks

The same friendly family have run this thatched 13th-c pub – in a pretty village – for over 20 years. The heavily beamed bar (mind your head on some of the beams) has comfortable seats, a handsome antique settle and a woodburning stove in the inglenook – there's also a good log fire in the big stone inglenook of the small lounge. A little back room has darts and pool; the three-legged cat is called Marmite. Country Life Old Appledore, Forge Litehouse and Otter Ale on handpump, local cider and ten wines by the glass; skittle alley (that doubles as a function room), piped music, games machine and occasional TV for sports. There are picnic-sets on the front terrace and in the side garden and some children's play equipment. The RHS garden Rosemoor is about 5 miles away and you can walk on the nearby moorland and along the beaches of Westward Ho! They have a holiday cottage to rent next to the pub.

Reasonably priced bar food includes sandwiches, pasties, fish and chips, steak in Guinness pie, chicken or vegetarian curry and pork tenderloin in a creamy peppercorn sauce. *Benchmark main dish: beef in Guinness pie £8.95. Two-course evening meal £14.90.*

Free house ~ Licensees Oliver and Nicola Wolfe ~ Real ale ~ Bar food (12-2, 6.30-9.30) ~ Restaurant ~ (01237) 451395 ~ Well behaved children welcome ~ Open 12-3, 5.30(6 Sun)-midnight

Recommended by Bob and Margaret Holder, Ewan and Moira McCall, Ryta Lyndley, the Didler, John Marsh

 BUCKLAND MONACHORUM Devon   SX4968   Map 1

Drake Manor

Off A386 via Crapstone, just S of Yelverton roundabout; PL20 7NA

Nice little village pub with snug rooms, popular food, quite a choice of drinks and pretty back garden; bedrooms

Originally built to house workers constructing the nearby church in the 12th century, this is a charming little village pub with a welcoming, long-serving landlady. The heavily beamed public bar on the left has brocade-cushioned wall seats, prints of the village from 1905 onwards, some horse tack and a few ship badges on the wall and a woodburning stove in a really big stone fireplace; a small door leads to a low-beamed cubbyhole. The snug Drakes Bar has beams hung with tiny cups and big brass keys, a woodburning stove in another stone fireplace, horsebrasses and stirrups and a mix of seats and tables (note the fine stripped pine high-backed settle with its hood). On the right is a small, beamed dining room with settles and tables on flagstones. Shove-ha'penny, darts, euchre and board games. Dartmoor Jail Ale, Otter Bitter, St Austell Tribute and Sharps Doom Bar on handpump, ten wines by the glass and several malt whiskies. There are picnic-sets in the prettily planted and sheltered back garden and the front floral displays are much admired. As well as offering bedrooms, there's also an attractive self-catering apartment.

Using their own home-reared pork and other local produce, the enjoyable bar food includes lunchtime filled baguettes, hake, ginger and lime fishcake with yoghurt and honey, minted lamb or steak and stilton burgers, chickpea, sweet potato and spinach curry, and specials like haddock with a cheese and herb crumb topping or venison steak topped with a fruit and port sauce. *Benchmark main dish: steak and kidney pie £8.95. Two-course evening meal £15.45.*

Punch ~ Lease Mandy Robinson ~ Real ale ~ Bar food (12-2, 7-10(9.30 Sun)) ~ Restaurant ~ (01822) 853892 ~ Children in restaurant and area off main bar ~ Dogs allowed in bar ~ Open 11.30-2.30(3 Sat), 6.30-11(11.30 Fri); 11.30-11.30 Sat; 12-11 Sun ~ Bedrooms: /£90B

Recommended by Martyn Williams, R and S Bentley, Maureen Wood, John and Gloria Isaacs

 CADGWITH Cornwall   SW7214   Map 1

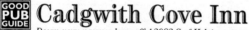 # Cadgwith Cove Inn
Down very narrow lane off A3083 S of Helston; no nearby parking; TR12 7JX

Fine walks in either direction from old-fashioned inn at the bottom of fishing cove; bedrooms

With fine coastal walks in either direction, this little local is just the place for a break and it's in a charming fishing cove position at the bottom of a pretty village. The two snugly dark front rooms have plain pub furnishings on their mainly parquet flooring, a log fire in one stripped-stone end wall, lots of local photographs including some of gig races, cases of naval hat ribands and of fancy knot-work and a couple of compass binnacles. Some of the dark beams have ships' shields and others have spliced blue rope hand-holds. Otter Bitter, Sharps Doom Bar and Skinners Betty Stogs on handpump. A back bar has a huge and colourful fish mural; piped music. There are green-painted picnic-sets on the good-sized front terrace, some under a fairy-lit awning, looking down to the fish sheds by the bay. The bedrooms overlook the sea and they make their own jams and marmalades for breakfast. While it's best to park at the top of the village and meander down through the thatched cottages, it's quite a steep hike back up again.

Well liked bar food using local produce includes sandwiches, crab pâté, popular pasty or fish with chips, aubergine charlotte, chicken curry, and specials such as bass fillet with bacon and garlic. *Benchmark main dish: fish and chips £10.50. Two-course evening meal £17.95.*

Punch ~ Lease David and Lynda Trivett ~ Real ale ~ Bar food (all day weekends; best to check food times in Dec and Jan) ~ (01326) 290513 ~ Well behaved children welcome away from main bar ~ Dogs welcome ~ Open 12-11 (10.30 Sun); 12-3, 7-11 in winter ~ Bedrooms: £45.25(£47.50S)/£60.50(£82.50S)

Recommended by Mayur Shah, Comus and Sarah Elliott, Peter Meister

> For those of you who use Sat Nav devices, we include a postcode for every entry in the *Guide*.

CERNE ABBAS Dorset   ST6601   Map 2

New Inn 🍴 ♀ 🛏

Long Street; DT2 7JF

DORSET DINING PUB OF THE YEAR

Fine old inn with hard-working hands-on licensees, a friendly atmosphere, three real ales, a good choice of wines and interesting food; bedrooms

Since Mr and Mrs Lee took over this charming 16th-c former coaching inn, we've had nothing but praise from our readers for the warm welcome and enjoyable food; it's a nice place to stay as well and the bedrooms are clean and comfortable. The simple bar has straightforward wooden tables and chairs on the patterned carpet, old photographs and prints on pink walls, logs to either side of the stone fireplace and a few high bar chairs by the duck egg blue-painted bar counter where they keep Palmers Best, Copper and 200 on handpump and a dozen good wines by the glass. The two rooms of the dining room have a happy mix of dark chairs around wooden tables, more old prints and mullioned window seats with a view down the main street of this attractive stone-built village. There are seats on the terrace and picnic-sets under mature fruit trees or parasols in the back garden. You can walk from the village up and around the prehistoric Cerne Abbas Giant chalk carving and on to other nearby villages. They are hoping to add more bedrooms.

 Good, imaginative food includes lunchtime sandwiches, seared local scallops with black pudding and rhubarb, baked courgette with blue vinney and chestnut stuffing and lemon and parmesan polenta, beer-battered haddock, a daily pasta, risotto and pie of the day, bass fillet with pak choi, crab dumplings and green curry sauce, and plum and almond tart with marmalade and liquorice blancmange. *Benchmark main dish: fillet of local venison wrapped in pancetta with stuffed savoy cabbage £14.00. Two-course evening meal £19.95.*

Palmers ~ Tenant Jeremy Lee ~ Real ale ~ Bar food (12-2.15, 6.30-8.45) ~ Restaurant ~ (01300) 341274 ~ Children welcome ~ Dogs welcome ~ Open 11-3, 6-11; closed Sun evening in winter ~ Bedrooms: £55S/£90S

Recommended by David and Sue Smith, Sue Demont, Tim Barrow, Tony and Gill Powell, T G Shaw, Alan Johnson

CHARLTON HORETHORNE Somerset   ST6623   Map 2

Kings Arms 🛏

B3145 Wincanton—Sherborne; DT9 4NL

Imposing and rather smart but with a good mix of drinkers and diners, relaxed bars and more formal restaurant, good choice of ales and wines, and enjoyable food; comfortable bedrooms

Although much emphasis in this imposing Edwardian inn is on the comfortable contemporary bedrooms and the first-rate food, there's a relaxed atmosphere and the cheerful drinkers and diners mix easily; both are made just as welcome by the friendly, helpful staff. The main bar has all manner of local modern art (all for sale) on the dark mulberry or cream walls, nice old carved wooden dining chairs and pine pews around a mix of tables on the slate floor, and a woodburning stove. Leading off here is a cosy room with sofas, and newspapers on low tables. Butcombe Bitter, Sharps Doom Bar and a beer named after the pub from Wadworths on handpump are served from the rather fine granite bar counter and they keep 13 wines by the glass and local draught cider. To the left of the main door is an informal dining room with Jacobean-style chairs and tables on the pale wooden floor and more local artwork. The back restaurant (you have to walk past the open kitchen which is quite fun to peek into) is smart with decorative wood and glass mirrors, wicker or black leather high-backed dining chairs around chunky polished pale wooden tables on the coir carpeting, and handsome striped curtains. At the back of the building, the attractive courtyard has plenty of chrome and wicker chairs around teak tables under green parasols and there is a good smokers' shelter overlooking the croquet lawn.

Using carefully sourced local produce and making their own breads, pasta and ice-creams, the very good modern food might include chicken liver parfait with bitter orange marmalade, lunchtime smoked hickory and honey sausages and steak in Guinness pie, and evening choices like duck breast with celeriac dauphinoise and nectarine chutney, and chicken breast with jerusalem artichoke risotto and truffled mascarpone. *Benchmark main dish: blade of beef £15.50. Two-course evening meal £20.20.*

Free house ~ Licensee Tony Lethbridge ~ Real ale ~ Bar food (12-2.30, 7-9.30(9 Sun, 10 Fri and Sat)) ~ Restaurant ~ (01963) 220281 ~ Children welcome ~ Dogs allowed in bar ~ Open 11-11(10.30 Sun) ~ Bedrooms: /£110S

Recommended by Charles Gysin, Edward Mirzoeff, John Branston, Mrs C Roe, Tim and Sue Halstead

CHICKSGROVE Wiltshire   ST9729   Map 2

Compasses ★ ⑪ ♀ ⮂

From A30 5.5 miles W of B3089 junction, take lane on N side signposted Sutton Mandeville, Sutton Row, then first left fork (small signs point the way to the pub, in Lower Chicksgrove; look out for the car park); can also be reached off B3089 W of Dinton, passing the glorious spire of Teffont Evias church; SP3 6NB

An excellent all-rounder with enjoyable food, a genuine welcome, four real ales and seats in the quiet garden; comfortable bedrooms

After enjoying one of the nearby walks, this ancient thatched house is just the place to head for – although as it's very popular with both locals and visitors it might be best to book a table in advance. The unchanging bar has plenty of real character: old bottles and jugs hanging from beams above the roughly timbered counter, farm tools and traps on the partly stripped-stone walls, and high-backed wooden settles forming snug booths around tables on the mainly flagstoned floor. Helpful and friendly young staff serve Butcombe Blonde, Keystone Bedrock, Plain Ales Inntrigue and a guest beer on handpump, eight wines by the glass and several malt whiskies. The quiet garden, terraces and flagstoned farm courtyard are very pleasant places to sit, and our readers have told us that this is a lovely place to stay overnight – smashing breakfasts, too.

Listed on blackboards and using as much local produce as possible, the splendid bar food includes sandwiches, ham hock terrine with home-made chutney, leek, mushroom and goats cheese pancakes, venison sausages with onion mash, lamb shank with bubble and squeak, and monkfish wrapped in parma ham with a mussel and lemon risotto. *Benchmark main dish: steak and kidney pudding £9.00. Two-course evening meal £19.50.*

Free house ~ Licensee Alan Stoneham ~ Real ale ~ Bar food ~ (01722) 714318 ~ Children welcome ~ Dogs welcome ~ Open 12-3, 6-11; 12-3, 7-10.30 Sun; closed Mon Jan-Easter ~ Bedrooms: £65B/£85S

Recommended by Mrs C Roe, Steve Whalley, Ross Balaam, Philip and Jan Medcalf, Ian Herdman, John Branston, Peter and Jan Humphreys, Helen and Brian Edgeley, David and Judy Robison, Mrs Susannah Riley, R and M Thomas, Roxanne Chamberlain

 CHIDEOCK Dorset — SY4292 Map 1

George

A35 Bridport—Lyme Regis; DT6 6JD

Comfortably traditional local with well liked food

As we went to press, enthusiastic new licensees took over this traditional thatched village pub and were making several changes. They've updated the restaurant furniture, have a new terrace with a wood-fired oven and have bought a food smoker. The cosy low-ceilinged carpeted bar has warm log fires, brassware and pewter tankards hanging from dark beams, wooden pews and long built-in tongue and groove wooden banquettes, tools on the cream walls and high shelves of bottles, plates and mugs. Palmers Copper, Best and 200 on handpump; piped music and board games. A garden room opens on to a pretty walled garden.

Using local seasonal produce, the popular bar food might include sandwiches, home-made chorizo scotch egg, devilled sprats, beer-battered fish, and specials such as beetroot, goats cheese and thyme tart, venison burger with red onion chutney, and smoked pollack with spinach and a poached egg. *Benchmark main dish: fish of the day £9.50. Two-course evening meal £15.00.*

Palmers ~ Tenants Mr and Mrs Steve Smith ~ Real ale ~ Bar food (12-2.30, 6-9.30) ~ Restaurant ~ (01297) 489419 ~ Children welcome ~ Dogs allowed in bar ~ Live music Sat evening during school holidays ~ Open 12-3, 6-11

Recommended by Dennis Jenkin, William Ruxton, Peter Salmon, David and Stella Martin, B and M Kendall

 CHURCHILL Somerset — ST4459 Map 1

Crown £

The Batch; in village, turn off A368 into Skinners Lane at Nelson Arms; BS25 5PP

Unspoilt and unchanging small cottage with friendly customers and staff, super range of real ales, and homely lunchtime food

For some, this quite unchanging and distinctly laid-back pub might not be spic and-span enough – it could perhaps do with a lick of paint – but you can be sure of a genuinely warm welcome, a roaring log fire and a fine choice of real ales. The small and rather local-feeling stone-floored and cross-beamed room on the right has a wooden window seat, an unusually sturdy settle, built-in wall benches and chatty, friendly customers; the left-hand room has a slate floor and some steps past the big log fire in a big stone fireplace lead to more sitting space. No noise from music or games (except perhaps dominoes) and up to ten real ales tapped from the cask: Bath Ales Gem Bitter, Butcombe Bitter, Cotleigh Batch, Palmers Best, RCH Hewish IPA, PG Steam, St Austell Tribute and changing guest beers. Several wines by the glass and local ciders. Outside lavatories are basic. There are garden tables at the front, a smallish back lawn and hill views; the Mendip morris men come in summer. There's no pub sign outside but no one ever seems to have a problem finding it. Some of the best walking on the Mendips is close by.

🍴 Using beef from the field next door, the straightforward and reasonably priced lunchtime bar food includes sandwiches (the rare roast beef is popular), good soup, cauliflower cheese, chilli con carne and tasty beef casserole. *Benchmark main dish: chilli con carne £6.20.*

Free house ~ Licensee Tim Rogers ~ Real ale ~ Bar food (12-2.30; not evenings) ~ No credit cards ~ (01934) 852995 ~ Children welcome away from bar ~ Dogs welcome ~ Open 11-11(midnight Fri and Sat); 12-10.30 Sun

Recommended by Barry and Anne, Bob and Margaret Holder, John and Gloria Isaacs, Tom Evans, Adrian Johnson, MLR, the Didler, Simon and Mandy King, Michael Doswell, Dr and Mrs A K Clarke, John and Joan Nash

CLAPTON-IN-GORDANO Somerset   ST4773 Map 1

Black Horse ◀ £

4 *miles from M5 junction 19; A369 towards Portishead, then B3124 towards Clevedon; in north Weston opposite school, turn left signposted Clapton, then in village take second right, may be signed Clevedon, Clapton Wick; BS20 7RH*

Nicely old-fashioned pub with lots of cheerful customers, friendly service, real ales and cider, and straightforward pub food; pretty garden

Although a new licensee has taken over this unspoilt local, readers have been quick to tell us that happily, little has changed and the pub remains popular with locals, farmers and walkers with their dogs; visitors are made just as welcome. The partly flagstoned and partly red-tiled main room has winged settles and built-in wall benches around narrow, dark wooden tables, window seats, a big log fire with stirrups and bits on the mantelbeam, and amusing cartoons and photographs of the pub. A window in an inner snug is still barred from the days when this room was the petty-sessions gaol; high-backed settles – one a marvellous carved and canopied creature, another with an art nouveau copper insert reading, East, West, Hame's Best – lots of mugs hanging from its black beams and plenty of little prints and photographs. There's also a simply furnished room which is the only place families are allowed; darts. Butcombe Bitter, Courage Best, Exmoor Gold, Otter Ale, Wadworths 6X and Wells & Youngs Bombardier on handpump or tapped from the cask, several wines by the glass and farm ciders. There are some old rustic tables and benches in the garden, with more to one side of the car park, and the summer flowers are really quite a sight. Paths from the pub lead up Naish Hill or along to Cadbury Camp.

🍴 Straightforward lunchtime bar food includes good filled baguettes and hot dishes like cauliflower and broccoli cheese, beef stew and paprika chicken. *Benchmark main dish: beef stew £7.25.*

Enterprise ~ Lease Nicholas Evans ~ Real ale ~ Bar food (not evenings, not Sun) ~ (01275) 842105 ~ Children in very plain family room only ~ Dogs welcome ~ Live music Mon evening ~ Open 11-11; 12-10.30 Sun

Recommended by Bob and Margaret Holder, Tom Evans, Dr D J and Mrs S C Walker, the Didler, Roy Hoing, Barry and Anne, Chris and Angela Buckell

---

The ◀ symbol shows pubs that keep their beer unusually well, have a particularly good range or brew their own.

CLAYHIDON Devon   ST1817   Map 1

Merry Harriers 🍴 ♈ 🍺

3 miles from M5 junction 26: head towards Wellington; turn left at first
roundabout signposted Ford Street and Hemyock, then after a mile turn left signposted
Ford Street; at hilltop T junction, turn left towards Chard – pub is 1.5 miles on right;
at Forches Corner NE of the village itself; EX15 3TR

DEVON DINING PUB OF THE YEAR

Bustling and friendly dining pub with imaginative food, several real ales
and quite a few wines by the glass; sizeable garden

Readers very much enjoy this well run, friendly pub and you will be
sure to get a genuinely warm welcome from the hardworking, hands-
on licensees. Several small linked green-carpeted areas have a cheerful,
bustling atmosphere, comfortably cushioned pews and farmhouse chairs,
a sofa beside the woodburning stove, candles in bottles, horsey and
hunting prints and local wildlife pictures. Two dining areas have a
brighter feel with quarry tiles and lightly timbered white walls. Cotleigh
Golden Seahawk, Exmoor Ale and Otter Head on handpump, 14 wines by
the glass, two local ciders, 25 malt whiskies and a good range of spirits;
skittle alley, chess and solitaire. There are plenty of tables and chairs in
the sizeable garden and on the terrace, and they have a wendy house and
other play equipment for children; there are good surrounding walks.

Growing some of their own vegetables, keeping their own hens and using
seasonal local produce from named suppliers, the imaginative bar food might
include lunchtime filled baguettes, pork and pistachio terrine with home-made fruit
chutney, mussels in a cider cream sauce, beer-battered cod and chips, organic pork
and apple sausages, black bream fillets on wild mushrooms, leeks and bacon, and
confit duck leg on onion marmalade. *Benchmark main dish: local scallops with*
lemon cream sauce and crispy parma ham salad £10.50. Two-course evening
meal £15.50.

Free house ~ Licensees Peter and Angela Gatling ~ Real ale ~ Bar food (not Sun evening
or Mon) ~ Restaurant ~ (01823) 421270 ~ Children welcome ~ Dogs allowed in bar ~
Open 12-3, 6.30-11; 12-4 Sun; closed Sun evening, all day Mon, 25 and 26 Dec
Recommended by Bob and Margaret Holder, Jenna Phillips, PLC, Brian Glozier, I H G Busby,
David Saunders, Katherine Bright, Ted and Charlotte Routley, Geoff and Linda Payne, John Prescott,
Patrick and Daphne Darley, Christine and Neil Townend, Mike Gorton

CLYST HYDON Devon   ST0201   Map 1

Five Bells

West of the village and just off B3176 not far from M5 junction 28; EX15 2NT

Attractive thatched pub with several distinctive areas, well liked food
and drink, and carefully planted cottagey garden

Tucked away down little lanes, this attractive thatched pub is quite a sight in
spring and summer when the immaculate cottagey front garden is full of
thousands of flowers and the big window boxes and hanging baskets are at their
prettiest. To the side and up some steps there are plenty of seats on a sizeable flat
lawn and pleasant country views. Inside, the bar is divided at one end into different
seating areas by brick and timber pillars: china jugs hang from big horsebrass-
studded beams, lots of plates line delft shelves, there's quite a bit of copper and
brass and a nice mix of dining chairs around small tables, with some comfortable
pink plush banquettes on a little raised area. Past the inglenook fireplace is another
big (but narrower) room they call the Long Barn which has a series of prints on the

walls, a pine dresser at one end and similar furnishings. Cotleigh Tawny, O'Hanlons Stormstay and Otter Bitter on handpump, ten wines by the glass, local farm cider and a wide range of soft drinks; piped music.

Well liked bar food includes sandwiches, duck, pheasant and chicken terrine with apple chutney, mussels in white wine and cream, beef and mushroom in Guinness pie, changing curries, aubergine crumble, lancashire hotpot, and fish pie; they also offer a good value two-course lunch menu. *Benchmark main dish: steak and kidney pudding £10.50. Two-course evening meal £16.70.*

Free house ~ Licensees Mr and Mrs R Shenton ~ Real ale ~ Bar food (not Mon lunchtime) ~ (01884) 277288 ~ Children welcome away from bar area ~ Live jazz second Weds of month ~ Open 11.30-3, 6.30-11; 12-3, 6.30-10.30 Sun; closed Mon lunchtime

Recommended by Bob and Angela Brooks, Bruce and Sharon Eden, Mr and Mrs W Mills, Ryta Lyndley, Mr and Mrs Richard Osborne

COLEFORD Devon   SS7701 Map 1

New Inn ♀ ⇐

Just off A377 Crediton—Barnstaple; EX17 5BZ

Ancient thatched inn with interestingly furnished areas, well liked food and real ales, and welcoming licensees; bedrooms

Both Mr and Mrs Cowie are genuinely friendly licensees who work hard to ensure their customers enjoy visiting this 800-year-old inn. Most people are here for the good food or to stay overnight in the comfortable bedrooms (the breakfasts are especially enjoyable) but you can drop in for a drink and the welcome will be just as warm. It's a U-shaped building with the servery in the 'angle' and interestingly furnished areas leading off it: ancient and modern settles, cushioned stone wall seats, some character tables – a pheasant worked into the grain of one – and carved dressers and chests. Also, paraffin lamps, antique prints on the white walls and landscape plates on one of the beams, with pewter tankards on another. Captain, the chatty parrot, may greet you with a 'hello' or even a 'goodbye'. Otter Ale, Sharps Doom Bar and a guest like Bath Ales Gem Bitter on handpump, local cider, 14 wines by the glass and a dozen malt whiskies; piped music, darts and board games. There are chairs and tables on decking under a pruned willow tree by the babbling stream and more in a covered dining area.

Using local produce where possible, the constantly changing bar food includes filled baguettes, moules marinière, butternut squash and red pepper risotto, sausages with rosemary mash, beef and mushroom pie, bass with ginger, chilli and soy on sesame noodles and stir-fried vegetables, and confit duck leg with orange and redcurrant sauce; they hold regular themed food weeks. *Benchmark main dish: rare breed beefburgers topped with stilton £10.25. Two-course evening meal £16.70.*

Free house ~ Licensees Carole and George Cowie ~ Real ale ~ Bar food (12-2, 6.30-9.30) ~ Restaurant ~ (01363) 84242 ~ Children welcome ~ Dogs allowed in bar ~ Open 12-3, 6-11(10.30 Sun); closed 25 and 26 Dec ~ Bedrooms: £67B/£89B

Recommended by P and J Shapley, Anthony Barnes, Dr A McCormick, Mrs P Sumner, B J Harding, Mike and Mary Carter, Jane Hudson, Simon and Philippa Hughes, S G N Bennett, John and Bryony Coles, Mr Yeldahn

---

We can always use photos of pubs on our website – do email one to us:
feedback@thegoodpubguide.co.uk

CORTON DENHAM Somerset   ST6322   Map 2

Queens Arms ⊗ ↤

Village signposted off B3145 N of Sherborne; DT9 4LR

Civilised stone inn, super choice of drinks, interesting food, and a sunny garden; refurbished bedrooms

New licensees have taken over this rather civilised country inn and have updated the bedrooms and are hoping to have added three more by the time this edition is published. They've also redecorated and refurbished the dining room. The plain high-beamed bar has a woodburning stove in the inglenook at one end, with rugs on flagstones in front of the raised fireplace at the other end, some old pews, barrel seats and a sofa, church candles and maybe a big bowl of flowers; a little room off here has just one big table – nice for a party of eight or so – which is where they serve breakfast for those who stay. Black Sheep, Manchester Marble, Moor Revival and Ramsgate Gadds No 3 Kent Pale Ale on handpump, 34 wines by the glass, 62 whiskies, six ciders and unusual bottled beers from Belgium, Germany and America. A south-facing back terrace has teak tables and chairs under parasols (or heaters if it's cool), with colourful flower tubs. There are some lovely surrounding walks.

Using their own pigs and chickens and local seasonal produce, the imaginative food might include sandwiches, some pubby staples, and specials like fresh seafood and tomato risotto, hickory smoked chicken burger with their own bacon, baked goats cheese in filo pastry with sweet and sour leeks and a roasted pepper dressing, and duck breast with orange, ginger and soy sauce. *Benchmark main dish: pork cutlets with parmesan and apple and cider sauce £12.50. Two-course evening meal £19.50.*

Free house ~ Licensees Jeanette and Gordon Reid ~ Real ale ~ Bar food (12-3, 6-10(9.30 Sun)) ~ Restaurant ~ (01963) 220317 ~ Children welcome ~ Dogs allowed in bar ~ Open 10am(midday Sun)-11.30pm ~ Bedrooms: £75S(£80B)/£105B

Recommended by Charles Gysin, David Hudd, Philip and Jan Medcalf, Dr Nigel Bowles, Victoria Bright, Patrick and Daphne Darley, Will Douglas German

CRAFTHOLE Cornwall   SX3654   Map 1

Finnygook ⚲

B3247, off A374 Torpoint road; PL11 3BQ

Carefully renovated and rather civilised former coaching inn, good mix of drinkers and diners, interesting furniture and décor in bar and dining room, enjoyable food, real ales, and friendly service; bedrooms

Civilised but with an informal and relaxed atmosphere, this is a 15th-c coaching inn with a good mix of both drinkers and diners. The bar has beams and joists, a central log fire that warms both sides of the room, really long pews set against the walls with attractive cushions and carved cushioned dining chairs around various wooden tables on the stripped floorboards. There's also a couple of high wooden tables with chairs to match near the bar counter, big bowls of lilies, black and white local photographs, big warship and other prints on the walls and, in one large window, an old compass. St Austell Dartmoor and Proper Job and Sharps Doom Bar on handpump and a decent choice of wines by the glass. The carefully lit dining room on the other side of the building has all manner of dining chairs and tables, rugs on floorboards, an unusual log-effect gas fire in a big glass cabinet, church candles and plants, black and white photographs of local people, houses and beaches, and some vinyl records on the walls; at one end, there's a library. Through the hop-hung windows are fine views across the Lynher and Tamar rivers. This is under the same ownership as the Turtley Corn Mill at Avonwick in Devon.

Good bistro-style bar food includes sandwiches, chicken liver parfait with chutney and brioche, crab spaghetti with chilli and coriander, aubergine, lentil and sweet potato moussaka, chicken with vermouth and tarragon, and cod loin with chorizo, spinach, pine nuts and peppers. *Benchmark main dish: haddock and chips with minted mushy peas £12.00. Two-course evening meal £17.95.*

Free house ~ Licensee David Colton ~ Real ale ~ Bar food (12-9.30(9 Sun)) ~ Restaurant ~ (01503) 230338 ~ Children welcome ~ Dogs allowed in bar and bedrooms ~ Open 11-11; 12-10.30 Sun; closed Mon Oct-March ~ Bedrooms: £55B/£75B

Recommended by Dennis Jenkin, Dr and Mrs M W A Haward, Colin and Maggie Fancourt, Dr D J and Mrs S C Walker, Olly Padbury, Evelyn and Derek Walter

 CRICKLADE Wiltshire   SU1093   Map 4

 # Red Lion 🍴 🍺 🛏

Off A419 Swindon—Cirencester; High Street; SN6 6DD

WILTSHIRE DINING PUB OF THE YEAR

16th-c inn with imaginative food in two dining rooms, up to ten real ales, lots of bottled beers, several wines by the glass, a friendly, relaxed atmosphere and big garden; bedrooms

After a walk along the nearby Thames path, this particularly well run former coaching inn is just the place to head for. The bar has stools by the nice old counter, wheelbacks and other solid dark wooden tables and chairs on the red patterned carpet, an open fire and all sorts of bric-a-brac, and old road or street signs on the stone walls. You can eat here or in the slightly more formal dining room which has pale wooden farmhouse chairs and tables on beige carpeting and a woodburning stove in the brick fireplace. They keep a fine range of up to ten real ales on handpump (and hope to start brewing their own beer soon), such as Arbor Breakfast Stout, Bristol Beer Factory Hefe, Butcombe Bitter, Cottage Champflower Ale, Forge Gold, Hop Back Entire Stout, Moles Best, Stonehenge Sign of Spring, Wadworths 6X and West Berkshire Mr Chubbs Lunchtime Bitter, around 63 interesting bottled beers, farm cider, eight wines by the glass and their own ginger beer and cordials. There are plenty of picnic-sets in the big back garden. Their bedrooms are attractive and comfortable.

Using local, organic produce, free-range meat and chicken, and fruit and vegetables from their neighbours in exchange for a pint or two, the much-enjoyed food includes lunchtime sandwiches, home-cooked ham, egg and triple-cooked chips, their own spicy bean or meaty burgers, home-salted line-caught pollack fishcakes with home-made garlic mayonnaise, pig's cheeks in cider and chicken with savoy cabbage, bacon and chicken broth; they suggest a beer for each course. *Benchmark main dish: haunch of venison, grilled liver, garlic mash and cherries £13.95. Two-course evening meal £18.90.*

Free house ~ Licensee Tom Gee ~ Real ale ~ Bar food (12-3(3.30 weekends), 6-9 (9.30 Sat; not Sun evening) ~ Restaurant ~ (01793) 750776 ~ Children welcome ~ Dogs welcome ~ Open 12-11(10.30 Sun); 12-midnight Fri and Sat ~ Bedrooms: /£75B

Recommended by Jenny and Peter Lowater, Robert W Buckle

CROCKERTON Wiltshire   ST8642 Map 2

Bath Arms
Off A350 Warminster—Blandford; BA12 8AJ

Attractively modernised dining pub with pretty gardens, relaxed atmosphere, real ales, and good food cooked by the landlord; bedrooms

Always busy and friendly, this attractive pub is run by a welcoming landlord and his helpful staff. The long, stylishly modernised two-roomed bar has lots of well spaced tables on the parquet floor, beams in the whitewashed ceiling and horsebrasses. There's a restaurant at one end and a log fire in a stone fireplace at the other. Wessex Crockerton Classic and Potters Ale on handpump, several wines by the glass and cider; piped music. There are plenty of inviting places to sit outside too, with various garden areas featuring plenty of picnic-sets. Longleat is close by so it does get crowded during school holidays.

Cooked by the landlord, the good, enjoyable food includes filled baguettes, crab mayonnaise, courgette, leek and tarragon risotto, burger with bacon and tomato salsa, cumberland sausage and champ, fillet of black bream with asparagus and artichoke, and calves liver with black pudding and chestnuts. *Benchmark main dish: sticky beef £14.95. Two-course evening meal £19.50.*

Wellington ~ Lease Dean Carr ~ Real ale ~ Bar food ~ Restaurant ~ (01985) 212262 ~ Children welcome ~ Dogs allowed in bar ~ Open 11-3, 6-11; 11-11 Sat; 12-11 Sun ~ Bedrooms: /£80S

Recommended by Douglas and Ann Hare, Gordon Tong, Edward Mirzoeff, Mrs C Roe, Richard and Judy Winn

CROSCOMBE Somerset   ST5844 Map 2

George
Long Street (A371 Wells—Shepton Mallet); BA5 3QH

Carefully renovated old coaching inn, warmly welcoming, informative canadian landlord, bar food cooked by landlady, good local beers, attractive garden; bedrooms

Mr Graham is a first-rate landlord who offers a genuinely warm and interested welcome to all his customers. The main bar has some stripped stone, dark wooden tables and chairs and more comfortable seats, winter log fires in inglenook fireplaces and the family grandfather clock; a snug area has recently been added with a stone fireplace and woodburning stove. The attractive dining room has more stripped stone, local artwork and photographs on the burgundy walls and high-backed cushioned dining chairs around a mix of tables. The back bar has canadian timber reclaimed from the local church and there's a family room with games and books for children. King George the Thirst (brewed exclusively for them by Blindmans), Butcombe Bitter, Cheddar Ales Totty Pot and Moor Revival on handpump or tapped from the cask, four farm ciders and ten wines by the glass. Darts, shut the box, a canadian wooden table game called crokinole, shove-hapenny, piped music and separate TV room. The friendly pub dog is called Tessa. The attractive, sizeable garden has seats on the heated and covered terrace, flower borders and a grassed area; children's swings.

Cooked by the landlady and using locally sourced produce, the enjoyable food includes filled baguettes, chicken liver pâté, lamb curry, sausages with onion gravy, smoked haddock fishcakes, and specials like crab au gratin, cashew nut terrine, bass with a wild garlic and vermouth sauce, and seasonal game dishes. *Benchmark main dish: steak in ale pie £7.95. Two-course evening meal £19.00.*

Free house ~ Licensees Peter and Veryan Graham ~ Real ale ~ Bar food (12-2, 6-9) ~ Restaurant ~ (01749) 342306 ~ Children welcome ~ Dogs allowed in bar ~ Live jazz bank holiday Sun ~ Open 12-2.30, 6-11 ~ Bedrooms: £35S/£70S

Recommended by Maureen Wood, Terry Buckland, Phyl and Jack Street, Peter Dearing, David and Sharon Collison, Rupert Handley, Bruce and Sharon Eden

CRUDWELL Wiltshire   ST9592   Map 4

Potting Shed ⊕ ♀ ☎

SOUTH WEST PUB OF THE YEAR

A429 N of Malmesbury; The Street; SN16 9EW

Appealing variation on the traditional country tavern theme, a fine choice of drinks, interesting food, and friendly staff

Rather than just another pub/restaurant, this highly enjoyable place is a proper country pub where people and dogs are genuinely welcomed by the cheerful young staff – and they have a fantastic range of drinks and often inventive food as well. Low-beamed rooms ramble around the bar with mixed plain tables and chairs on pale flagstones, log fires (one in a big worn stone fireplace, some well worn easy chairs in one corner, and a couple of blacktop daily papers. Four steps take you up into a high-raftered further area with coir carpeting, and there's one separate smaller room ideal for a lunch or dinner party. The rustic decorations are not overdone and quite fun: a garden-fork door handle, garden-tool beer pumps, rather witty big black and white photographs. Bath Ales Gem Bitter, Butcombe Bitter, Timothy Taylors Landlord and St Austell Tribute on handpump, as well as an excellent range of 30 wines and champagne by the glass, home-made seasonal cocktails using local or home-grown fruit, local fruit liqueurs, good coffees and popular winter mulled wine; visiting dogs may meet Barney and Rubbles (who belong to the owners) and be offered biscuits. Well chosen piped music and board games. They have summer barbecues on fine Saturdays; there are sturdy teak seats around cask tables as well as picnic-sets out on the side grass among weeping willows.

Imaginative food, using their own-grown fruit and vegetables and produce from the villagers to whom they've loaned allotments, might include sandwiches, marinated, seared duck with pomegranate seeds, orange and candied ginger, venison burger with onion marmalade, wild mushroom and truffle open lasagne, old spot pork belly and cider casserole, and halibut fillet with mussel broth, crispy leeks and capers. *Benchmark main dish: beer-battered haddock and triple-cooked chips £12.95. Two-course evening meal £20.20.*

Enterprise ~ Lease Jonathan Barry, Julian Muggridge and Laura Sheffield ~ Real ale ~ Bar food (12-2.30(3 Sun), 7-9.30(9 Sun)) ~ (01666) 577833 ~ Children welcome ~ Dogs welcome ~ Open 11am-midnight(11pm Sun)

Recommended by Peter and Audrey Dowsett, Richard Tilbrook, Mr and Mrs P R Thomas, MJVK, David Gunn, Paul Goldman, R J Herd, Sue Callard

Places with gardens or terraces usually let children sit there – we note in the text the very few exceptions that don't.

DALWOOD Devon   ST2400 Map 1

Tuckers Arms

Village signposted off A35 Axminster—Honiton; keep on past village;
EX13 7EG

**13th-c thatched inn with friendly, hard-working young licensees, real
ales and interesting bar food**

With welcoming and enthusiastic young licensees and particularly
good, interesting food, this pretty thatched longhouse is extremely
popular with our readers. The beamed and flagstoned bar has a relaxed
atmosphere, a good mix of locals and visitors, traditional furnishings
including various dining chairs, window seats and wall settles, and a log
fire in the inglenook fireplace with lots of horsebrasses above it. The
back bar has an enormous collection of miniature bottles and there's also
a more formal dining room; lots of copper implements and platters.
Branscombe Vale Branoc, Otter Bitter and a changing local guest beer on
handpump, several wines by the glass and up to 20 malt whiskies. Piped
music and a double skittle alley. In summer, the hanging baskets are
pretty and there are seats in the garden. Apart from the church, this is the
oldest building in the parish.

Using local produce, the popular often inventive food includes lunchtime filled
baguettes, roast tomato and goats cheese crème brûlée, moules marinière, a
lunchtime pork platter, a home-made burger topped with cheese, wild mushroom
pancakes with cream and spinach sauce, chicken with mascarpone sauce, couscous,
a pepper and rocket salad and a parmesan crisp, and bass with black pudding and
beetroot. *Benchmark main dish: pork belly with plum and star anise sauce £15.95.
Two-course evening meal £23.00.*

Free house ~ Licensee Tracey Pearson ~ Real ale ~ Bar food ~ Restaurant ~
(01404) 881342 ~ Children in restaurant but must be well behaved ~ Dogs allowed in bar
~ Open 11.30-3, 6.30(6 Sat)-11.30; 12-4, 7-10.30 Sun ~ Bedrooms: £45S/£70S
*Recommended by Bob and Margaret Holder, John Luckes, Michelle Gallagher, Shaun Holley,
Jane Hudson, Fiona Loram*

DARTMOUTH Devon   SX8751 Map 1

Floating Bridge

Opposite Upper Ferry, use Dart Marina Hotel car park; Coombe Road (A379);
TQ6 9PQ

**Quayside local with seats outside making the most of the position,
simple bar, neat dining room, friendly staff, and popular summer roof
terrace**

Under the same ownership as the nearby Dart Marina Hotel, this
quayside local is at its best when Ann the friendly landlady is behind
the bar. It's right by the ferry and the River Dart views can be enjoyed
through windows in the bar, from the picnic-sets by the water and from
the sizeable roof terrace. The simple bar has cushioned, wood-slatted
wall seats and wheelback chairs around straightforward pubby tables
(each with a little nightlight), some rather fine model boats, black and
white photographs of local boating scenes and ship's badges on the walls,
Otter Ale, St Austell Tribute and Sharps Doom Bar on handpump and
quite a few wines by the glass; piped music and TV. The dining room on
the left is lighter with more wheelback chairs around scrubbed kitchen
tables on bare boards and naïve gig rowing photographs and one of a big

old yacht on the white walls. The window boxes are pretty against the white-painted building.

 Pubby bar food includes sandwiches, deep-fried brie with cranberry sauce, ham and egg, popular burgers or beer-battered fish and chips, a changing vegetarian pasta dish, and bream in a white wine and cream sauce. *Benchmark main dish: beer-battered fish and chips £10.50. Two-course evening meal £17.00.*

Enterprise ~ Lease Ann Firmstone ~ Real ale ~ Bar food (12-2.30, 6-9.30) ~ Restaurant ~ (01803) 832354 ~ Children welcome but not in main bar in evening ~ Dogs welcome ~ Open 11-11; closed Sun evening, and all day Mon and Tues from end Oct to end March
Recommended by Ian Malone, Phil and Sally Gorton

 DARTMOUTH Devon SX8751 Map 1

Royal Castle Hotel
The Quay; TQ6 9PS

17th-c hotel with a lot of character in two quite different bars, a genuine mix of customers, real ales and good food served all day; comfortable bedrooms

Overlooking the inner harbour, this 17th-c hotel has a vibrant atmosphere and a really good mix of customers. There are two ground floor bars, each with their own identity. On the right is the traditional Galleon bar with lots of character, a Tudor fireplace, some fine antiques and maritime pieces and quite a bit of copper and brass. To the left of the flagstoned entrance hall is the Harbour Bar which is contemporary and rather smart with a big screen TV and regular live acoustic music on Thursday evenings. The more formal restaurant looks over the river. Dartmoor Jail Ale, Otter Amber and Sharps Doom Bar on handpump and several wines by the glass. The inn was originally two Tudor merchant houses (but has a Regency façade); they have their own secure parking.

Enjoyable food of some sort, using seasonal local produce, is served all day from 8am for breakfast: sandwiches, mussels in white wine and cream, chicken liver pâté with red onion marmalade, home-baked ham and eggs, spinach and ricotta ravioli, monkfish with lentils and mussels in a saffron, coconut and lemon grass cream, and oriental-style stir-fried beef with noodles. *Benchmark main dish: cod and chips £9.95. Two-course evening meal £18.00.*

Free house ~ Licensees Nigel and Anne Way ~ Real ale ~ Bar food (all day) ~ Restaurant ~ (01803) 833033 ~ Children welcome but not after 7pm in bar (can eat in restaurant then) ~ Dogs welcome ~ Live acoustic music Thurs evening ~ Open 8am-11pm(10.30 Sun) ~ Bedrooms: £110B/£160B
Recommended by Peter and Giff Bennett, Alison Ball, Ian Walton, Sandy Butcher

DODDISCOMBSLEIGH Devon SX8586 Map 1

Nobody Inn ♀
Off B3193; EX6 7PS

Busy old pub with plenty of character, a fine range of drinks, friendly staff, and well liked bar food; bedrooms

With welcoming licensees and a fine range of drinks, this is a popular old pub with plenty of character. The two rooms of the beamed lounge bar have handsomely carved antique settles, windsor and wheelback chairs, quite a mix of wooden tables, guns and hunting prints in a snug area by one of the big inglenook fireplaces and fresh flowers. The restaurant is more formal. A beer named for the pub from Branscombe Vale and two changing guests such as Branscombe Vale Branoc and Exe Valley Bitter on handpump, 240 whiskies and 28 wines by the glass. There are picnic-sets on the terrace with views of the surrounding wooded hill pastures. The medieval stained glass in the local church is some of the best in the west country.

Using local produce and naming their suppliers, bar food includes game terrine with red onion marmalade, moules marinière, nut roast with passata, pork, hickory and honey sausages, beer-battered fish and chips, steak in ale pie, and venison steak with mandarin and chocolate sauce. *Benchmark main dish: steak in ale pie £10.75. Two-course evening meal £16.50.*

Free house ~ Licensee Susan Burdge ~ Real ale ~ Bar food (12-2, 6.30-9(9.30 Fri and Sat); 12-3, 7-9 Sun; restaurant closed Sun and Mon) ~ Restaurant ~ (01647) 252394 ~ Children welcome away from main bar; no children under 5 in restaurant ~ Dogs allowed in bar ~ Open 11-11; 12-10.30 Sun; closed 25 and 26 Dec and 1 Jan ~ Bedrooms: £65S/£90S

Recommended by Robert Lorimer, Andrea Rampley, Mike and Monnie Jefferies, Michael Cooper, Barry Steele-Perkins, the Didler, Hugh Roberts, Mike Bartram

 DONHEAD ST ANDREW Wiltshire   ST9124 Map 2

Forester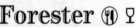

Village signposted off A30 E of Shaftesbury, just E of Ludwell; Lower Street; SP7 9EE

Attractive old thatched pub in a charming village, real ales, popular food, and fine views from the very pleasant big terrace

In a lovely little village, this 14th-c thatched pub places much emphasis on the appealing food – but there is a nice bar with a relaxed atmosphere and usually a few locals chatting around the servery. Butcombe Bitter and a changing guest beer on handpump, 15 wines (including champagne) by the glass, stripped tables on wooden floors and a log fire in a big inglenook fireplace. Off here is an alcove with a sofa, table and magazines to read. The comfortable main dining room has country-kitchen tables in varying sizes and there's also a second smaller and cosier dining room. Outside, seats on a good-sized terrace have fine country views. The neighbouring cottage used to be the pub's coach house. You can walk up White Sheet Hill and past the old and 'new' Wardour castles.

As well as lunchtime sandwiches, the good bar food might include provençale-style fish and shellfish soup, aberdeen angus steak burger with bacon and cheese, veal milanese, duck breast with redcurrant jus and dauphinoise potatoes, and cornish sea bream with wild mushrooms, spinach and sauce vierge; they also offer a two- and three-course set seafood menu (Tuesday-Friday). *Benchmark main dish: fritto misto of fish £14.00. Two-course evening meal £21.50.*

Free house ~ Licensee Chris Matthew ~ Real ale ~ Bar food (12-3, 7-9; not Sun evening) ~ Restaurant ~ (01747) 828038 ~ Children welcome ~ Dogs welcome ~ Open 12-3, 6.30-11; 12-4 Sun; closed Sun evenings

Recommended by Mrs C Roe, Robert Watt

We say if we know a pub allows dogs.

DULVERTON Somerset   SS9127 Map 1

Woods ★ ⊘ ♀

Bank Square; TA22 9BU

Smartly informal place with exceptional wines, real ales, first-rate food, and a good mix of customers

Comfortably relaxed and mildly upmarket in a country way, this bustling place always has a good mix of both locals and visitors and a good balance between drinkers and diners. It's run by a particularly charming landlord and his genuinely helpful and friendly staff who will open any of their 400 wines for just a glass from a quite extraordinarily good list; there's also an unlisted collection of some 500 well aged, new world wines which Mr Groves will happily chat about. St Austell Dartmoor Best, Otter Head and a changing guest beer tapped from the cask, a farm cider, many sherries and some unusual spirits. As the pub is on the edge of Exmoor, there are plenty of good sporting prints on the salmon pink walls, some antlers, other hunting trophies, stuffed birds and a couple of salmon rods. There are bare boards on the left by the bar counter and daily papers to read, tables partly separated by stable-style timbering and masonry dividers and a bit on the right which is carpeted and has a woodburning stove in the big fireplace; maybe unobjectionable piped music. Big windows keep you in touch with what's going on out in the quiet town centre (or you can sit out on the pavement at a couple of metal tables). A small suntrap back courtyard has a few picnic-sets.

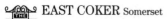 They breed their own pigs and chickens for the excellent food and as well as fair value light lunches like filled ciabatta rolls, honey-roast ham and egg, a good cheeseburger and seared steak with crispy bacon, the more pricey, restauranty choices include ballotine of chicken with confit leg rillettes and poultry sauce, lamb rump with slow-roast loin, crispy sweetbreads and thyme sauce, and skate wing with caper nut brown butter. *Benchmark main dish: belly of pork stuffed with black pudding with cider sauce £16.00. Two-course evening meal £24.00.*

Free house ~ Licensee Patrick Groves ~ Real ale ~ Bar food ~ Restaurant ~ (01398) 324007 ~ Children welcome ~ Dogs welcome ~ Open 11-3, 6-midnight; 12-3, 7-11 Sun

Recommended by Bob and Margaret Holder, Mr and Mrs B Cox, Richard, Anne and Kate Ansell, Sheila Topham, M G Hart, Guy Vowles, Jeremy Whitehorn, John and Jackie Chalcraft

EAST COKER Somerset   ST5412 Map 2

Helyar Arms ♀ 🛏

Village signposted off A37 or A30 SW of Yeovil; Moor Lane; BA22 9JR

Old pub in charming village with comfortable big bar, a fair range of drinks, and bar food cooked by the landlord; attractive bedrooms

This partly 15th-c inn is in a charming village. The heavy beamed, spacious and comfortable bar is carefully laid out to give a degree of intimacy to its various candlelit tables and there are a couple of high-backed settles and squashy leather sofas on the patterned carpet in front of a warm log fire. Also, lots of hunting and other country pictures, brass and copper ware, and daily papers to read. Steps lead up to a good-sized back high-raftered dining room. Butcombe Bitter, Dorset Jurassic and Sharps Doom Bar on handpump and nine wines by the glass; piped music, board games and skittle alley. There are a few picnic-sets out on a neat lawn.

🍴 Bar food cooked by the landlord includes sandwiches, game terrine with chutney, lasagne, toad in the hole, chicken breast with crispy parma ham and garlic butter, and slow-cooked leg of lamb with rosemary and cardamom jus; Monday night is steak night. *Benchmark main dish: steak sandwich £9.00. Two-course evening meal £17.00.*

Punch ~ Lease Mathieu Eke ~ Real ale ~ Bar food (12-2.30, 6.30-9.30(9 Sun)) ~ Restaurant ~ (01935) 862332 ~ Children welcome ~ Dogs welcome ~ Open 11-3, 6-11; 11am-midnight Sat; 12-10.30 Sun ~ Bedrooms: £65S/£89S

Recommended by Malcolm and Sue Scott, M G Hart

EAST KNOYLE Wiltshire ST8731 Map 2

Fox & Hounds 🍴 ♀

Village signposted off A350 S of A303; The Green (named on some road atlases), a mile NW at OS Sheet 183 map reference 872313; or follow signpost off B3089, about 0.5 miles E of A303 junction near Little Chef; SP3 6BN

Beautiful thatched village pub with splendid views, welcoming service, good beers, and popular food

Perhaps a bit tricky to find but so well worth it when you do, this is a charming country pub and loved by our readers. You can be sure of a friendly welcome and the three linked areas are on different levels around the central horseshoe-shaped servery with big log fires, plentiful oak woodwork and flagstones, comfortably padded dining chairs around big scrubbed tables with vases of flowers, and a couple of leather sofas; the furnishings are all very individual and uncluttered. There's also a small light-painted conservatory restaurant. Hop Back Summer Lightning, Plain Ales Sheep Dip and guests like Adnams Broadside and Purity Pure UBU on handpump, quite a few wines by the glass and farm cider. Piped music and skittle alley. The pub is in a lovely spot by the village green and there are marvellous views of the Blackmore Vale. The nearby woods are good for a stroll, and the Wiltshire Cycle Way passes through the village.

🍴 Consistently good food includes lunchtime ploughman's, home-made sausages with onion gravy, ricotta and parmesan tart, singapore-style laksa pork belly curry, stone-baked pizzas (they have a clay oven), lamb chump with a rosemary and mint jus, and crab and prawn risotto. *Benchmark main dish: beer-battered fish and chips £12.00. Two-course evening meal £17.50.*

Free house ~ Licensee Murray Seator ~ Real ale ~ Bar food (12-2.30, 6.30-9.30) ~ (01747) 830573 ~ Children welcome ~ Dogs welcome ~ Open 11.30-3, 5.30-11(10.30 Sun)

Recommended by R I Turner, Paul Goldman, Helen and Brian Edgeley, Michael Doswell, Martin and Karen Wake, R and M Thomas, Peter Dandy

FARNHAM Dorset ST9515 Map 2

Museum 🍴 ♀ 🛏

Village signposted off A354 Blandford Forum—Salisbury; DT11 8DE

Stylish civilised inn with appealing rooms including a bustling bar, inventive modern cooking, real ales and fine wines, and seats outside; lovely bedrooms

There's no doubt that most emphasis in this partly-thatched and rather smart 17th-c inn is on the highly thought-of food but they do keep Flack Manor Double Drop and Waylands Sixpenny 6D Best and Rushmore Gold on handpump, an excellent choice of wines with 15 by the glass and around 30 malt whiskies. The little bar has a bustling atmosphere, beams and flagstones, a big inglenook fireplace, good comfortably cushioned furnishings and plentiful windows that give the place a bright feel. To the right, a dining room has a fine antique dresser and off to the left is a cosier room. Yet another room feels rather like a contemporary baronial hall with dozens of antlers and a stag's head looking down on a long refectory table and church-style pews. This leads to an outside terrace with wooden tables and chairs. The bedrooms in the main building are very comfortable.

Beautifully presented (if not cheap) modern food includes lunchtime pork, leek and mustard sausages, beer-battered cod and slow-cooked pork belly with grain mustard mash and apple sauce with more elaborate choices like seared scallops with roasted cauliflower cream and crisp black pudding with apple, lamb three ways (roasted saddle, sweet breads, shepherd's pie with neeps and tatties, haggis and white onion purée), and fillet of bass with giant butter bean, mussel, clam and chorizo casserole. *Benchmark main dish: lamb three ways £19.50. Two-course evening meal £24.70.*

Free house ~ Licensee David Sax ~ Real ale ~ Bar food (12-2(2.30, 3 Sun), 7-9.30 (9 Sun)) ~ Restaurant (Fri and Sat evening and Sun lunch) ~ (01725) 516261 ~ Children welcome ~ Dogs welcome ~ Open 12-3, 6-11 ~ Bedrooms: £100S(£125B)/ £110S(£135B)
Recommended by Neil and Karen Dignan, Cathryn and Richard Hicks, Clare Mills

FONTHILL GIFFORD Wiltshire   ST9231   Map 2

Beckford Arms ⊕ ♀ 🛏

Off B3089 W at Fonthill Bishop; SP3 6PX

18th-c coaching inn with refurbished bar and restaurant, interesting food, real ales, and an informal but civilised atmosphere; bedrooms

On the edge of lovely rolling parkland, this is an elegant old coaching inn, recently re-opened after a bad fire. The main bar has a huge fireplace, bar stools beside the counter, various old wooden dining chairs and tables on parquet flooring, Butcombe Bitter, Keystone Large One and Milestone Lions Pride on handpump, several wines by the glass and local cider; staff are cheerful and helpful. The elegant sitting room has comfortable sofas facing each other across a low table of newspapers, a nice built-in window seat and other chairs and tables, and an open fire in the stone fireplace with candles in brass candlesticks and fresh flowers on the mantelpiece. There's also a separate restaurant and charming private dining room. Much of the artwork on the walls is by local artists; the pub dog is called Elsa. The mature rambling garden has seats on the brick terrace, hammocks under trees and boules. The bedrooms are stylish and the breakfasts with home-made jams, are enjoyable.

Good, bistro-style food includes sandwiches, pork terrine with piccalilli, goats cheese soufflé with tomato chutney, home-baked ham and free-range eggs, chicken and leek pie, salt marsh lamb breast with peas, broad beans and mint, skate with lemon and capers, and slow-roasted pork belly with creamed flageolet beans; they also offer proper afternoon tea and a Saturday brunch. *Benchmark main dish: fish and chips £11.00. Two-course evening meal £18.50.*

Free house ~ Licensees Dan Brod and Charlie Luxton ~ Real ale ~ Bar food (12-9) ~ Restaurant ~ (01747) 870385 ~ Children welcome ~ Dogs allowed in bar ~ Open 9am-11pm(11.30 Sat); 11-10.30 Sun ~ Bedrooms: /£75S(£95B)
Recommended by Mrs C Roe, Mr and Mrs A Curry, Susan Buchanan, Ian Herdman, Andrea Rampley, Michael Doswell, Shirley Mackenzie

GEORGEHAM Devon   SS4639 Map 1

Rock 🍴 �

Rock Hill, above village; EX33 1JW

Beamed family pub, good food cooked by the landlord, up to six real ales on handpump, plenty of room inside and out, and a relaxed atmosphere

There's a cheerful, relaxed atmosphere in this heavily beamed and popular 17th-c inn and a good balance between drinkers and diners – though to miss the food cooked by the hard-working chef/landlord would be a great shame. The sizeable bar is separated by a step and the pubby top part has an open woodburning stove in a stone fireplace, captain's and farmhouse chairs around wooden tables on the quarry tiles and half-planked walls; the lower bar has panelled wall seats, some built-in settles forming a cosy booth, old local photographs and ancient flat irons. Leading off here is a red-carpeted dining room with attractive black and white photographs of people from North Devon. Friendly young staff serve Exmoor Ale, Fullers London Pride, St Austell Tribute, Sharps Doom Bar and Timothy Taylors Landlord on handpump and they keep around a dozen wines by the glass; piped music and board games. The light and airy back dining conservatory has high-backed wooden or modern dining chairs around tables under the growing vine, and beyond that, there's a little terrace. They have wheelchair access. Beside the pretty hanging baskets and tubs in front of the pub are some picnic-sets.

Interesting food cooked by Mr Craddock might include sandwiches, mixed deli boards, honey-glazed ham with free-range eggs and home-made piccalilli, risotto of smoked haddock, grain mustard and peas and a poached egg, home-made venison burger with a blue cheese glaze, and specials such as local lobster and crayfish spaghetti with tarragon cream sauce, pavé of roe deer with red wine jus, and Exmoor beef stroganoff with brandy cream. *Benchmark main dish: beer-battered cod £9.50. Two-course evening meal £17.45.*

Punch ~ Lease Daniel Craddock ~ Real ale ~ Bar food (all day Jun-Sept; 12-2.30 (3 Sun), 6-9.30(9 Sun)) ~ Restaurant ~ (01271) 890322 ~ Children welcome away from public bar ~ Dogs welcome ~ Open 11am-11.30pm; 12-11 Sun
Recommended by Stephen Shepherd, Brian Glozier, Dr and Mrs S G Barber, Bob and Margaret Holder, Peter and Josie Fawcett, John and Joan Nash

GREAT BEDWYN Wiltshire   SU2764 Map 2

Three Tuns

Village signposted off A338 S of Hungerford, or off A4 W of Hungerford via Little Bedwyn; High Street; SN8 3NU

Thriving village pub with local real ales, helpful staff, nicely presented bar food, and eclectic décor

This bustling country pub has been trading since 1756 – part of the building was once a bakery and the cellar was the village morgue. The traditional décor in the beamed, bare-boards front bar is lifted out of the ordinary by some quirky touches and almost every inch of the walls and ceiling is covered by either the usual brasses, jugs, hops and agricultural implements, or more unusual collections such as ribbons from sailors' hats, showbiz photos and yellowing cuttings about the royal family. Moles Rucking Mole, Ramsbury Gold and a couple of guest beers (one named after the pub) on handpump and farm cider. There's an inglenook

fireplace and maybe evening candlelight. The raised back garden has
seats, tables and a heated smoking area. It can get pretty packed at
weekends.

Using some of their own-grown produce, the bar food might include hand-dived
scallops with bacon, basil and sweet pepper oil, butternut squash, goats cheese
and beetroot purée risotto, slow-roast lamb shoulder with red wine and redcurrant
jus, monkfish and prawn thai green curry and a proper cassoulet. *Benchmark main
dish: bouillabaise £12.95. Two-course evening meal £18.95.*

Free house ~ Licensees Alan and Jan Carr ~ Real ale ~ Bar food ~ Restaurant ~
(01672) 870280 ~ Children welcome ~ Dogs allowed in bar ~ Open 12-3, 6-11; 12-6 Sun;
closed Sun evening

Recommended by Phil Bryant

GRITTLETON Wiltshire   ST8680   Map 2

Neeld Arms

*Leave M4 junction 17, follow A429 to Cirencester and immediately left,
signed Stanton St Quinton and Grittleton; SN14 6AP*

**Bustling village pub with popular food and beer and friendly staff;
comfortable bedrooms**

Even on a chilly winter's day, the bar in this 17th-c stone inn has a
cheerful atmosphere and plenty of chatty customers – it's still very
much the centre of village life. Largely open-plan, there's a pleasant mix
of seats ranging from bar stools, a traditional settle, window seats and
pale wooden dining chairs around a mix of tables. The little brick
fireplace houses a woodburning stove, there's an inglenook fireplace on
the right, and Cotswold-stone walls. Wadworths IPA and 6X and guests
such as Bath Ales Gem Bitter and Plain Ales Sheep Dip on handpump,
served from the blue-painted panelled and oak-topped bar counter. The
back dining area has yet another inglenook with a big woodburning stove
and even back here, you still feel thoroughly part of the action. There's an
outdoor terrace with a pergola.

Popular food includes lunchtime ciabatta sandwiches, moules marinière, ham
and egg, a pie of the day, wild mushroom stroganoff, calves liver with black
pudding, and pork medallions with apple and calvados sauce. *Benchmark main
dish: pie of the day £10.95. Two-course evening meal £16.90.*

Free house ~ Licensees Charlie and Boo West ~ Real ale ~ Bar food ~ (01249) 782470 ~
Children welcome ~ Dogs allowed in bar ~ Open 12-3, 5.30(7 Sun)-11.30 ~
Bedrooms: £50B/£80B

Recommended by Ian Malone, W J Taylor, Sara Fulton, Roger Baker, MJVK, David Jackman

GURNARDS HEAD Cornwall   SW4337   Map 1

Gurnards Head Hotel

B3306 Zennor—St Just; TR26 3DE

CORNWALL DINING PUB OF THE YEAR

**Interesting, well run inn close to the sea, with real ales, lots of wines by
the glass and very good inventive food; comfortable bedrooms and fine
surrounding walks**

This is an informal and friendly dining pub with comfortable bedrooms
and in a wonderful position just 500 yards from the Atlantic. There are

glorious walks all around through the outstanding bleak National Trust scenery – both inland and along the cliffy coast. Inside, the bar rooms are painted in bold, strong colours, there are paintings by local artists, open fires and a happy mix of wooden dining chairs and tables on stripped boards. Skinners Betty Stogs, St Austell Tribute and a changing guest beer on handpump, several wines by the glass or carafe and a couple of ciders; piped music and board games. Seats in the large garden behind, and the recently refurbished bedrooms either have views of the rugged moors or of the sea. This is under the same ownership as the civilised Griffin at Felinfach (see our Wales chapter).

🍴 Excellent modern food from sensibly short seasonal menus and using the best local produce might include ham terrine with apple chutney, salt and pepper squid with saffron aioli, white asparagus, poached egg and truffle vinaigrette, gurnard with mousseline potatoes, braised leeks and orange, and duck with carrot and cardamom purée, pak choi, five spice and rice cake; good value set lunches. *Benchmark main dish: pollack, salsa verde, and crushed new potatoes £11.25. Two-course evening meal £23.00.*

Free house ~ Licensees Charles and Edmund Inkin ~ Real ale ~ Bar food (12(12.30 winter)-2.30, 6(6.30 winter)-9.30) ~ Restaurant ~ (01736) 796928 ~ Children welcome ~ Dogs allowed in bar and bedrooms ~ Live folk music Mon evenings ~ Open 11.30-11; closed 24 and 25 Dec and four days in Jan ~ Bedrooms: £80S/£95S(£165B)

Recommended by Peter Monk, S J and C C Davidson, Nicky Pallot, Laura Rosser, Robin Sykes, R T and J C Moggridge, John and Sharon Hancock, Mike and Sue Loseby

---

🏆 **HAYTOR VALE** Devon   SX7777 Map 1

Rock ★ 🍴 🛏

Haytor signposted off B3387 just W of Bovey Tracey, on good moorland road to Widecombe; TQ13 9XP

Civilised Dartmoor inn at its most informal at lunchtime; super food, real ales, and seats in pretty garden; comfortable bedrooms

Cleverly appealing to the more informal lunchtime customers (many then are walkers from Dartmoor National Park) as well as to those expecting a more formal evening meal and comfortable overnight stay, this is an especially well run and civilised inn. The two neatly kept communicating, partly panelled bar rooms have lots of dark wood and red plush, polished antique tables with candles and fresh flowers, old-fashioned prints and decorative plates on the walls and warming winter log fires (the main fireplace has a fine Stuart fireback). Dartmoor Jail Ale, Otter Bright and St Austell Dartmoor Best on handpump, ten wines (plus champagne) by the glass and several malt whiskies. A new light and spacious dining room has been added to the lower part of the inn and the residents' lounge is now larger and more comfortable. There are seats in the large, pretty garden opposite, with tables and chairs on a small terrace next to the pub itself. The bedrooms are comfortable with good facilities (some are up steep stairs) and the breakfasts are highly thought-of. There is a car park at the back.

🍴 Particularly good food (they name their local suppliers) includes lunchtime ploughman's, butternut squash risotto with crème fraîche and steak in ale pie, with evening choices such as steamed mussels in white wine and cream, duo of beef with spinach and truffle mash and bass fillet on niçoise salad with lemon and caper dressing; they also offer a two- and three-course set menu. *Benchmark main dish: rump steak with garlic butter and chunky chips £13.95. Two-course evening meal £23.45.*

Free house ~ Licensee Christopher Graves ~ Real ale ~ Bar food ~ Restaurant ~
(01364) 661305 ~ Children welcome ~ Dogs allowed in bedrooms ~ Open 11-11;
12-10.30 Sun; closed 25 and 26 Dec ~ Bedrooms: £75B/£85S(£103B)

*Recommended by Neil and Anita Christopher, Mayur Shah, Hugh Roberts, Revd R P Tickle, Paul and
Mary Walmsley, W K Wood, Mike and Mary Carter, Barry Steele-Perkins*

HELSTON Cornwall   SW6522   Map 1

Halzephron ♀ ⇔

*Gunwalloe, village about 4 miles S but not marked on many road maps; look
for brown sign on A3083 alongside perimeter fence of RNAS Culdrose; TR12 7QB*

**Bustling pub in lovely spot with tasty bar food, local beers, and
bedrooms; good nearby walks**

This popular inn may have changed hands by the time this edition is
printed so we are keeping our fingers crossed that things won't
change too much. The position will remain a strong draw as Gunwalloe
fishing cove is just 300 yards away and Church Cove with its sandy beach
is a mile away – as is the church of St Winwaloe (built into the dunes on
the seashore). Our readers very much enjoy the surrounding unspoilt
walks, too, with fine views of Mount's Bay. The neatly kept bar rooms
have an informal, friendly atmosphere, comfortable seating, copper on
the walls and mantelpiece, a warm winter fire in the woodburning stove
and St Austell Proper Job, Sharps Doom Bar and Skinners Betty Stogs on
handpump; also, nine wines by the glass and 40 malt whiskies. The dining
Gallery seats up to 30 people; darts and board games. Picnic-sets outside
look across National Trust fields and countryside.

As well as lunchtime sandwiches, the good bar food includes chicken liver pâté
with onion marmalade, pork sausages with mustard mash and onion gravy,
mediterranean vegetable tart with courgette fritters, a casserole of the day, and
mackerel fillets with seafood risotto. *Benchmark main dish: seafood chowder £5.95.
Two-course evening meal £19.00.*

Free house ~ Licensee Angela Thomas ~ Real ale ~ Bar food ~ Restaurant ~
(01326) 240406 ~ Children in family room ~ Dogs allowed in bar ~ Open 11-2.30, 6-11;
12-2.30, 6-10.30 Sun; 6.30 opening time in winter ~ Bedrooms: £52S/£94S

*Recommended by J B Taylor, Ray Carter, Mayur Shah, Mr and Mrs Gravener, Barry Collett,
Chris and Val Ramstedt, Ian and Rose Lock, Peter and Judy Frost*

HINTON ST GEORGE Somerset   ST4212   Map 1

Lord Poulett Arms ⊕ ♀ ⇔

*Off A30 W of Crewkerne and off Merriott road (declassified – former A356,
off B3165) N of Crewkerne; TA17 8SE*

SOMERSET DINING PUB OF THE YEAR

**Thatched 17th-c stone inn with charming antique-filled rooms, well
presented food, good choice of drinks, and a pretty garden; bedrooms**

Although most people come to this civilised old inn to enjoy the
excellent food or to stay in the pretty cottagey bedrooms, there's a
good mix of both diners and drinkers and they do keep Branscombe
Branoc, Otter Ale and a guest such as Moor Revival on handpump.
Several attractive cosy linked areas have rugs on bare boards or
flagstones, open fires (one in an inglenook and one in a raised fireplace
that separates two rooms), walls of honey-coloured stone or painted in

bold Farrow & Ball colours, hop-draped beams, antique brass candelabra, fresh flowers and candles, and some lovely old farmhouse, windsor and ladderback chairs around fine oak or elm tables. Fourteen wines by the glass, jugs of Pimms and home-made cordial; the pub cat is called Honey. Outside, under a wisteria-clad pergola, there are white metalwork tables and chairs in a mediterranean-style lavender-edged gravelled area and picnic-sets in a wild flower meadow; boules. This is a charming and peaceful village and there are walks nearby.

Using home-grown vegetables and other local organic produce, the first-rate food includes lunchtime filled baguettes, mackerel and poached rhubarb tart, burger with triple cooked chips and caramelised onion jam, beer-battered fish with gribiche sauce, slow-roasted pork shoulder with apple sauce and crackling, pigeon breast with parsnip purée, and a fish dish of the day. *Benchmark main dish: beer-battered fish £13.00. Two-course evening meal £21.00.*

Free house ~ Licensees Steve Hill and Michelle Paynton ~ Real ale ~ Bar food (12-9) ~ Restaurant ~ (01460) 73149 ~ Children welcome ~ Dogs allowed in bar ~ Live music 4-7 Sun mid-Jun to Sept ~ Open 12(11.45 Sun)-11; closed 25 and 26 Dec, 1 Jan ~ Bedrooms: £65B/£95B

Recommended by Guy Consterdine, Bob and Margaret Holder, Mr and Mrs W W Burke, Clare West, Stephen Colling, Dr A McCormick, Adrian Stear, Simon and Philippa Hughes, John Chambers

HONITON Devon

SY1198   Map 1

Holt

High Street, W end; EX14 1LA

Friendly, informal family-run pub with super tapas and other interesting food, and a fine range of Otter beers

Brewing has been in the McCaig family for three generations and indeed they founded the Otter Brewery, so it's not surprising that the full range of Otter beers are kept on handpump in this charming little pub: Ale, Amber, Bitter, Bright and Head. There's just one room downstairs with chunky pine chairs and tables (a pot of thyme on each one), a couple of brown leather sofas at one end facing each other across a circular table, a coal-effect woodburner in the brick fireplace with a shelf of books to one side, and a stone floor; the windows are shuttered (and one looks down on to a small stream). Upstairs, a bigger, brighter room has similar furniture on floorboards and small, very attractive musician prints, much larger contemporary pictures and an old Chamonix travel poster on the pale grey or maroon walls. Piped music and friendly staff. It's all very relaxed and informal. The black cat is called Dangermouse.

Listing their local growers and producers on a blackboard by the open kitchen, the short choice of interesting bar food includes lunchtime sandwiches and tapas, smoked prawns (they have their own smokehouse) with fresh herb mayonnaise, home-cured meats with celeriac toast, dolcelatte and watercress tart with pickled horseradish, smoked haddock with salsa verde and lemon and herb crumb, and chicken with serrano ham, mushrooms, parmesan polenta and red pesto. *Benchmark main dish: slow-roasted pork belly with white bean cassoulet £14.50. Two-course evening meal £21.50.*

Free house ~ Licensees Joe and Angus McCaig ~ Real ale ~ Bar food (not Sun or Mon) ~ Restaurant ~ (01404) 47707 ~ Well behaved children welcome ~ Dogs allowed in bar ~ Music festival four times a year ~ Open 11-3, 5.30-11; closed Sun and Mon; 25 and 26 Dec

Recommended by John and Dinah Waters, Paul Milican, Stephen Hunt, Jane Hudson, Alan Clark, Tim Gray, Derek and Sylvia Stephenson, Guy Vowles, M G Hart

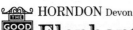 HORNDON Devon   SX5280 Map 1

Elephants Nest 🍷 ⬛ 🛏

If coming from Okehampton on A386, turn left at Mary Tavy Inn, then left after about 0.5 miles; pub signposted beside Mary Tavy Inn, then Horndon signposted; on the Ordnance Survey Outdoor Leisure Map it's named as the New Inn; PL19 9NQ

Isolated old inn surrounded by Dartmoor walks, some interesting original features, real ales and good food; comfortable bedrooms

With well appointed and attractively furnished bedrooms, this cosy old inn is an especially enjoyable place to stay – and the breakfasts are very highly thought of. The main bar has lots of beer pump clips on the beams, high bar chairs by the bar counter, Dartmoor Jail Ale, Palmers Best, Sharps Doom Bar and a guest beer such as Otter Bright on handpump, a couple of farm ciders and several wines by the glass. There are two other rooms with nice modern dark wood dining chairs around a mix of tables and throughout there are bare stone walls, flagstones and three woodburning stoves. The spreading, attractive garden has plenty of picnic-sets under parasols and from here you look over dry-stone walls to the pastures of Dartmoor's lower slopes and the rougher moorland above where there are plenty of walks.

Using local produce, the reliably good bar food includes lunchtime filled baguettes (not Sundays), ham hock terrine with wasabi mayonnaise, caramelised shallot and goats cheese tarte tatin, popular home-made burger with red onion marmalade, steak and kidney pudding, chicken breast stuffed with taleggio and rosemary, and whole lemon sole with prawns, capers and lemon butter. *Benchmark main dish: smoked haddock topped with welsh rarebit £13.95. Two-course evening meal £18.50.*

Free house ~ Licensee Hugh Cook ~ Real ale ~ Bar food ~ Restaurant ~ (01822) 810273 ~ Children welcome away from bar ~ Dogs welcome ~ Open 12-3, 6.30-11(10.30 Sun) ~ Bedrooms: £77.50B/£87.50B
Recommended by Viv Jameson, P and J Shapley, John and Bernadette Elliott, Bruce Adams

HORNS CROSS Devon   SS3823 Map 1

Hoops 🛏

A39 Clovelly—Bideford, W of village; EX39 5DL

Striking thatched inn with plenty of character, real ales and good bar and restaurant food, and a spacious garden; comfortable bedrooms

Particularly in summer when the window boxes are so pretty, this newly thatched 13th-c pub is a lovely sight. There are picnic-sets under parasols in the enclosed courtyard and plenty more seats on the terrace and in the two acres of surrounding gardens. Inside, the bar has solid mate's and other kitchen chairs around wooden tables, china hanging from the beams, log fires in sizeable fireplaces, and some standing timbers and partitioning creating separate areas. The more formal restaurant has an attractive mix of chairs and tables, some panelling and exposed stone and another open fire. Sharps Doom Bar and a couple of beers named for the pub, brewed by Forge, on handpump and over a dozen wines by the glass; piped music and board games. The two black labradors are called Sky and Scout. The bedrooms are well equipped and comfortable and the Coach House has family rooms.

Using seasonal local produce, the good bar food includes lunchtime sandwiches, moules marinière, vegetarian lasagne, beer-battered fresh fish, slow-cooked pork belly with apple and cider jus, seafood cassoulet, and duck breast with hot foie gras and endive tatin. *Benchmark main dish: beer-battered local cod £10.95. Two-course evening meal £20.50.*

Free house ~ Licensees Gerry and Dee Goodwin ~ Real ale ~ Bar food (all day) ~ Restaurant ~ (01237) 451222 ~ Children welcome ~ Dogs allowed in bar and bedrooms ~ Open 11-11; 12-10.30 Sun ~ Bedrooms: £65B/£70B
Recommended by John Urquhart

HUISH EPISCOPI Somerset ST4326 Map 1

Rose & Crown ¶ £
Off A372 E of Langport; TA10 9QT

Unchanging old place in the same family for over a century, local cider and beers, simple food, and a friendly welcome

This unpretentious and quite unspoilt old place has been in the same friendly family for over 140 years and the knowledgeable and helpful landlord is always willing to chat. There's no bar as such, just a central flagstoned still room with casks of Teignworthy Reel Ale and a couple of guests such as Branscombe Bitter and Palmers 200; also local Burrow Hill farm cider and cider brandy. This servery is the only thoroughfare between the casual little front parlours, with their unusual pointed-arch windows and genuinely friendly locals; good helpful service. Shove-ha'penny, dominoes, board games, bagatelle and cribbage, and a much more orthodox big back extension family room with pool, games machine and a juke box; skittle alley and popular quiz nights. There are tables in a garden and a second enclosed garden has a children's play area; you can camp (free by arrangement to pub customers) on the adjoining paddock. Summer morris men, fine nearby walks and the site of the Battle of Langport (1645) is close by.

Using local produce and free-range eggs, the simple, inexpensive food includes generously filled sandwiches, pork sausages with onion gravy, broccoli and stilton tart, steak in ale pie, and pork, apple and cider cobbler. *Benchmark main dish: steak in ale pie £7.95. Two-course evening meal £11.00.*

Free house ~ Licensee Stephen Pittard ~ Real ale ~ Bar food (12-2, 5.30-7.30; not Sun or Mon evenings) ~ No credit cards ~ (01458) 250494 ~ Children welcome ~ Dogs welcome ~ Live folk music third Sat of month (not Jun, July, Aug); irish music last Thurs of month ~ Open 11.30-3, 5.30-11; 11.30-11.30 Fri and Sat; 12-10.30 Sun
Recommended by Anthony and Vivienne Irons, the Didler

KING'S NYMPTON Devon SS6819 Map 1

Grove
Off B3226 SW of South Molton; EX37 9ST

Thatched 17th-c pub in remote village, local beers, interesting bar food, and cheerful licensees

Surrounded by quiet rolling and wooded countryside and in a lovely conservation village, this thatched 17th-c pub is run by friendly and cheerful licensees. The low-beamed bar has lots of bookmarks hanging from the ceiling, simple pubby furnishings on the flagstoned floor, bare stone walls, a winter log fire and Clearwater Real Smiler, Forge Maid in

Devon, Jollyboat Mainbrace and Exmoor Ale on handpump, 26 wines by the glass and 52 malt whiskies; darts, shove-ha'penny and dominoes. They have a self-catering cottage to rent.

 Naming their local suppliers and trading with regulars for their own-grown excess vegetables and fruit, the interesting bar food includes sandwiches, local trout pâté, all-day breakfast, chickpea, spinach and cauliflower curry, rabbit stew, fish pie, and chicken stuffed with devon blue, sage and parma ham. *Benchmark main dish: beef wellington £17.00. Two-course evening meal £15.75.*

Free house ~ Licensees Robert and Deborah Smallbone ~ Real ale ~ Bar food (not Sun evening or Mon (except bank hol Mon lunchtime)) ~ Restaurant ~ (01769) 580406 ~ Children welcome but must be seated and supervised ~ Dogs welcome ~ Open 12-3, 6-11; 12-4, 7-10.30 Sun; closed Mon lunchtime except bank holiday Mon
Recommended by Mark Flynn, Mrs Lorna Walsingham

KINGSBRIDGE Devon   SX7344   Map 1

Dodbrooke Inn 🍺 £
Church Street, Dodbrooke (parking some way off); TQ7 1DB

Chatty, bustling local, genuinely welcoming licensees, good mix of customers, and honest food and drink

Tucked away in a small street, this is a quaint little local with long-serving and welcoming licensees. There's always a mix of locals (and visitors) of all ages, the atmosphere is comfortably traditional and the bar has plush stools and straightforward built-in cushioned stall seats around pubby tables, ceiling joists, some horse harness, old local photographs and china jugs, and a log fire. Bass, Bath Ales Gem Bitter, Dartmoor IPA and Sharps Doom Bar on handpump and local farm cider. There's a simply furnished small dining room and a new covered eating area in the courtyard.

 Honest bar food includes sandwiches, a changing pâté, garlic mushrooms, home-cooked ham and egg and specials such as scallops with bacon, bass with red onions, and steaks topped with stilton; they offer takeaway fish and chips, too. *Benchmark main dish: charcoal steaks £12.50. Two-course evening meal £20.45.*

Free house ~ Licensees Michael and Jill Dyson ~ Real ale ~ Bar food (12-1.30, 5-8.30) ~ (01548) 852068 ~ Children welcome if over 5 ~ Dogs welcome ~ Open 12-2, 5-11; 12-2, 7-10.30 Sun; closed Mon and Tues lunchtimes; evening 25 and all day 26 Dec
Recommended by MP

LANLIVERY Cornwall   SX0759   Map 1

Crown 🍺
Signposted off A390 Lostwithiel—St Austell (tricky to find from other directions); PL30 5BT

Chatty atmosphere in nice old pub, traditional rooms, and well liked food and drink; the Eden Project is close by; bedrooms

This white-painted longhouse is one of Cornwall's oldest pubs and has some real character. The main bar has a warming log fire in the huge fireplace, traditional settles on big flagstones, some cushioned farmhouse chairs, a mix of wooden chairs and tables, and Sharps Doom Bar, Skinners Betty Stogs and a couple of changing guest beers on handpump, a dozen wines by the glass, several malt whiskies and summer farm cider.

A couple of other rooms are similarly furnished and there's another open fire; darts and board games. There's a huge lit-up well with a glass top by the porch and plenty of picnic-sets in the quiet garden. The Eden Project is only ten minutes away.

Nicely presented bar food includes lunchtime sandwiches and pasties, mini crab cakes with cauliflower purée, pea and mushroom risotto, popular fish pie, and specials like corn-fed chicken with garlic and mushroom cream, and local mussels in coconut milk, chilli and ginger. *Benchmark main dish: fish pie £12.50. Two-course evening meal £19.45.*

Wagtail Inns ~ Licensee Graham Hill ~ Real ale ~ Bar food (12-2.30, 6-9 (may offer shorter menu summer afternoons)) ~ Restaurant ~ (01208) 872707 ~ Children welcome but must be away from bar ~ Dogs allowed in bar and bedrooms ~ Open 11-11 ~ Bedrooms: /£79.95S

Recommended by Simon Le Fort, M Mossman, Nick Lawless, Norman and Sarah Keeping

LOSTWITHIEL Cornwall   SX1059   Map 1

Globe ♀ ◧

North Street (close to medieval bridge); PL22 0EG

Unassuming bar in traditional local, interesting food and drinks, and friendly staff; suntrap back courtyard with outside heaters

Whether you are a local or visitor, you'll get a genuinely friendly welcome from the cheerful staff in this well run old town pub – and customers do tend to return again and again. The unassuming bar is long and somewhat narrow with a bustling atmosphere and a good mix of pubby tables and seats. There are customers' photographs on pale green plank panelling at one end, nice, more or less local prints (for sale) on canary walls above a coal-effect stove at the snug inner end and a small red-walled front alcove. The ornately carved bar counter, with comfortable chrome and leatherette stools, dispenses Driftwood Red Mission, Skinners Betty Stogs and a couple of changing guest beers on handpump, plus a dozen reasonably priced wines by the glass, 20 malt whiskies and two farm ciders. Piped music, darts, board games and TV. The sheltered back courtyard is not large but has some attractive and unusual plants, and is a real suntrap (with an extendable overhead awning and outside heaters). You can park in several of the nearby streets. The 13th-c church is worth a look and the ancient river bridge, a few yards away, is lovely.

As well as lunchtime sandwiches, the good, enjoyable bar food includes moules marinière, steak and stilton pie, a trio of sausages with onion gravy, slow-roasted lamb shoulder, and daily specials like a vegetarian choice, lambs liver and bacon, curries, and fresh fish. *Benchmark main dish: bass with pesto, grilled asparagus and crushed new potatoes £13.95. Two-course evening meal £18.70.*

Free house ~ Licensee William Erwin ~ Real ale ~ Bar food ~ Restaurant ~ (01208) 872501 ~ Children welcome but no pushchairs in restaurant ~ Dogs allowed in bar ~ Live music Fri evening ~ Open 12-2.30, 6-11(midnight Fri and Sat) ~ Bedrooms: /£70B

Recommended by Tracey and Stephen Groves, Peter Salmon, B and M Kendall, Mike and Monnie Jefferies, R K Phillips, Alan Bowker, Dr and Mrs M W A Haward, Michelle, Graham Oddey, John Wooll

 LOWER CHUTE Wiltshire   SU3153   Map 2

Hatchet

The Chutes well signposted via Appleshaw off A342, 2.5 miles W of Andover; SP11 9DX

Unchanged, neatly kept, 13th-c thatched country pub with a friendly welcome from helpful staff; enjoyable food and real ales; comfortable bedrooms

This 16th-c thatched pub is a fine place to stay overnight – and dogs are welcome, too, in one bedroom; breakfasts are hearty. And whether you are a visitor or a regular, you can be sure of a warm welcome from the convivial landlord and his helpful staff. The very low-beamed bar has a splendid 17th-c fireback in the huge fireplace (and a roaring winter log fire), a mix of captain's chairs and cushioned wheelbacks around oak tables, and a peaceful local feel. Timothy Taylors Landlord, Otter Bitter and a guest like fff Pressed Rat & Warthog on handpump, nine wines by the glass, 20 malt whiskies and a farm cider; piped music and board games. There are seats out on a terrace by the front car park or on the side grass – as well as a smokers' hut and a children's sandpit.

Popular bar food includes lunchtime filled baguettes, chicken liver pâté with apricot chutney, haddock and spring onion fishcakes, spinach and ricotta lasagne, chicken with stilton sauce, and devilled kidneys with rice. *Benchmark main dish: steak in ale pie £8.95. Two-course evening meal £17.25.*

Free house ~ Licensee Jeremy McKay ~ Real ale ~ Bar food (12-2.15, 6.30-9.30; 12-3, 7-8.30 Sun) ~ Restaurant ~ (01264) 730229 ~ Children welcome ~ Dogs allowed in bar and one bedroom ~ Open 11.30-3, 6-11; 12-4, 7-10.30 Sun ~ Bedrooms: £60S/£70S

Recommended by Henry Midwinter, Ian Herdman, John Coatsworth, Mr and Mrs H J Langley, John Walker

LUCKINGTON Wiltshire   ST8384   Map 2

Old Royal Ship £

Off B4040 SW of Malmesbury; SN14 6PA

Friendly pub by the village green, with a fair choice of drinks and decent bar food

You can be sure of a genial welcome in this pleasant old pub right beside the village green. It's been opened up inside and there's effectively one long bar divided into three areas with a central counter serving Bass, Stonehenge Pigswill, Wadworths 6X and Wickwar Coopers WPA on handpump, a farm cider and a dozen wines by the glass. On the right are neat tables, spindleback chairs and small cushioned settles on dark bare boards, with a small open fireplace and some stripped masonry. Skittle alley, games machine and piped music. The garden beyond the car park has boules, a play area with a big wooden climbing frame and plenty of seats on the terrace or grass. Badminton House is close by.

Bar food includes sandwiches, garlic mushrooms, scampi, chicken with a white wine and stilton sauce, and specials such as sausage and eggs, steak in ale pie, and beer-battered cod. *Benchmark main dish: ham, egg and chips £8.75. Two-course evening meal £17.50.*

Free house ~ Licensee Helen Johnson-Greening ~ Real ale ~ Bar food (12-2.15, 6(7 Sun) -9.15) ~ Restaurant ~ (01666) 840222 ~ Live jazz second Weds of month ~ Open 11.30-3, 6-11; 11.30-11 Sat; 12-4, 7-10.30 Sun

Recommended by John and Gloria Isaacs

LUXBOROUGH Somerset   SS9837   Map 1

Royal Oak 🍴 ⇌

Kingsbridge; S of Dunster on minor roads into Brendon Hills – OS Sheet 181 map reference 983378; TA23 0SH

Smashing place in wonderful countryside, interesting bar and restaurant food, local beers and ciders and attentive, friendly staff; warm, comfortable bedrooms

In the heart of Exmoor, this is an exceptionally enjoyable place to stay for a few days and there are memorable nearby walks in the wonderful surrounding countryside; the Coleridge Way is popular. There's always a really good mix of chatty locals (often with their dogs) and visitors and you can be sure of a genuinely warm welcome from the landlord and his helpful staff. The compact bar, which has the most character and a relaxed, cheerful atmosphere, has lovely ancient flagstones, several rather fine settles (one with a very high back and one still with its book rest), scrubbed kitchen tables, lots of beer mats on beams, a cart horse saddle and a huge brick fireplace with a warm log fire; a simpler back room has an ancient cobbled floor, some quarry tiles and a stone fireplace. One room just off the bar is set for dining, with attractive old pine furniture and horse and hunting prints, and there are two dining rooms as well. One is green painted and a larger end one has stuffed fish in glass cabinets, fish paintings and fishing rods on the dark red walls, leather and brass-tack dining chairs and more formal ones around quite a mix of old tables, with turkish-style rugs on the black slate floor. Exmoor Ale and Gold and a couple of guests such as Cotleigh Tawny Owl and Old Hooker on handpump, 14 wines by the glass and Thatcher's and Rich's farmhouse cider; darts and board games. There are some seats out in the charming back courtyard.

Using lamb and beef from nearby farms and seasonal local game, the reliably good food might include lunchtime sandwiches, potted sea trout with crisp onion bread, fresh linguine with an oyster mushroom and sage cream, smoked haddock risotto, roast rump of salt marsh lamb with orange and coriander gremolata, and confit duck leg with watercress and smoked bacon. *Benchmark main dish: chilli-glazed belly of pork £14.25. Two-course evening meal £21.45.*

Free house ~ Licensees James and Sian Waller ~ Real ale ~ Bar food ~ Restaurant ~ (01984) 640319 ~ Children must be over 10 in evening and in bedrooms ~ Dogs allowed in bar and bedrooms ~ Open 12-2.30, 6-11 (all day weekends and school holidays); 12-11 Sat and Sun ~ Bedrooms: £60B/£90S(£65B)

Recommended by Barry and Anne, Bob and Margaret Holder, Ewan and Moira McCall, the Didler, M G Hart, Adrian Johnson, David Jackman, Stephen Bennett, S G N Bennett, Walter and Susan Rinaldi-Butcher, the Farmers, John and Joan Nash

---

'Children welcome' means the pub says it lets children inside without any special restriction. If it allows them in, but to restricted areas such as an eating area or family room, we specify this. Some pubs may impose an evening time limit. We do not mention limits after 9pm as we assume children are home by then.

MANTON Wiltshire   SU1768   Map 2

Outside Chance ♀

Village (and pub) signposted off A4 just W of Marlborough; High Street; SN8 4HW

Popular dining pub, civilised and traditional, nicely reworked with interesting sporting theme

Chatty drinkers and walkers (and their dogs) are just as welcome in this smart dining pub as those here to enjoy the popular food. The three small linked rooms have a thriving atmosphere, flagstones or bare boards, hops on beams, and mainly plain pub furnishings such as chapel chairs and a long-cushioned pew; one room has a more cosseted feel, with panelling and a comfortable banquette. The décor celebrates unlikely winners, such as 100-1 Grand National winners like Coughoo or Fuinavon, Mr Spooner's Only Dreams (a 100-1 winner at Leicester in 2007), or the odd-gaited little Seabiscuit who cheered many thousands of Americans with his dogged pursuit of victory during the Depression years. The lighting is soft (nightlights on tables), the pub is usually full of fresh flowers and there's a splendid log fire in the big main fireplace; piped music and board games. Wadworths IPA and 6X and guests such as Bishops Tipple and Swordfish on handpump, quite a few good wines by the glass, nicely served coffees, and neatly dressed young staff. A suntrap side terrace has contemporary metal-framed granite-topped tables and the good-sized garden has sturdy rustic tables and benches under ash trees. The garden opens into the local playing fields with a children's play area.

Good bar food includes sandwiches, lunchtime eggs benedict, home-made burger with cheese, chicken caesar salad, seafood tagliatelle and specials like venison steak with peppercorn sauce, and grilled sole with brown shrimp and chive butter. *Benchmark main dish: home-made burger £10.00. Two-course evening meal £16.95.*

Wadworths ~ Lease Hannah Lampard ~ Real ale ~ Bar food ~ Restaurant ~ (01672) 512352 ~ Children welcome ~ Dogs welcome ~ Bridge Mon evening ~ Open 12-3, 5.30-11.30; 12-11.30 Sat and Sun

Recommended by Guy Vowles, Andrew Tollington, Ian Herdman, Sheila and Robert Robinson, Ian and Rose Lock, Mr and Mrs A Curry

MEAVY Devon   SX5467   Map 1

Royal Oak

Off B3212 E of Yelverton; PL20 6PJ

Pleasant old pub with plenty of character, country furnishings, and popular food and drink

This partly 15th-c pub takes its name from the 800-year-old oak tree on the village green opposite. The heavy-beamed L-shaped bar has pews from the church, red plush banquettes, and old agricultural prints and church pictures on the walls; a smaller bar – where the locals like to gather – has flagstones, a big open hearth fireplace and side bread oven. There's also a separate dining room. Dartmoor Brewery Jail Ale and IPA, Sharps Doom Bar and a weekly guest like Wadworths 6X on handpump, farm ciders, a dozen wines by the glass and quite a few malt whiskies; piped music, cribbage and board games. This is a pretty Dartmoor-edge village and there are picnic-sets in front of the pub and on the green. They hold regular events.

Using Dartmoor lamb and beef, the well liked bar food includes filled baguettes, chicken liver pâté, steak in ale pie, mushroom and goats cheese tartlets, bangers and mash, and cajun chicken; they hold Wednesday pie nights and Friday fish and chips evenings. *Benchmark main dish: beer-battered cod and chips £9.95. Two-course evening meal £15.45.*

Free house ~ Licensee Steve Earp ~ Real ale ~ Bar food (12-3, 6-9) ~ Restaurant ~ (01822) 852944 ~ Children in lounge bar only ~ Dogs allowed in bar ~ Open 11-11 (midnight Sat); 11-3, 6-11 weekdays in winter
Recommended by Michael and Joan Johnstone, Peter Thornton, Jacquie Jones

 MIDDLEMARSH Dorset ST6607 Map 2

Hunters Moon
A352 Sherborne—Dorchester; DT9 5QN

Plenty of bric-a-brac in several linked areas, reasonably priced food and a good choice of drinks; comfortable bedrooms

This is a smashing place to stay overnight – with or without your dog – in warm and comfortable bedrooms and you can be sure of a genuinely friendly welcome from the hands-on licensees and their helpful staff; the breakfasts are excellent. It's a former coaching inn with comfortably traditional beamed bar rooms cosily filled with a great variety of tables and chairs on red patterned carpets and an array of ornamentation from horsebrasses up; lighting is by converted oil lamps. Booths are formed by some attractively cushioned settles, walls comprise exposed brick, stone and some panelling and there are three log fires (one in a capacious inglenook); piped music, children's books and toys and board games. Butcombe Bitter and Greene King Old Speckled Hen on handpump and farm cider, while all their wines are available by the glass. A neat lawn has circular picnic-sets as well as the more usual ones.

 Good bar food includes lunchtime filled baguettes, cheesy garlic mushrooms, pizzas, pasta with smoked salmon and black pepper or wild mushroom and oregano, a popular pie of the day, slow-roasted lamb shank in a rosemary and wine sauce, and daily specials; they do offer some dishes in smaller or larger sizes. *Benchmark main dish: home-made pie £9.95. Two-course evening meal £16.00.*

Enterprise ~ Lease Dean and Emma Mortimer ~ Real ale ~ Bar food (12-2, 6-9) ~ (01963) 210966 ~ Children welcome ~ Dogs welcome ~ Open 10.30-2.30, 6-11(10.30 in winter); 10.30-10.30(11 Sat in summer) weekends ~ Bedrooms: £65S/£75S
Recommended by Ann and Colin Hunt, Mr and Mrs W Mills

MORWENSTOW Cornwall SS2015 Map 1

Bush
Signed off A39 N of Kilkhampton; Crosstown; EX23 9SR

Friendly, ancient pub in fine spot, character bar and airy dining rooms, real ales, carefully sourced produce for well liked food, and seats outside; bedrooms

Much used by walkers, this ancient place is just off the South West Coast Path and only ten minutes from Vicarage Cliff, one of the grandest parts of the Cornish coast (with 400-ft precipices). The bar has some proper character with old built-in settles, flagstones, a woodburning stove in the big stone fireplace, horse tack, lots of brass and copper knick-knacks; St Austell HSD and Tribute and Skinners Betty

Stogs on handpump and farm cider. Other rooms are set for dining with pale wooden dining chairs and tables, pictures on creamy yellow walls, beams and fresh flowers; the dining room has big windows overlooking the picnic-sets on the grass outside and they now have a couple of heated dining huts overlooking the ocean. As well as bedrooms, they offer self-catering, too. This was once a monastic rest house on a pilgrim route between Wales and Spain.

Using beef from their own farm and other local produce, bar food includes sandwiches, sausages with onion gravy, red wine and blue cheese risotto, beer-battered pollack, john dory with capers and brown butter, and tarragon chicken wrapped in parma ham with jerusalem artichoke purée. *Benchmark main dish: beer battered fish and chips £10.50. Two-course evening meal £18.50.*

Free house ~ Licensees Rob and Edwina Tape ~ Real ale ~ Bar food (all day) ~ Restaurant ~ (01288) 331242 ~ Children welcome ~ Dogs allowed in bar and bedrooms ~ Occasional live music ~ Open 11-11 ~ Bedrooms: £47.50S/£85S

Recommended by Christian Mole, Barry and Anne, Anthony Bradbury, Dr and Mrs M W A Haward, the Didler, Mike and Sue Loseby, R K Phillips, Lois Dyer

 MUDEFORD Dorset   SZ1792   Map 2

Ship in Distress
Stanpit; off B3059 at roundabout; BH23 3NA

Wide choice of fish dishes, quirky nautical décor, and a friendly staff in cheerful cottage

Much more fun inside than the unassuming exterior suggests, this former smugglers' pub is full of entertaining nautical bits and pieces. There's everything from rope fancywork and brassware through lanterns, oars, to an aquarium, boat models (we particularly like the Mississippi steamboat) and the odd piratical figure; darts, games machine, board games, a big screen TV, piped music and a winter woodburning stove. Besides a good few boat pictures, the room on the right has tables with masses of snapshots of locals caught up in various waterside japes under the glass tabletops; Ringwood Best and guests such as Brains Rev James and St Austell Tribute on handpump alongside several wines by the glass. A spreading two-room restaurant area, as cheerful in its way as the bar, has a fish tank, contemporary works by local artists for sale, and a light-hearted mural sketching out the impression of a window open on a sunny boating scene. There are seats and tables out on the suntrap back terrace and a covered heated area for chillier evenings. The pub is near to Mudeford Quay and Stanpit Nature Reserve is close by.

As well as a good value two-course set lunch menu, the bar food includes lunchtime sandwiches, cottage pie and gammon, but most emphasis is on the good fresh local fish: fish soup, diver-caught scallops with a saffron cream sauce, beer-battered cod, lemon sole, and whole crab and lobster. *Benchmark main dish: bass with saffron cream sauce £16.50. Two-course evening meal £20.00.*

Punch ~ Lease Maggie Wheeler ~ Real ale ~ Bar food ~ Restaurant ~ (01202) 485123 ~ Children welcome ~ Dogs allowed in bar ~ Open 11am-midnight(11pm Sun)

Recommended by Victor Craven, Hans Becker, I D Barnett

Real ale to us means beer which has matured naturally in its cask –
not pressurised or filtered.

NETTLECOMBE Dorset   SY5195 Map 2

Marquis of Lorne ◀

Off A3066 Bridport—Beaminster, via West Milton; DT6 3SY

Attractive country pub with enjoyable food and drink, friendly licensees, and seats in the large mature garden; redecorated bedrooms

In deep and unspoilt countryside, this attractive pub is within walking distance of Eggardon Hill, one of Dorset's most spectacular Iron Age hill forts. The traditional bars and dining rooms are named after local hills and have been smartened up recently. The comfortable bustling main bar has a log fire, mahogany panelling and old prints and photographs around its neatly matching chairs and tables; two dining areas lead off, the smaller of which has another log fire. The wooden-floored snug (liked by locals) has board games, table skittles and piped music. Palmers Best, Copper and 200 on handpump and a dozen wines by the glass from a decent list. A lovely big mature garden is full of pretty herbaceous borders, there are picnic-sets under apple trees and a rustic-style play area. The bedrooms have been redecorated this year.

Popular bar food using local produce includes sandwiches, soft herring roes with capers and parsley on home-made fried sour dough bread, duck liver and pistachio pâté with spiced pears, lentil, cheese and spinach loaf with roast tomato sauce, lasagne, mustard and sugar-baked ham and eggs, and bass with creamed prawn velouté. *Benchmark main dish: lambs liver £11.00. Two-course evening meal £17.25.*

Palmers ~ Tenants Stephen and Tracey Brady ~ Real ale ~ Bar food (12-2, 6-9.30) ~ Restaurant ~ (01308) 485236 ~ Children welcome ~ Dogs allowed in bar ~ Open 12-3(2.30 winter), 6-11 ~ Bedrooms: £66B/£90S(£90B)

Recommended by Steve Derbyshire, Mike and Lynn Robinson, Mr and Mrs P R Thomas, Matthew Beard, David and Jane Hill, B and M Kendall

NEWTON TONY Wiltshire   SU2140 Map 2

Malet Arms 🍴 ◀

Village signposted off A338 Swindon—Salisbury; SP4 0HF

Smashing village pub with no pretensions, a good choice of local beers and highly thought-of food

Quite unpretentious and with plenty of character, this friendly place is run with much enthusiasm by the cheerful landlord. The two low-beamed interconnecting rooms have nice furnishings, including a mix of different-sized tables with high-winged wall settles, carved pews, chapel and carver chairs, and lots of pictures, mainly from imperial days. The main front windows are said to have come from the stern of a ship, and there's a log and coal fire in a huge fireplace. At the back is a homely dining room. Four real ales are well kept on handpump from breweries such as Andwell, Butcombe, Itchen Valley, Plain Ales, Ramsbury and Stonehenge; they also have 24 malt whiskies, 11 wines by the glass and Weston's Old Rosie cider. The small front terrace has old-fashioned garden seats and some picnic-sets on the grass, and there are more tables in the back garden, along with a wendy house. There's also a little aviary and a horse paddock behind. Getting to the pub takes you through a ford and it may be best to use an alternative route in winter, as it can be quite deep. There's now an all-weather cricket pitch on the village green.

Using lamb raised in the surrounding fields, lots of seasonal game (bagged by the landlord), their own pigs and baking their own bread, the enjoyable, interesting food might include pressed pork shoulder terrine with real ale chutney, popular breaded whitebait, pork, honey and watercress sausages, goats cheese and stinging nettle tart, beer-battered haddock with home-made tartare sauce, and spicy cajun chicken with sour cream; they hold monthly curry and pie nights. *Benchmark main dish: home-made burger £8.95. Two-course evening meal £17.00.*

Free house ~ Licensee Noel Cardew ~ Real ale ~ Bar food (12-2.30, 6.30-10 (6-9 Sun)) ~ Restaurant ~ (01980) 629279 ~ Children in restaurant only ~ Dogs allowed in bar ~ Open 11-3, 6-11; 12-3, 6 (7 in winter)-10.30 Sun; closed 25 and 26 Dec, 1 Jan

Recommended by P Waterman, John Prescott, B and M Kendall, Bren and Val Speed, Lois Dyer, Andrea Rampley, Paul Goldman, B J Harding, Peter Dandy, Ian Herdman, N R White, Richard and Sue Fewkes

NORTON Wiltshire   ST8884 Map 2

Vine Tree 🍴 ⅛

4 miles from M4 junction 17; A429 towards Malmesbury, then left at Hullavington, Sherston signpost, then follow Norton signposts; in village turn right at Foxley signpost, which takes you into Honey Lane; SN16 0JP

Civilised dining pub, beams and candlelight, big choice of seasonal food, super wines (including their own shop), and a sizeable garden

With so much to do and see nearby (from Westonbirt Arboretum and other fine gardens and houses to race courses and the county's official cycle route), it's not surprising that this well run pub is always pretty busy; they host all sorts of events, too. Three neatly kept little rooms open into each other, with aged beams, some old settles and unvarnished wooden tables on the flagstone floors, big cream church altar candles, a woodburning stove at one end of the restaurant and a large open fireplace in the central bar and limited edition and sporting prints; look out for Clementine, the friendly and docile black labrador. Butcombe Bitter and St Austell Tinners and a guest like Stonehenge Pigswill or Uley Bitter on handpump, 48 wines by the glass including sparkling wines and champagne (and they have their own wine shop, too), and quite a choice of malt whiskies and armagnacs. There are picnic-sets and a children's play area in a two-acre garden plus a pretty suntrap terrace with teak furniture under big cream umbrellas, and an attractive smoking shelter.

Quite a choice of interesting bar food might include sandwiches, home-made pork pies and duck scotch eggs, home-baked honey and mustard ham with eggs, pigeon and black pudding sausage with robust gravy, tomato and red onion tarte tatin with goats cheese, beer-battered whiting with minted pea purée, organic home-made chicken kiev, and all manner of fresh fish and seafood dishes. *Benchmark main dish: seared local venison steak with beetroot confit and game jus £18.95. Two-course evening meal £22.90.*

Free house ~ Licensees Charles Walker and Tiggi Wood ~ Real ale ~ Bar food (12-2.30(3.15 Sun), 7-9.30(10 Fri and Sat)) ~ Restaurant ~ (01666) 837654 ~ Well behaved children welcome ~ Dogs allowed in bar ~ Live jazz and blues on terrace some days in summer ~ Open 12-3-ish(4 Sat), 6-midnight; may open all day weekends

Recommended by Neil and Karen Dignan, Mr and Mrs A H Young, Peter and Audrey Dowsett, Rod Stoneman, Jennifer and Patrick O'Dell

You can send reports directly to us at **feedback@goodguides.com**

NORTON ST PHILIP Somerset   ST7755 Map 2

George ⇐

A366; BA2 7LH

Wonderful ancient building full of history and interest with well liked food, real ales, wines by the glass, and characterful bedrooms

It's worth visiting this exceptional building to take in the fine surroundings of a place that has been offering hospitality to travellers for 700 years. The central Norton Room, which was the original bar, has really heavy beams, an oak-panelled settle and solid dining chairs on the narrow strip wooden floor, a variety of 18th-c pictures, an open fire in the handsome stone fireplace and a low wooden bar counter. Wadworths IPA, Bishops Tipple, 6X and Swordfish on handpump and 25 wines by the glass. As you enter the building, there's a room on the right with high dark beams, squared dark half-panelling, a broad carved stone fireplace with an old iron fireback and pewter plates on the mantelpiece, a big mullioned window with leaded lights and a round oak 17th-c table reputed to have been used by the Duke of Monmouth who stayed here before the Battle of Sedgemoor; after their defeat, his men were imprisoned in what is now the Monmouth Bar. The Charterhouse Bar is mostly used by those enjoying a drink before a meal: a wonderful pitched ceiling with trusses and timbering, heraldic shields and standards, jousting lances and swords on the walls, a fine old stone fireplace, high-backed cushioned heraldic-fabric dining chairs on the big rug over the wood plank floor and an oak dresser with some pewter. The dining room (a restored barn with original oak ceiling beams, a pleasant if haphazard mix of early 19th-c portraits and hunting prints and the same mix of vaguely old-looking furnishings) has a good relaxing, chatty atmosphere; piped music. The bedrooms are very atmospheric and comfortable – some reached by an external Norman stone stair-turret and some across the cobbled and flagstoned courtyard and up into a fine half-timbered upper gallery (where there's a lovely 18th-c carved oak settle); note there's a £10 charge for dogs. A stroll over the meadow behind the pub (past the picnic-sets on the narrow grass pub garden) leads you to an attractive churchyard around the medieval church whose bells struck Pepys (here on 12 June 1668) as 'mighty tuneable'.

Under the new licensees, bar food includes filled ciabattas, duck and orange terrine, leek and mushroom bake, ham and egg with bubble and squeak, steak and mushroom in ale pie, lamb rump with rosemary and whisky gravy, and venison wellington. *Benchmark main dish: venison wellington £17.95. Two-course evening meal £17.50.*

Wadworths ~ Managers Eddy and Lisa Hoogervorst ~ Real ale ~ Bar food (11.30 (12 Sun) -9(9.30 Fri and Sat)) ~ Restaurant ~ (01373) 834224 ~ Children welcome ~ Dogs allowed in bar and bedrooms ~ Open 11-11; 12-10.30 Sun ~ Bedrooms: £65B/£90B

Recommended by Roger and Donna Huggins, John and Joan Nash, the Didler, Bruce and Sharon Eden

Bedroom prices normally include full english breakfast, VAT and any inclusive service charge that we know of. Prices before the '/' are for single rooms, after the '/' for two people in a double or twin (B includes a private bath, S a private shower). If there is no '/', the prices are only for twin or double rooms (as far as we know there are no singles). If there is no B or S, as far as we know no rooms have private facilities.

ODCOMBE Somerset   ST5015 Map 2

Masons Arms

Off A3088 or A30 just W of Yeovil; Lower Odcombe; BA22 8TX

Well run and pretty village pub with plenty of customers, friendly staff, own-brew beers, and well liked food; good bedrooms

Well worth a diversion from the A303 or A30, this pretty thatched cottage has a genuinely cheerful atmosphere and a good mix of customers. The homely little bar has joists and a couple of standing timbers, a mix of cushioned dining chairs around all sorts of tables (each with a little glass oil lamp, lit at night) on the cream and blue patterned carpet and a couple of tub chairs and a table in the former inglenook fireplace. Up a step is a similar area and more steps down lead to a dining room with a squashy brown sofa and a couple of cushioned dining chairs in front of the woodburning stove; the sandstone walls are hung with black and white local photographs and country prints. Friendly, chatty staff serve their own-brewed ales – Odcombe No 1, Spring, Roly Poly and seasonal beers on handpump – and they also make their own sloe and elderflower cordials. The garden has a good, thatched smokers' shelter and picnic-sets on some grass, and at the bottom there's a vegetable patch, some chickens and rabbits, and a campsite. The bedrooms are well equipped and comfortable and the breakfasts are hearty.

Well liked bar food includes open ciabattas, tom yum prawns with coconut bread, a pie of the day, ham and free-range duck egg, curried vegetable and sweet potato puff pastry parcel, pork fillet with wild mushroom sauce, and bass with chilli, lime and garlic. *Benchmark main dish: fishcakes £8.50. Two-course evening meal £18.75.*

Own brew ~ Licensees Drew Read and Paula Tennyson ~ Real ale ~ Bar food (12-2, 6.30-9.30) ~ (01935) 862591 ~ Dogs welcome ~ Open 12-3.30, 6-midnight ~ Bedrooms: £55S/£85B

Recommended by John Cunningham, Nigel Fortnam, Dennis Jenkin

 PENZANCE Cornwall   SW4730 Map 1

Turks Head

At top of main street, by big domed building (Lloyds TSB), turn left down *Chapel Street; TR18 4AF*

Cheerfully run pub with a good, bustling atmosphere and decent food and beer

This is the oldest pub in town and has always been popular with both locals and visitors – there's a friendly welcome for all. The bar has old flat irons, jugs and so forth hanging from the beams, pottery above the wood-effect panelling, wall seats and tables and a couple of elbow-rests around central pillars; piped music. Sharps Doom Bar, Skinners Betty Stogs and guest beers such as Hook Norton Old Hooky and Wychwood Hobgoblin on handpump served by helpful staff. The suntrap back garden has big urns of flowers. There has been a Turks Head here for over 700 years – though most of the original building was destroyed by a Spanish raiding party in the 16th century.

Tasty bar food includes lunchtime sandwiches, pork and leek sausages, honey and mustard ham with eggs, butternut squash, spinach and sweet potato curry, and local fish and chips. *Benchmark main dish: local fish and chips £7.95. Two-course evening meal £15.95.*

Punch ~ Lease Jonathan and Helen Gibbard ~ Real ale ~ Bar food ~ Restaurant ~
(01736) 363093 ~ Children welcome ~ Dogs welcome ~ Open 11am-midnight; 12-11 Sun

*Recommended by Richard Stanfield, B and M Kendall, Giles and Annie Francis, P Dawn, R T and
J C Moggridge, Alan Johnson*

 PERRANUTHNOE Cornwall   SW5329   Map 1

Victoria

Signed off A394 Penzance—Helston; TR20 9NP

**Carefully furnished inn close to Mount's Bay beaches, friendly welcome,
local beers, interesting fresh food, and seats in pretty garden; bedrooms**

Our readers enjoy their visits to this bustling and friendly village
pub very much – it's best to book a table in advance if dining. The
L-shaped bar is full of both regulars and visitors and there's an informal
atmosphere, various cosy corners, exposed joists, a woodburning stove,
an attractive mix of dining chairs around wooden tables on the oak
flooring, china plates, all sorts of artwork on the walls and fresh flowers.
The restaurant is separate. Sharps Doom Bar and Skinners Betty Stogs on
handpump and several wines by the glass; piped music. The pub labrador
is called Bailey. The pretty tiered garden has white metal furniture under
green parasols and the beaches of Mount's Bay are a couple of minutes'
stroll away.

Good, popular bar food includes lunchtime sandwiches, crispy pollack goujons
with spicy tomato ketchup, game pâté with port jelly and raisin toast,
mushroom, herb and rocket risotto with goats cheese, hake with garlic, parsley,
chorizo and chickpea stew, and pork fillet with black and hog's puddings, pork
cheek bubble and squeak. *Benchmark main dish: pork belly £14.95. Two-course
evening meal £20.95.*

Pubfolio ~ Lease Anna and Stewart Eddy ~ Real ale ~ Bar food (12-2(3 Sun), 6.30-9; not
Sun evening or winter Mon) ~ Restaurant ~ (01736) 710309 ~ Children welcome ~ Dogs
allowed in bar ~ Open 12-2.30(3.30 Sun), 5.30-midnight; closed Sun evening, winter Mon,
25 and 26 Dec, 1 Jan, one week in Jan ~ Bedrooms: £50S/£75S

Recommended by Clifford Blakemore, Ian Herdman, Roger and Donna Huggins, A J Ward, Jon B

 PERRANWELL Cornwall   SW7739   Map 1

Royal Oak ♀

*Village signposted off A393 Redruth—Falmouth and A39 Falmouth—Truro;
TR3 7PX*

**Welcoming and relaxed with helpful, friendly landlord, well presented
food, real ales, and thoughtful wines**

Mr Rudland is an excellent hands-on landlord who offers a warm
welcome to all. This is a pretty village pub with a gently upmarket
but relaxed atmosphere, enjoyable food and Sharps Doom Bar, IPA and
Skinners Betty Stogs on handpump, as well as good wines by the glass
and farm cider. The roomy, carpeted bar has horsebrasses and pewter
and china mugs on its black beams and joists, plates and country pictures
on the cream-painted stone walls and cosy wall and other seats around
candlelit tables. It rambles around beyond a big stone fireplace (with a
winter log fire) into a snug little nook of a room behind, with just a
couple more tables.

Listed on wooden boards in the shape of an oak tree, the good, interesting food includes lunchtime sandwiches and filled baguettes, various tapas and meze plates, home-made terrines and pâtés, a pie of the day, crab bake, and duck confit with a sweet orange and pepper marmalade; Sunday roasts are popular. *Benchmark main dish: crab bake £11.25. Two-course evening meal £20.00.*

Free house ~ Licensee Richard Rudland ~ Real ale ~ Bar food (12-2.30, 6.30-9.30) ~ Restaurant ~ (01872) 863175 ~ Children welcome ~ Dogs allowed in bar ~ Open 11-3, 6-11(midnight Sat); 12-4, 6-11 Sun

Recommended by J B Taylor, Gene and Tony Freemantle, Mr and Mrs Powers, A J Ward

PHILLEIGH Cornwall   SW8739 Map 1

GOOD PUB GUIDE

Roseland

Between A3078 and B3289, NE of St Mawes just E of King Harry Ferry; TR2 5NB

Bustling pub with real ales (and maybe their own brew), a wide mix of customers and well liked food

Handy for the King Harry Ferry and Trelissick Gardens, this is a busy little pub with quite a mix of holidaymakers and regulars of all ages. The two bar rooms (one with flagstones and the other carpeted) have wheelback chairs and built-in red cushioned seats, open fires, old photographs and some giant beetles and butterflies in glass cases. The tiny lower area is liked by regulars and there's a popular back restaurant, too. Skinners Betty Stogs, Sharps Doom Bar and maybe their own beer on handpump and several decent wines by the glass. There are seats on a pretty paved front courtyard.

Bar food includes lunchtime sandwiches, scallops with sweetcorn purée, local mussels in cider and cream, a changing risotto, liver and bacon, mackerel fillets with chorizo and salad, and chicken with spinach and wild mushroom in a tarragon cream sauce. *Benchmark main dish: beer-battered fish and chips £9.95. Two-course evening meal £17.50.*

Punch ~ Tenant Philip Heslip ~ Real ale ~ Bar food (12-2.30, 6(6.30 in winter)-9.30) ~ Restaurant ~ (01872) 580254 ~ Children welcome ~ Dogs allowed in bar ~ Open 11-3, 5-11 (all day school summer holidays)

Recommended by R K Phillips, Chris and Angela Buckell, Mrs Sheena and Emily Killick, R and S Bentley, John and Susan Miln, John and Jackie Chalcraft, Trevor Swindells

PITNEY Somerset   ST4527 Map 1

GOOD PUB GUIDE

Halfway House 🍺

Just off B3153 W of Somerton; TA10 9AB

Bustling, friendly local with up to ten real ales, local ciders, and good simple food

A new licensee has taken over this honest village local but luckily little seems to have changed. There's still an excellent range of beers tapped from the cask and changing regularly with up to ten to choose from: Art Brew Monkey IPA, Butcombe Bitter, Castle Rock Hemlock Bitter, Cheddar Ales Totty Pot, Hop Back Summer Lightning, Moor Northern Star and Union Pale, Otter Bright, RCH Pitchfork and Teignworthy Reel Ale. They also keep several local farm ciders, ten malt whiskies and several wines by the glass. No music or machines. A good mix of people are usually found chatting at communal tables in the three old-fashioned rooms, all with roaring log fires, and there's a homely feel underlined by a profusion of books, maps and newspapers; cribbage, dominoes and board games. There are tables outside.

As well as lunchtime sandwiches, the simple generous food includes filled baked potatoes, cheese and courgette bake, sausage and mash with onion gravy, lamb, chicken or beef curry, and pork in cider casserole. *Benchmark main dish: pork, bacon and apricot pie £7.95. Two-course evening meal £15.00.*

Free house ~ Licensee Mark Phillips ~ Real ale ~ Bar food (12-2.30, 7.30-9; not Sun evening) ~ (01458) 252513 ~ Children welcome ~ Dogs welcome ~ Open 11.30-3, 5.30-11(midnight Sat); 12-11 Sun

Recommended by Brian and Bett Cox, MLR, the Didler, Andrea Rampley, Bob and Margaret Holder, Patrick and Daphne Darley, B and M Kendall, Ted and Charlotte Routley, Liz and Jeremy Baker, Ken and Barbara Turner

PLUSH Dorset   ST7102 Map 2

Brace of Pheasants 🍴 ♀ 🛏

Village signposted from B3143 N of Dorchester at Piddletrenthide; DT2 7RQ

16th-c thatched pub with friendly service, three real ales, lots of wines by the glass, well liked food, and a decent garden; good nearby walks; comfortable bedrooms

Once the village smithy and two cottages, this handsome thatched place is tucked away in a pretty village. The beamed bar has a mix of locals (and maybe their dogs) and visitors, windsor chairs around good solid tables on the patterned carpet, a few standing timbers, a huge heavy-beamed inglenook at one end with cosy seating inside, and a good warming log fire at the other. Flack Manor Double Drop, Sharps Doom Bar and a guest like Palmers Copper tapped from the cask, a fine choice of wines with 18 by the glass and proper farm cider; friendly service. A decent-sized garden includes a terrace and a lawn sloping up towards a rockery. The pub is well placed for walks in beautifully folded countryside – an attractive bridleway behind goes to the left of the woods and over to Church Hill. The ensuite bedrooms are nicely fitted out and comfortable.

A shortish choice of bar food includes sandwiches, lambs kidneys with a mustard cream sauce, battered fish of the day, local faggots with onion gravy, portabello mushrooms with cream cheese and herb stuffing and red pepper yoghurt dressing, and baked hake in tomatoes, white wine and paprika. *Benchmark main dish: venison steak with red wine and redcurrant reduction £15.00. Two-course evening meal £18.00.*

Free house ~ Licensees Phil and Carol Bennett ~ Real ale ~ Bar food ~ (01300) 348357 ~ Children welcome ~ Dogs allowed in bar ~ Open 12-3, 7-11(10.30 Sun) ~ Bedrooms: £89B/£99B

Recommended by Mr and Mrs John Clifford, Tom and Rosemary Hall, D and J Ashdown, N R White, Mike and Sue Loseby, G Vyse, Phil Bryant, Mrs C Roe, John Ecklin, Barry Collett, the Didler

---

Please tell us if the décor, atmosphere, food or drink at a pub is different from our description. We rely on readers' reports to keep us up to date: **feedback@goodguides.com**, or (no stamp needed) The Good Pub Guide, FREEPOST TN1569, Wadhurst, E Sussex TN5 7BR.

POLKERRIS Cornwall   SX0952   Map 1

Rashleigh

Signposted off A3082 Fowey—St Austell; PL24 2TL

Fine beach-side spot, heaters on sizeable sun terrace, several real ales, and bar food

There's no doubt that in fine weather the biggest draw to this bustling pub is its position next to a splendid beach with its restored jetty and views towards the far side of St Austell and Mevagissey bays. The big front terrace with its heaters and awning (handy for less clement weather) makes the most of this. But on duller and colder days you can be sure of a warm welcome inside and up to five real ales on handpump: Otter Bitter, Sharps Doom Bar, Timothy Taylors Landlord and a couple of guests like St Austell HSD and Skinners Betty Stogs. The bar is cosy and the front part has comfortably cushioned seats, several wines by the glass, farm cider and organic soft drinks. The more basic back area has local photographs on brown panelling and a winter log fire, and in the restaurant, every table has a sea view. There's plenty of parking either in the pub's own car park or the large village one. The local section of the Cornish Coast Path is renowned for its striking scenery.

As well as sandwiches (the summer crab are popular), the choice of bar food might include tapas to share, steak in ale pie, chickpea, pepper and red onion curry, chicken caesar salad, and smoked haddock fishcakes. *Benchmark main dish: beer-battered cod and chips £9.50. Two-course evening meal £16.00.*

Free house ~ Licensees Jon and Samantha Spode ~ Real ale ~ Bar food (12-2, 6-9; cream teas and snacks during the afternoon) ~ Restaurant ~ (01726) 813991 ~ Children welcome ~ Dogs allowed in bar ~ Piano player Sat evening ~ Open 11-11; 12-11 Sun; may close at 10pm in winter

Recommended by Tracey and Stephen Groves, the Didler, Trevor Swindells, B and M Kendall, Anthony Wallace

POLPERRO Cornwall   SX2050   Map 1

Blue Peter

Quay Road; PL13 2QZ

Friendly pub overlooking pretty harbour, with fishing paraphernalia, and paintings by local artists

There's always a warm welcome for both locals and visitors from the licensees and their friendly staff in this bustling harbourside pub. The cosy low-beamed bar has a chatty, relaxed atmosphere, St Austell Tribute and Sharps Doom Bar and guests like Bays Gold and Otter Ale on handpump, and traditional furnishings that include a small winged settle and a polished pew on the wooden floor, fishing regalia, photographs and pictures by local artists, lots of candles and a solid wood bar counter. One window seat looks down on the harbour and another looks out past rocks to the sea; families must use the upstairs room. Piped music and TV. There are a few seats outside on the terrace and more in an upstairs amphitheatre-style area. The pub is quite small, so it does get crowded at peak times. They have a cash machine as there is no bank in the village.

Using carefully sourced produce, the well liked bar food includes sandwiches, caribbean crab cakes, popular goan chicken curry, moroccan mushrooms, enjoyable fish stew, beef in ale pie, and scallops with bacon and garlic. *Benchmark main dish: fish and chips £9.85. Two-course evening meal £15.35.*

Free house ~ Licensees Steve and Caroline Steadman ~ Real ale ~ Bar food (12-2.30, 6.30-8.30; food all day peak season) ~ (01503) 272743 ~ Children in upstairs family room only ~ Dogs welcome ~ Live music weekends ~ Open 10.30(11.30 Sun)-11.30

Recommended by Gordon Briggs, Barry Collett, the Didler, Edward Mirzoeff, Graham Oddey, Laura Rosser, Ryta Lyndley

 POOLE Dorset   SZ0391   Map 2

Cow ♀

Station Road, Ashley Cross, Parkstone; beside Parkstone Station; BH14 8UD

Interesting open-plan pub with contemporary décor, good modern food, and fine wines

Don't be put off this enjoyable pub by its slightly unpromising position by the railway station. You can be sure of a friendly welcome, some good food and up to four real ales on handpump: Fullers London Pride, Ringwood Best and Waylands Sixpenny 6D Best and a beer brewed for them by the same brewery called Cudweiser. There's also an extensive wine list with a dozen by the glass and many remarkable bottles. The pale walls of the airy bistro bar are hung with big modern cow prints done in bright pinks, yellows and blues and there are squashy sofas with huge colourful cushions and leather seating cubes arranged at low tables on stripped-wood floors; an exposed brick chimney has an open fire. Discreet flat screen TV in one corner, piped music, board games and a good array of newspapers. In the evening you can eat very well in the sizeable dining room where there are more heavy stripped tables on bare boards and plenty of wine bottles lining the window sills. Seats outside are on an enclosed and heated terrace area.

From a sensibly short menu, the good lunchtime bar food includes sandwiches, terrine of chinese spiced duck with plum chutney, haddock and chips and steak and mushroom in ale pie, with more elaborate restaurant choices like roast chicken breast, chicken and mushroom pie, smoked bacon mash and braised baby turnips, and halibut with celeriac purée, spring onion, mussels and white wine butter sauce. *Benchmark main dish: lamb two ways £16.95. Two-course evening meal £21.90.*

Free house ~ Licensee David Sax ~ Real ale ~ Bar food (12-2.30, 7-9.30; not Sun evening) ~ Restaurant ~ (01202) 749569 ~ Children allowed until 7.30pm ~ Dogs allowed in bar ~ Open 11-11.30; 12-midnight Sat; 12-10.30 Sun

Recommended by JDM, KM, Ian Herdman

PORT ISAAC Cornwall   SX0080   Map 1

Port Gaverne Inn ♀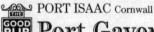

*Port Gaverne signposted from Port Isaac and from B3314 E of Pendoggett;
PL29 3SQ*

Lively bar with plenty of chatty locals in popular small hotel near the sea and fine cliff walks

There's always a good mix of both locals and visitors in the bustling small bar of this popular 17th-c inn – and many of our readers enjoy staying overnight, too. There are low beams, flagstones as well as carpeting, some exposed stone, a big log fire and a relaxed atmosphere; the lounge has some interesting antique local photographs. You can eat in the bar or the 'Captain's Cabin' – a little room where everything is shrunk to scale (old oak chest, model sailing ship, even the prints on the white stone walls). St Austell Tribute and Sharps Doom Bar and Cornish Coaster on handpump, a good wine list and several whiskies; cribbage and dominoes. There are seats in the terraced garden and splendid clifftop walks all around.

Bar food includes sandwiches, crab soup, fishcakes, vegetarian pasta, ham and eggs, battered fish of the day, and evening duck breast with herb mash and red wine and grain mustard jus. *Benchmark main dish: fish pie £9.50. Two-course evening meal £24.00.*

Free house ~ Licensee Graham Sylvester ~ Real ale ~ Bar food (12-2.30, 6.30-9) ~ Restaurant ~ (01208) 880244 ~ Children welcome ~ Dogs allowed in bar and bedrooms ~ Open 11-11; 12-10.30 Sun ~ Bedrooms: £67.50B/£115B

Recommended by Anne McCarthy, Sam Ward, Jeremy and Ruth Preston-Hoar, Peter and Judy Frost, Christopher Turner, Clifford Blakemore

PORTGATE Devon   SX4185   Map 1

Harris Arms ♀

Turn off A30 E of Launceston at Broadwoodwidger turn-off (with brown Dingle Steam Village sign), and head S; Launceston Road (old A30 between Lewdown and Lifton); EX20 4PZ

Enthusiastic, well travelled licensees in roadside pub with exceptional wine list and popular food

There are over 100 wines to choose from a fantastic wine list here – both Mr and Mrs Whiteman are qualified award-winning wine-makers. There are around 20 of their favourites by the glass and detailed, helpful notes with each wine; you can buy them to take home, too. The bar has burgundy end walls and cream ones in between, some rather fine photographs, afghan saddle-bag cushions scattered around a mixture of dining chairs and along a red plush built-in wall banquette, and a woodburning stove. On the left, steps lead down to the dining room with elegant beech dining chairs (and more afghan cushions) around stripped-wood tables, and some unusual paintings on the walls. Bays Best and Otter Ale or Sharps Doom Bar on handpump, local cider and Luscombe organic soft drinks; there may be a pile of country magazines. On a heated decked area there are seats among pots of lavender and plenty of picnic-sets in the sloping back garden looking out over the rolling wooded pasture hills. They are growing 24 vines.

Using seasonal produce from local suppliers and from their own vegetable garden and eggs from their own hens, the inventive food might include sandwiches, piri-piri prawns, twice-baked goats cheese soufflé, chicken in a beer, mushroom, shallot and cream sauce, 24-hour slow-cooked pork, and specials such as goat kid chop or coq au vin. *Benchmark main dish: slow-cooked pork belly with cider sauce £13.25. Two-course evening meal £19.45.*

Free house ~ Licensees Andy and Rowena Whiteman ~ Real ale ~ Bar food (12-2, 6.30-9; not Sun evening or Mon) ~ Restaurant ~ (01566) 783331 ~ Well behaved children welcome ~ Dogs allowed in bar ~ Open 12-3, 6.30-11; 12-3 Sun; closed Sun evening, Mon, 25 Dec, bank holidays

Recommended by Valerie and Michael Howard, Mayur Shah, Comus and Sarah Elliott, John Wooll

We include some hotels with a good bar that offers facilities comparable to those of a pub.

POSTBRIDGE Devon   SX6780 Map 1

Warren House

B3212 0.75 miles NE of Postbridge; PL20 6TA

Straightforward old pub, relaxing for a drink or meal after a Dartmoor hike

Deep in the heart of Dartmoor and built to serve the once busy tin mining community, this isolated pub is a valuable refuge after a walk. It's straightforward but friendly and the cosy bar has plenty of atmosphere. There are simple furnishings such as easy chairs and settles under the beamed ochre ceiling, old pictures of the inn on the partly panelled stone walls and dim lighting (fuelled by the pub's own generator); one of the fireplaces is said to have been kept alight almost continuously since 1845. There's also a family room. Adnams Broadside, Otter Ale and Sharps Doom Bar on handpump, local farm cider and malt whiskies; piped music, darts and board games. The picnic-sets on both sides of the road have moorland views.

 Decent bar food includes sandwiches, spinach and ricotta cannelloni, good rabbit or steak in ale pies, cajun chicken, and lamb shank in red wine and rosemary. *Benchmark main dish: rabbit pie £10.75. Two-course evening meal £15.00.*

Free house ~ Licensee Peter Parsons ~ Real ale ~ Bar food (all day but more restricted winter Mon and Tues) ~ (01822) 880208 ~ Children in family room ~ Dogs allowed in bar ~ Open 11-11; 11-5 Mon and Tues during Nov-Feb; 12-10.30 Sun
Recommended by Lois Dyer

RATTERY Devon   SX7461 Map 1

Church House

Village signposted from A385 W of Totnes, and A38 S of Buckfastleigh; TQ10 9LD

One of Britain's oldest pubs with plenty to look at, a friendly landlord, a good range of drinks, and popular bar food; peaceful views

As this is one of the country's oldest pubs there are some fine original features – notably the spiral stone steps behind a little stone doorway, on your left as you come in, that date from about 1030. It's a charming place with particularly helpful, friendly staff and plenty of character: massive oak beams and standing timbers in the homely open-plan bar, large fireplaces (one with a little cosy nook partitioned off around it), traditional pubby chairs and tables on the patterned carpet, some window seats and prints and horsebrasses on the plain white walls. The dining room is separated from this room by heavy curtains and there's a lounge area, too. Dartmoor Jail Ale and Legend, Otter Ale and Fullers Seafarers on handpump, several malt whiskies and ten wines by the glass. The garden has picnic-sets on the large hedged-in lawn and peaceful views of the partly wooded surrounding hills.

 Popular bar food includes sandwiches, crab cocktail, stilton and vegetable crumble, chicken breast wrapped in smoked bacon in a cheese and leek sauce, citrus and olive lamb shank and specials such as steak and kidney pudding, whole fresh plaice and scallops in garlic and butter. *Benchmark main dish: steak and kidney pie £9.60. Two-course evening meal £17.15.*

Free house ~ Licensee Ray Hardy ~ Real ale ~ Bar food (11.30-2, 6.30-9; not Sun

evening) ~ Restaurant ~ (01364) 642220 ~ Children welcome ~ Dogs allowed in bar ~
Open 11-2.30, 6-11; 12-3, 6-10.30 Sun

*Recommended by Geoff and Carol Thorp, Maureen Wood, Bob and Angela Brooks, Eryl and
Keith Dykes, David Jackman, Michael and Lynne Gittins, B J Harding, Hugh Roberts*

 SALISBURY Wiltshire   SU1429   Map 2

Haunch of Venison £
Minster Street, opposite Market Cross; SP1 1TB

**Ancient pub oozing history, with tiny beamed rooms, unique fittings and
a famous mummified hand; fine atmosphere and real ales**

Both the tiny downstairs rooms in this ancient pub have a great deal of
character and atmosphere and date back to 1320 when the place was
used by craftsmen working on the cathedral spire. There are massive
beams in the white ceiling, stout oak benches built into the timbered
walls, black and white floor tiles, and an open fire. A tiny snug (popular
with locals, but historically said to be where the ladies drank) opens off
the entrance lobby. Courage Best, Greene King IPA, Hop Back GFB and
Summer Lightning on handpump from a unique pewter bar counter, and
there's a rare set of antique taps for gravity-fed spirits and liqueurs.
They've also up to 100 malt whiskies and ten wines by the glass. Halfway
up the stairs is a panelled room they call the House of Lords, which has a
small-paned window looking down on to the main bar and a splendid
fireplace that dates back to the building's early years; behind glass in a
small wall slit is the smoke-preserved mummified hand of an 18th-c card
sharp still clutching his cards.

Bar food includes sandwiches, sausage and mash, stuffed aubergine and daily
specials like cottage pie, beefburger and battered cod and chips. *Benchmark
main dish: haunch of venison with rosemary and onion gravy £16.95. Two-course
evening meal £15.45.*

Scottish Courage ~ Lease Anthony Leroy and Justyna Miller ~ Real ale ~ Bar food
(12-2.30, 6-9(10 Fri and Sat)) ~ Restaurant ~ (01722) 411313 ~ Children welcome ~
Dogs allowed in bar ~ Open 11-11; 12-10.30 Sun
*Recommended by Maureen Wood, Ann and Colin Hunt, the Didler, Tim Loryman, Val and
Alan Green, A D Lealan*

 SHERBORNE Dorset   ST6316   Map 2

Digby Tap  £
Cooks Lane; park in Digby Road and walk round corner; DT9 3NS

**Regularly changing ales in simple alehouse, open all day with very
inexpensive beer and food**

Happily, nothing changes in this simple back street tavern – which is
just how our readers like it: incredibly cheap real ale, good value
food and a chatty, friendly atmosphere. The flagstoned bar is full of
character, the little games room has pool and a quiz machine and there's
also a TV room. Glastonbury Spring Loaded, Greene King IPA, Keystone
Gold Spice and Otter Bitter on handpump, several wines by the glass and
a choice of malt whiskies. There are some seats outside. Sherborne
Abbey is just a stroll away.

Good value, straightforward lunchtime food includes sandwiches, ham, egg and
chips, chilli beef and maybe liver and bacon, mixed grill, or plaice stuffed with

prawns. *Benchmark main dish: ham, egg and chips £4.20.*

Free house ~ Licensees Oliver Wilson and Nick Whigham ~ Real ale ~ Bar food (12-1.45, not Sun) ~ No credit cards ~ (01935) 813148 ~ Children welcome ~ Dogs welcome ~ Open 11-11; 12-11 Sun

Recommended by Phil and Sally Gorton, Maurice Ricketts, Mike and Sue Loseby, Ann and Colin Hunt, Tim and Sue Halstead

 SHERSTON Wiltshire　　　　　　　　　　　　　　　ST8585　Map 2

Rattlebone ♀

Church Street; B4040 Malmesbury—Chipping Sodbury; SN16 0LR

Village pub with lots of atmosphere in rambling rooms, good bar food and real ales, and friendly staff

Enjoyable and well run, this is a bustling old pub with attentive, friendly staff and a lot of character and atmosphere. The public bar has a good mix of locals and visitors and the other rambling rooms have beams, standing timbers and flagstones, pews, settles and country-kitchen chairs around a mix of tables, armchairs and sofas, and roaring fires. Bath Ales Gem Bitter, St Austell Tribute and Wells & Youngs Bitter on handpump and 14 wines by the glass. Piped music, board games, TV and games machine. Outside there's a skittle alley, two boules pitches, often in use by one of the many pub teams, a boules festival in July and mangold hurling (cattle turnip throwing). The two pretty gardens include an extended terrace where they hold barbecues and spit roasts. The pub is named after its ghost – the Saxon warrior John Rattlebone. They have wheelchair access.

Good bar food includes sandwiches, scallops with pea purée and crispy serrano ham, home-cooked ham with free-range eggs, goats cheese and roast vegetables en croûte with horseradish and beetroot relish, home-made burger with stilton and onion marmalade, rump of lamb with cucumber and olive salsa and tomato olive oil, and duck breast on spring onion mash with chilli, coriander and soy dressing. *Benchmark main dish: linguine with fresh crab, chilli and parmesan £13.50. Two-course evening meal £18.00.*

Youngs ~ Tenant Jason Read ~ Real ale ~ Bar food (12-2.30, 6-9.30; 12-3, 5.30-8 Sun) ~ Restaurant ~ (01666) 840871 ~ Children welcome (in bar until 7pm unless eating) ~ Dogs allowed in bar ~ Open 12-3, 5-11(midnight Fri); 12-midnight(11 Sun) Sat

Recommended by Tom and Ruth Rees, Bob and Angela Brooks, John and Gloria Isaacs, Chris and Angela Buckell, Barry and Anne

 SHROTON Dorset　　　　　　　　　　　　　　　ST8512　Map 2

Cricketers ◖

Off A350 N of Blandford (village also called Iwerne Courtney); follow signs; DT11 8QD

Well run country pub with friendly staff, well liked food, and four real ales; walks and nice views nearby

New licensees have taken over this red brick country pub and reports from our readers have been warmly enthusiastic. The bright divided bar has good quality old furniture, a big stone fireplace, alcoves and cricketing memorabilia and is kept pubby by serving Butcombe Bitter, St Austell Tribute and guests like Isle of Purbeck Best and Solar Power on handpump; eight wines by the glass and friendly, helpful service. The comfortable back restaurant overlooks the garden and has a fresh neutral décor; piped music. The garden is secluded and pretty with big sturdy tables under cocktail parasols, well tended shrubs and a well stocked (and well used) herb garden by the kitchen door. The pub sits right on the Wessex Ridgeway and is overlooked by the formidable Iron Age grassy ramparts of Hambledon Hill which gradually descends down to become the village cricket pitch in front of the pub. Walkers are welcome if they leave their walking boots outside. Please note, they no longer provide bedrooms.

Well liked bar food includes lunchtime sandwiches, creamy asparagus pasta, liver and bacon with chive mash and onion gravy, sausages of the week, beer-battered cod, honey-roast duckling and ballottine of chicken with a smoked bacon cream sauce. *Benchmark main dish: roast pork belly £10.95. Two-course evening meal £15.50.*

Heartstone Inns ~ Licensees Joe and Sally Grieves ~ Real ale ~ Bar food (12-2.30, 6.30-9.30(6-8 Sun)) ~ Restaurant ~ (01258) 860421 ~ Children welcome ~ Open 12-11(10.30 Sun); 12-3, 6-11 in winter

Recommended by Mrs C Roe, Clare West, Robert Watt, Bruce and Penny Wilkie, Dr and Mrs A K Clarke, Paul Goldman

SIDBURY Devon   SY1496 Map 1

Hare & Hounds ◖

3 miles N of Sidbury, at Putts Corner; A375 towards Honiton, crossroads with B3174; EX10 0QQ

Large, well run roadside pub with log fires, beams and attractive layout, popular daily carvery, efficient staff, and a big garden

Usefully serving food all day this sizeable roadside pub is a friendly, well run place.There are two log fires (and rather unusual wood-framed leather sofas complete with pouffes), heavy beams and fresh flowers, plenty of tables with red plush-cushioned dining chairs, window seats and a long bar with well used bar stools. It's mostly carpeted, with bare boards and stripped-stone walls at one end and they keep Branscombe Vale Branoc and Otter Ale and Bitter tapped from the cask. At the opposite end, on the left, another dining area has french windows leading out to a large marquee providing extra seating. The big garden, giving marvellous views down the Sid Valley to the sea at Sidmouth, has picnic-sets and a children's play area.

Using locally sourced produce, the extensive choice of bar food includes sandwiches, a popular and very good carvery (nut roast is the vegetarian alternative), duck and orange pâté, beef or lamb and mint burgers, smoked haddock and leek fishcakes, a curry of the day and specials such as grilled mackerel or beef stroganoff. *Benchmark main dish: carvery £9.15. Two-course evening meal £14.40.*

Heartstone Inns ~ Managers Graham Cole and Lindsey Chun ~ Real ale ~ Bar food (all day) ~ (01404) 41760 ~ Children welcome ~ Dogs allowed in bar ~ Open 10am-11pm(10.30pm Sun)

Recommended by Dr Phil Putwain, Derek and Maggie Washington

People named as recommenders after top pub entries have told us that the pub should be included. But they haven't written the report – we have, after anonymous on-the-spot inspection.

SIDFORD Devon   SY1389   Map 1

Blue Ball ◖

A3052 just N of Sidmouth; EX10 9QL

Big, popular inn with friendly staff, four real ales, well liked food and a neat garden; bedrooms

This bustling and handsome thatched pub has been in the same friendly family since 1912. The central bar covers three main areas: light beams, bar stools and a nice mix of wooden dining chairs around circular tables on the patterned carpet, three log fires, prints, horsebrasses and plenty of bric-a-brac on the walls, and Bass, Otter Bitter, St Austell Tribute and Sharps Doom Bar on handpump; attentive service. The public bar has darts, games machine and board games; skittle alley and piped music. There are seats on a terrace and in the flower-filled garden and a well designed wooden smokers' gazebo. Coastal walks are only about ten minutes away.

 As well as opening early for breakfasts, the well liked bar food includes sandwiches, potted crab with cucumber salad, lentil and vegetable chilli, burger with bacon and cheese, beer-battered fish of the day, and specials like ham hock and asparagus terrine and T-bone steak with mustard, tomato and herb butter. *Benchmark main dish: steak and kidney pudding £10.50. Two-course evening meal £16.50.*

Punch ~ Lease Roger Newton ~ Real ale ~ Bar food (8-10 for breakfast, 12-2.30, 6-9; 12-3, 5-8.30 Sun) ~ Restaurant ~ (01395) 514062 ~ Children welcome away from bar ~ Dogs allowed in bar ~ Open 11-11(midnight Sat); 12-11 Sun ~ Bedrooms: £60B/£95B

Recommended by Joan and Michel Hooper-Immins, Dennis Jenkin, George Atkinson, Geoff and Carol Thorp, Sara Fulton, Roger Baker, Pat and Roger Davies, M G Hart

STANTON WICK Somerset   ST6162   Map 2

Carpenters Arms ♨ ♀ ⇌

Village signposted off A368, just W of junction with A37 S of Bristol;
BS39 4BX

Bustling warm-hearted dining pub in country setting with quite a choice of bar food, friendly staff and good drinks; comfortable bedrooms

Only ten minutes' drive to the Chew Valley, this attractive little stone inn is on a quiet country lane. There are picnic-sets on the front terrace and pretty flower beds, hanging baskets and tubs. Inside, Coopers Parlour on the right has one or two beams, seats around heavy tables on the tartan carpet and attractive curtains and window plants; on the angle between here and the bar area, there's a fat woodburning stove in an opened-through corner fireplace. The bar has wood-backed wall settles with cushions, stripped-stone walls and a big log fire in an inglenook. There's also a snug inner room (lightened by mirrors in arched 'windows') and a restaurant with leather sofas and easy chairs in a comfortable lounge area. Butcombe Bitter, Courage Best and Sharps Doom Bar on handpump, good wines by the glass and several malt whiskies; TV in the snug. The bedrooms are comfortable and well equipped.

 As well as lunchtime pubby staples like sandwiches, ham and free-range eggs and beefburger with bacon and blue cheese, the choice of food might include chicken liver and wild mushroom pâté with plum and apple chutney, prawn, mussel

and crayfish risotto, thai vegetable and coconut curry, beer-battered haddock and confit duck leg on thyme rösti with red wine sauce. *Benchmark main dish: chicken filled with Boursin and wrapped in parma ham with mushroom and chestnut cream sauce £14.95. Two-course evening meal £19.90.*

Free house ~ Licensee Simon Pledge ~ Real ale ~ Bar food (12-2, 6-9.30(10 Fri and Sat); 12-9 Sun) ~ Restaurant ~ (01761) 490202 ~ Children welcome ~ Dogs allowed in bar ~ Open 11-11; 12-10.30 Sun; closed evenings 25 and 26 Dec and 1 Jan ~ Bedrooms: £72.50B/£105B

Recommended by JCW, Michael Doswell, Bob and Angela Brooks, Ian Malone, M G Hart, Dick Withington

 STAVERTON Devon   SX7964 Map 1

Sea Trout
Village signposted from A384 NW of Totnes; TQ9 6PA

Hard-working, enthusiastic licensees in bustling village inn, real ales, enjoyable food and seats in garden; comfortable bedrooms

Our readers have very much enjoyed staying overnight in the spotless and attractively decorated bedrooms in this partly 15th-c village inn – and the breakfasts are good and generous. The licensees and their staff are genuinely welcoming and the atmosphere throughout is friendly and bustling. The neatly kept and rambling beamed lounge bar has sea trout and salmon flies and stuffed fish on the walls and elegant armed wheelbacks around a mix of wooden tables on the part-carpeted, part-wooden floor. The locals' bar is simpler with wooden wall and other seats, a stag's head, a gun and horsebrasses on the walls, a large stuffed fish in a cabinet above the woodburning stove and a cheerful mix of locals and visitors. Palmers Best, Copper Ale and 200 on handpump and nine wines by the glass. The panelled restaurant and conservatory are both furnished with smart high-backed fabric dining chairs around more wooden tables. There are seats in the terraced garden and the bedrooms either overlook this or the country lane; lots to do and see nearby. They are kind to dogs with treats and water bowls dotted about the garden. You can fish on the nearby River Dart and the inn offers packages to fishermen that include accommodation and daily tickets.

Enjoyable bar food includes lunchtime sandwiches, confit duck terrine with plum and fig chutney and toasted date and walnut bread, wild mushroom tortellini with tomato and herb sauce, beer-battered fish and chips, venison and ale suet pudding and sea trout fillet with asparagus, leek and sunblush tomato risotto. *Benchmark main dish: slow-cooked pork belly with chorizo and apple and ginger relish £13.95. Two-course evening meal £19.50.*

Palmers ~ Tenants Jason and Samantha Price ~ Real ale ~ Bar food (12-2(3 Sun), 6(7 Sun)-9) ~ Restaurant ~ (01803) 762274 ~ Children welcome ~ Dogs allowed in bar and bedrooms ~ Open 9am-11pm(midnight Sat, 10.30 Sun) ~ Bedrooms: £65S/£102S

Recommended by Danny Savage, Bob Duxbury, Alan Sutton, George Price, Karen Skinner

---

'Children welcome' means the pub says it lets children inside without any special restriction. If it allows them in, but to restricted areas such as an eating area or family room, we specify this. Places with separate restaurants often let children use them, and hotels usually let them into public areas such as lounges. Some pubs impose an evening time limit – let us know if you find one earlier than 9pm.

STOKE ST GREGORY Somerset

ST3527   Map 1

Rose & Crown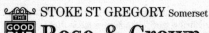

Woodhill; follow North Curry signpost off A378 by junction with A358 – keep on to Stoke, bearing right in centre, passing church and follow lane for 0.5 miles; TA3 6EW

Friendly, family-run pub with particularly good food and a fine choice of drinks; comfortable bedrooms and smashing breakfasts

The same welcoming and hard-working family have run this popular pub for over 30 years now. It's more or less open-plan and the bar area has wooden stools by a curved brick and pale wood-topped counter with Exmoor Ale and Otter Ale or Bitter on handpump, local farm cider and several wines by the glass. This leads into a long, airy dining room with all manner of light and dark wooden dining chairs and pews around a mix of tables under a high-raftered ceiling. There are two other beamed dining rooms as well, with similar furnishings and photographs on the walls of the village and the recent fire damage to the pub; one room has a woodburning stove and another has an 18th-c glass-covered well in one corner. Throughout, there are flagstoned or wooden floors. The sheltered front terrace has plenty of seats. They have three ensuite bedrooms, two of which can connect to make a family room; breakfasts are highly thought-of.

Making their own bread, jams, chutneys, sausages and salami, the generous helpings of impressive food includes lunchtime sandwiches, beer-battered haddock, stilton and mushroom vol-au-vent and steak and kidney pie, with evening choices such as somerset mussels, crispy pork belly with spiced apple and gravy, duck in an orange and Grand Marnier sauce, and bass with sweet chilli and lime. *Benchmark main dish: honey-roast ribs with barbecue sauce £11.95. Two-course evening meal £18.00.*

Free house ~ Licensees Stephen, Sally, Richard and Leonie Browning ~ Real ale ~ Bar food ~ Restaurant ~ (01823) 490296 ~ Children welcome ~ Dogs allowed in bar ~ Open 11-3, 6-11(10.30 Sun) ~ Bedrooms: £55B/£85B

Recommended by Bob and Margaret Holder, Edward Delling-Williams, Mike and Mary Carter, M G Hart, Sara Fulton, Roger Baker, Richard Cole, Dr Brian and Mrs Anne Hamilton, Dr and Mrs C W Thomas, Richard and Judy Winn, R T and J C Moggridge, Derek Goldrei

SYDLING ST NICHOLAS Dorset

SY6399   Map 2

Greyhound

Off A37 N of Dorchester; High Street; DT2 9PD

New licensees for this charming former coaching inn, country décor, real ales, wines by the glass, and imaginative food; refurbished bedrooms

Enthusiastic new licensees have taken over this charming pub in a pretty streamside village. There's a beamed and flagstoned serving area with plenty of bar stools and a carpeted bar with a comfortable mix of straightforward tables and chairs, some country decorations and a warm fire in a handsome Portland stone fireplace. Butcombe Bitter, Sydling Bitter (brewed for them by St Austell) and a changing guest such as Hop Back Summer Lightning on handpump, a farm cider, around 14 wines by the glass and several malt whiskies. The cosy, smarter dining room has a glass-covered well set into the floor (coachmen used it to pull up buckets of water for the horses during stagecoach stops) and the recently refurbished conservatory has attractive rustic furniture around scrubbed wooden tables and a green leather chesterfield. The small front garden has picnic-sets and a children's play area. The bedrooms have all been upgraded.

 Using lots of local fish and seafood, baking their own bread and making their own pasta, the imaginative food might include sandwiches, a proper bouillabaisse, rabbit terrine with red onion marmalade, tea-smoked mackerel with horseradish panna cotta, pigeon caesar salad with caramelised chicory and anchovy aioli, blue lobster and maize-fed chicken ravioli with a mussel and saffron broth, and fillet steak with a veal kidney pie and celeriac purée. *Benchmark main dish: wild bass with samphire £17.50. Two-course evening meal £21.00.*

Free house ~ Licensees Alice Draper and Helena Boot ~ Real ale ~ Bar food (12-2(2.30 Sun), 6.30-9; not Sun evening) ~ Restaurant ~ (01300) 341303 ~ Children welcome ~ Dogs allowed in bar ~ Open 12-3, 6-11; 12-3 Sun; closed Sun evening ~ Bedrooms: /£90B

Recommended by Roy Fox, Dave Hollins, Lois Dyer, Dr A McCormick, M G Hart, T R and B C Jenkins, Mr and Mrs John Clifford, John Branston, Tracey and Stephen Groves

TARRANT MONKTON Dorset   ST9408   Map 2

 # Langton Arms 🍴 🍺 🛏

Village signposted from A354, then head for church; DT11 8RX

Charming thatched pub in pretty village, with real ales in airy bars, good, popular food, friendly staff, and seats outside; comfortable bedrooms

Consistently warm praise from our readers, a delightful setting and friendly licensees all combine to make this 17th-c thatched inn a real winner. There are two comfortable bars for drinking or dining and the beamed bar has wooden tables and chairs on flagstones, plenty of old black and white photos, a light oak counter with recessed lighting, and three local real ales such as Flack Manor Double Drop, Plain Ales Inntrigue and Ringwood Best on handpump; TV in the public bar. The restaurant and conservatory are in an attractively reworked stable and the skittle alley doubles as a family room during the day; piped music. Dogs are allowed only in the Carpenters Bar and in the comfortable ensuite bedrooms (in a modern block at the back). In fine weather, you can sit out in front or at teak tables with seats in the back garden; there's also a wood-chip children's play area. The pub is next to the church and this is a charming village with a ford.

Making their own bread, ice-cream and petits fours, the interesting and carefully prepared food might include good filled baguettes, duck liver parfait and home-smoked duck breast with plum chutney, twice-baked three-cheese soufflé, venison burger with coleslaw and tomato salsa, smoked haddock and prawn gratin, and free-range chicken stuffed with leek and lemon thyme. *Benchmark main dish: steak pie £14.50. Two-course evening meal £19.45.*

Free house ~ Licensees Barbara and James Cossins ~ Real ale ~ Bar food (12-2.30, 6-9(10 Fri); all day weekends) ~ Restaurant ~ (01258) 830225 ~ Children welcome ~ Dogs allowed in bar and bedrooms ~ Open 11am-midnight; 12-11 Sun ~ Bedrooms: £70B/£90B

Recommended by Mark Sykes, Robert Watt, Leslie and Barbara Owen, Rob and Catherine Dunster, Mr and Mrs P R Thomas, Michael Doswell, Mrs C Roe

There are report forms at the back of the book.

TIPTON ST JOHN Devon   SY0991 Map 1

Golden Lion

Pub signed off B3176 Sidmouth—Ottery St Mary; EX10 0AA

Friendly village pub with three real ales, well liked bar food, a good mix of customers and plenty of seats in the attractive garden

A good mix of villagers and diners from further afield mingle quite happily in this bustling village pub – they do keep a few tables for those just wanting a pint and a chat, and have Bass and Otter Ale and Bitter on handpump and 16 wines by the glass. The main bar – which is split into two – has a comfortable, relaxed atmosphere, as does the back snug, and throughout the building there are paintings from west country artists, art deco prints, tiffany lamps, and hops, copper pots and kettles hanging from the beams; maybe piped music and board games. There's a verandah for dog walkers and smokers, seats on the terracotta-walled terrace with outside heaters and grapevines and more seats on the grass edged by pretty flowering borders; summer Sunday evening jazz out here.

 As well as lunchtime sandwiches and their popular chunky fish soup, the bar food includes moules frites, steak and kidney pudding, breast of duck with oriental sauce and specials such as whitebait, cod with tomato, feta and olives, and venison with chocolate sauce. *Benchmark main dish: chunky fish soup £7.50. Two-course evening meal £21.00.*

Heavitree ~ Tenants François and Michelle Teissier ~ Real ale ~ Bar food (12-2, 6.30-8.30; not winter Sun evening) ~ (01404) 812881 ~ Children welcome ~ Jazz summer Sun evenings ~ Open 10.30-2.30, 6-10.30; 12-3, 6.30-10 Sun; closed winter Sun evening Sept-Mar

Recommended by Roy Fox, Jane Hudson, Mrs C Roe, Mr and Mrs W Mills

TOTNES Devon   SX8059 Map 1

Steam Packet

St Peters Quay, on W bank (ie not on Steam Packet Quay); TQ9 5EW

Seats outside overlooking quay, interesting layout and décor inside, and popular food and drink; bedrooms

The seats and tables under parasols amongst the pretty flowering tubs in front of this busy pub are extremely popular in fine weather as they overlook the River Dart; there are walks along the river bank. Inside, it's interestingly laid out with bare stone walls and wooden flooring and one end has an open log fire, a squashy leather sofa with lots of cushions against a wall of books, a similar seat built into a small curved brick wall (which breaks up the room) and a TV. The main bar has built-in wall benches and plenty of stools and chairs around traditional pub tables and a further area has a coal fire and dark wood furniture. Dartmoor Jail Ale, Sharps Doom Bar and maybe a summer guest beer on handpump and several wines by the glass. The conservatory restaurant has high-backed leather dining chairs around wooden tables and smart window blinds.

 Good bar food includes lunchtime sandwiches, salmon and dill fishcakes with tomato salsa, nut roast terrine, moroccan-style chicken, a beer-battered fish of the day, and specials like thai prawn curry and gammon and egg. *Benchmark main dish: belly of pork with onion gravy £10.95. Two-course evening meal £16.45.*

Buccaneer Holdings ~ Manager Richard Cockburn ~ Real ale ~ Bar food (12-2.30(3 Sat and Sun); 6-9.30(9 Sun)) ~ Restaurant ~ (01803) 863880 ~ Children welcome ~

Dogs allowed in bar ~ Open 11-11; 12-10.30 Sun ~ Bedrooms: £59.50B/£79.50B

Recommended by Peter and Heather Elliott, Bob Duxbury, Mrs P Bishop, George Atkinson, P Dawn, Mike Gorton, Malcolm and Barbara Southwell

TREVAUNANCE COVE Cornwall   SW7251   Map 1

Driftwood Spars

Off B3285 in St Agnes; Quay Road; TR5 0RT

Friendly old inn, plenty of history, own-brew beers and wide range of other drinks, popular food, and beach nearby; attractive bedrooms

With a dramatic cove and beach just a stone's throw away and fine surrounding coastal walks, it's not surprising that this 17th-c inn is so popular with walkers and their dogs, cheerful surfers and summer families. The fine choice of real ales also remains quite a draw and includes their own Driftwood Dek, Lou's Brew and Red Mission and guests such as Bays Gold, St Austell Tribute, Sharps Doom Bar and Skinners Ginger Tosser on handpump. Also, 30 malt whiskies, 11 rums, several wines by the glass and home-made alcoholic ginger beer. The bustling bars are timbered with massive ships' spars – the masts of great sailing ships, many of which were wrecked along this coast – and there are dark wooden farmhouse and tub chairs and settles around a mix of tables, padded bar stools by the counter, old ship prints and lots of nautical and wreck memorabilia, and woodburning stoves; there's said to be an old smugglers' tunnel leading from behind the bar, up through the cliff. The modern dining room overlooks the cove; service is friendly and helpful. The summer hanging baskets are pretty and there are seats in the garden. Many of their attractive bedrooms overlook the coast.

Good, seasonally changing bar food might include filled ciabatta rolls, beer-battered fish and chips, three-bean chilli, popular home-made burger with emmenthal and red onion chutney, venison sausages, and specials like rabbit fricassée. *Benchmark main dish: home-made burger £9.75. Two-course evening meal £16.75.*

Free house ~ Licensee Louise Treseder ~ Real ale ~ Bar food (12-2.30, 6.30-9) ~ Restaurant ~ (01872) 552428 ~ Children welcome away from bar ~ Dogs allowed in bar and bedrooms ~ Live music Sat evenings ~ Open 11-11(1am Sat) ~ Bedrooms: £45S(£58B)/£86S

Recommended by the Didler, Comus and Sarah Elliott, Kev and Gaye Griffiths, Peter Salmon, Stanley and Annie Matthews, Alan Bowker, David Uren, Christopher Turner

WATERROW Somerset   ST0525   Map 1

Rock

A361 Wiveliscombe—Bampton; TA4 2AX

Welcoming family-run inn, local ales, interesting food, and a nice mix of customers; bedrooms

Run by a mother and son team, this is a 15th-c black and white inn where you can be sure of a warm welcome. The bar area has a dark brown leather sofa and low table with newspapers and books in front of the stone fireplace with its log fire, and big blackboard menus. There's a mix of dining chairs and wooden tables on the partly wood and partly red carpeted floor, a few high-backed bar chairs, hunting paintings and photographs and a couple of built-in cushioned window seats. Cotleigh

Tawny, Exmoor Ale and Otter Ale on handpump, several wines by the glass and farm cider. A back room has a pool table; darts and piped music. Up some steps from the bar is the heavily beamed restaurant. The welsh collie is called Meg. There are a few seats under umbrellas by the road.

 Using local produce and beef from their own farm, the particularly good bar food might include lunchtime sandwiches, thai crab cakes with bean sprout and pak choi salad, spinach, ricotta and pine nut pancakes, steak and kidney pie, creamy fish pie, and venison steak with a red wine and port sauce. *Benchmark main dish: rib-eye steak £15.50. Two-course evening meal £18.50.*

Free house ~ Licensees Matt Harvey and Joanna Oldman ~ Real ale ~ Bar food (12-2.30, 6-9.30) ~ Restaurant ~ (01984) 623293 ~ Children welcome ~ Dogs allowed in bar and bedrooms ~ Open 12-3, 6-11 ~ Bedrooms: £55B/£80B

Recommended by David and Julie Glover, Dr A McCormick, M G Hart, John Urquhart, David Saunders, Mike and Mary Carter, Liz and Jeremy Baker, Guy Vowles

WELLS Somerset ST5546 Map 2
Fountain
St Thomas Street; BA5 2UU

Friendly and attractive small pub in town centre, with plenty of room and a bustling atmosphere

Built in the 18th c to house builders working on the nearby cathedral, this attractive little pub, with blue shutters and pretty window boxes, is busy and friendly. There are lots of customers popping in and out but plenty of room in the big comfortable bar which has a large open fire, some interesting bric-a-brac, Butcombe Bitter and Sharps Doom Bar on handpump and several wines by the glass; unobtrusive piped music and board games. There's an upstairs restaurant, too.

 Traditional bar food at lunchtime includes sandwiches, pork, apple and sage terrine with apple chutney, a quiche of the day and sausages with onion gravy, with evening choices like lamb shank in cranberry, wine and garlic, and pork tenderloin with a creamy sherry and stilton sauce. *Benchmark main dish: 10oz rump steak with beer-battered onion rings £14.50. Two-course evening meal £17.25.*

Punch ~ Tenants Adrian and Sarah Lawrence ~ Real ale ~ Bar food ~ Restaurant ~ (01749) 672317 ~ Children welcome ~ Open 12-2.30, 6-11; 12-2.30, 7-10.30 Sun; closed 25 and 26 Dec

Recommended by N R White

WIDECOMBE Devon SX7276 Map 1
Rugglestone
Village at end of B3387; pub just S – turn left at church and NT church house, OS Sheet 191 map reference 720765; TQ13 7TF

Unspoilt local near busy tourist village, with a couple of bars, cheerful customers, friendly staff, four real ales and traditional pub food

Tucked away from the busy tourist village, this friendly little local is much loved by our readers – and both you – and your dog – can be sure of a warm welcome. The unspoilt bar has just four tables, a few window and wall seats, a one-person pew built into the corner by the nice old stone fireplace, and a good mix of customers. The rudimentary bar counter dispenses Butcombe Bitter, St Austell Dartmoor Best and a couple of guests like Otter Bright and Teignworthy Gun Dog tapped from the cask; local farm cider and a decent small wine list. The room on the right is a bit bigger and lighter-feeling with another stone fireplace, beamed ceiling, stripped-pine tables and a built-in wall bench, and there's also a small dining room. There are seats across the little moorland stream in the field and tables and chairs in the garden. They have a holiday cottage to rent out.

Popular, hearty bar food includes sandwiches, deep-fried brie with redcurrant jelly, vegetarian or meaty lasagne, beer-battered fresh haddock, chicken and leek pie, and lambs liver with bacon and onion gravy. *Benchmark main dish: luxury fish pie £10.50. Two-course evening meal £16.00.*

Free house ~ Licensees Richard and Vicky Palmer ~ Real ale ~ Bar food ~ Restaurant ~ (01364) 621327 ~ Children allowed but must be away from bar area ~ Dogs welcome ~ Open 11.30-3, 6-11.30(5-midnight Fri); 11.30am-midnight Sat; 12-11 Sun
Recommended by Alan Sutton, Bob and Angela Brooks, Mayur Shah, Helen Rawsthorn, Mike Beasley, Tim Maddison, Mike Gorton

WIMBORNE MINSTER Dorset   SZ0199   Map 2
Green Man ◀ £
Victoria Road at junction with West Street (B3082/B3073); BH21 1EN

Cosy, warm-hearted town pub with bargain simple food

The award-winning summer window boxes, flowering tubs and hanging baskets at the front of this cheerful local are a fantastic sight – there are more on the heated back terrace as well. This is a proper community pub with regulars popping in and out throughout the day, but as a visitor you'll get just as warm a welcome from the friendly landlord. The four small linked areas have maroon plush banquettes and polished dark pub tables, copper and brass ornaments, dark red walls and Wadworths IPA, 6X and Bishops Tipple on handpump. One room has a log fire in a biggish brick fireplace, another has a coal-effect gas fire, and they have two darts boards, a silenced games machine, piped music and TV; the Barn houses a pool table in the summer months. The little border terrier is called Cooper.

As well as a popular breakfast, the bargain-priced traditional food includes sandwiches, lasagne, vegetable burger, sausages, chips, beans and egg, and a well liked Sunday roast. *Benchmark main dish: Sunday roast £7.95.*

Wadworths ~ Tenant Andrew Kiff ~ Real ale ~ Bar food (10-2; not evenings) ~ Restaurant ~ (01202) 881021 ~ Children allowed until 7.30pm ~ Dogs allowed in bar ~ Live music Sat evening ~ Open 10am-11.30pm(12.30 Sat)
Recommended by Jenny and Brian Seller, Mrs Blethyn Elliott, Dr and Mrs A K Clarke, B and M Kendall

---

A very few pubs try to make you leave a credit card at the bar, as a sort of deposit if you order food. They are not entitled to do this. The credit card firms and banks that issue them warn you not to let your card out of your sight. If someone behind the counter used your card fraudulently, the card company or bank could in theory hold you liable, because of your negligence in letting a stranger hang on to your card. Suggest instead that if they feel the need for security, they 'swipe' your card and give it back to you. And do name and shame the pub to us.

WINSLEY Wiltshire   ST7960 Map 2

Seven Stars 🍴 🍺

Off B3108 bypass W of Bradford-on-Avon (pub just over Wiltshire border);
BA15 2LQ

**Handsome old stone pub with attractive bars, imaginative food, good
real ales, and friendly staff; seats outside**

On a quiet lane in an attractive village, this handsome early 18th-c
stone building has plenty of picnic-sets and tables and chairs under
parasols on the terrace or on neat grassy surrounds with pretty flowering
borders. Inside, the low-beamed linked areas have stripped stone and
light pastel paintwork, candlelight, farmhouse chairs and wooden tables
on flagstones and carpeting and a couple of stone fireplaces – one with a
sizeable hearth. Cheerful young staff serve Cheddar Ales Potholer,
Devilfish Best (one of the landlords, Mr Metz, also co-owns the Devilfish
Brewery), Otter Bitter and Wadworths 6X on handpump, several wines by
the glass and Sheppy's farm cider; piped music. The village bowling green
is opposite.

Using locally sourced seasonal produce, smoking and curing their own fish and
meat and making everything in-house (ice-creams, bread, pickles and
chutneys), the highly thought-of, imaginative food includes sandwiches, home-made
corned beef, pickled mushrooms, blue cheese fritter and candied walnuts, haddock
rarebit, wild garlic and celeriac rémoulade, samphire and brown shrimp vinaigrette,
home-cooked ham and free-range eggs, home-made burger with their own relish and
specials like roast turbot, braised ox cheek, smoked mashed potato and wild garlic.
Benchmark main dish: lamb fillet, crispy belly, tapenade and anchovy dressing
£17.50. Two-course evening meal £19.00.

Free house ~ Licensees Claire Spreadbury and Evan Metz ~ Real ale ~ Bar food
(12-2(2.30 Sun), 6-9; not winter Sun evening) ~ Restaurant ~ (01225) 722204 ~
Children welcome ~ Dogs allowed in bar ~ Open 12-2.30(3 Sat), 6-10.30(11 Sat); 12-3.30,
6-10 Sun; closed winter Sun evening

Recommended by John and Angela Main, Nigel Long

WOODBURY SALTERTON Devon   SY0189 Map 1

Diggers Rest

3.5 miles from M5 junction 30: A3052 towards Sidmouth, village signposted
on right about 0.5 miles after Clyst St Mary; also signposted from B3179 SE of Exeter;
EX5 1PQ

**Bustling village pub with real ales, well liked food, and lovely views
from the terraced garden**

A friendly new landlord had taken over this thatched village pub just as
we went to press and reports from readers were warm and
enthusiastic. The main bar has antique furniture, local art on the walls
and a cosy seating area by the open fire with its extra large sofa and
armchair. The modern extension is light and airy and opens on to the
garden which has contemporary garden furniture under canvas parasols
on the terrace and lovely countryside views. Otter Ale and Bitter and
St Austell Tribute on handpump, several wines by the glass and farm
cider; piped music. The window boxes and flowering baskets are pretty.

Using seasonal local produce, the enjoyable bar food includes lunchtime
sandwiches, fried mackerel on toast with gooseberry chutney, roast vegetable

terrine with apricots, spiced couscous and mint yoghurt, crispy pork belly with mustard and apple sauce, and grilled fish of the day in lemon and caper butter. *Benchmark main dish: steak in ale pie £9.95. Two-course evening meal £15.00.*

Heartstone Inns ~ Licensee Ben Thomas ~ Real ale ~ Bar food (12-2.15, 6.30-9.15) ~ (01395) 232375 ~ Well behaved children welcome ~ Dogs allowed in bar ~ Open 11-3, 5.30-11; 12-3.30, 5.30-10.30 Sun

Recommended by John and Susan Miln, Colin and Louise English, Ian and Joan Blackwell, Douglas and Ann Hare

 WORTH MATRAVERS Dorset   SY9777   Map 2

Square & Compass ★ ◖

 *At fork of both roads signposted to village from B3069; BH19 3LF*

Unchanging country tavern with masses of character, in the same family for many years; lovely sea views and fine nearby walks

The Newman family first took on this fine old pub over a hundred years ago and to this day, there's no bar counter. Palmers Copper and guests such as Bays Gold and Penpont Cornish Arvor and up to 13 ciders are tapped from a row of casks and passed to you in a drinking corridor through two serving hatches; several malt whiskies. A couple of basic unspoilt rooms have simple furniture on the flagstones, a woodburning stove and a loyal crowd of friendly locals; darts and shove-ha'penny. From benches (made from local stone) out in front there's a fantastic view down over the village rooftops to the sea around St Aldhelm's Head and there may be free-roaming hens, chickens and other birds clucking around your feet. A little museum (free) exhibits local fossils and artefacts, mostly collected by the current friendly landlord and his father. There are wonderful walks from here to some exciting switchback sections of the coast path above St Aldhelm's Head and Chapman's Pool – you will need to park in the public car park 100 yards along the Corfe Castle road (which has a £1 honesty box).

Bar food is limited to tasty home-made pasties and pies which are served till stocks run out. *Benchmark main dish: pasties £3.20.*

Free house ~ Licensee Charlie Newman ~ Real ale ~ Bar food (all day) ~ No credit cards ~ (01929) 439229 ~ Children welcome ~ Dogs welcome ~ Occasional live music on Fri and Sat ~ Open 12-11; 12-3, 6-11 weekdays in winter

Recommended by Mrs Carolyn Dixon, Steve Derbyshire, Richard Stanfield, Ian and Barbara Rankin, S J and C C Davidson, Theocsbrian, N R White, Tich Critchlow, the Didler, Mike and Sue Loseby, Robert Wivell, John and Gloria Isaacs, Ewan and Moira McCall, P Dawn, Tony and Wendy Hobden, Steve and Sue Griffiths, David Lamb

Bedroom prices normally include full english breakfast, VAT and any inclusive service charge that we know of. Prices before the '/' are for single rooms, after the '/' are for two people in a double or twin (B includes a private bath, S a private shower). If there is no '/', the prices are only for twin or double rooms (as far as we know there are no singles).

ALSO WORTH A VISIT IN CORNWALL

Besides the region's top pubs, we recommend the following. Do tell us
what you think of them: **feedback@goodguides.com**

ALTARNUN SX2280   PL15 7RX
Kings Head
Five Lanes

Old stone-built beamed roadside pub under newish management, Greene King Abbot,
Skinners Betty Stogs and a couple of guests, real ciders, reasonably priced pubby food
from sandwiches and baguettes up including good Sun carvery, carpeted lounge with big
log fire, slate floor restaurant and public bar with another fire; darts, pool and TV;
children and dogs welcome, picnic-sets on front terrace and in garden behind, four
bedrooms, open all day. *Recommended by Frank Willy*

ALTARNUN SX2083   PL15 7SN
☆ Rising Sun
NW; village signed off A39 just W of A395 junction

Tucked-away 16th-c pub with traditionally furnished L-shaped main bar, low beams, slate
flagstones, coal fires, local Penpont and Skinners ales, farm cider, food from sandwiches
up; piped music; dogs and well behaved children allowed in bar but not in restaurant,
seats on suntrap terrace and in garden, pétanque, camping field, beautiful church in nice
village, open all day weekends. *Recommended by Mr and Mrs P D Titcomb, Tracey and Stephen Groves,
Dennis Jenkin, Comus and Sarah Elliott, the Didler*

BODMIN SX0467   PL31 2RD
Borough Arms
Dunmere (A389 NW)

Roomy 19th-c roadside pub with good value food including daily carvery (all day Sun),
St Austell and Bass, cheerful staff, partly panelled stripped-stone walls, lots of railway
photographs and posters, open fire, side family room and separate dining room; piped
music, quiz machine; dogs allowed in bar, picnic-sets out among shady apple trees, play
area, on Camel Trail, open all day. *Recommended by Norman and Sarah Keeping*

BOSCASTLE SX0990   PL35 0BD
☆ Napoleon
High Street, top of village

Welcoming 16th-c thick-walled white cottage at top of steep quaint village (fine views
halfway up); slate floors and cosy rooms on different levels including small evening
bistro, oak beams and log fires, interesting Napoleon prints and lots of other knick-
knacks, well kept St Austell tapped from the cask, decent wines and coffee, wholesome
generous pub food, traditional games; piped music – live music Fri, sing-along Tues;
children and dogs welcome, small covered terrace and large sheltered garden, open all
day. *Recommended by Ted George, the Didler, Stanley and Annie Matthews, Christopher Turner*

BOTALLACK SW3632   TR19 7QG
☆ Queens Arms
B3306

Friendly old pub with good home-made food including local seafood, meat sourced within
3 miles, well kept Sharps and Skinners ales, good service, log fire in unusual granite
inglenook, dark wood furniture, tin mining and other old local photographs on stripped-
stone walls, family extension; dogs welcome, tables out in front and pleasant back
garden, wonderful clifftop walks nearby, lodge accommodation, open all day. *Recommended
by Richard Stanfield, Kirsty Wilson*

> We say if we know a pub has piped music.

BOTUSFLEMING SX4061   PL12 6NJ
Rising Sun
Off A388 near Saltash

Convivial low-ceilinged rural local, lively games bar, smaller quieter stripped-stone room with two good coal fires, well kept changing ales; picnic-sets in garden looking over quiet valley to church, has been closed Mon-Thurs lunchtimes, open all day weekends.
Recommended by the Didler, Phil and Sally Gorton

☆ BREAGE SW6128   TR13 9PD
Queens Arms
3 miles W of Helston just off A394

Friendly pub with L-shaped bar and smallish restaurant, six well kept ales including Sharps Doom Bar and Skinners Betty Stogs, farm cider, decent wines by the glass, good well priced food from baguettes with cornish brie and cranberry to seafood and steaks, nice coal fires, plush banquettes, brass-topped tables, daily papers, games area with pool; piped music; children and dogs welcome, some picnic-sets outside, covered smokers' area, two bedrooms, medieval wall paintings in church opposite, open all day Sun.
Recommended by Dennis Jenkin, Andy Beveridge

BUDE SS2006   EX23 8SD
Brendon Arms
Falcon Terrace

Popular (particularly in summer) canalside pub, with two big friendly pubby bars, back family room, well kept ales such as St Austell and Sharps, enjoyable bargain food including good crab sandwiches and interesting specials, OAP lunch Tues, nice coffee, hot spicy apple juice, good cheery service; juke box, sports TV, pool and darts; children welcome, dogs in public bar, disabled access, picnic-sets on front grass, heated smokers' shelter, bedrooms and holiday apartments, good walks nearby. *Recommended by Barry and Anne, Ryta Lyndley, Michael Tack*

CALLINGTON SX3569   PL17 7AQ
Bulls Head
Fore Street

Ancient unspoilt local with relaxed friendly atmosphere, handsome black timbering and stonework, well kept St Austell; erratic opening times. *Recommended by Giles and Annie Francis*

☆ CALSTOCK SX4368   PL18 9QA
Tamar
Quay

Cheerful local dating from 17th c, just opposite the Tamar with its imposing viaduct, dark stripped stone, flagstones, tiles and bare boards, pool room with woodburner, more modern fairy-lit back dining room, good generous straightforward food at bargain prices, summer cream teas, well kept ales such as Otter and Sharps Doom Bar, good service, darts, some live music; children away from bar and well behaved dogs welcome, nicely furnished terrace, heated smokers' shelter, hilly walk or ferry to Cotehele (NT).
Recommended by Phil and Sally Gorton

☆ CAWSAND SX4350   PL10 1PF
Cross Keys
The Square

Slate-floored traditional local with lots of matchboxes, banknotes and postcards, some cask tables, steps up to carpeted dining room with nautical décor, wide range of enjoyable generous food especially seafood (worth booking in season), reasonable prices, changing ales such as Hop Back Summer Lightning and Skinners Best, flexible helpful service; pool, may be piped music, no nearby parking; children and dogs welcome, seats outside, pleasant bedrooms. *Recommended by Dr D J and Mrs S C Walker*

CHAPEL AMBLE SW9975   PL27 6EU
Maltsters Arms
Off A39 NE of Wadebridge

More busy country restaurant than pub and they like you to book, good food and thriving atmosphere, drinkers confined to bar counter or modern back extension (if not used by diners), St Austell Tribute and Sharps Doom Bar served very cold; contemporary styling with splendid fire, beams, painted half-panelling, stripped stone and partly carpeted flagstones, light wood furniture; picnic-sets out in sheltered sunny corner. *Recommended by Mr and Mrs Mason, Fiona Loram, David Hoult*

CHARLESTOWN SX0351   PL25 3NX
Rashleigh Arms
Quay Road

Modernised early 19th-c pub with nautical touches, public bar, lounge and dining area, well kept St Austell ales and two guests, good wine choice and coffee, enjoyable competitively priced food all day including good crab sandwiches and popular Sun carvery, friendly obliging service; piped music – live music Fri, free wi-fi; children welcome, dogs in bar, disabled facilities, front terrace and garden with picnic-sets, eight bedrooms (some with sea views), open all day. *Recommended by Robert Watt*

CONSTANTINE SW7328   TR11 5RP
☆ Trengilly Wartha
Nancenoy; A3083 S of Helston, signposted Gweek near RNAS Culdrose, then fork right after Gweek; OS Sheet 204 map reference 731282

Popular friendly inn in several acres of gardens, long low-beamed main bar with woodburner, cornish beers, good wines by the glass, 50 malt whiskies, enjoyable food using local fish and shellfish, cosy bistro, conservatory family room, table football, folk night every other Weds; dogs welcome, seats under large parasols, lots of surrounding walks, bedrooms. *Recommended by Mark Evans, M Mossman, Rupert Sligh, Chris and Angela Buckell, Eamonn and Natasha Skyrme and others*

COVERACK SW7818   TR12 6SX
Paris
The Cove

Edwardian seaside inn above harbour in beautiful fishing village, comfortable carpeted L-shaped bar, St Austell ales and Skinners Betty Stogs, large relaxed dining room with white tablecloths and spectacular bay views, enjoyable food including good fresh fish, large model of namesake ship (wrecked nearby in 1899); more sea views from garden, four bedrooms. *Recommended by Peter Meister*

CREMYLL SX4553   PL10 1HX
☆ Edgcumbe Arms
End of B3247

Super setting by Plymouth foot-ferry, good Tamar views, picnic-sets out by water; attractive layout and décor, with slate floors, big settles, comfortably old-fashioned furnishings including fireside sofas, old pictures and china, well kept St Austell ales, cheerful staff, reasonably priced food from doorstep sandwiches up, weekend carvery, good family room/games area; pay car park some way off; children in eating area, dogs allowed in one bar (most tables here too low to eat at), bedrooms, open all day. *Recommended by Gordon Briggs, Peter Salmon, Dr D J and Mrs S C Walker*

CRIPPLES EASE SW5037   TR26 3JB
Balnoon
Balnoon; N, right off B3311 after 1.2 miles

Modern inn with good selection of real ales and good carvery (Sun lunch, summer evenings, Fri-Sun evenings in winter); children welcome, terrace tables, bedrooms. *Recommended by J A Snell*

CROWS NEST SX2669   PL14 5JQ

☆ **Crows Nest**

Signed off B3264 N of Liskeard; OS Sheet 201 map reference 263692

Old-fashioned 17th-c pub with enjoyable food from chef/landlord, well kept St Austell ales and a guest like Dartmoor, decent wines by the glass, prompt friendly service, attractive furnishings under bowed beams, big log fire, chatty locals; children welcome, picnic-sets on terrace by quiet lane, handy for Bodmin Moor walks. *Recommended by Henry Fryer, Peter Salmon, Dr and Mrs M W A Haward*

EDMONTON SW9672   PL27 7JA

☆ **Quarryman**

Off A39 just W of Wadebridge bypass

Welcoming three-room beamed bar, part of a small holiday courtyard complex; some good individual cooking besides generous pubby lunchtime food including nice baguettes, salads and fish and chips, good curry night (first Tues of month), quick friendly service, Sharps (summer only), Skinners and a couple of guest beers, good choice of wines by the glass, interesting decorations including old sporting memorabilia, cribbage and dominoes, no mobiles; well behaved dogs and children welcome, disabled facilities, courtyard with picnic-sets, open all day. *Recommended by Robert Kibble, the Didler, Dr and Mrs M W A Haward*

FALMOUTH SW8132   TR11 3HH

☆ **Chain Locker**

Custom House Quay

Busy place in fine spot by inner harbour with window tables and lots outside, Sharps and Skinners ales, good value generous food from sandwiches and baguettes to fresh local fish and interesting vegetarian choices (they also cater for smaller appetites), cheery young staff, bare boards and masses of nautical bric-a-brac, darts alley; games machine, piped music; well behaved children and dogs welcome, self-catering accommodation, open all day. *Recommended by David Crook*

FALMOUTH SW8032   TR11 3QA

☆ **Seven Stars**

The Moor (centre)

Quirky 17th-c local, unchanging and unsmart (not to everyone's taste), with long-serving and entertaining vicar-landlord, no gimmicks, machines or mobile phones, warm welcome, half a dozen ales tapped from the cask, home-made rolls, chatty regulars, big key-ring collection, quiet back snug; corridor hatch serving roadside courtyard. *Recommended by Henry Fryer, the Didler, Dennis Jones*

FOWEY SX1251   PL23 1AQ

Galleon

Fore Street; from centre follow Car Ferry signs

Superb spot by harbour and estuary, good ale range including local microbrews, good generous straightforward food, reasonable prices, nice choice of wines, fast friendly service, fresh modern nautical décor, lots of solid pine, dining areas off, jazz Sun lunchtime; pool, big screen TV, evenings can get loud with young people; children welcome, disabled facilities, attractive extended waterside terrace and sheltered courtyard with covered heated area, estuary-view bedrooms. *Recommended by Nick Lawless, Alain and Rose Foote, JPR, Dave Webster, Sue Holland, David Crook*

FOWEY SX1251   PL23 1AT

☆ **King of Prussia**

Town Quay

Handsome quayside building with good welcoming service in roomy neat upstairs bar, bay windows looking over harbour to Polruan, enjoyable pubby food including good crab sandwiches and carve your own Sun roasts, St Austell ales kept well, sensibly priced wines, side family restaurant; piped music, pool; seats outside, open all day in summer, six pleasant bedrooms. *Recommended by Edward Mirzoeff, Alan Johnson*

FOWEY SX1251   PL23 1BP
Safe Harbour
Lostwithiel Street

Redecorated 19th-c former coaching inn set away from main tourist area, lounge/dining area and regulars' bar, good value locally sourced home-made food, well kept St Austell ales, welcoming landlord, old local prints, upstairs overflow dining room; pool, darts, games machine; heated side terrace, seven bedrooms, self-catering apartment, open all day till midnight. *Recommended by JPR, Dave Webster, Sue Holland*

FOWEY SX1251   PL23 1AZ
☆ Ship
Trafalgar Square

Bustling local with friendly staff, good choice of well priced generous food from sandwiches up including fine local seafood, well kept St Austell ales, coal fire and banquettes in tidy bar with lots of yachting prints and nauticalia, newspapers, steps up to family dining room with big stained-glass window, pool/darts room; piped music, small sports TV; dogs allowed, comfortably old-fashioned bedrooms, some oak-panelled. *Recommended by Nick Lawless*

GOLANT SX1254   PL23 1LN
☆ Fishermans Arms
Fore Street (B3269)

Bustling partly flagstoned small waterside local with lovely views across River Fowey from front bar and terrace, good value generous home-made food including good crab sandwiches and seafood, efficient friendly service, well kept cornish ales, good wines by the glass, log fire, interesting pictures; dogs welcome, pleasant garden, closed Sun afternoon. *Recommended by Charles Meade-King, the Didler, Nick Lawless, Stuart Paulley*

GORRAN CHURCHTOWN SW9942   PL26 6HN
Barley Sheaf
Follow Gorran Haven signs from Mevagissey

Old pub reopened after extensive refurbishment by new owner; enjoyable food, Sharps Doom Bar and guests, friendly staff; garden, nice village. *Recommended by Julian Able*

GULVAL SW4831   TR18 3BB
Coldstreamer
Centre of village by drinking fountain

Under welcoming new ownership, good imaginative sensibly priced food using local produce, good wine choice, several well kept local ales, bar with old local photographs, woodburner and traditional games, freshly updated restaurant with modern pine furniture on wood floor, friendly helpful service; quiet pleasant village very handy for Trengwainton Gardens and Scillies heliport, comfortably refurbished bedrooms, open all day. *Recommended by Mrs B H Adams*

GUNNISLAKE SX4371   PL18 9BX
Rising Sun
Lower Calstock Road, just S of village

Attractive 17th-c two-room pub under newish licensees, beams, stripped stone, panelling and flagstones, lovely fireplaces, cheerful service, six real ales, enjoyable food (not Mon); pleasant valley views from terraced garden, open all day. *Recommended by Les Last*

GWEEK SW7026   TR12 6TU
Gweek Inn
Back roads E of Helston

Cheerful family chain pub, large comfortable open-plan bar with low beams, brasses, lots of motoring trophies (enthusiast licensees) and woodburner in big stone fireplace, well kept Greene King Old Speckled Hen, Sharps Doom Bar and Skinners Betty Stogs, decent wines, enjoyable reasonably priced standard food including good sandwiches (may try to keep your credit card while you eat), bright and roomy back restaurant, live music Fri; tables on grass (safe for children), summer kiosk with all-day snacks, short walk from seal sanctuary. *Recommended by Clifford Blakemore*

HARROWBARROW SX4069   PL17 8BQ
Cross House
Off A390 E of Callington; School Road – over towards Metherell

Substantial stone building, spreading carpeted bar with some booth seating, cushioned wall seats and stools around pub tables, enjoyable home-made food, well kept ales such as Hancocks HB, friendly smiling service, open fire and woodburner, darts area, restaurant; children and dogs welcome, disabled facilities, plenty of picnic-sets on good-sized lawn, play area. *Recommended by Les Last, Dennis Jenkin*

HELFORD SW7526   TR12 6JX
Shipwrights Arms
Off B3293 SE of Helston, via Mawgan

Thatched pub of great potential by beautiful wooded creek, at its best at high tide, terraces making the most of the view, plenty of surrounding walks, and summer foot-ferry from Helford Passage; nautical décor, open fire, Sharps, Skinners and a summer guest, decent wines, friendly staff, bar food including summer barbecues and lunchtime buffet platters; children and dogs welcome, quite a walk from nearest car park, open all day summer, closed winter Sun and Mon evenings; still up for sale as we go to press. *Recommended by the Didler, Richard Martin, Geoff and Linda Payne*

HELSTON SW6527   TR13 8EL
☆ ## Blue Anchor
Coinagehall Street

Many (not all) love this 15th-c no-nonsense, highly individual, thatched local; quaint rooms off corridor, flagstones, stripped stone, low beams and well worn furniture, traditional games, family room, limited bargain lunchtime food (perhaps best time for a visit), ancient back brewhouse still producing distinctive and very strong Spingo IPA, Middle and seasonals like Bragget with honey and herbs; seats out behind, bedrooms, open all day. *Recommended by Richard Stanfield, Steve and Liz Tilley, the Didler, Giles and Annie Francis*

HESSENFORD SX3057   PL11 3HJ
Copley Arms
A387 Looe—Torpoint

Village pub with slightly old-fashioned feel, popular with families and passing tourists, reasonably priced food from baguettes to enjoyable Sun lunch and restaurant dishes in linked areas, well kept St Austell ales, nice wine choice, variety of teas and coffee, log fires, tables in cosy booths, one part with sofas and easy chairs, big family room; piped music, dogs allowed in one area; sizeable and attractive streamside garden and terrace (but by road), play area, bedrooms. *Recommended by Dr D J and Mrs S C Walker*

HOLYWELL SW7658   TR8 5PP
St Pirans
Holywell Road

Great location backing on to dunes and popular with holidaymakers, friendly helpful staff, well kept ales including St Austell, decent wines, enjoyable pub food with blackboard specials; children and dogs welcome, tables on large back terrace. *Recommended by David and Jill Hunter, Dennis Jenkin*

LANNER SW7339   TR16 6AX
☆ ## Fox & Hounds
Comford; A393/B3298

Cosily comfortable rambling low-beamed pub under welcoming new licensees, fresh food from good sandwiches up, well kept St Austell ales tapped from the cask, decent wines, friendly helpful service, warm fires, high-backed settles and cottagey chairs on flagstones, stripped stone and dark panelling, newspapers and books, pub games; piped music; children welcome in dining room, dogs in bar, disabled facilities, great floral displays in front, picnic-sets in neat back garden with pond and play area, open all day weekends. *Recommended by Dennis Jenkin, R K Phillips*

LERRYN SX1356   PL22 0PT
☆ **Ship**
Signed off A390 in Lostwithiel; Fore Street

Lovely spot especially when tide's in, well kept local ales, farm cider, good wines (including country ones) and whiskies, imaginative sensibly priced food as well as more traditional things, huge woodburner, attractive adults-only dining conservatory (booked quickly evenings and weekends), games room with pool; children welcome, dogs on leads, picnic-sets and pretty play area outside, near famous stepping-stones and three well signed waterside walks, decent bedrooms in adjoining building and self-catering cottages, open all day weekends. *Recommended by Nick Lawless*

LIZARD SW7012   TR12 7NQ
Top House
A3083

Neat clean pub under new ownership, good local food (some quite pricey) from sandwiches and snacks up including fresh fish, children's meals and cream teas, well kept ales such as St Austell Tribute and Skinners Betty Stogs, lots of good local sea pictures, fine shipwreck relics and serpentine craftwork (note the handpumps), good log fire, friendly staff; sheltered terrace, interesting nearby serpentine shop, eight bedrooms in adjoining building (three with sea views), open all day summer, all day weekends in winter. *Recommended by Clifford Blakemore, Andy Beveridge*

LIZARD SW7012   TR12 7NJ
Witchball
Lighthouse Road

Good food including fresh local fish and seafood (booking advised), ales such as Choughs, St Austell and Skinners, cornish cider, helpful friendly staff; children and dogs welcome, terrace tables, open all day. *Recommended by Clifford Blakemore*

LOOE SX2553   PL13 1AE
Olde Salutation
Fore Street, East Looe

Good welcoming local bustle in big squareish slightly sloping beamed and tiled bar, reasonably priced food from notable crab sandwiches to wholesome specials and Sun roasts, fast friendly service, well kept ales including Sharps Doom Bar, red leatherette seats and neat tables, blazing fire in nice old-fashioned fireplace, lots of local fishing photographs, side snug with olde-worlde harbour mural, step down to simple family room; may be piped music, forget about parking; open all day, handy for coast path. *Recommended by Gordon Briggs, Dr D J and Mrs S C Walker*

LUDGVAN SW5033   TR20 8EY
☆ **White Hart**
Off A30 Penzance—Hayle at Crowlas

Appealing old-fashioned 19th-c pub, friendly and welcoming, with well kept Sharps, Skinners and a changing guest tapped from the cask, enjoyable food from sandwiches and pub standards up, vegetarian menu too, small unspoilt beamed rooms with wood and stone floors, nooks and crannies, woodburners; children welcome, beer garden and little decked area at back, interesting church next door, bedrooms. *Recommended by David Crook, Richard Stanfield, the Didler, John and Jackie Chalcraft*

Every entry includes a postcode for use in Sat Nav devices.

MALPAS SW8442   TR1 1SL
☆ **Heron**
Trenhaile Terrace, off A39 S of Truro

Idyllically placed creekside pub with seats on heated terrace, light and airy long narrow bar with areas leading off, flagstones and wood flooring, blue and white décor, modern yacht and heron paintings on wood-planked walls, brass nautical items, stuffed heron in cabinet, gas-effect coal fires, St Austell beers, enjoyable often interesting food; piped music, parking difficult in high season; children welcome, open all day in summer.
Recommended by Norman and Sarah Keeping, Mr and Mrs P D Titcomb, Chris and Angela Buckell, Adrian Johnson, Anthony Barnes, Sarah Flynn

MARAZION SW5130   TR17 0EN
Godolphin Arms
West End

Former coaching inn with great views across beach and Mount's Bay towards St Michael's Mount, traditional food including good crab sandwiches and popular Sun carvery, St Austell and Sharps ales, helpful friendly staff, upper lounge bar and dining area, informal lower bar with pool table, sports TV and live music (Fri); children and dogs welcome, decked beach-side terrace, ten bedrooms, most with sea view, good breakfast, open all day.
Recommended by Norman and Sarah Keeping, Roger and Donna Huggins, Christopher Turner

MARHAMCHURCH SS2203   EX23 0HB
Bullers Arms
Old Orchard Close

Oak beams and settles in pleasant rambling L-shaped bar, well prepared food from extensive menu, Sun carvery, three well kept local ales (takeaway cartons available), wide choice of wines by the glass, obliging staff, darts in flagstoned back part, restaurant, some live music including late summer Bude Jazz Festival; children and dogs welcome; picnic-sets in sizeable garden, a mile's walk to the sea, bedrooms, open all day in summer. *Recommended by Andy and Jill Kassube, JJW, CMW*

MAWNAN SMITH SW7728   TR11 5EP
☆ **Red Lion**
W of Falmouth, off former B3291 Penryn—Gweek; The Square

Old thatched and beamed pub, popular and chatty, with cosy series of dimly lit lived-in rooms, open-view kitchen doing wide choice of good food from interesting menu especially seafood (should book summer evenings), quick friendly service, lots of wines by the glass, real ales such as Sharps kept well, good coffee, daily papers, fresh flowers, woodburner, dark woodwork, country pictures, plates and bric-a-brac; piped music, TV; children and dogs welcome, picnic-sets outside, handy for Glendurgan and Trebah Gardens, open all day. *Recommended by Norman and Sarah Keeping, J B Taylor, Clifford Blakemore*

MEVAGISSEY SX0144   PL26 6QH
☆ **Fountain**
Cliff Street, down alley by Post Office

Popular low-beamed fishermen's pub, slate floor, some stripped stone, good coal fire, old local pictures, St Austell ales, enjoyable food, back locals' bar with glass-topped cellar, upstairs restaurant; pretty frontage with picnic-sets, bedrooms, open all day in summer.
Recommended by R K Phillips, the Didler

MEVAGISSEY SX0144   PL26 6UQ
☆ **Ship**
Fore Street, near harbour

16th-c pub with interesting alcove areas in big open-plan bar, low beams and flagstones, nice nautical décor, woodburner, cheery uniformed staff, wide range of fairly priced pubby food including good fresh fish, small helpings available, full St Austell range kept well, back pool table; games machines, piped and occasional live music; dogs allowed,

children welcome in two front rooms, comfortable bedrooms, open all day in summer.
Recommended by Stanley and Annie Matthews, George Atkinson

MINIONS SX2671   PL14 5LE
Cheesewring
Overlooking the Hurlers

Popular well run village pub useful for Bodmin Moor walks, real ales including Sharps
Doom Bar and Special, good choice of reasonably priced home-made food, lots of brass
and ornaments. *Recommended by Jenny and Peter Lowater, Anthony Wallace*

MITCHELL SW8554   TR8 5AX
☆ Plume of Feathers
Off A30 Bodmin—Redruth, by A3076 junction; take southwards road then first right

Busy dining pub with appealing contemporary décor in several rooms, old stripped
beams, painted wooden dado, paintings by local artist, open fires, food all day from
sandwiches to restaurant-style dishes, cornish beers, friendly service, dining
conservatory; children allowed away from bar, dogs welcome, plenty of seats in well
planted garden areas, bedrooms, open 9am-midnight. *Recommended by M Mossman, Steve and
Liz Tilley, Barry and Anne, Gerry and Rosemary Dobson*

MITHIAN SW7450   TR5 0QF
☆ Miners Arms
Off B3285 E of St Agnes

Cosy pub with traditional small rooms and passages, pubby furnishings, fine old wall
painting of Elizabeth I in squint-walled, irregular beam and plank ceilinged back bar,
open fires, popular good value food, Sharps and Skinners ales, friendly staff, board games;
piped music; children and dogs welcome, seats on back terrace, in garden and on
sheltered front cobbled forecourt, open all day. *Recommended by Dennis Jenkin, Ted George,
Mr and Mrs Gravener, Barry and Anne, John and Jackie Chalcraft, Barrie and Mary Crees*

MOUSEHOLE SW4626   TR19 6QX
☆ Ship
Harbourside

Bustling harbourside local with opened-up dimly lit main bar, black beams, flagstones,
open fire, panelling, built-in wooden wall benches and stools around low tables, sailors'
fancy ropework, darts, well kept St Austell ales, pubby food including good local fish;
piped music, TV, games machine, upstairs lavatories; children and dogs welcome, lovely
village (best to park at top and walk down), elaborate Christmas harbour lights worth a
visit, bedrooms, open all day. *Recommended by Paul Goldman, Adrian Johnson, Martin and
Anne Muers, John and Sharon Hancock*

MULLION SW6719   TR12 7HN
Old Inn
Near church – not down in the cove

Thatched and beamed pub with central servery doing generous good value food (all day
July/Aug) from doorstep sandwiches to pies and evening steaks, well kept ales and
decent wines (lots by the glass), fast friendly service in linked eating areas with lots of
brasses, plates, clocks, nautical items and old wreck pictures, big inglenook fireplace;
children welcome, picnic-sets on terrace and in garden, good bedrooms, open all day
weekends and in Aug. *Recommended by Ian and Rose Lock*

MULLION COVE SW6618   TR12 7EP
Mullion Cove Hotel
End of Cove Road

Imposing Victorian cliff-top hotel overlooking sea and harbour, friendly and hospitable,
with good food in bistro bar, ales such as Sharps Doom Bar, more formal and expensive
sea-view restaurant; children welcome, 30 bedrooms, useful coastal path stop.
Recommended by Clifford Blakemore

MYLOR BRIDGE SW8137   TR11 5ST

☆ **Pandora**

Restronguet Passage: from A39 in Penryn, take turning signposted Mylor Church,
Mylor Bridge, Flushing and go straight through Mylor Bridge following Restronguet
Passage signs; or from A39 further N, at or near Perranarworthal, take turning
signposted Mylor, Restronguet, then follow Restronguet Weir signs, but turn left down
hill at Restronguet Passage sign

Sadly, this idyllically placed medieval thatched pub suffered a catastrophic fire in the
spring which destroyed the roof and the first floor; we've no doubt it will be restored to
its former glory – several rambling interconnecting rooms with low wooden ceilings, big
polished flagstones, cosy alcoves and three large log fires in high hearths; picnic-sets in
front or on the long floating jetty; news please. *Recommended by K Hunt, M Smith, M Mossman,*
Chris and Angela Buckell, Gene and Tony Freemantle, Guy Vowles, David Rule and others

NEWLYN SW4629   TR18 5PR

Tolcarne

Tolcarne Place

Traditional 17th-c quayside pub, cosy and lived in with open fire, local fishing photos,
wide choice of good value home-made food including good seafood, friendly staff and
locals, well kept Brakspears and Sharps; terrace (harbour wall cuts off view), good
parking. *Recommended by Jane and Alan Bush, M and GR*

PADSTOW SW9175   PL28 8AN

☆ **Golden Lion**

Lanadwell Street

Old inn dating to the 14th c, cheerful black-beamed locals' bar, high-raftered back lounge
with plush banquettes, three well kept ales such as Sharps Doom Bar, reasonably priced
simple bar lunches including good crab sandwiches, evening steaks and fresh fish,
friendly staff, coal fire and woodburner; pool in family area, piped music, sports TV; dogs
welcome, colourful floral displays at front, terrace tables, three bedrooms, open all day.
Recommended by Adrian Johnson, the Didler, Sally and John Quinlan, Dennis Jones

PADSTOW SW9275   PL28 8BL

Old Custom House

South Quay

Large, bright and airy open-plan seaside bar, comfortable and well divided, with rustic
décor and cosy corners, beams, exposed brickwork and bare boards, raised section, big
family area and conservatory, good food choice from baguettes to bargain deals for two,
four local ales including St Austell, good friendly service, adjoining fish restaurant; piped
and live music, TV, machines, pool; good spot by harbour, open all day, attractive sea-view
bedrooms. *Recommended by Ted George, Dennis Jones*

PADSTOW SW9175   PL28 8AF

Shipwrights

North Quay; aka the Blue Lobster

Long narrow quayside building with open-plan low-ceilinged bar, stripped brick, lots of
wood, flagstones, lobster pots and nets, quick popular food, well kept St Austell ales,
friendly polite service, further upstairs eating area; piped music, TV, machines, busy with
young people in evenings; dogs welcome, a few tables out by water, more in back suntrap
garden. *Recommended by Dave Irving, Jenny Huggins, Eddie Edwards, Dennis Jones, Robert Watt*

PAUL SW4627   TR19 6TZ

☆ **Kings Arms**

Mousehole Lane, opposite church

Friendly beamed local with cosy bustling atmosphere, enjoyable sensibly priced food from
sandwiches up, well kept St Austell ales, local artwork, darts, live bluegrass Tues
evenings; children and dogs welcome, five bedrooms, open all day in summer. *Recommended*
by Mike Proctor

☆ **PELYNT** SX2054   PL13 2JZ
Jubilee
B3359 NW of Looe

Popular early 17th-c beamed inn with wide range of locally sourced home-made food
(best to book in season) from good sandwiches up including Sun roasts, well kept
St Austell ales, good wines by the glass, friendly helpful staff, interesting Queen Victoria
mementoes (pub renamed 1897 to celebrate her diamond jubilee), some handsome
antique furnishings, log fire in big stone fireplace, separate bar with darts, pool and
games machine; sparkling new lavatories; children and dogs welcome, disabled facilities,
large terrace, 11 comfortable bedrooms, open all day weekends. *Recommended by*
Dennis Jenkin, Dudley and Moira Cockroft, Stanley and Annie Matthews and others

PENDOGGETT SX0279   PL30 3HH
Cornish Arms
B3314

Picturesque old coaching inn with traditional oak settles on front bar's polished slate
floor, fine prints, above-average food from good sandwiches and fresh fish to splendid
steaks and Sun lunch (best to book), also good authentic thai food from resident thai
chefs, well kept Bass and Sharps Doom Bar, good wines by the glass, comfortably spaced
tables in small dining room, proper back locals' bar with woodburner and games;
provision for children, disabled access (staff helpful), terrace with distant sea view,
bedrooms, open all day. *Recommended by Henry Fryer*

PENZANCE SW4730   TR18 4AF
Admiral Benbow
Chapel Street

Well run rambling pub, full of life and atmosphere and packed with interesting nautical
gear, friendly thoughtful staff, good value above-average food including local fish, real
ales such as Sharps, Skinners and St Austell, cosy corners, fire, downstairs restaurant in
captain's cabin style, upper floor with pool, pleasant view from back room; children
welcome, open all day in summer. *Recommended by Clifford Blakemore, Richard Stanfield, P Dawn,*
John and Sharon Hancock

☆ **PENZANCE** SW4729   TR18 4EF
Dolphin
Barbican; Newlyn road, opposite harbour after swing-bridge

Part old-fashioned pub and part bistro, good value food especially fresh fish (landlady's
husband is a fisherman), St Austell ales, good wines by the glass, friendly helpful service,
roomy bar, great fireplace, dining area a few steps down, cosy family room; big pool room
with juke box etc, no obvious nearby parking; pavement picnic-sets, open all day.
Recommended by the Didler, P Dawn, Roger and Donna Huggins, Christopher Turner

☆ **PERRANARWORTHAL** SW7738   TR3 7NU
Norway
A39 Truro—Penryn

Large pub doing well under enterprising licensees, helpful friendly service, wide choice
of generous carefully prepared food using local produce including vegetarian options, all-
day Sun carvery, morning coffee and afternoon tea, good selection of St Austell ales and
of wines by the glass, unusual sherry menu with accompanying nibbles, half a dozen
linked areas, beams hung with farm tools, lots of prints and rustic bric-a-brac, old-style
wooden seating and big tables on slate flagstones, open fires, Mon night quiz; children
well catered for, tables outside, open all day. *Recommended by Gene and Tony Freemantle,*
Peter Salmon, Chris and Angela Buckell

The price we give for a two-course evening meal in the featured top pub entries is
the mean (average of cheapest and most expensive) price of a starter
and a main course – no drinks.

PILLATON SX3664   PL12 6QS

Weary Friar
Off Callington—Landrake back road

Tucked-away welcoming 12th-c pub, good food in bar and restaurant served by friendly attentive staff, well kept ales, farm cider, knocked-together carpeted rooms, dark beams, copper and brass, log fires in stone fireplaces; no dogs inside; children welcome, tables outside, church next door (Tues evening bell-ringing), comfortable bedrooms.
Recommended by Ted George, Tom Bray, J F Stackhouse

POLGOOTH SW9950   PL26 7DA

Polgooth Inn
Well signed off A390 W of St Austell; Ricketts Lane

Big welcoming country pub, separate servery for enjoyable generous food from doorstep sandwiches up (only roasts on Sun), children's helpings and reasonable prices, well kept St Austell ales, good wine choice, eating area around sizeable bar with woodburner, good big family room; fills quickly in summer (handy for nearby caravan parks); dogs welcome, steps up to play area, tables out on grass, pretty countryside. *Recommended by Andrew Scott*

POLRUAN SX1250   PL23 1PJ

Russell
West Street

No-frills fishermen's local, sensibly priced food including curries and enjoyable Sun lunch, St Austell beers, friendly staff, large bar with interesting old local photographs, log fire; piped radio; children and dogs welcome, pavement tables, open all day Easter-Nov.
Recommended by Nick Lawless, Ian Phillips, Dave Webster, Sue Holland

PORTHLEVEN SW6225   TR13 9JB

Harbour Inn
Commercial Road

Large neatly kept pub/hotel in outstanding harbourside setting, pleasant well organised service, expansive lounge and bar with impressive dining area off, big public bar with panelling and leather seating, St Austell ales, comprehensive wine list, enjoyable generous food from fresh fish to steaks, quiet piped music, Thurs quiz; picnic-sets on big quayside terrace, well equipped bedrooms, some with harbour view, good breakfast.
Recommended by Tracey and Stephen Groves, Stanley and Annie Matthews

PORTHLEVEN SW6225   TR13 9JS

Ship
Mount Pleasant Road (harbour) off B3304

Friendly fishermen's pub built into cliffs, fine harbour views (interestingly floodlit at night) from seats on terrace and in knocked-through bar, well kept Courage Best, St Austell Tribute and Sharps Doom Bar, honest bar food including good crab sandwiches and home-made pies, log fires in big stone fireplaces, some genuine individuality, family room (converted from old smithy) with huge log fire, candlelit dining room also looking over sea; piped music, games machine; dogs welcome in bar, open all day. *Recommended by K Hunt, M Smith, Adrian Johnson, the Didler, Clifford Blakemore, Roger and Donna Huggins and others*

PORTHTOWAN SW6948   TR4 8AW

☆ Blue
Beach Road, East Cliff; car park (fee in season) advised

Informal busy bar (not a traditional pub) right by wonderful beach, so immensely popular with customers of all ages and their dogs; St Austell ales, several wines by the glass, cocktails, giant cups of coffee, good modern food all day (reduced from 3-6pm), lively friendly staff and easy informal atmosphere; big picture windows looking across the terrace to the huge expanse of sand and sea, mix of built-in pine seats, chrome and wicker furniture on stripped-wood floor, powder-blue walls, ceiling fans, big plants; quiet piped music, live bands Sat evening, pool; open all day in summer, closed 6pm winter Mon and Tues and two weeks in Jan. *Recommended by anon*

PORTLOE SW9339   TR2 5RA
☆ **Ship**
At top of village

Bright unspoilt L-shaped local, popular generous food including fresh fish (good if pricey crab sandwiches), well kept St Austell ales, Healey's cider/perry, good choice of wines, friendly welcoming service, interesting nautical and local memorabilia and photographs, amazing beer bottle collection; piped music; children and dogs welcome, disabled access to main bar (road very steep though), smokers' gazebo, sheltered and attractive streamside picnic-sets over road, pretty fishing village with lovely cove and coast path above, bedrooms, open all day Fri-Sun summer. *Recommended by Chris and Angela Buckell, Lawrence Pearse, Trevor Swindells, Barry Collett*

PORTSCATHO SW8735   TR2 5HW
Plume of Feathers
The Square

Cheerful largely stripped-stone pub in pretty fishing village, well kept St Austell and other ales, Healey's cider, pubby food from sandwiches and huge ploughman's up, bargain fish night Fri, sea-related bric-a-brac in comfortable linked room areas, small side locals' bar (can be very lively evenings), restaurant; very popular with summer visitors, warm local atmosphere out of season; piped music; children, dogs and boots welcome, disabled access, lovely coast walks, open all day in summer (other times if busy). *Recommended by Chris and Angela Buckell, David Crook*

PRAZE AN BEEBLE SW6335   TR14 0JR
St Aubyn Arms
The Square

Welcoming place with well kept ales and enjoyable sensibly priced pubby food in bar and dining areas (one upstairs), games in public bar; piped music; children welcome, picnic-sets in large attractive garden. *Recommended by Ernie Williams*

RUAN LANIHORNE SW8942   TR2 5NX
☆ **Kings Head**
Village signed off A3078 St Mawes road

Country pub in quiet hamlet, relaxed small bar with log fire, Skinners and a guest, maybe farm cider, good food especially local fish, friendly service, two dining areas, lots of china cups hanging from ceiling joists, plenty of copper and brass, hunting prints, cabinet filled with old glass bottles, separate restaurant; piped music; well behaved children allowed in dining areas only, dogs in bar; terrace across road and lower beer garden; interesting nearby church and walks along Fal estuary, closed winter Sun evening, Mon. *Recommended by Nick Lawless, R K Phillips, Mr and Mrs P D Titcomb, Philip and Jan Medcalf, Comus and Sarah Elliott and others*

ST AGNES SW7250   TR5 0TJ
Railway Inn
Vicarage Road, via B3277

Friendly low-ceilinged village local with well kept Greene King Abbot and Sharps Doom Bar, coal fire; sports TV; children in eating area, terrace. *Recommended by Barry and Anne*

ST GERMANS SX3557   PL12 5NR
Eliot Arms
Fore Street

Stone-built slate-roofed pub with reasonably priced food from filled rolls up; picnic-sets out in front walled area with flowers and hanging baskets, seven chintzy bedrooms. *Recommended by Chris and Angela Buckell, Charles Gysin, Dr D J and Mrs S C Walker*

If you know a pub's ever open all day, please tell us.

ST IVES SW5140   TR26 1LF
Lifeboat
Wharf Road

Thriving family-friendly beamed quayside pub, wide choice of good value food all day, three St Austell ales, friendly helpful staff, well spaced harbour-view tables and cosier corners, nautical theme including lifeboat pictures; sports TV; dogs welcome, good disabled access and facilities, open all day. *Recommended by George Atkinson*

ST IVES SW5140   TR26 1LP
Sloop
The Wharf

Busy low-beamed, panelled and flagstoned harbourside pub with bright St Ives School pictures and attractive portrait drawings in front bar, booth seating in back bar, good value food from sandwiches and interesting baguettes to lots of fresh local fish, quick friendly service even though busy, Greene King and Sharps, good coffee; piped music, TV; children in eating area, a few beach-view seats out on cobbles, open all day (breakfast from 9am), cosy bedrooms, handy for Tate Gallery. *Recommended by Robert Kibble, Richard Stanfield, Peter Salmon, the Didler, P Dawn, Stanley and Annie Matthews and others*

ST IVES SW5140   TR26 1AB
Union
Fore Street

Popular friendly low-beamed local, roomy but cosy, with good value food from sandwiches to local fish, well kept Sharps Doom Bar, decent wines, coffee, small fire, leather sofas on carpet, dark woodwork and masses of ship photographs; piped music; dogs welcome. *Recommended by David Crook, George Atkinson, Alan Johnson*

ST JUST IN PENWITH SW3731   TR19 7HF
Kings Arms
Market Square

Under newish welcoming management, well kept St Austell ales, home-made food (not Sun evening) including good fish and chips, three separate areas, granite walls and beamed and boarded ceilings, open fires; live music Sun, Weds quiz night; children and dogs welcome, tables out in front*Recommended by the Didler, Richard Stanfield, Robin Sykes, Alan Johnson*

ST KEW SX0276   PL30 3HB
St Kew Inn
Village signposted from A39 NE of Wadebridge

Grand-looking 15th-c pub with neat beamed bar, St Austell beers tapped from the cask, much enjoyed bar food (not winter Sun evenings) using some produce grown by locals, stone walls, winged high-backed settles and more traditional furniture on tartan carpeting, all sorts of jugs dotted about, woodburner in stone fireplace, three dining areas, live music every other Fri; children (away from bar) and dogs welcome, pretty flowering tubs and baskets, open all day. *Recommended by David Eberlin, Anthony Barnes, Henry Fryer, the Didler, David Hoult and others*

ST MAWES SW8433   TR2 5AN
Idle Rocks
Tredenham Road (harbour edge)

Comfortable, old-fashioned waterfront hotel with lovely sea views, Skinners Betty Stogs and decent wines by the glass (at a price), enjoyable lunchtime food in two-tier restaurant looking on to terrace and harbour (more formal in evening but still relaxed), also nice snacks in pleasant small bar area and separate lounge, daily papers, friendly helpful young staff; well behaved dogs (but no small children) allowed on sun terrace over harbour, smallish bedrooms overlooking the water are the best bet. *Recommended by Dennis Jenkin, R and S Bentley and others*

ST MAWES SW8433   TR2 5DJ
Rising Sun
The Square

Light and airy, with relaxed nicely redone bar on right with end woodburner, sea-view
bow window opposite, rugs on stripped wood, a few dining tables, sizeable carpeted left-
hand bar with dark wood furniture, standard food, St Austell ales, good wines by the
glass, friendly staff, wood-floored conservatory; piped music; awkward wheelchair access,
sunny terrace with picnic-sets just across road from harbour wall, bedrooms. *Recommended
by Comus and Sarah Elliott, Stanley and Annie Matthews, R and S Bentley*

ST MAWES SW8433   TR2 5DQ
Victory
Victory Hill

Currently up for sale but carrying on as usual; locals' bare-boards bar on left, carpeted
dining area on right with partitions, upstairs room with balcony, well kept Sharps and
perhaps Cornish Shag (brewed at sister pub, the Roseland in Philleigh), good pubby food
including local fish, log fires, welcoming attentive staff, plain wooden seating, board
games; piped music, no wheelchair access; one or two picnic-sets outside, two good value
bedrooms, open all day. *Recommended by R K Phillips, AEB, Barry Collett, Comus and Sarah Elliott,
Geoff and Linda Payne and others*

ST MAWGAN SW8765   TR8 4EP
☆ Falcon
NE of Newquay, off B3276 or A3059

Attractive old wisteria-clad stone inn, log-fire bar with antique coaching prints and falcon
pictures, St Austell ales kept well, pubby food, good friendly service, compact stone-
floored dining room, darts; children welcome, front cobbled courtyard and peaceful back
garden with wishing well (they ask to keep a credit card if you eat outside), pretty village,
bedrooms, has been open all day in summer. *Recommended by Peter Jacobs, David Eberlin,
James House, Mayur Shah, Eddie Edwards*

ST MERRYN SW8874   PL28 8ND
Cornish Arms
Churchtown (B3276 towards Padstow)

Managed by Rick Stein as a traditional local rather than gastropub; enjoyable inexpensive
food such as mussels and chips, steak and ale pie and scampi in a basket (can be a wait
for a table and food at peak times), friendly staff, well kept St Austell ales, good choice of
wines by the glass, log fire, fine slate floor, some 12th-c stonework and RNAS
memorabilia; popular with families, dogs welcome, picnic-sets at front and on sunny side
terrace under large heated parasols, nice views, open all day in summer from breakfast.
Recommended by Nigel and Kath Thompson, Peter and Judy Frost, Phil and Gill Wass

ST NEOT SX1867   PL14 6NG
☆ London
N of A38 Liskeard—Bodmin

Popular 16th-c beamed country pub on Bodmin Moor, open-plan but well divided, with
soft lighting, two log fires and some stripped stone, cheerful efficient staff, good
reasonably priced home-made food, good choice of real ales, decent house wines, dining
area behind timber divider; piped music; children welcome, picnic-sets on small front
terrace below 15th-c church with outstanding medieval stained glass, attractive village in
wooded valley, three bedrooms. *Recommended by Richard Fulbrook, Robert Watt*

STITHIANS SW7640   TR4 8RP
Cornish Arms
*Frogpool, which is not shown on many roadmaps but is NE of A393 – ie opposite side
to Stithians itself*

Unspoilt 18th-c village pub under newish brother and sister team (he cooks), long
beamed bar with fires either end, cosy snug, good value wholesome food, local ales and

ciders; pool, euchre, piped radio; well behaved children and dogs welcome, closed Mon lunchtime. *Recommended by John Marsh*

STRATTON SS2306   EX23 9DA
Tree
Just E of Bude; Fore Street

Rambling softly lit 16th-c beamed local with interesting old furniture and colourful décor, log fire and woodburner, well kept ales including Sharps Doom Bar, home-made food using local supplies, Sun carvery, character Elizabethan-style restaurant with old paintings; big-screen sports TV, machines, pool, darts; children welcome in back bar, seats alongside unusual old dovecote in ancient coachyard with post office, six bedrooms, open all day Fri-Sun. *Recommended by Ryta Lyndley*

TIDEFORD SX3459   PL12 5HW
Rod & Line
Church Road

Small old-fashioned local set back from road up steps, friendly lively atmosphere, Greene King Abbot and St Austell Tribute, lots of fish from local market including good crab (huge baguettes), angling theme with rods etc, low-bowed ceiling, settles, good log fire; children and dogs welcome, tables outside. *Recommended by Ian Phillips, Dr D J and Mrs S C Walker*

TREBARWITH SX0585   PL34 0HB
Port William
Trebarwith Strand

Lovely seaside setting with glorious views and sunsets, waterside picnic-sets across road and on covered terrace, fishing nets, fish tanks and maritime memorabilia inside, gallery with local artwork, well kept St Austell Tinners and HSD, farm cider, enjoyable pub food (may be a wait for a table at busy times); pool and other games, piped music; children in eating area, well equipped comfortable bedrooms, open all day. *Recommended by Mr and Mrs E Hughes*

☆ TREEN SW3923   TR19 6LG
Logan Rock
Just off B3315 Penzance—Land's End

Low-beamed traditional bar with well kept St Austell ales, enjoyable generous home-made food from sandwiches up, inglenook fire, small back snug with excellent cricket memorabilia – welcoming landlady eminent in county's cricket association, family room; no under-14s in bar, pretty split-level garden behind with covered area, good coast walks, open all day in season and can get very busy. *Recommended by the Didler, Clifford Blakemore*

☆ TREGADILLETT SX2983   PL15 7EU
Eliot Arms
Village signposted off A30 at junction with A395, W end of Launceston bypass

Creeper-covered with series of small rooms, interesting collections including 72 antique clocks, 400 snuffs, hundreds of horsebrasses, barometers, old prints and shelves of books/china, fine mix of furniture on Delabole slate from high-backed settles and chaises longues to more modern seats, open fires, well kept Courage and Sharps, decent good value food, friendly service; piped music, games machine and darts; children and dogs welcome, seats out front and back, lovely hanging baskets and tubs, bedrooms, open all day. *Recommended by John and Bernadette Elliott, the Didler, Giles and Annie Francis, Suedinley, Jacquie Jones*

TREGONY SW9244   TR2 5RW
Kings Arms
Fore Street (B3287)

Light and airy 16th-c coaching inn, long traditional main bar and two beamed and panelled front dining areas, St Austell ales, Healey's cider/perry, good quality reasonably priced food using local produce including sandwiches, tea and coffee, welcoming prompt service and chatty landlord, two fireplaces, one with huge cornish range, pubby furniture on carpet or flagstones, old team photographs, back games room; children welcome, disabled access, tables in pleasant suntrap garden, charming village. *Recommended by Chris and Angela Buckell*

TREVARRIAN SW8566   TR8 4AQ
Travellers Rest
B3276 NE of Newquay

Good choice of enjoyable food, RAF memorabilia, large open fire; dogs welcome. *Recommended by Eddie Edwards*

☆ TRURO SW8244   TR1 2HD
Old Ale House
Quay Street

Bustling town-centre pub with eight mainly local changing ales, some tapped from casks behind bar, several wines by the glass and country ones, bargain food from open kitchen, dimly lit beamed bar with engaging mix of furnishings, some interesting 1920s bric-a-brac, beer mats, matchbox collection, daily papers, upstairs room with juke box, pool and table football, beer festivals; children allowed away from bar, open all day. *Recommended by Ted George, Henry Fryer, Barry Collett, the Didler, Comus and Sarah Elliott, Peter Salmon and others*

TRURO SW8244   TR1 2LW
Try Dower
Lemon Quay

Busy Wetherspoons in former newspaper offices on the quay, up to eight real ales at bargain prices, their usual meal deals, efficient service, pastel décor, sofas, family tables and quiet areas; TV news; good market outside on Weds, Sat. *Recommended by David Crook*

TRURO SW8244   TR1 2AA
White Hart
New Bridge Street (aka Crab & Ale House)

Compact old city-centre pub with nautical theme, friendly landlord and locals, three well kept ales, decent pub food including sandwiches. *Recommended by Stanley and Annie Matthews*

VERYAN SW9139   TR2 5QA
New Inn
Village signed off A3078

Comfortable homely one-bar beamed local thriving under present landlord, straightforward good value food from sandwiches up (can get busy evenings so worth booking), St Austell ales, Healey's cider, good wines, friendly attentive service, inglenook woodburner, polished brass and old pictures; piped music, nearby parking unlikely in summer; dogs and well behaved children welcome, wheelchair access with help, secluded beer garden behind, bedrooms, interesting partly thatched village not far from nice beach. *Recommended by R K Phillips, Norman and Sarah Keeping, Chris and Angela Buckell, Lawrence Pearse and others*

WATERGATE BAY SW8464   TR8 4AA
Beach Hut
B3276 coast road N of Newquay

Great views from bustling modern beach bar with good mix of customers of all ages, surfing photographs on planked walls, cushioned wicker and cane armchairs around green and orange tables, weathered stripped-wood floor, unusual sloping bleached-board ceiling, big windows and doors opening to glass-fronted deck looking across sand to the sea, simpler end room, decent wines by the glass, possibly real ale, lots of coffees and teas, good modern food served by friendly young staff; piped music; dogs welcome in bar, open 8.30am-11pm, 10.30am-5pm in winter. *Recommended by Chris and Val Ramstedt, Eddie Edwards, Christopher Turner*

WATERGATE BAY SW8464   TR8 4AB
Phoenix
Trevarrian Hill

Popular surfers' haunt with great coast and sunset views from open balcony, bar/restaurant upstairs with enjoyable food including interesting fish dishes, downstairs bistro bar, well kept St Austell Tribute, Sharps Doom Bar and Skinners Betty Stogs, decent wines, sensible prices, friendly efficient staff; live music; TV, pool; well behaved children and dogs welcome, disabled facilities, plenty of outside seating, open all day weekends. *Recommended by Eddie Edwards*

ZELAH SW8151   TR4 9HU
Hawkins Arms
A30

Homely 18th-c stone-built beamed local with enjoyable good value food including freshly cooked pies, well kept Bays and a guest such as Skinners, friendly landlord and staff, copper and brass in bar and dining room, woodburners; children welcome, pleasant back terrace. *Recommended by Paul and Dawn Rundle, Mike and Kathryn Budd*

ZENNOR SW4538   TR26 3BY
☆  # Tinners Arms
B3306 W of St Ives

Friendly welcome and honest good value food including enjoyable ploughman's with three cornish cheeses and home-baked bread, long unspoilt bar with flagstones, granite, stripped pine and real fires each end, back dining room, well kept ales such as St Austell Tinners, Sharps Doom Bar and Wadworths 6X from casks behind counter, farm cider, sensibly priced wines, decent coffee, friendly mix of locals and visitors; muddy walkers welcome, tables in small suntrap courtyard, lovely peaceful windswept setting by church near coast path. *Recommended by Tracey and Stephen Groves, Dr A McCormick, S J and C C Davidson, the Didler, M and GR, Chris and Libby Allen and others*

SCILLY ISLES

ST AGNES SV8808   TR22 0PL
☆ # Turks Head
The Quay

One of the UK's most beautifully placed pubs, idyllic sea and island views from garden terrace, can get very busy on fine days, good food from pasties to popular fresh seafood (best to get there early), friendly licensees and good cheerful service, well kept ales and cider; closed winter, otherwise open all day. *Recommended by Bob and Margaret Holder, Michael Sargent, Tony and Jill Radnor, Nigel Morton*

ST MARY'S SV9010   TR21 0HY
☆ # Atlantic Inn
The Strand; next to but independent from Atlantic Hotel

Spreading and hospitable dark bar with well kept St Austell ales, good range of food including daily specials, sea-view restaurant, low beams, hanging boat and other nauticalia, mix of locals and tourists – busy evenings, quieter on sunny lunchtimes; darts, pool, games machines, piped and live music; nice raised verandah with wide views over harbour, good bedrooms in adjacent hotel. *Recommended by Neil and Anita Christopher, Bob and Margaret Holder, G M Hollington, Nigel Morton*

Most pubs with any outside space now have some kind of smokers' shelter. There are regulations about these – for instance, they have to be substantially open to the outside air. The best have heating and lighting and are really quite comfortable.

TRESCO SV8815 TR24 0QG
☆ New Inn
New Grimsby

Attractive inn close to quay and ferries and handy for famous gardens; little locals' bar but most visitors head for main bar with its standing timbers, mix of comfortable old sofas and banquettes, farmhouse chairs and tables, boat pictures, large model sailing boat, collection of old telescopes and plates, light airy dining extension with cheerful yellow walls and blue wooden floors, enjoyable food, cornish beers, good wines by the glass; piped music, pool; children and dogs welcome, teak furniture under huge parasols on flower-filled terrace, views of the sea, bedrooms, open all day in summer. *Recommended by Neil and Anita Christopher, Bernard Stradling, Michael Sargent, R J Herd, R T and J C Moggridge*

ALSO WORTH A VISIT IN DEVON

Besides the region's top pubs, we recommend the following. Do tell us
what you think of them: **feedback@goodguides.com**

ABBOTSKERSWELL SX8568 TQ12 5NY
☆ Court Farm
Wilton Way; look for the church tower

Attractive neatly extended 17th-c longhouse tucked away in picturesque hamlet, various rooms off long crazy-paved main beamed bar, good mix of furnishings, good well priced food from sandwiches to steaks, friendly helpful staff, several ales including Otter, farm cider, decent wines, woodburners; piped music; children welcome, picnic-sets in pretty lawned garden, open all day. *Recommended by Tom and Ruth Rees*

APPLEDORE SS4630 EX39 1RY
☆ Beaver
Irsha Street

Relaxed harbourside pub, good choice of enjoyable well priced food especially fresh local fish, friendly helpful staff, ales such as St Austell Tribute and Sharps, farm cider, decent house wines, great range of whiskies, lovely estuary view from popular raised dining area; pool in smaller games room; children and dogs welcome, disabled access (but no nearby parking), tables on small sheltered water-view terrace. *Recommended by Andy and Jill Kassube, Peter Thornton, Ryta Lyndley, Richard Tilbrook*

ASHBURTON SX7569 TQ13 7DU
Exeter Inn
West Street

Welcoming pleasantly old-fashioned beamed pub, straightforward low-priced food, well kept Dartmoor and a guest such as Teignworthy, local cider and decent wines, log fire; attractive little suntrap courtyard. *Recommended by Patricia Wood, Clive and Fran Dutson, Jeremy King*

ASHPRINGTON SX8056 TQ9 7EG
Watermans Arms
Bow Bridge, on Tuckenhay Road

Busy quarry-tiled heavy-beamed 17th-c pub in great waterside spot, high-backed settles and other sturdy furnishings, stripped stonework, roaring log fires, chatty and helpful landlord, friendly staff, well kept Palmers ales, decent wines, Thatcher's cider, wide choice of enjoyable food including children's, three eating areas, darts and dominoes; piped music, TV; dogs welcome (pub has two), heated covered dining terrace, close-set tables over road by creek, 15 comfortable bedrooms, open all day. *Recommended by Graeme Roberts, Ian Shorthouse, Theocsbrian, Roger and Donna Huggins*

ASHWATER SX3895   EX21 5EY
Village Inn
Overlooking village green

Roomy and well decorated slate-floored pub, wide choice of good generous food from
sandwiches up, welcoming efficient service, well kept Dartmoor and a guest, dining room,
conservatory with venerable grapevine, pool room; piped music; children welcome,
terrace tables. *Recommended by John and Bernadette Elliott, JJW, CMW, Reg Fowle, Helen Rickwood*

BAMPTON SS9520   EX16 9DY
Exeter Inn
A396 some way S, at B3227 roundabout

Long low roadside pub, stone-built with several updated linked rooms, mainly flagstoned,
two log fires and woodburner, large restaurant, wide choice of good generous food at
sensible prices including plenty of fresh fish, friendly helpful staff, up to six well kept ales
tapped from the cask such as Exmoor and Sharps, decent coffee, daily papers, no piped
music; children and dogs welcome, disabled facilities, tables out in front, ten revamped
bedrooms, fairly handy for Knightshayes, open all day. *Recommended by Dennis and
Doreen Haward*

BANTHAM SX6643   TQ7 3AJ
Sloop
Off A379/B3197 NW of Kingsbridge

Friendly 14th-c pub close to fine beach and walks, good mix of customers in black-
beamed bar with stripped-stone walls and flagstones, country chairs and tables,
woodburner, well kept St Austell and a guest ale, well liked reasonably priced food,
restaurant; piped music; children and dogs welcome, seats out at back, five bedrooms,
open all day in summer. *Recommended by Danny Savage, Bob and Angela Brooks, Maurice Ricketts, MP,
Geoff and Carol Thorp and others*

BARBROOK SS7248   EX35 6LD
Beggars Roost
A39 NE of village

Welcoming 17th-c pub adjoining Exmoor Manor Hotel, enjoyable freshly prepared local
food including traditional Sun lunch, good beer and cider choice, log fire, theme nights
and live music including June jazz weekend; children and dogs welcome, garden tables,
campsite next door. *Recommended by Tim Mountain, Helen Farrow, Jeff Sandford*

BARNSTAPLE SS5533   EX31 1RX
Panniers
Boutport Street

Centrally placed Wetherspoons, busy and reliable, with good value beers and food.
Recommended by MLR

BEER ST2289   EX12 3ET
Anchor
Fore Street

Friendly sea-view dining pub with wide choice of enjoyable food including good local fish,
Greene King and Otter, good value wines, coffee, rambling open-plan layout with old local
photographs, large eating area; sports TV, piped music; children well looked after, lots of
tables in attractive clifftop garden over road, delightful seaside village, reasonably priced
bedrooms. *Recommended by Bob and Margaret Holder, Peter and Giff Bennett*

BEER SY2289   EX12 3EQ
Dolphin
Fore Street

Hotel's comfortable old-fashioned lounge bar with oak panelling and interesting nooks,
marvellous old distorting mirrors, nautical bric-a-brac and antique boxing prints, and
long public bar (open all day) with darts, pool and machines, well kept Branscombe Vale,

Butcombe, Fullers and Skinners, decent wine and coffee, enjoyable food including fresh local fish (scallops and bacon the signature dish), large back restaurant; piped and some live music; children and dogs welcome, back suntrap terrace, 22 bedrooms. *Recommended by Derek and Maggie Washington, Joan and Michel Hooper-Immins*

BELSTONE ST61293   EX20 1QZ
Tors
A mile off A30

Small family-run Victorian granite pub/hotel in peaceful Dartmoor-edge village, long carpeted bar divided by settles, changing well kept ales such as Sharps, Otter and Palmers, over 50 malt whiskies, good choice of wines, enjoyable well presented food from sandwiches to specials, cheerful prompt service, restaurant; children and dogs welcome, disabled access, seats out on nearby grassy area overlooking valley, good walks, bedrooms, open all day in summer. *Recommended by Chris and Angela Buckell, Jon Wort*

BERRYNARBOR SS5546   EX34 9SG
Olde Globe
Off A399 E of Ilfracombe

Rambling dimly lit rooms geared to family visitors (cutlasses, swords, shields and rustic oddments), good choice of reasonably priced straightforward food, real ales, friendly service, games area – and genuine age behind the trimmings, with ancient walls and flagstones, high-backed oak settles and antique tables, lots of old pictures; piped music; children looked after well, dogs welcome, crazy-paved front terrace, play area, pretty village. *Recommended by Adrian Johnson*

BISHOPSTEIGNTON SX9073   TQ14 9RF
Cockhaven Manor
Off A380 Teignmouth—Newton Abbot; Cockhaven Road

Friendly family and staff in 16th-c former manor with 18th-c additions, enjoyable food including good value set lunch, Dartmoor Jail and two from Red Rock (brewed in the village), carpeted black-beamed bar with open fire, restaurant, conservatory; bedrooms. *Recommended by Joan and Michel Hooper-Immins*

BLACK DOG SS8009   EX17 4QS
Black Dog
Off B3042 at Thelbridge

Popular thatched and beamed village pub with friendly hard-working landlord, enjoyable food including good Sun carvery using local meat, cosy bar area with log fire. *Recommended by Mrs P Sumner*

BLACKAWTON SX8050   TQ9 7BG
George
Signed off A3122 and A381

Friendly bow-windowed village local with enjoyable reasonably priced pubby food (not Sun evening, Mon lunchtime) from baguettes up, well kept Dartmoor, Teignworthy and guests, chatty traditional bar, lounge with leather-backed dining chairs, woodburners, Mon quiz; children and dogs welcome, nice views from garden behind, play area, four bedrooms. *Recommended by MP*

BLACKAWTON SX8050   TQ9 7BN
☆ ## Normandy Arms
Signposted off A3122 W of Dartmouth

Clean and airy dining pub under newish friendly landlord, good food in two main dining areas with high-backed leather chairs around wooden tables on slate floors, drinkers' area with tub leather chairs and sofas by woodburner, up to three local ales, pictures of village and the pub over the years; piped music; children and dogs welcome, benches outside in front and picnic-sets in small garden across lane, pretty village, four bedrooms, closed Sun evening. *Recommended by M G Hart, Mr and Mrs W Mills*

BRAMPFORD SPEKE SX9298 EX5 5DP

 Lazy Toad

Off A377 N of Exeter

Welcoming carefully restored dining pub, beams and flagstones, settles and log fire, good interesting food from locally sourced ingredients including own lamb, herbs and soft fruits, smokery, good friendly service, well kept Otter, Sharps Doom Bar and a guest, good choice of wines by the glass; dogs welcome in bar (friendly resident cocker spaniel called Sam), disabled facilities, courtyard and garden, closed Sun evening, Mon. *Recommended by Nigel Clifton, John and Bryony Coles, Roy and Jean Russell, John Andrew, Gene and Tony Freemantle*

BRAYFORD SS7235 EX36 3HA

☆ Poltimore Arms

Yarde Down; 3 miles towards Simonsbath

Unspoilt 17th-c beamed local – so remote it generates its own electricity – freshened up under new licensees, popular home-made food from local produce (best to book), well kept Skinners Betty Stogs and a guest tapped from the cask, basic traditional furnishings, fine woodburner in inglenook, interesting ornaments and murals, two attractive restaurant areas separated by another woodburner; children and dogs welcome (pub has two labradors), picnic-sets in side garden, closed Sun evening, Mon. *Recommended by Tony and Gill Powell, B M Eldridge*

BRENDON SS7547 EX35 6PT

☆ Rockford Inn

Rockford; Lynton—Simonsbath Road, off B3223

Welcoming unspoilt and interesting 17th-c beamed inn by East Lyn River (pub has fishing permits), enjoyable home-made food including popular Sun roasts, Cotleigh and Exmoor ales, Thatcher's farm cider, interesting wines; small linked rooms with mix of padded settles and chairs around sturdy tables, open fire and three woodburners, fishing books, board games; piped music; children and dogs welcome, good walks, five bedrooms (some sharing bathrooms), open all day but closed Mon lunchtime (and evening in winter). *Recommended by Richard, Anne and Kate Ansell*

BRIXHAM SX9256 TQ5 9TH

☆ Maritime

King Street (up steps from harbour – nearby parking virtually non-existent)

Single bar packed with bric-a-brac, chamber-pots hanging from beams, hundreds of key fobs, cigarette cards, pre-war ensigns, toby jugs, mannequins, astronomical charts, even a binnacle by the door, friendly landlady, Bays Best and St Austell, 78 malts, no food or credit cards, lively terrier called George and Mr Tibbs the parrot (watch your fingers); piped music, small TV, darts and board games; well behaved children and dogs allowed, fine views over harbour, bedrooms sharing bathroom, closed lunchtime. *Recommended by the Didler*

BROADHEMBURY ST1004 EX14 3NF

Drewe Arms

Off A373 Cullompton—Honiton

Extended ancient pub with carved beams and handsome stone-mullioned windows, log fire, furniture perhaps not matching age of building, Otter beers, basic food in bar and modernised dining room; piped music, outside gents'; children and dogs welcome, seats on lawn under chestnut trees, pretty village, open all day Sun, closed Mon. *Recommended by Nick Wallis, Andrea Rampley, Colin and Louise English, Alistair Forsyth*

BUCKFAST SX7467 TQ11 0EA

☆ Abbey Inn

Buckfast Road off B3380

On a sunny day, best to arrive early to get a table on the terrace overlooking River Dart; partly panelled bar with woodburner and local paintings, St Austell ales and local cider, decent food, big dining room with more panelling and river views; piped music; children and dogs welcome, bedrooms, open all day. *Recommended by George Atkinson, Dr and Mrs A K Clarke, Edward Mirzoeff, Patrick and Daphne Darley, Pat and Tony Martin, Mike Gorton and others*

BUDLEIGH SALTERTON SY0681 EX9 6LE
Feathers
High Street

Long beamed room with nice bustling local atmosphere, decent well presented/priced food (not Sun evening) from good sandwiches to Sun roasts, friendly prompt service, well kept Branscombe Vale Branoc and guests, good mix of customers; children welcome, bedrooms, open all day. *Recommended by George Atkinson, Martin and Judith Tomlinson, PL*

BURGH ISLAND SX6444 TQ7 4BG
Pilchard
300 yards across tidal sands from Bigbury-on-Sea; walk, or summer Sea Tractor if tide's in – unique bus on stilts

Sadly, the splendid beamed and flagstoned upper bar with its lanterns and roaring log fire is now reserved for guests at the associated flamboyantly art deco hotel, but the more utilitarian lower bar is still worth a visit for the unbeatable setting high above the sea swarming below this tidal island; well kept Sharps, Thwaites Lancaster Bomber and an ale brewed for the pub, local farm cider, lunchtime baguettes; dogs welcome, tables outside, some down by beach. *Recommended by Brian Glozier, Mike and Eleanor Anderson*

BUTTERLEIGH SS9708 EX15 1PN
Butterleigh Inn
Off A396 in Bickleigh

Small-roomed heavy-beamed country pub, friendly and relaxed, with enjoyable reasonably priced food including Sun carvery, four real ales, good choice of wines, two big fireplaces, back dining room; children welcome, picnic-sets in large garden, four comfortable bedrooms. *Recommended by N Scattergood, Dawn and Ian Robertson, Jeremy Whitehorn*

☆ CADELEIGH SS9107 EX16 8HP
Cadeleigh Arms
Village signed off A3072 W of junction with A396 Tiverton—Exeter at Bickleigh

Attractive old pub with friendly civilised atmosphere and emphasis on nicely presented often interesting food, well kept Otter beer, bar to left with high-backed farmhouse and church chairs, bay window seat, ornamental stove in stone fireplace, striking hound paintings, flagstoned room with high-backed settle, log fire in big fireplace, newspapers and magazines, airy dining room down a couple of steps with valley views; unobtrusive piped music; children and dogs welcome, picnic-sets on gravel terrace, more on sloping lawn, closed Sun evening, Mon. *Recommended by John and Susan Miln, Anthony Barnes, Jane Hudson, Adrian and Dawn Collinge*

☆ CALIFORNIA CROSS SX7053 PL21 0SG
California
Brown sign to pub off A3121 S of A38 junction

Neatly modernised 18th-c or older dining pub with beams, panelling, stripped stone and log fire, wide choice of sensibly priced food from good crab baguettes to steaks in dining bar and family area, restaurant menu, popular Sun lunch (best to book), sofa in small separate snug, Coach House, Fullers and Greene King ales, decent wines, local farm cider; piped music; dogs welcome, attractive garden, back terrace, open all day. *Recommended by Helen and Brian Edgeley, S Holder*

CHAGFORD SX7087 TQ13 8AH
Ring o' Bells
Off A382

Welcoming old pub with beamed and panelled bar, four well kept ales including Dartmoor, traditional fairly priced home-made food, good friendly service, woodburner in big fireplace, some live music; dogs and well behaved children welcome, sunny walled garden, nearby moorland walks, four bedrooms, open all day. *Recommended by Sarah Moore*

CHAGFORD SX7087   TQ13 8AJ
Three Crowns
High Street

Comfortably refurbished 13th-c inn, big dimly lit bar with hunting pictures and big fireplace, separate dining room, well kept St Austell ales, enjoyable food from sandwiches to good ploughman's using local cheeses and game pie, efficient pleasant service; games room with pool. *Recommended by Mark Flynn, Pat and Tony Martin*

CHALLACOMBE SS6941   EX31 4TT
Black Venus
B3358 Blackmoor Gate—Simonsbath

Low-beamed 16th-c pub with friendly helpful landlady, two well kept changing ales, Thatcher's farm cider, enjoyable fairly priced generous food from sandwiches to popular Sun lunch, pews and comfortable chairs, woodburner and big fireplace, roomy and attractive dining area, games room with pool and darts; children welcome, garden tables, play area, grand countryside. *Recommended by Matthew Shackle, Sheila Topham, Alan A Newman, B M Eldridge*

CHUDLEIGH SX8679   TQ13 0HY
Bishop Lacey
Fore Street, just off A38

Unpretentious and interesting partly 14th-c low-beamed church house, cheerful obliging landlady and staff, characterful locals, well kept O'Hanlons, Sharps and changing west country microbrews, farm cider, home-made food including good curries, log fires, dark décor, two bars, dining room; live bands in next-door offshoot; children welcome, garden tables, good value bedrooms, open all day. *Recommended by Hugh Roberts, Sue and Mike Todd, the Didler*

CHURCHSTOW SX7145   TQ7 3QW
Church House
A379 NW of Kingsbridge

Well cared for refurbished pub dating from the 13th c under friendly licensees, heavy black beams and stripped stone, wide choice of enjoyable home-made food including popular evening carvery (Weds-Sat), well kept local ales, decent wines, back conservatory with floodlit well; children welcome, dogs in certain areas, tables on big terrace. *Recommended by Michael and Joan Johnstone, David Eberlin*

CLAYHIDON ST1615   EX15 3TJ
Half Moon
On main road through village

Attractive old village pub with pleasant staff and warm friendly atmosphere, wide choice of good home-made food including imaginative snacks, well kept Cotleigh and a guest such as Otter, farm cider, good wine list, comfortable bar with good inglenook log fire; children and dogs welcome, picnic-sets in tiered garden over road, valley views. *Recommended by Mike Gorton, Derek and Karin Churchman*

CLOVELLY SS3225   EX39 5TQ
New Inn
High Street; car-free village, visitors charged £5.95 (£3.75 children) to park and enter

Quaint peaceful 17th-c inn halfway down the steep cobbled street, Arts & Crafts décor, simple lower bar with flagstones and bric-a-brac (narrow front part has more character than back eating room), well kept Sharps Cornish Coaster and a beer brewed for the pub by local Country Life, short choice of good value bar food, upstairs restaurant; great views, small garden behind, good bedrooms. *Recommended by Andy and Jill Kassube, Michael Tack*

COCKINGTON SX8963   TQ2 6XA
Drum
Cockington Lane

Cheerfully bustling Vintage Inn in thatched and beamed tavern (designed by Lutyens to match the quaintly touristy Torquay-edge medieval village), Butcombe and St Austell ales, good choice of wines by the glass, roomy well divided wood-floor bar with open fires and family eating areas, decent food, good service; tables on terrace and in attractive back garden by 500-acre park, open all day. *Recommended by Roger and Donna Huggins*

COCKWOOD SX9780   EX6 8RA
☆ Anchor
Off, but visible from, A379 Exeter—Torbay

Extremely popular dining pub specialising in seafood (including 29 choices of mussels), food all day with two restaurant sittings summer evenings and winter weekends to cope with crowds, six real ales, a dozen wines by the glass, 130 malt whiskies and quite a few brandies and ports, several low-ceilinged small rooms with panelling, coal fire in snug, extension made mainly of reclaimed timber with over 300 ship emblems, brass and copper lamps and nautical knick-knacks, live music including Weds jazz night; children welcome seated away from bar, dogs allowed in bar, tables on verandah looking across road to inlet, open all day. *Recommended by B and M Kendall, Peter and Giff Bennett, the Didler, Mike and Monnie Jefferies, Guy Vowles, Mike Gorton and others*

COCKWOOD SX9780   EX6 8NU
☆ Ship
Off A379 N of Dawlish

Comfortable traditional 17th-c pub overlooking estuary and harbour, good value generous food including good fish dishes and puddings (freshly made by landlady so takes time), Butcombe and Sharps Doom Bar, friendly helpful staff, partitioned beamed bar with big log fire and ancient oven, decorative plates and seafaring memorabilia, small restaurant; piped music; children and dogs welcome, nice steep-sided garden. *Recommended by Bob Jones, J D O Carter*

COLYFORD SY2592   EX24 6QQ
☆ Wheelwright
Swan Hill Road (A3052 Sidmouth—Lyme Regis)

Attractive 17th-c thatched dining pub, welcoming and civilised, with high beamed ceiling, cream stone walls and flagstones, lots of knick-knacks, woodburner, really good well priced food from lunchtime sandwiches and deli boards to fresh fish/seafood, well kept Badger ales and a guest from a panelled and thatched bar, lots of bottled beer, nice wines, friendly service from aproned staff, snug area leading to more modern dining room with light furniture on wood floor, further restaurant with interesting stained-glass ceiling piece, little shop; children and dogs welcome, tables in small paved front garden, open all day. *Recommended by Roy Fox, A M Falconer, B D Jones, Tim Gray, Bart Leonard*

COLYTON SY2494   EX24 6JN
Gerrard Arms
St Andrews Square

Friendly unpretentious open-plan local, Bass, Branscombe Vale Branoc and a guest tapped from the cask, good value home-made food, skittle alley; courtyard and garden. *Recommended by the Didler*

COMBE MARTIN SS5747   EX34 0AW
Dolphin
Seaside

Well placed one-room pub with nice beach views, good friendly staff, Sharps Doom Bar and another well kept ale, good log fire, upstairs restaurant; bedrooms. *Recommended by MLR, Rob Schofield*

COMBEINTEIGNHEAD SX9072   TQ12 4RT
Coombe Cellars
Shaldon Road, off A380 opposite main Newton Abbot roundabout

Great estuary views from big waterside pub well reworked by M&B, comfortable modern feel with mix of new and traditional furnishings, well kept changing ales, lots of wines by the glass, food all day (mixed reports), friendly well trained young staff, open fire; good disabled facilities, terrace, open all day. *Recommended by Simon Cohen, Roger and Donna Huggins*

COMBEINTEIGNHEAD SX9071   TQ12 4RA
 ☆ **Wild Goose**
Off unclassified coast road Newton Abbot—Shaldon, up hill in village

Rambling pub with good choice of up to seven real ales in spacious back beamed lounge, wheelbacks and red plush dining chairs, agricultural artefacts, pubby food, front bar with beams, standing timbers and some flagstones, step down to area with big old fireplace and another cosy room with comfortable sofa and armchairs, bar billiards, darts and board games; piped music (live music Fri), games machine, TV; children in dining area only, dogs in bar, garden with nice country views. *Recommended by J D O Carter, P and J Shapley, B and M Kendall, John and Fiona McIlwain, Mike and Monnie Jefferies, Patrick and Daphne Darley*

CREDITON SS8300   EX17 1EZ
Crediton Inn
Mill Street (follow Tiverton sign)

Small friendly local with long-serving landlady, well kept Fullers London Pride, Sharps Doom Bar and quickly changing guests (Nov beer festival), cheap well prepared weekend food, back games room; free bookable skittle alley, open all day Mon-Sat. *Recommended by the Didler*

CULMSTOCK ST1013   EX15 3JJ
☆ **Culm Valley**
B3391, off A38 E of M5 junction 27

Quirky old dining pub with friendly lively atmosphere, good imaginative food (not Sun evening), interesting real ales and spirits, wines imported by landlord from smaller french vineyards, hotchpotch of modern and unrenovated furnishings (some find housekeeping a bit lapse), horse-racing paintings and knick-knacks, big fireplace, dining room and small front conservatory, larger back room with paintings by local artists for sale; no credit cards, outside gents'; children allowed away from main bar, dogs welcome (there are several pub dogs), outside seats overlooking River Culm, bedrooms, open all day Fri-Sun. *Recommended by Jenna Phillips, Dr and Mrs A K Clarke, Andrea Rampley, John Prescott, Gary Marchant, Tony Winckworth and others*

DARTMOUTH SX8751   TQ6 9RB
☆ **Cherub**
Higher Street; walk along river front, right into Hauley Road and up steps at end

Handsome timbered building (Dartmouth's oldest) with two heavily timbered upper floors jutting over the street and many original interior features, oak beams, leaded lights, tapestried seats, big stone fireplace, Otter, St Austell, Sharps Doom Bar and one or two guests in bustling bar, low-ceilinged upstairs restaurant, food from pubby favourites to more imaginative dishes (not Mon or Tues evenings in winter), good service; piped music; no children; dogs in bar, open all day in summer, closed winter afternoons Mon-Thurs. *Recommended by Peter and Heather Elliott, Alan Sutton, Alun and Jennifer Evans, Guy Vowles, the Didler, P Dawn and others*

DARTMOUTH SX8751   TQ6 9AN
Dartmouth Arms
Lower Street, Bayard's Cove

Friendly local with tables out in prime harbour-wall spot overlooking estuary – the Pilgrim Fathers set sail from here, well kept beer, enjoyable bar food, panelling and boating memorabilia, log fire. *Recommended by Simon Cohen*

DARTMOUTH SX8751   TQ6 9RT
Windjammer
Victoria Road

Family-run pub with good substantial home-made food and well kept local ales, cosy woodburner; market nearby. *Recommended by Phil and Sally Gorton*

DITTISHAM SX8654   TQ6 0EX
☆ # Ferry Boat
Manor Street

Cheerful riverside pub with lively mix of customers, beamed bar with log fires and straightforward pubby furniture, lots of boating bits and pieces, tide times chalked on wall, Otter, St Austell, Sharps and Wells & Youngs, a dozen wines by the glass, pubby food; piped music; children and dogs welcome, moorings for visiting boats on adjacent pontoon and bell to summon ferry, good walks, open all day. *Recommended by Wendy and Carl Dye, Peter and Giff Bennett, Sandy Butcher, Phil and Sally Gorton*

DREWSTEIGNTON SX7390   EX6 6QN
☆ # Drewe Arms
Off A30 NW of Moretonhampstead

Pretty thatched pub in lovely village, unspoilt room on left with basic wooden wall benches, stools and tables, original serving hatch, Hop Back, Otter and Sharps tapped from casks in tap room, local cider, tasty bar food in three dining areas, one with Rayburn and history of Britain's longest serving and oldest landlady, another with woodburner, back room with lots of prints, pictures and copper saucepans; children and dogs welcome, seats under umbrellas on front terrace and in garden, pretty flowering tubs and baskets, bedrooms and bunk rooms, handy for Castle Drogo, open all day in summer. *Recommended by B and M Kendall, Adrian Johnson, Gene and Tony Freemantle, Alison Ball, Ian Walton, Jane Hudson, Tich Critchlow and others*

DUNSFORD SX8189   EX6 7DA
☆ # Royal Oak
Signed from Moretonhampstead

Comfortably worn-in village inn, good generous food cooked to order, changing ales including Dartmoor and Sharps, local cider, friendly landlord, airy lounge with woodburner and view from sunny dining bay, simple dining room, steps down to pool room; piped music, quiz nights; children well looked after, sheltered tiered garden, good value bedrooms in converted barn. *Recommended by the Didler*

EAST ALLINGTON SX7648   TQ9 7RA
☆ # Fortescue Arms
Village signed off A381 Totnes—Kingsbridge, S of A3122 junction

Pretty village pub with two-room bar, nice mix of cushioned dining chairs and wooden tables on black slate floor, log fire, church candles in main part and similarly furnished second room used more for dining, inventive food cooked by austrian landlord, Butcombe, Dartmoor and a guest, several wines by the glass, separate contemporary restaurant; children (over 6) in one area, dogs in bar, sheltered courtyard with picnic-sets, teak steamer chairs under pair of marquees on terrace, bedrooms, closed Mon lunchtime. *Recommended by Peter and Heather Elliott, M G Hart*

EAST PRAWLE SX7836   TQ7 2BY
Pigs Nose
Prawle Green

Relaxed quirky three-room 16th-c inn with low beams and flagstones, local ales tapped from the cask, farm ciders, simple pubby food, open fire, mix of old furniture, lots of interesting bric-a-brac and pictures, jars of wild flowers and candles on tables, darts, small family area with unusual toys, nice dogs, laid-back service; unobtrusive piped music, hall for live bands (friendly landlord was 60s tour manager); tables outside, pleasant spot on village green. *Recommended by Tich Critchlow, the Didler, Sally and John Quinlan*

ERMINGTON SX6353   PL21 9LP
Crooked Spire
The Square

Cheerful scots landlord, well kept Sharps Doom Bar, enjoyable straightforward food (not Mon), no-frills open-plan layout with warm open fire, pool; children and dogs welcome, pleasant heated back courtyard, open all day Thurs-Sat. *Recommended by MP*

EXETER SX9390   EX2 6LT
Double Locks
Canal Banks, Alphington, via Marsh Barton Industrial Estate; OS Sheet 192 map ref 933901

Unchanging, unsmart and individual, by ship canal, remote yet busy, Wells & Youngs and guest ales, Gray's farm cider in summer, hearty home-made bar food all day including Sun roast, friendly service (can get swamped); piped music, live at weekends; children and dogs welcome, seats out on grass or decking with distant view to city and cathedral (nice towpath walk out – or hire a canoe at The Quay), big play area, summer barbecues, camping, open all day. *Recommended by the Didler, John Prescott, Mr and Mrs Alesbrook, Phil and Sally Gorton, Richard Mason and others*

EXETER SX9192   EX1 1BL
Fat Pig
John Street

Refurbished Victorian pub, welcoming and relaxed, with several local ales including Exeter, good wine choice, imaginative blackboard food, nice fire; tables in heated courtyard. *Recommended by Elizabeth Saunders, M J Winterton*

EXETER SX9193   EX4 4NU
Great Western
St David's Hill

Regulars enjoy up to a dozen or so well kept changing ales including some rarities in this large commercial hotel's comfortably worn-in plush-seated bar, friendly efficient staff, fresh good value pubby food all day from sandwiches up (kitchen also supplies hotel's restaurant), daily papers; may be piped music, sports TV, pay parking; children welcome, 35 bedrooms, open all day. *Recommended by Phil and Sally Gorton, the Didler*

EXETER SX9292   EX2 4AU
☆ # Hour Glass
Melbourne Street; off B3015 Topsham Road

Old-fashioned corner local with enjoyable surprisingly inventive food, Branscombe Vale, Exeter and St Austell beers and good range of wines by the glass, comfortable atmosphere (fine either for meeting friends or on a lone visit), beams and nice mix of furnishings, open fire in small brick fireplace, dark red walls, resident cats; piped music; children (away from bar) and dogs welcome, open all day Fri-Sun, closed Mon lunchtime. *Recommended by the Didler, Mike Gorton*

EXETER SX9193   EX4 4AH
Imperial
New North Road (above St David's Station)

Impressive 19th-c mansion in own six-acre hillside park with sweeping drive, various different areas including two clubby little side bars, fine former ballroom with elaborate plasterwork and gilding, light and airy former orangery with unusual mirrored end wall, interesting pictures, up to 14 real ales, standard good value Wetherspoons' menu; can get very busy and popular with students; plenty of picnic-sets in grounds and elegant garden furniture in attractive cobbled courtyard. *Recommended by Bob and Margaret Holder, Tony and Wendy Hobden, B and M Kendall, the Didler, Mike Gorton, Giles and Annie Francis and others*

Tipping is not normal for bar meals, and not usually expected.

EXETER SX9292   EX4 4EP
Old Fire House
New North Road

Compact relaxed city-centre pub in Georgian building behind high arched wrought-iron
gates, up to eight ales including Otter (regular beer festivals), several real ciders and
good choice of bottled beers and wines, bargain food including late evening pizzas,
friendly efficient staff, dimly lit beamed rooms with simple furniture; piped music, live
folk and jazz weekends, popular with young crowd in evenings; picnic-sets in front
courtyard, open all day. *Recommended by the Didler, P Dawn, L Stevens*

EXETER SX9292   EX2 4AN
Prospect
The Quay (left bank, near rowing club)

Early 19th-c pub in good quayside position, enjoyable simple all-day food generously
served, well kept Otter, St Austell Tribute and Skinners Betty Stogs, friendly efficient
young staff, plenty of comfortable tables including raised river-view dining area; gentle
piped music, live bands Mon, Tues; children welcome, tables out by historic ship-canal
basin, open all day. *Recommended by Dave Irving, Jenny Huggins, Tony and Wendy Hobden,
David Crook*

EXETER SX9293   EX4 4LZ
Rusty Bike
Howell Road

Comfortably refurbished backstreet pub with bistro feel (same owners as Fat Pig in
John Street), pine tables on stripped boards in large open bar, big black and white
photographs, adjoining dining area, four changing ales, farm cider, good wine choice,
enjoyable interesting blackboard food; piped music, popular with students, limited
parking; walled beer garden with projector for live sport and film nights. *Recommended by
Mike Gorton, Becky Moore*

EXETER SX9291   EX2 8DU
Welcome
*Haven Banks, off Haven Road (which is first left off A377 heading S after Exe
crossing)*

Two-room pub little changed since the 60s (ditto the juke box), gas lighting and
flagstones, very friendly old-school landlady, changing ales; a few tables out overlooking
basin on Exeter Ship Canal, can be reached on foot via footbridges from The Quay;
limited opening times. *Recommended by Phil and Sally Gorton, the Didler*

EXETER SX9292   EX1 1HB
Well House
Cathedral Yard (attached to Royal Clarence Hotel)

Good position with big windows looking across to cathedral in partly divided open-plan
bar, good choice of west country ales, real cider, quick service, enjoyable food from
hotel's kitchen, lots of Victorian prints, daily papers, Roman well below (can be viewed
when pub not busy), live music (last Sun of month), beer/cider festivals; open all day.
Recommended by the Didler

EXMINSTER SX9686   EX6 8EE
☆ ## Turf Hotel
*Follow the signs to the Swan's Nest, signed from A379 S of village, then continue to end
of track, by gates; park and walk right along canal towpath – nearly a mile*

Remote but very popular waterside pub reached by 30-minute towpath walk, cycle ride or
60-seater boat from Topsham quay (15-minute trip), also visitor moorings; three simply
furnished informal rooms, built-in seats, wood-strip floors, lots of photographs of the pub,
woodburner, up to five real ales, local cider, decent wines by the glass, good food (not Sun
evening) using organic produce, summer barbecues, efficient friendly staff even when
packed (queues at peak summer times); children and dogs welcome, plenty of picnic-sets

in big garden, sea and estuary birds to watch at low tide, open all day in summer, closed weekdays in Oct, Nov, Feb, Mar, all Dec and Jan. *Recommended by the Didler, Richard Tilbrook, Dr and Mrs A K Clarke, Mike Gorton*

EXMOUTH SY9980   EX8 1BJ
Grove
Esplanade

Roomy unpretentious old-fashioned family pub set back from beach, basic traditional furnishings, caricatures and local prints, good value food all day from sensibly short menu, specials including local fish, all cooked to order so may be a wait at peak times, friendly staff, Wells & Youngs and guests, decent house wines, good coffee, attractive fireplace at back, sea views from appealing upstairs dining room and balcony; piped music, live music on Fri; picnic-sets in big garden (no view) with play area. *Recommended by PL, M J Winterton, Richard Tilbrook, Michael and Lynne Gittins*

FROGMORE SX7742   TQ7 2NR
Globe
A379 E of Kingsbridge

Extended and refurbished pub with friendly staff and regulars, well kept Otter, Skinners and South Hams, local farm cider in summer, good wine by the glass, enjoyable well priced food from baguettes to steak, airy bar, fine log fire in cosy restaurant, monthly folk music evenings; piped music, TV, games machine, darts; dogs welcome, terrace tables, creek and coast walks, eight well appointed modern bedrooms, good breakfast.
Recommended by Dennis Jenkin, Geoff and Carol Thorp, Roxanne Chamberlain

GALMPTON SX8856   TQ5 0NL
Manor
Village and pub signed off A3022; Stoke Gabriel Road

Large friendly open-plan Edwardian local with well kept ales such as Otter, St Austell Dartmoor and Sharps Doom Bar, good choice of sensibly priced food including local fish, two-part bar and family dining area, games room with sports TV, some live music; tables outside, conker tournament and gooseberry pie fair, new bedrooms, open all day.
Recommended by Mrs J King, Sam Mitchel, Tom Ben

HARBERTON SX7758   TQ9 7SF
☆ # Church House
Off A381 S of Totnes

Ancient partly Norman village pub with unusually long bar, well kept ales such as Butcombe, Courage, Marstons and St Austell, good choice of wines by the glass, farm cider, wide range of good well priced local food, friendly efficient service, blackened beams, medieval latticed glass and oak panelling, attractive 17th- and 18th-c pews and settles, woodburner in big inglenook, family room; bedrooms. *Recommended by Dr Nigel Bowles, David and Pamela White, F A Ashley, Mrs Gillian McAllen, Paul and Karen Cornock*

HATHERLEIGH SS5404   EX20 3JN
George
A386 N of Okehampton; Market Street

Completely rebuilt after original 15th-c thatched and timbered pub burnt down in 2008; old-style interior with lots of reclaimed beamery and other old materials, mix of furniture (old and new) on carpet, wood and tiled floors, open fires, good range of enjoyable food including sharing boards and pizzas, real ales such as Fullers London Pride, good coffee, friendly staff; bedrooms. *Recommended by Ryta Lyndley*

HATHERLEIGH SS5404   EX20 3JN
☆ # Tally Ho
Market Street (A386)

Good generous uncomplicated food (not Sun evening) from lunchtime sandwiches up, good value wines, real ales such as local Clearwater and St Austell, quick friendly service, attractive heavy-beamed and timbered linked rooms, sturdy furnishings, big log fire and woodburner, traditional games, restaurant, busy Tues market day (beer slightly cheaper then); unobtrusive piped music; dogs welcome, tables in nice sheltered garden, three good value pretty bedrooms, open all day. *Recommended by the Didler, Ron and Sheila Corbett, Reg Fowle, Helen Rickwood*

HEANTON PUNCHARDON SS5034   EX31 4AX
Tarka
A361 SE of village

Castle-look Vintage Inn overlooking estuary (lovely sunsets), enjoyable sensibly priced food including nice specials, a couple of well kept ales such as St Austell Tribute, good staff particularly helpful with children. *Recommended by Barrie and Mary Crees, John and Fiona McIlwain, Sue Rowland*

HELE SS5347   EX34 9QY
Billys
Watermouth Road

Friendly refurbished bar/restaurant with well kept St Austell Tribute and guests, enjoyable home-made food from snacks up including fresh fish, good choice of sensibly priced wines, open fire, friendly cat called Thumbelina; piped music, machines, pool; well behaved children and dogs welcome, front terrace with big heated umbrella, open all day. *Recommended by Reg Fowle, Helen Rickwood, MLR*

HEMBOROUGH POST SX8352   TQ9 7DE
Sportsmans Arms
B3207 Dartmouth—Halwell

Spacious family pub with good value carvery, well kept ales such as St Austell Tribute, helpful friendly service; play area outside. *Recommended by M G Hart, Vicky Barron*

HOLBETON SX6150   PL8 1NE
Dartmoor Union
Off A379 W of A3121 junction; Fore Street

Changed hands in 2010 and once again brewing own Union ales, civilised bare-boards bar with leather sofas and armchairs by open fire, good food here or more choice in smart restaurant, friendly staff; closed Mon, Tues. *Recommended by P R Light, Geoff and Carol Thorp*

HOLNE SX7069   TQ13 7SJ
☆ # Church House
Signed off B3357 W of Ashburton

Newish owners for two-room medieval inn in lovely moorland village; lower bar with stripped-pine panelling and 18th-c curved elm settle, heavy 16th-c oak partitioning separating it from lounge, open log fires, Dartmoor and Teignworthy ales, farm cider, decent traditional food (not Sun evening); piped music; children and dogs welcome, good walks, bedrooms, open all day in summer. *Recommended by John Butcher, Val Offer, P and J Shapley, Bob and Angela Brooks, R K Phillips, Sally and John Quinlan*

HOPE COVE SX6740   TQ7 3HQ
Hope & Anchor
Tucked away by car park

Bustling unpretentious inn, friendly and comfortably unfussy, in lovely seaside spot, good open fire, quick helpful service, good value straightforward food including lots of fish, well kept St Austell Dartmoor and a beer brewed for the pub, reasonably priced wines, flagstones and bare boards, dining room views to Burgh Island, big separate family room; piped music; children and dogs welcome, sea-view tables out on decking, great coast walks, bedrooms, good breakfast, open all day. *Recommended by Richard Fendick, Sally and John Quinlan, Theocsbrian*

IDE SX8990

EX2 9RW

☆ **Poachers**

3 miles from M5 junction 31, via A30; High Street

Nice beamed inn in quaint village, good home-made food, Bass, Branscombe Vale Branoc, Otter and guests from ornate curved wooden bar, non-standard mix of old chairs and sofas, big log fire, restaurant; tables in pleasant garden with barbecue, three comfortable bedrooms. *Recommended by the Didler*

IDEFORD SX8977

TQ13 0AY

☆ **Royal Oak**

2 miles off A380

Unpretentious 16th-c thatched and flagstoned village local, friendly helpful service, Greene King, Otter and guests, basic pub snacks, navy theme including interesting Nelson and Churchill memorabilia, panelling, big open fireplace; children and dogs welcome, tables out at front and by car park over road. *Recommended by the Didler*

INSTOW SS4730

EX39 4JJ

Boat House

Marine Parade

Airy modern high-ceilinged place with huge tidal beach just across lane and views to Appledore, well kept ales and decent wines, wide choice of good food including plenty of fish/seafood, friendly prompt service, lively family bustle; piped music; roof terrace. *Recommended by Ryta Lyndley*

INSTOW SS4730

EX39 4LB

Wayfarer

Lane End

Unpretentious locals' pub tucked away near dunes and beach, well kept ales tapped from the cask, winter mulled wine, good choice of enjoyable generous home-made food using local fish and meat, quick cheerful service; children and dogs welcome, enclosed garden behind, six well presented bedrooms (some with sea view), open all day. *Recommended by Mrs V A Taylor, Stephen Haynes*

KENTISBEARE ST0608

EX15 2AA

Wyndham Arms

3.5 miles from M5 junction 28, via A373

Village pub rescued from closure and refurbished by enthusiastic local volunteers, well kept Otter and guests, traditional food and specials, friendly helpful staff, big log fire in long beamed main bar, restaurant, games room, live music; children welcome, tables in sheltered back courtyard. *Recommended by the Head family*

KILMINGTON SY2798

EX13 7RB

☆ **Old Inn**

A35

Thatched 16th-c pub, beams and flagstones, welcoming licensees and nice bustling atmosphere, enjoyable good value food using local supplies, well kept Cotleigh and Otter, good choice of wines, small character front bar with traditional games, back lounge with leather armchairs by inglenook log fire, small restaurant; children welcome, skittle alley, beer gardens. *Recommended by John Butcher, Val Offer, Nigel Fortnam, Geoff and Linda Payne*

KINGSBRIDGE SX7343

TQ7 1JZ

Crabshell

Embankment Road, edge of town

Lovely waterside position, charming when tide is in, with big windows and tables outside; popular and improved under new owners with emphasis on food, friendly staff, well kept local Quercus ales, feature open fire, good upstairs views; children welcome. *Recommended by Geoff and Carol Thorp, MP*

KINGSTON SX6347 TQ7 4QE

☆ **Dolphin**

Off B3392 S of Modbury (can also be reached from A379 W of Modbury)

Cosy peaceful old pub with knocked-through beamed rooms, traditional furnishings on red patterned carpet, amusing drawings on stone walls, open fire and woodburner, Courage, Otter and Sharps ales, summer farm cider, pubby food (not winter Sun evening); gents' across road; children and dogs welcome, seats outside, walks down to sea, bedrooms. *Recommended by John Butcher, Val Offer, Geoff and Carol Thorp, Bob and Angela Brooks, S Holder and others*

KINGSWEAR SX8851 TQ6 0AG

☆ **Ship**

Higher Street

Simple attractive beamed local with kind friendly family service, five well kept ales including Otter from horseshoe bar, farm cider, nice wines, well liked food including good fresh fish (best views from restaurant up steps), nautical bric-a-brac and local photographs, open fire; big-screen TV; a couple of river-view tables outside, open all day Fri-Sun and in summer (when it can get very busy). *Recommended by Mrs P Bishop, Alun and Jennifer Evans, Tony and Wendy Hobden, Richard Tilbrook, the Didler, P Dawn and others*

KINGSWEAR SX8851 TQ6 0AD

Steam Packet

Fore Street

Small friendly traditional local, well kept Bays and guests, pasties and pubby food in bar and restaurant; outside tables overlooking steam railway, good views across to Dartmouth, too. *Recommended by the Didler, P Dawn*

LAKE SX5288 EX20 4HQ

☆ **Bearslake**

A386 just S of Sourton

Rambling low thatched stone pub, leather sofas and high bar chairs on crazy-paved slate floor at one end, three more smallish rooms with woodburners, toby jugs, farm tools and traps, stripped stone, well kept Otter and Teignworthy, good range of spirits and whiskies, decent wines and enjoyable food, beamed restaurant; children allowed, large sheltered streamside garden, Dartmoor walks, six comfortably olde-worlde bedrooms, generous breakfast. *Recommended by Peter Bunting, Paul Smart*

LANDKEY SS5931 EX32 0NF

Castle Inn

Signed off A361 E of Barnstaple; Blakeshill Road

Cosy welcoming pub with wood-floored bar and separate restaurant, enjoyable pubby food including good cod and chips, local real ales; dogs welcome in bar, tables in good-sized side garden. *Recommended by Lesley Lane*

LEE SS4846 EX34 8LR

Grampus

Signed off B3343/A361 W of Ilfracombe

Attractive unpretentious 14th-c beamed pub, well kept ales such as local Jollyboat, well priced pubby food, friendly efficient service even when busy, nice relaxed atmosphere, pool; dogs very welcome, lots of tables in appealing sheltered garden, short stroll from sea – superb coast walks. *Recommended by Sue Addison*

LIFTON SX3885 PL16 0AA

☆ **Arundell Arms**

Fore Street

Good interesting lunchtime food in substantial country-house fishing hotel, warmly welcoming and individual, with rich décor, nice staff and sophisticated service, good choice of wines by the glass, morning coffee with home-made biscuits, afternoon tea, restaurant; also adjacent Courthouse bar (complete with original cells) doing fairly priced pubby food (not Mon evening), well kept St Austell Tribute and Dartmoor Jail; can arrange fishing tuition – also shooting, deer-stalking and riding; pleasant bedrooms, useful A30 stop. *Recommended by Mayur Shah, Clifford Blakemore*

LUPPITT ST1606   EX14 4RT

☆ ## Luppitt Inn
Back roads N of Honiton

Unspoilt basic farmhouse pub tucked away in lovely countryside, an amazing survivor, with chatty long-serving landlady, tiny room with corner bar and a table, another not much bigger with fireplace, cheap Otter tapped from the cask, intriguing metal puzzles made by a neighbour, no food or music, lavatories across the yard; closed lunchtime and Sun evening. *Recommended by Phil and Sally Gorton, the Didler*

LUSTLEIGH SX7881   TQ13 9TJ

☆ ## Cleave
Off A382 Bovey Tracey—Moretonhampstead

Beautifully set thatched country pub with welcoming newish landlord, enjoyable well priced food all day from baguettes up, real ales such as Otter, traditional low-ceilinged front bar with log fire, modernised back rooms, film and live music nights; children welcome, sheltered cottagey garden, good circular walks, open all day. *Recommended by Alan Sutton, Bob and Angela Brooks, Suzy Miller, Barry Steele-Perkins*

LUTON SX9076   TQ13 0BL

☆ ## Elizabethan
Haldon Moor

Charming low-beamed old-world dining pub once owned by Elizabeth I, welcoming owners and friendly efficient staff, wide choice of good well presented food including popular Sun lunch, five well kept ales, several reasonably priced wines by the glass, thriving atmosphere; tables on neat lawn. *Recommended by Mike Gorton*

LYDFORD SX5184   EX20 4BH
Castle Inn
Off A386 Okehampton—Tavistock

Tudor inn owned by St Austell, friendly chatty staff, traditional twin bars, big slate flagstones, bowed low beams, granite walls, four inglenook log fires, notable stained-glass door, generous food (all day Thurs-Sun), restaurant; beer garden, lovely nearby NT river gorge, open all day. *Recommended by Mrs Ann Gray, Edward Leetham, Reg Fowle, Helen Rickwood*

LYDFORD SX5285   EX20 4AY
Dartmoor Inn
Downton, A386

Attractive restaurant-with-rooms rather than pub, several small civilised and relaxed stylishly decorated contemporary areas, interesting and imaginatively presented expensive food, separate bar menu (not Fri, Sat evenings), good wines by the glass, well kept ales, competent service; children welcome, dogs allowed in small front log-fire bar, terrace tables, three spacious comfortable bedrooms, good breakfast, closed Sun evening, Mon. *Recommended by Bob and Angela Brooks, Henry Midwinter, Angela Nicholson, Oli Coryton*

LYMPSTONE SX9884   EX8 5ET
Swan
The Strand

Pleasant old-fashioned décor, split-level panelled dining area with leather sofas by big fire, traditional food including fresh local fish and Sun roasts, well kept Marstons and guests such as Otter, short interesting wine list, friendly staff, games room with pool; small front garden with smokers' area. *Recommended by Jo Rees, the Didler, Richard Tilbrook*

☆ **MARLDON** SX8663   TQ3 1SL
Church House
Off A380 NW of Paignton

Friendly landlord and hard-working staff in attractive village pub, spreading bar with beams, dark pine chairs and solid tables, unusual Georgian windows, Bass, Bays, Otter and St Austell, 15 wines by the glass, good range of well presented imaginative food from sandwiches up, cosy candlelit room with big stone fireplace, restaurant with another fireplace and two-part room off, second restaurant in old barn, local artwork; piped music; children and dogs welcome, picnic-sets on three carefully maintained grassy terraces behind. *Recommended by Alan Sutton, Peter Salmon, Michael and Joan Johnstone, Mike and Mary Carter, Mike Gorton and others*

☆ **MERRIVALE** SX5475   PL20 6ST
Dartmoor Inn
B3357, 4 miles E of Tavistock

17th-c beamed inn in tranquil spot with high Dartmoor views, big beamed lounge with smaller adjoining bar (dogs allowed here), generous lunchtime food from good baguettes up, more evening choice, quick friendly service, ales such as Sharps Doom Bar and Skinners Betty Stogs, decent wines (including country ones), water from their 36-metre well, log fire; far-reaching views from tables out in front, good walks – near Bronze Age hut circles, stone rows and pretty river, four bedrooms, open all day in summer, closed Mon and weekday lunchtimes in winter, and first three weeks of Jan. *Recommended by Gene and Tony Freemantle*

MOLLAND SS8028   EX36 3NG
London
Village signed off B3227 E of South Molton

This proper old Exmoor inn has shut – news please.

MORETONHAMPSTEAD SX7586   TQ13 8LN
Union
Fore Street

Cosy flower-decked beamed and timbered village pub, welcoming, clean and well run, with Fullers London Pride and three low-priced house beers brewed by local Red Rock, farm cider, good value home-made traditional food, several rooms including stables dining area; sports TV. *Recommended by Giles and Annie Francis, Martin and Judith Tomlinson, Ann, Jilly and Don Huish*

MORETONHAMPSTEAD SX7586   TQ13 8NF
White Horse
George Street

Nicely refurbished old pub with mediterranean-influenced food from chef/landlord including home-made pizzas, extensive wine list with good choice by the glass, well kept beers; some live music, courtyard tables, open all day in summer, closed lunchtime in winter. *Recommended by Giles and Annie Francis, Dr and Mrs A K Clarke*

MORTEHOE SS4545   EX34 7DU
Chichester Arms
Off A361 Ilfracombe—Braunton

Welcoming former 16th-c vicarage, varied choice of enjoyable local food, quick friendly service, well kept St Austell, Sharps and Wizard, reasonably priced wine, plush and leatherette panelled lounge, comfortable dining room, pubby locals' bar with darts and pool, interesting old local photographs; skittle alley and games machines in summer children's room, tables out in front and in shaded pretty garden, good coast walk. *Recommended by Andy and Jill Kassube, Stuart Paulley*

MUDDIFORD SS5638 EX31 4EY
Muddiford Inn
B3230 Barnstaple—Ilfracombe

Family pub dating from the 16th c, plenty of character, enjoyable reasonably priced
generous food, local real ale, open fire, fancier menu for pleasant separate restaurant,
friendly service; pool, car park over road; big garden with terrace, handy for Marwood
Gardens. *Recommended by Mr and Mrs D Mackenzie, Sue Rowland, Stephen Haynes*

NEWTON ABBOT SX8571 TQ12 2JP
Dartmouth
East Street

Genuine friendly old place, no longer brewing its own beers but good choice of changing
ales and farm ciders, decent wines, low ceilings, dark woodwork, roaring log fire; children
welcome till 7pm, nice outside area, open all day. *Recommended by the Didler*

NEWTON ABBOT SX8571 TQ12 2JP
Locomotive
East Street

Cheerful traditional town pub, well kept Adnams and guests, linked rooms including
games room with pool; TV, juke box; open all day. *Recommended by the Didler*

☆ NEWTON ABBOT SX8671 TQ12 2LD
Olde Cider Bar
East Street

Basic old-fashioned cider house, casks of interesting low-priced farm ciders (helpful long-
serving landlord may give tasters), a couple of perries, more in bottles, good country
wines from the cask too, baguettes and pasties etc, great atmosphere, dark stools made
from cask staves, barrel seats and wall benches, flagstones and bare boards; small back
games room with machines; terrace tables, open all day. *Recommended by the Didler,
Paul Herbert*

NEWTON ABBOT SX8671 TQ12 2EH
Richard Hopkins
Queen Street

Big partly divided open-plan Wetherspoons, busy and friendly, with ten beers including
Bays, Exmoor, O'Hanlons and Red Rock, real cider, usual food; covered tables out at front,
open all day. *Recommended by the Didler*

NEWTON ABBOT SX8468 TQ12 6DF
Two Mile Oak
A381 2 miles S, at Denbury/Kingskerswell crossroads

Appealing beamed coaching inn, log fires, traditional furnishings, black panelling and
candlelit alcoves, well kept Bass, Otter and guests tapped from the cask, straightforward
bar food including weekday lunchtime bargains, decent coffee, cheerful staff; piped
music, TV and games machine; children in lounge, dogs in bar, terrace and lawn, open all
day. *Recommended by the Didler, George Atkinson*

NEWTON ABBOT SX8571 TQ12 1JQ
Wolborough
Wolborough Street

Popular simple town local, compact wood-floored bar with etched windows, well kept
Teignworthy and some interesting cask-tapped guests, good friendly service; small
terrace, open all day, closed Mon lunchtime. *Recommended by the Didler*

If we know a pub has an outdoor play area for children, we mention it.

NEWTON ST CYRES SX8798   EX5 5AX
Beer Engine
Off A377 towards Thorverton

Friendly former railway hotel brewing its own beers since the 1980s, wide choice of good home-made food including local fish and popular Sun lunch; children welcome, decked verandah, steps down to garden, open all day. *Recommended by the Didler, Gene and Kitty Rankin*

NEWTON TRACEY SS5226   EX31 3PL
Hunters
B3232 Barnstaple—Torrington

Extended 15th-c pub with massive low beams and two inglenooks, good reasonably priced food from pub standards to more imaginative dishes, two well kept St Austell ales and Jollyboat Mainbrace, decent wines, friendly prompt service; soft piped music; children and dogs welcome, disabled access using ramp, skittle alley popular with locals, tables on small terrace behind, open all day. *Recommended by Roger and Pauline Pearce*

NOMANSLAND SS8313   EX16 8NN
Mount Pleasant
B3137 Tiverton—South Molton

Informal country local, huge fireplaces in long low-beamed main bar, well kept Cotleigh, St Austell and Sharps, several wines by the glass, Weston's Old Rosie cider, good freshly cooked generous food, good friendly service, nice mix of furniture including comfy old sofa, candles on tables, country pictures, daily papers, cosy dining room (former smithy), darts in public bar; piped music; well behaved children and dogs welcome, picnic-sets in back garden, open all day. *Recommended by Nick Townsend, Adrian and Dawn Collinge, David Saunders, Ron Logie*

NORTH BOVEY SX7483   TQ13 8RB
☆ # Ring of Bells
Off A382/B3212 SW of Moretonhampstead

Bulgy-walled thatched inn dating from the 13th c doing well under present licensees, low beams, flagstones, big log fire, sturdy rustic tables and winding staircases, good imaginative local food, well kept Otter, St Austell and guests, friendly staff, carpeted dining room and overspill room; children and dogs welcome, garden by lovely tree-covered village green below Dartmoor, good walks, five big clean bedrooms, open all day. *Recommended by Peter Thornton, Elven Money, Sue Saunders, Adrian Edmondson*

NOSS MAYO SX5447   PL8 1EW
☆ # Ship
Off A379 via B3186, E of Plymouth

Charming setting overlooking inlet and visiting boats, thick-walled bars with bare boards and log fires, six west country beers, 25 malt whiskies and 12 wines by the glass, popular often interesting food, lots of local pictures and charts, books, newspapers and board games, restaurant upstairs; can get crowded in good weather, parking restricted at high tide; children and dogs welcome, plenty of seats on heated waterside terrace. *Recommended by Geoff and Carol Thorp, Roy Hoing, Richard Fendick, S Holder, John Andrew and others*

PAIGNTON SX8860   TQ3 3AA
Isaac Merritt
Torquay Road

Spacious well run Wetherspoons conversion of former shopping arcade, particularly good range of west country ales (regular festivals), usual low-priced food all day, friendly welcoming service, low prices, cosy alcoves, comfortable family dining area, air conditioning; good disabled access. *Recommended by the Didler*

PARKHAM SS3821   EX39 5PL
Bell
Rectory Lane

Cheerful old thatched village pub, well run and spotless, with large comfortable family eating areas, good home-made food at reasonable prices including fresh fish and Aga-cooked Sun roasts, friendly efficient service, well kept ales such as Sharps Doom Bar and Skinners Betty Stogs, decent choice of wine, nice coffee, lots of nooks and crannies, log fire. *Recommended by Andy and Jill Kassube, Peter Thornton, Michael Snaith*

PARRACOMBE SS6644   EX31 4PE
 ## ☆ Fox & Goose
Off A39 Blackmoor Gate—Lynton

Popular rambling village pub, hunting and farming memorabilia and interesting photographs, well kept ales such as Cotleigh and Exmoor, good choice of wines by the glass, farm cider, good well presented food from imaginative menu, friendly staff, log fire, separate dining room; children and dogs welcome, small front verandah, terraced garden leading to garden room. *Recommended by V Brogden, John Pawson, A and H Piper, John Sharpe, B M Eldridge*

PETER TAVY SX5177   PL19 9NN
☆ Peter Tavy Inn
Off A386 near Mary Tavy, N of Tavistock

Old stone inn with bustling low-beamed bar, high-backed settles on black flagstones, stone-mullioned windows, good log fire in big stone fireplace, snug dining area with carved wooden chairs, hops on beams and plenty of pictures, three or four well kept west country ales, good wine choice, well liked fairly priced food, friendly service, separate restaurant; children and dogs welcome, picnic-sets in pretty garden, peaceful moorland views. *Recommended by Dr and Mrs M W A Haward, Andrea Rampley, Bob and Angela Brooks, Jacquie Jones, Chris and Libby Allen, Mick and Moira Brummell and others*

PLYMOUTH SX4854   PL4 0DW
☆ China House
Sutton Harbour, via Sutton Road off Exeter Street (A374)

Attractive conversion of Plymouth's oldest warehouse, lovely boaty views, dimly lit and inviting interior with beams and flagstones, bare slate and stone walls, two good log fires, interesting photographs, enjoyable pubby food, good choice of real ales and wines by the glass, friendly attentive staff; piped music, no dogs; good parking and disabled access/facilities, tables out on waterside balconies, open all day. *Recommended by Alain and Rose Foote, Sally and John Quinlan, Allan Macpherson*

PLYMOUTH SX4854   PL1 2LS
Dolphin
Barbican

Basic unchanging chatty local, good range of beers including cask-tapped Bass, coal fire (not always lit), Beryl Cook paintings including one of the friendly landlord; open all day. *Recommended by the Didler*

PLYMOUTH SX4555   PL1 4QT
Lounge
Stopford Place, Stoke

Old-fashioned panelled corner local, friendly landlord and chatty regulars, well kept Bass and guest ales, popular lunchtime food (not Mon), busy on match days; open all day Sat, Sun. *Recommended by the Didler*

> If you stay overnight in an inn or hotel, they are allowed to serve you an alcoholic drink at any hour of the day or night.

PLYMOUTH SX4853   PL4 0LE
Thistle Park
Commercial Road

Welcoming bare-boards pub near National Maritime Aquarium, full range of well kept South Hams ales (used to be brewed on premises), Thatcher's cider, friendly service, lunchtime bar food, evening upstairs thai restaurant, interesting décor, open fire, back pool room, juke box, live music at weekends; no children; dogs in bar, roof garden, smokers' shelter, open all day till late. *Recommended by the Didler*

PLYMOUTH SX4753   PL1 3DQ
Waterfront
Grand Parade

Restaurant/bar (former 19th-c yacht club) in good spot by Plymouth Sound, enjoyable fairly priced food served quickly by friendly staff including Sun roasts, St Austell, Sharps and Skinners from long central bar, dining areas with light wood tables on bare boards, Sun afternoon jazz, Weds quiz; children and dogs welcome, café-style seating on big decked waterside terrace with superb views. *Recommended by Steve Whalley*

POUNDSGATE SX7072   TQ13 7NY
☆ ## Tavistock Inn
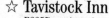
B3357 continuation

Friendly and picturesque, liked by walkers (plenty of nearby hikes), beams and other original features like narrow-stepped granite spiral staircase, original flagstones, ancient log fireplaces, Courage Best, Otter and Wychwood Hobgoblin, traditional bar food (all day in summer); children and dogs welcome, tables on front terrace and in quiet back garden, pretty summer flower boxes, open all day in summer. *Recommended by Elven Money*

RACKENFORD SS8518   EX16 8DT
Stag
Pub signed off A361 NW of Tiverton

12th-c thatched pub with ancient cobbled 'tunnel' entry passage between massive walls, Cotleigh, Exmoor and occasional guest ales, food from sandwiches up, scrubbed pine tables and country furnishings, huge inglenook fireplace, low beams, Jacobean panelling, flagstones, separate oak-floor white-tablecloth restaurant with woodburner, darts, skittle alley, highwayman ghost; children and dogs welcome, disabled facilities, two picnic-sets out in front, decking and enclosed garden behind, open all day, closed Sun evening. *Recommended by Sue Addison, Stuart Paulley*

RINGMORE SX6545   TQ7 4HL
Journeys End
Signed off B3392 at Pickwick Inn, St Ann's Chapel, near Bigbury; best to park opposite church

Ancient village inn with friendly chatty licensees, character panelled lounge and other linked rooms, well kept changing local ales tapped from the cask, farm cider, decent wines, pubby food from sandwiches up, log fires, bar billiards (for over-16s), family dining conservatory with board games; pleasant big terraced garden with boules, attractive setting near thatched cottages not far from the sea. *Recommended by John Butcher, Val Offer, Bob and Angela Brooks, the Didler, Mike and Eleanor Anderson*

ROCKBEARE SY0195   EX5 2EE
☆ ## Jack in the Green
Signed from A30 bypass E of Exeter

Neat welcoming dining pub with long-serving owner, tidy bar with comfortable sofas, Butcombe, Otter and Sharps, local cider, a dozen wines by the glass, popular food and most emphasis on larger similarly traditional dining side with old hunting/shooting photographs and leather chesterfields by big woodburner, live jazz May-Sept; piped music; well behaved children in one part only, plenty of seats in courtyard, open all day

Sun, closed 25 Dec-6 Jan. *Recommended by David and Sue Medcalf, Gene and Tony Freemantle, Mrs P Sumner, Cathryn and Richard Hicks, Ted and Charlotte Routley and others*

SALCOMBE SX7439   TQ8 8BU

☆ **Victoria**

Fore Street

Neat and attractive 19th-c family pub opposite harbour car park, nautical décor, comfortable furnishings and big open fires, enjoyable reasonably priced food from open sandwiches up, well kept St Austell ales, decent wines, friendly enthusiastic service, separate family area; busy at weekends, piped music; large sheltered tiered garden behind with good play area and chickens, bedrooms. *Recommended by Richard Fendick, Bob and Angela Brooks, Neil and Anita Christopher, Pat and Tony Martin, Sally and John Quinlan*

SAMPFORD PEVERELL ST0314   EX16 7BJ

☆ **Globe**

A mile from M5 junction 27, village signed from Tiverton turn-off; Lower Town

Spacious comfortable village pub backing on to Grand Western Canal, popular with walkers and locals, enjoyable good value home-made food from sandwiches to massive mixed grill and popular carvery (Fri, Sat evenings, all day Sun, Mon lunch), breakfast (8-11am), coffee and cream teas, seven well kept ales including Cotleigh, Exmoor and Otter (Nov beer festival), good wine choice, friendly efficient staff, cosy beamed lounge with boothed eating area, back restaurant; big-screen sports TV in bar, piped music; children and dogs welcome, disabled facilities, courtyard and enclosed garden with play equipment, six bedrooms, open all day. *Recommended by Tony Hobden, Adrian and Dawn Collinge, Andrew Bosi*

SANDFORD SS8202   EX17 4LW

☆ **Lamb**

The Square

Relaxed homely local with small choice of good reasonably priced interesting food (bar snacks all day – from 9.30am weekdays), well kept O'Hanlons Royal Oak and Palmers Copper, village farm cider, good value wines, friendly efficient service, cheery regulars, sofas by log fire, fresh flowers, daily papers, books and magazines, skittle alley/cinema – live music here too (last Fri of month); dogs very welcome (they have their own), tables in attractive sheltered garden, three good bedrooms, generous breakfast, open all day. *Recommended by Kate Wheeldon, Elaine Lee*

SANDY PARK SX7189   TQ13 8JW

☆ **Sandy Park Inn**

A382 Whiddon Down—Moretonhampstead

Welcoming little thatched inn under new licensees, beams, flagstones, varnished built-in wall settles around nice tables, high stools by counter, Dartmoor, Otter and a guest ale, good food from sensibly short menu including pizzas and vegetarian choices, small dining room on left, inner snug; open mike nights (third Sun of month); children and dogs welcome, big garden with fine views and smokers' shelter, five bedrooms, open all day. *Recommended by Jane Hudson, Barry Steele-Perkins, Roger and Donna Huggins*

SCORRITON SX7068   TQ11 0JB

Tradesmans Arms

Main road through village

Welcoming open-plan Dartmoor-edge pub, good choice of ales, enjoyable locally sourced food, friendly service, wonderful rolling hill views from conservatory and garden. *Recommended by Geoff and Marianne Millin, Elven Money*

Though we don't usually mention it in the text, most pubs now provide coffee or tea – so it's always worth asking.

SHEBBEAR SS4309   EX21 5RU

☆ Devils Stone Inn

Off A3072 or A388 NE of Holsworthy

Up for sale so this neatly kept beamed village pub is likely to change; has had brown leather armchairs in front of open woodburner, long L-shaped pew and second smaller one, old photographs of pupils from Shebbear school, bar counter with smart creaky high-backed leather chairs, Sharps and St Austell beers, dining room across corridor, plain back games room with pool, juke box, fruit machine; picnic-sets on back terrace and lawn, right by actual Devils Stone, bedrooms, has been open all day Fri-Sun. *Recommended by Ryta Lyndley, Reg Fowle, Helen Rickwood*

SHEEPWASH SS4806   EX21 5NE

☆ Half Moon

Off A3072 Holsworthy—Hatherleigh at Highampton

Ancient inn loved by anglers for its 12 miles of River Torridge fishing (salmon, sea trout and brown trout), small tackle shop and rod room with drying facilities; simply furnished main bar, lots of beams, log fire in big fireplace, well kept Nottingham, St Austell and Sharps, several wines by the glass, good choice of popular local food, friendly service, separate extended dining room, bar billiards; children and dogs welcome, bedrooms in converted stables, tiny Dartmoor village off the beaten track. *Recommended by J V Dadswell, Roy Hoing, Mike and Sue Loseby, Stephen Bennett, David Saunders, Reg Fowle, Helen Rickwood and others*

SIDMOUTH ST1287   EX10 8LP

Anchor

Old Fore Street

High-ceilinged pub on two floors popular for its seafood and other good value food, Courage Best and Sharps Doom Bar, good service; tables in nice outdoor area, open all day. *Recommended by Derek and Sylvia Stephenson*

SIDMOUTH SY1287   EX10 8LP

☆ Old Ship

Old Fore Street

Friendly traditional pub in pedestrian zone near sea (local parking limited to 30 minutes), partly 14th c with low beams, mellow black woodwork including early 17th-c carved panelling, nautical theme, good value food (not Sun evening) including local fish and some adventurous dishes, well kept Branscombe Vale Branoc, Fullers London Pride and Otter, decent wine choice, prompt service even when busy, newspapers, no piped music; close-set tables – raftered upstairs family area is more roomy; dogs allowed. *Recommended by Phil and Sally Gorton*

SIDMOUTH SY1287   EX10 8BY

☆ Swan

York Street

Cheerful old-fashioned town-centre local, well kept Wells & Youngs, good value food from splendid sandwiches up, helpful long-serving licensees, lounge bar with interesting pictures and memorabilia, darts and warm coal fire in bigger light and airy public bar with boarded walls and ceilings, separate dining area; no credit cards; dogs welcome, nice small flower-filled garden. *Recommended by Mike Gorton*

SILVERTON SS9503   EX5 4HZ

Lamb

Fore Street

Flagstoned local run well by friendly landlord, Dartmoor, Exe Valley, Otter and guests tapped from casks, inexpensive home-made pubby food, separate eating area; handy for Killerton (NT), open all day weekends. *Recommended by the Didler*

SLAPTON SX8245 TQ7 2PN
☆ **Queens Arms**
Sands Road corner, before church

Neatly modernised one-room village local with welcoming landlady, good straightforward inexpensive food, well kept Dartmoor, Otter and Teignworthy, snug comfortable corners, World War II mementoes, dominoes and draughts; parking needs skill; children and dogs welcome, lots of tables in lovely suntrap stepped garden. *Recommended by MP*

SLAPTON SX8245 TQ7 2PN
Tower
Off A379 Dartmouth—Kingsbridge

Old low-beamed pub doing well under current owners, good locally sourced food from traditional to more enterprising things, attentive friendly service, ales such as Butcombe, Otter, St Austell and Quercus, good choice of wines, flagstones, bare boards and log fires; children and dogs welcome, lovely garden overlooked by imposing 14th-c ivy-covered tower (remains of an ecclesiastical college), three comfortable bedrooms, closed Sun evening in winter, and first two weeks of Jan. *Recommended by the Didler, Nick Lawless, Mr and Mrs John Clifford, Daniel Murphy*

SOURTON SX5390 EX20 4HN
☆ **Highwayman**
A386, S of junction with A30

A fantasy of dimly lit stonework and flagstone-floored burrows and alcoves, all sorts of things to look at, one room a make-believe sailing galleon; local farm cider (perhaps a real ale in summer), organic wines, good proper sandwiches or pasties, friendly chatty service, nostalgic piped music; outside fairy-tale pumpkin house and an old-lady-who-lived-in-the-shoe house – children allowed to look around pub but can't stay inside; period bedrooms with four-posters and half-testers, bunkrooms for walkers/cyclists. *Recommended by Andrea Rampley, the Didler*

SOUTH BRENT SX6960 TQ10 9BE
Royal Oak
Station Road

Friendly village pub with well priced traditional and modern food, three well kept local ales, good choice of wines by the glass, welcoming helpful service, comfortable open-plan bar with some leather sofas, restaurant, Weds folk music night; children and dogs welcome, small courtyard, five good bedrooms. *Recommended by Dr and Mrs John Fripp, Geoff and Carol Thorp, Richard Pethybridge*

SOUTH MOLTON SS7425 EX36 3QF
Mill Inn
Just off A361 at Bish Mill roundabout

Large dining room and cosy little bar with log fire, beams hung with farm tools, Barum Original, Fullers London Pride and Sharps Doom Bar, decent pub food, good friendly service even when busy; dogs welcome. *Recommended by Stuart Paulley*

SOUTH POOL SX7740 TQ7 2RW
Millbrook
Off A379 E of Kingsbridge

Charming little creekside pub with more of a bistro flavour at night, dining area off cheerful compact bar, good generous if not cheap food from lunchtime crab sandwiches up (they add a service charge), well kept ales such as Palmers and South Hams tapped from the cask, local farm cider, log fires, newspapers, no piped music; children welcome, covered seating and heaters for front courtyard and waterside terrace. *Recommended by Diana Hunt, Nick Lawless*

SOUTH ZEAL SX6593   EX20 2JT
☆ **Oxenham Arms**
Off A30/A382

Stately interesting 12th-c building doing well under present management, elegant
mullioned windows and Stuart fireplaces in beamed and partly panelled flagstoned front
bar, small beamed inner room with open fire and remarkable old monolith, well kept ales
tapped from the cask, quite a few wines by the glass, good reasonably priced food using
meat from landlord's farm and fresh fish from Cornwall, contemporary dining room;
imposing garden with lovely views, seven bedrooms. *Recommended by Viv Jameson, Phil and
Sally Gorton, Andrea Rampley, David and Fiona Sweeting, Roxanne Chamberlain, Sue Gray*

SPREYTON SX6996   EX17 5AL
☆ **Tom Cobley**
Dragdown Hill; W out of village

Fantastic range of up to 22 ales (some tapped from the cask) and local ciders at this busy
village pub; warm welcome from landlord, decent well priced bar food, straightforward
pubby furnishings in small bar, surprisingly large back restaurant with beams and piped
music; children welcome, dogs in bar, seats out in front by quiet street, more in tree-
shaded garden, bedrooms, open till 1am Fri, Sat, closed Mon lunchtime. *Recommended by
Dr D J and Mrs S C Walker, Peter Thornton, D P and M A Miles, David Saunders, Peter Hill, KJ French*

STICKLEPATH SX6494   EX20 2NW
☆ **Devonshire**
Off A30 at Whiddon Down or Okehampton

Warmly welcoming licensees in old-fashioned 16th-c thatched village local next to
foundry museum (NT), low-beamed slate-floor bar with big log fire, longcase clock and
easy-going old furnishings, key collection, sofa in small snug, well kept low-priced ales
tapped from the cask, farm cider, good value sandwiches and home-made pasties from
the Aga, games room, lively folk music night (first Sun of month); dogs welcome (pub has
its own), good walks, bedrooms, open all day Fri, Sat. *Recommended by Phil and Sally Gorton,
the Didler, Reg Fowle, Helen Rickwood*

STOKE FLEMING SX8648   TQ6 0PX
Green Dragon
Church Street

Popular village pub with yachtsman landlord, well worn-in with beams and flagstones,
boat pictures, friendly dogs and cats, snug with sofas and armchairs, grandfather clock,
open fire, well kept Otter ales, Addlestone's and Aspall's ciders, good choice of wines by
the glass, bargain food; tables out on partly covered heated terrace, lovely garden.
Recommended by Guy Vowles, Richard Tilbrook, Sally and John Quinlan, Nick Lawless

STOKE GABRIEL SX8457   TQ9 6SD
☆ **Church House**
Off A385 just W of junction with A3022; Church Walk

Friendly early 14th-c pub, lounge bar with fine medieval beam-and-plank ceiling, black
oak partition wall, window seats cut into thick butter-coloured walls, huge log fireplace,
ancient mummified cat, Bass, Hancocks HB and a guest, enjoyable good value food, little
locals' bar; piped music, no children; dogs welcome in bar, picnic-sets on small front
terrace, limited parking, open all day. *Recommended by B J Harding, Mrs P Bishop, Malcolm and
Barbara Southwell, Barbarrick*

STOKEINTEIGNHEAD SX9170   TQ12 4QA
Church House
Signed from Combeinteignhead, or off A379 N of Torquay

Relaxed 13th-c thatched pub in unspoilt village, heavy beams, antique furnishings,
ancient spiral stairs and inglenook fireplace, well kept ales and decent wines, enjoyable
food served by friendly helpful staff, smart extended dining room, simple public bar;
piped music; children welcome in eating area, back garden. *Recommended by Bob Jones*

STOKENHAM SX8042   TQ7 2SZ
☆ **Church House**
Opposite church, N of A379 towards Torcross

Attractive extended old pub overlooking common, three low-beamed open-plan areas, mix of seating on flagstones, lots of knick-knacks, Greene King, Otter and guest ales, local cider, several wines by the glass, enjoyable food using local produce, pleasant helpful service, dining conservatory, jazz Weds evening; children and dogs welcome, picnic-sets on lawn with play area, interesting church next door. *Recommended by Torquil MacLennan, Richard Fendick, Dennis Jenkin, MP, Alistair Stanier and others*

STRETE SX8446   TQ6 0RW
Kings Arms
A379 SW of Dartmouth

Unusual cross between village local and seafood restaurant, same good generous food in country-kitchen bar and more contemporary restaurant up steps, prompt friendly service, real ales such as Otter, good wines by the glass; piped music; children and dogs welcome, back terrace and garden with lovely views over Start Bay, open all day, closed Sun evening. *Recommended by Wendy and Carl Dye, Alan Sutton, Guy Vowles, Jonathan Tate*

TOPSHAM SX9688   EX3 0QQ
☆ **Bridge Inn**
2.5 miles from M5 junction 30: Topsham signposted from exit roundabout; in Topsham follow signpost (A376) Exmouth, on the Elmgrove Road, into Bridge Hill

Very special old drinkers' pub (16th-c former maltings) with up to eight real ales and in landlady's family for five generations; quite unchanging and completely unspoilt with friendly staff and locals, character small rooms and snugs, traditional furniture including a nice high-backed settle, woodburner, the 'bar' is landlady's front parlour (as notice on the door politely reminds customers), simple lunchtime food, live folk and blues music; no piped music, mobile phones or credit cards; children and dogs welcome, picnic-sets overlooking weir. *Recommended by Phil and Sally Gorton, Julia Mann, John Prescott, Maurice Ricketts, John and Sarah Perry, the Didler and others*

TOPSHAM SX9688   EX3 0DY
Exeter Inn
High Street

Friendly well run 17th-c local with enthusiastic landlord, well kept Teignworthy Beachcomber and interesting guests, farm ciders, long bar and front area with pool, reasonable prices; big-screen sports TV; bedrooms, open all day. *Recommended by the Didler*

TOPSHAM SX9687   EX3 0HR
* **Globe**
Fore Street; 2 miles from M5 junction 30

Substantial traditional inn dating from the 16th c, welcoming chatty landlord, six west country ales in heavy-beamed bow-windowed bar (popular with locals), good interesting home-made food from sandwiches and snacks up, reasonable prices, friendly helpful service, log-effect gas fire, compact dining lounge, restaurant, nice relaxed atmosphere; children in eating areas, well priced attractive bedrooms, parking can be tricky, open all day. *Recommended by the Didler, George Atkinson, Adrian and Dawn Collinge, Barry Steele-Perkins*

TOPSHAM SX9687   EX3 0HZ
☆ **Lighter**
Fore Street

Big, busy well run pub looking out over quay, quickly served food from good sandwiches and light dishes to fresh fish, Badger ales, nautical décor, panelling and large central log fire, friendly staff, good children's area; games machines, piped music; lots of waterside tables outside – good bird views at half tide, handy for antiques centre. *Recommended by J D O Carter, the Didler*

TOPSHAM SX9688   EX3 0JN
Passage House
Ferry Road, off main street

18th-c pub with traditional black-beamed bar and slate-floored lower dining area, well
kept ales and decent wines, enjoyable food from sandwiches up, good friendly service;
peaceful terrace looking over moorings and river (lovely at sunset) to nature reserve
beyond. *Recommended by Douglas and Ann Hare*

TORBRYAN SX8266   TQ12 5UR
☆ Old Church House
Off A381

Friendly 14th-c inn, particularly attractive right-hand bar with benches built into fine old
panelling, cushioned high-backed settle and leather-backed small seats, big log fire,
series of comfortable and discreetly lit lounges, one with splendid deep inglenook and
bread oven, Skinners ales, 35 malt whiskies, enjoyable generous food, good service; piped
music – live on Sun evening; children (away from bar) and dogs welcome, part-Saxon
church next door, plenty of nearby walks, 16 bedrooms, open all day. *Recommended by
Peter Salmon, Gene and Tony Freemantle, Malcolm and Barbara Southwell*

TORCROSS SX8242   TQ7 2TQ
☆ Start Bay
A379 S of Dartmouth

More fish and chip restaurant than pub but does sell Bass, Otter, local wine and cider;
very much set out for eating and exceptionally busy at peak times with staff coping well,
wheelback chairs around dark tables, country pictures, some photographs of storms
buffeting the pub, winter coal fire, small drinking area by counter, large family room; no
dogs during food times; seats outside (highly prized) looking over pebble beach and
wildlife lagoon, open all day. *Recommended by Bruce and Sharon Eden, Mike Gorton, Barbarrick*

TORQUAY SX9265   TQ1 3LX
☆ Cary Arms
*Beach Road: off B3199 Babbacombe Road, via Babbacombe Downs Road; turn steeply
down near Babbacombe Theatre*

Secluded and unusual higgledy-piggledy hotel with lovely sea and cliff views, beamed,
grotto-effect bar with alcoves, rustic red leather chairs around carved tables, open
woodburner, Bays, Dartmoor, Otter and St Austell, local cider, decent wines, good food
(meals for dogs too), cheerful young staff, small glass-enclosed entrance room with large
ship lanterns and cleats, civilised residents' lounge, monthly jazz; children welcome, well
tended terraces leading down to quay, outside bar, barbecue and pizza oven, eight sea-
facing bedrooms, three self-catering cottages, open all day. *Recommended by Christopher and
Victoria Wren, Ben Gooder, Mrs M B Gregg*

TORQUAY SX9166   TQ1 4QA
Crown & Sceptre
Petitor Road, St Marychurch

Friendly two-bar local in 18th-c stone-built beamed coaching inn, wide choice of well
kept ales, interesting naval memorabilia and chamber-pot collection, friendly long-
serving landlord, basic good value lunchtime food (not Sun), snacks any time, live jazz
(Tues), folk music (Fri); dogs and children welcome, two gardens. *Recommended by
the Didler*

TORQUAY SX9163   TQ1 2AU
Hole in the Wall
Park Lane, opposite clock tower

Ancient two-bar local near harbour, reasonably priced usual food including good steaks,
several well kept ales such as Bays and Sharps, Blackawton cider, proper old-fashioned
landlord and friendly service, smooth cobbled floors, low beams and alcoves, lots of

nautical brassware, ship models, old local photographs, chamber-pots, restaurant/function room (band nights); can get very busy weekends; some seats out at front, open all day. *Recommended by the Didler, Roger and Donna Huggins*

TORQUAY SX9263 TQ1 2BW
Meadfoot
Meadfoot Lane

Friendly pub popular with the gay community, walls decorated with film posters, ceiling with gold discs including Diana Ross and Will Young, a beer from Bays; quiz nights, bingo and karaoke; open all day Fri-Sun, closed weekday lunchtimes. *Recommended by Roger and Donna Huggins*

TOTNES SX8060 TQ9 5AD
Albert
Bridgetown

Two-room roadside pub with low beams, flagstones, panelling and lots of knick-knacks, friendly landlord brewing own Bridgetown ales, good local atmosphere; neat garden. *Recommended by the Didler, Roger and Donna Huggins*

TOTNES SX7960 TQ9 5SP
Bay Horse
Cistern Street

Popular traditional two-bar inn dating from the 15th c, friendly landlord, good value home-made food, well kept Dartmoor, Otter, South Hams and guests, may be winter mulled cider, regular beer festivals; piped and live music including good Sun jazz; children and dogs welcome, garden, two nice bedrooms, open all day. *Recommended by the Didler, Celia Minoughan*

TOTNES SX8060 TQ9 5DD
☆ # Royal Seven Stars
Fore Street, The Plains

Exemplary town-centre bar and coffee bar in well run civilised old hotel, friendly and easy-going, with well kept ales such as Bays Gold, Courage Best, Princetown Jail and Sharps Doom Bar, enjoyable good value food all day from breakfast on, plenty of seating variety, pretty restaurant; heated tables out in front, river across busy main road, bedrooms, open all day. *Recommended by Bob Duxbury, the Didler, Michael and Lynne Gittins*

TOTNES SX8060 TQ9 5RY
Rumour
High Street

Spotless up-to-date bar-bistro, well kept Greene King, Skinners and guests, bottled belgian beers, wide-ranging wines by the glass, local fruit juices, enjoyable food from pizzas to some enterprising dishes using local produce, bare-boards dining area with bentwood chairs and informal contemporary décor, good service; open all day. *Recommended by the Didler*

TUCKENHAY SX8156 TQ9 7EQ
Maltsters Arms
Ashprington Road, off A381 from Totnes

Charmingly worn-in old pub in lovely quiet spot by wooded creek, great range of wines by the glass, good beer choice and farm cider, food from snacks to restaurant dishes; children and dogs allowed, waterside terrace with open-air bar and summer barbecues, individually styled bedrooms, open all day. *Recommended by B J Harding, Tim Maddison, MP*

All *Guide* inspections are anonymous. Anyone claiming to be a *Good Pub Guide* inspector is a fraud. Please let us know.

UGBOROUGH SX6755   PL21 0NS
Ship
Off A3121 SE of Ivybridge

Quietly chatty well run dining pub extended from cosy 16th-c flagstoned core, nicely
divided open-plan eating areas a step down from neat bar, wide choice of good home-
made food including fresh fish, willing pleasant service, well kept Palmers and St Austell
ales, good house wines; piped music; tables out in front. *Recommended by S Holder, MP*

WEMBWORTHY SS6609   EX18 7SA
☆ Lymington Arms
Lama Cross

Large early 19th-c beamed dining pub, clean and bright, with wide choice of reliably good
food (not Sun evening or Mon) including some interesting specials, good service from
character landlady and friendly staff, well kept Sharps Doom Bar and Skinners Betty
Stogs, Winkleigh farm cider, decent wines, comfortably plush seating and red tablecloths
in partly stripped-stone bar, big back evening restaurant (not Sun, Mon); children
welcome, picnic-sets outside, pleasant country setting, bedrooms. *Recommended by
Mark Flynn, Mrs P Sumner, Justin Beament*

WEST DOWN SS5142   EX34 8NF
Crown
Centre of village, off West Pool

17th-c village pub with enjoyable good value home-made food including some vegetarian
options, well kept local beers, friendly staff, log fires; children welcome, nice back
garden. *Recommended by David Saunders*

WESTLEIGH SS4728   EX39 4NL
Westleigh Inn
0.5 miles off A39 Bideford—Instow

Popular and comfortable beamed pub, well kept ales such as Sharps Doom Bar, enjoyable
usual food from sandwiches and baguettes up, friendly prompt service, inglenook log fire,
brass and knick-knacks, sleepy pub cat, darts; well behaved children and dogs welcome,
play area in big garden overlooking Torridge estuary, Tarka Trail walks. *Recommended by
Eamonn and Natasha Skyrme*

WESTON ST1400   EX14 3NZ
☆ Otter
Off A373, or A30 at W end of Honiton bypass

Big busy family pub with heavy low beams, enjoyable food from light dishes up including
good Sun carvery, OAP specials and perhaps other deals, cheerful helpful staff, Cotleigh
and Otter, good log fire; piped music; children welcome, disabled access, picnic-sets on
big lawn leading to River Otter, play area. *Recommended by Bob and Margaret Holder*

WHIMPLE SY0497   EX5 2TA
New Fountain
Off A30 Exeter—Honiton; Church Road

Attractive two-bar beamed pub with friendly local atmosphere, good inexpensive food,
well kept changing beers including O'Hanlons brewed in the village, woodburner; well
behaved dogs welcome. *Recommended by Sam*

WIDECOMBE SX7176   TQ13 7TA
Old Inn
B3387 W of Bovey Tracey

Busy comfortably refurbished dining pub, large eating area and roomy side conservatory
with central fire – get there before about 12.30pm in summer to miss the coach-loads,
enjoyable standard food served promptly by friendly staff, well kept beers; children and
dogs welcome, nice garden with water features and pleasant terrace, great walks from

this pretty moorland village. *Recommended by Chris and Angela Buckell, Mike and Mary Carter, J F Stackhouse*

☆ WINKLEIGH SS6308   EX19 8HQ
Kings Arms
Fore Street; off B3220 Crediton—Torrington

Cheery timeless-feeling thatched village pub, cosy beamed main bar with old-fashioned built-in wall settles and benches, scrubbed pine tables on flagstones, woodburner in cavernous fireplace, green or red-painted dining rooms (one with military memorabilia and glass-covered mine shaft), Butcombe, Otter and Sharps Doom Bar, traditional food all day, darts and board games; children welcome, dogs in bar, small sheltered side garden. *Recommended by Peter Thornton, Mark Flynn, Mrs P Sumner, Jeremy Whitehorn*

☆ WONSON SX6789   EX20 2JA
Northmore Arms
Between Throwleigh and Gidleigh

Far from smart and a favourite with those who take to its idiosyncratic style (not everyone does); two simple old-fashioned rooms, log fire and woodburner, low beams and stripped stone, well kept Adnams, Cotleigh and Exe Valley tapped from the cask, good house wines, cheap plain food (all day Mon-Sat), darts and board games; children and dogs welcome, picnic-sets outside, bedrooms, beautiful remote walking country, normally open all day. *Recommended by the Didler, Howard and Lorna Lambert, Anthony Longden*

☆ WOODLAND SX7869   TQ13 7JT
Rising Sun
Village signed off A38 just NE of Ashburton, then pub usually signed, near Combe Cross

Surprisingly plush and expansive, with friendly attentive staff, wide choice of good food from open sandwiches to home-made pies and local seafood, well kept Dartmoor Jail and a local guest, good choice of wines by the glass, farm cider, beams and soft lighting, snug corner by log fire, family area, restaurant; children and dogs welcome, picnic-sets and play area in spacious garden, four comfortable good value bedrooms. *Recommended by Barry Cross, Col and Mrs Patrick Kaye*

ALSO WORTH A VISIT IN DORSET

Besides the region's top pubs, we recommend the following. Do tell us what you think of them: **feedback@goodguides.com**

BLANDFORD FORUM ST8806   DT11 7AJ
Crown
West Street

Civilised red-brick Georgian hotel on edge of town, spacious refurbished bar area with Badger ales from nearby brewery, good choice of wines, teas and coffee, appetising food from sandwiches to daily specials, restaurant; children welcome, sturdy tables on big terrace with formal garden beyond, 32 bedrooms. *Recommended by Mrs C Roe, Michael Doswell*

BLANDFORD ST MARY ST8805   DT11 9LS
Hall & Woodhouse
Bournemouth Road

Visitor centre for Badger brewery, their full beer range in top condition including interesting bottled beers, traditional lunchtime food from well filled baguettes up, friendly staff; spectacular chandelier made of beer bottles, lots of memorabilia in centre and upper gallery; popular brewery tours, open lunchtimes, closed Sun; new brewery currently under construction. *Recommended by Joan and Michel Hooper-Immins*

BOURNEMOUTH SZ0991   BH2 6NB
Dean Park
A347 Wimborne Road

White gabled two-bar Wadworths inn, their ales and a guest like Brains kept well, good
value pubby food from baguettes up, friendly staff, Thurs quiz; pool, darts and sports TV
in public bar; quiet part of town, 12 bedrooms, open all day. *Recommended by Joan and*
Michel Hooper-Immins

BOURTON ST7731   SP8 5AT
☆ # White Lion
High Street, off old A303 E of Wincanton

Lively 18th-c low-beamed and stripped-stone dining pub with welcoming energetic
landlord, appealing place with fine inglenook fire in pubby bar, two cosy rooms off and
good-sized restaurant, bar snacks and enjoyable good value main meals, good service,
beers such as Butcombe and Sharps Doom Bar, Thatcher's cider, nice wines; picnic-sets
on back paved area and raised lawn, two neat bedrooms. *Recommended by Mrs C Roe*

BRIDPORT SY4692   DT6 3LY
Tiger
Barrack Street, off South Street

Cheerful open-plan Victorian beamed pub with well kept range of changing ales, real
ciders, enjoyable food, skittle alley; two outside areas. *Recommended by Bill Stanley,*
Roger Scammell

BRIDPORT SY4692   DT6 3NZ
Woodman
South Street

Welcoming traditional little local with well kept Branscombe Vale and interesting guests,
decent straightforward home-made food, skittle alley, live music, Sun quiz; seats out on
pavement, attractive garden behind, open all day. *Recommended by the Didler, Roger Scammell,*
Carole Masset

BUCKHORN WESTON ST7524   SP8 5HS
☆ # Stapleton Arms
Church Hill; off A30 Shaftesbury—Sherborne via Kington Magna

Upmarket dining pub in handsome Georgian building, sizeable bar divided by glazed-in
entrance lobby, farmhouse and pew chairs around scrubbed table on slate flagstones,
comfortable sofas, log fire in fine stone fireplace, four real ales including Butcombe,
Cheddar Valley cider, imaginative daily-changing seasonal menu using locally sourced
produce, dining room with mahogany tables on coir, church candles in fireplace; children
welcome, dogs in bar, elegant metal tables and chairs out on York flagstones and gravel,
good comfortable bedrooms, open all day weekends. *Recommended by Mrs C Roe, Joan and*
Michel Hooper-Immins, Ian Malone

BUCKLAND NEWTON ST6804   DT2 7BS
☆ # Gaggle of Geese
Locketts Lane; E end of village

19th-c country pub with relaxed atmosphere, sofas and armchairs next to log fire, books
and games, enjoyable locally sourced modern pub food, Sun roasts, Ringwood, St Austell
and two west country guest ales, good wine choice, nice coffee, red candlelit dining room
with persian rugs and mix of old and new furniture, darts, skittle alley; children and dogs
welcome, garden with terrace, orchard and pond, paddock with chickens and goats,
charity poultry auction May and Sept, open all day weekends. *Recommended by*
Tim Carron-Brown, Peter Salmon

It's very helpful if you let us know up-to-date food prices when you report on pubs.

BURTON BRADSTOCK SY4889 DT6 4QF
Anchor
B3157 SE of Bridport

Cheerful landlord and staff in pricey but good seafood restaurant, other generous food including nice steaks, lively village pub part too, several real ales, Thatcher's cider, lots of malt whiskies and decent wines by the glass; children and dogs welcome, bedrooms, open all day. *Recommended by Penny Royle*

BURTON BRADSTOCK SY4889 DT6 4QZ
☆ Three Horseshoes
Mill Street

Busy old thatched place 400 yds from Chesil Beach and coastal path; array of pictures and local photographs in pleasant low-ceilinged carpeted bar, inglenook woodburner, welcoming staff, full range of Palmers beers (under light blanket pressure in winter), generous food including local fish and game (booking advised at peak times), dining room; piped music; children welcome, dogs in bar, suntrap back garden with heaters on large partly covered terrace, open all day. *Recommended by Bob and Margaret Holder, M G Hart, George Atkinson, John and Gloria Isaacs, Phil and Jane Hodson and others*

CERNE ABBAS ST6601 DT2 7JG
Royal Oak
Long Street

Village-centre position with low beams, flagstones and all sorts of rustic memorabilia, well kept Badger ales, friendly staff, mixed reports on food; children welcome, small back garden. *Recommended by John and Gloria Isaacs, Ann and Colin Hunt, Joan and Michel Hooper-Immins*

CHEDINGTON ST4805 DT8 3HY
Winyards Gap
A356 Dorchester—Crewkerne

Attractive dining pub surrounded by NT land with spectacular view over Parrett Valley and into Somerset, enjoyable good value food from sandwiches to some unusual choices, bargain two-course OAP weekday lunch, well kept beers such as Sharps Doom Bar, friendly staff and dog, stylish dining room, skittle alley; children and dogs welcome, tables on front lawn under parasols, good walks, open all day weekends. *Recommended by Mr and Mrs N Davies, Robert Watt, B and M Kendall*

CHETNOLE ST6008 DT9 6NU
☆ Chetnole Inn
Village signed off A37 S of Yeovil

Attractive well run inn with beams, huge flagstones and country kitchen décor, friendly staff, Otter, Sharps Doom Bar and a guest such as Dorset Piddle, 16 malt whiskies, central woodburner and modern leather seats in minimalist snug, open fire and pale wood tables on stripped boards in attractive dining room with fresh flowers, candles and linen napkins, well liked food using local produce including own duck eggs, deli with small tearoom in one corner; dogs welcome in bar, picnic-sets out in front and in delightful back garden (with ducks), three bedrooms overlooking old church, good breakfast, closed Sun evening and Mon in winter. *Recommended by Michael Dandy, Mrs A A Loukes, M G Hart, Ian Malone*

CHIDEOCK SY4191 DT6 6JU
☆ Anchor
Off A35 from Chideock

Arrive early in summer for table on spacious front terrace, a few steps from cove beach nestling dramatically beneath 188-metre Golden Cap pinnacle; snug little bars with low white-planked ceilings, neatly simple furnishings and seaside bric-a-brac, open fires, well kept Palmers (under light blanket pressure in winter), tasty bar food, friendly efficient staff; piped mainly classical music; children and dogs welcome, near Dorset Coast Path, open all day in summer (food all day then too). *Recommended by Lawrence Pearse, Peter Salmon, the Didler, George Atkinson, John and Gloria Isaacs, Jonathan Weedon and others*

CHIDEOCK SY4192   DT6 6JW
Clockhouse
A35 W of Bridport

Attractive open-plan thatched village local with friendly landlord, well kept Otter and Palmers, enjoyable straightforward food including bargain deals, huge collection of clocks; bedrooms. *Recommended by Lawrence Pearse, Terry and Nickie Williams*

CHILD OKEFORD ST8213   DT11 8HD
☆ Saxon
Signed off A350 Blandford—Shaftesbury and A357 Blandford—Sherborne; Gold Hill

Welcoming 17th-c village pub, quietly clubby snug bar with log fire, two dining rooms, Butcombe, Ringwood and guests, good choice of wines, enjoyable reasonably priced home-made food, good service; children welcome, dogs in bar, attractive back garden with wooden shelter, good walks on neolithic Hambledon Hill, four comfortable bedrooms. *Recommended by Robert Watt, Keith Sale*

CHRISTCHURCH SZ1592   BH23 1DT
☆ Olde George
Castle Street

Bustling and cheerfully old-fashioned two-bar low-beamed pub dating from the 15th c, Dorset Piddle ales and a guest, real ciders and nice wine, enjoyable sensibly priced food all day using local suppliers, Sun carvery and different evening menu, friendly staff; dogs welcome (they provide food), lots of teak seats and tables in heated character coachyard, open all day. *Recommended by Joan and Michel Hooper-Immins, Hans Becker, Hugh Roberts, A D Lealan*

CHURCH KNOWLE SY9381   BH20 5NQ
☆ New Inn
Village signed off A351 N of Corfe Castle

Pleasantly furnished 16th-c stone and partly thatched dining pub, good food with emphasis on fresh fish, choose your own wine from walk-in cellar, three real ales including Greene King Old Speckled Hen; jolly staff and entertaining mix of bric-a-brac, old tables and chairs on red patterned carpet in two stone-walled areas, open fires; children welcome, disabled facilities, fine surrounding walks and views from nice garden, camping. *Recommended by Pamela and Alan Neale, Adrian and Dawn Collinge, Adrian Johnson, Tony Brace, Barrie and Mary Crees, Robert Watt and others*

COLEHILL SU0302   BH21 7AH
Barley Mow
Colehill signed from A31/B3073 roundabout; Long Lane

Welcoming part-thatched, part-tiled family-managed 17th-c pub, enjoyable food and well kept Badger ales, low-beamed main bar, open fire in brick inglenook, attractive oak panelling, carpeted restaurant; piped music; children and dogs welcome, tethering for horses, seats out at front and in pleasant enclosed lawn behind with terrace, open all day in summer. *Recommended by James Palmer*

CORFE CASTLE SY9681   BH20 5EE
Castle Inn
East Street

Small two-room pub mentioned in Hardy's *Hand of Ethelberta*, enjoyable fairly priced food using local supplies including popular Fri fish night, Dorset and Ringwood ales, heavy black beams, exposed stone walls, flagstones and open fire; children welcome, back terrace and big sunny garden with mature trees. *Recommended by Susan and Jeremy Arthern, Mike and Sue Loseby, Dawn Viner, Richard Stanfield, the Didler*

Post Office address codings confusingly give the impression that some pubs are in Dorset, when they're really in Somerset (which is where we list them).

CORFE CASTLE SY9682   BH20 5EZ

☆ **Greyhound**

A351; The Square

Bustling and picturesque old pub in centre of tourist village, three small low-ceilinged panelled rooms, steps and corridors, well kept ales such as Everards and Ringwood, local cider, good choice of fairly priced food from sandwiches and light dishes up, friendly helpful staff, traditional games including Purbeck long board shove-ha'penny, family room; piped music, live music Fri; garden with large decked area, great views of castle and countryside, pretty courtyard opening on to castle bridge, open all day weekends and in summer. *Recommended by Christine Vallely, L Bond, Nigel Clifton, Tony Brace, the Didler and others*

CORFE MULLEN SY9798   BH21 3RH

☆ **Coventry Arms**

Mill Street (A31 W of Wimborne)

New licensees at this 15th-c shabby-chic-style pub, bar and four dining rooms, low ceilings, eclectic mix of furniture on flagstones or parquet flooring, large central open fire, Timothy Taylors Landlord and Ringwood tapped from cooled casks, affordable traditional food including Sun roasts, friendly helpful staff; stuffed fish and a mummified cat (to ward off evil spirits); piped and occasional live music; children and dogs welcome, big waterside garden with terrace, open all day. *Recommended by Roger and Kathy Elkin, Louise Goodison*

DORCHESTER SY6990   DT1 1JN

☆ **Blue Raddle**

Church Street, near central short stay car park

Cheery pubby atmosphere in long carpeted and partly panelled bar, well kept ales including one brewed for them, Weston's farm cider, good wines and coffee, enjoyable reasonably priced simple home-made food from sandwiches up, open fire; piped music; disabled access (but one step), closed Mon lunchtime. *Recommended by Karen Holland, Pam and John Smith, the Didler, John Ecklin, Rob and Catherine Dunster, B and M Kendall and others*

DORCHESTER SY6790   DT1 3GW

☆ **Poet Laureate**

Pummery Square, Poundbury

Substantial building in the Prince of Wales's Poundbury development, enjoyable if not particularly cheap food including some interesting dishes, Fullers London Pride, Palmers Copper and Ringwood Fortyniner, decent wines by the glass, proper coffee, top-notch service, light and airy L-shaped bar with good décor, lots of chandeliers, good solid tables and chairs, daily papers, flame-effect stove, nice restaurant area; unobtrusive piped music; wheelchair access (step up at entrance), a few picnic-sets on side terrace. *Recommended by Paul Goldman, Joan and Michel Hooper-Immins*

EAST MORDEN SY9194   BH20 7DL

☆ **Cock & Bottle**

B3075 W of Poole

Popular dining pub with wide choice of good if not cheap food (best to book), well kept Badger ales, nice selection of wines by the glass, efficient cheerful service, two dining areas with heavy rough beams; children and dogs allowed in certain areas, garden and adjoining field, pleasant pastoral outlook. *Recommended by Neil and Karen Dignan, Peter Veness, Howard and Margaret Buchanan*

EAST STOUR ST8123   SP8 5NB

Kings Arms

B3095, 3 miles W towards Shaftesbury; The Common

Emphasis on above-average very good value pubby food including all-day Sun roasts (best to book), Palmers and guests such as St Austell and Wadworths 6X, decent wines, friendly efficient staff, large bar with light airy dining area; children welcome, good disabled access, big garden, bluebell walks nearby, bedrooms. *Recommended by Paul Goldman, Robert Watt, Jeremy King*

EVERSHOT ST5704   DT2 0JW
Acorn
Off A37 S of Yeovil

16th-c coaching inn (Sow & Acorn in *Tess of the d'Urbevilles*), two well kept changing ales, good choice of wines by the glass including champagne, real ciders, decent food in restaurant front part with up-to-date décor as well as log fires and oak panelling, bar snacks from good open sandwiches to salads and pubby hot dishes in beamed and flagstoned back bar with darts and pool, skittle alley; piped music; children allowed in eating areas, dogs in bar, terrace with dark oak furniture, ten bedrooms, pretty village, good walks, open all day. *Recommended by Michael Dandy, Bruce Jamieson, Alan Johnson*

GUSSAGE ALL SAINTS SU0010   BH21 5ET
☆ Drovers
8 miles N of Wimborne

Partly thatched pub with good proper home-made food at sensible prices, friendly service, Ringwood ales and guests kept well, good wines by the glass, log fire and pleasantly simple country furnishings, public bar with piano and darts; well behaved children and dogs welcome, tables on pretty front lawn with views across the Dorset hills, adjoining farm shop, peaceful village. *Recommended by Leslie and Barbara Owen, Robert Watt, Michael Doswell, Howard and Margaret Buchanan*

KINGSTON SY9579   BH20 5LH
☆ Scott Arms
West Street (B3069)

Extensively modernised pub rambling through several levels, some sofas and easy chairs, beams, stripped stone, bare boards and log fires, good choice of enjoyable reasonably priced local food including fresh fish, well kept Dorset and Ringwood ales, decent wines, family dining area; dogs welcome, large attractive garden with outstanding views of Corfe Castle and the Purbeck Hills, summer barbecues, two well equipped bedrooms, good walks, open all day. *Recommended by Matthew Shackle, Dr A J and Mrs Tompsett, Mike and Sue Loseby, Paul and Elizabeth Wright, Ewan and Moira McCall, William Henderson and others*

LODERS SY4994   DT6 3SA
Loders Arms
Off A3066 just N of Bridport

Unspoilt 17th-c stone-built pub in pretty thatched village, well kept Palmers ales, Thatcher's cider, good choice of wines by the glass, home-made food from varied menu, log fire, dining room, skittle alley; children and dogs welcome, pleasant views from picnic-sets in small garden behind, good surrounding walks, closed Sun evenings in winter. *Recommended by Tony and Gill Powell*

LYME REGIS SY3391   DT7 3JF
☆ Harbour Inn
Marine Parade

More eating than pubby with thriving family atmosphere, friendly efficient service even at busy times, enjoyable food from lunchtime sandwiches to local fish, good choice of wines by the glass, well kept Otter and local Town Mill, tea and coffee, clean-cut modern décor keeping original flagstones and stone walls (lively acoustics), paintings for sale, sea views from front windows; piped music; disabled access from street, verandah tables. *Recommended by Mr and Mrs D Hammond, P Dawn, Nick Birtley, Guy Vowles*

LYME REGIS SY3391   DT7 3JF
☆ Royal Standard
Marine Parade, The Cobb

Right on broadest part of beach, properly pubby bar with log fire, fine built-in stripped high settles, local photographs and even old-fashioned ring-up tills, quieter eating area with stripped-brick and pine, friendly helpful service, four well kept Palmers ales, good choice of wines by the glass, food from massive crab sandwiches up including local fish;

darts, prominent pool table, free wi-fi; piped and some live music, gets very busy in season – may be long waits then; children and dogs welcome, good-sized suntrap courtyard with own servery and harbour views, open all day. *Recommended by Dave Irving, Jenny Huggins, Joan and Michel Hooper-Immins*

MORETON SY7789   DT2 8BB
Frampton Arms
B3390 near station

Neatly kept 19th-c railway inn, enjoyable food from baguettes up, Dorset and Ringwood ales, decent wines, friendly service, steam railway pictures in lounge bar, Warmwell Aerodrome theme in public bar, conservatory restaurant, family room with pool and machines, skittle alley; disabled facilities, tables on front terrace, bedrooms. *Recommended by Rob and Catherine Dunster*

MOTCOMBE ST8426   SP7 9HW
Coppleridge
Signed from The Street, follow to Mere/Gillingham

Good food from sandwiches to speciality steaks and fresh fish, real ales including Butcombe, decent wines and welcoming service in former 18th-c farmhouse's bar and various dining rooms, some live music; children welcome, ten spacious courtyard bedrooms, 15-acre grounds, play area. *Recommended by Mrs C Roe, Mr and Mrs A Curry*

MUDEFORD SZ1792   BH23 3NJ
Nelson
75 Mudeford

Friendly well run local, good service, four well kept ales, wide range of food from bar meals to authentic thai dishes (takeaways available), bright modern back dining area; Thurs quiz, some live music including jazz, sports TV; pleasant back terrace, open all day. *Recommended by Malcolm Derrick*

OSMINGTON MILLS SY7381   DT3 6HF
☆ Smugglers
Off A353 NE of Weymouth

Bustling old partly thatched family-oriented inn under newish management, well extended, with cosy timber divided areas, woodburners, old local pictures, Badger ales, good choice of wines by the glass, all-day food from varied well priced menu; picnic sets on crazy paving by little stream, thatched summer bar, play area, useful for coastal path, four bedrooms, open all day. *Recommended by Joan and Michel Hooper-Immins, Mrs Joyce Robson*

PAMPHILL ST9900   BH21 4EE
☆ Vine
Off B3082 on NW edge of Wimborne: turn on to Cowgrove Hill at Cowgrove sign, then left up Vine Hill

Simple old-fashioned place run by same family for three generations and part of Kingston Lacy estate (NT); two tiny bars with coal-effect gas fire, handful of tables and seats on lino floor, some under narrow wooden stairs up to games room (darts and board games), local photographs and notices on painted panelling, two real ales (usually Fullers London Pride), local cider and bottled beers, lunchtime bar snacks; quiet piped music, no credit cards, outside lavatories; children allowed away from bar, dogs welcome, heated verandah with fairy lights and grapevine, sheltered gravel terrace, grassy area with climbing frame. *Recommended by Theocsbrian, N R White, the Didler, Richard, Anne and Kate Ansell*

PIDDLETRENTHIDE SY7099   DT2 7QF
☆ Piddle
B3143 N of Dorchester

Family-run village pub with good popular food including fresh fish and daily specials, also enjoyable sandwiches and ploughman's, polite helpful staff, well kept Dorset Piddle, St Austell Tribute and a local guest tapped from the cask, well chosen wines, comfortable leatherette sofas in bar, two separate dining areas; pool, darts, TV; children and dogs welcome, picnic-sets on sunny terrace by River Piddle, three good bedrooms, open all day. *Recommended by Lois Dyer, Phil Bryant, Ian Herdman*

PIDDLETRENTHIDE ST7000   DT2 7QX
Poachers
B3143 N of Dorchester

Bright up-to-date décor, comfortable lounge end, well kept Palmers Copper, Ringwood Fortyniner and St Austell, good wine, generous food from good ciabattas up, smiling service, three linked beamed dining areas; piped music; dogs welcome in bar, garden with tables on decking and stream at bottom, 21 comfortable good value motel-style bedrooms around residents' heated swimming pool, good breakfast, open all day. *Recommended by Dennis Jenkin*

POWERSTOCK SY5196   DT6 3TF
☆ ## Three Horseshoes
Off A3066 Beaminster—Bridport via West Milton

Friendly village inn with stripped panelling, country furniture and good log fires, Palmers ales in traditional bar, enterprising food in dining room with local paintings for sale; piped music; children and dogs welcome, fine uninterrupted valley view from back terrace and big sloping garden, good walks, bedrooms (two with view). *Recommended by Steve Derbyshire, SRD, Roger and Donna Huggins, Ken and Barbara Turner*

SHAFTESBURY ST8722   SP7 8BS
Half Moon
Salisbury Road, Ludwell (A30 E, by roundabout)

Comfortable and pleasantly extended Badger family dining pub with their usual food including popular Sun lunch, well kept ales, quick helpful service, spotless housekeeping, low ceilings, tiled and wood floors on different levels, mixed tables and chairs, old local photographs; disabled parking, garden with adventure playground. *Recommended by Robert Watt, Michael and Jenny Back, Mrs C Roe, Edward Mirzoeff*

SHAFTESBURY ST8622   SP7 8JE
Mitre
High Street

Imposing ancient building, unpretentious inside, with friendly efficient service, well kept Wells & Youngs ales, good range of wines, decent pub food served all day (till 6pm Sun) including good burgers, fine log fire, daily papers, varied mix of tables, Blackmore Vale views from back dining room and three-tier suntrap back decking; piped music; children and dogs welcome, open all day. *Recommended by Jonathan Weedon*

SHAVE CROSS SY4198   DT6 6HW
Shave Cross Inn
On back lane Bridport—Marshwood, signposted locally; OS Sheet 193 map reference 415980

Former medieval monks' lodging, small character timbered and flagstoned bar with huge inglenook, Branscombe Vale Branoc, Dorset Marshwood Vale and pub's own-label 4Ms, farm ciders, vintage rums, attractive restaurant with grandfather clock, pricey caribbean influenced food, ancient skittle alley with bar billiards, pool, darts and a juke box; piped music; children and dogs welcome, sheltered pretty garden with thatched wishing-well, carp pool and play area, seven newly built boutique bedrooms, closed Mon. *Recommended by Bob and Angela Brooks, the Didler, Guy Vowles, Matthew Beard*

STOBOROUGH SY9286   BH20 5AB
Kings Arms
B3075 S of Wareham; Corfe Road

Up to four well kept changing ales, Thatcher's farm cider, good choice of enjoyable reasonably priced food in bar and restaurant, live music Sat; children welcome, disabled access, views over marshes to River Frome from big terrace tables, open all day weekends. *Recommended by Maria Preece, David Lamb, Robert Wivell*

 STOKE ABBOTT ST4500   DT8 3JW
New Inn
Off B3162 and B3163 2 miles W of Beaminster

Spotless 17th-c thatched pub with friendly helpful licensees and pleasant efficient service, well kept Palmers ales, good fairly priced food, woodburner in big inglenook, beams, brasses and copper, some handsome panelling, paintings for sale, flagstoned dining room, fresh flowers on tables; occasional piped music; children welcome, wheelchair access, two lovely gardens, unspoilt quiet thatched village, good walks, bedrooms, closed Sun evening, Mon. *Recommended by John Wymer, the Farmers, Michael David Doyle, Rupert Dick, Patricia and Anthony Daley*

STOURPAINE ST8609   DT11 8TA
White Horse
Shaston Road; A350 NW of Blandford

Traditional country local carefully extended from original core, landlord/chef doing good choice of food from lunchtime sandwiches and bar meals to ambitious dishes (particularly evenings), bargain deals midweek lunchtime, friendly prompt service, well kept Badger ales, sensible wine list, nice layout and décor, scrubbed tables; pool; bedrooms. *Recommended by Robert Watt*

☆ STOURTON CAUNDLE ST7115   DT10 2JW
Trooper
Village signed off A30 E of Milborne Port

Pretty little stone-built pub in lovely village setting, friendly staff and atmosphere, good simple food, well kept ales, reasonable prices, spotless tiny low-ceilinged bar, stripped-stone dining room, darts, cribbage, dominoes, shove-ha'penny, skittle alley; piped music, TV, outside gents'; children and dogs welcome, a few picnic-sets out in front, pleasant side garden with play area, has been open all day on summer weekends, closed Mon lunchtime. *Recommended by Dr A McCormick, Ann and Colin Hunt*

STRATTON SY6593   DT2 9WG
Saxon Arms
Off A37 NW of Dorchester; The Square

Traditional but recently built flint-and-thatch local, open-plan, bright and spacious with light oak tables and comfortable settles on flagstones or carpet, open fire, well kept Otter, Ringwood and Timothy Taylors Landlord, good value wines, tasty generous food including good choice of specials and lunchtime set deals, large comfortable dining section on right, traditional games; piped music; children and dogs welcome, terrace tables overlooking village green, open all day weekends. *Recommended by M G Hart*

☆ STUDLAND SZ0382   BH19 3AU
Bankes Arms
Off B3351, Isle of Purbeck; Manor Road

Very popular spot above fine beach, outstanding country, sea and cliff views from huge garden over road with lots of seating; comfortably basic big bar with raised drinking area, beams, flagstones and good log fire, nine well kept changing ales including own Isle of Purbeck brews, local cider, good wines by the glass, wide choice of food all day from baguettes to local fish and good crab salad (they ask to keep a credit card while you eat), swift service from friendly young staff, darts and pool in side area; piped music, machines, sports TV, can get very busy with trippers at weekends and in summer, parking complicated (NT car park); over-8s and dogs welcome, just off Coast Path, big comfortable bedrooms. *Recommended by Richard Stanfield, Jenny and Brian Seller, Mike and Sue Loseby, John Faircloth*

You can send reports directly to us at **feedback@goodguides.com**

STURMINSTER MARSHALL SY9500
BH21 4BU

Red Lion

Opposite church; off A350 Blandford—Poole

Attractive proper village pub opposite handsome church, welcoming bustling local atmosphere, wide choice of enjoyable imaginative home-made food including good value weekday set lunches and Sun roasts, efficient service, well kept Badger ales, nice wines, old-fashioned roomy U-shaped bar with nice log fire, good-sized lived-in dining room in former skittle alley; piped music; children and dogs welcome, disabled access, back garden with wicker furniture and picnic-sets, open all day Sun. *Recommended by John Branston, Robert Watt*

STURMINSTER NEWTON ST7813
DT10 2BS

 # Bull

A357, S of centre

Friendly thatched 16th-c country pub by River Stur, low beams and plenty of character, enjoyable home-made food, Badger ales, soft lighting; children welcome in compact eating area, roadside picnic-sets, more in secluded back garden. *Recommended by Ann and Colin Hunt*

STURMINSTER NEWTON ST7814
DT10 1AR

Swan

Off A357 Blandford—Sherborne, via B3092; Market Place

Comfortable market-town inn with panelled and stripped-brick bar, fireside sofa, well kept Badger ales, pleasant all-day dining area, good choice of usual food, decent coffee, friendly service; piped music, sports TV; terrace and garden, bedrooms, open all day. *Recommended by Ian Jones, Ann and Colin Hunt*

SWANAGE SZ0378
BH19 2LT

White Swan

High Street

Three ales including Dorset Piddle, enjoyable reasonably priced standard food, cheerful helpful service; children very welcome. *Recommended by Sue and Mike Todd*

SYMONDSBURY SY4493
DT6 6HD

Ilchester Arms

Signed off A35 just W of Bridport

Welcoming 16th-c thatched pub under newish friendly landlord, three well kept Palmers ales, traditional food from lunchtime sandwiches to fresh fish, cosy rustic open-plan low-beamed bar with high-backed settle built in by inglenook, pretty restaurant with another fire, pub games, skittle alley doubling as family room; dogs welcome in bar, level entrance (steps from car park), tables in nice brookside back garden with play area, peaceful village, good walks, three new bedrooms, may be open all day weekends. *Recommended by Martin and Sue Radcliffe*

TARRANT KEYNSTON ST9204
DT11 9JG

True Lovers Knot

B3082 Blandford—Wimborne

Neatly kept corner pub with modernised largely carpeted bar, some beams and flagstones, woodburner, uncluttered dining extension, good fresh food from traditional things to the more imaginative, well kept Badger ales, good wines by the glass; children and dogs welcome, picnic-sets in big garden overlooking fields, four well equipped bedrooms, good breakfast, campsite. *Recommended by Jill Richardson, David Lamb*

TRENT ST5818
DT9 4SL

Rose & Crown

Opposite the church

Thatched former farmhouse with good variety of enjoyable food, well kept Wadworths and guests, welcoming helpful service, log fires, oak settles, grandfather clock, dining conservatory; children welcome, picnic-sets behind – lovely peaceful surroundings, good walks, open all day weekends. *Recommended by Adrian Lawrence*

UPLODERS SY5093   DT6 4NU

☆ ## Crown
Signed off A35 E of Bridport

Inviting homely village pub, log fires, dark low beams, flagstones and lots of bric-a-brac, cheery locals, good food and well kept Palmers ales, friendly caring service; piped music; dogs welcome, tables in attractive two-tier garden. *Recommended by JPR, Mark Flynn, John and Gloria Isaacs, Phil and Jane Villiers, Matthew Beard, Douglas Baldwin and others*

WAREHAM SY9287   BH20 4NN

Duke of Wellington
East Street

Small traditional 18th-c beamed pub, half a dozen mainly local ales kept well, wide choice of reasonably priced food especially fish, some original features including panelling, fire, copper ornaments, old local photographs; piped music; back courtyard tables, bedrooms, open all day. *Recommended by Richard Stanfield, Mrs Joy Griffiths, the Didler, Robert W Buckle*

WAREHAM SY9287   BH20 4LP

Old Granary
The Quay

Fine old brick building with riverside terrace, emphasis on the enjoyable food but two small beamed rooms by main door for drinkers, well kept Badger ales, good wines by the glass, neat efficient young staff, airy dining room with leather high-backed chairs and pews around pale wood tables, brick walls and new oak standing timbers, two further rooms with big photographs of the pub, woodburners, nice relaxed atmosphere; quiet piped jazz; boats for hire over bridge. *Recommended by Dave Hollins*

WAREHAM SY9287   BH20 4LP

Quay Inn
The Quay

Comfortable 18th-c inn in great spot by the water, enjoyable food including pubby favourites and cook your own meat on a hot stone, attentive service, well kept Otter, Isle of Purbeck and Ringwood, reasonably priced wine list, flagstones and open fires; children welcome, terrace area and picnic-sets out on quay, boat trips, bedrooms, parking nearby can be difficult, open all day in summer. *Recommended by John and Gloria Isaacs, Carol Robertson, Richard Stanfield*

WAREHAM FOREST SY9089   BH20 7PA

☆ ## Silent Woman
Wareham—Bere Regis

Long neatly kept Badger dining pub divided by doorways and standing timbers, enjoyable home-made food, well kept Best, Tanglefoot and a seasonal beer, country wines, pleasant staff, traditional furnishings, farm tools and stripped masonry on left; piped music, no children inside; dogs welcome, wheelchair access, plenty of picnic-sets outside including a covered area, walks nearby. *Recommended by S Holder, Richard Stanfield*

WEST BAY SY4690   DT6 4EW

☆ ## West Bay
Station Road

18th-c harbourside pub, island servery separating fairly simple bare-boards front part with coal-effect gas fire from cosier country-kitchen-feel dining area, candles, local pictures and posters, good locally sourced food including plenty of seafood, helpful efficient service, well kept Palmers ales, skittle alley; piped music; dogs welcome, disabled facilities, tables in side and back gardens, three bedrooms, good breakfast, open all day Fri-Sun.
Recommended by David and Julie Glover, B and M Kendall, Matthew Beard, Mr and Mrs Gordon Turner

WEST LULWORTH SY8280   BH20 5RN
Castle Inn
B3070 SW of Wareham

Pretty 16th-c thatched inn in lovely spot near Lulworth Cove, good walks and lots of
summer visitors; beamed flagstoned bar concentrating on wide choice of enjoyable
generous food, friendly chatty staff, well kept changing local ales, 12 ciders/perries,
decent house wines, maze of booth seating divided by ledges, cosy more modern-feeling
lounge bar, pleasant restaurant; piped music; children and dogs welcome, front terrace,
long attractive garden behind on several levels, boules and barbecues, 12 bedrooms.
Recommended by Richard Stanfield, Dave Hollins, N R White, David Bizzell

WEST LULWORTH SY8280   BH20 5RQ
Lulworth Cove
Main Road

Fairly modern place with good range of enjoyable food including local fish/seafood and
Sun carvery, reasonable prices, well kept Badger ales, several wines by the glass, efficient
service even at busy times; sizeable attractive terrace, short stroll down to cove.
Recommended by Jenny and Brian Seller, David and Gill Carrington, John Faircloth

WEST PARLEY SZ0898   BH22 8SQ
Curlew
Christchurch Road

Vintage Inn in early 19th-c farmhouse, informal beamed areas around central bar, mixed
furnishings, candles on tables, two log fires, wide choice of enjoyable food with plenty for
vegetarians, three well kept ales including Ringwood BB, plenty of good value wines,
friendly well trained staff; picnic-sets in well tended front garden. *Recommended by
Ian Malone, Val and Alan Green, David and Sally Frost*

WEST STOUR ST7822   SP8 5RP
☆ ## Ship
A30 W of Shaftesbury

Civilised pleasantly updated 18th-c roadside dining inn, smallish bar on left with big sash
windows and chunky farmhouse furniture on dark boards, smaller low-ceilinged public
bar with flagstones and a good log fire, two stripped-stone dining rooms on right, friendly
neatly dressed staff, good choice of enjoyable generous food (not Sun evening) from
lunchtime baguettes up, Palmers Best and a couple of guests, summer farm cider, good
wines by the glass; piped music, TV, darts and board games; children welcome, dogs in
bar (resident bedlington terriers), terrace and garden behind, car park across road, five
bedrooms, open all day Sun (7pm in winter). *Recommended by Mrs C Roe, Douglas and Ann Hare,
Robert Watt, Steve Jackson, Tracey and Stephen Groves and others*

WEYMOUTH SY6878   DT4 8TZ
☆ ## Nothe Tavern
Barrack Road

Roomy and comfortable early 19th-c pub near Northe Fort, wide range of enjoyable food
including local fresh fish and good value Sun carvery, OAP weekday deals too, friendly
staff coping at busy times, well kept ales such as Courage, Ringwood, Otter and
Wadworths, decent wines, good choice of malt whiskies, lots of dark wood, whisky-water
jugs on ceiling, interesting prints and photographs, restaurant with distant harbour
glimpses; may be quiet piped music; children welcome, more views from terrace.
Recommended by Phil and Jane Hodson, Rob Winstanley, Joan and Michel Hooper-Immins

WEYMOUTH SY6878   DT4 8TR
Red Lion
Hope Square

Small bare-boards 19th-c pub in pedestrianised area, five well kept ales including
Butcombe, Dorset (brewery opposite pub) and Hop Back Summer Lightning, fine whisky

and rum collection, pubby food, friendly capable staff, coal fire, darts; piped music; children welcome, plenty of picnic-sets on sunny front terrace, open all day. *Recommended by Matthew Beard, Rob Winstanley*

WEYMOUTH SY6778 DT4 8BE
Ship
Custom House Quay

Neatly modern extended waterfront pub with several nautical-theme open-plan levels, three well kept Badger ales from long bar, good choice of wines by the glass, enjoyable good value usual food (only upstairs at night) from sandwiches, baguettes and ciabattas up; unobtrusive piped music; wheelchair access downstairs, some quayside seating and pleasant back terrace. *Recommended by Phil and Jane Hodson, David and Gill Carrington*

WEYMOUTH SY6778 DT4 8PY
Wellington Arms
St Alban Street

Handsome green and gold 19th-c tiled façade, well restored panelled interior, carpets, banquettes, mirrors and lots of old local photographs, well kept Ringwood ales, bargain pubby food from sandwiches up including daily roast, friendly landlord and family, some live music; children welcome in back dining room, disabled access, open all day from 10am. *Recommended by Joan and Michel Hooper-Immins, the Didler*

WIMBORNE MINSTER SU0100 BH21 1PF
☆ ## Olive Branch
East Borough, just off Hanham Road (B3073, just E of its junction with B3078); has good car park

Handsome opened-up townhouse, contemporary décor throughout but bar area more traditional with Jacobean panelling, squashy sofas, butcher's block with daily papers, log fire, spreading dining areas divided by standing timbers, modern furniture on wood-strip floors, framed Penguin books, lots of dog latin mottoes, Badger beers, enjoyable bistro-style food, friendly service; teak tables and chairs on terrace. *Recommended by Joan and Michel Hooper-Immins, Paul Goldman*

WIMBORNE ST GILES SU0212 BH21 5NF
Bull
Off B3078 N of Wimborne

Nicely refurbished open-plan Edwardian dining pub, good original restaurant food using fresh local ingredients (organic where possible), fine choice of wines by the glass, Badger ales, friendly staff, garden room, daily papers; children and dogs welcome, tables outside, five stylish bedrooms, open all day summer weekends. *Recommended by Robert Watt*

WINKTON SZ1696 BH23 7AS
Fishermans Haunt
B3347 N of Christchurch

Comfortable big-windowed riverside inn on fringes of New Forest and under newish management, three well kept Fullers/Gales beers, food from sandwiches up including good value weekday lunch menu, two log fires, restaurant views of River Avon; piped music; children welcome, dogs in bar (may be biscuits), disabled facilities, tables among shrubs in quiet back garden, heaters in covered area, 12 comfortable bedrooms, good breakfast, open all day. *Recommended by Stuart Price, Sara Fulton, Roger Baker, Comus and Sarah Elliott, Joan and Michel Hooper-Immins*

WINTERBORNE WHITECHURCH ST8300 DT11 0HW
Milton Arms
A354 Blandford—Dorchester

Enjoyable food and local beers in this refurbished village pub, pleasant staff and atmosphere. *Recommended by Christopher Turner*

WOOL SY8486   BH20 6EQ
Ship
Dorchester Road (A352)

Roomy open-plan thatched and timbered family pub, good choice of enjoyable reasonably priced food all day from baguettes and baked potatoes up, small helpings available, friendly prompt service, well kept Badger ales, decent wines, good coffee, low-ceilinged linked areas and plush back restaurant; quiet piped music; picnic-sets overlooking railway in attractive fenced garden with terrace and play area, handy for Monkey World and Tank Museum, pleasant village. *Recommended by Steve and Sue Griffiths*

ALSO WORTH A VISIT IN SOMERSET

Besides the region's top pubs, we recommend the following. Do tell us what you think of them: **feedback@goodguides.com**

ASHILL ST3116   TA19 9NX
☆ ## Square & Compass
Windmill Hill; off A358 between Ilminster and Taunton; up Wood Road for 1 mile behind Stewley Cross service station; OS Sheet 193 map reference 310166

Well run simple pub overlooking Blackdown Hills, small beamed bar with upholstered window seats taking in the fine view, heavy hand-made furniture, open winter fire and maybe Lilly the pub cat, Butcombe, St Austells and a guest, tasty bar food served by friendly staff; piped music (live music in sound-proofed barn); children and dogs welcome, large glass-covered walled terrace, garden picnic-sets, bedrooms. *Recommended by Roy Hoing, Adrian and Dawn Collinge, Max Benson, Glenwys and Alan Lawrence*

BACKWELL ST4767   BS48 3BE
New Inn
West Town Road (A370 W of Bristol)

Refurbished dining pub with imaginative well presented modern food (not Sun evening) from owner/chef including good value lunchtime set menu, well kept ales and good wines; disabled access with help, big back garden, open all day. *Recommended by Steve and Liz Tilley*

BATH ST7564   BA1 5AR
☆ ## Coeur de Lion
Northumberland Place; off High Street by W H Smith

Tiny stained-glass fronted single-room pub, perhaps Bath's prettiest, simple, cosy and jolly, with candles and log-effect gas fire, well kept Abbey ales and guests, good well priced food from huge baps to roasts (vegetarian options too), good Christmas mulled wine; may be piped music, stairs to lavatories; tables out in charming flower-filled flagstoned pedestrian alley, open all day. *Recommended by the Didler, Michael Dandy, Roger and Donna Huggins, Colin and Peggy Wilshire, David Crook, TB and others*

BATH ST7564   BA1 1NW
Crystal Palace
Abbey Green

Spacious two-room pub with something of a winebar feel, dark panelling and tiled floors, freshly prepared straightforward food (not Sun evening) including lunchtime snacks, speedy friendly service, well kept Marstons related ales, log fire, family room and conservatory; piped music; sheltered heated courtyard with lovely hanging baskets, handy for main shopping areas. *Recommended by Alan Thwaite, Michael Dandy, Dr and Mrs A K Clarke, Roger and Donna Huggins*

BATH ST7464   BA1 1ET
☆ Garricks Head
St Johns Place/Westgate, beside Theatre Royal

Civilised and relaxed pub with high-windowed bar, gingham-covered wooden armchairs by gas-effect coal fire, church candles on mantelpiece and fine silver meat domes on wall above, wheelback and other dining chairs around wooden tables on bare boards, big black squashy sofa and more armchairs at far end, sizeable brass chandeliers, Palmers and a couple of guests, good choice of wines by the glass, proper cocktails, good food including pre-theatre set meals, separate dining room smartly set for eating; may be soft piped jazz; children welcome, dogs in bar, pavement tables, open all day. *Recommended by Edward Mirzoeff, George Atkinson, Michael Dandy, David Crook*

BATH ST7465   BA1 3AR
☆ Hop Pole
Albion Buildings, Upper Bristol Road

Bustling family-friendly Bath Ales pub with guest beers, decent wines by the glass, enjoyable food (not Sun evening or Mon lunchtime) from sandwiches to full meals in bar and former skittle alley restaurant, traditional settles and other pub furniture on bare boards in four tastefully reworked linked areas, lots of black woodwork, ochre walls, some bric-a-brac, board games, daily papers; Mon quiz night, piped music, discreet sports TV; wheelchair accessible, attractive two-level back courtyard with boules, fairy-lit vine arbour and summer houses with heaters, opposite Victoria Park with its great play area, open all day. *Recommended by the Didler, Taff Thomas*

BATH ST7564   BA1 2JZ
☆ Old Green Tree
Green Street

Much loved atmospheric tavern, unchanging and always packed, with three cosy low-ceilinged oak-panelled rooms including comfortable lounge with wartime aircraft pictures (local artwork in summer), back bar with big skylight, up to six interesting changing ales, a dozen wines by the glass (helpful notes on list) and 35 malt whiskies, generous lunchtime bar food, lots of board games; basic gents' down steep steps, no credit cards or children; open all day but closed Sun lunchtime in summer. *Recommended by Terry and Nickie Williams, Alan Thwaite, Rob and Catherine Dunster, the Didler, N R White, Michael Dandy and others*

BATH ST7565   BA1 5BR
Pig & Fiddle
Saracen Street

Lively, not smart, with half a dozen good sensibly priced local ales, friendly staff, two big open fires, bare boards and bright paintwork, clocks on different time zones, steps up to darker bustling servery and little dining area, games area and several TVs for sport; lots of students at night, piped trendy music then; picnic-sets on big heated front terrace, open all day. *Recommended by the Didler, Taff Thomas, Roger and Donna Huggins*

BATH ST7464   BA1 1HE
Raven
Queen Street

Small buoyant city-centre local, two well kept ales for the pub from Blindmans and local guests, a changing farm cider, limited food including good reasonably priced pies, quick friendly service, bare boards, some stripped stone and an open fire, newspapers, upstairs area, live acoustic music; open all day. *Recommended by Colin Campbell, Ian Phillips, the Didler, Andy Lickfold, Michael Dandy, TB and others*

BATH ST7364   BA2 3BW
Royal Oak
Lower Bristol Road

Basic bare-boards pub with great choice of beer including their own, local ciders, friendly licensees, live music; open all day. *Recommended by Taff Thomas*

BATH ST7464   BA1 2JL
Salamander
John Street

Busy city local tied to Bath Ales, their full range and guests kept well, good choice of wines by the glass, bare boards, black woodwork and dark ochre walls, popular food including some unusual choices, friendly young staff, two rooms downstairs, open-kitchen restaurant upstairs, daily papers, Sun quiz; piped music, no dogs; children till 8pm, open all day. *Recommended by Alan Thwaite, Steve Jackson, the Didler, Michael Dandy, N R White and others*

BATH ST7565   BA1 5NA
☆ Star
Vineyards; The Paragon (A4), junction with Guinea Lane

Unspoilt city-centre pub with a real sense of its past, now tap for Abbey Ales with guests including Bass poured from a jug, four small linked rooms served from single bar, many original features, traditional wall benches (one hard one known as Death Row), panelling, dim lighting and open fires, no food apart from rolls and Sun bar nibbles, free snuff, shove-ha'penny and cribbage, live folk nights; children and dogs welcome, open all day weekends when it gets packed. *Recommended by the Didler, N R White, Taff Thomas*

BATH ST7766   BA1 7DD
Wagon & Horses
London Road W

Roomy pub popular for bargain OAP lunch and other deals, well kept ales, pleasant décor and stunning Avon Valley views; piped music, Sun quiz. *Recommended by Meg and Colin Hamilton, Dr and Mrs A K Clarke*

BATH ST7564   BA2 6AA
White Hart
Widcombe Hill

Bare-boards bistro-style pub popular for its food, quick friendly service even when busy, well kept Butcombe from attractive panelled bar, farm cider, helpful staff, fresh flowers; pretty beer garden, bedrooms and self-catering hostel. *Recommended by Dr and Mrs A K Clarke*

BATHFORD ST7866   BA1 7SL
Crown
Bathford Hill, towards Bradford-on-Avon, by Batheaston roundabout and bridge

Recently reopened bistro pub, decent choice of blackboard food including weekday set deals, ales such as Bath and Fullers London Pride; children and dogs welcome, tables out in front and in back garden with pétanque, open all day. *Recommended by anon*

BISHOP'S WOOD ST2512   TA20 3RS
☆ Candlelight
Off A303/B3170 S of Taunton

Renovated dining pub, roomy yet cosy, with beams and log fires, food has been good and varied but new chef – reports please, good wine list, well kept beers such as Exmoor and Otter, competent service; children and dogs welcome, disabled access, nice side garden and back terrace by fish pond. *Recommended by Patrick and Daphne Darley, Bob and Margaret Holder and others*

BLAGDON ST5058   BS40 7SB
☆ New Inn
Off A368; Park Lane/Church Street

Lovely view over Blagdon Lake (where they get their trout) from seats in front of this friendly pub; Wadworths ales, tasty fairly priced bar food, cheerful service, bustling bars with two inglenook log fires, heavy beams hung with horsebrasses and tankards, comfortable antique settles and mate's chairs among more modern furnishings, old prints and photographs, plainer side bar; children (over 10) and dogs welcome, wheelchair access (best from front). *Recommended by Dr and Mrs A K Clarke, Dennis Jenkin, Jim and Frances Gowers, Chris and Angela Buckell, Jennifer Norie*

BLAGDON ST5059   BS40 7RA
Queen Adelaide
High Street

Cosy unpretentious pub in lovely spot overlooking Blagdon Lake, chunky tables and settles, local real ales, traditional pub food plus some interesting additions from smallish blackboard menu, enjoyable and reasonably priced. *Recommended by Jane and Alan Bush*

BLEADON ST3457   BS24 0NF
 ## Queens Arms
Just off A370 S of Weston; Celtic Way

Popular 16th-c village pub with informal chatty atmosphere in carefully divided areas, candles on sturdy tables flanked by winged settles, solid fuel stove, old hunting prints, generous reasonably priced food (not Sun evening) from lunchtime baguettes to steaks, friendly service, well kept Butcombe and guests tapped from the cask, local cider, several wines by the glass, flagstoned restaurant and stripped-stone back bar with woodburner, darts, clean lavatories (mind the steps); children (away from bar) and dogs welcome, picnic-sets on pretty heated terrace, open all day. *Recommended by Dennis Jenkin, M Mossman, Tom Evans, Ian and Nita Cooper, Michael Doswell*

BRADFORD-ON-TONE ST1721   TA4 1ET
Worlds End
S of village, towards Silver Street; on A38 NE of Wellington

Neat, comfortable and spacious roadside pub, wide choice of imaginative good value food including vegetarian options, friendly efficient staff. *Recommended by Heather Coulson, Neil Cross*

BRADLEY GREEN ST2438   TA5 2NE
Malt Shovel
Off A39 W of Bridgwater, near Cannington

Low-beamed pub with interconnecting rooms, mix of old and new furniture on quarry-tiles and carpet, some stripped stone, old hunting prints, woodburner, enjoyable food from snacks up including good value lunchtime carvery, weekend breakfast till 10.30am, helpful staff, well kept Butcombe ales, real cider and decent wines by the glass, sizeable skittle alley; piped music; children in eating areas, disabled access (highish door sills into restaurant) and facilities, picnic-sets on paved laneside area, bedrooms. *Recommended by Chris and Angela Buckell*

BRISTOL ST5873   BS1 2HR
Bank
John Street

Small proper single-bar pub doing well under current landlord, centrally placed and popular with office workers, four or five changing local ales, Thatcher's cider, some lunchtime food including Sun roasts; wheelchair access, tables under umbrellas in large paved courtyard. *Recommended by Chris and Angela Buckell*

BRISTOL ST5873   BS1 5BD
Colston Yard
Upper Maudlin Street/Colston Street

Popular Butcombe pub on two floors (site of old Smiles Brewery), their full range and guests kept well, interesting bottled beers, good choice of wines and spirits, enjoyable food from lunchtime sandwiches to grills and evening restaurant menu; disabled facilities, open all day (till 1am Fri, Sat). *Recommended by Chris and Angela Buckell, Paul Hillier*

We say if we know a pub allows dogs.

BRISTOL ST5872   BS1 6EN
Cornubia
Temple Street

18th-c backstreet real ale pub with good range including Hidden and several recherché regional guests, interesting bottled beers, farm cider and perry, limited weekday pubby food till 7.30pm (Sun till 6pm), friendly service, small woody seating areas; can be crowded evenings, not for wheelchairs; picnic-sets on cobbles outside. *Recommended by John and Gloria Isaacs, the Didler, Jeremy King*

BRISTOL ST5872   BS1 1UB
Elephant
St Nicholas Street

Nicely refurbished 18th-c city-centre pub with chunky tables, chairs and benches on bare boards, high ceilings, big mirrors, log fire, Bath, Otter, Timothy Taylors Landlord and a guest, extensive and interesting choice of wines by the glass, enjoyable home-made food including pub staples and pizzas, friendly staff; open all day (till 2am Fri, Sat). *Recommended by Bep Bartrip, Ann Smith, Pamela Rogers*

BRISTOL ST5772   BS8 4RU
Grain Barge
Hotwell Road

Floating 100-ft barge tied to Bristol Beer Factory, their ales kept well, good well priced freshly made food including Sun roasts, friendly staff, seats out on top deck, sofas and tables on wood floor below; live music Fri night, open all day. *Recommended by the Didler, Steve Price*

BRISTOL ST5772   BS8 1DR
☆ ## Hope & Anchor
Jacobs Wells Road, Clifton

Friendly recently refurbished 18th-c pub, half a dozen good changing ales such as Cheddar, Otter, Timothy Taylors and Wadworths from central bar, nice wines and good choice of malts, tables of various sizes (some shaped to fit corners) on bare boards, darker back area, flowers and candles, sensibly priced hearty food all day – very popular lunchtime, friendly staff; soft piped music, occasional live music, can get crowded late evening; children welcome, disabled access, barbecues in good-sized tiered back garden with interesting niches, nearby parking can be tricky. *Recommended by Simon and Amanda Southwell, Dr and Mrs A K Clarke, Jeremy King, the Didler, Chris and Angela Buckell*

BRISTOL ST5874   BS6 6NP
☆ ## Kensington Arms
Stanley Road

Smart dining pub in discreet shades of grey and cream, nice relaxed atmosphere with cheerful accommodating bar staff, good food from light pub lunches to bigger pricier evening dishes, well kept beers and good if not cheap wine choice, interesting rums etc, flowers and lit candles; may be piped music; disabled facilities and access (not to dining room/upstairs dining room), well behaved children and dogs welcome, heated terrace. *Recommended by Susanna Wadeson, Paul Hillier*

BRISTOL ST5976   BS7 9JR
Lazy Dog
Ashley Down Road

Refurbished local with two bar areas (one upstairs), Bath and Bristol Beer Factory ales, real ciders, good choice of wines and malt whiskies, well priced food all-day from snacks and sharing plates up, dark green interior with wood panelled alcoves, white marble-effect bar counter, leather wall benches, sofas and armchairs on light wood floors, lots of mirrors, family room with metal furniture (children welcome till 7pm), vintage juke box,

Tues quiz; dogs welcome, wheelchair access, seats out at front and in decked garden behind. *Recommended by Chris and Angela Buckell*

BRISTOL ST5772   BS8 4PZ
Merchants Arms
Merchants Road, Hotwells

Tiny two-room pub close to historic dockside, welcoming landlord and friendly locals, well kept Bath ales and their Bounders cider, guest beers, modest choice of well chosen wines, limited food, open fire; popular Thurs quiz, singalongs/karaoke; sports TV; wheelchair access with help (narrow door and steps). *Recommended by Simon and Amanda Southwell, Dr and Mrs A K Clarke, Chris and Angela Buckell, John and Gloria Isaacs and others*

BRISTOL ST5772   BS1 6XJ
Nova Scotia
Baltic Wharf, Cumberland Basin

Unreconstructed old local on S side of Floating Harbour, views to Clifton and Avon Gorge, Bass, Courage Best and guest beers, real ciders, bargain hearty food from good doorstep sandwiches to Sun roasts, pubby seats in four linked areas, snob screen, mahogany and mirrors, nautical charts as wallpaper, character locals; wheelchair access (easiest through snug), plenty of tables out by water, bedrooms sharing bathroom. *Recommended by Chris and Angela Buckell*

BRISTOL ST5672   BS8 4LE
Portcullis
Wellington Terrace

Compact two-storey pub in Georgian building with spectacular views, well kept Dawkins and several changing guests, farm ciders, fine range of wines by the glass and spirits, friendly service, basic cheap bar food (not Mon) including well filled rolls; flame-effect gas fire, dark wood and usual pubby furniture; tricky wheelchair access. *Recommended by Roger and Donna Huggins*

BRISTOL ST5972   BS1 6JG
Seven Stars
Thomas Lane

Unpretentious one-room real ale pub near harbour (and associated with Thomas Clarkson and slave trade abolition), much enjoyed by students and local office workers, up to eight ales including Absolution brewed for them by Sharps, beer, cider and perry festivals, interesting malts and bourbons, dark wood, bare boards, old local prints and photographs, you can bring in take-aways, regular irish music; juke box, pool, games machines; disabled access (but narrow alley with uneven cobbles and cast-iron kerbs). *Recommended by Chris and Angela Buckell, Jeremy King*

BRISTOL ST5872   BS1 5UR
Three Tuns
St Georges Road

Now owned by local Arbor with their ales and guests such as Bristol Beer Factory and Dark Star, interesting selection of US beers, Thatcher's cider and decent choice of wines, cheerful knowledgeable staff, extended bar area with mix of pubby furniture on bare boards, a couple of armchairs in alcoves, open fire, lunchtime rolls; very busy weekends when live music; garden with smokers' area, near cathedral. *Recommended by Chris and Angela Buckell and others*

BRISTOL ST5873   BS1 5BB
Urban Wood
Colston Street

Relaxed two-room bar with bohemian feel, mix of old wooden furniture and chesterfields on wood floors, standard lamps, candles, modern art and fresh flowers, enjoyable home-made food from brunch dishes to risotto and steaks, a real ale and interesting bottled beers, cocktails, friendly staff; downstairs lavatories, piped music and some live; closed Sun otherwise open all day (till late Thurs-Sat). *Recommended by Edd Hetherington*

BRISTOL ST5773   BS8 2BH
Victoria
Southleigh Road, Clifton

Modest little two-room pub, popular and can get crowded, with half a dozen or more changing ales (mostly from small brewers), interesting lagers and belgian beers, local ciders/perries, dozens of malt whiskies, good wines by the glass including organic, knowledgeable cheerful staff, basic snacks, big mirrors and open fire, cards and board games, old silent movies some nights; dogs welcome, disabled access improved now outside area pedestrianised, opens mid-afternoon (all day weekends). *Recommended by Chris and Angela Buckell*

BRISTOL ST5976   BS7 8UR
Wellington
Gloucester Road, Horfield (A38)

Lively and roomy 1920s pub refitted in traditional style and continuing well under newish management, well kept Bath Ales and guests, good choice of bottled beers, enjoyable traditional food including Sun roasts, large horseshoe bar, sofas and low tables in extended lounge with dining area overlooking sunny terrace; very busy on home match days for Bristol RFC or Rovers; children welcome, disabled facilities, bedrooms, open all day. *Recommended by Chris and Angela Buckell*

BURROW BRIDGE ST3530   TA7 0RB
King Alfred
Main Road, by the bridge

Proper old-fashioned friendly local, enjoyable unpretentious fresh food (meat all from Somerset) including popular Sun lunch, reasonable prices, pleasant efficient service, four well kept ales and local cider, games, some live music. *Recommended by Bob and Margaret Holder, J S Hurst, Hugh Roberts*

CATCOTT ST3939   TA7 9HU
King William
Signed off A39 Street—Bridgwater

Rugs on flagstones, traditional furnishings, old prints and big stone fireplaces, good choice of enjoyable generous food, well kept Palmers ales, decent wines, good service, big back extension with skittle alley and glass-topped well, pub games; piped music; children welcome. *Recommended by Shirley and Bob Gibbs*

CHARLTON ADAM ST5328   TA11 7AU
Fox & Hounds
Broadway Road, just off A37 about 3 miles N of Ilchester

Big neatly refurbished village pub, tankards on low black beams, carpeted or parquet floors, some bare stone walls, cricketing and hunting prints, old Guinness ads, usual pubby furniture, woodburner, well kept Butcombe from stone bar, enjoyable home-made food, prompt pleasant service; children welcome, disabled access, verandah-style area and garden with wendy house, campsite. *Recommended by David and Stella Martin, Chris and Angela Buckell*

CHEDDAR ST4553   BS27 3LE
Gardeners Arms
Silver Street

Tucked away in the old part (originally four farmworkers' cottages) and under newish management, enjoyable food including good Sun roasts, well kept real ales, attractive two-room beamed dining area, interesting old local photographs, woodburner; children and dogs have been welcome, quiet back garden, open all day weekends. *Recommended by Jo Greenman*

CHEW MAGNA ST5763   BS40 8SL
☆ Bear & Swan
B3130 (South Parade)

Open-plan Fullers pub with much emphasis on food, their ales and guests such as Butcombe, good choice of wines, helpful attentive staff, mix of pine tables, pews and big log fire, L-shaped dining room with stripped stone, bare boards and woodburner; piped music, TV, small car park (street parking not easy); children and dogs welcome, wheelchair access from car park, secluded beer garden, smokers' area with big heated parasol, old-fashioned bedrooms, closed Sun evening. *Recommended by D R Grossmark, Dr and Mrs A K Clarke, Steve and Liz Tilley, Chris and Angela Buckell, Mrs Susannah Riley*

CHEW MAGNA ST5861   BS40 8TQ
☆ Pony & Trap
Knowle Hill, New Town; from B3130 in village, follow Bishop Sutton, Bath signpost

Dining pub in nice rural spot near Chew Valley Lake, very good imaginative food from sandwiches through to restaurant dishes, friendly service, Butcombe, Courage Best and Otter, front bar with cushioned wall seats and built-in benches on parquet, snug area on left with old range, dark plank panelling and housekeeper's chair in corner, lovely pasture views from two-level back dining area, rush-seated chairs around white tables on slate flagstones; children welcome, dogs in bar, modern metal and wood furniture on back terrace, picnic-sets on grass with chickens pottering in runs below, front smokers' shelter, good walks, closed Sun evening. *Recommended by Dr and Mrs A K Clarke, John Urquhart, John and Gloria Isaacs, Michael Doswell, A Helme and others*

CHILCOMPTON ST6451   BA3 4JW
Somerset Wagon
B3139; Broadway

Cosy and friendly with well kept Wadworths ales, enjoyable reasonably priced food including speciality ribs, good service, pleasant olde-worlde areas off central bar, lots of settles, newspapers, log fire; small front garden. *Recommended by Ian Phillips*

CHISELBOROUGH ST4614   TA14 6TT
☆ Cat Head
Cat Street; leave A303 on A356 towards Crewkerne; take the third left (at 1.4 miles), Signed Chiselborough, then left after 0.2 miles

Well run and much enjoyed old sandstone pub, neat attractive bars with traditional light-wood tables and chairs, some high-backed cushioned settles, flagstones and mullioned windows, woodburner in fine fireplace, Butcombe and Sharps, local cider, several wines by the glass, good well presented food from lunchtime sandwiches up (more elaborate evening choice), friendly helpful service, darts, skittle alley; piped music; children and dogs welcome, seats on terrace, pretty garden, closed Sun evening. *Recommended by Guy Consterdine, Bob and Margaret Holder, Stephen Colling, Ian Scott-Thompson, Dr A McCormick, Maurice Ricketts and others*

CLEVEDON ST4071   BS21 7QU
Moon & Sixpence
The Beach

Substantial seafront Victorian family dining pub, large bar area, balconied mezzanine floor with good view of pier and over to Brecon Beacons, reasonably priced food with some mediterranean touches including mezze, helpful friendly staff, well kept Greene King ales; may be piped music; terrace seating, bedrooms. *Recommended by Dave Braisted, John Wooll*

CLEVEDON ST4071   BS21 6AE
☆ Old Inn
Walton Road (B3124 on outskirts)

Friendly mix of regulars and visitors in neatly extended beamed pub, good value generous pubby food (not Mon lunchtime) from baguettes up, well kept changing ales such as

Cotswold Spring, Cottage and Otter, half a dozen wines by the glass, seating from cushioned settles and stools to sofas, carpeted floors, white german shepherd called Polar Bear; piped music, silent TV; children welcome, pleasant secluded back garden with boules, bedrooms. *Recommended by Tom Evans, Chris and Angela Buckell, Jim and Frances Gowers*

COMBE FLOREY ST1531   TA4 3HZ
☆ Farmers Arms
Off A358 Taunton—Williton, just N of main village turn-off

Neatly kept thatched and beamed dining pub, popular and can get packed lunchtime, welcoming helpful staff, wide choice of good reasonably priced food using prime local produce, well kept ales such as Cotleigh and Exmoor, local farm cider, comfortable drinking area with log fire; children welcome, plenty of tables in attractive garden, by summer steam line. *Recommended by Bob and Margaret Holder, W N Murphy, Christine and Neil Townend*

COMBE HAY ST7359   BA2 7EG
☆ Wheatsheaf
Off A367 or B3110 S of Bath

Good upscale food from short changing menu (not cheap), lunchtime set meals, Butcombe beers, local farm cider, good if pricey wine choice, quick friendly service, plush fireside sofas, big fresh and airy dining area with trendy light modern furnishings (a radical change for this 1576 pub); tables in attractive terraced garden overlooking church and steep valley, dovecotes built into the walls, plenty of good nearby walks, comfortable bedrooms in outbuildings, closed Mon. *Recommended by Ian Phillips, Dr and Mrs A K Clarke, Taff Thomas*

COMPTON MARTIN ST5457   BS40 6JE
Ring o' Bells
A368 Bath—Weston

Popular country pub in attractive spot, traditional front part with rugs on flagstones, inglenook seats by log fire, up step to spacious carpeted back part, stripped stone, Butcombe ales and guests, reasonably priced wine, tasty pub food with some south african influences (licensees from there), cheerful helpful young staff, newspapers; well behaved children and dogs welcome, charming big garden with play area, open all day weekends. *Recommended by Bob and Angela Brooks, C and R Bromage, Stuart Paulley*

CONGRESBURY ST4363   BS49 5JA
Plough
High Street (B3133)

Old-fashioned local (a pub since 1800s) and full of life, usually five well kept changing west country ales including Bath, Butcombe and St Austell, quick smiling service, decent well priced bar food including specials, several small interconnecting rooms off flagstoned main bar, mix of furniture old and new, built-in pine wall benches, old prints, photos, farm tools and sporting memorabilia, log fire; Sun quiz; garden with rustic furniture and boules. *Recommended by Chris and Angela Buckell*

CONGRESBURY ST4363   BS49 5JA
Ship & Castle
High Street (just off A370 from lights at W end of bypass)

Old family-run inn with series of revamped contemporary rooms, enjoyable food from lunchtime sandwiches and baked potatoes up at solid tables, open fire and soft seats, Greene King ales; children welcome, garden, boules, six individually styled bedrooms. *Recommended by M Mossman, Jim and Frances Gowers*

> For those of you who use Sat Nav devices, we include a postcode for
> every entry in the *Guide*.

CRANMORE ST6643 BA4 4QJ
☆ Strode Arms
West Cranmore; signed with pub off A361 Frome—Shepton Mallet

Originally a 15th-c farmhouse, now a pretty dining pub with most customers here for the often interesting food (not Sun evening), rambling rooms with country furnishings, fresh flowers and pot plants, grandfather clock on flagstones, remarkable old locomotive engineering drawings and big black and white steam train murals in central lobby, log fires in handsome fireplaces, Wadworths ales, several wines by the glass, daily papers; children welcome lunchtimes/early evening, dogs allowed, pretty tubs and hanging baskets on front terrace, more seats in back garden, may be vintage car meetings (first Tues of month), handy for East Somerset Light Railway. *Recommended by David and Diane Young, Ted George, Neil and Karen Dignan, M G Hart, Mrs Ann Gray, Bob and Margaret Holder and others*

DINNINGTON ST4013 TA17 8SX
Dinnington Docks
aka Rose & Crown; Fosse Way

Good cheery atmosphere in large old-fashioned country local, unspoilt and unfussy, with good choice of inexpensive genuine home cooking, Butcombe and guest ales, farm ciders, log fire, friendly attentive staff, memorabilia to bolster the myth that there was once a railway line and dock here, sofas in family room, skittle alley in adjoining building; large garden behind. *Recommended by Maurice Ricketts, Michael Lamm*

DITCHEAT ST6236 BA4 6RB
☆ Manor House
Signed off A37 and A371 S of Shepton Mallet

Pretty 17th-c red-brick village inn, buoyant atmosphere, often full of jockeys from nearby racing stables, enjoyable home-made food from sandwiches and pubby bar meals to more sophisticated choices, Butcombe and guests, unusual arched doorways linking big flagstoned bar to comfortable lounge and restaurant, open fires, skittle alley; children welcome, tables on back grass, handy for Royal Bath & West showground, three mews bedrooms, open all day. *Recommended by Carey Smith*

DOULTING ST6444 BA4 4PY
Poachers Pocket
Chelynch Road, off A361

Popular modernised local, flagstones with some carpet, good hearty food, well kept Wadworths ales and Butcombe as guest, local farm cider, log fire in stripped-stone end wall, dining conservatory; children in eating area and large family room/skittle alley, nice back garden with country views. *Recommended by Susan and Nigel Wilson*

DULVERTON SS9127 TA22 9HJ
Bridge Inn
Bridge Street

Unpretentious local with Lorna Doone connections, enjoyable home-made food from local suppliers, well kept ales including Exmoor and St Austell, some unusual imported beers, Addlestone's cider, decent wine choice and 30 malt whiskies, comfortable sofas, log fire, folk night third Sat of month, Sun quiz; children welcome and dogs (resident one called Molly), riverside terrace, open all day Fri-Sun, closed Mon evening. *Recommended by JJW, CMW, Peter Dearing, Mr and Mrs G Prisk*

DUNSTER SS9943 TA24 6SG
☆ Luttrell Arms
High Street; A396

Small hotel in 15th-c timber-framed abbey building, well used high-beamed back bar hung with bottles, clogs and horseshoes, stag's head and rifles on walls above old settles and more modern furniture, big log fires, enjoyable generous food including substantial sandwiches with home-baked bread, small helpings available, friendly attentive staff, well kept ales including Exmoor, good wines in three glass sizes, more formal restaurant; dogs welcome in bar, ancient glazed partition dividing off small galleried and flagstoned courtyard, upstairs access to quiet attractive garden with Civil War cannon emplacements and great views, comfortable if pricey bedrooms – some with four-posters. *Recommended by Kay Wheat, David and Julie Glover*

EAST LAMBROOK ST4218   TA13 5HF

☆ Rose & Crown

Neatly kept stone-built dining pub spreading extensively from compact 17th-c core with inglenook log fire, efficient friendly staff and relaxed atmosphere, good generous inexpensive food freshly made using local supplies including very popular weekday OAP lunches, full Palmers range kept well, farm cider, decent wines by the glass, restaurant extension with old glass-covered well; picnic-sets on neat lawn, opposite East Lambrook Manor Garden. *Recommended by Mrs C Roe, Cliff Sparkes, Mr and Mrs B Cox*

EAST WOODLANDS ST7944   BA11 5LY

☆ Horse & Groom

Off A361/B3092 junction

Small pretty pub tucked away down country lanes, enjoyable well priced fresh food (not Sun evening), friendly service, Butcombe, Wadworths and a guest tapped from the cask, pews and settles in flagstoned bar, woodburner in comfortable lounge, big dining conservatory, traditional games; dogs welcome away from restaurant, children in eating areas, disabled access, tables out in nice front garden with more seats behind, handy for Longleat. *Recommended by Edward Mirzoeff*

EVERCREECH ST6336   BA4 6NA

Natterjack

A371 Shepton Mallet—Castle Cary

Wide choice of popular generous food at reasonable prices, three local ales including one for the pub from Box Steam, good wine choice, welcoming landlord and cheerful efficient staff, long bar with eating areas off; lots of tables under parasols in big neatly kept garden. *Recommended by Col and Mrs Patrick Kaye*

EXEBRIDGE SS9324   TA22 9AZ

Anchor

B3222 S of Dulverton; pub itself actually over the river, in Devon

Comfortable child-friendly pub in idyllic Exmoor-edge spot, some attractive furnishings, oak panelling and pictures, enjoyable well presented food from varied menu, friendly service (can be slow when busy), well kept Greene King ales, local farm cider, above-average wines, woodburner, family eating area and restaurant, smaller back games bar, skittle alley; dogs welcome, nice big riverside garden with plenty of tables and play area, fishing rights, opposite Exe Valley trout smokery, six bedrooms, good breakfast, open all day at least in summer. *Recommended by David and Julie Glover, Rosemary Budgell*

EXFORD SS8538   TA24 7PY

☆ White Horse

B3224

Popular and welcoming three-storey creeper-clad inn, more or less open-plan bar, high-backed antique settle among more conventional seats, scrubbed deal tables, hunting prints and local photographs, good log fire, Exmoor ales and Sharps Doom Bar, over 100 malt whiskies, Thatcher's cider, hearty food from sandwiches to good value Sun carvery, Land Rover Exmoor safaris; children and dogs welcome, play area and outside tables, comfortable bedrooms, pretty village, open all day from 8am. *Recommended by Peter and Giff Bennett*

FAILAND ST5171   BS8 3TU

Failand Inn

B3128 Bristol—Clevedon

Refurbished welcoming old coaching inn with wide choice of popular pub food, well kept

Butcombe, Courage and Theakstons, good wines by the glass, large bright dining areas either side of entrance, two bars, low beams, toby jugs, decorative plates and brasses; gentle piped music; children and dogs welcome, garden with decking and heated smokers' shelter, open all day. *Recommended by Dr and Mrs C W Thomas*

FAULKLAND ST7555   BA3 5XF

 ## Tuckers Grave
A366 E of village

Sadly this unspoilt tiny cider house (a great favourite with readers) has closed.

FRESHFORD ST7960   BA2 7WG
Inn at Freshford
Off A36 or B3108

Roomy beamed stone-built dining pub prospering under current management, well kept Box Steam ales and guests, real ciders and a draught perry, decent wines by the glass, good choice of malts, food from lunchtime sandwiches up, more evening choice, helpful attentive service; wheelchair access from car park, pretty hillside garden, attractive spot near river. *Recommended by Chris and Angela Buckell*

FROME ST7747   BA11 1BH
Arcangel
King Street

Newly and imaginatively renovated old coaching inn, bars either side of entrance, one with big renaissance angel wall print and comfortable sofas next to open stone fireplace, high-raftered stable restaurant with original rough walls and modern seating areas including a mezzanine with glass side panels and higher 'floating' section with single table, adventurous food as well as pub favourites, well kept ales; courtyard tables, six stylish bedrooms some with stand-alone zinc baths. *Recommended by Dr and Mrs A K Clarke*

HALLATROW ST6357   BS39 6EN
 ## Old Station
A39 S of Bristol

Good fresh food and well kept ales such as Brains and Butcombe in idiosyncratic bar packed with cluttered railway, musical and other bric-a-brac, also italian evening dishes in *Flying Scotsman* railcar restaurant (you can look in during daytime), friendly welcoming service; piped music; children in eating areas, big garden with barbecue, pizza oven and well equipped play area, five bedrooms (may not serve breakfast). *Recommended by Ken Marshall, John and Sheena Radnedge*

HARDWAY ST7234   BA10 0LN
Bull
Off B3081 Bruton—Wincanton at brown sign for Stourhead and King Alfred's Tower; Hardway

Charming beamed 17th-c country dining pub popular locally, especially with older people weekday lunchtimes, good food (not Sun evening) in comfortable bar and character dining rooms, good informal service, well kept Butcombe and Otter, farm cider, nice wines by the glass, log fire; unobtrusive piped music; tables and barbecues in garden behind, more in rose garden over road, bedrooms. *Recommended by SRD, Mrs C Roe*

HINTON CHARTERHOUSE ST7758   BA2 7SN
Rose & Crown
B3110 about 4 miles S of Bath

Reliable 18th-c village pub with friendly young licensees, partly divided bar with panelling, blue plush cushioned wall seats and mix of wooden tables and chairs on carpet, candles in bottles, ornate carved stone fireplace (smaller brick one on other side), Butcombe, Fullers and a guest, good straightforward bar food, long dining room with steps to lower area with unusual beamed ceiling; piped music, TV; children welcome, dogs in bar (pub's dog is called Tia Maria), picnic-sets under parasols in terraced garden, pretty window boxes, bedrooms, open all day weekends. *Recommended by Frank Willy, Simon Rodway, Meg and Colin Hamilton*

HOLCOMBE ST6648
BA3 5HQ
Duke of Cumberland
Edford Hill

Modernised under newish hard-working licensees, good choice of reasonably priced food including home-made pizzas, local ales such as Bath, Butcombe, Dawkins and Wadworths, Ashton Press and Cheddar Vale ciders, skittle alley; piped music, TV; children welcome, riverside garden with picnic-sets, open all day. *Recommended by Ian Phillips*

HOLYWELL LAKE ST1020
TA21 0EJ
Holywell Inn
Off A38

Comfortable and relaxed old pub in tiny hamlet, good value food including remarkable vegetarian range with their popular Sun carvery, good local ales and a potent cider from unusual canal boat counter, three dining areas; darts, pool and TV; children over 5 allowed away from bar and main dining area, well behaved dogs welcome in bar, garden picnic-sets, closed Mon, Tues-Sat lunchtimes and Sun evening. *Recommended by Dr E Scarth and Miss A Pocock*

HORTON ST3214
TA19 9QH
Five Dials
Hanning Road; off A303

Reopened local run by friendly helpful young couple, popular reasonably priced food, restaurant; children and dogs welcome, bedrooms. *Recommended by Evelyn and Derek Walter, Ted and Charlotte Routley*

KELSTON ST7067
BA1 9AQ
Old Crown
Bitton Road; A431 W of Bath

Four small traditional rooms with beams and polished flagstones, carved settles and cask tables, logs burning in ancient open range, two more coal-effect fires, Bath, Butcombe, Fullers and Wadworths (some cask tapped), Thatcher's cider, good choice of wines by the glass and whiskies, friendly helpful staff, enjoyable food from new chef in bar (not Sun or Mon evenings) and small restaurant (not Sun); dogs welcome on leads, children in eating areas, wheelchair accessible with help, picnic-sets under apple trees in sunny sheltered back garden, bedrooms in converted outbuildings, open all day weekends. *Recommended by Dr and Mrs A K Clarke, Ian and Rose Lock, Chris and Angela Buckell*

KEYNSHAM ST6669
BS31 2DD
☆ # Lock-Keeper
Keynsham Road (A4175 NE of town)

Friendly riverside pub with plenty of character, bare boards and relaxed worn-in feel, simple left-hand bar with big painted settle, cushioned wall benches, trophy cabinet and old local photographs, two more little rooms with all manner of cushioned dining chairs, more photographs and rustic prints, Wells & Youngs and guests, good choice of wines and coffees, reasonably priced bar food and cheerful, friendly young staff, light modern conservatory (quite different in style), live music Fri, Sat; children welcome, dogs in bar, disabled facilities, teak furniture under giant parasols on big heated decked terrace overlooking water, steps down to plenty of picnic-sets on grass, outside bar and barbecue, pétanque pitch, open all day. *Recommended by Chris and Angela Buckell, Dr and Mrs A K Clarke*

KILMERSDON ST6952
BA3 5TD
Jolliffe Arms
High Street

Large attractive stone-built Georgian local overlooking pretty churchyard, Butcombe and Fullers London Pride, good wines by the glass, reasonably priced home-made pub food, friendly service, four linked areas (three mainly for dining) reminiscent of unpretentious farmhouse parlour, some huge black flagstones, skittle alley; piped music; front picnic-sets. *Recommended by Dr and Mrs A K Clarke*

KINGSDON ST5126   TA11 7LG
Kingsdon Inn
Off B3151

This pretty 18th-c thatched dining pub has reopened under same management after being badly damaged by 2010 fire; busy friendly atmosphere in attractively decorated beamed rooms, open fires, enjoyable food (more evening choice), well kept local ales, good service; children and dogs welcome, picnic-sets on front grass, three bedrooms and holiday cottage, handy for Lytes Cary (NT) and Fleet Air Arm Museum. *Recommended by Patric Hosier*

KINGSTON ST MARY ST2229   TA2 8HW
Swan
Lodes Lane, in centre of village

Cosy 17th-c roadside pub doing well under present welcoming team, clean and tidy, with long knocked-through panelled bar, modern furniture on carpets, rough plastered walls with local artwork for sale, fresh flowers, big stone fireplaces, home-made mostly pubby food (not Sun evening), well kept Exmoor, Fullers London Pride, Sharps Doom Bar and Skinners Betty Stogs, Thatcher's cider, well priced wines; unobtrusive jazz-based piped music; children and dogs welcome, disabled access, garden with play area, handy for Hestercombe Gardens. *Recommended by Chris and Angela Buckell*

LANGFORD BUDVILLE ST1122   TA21 0QZ
☆ Martlet
Off B3187 NW of Wellington

Cosy, comfortable cottagey pub with friendly landlady and staff, good generously served food popular at lunchtime with older diners, well kept ales including Exmoor, inglenook, beams and flagstones, central woodburner, steps up to carpeted lounge with another woodburner; skittle alley. *Recommended by Stephen Bennett, Paul Sayers*

LANSDOWN ST7268   BA1 9BT
Blathwayt Arms
Near Bath Racecourse

Interesting old hilltop building with enjoyable food including some unusual dishes and good Sun roast, well kept ales, decent wines, good service; children welcome, racecourse view from garden, open all day. *Recommended by Meg and Colin Hamilton, Dr and Mrs A K Clarke*

LONG SUTTON ST4625   TA10 9LP
☆ Devonshire Arms
B3165 Somerton—Martock, off A372 E of Langport

Handsome gabled inn (former hunting lodge) with civilised atmosphere, simple back bar with modern metal and leather bar stools, rush-seated high-backed chairs around dark tables on flagstones, Moor and guest ales tapped from the cask, local cider brandy and several wines by the glass, stylish main room with comfortable leather sofas and modern glass-topped log table by fire, long wall bench with lots of scatter cushions, chunky black church candles, elegant dining room with brown wicker chairs around pale wood tables on broad stripped boards, interesting food (local suppliers listed on board) from lunchtime sandwiches up, charming efficient service, evening pianist; teak furniture out at front, pretty box-enclosed courtyard with unusual water-ball feature, more seats on raised terraces, bedrooms. *Recommended by Edward Mirzoeff, Fergus Dowding, William and Ann Reid*

LOVINGTON ST5831   BA7 7PT
☆ Pilgrims
B3153 Castle Cary—Keinton Mandeville

Decidedly more restaurant than pub but does have a pubby corner serving local Cottage, farm cider and 16 wines by the glass, good imaginative food (not cheap) using local produce, efficient friendly service, cosy flagstoned inner area with modern prints, bookshelves, china and some sofas by big fireplace, compact eating area with candles on tables and more formal carpeted dining room; children welcome, dogs in bar, decked terrace in enclosed garden, car park exit has own traffic lights, bedrooms (no children), closed Sun evening, Mon, Tues lunchtime. *Recommended by John and Gloria Isaacs*

MARK ST3747   TA9 4NF
Pack Horse
B3139 Wedmore—Highbridge; Church Street

Attractive traditional 16th-c village pub run by welcoming greek cypriot family, very popular weekends for its wide food choice including good Sun roasts, fresh Brixham fish and delicious puddings, well kept Butcombe and Fullers London Pride, good friendly service; next to church. *Recommended by MP*

MELLS ST7249   BA11 3PN
☆ ## Talbot
W of Frome, off A362 or A361

Interesting old inn, austere public bar in carefully restored tithe barn, farm tools on stone walls, big mural behind counter, dining room in main building with solid tables and chairs, sporting and riding pictures, enjoyable food, Butcombe tapped from cask, helpful pleasant staff, darts; piped music, TV; children and dogs welcome, nice cobbled courtyard, comfortable bedrooms. *Recommended by Meg and Colin Hamilton, M G Hart, Felicity Bromby, Chris and Angela Buckell*

MIDDLEZOY ST3732   TA7 0NN
George
Off A372 E of Bridgwater

Friendly 17th-c village pub, well kept Butcombe and guests, proper ciders, simple home-made lunchtime food, more evening choice including grills using local and exotic meats, attentive welcoming staff, low ceilings, bare stone walls, flagstones, open fire and woodburner, pool, darts, skittle alley, Easter beer festival; children welcome, tables outside, closed Mon, no food Tues evening, Sun. *Recommended by Liz and Jeremy Baker*

MIDFORD ST7660   BA2 7DD
☆ ## Hope & Anchor
Bath Road (B3110)

Open-plan roadside pub with wide choice of good generous home-made food from traditional to more imaginative dishes, civilised bar, heavy-beamed and flagstoned restaurant end, new back conservatory, six well kept changing ales such as Butcombe, Hidden and Wadworths, good house wines, proper coffee, relaxed atmosphere, log fire; children welcome, tables on sheltered back terrace with upper tier beyond, pleasant walks on disused Somerset & Dorset rail track, open all day. *Recommended by M G Hart, Ian and Helen Stafford, Taff Thomas, David Hoult*

MILVERTON ST1225   TA4 1JX
Globe
Fore Street

Smartly reworked pub/restaurant, good food from interesting lunchtime baguettes and ciabattas up, well kept Exmoor ale, friendly polite staff. *Recommended by Bob and Margaret Holder, David Leyland*

MONKTON COMBE ST7761   BA2 7HB
Wheelwrights Arms
Just off A36 S of Bath; Church Cottages

Compact old stone-built pub with clean modern uncluttered feel, competently prepared food including sharing plates and good value lunchtime set menu (Tues-Thurs), friendly attentive service, well kept Butcombe and Sharps Doom Bar from high green-painted wood counter, good choice of wines, some stripped-stone walls, ladder-back chairs around modern tables, an old settle, wood or carpeted floors, log fire in big stone fireplace; children welcome, attractively expanded garden with valley view, seven good annexe bedrooms. *Recommended by Michael Doswell, Hugo Jeune*

NORTH FITZWARREN ST3936   TA7 9BT
Ring o' Bells
Signed off A39

Fine old building, carpeted throughout, with black beams, stone and rough plaster walls, modern furniture, grandfather clock, woodburners and open fires, keen chef/landlord doing good value hearty food including good Sun roasts, vegetarian options too, well kept changing ales such as Butcombe, Greene King and St Austell, local ciders, helpful staff; sports TV in public bar, darts pool and skittles; children welcome, wheelchair access from back, garden tables, open all day weekends, closed Mon and lunchtimes Tues-Thurs. *Recommended by Chris and Angela Buckell, Heather Coulson, Neil Cross*

NAILSEA ST4669   BS48 4NQ
Ring O'Bells
St Mary's Grove

Well kept ales such as Butcombe, Courage and Sharps Doom Bar (Easter beer festival), real ciders, good value traditional food including meal deals and Sun carvery, folk music nights, skittle alley; sports TV; children and dogs welcome, garden with floodlit boules pitches and play area, open all day. *Recommended by Steve and Liz Tilley, Tom Evans*

NEWTON ST LOE ST7065   BA2 9BB
☆ ## Globe
A4/A36 roundabout

Popular 17th-c Vintage Inn, large and rambling, with pleasant décor and dark wood partitions, pillars and timbers giving secluded feel, enjoyable mainly pubby food all day, well kept Butcombe, St Austell Tribute and a guest, prompt friendly uniformed staff, good atmosphere; pleasant back terrace. *Recommended by Dr and Mrs A K Clarke, Nigel Long*

NORTH CURRY ST3125   TA3 6LT
Bird in Hand
Queens Square; off A378 (or A358) E of Taunton

Friendly village pub, cosy main bar with old pews, settles, benches and yew tables on flagstones, some original beams and timbers, locally woven willow work, cricket memorabilia, good inglenook log fire, well kept real ales and decent wines by the glass; some reader concerns over food, prices and service, piped music; children and dogs welcome, open all day Sun. *Recommended by Bob and Margaret Holder, Gillian Hunter, Richard Tilbrook, Peter and Giff Bennett, Ted and Charlotte Routley and others*

NORTON FITZWARREN ST2026   TA2 6NR
Cross Keys
A358 roundabout NW of Taunton

Comfortably extended and refurbished 19th-c stone-built beamed pub, good value promptly served food all day, four changing ales, decent wines by the glass, friendly cheerful staff, stone-tiled bar and carpeted dining area with some plank panelling, log fire in big hearth, skittle alley; children welcome, riverside garden with picnic-sets, open all day. *Recommended by Ian Phillips, Andrew Bosi, Brenda and Stuart Naylor*

NORTON SUB HAMDON ST4715   TA14 6SP
Lord Nelson
Off A356 S of Martock

Homely and welcoming old corner pub in picturesque village, enthusiastic helpful licensees and staff, generally good fairly priced food, well kept Wadworths ales, beams, flagstones and log fires, restaurant, live music and quiz nights; some tables outside. *Recommended by Stephen Colling, David and Sue Smith, Ken and Barbara Turner*

OAKE ST1526   TA4 1DS

Orchard
Hillcommon, N; B3227

Refurbished village pub under new management (was the Royal Oak); enjoyable food including lunchtime deals (carvery Tues, Thurs), well kept ales such as Exmoor, Otter and Sharps from central servery, friendly service; children welcome, pleasant walled garden with play area. *Recommended by Michelle and Graeme Voss, Roddy Kane*

OAKHILL ST6347   BA3 5HU

Oakhill Inn
A367 Shepton Mallet—Radstock

Dining pub with sofas and easy chairs among candlelit tables around bar, friendly atmosphere and welcoming staff, decent if not particularly cheap food including some interesting choices, ales such as Butcombe, dining extension in former skittle alley, rugs on bare boards, wall of clocks, log fires; piped music; nice views from garden, five bedrooms, open all day weekends. *Recommended by Ian Phillips, Dr and Mrs A K Clarke*

PANBOROUGH ST4745   BA5 1PN

Panborough Inn
B3139 Wedmore—Wells

Large well run 17th-c beamed dining pub, good welcoming staff, enjoyable traditional food, ales such as Boddingtons and Butcombe in cosy bar with wall benches, polished tables and roaring log fire, restaurant, skittle alley; views from tables on front terrace. *Recommended by Dr and Mrs C W Thomas*

PORLOCK WEIR SS8846   TA24 8QD

☆ # Ship
Porlock Hill (A39)

Unpretentious thatched bar in wonderful spot by peaceful harbour (so can get packed), long and narrow with dark low beams, flagstones and stripped stone, simple pub furniture, woodburner, Cotleigh, Exmoor, Otter and a guest like Clearwater Proper Ansome, real ciders and a perry, good whisky and soft drinks choice, friendly prompt staff, bargain simple food from thick sandwiches up, games rooms across small back yard, tea room; piped music, big-screen TV, little free parking but pay & display opposite; children and dogs welcome, sturdy picnic-sets out at front and side, good coast walks, three decent bedrooms; calls itself the Bottom Ship to distinguish from nearby Ship at Porlock. *Recommended by Peter Dearing, Adrian and Dawn Collinge*

PORTISHEAD ST4576   BS20 6JZ

☆ # Windmill
M5 junction 19; A369 into town, then follow Sea Front sign and into Nore Road

Busy dining pub making most of terrific panorama over Bristol Channel; completely re-styled with curving glass frontage rising two storeys (adjacent windmill remains untouched), contemporary furnishings, Bass, Butcombe, Courage and local guests, traditional bar food; children welcome in lower family floor, dogs allowed in bar, disabled access including lift, picnic-sets on tiered lantern-lit terraces and decking, open all day. *Recommended by Tom Evans, Steve and Claire Harvey, Irene and Derek Flewin and others*

PRIDDY ST5450   BA5 3AR

☆ # Hunters Lodge
From Wells on A39 pass hill with TV mast on left, then next left

Welcoming and unchanging farmers', walkers' and potholers' pub above Ice Age cavern, in same family for generations, well kept beers such as Blindmans and Cheddar tapped from casks behind bar, Wilkins' farm cider, simple cheap food, log fires in huge fireplaces, low beams, flagstones and panelling, old lead mining photographs, perhaps live folk music; no mobiles or credit cards; children and dogs in family room, wheelchair access, garden picnic-sets. *Recommended by MLR, the Didler, Chris and Angela Buckell, M G Hart*

PRIDDY ST5250   BA5 3BA
☆ **Queen Victoria**
Village signed off B3135; Pelting Drove

Character stone-built country local in lovely position and continuing well under present
management, friendly staff and regulars, well kept Butcombe and guests tapped from
casks, local ciders, several wines by the glass, enjoyable locally sourced food, three good
log fires (one open on two sides), beams, stripped stone and flagstones, some dark
panelling, mixed furniture including pews, interesting bric-a-brac, occasional folk music;
well behaved children and dogs welcome, disabled facilities, garden with play area and
car park over road, great walks, open all day Fri-Sun. *Recommended by Chris and Angela Buckell,*
Tom Evans, M Mossman

RODE ST8053   BA11 6PW
Bell
Frome Road (A361)

Sister pub to the Castle in Bradford-on-Avon, extensive refurbishment including many
quirky touches, bare boards or flagstones, oak-panelling, log fires, old club portraits on
green flock or fish-printed wallpaper, various stuffed animals, mishmash of furniture –
scrub-top painted pine tables, chapel chairs and old rescued leather sofas/armchairs,
1930s standard lamps, six well kept mainly local beers including Flatcapper brewed for
the pub by Three Castles, enjoyable food all day, good service; big terrace and lawned
garden. *Recommended by John Martin, Hugo Jeune*

RODE ST8054   BA11 6AG
Mill
NW off Rode Hill

Popular family pub in beautifully set former watermill, smart restauranty layout and up-
to-date décor, good quality food including early evening deals, good choice of real ales
and of wines by the glass, children's room with impressive games, live music Fri; garden
and decks overlooking River Frome, big play area. *Recommended by Mr and Mrs A Curry*

ROWBERROW ST4458   BS25 1QL
☆ **Swan**
Off A38 S of A368 junction

Neat and spacious dining pub opposite pond, olde-worlde beamery and so forth, good log
fires, friendly atmosphere especially in nicely unsophisticated old bar part, good
reasonably priced food (small helpings available), prompt pleasant service, well kept
Butcombe and a guest, decent choice of wines by the glass, Thatcher's cider, live music
(first Sun of month); children welcome, good-sized garden over road, open all day
weekends. *Recommended by Tom Evans, Bob and Angela Brooks, Hugh Roberts*

RUMWELL ST1923   TA4 1EL
Rumwell Inn
A38 Taunton—Wellington, just past Stonegallows

Roomy roadside pub with welcoming landlord and friendly staff, comfortable and clean
with old beams and cosy corners, well priced enjoyable food from good lunchtime
sandwiches up, changing well kept ales, roaring log fire, family room; tables in nice
garden, handy for Sheppy's Cider, closed Sun evening. *Recommended by Bob and*
Margaret Holder, Meg and Colin Hamilton, John Gould, Peter Salmon

SALTFORD ST6867   BS31 3EJ
Bird in Hand
High Street

Comfortable and friendly, with lively front bar, good range of beers such as Blindmans,
Butcombe, Courage and Sharps, farm cider, attractive back conservatory dining area,
good choice of popular fairly priced fresh food from snacks up, friendly staff, pubby
furniture including settles, carpets throughout, lots of bird pictures and old plates, small

family area; live entertainment, fruit machine; wheelchair access at front (not from car park), picnic-sets down towards river, handy for Bristol—Bath railway path. *Recommended by Chris and Angela Buckell, Dr and Mrs A K Clarke, Colin and Peggy Wilshire*

☆ **Jolly Sailor**   SALTFORD ST6968   BS31 3ER
Off A4 Bath—Keynsham; Mead Lane

Great spot by lock and weir on River Avon, with dozens of picnic-sets, garden heaters and own island between lock and pub; enjoyable generous standard food all day, Wadworths ales and a guest like Butcombe, flagstones, low beams, two roaring log fires, daily papers, conservatory dining room; piped music; children allowed, disabled facilities, open all day. *Recommended by Chris and Angela Buckell, Dr and Mrs A K Clarke, Colin and Peggy Wilshire*

☆ **Montague Inn**   SHEPTON MONTAGUE ST6731   BA9 8JW
Village signed off A359 Bruton—Castle Cary

Simply but tastefully furnished dining pub with welcoming licensees, popular for a civilised meal or just a drink, stripped wood tables, kitchen chairs and log fire in nice inglenook, Bath Ales, Wadworths and local guest tapped from the cask, farm ciders, good wine and whisky choice, good interesting food from lunchtime open sandwiches up, friendly service, bright spacious restaurant extension; children welcome, dogs in bar, garden and terrace with smart teak furniture, closed Sun evening. *Recommended by Edward Mirzoeff, Richard Wyld, G Vyse, Mrs C Roe, Mr and Mrs J J A Davis and others*

☆ **Exmoor Forest Inn**   SIMONSBATH SS7739   TA24 7SH
B3223/B3358

Beautifully placed inn under friendly licensees, circular tables by the bar counter, larger area with cushioned settles, upholstered stools and mate's chairs around mix of dark tables, hunting trophies, antlers and horse tack, woodburner, enjoyable local food including game, well kept ales such as Cotleigh, Dartmoor, Exmoor and a guest, real cider, good choice of wines by the glass and malt whiskies, residents' lounge, airy dining room; children and clean dogs (towels provided) welcome, seats in front garden, fine walks along River Barle, own trout and salmon fishing, ten comfortable bedrooms, open all day in full season. *Recommended by Melvyn Owen, Steve and Liz Tilley, Sheila Topham*

☆ **Pack Horse**   SOUTH STOKE ST7461   BA2 7DU
Off B3110, S edge of Bath

Former medieval priory with passageway running through its centre (route along which the dead were carried to church cemetery); ancient main room with good local atmosphere, heavy black beam-and-plank ceiling, stone-mullioned windows with rough black shutters (put up in World War I), antique oak settles (two well carved) and other seats on quarry tiles, royalty pictures, log fire in handsome stone inglenook, another bar down on left with open fire and shove-ha'penny slates, Butcombe, Sharps and a guest, four local ciders, well liked bar food (not Mon); piped music; children and dogs welcome, seats in nice garden with roses and boules, good walks along traces of long-defunct canal, open all day weekends, closed Mon lunchtime. *Recommended by Colin McKerrow, Guy Vowles, Roger and Donna Huggins, Taff Thomas*

☆ **Greyhound**   STAPLE FITZPAINE ST2618   TA3 5SP
Off A358 or B3170 S of Taunton

Light rambling country pub with wide range of good food (best to book evenings), changing ales, good wines by the glass, welcoming atmosphere and attentive staff, flagstones, inglenooks, pleasant mix of settles and chairs, log fires throughout, olde-worlde pictures, farm tools and so forth; children and dogs welcome, comfortable bedrooms, good breakfast. *Recommended by A H Latham, Bob and Margaret Holder, Graham Quinn*

STOKE ST MARY ST2622
TA3 5BY
Half Moon
From M5 junction 25 take A358 towards Ilminster, first right, right in Henlade

Much-modernised village pub very popular lunchtime for wide choice of hearty good value food including daily carvery, pleasant staff, Butcombe, Fullers London Pride and Greene King Abbot, nice coffee, quite a few malt whiskies, thriving local atmosphere in several comfortable open-plan areas including restaurant; children welcome, well tended garden. *Recommended by Bob and Margaret Holder, Ted and Charlotte Routley*

TARR SS8632
TA22 9PY
Tarr Farm
Tarr Steps – narrow road off B3223 N of Dulverton; deep ford if you approach from the W (inn is on E bank)

Lovely Exmoor setting above River Barle's medieval clapper bridge; compact unpretentious bar rooms with good views, stall seating, wall seats and leather chairs around slabby rustic tables, game bird pictures on wood-clad walls, three woodburners, Exmoor ales and several wines by the glass, good food, residents' end with smart evening restaurant (a mix of bar or restaurant choices using local produce), pleasant log-fire lounge with dark leather armchairs and sofas; children and dogs welcome slate-topped stone tables outside making most of setting, bedrooms (no under-10s), open all day but closed 1-10 Feb. *Recommended by Sheila Topham, JJW, CMW, Dominic McGonigal, Adrian Johnson, John and Jackie Chalcraft and others*

TAUNTON ST2525
TA1 2LR
☆ Hankridge Arms
Hankridge Way, Deane Gate (near Sainsbury); just off M5 junction 25 – A358 towards city, then right at roundabout, right at next roundabout

Well appointed Badger dining pub based on 16th-c former farm, splendid contrast to the modern shopping complex around it, different-sized linked areas, well kept ales, generous enjoyable food from interesting soups and sandwiches through pubby things to restaurant dishes, quick friendly young staff, decent wines, big log fire; piped music; dogs welcome, plenty of tables in pleasant outside area. *Recommended by John Gould, Andy West, Dr and Mrs A K Clarke*

TAUNTON ST2223
TA1 3JR
Vivary Arms
Wilton Street; across Vivary Park from centre

Pretty low-beamed 18th-c local (Taunton's oldest), good value fresh food from light lunches up in snug plush lounge and small dining room, friendly helpful young staff, relaxed atmosphere, well kept ales including Butcombe, decent wines, interesting collection of drink-related items; lovely hanging baskets and flowers. *Recommended by John Gould, Bob and Margaret Holder*

TIMBERSCOMBE SS9542
TA24 7TP
Lion
Church Street

Refurbished Exmoor-edge coaching inn dating from 15th c, thriving village-pub atmosphere in comfortable flagstoned main bar with rooms off, scrubbed pine tables in dining area, enjoyable pub food from good fresh ciabattas up, friendly service, well kept Exmoor tapped from the cask, nice wines, good log fire; children and dogs welcome, bedrooms. *Recommended by Dennis Jenkin, Richard*

TINTINHULL ST5019
BA22 8PZ
Crown & Victoria
Farm Street, village signed off A303

Roomy, light and airy carpeted main bar with nice log fire, good fairly priced well presented food cooked to order, Sun roasts, well kept ales such as Butcombe, Cheddar and Cotleigh, good choice of wines, attentive friendly service, pleasant conservatory;

children welcome, disabled facilities, big garden with play area, five bedrooms, handy for Tintinhull House (NT). *Recommended by David and Sue Smith, Andy Flowers, Patrick and Daphne Darley*

TRISCOMBE ST1535   TA4 3HE
☆ Blue Ball
Village signed off A358 Crowcombe—Bagborough; turn off opposite sign to youth hostel; OS Sheet 181 map reference 155355

Smartly refurbished old place tucked beneath the Quantocks and again under new management; on first floor of original stables sloping down gently on three levels, each with own fire and cleverly divided into seating by hand-cut beech partitions, Cotleigh and two guests, local farm cider and several wines by the glass, enjoyable food from sandwiches up including walkers' breakfast; piped music; children and dogs welcome, chair lift to bar/restaurant area for disabled customers, decking at top of woodside, terraced garden makes most of views, bedrooms, closed Sun evening, Mon. *Recommended by Neil and Anita Christopher, Martin Hatcher, Mike and Mary Carter, John and Sharon Hancock, Kevin Chamberlain, Bob and Margaret Holder*

UPTON ST0129   TA4 2DB
☆ Lowtrow Cross Inn
A3190 E of Upton

Well run by cheery landlord and staff, good fresh home-made food, nice relaxed mix of locals and diners, character low-beamed bar with log fire, bare boards and flagstones, two carpeted country-kitchen dining areas, one with enormous inglenook, plenty of atmosphere, well kept ales such as Cotleigh Tawny and Exmoor Fox; no dogs; children welcome, attractive surroundings, bedrooms. *Recommended by Richard, Anne and Kate Ansell*

VOBSTER ST7049   BA3 5RJ
☆ Vobster Inn
Lower Vobster

Roomy old stone-built dining pub with good reasonably priced food including some spanish dishes (chef/landlord is from Spain) and fresh fish daily from Cornwall, good service, Butcombe and a Blindmans seasonal ale, good wines by the glass, three comfortable open-plan areas with antique furniture, plenty of room for just a drink; dogs allowed in bar, side lawn, peaceful views, boules, adventure playground behind, bedrooms. *Recommended by Sue Cane, Bob and Angela Brooks, Sophie Holborow*

WATCHET ST0643   TA23 0BZ
Star
Mill Lane (B3191)

Late 18th-c pub near seafront, main flagstoned bar with other low-beamed side rooms and nooks and crannies, pubby furniture including oak settles, window seats, lots of bric-a-brac, ornate fireplace with woodburner, good choice of enjoyable straightforward food, well kept ales such as Cottage, Exmoor and Otter, Thatcher's cider, some interesting whiskies, cheerful efficient staff; no credit cards; children and dogs welcome, picnic-sets out in front and in beer garden. *Recommended by Joan and Michel Hooper-Immins, Chris and Angela Buckell*

WELLOW ST7358   BA2 8QG
☆ Fox & Badger
Signed off A367 SW of Bath

Opened-up village pub, flagstones one end, bare boards the other, some snug corners, woodburner in massive hearth, decent choice of ales including local ones, Weston's cider, wide range of enjoyable bar food from doorstep sandwiches and generous ploughman's up, prompt good-humoured service; children and dogs welcome, picnic-sets in covered courtyard, open all day Fri-Sun. *Recommended by Maureen Wood, Guy Vowles*

WELLS ST5445   BA5 2AG

☆ City Arms

High Street

Bustling town centre pub with up to seven real ales, four ciders and decent reasonably priced food from breakfast on; main bar with leather sofas and chairs around assorted tables, plenty of prints and paintings, gas-effect log fire, upstairs restaurant with vaulted-ceiling, red walls and chandeliers; piped music; children and dogs welcome, cobbled courtyard and some reminders that the building was once a jail, first floor terrace, open all day from 9am (10am Sun). *Recommended by Jim and Frances Gowers, Bruce Ashmore, Bob and Angela Brooks, Terry Buckland, Richard and Judy Winn and others*

WEST BAGBOROUGH ST1733   TA4 3EF

☆ Rising Sun

Village signed off A358 NW of Taunton

Charming village pub lit up with evening candles; small flagstoned bar to right of massive main door with settles and carved dining chairs around polished tables, daily papers on old-fashioned child's desk, fresh flowers and some quirky ornaments dotted about, well kept Butcombe, Exmoor and St Austell, good if not cheap food, friendly service, smart cosy dining room with attractive mix of Chippendale and other dining chairs around a few dark wood tables, attractive back snug room with coal-effect gas fire and big modern photographs, upstairs room with trusses in high pitched ceiling, refectory tables and an oriental rug on wood floor, large prints of cathedral cities; children and dogs welcome; teak seats outside by lane, closed Sun evening and Mon in winter. *Recommended by Bob and Margaret Holder, Patrick and Daphne Darley, R T and J C Moggridge*

WEST BUCKLAND ST1621   TA21 9HX

Blackbird

A38 N of village, 3 miles E of Wellington and handy for M5 junction 26

Partly 16th-c roadside inn, enjoyable good value local food including Sun roasts, well kept ales such as Cotleigh and Exmoor, friendly service, large restaurant, open fires; pleasant garden, bedrooms. *Recommended by John Gould, Dr E Scarth and Miss A Pocock*

WEST HUNTSPILL ST3145   TA9 3RA

Crossways

A38, between M5 exits 22 and 23

Rambling beamed pub brightened up and improved by present licensees, six well kept real ales, good choice of enjoyable reasonably priced food, friendly staff, dining area extending into skittle alley; children welcome, fruit trees in sizeable garden with play area. *Recommended by R K Phillips, David Dean*

WEST MONKTON ST2628   TA2 8NP

☆ Monkton

Blundells Lane; signed from A3259

Comfortable dining pub very popular for its good low-priced fresh food including set deals (best to book), linked areas with smallish bar serving well kept local beers, good value wines; wheelchair access from car park, lots of tables in streamside meadow, peaceful spot, closed Sun evening. *Recommended by Patrick and Daphne Darley, Chris and Angela Buckell, Bob and Margaret Holder, Shirley and Bob Gibbs*

WESTON-IN-GORDANO ST4474   BS20 8PU

White Hart

B3124 Portishead—Clevedon, between M5 junctions 19 and 20

Friendly neatly kept roadside pub with lots of old photographs and bric-a-brac in lower room, large pleasant dining area, enjoyable straightforward home-made food including deals, good service, well kept ales such as Sharps Doom Bar; children welcome, Gordano Valley views from fine back lawn with play area, open all day. *Recommended by Tom Evans*

WESTON-SUPER-MARE ST3062   BS23 2EF
Captains Table
Birnbeck Road

Unpretentious local atmosphere, wide choice of good food in bar and sea-view restaurant including fresh fish/seafood, good service, real ales; disabled access, terrace. *Recommended by Andrew O'Brien, Dave Webster, Sue Holland*

WESTON-SUPER-MARE ST3762   BS22 7XE
Woolpack
St George's, just off M5 junction 21

Opened-up and extended 17th-c coaching inn with full Butcombe range and a guest ale kept well, decent wines, enjoyable pubby food including carvery, friendly local atmosphere, pleasant window seats and library-theme area, small attractive restaurant, conservatory, skittle alley; no dogs; children welcome, disabled access, terrace areas with rustic furniture. *Recommended by Bob and Angela Brooks, Rod Dykeman, Dave Webster, Sue Holland*

WINCANTON ST7028   BA9 9DL
Nog
South Street

Welcoming pub with good changing ales such as Evan Evans, Purity and Otter, real cider, reasonably priced traditional food from lunchtime sandwiches and baked potatoes up, Sun carvery, old photographs, open fires, charity quiz (last Thurs); well behaved children and dogs welcome, pleasant terrace garden with heated smokers' shelter, open all day. *Recommended by Joan and Michel Hooper-Immins*

WINSCOMBE ST4257   BS25 1HD
☆ ## Woodborough
Sandford Road

Big 1930s mock-Tudor village dining pub, smart, comfortable and busy, with wide choice of good generous local food, Butcombe and Sharps Doom Bar, good wine choice, helpful friendly staff, large public bar, skittle alley; disabled access, bedrooms. *Recommended by Michelle Cottis, Hugh Roberts, Bruce and Sharon Eden*

WINSFORD SS9034   TA24 7JE
☆ ## Royal Oak
Off A396 about 10 miles S of Dunster

Prettily placed thatched and beamed Exmoor inn, wide choice of good locally sourced food, friendly staff, well kept Exmoor ales, Addlestone's cider, good wines by the glass, lounge bar with big stone fireplace and large bay-window seat looking across towards village green and foot and packhorse bridges over River Winn, more eating space in second bar, several comfortable lounges; children welcome and dogs (they have three), disabled facilities, good bedrooms. *Recommended by Johnn and Jennifer Wright, Sheila Topham*

WITHYPOOL SS8435   TA24 7QP
☆ ## Royal Oak
Village signed off B3233

Well run prettily placed country inn – where R D Blackmore stayed while writing *Lorna Doone*; lounge with raised working fireplace, comfortably cushioned wall seats and slat-backed chairs, sporting trophies, paintings and copper/brass ornaments, good food here and in restaurant, particularly well kept Exmoor ales, friendly service, character locals' bar; children in eating areas, dogs welcome, wooden benches on terrace, attractive riverside village with lovely walks, grand views from Winsford Hill just up the road, eight bedrooms, open all day. *Recommended by Bob and Margaret Holder, David Treherne Pollock, J L Wedel, Andrew Scott, Sheila Topham and others*

WOOKEY ST5245 BA5 1NJ

☆ **Burcott**

B3139 W of Wells

Unspoilt beamed roadside pub with two simply furnished old-fashioned front bar rooms, flagstones, lantern wall lights, woodburner, three changing ales such as Hop Back, Otter and RCH, several wines by the glass, enjoyable food (not evenings Sun, Mon, or Mon lunchtime in winter) from substantial sandwiches up in bar and restaurant, small games room with built-in wall seats; soft piped music, no dogs; well behaved children allowed in restaurant, front window boxes and tubs, picnic-sets in sizeable garden with Mendip Hill views, four self-catering units in converted stables. *Recommended by M G Hart, John Gould*

WRANTAGE ST3022 TA3 6DF

☆ **Canal Inn**

4 miles from M5 junction 25; A358E, then left on to A378

Pleasant roadside pub with two bar rooms separated by stable-style partitioning, sofa, green leather dining chairs and granite or wood-topped tables on flagstones, adjoining room with sporting prints and picture of African Grey parrots, ales from Exmoor, Moor and Otter, formal back dining room with heavy beams and ambitious food, occasional live music; children welcome, dogs in bar, picnic-sets in fenced-off garden, nicely done smokers' shelter, open all day. *Recommended by Bob and Margaret Holder, PLC*

WRAXALL ST4971 BS48 1LQ

Battleaxes

Bristol Road

Interesting Victorian building now part of the small Flatcappers group and nicely refurbished, well kept local ales including one brewed for them by Three Castles, good choice of food from snacks up (they ask to keep a credit card if you run a tab), spacious interior split into two main areas, bare boards, painted panelling and good mix of old furniture; children welcome. *Recommended by Steve and Liz Tilley*

WRAXALL ST4971 BS48 1LQ

☆ **Old Barn**

Just off Bristol Road (B3130)

Idiosyncratic gabled barn conversion, scrubbed tables, school benches and soft sofas under oak rafters, stripped boards and flagstones, welcoming atmosphere and friendly service, well kept Butcombe, Fullers, St Austell, Sharps and a guest tapped from the cask (plans for their own brews too), farm ciders, good wines by the glass, simple sandwiches, unusual board games; occasional piped music and sports TV; children and dogs welcome, nice garden with terrace barbecue (bring your own meat), smokers' shelter, closed Mon lunchtime otherwise open all day. *Recommended by Steve and Liz Tilley, the Didler*

YARLINGTON ST6529 BA9 8DG

Stags Head

Pound Lane

Old low-ceilinged and flagstoned country pub tucked away in rustic hamlet, Bass, Greene King IPA and a local guest from small central bar, woodburner, chapel chairs and mixed pine tables on left, carpeted dining area on right with big log fire, modern landscape prints and feature cider-press table, second dining room with doors on to terrace, food from traditional choices up including OAP lunchtime menu; piped music; well behaved children welcome, dogs in bar, picnic-sets in sheltered back garden, three bedrooms, closed Sun evening. *Recommended by Mr Stan Lea*

When you report on a pub, please tell us any lunchtimes or evenings when
it doesn't serve bar food.

ALSO WORTH A VISIT IN WILTSHIRE

Besides the region's top pubs, we recommend the following. Do tell us
what you think of them: **feedback@goodguides.com**

ALVEDISTON ST9723   SP5 5JY
Crown
Off A30 W of Salisbury

Refurbished 15th-c thatched inn, three cosy very low-beamed partly panelled rooms, two
inglenook fireplaces, good varied choice of fair-priced home-made food, pleasant service;
children and dogs welcome, pretty views from attractive garden with terrace, bedrooms,
open all day Fri and Sat, till 8.30pm Sun (all week July, Aug). *Recommended by Lady Keith*

AMESBURY SU1541   SP4 7EU
☆ Antrobus Arms
Church Street

Handsome hotel, quiet, comfortable and relaxed, with good food, friendly helpful staff,
changing real ales, log fires in warmly welcoming smart yet pubby bar and
communicating lounge overlooking beautiful walled garden, two dining rooms; children
and dogs welcome, 17 attractive bedrooms, open all day. *Recommended by anon*

AXFORD SU2470   SN8 2HA
☆ Red Lion
Off A4 E of Marlborough

Pretty beamed and panelled pub with big inglenook, comfortable sofas, cask seats and
other solid chairs, good popular food from pub staples to pricier fish etc, welcoming
attentive staff, well kept ales such as Ramsbury, good choice of wines by the glass,
picture-window restaurant; valley views from nice terrace, children welcome, closed Sun
evening. *Recommended by Henry Midwinter, John Redfern, Joy and Gordon Kellam, Michael Rowse,
Jennifer and Patrick O'Dell and others*

BADBURY SU1980   SN4 0EU
Bakers Arms
1 mile from M4 junction 15, off A346 S

Proper unassuming village local, a relaxing motorway escape, friendly licensees, wide
choice of sensibly priced pubby food (not Sun evening) including doorstep sandwiches,
Arkells ales, generous coffee, warm fire, three small old-fashioned rooms, pool and darts
area; piped music, TV, silenced games machine, no under-10s; picnic-sets in garden with
heated smokers' area. *Recommended by Bill and Sally Leckey, Peter Hayman, JJW, CMW,
Paul Humphreys*

BADBURY SU1980   SN4 0EP
☆ Plough
A346 (Marlborough Road) just S of M4 junction 15

Popular good value pub food all day including Sun roasts, friendly helpful staff, well kept
Arkells and Donnington SBA, decent wines, coffee from 10am, large rambling bar area
(dogs welcome), light and airy dining room (children allowed), daily papers, big Mucha
prints; piped music; tree-shaded garden with terrace and good play area (trunk road
noise), open all day. *Recommended by JJW, CMW, Mary Rayner*

BARFORD ST MARTIN SU0531   SP3 4AB
☆ Barford Inn
B3098 W of Salisbury (Grovely Road), just off A30

Welcoming 16th-c coaching inn, dark panelled front bar with big log fire, other
interlinking rooms, old utensils and farming tools, beamed bare-brick restaurant, wide

choice of generous food including fish and game, OAP lunch deals, take-aways, prompt service, well kept Badger ales, lots of wines by the glass; children and dogs welcome, disabled access (not to bar) and facilities, terrace tables, more in back garden, four charming comfortable bedrooms, good walks, open all day. *Recommended by Chris and Angela Buckell, Edward Mirzoeff, S J and C C Davidson, Dennis Jenkin*

BECKHAMPTON SU0868   SN8 1QJ

 ## Waggon & Horses
A4 Marlborough—Calne

Handsome stone-and-thatch coaching inn continuing well under new management, old-fashioned settles and comfortably cushioned wall benches in open-plan beamed bar, dining area, generous unfussy fair-priced food (not Sun evening), prompt friendly service, well kept Wadworths and a guest, pool and pub games; unobtrusive piped music; children in restaurant, pleasant raised garden with good play area, bedrooms, handy for Avebury, open all day. *Recommended by Sheila and Robert Robinson*

BERWICK ST JAMES SU0739   SP3 4TN

 ## Boot
High Street (B3083)

Welcoming flint and stone pub not far from Stonehenge with friendly efficient staff, well kept Wadworths, huge log fire in inglenook one end, sporting prints over small brick fireplace at other, lit candles, small back dining room with collection of celebrity boots, food can be good; children welcome, sheltered side lawn. *Recommended by Dennis Parnham, Mark Davies*

BERWICK ST JOHN ST9422   SP7 0HA

 ## Talbot
Village signed from A30 E of Shaftesbury

Unspoilt pub in attractive village, heavily beamed simply furnished bar with huge inglenook and bread ovens, solid wall and window seats, spindlebacks and high-backed built-in settle, Ringwood, Wadworths and a guest, popular bar food, friendly hands-on landlord, restaurant; children and dogs welcome, seats outside, good walks nearby, closed Sun evening, Mon. *Recommended by JDM, KM, D and J Ashdown, Ian Herdman, Mrs C Roe and others*

BIDDESTONE ST8673   SN14 7DG
White Horse
The Green

Popular 16th-c local overlooking duckpond in picturesque village, wide choice of sensibly priced hearty pub food (all day Sun) including interesting specials, well kept Butcombe, Bath Gem Courage Best and Wadworths 6X, quick cheerful service, lounge and dining area, small hatch-served bar with shove-ha'penny, board games and table skittles; children and dogs welcome, tables in good garden with play area and guinea pigs, open all day. *Recommended by Michael Doswell, Taff Thomas*

BISHOPSTONE SU2483   SN6 8PP
 ## Royal Oak
Cues Lane; near Swindon; at first exit roundabout from A419 N of M4 J15, follow Wanborough sign, then keep on to Bishopstone, at small sign to pub turn right

Informal dining pub run by local farmers using seasonal organic produce including properly hung home-reared steaks (farm shop too), mainly scrubbed wood furnishings on bare boards or parquet, animal pictures for sale, log fire on left and little maze of dark pews, well kept Arkells ales, organic wines, maybe home-made elderflower cordial, decent whiskies, charity shelves and window sills of paperbacks; children and dogs welcome, picnic-sets dotted through a bit of a copse with more on grass, smarter modern tables on front decking, cheap serviceable bedrooms in back cabins, pretty village below Ridgeway and White Horse. *Recommended by John Hickman, Frank Blanchard, Mary Rayner, Dave Snowden*

BOX ST8168　　　　　　　　　　　　　　　　　　　　　　　　SN13 8AE
Northey Arms
A4, Bath side

Stone-built 19th-c dining pub with enjoyable food all day, Wadworths ales, decent wines by the glass, simple contemporary décor with chunky modern furniture on pale hardwood floor; piped music; children welcome, garden tables. *Recommended by Mr and Mrs P R Thomas*

BOX ST8369　　　　　　　　　　　　　　　　　　　　　　　　SN13 8HN
☆ Quarrymans Arms
Box Hill; from Bath on A4 right into Bargates 50 yards before railway bridge, left up Quarry Hill at T junction, left again at grassy triangle; from Corsham, left after Rudloe Park Hotel into Beech Road, third left on to Barnetts Hill, and right at top of hill; OS Sheet 173 map reference 834694

Enjoyable unpretentious pub with friendly staff and informal relaxed atmosphere, comfortable rather than overly smart (even mildly untidy in parts), plenty of mining-related photographs and memorabilia dotted around (once the local of Bath-stone miners – licensees run interesting guided trips down mine itself), one modernised room with open fire set aside for drinking, Butcombe, Moles, Wadworths and York, 60 malt whiskies, several wines by glass, tasty bar food at fair prices; children and dogs welcome, picnic-sets on terrace with sweeping views, popular with walkers and potholers, bedrooms, open all day. *Recommended by Dr and Mrs A K Clarke, Stephen Turpin, Gordon Tong, Richard and Madeleine Wagner, Ian Herdman, Guy Vowles and others*

BRADFORD-ON-AVON ST8260　　　　　　　　　　　　　　　　BA15 2EA
Barge
Frome Road

Large open-plan modernised pub set down from canal, well kept ales such as Brewsters, Fullers and Moles, generous homely food, friendly service, stripped stone and flagstones, solid furniture, log fire; children welcome, garden with smokers' pavilion, steps up to canalside picnic-sets, moorings. *Recommended by Ian Phillips, Taff Thomas, Ken and Barbara Turner*

BRADFORD-ON-AVON ST8060　　　　　　　　　　　　　　　　BA15 2HB
Cross Guns
Avoncliff, 2 miles W; OS Sheet 173 map reference 805600

Congenial bustle on summer days with swarms of people in floodlit partly concreted areas steeply terraced above the bridges, aqueducts and river; appealingly quaint at quieter times, with stripped-stone low-beamed bar, 16th-c inglenook, full Box Steam range kept well and a guest, several ciders, lots of malt whiskies, interesting wines by the glass including country ones, comprehensive choice of enjoyable food, good friendly service, upstairs river-view restaurant; children and dogs welcome, wheelchair accessible, bedrooms, open all day. *Recommended by Alan Bulley, Chris and Angela Buckell*

BREMHILL ST9772　　　　　　　　　　　　　　　　　　　　SN11 9LJ
Dumb Post
Off A4/A3102 just NW of Calne

The long-serving licensee at this quirky unspoilt place has retired but new management running it as before; mismatched no-frills décor with odds and ends hanging from beams, guns and stuffed animal heads on walls, working model waterwheel, Oscar the parrot, homely armchairs and plush banquettes, big woodburner in brick fireplace and log fire at other end, fine country views from big windows, Wadworths 6X and a changing guest, simple hearty bar food, tap room with pool and darts; piped music; children and dogs welcome, couple of picnic-sets outside and some wooden play equipment, currently closed Mon-Weds lunchtimes, open all day weekends. *Recommended by Giles*

We accept no free drinks or meals and inspections are anonymous.

BROMHAM ST9665
SN15 2HA
Greyhound
Off A342; High Street

Popular old beamed dining pub with light modern décor, comfortable sofas and log fires, walk-across well in back bar, wide choice of good reasonably priced food, efficient friendly service, well kept Wadworths, good wine choice, upstairs skittle alley for extra dining space; pretty hanging baskets in front, big enclosed garden (dogs allowed here) with decking and boules. *Recommended by Mr and Mrs P R Thomas, Neil and Anita Christopher, David Coe*

BROUGHTON GIFFORD ST8764
SN12 8LX
Bell on the Common
The Common

New licensees but few changes for this imposing rose-draped stone local on village common, lounge with well kept Wadworths from handpumps on back wall, big open fire, enjoyable good value food, dining room full of copper and brass, rustic bar with local photographs, small pool room with darts, live irish music (last Sun of month); children welcome, dogs in public bar, charming flower-filled crazy-paved garden, boules, bowls club next door, open all day Fri-Sun. *Recommended by Michael Doswell, Taff Thomas*

BULKINGTON ST9458
SN10 1SJ
Well
High Street

Roomy and attractively modernised under new licensees, good food, quick friendly service, real ales such as Sharps, Timothy Taylors and Wadworths. *Recommended by Mrs Blethyn Elliott*

BURCOMBE SU0631
SP2 0EJ
 # Ship
Burcombe Lane; brown sign to pub off A30 W of Salisbury, then turn right

Busy pub and most customers here for the food – pubby dishes through to elaborate pricey restaurant-style meals; area by entrance with log fire, beams and leather-cushioned wall and window seats on dark slate tiles, steps up to spreading area of pale wood dining chairs around bleached tables on neat dark-brown woodstrip floor, more beams (one supporting a splendid chandelier), small modern pictures and big church candles, Butcombe, Ringwood and Wadworths, good choice of wines by the glass and whiskies; piped music; children welcome, dogs in bar, picnic-sets in informal back garden sloping down to willows by safely fenced-off River Nadder. *Recommended by Ken Marshall, David Hunt*

BURTON ST8179
SN14 7LT
Old House At Home
B4039 Chippenham—Chipping Sodbury

Spacious stone-built dining pub, enjoyable food including fresh fish and game, friendly efficient service, well kept ales and good choice of wines by the glass, log fire. *Recommended by Taff Thomas*

CASTLE COMBE ST8477
SN14 7HN
Castle Inn
Off A420

Handsome inn in remarkably preserved Cotswold village, beamed bar with big inglenook, padded bar stools and fine old settle, hunting and vintage motor racing pictures, Butcombe Bitter and a guest, decent wines by the glass, two snug and comfortable olde-worlde sitting rooms, formal dining rooms and big upstairs eating area opening on to charming little roof terrace; no dogs; children welcome, tables out at front looking down idyllic main street, fascinating medieval church clock, 11 bedrooms, limited parking, open all day. *Recommended by Peter and Giff Bennett*

CHARLTON ST9688   SN16 9DL

☆ **Horse & Groom**

B4040 towards Cricklade

Smartly refurbished stone-built village pub, appealing and relaxing, keeping flagstones and log fire in proper bar (dogs welcome), interlinked dining areas with stylish understated décor, well liked good value food from pub standards to upscale modern cooking such as scallops with black pudding, pancetta and butternut squash purée, polished friendly service, well kept Moles and Wadworths 6X, good choice of wines by the glass; tables out under trees, five well appointed bedrooms, good breakfast. *Recommended by Peter and Audrey Dowsett, Michael Doswell*

CHIRTON SU0757   SN10 3QN

☆ **Wiltshire Yeoman**

Andover Road (A342 SE of Devizes)

Chef/landlord doing some imaginative cooking including good seafood and two-course lunch deals, neat friendly young staff, well kept Wadworths IPA and 6X, Stowford Press cider, good value wines, proper bar with log fire and well lit games room (pool, darts, machines), separate carpeted dining room; unobtrusive piped pop music, some live; garden with heated shelter, closed Mon, no food Sun evening. *Recommended by KC, M and GR, Michael Doswell*

COLLINGBOURNE DUCIS SU2453   SN8 3ED

Shears

Cadley Road

Attractive 18th-c flint and brick thatched pub, enjoyable freshly cooked food in bar and comfortable bare-boards restaurant with open fire, ales such as Brakspears and Wychwood, friendly service; courtyard garden, six bedrooms. *Recommended by Rachel Arnold, Mrs J P Cleall*

COMPTON BASSETT SU0372   SN11 8RG

White Horse

At N end of village

Good fairly priced home-made food in bar and popular restaurant, welcoming attentive service, four real ales including Bath Gem and Wadworths 6X, good choice of wines, woodburner; children and dogs welcome, garden, good walks, refurbished bedrooms, closed Sun evening, Mon. *Recommended by Helen Carby, T R and B C Jenkins, Alastair Muir*

CORSHAM ST8670   SN13 0HY

Hare & Hounds

Pickwick (A4 E)

Clean friendly local with well kept changing ales such as Bass, Caledonian Deuchars IPA, Fullers London Pride and Marstons Pedigree (annual beer festival), usual food, log fire; dogs welcome but not in garden, open all day Fri-Sun. *Recommended by Dr and Mrs A K Clarke, Denis Taylor*

CORSHAM ST8670   SN13 0HB

Methuen Arms

High Street

Extensively refurbished dining pub (former priory) under new owners (previously at the Pear Tree at Whitley), good food including set menus; tables in attractive courtyard, newly done bedrooms. *Recommended by James McAninch, Mr and Mrs P R Thomas*

CORSHAM ST8670   SN13 0HY

☆ **Two Pigs**

Pickwick (A4)

Cheerfully eccentric little beer lovers' pub run by character landlord – at its liveliest Mon evenings when live blues/rock; zany collection of bric-a-brac in narrow dimly lit flagstoned bar and good mix of customers around long dark wood tables, Stonehenge and a couple of guests; no food, credit cards or under-21s, piped blues; covered yard outside (called the Sty), closed lunchtimes except Sun. *Recommended by Dr and Mrs A K Clarke, Taff Thomas*

CORTON ST9340   BA12 0SZ

☆ **Dove**

Off A36 at Upton Lovell, SE of Warminster

Good food from ciabattas and pub favourites to more enterprising dishes, efficient charming service, up to five well kept ales such as Butcombe, Fullers/Gales and Wychwood, good wines by the glass, renovated linked rooms with flagstones and oak boards, woodburner in bar, flowers on dining room tables, conservatory; children welcome, wheelchair access, rustic furniture in garden, lovely valley, five comfortable courtyard bedrooms, open all day Sun. *Recommended by Edward Mirzoeff, Chris and Angela Buckell*

DEVIZES SU0061   SN10 1HS

Bear

Market Place

Comfortable ancient coaching inn with carpeted big main bar, log fires, black winged wall settles and upholstered bucket armchairs, steps up to room named after portrait painter Thomas Lawrence with oak-panelled walls and big open fireplace, Wadworths ales and a guest, up to 15 wines by the glass, several malt whiskies, food from sandwiches and light dishes up; wheelchair access, mediterranean-style courtyard, bedrooms. *Recommended by the Didler, Nigel Long, Mary Rayner*

DEVIZES SU0262   SN10 2RH

☆ **Hourglass**

Horton Avenue; follow boat brown sign off A361 roundabout, N edge of town

Modern pub featuring sturdy beams, broad bare boards, cream and terracotta décor, wall of windows looking across canalside terrace to fields beyond, enjoyable enterprising food at reasonable prices, well kept Marstons-related ales, good coffees and wine list, cheerful efficient young staff, daily papers and magazines; unobtrusive piped music. *Recommended by Robert Kibble*

EAST CHISENBURY SU1352   SN9 6AQ

☆ **Red Lion**

At S end of village

Pretty thatched pub with welcoming licensees, good enterprising food (not Sun evening, booking advised) including fixed-price weekday lunch, children's helpings, friendly competent service, well kept local Stonehenge and Three Castles, good wine choice, bare boards or flagstones, mixed tables and chairs, large fireplace with woodburner, area with black leather sofa and armchairs, daily papers, dining room; soft piped music; dogs welcome, play area on lawn, open all day weekends, closed Mon. *Recommended by Rochelle Seifas, Antony Willman, Nick Hall, Agusti Jausas*

EBBESBOURNE WAKE ST9924   SP5 5JF

☆ **Horseshoe**

On A354 S of Salisbury, right at signpost at Coombe Bissett; village about 8 miles further

Unspoilt country pub in pretty village with plenty of regular customers, friendly long-serving licensees, Bowman, Otter, Palmers and guests tapped from the cask, farm cider, good traditional bar food (not Sun evening, Mon), neatly kept and comfortable character bar, collection of farm tools and bric-a-brac on beams, conservatory extension and small restaurant; children welcome (not in bar), dogs allowed, seats in pretty little garden with views over River Ebble valley, chickens and a goat in paddock, good nearby walks, bedrooms closed Sun evening, Mon lunchtime. *Recommended by Tom and Rosemary Hall, Chris Wall, Ian Herdman, Peter Dandy, the Didler, Col and Mrs Patrick Kaye and others*

FARLEIGH WICK ST8063   BA15 2PU
Fox & Hounds
A363 NW of Bradford-on-Avon

Rambling low-beamed 18th-c pub, welcoming and clean, with enjoyable food including good value lunchtime set deals (Tues-Fri), real ales, log fire in big oak-floored dining area; attractive garden. *Recommended by Philip and Jan Medcalf*

FORD ST8474   SN14 8RP
☆ White Hart
Off A420 Chippenham—Bristol

Attractive 16th-c stone-built Marstons country inn, their ales and guest such as Otter, wide choice of enjoyable food (especially puddings) all day, lovely home-baked bread, smart friendly staff, heavy black beams and good log fire in ancient fireplace, separate dining room, nice relaxed atmosphere; dogs welcome, plenty of tables outside, attractive stream-side grounds, on the Palladian Way trail, comfortable bedrooms (some in annexe), good breakfast. *Recommended by Dr D Jeary, Ian Malone, Guy Vowles, Taff Thomas*

GIDDEAHALL ST8574   SN14 7ER
Crown
A420 Chippenham—Ford; keep eyes skinned as no village sign

Tudor pub with rambling beamed and flagstoned bar, dining areas in several small rooms on various levels, enjoyable food, three changing ales, good local feel. *Recommended by Roger and Donna Huggins*

GREAT HINTON ST9059   BA14 6BU
Linnet
3.5 miles E of Trowbridge, village signed off A361 opposite Lamb at Semington

Has been popular dining pub but up for sale; comfortable bar on right with Wadworths 6X, two dozen malt whiskies, bookshelves in snug part, candles in restaurant, food has been interesting; piped music; children and dogs welcome, pretty window boxes and flowering tubs, closed Mon. *Recommended by Martin Clifton, Michael Doswell, Maureen Wood, Mr and Mrs A Curry, Mr and Mrs P R Thomas*

HAMPTWORTH SU2419   SP5 2DU
Cuckoo
Hamptworth Road

17th-c thatched New Forest pub, peaceful and unspoilt, with welcoming landlord, friendly mix of customers from famers in families in four compact rooms around tiny servery, well kept Bowman, Hop Back, Ringwood and guests tapped from the cask (Sept beer festival), real cider, pasties and ploughman's (no evening food), mugs and jugs hanging from ceiling, beer memorabilia, basic wooden furniture, open fire; big garden (adults area with view of golf course), open all day weekends. *Recommended by the Didler, Joan and Michel Hooper-Immins*

HEDDINGTON ST9966   SN11 0PL
☆ Ivy
Off A3102 S of Calne

Picturesque thatched 15th-c village local, good inglenook log fire in old-fashioned L-shaped bar, heavy low beams, timbered walls, assorted furnishings on parquet floor, brass and copper, well kept cask-tapped Wadworths ales, popular freshly made food (not Mon or evenings Sun, Tues), friendly service, back family eating room, sensibly placed darts, piano; may be piped music; disabled access, front garden, closed Mon lunchtime. *Recommended by the Didler, Taff Thomas*

Children – if the details at the end of a featured top pub don't mention them, you should assume that the pub doesn't allow them inside.

HINDON ST9032   SP3 6DJ
Angel
B3089 Wilton—Mere

Smartened-up dining pub with big log fire, flagstones and other coaching-inn survivals, sensibly priced food from pub favourites to more unusual dishes, good service, nice choice of wines, ales such as Bass, Ringwood and Sharps; children welcome, dogs in bar, courtyard tables, seven comfortable bedrooms, open all day in summer. *Recommended by Jill Bickerton, Ian Scott-Thompson, Mike Mingars, David Zackeim, Helen and Brian Edgeley, David Zackheim*

HINDON ST9132   SP3 6DP
Lamb
B3089 Wilton—Mere

Smart attractive old hotel with long roomy log-fire bar, two flagstoned lower sections with very long polished table, high-backed pews and settles, plus a third, bigger area up steps, well kept ales such as Butcombe and St Austell Tribute, several wines by the glass and over 100 malt whiskies, cuban cigars, enjoyable bar and restaurant food, polite friendly service from smartly dressed staff; can get very busy; children and dogs welcome, tables on roadside terrace and in garden across road with boules, 19 refurbished bedrooms, good breakfast, open all day from 7.30am. *Recommended by Edward Mirzoeff, John Coatsworth, J Harvey*

HOLT ST8561   BA14 6PY
Old Ham Tree
Ham Green

Refurbished and under new management, locals' bar, beamed restaurant/lounge, Wadworths ales, friendly helpful staff; handy for the lovely gardens of The Courts (NT). *Recommended by Philip and Jan Medcalf*

☆ HOLT ST8561   BA14 6PX
Toll Gate
Ham Green; B3107 W of Melksham

Appealing individual décor and furnishings and thriving atmosphere in comfortable bar, good friendly service, three interesting well kept changing ales, farm cider, popular imaginative food from good lunchtime sandwiches and reasonably priced light meals up, daily papers, log fire, another in more sedate high-raftered former chapel restaurant up steps; piped music; no under-12s, dogs welcome, pretty back terrace, compact bedrooms, closed Sun evening, Mon. *Recommended by Philip and Jan Medcalf, Mr and Mrs A H Young, Michael Doswell, Dr and Mrs A K Clarke and others*

HOOK SU0785   SN4 8DZ
Bolingbroke Arms
B4041, off A420 just W of M4 junction 16

Airy bare-boards bar with lots of light pine, lounge and pleasantly decorated restaurant popular with older lunchers, enjoyable freshly prepared food from sandwiches up including good range of puddings, Arkells ales, good service; piped music; children welcome, garden with pond and fountain, bedrooms, closed Sun evening. *Recommended by Fr Robert Marsh*

HORNINGSHAM ST8041   BA12 7LY
Bath Arms
By entrance to Longleat House

Handsome old stone-built inn on pretty village's sloping green, stylishly opened up as welcoming dining pub with several linked areas including a proper bar, polished wood floors and open fires, good well presented local food, well kept Wessex ales and a guest such as Northumberland Sheepdog, local cider, good choice of wines and other drinks, charming efficient staff, side restaurant and conservatory; can get very busy; wheelchair access through side door, attractive garden with neat terraces, smokers' gazebo, 15 good bedrooms. *Recommended by Michael Doswell, Ian Herdman, Chris and Angela Buckell*

HORTON SU0363   SN10 2JS
☆ **Bridge Inn**
Horton Road; village signed off A361 London Road, NE of Devizes

Former flour mill and bakery by Kennet & Avon Canal, half a dozen cask-tapped
Wadworths ales, generous well prepared traditional food (not Sun evening) including all-
day breakfasts and specials, good service, carpeted log-fire area on left with tables set for
dining, pubby bit to right of bar with some stripped brickwork and country kitchen
furniture on reconstituted flagstones, old bargee photographs and country pictures; piped
music, TV; well behaved children welcome, dogs in bar, disabled facilities, safely fenced
garden with picnic-sets, original grinding wheel, aviary and fantail doves, canal walks
and moorings, bedrooms, closed Mon. *Recommended by Elen Matthews, P and J Shapley, Mr and
Mrs A H Young, Sheila and Robert Robinson, Taff Thomas*

KILMINGTON ST7835   BA12 6RP
☆ **Red Lion**
B3092 Mere—Frome, 2.5 miles S of Maiden Bradley; 3 miles from A303 Mere turn-off

No-nonsense country inn owned by NT with long-serving professional licensees, convivial
atmosphere in low-ceilinged bar, curved high-backed settle and red leatherette wall and
window seats on flagstones, photos of locals pinned to beams, log fires in big fireplaces
(fine iron fireback in one), Butcombe, Butts and a guest, Thatcher's cider, traditional
food (till 1.50pm, not evenings), newer big-windowed eating area decorated with brasses,
large leather horse collar and hanging plates, shove-ha'penny; no credit cards; children
welcome, dogs in bar (not lunchtime), picnic-sets in big attractive garden, smokers'
shelter, White Sheet Hill (radio-controlled gliders, hang-gliding) and Stourhead Gardens
nearby. *Recommended by Joan and Michel Hooper-Immins, Andrea Rampley, Steve Jackson, SRD,
Chris and Angela Buckell, Edward Mirzoeff and others*

KINGTON ST MICHAEL ST9077   SN14 6JB
Jolly Huntsman
Handy for M4 junction 17

Roomy welcoming stone-built pub, six ales including Greene King, popular home-made
food from pub standards to unusual things like bison steaks, prompt service, lit candles
on scrubbed tables, comfortable sofas, pleasant décor and good log fire; seven well
equipped bedrooms in separate block. *Recommended by Michael Doswell, Chris Bell*

LACOCK ST9268   SN15 2PJ
Bell
E of village

Extended cottagey pub with warm welcome from enthusiastic owners, wide choice of
enjoyable food, changing ales such as Bath, Ramsbury and Palmers (beer festivals), real
ciders, decent wines by the glass, lots of malt whiskies, linked rooms off bar including
pretty restaurant, conservatory; children welcome away from bar, disabled access, well
kept sheltered garden with smokers' shelter, open all day weekends. *Recommended by
Jean and Douglas Troup, Taff Thomas, Chris and Angela Buckell*

LACOCK ST9168   SN15 2LH
☆ **George**
West Street; village signed off A350 S of Chippenham

Rambling inn at centre of busy NT tourist village, low-beamed bar with upright timbers
creating cosy corners, armchairs and windsor chairs around close-set tables, seats in
stone-mullioned windows, some flagstones, dog treadwheel in outer breast of central
fireplace, walls covered with vintage cameras (small exhibition on William Henry Fox
Talbot), souvenirs from filming *Cranford* and *Harry Potter* in village, Wadworths beers,
tasty bar food, pleasant attentive staff; piped music; children welcome, dogs in bar,
picnic-sets under parasols in attractive courtyard, open all day in summer. *Recommended by
Chris and Jeanne Downing, Bob and Angela Brooks, PL, D and J Ashdown, Roger and Donna Huggins,
Maureen Wood and others*

☆ **Red Lion**

LACOCK ST9168   SN15 2LQ

High Street

Busy NT-owned Georgian inn, sizeable bar with log fire, heavy tables and oriental rugs on flagstones, cosy snug with leather armchairs, well kept Wadworths, good choice of enjoyable food (all day weekends), pleasant service; piped music; children and dogs welcome, seats outside, bedrooms, open all day. *Recommended by Susan and Nigel Brookes, Ellie Weld, David London, Roger and Donna Huggins, Taff Thomas*

☆ **Rising Sun**

LACOCK ST9367   SN15 2PP

Bewley Common, Bowden Hill – out towards Sandy Lane, up hill past Abbey; OS Sheet 173 map reference 935679

Unassuming stone pub with three knocked-together simply furnished rooms, mix of wooden tables and chairs on stone floors, country pictures and open fires, Moles and a guest beer, Black Rat cider, decent generously served bar food (all day weekends July/Aug, not Sun evening in winter), cheery chatty staff, conservatory, live entertainment Weds evening; children and dogs welcome (there are two pub dogs), big two-level terrace with plenty of modern steel and wood furniture, fantastic views – on a clear day you can see up to 25 miles over the Avon Valley (stunning sunsets), open all day Sat in summer. *Recommended by P Waterman, Chris and Angela Buckell, Martin and Karen Wake, Taff Thomas, Andy Jones*

Village Inn

LIDDINGTON SU2081   SN4 0HE

Handy for M4 junction 15, via A419 and B4192; Bell Lane

Comfortable, warm and welcoming, enjoyable good value food including weekday OAP bargains and Sun roasts, well kept Arkells ales, linked bar areas, stripped-stone and raftered back dining extension, conservatory, log fire in splendid fireplace; well behaved children welcome in restaurant area, disabled facilities, terrace tables. *Recommended by KC*

George

LONGBRIDGE DEVERILL ST8640   BA12 7DG

A350/B3095

Friendly extended roadside pub with well kept ales including Deverill Advocate brewed locally for them, reasonably priced usual food, popular Sun carvery; children welcome, big riverside garden with play area, open all day. *Recommended by Dave Braisted*

☆ **Wheatsheaf**

LOWER WOODFORD SU1235   SP4 6NQ

Signed off A360 just N of Salisbury

Recently refurbished and extended 18th-c Badger dining pub, open airy feel, with good choice of fairly priced traditional food from sharing boards up, well kept ales, good wines and coffee, well trained genial staff, beams, mix of old furniture, log fire and woodburner; piped music; children welcome, dogs in bar, disabled access and parking, tree-lined fenced garden with play area, pretty setting, open all day. *Recommended by I D Barnett*

Somerset Arms

MAIDEN BRADLEY ST8038   BA12 7HW

Church Street

Large Victorian pub (originally built as railway hotel) under new friendly management, bar with bare boards and black marble floor, painted panelling, unusual bookshelf wallpaper (write your own title on a spine), traditional cast-iron tables and log fire, daily newspapers, Wadworths ales, good interesting seasonal food using local and own produce, restaurant, live music including Tues folk night; children and dogs welcome, nice garden, skittle alley in barn, five bedrooms, open all day Fri-Sun. *Recommended by Chris Brickell*

MARDEN SU0857   SN10 3RH
Millstream
Village signposted off A342 SE of Devizes

Formerly the Triple Crown, this well liked Wadworths country pub has been closed for
some months and was still shut as we went to press; appealing layout of linked cosy areas,
beams and log fires, red-cushioned dark pews and small padded dining chairs around
sturdy oak and other good tables, more formal dining area; children and dogs have been
welcome, garden down to tree-lined stream – news please. *Recommended by anon*

MARKET LAVINGTON SU0154   SN10 4AG
Green Dragon
High Street

Rambling early 17th-c pub, well kept Wadworths and guests, good value wines and nice
jugs of summer Pimms, enjoyable food including good deli platters; children welcome,
wheelchair access, garden with play area and aunt sally. *Recommended by Trevor Brown*

MARLBOROUGH SU1869   SN8 1LZ
Castle & Ball
High Street

Georgian coaching inn with nicely worn-in lounge bar, unusually wide choice of decent
food including good speciality pie, quieter and slightly simpler eating area, Greene King
ales, good range of well listed wines by the glass, young enthusiastic staff; seats out under
projecting colonnade, good value bedrooms. *Recommended by Peter Dandy, Comus and
Sarah Elliott, Mary Rayner*

☆ MARLBOROUGH SU1869   SN8 1NE
Lamb
The Parade

Well worn in old-fashioned 17th-c coaching inn with further stable-block eating area,
good up-to-date food at reasonable prices, well kept Wadworths tapped from the cask,
decent choice of wines, amiable landlord and good service, popular place especially
weekends; pretty courtyard, six comfortable clean bedrooms, hearty breakfast.
Recommended by Frank Blanchard, Tony Baldwin

MARLBOROUGH SU1868   SN8 1HF
Sun
High Street

Welcoming 15th-c pub, heavy sloping beams, wonky floors, dim lighting, benches built
into panelling, log fires, enjoyable food especially seafood, well kept real ales and good
choice of wines; back courtyard, bedrooms. *Recommended by Mike and Corinne Tomkins*

MERE ST8131   BA12 6BH
Walnut Tree
Shaftesbury Road

Newly built pub with good value home-made food all day including Sun, Weds carvery.
Recommended by J Stickland

MONKTON FARLEIGH ST8065   BA15 2QH
Kings Arms
Signed off A363 Bradford—Bath

Imposing 17th-c stone building with sofas, open fire and dining tables in one bar, huge
inglenook and more dining tables in L-shaped beamed lounge, good if not cheap food (all
day weekends) using local supplies, efficient friendly service, well kept changing ales,
good wine and whisky choice; piped music; front partly flagstoned courtyard, well tended
two-level back garden, lovely village, three bedrooms. *Recommended by John and Gloria Isaacs,
Mr and Mrs A H Young, Philip and Jan Medcalf, Guy Vowles*

NETHERHAMPTON SU1129   SP2 8PU

☆ **Victoria & Albert**

Just off A3094 W of Salisbury

Cosy black-beamed bar in simple thatched cottage, good generous food from nicely presented sandwiches up, sensible prices and local supplies, four well kept changing ales, farm cider, decent wines, friendly staff, nicely cushioned old-fashioned wall settles on ancient floor tiles, restaurant; children welcome, hatch service for sizeable terrace and garden behind, handy for Wilton House and Nadder Valley walks. *Recommended by Peter Salmon*

NOMANSLAND SU2517   SP5 2BP

Lamb

Signed off B3078 and B3079

Lovely New Forest village-green setting, welcoming unpretentious local feel, good value food including lots of pasta and fish, popular Sun roasts, four changing ales such as Gales HSB, Ringwood Fortyniner, Skinners and Timothy Taylors Landlord, sensibly priced wine list, fast friendly service, log fire, small dining room, games room with pool; TV; children and dogs welcome, tables on terrace, green and garden behind, open all day. *Recommended by Sally Matson*

PITTON SU2131   SP5 1DU

☆ **Silver Plough**

Village signed from A30 E of Salisbury (follow brown tourist signs)

Bustling country dining pub with comfortable front bar, beams strung with hundreds of antique boot-warmers and stretchers, pewter and china tankards, copper kettles, toby jugs, rolling pins and so forth, cushioned antique settles (one elaborately carved), timbered walls hung with Thorburn and other game bird prints (and big naval battle glass-painting), simpler back bar with big winged high-backed settle, cased antique guns, and substantial pictures, Badger ales and several wines by the glass, tasty bar food (they stop serving promptly), skittle alley next to snug (children allowed here); piped music; dogs welcome in bar, picnic-sets and other seats on lawn, more on terrace with heated smokers' area, good nearby woodland and downland paths including Clarendon Way, bedrooms. *Recommended by JDM, KM, Glenwys and Alan Lawrence, George Atkinson, Ian Herdman, Dave Braisted*

POULSHOT ST9760   SN10 1RW

☆ **Raven**

Off A361

Friendly half-timbered pub across from village green, well kept Wadworths tapped from cask, wide range of popular home-made pubby food, two cosy black-beamed rooms, comfortable banquettes, open fire, obliging service; children and dogs welcome, garden picnic-sets, closed Mon. *Recommended by Mrs Blethyn Elliott, Mr and Mrs P R Thomas*

RAMSBURY SU2771   SN8 2PT

Crown & Anchor

Crowood Lane/Whittonditch Road

Friendly and relaxed beamed village pub, popular for good value simple food, well kept Bass, Wadworths, Ramsbury and a guest, good house wine, helpful service, open fires; children welcome, hanging baskets and small garden with terrace, two new bedrooms, closed Mon. *Recommended by Anne Morris, Mary Rayner*

ROWDE ST9762   SN10 2PN

☆ **George & Dragon**

A342 Devizes—Chippenham

Plenty of character in this 16th-c former coaching inn, two low-beamed rooms with large open fireplaces, wooden dining chairs around candlelit tables, antique rugs and walls covered with old pictures and portraits, Butcombe, Fullers and a guest, well liked if not cheap food; piped music; children and dogs welcome, seats in pretty back garden, Kennet & Avon canal nearby, bedrooms, closed Sun evening. *Recommended by Mr and Mrs P R Thomas, Peter and Jan Humphreys*

SALISBURY SU1429   SP1 2DH

Cloisters
Catherine Street/Ivy Street

Olde worlde city pub, comfortable and rambling, with low beams and bare boards, friendly buoyant atmosphere, good value food including generous Sun roasts, ales such as Ringwood, Hop Back and Sharps, helpful staff; open all day. *Recommended by Ann and Colin Hunt*

SALISBURY SU1429   SP1 2PH

☆ New Inn
New Street

Much extended old building with massive beams and timbers, good choice of well prepared standard food from snacks up, well kept Badger ales, decent house wines, cheerful staff, flagstones, floorboards and carpet, quiet cosy alcoves, inglenook log fire; children welcome, attractive walled garden with striking view of nearby cathedral spire, bedrooms, open all day summer weekends. *Recommended by Tony and Wendy Hobden, Richard Stanfield*

SALISBURY SU1329   SP2 8EU

☆ Old Mill
Town Path, West Harnham

Charming 17th-c pub/hotel in tranquil setting, unpretentious beamed bars with prized window tables, decent good value food from sandwiches up, local ales, good wines and malt whiskies, attractive restaurant showing mill race; children welcome, small floodlit garden by duck-filled millpond, delightful stroll across water meadows from cathedral (classic view of it from bridge beyond garden), 11 bedrooms. *Recommended by Ian and Helen Stafford, Tim Loryman, Mr and Mrs P D Titcomb*

SALISBURY SU1429   SP1 1DT

Pheasant
Near bus station

Spaciously refurbished 16th-c timbered inn, enjoyable well priced food (all day Sat) from baguettes and sharing plates to steaks and grills, Ringwood and a couple of guests, good service and housekeeping, open fire, live music; four newly done bedrooms, open all day (Sun till 6pm). *Recommended by Jackie Craker*

SANDY LANE ST9668   SN15 2PX

☆ George
A342 Devizes—Chippenham

Old mellow-stone Wadworths dining pub, good competently cooked food from newish landlord/chef using local meat and freshly delivered fish from Cornwall, own-baked bread too, well kept ales and good choice of wines by the glass, efficient friendly service, bar, restaurant and conservatory; tables out at front, more in garden behind, open all day, closed Sun evening. *Recommended by Neil and Anita Christopher, Mrs Pickwick*

SEEND ST9361   SN12 6QB

☆ Barge
Seend Cleeve; signed off A361 Devizes—Trowbridge

Plenty of seats in garden making most of boating activity on Kennet & Avon Canal, unusual seating in bar including milk churns, an upturned canoe and high-backed chairs made from old boat parts, small oak settle among the rugs on parquet floor, well stocked aquarium, pretty Victorian fireplace, Wadworths ales and 30 wines by the glass, standard bar food (not the highlight), good service; piped music; children and dogs welcome, open all day. *Recommended by Meg and Colin Hamilton, Robert Watt*

SEEND ST9562   SN12 6RN

Three Magpies

Sells Green – A365 towards Melksham

Unpretentious partly 18th-c pub popular for its good value straightforward home-made food including children's choices and Sun roasts, two warm fires, welcoming efficient service, well kept Wadworths ales, decent choice of wines by the glass; dogs allowed in bar, big garden with play area, campsite next door, open all day Fri-Sun. *Recommended by Paul and Claudia Dickinson, David and Gill Carrington*

SEMINGTON ST9259   BA14 6LL

Lamb

The Strand; A361 Devizes—Trowbridge

Refurbished ivy-covered pub, wood-strip floor in bar with log fire, traditional carpeted dining room, beers from Bath, Butcombe and Moles, decent bar food, efficient friendly staff; piped music; pleasant colourfully planted walled garden with tables under parasols and views to the Bowood Estate. *Recommended by Taff Thomas*

SEMINGTON ST8960   BA14 6JR

☆ Somerset Arms

Off A350 bypass 2 miles S of Melksham

Well refurbished 16th-c coaching inn, heavy-beamed long bar opening into comfortable seating area with sofas and armchairs by open fire, restaurant, good food (not Sun evening) from sandwiches and panini to more ambitious things including nice fresh fish, enthusiastic landlord and efficient young staff, four well kept ales including Bath and Box Stream, real ciders, coffees and teas, newspapers; children welcome, small garden behind, good bedrooms, short walk from Kennet & Avon Canal, open all day. *Recommended by Stephen Turpin, Dr A J and Mrs Tompsett, Taff Thomas, M J K and F A Ronald, Dr and Mrs A K Clarke, B and F A Hannam*

SHALBOURNE SU3162   SN8 3QF

Plough

Off A338

Low-beamed traditional village pub on green, good choice of enjoyable fairly priced blackboard food including vegetarian options, Butcombe and Wadworths, friendly helpful landlady, neat tiled-floor bar with sofa and armchairs in snug; disabled access, small garden with play area. *Recommended by Tighe Reeves, David Gray*

SOUTH WRAXALL ST8364   BA15 2SB

☆ Long Arms

Upper S Wraxall, off B3109 N of Bradford-on-Avon

Partly 17th-c small open-plan country pub with good value fresh food including bargain daily roast, fish and homely puddings, Wadworths, good range of wines by the glass, friendly efficient staff, cheerful atmosphere, characterful dark décor with beams, flagstones and some stripped stone, log fire; dogs welcome in bar areas, pretty little back garden. *Recommended by Simon Rodway*

STEEPLE ASHTON ST9056   BA14 6EU

Longs Arms

High Street

Friendly 17th-c renovated coaching inn, good locally sourced home-made food, well kept real ales, open fire; children and dogs welcome, big garden with play area, delightful village. *Recommended by Roly Hill, Taff Thomas*

Virtually all pubs in the *Good Pub Guide* sell wine by the glass. We mention wines if they are a cut above the average.

STOURTON ST7733   BA12 6QE

☆ Spread Eagle

Church Lawn; follow Stourhead brown signs off B3092, N of junction with A303 W of Mere

Georgian inn, always packed as at entrance to magnificent Stourhead Estate and handy for A303; old-fashioned, rather civilised interior with antique panel-back settles, new and old solid tables and chairs, log fires in handsome fireplaces, smoky old sporting prints, room by entrance with armchairs, longcase clock and corner china cupboard, Butcombe and a guest such as Great Western, nice wines by the glass, good food (must book), cream teas, friendly helpful service, restaurant; piped music; children welcome, wheelchair access (step down to dining areas), benches in back courtyard, bedrooms (guests can wander freely around famous NT gardens outside normal opening hours), open all day. *Recommended by Michael Doswell, V Brogden, Peter and Heather Elliott, Sheila Topham and others*

SUTTON VENY ST8941   BA12 7AW

Woolpack

High Street

Small resurrected village pub nicely refurbished by landlord/chef, good mainstream food using local ingredients (best to book), sensibly priced wines by the glass, charming service, compact side restaurant, friendly busy atmosphere. *Recommended by Edward Mirzoeff, Mrs Blethyn Elliott*

TOLLARD ROYAL ST9317   SP5 5PS

☆ King John

B3081 Shaftesbury—Sixpenny Handley

Busy refurbished red-brick Victorian dining pub, well liked interesting food in stylish open-plan country-style interior with old pine tables on terracotta and coir floors, black and white hunting photographs and old etchings, logs stacked by woodburner, Ringwood and two changing guests from long oak counter with wine bottles racked behind (pub also has a wine shop), charming helpful service; well behaved children and clean dogs welcome, solid tables out in front under cream parasols, picnic-sets in terraced garden, eight comfortable bedrooms (three in barn opposite), good breakfast, nice walks. *Recommended by Robert Whitaker, Mrs C Roe, Peter Meister, Paul and Marion Watts*

UPPER CHUTE SU2953   SP11 9ER

☆ Cross Keys

N of Andover; best reached off A343 via Tangley, or off A342 in Weyhill via Clanville

Country pub run by hospitable landlord but up for sale; open-plan rooms with beams, pubby tables and chairs, some sofas, cushioned built-in window seat, log fire and woodburner, Arkells, Fullers and Hop Back, well liked proper pies and other bar food (not Sun evening), shut the box; piped music, TV; children welcome and dogs (they have three staffies), picnic-sets on grass and terrace with far-reaching rural views, play fort, stables at back for visiting horses, bedrooms, good breakfast, open all day weekends. *Recommended by Martin Hatcher, Phyl and Jack Street, Don Faskle, Derek Goldrei and others*

WANBOROUGH SU2183   SN4 0AE

Brewers Arms

High Street

Extended Victorian village pub with modern décor, good range of enjoyable food including Sun evening tapas, well kept Arkells, friendly service, conservatory; children welcome, covered terrace, big garden with play area. *Recommended by Mary Rayner*

WARMINSTER ST8745   BA12 8JA

Weymouth Arms

Emwell Street

Nicely refurbished old backstreet pub with bar, two dining areas and charming snug, dark panelling, wide old floorboards and fine fireplaces, more modern feel at back with view into kitchen, good imaginative cooking, Butcombe and Wadworths 6X, water from own well, friendly staff; garden tables. *Recommended by Edward Mirzoeff*

☆ **WEST LAVINGTON** SU0052   SN10 4LD
Bridge Inn
Church Street (A360)

Most emphasis on good imaginative food at this busy dining pub (must book), comfortable spacious bar with timbers and steps dividing various areas, tables all set for eating, logs and candles in huge brick inglenook, smaller modern fireplace at other end, pictures for sale on brick or cream walls, fresh flowers, Wadworths and two guests, several wines by the glass; evening piped music; children welcome, seats under big tree on raised back lawn, boules, closed Sun evening, Mon and two weeks in Feb.
Recommended by Robert Kibble, Mr and Mrs P R Thomas, Colin Wood, B and F A Hannam, Mr and Mrs A Curry

WEST OVERTON SU1368   SN8 1QD
Bell
A4 Marlborough—Calne

Former coaching inn reopened after extensive refurbishment, enjoyable food from sandwiches up in bar with woodburner, Wadworths and local guests, good modern restaurant food including fixed-price menus in spacious dining part (closed evenings Sun and Mon), uniformed staff; piped music; disabled access, tables in back garden with country views. *Recommended by T R and B C Jenkins, Sheila and Robert Robinson*

WESTWOOD ST8159   BA15 2AE
New Inn
Off B3109 S of Bradford-on-Avon

Traditional country pub with friendly landlord and good staff, several linked rooms, beams and stripped stone, scrubbed tables on slate floor, imaginative good value food in bar and spacious restaurant, well kept Wadworths, buzzy atmosphere; a few tables out behind, lovely hanging baskets, walks nearby, pretty village, closed Mon. *Recommended by Philip and Jan Medcalf, Taff Thomas*

WILTON SU2661   SN8 3SS
Swan
S of Great Bedwyn

Light and airy 1930s pub, good food including fresh fish (not Sun evening), efficient service, reasonably priced wines, two Ramsbury ales and a local guest, farm ciders, stripped pine tables, high-backed settles, pews and a woodburner; children and dogs welcome, disabled access, front garden with picnic-sets, picturesque village with windmill, open all day weekends. *Recommended by Andrew Gardner, Terry Davis, Mary Rayner*

☆ **WINGFIELD** ST8256   BA14 9LN
Poplars
B3109 S of Bradford-on-Avon (Shop Lane)

Attractive country pub with beams and log fires, very popular for its good interesting sensibly priced food, especially with older people at lunchtime, Wadworths ales, friendly fast service even when busy, warm atmosphere, light and airy family dining extension; nice garden, own cricket pitch. *Recommended by Mr and Mrs A Curry, Taff Thomas*

☆ **WINTERBOURNE BASSETT** SU1075   SN4 9QB
White Horse
Off A4361 S of Swindon

Neatly kept roadside dining pub with gently old-fashioned feel, carpeted bar with plenty of wood, wrought-iron plush-topped stools and cushioned dining chairs, Wadworths ales and quite a few wines by the glass, popular homely food served by friendly helpful staff, dining rooms with country kitchen furniture on light wood floors, old prints and paintings, assorted plants, woodburner in little brick fireplace, conservatory; piped music; children welcome, tables on good-sized lawn, pretty hanging baskets. *Recommended by Michael Doswell, Tony Baldwin, Bruce and Sharon Eden, Ian and Julie Campbell, Frank Blanchard*

WOODBOROUGH SU1159   SN9 6LW
Seven Stars
Off A345 S of Marlborough; Bottlesford

Welcoming pretty 16th-c thatched pub, enjoyable reasonably priced freshly prepared food including some imaginative dishes, Timothy Taylors Landlord, Wadworths 6X and a changing guest, good choice of wines, pews and country furniture, attractively moulded panelling, hunting prints, open fire one end, woodburner the other, cosy nooks; piped music; children and dogs welcome, extensive gardens bordered by small River Bottle, roaming chickens, three bedrooms, camping, open all day Sun, closed Mon, Tues lunchtime. *Recommended by P R and D C Groves*

WOOTTON BASSETT SU0682   SN4 7BD
Five Bells
Wood Street

Friendly town local with great atmosphere, well kept Fullers London Pride and changing guests, farm cider, good food a cut above usual pub style including special menus/theme nights and well liked Sun lunch, board games, darts; TV; shaded courtyard, open all day Fri-Sun. *Recommended by DT and Sue, Ric Mason, John Hickman*

WOOTTON RIVERS SU1963   SN8 4NQ
Royal Oak
Off A346, A345 or B3087

Cosy 16th-c beamed and thatched pub, good food from lunchtime sandwiches to nice fish dishes, ales such as Ramsbury and Wadworths 6X, good choice of wines by the glass, comfortable L-shaped dining lounge with woodburner, timbered bar with small games area; children and dogs welcome, tables out in yard, pleasant village, bedrooms in adjoining house. *Recommended by John and Gloria Isaacs, Rachel Arnold*

If a pub tries to make you leave a credit card behind the bar, be on your guard. The credit card firms and banks that issue them condemn this practice. After all, the publican who asks you to do this is in effect saying: 'I don't trust you'. Have you any more reason to trust his staff? If your card is used fraudulently while you have let it be kept out of your sight, the card company could say you've been negligent yourself – and refuse to make good your losses. So say that they can 'swipe' your card instead, but must hand it back to you. Please let us know if a pub does try to keep your card.

The South East
& London

Berkshire

Buckinghamshire

Hampshire

Isle of Wight

Kent

Oxfordshire

Surrey

Sussex

London

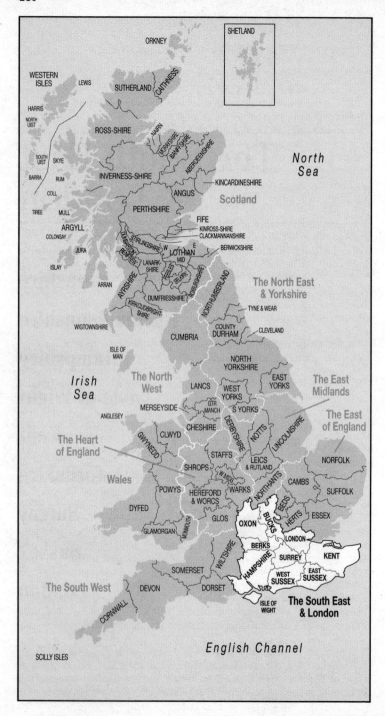

EDITORS' FAVOURITES
THE SOUTH EAST & LONDON

This region's top pub for 2012 is the Cat at West Hoathly in **Sussex** (warmly friendly hands-on landlord). Other special pubs in this county are the smashing old Rose Cottage at Alciston, Jolly Sportsman at East Chiltington (**Sussex Dining Pub of the Year**, plus lovely little bar), charming Tiger by cottage-lined East Dean green, Partridge in Singleton (a fine newcomer) and timeless Royal Oak at Wineham. Also particularly worth a visit are the Cricketers Arms at Berwick, Hatch in Colemans Hatch, Three Horseshoes at Elsted, Bulls Head at Fishbourne, Queens Head at Icklesham, Lewes Arms in Lewes, Chalk Pit in Offham, Green Man at Partridge Green and Horse Guards at Tillington.

Top picks in **Berkshire** are the Hinds Head at Bray (**Berkshire Dining Pub of the Year**), Pot Kiln in Frilsham (super country dining pub), newly opened Horse & Groom at Hare Hatch (a model refurbishment), Hobgoblin in Reading (great beers), Royal Oak at Ruscombe (good all round), village-owned Shurlock Inn at Shurlock Row (another new entry) and Beehive at White Waltham (deservedly enormously popular). Also worth a visit are the Bell at Aldworth, Flower Pot in Aston, Bel & the Dragon in Cookham, Magpie & Parrot at Shinfield and the Royal Oak in Yattendon.

The best **Buckinghamshire** pubs include the Royal Oak at Bovingdon Green (**Buckinghamshire Dining Pub of the Year**), properly traditional Red Lion at Chenies, Royal Standard of England in Forty Green (great character), White Horse at Hedgerley (unchanging gem), Queens Head in Little Marlow (smashing all-rounder) and the Eight Bells at Long Crendon (another unspoilt charmer). Also well worth a visit are the Three Crowns in Askett, Three Horseshoes at Bennett End, Pheasant in Brill, Hampden Arms at Great Hampden, Full Moon in Hawridge Common, Red Lion at Marsworth, Chandos Arms in Oakley and the Bull & Butcher at Turville.

Pubs we've particularly enjoyed in **Hampshire** are the friendly and chatty Sun in Bentworth, Anchor at Lower Froyle (**Hampshire Dining Pub of the Year**), Yew Tree at Lower Wield (exceptional landlord), White Horse near Petersfield (remote, unspoilt), Plough at Sparsholt (hands-on licensees, nice food), Harrow at Steep (quite unchanging, in the same family for 82 years), and a great clutch of new finds, all with good food: smartly updated Hurdles at Droxford, bustling Hogget in Hook, warmly traditional Fox at North Waltham, waterside Mill House at North Warnborough and gently stylish Purefoy Arms in Preston Candover. Also worth a visit are the Flower Pots at Cheriton, Hampshire Bowman in Dundridge, Mill at Gordleton in Hordle, Running Horse at Littleton, Jolly Farmer at Locks Heath, Ship in Lymington and the Old Vine in Winchester.

Top pubs on the **Isle of Wight** are the Red Lion at Freshwater (happy balance between bar and dining) and rambling old New Inn in Shalfleet (**Isle of Wight Dining Pub of the Year**). Also worth a visit are the Folly in Cowes, Taverners at Godshill and the Seaview Hotel at Seaview.

Pubs that stand out in **Kent** include the lovely old Three Chimneys at Biddenden (**Kent Dining Pub of the Year**), Royal Oak at Brookland and Bottle House at Penshurst (both welcoming places for good meals), Dering Arms in Pluckley and Sankeys in Tunbridge Wells (very good fish and seafood at both), and the Tiger near Stowting (super country pub). Of five new top pubs this year, three that particularly stand out are the Pearsons Arms in Whitstable (great sea views from the restaurant) and two Brunning & Price pubs – the Nevill Crest & Gun at Eridge Green and the White Hart in Sevenoaks. Also worth a visit are the Timber Batts in Bodsham, Gate Inn at Boyden Gate, Shipwrights Arms in Oare, Crown at Stone in Oxney, Spotted Dog at Penshurst, Chaser in Shipbourne, Red Lions at Snargate and Stodmarsh, and the Fox & House at Toys Hill.

First-class **Oxfordshire** choices are the Lamb at Burford (civilised and friendly), Chequers tucked away in Chipping Norton, Blowing Stone at Kingston Lisle (**Oxfordshire Dining Pub of the Year**, a newcomer to the *Guide*), Blue Boar at Longworth (smashing old place), beautiful Old Swan & Minster Mill at Minster Lovell, Turf Tavern in Oxford (excellent city-centre pub), and the Swan at Swinbrook (civilised, good, inventive food). Half a dozen other memorable newcomers are the Black Boy at Headington (great Oxford oasis), civilised Oxford Arms in Kirtlington (good food), bustling well run George & Dragon at Long Hanborough, lovely Chilterns Maltsters Arms at Rotherfield Greys, Horse & Jockey at Stanford in the Vale (great all-rounder), and the charmingly updated White Horse at Stonesfield. Also worth a visit are the Saye & Sele Arms at Broughton, Black Horse in Checkendon, Chequers at Churchill, Duke of Cumberlands Head at Clifton, Radnor Arms at Coleshill, White Hart in Fyfield, King William IV at Hailey, and the Bell at Hampton Poyle.

A good batch of new top pubs in **Surrey** includes the thriving Richard Onslow at Cranleigh, Red Lion in Horsell (popular bistro-style food), handsome Refectory at Milford and the warmly welcoming Flower Pot in Sunbury. The Seven Stars at Leigh (enjoyable food) is on good form, as is the Inn at West End (fabulous wines and food) and the Three Horseshoes at Thursley (**Surrey Dining Pub of the Year**). Also worth a special visit are the Barley Mow at West Horsley and the Running Horses at Mickleham.

Unchanging old-world pubs in **London** are a timeless success with readers, especially the waterside Grapes in East London, cosy Harp, Old Mitre and nicely eccentric Seven Stars (all Central London). The Royal Oak in South London is a clever historical re-creation by Harveys and carries their full beer range. Great food pubs include the Thames-side Gun in East London (**London Dining Pub of the Year**), Old Orchard in Haresfield, Outer London (Brunning & Price's usual great all-round package) and for an outstanding burger the Bountiful Cow in Central London. Also worth a visit are the Black Friar, Chandos, Cittie of Yorke, Jerusalem Tavern and Olde Cheshire Cheese in Central London, the Doric Arch in North London and the Anglesea Arms (Wingate Road), Dove and the Windsor Castle in West London.

ADSTOCK Buckinghamshire   SP7330   Map 4

Old Thatched Inn
Main Street, off A413; MK18 2JN

Pretty thatched dining pub with keen landlord, friendly staff, real ales, and enjoyable food

This is a pretty, thatched dining pub in an attractive village and run by an enthusiastic landlord. The pubby front bar has low beams, flagstones, high bar chairs and an open fire and leads on to a dining area with more beams and a mix of pale wooden dining chairs around miscellaneous tables on the stripped wooden floor. There's a modern conservatory restaurant at the back. Fullers London Pride, Hook Norton Hooky Bitter and Timothy Taylors Landlord on handpump, several wines by the glass and 15 malt whiskies served by friendly staff. The sheltered terrace has tables and chairs under a gazebo.

Making everything in-house including bread and ice-cream, the inventive food includes various appetisers, grilled black pudding and bacon salad with a poached duck egg and grain mustard dressing, asian-spiced cured salmon with sesame oil and bean sprout salad, home-made burger with blue cheese mayonnaise, courgette, lemon, spinach and parmesan risotto, pork fillet with a cider apple cream sauce, and slow-cooked lamb fillet with celeriac purée and a rosemary and redcurrant sauce. *Benchmark main dish: local sausages with onion gravy £11.95. Two-course evening meal £19.95.*

Free house ~ Licensee Andrew Judge ~ Real ale ~ Bar food (12-2.30, 6-9.30; 12-8 Sun) ~ Restaurant ~ (01296) 712584 ~ Children welcome ~ Dogs allowed in bar ~ Open 12-midnight

Recommended by Sue Vincent, Michael Dandy, Richard Inman

ALCISTON Sussex   TQ5005   Map 3

Rose Cottage
Village signposted off A27 Polegate—Lewes; BN26 6UW

Old-fashioned cottage with cosy fires and country bric-a-brac, several wines by the glass, well liked food and local beers; bedrooms

This is a smashing old pub with a landlord of some character. It's extremely popular (get there early on Sunday lunchtimes especially) and many of our readers count it among their favourites. There are half a dozen tables with cushioned pews, winter log fires and quite a forest of harness, traps, a thatcher's blade and lots of other black ironware; more bric-a-brac on the shelves above the stripped pine dado or in the etched-glass windows and maybe Jasper the parrot (only at lunchtimes – he gets too noisy in the evenings). The restaurant area has a lunchtime overflow as they don't take bookings in the bar then. Dark Star Hophead, Harveys Best and a guest beer on handpump and several wines by the glass. Piped music, darts and board games. For cooler evenings, there are heaters outside and the small paddock in the garden has ducks and chickens; boules. Nearby fishing and shooting. They take self-catering bedroom bookings for a minimum of two nights. The charming small village (and local church) are certainly worth a look and there are bracing South Downs walks nearby.

Popular bar food (they also have an evening restaurant menu) includes potted shrimps, farmhouse-style pâté with apple and plum chutney, local sausages

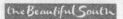

with onion gravy, battered local cod, rabbit and bacon pie, lamb tagine with apricots, chickpeas and chilli, and crispy gressingham duck with orange and peppercorn sauce. *Benchmark main dish: fish pie £11.50. Two-course evening meal £18.00.*

Free house ~ Licensee Ian Lewis ~ Real ale ~ Bar food ~ Restaurant ~ (01323) 870377 ~ Children allowed if over 10 ~ Dogs allowed in bar ~ Open 11.30-3, 6.30-11; 12-3, 6.30-10.30 Sun; closed 25 and 26 Dec, evening 1 Jan ~ Bedrooms: /£60S

Recommended by the Didler, PL, Ian and Nita Cooper, Ron and Sheila Corbett, Terry and Nickie Williams, Gene and Tony Freemantle, Simon Watkins, Peter Meister, Phil and Jane Villiers, Alan Franck, R and S Bentley, Mike Gorton, Tracey and Stephen Groves

 ALFRISTON Sussex   TQ5203   Map 3

George
High Street; BN26 5SY

Venerable inn in lovely village with comfortable, heavily beamed bars, good wines and several real ales; fine nearby walks; bedrooms

Much enjoyed by our readers, this is an ancient and very well run village inn. The busy long bar has massive hop-hung low beams, appropriately soft lighting and a log fire (or summer flower arrangement) in a huge stone inglenook fireplace that dominates the room, with lots of copper and brass around it. There are settles and chairs around sturdy stripped tables, Greene King IPA and Abbot, Hardys & Hansons Old Trip and a guest like Goddards Fuggle-Dee-Dum on handpump, decent wines including champagne by the glass, board games and piped music; good service. The lounge has comfortable sofas, standing timbers and rugs on the wooden floor and the restaurant is cosy and candlelit. There are seats in the spacious flint-walled garden and two long-distance paths, the South Downs Way and Vanguard Way, cross here; Cuckmere Haven is close by. The beamed bedrooms are comfortable; they don't have a car park but there is parking a couple of minutes away.

Good, interesting food includes lunchtime sandwiches, rustic sharing boards, grilled field mushrooms with manchego and chorizo, smoked salmon and mackerel terrine, sausage and mash with onion gravy, a changing risotto, game casserole, and corn-fed chicken with a roasted tomato and olive sauce. *Benchmark main dish: seared salmon fillet and prawns with chilli, garlic white wine and cream on pasta £14.50. Two-course evening meal £20.95.*

Greene King ~ Lease Roland and Cate Couch ~ Real ale ~ Bar food (all day) ~ Restaurant ~ (01323) 870319 ~ Children welcome ~ Dogs allowed in bar and bedrooms ~ Open 11-11(midnight Sat) ~ Bedrooms: £70S/£100B

Recommended by Phil Bryant, Andy West, Tracey and Stephen Groves, Ian and Nita Cooper, Phil and Jane Villiers

 ARRETON Isle of Wight   SZ5386   Map 2

White Lion £
A3056 Newport—Sandown; PO30 3AA

Friendly local with pubby food

A genuinely warm welcome awaits at this white-painted village house. The neatly kept beamed lounge is comfortably old fashioned and cosy, with dark pink walls or stripped brick above a stained pine dado, gleaming brass and horse tack and lots of cushioned wheelback chairs on the patterned red carpet. The piped music tends to be very quiet, and the public bar has a TV, games machine, darts and board games.Three changing real ales on handpump might be Wells & Youngs Eagle, Sharps Doom Bar and Wadworths 6X and they've a farm cider and draught pear cider. There's also a restaurant (no children in here), family room and stable room. The pleasant garden has a small play area.

Traditional tasty food, served in generous helpings, runs from sandwiches and ploughman's to whitebait and breaded brie with vegetable curry, stews, seasonal local game, fish and seafood as main courses. *Benchmark main dish: pie of the day £9.95. Two-course evening meal £15.45.*

Enterprise ~ Lease Chris and Kate Cole ~ Real ale ~ Bar food (12-9) ~ Restaurant ~ (01983) 528479 ~ Children welcome away from bar ~ Dogs allowed in bar ~ Open 11(12 Sun)-11

Recommended by Simon Collett-Jones, Terry and Nickie Williams

BANK Hampshire   SU2806   Map 2

Oak

Signposted just off A35 SW of Lyndhurst; SO43 7FE

Tucked-away and very busy New Forest pub with well liked food and interesting décor

Given its peaceful and tucked-away location, it's quite a surprise how busy this pub always is; to be sure of a table, it's best to book in advance. On either side of the door in the bay windows of the L-shaped bar are built-in red-cushioned seats, and on the right there are two or three little pine-panelled booths with small built-in tables and bench seats. The rest of the bare-boarded bar has some low beams and joists, candles in individual brass holders on a line of stripped old and newer blond tables set against the wall and all manner of bric-a-brac: fishing rods, spears, a boomerang, old ski poles, brass platters, heavy knives and guns. There are cushioned milk churns along the bar counter and little red lanterns among hop bines above the bar. Fullers London Pride and Gales HSB and Seafarers on handpump; piped music. The pleasant side garden has picnic-sets, long tables and benches by the big yew trees.

Popular bar food includes sandwiches, whole baked camembert with fruit chutney, maple syrup-roasted ham with free-range eggs, pasta parcels filled with cheese and pear in a creamy basil sauce, steak in ale pie, pork chop with five bean rice salad and citrus and sweet chilli sauce, and a steak of the day. *Benchmark main dish: steak in ale pie £10.95. Two-course evening meal £17.00.*

Fullers ~ Manager Martin Sliva ~ Real ale ~ Bar food (12-2.30, 6-9.30; all day weekends) ~ (023) 8028 2350 ~ Children welcome but all under-10s must leave by 6pm ~ Dogs welcome ~ Open 11.30-11; 12-10.30 Sun; 11.30-3, 6-11 weekdays in winter

Recommended by Terry and Nickie Williams, Laurence Smith, the Shiread family, Lois Dyer, Leslie and Barbara Owen, Phyl and Jack Street, Mike and Sue Loseby, Mr and Mrs D Hammond, Peter Meister, Ian and Rose Lock, Mr and Mrs P D Titcomb, Phil and Jane Villiers, N R White, Steven King and Barbara Cameron

---

If a service charge is mentioned prominently on a menu or accommodation terms, you must pay it if service was satisfactory. If service is really bad, you are legally entitled to refuse to pay some or all of the service charge as compensation for not getting the service you might reasonably have expected.

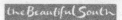

 BEMBRIDGE Isle of Wight   SZ6587 Map 2

Crab & Lobster

Foreland Fields Road, off Howgate Road (which is off B3395 via Hillway Road); PO35 5TR

Clifftop views from terrace and some bedrooms

Perched on low cliffs within yards of the shore, the relaxed waterside terrace here enjoys terrific Solent views – not surprisingly, it's a very popular summer destination (service can slow down at peak times) and the picnic-sets fill up quickly; the dining area and some of the bedrooms share the same views. Inside it's roomier than you might expect and is done out in an almost parlourish style, with lots of yachting memorabilia, old local photographs and a blazing winter fire; darts, dominoes and cribbage. Goddards Fuggle-Dee-Dum, Greene King IPA and Sharps Doom Bar are on handpump, with a dozen wines by the glass, 16 malt whiskies and good coffee.

As well as curries, lasagne and daily specials, they do seafood dishes including lobster; they may keep your credit card if you run a tab. *Benchmark main dish: crab cakes £10.95. Two-course evening meal £20.90.*

Enterprise ~ Lease Caroline and Ian Quekett ~ Real ale ~ Bar food (12-2.30, 6-9(9.30 Fri, Sat) with limited menu 2.30-5.30 weekends and holidays) ~ Restaurant ~ (01983) 872244 ~ Children welcome ~ Dogs allowed in bar ~ Open 11-11; 12-10.30 Sun ~ Bedrooms: £50S(£55B)/£85S(£90B)

Recommended by Guy Consterdine, Thomas Moore, George Atkinson, Simon Collett-Jones, Paul Humphreys, Tony and Maggie Harwood, Anne and Jeff Peel, Mark Seymour, Jackie Roberts

 BENTWORTH Hampshire   SU6740 Map 2

Sun ◖

Sun Hill; from the A339 coming from Alton, the first turning takes you there direct; or in village follow Shalden 2¼, Alton 4¼ signpost; GU34 5JT

Smashing choice of real ales and welcoming landlady in popular country pub; nearby walks

Even on a wet and windy winter's day, this bustling 17th-c country pub will be full of chatty customers – all warmly welcomed by the friendly landlady and her helpful staff. The two little traditional communicating rooms have high-backed antique settles, pews and schoolroom chairs, olde-worlde prints and blacksmith's tools on the walls, and bare boards and scrubbed deal tables on the left; three big fireplaces with log fires make it especially snug in winter. An arch leads to a brick-floored room with another open fire. There's a fine choice of seven real ales on handpump: Andwell Resolute Bitter, Bowman Wallops Wood, Fullers London Pride, Hogs Back TEA, Otter Amber, Sharps Doom Bar and Stonehenge Pigswill. There are seats out in front and in the back garden; pleasant nearby walks.

Generous helpings of carefully cooked, good food might include sandwiches, filo prawns with a sweet chilli or garlic mayonnaise dip, chicken curry, avocado and stilton bake, game or steak and mushroom in ale pies, gammon and egg, calves liver and bacon with onion gravy, and chicken in honey and wholegrain mustard sauce. *Benchmark main dish: beer-battered cod £11.95. Two-course evening meal £19.40.*

Free house ~ Licensee Mary Holmes ~ Real ale ~ Bar food ~ (01420) 562338 ~ Children welcome ~ Dogs welcome ~ Open 12-3, 6-11; 12-11 Sun

Recommended by Phyl and Jack Street, Ann and Colin Hunt, Mrs Jill Rich, Neil and Karen Dignan, the Didler, Mr and Mrs D Hammond, Mr and Mrs H J Langley, Martin and Karen Wake, Tony and Jill Radnor, Stephen Saunders, Margaret Grimwood

BESSELS LEIGH Oxfordshire   SP4501   Map 4

Greyhound ⓎⒶ◀

A420 Faringdon—Botley; OX13 5PX

400-year-old handsome stone pub with knocked-through rooms, plenty of character and interest, individual furnishings, half a dozen real ales and lots of wines by the glass, good service, and enjoyable food

Dating back 400 years, this is a handsome golden-stone building and a former coaching inn. The knocked-through rooms give plenty of space and interest and the half-panelled walls are covered in all manner of old photographs and pictures. The individually chosen cushioned dining chairs, leather-topped stools and dark wooden tables are grouped on the carpeting or rug-covered floorboards and there are books on shelves, glass and stone bottles on windowsills, big gilt mirrors, three fireplaces (one housing a woodburning stove), and sizeable pot plants dotted about. Wooden bar stools sit against the counter where they serve Adnams Southwold, Brunning & Price Original (brewed for the company by Phoenix), Everards Coppernob, Hook Norton Hooky Bitter, Loose Cannon Pale Ale and White Horse Wayland Smithy on handpump, 15 wines by the glass and 80 malt whiskies, and staff are friendly and helpful. By the back dining extension there's a white picket fence-enclosed garden with picnic-sets under green parasols.

Modern bar food includes good sandwiches and light meals as well as interesting dishes such as pigeon and thyme wellington with celeriac purée and juniper jus, wild mushroom, leek and walnut quiche, venison faggots with bubble and squeak and onion gravy, king prawn, pineapple and cashew nut salad, and chicken, pearl barley and vegetable broth with bacon and thyme dumplings. *Benchmark main dish: steak burger topped with bacon and cheese £10.95. Two-course evening meal £17.70.*

Brunning & Price ~ Manager Emily Waring ~ Real ale ~ Bar food (12-10(9.30 Sun)) ~ (01865) 862110 ~ Children welcome ~ Dogs allowed in bar ~ Open 12-11(10.30 Sun)
Recommended by Jan and Roger Ferris, Derek Goldrei

BIDDENDEN Kent   TQ8238   Map 3

Three Chimneys ⓎⒶ

A262, 1 mile W of village; TN27 8LW

KENT DINING PUB OF THE YEAR

Pubby beamed rooms of considerable individuality, log fires, imaginative food, and pretty garden

The little low-beamed rooms at this appealingly civilised place have a charmingly timeless feel – as one reader put it 'spend more than a couple of pints here and you will cheerfully let slip which decade you are in'. They are simply done out with plain wooden furniture and old settles on flagstones and coir matting, some harness and sporting prints on the stripped-brick walls and good log fires. The public bar on the left is quite down-to-earth, with darts, dominoes and cribbage. Adnams Best, St Austell Tribute and a guest tapped straight from casks racked behind the counter, several wines by the glass, local Biddenden cider and apple juice and several malt whiskies. But don't be misled into thinking this place is in any way old fashioned. In fact, the candlelit bare-boards restaurant though rurally rustic in its decor is chatty and alive with customers and the style of dining is completely up to date. French windows open from the restaurant to a conservatory and garden. Sissinghurst Gardens are nearby.

🍴 Excellent (if not cheap) food changes daily but might include french onion soup, smoked haddock, creamed leek and bacon tart, baked mushrooms topped with caramelised red onions, duck leg confit, sun-dried tomato couscous with potato wedge, and grilled brie with balsamic roast vegetables. *Benchmark main dish: smoked haddock with creamed leeks and chive velouté £18.95. Two-course evening meal £23.70.*

Free house ~ Licensee Craig Smith ~ Real ale ~ Bar food (12-2(2.30 Sat, Sun), 6.30-9 (9.30 Sat)) ~ (01580) 291472 ~ Children welcome ~ Dogs allowed in bar ~ Open 11.30-3.30, 5.30-11; 12-4, 6-11.30 Sun

Recommended by Robert Kibble, A and H Piper, Jill and Julian Tasker, John and Enid Morris, Colin and Louise English, Cathryn and Richard Hicks, the Didler, Mrs J Ekins-Daukes, Bill Adie, Anthony Longden, Gordon and Margaret Ormondroyd, Malcolm and Barbara Southwell, Derek Thomas

BLINDLEY HEATH Surrey   TQ3645 Map 3

Red Barn ♀

Tandridge Lane, just off B2029, which is off A22; RH7 6LL

Splendidly converted spacious farmhouse and barn with plenty of character, food all day starting with breakfast

The chief glory at this 300-year-old farmhouse is its huge raftered barn conversion that features a central glassed woodburning stove with a chimney that soars up into the roof timbers. Contemporary décor with bright red and green splashes of colour works well against a plethora of stripped beams and timbers. Funky round modern lights and a large model plane hang from the elevated rafters and one wall is dominated by shelves of books stretching high above a window and a wall hung with antlers. An eclectic mix of modern furnishings includes everything from leather or wicker chairs to cow-print pouffes. Clever partitioning creates cosier areas too, each with their own character and comfortably intimate feel. A lighter farmhouse-style room that they call the pantry has big wooden tables and a red cooking range; it's where they serve breakfast. Efficient smartly dressed staff take your order at the table, but this is very much a pub, with bar billiards and a pile of board games in the adjacent bar, along with sofas by another sizeable fireplace; piped music. Two real ales might be from Adnams, Harveys or Sharps and there's a good wine list. A big farmer's market is held here the first Saturday morning of each month and they may also have summer barbecues and hold various foodie events. Out on the lawn, you'll find solid granite tables.

🍴 Well presented bar food relies on fresh local ingredients, which, from a daily changing menu, might include filled baguettes, ham hock and parsley terrine, roast courgette and dried tomato tart, black pudding salad with hard-boiled egg, battered haddock, chicken caesar salad, pea, broad bean and mint risotto, cumberland sausage and mash, fried bream with tomato salsa and white wine sauce, and steak, Guinness and mushroom pie. *Benchmark main dish: home-made burger £10.75. Two-course evening meal £20.00.*

Geronimo Inns ~ Manager Sacha Dickinson ~ Real ale ~ Bar food (12-3, 6-9.30(10 Fri, Sat); 12-8 Sun; breakfast 9.30am-11am Sat, Sun) ~ Restaurant ~ (01342) 830820 ~ Children welcome ~ Dogs allowed in bar ~ Live music last Fri of month ~ Open 10-11; 9.30-11 Sat; 9.30-11 Sun

Recommended by Derek Thomas, John Branston, Grahame Brooks

BOUGH BEECH Kent   TQ4846   Map 3

Wheatsheaf ♀ ◖

B2027, S of reservoir; TN8 7NU

Former hunting lodge with lots to look at, fine range of local drinks, popular food, and plenty of seats in appealing garden

Said to have been built as a medieval royal hunting lodge, this ancient ivy-clad building is full of characterful features and historic detail. Its neat central bar and long front bar (which has an attractive old settle carved with wheatsheaves) have unusually high ceilings with lofty oak timbers, a screen of standing timbers and a revealed king post. Divided from the central bar by two more rows of standing timbers – one formerly an outside wall to the building – are the snug and another bar. On the walls and above the massive stone fireplaces, there are quite a few horns and heads as well as african masks, a sword from Fiji, crocodiles, stuffed birds, swordfish spears and a matapee. Look out, too, for the piece of 1607 graffiti, 'Foxy Holamby', who is thought to have been a whimsical local squire. Thoughtful touches include piles of smart magazines, board games, tasty nibbles and winter chestnuts to roast. Harveys Best, Westerham Brewery Grasshopper and a guest are on handpump and they've three ciders (including one from local Biddenden), a decent wine list, several malt whiskies, summer Pimms and winter mulled wine. Outside is appealing too, with plenty of seats, flowerbeds and fruit trees in the sheltered side and back gardens. Shrubs help divide the garden into various areas, so it doesn't feel too crowded even when it's full.

Bar food (there may be a wait at busy times) might include breaded whiting with sweet chilli sauce, lamb kofta kebab with chickpea and feta salad and minted yoghurt, potted crab and brown shrimps with harissa, battered whiting, chicken fillet in honey and wholegrain mustard sauce, mexican bean burger with spicy tomato sauce, and fried rump of lamb with sweet potatoes and redcurrant and mint gravy. *Benchmark main dish: shepherd's pie £12.95. Two-course evening meal £18.75.*

Enterprise ~ Lease Liz and David Currie ~ Real ale ~ Bar food (10-12) ~ (01732) 700254 ~ Children welcome in one area of bar ~ Dogs welcome ~ Folk night monthly ~ Open 11-11

Recommended by David and Sue Atkinson, Mrs B Forster, Bob and Margaret Holder, D P and M A Miles, Andrea Rampley, John Branston, Nigel and Jean Eames, Kevin Thomas, Nina Randall

---

'Children welcome' means the pub says it lets children inside without any special restriction. If it allows them in, but to restricted areas such as an eating area or family room, we specify this. Places with separate restaurants often let children use them, and hotels usually let them into public areas such as lounges. Some pubs impose an evening time limit – let us know if you find one earlier than 9pm.

BOVINGDON GREEN Buckinghamshire   SU8386   Map 2

Royal Oak ⚓ ♀

0.75 miles N of Marlow, on back road to Frieth signposted off West Street (A4155) in centre; SL7 2JF

BUCKINGHAMSHIRE DINING PUB OF THE YEAR

Civilised dining pub with nice little bar, excellent choice of wines by the glass, real ales, good service, and excellent food

This is a smashing all-rounder and much enjoyed by our readers. Of course, much emphasis is placed on the delicious food but the friendly and helpful staff will make you just as welcome if you only want a drink – they keep Rebellion IPA, Mutiny and Smuggler on handpump, 21 wines by the glass (all from Europe), nine pudding wines and a good choice of liqueurs. Locals tend to head for the low-beamed cosy snug, closest to the car park, which has three small tables, a woodburning stove in an exposed brick fireplace, and a big pile of logs. Several attractively decorated areas open off the central bar: the half-panelled walls variously painted in pale blue, green or cream (though the dining room ones are red). Throughout, there's a mix of church chairs, stripped wooden tables and chunky wall seats, with rugs on the partly wooden, partly flagstoned floors, co-ordinated cushions and curtains, and a very bright, airy feel; thoughtful extra touches enhance the tone: a bowl of olives on the bar, carefully laid-out newspapers and fresh flowers or candles on the tables. Board games and piped music. A terrace with good solid tables leads to an appealing garden, and there's a smaller side garden; pétanque. Civilised dining pub with nice little bar, excellent choice of wines by the glass, real ales, good service and excellent food.

Beautifully presented and imaginative, the food includes lunchtime sandwiches, much-liked bubble and squeak with smoked bacon, free-range poached egg and hollandaise, oak-smoked salmon, soused shallot and potato salad and caviar and dill dressing, rabbit, pearl barley and mustard pie with carrot hash, filo-baked sweet potato, celeriac and double gloucester dauphinoise with dandelion and fennel salad, and roast and braised baby chicken with chorizo and vegetable minestrone. *Benchmark main dish: coley fillet with ham hock and pea risotto and lemon mascarpone £13.75. Two-course evening meal £20.00.*

Salisbury Pubs ~ Lease James Penlington ~ Real ale ~ Bar food (12-2.30(3 Sat, 4 Sun), 6.30-9.30(10 Fri, Sat)) ~ Restaurant ~ (01628) 488611 ~ Children welcome ~ Dogs allowed in bar ~ Open 11-11; 12-10.30 Sun; closed 25 and 26 Dec

Recommended by Serkan Ibrahim, Chris Smith, Jeff and Wendy Williams, Tracey and Stephen Groves, C and R Bromage, Doug Kennedy, Neil and Karen Dignan, Martin and Karen Wake, Gordon Maddocks, Jonathan Holloway, Neil and Anne McDougall

BRAMLEY Surrey   TQ0044   Map 3

Jolly Farmer ◗

High Street; GU5 0HB

Relaxed village inn near Surrey hills with great selection of beers

The eight handpumps at this family-owned free house serve Hogsback HBB and Sharps Doom Bar alongside half a dozen guests – they can go through up to 20 different ales a week – typically from brewers such as Ballards, Milestone and Vale. They also keep three changing belgian draught beers and a dozen wines by the glass. The traditional interior is filled with a miscellany of homely wooden tables and chairs, with various collections of plates, enamel advertising signs, sewing machines, antique bottles, prints and old tools filling the walls and surfaces. Timbered semi-partitions, a mixture of brick and timbering and an open fireplace give it a snug cosy feel; piped music, TV (which can be loud), dominoes and board games. There are tables out by the car park and the village is handy for Winkworth Arboretum and walks up St Martha's Hill.

As well as lunchtime sandwiches, bar food includes whitebait, smoked haddock fishcakes, ploughman's, home-made burger, fried cod fillet with citrus and saffron butter, pie of the day, with daily specials such as fried calves liver with red wine jus, fried duck breast with port and redcurrant sauce, mushroom risotto, and baked trout with lemon and dill. *Benchmark main dish: fish and chips £10.00. Two-course evening meal £20.50.*

Free house ~ Licensees Steve and Chris Hardstone ~ Real ale ~ Bar food (12-2.30, 6.30(7 Sun)-9.30) ~ Restaurant ~ (01483) 893355 ~ Children welcome ~ Dogs allowed in bar and bedrooms ~ Open 11-11; 12-11 Sun ~ Bedrooms: £60S(£65B)/£70S(£75B)

Recommended by Brian and Anna Marsden, Revd R P Tickle, LM, John Branston

---

BRANSGORE Hampshire   SZ1997   Map 2

Three Tuns

Village signposted off A35 and off B3347 N of Christchurch; Ringwood Road, opposite church; BH23 8JH

Interesting food in pretty thatched pub with proper old-fashioned bar and good beers, as well as a civilised main dining area

In summer, this 17th-c thatched pub with its lovely hanging baskets looks quite charming and there's an attractive, extensive shrub-sheltered terrace with picnic-sets on its brick pavers; beyond are more tables out on the grass looking over pony paddocks. But whatever time of year, you can be sure of a friendly welcome from the cheerful landlord and his staff and there are always plenty of happy customers. The roomy low-ceilinged and carpeted main area has a fireside 'codgers' corner', as well as a good mix of comfortably cushioned low chairs around a variety of dining tables. On the right is a separate traditional regulars' bar that seems almost taller than it is wide, with an impressive log-effect stove in a stripped brick hearth, some shiny black panelling and individualistic pubby furnishings. Ringwood Best and Fortyniner and Timothy Taylors Landlord and guests like Otter Bitter and Sharps Doom Bar on handpump and a good choice of wines by the glass. The pub is on the edge of the New Forest Country Park. The Grade II listed barn is popular for parties.

Using local produce and making everything in-house, the wide choice of popular food includes lunchtime sandwiches, dorset snails in garlic and tarragon butter, foie gras terrine with crab apple jam, truffle risotto, bangers and mash, rabbit pie, and rack of lamb with aubergine moussaka. *Benchmark main dish: bass with asparagus, tomatoes, shaved fennel and a lemon fish sauce £14.95. Two-course evening meal £20.25.*

Enterprise ~ Lease Nigel Glenister ~ Real ale ~ Bar food (12-2.15, 6-9.15; all day weekends) ~ Restaurant ~ (01425) 672232 ~ Children welcome ~ Dogs allowed in bar ~ Open 11(11.30 Sat)-11.30; 12-11 Sun

Recommended by Laurence Smith, Phyl and Jack Street, N R White, Terry and Nickie Williams, Henry Fryer, Caz Brant, Roger Baynes

BRAY Berkshire   SU9079   Map 2

Crown 🍴 🍷

1.75 miles from M4 junction 9; A308 towards Windsor, then left at Bray signpost on to B3028; High Street; SL6 2AH

Low-beamed pub with refurbished, knocked-through rooms, surprisingly pubby food (given the owner), real ales and plenty of outside seating

Now that this 16th-c pub is owned by Heston Blumenthal, many customers are here for the good, surprisingly pubby food. But drinkers drop in, too, and they keep Courage Best and Directors and Sharps Doom Bar on handpump and several wines by the glass. The partly panelled main bar has heavy old beams – some so low you may have to mind your head – plenty of timbers handily left at elbow height where walls have been knocked through, three winter log fires and newly upholstered dining chairs and cushioned settles. There are modern slatted chairs and tables in the courtyard with plenty of picnic-sets in the large, enclosed back garden.

Popular food now includes lunchtime sandwiches, potted duck with grilled bread, moules marinière, macaroni with leeks and chanterelle mushrooms, steak burger with fries, steak in ale suet pie and lemon sole with potted shrimps, cucumber and dill; vegetables are extra which bumps the price up. *Benchmark main dish: hereford sirloin steak with marrowbone sauce £19.50. Two-course evening meal £21.75.*

Scottish Courage ~ Manager Tony Carson ~ Real ale ~ Bar food (12-2.30(3 weekends), 6(7 Sun)-9.30(6.30-10 Fri and Sat)) ~ Restaurant ~ (01628) 621936 ~ Children welcome ~ Dogs welcome ~ Open 11-11; 12-10.30 Sun; closed 25-27 Dec
Recommended by Ron and Sheila Corbett, Hunter and Christine Wright

BRAY Berkshire   SU9079   Map 2

Hinds Head 🍴 🍷

High Street; car park opposite (exit rather tricky); SL6 2AB

BERKSHIRE DINING PUB OF THE YEAR

Top-notch gastropub with excellent food, traditional surroundings and a fine choice of drinks

Under the same ownership as the nearby Crown and the renowned Fat Duck restaurant, this handsome old pub is exceedingly popular for its excellent food. They do keep Rebellion IPA and Smuggler and Windsor & Eton Guardsman on handpump, 14 wines by the glass from an extensive list and quite a few malt whiskies, but there's no doubt that most customers are here to eat. The thoroughly traditional L-shaped bar has dark beams and panelling, polished oak parquet, blazing log fires, red-cushioned built-in wall seats and studded leather carving chairs around small round tables, and latticed windows.

First class, if not cheap, food might include devils on horseback, ham hock and foie gras terrine with piccalilli, venison cheeseburger, chicken, smoked guinea fowl and mushroom pie, fillet of bream with wild garlic and mussel broth and steak with bone marrow sauce. *Benchmark main dish: oxtail and kidney pudding £17.50. Two-course evening meal £25.45.*

Free house ~ Licensee Kevin Love ~ Real ale ~ Bar food (12-2.30, 6.30-9.30; 12-4 Sun; not Sun evening) ~ Restaurant ~ (01628) 626151 ~ Children welcome ~ Dogs allowed in bar ~ Open 11-11; 12-10.30 Sun

 BRIGHTWELL BALDWIN Oxfordshire   SU6594 Map 4

Lord Nelson ⊕ ♀

Off B480 Chalgrove—Watlington, or B4009 Benson—Watlington; OX49 5NP

Attractive inn with several different character bars, real ales, good wines by the glass and enjoyable food; bedrooms

Most customers come to this busy 300-year-old inn to enjoy the interesting food but they do keep Adnams Bitter, Black Sheep Best and Brakspears Bitter on handpump and around 14 wines by the glass. There are wheelback and other dining chairs around a mix of dark tables, candles and fresh flowers, wine bottles on window sills, horsebrasses on standing timbers, lots of paintings on the white or red walls and a big brick inglenook fireplace. One cosy room has cushions on comfortable sofas, little lamps on dark furniture, ornate mirrors and portraits in gilt frames; piped music. There are seats on the back terrace with more in the willow-draped garden and the pub is prettily placed on a quiet lane opposite the church.

As well as sandwiches, the well thought-of food includes coarse pâté with home-made chutney, thai fishcakes with sesame and lime dipping sauce, asparagus, mint and lemon risotto, beer-battered fresh haddock with triple-cooked chips, calves liver with onion rings and red wine sauce, and half a slow-roasted duck with spiced plum sauce. *Benchmark main dish: local free-range pork sausages with onion gravy £12.95. Two-course evening meal £21.20.*

Free house ~ Licensees Roger and Carole Shippey ~ Real ale ~ Bar food (12-2.30, 6-10) ~ Restaurant ~ (01491) 612497 ~ Children welcome ~ Dogs allowed in bar ~ Open 12-3, 6-11; 12-10.30 Sun ~ Bedrooms: £70B/£90B

Recommended by Hugh Roberts, Neil and Karen Dignan, D and M T Ayres-Regan, Roy Hoing

BROOKLAND Kent   TQ9825 Map 3

Royal Oak ⊕ ⇌

Just off A259 Rye—New Romney; High Street; TN29 9QR

Lovely old building with gently modernised rooms, comfortable atmosphere, delicious food, and seats in garden; bedrooms

Such are the sensitive alterations at this welcoming 17th-c inn on Romney Marsh that it retains an attractive timeless feel. The bar is light and airy with big windows, one nice old pew and leather upholstered chairs around oak tables on flagstones, oak boards and bricks. Locals pop in to sit on the high bar chairs by the granite-topped counter for a chat and a pint: Adnams Best, Harveys and Woodfordes Wherry on handpump, 17 wines by the glass. The friendly landlord knows a lot about the local area and his equestrian interests are manifest in a lovely set of racing watercolours and a couple of signed photographs on the lime white wall panelling in the bar and in a rather special set of Cecil Aldin prints displayed in the beamed restaurant (with its well spaced tables and big inglenook fireplace). French windows from here open on to a terrace with metal chairs and there are picnic-sets in the narrow garden beyond and quaint views of the ancient church and graveyard next door; piped music and a woodburning stove.

the Beautiful South

¶¶ Lovingly sourced and prepared food includes filled baps, ploughman's, chargrilled beefburger, fish and chips, and specials such as seared wood pigeon breasts with rhubarb compote, grilled mackerel with chilli jam glaze and wild garlic mash, chicken breast wrapped in air-dried ham and stuffed with mozzarella and basil and roast pork chop with crumbled black pudding and celeriac and apple mash; they do spit roasts in the inglenook on Wednesday evenings. *Benchmark main dish: grilled rump of lamb £15.95. Two-course evening meal £20.00.*

Enterprise ~ Lease David Rhys Jones ~ Real ale ~ Bar food (12-2(2.30 Fri-Sun), 6.30-9) ~ Restaurant ~ (01797) 344215 ~ No children under 12 in evening restaurant ~ Dogs allowed in bar ~ Open 12-3, 6-11; closed Sun and Mon evenings ~ Bedrooms: /£75(£95B)

Recommended by Sue Fincham, Colin and Louise English, Sara Fulton, Roger Baker, V Brogden, B and M Kendall, John Peppitt, Kevin Thomas, Nina Randall

BROOKLAND Kent
TQ9724   Map 3

THE GOOD PUB GUIDE

Woolpack £

On A259 from Rye, about 1 mile before Brookland, take the first right turn signposted Midley where the main road bends sharp left, just after the expanse of Walland Marsh; OS Sheet 189 map reference 977244; TN29 9TJ

15th-c pub with simple furnishings, massive inglenook fireplace, big helpings of tasty food and large garden

Steeped in the atmosphere of days gone by, this crooked early 15th-c cottage is said to have been the haunt of local smugglers. Its ancient entrance lobby has an uneven brick floor and black-painted pine-panelled walls, and to the right, the simple quarry-tiled main bar has basic cushioned plank seats in the massive inglenook fireplace and a painted wood-effect bar counter hung with lots of water jugs. Low-beamed ceilings include some very early ships' timbers (maybe 12th c) thought to be from local shipwrecks. A long elm table has shove-ha'penny carved into one end and there are other old and newer wall benches, chairs at mixed tables with flowers and candles and photographs of locals on the walls. The two pub cats, Liquorice and Charlie Girl, are often toasting themselves around the log fire. To the left of the lobby is a sparsely furnished little room and an open-plan family room; piped music. Shepherd Neame Master Brew, Spitfire and two seasonal brews on handpump. In summer, the award-winning hanging baskets are really quite a sight and there are plenty of picnic-sets under parasols in the garden with its barbecue area; it's all nicely lit up in the evenings.

¶¶ Reasonably priced, the pubby food includes sandwiches and baguettes, filled baked potatoes, ploughman's, soup, steak pie, stilton and vegetable bake, battered cod, generous moules marinière and mixed grill. *Benchmark main dish: mixed grill £13.95. Two-course evening meal £15.45.*

Shepherd Neame ~ Tenant Scott Balcomb ~ Real ale ~ Bar food (12-2.30, 7-9; all day Sat, Sun) ~ Restaurant ~ (01797) 344321 ~ Children in family room ~ Dogs welcome ~ Open 11-3, 6-11; 12-11 Sat, Sun

Recommended by Colin and Louise English, John Prescott, Mr and Mrs Price

---

Please tell us if the décor, atmosphere, food or drink at a pub is different from our description. We rely on readers' reports to keep us up to date: **feedback@goodguides.com**, or (no stamp needed) The Good Pub Guide, FREEPOST TN1569, Wadhurst, E Sussex TN5 7BR.

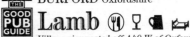

BURFORD Oxfordshire   SP2412   Map 4

Lamb 🍴 ♀ 🍺 🛏

Village signposted off A40 W of Oxford; Sheep Street (B4425, off A361);
OX18 4LR

**Proper pubby bar in civilised inn, real ales and an extensive wine list,
interesting bar and restaurant food, and pretty gardens; bedrooms**

This is a lovely 15th-c inn, very much enjoyed by our readers for its
civilised but friendly and relaxed atmosphere and its genuine mix of
customers – hotel guests, diners and chatty locals. The cosy bar remains
the heart of the place with high-backed settles and old chairs on
flagstones in front of the log fire, Hook Norton Bitter and Old Hooky on
handpump and an extensive wine list with 16 by the glass; board games.
The roomy beamed main lounge is charmingly traditional, with
distinguished old seats including a chintzy high-winged settle, ancient
cushioned wooden armchairs, seats built into its stone-mullioned
windows and fresh flowers on polished oak and elm tables; also, rugs on
the wide flagstones and polished oak floorboards, a winter log fire under
its fine mantelpiece and plenty of antiques and other decorations
including a grandfather clock. Service is impeccable. A pretty terrace
with teak furniture leads down to small neatly kept lawns surrounded by
flowers, shrubs and small trees, and the garden itself is a real suntrap,
enclosed as it is by the warm stone of the surrounding buildings.

Under the new licensee, the good, often interesting food might include open
sandwiches, sharing deli boards (charcuterie, fish or antipasti), crayfish and
chive risotto, lamb burger with mint sauce and chips, confit duck leg with plum
chutney, braised pig's trotter with ham and morels with potato truffle purée and
apple and black pudding salad, and salmon and scallops with aubergine caviar,
sundried tomato purée and pesto dressing; they offer a two- and three-course set
evening menu. *Benchmark main dish: lamb burger with home-made mint sauce
£12.50. Two-course evening meal £20.45.*

Cotswold Inns & Hotels ~ Manager Bill Ramsay ~ Real ale ~ Bar food (12-2.30(3 Sun),
6.30-9.30) ~ Restaurant ~ (01993) 823155 ~ Children welcome ~ Dogs welcome ~ Open
12-11(midnight weekends) ~ Bedrooms: £120B/£155B
*Recommended by MDN, David and Sue Smith, the Didler, Eithne Dandy, Michael Dandy,
Peter Dandy, Graham Oddey, Malcolm Greening, George Atkinson, David Glynne-Jones,
Simon Collett-Jones*

CAULCOTT Oxfordshire   SP5024   Map 4

Horse & Groom 🍺

Lower Heyford Road (B4030); OX25 4ND

**Bustling and friendly with an obliging licensee, enjoyable bar food, and
changing beers**

The attentive french chef/patron of this thatched 16th-c cottage keeps
everything running smoothly and with genuine friendliness. It's not a
huge place: an L-shaped red-carpeted room angles around the servery,
with plush-cushioned settles, chairs and stools around a few dark tables at
the low-ceilinged bar end and a blazing fire in the big inglenook, with
brassware under its long bressumer beam; shove-ha'penny and board
games. The far end, up a shallow step, is set for dining with lots of
decorative jugs hanging on black joists, some decorative plates and
attractive watercolours and original drawings. Hook Norton Hooky Bitter

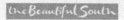

and three changing guests such as Sharps Special, Slaters Why Knot and White Horse Epona on handpump and decent house wines. There's a small side sun lounge and picnic-sets under cocktail parasols on a neat lawn.

As well as ten different types of speciality sausages, the lunchtime bar food includes filled baguettes, croque monsieur, ham and egg, and home-made burgers with bacon and cheese, with evening choices like pâté with baby onion chutney, fresh pasta with goats cheese, asparagus, artichokes and roasted peppers and olives, steak and mushroom pie, and a proper paella. *Benchmark main dish: moules marinière £12.50. Two-course evening meal £20.00.*

Free house ~ Licensee Jerome Prigent ~ Real ale ~ Bar food (not Sun evening or Mon) ~ Restaurant ~ (01869) 343257 ~ Children must be over 7 and well behaved ~ Open 12-3, 6-11; 12-3, 7-10.30 Sun
Recommended by Jane Hudson, Roger and Anne Newbury, Ian Herdman, David Lamb

CHARLTON Sussex   SU8812   Map 2

Fox Goes Free

Village signposted off A286 Chichester—Midhurst in Singleton, also from Chichester—Petworth via East Dean; PO18 0HU

Comfortable old pub with beamed bars, popular food and drink, and big garden; bedrooms

Handy for the Weald and Downland Open Air Museum, West Dean Gardens and Goodwood, this bustling pub is also usefully open all day. The bar is the first of the dark and cosy series of separate rooms: old irish settles, tables and chapel chairs and an open fire. Standing timbers divide a larger beamed bar which has a huge brick fireplace with a woodburning stove and old local photographs on the walls. A dining area with hunting prints looks over the garden. The family extension is a clever conversion from horse boxes and the stables where the 1926 Goodwood winner was housed; darts, games machine and piped music. Ballards Best, a beer named for the pub brewed by Arundel and a guest such as Harveys Best or Sharps Doom Bar on handpump and several wines by the glass. You can sit at one of the picnic-sets under the apple trees in the attractive back garden with the downs as a backdrop and there are rustic benches and tables on the gravelled front terrace, too. There are good surrounding walks including one up to the prehistoric earthworks on the Trundle.

Bar food includes lunchtime filled baguettes (not Sunday), whole roast camembert with toasted fingers, roasted garlic and quince jelly, wild mushroom risotto, honey-roast ham and egg, salmon fillet with pea purée and tomato coulis, a pie of the day, and crispy confit duck leg with hoisin jus. *Benchmark main dish: steak and kidney pie £10.95. Two-course evening meal £22.00.*

Free house ~ Licensee David Coxon ~ Real ale ~ Bar food (12-2.30, 6.30-9.30; all day weekends) ~ Restaurant ~ (01243) 811461 ~ Children welcome ~ Dogs allowed in bar ~ Live music Weds evenings ~ Open 11-11(11.30 Sat); 12-10.30 Sun ~ Bedrooms: £65S/£90S
Recommended by Nick Lawless, Bernard Stradling, Helen and Brian Edgeley, Miss A E Dare

Stars after the name of a pub show exceptional character and appeal. They don't mean extra comfort. And they are nothing to do with food quality, for which there's a separate knife-and-fork symbol. Even quite a basic pub can win stars, if it's individual enough.

CHENIES Buckinghamshire   TQ0298   Map 3

Red Lion ★

2 miles from M25 junction 18; A404 towards Amersham, then village signposted on right; Chesham Road; WD3 6ED

Delightful pub with long-serving licensees, a bustling atmosphere, real ales, and good food

Extremely popular locally – always a good sign – but with a genuine welcome for visitors too, this white-painted brick pub has now been run by the same friendly licensees for 25 years. The L-shaped bar is very traditional and unpretentious (no games machines or piped music) and has comfortable built-in wall benches by the front windows, other straightforward seats and tables, and original photographs of the village and traction engines. There's also a small back snug and a neat dining extension with more modern décor. Well kept Lion Pride is brewed for the pub by Rebellion and served on handpump alongside Vale Best Bitter and a changing guest and Wadworths 6X, and they have up to ten wines by the glass and some nice malt whiskies. The hanging baskets and window boxes are pretty in summer, there are picnic-sets on a small side terrace, and good local walks. No children.

A good range of well liked bar food includes sandwiches, field mushrooms with garlic, mint and chilli, home-made pâté, pasta with sunblush tomatoes, feta, olives and parmesan, their famous pies (lamb is the favourite), mixed seafood in a creamy white sauce with a crumble topping, a changing curry, and lamb with a red wine and rosemary gravy. *Benchmark main dish: lamb pie £11.00. Two-course evening meal £16.60.*

Free house ~ Licensee Mike Norris ~ Real ale ~ Bar food (12-2,7-10; 12-8 Sun) ~ Restaurant ~ (01923) 282722 ~ Dogs allowed in bar ~ Open 11-2.30, 5.30-11; 12-10.30 Sun

Recommended by Roy Hoing, J V Dadswell, John and Victoria Fairley, LM, William Ruxton, Ian Phillips, Peter and Giff Bennett, N J Roberts, Val and Alan Green

CHIPPING NORTON Oxfordshire   SP3127   Map 4

Chequers ★ ♀

Goddards Lane; OX7 5NP

Busy, friendly town pub open all day with several real ales, popular bar food, a cheerful mix of customers and simple bars

Much enjoyed for its efficiently served pre-theatre suppers (the theatre is next door) and for its six well kept real ales, this tucked-away pub has a cheerful and relaxed atmosphere. There's a mix of both locals and visitors and the three softly lit beamed rooms have no frills, but are clean and comfortable with low ochre ceilings, lots of character, and a blazing log fire. Quick staff serve Fullers Chiswick, London Pride, ESB and two guest beers on handpump, and they have good house wines – 15 by the glass. The conservatory restaurant is light and airy and used for more formal dining.

Popular bar food includes sandwiches, pork and rabbit terrine with pear and star anise chutney, chicken caesar salad, local sausages of the day with onion gravy, honey and cider roast gammon and eggs, pumpkin, sundried tomato and olive risotto, and chicken breast in a mushroom and white wine velouté. *Benchmark main dish: home-made pies £9.95. Two-course evening meal £15.45.*

the Beautiful South

Fullers ~ Lease Jim Hopcroft ~ Real ale ~ Bar food (12-2.30, 6-9.30; 12-4 Sun; not Sun evening) ~ Restaurant ~ (01608) 644717 ~ Children welcome ~ Dogs allowed in bar ~ Live music monthly and Sun evening quiz ~ Open 11(11.30 Sun)-11(midnight Sat)

Recommended by Stuart Turner, Derek and Sylvia Stephenson, Chris Glasson, MP, Barry Collett, the Didler, Steve Whalley, Richard Tilbrook

COLESHILL Buckinghamshire   SU9594 Map 4

Harte & Magpies

E of village on A355 Amersham—Beaconsfield, by junction with Magpie Lane; HP7 0LU

Friendly, professionally run roadside dining pub with enjoyable food all day, well kept local ales, and seats in big garden

Just the place to end a walk across the Chiltern Hills, this is well run and enjoyable for both a drink or a meal. It's big and open-plan but its rambling collection of miscellaneous pews, high-backed booths and some quite distinctive tables and chairs and cosy boltholes over to the right give it a pleasantly snug feel. There's a profusion of vigorously patriotic antique prints, candles in bottles and Scrumpy Jack the self-possessed young labrador who adds a relaxed country touch – as does the jar of dog treats. Brakspears Bitter, Chiltern Ale and Rebellion Smuggler on handpump and a good choice of other drinks, too; service is friendly and civilised. Outside, a terrace has picnic-sets by a tree picturesquely draped with wisteria and a big sloping informal garden has more trees and more tables on wood chippings.

As well as filled baguettes and an all-day breakfast, the tasty food includes pork terrine with red onion marmalade, gammon and eggs, shepherd's pie, vegetable risotto, rare-breed burger and chips, and steak and kidney pudding. *Benchmark main dish: fish and chips £12.50. Two-course evening meal £16.50.*

Free house ~ Licensee Stephen Lever ~ Real ale ~ Bar food (10-9.45; 12-8 Sun) ~ (01494) 726754 ~ Children welcome ~ Dogs welcome ~ Live music Sat evening ~ Open 10am-11pm; 11-10 Sun

Recommended by Tracey and Stephen Groves, Mrs Ann Gray, Phil Harrison

CRANLEIGH Surrey   TQ0539 Map 3

Richard Onslow

High Street; GU6 8AU

Well run pub with a good mix of customers in several bar rooms, friendly, efficient staff, real ales, and interesting all-day food

As this pub is right in the middle of a large village and usefully open all day for breakfast (from 9am), morning coffee, lunch and afternoon tea, it's always packed with a wide mix of customers. There's a busy little public bar with stools by the counter, leather tub chairs and a built-in sofa and a slate-floored drinking area where efficient and friendly staff serve Surrey Hills Shere Drop, Wells & Youngs Bombardier and a guest like Dark Star Hophead on handpump, several wines by the glass from a shortish list and home-made summer lemonade and fresh lime soda. Two dining rooms off here have a mix of tartan tub chairs around wooden tables, a rather fine long leather-cushioned church pew, local photographs on mainly pale paintwork and a couple of open fires – one in a nice brick fireplace. The sizeable restaurant, with pale tables and chairs on the wooden floor and modern flowery wallpaper, has big windows overlooking the street; piped music and board games. There are a few tables and chairs on the front pavement. By the time this edition is published, they will have opened eight bedrooms and created some parking space – nearby parking is currently restricted.

A wide choice of interesting food using free-range meat might include sandwiches, chicken and spring onion terrine with apple chutney, deli or veggie boards, leek, pea and dill pancake with gruyère sauce, sausages with onion gravy, fishcakes with lemon butter sauce, chicken with crispy parma ham and roast garlic and basil tagliatelle, and pork tenderloin with potato and beetroot salad. *Benchmark main dish: sustainable yellowfin tuna, cucumber, mooli and edamame bean with soy and sesame dressing £14.50. Two-course evening meal £18.50.*

Peach Pub Company ~ Licensee John Taylor ~ Real ale ~ Bar food (all day from 9am) ~ Restaurant ~ (01483) 274922 ~ Children welcome ~ Dogs allowed in bar ~ Open 9-11
Recommended by Phil Bryant

DANEHILL Sussex   TQ4128   Map 3

Coach & Horses ⊕ ♀

Off A275, via School Lane towards Chelwood Common; RH17 7JF

Country dining pub with bustling bars, welcoming staff, enjoyable food and ales, and a big garden

You can be sure of a warm welcome from the friendly staff in this cottagey dining pub. There's a little bar to the right with half-panelled walls, simple furniture on polished floorboards, a small woodburner in the brick fireplace and a big hatch to the bar counter: Harveys Best, Kings Horsham Best and a guest from Hepworth or Hammerpot on handpump and several wines by the glass including prosecco and champagne. A couple of steps lead down to a half-panelled area with a mix of dining chairs around characterful wooden tables (set with flowers and candles) on the fine brick floor and some large Victorian prints. Down another step to a dining area with stone walls, beams, flagstones and a woodburning stove. There's an adult-only terrace under a huge maple tree and picnic-sets and a children's play area in the big garden which has fine views of the South Downs.

Using local meat and game, the interesting food includes sandwiches, welsh rarebit, guinea fowl gateau with redcurrant glaze, courgette croquettes with roasted onion aioli and rocket and courgette frites, beer-battered fish, duck breast with roast cherries and balsamic jus, and soy and honey-glazed salmon fillet with pickled mooli. *Benchmark main dish: crisp pork belly with bramley boulangère £13.75. Two-course evening meal £21.00.*

Free house ~ Licensee Ian Philpots ~ Real ale ~ Bar food (12-2(2.30 Sat, 3 Sun), 7-9(9.30 Sat); not Sun evening) ~ Restaurant ~ (01825) 740369 ~ Well behaved children welcome but not on adult terrace ~ Dogs allowed in bar ~ Open 12-3, 6-11.30; 12-11.30(10.30 Sun) Sat
Recommended by Mr and Mrs R A Bradbrook, Rebecca Gould, Peter Gartrell

We mention bottled beers and spirits only if there is something unusual about them – imported belgian real ales, say, or dozens of malt whiskies; so do please let us know about them in your reports.

 DENHAM Buckinghamshire   TQ0487 Map 3

 Swan (♥♦) ♀

Village signed from M25 junction 16; UB9 5BH

Handsome and civilised dining pub in pretty village; stylish furnishings in several bars, open fires, interesting food, and fine choice of drinks

Handsome, Georgian pub in a pretty village and particularly popular for its fresh, interesting bar food. The rooms are stylishly furnished with a nice mix of antique and old-fashioned chairs and solid tables, individually chosen pictures on the cream and warm green walls, rich heavily draped curtains, inviting open fires, newspapers to read and fresh flowers. Courage Best, Rebellion IPA, and Wadworths 6X on handpump, 21 european wines by the glass, plus nine pudding wines and a good choice of liqueurs; piped music. The extensive garden is floodlit at night, and leads from a sheltered terrace with tables to a more spacious lawn; the wisteria is lovely in May. It can get busy at weekends and parking may be not be easy then.

🍴 Impressive bar food using seasonal produce includes rabbit rillettes with home-baked rosemary focaccia, duck livers and hearts with crispy bacon and dandelion and gooseberry salad, beer-battered haddock, free-range chicken tagine with fig couscous and toasted almonds, and gurnard fillet with flageolet bean, chorizo and roast tomato cassoulet. *Benchmark main dish: pork loin chop with braised baby gem and cider cream sauce £14.75. Two-course evening meal £20.00.*

Salisbury Pubs ~ Lease Mark Littlewood ~ Real ale ~ Bar food (12-2.30(3 Sat, 4 Sun), 6.30-9.30(10 Fri and Sat)) ~ Restaurant ~ (01895) 832085 ~ Children welcome ~ Dogs allowed in bar ~ Open 11-11; 12-10.30 Sun; closed 25 and 26 Dec

Recommended by Brian Glozier

 DIAL POST Sussex   TQ1519 Map 3

Crown

Worthing Road (off A24 S of Horsham); RH13 8NH

Extended village pub with good food, real ales and plenty of space in the bar and two dining rooms; bedrooms

It's the interesting food cooked by the landlord that draws in most customers here – though the bar is a friendly and relaxing place if you just want a drink and a chat. It's a beamed room with a couple of standing timbers, brown squashy sofas and pine tables and chairs on the stone floor, a small woodburning stove in the brick fireplace, and Dark Star Best and Harveys Best and a Harveys guest beer on handpump from the attractive herringbone brick counter. The pub dog is called Chops. The straightforwardly furnished dining conservatory, facing the village green, is light and airy; board games and shove-ha'penny. To the right of the bar, the restaurant (with more beams) has an ornamental woodburner in a brick fireplace, a few photographs on the walls, chunky pine tables, chairs and a couple of cushioned pews on the patterned carpet, and a shelf of books; steps lead down to a further dining room. The bedrooms are in the converted stables and there are picnic-sets on grass behind the pub.

🍴 Using carefully sourced produce, the highly thought-of food might include sandwiches, potted brown shrimps and crayfish with rosemary crostini, beer-battered fish and chips, home-made steak burger with spicy relish and coleslaw, a changing pie and salmon fillet on roasted mediterranean vegetables with pesto;

there's also an early bird menu. *Benchmark main dish: crispy local pork belly £15.00. Two-course evening meal £21.00.*

Free house ~ Licensees James and Penny Middleton-Burn ~ Real ale ~ Bar food (12-2(2.30 Sun), 6-9(9.30 Fri and Sat); not Sun evening) ~ Restaurant ~ (01403) 710902 ~ Children welcome but must be dining after 7pm ~ Dogs welcome ~ Open 11.30-3, 6(5.30 Fri)-11; 12-4 Sun; closed Sun evening ~ Bedrooms: £50S/£60S

Recommended by David and Sharon Collison

DROXFORD Hampshire

SU6118   Map 2

Hurdles ⑪ ⏛

Brockbridge, just outside Soberton; from A32 just N of Droxford take B2150 towards Denmead; SO32 3QT

Roomy smartly updated country dining pub, food interesting and good value

Surprisingly grand for such a tucked-away country pub, this handsome brick building is a reminder that the Meon Valley has long had quite a touch of class. It's been brought very suitably up to date inside, from the dark grey leather chesterfield and armchairs by the log fire in one room with elegant columnar lamps in its big windows, to the dining areas on the right, with their stylish figured wallpaper, toning stripy chairs around shiny modern tables, and glittering mirrors. There are high ceilings and stripped boards throughout. Service by attentive young staff is prompt, and they have decent wines by the glass, good coffee, and Bowmans Wallops Wood and a guest beer such as Otter on handpump; unobtrusive piped pop music. It's a peaceful spot, with wood and metal tables on neat terraces (one covered and heated), and a long flight of steps up to picnic-sets on a sloping lawn by tall trees.

Good interesting food includes filled baguettes, potted crab pâté with orange, basil and red onion, burger with smoked applewood cheese, beetroot and horseradish chutney, hake fillet wrapped in parma ham with basil, sunblush tomato and mozzarella risotto, burger with smoked applewood cheese, beetroot and horseradish chutney, chicken breast with wild mushroom and pancetta tagliatelle carbonara, and lamb rump with mint pea purée, honey carrots and red wine jus; they also offer a two- and three-course set menu (Mon-Fri lunchtimes and Mon-Thurs evenings 6-7pm) and cream teas. *Benchmark main dish: hake fillet wrapped in parma ham and basil with a sunblush tomato and mozzarella risotto £14.95. Two-course evening meal £19.45.*

Enterprise ~ Lease Gareth and Sarah Cole ~ Real ale ~ Bar food (12-3, 6-9.30; 12-8 Sun) ~ Restaurant ~ (01489) 877451 ~ Children welcome ~ Dogs allowed in bar ~ Open 11-11; 12-10.30 Sun

Recommended by Phyl and Jack Street, Roger and Anne Mallard, Susan Robinson

DUNCTON Sussex

SU9517   Map 3

Cricketers

Set back from A285; GU28 0LB

Charming old coaching inn with friendly licensees, real ales, popular food, and suntrap back garden

Doing particularly well under its present licensees, this is a pretty 16th-c coaching inn close to Goodwood. The friendly, traditional bar has a few standing timbers, simple seating, cricketing memorabilia and an open woodburning stove in the inglenook fireplace. Steps lead down to the dining room with wooden tables and chairs. Dark Star Hophead, King Horsham Best Bitter and Skinners Betty Stogs on handpump, several wines by the glass and Thatcher's cider. There are some picnic-sets out in front beneath the flowering window boxes and more on decked areas and under parasols on the grass in the back garden.

Enjoyable food includes lunchtime sandwiches, crab, prawn and leek gratin, cheese risotto topped with a poached egg, toad in the hole with onion gravy, a pie of the day, beer-battered fresh haddock, steak and kidney pudding, and chicken stuffed with brie and wrapped in pancetta. *Benchmark main dish: steak and mushroom in ale pie £10.95. Two-course evening meal £17.20.*

Inn Company ~ Lease Martin Boult ~ Real ale ~ Bar food (12-2.30, 6-9 (some hot snacks in afternoon); 12-9 weekends) ~ Restaurant ~ (01798) 342473 ~ Children welcome ~ Dogs welcome ~ Open 11-11; 12-10.30 Sun
Recommended by Bruce Bird, Derek and Maggie Washington

EASINGTON Buckinghamshire   SP6810 Map 4

Mole & Chicken

From B4011 in Long Crendon follow Chearsley, Waddesdon signpost into Carters Lane opposite indian restaurant, then turn left into Chilton Road; HP18 9EY

Country views from decking and garden, an inviting interior, real ales, and much emphasis on restauranty food; nice bedrooms

This is a lovely place to stay in cosy and comfortable bedrooms and the breakfasts are good, too. It's very much a dining pub with upmarket food and prices to match but they do still keep Hook Norton Bitter and Vale Best Bitter on handpump, lots of wines by the glass and quite a few malt whiskies. The opened-up interior is arranged so that its different parts seem quite snug and self-contained without being cut off from the relaxed sociable atmosphere. The beamed bar curves around the serving counter in a sort of S-shape, and there are cream-cushioned chairs and high-backed leather dining chairs at oak and pine tables on flagstones or tiles, a couple of dark leather sofas, and fabric swatches stylishly hung as decorations on creamy walls, lit candles and good winter log fires; piped music. The attractive raised terrace, with views over fine rolling countryside, is a lovely place for a summer's lunch or sunset drink.

As well as lunchtime sandwiches, ham and free-range eggs and pork and leek sausages, there's a good value two- or three-course set menu as well as chilli fried squid with garlic and lemon, liver, maple-cured bacon, kidneys, grilled onions and mash, gnocchi with butternut squash, feta, pine nuts and balsamic, and lamb shank with bubble and squeak. *Benchmark main dish: duck salad with thai herbs and cashew nuts £9.50. Two-course evening meal £22.00.*

Free house ~ Licensees Alan Heather and Steve Bush ~ Real ale ~ Bar food ~ (01844) 208387 ~ Children welcome ~ Dogs allowed in bar ~ Occasional jazz evenings ~ Open 12-2.30(4 Sun), 6-9.30(9 Sun) ~ Bedrooms: £70B/£95B
Recommended by Richard and Sissel Harris, John Wheeler, David and Lexi Young, Di and Mike Gillam, Karen Eliot

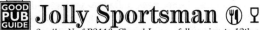

EAST CHILTINGTON Sussex   TQ3715 Map 3

Jolly Sportsman 🍴 🍷

2 miles N of B2116; Chapel Lane – follow sign to 13th-c church; BN7 3BA

SUSSEX DINING PUB OF THE YEAR

Excellent modern food in civilised, rather smart place, small bar for drinkers, contemporary furnishings, fine wine list, and huge range of malt whiskies; nice garden

Extremely well run and a favourite with many of our readers, this is a civilised dining pub with first-class food. The bar may be small but it's full of character and has a roaring winter fire, a mix of furniture on the stripped wood floors and Dark Star Hophead and Harveys Best tapped from the cask. They also have a remarkably good wine list with around a dozen by the glass, over 100 malt whiskies, an extensive list of cognacs, armagnacs and grappa and quite a choice of bottled belgian beers; well trained, charming staff. The larger restaurant is smart but informal with contemporary light wood furniture and modern landscapes on coffee-coloured walls; there's also a new garden room. The cottagey front garden is pretty with rustic tables and benches under gnarled trees, on the terrace and on the front bricked area, and there are more on a large back lawn, a children's play area and views towards the downs; good walks and cycle rides nearby.

As well as good value two- and three-course set menus, the exceptional food might include lunchtime sandwiches, venison carpaccio with horseradish aioli and pickled onion, pike and trout terrine with prawn sauce, chicken breast with chorizo, chickpea and vegetable ragu, beef cheek bourguignon, sea bream fillet with coriander rice, pak choi and black bean salsa, and 28-day-aged rib-eye steak with béarnaise sauce. *Benchmark main dish: rump of local lamb with minted peas and beans £16.85. Two-course evening meal £22.50.*

Free house ~ Licensee Bruce Wass ~ Real ale ~ Bar food (12-2.30(3.30 Sun), 6.30-10) ~ Restaurant ~ (01273) 890400 ~ Children welcome ~ Dogs allowed in bar ~ Open 12-11(10.30 Sun); 12-3, 6-11 weekdays in winter; closed winter Sun evening

Recommended by Susan and John Douglas, Nick Lawless, John Redfern, Terry and Nickie Williams, David Sizer, Laurence Smith, Kelvin Meade, N R White

EAST DEAN Sussex   TV5597 Map 3

Tiger 🍷 🛏

Off A259 Eastbourne—Seaford; BN20 0DA

Charming old pub by cottage-lined village green, two little bars and a dining room, and an informal and friendly atmosphere; bedrooms

This is a lovely pub and as popular with drinkers as it is with diners so the atmosphere is always chatty and relaxed. The focal point of the little beamed main bar is the open woodburning stove in its brick inglenook surrounded by polished horsebrasses, and there are just a few rustic tables with benches, simple wooden chairs, a window seat and a long cushioned wall bench. The walls are hung with fish prints and a stuffed tiger's head, there are a couple of hunting horns above the long bar counter, Harveys Best and Old and their own-brewed Beachy Head Legless Rambler and Original on handpump and several wines by the glass. Down a step on the right is a second small room with an exceptionally fine high-backed curved settle and a couple of other old

the Beautiful South

settles, nice old chairs and wooden tables on the coir carpeting, and an ancient map of Eastbourne and Beachy Head and photographs of the pub on the walls. The dining room to the left of the main bar has a cream woodburner and hunting prints. With such a premium on space, it does pay to get here early if you want a seat. There are picnic-sets on the terrace among the window boxes and flowering climbers or you can sit on the delightful cottage-lined village green. The South Downs Way is close by so the pub is naturally popular with walkers, and the lane leads on down to a fine stretch of coast culminating in Beachy Head. The bedrooms are comfortable and the breakfasts good.

As well as lunchtime sandwiches, the much-liked food includes a meat, seafood or cheese platter, chicken or king prawn caesar salad, braised lamb shoulder with fennel and spring onion and a chilli, ginger and anise jus, salmon fillet on minted pea and spinach risotto with a yellow pepper and lemon coulis, and slow-roast pork belly with bubble and squeak and a mustard, cream and bramley apple dressing. *Benchmark main dish: home-made burger with bacon and cheese £8.95. Two-course evening meal £17.45.*

Free house ~ Licensee Jo Staveley ~ Real ale ~ Bar food (12-3, 6-9) ~ (01323) 423209 ~ Children welcome ~ Dogs allowed in bar ~ Open 11-11(10.30 Sun) ~ Bedrooms: /£95S
Recommended by Kevin Thorpe, B and M Kendall

EAST GARSTON Berkshire — SU3676 Map 2

Queens Arms ♀ 🛏

3.5 miles from M4 junction 14; A338 and village signposted Gt Shefford; RG17 7ET

Smart but chatty dining pub with good food and friendly country bar

Right at the heart of racehorse-training country, this busy pub is especially popular locally and much of the chat will be to do with horse racing. The roomy opened-up bar has plenty of antique prints (many featuring jockeys), daily papers on a corner table (the most prominent being the *Racing Post*), wheelbacks and other dining chairs around well spaced tables on the wooden floor, Wadworths IPA and 6X and a changing local guest on handpump, several wines by the glass and a fair choice of whiskies. Friendly staff, piped music and live horse-racing on TV. Opening off on the right is a lighter dining area with bigger horse and country prints and a pleasing mix of furniture. There are seats on a sheltered terrace. The bedrooms are attractive, the breakfasts tasty and they can arrange fly fishing and shooting; plenty of surrounding downland walks.

Using seasonal local produce, the enjoyable food might include lunchtime sandwiches, pigeon breast with bacon, black pudding and lentils, goats cheese and roast beetroot salad with pine nuts, croutons and balsamic, bass fillet with creamed black cabbage and caper jus, and rare roast loin of venison with red wine jus. *Benchmark main dish: bass fillet with chorizo £14.50. Two-course evening meal £21.00.*

Free house ~ Licensee Adam Liddiard ~ Real ale ~ Bar food (12-2.30(3 Sun), 6.30-9.30(7-9 Sun)) ~ Restaurant ~ (01488) 648757 ~ Children welcome ~ Dogs welcome ~ Open 11-11(10.30 Sun) ~ Bedrooms: /£90S
Recommended by Phyl and Jack Street

There are report forms at the back of the book.

EAST HENDRED Oxfordshire — SU4588 Map 2

Eyston Arms ♨

Village signposted off A417 E of Wantage; High Street; OX12 8JY

Attractive bar areas with low beams, flagstones, log fires and candles, imaginative food, and helpful service

Always busy and welcoming, this is a well run and pleasant dining pub – although locals do pop in for a drink and a chat. There are several separate-seeming areas with contemporary paintwork and modern country-style furnishings: low ceilings and beams, stripped timbers, the odd standing timber, an inglenook fireplace, nice tables and chairs on the flagstones and carpet, some cushioned wall seats, candlelight and a piano; piped music. Cheerful staff serve Fullers London Pride and Wadworths 6X on handpump and several wines by the glass. Picnic-sets outside overlook the pretty lane and there are seats in the back courtyard garden.

As well as lunchtime sandwiches, the imaginative food includes bruschetta of foie gras, madeira, wild mushrooms and shallots, meat or fish antipasti, trio of local hog (loin, belly and black pudding) with apple mash and cider jus, broad bean, pea and mint risotto, tandoori lamb with shredded mango and cucumber and a yoghurt and lime dressing, and corn-fed chicken with sage and lemon butter and butternut squash. *Benchmark main dish: seafood linguine £16.50. Two-course evening meal £22.20.*

Free house ~ Licensees George Dailey and Daisy Barton ~ Real ale ~ Bar food (not Sun evening) ~ Restaurant ~ (01235) 833320 ~ Children welcome but must be well behaved ~ Dogs allowed in bar ~ Open 11-3, 6-11; 11-7 Sun; closed Sun evening

Recommended by Robert Lorimer, William Goodhart, Jane Hudson, Barry Jackson, Bob and Margaret Holder

EAST STRATTON Hampshire — SU5339 Map 2

Northbrook Arms

Brown sign to pub off A33 4 miles S of A303 junction; SO21 3DU

Easy-going camaraderie in nicely placed village pub; good all round

Just as welcoming if you want a meal or a chatty drink, this is a pleasantly unassuming pub with polite, hard-working staff. There's a relaxed traditional tiled-floor bar on the right, with Flower Pots Perridge Pale, Otter Bitter and maybe a guest like Bowman Swift One on handpump and ten wines by the glass; also, a mix of pubby chairs around sturdy stripped-top tables, a collection of regulars' snapshots, reference books and bric-a-brac on the sills of the big windows and a log fire. Piped pop music is not too obtrusive. On the left, it's carpeted, and progressively rather more formal, ending in a proper dining room beyond a little central hall. There are picnic-sets out on the green across the quiet village road, with more in the good-sized back courtyard – which has a skittle alley, as well as the gents', on the far side. There are fine walks nearby. This is owned by the same good people as the Yew Tree at Lower Wield.

As well as a good value two- and three-course set lunch menu, the enjoyable bar food includes sandwiches, chilli crab soufflé with parmesan cream, a risotto of the day, a proper burger with cheddar or stilton and onion marmalade, fish and chips, bacon steak with egg and chips, and confit of duck with an orange and rosemary jus. *Benchmark main dish: pie of the day £11.95. Two-course evening meal £17.00.*

Free house ~ Licensees Tim Gray and Wendy Nichols ~ Real ale ~ Bar food (not Sun evening or Mon) ~ Restaurant ~ (01962) 774150 ~ Children welcome ~ Dogs allowed in bar and bedrooms ~ Open 12-3, 6-11; 12-10.30 Sun; closed Mon and winter Sun evening from 4pm ~ Bedrooms: £60S/£65S

Recommended by Ann and Colin Hunt

 EASTON Hampshire   SU5132 Map 2

Chestnut Horse 🍴 ♀

3.6 miles from M3 junction 9: A33 towards Kings Worthy, then B3047 towards Itchen Abbas; Easton then signposted on right – bear left in village; SO21 1EG

Cosy dining pub with log fires, fresh flowers and candles, deservedly popular food and friendly staff; Itchen Valley walks nearby

Run by a professional, hands-on landlady, this is a smart 16th-c dining pub and the hub of this pretty village of thatched cottages. The open-plan interior manages to have a pleasantly rustic and intimate feel with a series of cosily separate areas, and the snug décor takes in candles and fresh flowers on the tables, log fires in cottagey fireplaces and comfortable furnishings. The black beams and joists are hung with all sorts of jugs, mugs and chamber-pots, and there are lots of attractive pictures of wildlife and the local area. Badger K&B and Hopping Hare on handpump, several wines by the glass and 30 malt whiskies. There are seats and tables out on a smallish sheltered decked area with colourful flower tubs and baskets, and some picnic-sets in front; plenty of nearby walks in the Itchen Valley.

As well as a good value two-course set lunch (not Sunday), the sensibly short choice of interesting food might include lunchtime sandwiches, ham hock terrine, tian of crab and crayfish tails, thai green vegetable curry, sausage and mash with onion gravy, irish stew with Guinness bread, and pork tenderloin with apple and black pudding. *Benchmark main dish: beer-battered fresh cod and chips £12.00. Two-course evening meal £20.00.*

Badger ~ Tenant Karen Wells ~ Real ale ~ Bar food (12-2.30, 6-9.30; 12-8 Sun (not winter)) ~ Restaurant ~ (01962) 779257 ~ Children welcome ~ Dogs allowed in bar ~ Open 12-3.30, 5.30-11; 12-11(10 Sun) Sat; closed winter Sun evening

Recommended by Ann and Colin Hunt, Gene and Tony Freemantle, Neil and Karen Dignan, Helen and Brian Edgeley, Phyl and Jack Street, A M Falconer

 ELSTEAD Surrey   SU9044 Map 2

Mill at Elstead

Farnham Road (B3001 just W of village, which is itself between Farnham and Milford); GU8 6LE

Fascinating building, big attractive waterside garden, Fullers beers

Inside this largely 18th-c four-storey watermill you'll see the great internal waterwheel turning and hear the gentle rush of the stream running below your feet. Big windows throughout make the most of the charming setting above the prettily banked River Wey. The building has been sensitively converted, with a series of rambling linked bar areas on the spacious ground floor, and a restaurant upstairs, that change in mood from one part to the next. You'll find brown leather armchairs and antique engravings by a longcase clock, neat modern tables and dining chairs on dark woodstrip flooring, big country tables on broad ceramic tiles, iron pillars and stripped masonry, and a log fire in a huge inglenook. They have four Fullers beers on handpump, and a good range of wines by the glass; piped music, board games. Outside there are plenty of picnic-sets dotted around by the water, with its lovely millpond, swans and weeping willows, and the entire scene is well floodlit at night.

The menu here includes sautéed king prawns, welsh rarebit, chicken caesar salad, duck leg confit with raspberry sauce, battered cod, rabbit stew with herb dumplings, smoked haddock and pea risotto, breaded scampi, sausage and mash and well hung sirloin steak; Sunday and Wednesday evening carvery from autumn through to spring. *Benchmark main dish: bass fillet with roast peppers, garlic and tomato £13.50. Two-course evening meal £17.00.*

Fullers ~ Managers Kate and Richard Williams ~ Real ale ~ Bar food (12-9.30(8 Sun, 9 winter Mon-Thurs)) ~ Restaurant ~ (01252) 703333 ~ Children welcome ~ Dogs allowed in bar ~ Open 11-11; 11.30-10.30 Sun
Recommended by Ian Wilson, Ian Herdman, Rosemary and Mike Fielder, Gordon Stevenson

ERIDGE GREEN Sussex   TQ5535   Map 3

Nevill Crest & Gun ♀

A26 Tunbridge Wells—Crowborough; TN3 9JR

Handsome 500-year-old building with lots of character, beams and standing timbers, hundreds of pictures and photographs, three real ales, enjoyable modern food, and friendly, efficient staff

This is a fine former farmhouse – around 500 years old – adorned by the crest of the Nevill family on whose estate the building stands. There's plenty of interesting history and it's been carefully and cleverly opened up inside with standing timbers and doorways keeping some sense of separate rooms. Throughout there are heavy beams (some carved), panelling, rugs on wooden floors, woodburning stoves and an open fire in three fireplaces (the linenfold carved bressumer above one is worth seeking out), all manner of individual dining chairs around dark wood or copper-topped tables and lots of pictures, maps and photographs, many of them local to the area. The window sills are full of toby jugs, stone and glass bottles and plants, there are daily papers, board games and a happy mix of customers of all ages; the atmosphere is civilised but informal. Beers from Tunbridge Wells, Westerham and Phoenix Brunning & Price on handpump and good wines by the glass; efficient, friendly staff. In front of the building are a few picnic-sets with teak furniture on a back terrace beside the new dining extension (light oak rafters, beams and coir flooring).

With something for every taste, the modern brasserie food might include roquefort and spring onion fritter with beetroot relish, charcuterie, ploughman's, bouillabaisse, good moroccan-style lamb with apricot and date salad and chickpea cakes, braised pig's cheek with apples, bacon, sage and celeriac mash, tempting puddings and a british cheeseboard. *Benchmark main dish: battered haddock and chips £11.95. Two-course evening meal £18.60.*

Brunning & Price ~ Manager Jamie Rose ~ Real ale ~ Bar food (12-10(9 Sun)) ~ (01892) 864209 ~ Children welcome ~ Dogs allowed in bar ~ Open 11.30-11; 12-10.30 Sun
Recommended by Alan Franck

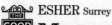

ESHER Surrey   TQ1566   Map 3

Marneys £

Alma Road (one-way only), Weston Green; heading N on A309 from A307 roundabout, after Lamb & Star pub turn left into Lime Tree Avenue (signposted to All Saints Parish Church), then left at T junction into Chestnut Avenue; KT10 8JN

Country feeling pub with good value food and attractive garden

Just a mile from Hampton Court Palace and a surprisingly rural haven for this area, this cottagey little place consists of just two rooms. The small snug bar has a low-beamed ceiling, Fullers London Pride, Youngs and a guest such as Twickenham Original on handpump, about a dozen wines by the glass and perhaps horseracing on the unobtrusive corner TV. To the left, past a little cast-iron woodburning stove, a dining area has big pine tables, pews, pale country kitchen chairs and cottagey blue-curtained windows; piped music. The front terrace has wooden tables with table lighting and views over the rural-feeling wooded common, village church and duck pond, and the pleasantly planted sheltered garden has a decked area.

As well as sandwiches, the very reasonably priced traditional bar food might include whitebait, thai prawns, goats cheese tart, liver and bacon, vegetable lasagne, chicken curry, and fresh fish. *Benchmark main dish: steak and ale pie £8.95. Two-course evening meal £13.90.*

Free house ~ Licensee Thomas Duxberry ~ Real ale ~ Bar food (12-2.30(3 Sun), 6-9; not Fri-Sun evenings) ~ (020) 8398 4444 ~ Children welcome away from bar ~ Dogs welcome ~ Open 11-11; 12-10.30 Sun

Recommended by C and R Bromage, LM, Ian Phillips

EWHURST GREEN Sussex   TQ7924   Map 3

White Dog

Turn off A21 to Bodiam at S end of Hurst Green, cross B2244, pass Bodiam Castle, cross river then bear left uphill at Ewhurst Green sign; TN32 5TD

Comfortable pub with a nice little bar, several real ales and popular food

The garden behind this partly 17th-c pub has lots of picnic-sets and a new children's play area and looks over to Bodiam Castle. The bar on the left has a proper pubby feel with a fine inglenook fireplace, hop-draped beams, wood-panelled walls, farm implements and horsebrasses, just a few tables with high-backed, rush-seated dining chairs and red plush-topped bar stools on the old brick or flagstoned floor. There's also a high-backed cushioned settle by the counter and Dark Star Hophead, Harveys Best and Skinners Betty Stogs on handpump and several wines by the glass. To the right of the door is the busy but fairly plain dining room with more big flagstones, the same tables and chairs as the bar, fresh flowers, black joists and hops, paintings by local artists for sale, and again, one high-backed settle by the bar; piped music. There's also a games room with darts, pool and a games machine.

Well liked bar food includes sandwiches, scallops with cauliflower purée and bacon, duck terrine, tempura prawns with dipping sauce, lunchtime burgers and sausage and mash, bass with crab and spring onion mash and a sun-dried tomato sauce, and pork tenderloin wrapped in pancetta and sage. *Benchmark main dish: fish and chips £10.95. Two-course evening meal £18.00.*

Free house ~ Licensee Mrs Danni Page ~ Real ale ~ Bar food (12-2.30, 6.30-9; 12-4; not Sun or Mon evenings) ~ Restaurant ~ (01580) 830264 ~ Children welcome ~ Dogs allowed in bar ~ Open 12-3, 5.30-11; 12-11.30 Sat; 12-6 Sun; closed Sun and Mon evenings ~ Bedrooms: /£75B

Recommended by Philip and Cheryl Hill, Dr Martin Owton, Leslie and Barbara Owen, V Brogden, Michael Butler, Arthur Pickering

FERNHAM Oxfordshire

SU2991 Map 4

Woodman

A420 SW of Oxford, then left into B4508 after about 11 miles; village a further 6 miles on; SN7 7NX

A good choice of real ales and interesting bar food in a charming old-world country pub

With consistently good food, several real ales and a genuine welcome from attentive staff, this smashing pub, not surprisingly, remains as popular as ever. The heavily beamed main rooms have the most character and are full of an amazing assortment of old objects like clay pipes, milkmaids' yokes, leather tack, coach horns, an old screw press, some original oil paintings and good black and white photographs of horses. Comfortable seating includes cushioned benches, pews and windsor chairs, and the candlelit tables are simply made from old casks; a big wood fire, too. As well as some comfortable newer areas, there's a large room for Sunday lunches. Greene King Old Speckled Hen, Oakham JHB, Timothy Taylors Landlord and Wadworths 6X tapped from the cask and several wines by the glass; piped music. There are seats outside on the terrace. Disabled lavatories.

Highly thought-of food includes filled baguettes, duck liver and orange pâté, rosemary-studded baked camembert, local sausages with red wine onion gravy, a curry of the day, pasta with wild mushroom and white wine sauce, crispy duck with stir-fried vegetables, noodles and plum sauce, and bass fillets with tomatoes, capers and chives. *Benchmark main dish: lamb shank with redcurrant mint jus £16.95. Two-course evening meal £20.90.*

Free house ~ Licensee Steven Whiting ~ Real ale ~ Bar food (12-2, 6.30-9.30) ~ Restaurant ~ (01367) 820643 ~ Children welcome ~ Dogs welcome ~ Open 11-11(10.30 Sun)

Recommended by William Goodhart, Lesley and Peter Barrett, Mary Rayner

FLETCHING Sussex

TQ4223 Map 3

Griffin

Village signposted off A272 W of Uckfield; TN22 3SS

Busy, gently upmarket inn with a fine wine list, bistro-style bar food, real ales, and big garden with far-reaching views; bedrooms

There's a genuinely warm welcome for all – children and dogs, too – in this civilised and very well run inn. The beamed and quaintly panelled bar rooms have blazing log fires, old photographs and hunting prints, straightforward close-set furniture including some captain's chairs and china on a delft shelf. There's a small bare-boarded serving area off to one side and a snug separate bar with sofas and a TV. Harveys Best, Hepworths Iron Horse, Hogs Back TEA and Kings Horsham Best on handpump, a fine wine list with 16 (including champagne and sweet wine) by the glass and farm cider. The very spacious two-acre back garden has plenty of seats on the sandstone terrace and on the grass and lovely views of rolling countryside. The bedrooms are comfortable and the breakfasts particularly good and the pub is handy for Glyndebourne. There are ramps for wheelchairs.

🍴 Using carefully sourced local produce, the imaginative and extremely good – if not cheap – food might include scallops with aubergine caviar, crispy pancetta and truffle oil, slow-braised oxtail ravioli with red wine jus, wild garlic and brie risotto with toasted hazelnuts, organic chicken and ham hock pie, confit duck leg with tomato, rosemary and chickpea stew, and crab linguine with chilli, garlic, white wine and parsley; summer barbecues. *Benchmark main dish: cod and chips with pea and mint purée £13.00. Two-course evening meal £22.50.*

Free house ~ Licensees James Pullan, J Gatti and Emma Barlow ~ Real ale ~ Bar food (12-2.30(3 weekends), 7-9.30) ~ Restaurant ~ (01825) 722890 ~ Children welcome ~ Dogs allowed in bar ~ Open 12am-midnight (1am Sat, 11 Sun) ~ Bedrooms: £80B/£85S(£95B)

Recommended by Hugh Roberts, Charles Kingsley Evans, Ann and Colin Hunt, Sheila Topham, Michael Pelham, Charles Gibbs, Simon and Mandy King, David and Jenny Reed, Grahame Brooks, Alan Franck, Harriet Tarnoy, John Ralph

FORTY GREEN Buckinghamshire   SU9291 Map 2

Royal Standard of England ◀

3.5 miles from M40 junction 2, via A40 to Beaconsfield, then follow sign to Forty Green, off B474 0.75 miles N of New Beaconsfield; keep going through village; HP9 1XT

Ancient place with fascinating antiques in rambling rooms, and good choice of drinks and food

Often used for filming programmes such as *Midsomer Murders*, this fine old place has been trading for nearly 900 years; they have an interesting leaflet documenting the pub's history. It's a favourite with many of our readers who come back on a regular basis and you can always be sure of a friendly welcome. The rambling rooms have huge black ship's timbers, lovely worn floors, finely carved old oak panelling, roaring winter fires with handsomely decorated iron firebacks and cluttered mantelpieces, and there's a massive settle apparently built to fit the curved transom of an Elizabethan ship. Nooks and crannies are filled with a fascinating collection of antiques, including rifles, powder-flasks and bugles, ancient pewter and pottery tankards, lots of tarnished brass and copper, needlework samplers and richly coloured stained glass. Brakspears, Chiltern Ale and Beechwood Bitter, Rebellion IPA and Mild and Theakstons Old Peculier on handpump, a carefully annotated list of bottled beers and malt whiskies, farm ciders, perry, somerset brandy and around a dozen wines by the glass; board games. You can sit outside in a neatly hedged front rose garden or under the shade of a tree.

🍴 Traditional, popular bar food includes lunchtime sandwiches, devilled lamb kidneys on fried toast, chicken caesar salad, vegetable risotto, fish pie, steak and kidney pudding, seasonal game dishes, and pork belly with bubble and squeak with apple sauce. They still ask to keep your card behind the bar. *Benchmark main dish: fish and chips £12.50. Two-course evening meal £17.00.*

Free house ~ Licensee Matthew O'Keeffe ~ Real ale ~ Bar food (12-10) ~ Restaurant ~ (01494) 673382 ~ Children welcome ~ Dogs welcome ~ Open 11-11; 12-10.30 Sun

Recommended by Paul Humphreys, D and M T Ayres-Regan, June and Robin Savage, Tracey and

Stephen Groves, the Didler, Richard and Liz Thorne, Roy Hoing, Susan and John Douglas,
Anthony Longden, Mark Wilson

FRESHWATER Isle of Wight   SZ3487   Map 2

Red Lion ♀

Church Place; from A3055 at E end of village by Freshwater Garage mini-
roundabout follow Yarmouth signpost, then take first real right turn signed to Parish
Church; PO40 9BP

**Good mix of locals and visiting diners, decent food, and composed
atmosphere**

Steady and reliable, this civilised place is a longstanding stalwart of the
Guide. The not over-done but comfortably furnished open-plan bar
has fires, low grey sofas and sturdy country-kitchen-style furnishings on
mainly flagstoned floors and bare boards. Although the food is quite a
draw, chatting locals, occupying stools along the counter and enjoying
the Flowers Original, Goddards, Shepherd Neame Spitfire and Wadworths
6X, maintain the grown-up pubby atmosphere. Outside, there are tables
(some under cover) in a carefully tended garden and beside the kitchen's
herb and vegetable garden. A couple of picnic-sets in a quiet square at the
front have pleasant views of the church. The pub is virtually on the
Freshwater Way footpath that connects Yarmouth with the southern
coast at Freshwater Bay.

Food, listed on blackboards behind the bar, includes a sensible cross-section of
dishes from lunchtime filled baguettes and ploughman's to crab and avocado
cocktail, sausage and mash, salmon fillet with dill sauce, goats cheese nut roast and
several pies; they also do takeaways. *Benchmark main dish: fishcakes £11.50. Two-
course evening meal £18.90.*

Enterprise ~ Lease Michael Mence ~ Real ale ~ Bar food (12-2, 6.30-9 (not every Sun
evening Jan-March)) ~ (01983) 754925 ~ Children over 10 ~ Dogs welcome ~ Open
11.30-3, 5.30-11; 11.30-4, 6-11 Sat; 12-3, 7-10.30 Sun

*Recommended by Stuart Paulley, Paul Humphreys, Geoff and Linda Payne, Denise Bowes,
D M and B K Moores*

FRILSHAM Berkshire   SU5573   Map 2

Pot Kiln ⊕ ◀

From Yattendon take turning S, opposite church, follow first Frilsham
signpost, but just after crossing motorway go straight on towards Bucklebury ignoring
Frilsham signposted right; pub on right after about half a mile; RG18 0XX

**Country dining pub, bustling little bar, local beers, and imaginative bar
and restaurant dishes; suntrap garden and nearby walks**

With plenty of walks in the nearby woods and seats in a big suntrap
garden looking across the valley, this particularly well run country
pub is very popular in fine weather. But on colder days, too, there are lots
of locals and visitors who crowd inside, keen to enjoy the good,
interesting food served by warmly friendly staff. The little bar has West
Berkshire Brick Kiln Bitter, Mr Chubbs Lunchtime Bitter and Maggs
Magnificent Mild, and a weekly changing guest beer on handpump, wines
by the glass and a couple of ciders. The main bar area has dark wooden
tables and chairs on bare boards, and a winter log fire and the extended
lounge is open-plan at the back and leads into a large, pretty dining room

with a nice jumble of old tables and chairs, and an old-looking stone fireplace; darts and board games.

🍴 Using home-made bread, some home-grown vegetables, and venison shot by the landlord, the food includes lunchtime sandwiches, venison burger and pork and leek sausages with onion marmalade, with imaginative restaurant choices like ragoût of muntjac with pasta and aged parmesan, wild mushroom risotto with a pheasant egg salad, pork belly with pearl barley broth and wild garlic leaves, and bass with braised gem lettuce, asparagus and saffron sauce. *Benchmark main dish: venison steak sandwich £8.95. Two-course evening meal £22.45.*

Free house ~ Licensees Mr and Mrs Michael Robinson ~ Real ale ~ Bar food (12-2.30, 6.30-8.30; not Tues) ~ Restaurant ~ (01635) 201366 ~ Children welcome ~ Dogs allowed in bar ~ Open 12-2.30, 6-11; 12-11 Sat; 12-10.30 Sun; closed Tues

Recommended by Graham and Toni Sanders, Robert Watt, the Didler, Neil and Karen Dignan, Angela Crum Ewing, Peter Chapman, Dick and Madeleine Brown

FULMER Buckinghamshire   SU9985 Map 2

🍴 Black Horse ⛱ 🍷

Village signposted off A40 in Gerrards Cross, W of its junction with A413; Windmill Road; SL3 6HD

Appealingly reworked dining pub, friendly and relaxed, with enjoyable up-to-date food, exemplary service, and pleasant garden

Right at the heart of a charming conservation village, this is a bustling dining pub with a warm welcome for drinkers, too. There's a proper bar area on the left – three smallish rooms with low black beams, parquet floor or a rug on bare boards, very mixed tables and chairs, Greene King IPA and Old Speckled Hen and a changing guest beer on handpump, 21 european wines by the glass, nine pudding wines and a good range of liqueurs; service is prompt, friendly and efficient. The main area on the right is set for dining with comfortable, modern dining chairs on a beige carpet and the rest of the pub has a warm, relaxed and contented atmosphere; piped music. The good-sized back terrace, below the church, has teak and wrought-iron tables and chairs, with picnic-sets on the sheltered grass beyond.

🍴 Interesting food includes sandwiches, ham hock terrine with pineapple relish, cornish crab with a watercress and pea shoot salad and crab fritter, pork tenderloin with minestrone, chorizo and crispy salt and pepper squid, corn-fed chicken stuffed with fontina on a tomato, fennel and roast garlic stew with parmesan crackling, and whole lemon sole with a sorrel cream sauce. *Benchmark main dish: slow-roast rabbit with black pudding ravioli, celeriac purée and crispy nettles £13.50. Two-course evening meal £20.25.*

Salisbury Pubs ~ Lease Richard Coletta ~ Real ale ~ Bar food (12-2.30(3 Sat, 4 Sun), 6.30-9.30(10 Fri and Sat)) ~ Restaurant ~ (01753) 663183 ~ Children welcome ~ Dogs allowed in bar ~ Open 11-11; 12-10.30 Sun; closed 25 and 26 Dec

Recommended by Richard Gibbs

GREAT MISSENDEN Buckinghamshire   SP9000   Map 4

Nags Head 🍷 🛏
Old London Road, E – beyond Abbey; HP16 0DG

Well run and pretty inn with beamed bars, an open fire, a good range of drinks and good modern cooking; comfortable bedrooms

Roald Dahl used this pretty brick and flint inn – once three cottages – as his local and the Roald Dahl Museum and Story Centre is just a stroll away. It's quietly civilised and neatly kept with a low beamed area on the left, a loftier part on the right, a mix of small pews, dining chairs and tables on the carpet, Quentin Blake prints on the cream walls and a log fire in a handsome fireplace. Fullers London Pride, Rebellion IPA and Tring Monks Gold on handpump from the unusual bar counter (the windows behind face the road) and a dozen wines by the glass from an extensive list. There's a new outside dining area under a pergola and seats on the extensive back lawn. The beamed bedrooms are well equipped and attractive.

Skilfully cooked modern food includes blinis with crab, home-smoked salmon and a chive cream sauce, wild mushroom, leek and pea risotto, steamed haddock with a chardonnay and tarragon sauce, coq au vin-style cockerel leg with beetroot coulis, sausages of the day with red wine gravy and breast of barbary duck with confit onion mash and dry sherry jus; they also have a two- and three-course set menu. *Benchmark main dish: sliced leg of lamb with shredded shoulder on a rosemary stick with ratatouille £18.95. Two-course evening meal £21.90.*

Free house ~ Licensee Adam Michaels ~ Real ale ~ Bar food (12-2.30(3.30 Sun), 6.30-9.30(8.30 Sun)) ~ (01494) 862200 ~ Children welcome ~ Dogs allowed in bar ~ Open 12-11(midnight Fri and Sat); 12-10.30 Sun ~ Bedrooms: /£95B
Recommended by Tracey and Stephen Groves, D and M T Ayres-Regan

GROVE Buckinghamshire   SP9122   Map 4

Grove Lock 🍷 🍴 £
Pub signed off B488, on left just S of A505 roundabout (S of Leighton Buzzard); LU7 0QU

By Grand Union Canal Lock 28, with plenty of room inside, fair value food and real ales, and lots of seats overlooking the water

In fine weather, the seats and picnic-sets in the terraced garden and on the canopied decking overlooking the Grand Union Canal here are much prized. Inside, it's open-plan and the bar has a lofty high-raftered pitched roof, terracotta and wallpapered walls, squashy brown leather sofas on diagonal oak floor boarding, an eclectic mix of tables and chairs, a couple of butcher's block tables by the bar, a big open-standing winter log fire and canal-themed artwork. Steps take you up to the original lock-keeper's cottage (now a three-room restaurant area) which is partly flagstoned, has more winter log fires and looks down on the narrow canal lock. Fullers London Pride and a couple of Fullers seasonal beers on handpump, several wines by the glass, and friendly staff; piped music and newspapers.

Fair value bar food includes sandwiches, wraps and baps, lamb kofta with tzatziki dip, leek, cheese and white wine risotto, ham hash with a poached egg and bloody mary ketchup, beer-battered cod and a steak burger with bacon and cheese. *Benchmark main dish: treacle-glazed ham £9.95. Two-course evening meal £15.00.*

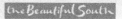

Fullers ~ Managers Gregg and Angela Worrall ~ Real ale ~ Bar food (12-9(7 Sun)) ~ (01525) 380940 ~ Children welcome ~ Open 11-11; 12-10.30 Sun

Recommended by Mr and Mrs John Taylor, Tony and Wendy Hobden

 HARE HATCH Berkshire   SU8077 Map 2

Horse & Groom

A4 Bath Road W of Maidenhead; RG10 9SB

Spreading pub, very well refurbished recently, good staff, good all round

One of the newest – and biggest – in the small Brunning & Price group: their typical style, spacious linked areas with a pleasing variety of well spread tables and chairs on mahogany-stained boards, plenty of oriental rugs and some carpet to soften the acoustics, open fires in attractive tiled fireplaces, and a profusion of mainly old or antique prints. The long bar counter has a splendid choice of drinks, including a good changing range of wines by the glass, Brakspears Bitter and Oxford Gold, Marstons and a couple of changing specials on handpump, 15 wines by the glass, two Weston's farm ciders, lots of spirits including malts of the week, and good coffees; also several different daily papers. Busy well trained staff are kind and friendly. A sheltered back terrace has teak tables under square canvas parasols.

 As well as sandwiches, the interesting modern food includes duck liver pâté with rhubarb chutney, beetroot and chickpea fritters with moroccan coleslaw and minted yoghurt, potato, thyme and parmesan gnocchi with roast pumpkin, figs, spinach and sage velouté, pork and leek sausages with onion gravy, salad of slow-roasted duck leg with toulouse sausage, butter beans and red wine dressing, and braised lamb shoulder with dauphinoise potatoes. *Benchmark main dish: battered haddock and chips £11.95. Two-course evening meal £17.70.*

Brunning & Price ~ Manager Paul Boden ~ Real ale ~ Bar food (12-10(9.30 Sun)) ~ (0118) 940 3136 ~ Children welcome ~ Dogs allowed in bar ~ Open 11-11(10.30 Sun)

Recommended by Danny Thompson

 HEADINGTON Oxfordshire   SP5407 Map 4

Black Boy

Old High Street/St Andrews Road; off A420 at traffic lights opposite B4495; OX3 9HT

Stylish and enterprising modern dining pub with good, enjoyable food, and useful summer garden

Black leather seating on dark parquet, big mirrors, silvery patterned wallpaper, nightlights in fat opaque cylinders and glittering bottles behind the long bar counter add up to a cool contemporary look for this friendly place, its neat young black-aproned staff well schooled by the charming landlady. It's all light and airy, particularly for the two tables in the big bay window; just to the side is an open fire, with lower softer seats by it. Crisp white tablecloths and bold black and white wallpaper lend the area on the left a touch of formality. Behind is an appealing terrace, with picnic-sets under alternating black and white parasols on smart pale stone chippings, and a central seat encircling an ash tree. They have Greene King London Glory and Roosters Leghorn on handpump, good coffee and tea, and a good choice of wines by the glass; one enterprising programme is the Sunday morning kitchen class, adults and children alternate weeks.

the Beautiful South

🍴 Using only local produce and making their own bread and ice-cream, the interesting food might include a grazing menu, prawn and cod fishcake with a soy, mirin and lime dressing, gnocchi with fresh basil pesto, a proper burger with cheese, onion and gherkins, beer-battered fish and chips with a pea and mint purée, and confit gressingham duck leg with beetroot, radicchio and an orange and chilli gastrique (a vinegar and sugar caramelised reduction). *Benchmark main dish: roast pork belly with garlic mash and cider jus £12.95. Two-course evening meal £16.75.*

Greene King ~ Lease Abi Rose and Chris Bentham ~ Real ale ~ Bar food (12-2.45, 6-9.15) ~ (01865) 741137 ~ Children welcome ~ Open 12-3, 5-11; 12-10 Sun
Recommended by Richard Gibbs

HEDGERLEY Buckinghamshire   SU9687   Map 2

GOOD PUB GUIDE

White Horse ★ 🍺 £

2.4 miles from M40 junction 2; at exit roundabout take Slough turn-off following alongside M40; after 1.5 miles turn right at T junction into Village Lane; SL2 3UY

Old-fashioned drinkers' pub with lots of beers tapped straight from the cask, regular beer festivals, and a cheery mix of customers

Locals and visitors mix happily in this smashing little pub – all drawn in by the friendly welcome and marvellous choice of real ales. As well as Rebellion IPA they keep up to seven daily changing guests, sourced from all over the country and tapped straight from casks kept in a room behind the tiny hatch counter. Their Easter, May, Spring and August bank holiday beer festivals (they can get through about 130 beers during the May one) are a highlight of the local calendar. This fine range of drinks extends to three farm ciders, still apple juice, a perry, belgian beers, ten or so wines by the glass and winter mulled wine. The cottagey main bar has plenty of unspoilt character, with lots of beams, brasses and exposed brickwork, low wooden tables, standing timbers, jugs, ballcocks and other bric-a-brac, a log fire, and a good few leaflets and notices about village events. A little flagstoned public bar on the left has darts and board games. A canopy extension leads out to the garden where there are tables and occasional barbecues, and there are lots of hanging baskets and a couple more tables in front of the building overlooking the quiet road. Good walks nearby, and the pub is handy for the Church Wood RSPB reserve and popular with walkers and cyclists; it can get crowded at weekends.

🍴 Lunchtime bar food such as sandwiches, cold meats and quiches, and changing straightforward hot dishes (their steak and mushroom pie is popular). *Benchmark main dish: steak and mushroom pie £7.25.*

Free house ~ Licensees Doris Hobbs and Kevin Brooker ~ Real ale ~ Bar food (lunchtime only) ~ (01753) 643225 ~ Children in canopy extension area ~ Dogs allowed in bar ~ Open 11-2.30, 5-11; 11-11 Sat; 12-10.30 Sun; closed evenings 25 and 26 Dec
Recommended by D and M T Ayres-Regan, Tracey and Stephen Groves, Nigel and Sue Foster, Gavin Robinson, the Didler, LM, Roy Hoing, N R White, Susan and John Douglas, Kevin Thomas, Nina Randall, Anthony Longden, Dave Braisted, Mark Wilson, Ian and Jane Irving

---

Stars after the name of a pub show exceptional quality. One star means most people (after reading the report to see just why the star has been won) would think a special trip worth while. Two stars mean that the pub is really outstanding – for its particular qualities it could hardly be bettered.

HENLEY Berkshire   SU7682 Map 2

Little Angel ⑩ ♀

Remenham Lane (A4130, just over bridge E of Henley); RG9 2LS

Relaxed linked contemporary areas plus attractive conservatory, modern bar and restaurant food, helpful service, real ales, and several wines by the glass

After a smart refurbishment, this civilised place is more popular than ever and the genuine mix of customers keeps the atmosphere informal and chatty. The rooms are more or less open plan but with quite distinct seating areas. There are bare boards throughout and the little bar has leather cube stools, some tub and farmhouse chairs and a squashy sofa, high chairs beside the panelled, carved counter and a woodburning stove. Elsewhere, there are all sorts of dining chairs and tables, quite a bit of artwork on Farrow & Ball paintwork and an airy conservatory. Brakspears Bitter and Special, lots of wines (and champagne) by the glass, unobtrusive piped music and board games; helpful, friendly staff. A sheltered floodlit back terrace has tables under cocktail parasols looking over to the local cricket ground.

🍴 As well as sharing plates and daily specials, the particularly good food might include lunchtime sandwiches, salt and pepper squid with tomato, red onion and lime and dill salsa, smoked chicken, spring onion and pine nut terrine with avocado cream, creamy wild mushrooms topped with a herb and brioche crumble, confit duck hash with a free-range egg, and maize-fed chicken on spring greens with a red wine jus. *Benchmark main dish: steak burger £11.25. Two-course evening meal £20.00.*

Brakspears ~ Lease Douglas and Lolly Green ~ Real ale ~ Bar food (12-3, 7-9; all day weekends) ~ Restaurant ~ (01491) 411008 ~ Children allowed but must be well behaved ~ Dogs allowed in bar ~ Open 11-11(midnight Fri and Sat); 12-10 Sun

Recommended by Simon Collett-Jones, Neil and Karen Dignan, Chris Glasson, Tom and Ruth Rees, Kim Upton

HIGHMOOR Oxfordshire   SU6984 Map 2

Rising Sun

Witheridge Hill, signposted off B481; OS Sheet 175 map reference 697841; RG9 5PF

Thoughtfully run, pretty pub with a mix of diners and drinkers

This pretty black and cream village pub is usually packed out with cheerful customers but the friendly licensees and their pleasant staff are sure to make you welcome – no matter how busy they are. The two front rooms are for those just wanting a drink as the rest of the place is laid out for dining. On the right by the bar, there are wooden tables and chairs and a sofa on the stripped wooden floors, cream and terracotta walls and an open fire in the big brick inglenook fireplace. The main area spreading back from here has shiny bare boards and a swathe of carpeting with well spaced tables and attractive pictures on the walls. Brakspears Bitter and Oxford Gold on handpump, ten wines by the glass and Weston's cider; piped music and board games. There are seats and tables in the pleasant back garden; boules. As this is the heart of the Chilterns, there are plenty of surrounding walks.

Well liked bar food includes sandwiches, crab and prawn tartlet with tomato coulis, honey-roast gammon and poached egg salad with croûtons, pasta with a creamy courgette sauce and parmesan, pork and leek sausages with onion jus, venison casserole and bass with sweet potato and sticky red onion and tomato dressing. *Benchmark main dish: slow-cooked pork belly with black pudding mash £11.50. Two-course evening meal £18.25.*

Brakspears ~ Tenant Simon Duffy ~ Real ale ~ Bar food (not Sun evening) ~ Restaurant ~ (01491) 640856 ~ Children allowed under strict supervision in dining areas only ~ Dogs allowed in bar ~ Open 12-3, 5.30-11; 12-11(7 Sun) Sat; closed Sun evening
Recommended by Martin and Karen Wake, John Roots, Roy and Jean Russell, Bob and Margaret Holder

HOOK Hampshire   SU7153   Map 2

Hogget ☜

1.1 miles from M3 junction 5; A287 N, at junction with A30 (car park just before traffic lights); RG27 9JJ

Well run and accommodating, a proper pub moving with the times and giving good value

On a Friday morning this bustling place opens from 7.30 for breakfast – so helpful for travellers wanting early morning refreshment. Locally popular and chatty, the rooms ramble right round the central servery. The lighting, wallpaper and carpet pattern, and the leather sofas and tub chairs over on the right at the back, give a friendly and homely feel, as does the way it provides several smallish distinct areas. They have well kept Jennings Cumberland and Marstons Best and EPA on handpump, decent wines by the glass, and plenty of staff in neat but informal black uniforms. A sizeable terrace had sturdy tables and chairs, with some in a heated covered area.

Good food using local ingredients and including fair value lunchtime deals includes sandwiches, antipasti boards for sharing, crispy baby squid on crunchy salad with chilli, lime and mango dressing, chicken caesar salad, ham and free-range eggs, home-made burger with bacon and cheese, wild mushroom risotto and slow-roast pork belly with sun-dried tomato mash and a tangy tomato salad. *Benchmark main dish: local sausages with colcannon £10.00. Two-course evening meal £20.90.*

Marstons ~ Lease Tom Faulkner ~ Real ale ~ Bar food (12-2.30, 6.30-9; all day Sat; 12-6 Sun; not Sun evening) ~ Restaurant ~ (01256) 763009 ~ Children welcome ~ Dogs allowed in bar ~ Open 12-3, 5-11; 12-11(10.30 Sun) Sat
Recommended by David and Sue Smith, Jennifer Banks

HORSELL Surrey   SU9959   Map 2

Red Lion

High Street; GU21 4SS

Contemporary and popular with good food

Plenty of upholstered and leather sofas and chairs give this pleasantly spruced-up place a comfortable relaxed atmosphere. Lots of polished light wood, flowers and plants and cream-painted walls with clusters of pictures keep it feeling light and airy. The long solid wood counter (topped off by a row of metal café lights) serves Courage Best, Fullers

London Pride and a guest such as Sharps Doom Bar and a dozen wines by the glass – bar chairs lined up here keep the place feeling pubby. Feeling just special enough, the big dining room has old church pews, exposed brickwork and food listed on blackboards. Outside, the attractive terrace is particularly inviting, with its good quality furnishings, smart umbrellas and big shady tree in the middle; piped music, TV and board games.

As well as sandwiches, the bistro-style food includes potato gnocchi with mushroom, pesto and parmesan, fish and chips, goats cheese, sweet potato and spring onion tart, well hung ribeye steak, and daily specials such as fish pie, grilled mackerel fillets with herb couscous and harissa dressing, fried duck breast with oriental vegetables and teriyaki sauce, and free-range pork chop with black pudding and apple sauce. *Benchmark main dish: rotisserie chicken with pancetta and mushroom sauce £12.95. Two-course evening meal £18.50.*

S&N ~ Licensee Richard Brown ~ Real ale ~ Bar food (12-9.30(10 Fri, Sat)) ~ Restaurant ~ (01483) 768497 ~ Seated children welcome in bar till 6pm and restaurant till 7.30pm ~ Open 11-11(11.30 Sat); 12-10.30 Sun
Recommended by Ian Phillips

HORSHAM Sussex   TQ1730   Map 3

Black Jug ☑
North Street; RH12 1RJ

Bustling town pub with wide choice of drinks, efficient staff, and good bar food

Always busy with a wide mix of customers, this is a well run town pub with friendly, knowledgeable staff. The one large open-plan, turn-of-the-century room has a large central bar, a nice collection of sizeable dark wood tables and comfortable chairs on the stripped-wood floor, board games and interesting old prints and photographs above a dark wood panelled dado on the cream walls. A spacious conservatory has similar furniture and lots of hanging baskets. Caledonian Deuchars IPA, Harveys Best, Jennings Cumberland, Theakstons Old Peculier and Thwaites Wainwright on handpump, 20 wines by the glass, around 100 malt whiskies and Weston's cider. The pretty flower-filled back terrace has plenty of garden furniture. The small car park is for staff and deliveries only but you can park next door in the council car park.

Good, bistro-style food includes sandwiches, ham hock terrine with piccalilli, a charcuterie plate (for two), smoked haddock and salmon fishcakes, lamb, leek and potato hash with a fried egg, potato, thyme and parmesan gnocchi with roast pumpkin, figs, spinach and sage velouté, and venison steak with braised chicory and a blueberry and star anise jus. *Benchmark main dish: beer-battered fish and chips £11.95. Two-course evening meal £17.70.*

Brunning & Price ~ Tenant Alastair Craig ~ Real ale ~ Bar food (12-10(9.30 Sun)) ~ (01403) 253526 ~ Children welcome ~ Dogs allowed in bar ~ Open 11.30-11; 12-10.30 Sun
Recommended by Derek and Maggie Washington, Mike and Eleanor Anderson

---

> The price we give for a two-course evening meal in the featured top pub entries is the mean (average of cheapest and most expensive) price of a starter and a main course – no drinks.

HUNGERFORD Berkshire   SU3368   Map 2

Plume of Feathers

High Street; street parking opposite; RG17 0NB

Right at the heart of a bustling little town with well liked bar food and a relaxed family atmosphere

Since it's in an appealing small town, there's always a happy mix of both visitors and locals here. It's all open-plan and stretches from its smallish bow-windowed façade around the island bar to an open fire in the stripped fireplace right at the back. There are armchairs and a black leather sofa around low tables under lowish beams on the left at the front and a mix of tables with padded chairs or cushioned small pews on the bare boards elsewhere. They have a fair choice of wines by the glass alongside Greene King IPA and Ruddles Best on handpump and good coffee, and the scottish landlord and his staff are friendly and helpful. The sheltered back courtyard isn't large but is well worth knowing on a warm day: prettily planted, and with a swing seat as well as green-painted metal tables and chairs.

Well liked food includes lunchtime filled panini, black pudding fritters with apple sauce, brie in filo pastry with red wine and cranberry sauce, ham and free-range eggs, beer-battered haddock, portobello mushroom, spring onion and parmesan risotto, and venison stew with herb dumplings. *Benchmark main dish: beer-battered fresh haddock £11.20. Two-course evening meal £17.00.*

Greene King ~ Lease Haley and James Weir ~ Real ale ~ Bar food (12-2.30(4 Sun), 7-9; not Sun evening) ~ (01488) 682154 ~ Children welcome ~ Dogs welcome ~ Open 11-3, 5.30(6 Sat)-11(midnight Fri); 12-4 Sun; closed Sun evening; 25 and 26 Dec
Recommended by I D Barnett, Chris and Martin Taylor, Richard Tilbrook, Clive and Fran Dutson, Mike and Mary Carter

---

HURST GREEN Sussex   TQ7326   Map 3

White Horse ♀

Silverhill (A21); TN19 7PU

Friendly, well run pub with relaxed bar, elegant dining room, enjoyable food, and seats in garden

A former Georgian farmhouse, this is a friendly and civilised place for a drink or a meal. The relaxed bare-boards bar has a few leather armchairs and white-painted dining chairs around various wooden tables (laid with nightlights and wooden candlesticks), game trophies, prints and photographs on the walls, fresh flowers and an open fire. Harveys Best on handpump and 14 nice wines by the glass; piped music. An open doorway leads through to a second bar room with built-in leather wall seats and similar tables and then through again to the dining room. This is an elegant but informal room with similar furniture, oil paintings and ornate mirrors on modern paintwork, chandeliers and some panelling. Outside, there's a sizeable terrace with attractive white metal tables and chairs looking across a lawn and over the Weald.

Enjoyable bar food includes sandwiches, chicken terrine with home-made chutney, tempura prawns with sweet chilli jam, beef and bacon in ale pie, chicken breast wrapped in pancetta with a caper and beurre blanc sauce, open mushroom ravioli with truffle oil, and pork medallions with mustard sauce and garlic-sautéed potatoes. *Benchmark main dish: confit duck with cranberry jus*

£15.50. Two-course evening meal £21.00.

Free house ~ Licensee Anthony Panic ~ Real ale ~ Bar food (12-3, 6-10) ~ Restaurant ~ (01580) 860235 ~ Children welcome ~ Dogs allowed in bar ~ Live jazz last Fri of month ~ Open 12-3, 6-11; 12-8 Sun

Recommended by David and Jenny Reed, Richard Mason

ICKHAM Kent   TR2258 Map 3

Duke William
Off A257 E of Canterbury; The Street; CT3 1QP

Relaxing family-owned village pub with airy bar, dining conservatory, enjoyable bar food, and plenty of seats outside; bedrooms

The big spreading bar at this friendly village pub has huge new oak beams and stripped joists, a fine mix of seats from settles to high-backed cushioned dining chairs, dark wheelback and bentwood chairs around all sorts of wooden tables on the stripped wooden floor, a log fire with a couple of settles and a low barrel table in front of it, a central bar counter with high stools and brass coat hooks and a snug little area with one long table, black leather high-backed dining chairs, a flat-screen TV and a computer if you need it; daily papers, quiet piped music, cheerful modern paintings and large hop bines. Adnams, Harveys and Shepherd Neame Master Brew are on handpump alongside some decent wines and Happy Hour is 4-6pm. Staff are chatty and attentive. A low-ceilinged dining room leads off to the left with dark wood chairs, tables and more cushioned settles, with paintings and mirrors on the walls. At the back of the pub, there's a light dining conservatory with all manner of interesting paintings, prints and heraldry on the walls and similar furniture on the stone floor. Doors lead from here to a big terrace with a covered area to one side, plenty of wooden and metal tables and chairs, and a lawn with picnic-table sets, some swings and a slide.

Tasty bar food includes filled baguettes, chicken liver pâté, whitebait, field mushroom topped with goats cheese and prawns, steak and ale pie, calves liver and bacon, slow-roasted belly of pork with cider and apple sauce, and chicken with tarragon and mushrooms; there's also a good value two-course lunch menu and Sunday roasts (booking advised). *Benchmark main dish: beef and ale pie £11.50. Two-course evening meal £20.80.*

Free house ~ Licensee Louise White ~ Real ale ~ Bar food (12-3, 6-9.30) ~ Restaurant ~ (01227) 721308 ~ Children welcome ~ Dogs allowed in bar ~ Open 11-11(midnight Sat, 10 Sun) ~ Bedrooms: /£65S

Recommended by David Heath, Dr Kevan Tucker

IGHTHAM COMMON Kent   TQ5855 Map 3

Harrow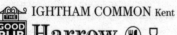
Signposted off A25 just W of Ightham; pub sign may be hard to spot;
TN15 9EB

Emphasis on good food in friendly, smart dining pub, fresh flowers and candles; pretty back terrace

The amiable landlord and his attentive staff extend a warm welcome at this comfortably genial pub and while most customers visit to enjoy the particularly good food, there's a tiny bar inside the door. The larger relaxed-feeling bar area to the right, painted a cheerful sunny yellow above the wood-panelled dado, is attractively finished with fresh flowers and candles on tables, smart dining chairs on the herringbone-patterned wood floor and there's a winter fire. There's a charming little antiquated conservatory and a more formal dining room; piped music. Gravesend Shrimpers and Loddon Hoppit are on handpump and they offer several wines by the glass. There are tables and chairs out on a pretty little pergola-enclosed back terrace and the pub is handily placed for Ightham Mote (National Trust).

Good, popular food includes pork sausages with onion gravy, home-baked ham and eggs, risotto verde, thai-style prawn curry, salmon and chive fishcake with citrus cream sauce, goats cheese and caramelised red onion tart with grape salad, duck suprême with dauphinoise potatoes and plum tarte tatin, king scallops wrapped in pancetta with a garlic and herb dressing, and seasonal game like venison or pheasant; Sunday roasts. *Benchmark main dish: fishcakes £13.50. Two-course evening meal £19.00.*

Free house ~ Licensees John Elton and Claire Butler ~ Real ale ~ Bar food (12-2, 6-9) ~ Restaurant ~ (01732) 885912 ~ Children welcome but not in dining room on Sat evening ~ Open 12-3, 6-11; 12-4 Sun; closed Sun evening and all day Mon
Recommended by Derek Thomas, Nick and Carolyn Carter

INKPEN Berkshire SU3764 Map 2

Crown & Garter

Inkpen Common: Inkpen signposted with Kintbury off A4; in Kintbury turn left into Inkpen Road, then keep on into Inkpen Common; RG17 9QR

Remote-feeling pub with appealing layout, lovely garden and nearby walks, local ales, nicely lit bars, and especially friendly landlady

Tucked away up a country lane, this is an attractive 16th-c pub run by a friendly and helpful landlady. The low-ceilinged and relaxed panelled bar has West Berkshire Good Old Boy and a guest such as Fullers London Pride on handpump, decent wines by the glass and several malt whiskies. Three areas radiate from here; our pick is the parquet-floored part by the raised woodburning stove which has a couple of substantial old tables and a huge old-fashioned slightly curved settle. Other parts are slate and wood with a good mix of well spaced tables and chairs, and nice lighting. There's a front terrace for outside eating, a lovely long side garden with picnic-sets, and plenty of good downland walks nearby. In a separate single-storey building, the bedrooms (many have been redecorated recently) form an L around a pretty garden. James II is reputed to have used the pub on his way to visit his mistress who lived locally.

From a varied menu, the choice of food might include sandwiches, twice-baked natural smoked haddock and cheese soufflé, poached pear, walnut and stilton salad, chicken curry with an onion bhaji, leek and goats cheese tart, steak and kidney pudding, and venison casserole with dumplings. *Benchmark main dish: steak and kidney pudding £11.25. Two-course evening meal £18.20.*

Free house ~ Licensee Gill Hern ~ Real ale ~ Bar food (not Sun evening or Mon and Tues lunchtimes) ~ Restaurant ~ (01488) 668325 ~ Children allowed in bar only but must be over 7 evenings and in bedrooms ~ Dogs allowed in bar ~ Open 12-3, 5.30-11; 12-5.30, 7-10.30 Sun; closed Mon and Tues lunchtimes ~ Bedrooms: $79.50B/$99B
Recommended by I H G Busby, Julia and Richard Tredgett, Mr and Mrs H J Langley, Mr and Mrs P R Thomas, N R White

INKPEN Berkshire   SU3564 Map 2

Swan

Lower Inkpen; coming from A338 in Hungerford, take Park Street (first left after railway bridge, coming from A4); RG17 9DX

Extended country pub with rambling rooms, traditional décor, friendly staff, real ales and plenty of seats outside; bedrooms

This is a much-extended country pub with a 17th-c heart. The rambling beamed rooms have cosy corners, traditional pubby furniture, eclectic bric-a-brac and three log fires and there's a flagstoned games area and a cosy restaurant, too; piped music. Friendly helpful staff serve Butts and West Berkshire ales on handpump and local farm cider. There are picnic-sets outside on tiered front terraces overlooking a footpath; the quiet bedrooms are set away from the pub in a courtyard. The interesting farm shop next door sells their own organic beef and ready-made meals, as well as groceries, dairy products and so forth.

Popular bar food using their own farmed organic produce and home-made bread and pasta includes sandwiches, beef ravioli with basil tomato sauce and parmesan, brie and beetroot tatin with caramelised red onion, various home-made sausages, chicken in a creamy mushroom sauce, lamb shoulder in red wine and orange, and mixed seafood risotto. *Benchmark main dish: beef curry £12.95. Two-course evening meal £19.45.*

Free house ~ Licensees Mary and Bernard Harris ~ Real ale ~ Bar food (12-2(4 Sun), 7-9; not Sun evening or winter Mon) ~ Restaurant ~ (01488) 668326 ~ Children welcome ~ Open 12-2.30, 6-11; 12-11(4.30 Sun) Sat; closed Sun evening and winter Mon ~ Bedrooms: £70S/£90S

Recommended by John Robertson, CP

KINGHAM Oxfordshire   SP2624 Map 4

Plough 🍴 ♀ 🛏

Village signposted off B4450 E of Bledington; or turn S off A436 at staggered crossroads a mile SW of A44 junction – or take signed Daylesford turn off A436 and keep on; The Green; OX7 6YD

Friendly dining pub combining an informal pub atmosphere with upmarket food; bedrooms

More of a restaurant-with-rooms than a straightforward pub, this busy place continues to draw in plenty of cheerful customers. But despite the emphasis on dining, there's a properly pubby bar with some nice old high-backed settles, as well as brightly cushioned chapel chairs on its broad dark boards, candles on stripped tables and cheerful farmyard animal and country prints; at one end there's a big log fire and at the other (by an unusual cricket table), a woodburning stove. There's a piano in one corner and a snug separate one-table area opposite the servery which has Goffs Jouster and Hook Norton Hooky Bitter on handpump and good wines by the glass. The fairly spacious and raftered two-part dining room is up a few steps. If you stay, the breakfast is good. The heated smokers' shelter is at the back of the building.

Ambitious and inventive food might include scotched quails eggs, duck terrine with duck liver parfait and rhubarb toast, wild vegetable and potato casserole with a green pastry wafer, cock-a-leekie pie with mash, lemon sole with razor clams, tomatoes and potato pancake, and pork loin with crispy trotters, onion tart and sage and onion; interesting local cheeses. *Benchmark main dish: hereford beef with triple-cooked chips and horseradish butter £23.00. Two-course evening meal £22.00.*

Free house ~ Licensees Emily Watkins and Miles Lampson ~ Real ale ~ Bar food (all day) ~ Restaurant ~ (01608) 658327 ~ Children welcome ~ Dogs allowed in bar and bedrooms ~ Open 12-11(10.30 Sun) ~ Bedrooms: /£90S(£130B)

Recommended by Keith and Sue Ward, Myra Joyce, Richard Tilbrook, Anthony and Pam Stamer, George Atkinson, Richard Greaves, Edward Mirzoeff, Anthony Longden, Michael Doswell, David Glynne-Jones, Dr Martin Owton

KINGSTON LISLE Oxfordshire   SU3287   Map 4

Blowing Stone 🍴 ♟ 🍺

Village signposted off B4507 W of Wantage; OX12 9QL

OXFORDSHIRE DINING PUB OF THE YEAR

Easy-going chatty country pub with up-to-date blend of simple comfort, good food and drink

The Tuckers delighted us and our readers at their previous pub, the White Horse over at Woolstone, and have brought the same winning mix of easy country informality with good food and drink to this friendly village pub. Its heart is the central bar, where broad tiles by the log fire suit the muddy riding boots of the cheerful young people in from nearby training stables. They have the *Racing Post* alongside other daily papers, and most of the photographs on the pale sage walls are of racehorses, often spectacularly coming to grief over jumps. Several separate areas radiate off, most of them carpeted, quite small and snug, though a back dining conservatory is more spacious. Apart from a couple of high-backed winged settles, most of the furniture is an unfussy mix of country dining tables each with its own set of matching chairs, either padded or generously cushioned. Decent wines by the glass and Greene King Morland Original, Hook Norton Hooky Bitter, Ringwood Fortyniner and perhaps a White Horse ale named after the pub; service is quick and friendly and there may be unobtrusive piped music. The pretty front terrace has a couple of picnic-sets under cocktail parasols with more on the back lawn by a rockery; the Ridgeway and Uffington White Horse are both nearby. Many years ago one of your editors, in his teens, was proud of being able to 'sound' the blowing stone itself, a hole-filled boulder outside a cottage down just beyond the crossroads, which can be induced to produce a spine-tingling far-carrying horn blast. Alas, on his re-visit this year, he seemed to have lost the knack – or perhaps he'd just lunched too well here!

Sturdy lunchtime bar food (not Sunday) includes home-baked baguettes with soup or chips, generous ham and eggs and kedgeree, with more elaborate main menu choices like mixed game and foie gras terrine with rosemary toast and chutney, salami with cheeses, home-made sausages, vegetable wellington, spicy monkfish and king prawn curry with aubergine bhaji, and pork cassoulet with confit of duck, toulouse sausages and haricot beans; there's also a good value two-course Tuesday evening menu. *Benchmark main dish: chicken kiev with greek salad £13.50. Two-course evening meal £22.00.*

Free house ~ Licensees Angus and Steph Tucker ~ Real ale ~ Bar food (not Sun evening) ~ Restaurant ~ (01367) 820288 ~ Children welcome ~ Dogs allowed in bar ~ Open 12-11

Recommended by Michael Sissons, Mrs J M Robinson

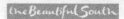

KIRTLINGTON Oxfordshire   SP4919 Map 4

Oxford Arms 🍴 🍷

Troy Lane, junction with A4095 W of Bicester; OX5 3HA

Civilised and friendly stripped-stone pub with enjoyable food and good wine choice

A long line of linked rooms are divided by a central stone hearth with a great round stove – and by the servery itself, with Brakspears and Hook Norton Old Hooky on handpump, an interesting range of wines in two glass sizes, and a good choice of soft drinks. The chef/landlord and his charming young staff ensure a genial atmosphere, helped by the tables' fat church candles and flower bunches. Past the bar area with its cushioned wall pews, creaky beamed ceiling and age-darkened flooring tiles, dining tables on parquet have neat red chairs, and beyond that leather sofas cluster round an end log fire; there is stripped stone throughout. A sheltered back terrace has teak tables under giant parasols with heaters, and beyond are picnic-sets on pale gravel.

Hearty well prepared food using good local ingredients, especially from Kelmscott, includes lunchtime sandwiches, wild garlic and goats cheese tart, salmon and prawn fishcakes, ham and eggs, a risotto of the day, venison burgers with triple-cooked chips, barbary duck leg confit with sweet chilli sauce, and well aged steaks; good cheeses, too. *Benchmark main dish: wild mushroom tagliatelle with parmesan and truffle oil £12.00. Two-course evening meal £18.50.*

Punch ~ Lease Bryn Jones ~ Real ale ~ Bar food (12-2.30, 6.30-9.30) ~ (01869) 350208 ~ Well behaved children welcome ~ Dogs allowed in bar ~ Open 12-3, 6-11; 12-3 Sun; closed Sun evening

Recommended by D C T and E A Frewer, Oxana Mishina, Veronica Hall

---

WELCOME TO THE INSPIRING SOUTH EAST OF ENGLAND

With mile upon mile of stunning coastline and unsurpassed countryside, and a rich history that is embellished with royal connections, the South East is a major player when it comes to day trips, short breaks and extended holidays. Added to this, you're spoilt for choice when looking for an outstanding pub where you can indulge in good quality fare that makes the most of local produce or somewhere to rest your weary head after a long day discovering all the exciting things the South East has to offer.

Each of the counties in the region has its own enthralling history for you to unravel. From Hastings in East Sussex to Windsor Castle in Berkshire, you're surrounded by Britain's proud heritage. The jewel in the crown is Winchester Cathedral, to be found in a city that was once England's capital, while the Royal Pavilion in Brighton is one of the most dazzling buildings that Britain has ever produced.

Leeds Castle, just four miles from Maidstone, is the ideal spot for long relaxing strolls and picnics, while the South Downs Way and Test Way are two of the country's most outstanding trails for a hiking or cycling day out. And don't overlook palatial Goodwood House, which is always worth a visit for its world-class horse-racing track and motor-racing circuit.

If you're taking the family along, head to a theme park such as Paultons Park on the edge of the New Forest National Park, where kids will delight in the ponies wandering free, or take them on safari at Port Lympne. If you still haven't had your fill of furry friends, there is always Howletts Wild Animal Park, or perhaps hop on a ferry to the Isle of Wight Zoo.

To locate the perfect pub for a stop over when you're on a tour of South East England visit
www.greatcountrypubs.com

For more information about even more things to do in the South East visit
www.visitsoutheastengland.com

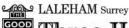

LALEHAM Surrey   TQ0568   Map 3

Three Horseshoes

Shepperton Road (B376); TW18 1SE

Contemporary styling in aged pub with popular food

Rich deep blue paintwork on the front of the long counter, on some table pedestals and on the dado lends a striking contrast to the white walls at this much freshened-up extending pub. Good natural light and clever lighting keep it airy and spacious while bare boards and a nice mix of farmhouse furniture give a relaxed and pubby feel. Efficient bar staff serve Sharps Doom Bar and a couple of guests such as Hogs Back TEA and Ringwood Best from handpumps and over a dozen wines by the glass; piped music. The dining areas are a little smarter with their grey woodwork and caramel leather chairs. There are tables out on a flagstoned terrace and picnic-sets on grass.

 Bar food includes sandwiches with chips or soup, smoked haddock and spinach tart with cheese sauce, caesar salad, duck liver and pistachio terrine with onion marmalade, devilled lambs kidneys, roast butternut and broad bean risotto, crispy duck with peppercorn sauce, lemon and thyme rotisserie chicken with mushroom and pancetta sauce, and well hung fillet steak. *Benchmark main dish: fish and chips £12.50. Two-course evening meal £19.50.*

Unique (Enterprise) ~ Lease Richard Brown ~ Real ale ~ Bar food (12-9.30(10 Fri, Sat)) ~ Restaurant ~ (01784) 455014 ~ Children welcome till 7.30pm ~ Open 11-11(11.30 Fri, Sat, 10.30 Sun)
Recommended by Susan and Neil McLean, M Ross-Thomas

LANGFORD Oxfordshire   SP2402   Map 4

Bell ♀ ◗

Village signposted off A361 N of Lechlade, then pub signed; GL7 3LF

Civilised pub with beams, flagstones, a good log fire, well chosen wines and beer, and quite a choice of bar food

In a quiet and charming village, this country dining pub is tucked away near the church. It's a friendly place with an informal country atmosphere and the simple low-key furnishings and décor add to the appeal. The main bar has just six sanded and sealed mixed tables on grass matting, a variety of chairs, three nice cushioned window seats, an attractive carved oak settle, polished broad flagstones by a big stone inglenook fireplace with a good log fire, low beams and butter-coloured walls with two or three antique engravings. A second even smaller room on the right is similar in character; daily papers on a little corner table. Hook Norton Hooky Bitter, Sharps Doom Bar and St Austell Tribute on handpump and a dozen wines by the glass. The bearded collie is called Madison. There are two or three picnic-sets out in the small garden with a play house; aunt sally.

 As well as fish specials such as crab and leek risotto and calamari with a parmesan crust and garlic and lemon mayonnaise, the well liked food might include sandwiches, eggs benedict, beefburger in a rustic roll, nut roast with tomato and basil sauce, thai green chicken curry, steak and kidney pie and rump of lamb on honey-roasted root vegetables with a red wine jus. *Benchmark main dish: seared king scallops with chorizo and rocket and parmesan salad £15.95. Two-course evening meal £20.00.*

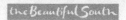

Free house ~ Licensees Paul and Jackie Wynne ~ Real ale ~ Bar food (12-1.45, 7-9; not Sun evening or Mon) ~ Restaurant ~ (01367) 860249 ~ Children welcome but no under-4s after 7pm ~ Dogs allowed in bar ~ Open 12-3, 7-11(midnight Fri, 11.30 Sat); 12-3.30 Sun; closed Sun evening, all day Mon

Recommended by Mrs L James, P and J Shapley, Grahame and Myra Williams, Henry Midwinter, Phil and Jane Hodson, Mrs Jean Lewis, KN-R, R K Phillips, Neil and Diane Williams, Graham Oddey, Jennifer and Patrick O'Dell

 LANGTON GREEN Kent   TQ5439   Map 3

Hare ♀

A264 W of Tunbridge Wells; TN3 0JA

Interestingly decorated Edwardian pub with a fine choice of drinks and popular food

With Kent now boasting three Brunning and Price pubs, this roomy mock-Tudor former hotel, dating from 1901, was one of the first in this much-liked chain to open in the South East. Inside, it's high-ceilinged and the rooms have been knocked through, with plenty of light flooding through large windows, especially in the front bar where drinkers tend to gather. Décor, more or less in period with the building, runs from dark-painted dados below light walls, 1930s oak furniture, light brown carpet and turkish-style rugs on stained wooden floors to old romantic pastels and a huge collection of chamber-pots hanging from beams. Greene King IPA, Abbot, Morland Original and Ruddles, alongside a couple of guests on handpump, lots of wines by the glass, over 100 whiskies and a fine choice of vodkas and other spirits; board games. French windows open on to a big terrace with picnic-sets and pleasant views of the tree-ringed village green. Parking is limited.

From a frequently changing menu, interesting modern bistro-style food might include devilled whitebait with lemon and caper mayonnaise, fried scallops with chorizo and chickpeas, sandwiches, steak, venison and mushroom suet pudding, wild mushroom and lentil pie with sweet potato mash, and fried bass with teriyaki noodles. *Benchmark main dish: steak, Guinness and stilton pie £11.95. Two-course evening meal £18.50.*

Brunning & Price ~ Manager Rob Broadbent ~ Real ale ~ Bar food (12-9.30(10 Fri, Sat; 9 Sun)) ~ Restaurant ~ (01892) 862419 ~ Children welcome (away from bar after 6pm) ~ Dogs allowed in bar ~ Open 12-11(midnight Fri and Sat, 10.30 Sun)

Recommended by B J Harding, Vernon Rowe, Ian Phillips

 LEIGH Surrey   TQ2147   Map 3

Seven Stars ♀

Dawes Green, S of A25 Dorking—Reigate; RH2 8NP

Popular country dining pub with enjoyable food and good wines

Many readers enjoy the child-free atmosphere (no piped music or games either) at this tile-hung 17th-c tavern. What's more, it's beautifully kept, welcoming, serves well kept beer and jolly good food. The comfortable saloon bar has a 1633 inglenook fireback showing a royal coat of arms, and there's a plainer public bar. The sympathetically done restaurant extension at the side incorporates 17th-c floor timbers imported from a granary. Greene King Old Speckled Hen, Fullers London Pride and Wells & Youngs Bitter are served from handpump, alongside decent wines with about a dozen by the glass. Outside, there's plenty of room in the beer garden at the front, on the terrace and in the side garden.

🍴 The nicely varied menu includes lunchtime ciabattas, breaded whitebait with caper and lemon mayonnaise, pheasant pâté, mushroom, leek and stilton risotto, curry and rice, porcini ravioli in creamy parmesan sauce with mushrooms, leeks and peas, home-smoked hickory ribs, roast chicken stuffed with brie, and confit duck leg with parsley mash. They do two sittings for Sunday lunch and it's advisable to book at all times. *Benchmark main dish: ham, egg and chips £10.95. Two-course evening meal £19.75.*

Punch ~ Lease David and Rebecca Pellen ~ Real ale ~ Bar food (12-2.30(4 Sun), 6-9(6.30-9.30 Fri, Sat); not Sun evening) ~ Restaurant ~ (01306) 611254 ~ Dogs allowed in bar ~ Open 12-10(11 Sat, 8 Sun)

Recommended by Michael and Margaret Cross, Tony and Jill Radnor, Ian and Barbara Rankin, J R Osborne, Mr and Mrs Price, Nick Lawless, M G Hart, Peter Loader, Simon and Mandy King

---

 LEY HILL Buckinghamshire   SP9901   Map 4

Swan 🍺

Village signposted off A416 in Chesham; HP5 1UT

Charming, old-fashioned pub with chatty customers, four real ales, and quite a choice of popular food

The professional and friendly licensees run a tight ship here and you can be sure of attentive, helpful service and good food and beer. It's all kept spic and span – not easy given the antiquity of the interior – and the atmosphere is chatty and relaxed. The main bar is cosily old fashioned with black beams (mind your head) and standing timbers, an old range, a log fire, a nice mix of old furniture and a collection of old local photographs. Brakspears Bitter, Greene King Old Speckled Hen, St Austell Tribute and Timothy Taylors Landlord on handpump and several wines by the glass. The dining area is light and airy with a raftered ceiling, cream walls and curtains and a mix of old tables and chairs on timber floors. It's worth wandering over the common (where there's a cricket pitch and a nine-hole golf course) opposite this little timbered 16th-c pub to turn back and take a look at the very pretty picture it makes, with its picnic-sets among flower tubs and hanging baskets (there are more in the large back garden).

🍴 Good, enjoyable food includes lunchtime sandwiches, black pudding with bubble and squeak, a poached egg and hollandaise, home-made burger with cheese and mustard mayonnaise, pork and leek sausages with onion gravy, bass with a sun-dried tomato, crayfish and herb sauce, and slow-cooked and crackled pork belly with apple purée and jus. *Benchmark main dish: seafood casserole £13.50. Two-course evening meal £20.50.*

Free house ~ Licensee Nigel Byatt ~ Real ale ~ Bar food (12-2.30(3 Sun), 6.30-9.30; not Sun or Mon evenings) ~ Restaurant ~ (01494) 783075 ~ Live music twice a month ~ Open 12-3, 5.30-11; 12-10.30 Sun; closed Mon evening

Recommended by Roy Hoing, LM, Ashley Frost, Peter and Giff Bennett, Jennifer Beeston and Julian Browne, Tracey and Stephen Groves, John Holroyd

---

> Half pints: by law, a pub should not charge more for half a pint than half the price of a full pint, unless it shows that half-pint price on its price list.

the Beautiful South

LISS Hampshire SU7826 Map 2

Jolly Drover 🛏

London Road, Hill Brow; B2070 S of town, near B3006 junction; GU33 7QL

Particularly well run traditional pub, comfortable and friendly, with real ales and pubby food; good bedrooms

Smiling quick service and generous helpings of traditional bar food continue to draw customers into this well run pub. The neatly carpeted low-beamed bar includes leather tub chairs and a couple of sofas in front of the inglenook log fire and they keep Bowman Swift One, Fullers London Pride and Sharps Doom Bar on handpump; daily papers, a silenced games machine in one alcove and board games. Several areas, with a gentle décor mainly in muted terracotta or pale ochre, include two back dining areas, one of which opens on to a sheltered terrace with teak furniture, and a lawn with picnic-sets beyond. The neat bedrooms are in a barn conversion.

Generous helpings of well liked pubby food include sandwiches, pollack goujons with tartare sauce, vegetable lasagne, steak and kidney in ale pie, sausages and mash, chicken curry, and a mixed grill. *Benchmark main dish: steak and kidney pie £10.50. Two-course evening meal £17.00.*

Enterprise ~ Lease Barry and Anne Coe ~ Real ale ~ Bar food (12-2(2.30 Sun), 7-9.30; not Sun evening) ~ Restaurant ~ (01730) 893137 ~ Children welcome ~ Open 11-2.30, 6-11; 12-4 Sun; closed Sun evening ~ Bedrooms: £70S/£80S
Recommended by Neil and Pippa King, Tony and Wendy Hobden, Tony and Jill Radnor

LITTLE MARLOW Buckinghamshire SU8787 Map 2

Queens Head 🍴

Village signposted off A4155 E of Marlow near Kings Head; bear right into Pound Lane cul-de-sac; SL7 3SR

Charmingly tucked away, with good food and beers, and an appealing garden

Thoroughly enjoyable all round, this is an unpretentious country pub that our readers like very much. The main bar, with a table of magazines by the door, has simple but comfortable furniture on its polished boards and leads back to a sizeable squarish carpeted dining extension with good solid tables. Throughout are old local photographs on the cream or maroon walls, panelled dados painted brown or sage, and lighted candles. On the right is a small, quite separate, low-ceilinged public bar with Brakspears Bitter, Fullers London Pride and a weekly changing guest on handpump, several wines by the glass, quite a range of whiskies and good coffee; neatly dressed efficient staff and unobtrusive piped music. On a summer's day, the garden of this pretty tiled cottage – though not large – is a decided plus, sheltered and neatly planted, with some teak tables, some quite close-set picnic-sets, and some white-painted metal furniture in a little wickerwork bower.

Enjoyable bar food includes lunchtime sandwiches, potted rabbit and pheasant pâté with home-made chutney, roast artichoke and red pepper lasagne, stuffed corn-fed chicken with leek and potato hash with pearl onion, pancetta and jus, and seafood casserole with rouille and gruyère croûton. *Benchmark main dish: fish and chips £10.95. Two-course evening meal £20.45.*

Punch ~ Lease Daniel O'Sullivan and Chris Rising ~ Real ale ~ Bar food (12-2.30 (4 weekends), 6.30-9.30) ~ Restaurant ~ (01628) 482927 ~ Children welcome ~ Open 12-11(10 Sun); closed 24-26 Dec

Recommended by D and M T Ayres-Regan, Doug Kennedy, Martin and Karen Wake, Roy Hoing, Tracey and Stephen Groves, Betsy and Peter Little, Mrs Shirley Hughes, Jamie and Sue May, Samantha Baxendale

 **LITTLE MISSENDEN** Buckinghamshire   SU9298   Map 4

Crown ◖ £

Crown Lane, SE end of village, which is signposted off A413 W of Amersham; HP7 0RD

Long-serving licensees and pubby feel in little brick cottage, with several real ales and traditional food; attractive garden

Sadly, it's rare nowadays to find a classic Chilterns local like this small brick cottage – which makes coming here all the more special. It's been in the same family for over 90 years and the friendly landlord keeps it spotless and deliberately traditional. There are old red flooring tiles on the left, oak parquet on the right, built-in wall seats, studded red leatherette chairs and a few small tables and a winter fire. A good mix of customers, including a loyal bunch of regulars, adds to the cheerfully chatty atmosphere. Adnams Bitter, Hook Norton Bitter, St Austell Tribute, and a guest or two such as Hogs Back Hop Garden Gold or Sharps Doom Bar on handpump or tapped from the cask, farm cider, summer Pimms and several malt whiskies; darts, bar billiards and board games. The large attractive sheltered garden behind has picnic-sets and other tables, and there are also seats out in front. The interesting church in the pretty village is well worth a visit. Bedrooms are in a converted barn (continental breakfasts in your room only).

 Straightforward lunchtime bar food such as good fresh sandwiches, soup, buck's bite (a special home-made pizza-like dish), filled baked potatoes, ploughman's, and steak and kidney pie. *Benchmark main dish: buck's bite £5.50.*

Free house ~ Licensees Trevor and Carolyn How ~ Real ale ~ Bar food (12-2; not evenings, not Sun) ~ (01494) 862571 ~ Open 11-2.30(3 Sat), 6-11; 12-3, 7-11 Sun ~ Bedrooms: £65S/£75S

Recommended by Patrick and Daphne Darley, Anthony Longden, Tracey and Stephen Groves, Roy Hoing, Peter and Lois McDonald

 **LODSWORTH** Sussex   SU9321   Map 2

Halfway Bridge Inn ⊕ ♀ ⇌

Just before village, on A272 Midhurst—Petworth; GU28 9BP

Restauranty coaching inn with contemporary décor in several dining areas, log fires, local real ales and modern food; lovely bedrooms

There's no doubt that most customers are here to eat and, although the tables are set for dining, there are regulars who do pop in for a chat and a pint. It's a smart place and the various bar rooms have plenty of intimate little corners and are carefully furnished with good oak chairs and an individual mix of tables; one of the log fires is a well polished kitchen range. The interconnecting restaurant rooms have beams, wooden floors and a cosy atmosphere. Sharps Doom Bar, Skinners Betty Stogs and Triple fff Moondance on handpump and 14 wines by the glass; piped music. At the back, there are seats on a small terrace. The bedrooms in the former stable yard are extremely stylish and comfortable.

Well presented – if not particularly cheap – the interesting food includes lunchtime filled ciabattas, spiced crab and crayfish gateaux with avocado salad and dill dressing, honey-roasted root vegetable tagine with chargrilled polenta, chicken and smoked ham pie, venison steak with bitter chocolate jus and sweet potato fondant, and jerk and herb-crusted lamb loin with minted and chilli couscous and mango relish. *Benchmark main dish: chicken and ham pie £13.75. Two-course evening meal £21.00.*

Free house ~ Licensee Paul Carter ~ Real ale ~ Bar food (12-2.30, 6.30-9.15) ~ Restaurant ~ (01798) 861281 ~ Children welcome ~ Dogs allowed in bar ~ Open 11-11; 12-10.30 Sun ~ Bedrooms: £85B/£120B

Recommended by Colin McKerrow, Tracey and Stephen Groves, Ian Wilson, Mrs Lorna Walsingham, Martin and Karen Wake

LONG CRENDON Buckinghamshire   SP6908   Map 4

Eight Bells ⚓ £

High Street, off B4011 N of Thame; car park entrance off Chearsley Road, not 'Village roads only'; HP18 9AL

Good beers and sensibly priced pubby food in nicely traditional village pub with charming garden

This pub's unchanging character fits well with the interesting old village, known to many from TV's *Midsomer Murders*. The little bare-boards bar on the left has two cool well kept regular beers on handpump, Hel's Bells (brewed for the pub) and Wadworths IPA, and two or three changing guests tapped from the cask such as Tring Jack o' Legs and Vale P&Q; they also have a decent choice of wines by the glass. A bigger low-ceilinged room on the right has a log fire, daily papers, darts, and a pleasantly haphazard mix of tables and simple seats on its ancient red and black tiles; one snug little hidey-hole with just three tables is devoted to the local morris men – frequent visitors. Service is cheerful, and full marks to the landlady not just for the excellent quality of her beers but for the way she's preserved the pub's unassuming and welcoming style in an area where pressure to move upmarket is so strong. The quiet garden behind is a particular joy in summer: well spaced picnic-sets among a colourful variety of shrubs and flowers; they play aunt sally.

Enjoyable modestly priced home-made pubby food includes lunchtime sandwiches, lemon and garlic field mushrooms with a rich tomato sauce and mozzarella, corned beef hash with a duck egg, beef or vegetarian lasagne, steak burger topped with cheddar or stilton, pork ribs in barbecue sauce, and chicken enchilada with salsa, guacamole and sour cream. *Benchmark main dish: home-made pie £9.25. Two-course evening meal £13.90.*

Free house ~ Licensee Helen Copleston ~ Real ale ~ Bar food (12-2(2.30 Sun), 6-9; not Sun evening or all day Mon) ~ (01844) 208244 ~ Children welcome ~ Dogs allowed in bar ~ Open 12-3, 5.30-11; 12-11 Sat and Sun; closed Mon lunchtime

Recommended by Doug Kennedy, David Lamb

Most pubs with any outside space now have some kind of smokers' shelter. There are regulations about these – for instance, they have to be substantially open to the outside air. The best have heating and lighting and are really quite comfortable.

LONG HANBOROUGH Oxfordshire   SP4214   Map 4

George & Dragon

A4095 Bladon—Witney; Main Road; OX29 8JX

Substantial well organised pub, something for everyone

This is almost best thought-of as two separate places – even three, if you count the peaceful back garden, with cream-painted picnic-sets among attractive shrubs, tables under a big dark canopy on a separate sheltered terrace, and further areas where you'll find rabbits and guinea-pigs. The original two-room bar, 17th-c or older, is all stripped stone, low beams, soft lighting, two stoves (one very elaborate), and a thoroughly traditional pubby feel with furnishings to suit. It then forms an L with a roomy thatched restaurant extension, which has comfortably padded dining chairs around the sturdy tables on its boards, plenty of pictures on deep pink walls, and decorative plates on the beams. Neat black-uniformed staff are friendly and efficient; they have well kept Courage Directors and Wells & Youngs Bombardier and Eagle on handpump, Weston's farm cider and a good range of wines; there may be soft piped music.

A very wide choice of good generous food (best to book at weekends) includes plenty of sandwiches and baguettes, duck and orange pâté, a brunch, cottage pie, a full rack of barbecue ribs, cherry tomato and mixed vegetable tarte tatin topped with cheese, lambs liver and bacon with onion gravy, and half a duck with creamy apple and calvados sauce; they also offer a two-course set menu on Monday and Tuesday and for OAPs at lunchtime on Wednesday and Thursday. *Benchmark main dish: steak in ale pie £12.95. Two-course evening meal £20.45.*

Charles Wells ~ Lease Mr A and Mrs J Wright ~ Real ale ~ Bar food (12-2(3 Sun), 6.30-9 (9.30 Fri and Sat); not Sun evening) ~ Restaurant ~ (01993) 881362 ~ Children welcome ~ Dogs allowed in bar ~ Open 12-3, 6-midnight; 12-4, 6.30-11 Sun
Recommended by Peter Grant, P M Newsome

LONGSTOCK Hampshire   SU3537   Map 2

Peat Spade

Off A30 on W edge of Stockbridge; SO20 6DR

Former coaching inn with boldly painted rooms, shooting and fishing themed décor, imaginative food and real ales; stylish bedrooms

In a pretty village and right by the River Test, this is well run pub where locals, diners and residents all mix easily together. There's quite a sporting feel – they arrange fishing and shooting – and there are stuffed fish, lots of hunting pictures and prints on the dark red or green walls and even a little fishing shop at the end of the garden. Both the bar and dining room have pretty windows, an interesting mix of dining chairs around miscellaneous tables on bare boards, standard lamps and candlelight, wine bottles, old stone bottles and soda siphons, a nice show of toby jugs and shelves of books. The atmosphere is chatty and informal. There's also an upstairs room with comfortable sofas and armchairs. Ringwood Best and local Flack Manor Double Drop on handpump and several wines by the glass; piped music. The terrace and garden have plenty of seats and there are lots of surrounding walks. The contemporary bedrooms are stylish and comfortable.

🍴 Highly thought-of food includes lunchtime sandwiches, earl grey smoked duck with pea shoots, honeycomb and shaved radish, chicken liver and foie gras parfait with plum compote, various sharing boards and platters, pumpkin and herb risotto, gammon with a fried duck egg, and bass with scallops, samphire and a brown shrimp and dill butter. *Benchmark main dish: trio of lamb £18.50. Two-course evening meal £21.00.*

Free house ~ Licensee Tracy Levett ~ Real ale ~ Bar food (12-2.30(4 Sun), 6-9.30) ~ Restaurant ~ (01264) 810612 ~ Well behaved children welcome ~ Dogs allowed in bar ~ Open 11-11 ~ Bedrooms: /£145S

Recommended by Phyl and Jack Street, David and Nicola Stout, Ann and Colin Hunt

LONGWORTH Oxfordshire   SU3899   Map 4

Blue Boar 🍴

Tucks Lane; OX13 5ET

Smashing old pub with a friendly welcome for all, good wines and beer, and fairly priced good food; Thames-side walks nearby

Mr Dailey has been running this 17th-c thatched stone pub for 32 years now (though his friendly staff tend to be more in evidence) and the atmosphere remains bustling and relaxed – helped by the genuine mix of both diners and chatty locals. The three low-beamed, characterful little rooms are warmly traditional with well worn fixtures and furnishings and two blazing log fires, one beside a fine old settle. Brasses, hops and assorted knick-knacks like skis and an old clocking-in machine line the ceilings and walls, there are fresh flowers on the bar and scrubbed wooden tables, and faded rugs on the tiled floor; benches are firmly wooden rather than upholstered. The main eating area is the red-painted room at the end and there's a quieter restaurant extension, too. Brakspears Bitter, Fullers London Pride and a guest like Prescott Hill Climb on handpump, 20 malt whiskies, nine wines by the glass, summer Pimms and quite a few brandies and ports. There are tables in front and on the back terrace, and the Thames is a short walk away.

🍴 As well as pizzas served all day, the reliably good food includes sandwiches, a changing terrine with home-made chutney, szechuan pepper and ginger squid, potato and rocket salad, beefburger with bacon, cheese and aioli, steak and kidney pudding, seasonal risotto with parmesan, roast wild salmon with wild mushrooms and a red wine sauce, and malaysian prawn or chicken curry. *Benchmark main dish: beer-battered fresh fish and chips £10.50. Two-course evening meal £18.45.*

Free house ~ Licensee Paul Dailey ~ Real ale ~ Bar food (12-2.30(3 Sun), 7-9; pizzas all day) ~ Restaurant ~ (01865) 820494 ~ Children welcome ~ Dogs allowed in bar ~ Open 11.30-11(midnight Sat)

Recommended by Tina and David Woods-Taylor, R K Phillips, Jennifer and Patrick O'Dell, Dick and Madeleine Brown

---

LOWER FROYLE Hampshire SU7643 Map 2

Anchor 🍴 🛏

Village signposted N of A31 W of Bentley; GU34 4NA

HAMPSHIRE DINING PUB OF THE YEAR

Civilised pub, lots to look at, real ales, good wines and imaginative bar food; comfortable bedrooms

There's always a really good mix of customers in this civilised but informal old pub – locals (often with their dogs) enjoying a pint and a chat and groups of friends, families and couples appreciating the particularly good food; all are made welcome by the friendly and efficient staff. There are low beams and standing timbers, flagstones in the bar and wood stripped floors elsewhere, sofas and armchairs dotted here and there, a mix of nice old tables and dining chairs, lit candles in candlesticks, an open fire and high bar chairs at the counter. Throughout there are all sorts of interesting knick-knacks, books, lots of copper, horsebrasses, photographs (several of Charterhouse School) and all manner of pictures and prints; paint colours are fashionable, values are traditional and they keep Andwells King John and Triple fff Altons Pride and Pale Ale on handpump, nine wines by the glass (including fizz) and interesting pressés. The bedrooms are stylish and breakfasts are good.

🍴 Imaginative and highly thought-of food might include sandwiches, pork and sage pâté with rhubarb chutney, hand-picked crab mayonnaise with chilli and lime, avocado purée and brown crab pâté on toast, wild mushroom risotto with parmesan and tarragon butter, local sausages with colcannon, free-range chicken kiev with haricot beans and chorizo, and halibut fillet with lentils, ham hock and spinach gnocchi. *Benchmark main dish: pork five ways £17.50. Two-course evening meal £22.00.*

Free house ~ Licensee Tracy Levett ~ Real ale ~ Bar food (12-2.30(3 Sat), 6.30-9.30 (10 Fri and Sat); 12-4, 7-9 Sun) ~ Restaurant ~ (01420) 23261 ~ Children welcome ~ Dogs allowed in bar and bedrooms ~ Open 11-11(midnight Sat; 10.30 Sun) ~ Bedrooms: £100S/£120S

Recommended by Martin and Karen Wake, John Branston, Tony and Jill Radnor, Dave Braisted

LOWER WIELD Hampshire SU6339 Map 2

Yew Tree 🍴 ♀ £

Turn off A339 NW of Alton at Medstead, Bentworth 1 signpost, then follow village signposts; or off B3046 S of Basingstoke, signposted from Preston Candover; SO24 9RX

Bustling country pub with smashing landlord, relaxed atmosphere and super choice of wines and good food; sizeable garden and nearby walks

As always, the enthusiastic Mr Gray and his friendly staff will give you a genuinely warm welcome here – whether you want just a drink and a chat or a full meal. There's a small flagstoned bar area on the left with pictures above its stripped-brick dado, a steadily ticking clock and a log fire. Around to the right of the serving counter – which has a couple of stylish wrought-iron bar chairs – it's carpeted; throughout there is a mix of tables, including some quite small ones for two, and miscellaneous chairs. Twelve wines by the glass from a well chosen list which may include summer rosé and Louis Jadot burgundies from a shipper based just along the lane. Bowman Eldorado and a beer from Triple fff named after the pub on handpump. There are solid tables and chunky seats out on the front terrace, picnic-sets in a sizeable side garden, pleasant views and a cricket field across the quiet lane; nearby walks.

🍴 Top quality food from an interesting menu includes sandwiches, smoked duck breast and pear salad with a beetroot and apricot compote, thyme and blue cheese creamy mushrooms on herbed toast, sausages of the week with spring onion and parsley mash and onion gravy, thai red chicken and baby corn curry, pork belly on caramelised apple with a calvados and apple sauce, and whole bass dressed with orange, fennel and rosemary. *Benchmark main dish: honey-roasted haddock with leeks and parsley sauce £10.50. Two-course evening meal £16.45.*

Free house ~ Licensee Tim Gray ~ Real ale ~ Bar food (not Mon) ~ Restaurant ~ (01256) 389224 ~ Children welcome ~ Dogs allowed in bar ~ Quiz night first Weds of month in winter ~ Open 12-3, 6-11; 12-10.30 Sun; closed Mon; first two weeks in Jan

Recommended by Margaret Ball, Darryl and Lindy Hemsley, Phyl and Jack Street, Ian Herdman, Tony and Jill Radnor, Richard and Stephanie Foskett, Martin and Karen Wake, John Walker, Philip and June Caunt, Stevie Joy, Glen and Nola Armstrong, Margaret Grimwood

LURGASHALL Sussex   SU9327 Map 2

Noahs Ark

Off A283 N of Petworth; GU28 9ET

Busy old pub in nice spot with neatly kept rooms, real ales and pleasing food

The position of this 15th-c tile-hung pub is charming as it overlooks the village green and cricket pitch; picnic-sets make the most of this and there are more in the large side garden. The simple, traditional bar is popular locally and has leather-topped bar stools by the counter where they serve Greene King IPA and Abbot and a guest such as Thwaites Wainwright on handpump, several wines by the glass, farm cider and a special bloody mary; also, beams, a mix of wooden chairs and tables on the parquet flooring and an inglenook fireplace. Open right up to its apex, the dining room is spacious and airy with church candles and fresh flowers on light wood tables; a couple of comfortable sofas face each other in front of an open woodburning stove. The pub border terrier is called Gillie and visiting dogs may get a dog biscuit.

🍴 To be sure of a meal, it's best to book a table beforehand: sandwiches (not Sunday), home-cured beetroot gravadlax with horseradish mousse, an antipasti plate, burger with cheese and bacon, shrimp, clam and smoked haddock risotto, free-range chicken caesar salad, and seared tuna steak with niçoise salad. *Benchmark main dish: home-made burger £9.95. Two-course evening meal £17.75.*

Greene King ~ Lease Henry Coghlan and Amy Whitmore ~ Real ale ~ Bar food (12-2.30, 7-9.30; 12-3.30 Sun; not Sun evening) ~ Restaurant ~ (01428) 707346 ~ Children allowed but not in bar after 7pm ~ Dogs allowed in bar ~ Open 11-11(midnight Sat); 12-10 Sun; 11-3.30, 5.30-11 in winter

Recommended by Ann and Colin Hunt

MARLOW Buckinghamshire   SU8586 Map 2

Two Brewers

St Peter Street, first right off Station Road from double roundabout; SL7 1NQ

Bustling, neatly kept pub close to the Thames with plenty of seating areas, quite an emphasis on dining, real ales and decent wines, and seats outside

As well as being right on the Thames Path, cheerfully painted picnic-sets at the front of this bustling pub have a glimpse of the river; there's also a sheltered back courtyard with more seats and tables – and a covered area, too. Inside, the interesting layout has low beams, shiny black woodwork, a nice mix of wooden tables and chairs on bare floorboards, nautical pictures and gleaming brassware. The River View Room and Cellar are set for dining. Brakspears Bitter, Fullers London Pride and Rebellion IPA and Mutiny on handpump, nice wines and coffee and good friendly service.

Enjoyable food includes lunchtime sandwiches, duck liver parfait with red onion chutney, fresh crab in lemon mayonnaise with red pepper coulis, wild mushroom risotto, a pie of the day, free-range chicken with potato and leek sauté and smoked salmon and prawn fishcake with chive butter sauce; they offer a two- and three-course set menu and may have summer Sunday barbecues. *Benchmark main dish: roast lamb £17.95. Two-course evening meal £20.90.*

Enterprise ~ Lease Anthony Burnham ~ Real ale ~ Bar food (12-3, 6.30-9.30; all day Sat; 12-4 Sun; not Sun evening) ~ Restaurant ~ (01628) 484140 ~ Children welcome ~ Dogs allowed in bar ~ Open 11-11(midnight Fri and Sat, 10.30 Sun)

Recommended by Robert Kibble

MILFORD Surrey   SU9542 Map 2

Refectory ⚑

Portsmouth Road; GU8 5HJ

Handsome building with plenty of interest inside, beams, timbering, fine stone fireplaces and so forth, plenty of room, real ales, and well liked food

The frontage of this interesting building is most appealing with its golden stone and timbering and it's thought to have been a former cattle barn, and a tea and antique shop. There are teak tables and chairs in the back courtyard by the newer extension and adjacent to the characterful pigeonry. Inside, it's L-shaped and mainly open-plan and throughout there are heavy beams and timbering, exposed stone walls, stalling and standing timbers creating separate seating areas and a couple of big log fires in handsome stone fireplaces. A two-tiered and balconied part at one end has a wall covered with huge brass platters and the rest of the walls are hung with some nice old photographs and various paintings. Individual dining chairs and dark wooden tables are grouped on the wood, quarry-tiled or carpeted flooring and there are rugs, bookshelves, big pot plants, stone bottles on window sills and fresh flowers. High wooden bar stools line the long counter where they serve Hogsback TEA, Phoenix Brunning & Price and four guests from brewers such as Adnams, Andwell and Hammerpot on handpump, around 16 wines by the glass and over 80 malt whiskies.

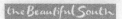

 As well as a good range of sandwiches and light meals, the popular food might include carrot and coriander soup, cracked wheat and chickpea cake with moroccan coleslaw and cinnamon yoghurt, star anise poached chicken with blood orange and toasted fennel salad, crab linguine, battered haddock, black cardamom braised beef with tropical fruit curry, red wine braised cuttlefish and calamari with poached garlic risotto, and spinach and onion pie. *Benchmark main dish: ham, egg and chips £9.95. Two-course evening meal £17.75.*

Brunning & Price ~ Manager Benjamin Redwood ~ Real ale ~ Bar food (12-10) ~ (01483) 413820 ~ Children welcome ~ Dogs welcome ~ Open 11.30-11; 12-10.30 Sun
Recommended by Richard Gibbs

MINSTER LOVELL Oxfordshire SP3211 Map 4

 # Old Swan & Minster Mill

Just N of B4047 Witney—Burford; OX29 0RN

Carefully restored ancient inn with old-fashioned bar, lots of beamed, comfortable antique-filled rooms, real ales, a thoughtful wine list and acres of gardens and grounds with fishing; exceptional bedrooms

Civilised and rather lovely, this newly restored old inn – with a history going back 600 years – is back in the *Guide* after a break. Of course, much emphasis is placed on the hotel and restaurant side but at its heart is the restful and unchanging small bar with stools by the ancient wooden counter; Brakspears Bitter, Oxford Gold and a guest beer on handpump and several wines by the glass from a fine list. Leading off here is a myriad of attractive low-beamed rooms with big log fires in huge fireplaces, red and green leather tub chairs, all manner of comfortable armchairs, sofas, dining chairs and wooden tables, rugs on bare boards or ancient flagstones, antiques and prints and lots of horsebrasses, bed-warming pans, swords, hunting horns and even a suit of armour; fresh flowers everywhere. Seats are dotted around the 65 acres of grounds (the white metal ones beside the water are much prized) and they have a mile of fishing on the River Windrush, tennis courts, boules and croquet. The bedrooms have a lot of character and some are luxurious.

 Using produce from their kitchen garden and other local, seasonal ingredients, the excellent food might include sandwiches, home-baked ham hock, crab apple and mustard seed terrine with home-made piccalilli, roast pumpkin risotto with truffle oil, steak in ale pie, fresh crab with celeriac and fennel rémoulade and cucumber spaghetti, coq au vin, and slow-roasted pork belly with white pudding and cider apple jus. *Benchmark main dish: 28-day-aged hung rib-eye steak £21.95. Two-course evening meal £22.45.*

Free house ~ Licensee Ian Solkin ~ Real ale ~ Bar food (12(12.30 weekends)-3, 6.30-9) ~ (01993) 774441 ~ Children welcome ~ Dogs allowed in bar and bedrooms ~ Open 12(12.30 weekends)-11(10.30 Sun) ~ Bedrooms: £145S/£165S
Recommended by Richard Gibbs

'Children welcome' means the pub says it lets children inside without any special restriction; some may impose an evening time limit earlier than 9pm – please tell us if you find this.

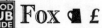

NORTH WALTHAM Hampshire　　　　SU5645　Map 2

Fox ✦ £

3 miles from M3 junction 7: A30 southwards, then turn right at second North Waltham turn, just after Wheatsheaf; pub also signed from village centre; RG25 2BE

Traditional flint country pub, very well run, with good food and drink, nice garden

Relaxed and chatty, the low-ceilinged bar on the left has lots of bottled ciders as well as Thatcher's on draught, and a well kept guest beer such as Saxon Archer along with Brakspears, Ringwood Best and West Berkshire Good Old Boy at attractive prices on handpump; ten wines by the glass, 22 malt whiskies and quite a collection of miniatures. The big woodburning stove, parquet floor, simple padded country-kitchen chairs, and poultry and 'Beer is Best' prints above the dark dado, all give a comfortably old-fashioned feel – in which perhaps the vital ingredient is the polite and friendly efficiency of the hands-on landlord. There may be very faint piped music. The separate dining room, with high-backed leather chairs on a blue tartan carpet, is rather larger. The garden, colourful in summer with its pergola walkway up from the gate on the lane, and with immaculate flower boxes and baskets, has picnic-sets under cocktail parasols in three separate areas, and overlooks rolling farmland (with a glimpse of the distant M3). Walks include a nice one to Jane Austen's church at Steventon.

Good home-made food includes a bargain bacon butty and other sandwiches, good value bar meals such as ham and eggs, a pie of the day or their speciality cheese soufflé, and restaurant dishes (which you can also eat in the bar) such as ham hock terrine with home-made chutney, gressingham duck breast with a black cherry and red wine sauce and local venison with a port glaze, shallots, field mushrooms, spinach and creamed swede; it's best to book for their Sunday roasts. *Benchmark main dish: cheese soufflé £12.50. Two-course evening meal £20.75.*

Free house ~ Licensees Rob and Izzy MacKenzie ~ Real ale ~ Bar food (12-2.30(3 Sun), 6.30-9.30(9 Sun)) ~ Restaurant ~ (01256) 397288 ~ Children welcome ~ Dogs allowed in bar ~ Open 11-11(midnight Sat)
Recommended by Patrick Spence, John Branston

NORTH WARNBOROUGH Hampshire　　　　SU7352　Map 2

Mill House ⊕ ♀ ✦

A mile from M3 junction 5: A287 towards Farnham, then right (brown sign to pub) on to B3349 Hook Road; RG29 1ET

Attractive layout, lovely waterside terraces, good food and drink

Newly done out in the Brunning & Price fashion – lots of well spaced tables in a variety of sizes and styles, rugs on polished boards or beige carpet, coal-effect gas fires in pretty fireplaces, a profusion of often interesting pictures – this old heavy-beamed and raftered mill building has several linked areas on its main upper floor. A section of glass floor shows the rushing water and mill wheel below, and a galleried part on the left looks down into a dining room on that level, given a more formal feel by its panelling. In warm weather a very big plus is the extensive garden, attractively landscaped around a sizeable millpond, with plenty of solid tables and chairs on various terraces; there are swings on a neatly kept stretch of grass. The well stocked bar has an interesting changing range of malt whiskies, a good choice of wines, and well kept B&P Original (the house beer, brewed by Phoenix), Andwells King John, Saxon Archer, Skinners Porthleven and Stonehenge Heel Stone and Pigswill on handpump; the young staff are cheerful and effective, and the atmosphere is relaxed and comfortable.

 Good modern food includes sandwiches, duck liver pâté with rhubarb chutney, ham and free-range eggs, aubergine, lentil and chestnut mushroom moussaka, chicken, pearl barley and vegetable broth with tarragon dumplings, citrus-cured bass, scallop and prawn salad, crispy wasabi rice balls and pickled ginger, and venison rump with venison faggot, bubble and squeak and juniper jus. *Benchmark main dish: braised lamb shoulder with dauphinoise potatoes £16.95. Two-course evening meal £17.70.*

Brunning & Price ~ Lease Ashley Harlow ~ Real ale ~ Bar food (all day) ~ Restaurant ~ (01256) 702953 ~ Children welcome ~ Dogs allowed in bar ~ Open 12-11.30(10.30 Sun)
Recommended by Richard Gibbs

OXFORD Oxfordshire   SP5106   Map 4

Bear

Alfred Street/Wheatsheaf Alley; OX1 4EH

Delightful pub with friendly staff, two cosy rooms, six real ales, and well liked bar food

Just off the busy High Street, this charming little pub is the oldest in the city. There are two small low-ceilinged, beamed and partly panelled ancient rooms, not over-smart and often packed with students, with a bustling chatty atmosphere, winter coal fires, thousands of vintage ties on walls and up to six real ales from handpump on the fine pewter bar counter: Fullers Chiswick, ESB, Gales HSB and London Pride and a couple of guests beers such as Butcombe Bitter and Prospect Gold Rush. Staff are friendly and helpful. There are seats under parasols in the back terraced garden where they hold summer barbecues.

 Bar food includes sandwiches, nibbles like olives and hummus with local bread, a proper ploughman's, various burgers including a vegetarian one, fish and chips, garlic tiger prawns, sausage and colcannon mash and belly of pork, and steak in ale pie. *Benchmark main dish: battered fish and chips £9.75. Two-course evening meal £15.00.*

Fullers ~ Manager Stuart Scott ~ Real ale ~ Bar food (all day) ~ (01865) 728164 ~ Children allowed in back room ~ Open 11-11(midnight Fri and Sat, 10.30 Sun)
Recommended by Andrea Rampley, Gordon Stevenson, Tim Williams, Pippa Manley, the Didler, Michael Dandy, Alasdair Mackay

OXFORD Oxfordshire   SP5107   Map 4

Rose & Crown

North Parade Avenue; very narrow, so best to park in a nearby street; OX2 6LX

Long-serving licensees in this lively friendly local, a good mix of customers, fine choice of drinks, and proper home cooking

Well behaved customers (no children or dogs) are still warmly welcomed by the sharp-witted Mr Hall and his wife – who have now run this straightforward local for 28 years – and there's always a good mix of undergraduates and more mature customers. The front door opens into a passage by the bar counter and the panelled back room, with traditional pub furnishings, is slightly bigger with reference books for crossword buffs; no mobile phones, piped music or noisy games machines, but they do have board games. Adnams Bitter, Hook Norton Old Hooky and a couple of guest beers on handpump, 26 malt whiskies and 14 wines by the glass. The pleasant walled and heated backyard can be covered with a huge awning; at the far end is a 12-seater dining/meeting room. The lavatories are pretty basic.

Traditional but enjoyable food includes interesting sandwiches and baguettes, omelettes, sausage and mash, all-day breakfast, and a hot dish of the day such as honeyed chicken or beef stew with herb dumplings. *Benchmark main dish: sausage and mash £7.00. Two-course evening meal £14.00.*

Free house ~ Licensees Andrew and Debbie Hall ~ Real ale ~ Bar food (12-2.15, 6-9) ~ No credit cards ~ (01865) 510551 ~ Open 11-midnight
Recommended by Robert Lorimer, Tony and Jill Radnor, the Didler, Chris Glasson

---

OXFORD Oxfordshire   SP5106   Map 4

Turf Tavern ⬤ £

Tavern Bath Place; via St Helen's Passage, between Holywell Street and New College Lane; OX1 3SU

Interesting character pub hidden away behind high walls, with a dozen ales, regular beer festivals, nice food, and knowledgeable staff

Hidden behind the high stone walls of some of the city's oldest buildings, this is arguably Oxford's most characterful pub. It's certainly one of the city's busiest but the helpful, knowledgeable young staff manage to deal quickly and efficiently with the wide mix of customers of all ages. The two dark-beamed and low-ceilinged small bars fill up quickly, though many prefer (whatever the time of year) to sit outside in the three attractive walled-in flagstoned or gravelled courtyards (one has its own bar); in winter, they have coal braziers so you can roast chestnuts or toast marshmallows and there are canopies with lights and heaters. Up to a dozen constantly changing real ales on handpump might include Greene King IPA, Abbot, Morlands Old Speckled Hen and Ruddles Best and maybe Black Country Fireside, Great Oakley Wot's Occurring, Rebellion IPA and Mutiny, Thwaites Lancaster Bomber and Wainwright and White Horse Wayland Smithy. They hold a spring and summer beer festival, keep Weston's Old Rosie cider and offer winter mulled wine.

Enjoyable and reasonably priced, the food includes sandwiches, crab cakes in coriander breadcrumbs with red pepper and chilli dipping sauce, various sharing platters, honey-roast ham and free-range eggs, beef in ale pie with chive mash and gravy, beef and vegetarian burgers, and hunter's chicken (cooked with bacon, barbecue sauce and cheese). *Benchmark main dish: battered cod and chips £8.45. Two-course evening meal £12.70.*

Greene King ~ Manager Stella Berry ~ Real ale ~ Bar food (11-9) ~ (01865) 243235 ~ Children welcome ~ Dogs welcome ~ Open 11-11(10.30 Sun); 12-10.30 Sun
Recommended by Colin and Louise English, Andrea Rampley, Michael Dandy, LM, G Jennings, MP, the Didler, David and Sue Smith, Clive and Fran Dutson, Roger and Donna Huggins, Malcolm Greening, Tim and Ann Newell, Barry Collett

---

Tipping is not normal for bar meals, and not usually expected.

PENN Buckinghamshire   SU9093 Map 4

Old Queens Head ♀

Hammersley Lane/Church Road, off B474 between Penn and Tylers Green;
HP10 8EY

Smartly updated pub with a good choice of drinks, and interesting modern cooking

They've opened up a new sunny terrace here that overlooks the church of St Margaret's and there are picnic-sets on the sheltered L-shaped lawn; just the place to relax after a walk on the nearby common or in the Penn woods. Inside, it's open-plan and decorated in a stylish mix of contemporary and chintz, with well spaced tables in a variety of linked areas, a modicum of old prints, and comfortably varied seating on flagstones or broad dark boards. Stairs take you up to an attractive (and popular) two-level dining room, part carpeted, with stripped rafters. The active bar side has Greene King IPA and Ruddles County on handpump, 21 wines by the glass, nine pudding wines and quite a few liqueurs; the turntable-top bar stools let you swivel to face the log fire in the big nearby fireplace. There are lots of daily papers and well reproduced piped music.

Enjoyable modern food includes weekday lunchtime sandwiches, pigeon breast with thyme rösti and a red wine and shallot dressing, free-range chicken liver parfait with wild mushroom pâté and onion marmalade, goats cheese and sweet potato cannelloni, trout fillet with warm artichoke and griddled fennel stew, and honey-glazed pork belly with black pudding beignets and sage cream. *Benchmark main dish: free-range chicken stuffed with chorizo on roast sweet peppers with wild garlic gnocchi £13.50. Two-course evening meal £20.75.*

Salisbury Pubs ~ Lease Tina Brown ~ Real ale ~ Bar food (12-2.30(3 Sat, 4 Sun), 6.30-9.30(10 Fri, Sat)) ~ Restaurant ~ (01494) 813371 ~ Children welcome ~ Dogs allowed in bar ~ Open 11-11; 12-10.30 Sun; closed 25 and 26 Dec
Recommended by Tracey and Stephen Groves

PENSHURST Kent   TQ5142 Map 3

Bottle House ⊗ ♀

Coldharbour Lane; leaving Penshurst SW on B2188 turn right at Smarts Hill signpost, then bear right towards Chiddingstone and Cowden; keep straight on;
TN11 8ET

Low-beamed, connected bars in country pub, friendly service, chatty atmosphere, real ales and decent wines, popular bar food and sunny terrace; nearby walks

Plenty of cosy nooks, with standing timbers separating the open-plan rooms into intimate areas, keep this chatty dining pub feeling pubby. There are beams and joists (one or two of the especially low ones are leather padded), an attractive mix of old wheelback and other dining chairs around all sorts of wooden tables, photographs of the pub and local scenes on the walls (some of which are stripped stone), an old brick floor by the copper-topped wooden bar counter with dark wooden boarding elsewhere; the fireplace houses a woodburning stove and most of the tables are set with fresh flowers. Harveys Best and Larkins Traditional on handpump, a local bottled ale, local apple juice and nearly a dozen wines by the glass from a good list; friendly, helpful young service and piped music. The sunny, brick-paved terrace has green-painted picnic-sets under parasols and some olive trees in white pots; parking is limited. Good surrounding walks in this charming area of rolling country.

From a monthly changing seasonal menu featuring local produce and a daily changing specials board, popular bar food might include ploughman's, fried scallops with pea purée and pancetta, duck liver and orange parfait with toasted brioche, poached pear and stilton salad with walnut dressing, chicken breast stuffed with goats cheese, salami and sun-dried tomatoes with spiced tomato and caper sauce, steak and kidney pudding, fillet of cod with spring onion and ginger sauce, roast pork belly with butternut squash and sage mash and apple and cider sauce, and well hung steak *Benchmark main dish: belly of pork £12.50. Two-course evening meal £19.60.*

Free house ~ Licensee Paul Hammond ~ Real ale ~ Bar food (12-10(9 Sun)) ~ Restaurant ~ (01892) 870306 ~ Children welcome ~ Dogs allowed in bar ~ Open 11-11 (10.30 Sun)

Recommended by LM, Bob and Margaret Holder, Tina and David Woods-Taylor, R and S Bentley, Ann and Colin Hunt, Gerry and Rosemary Dobson, Steve Coates, Simon and Helen Barnes, Heather and Dick Martin, Christian Mole, Derek Thomas

---

PETERSFIELD Hampshire   SU7227   Map 2

Trooper ⓘ 🍺 🛏

From A32 (look for staggered crossroads) take turning to Froxfield and Steep; pub 3 miles down on left in big dip; GU32 1BD

Charming landlord, popular food, decent drinks, and little persian knick-knacks and local artists' work; comfortable bedrooms

Our readers enjoy staying in the comfortable bedrooms of this well run pub whilst walking in the area and the warmly friendly Mr Matini is always on hand to ensure things run smoothly. The bar has a mix of cushioned dining chairs around dark wooden tables, old film star photos and paintings by local artists (for sale) on the walls, little persian knick-knacks here and there, quite a few ogival mirrors, lots of lit candles, fresh flowers and a log fire in the stone fireplace; there's a sun room with lovely downland views, carefully chosen piped music and newspapers and magazines to read. Bowman Swift One and Ringwood Best on handpump and several wines by the glass or carafe. The attractive raftered restaurant has french windows to a paved terrace with views across the open countryside, and there are lots of picnic-sets on an upper lawn. The horse rail in the car park is reserved 'for horses, camels and local livestock'.

Good, popular food includes filled lunchtime rolls, warm chicken liver salad, lime and ginger prawns with sweet chilli dip, hazelnut and mushroom parcel with roasted red pepper sauce, cumberland sausages with onion gravy, spicy thai-glazed salmon with sesame noodles, and chicken, pork and chorizo stew; Tuesday is pie day. *Benchmark main dish: lamb shoulder in honey and mint £15.00. Two-course evening meal £20.00.*

Free house ~ Licensee Hassan Matini ~ Real ale ~ Bar food (not Sun evening or Mon lunchtime) ~ Restaurant ~ (01730) 827293 ~ Children must be seated and supervised by an adult ~ Dogs allowed in bar ~ Open 12-3, 6-11; 12-3.30 Sun; closed Sun evening, Mon lunchtime, 25 and 26 Dec, 1 Jan ~ Bedrooms: £69B/£89B

Recommended by Keith and Chris O'Neill, Henry Fryer, Geoff and Linda Payne, Jenny and Peter Lowater, Mike and Mary Carter, John and Jackie Chalcraft, Richard Mason

PETERSFIELD Hampshire SU7129 Map 2

White Horse

Up on an old downs road about halfway between Steep and East Tisted, near Priors Dean – OS Sheet 186 or 197 map reference 715290; GU32 1DA

Unchanging and much-loved old place with a great deal of simple character, a cheerful, relaxed atmosphere, friendly licensees and up to ten real ales

A favourite with a great many of our readers, this remote 17th-c country pub has remained almost unchanged for 30 years. The two charming and idiosyncratic parlour rooms (candlelit at night) have open fires, oak settles and a mix of dark wooden dining chairs, nice old tables (including some drop-leaf ones), various pictures, farm tools, rugs, a longcase clock, a couple of fireside rocking chairs, and so forth. The beamed dining room is smarter with lots more pictures on the white or pink walls. They keep a fantastic range of up to ten real ales on handpump – such as two beers named for the pub, plus Butcombe Bitter, Caledonian Deuchars IPA, Fullers London Pride, Ringwood Best and Fortyniner and guests such as Elgoods Cambridge Bitter and Ossett Yorkshire Blonde, and lots of country wines. They hold a beer festival in June and a cider festival in September. There are some rustic seats outside and they have camping facilities. If trying to find it for the first time, keep your eyes skinned – not for nothing is this known as the Pub With No Name.

Using local produce and free-range meat the well liked food includes sandwiches, steak in ale pie, home-cooked honey-roast ham and free-range eggs, sausages with colcannon and onion gravy, prawn and salmon fishcakes with a mustard cream sauce, and winter game dishes. *Benchmark main dish: beer-battered fish and chips £11.95. Two-course evening meal £16.00.*

Gales (Fullers) ~ Managers Georgie and Paul Stuart ~ Real ale ~ Bar food (12-2.30, 6-9.30; some cold food all day weekdays; all day weekends) ~ Restaurant ~ (01420) 588387 ~ Children welcome ~ Dogs allowed in bar ~ Open 12-11

Recommended by Ann and Colin Hunt, Jack Matthew, Jenny and Peter Lowater, Mike and Eleanor Anderson, the Didler, W A Evershed

PLUCKLEY Kent TQ9243 Map 3

Dering Arms

Pluckley Station, which is signposted from B2077; or follow Station Road (left turn off Smarden Road in centre of Pluckley) for about 1.3 miles S, through Pluckley Thorne; TN27 0RR

Fine fish dishes plus other good food in handsome building, stylish main bar, carefully chosen wines, and roaring log fire; comfortable bedrooms

This former hunting lodge, originally part of the Dering Estate, was built in the 1840s as a mini replica of the manor house. Hence its imposing frontage, mullioned arched windows and dutch gables. Though emphasis is very much on the fish and seafood, the bar is characterful and comfortable and they do keep a beer named for the pub from Goachers on handpump as well as a good wine list of around 100 wines, 50 malt whiskies and an occasional local cider. High-ceilinged and stylishly plain, this main bar has a solid country feel with a variety of wooden furniture on the flagstone floors, a roaring log fire in the great fireplace, country prints and some fishing rods. The smaller half-panelled back bar has similar dark wood furnishings, and an extension to this area has a woodburning stove, comfortable armchairs, sofas and a grand piano; board games. Classic car meetings (the long-serving landlord has a couple of classics) are held here on the second Sunday of the month. Readers very much enjoy staying here – and the breakfasts are excellent.

The landlord himself buys fish straight from the boats in Folkestone and oversees the kitchen at all times. Dishes might include half a pint of prawns, oysters, provençale fish soup, pie of the day, whole crab salad, fried scallops with basil spaghetti and saffron sauce, fillet of black bream with marsh samphire and beurre blanc, and guinea fowl casseroled in sherry and tarragon sauce; seafood platter for two (24 hours' notice). *Benchmark main dish: fillet of turbot meunière £18.95. Two-course evening meal £24.90.*

Free house ~ Licensee James Buss ~ Real ale ~ Bar food ~ Restaurant ~ (01233) 840371 ~ Children welcome ~ Dogs allowed in bar ~ Open 11.30(12 Sun)-3.30, 6-11; closed Sun evening ~ Bedrooms: £55(£75S)/£65(£85S)

Recommended by Philip and Cheryl Hill, Patrick Noble, John Prescott, Simon Collett-Jones, Colin and Louise English

PRESTON CANDOVER Hampshire — SU6041 Map 2

Purefoy Arms ⊕ ♀

B3046 Basingstoke—Alresford; RG25 2EJ

Good food and wines in gently upmarket village pub

Reopened after refurbishment a couple of years ago, this has two pairs of smallish linked rooms. On the left, the airy front bar has chunky tables, including ones so tall as to need bar stools, and a corner counter serving a fine changing choice of wines, as well as Andwells and Black Sheep Best on handpump; this opens into a jute-floored back area with four dining tables and characterful mixed seats including old settles. The right-hand front room has red leather sofas and armchairs by a log fire, and goes back into a bare-boards area with three or four sturdy pale pine tables. An understated contemporary décor in grey and puce goes nicely with the informal friendliness of the service; there may be unobtrusive piped pop music. The sizeable sloping garden has well spaced picnic-sets, a wendy house and perhaps a big hammock slung between two of its trees; there are teak tables on a terrace sheltered by the pub. This is an attractive village, with nearby snowdrop walks in February.

Good food changing daily includes lunchtime sandwiches, quality tapas and other inventive dishes such as a crayfish and blood orange salad, ballottine of quail and foie gras with madeira jelly, burgers made with well hung rare-breed steak, butternut squash risotto with sage and aged parmesan, and specials like slow-roasted shoulder of rare-breed pork with white beans and pata negra (cured spanish ham), and whole plaice with cornish crab gratin. *Benchmark main dish: cider-baked ham, duck eggs and proper chips £10.00. Two-course evening meal £18.00.*

Free house ~ Licensees Andres and Marie-Louise Alenany ~ Real ale ~ Bar food (12-3, 6-10; 12-4 Sun; not Sun evening or Mon) ~ Restaurant ~ (01256) 389777 ~ Well behaved children welcome ~ Dogs allowed in bar ~ Open 12-3, 6-11.30; 12-6 Sun; closed Mon

Recommended by Ann and Colin Hunt, Jill Hurley

The ⊕ symbol distinguishes pubs where the food is of exceptional quality.

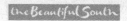

 PRESTWOOD Buckinghamshire   SP8799 Map 4

Polecat

170 Wycombe Road (A4128 N of High Wycombe); HP16 0HJ

Enjoyable food, real ales and a chatty atmosphere in several smallish civilised rooms; attractive sizeable garden

An evening favourite with several of our readers, this smart country pub has a quietly chatty atmosphere and helpful, friendly staff. Several smallish rooms, opening off the low-ceilinged bar, have a slightly chintzy décor: an assortment of tables and chairs, various stuffed birds, stuffed white polecats in one big cabinet, small country pictures, rugs on bare boards or red tiles, and a couple of antique housekeeper's chairs by a good open fire. Brakspears Bitter, Greene King Old Speckled Hen, Marstons Pedigree and Ringwood Best on handpump, 18 wines by the glass and 20 malt whiskies; may be piped music. The garden is most attractive with lots of spring bulbs and colourful summer hanging baskets and tubs, and herbaceous plants; quite a few picnic-sets under parasols on neat grass out in front beneath a big fairy-lit pear tree, with more on a big well kept back lawn. They don't take bookings at lunchtime (except for tables of six or more) so you do need to arrive promptly at weekends to be sure of a table.

 As well as lunchtime sandwiches, the popular food includes smoked salmon terrine with lime crème fraîche, chicken curry, chickpea, sweet potato and apricot tagine, seafood bake and specials such as ham hock terrine with apple chutney, bass with cherries and kirsch, and pork medallions with caramelised prune and chestnut stuffing and calvados sauce. *Benchmark main dish: steak and kidney pie £10.95. Two-course evening meal £17.00.*

Free house ~ Licensee John Gamble ~ Real ale ~ Bar food (12-2, 6.30-9 (not Sun evening)) ~ (01494) 862253 ~ Children in gallery or drovers' bar only ~ Dogs allowed in bar ~ Open 11.30-2.30, 6-11; 12-3 Sun; closed Sun evening; evenings 24 and 31 Dec, all day 25 and 26 Dec

Recommended by Simon Collett-Jones, Gordon Tong, Tracey and Stephen Groves, Roy Hoing, Peter and Jan Humphreys, Mel Smith

---

RAMSDEN Oxfordshire   SP3515 Map 4

Royal Oak 🍴 ⚲ 🍺

Village signposted off B4022 Witney—Charlbury; OX7 3AU

Busy pub with long-serving licensees, large helpings of varied food, a carefully chosen wine list, and seats outside; bedrooms

Facing the church and the war memorial in a peaceful village, this 17th-c Cotswold stone pub's unpretentious rooms have a mix of wooden tables, chairs and settles, cushioned window seats, exposed stone walls, fresh flowers, bookcases with old and new copies of *Country Life* and, when the weather gets cold, a cheerful log fire. Hook Norton Hooky Bitter, Wye Valley HPA and a guest from breweries like Stonehenge and Wickwar on handpump, and ten wines by the glass from a carefully chosen list. There are tables and chairs out in front and on the terrace behind the restaurant (folding back doors give easy access). The bedrooms are in separate cottages and there are some fine surrounding walks.

Quite a choice of food served in large helpings includes lunchtime sandwiches (if they are not too busy), baked baby brie with a tomato and herb crust, pasta with a wild mushroom and truffle sauce, home-made burgers with cheese or bacon, a pie of the week, a sri lankan curry, and daily specials like gloucester old spot sausages with haricot beans and onion gravy and pot-roasted local pheasant. *Benchmark main dish: fillet steak with peppercorn sauce £24.00. Two-course evening meal £18.25.*

Free house ~ Licensee Jon Oldham ~ Real ale ~ Bar food (12-2, 7-9.45) ~ Restaurant ~ (01993) 868213 ~ Children in restaurant with parents ~ Dogs allowed in bar and bedrooms ~ Open 11.30-3, 6.30-11; 12-3, 7-10.30 Sun ~ Bedrooms: £50S/£70S

Recommended by Dennis and Doreen Haward, Malcolm and Jo Hart, Roy Harding, Jane Hudson, Chris Glasson, Garry and Hannah Mortimer, Richard and Laura Holmes, Phil and Jane Hodson, Rob and Catherine Dunster, Mike and Mary Carter, JJW, CMW, Colin McKerrow

 READING Berkshire   SU7173   Map 2

Hobgoblin

2 Broad Street; RG1 2BH

No-frills pub with small panelled rooms, cheerful atmosphere, and eight quickly changing ales

With such a fine choice of up to eight real ales on handpump, this cheerfully basic town pub is as popular as ever. As well as three from the West Berkshire Brewery, the constantly changing choice might include Box Steam Tunnel Vision, Cottage Ambassador, Dark Star Summer Meltdown, Windsor & Eton Guardsman and Wooden Hand Cornish Mutiny. Pump clips cover practically every inch of the walls and ceiling of the simple bare-boards bar – a testament to the enormous number of brews that have passed through the pumps over the years (now over 6,378). They've also lots of different bottled beers, czech lager on tap, farm ciders, perry and country wines. Up a step is a small seating area, but the best places to sit are the three or four tiny panelled rooms reached by a narrow corridor leading from the bar; cosy and intimate, each has barely enough space for one table and a few chairs or wall seats, but they're very appealing if you're able to bag one; the biggest also manages to squeeze in a fireplace; piped music and TV.

 No food.

Community Taverns ~ Manager Katrina Fletcher ~ Real ale ~ No credit cards ~ (0118) 950 8119 ~ Children allowed in booths only ~ Open 11-11; 12-10.30 Sun

Recommended by Simon Collett-Jones, Dr and Mrs A K Clarke, the Didler, Nigel and Sue Foster, Paul Humphreys

 RINGMER Sussex   TQ4313   Map 3

Cock £

Uckfield Road – blocked-off section of road off A26 N of village turn-off; BN8 5RX

16th-c country pub with a wide choice of popular bar food, real ales in character bar, and plenty of seats in the garden

Particularly on a chilly evening, the unspoilt bar of this 16th-c weatherboarded pub is a cosy and friendly refuge. There's a log fire in the inglenook fireplace (lit from October to April), traditional pubby furniture on flagstones, heavy beams and Fullers London Pride, Harveys Best and a guest like Hogs Back Spring Ale on handpump, up to a dozen wines by the glass, 12 malt whiskies and Weston's summer cider; piped music. There are three dining areas. Outside on the terrace and in the garden are lots of picnic-sets with views across open fields to the South Downs; the sunsets are pretty. Visiting dogs are offered a bowl of water and a chew, and their own dogs are called Fred and Tally.

From an extensive menu and using local produce, the well liked food might include sandwiches, chicken liver pâté, deep-fried camembert with cranberry sauce, home-cooked ham and free-range eggs, mushroom and red pepper stroganoff, liver and bacon with mash and onion gravy, local venison burger with spicy relish, and chicken breast with a cheese and spinach sauce. *Benchmark main dish: steak in ale pie £10.25. Two-course evening meal £15.70.*

Free house ~ Licensees Ian, Val and Matt Ridley ~ Real ale ~ Bar food (12-2.15(2.30 Sat), 6-9.30; all day Sun) ~ Restaurant ~ (01273) 812040 ~ Well behaved children welcome away from bar ~ Dogs allowed in bar ~ Open 11-3, 6-11.30; 11-11.30 Sun
Recommended by Tony and Shirley Albert, Mike and Eleanor Anderson, Alan Franck

 ROCKBOURNE Hampshire   SU1118 Map 2

Rose & Thistle 🍽 ♀

Signed off B3078 Fordingbridge—Cranborne; SP6 3NL

Pretty pub with hands-on landlady and friendly staff, informal bars, real ales, good food, and seats in garden

Kerry Dutton is a first-class, hands-on landlady and runs her 16th-c thatched pub with great efficiency and friendliness. The bar has homely dining chairs, stools and benches around a mix of old pubby tables and there's a two-roomed restaurant with a log fire in each (one is a big brick inglenook), old engravings and cricket prints and an informal and relaxed atmosphere. Fullers London Pride, Palmers Copper Ale and Timothy Taylors Landlord on handpump, a dozen wines (and prosecco) by the glass and Weston's cider. There are benches and tables under the pretty hanging baskets at the front of the building, with picnic-sets under parasols on the grass; good nearby walks. This is a pretty village on the edge of the New Forest.

Using local, seasonal produce, the reliably good food includes sandwiches, smoked fish platter, lunchtime welsh rarebit and local pork and leek sausages with wholegrain mustard mash and onion gravy, slow-cooked pork belly with bacon, black pudding and apple, confit of duck leg on braised flageolet beans, pancetta and tarragon, and fish and game specials. *Benchmark main dish: steak and kidney pudding £13.95. Two-course evening meal £21.90.*

Free house ~ Licensee Kerry Dutton ~ Real ale ~ Bar food (12-2.30, 7-9.30; 12-3 Sun; not Sun evening) ~ Restaurant ~ (01725) 518236 ~ Children welcome ~ Dogs allowed in bar ~ Open 11-3, 6-11; 11-11 Sat; 12-10.30(8 in winter) Sun
Recommended by Nick Lawless, Peter Barnwell, Mrs J Butler, Mr and Mrs P R Thomas

---

Anyone claiming to arrange or prevent inclusion of a pub in the *Guide* is a fraud. Pubs are included only if recommended by genuine readers and if our own anonymous inspection confirms that they are suitable.

ROLVENDEN Kent   TQ8431   Map 3

Bull

Regent Street; TN17 4PB

Cottagey pub with relaxed bar, friendly atmosphere and bar food

This small tile-hung cottage has a chatty informal main bar with a woodburning stove in the fine old brick ingelnook, dark brown high-backed leather dining chairs around rustic tables on stripped floorboards, some grey-painted built-in panelled wall seats and a few high bar chairs by the counter where they serve Fullers London Pride, Harveys and Larkins on handpump and just under a dozen wines by the glass. There's a flatscreen TV in one corner and plenty of fresh flowers. The dining room – with less character – has similar chairs around pale oak tables and a decorative fireplace. Helpful service and piped music. There are seats in the back garden and a few picnic-sets in front.

Bar food might include aubergine pâté with roast tomato chutney, ploughman's, sandwiches, steak and stilton pie, roast vegetable tagine, roast salmon fillet in crayfish and sorrel sauce, home-made burger, and rib-eye steak. *Benchmark main dish: chicken and bacon pie £9.95. Two-course evening meal £17.45.*

Free house ~ Licensee Peter Hughes-Smith ~ Real ale ~ Bar food (12-2.30(6 Sun), 6-9; not Sun evening) ~ Restaurant ~ (01580) 241212 ~ Children welcome ~ Dogs allowed in bar ~ Open 11(12 Sun)-11
Recommended by Richard Gibbs

ROTHERFIELD GREYS Oxfordshire   SU7282   Map 2

Maltsters Arms ♀

Can be reached off A4155 in Henley, via Greys Road passing Southfields long-stay car park; or follow Greys Church signpost off B481 N of Sonning Common; RG9 4QD

Well run, civilised Chilterns country pub, nice scenery and walks

Friendly helpful staff make you feel quickly at home here, and they have a winter open fire, decent coffee and a dozen wines by the glass as well as well kept Brakspears Bitter and Old and a guest such as Jennings Cumberland on handpump. The maroon-carpeted front room has comfortable wall banquettes and lots of horsebrasses on its black beams; there may be soft piped music. Beyond the serving area, which has hop bines and pewter tankards hanging from its joists, a back room has cricketing prints on dark red walls over a shiny panelled dado, and a mix of furnishings from pink-cushioned pale wooden dining chairs to a pair of leatherette banquettes forming a corner booth. The chocolate labradors have been here as long as the licensees – 13 years. Terrace tables under a big heated canopy are set with linen for meals, and the grass behind has picnic-sets under green parasols, looking out over paddocks to rolling woodland beyond. Greys Court (NT) is not far and two good walks pass close by.

A wide choice of reasonably priced home-made food runs from from paninis through chicken liver mousse, a daily pie, spinach gnocchi on tomato passata, baked smoked haddock florentine with béchamel sauce, crispy belly of pork chinese style and slow-roasted half shoulder of lamb with mint gravy; it's best to book for weekends. *Benchmark main dish: chicken and mushroom pancake £8.95. Two-course evening meal £16.25.*

Brakspears ~ Tenants Peter and Helen Bland ~ Real ale ~ Bar food (12-2.15(2.30 Sun),
6.15-9.15; not Sun evening) ~ Restaurant ~ (01491) 628400 ~ Children welcome ~ Dogs
allowed in bar ~ Open 11.45-3, 6-11(midnight Sat); 12-9(5pm in winter) Sun

*Recommended by Roy and Jean Russell, Sharon Oldham, Ross Balaam, Roy Hoing, Tony and
Gill Powell, Simon Collett-Jones*

 RUSCOMBE Berkshire   SU7976   Map 2

Royal Oak

Ruscombe Lane (B3024 just E of Twyford); RG10 9JN

**Wide choice of popular food at welcoming pub with interesting
furnishings and paintings, and adjoining antiques and collectables shop**

The new Binghams Brewery is just across the road from this
welcoming, well run pub (known locally as Buratta's) and the Space
Hoppy and Twyford Tipple arrive on a barrow; they also have Fullers
London Pride on handpump and stock wines from the Stanlake Park
Vineyard (also in the village). The open-plan carpeted interior is well laid
out so that each bit is fairly snug, but still manages to keep the overall
feel of a lot of people enjoying themselves. A good variety of furniture
runs from dark oak tables to big chunky pine ones with mixed seating to
match – the two sofas facing one another are popular. Contrasting with
the old exposed ceiling joists, mostly unframed modern paintings and
prints decorate the walls – mainly dark terracotta over a panelled dado.
Picnic-sets are ranged around a venerable central hawthorn in the garden
behind (where there are ducks and chickens); summer barbecues. The
landlady's antiques and collectables shop is open during pub hours. The
pub is on the Henley Arts Trail.

Using their own eggs and some local produce, the good, popular food includes
sandwiches, chicken liver pâté with red onion marmalade, feta cheese, sun-
dried tomato and olive salad with parma ham, mushroom and leek stroganoff, saddle
of rabbit with garlic and mashed potato, beef stroganoff, and salmon and prawn
linguine. *Benchmark main dish: black pudding stack £9.95. Two-course evening
meal £21.45.*

Enterprise ~ Lease Jenny and Stefano Buratta ~ Real ale ~ Bar food (12-2.30, 6.30-9.30;
12-4 Sun; not Sun or Mon evenings) ~ Restaurant ~ (0118) 934 5190 ~ Children welcome
~ Dogs welcome ~ Open 12-3, 6-11; 12-4 Sun; closed Sun and Mon evenings

Recommended by Paul Humphreys, John Branston, Tracey and Stephen Groves

 RYE Sussex   TQ9120   Map 3

Ship

The Strand, at the foot of Mermaid Street; TN31 7DB

**Informal and prettily set old inn with a relaxed atmosphere,
straightforward furnishings, local ales, and often inventive food**

There's an easy-going atmosphere and a friendly welcome from the
pleasant staff in this 16th-c pub. The ground floor is all opened up,
from the sunny big-windowed front part to a snugger part at the back,
with a log fire in the stripped-brick fireplace below a stuffed boar's head,
and a feeling of separate areas is enhanced by the varied flooring:
composition, stripped boards, flagstones, a bit of carpet in the armchair
corner. There are beams and timbers, a mixed bag of rather second-hand-
feeling furnishings – a cosy group of overstuffed leather armchairs and

sofa, random stripped or Formica-topped tables and various café chairs – that suit it nicely, as do the utilitarian bulkhead wall lamps. Harveys Best and a couple of local guest beers such as Old Dairy Blue Top and Whitstable Oyster Stout on handpump, local farm cider and perry, and lots of wines by the glass; piped music and board games. Out by the quiet lane are picnic-sets and one or two cheerful oilcloth-covered tables.

🍴 Interesting food using local ingredients includes sandwiches, duck, fig and prune terrine with red onion marmalade, smoked haddock fishcake with spinach, a poached egg and grain mustard sauce, rabbit stew, lamb with jerusalem artichoke gratin and quince aioli, and specials like chicken with a pea, broad bean and dill risotto. *Benchmark main dish: toad in the hole £10.75. Two-course evening meal £19.00.*

Enterprise ~ Lease Karen Northcote ~ Real ale ~ Bar food (12-3(3.30 weekends), 6.30-10; they serve breakfast from 8.30am) ~ (01797) 222233 ~ Children welcome ~ Dogs welcome ~ Open 10am-11pm; 12-10.30pm Sun ~ Bedrooms: £80B/£90S(£100B)

Recommended by Barry Collett, Mike Gorton, Mike and Eleanor Anderson

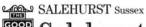

SALEHURST Sussex   TQ7424   Map 3

Salehurst Halt

Village signposted from Robertsbridge bypass on A21 Tunbridge Wells—Battle; Church Lane; TN32 5PH

Relaxed small local in quiet hamlet, chatty atmosphere, real ales, well liked bar food, and seats in pretty back garden

Always bustling and friendly, this informal little pub is very much enjoyed by both locals and visitors. To the right of the door, there's a small stone-floored area with a couple of tables, a piano, a settle, TV and an open fire. To the left, there's a nice long scrubbed-pine table with a couple of sofas, a mix of more ordinary pubby tables and wheelback and mate's chairs on the wood-strip floor and may be piped music; board games. Dark Star American Pale Ale, Harveys Best and Old Dairy Silver Top on handpump, several malt whiskies and decent wines by the glass. The back terrace has metal chairs and tiled tables and there are more seats in the landscaped garden with views out over the Rother Valley; outdoor table tennis.

🍴 As well as a fair weather wood-fired pizza oven, the popular bar food includes filled baguettes, smashing burgers, faggots and mushy peas, venison sausages, various pies, lemon sole with brown butter, and onglet steaks. *Benchmark main dish: goat curry £10.00. Two-course evening meal £15.00.*

Free house ~ Licensee Andrew Augarde ~ Real ale ~ Bar food (not Mon) ~ (01580) 880620 ~ Children welcome ~ Dogs welcome ~ Open 12-3, 6-11; 12-11 Sat; closed Mon

Recommended by Geoff and Linda Payne, Tony and Wendy Hobden, Ellie Weld, David London, Robert Mitchell

---

The letters and figures after the name of each town are its Ordnance Survey map reference. 'Using the *Guide*' explains how it helps you find a pub, in road atlases or on large-scale maps as well as in our own maps.

SEVENOAKS Kent   TQ5352 Map 3

White Hart ♀

Tonbridge Road (A225 S, past Knole); TN13 1SG

Well run and bustling old coaching inn with a civilised atmosphere in many bar rooms, a thoughtful choice of drinks, enjoyable modern food and friendly, helpful staff

Part of the Brunning & Price group, this sizeable early 18th-c coaching inn is extremely popular with both drinkers and diners. The many rooms are interconnected by open doorways and steps and there are several open fires and woodburning stoves. All manner of nice wooden dining chairs around tables of every size sit on rugs or varnished bare floorboards, the cream walls are hung with lots of prints and old photographs (many of local scenes or schools) and there are fresh flowers and plants, daily papers to read, board games and a bustling, chatty atmosphere. Friendly, efficient staff serve Brunning & Price Original (brewed for the pub by Phoenix), Fullers London Pride, Harveys Best, Shepherd Neame Spitfire and two or three guests from brewers such as Adnams and BrewDog, and they keep over 20 good wines by the glass, a fair choice of ciders and over 60 whiskies. It's all very civilised. At the front of the building there are picnic-sets under parasols.

Interesting and enjoyable modern bar food includes lamb patty on toasted muffin with welsh rarebit and carrot relish, crab and horseradish tart, charcuterie, ploughman's, sandwiches, crab linguine, battered haddock, fried bass with stir-fried vegetables and noodle salad, rump of lamb with lavender crust, spring vegetable casserole with wild garlic dumplings and braised beef in port and cranberry. *Benchmark main dish: beef and ale pie £11.50. Two-course evening meal £17.25.*

Brunning & Price ~ Manager Chris Little ~ Real ale ~ Bar food (12-10(9.30 Sun)) ~ Restaurant ~ (01732) 452022 ~ Children welcome away from bar until 7pm ~ Dogs allowed in bar ~ Open 11-11; 12-10.30 Sun

Recommended by Derek Thomas, Richard Green

SHALFLEET Isle of Wight   SZ4089 Map 2

New Inn ⊛ ♀

A3054 Newport—Yarmouth; PO30 4NS

ISLE OF WIGHT DINING PUB OF THE YEAR

Cheerful pub with seafood specialities, good beers and wines, too

Going from strength to strength, this nice old 18th-c former fishermen's haunt offers a genuinely happy atmosphere, great seafood and well kept beer. Its rambling rooms have plenty of character with warm fires, yachting photographs and pictures, boarded ceilings and scrubbed-pine tables on flagstone, carpet and slate floors. Goddards Fuggle-Dee-Dum, and Sharps Doom Bar are kept under light blanket pressure, and they stock over 60 wines; piped music. As it's popular, you will need to book and there may be double sittings in summer.

Their famous crab sandwich, seafood platter and crab and lobster salads are served alongside a good choice of fish dishes and pubbier options such as sandwiches, ploughman's, steak and ale pie, gnocchi with mushroom, parsley and walnut cream sauce, and various steaks. *Benchmark main dish: seafood platter £27.50. Two-course evening meal £18.30.*

Enterprise ~ Lease Mr Bullock and Mr McDonald ~ Real ale ~ Bar food (12-2.30, 6-9.30) ~ (01983) 531314 ~ Children welcome ~ Dogs allowed in bar ~ Open 12-11(10.30 Sun)

Recommended by Rochelle Seifas, Gareth James, David Glynne-Jones, Mike Tucker, George Atkinson, Paul Humphreys, David Hoult, Bruce and Sharon Eden, Mr and Mrs P D Titcomb, Joshua Fancett, Penny and Peter Keevil, Mrs Joyce Robson

SHAMLEY GREEN Surrey   TQ0343 Map 3

Red Lion
The Green; GU5 0UB

Pleasant dining pub with tasty food and pleasant gardens

The front garden of this prettily positioned pub overlooks the village green and is quite delightful in summer when there's a cricket match underway. Inside, it's fairly traditional with real fires in its two bars, a mix of new and old wooden tables and chairs on bare boards and red carpeting, stripped standing timbers, fresh white walls and deep red ceilings; piped music. They serve well kept Youngs and a couple of guests such as Hogs Back TEA and Sharps Doom Bar and over a dozen wines by the glass. At the back, hand-made rustic tables and benches are closely set on a terrace, and there are more on a lawn beyond.

As well as sandwiches and ploughman's, bar food includes mushrooms stuffed with brie, garlic king prawns, warm bacon and scallop salad, chicken caesar salad, wild mushroom risotto, spiced pork belly with chinese stir-fried vegetables, lamb shank cooked in red wine, sausage and mash, fish and chips, and daily specials such as malaysian chicken curry. *Benchmark main dish: fried bass £13.50. Two-course evening meal £20.00.*

Punch ~ Lease Debbie Ersser ~ Real ale ~ Bar food (12-2.30(3 Sat, Sun), 6.30-9.30(8.30 Sun)) ~ Restaurant ~ (01483) 892202 ~ Children welcome ~ Dogs allowed in bar ~ Open 11.30-11; 12-10.30 Sun; closed Sun evening Christmas-Easter

Recommended by Shirley Mackenzie

SHANKLIN Isle of Wight   SZ5881 Map 2

Fishermans Cottage £
Bottom of Shanklin Chine; PO37 6BN

On the beach at the foot of Shanklin Chine, simple food

Just a few minutes' walk from busy Shanklin's Esplanade, this unchanging thatched cottage, peacefully tucked into the cliffs and quite literally on Appley beach, enjoys one of the nicest and most unusual settings of any pub we know. Tables on the terrace soak up the sun by day and, later, moonlight shimmers on the sea. It's a lovely walk to get here along the zigzagged path down the steep and sinuous chine, the beautiful gorge that was the area's original tourist attraction. Inside, the clean little flagstoned rooms have an eclectic mix of bric-a-brac including skulls hanging from the low beams and navigation lamps in the windows, with photographs, paintings and engravings on the stripped-stone walls. Goddards Fuggle-Dee-Dum and Yates Undercliff are on handpump; piped music and wheelchair access. Do take note that the pub is closed out of season.

Pubby food includes sandwiches, ploughman's, vegetable lasagne, cottage or fisherman's pie, and scampi. *Benchmark main dish: seafood pancake £10.95. Two-course evening meal £17.90.*

Free house ~ Licensees Ann Springman and Eric Wright ~ Real ale ~ Bar food (11-2, 6-8) ~ (01983) 863882 ~ Children welcome ~ Dogs welcome ~ Live entertainment Tues, Fri, Sat evening ~ Open 11-11; closed end Oct-early Mar
Recommended by anon

SHILTON Oxfordshire   SP2608   Map 4

Rose & Crown
Just off B4020 SE of Burford; OX18 4AB

Simple and appealing little village pub, with a relaxed civilised atmosphere, real ales and good food

Unspoilt – but in a subtly upmarket way – this pretty 17th-c stone-built pub is cosy and friendly with a good mix of customers. The small front bar has low beams and timbers, exposed stone walls, a log fire in a big fireplace and half a dozen or so kitchen chairs and tables on the red tiled floor. There are usually a few locals at the planked counter where they serve Hook Norton Old Hooky, Wells & Youngs Bitter and Wye Valley Dorothy Goodbody's Golden Ale on handpump and 10 wines by the glass; big cafetières of coffee. A second room, similar but bigger, is used mainly for eating, with flowers on the tables and another fireplace. At the side, an attractive garden has picnic-sets.

Cooked by the landlord, the highly thought-of food includes lunchtime filled ciabattas, pigeon terrine with red onion marmalade, aubergine parmigiana baked with mozzarella, steak and mushroom in ale pie, chicken milanese with gremolata, and roast venison with celeriac purée and cumberland sauce. *Benchmark main dish: fish pie £12.50. Two-course evening meal £17.75.*

Free house ~ Licensee Martin Coldicott ~ Real ale ~ Bar food (12-2(2.45 weekends and bank hols), 7-9; maybe not winter Sun evenings) ~ (01993) 842280 ~ Well behaved children welcome until 7pm ~ Dogs allowed in bar ~ Open 11.30-3, 6-11; 11.30-11 Fri and Sat; 12-10 Sun

Recommended by Jean and Douglas Troup, William Goodhart, Anthony Barnes, Martin and Karen Wake, David Lamb, Richard Wyld, Glenwys and Alan Lawrence, R K Phillips, T R Austin, Guy Vowles

SHIPLAKE Oxfordshire   SU7779   Map 2

Baskerville
Station Road, Lower Shiplake (off A4155 just S of Henley); RG9 3NY

Emphasis on imaginative food though a proper public bar too; real ales, several wines by the glass, interesting sporting memorabilia, and a pretty garden; bedrooms

Although the exterior here is slightly plain looking, it fronts a particularly well run pub which is very much the hub of the village, offering a warm welcome from friendly staff and top quality imaginative food. There are some bar chairs around the light, modern bar counter (used by the chatty locals), a few beams, pale wooden dining chairs and tables on the light wood or patterned carpeted floors, plush red banquettes around the windows and a couple of log fires in brick fireplaces. A fair amount of sporting memorabilia and pictures, especially old rowing photos (the pub is very close to Henley) and signed rugby shirts and photographs (the pub runs its own rugby club), plus some maps of the Thames are hung on the red walls, and there are flowers and large house plants dotted about. It all feels quite homely, but in a smart way, with some chintzy touches such as a shelf of china cow jugs. Fullers London Pride, Loddon Hoppit and Timothy Taylors Landlord on handpump, 40 malt whiskies and a dozen wines by the glass. There's a separate dining room and a small room for private family or business groups. The pretty garden has a proper covered barbecue area, smart teak furniture under huge parasols and some rather fun statues made out of box. There's a timber play frame for children. The bedrooms are well equipped and comfortable. We'd love to hear from readers who have stayed here.

Usefully open for food all day including a fine breakfast from 9.30am, there might be open sandwiches, goats cheese and rosemary panna cotta with a sweet and spicy tomato relish, steak and kidney in ale pie, chicken saltimbocca with spring onion mash and smoked aubergine caponata, rolled, slow-cooked lamb with apricots, paprika and mustard, and scallops and tiger prawns with pasta, garlic, Pernod, cream and herbs; they also offer a two- and three-course set menu. *Benchmark main dish: fish and chips £12.95. Two-course evening meal £21.70.*

Free house ~ Licensee Allan Hannah ~ Real ale ~ Bar food (9.30am-9.30pm) ~ Restaurant ~ (0118) 940 3332 ~ Children welcome but not in restaurant after 7pm Fri and Sat ~ Dogs allowed in bar and bedrooms ~ Open 9.30am-11pm; 12-4.30, 7-10.30 Sun ~ Bedrooms: £77S/£97.50S(£87.50B)
Recommended by Paul Humphreys, Neil and Karen Dignan, David O'Shaughnessy, Mrs Susan Lines, Ian Herdman

SHORWELL Isle of Wight   SZ4582   Map 2

Crown ♠ £
B3323 SW of Newport; PO30 3JZ

Popular pub with appealing streamside garden and play area

They serve a particularly good pint at this pretty inland pub, with their five or six real ales on handpump usually including Adnams Broadside, Goddards Fuggle-Dee-Dum, Ringwood Fortyniner, St Austell Tribute and Sharps Doom Bar. The other main draw here is the appealing tree-sheltered garden with its sweet little stream that broadens into a small trout-filled pool, decent children's play area within easy view of closely spaced picnic-sets and white garden chairs and tables set out on the grass. Inside, four pleasant opened-up rooms spread around a central bar, with either carpet, tiles or flagstones, and chatty regulars lending some local character. The beamed knocked-through lounge has blue and white china on an attractive carved dresser, old country prints on stripped-stone walls and a winter log fire with a fancy tile-work surround. Black pews form bays around tables in a stripped-stone room off to the left with another log fire; piped music and board games.

Pubby bar food runs from starters such as half a pint of prawns and pâté of the day to main courses such as fish and chips, chicken curry, venison curry, nut roast, burgers and pies. *Benchmark main dish: fish and chips £10.25. Two-course evening meal £15.70.*

Enterprise ~ Lease Nigel and Pam Wynn ~ Real ale ~ Bar food (12-9.30) ~ (01983) 740293 ~ Children welcome ~ Dogs welcome ~ Open 10.30(11.30 Sun)-11
Recommended by Quentin and Carol Williamson, Terry and Nickie Williams

SHURLOCK ROW Berkshire   SU8374 Map 2

Shurlock Inn ♀ ◀

Just off B3018 SE of Twyford; The Street; RG10 0PS

Comfortable village-owned pub with warm atmosphere, enjoyable food and drinks

Bought and refurbished by a consortium of 17 locals, this has the splendid atmosphere of a place that's run for the sheer enjoyment of doing a good job really well rather than for making pots of money. Décor is simple and clean-cut, with fitted carpet, just a few pictures on plain cream walls, russet curtains, one or two beams in the low ceiling, and a brick hearth with a log-effect gas fire dividing the main area, set for dining, from a small bar. The little corner counter serves three well kept changing ales such as Binghams Brickworks and Marlow Rebellion IPA and Zebedee from handpump, and good wines by the glass; the radio may be on quietly. A side terrace has black metal tables and chairs, with more in a garden with shrubs, sycamore, a big weeping willow, picnic-sets under canvas parasols, and a play area.

Good, interesting food includes lunchtime sandwiches, crab and avocado tian, smoked haddock risotto with a poached egg, a popular burger, sausages of the week with onion gravy, moules marinière, and pork belly with spiced apple, cider and mustard sauce. *Benchmark main dish: sea trout with samphire and new potato chowder £13.95. Two-course evening meal £17.30.*

Free house ~ Licensee Andrew Norman ~ Real ale ~ Bar food (12-2.30, 6-9(9.30 Fri and Sat); 12-8 Sun) ~ Restaurant ~ (0118) 934 9094 ~ Children welcome ~ Dogs allowed in bar ~ Open 12-3, 6-11; 10am-11pm Sat; 10-8 Sun
Recommended by Paul Humphreys

SINGLETON Sussex   SU8713 Map 2

Partridge

Just off A286 Midhurst—Chichester; PO18 0EY

Well run, friendly village pub with daily papers and log fires, real ales, good pubby food, and a pretty walled garden

Handy for the Weald & Downland Open Air Museum and not far from Goodwood, this pretty black and cream 16th-c pub is doing especially well at the moment. It's now run by a former executive head chef of the Ritz and, not surprisingly, the food is extremely good. But despite the emphasis on dining, they keep Ballards Golden Bine, Fullers London Pride and Harveys Best on handpump and several wines by the glass, and there's a friendly, relaxed atmosphere. There are all sorts of light and dark wooden tables and dining chairs on polished wooden floors, flagstones and carpet, daily papers, a woodburning stove and winter log fires, and a modicum of country knick-knacks. Piped music, board games and summer table tennis. Both the terrace and walled garden have plenty of picnic-sets under parasols.

Enjoyable food using local produce includes sandwiches, chicken liver, smoked bacon and port pâté with a berry compote, house-potted brown shrimps, risotto of wild mushrooms with truffle oil, sausage and mash with red onion gravy, steak and mushroom in ale pie, and salmon, smoked haddock and chive fishcakes with lemon mayonnaise. *Benchmark main dish: steak in ale pie £11.95. Two-course evening meal £18.70.*

Enterprise ~ Lease Giles Thompson ~ Real ale ~ Bar food (12-2(3 Sun), 6-9(9.30 Fri and Sat)) ~ Restaurant ~ (01243) 811251 ~ Children welcome ~ Dogs allowed in bar and bedrooms ~ Open 11-11(11.30 Sat); 12-11 Sat

Recommended by G Dobson, Nick Lawless, J A Snell, Tim and Sue Halstead

SKIRMETT Buckinghamshire   SU7790   Map 2

Frog 🍴 🍷 🛏

From A4155 NE of Henley take Hambleden turn and keep on; or from B482 Stokenchurch—Marlow take Turville turn and keep on; RG9 6TG

Bustling pub with modern cooking in a traditional atmosphere, fine choice of drinks, lovely garden, and nearby walks; bedrooms

The long-serving licensees and their friendly staff are sure to make you welcome in this 18th-c coaching inn and although much emphasis is placed on the good, interesting food, the public bar is still very much the heart of the place. There's a winter log fire in the brick fireplace with lots of little framed prints above it, a cushioned sofa and leather-seated bar stools around a low circular table on the wooden floor, and high bar chairs by the counter; piped music. Rebellion IPA and guests like Gales Seafarer and Sharps Atlantic IPA on handpump, a dozen wines by the glass (including champagne) and around two dozen carefully sourced malt whiskies. The two dining rooms are quite different in style – one is light and airy with country kitchen tables and chairs and the other is more formal with dark red walls, smarter dining chairs and tables and candlelight. Outside, a side gate leads to a lovely garden with a large tree in the middle and the unusual five-sided tables are well placed for attractive valley views. Plenty of nearby hikes (Henley is close by) and just down the road is the delightful Ibstone windmill. There's a purpose-built outdoor heated area for smokers. The breakfasts are good (though it might be worth having a room not right above the bar).

Imaginative and extremely good, the food might include grilled mackerel with marinated cucumber and mustard crème fraîche, ham hock terrine with pickled vegetables, a trio of sausages with chive mash and onion gravy, gnocchi with asparagus, sunblush tomatoes and chargrilled peppers in tomato sauce, plaice with brown shrimps and lemon butter sauce, and pork wellington with fruit stuffing wrapped in parma ham and filo pastry. *Benchmark main dish: fish and chips with mushy peas £12.45. Two-course evening meal £18.50.*

Free house ~ Licensees Jim Crowe and Noelle Greene ~ Real ale ~ Bar food (12-2.30, 6.30-9.30; not winter Sun evenings) ~ Restaurant ~ (01491) 638996 ~ Children welcome ~ Dogs allowed in bar ~ Open 11.30-3, 6-11; 12-4, 6-10.30 Sun; closed Sun evening Oct-May ~ Bedrooms: £60B/£80B

PORTSMOUTH, THE WATERFRONT CITY

Portsmouth has miles of sea views and centuries of history. Explore Portsmouth Historic Dockyard, scale the Spinnaker Tower and be inspired by the city's many museums. Enjoy waterfront shopping and dining at Gunwharf Quays, visit art galleries and cathedrals or catch a performance at one of the many theatres. Discover green open spaces, four miles of seafront promenade and get active with a range of cycle trails and walks.

Portsmouth is home to more than 160 pubs ranging from cosy, historic pubs to modern waterfront establishments. With its diverse range of watering holes and fascinating attractions, you'll need more than a day. For more information contact:
www.visitportsmouth.co.uk

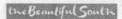

Recommended by Martin and Karen Wake, Tracey and Stephen Groves, Richard and Liz Thorne, Ian Wilson, Paul Humphreys, Colin and Louise English, Brian and Anna Marsden, John and Sharon Hancock

SONNING Berkshire   SU7575 Map 2

Bull 🛏

Off B478, by church; village signed off A4 E of Reading; RG4 6UP

Pretty timbered inn in attractive spot near Thames, plenty of character in old-fashioned bars, Fullers beers, friendly staff and good food; bedrooms

The two old-fashioned bar rooms in this pretty 16th-c black and white timbered inn have a good bustling atmosphere and plenty of chatty locals. There are low ceilings and heavy beams, cosy alcoves, leather armchairs and sofas, cushioned antique settles and low wooden chairs on bare boards, and open fireplaces. The dining room has a mix of wooden chairs and tables, rugs on parquet flooring and shelves of books. Fullers Chiswick, Discovery, HSB, London Pride and a couple of guests on handpump, served by friendly staff. When the wisteria is flowering, the inn looks especially pretty and the courtyard is bright with tubs of flowers. If you bear left through the ivy-clad churchyard opposite, then turn left along the bank of the River Thames, you come to a very pretty lock.

Good, if not cheap, bar food includes sandwiches, home-made mackerel pâté with gooseberry compote, gratin of smoked haddock, pork and leek sausages with onion gravy, corn-fed chicken with thyme and garlic sweet potatoes and a berry sauce, steak and venison pie, and cinnamon and apple-spiced pork belly with cider gravy and mustard mash. *Benchmark main dish: fish casserole £15.00. Two-course evening meal £22.00.*

Gales (Fullers) ~ Manager Dennis Mason ~ Real ale ~ Bar food (all day) ~ Restaurant ~ (0118) 969 3901 ~ Children welcome ~ Dogs allowed in bar ~ Open 11-11; 12-10.30 Sun ~ Bedrooms: /£99S(£125B)

Recommended by Jennifer Banks, Jack and Sandra Clarfelt, Simon Collett-Jones, Susan and John Douglas, John Saville, David and Sue Atkinson

SOUTHSEA Hampshire   SZ6499 Map 2

Wine Vaults 🍺

Albert Road, opposite King's Theatre; PO5 2SF

Bustling pub with a fine choice of real ales and reasonably priced pubby food

The fine range of eight changing real ales continues to pack in the customers at this well run and extremely busy pub. On handpump these might include Fullers London Pride, Discovery, ESB, London Porter and Organic Honey Dew, Gales HSB and guests such as Windsor & Eton Guardsman or Knight of the Garter and Wells & Youngs Bombardier. There are several rooms on different floors – all fairly straightforward and chatty – and the main bar has wood-panelled walls, pubby tables and chairs on the wooden floor, and bar stools by the long plain bar counter; there's a newly smartened-up restaurant area away from the hustle and bustle of the bars. Maybe newspapers to read, piped music and TV for sports events. There's a heated roof terrace for smokers.

🍴 Some sort of food is offered all day: sandwiches, garlic mushrooms, champagne pâté with red onion marmalade, beer-battered haddock, vegetable lasagne, steak in ale pie, and minted lamb steak. *Benchmark main dish: beef en croûte £10.95. Two-course evening meal £20.00.*

Fullers ~ Manager Sophie Mannering ~ Real ale ~ Bar food (all day) ~ Restaurant ~ (023) 9286 4712 ~ Children welcome ~ Dogs allowed in bar ~ Open 12-11(1am Fri and Sat; 10.30 Sun)

Recommended by Andy West, the Didler, Ann and Colin Hunt

SPARSHOLT Hampshire · SU4331 Map 2

Plough 🍴 ♀

Village signposted off B3049 (Winchester—Stockbridge), a little W of Winchester; SO21 2NW

Neat, well run dining pub with interesting furnishings, an extensive wine list, and popular bar food; garden with children's play fort

Particularly well run by friendly, polite licensees and their well trained staff, this country pub is always deservedly busy; you must book in advance to be sure of a table. Of course most customers are here to enjoy the wide choice of reliably good food but they do keep Wadworths IPA, 6X, Bishops Tipple and Horizon on handpump, and have an extensive wine list with a fair selection by the glass including champagne and pudding wine. The main bar has an interesting mix of wooden tables and chairs with farm tools, scythes and pitchforks attached to the ceiling. Disabled access and facilities. Outside, there are plenty of seats on the terrace and lawn and a children's play fort.

🍴 Well presented, much-liked food includes lunchtime sandwiches, chicken liver and bacon in a mushroom cream sauce, grilled mackerel on crostini with a tomato and garlic compote, beef and mushroom in ale pie with mustard mash, butternut squash risotto with a pine nut crumb, thai chicken curry, steak burgers with pepper sauce, and pork loin with stilton sauce, glazed apples and dauphinoise potatoes. *Benchmark main dish: salmon and crab fishcakes with saffron sauce £11.95. Two-course evening meal £18.50.*

Wadworths ~ Tenants Richard and Kathryn Crawford ~ Real ale ~ Bar food (12-2, 6-9 (9.30 Fri and Sat)) ~ (01962) 776353 ~ Children welcome except in main bar area ~ Dogs allowed in bar ~ Open 11-3, 6-11

Recommended by Phyl and Jack Street, John Michelson, Henry Fryer, John and Joan Calvert, Jill and Julian Tasker, David Jackson, Tony and Jill Radnor

ST MARGARET'S BAY Kent · TR3744 Map 3

Coastguard ♀ 🍺

Off A256 NE of Dover; keep on down through the village to the bottom of the bay, pub off on right by the beach; CT15 6DY

Great views, nautical décor, fine range of drinks and well liked food

This terrifically positioned pub in a cosy bay beneath the white cliffs of Dover has tables out on its prettily planted balcony from where you can look across the Straits of Dover, and there are more seats down by the beach. Inside, the warm, carpeted, wood-clad bar has some shipping memorabilia, Gadds No 5 and Goachers Dark alongside a couple of guests from brewers such as Fyne and Orkney on handpump, over 40 whiskies, Weston's cider and a carefully chosen wine list including

some from Kent vineyards; good service even when busy. The restaurant has wooden dining chairs and tables on a wood-strip floor and more fine views; piped music.

Ⅱ Well presented bar food typically includes scallops in garlic butter, curried cauliflower and mediterranean vegetable soup, roast lemon sole, chicken on blue cheese, bacon and walnut salad, and sirloin steak with garlic butter. *Benchmark main dish: cod and chips £12.50. Two-course evening meal £18.50.*

Free house ~ Licensee Nigel Wydymus ~ Real ale ~ Bar food (12.30-2.45, 6.30-8.45) ~ Restaurant ~ (01304) 853176 ~ Children welcome away from bar ~ Dogs allowed in bar ~ Open 11-11(10.30 Sun)

Recommended by Christopher Turner, David Jackman, Richard Mason, N R White

STALISFIELD GREEN Kent   TQ9552 Map 3

Plough

Off A252 in Charing; ME13 0HY

Ancient country pub with rambling rooms, open fires, interesting local ales, smashing bar food, and friendly licensees

Perched on the Downs and surrounded by farmland, parts of this ancient country pub are said to date back to 1350. Its several hop-draped rooms, relaxed and easy-going, ramble around, up and down, with open fires in brick fireplaces, interesting pictures on green- or maroon-painted walls, books on shelves, farmhouse and other nice old dining chairs around a mix of pine or dark wood tables on bare boards and the odd milk churn dotted about. Dixie, the pub cat, likes to find a cosy lap to lie on. The cheery, helpful landlord stocks local ales from kentish brewers such as Gadds, Goachers, Old Dairy and Whitstable; he keeps kentish lager as well as local wines, water, fruit juices and cider. Picnic-sets on a simple terrace overlook the village green. They also have a site for caravans.

Ⅱ Using seasonal fruit and vegetables direct from local farms, local meat and game (they hang their own) and making their own sausages, ketchup, bread and ice-creams, the very good food includes sandwiches, walnut and stilton cheesecake with poached pear and a port and redcurrant sauce, steak in ale suet pudding, mackerel fillets with butternut squash, bacon, wilted spinach and paprika roasted potatoes with a cold-smoked butter sauce. *Benchmark main dish: locally reared rump steak £14.95. Two-course evening meal £20.50.*

Free house ~ Licensee Robert and Amy Lloyd ~ Real ale ~ Bar food (12-2, 7-9; 12-9 Sat; 12-4 Sun) ~ Restaurant ~ (01795) 890256 ~ Children welcome on left ~ Dogs allowed in bar ~ Live music Fri monthly ~ Open 12-3, 6-11; 12-12.30(6 Sun) Sat; closed Mon, Tues lunchtime, Sun evening

Recommended by Joan and Alec Lawrence, N R White

STANFORD DINGLEY Berkshire   SU5771 Map 2

Old Boot

Off A340 via Bradfield, coming from A4 just W of M4 junction 12; RG7 6LT

Country furnishings and open fires in welcoming beamed bars, a choice of bar food, real ales, and rural garden views

The beamed bar in this stylish 18th-c pub has two welcoming fires (one in an inglenook) and is just the place for a cosy winter drink. There are fine old pews, settles, old country chairs and polished tables, as well as some striking pictures and hunting prints, boot ornaments and fresh flowers. There's also a conservatory-style restaurant. West Berkshire Good Old Boy and a guest, plus Wadworths 6X on handpump and several wines by the glass. There are seats in the quiet sloping back garden or on the terrace and pleasant rural views; more tables out in front. Please note, they no longer have bedrooms.

 Changing bar food includes sandwiches, scallops with celeriac purée, a pie of the week, a proper burger, linguine with cherry tomatoes, pesto and spinach, sesame chicken with a creamy curry sauce, and bass with thai-spiced vegetables. *Benchmark main dish: duck with apple and cider sauce £12.95. Two-course evening meal £20.95.*

Free house ~ Licensee John Haley ~ Real ale ~ Bar food ~ Restaurant ~ (0118) 974 4292 ~ Children welcome ~ Dogs allowed in bar ~ Open 11-3, 6-11; 11-11 Sat and Sun
Recommended by Neil and Karen Dignan

STANFORD IN THE VALE Oxfordshire   SU3393 Map 4

Horse & Jockey ♀

A417 Faringdon—Wantage; Faringdon Road; SN7 8NN

Friendly traditional village local with real character, good value pubby food and a good wine choice

They take trouble with their wines here, serving a fairly priced range in a sensible choice of glass sizes, and have Greene King Morlands Original, Old Speckled Hen and Ruddles County on handpump. Big Alfred Munnings' racecourse prints, Grand National winner-card collections and other horse and jockey pictures reflect not just the pub's name but the fact that this is racehorse training country – which so often seems to guarantee a relaxed and comfortably welcoming atmosphere. The main area, with flagstones, low ochre ceiling and a woodburning stove in its big fireplace, has several old high-backed settles and a couple of bucket armchairs. On the right is a carpeted area with a lofty raftered ceiling, a lattice-windowed inner gallery and some stripped stone, and at the back a spacious bare-boards dining room. Besides the tables out under a heated courtyard canopy, the separate enclosed and informal family garden has a play area; aunt sally. We have not yet heard from readers using the bedrooms here, but would expect an enjoyable stay.

 As well as fair value lunchtime choices like sandwiches, sausages with garlic and herb mash and onion gravy, and spinach and ricotta tortellini in white wine and herb cream, the highly thought-of food includes moules marinière, lamb rump with rosemary and redcurrant sauce, bass fillet on spiced potato cake with lobster beurre blanc and slow-roasted pork belly with thyme jus and dauphinoise potatoes. *Benchmark main dish: steak in Guinness casserole £8.95. Two-course evening meal £19.25.*

Greene King ~ Lease Charles and Anna Gaunt ~ Real ale ~ Bar food (12-2.30, 6.30-9(9.30 Fri and Sat)) ~ Restaurant ~ (01367) 710302 ~ Children welcome ~ Dogs allowed in bar ~ Thurs evening quiz and monthly open mike first Weds evening of month ~ Open 11-3, 5-midnight; 11am-12.30am Fri and Sat; midday-midnight Sun ~ Bedrooms: £50S/£60S
Recommended by R K Phillips, Valerie Bone

You can send reports directly to us at **feedback@goodguides.com**

the Beautiful South

STANTON ST JOHN Oxfordshire   SP5709 Map 4

Talk House ♀ ☞

Middle Road/Wheatley Road (B4027 just outside village); OX33 1EX

Attractive thatched dining pub with interesting food from a varied menu in several separate areas, real ales, friendly staff, and seats in a sheltered courtyard; bedrooms

Although the inventive modern food remains the main draw to this partly 16th-c dining pub, they do keep Fullers London Pride, Discovery and Seafarers Ale on handpump, and several wines by the glass; also daily papers. The thatched part, at the front on the left, dates from about 1550, giving a splendid dining area with steeply pitched rafters soaring above stripped-stone walls, a mix of old dining chairs around big stripped tables, and large rugs on flagstones. Most of the rest of the building has been well converted more recently, keeping a similar style – fat candles on stripped tables, massive beams, flagstones or stoneware tiles, log fires below low mantelbeams, and a relaxed and leisurely feel. At the front on the right are dark leather button-back settees and leather-cushioned easy chairs, with two more dining areas at the back. An inner courtyard has comfortable teak tables and chairs, with a few picnic-sets on side grass. The snug ground-floor bedrooms are behind here and they serve good breakfasts.

Using produce from local farms, the well liked food includes sandwiches, smoked salmon roulade, seared scallops with a mustard potato salad and beetroot, gnocchi with asparagus, peas and a salsa verde, battered haddock and chips, steak hash burger with triple-cooked chips and a tomato salsa, and chicken breast stuffed with sunblush tomatoes and a garlic potato rösti. *Benchmark main dish: roasted rump of lamb with red pepper and butternut crush £16.95. Two-course evening meal £19.95.*

Fullers ~ Manager John McKay ~ Real ale ~ Bar food (12-3, 6-9; all day Sat, Sun and bank hols) ~ Restaurant ~ (01865) 351648 ~ Children welcome ~ Dogs allowed in bar ~ Live jazz first Fri of month ~ Open 10am-midnight(1.30am Fri and Sat); 10am-11pm Sun ~ Bedrooms: /£65S
Recommended by Franklyn Roberts

STEEP Hampshire   SU7525 Map 2

Harrow ◖ £

Take Midhurst exit from Petersfield bypass, at exit roundabout take first left towards Midhurst, then first turning on left opposite garage, and left again at Sheet church; follow over dual carriageway bridge to pub; GU32 2DA

Unchanging, simple place with long-serving landladies, beers tapped from the cask, unfussy food and a big free-flowering garden; no children inside

There's no pandering to modern methods here – no credit cards, no waitress service, no restaurant, no music and outside lavatories. And our readers love it. The same family have been running it for 82 years now and as a pub it remains quite unchanged and unspoilt. Everything revolves around village chat and the friendly locals who will probably draw you into light-hearted conversation. There are adverts for logs next to calendars of local views being sold in support of local charities and news of various quirky competitions. The cosy public bar has hops and dried flowers hanging from the beams, built-in wall benches on the tiled floor, stripped-pine wallboards, a good log fire in the big inglenook, and wild flowers on the scrubbed deal tables; board games. Ringwood Best and Bowman Swift One are tapped straight from casks behind the counter, and they've local wine, and apple and pear juice; staff are polite and friendly, even when under pressure. The big garden is left free-flowering so that goldfinches can collect thistle seeds from the grass, but there are some seats on paved areas now. The Petersfield bypass doesn't intrude on this idyll, though you will need to follow the directions above to find the pub. No children inside and dogs must be on leads.

Good helpings of unfussy bar food include sandwiches, home-made scotch eggs, hearty ham, split pea and vegetable soup, ploughman's, cottage pie, flans and quiches, and puddings such as treacle tart or seasonal fruit pies. *Benchmark main dish: home-cooked beef ploughman's £5.00.*

Free house ~ Licensees Claire and Denise McCutcheon ~ Real ale ~ Bar food (not Sun evening; limited Mon evening) ~ No credit cards ~ (01730) 262685 ~ Dogs welcome ~ Open 12-2.30, 6-11; 11-3, 6-11 Sat; 12-3, 7-10.30 Sun; closed winter Sun evenings

Recommended by Ian Phillips, David Gunn, Tony and Jill Radnor, Neil and Karen Dignan, the Didler, Phil and Sally Gorton, W A Evershed, Prof James Stevens Curl, John and Anne Mackinnon, John and Jackie Chalcraft

STOKE MANDEVILLE Buckinghamshire SP8310 Map 4

Woolpack ♀

Risborough Road (A4010 S of Aylesbury); HP22 5UP

Boldy decorated pub with contemporary and stylish bar rooms, imaginative food, a good choice of drinks, and seats outside

Decorated throughout in a thoroughly modern style, this partly thatched pub has plenty of room in its spreading open-plan rooms. Bold red and cream paintwork team up with plenty of contemporary art, high-backed black or beige leather dining chairs around a mix of chunky pale wooden tables on red and beige rugs or stone flooring, high white-seated stools against the bar counter and comfortably cushioned wall seats; there's an open fire in the bar. Brakspears, Purity Pure UBU and Timothy Taylors Landlord on handpump and a good choice of wines by the glass. There are seats and tables in the back garden or on the heated front terrace.

Interesting up-to-date food includes scallops of the day, duck rillettes with rhubarb and ginger chutney, pasta with tiger prawns, crab, chorizo, chilli, tomato and white wine, various pizzas, a proper burger with mustard mayo, curried smoked haddock and leek fishcake with a poached egg, mango salad and hollandaise sauce, and spit-roasted chicken with lemon, garlic and thyme. *Benchmark main dish: crispy duck salad £11.95. Two-course evening meal £17.45.*

Mitchells & Butlers ~ Manager Chloe Godridge ~ Real ale ~ Bar food (12-3, 6-10(10.30 Sun); Sun 12-9) ~ Restaurant ~ (01296) 615970 ~ Well behaved children allowed but not Fri or Sat evenings ~ Open 11-11(midnight Sat;10.30 Sun)

Recommended by John Faircloth, Mel Smith

'Children welcome' means the pub says it lets children inside without any special restriction. If it allows them in, but to restricted areas such as an eating area or family room, we specify this. Some pubs may impose an evening time limit. We do not mention limits after 9pm as we assume children are home by then.

STONESFIELD Oxfordshire   SP3917   Map 4

White Horse

Village signposted off B4437 Charlbury—Woodstock; Stonesfield Riding;
OX29 8EA

**Attractively upgraded small country pub with enjoyable food and a
relaxed atmosphere**

Contemporary artworks, restful colours (grey or near-white in the snug
little bar, dark pink over a grey dado in the dining room) and nicely
chosen furniture all show that the couple who reopened this in 2009 have
a real eye for detail. One of their best touches is the little inner room with
just a pair of Sheraton-style chairs around a single mahogany table.
Service is cheerful and efficient. The corner bar counter, with padded
stools, has White Horse ale on handpump; open fire, daily papers, faint
piped pop music. The dining room's french windows open on to a neat
walled garden with picnic-sets; there's a skittle alley in the separate stone
barn. There are good local walks (the pub is on the Oxfordshire Way) and
is handy for the Roman villa (EH) at nearby North Leigh.

Good food cooked by the landlady using carefully sourced local produce
includes lunchtime sandwiches, smoked salmon pâté, minted pea risotto, steak
and mushroom puff pie, lamb cutlets with pea purée, salmon with a parmesan and
parsley crust and a white wine and mushroom sauce, and braised lamb shank with
honey and rosemary. *Benchmark main dish: steak and mushroom pie £9.95. Two-
course evening meal £14.00.*

Free house ~ Licensees John and Angela Lloyd ~ Real ale ~ Bar food (No food Mon-
Thurs (phone to check)) ~ Restaurant ~ (01993) 891063 ~ Children welcome ~ Dogs
allowed in bar ~ Open 12-3, 5(6 Fri and Sat)-11; closed Mon; first week Jan
Recommended by Guy Vowles

STOWTING Kent   TR1241   Map 3

Tiger ◀

*3.7 miles from M20 junction 11; B2068 N, then left at Stowting signpost,
straight across crossroads, fork left after 0.25 miles and pub is on right; coming from
N, follow Brabourne, Wye, Ashford signed to right at fork, then turn left towards
Posting and Lyminge at T junction; TN25 6BA*

**Peaceful pub with friendly staff, traditional furnishings, well liked food,
several real ales and open fires; good walking country**

Tucked away down leafy lanes, this 17th-c inn is cosily traditional with
a happy mix of wooden tables and chairs and built-in cushioned wall
seats on wooden floorboards and woodburning stoves at each end of the
bar. There's an array of books, board games, candles in bottles, brewery
memorabilia and paintings, lots of hops and some faded rugs on the stone
floor towards the back of the pub. Fullers London Pride, Harveys Best
and Old Dairy Brewery, Shepherd Neame Master Brew and a guest on
handpump, lots of malt whiskies, several wines by the glass, local
Biddenden cider and local fruit juice. On warmer days you can sit out on
the front terrace and there are plenty of nearby walks along the Wye
Downs or North Downs Way.

Enjoyable bar food from a daily changing menu, using seasonal local produce,
might include items such as sandwiches, caramelised goats cheese with grilled
sweet and sour strawberries, steamed asparagus topped with poached egg and

lemon hollandaise, red onion, mushroom and gorgonzola tart, dover sole with caper butter, chicken, ham and leek pie, tuna steak niçoise, rack of lamb on courgette provençale with sweet potato dauphinoise, and honey and mustard sausages. *Benchmark main dish: roast pork belly with smoked bacon £15.00. Two-course evening meal £21.00.*

Free house ~ Licensees Emma Oliver and Benn Jarvis ~ Real ale ~ Bar food (12(4 Mon)-9(9.30 Fri, Sat, 8 Sun)) ~ Restaurant ~ (01303) 862130 ~ Children welcome ~ Dogs allowed in bar ~ Jazz every second Mon evening ~ Open 12(4 Mon)-11; 12-11 Sat; 12-10.30 Sun; closed Mon lunchtime, Tues

Recommended by Brian and Anna Marsden, Jill and Julian Tasker, Paul Goldman, N R White, Matthew Lonergan, Michael Butler, Julie and Bill Ryan

SUNBURY Surrey   TQ1068   Map 3

Flower Pot ◀

1.6 miles from M3 junction 1; follow Lower Sunbury sign from exit roundabout, then at Thames Street turn right; pub on next corner, with Green Street; TW16 6AA

Appealing contemporary update of small 18th-c inn near the Thames

Though it's not actually on the river, the pub is really just across the road from an attractive reach of the Thames, in quite a villagey area with waterside walks. The building's façade, complete with elegant wrought-iron balconies, makes the bar something of a surprise: modern pale chunky tables on pale boards, a contemporary colour scheme of lavender-grey and deep claret-purple, and round the corner of the horseshoe-shaped bar an aquarium wall. Service, though, is thoroughly old-fashioned in the best helpful sense, and the Brakspears, Jennings Bitter, Ringwood Best and Wychwood Hobgoblin on handpump are kept in fine condition; we particularly liked the comfortable swivelling bar chairs. The atmosphere, suiting the area, is relaxed and uncitified, with a rack of daily papers, unobtrusive piped music, and perhaps locals watching TV racing. We have not yet heard from readers staying here, but would expect good value.

As well as lunchtime sandwiches and filled panini, good value food, changing monthly, might include tempura prawns with sweet chilli dip, baked goats cheese with honey and mustard dressing with smoked salmon and walnut salad, breaded cheese platter with dips, salmon fishcakes, thai fish curry, pie of the day, penne carbonara, chicken caesar salad, mushroom stroganoff, and well hung steak. *Benchmark main dish: fish and chips £9.95. Two-course evening meal £15.00.*

Brakspears ~ Tenant Faye Wood ~ Real ale ~ Bar food (12-2.30(5.30 Sun), 6-9; not Sun evening) ~ Restaurant ~ (01932) 780741 ~ Children welcome ~ Dogs welcome ~ Open 12-11(11.30 Fri, Sat) ~ Bedrooms: £55B/£70B

Recommended by Edward Mirzoeff, Gerry and Rosemary Dobson

SWALLOWFIELD Berkshire   SU7364   Map 2

George & Dragon ♀

Church Road, towards Farley Hill; RG7 1TJ

Busy country pub with good nearby walks, enjoyable bar food, real ales, friendly service, and seats outside

Run by long-serving licensees, this popular pub is just the place to head for after enjoying one of the nearby walks. The various interconnected rooms have a thriving atmosphere and plenty of character – as well as beams and standing timbers, ladder-back chairs and stools around individual wooden tables, rugs on flagstones, lit candles, a big log fire and country prints on the red walls; piped music. Bingham Brewery Twyford Tipple, Fullers London Pride and Itchen Valley Pure Gold on handpump and quite a few wines by the glass served by friendly staff. There are picnic-sets on gravel or paving in the garden.

Well liked bistro-style bar food includes sandwiches, flambéed devilled kidneys, battered fish and chips, burger with bacon, guacamole and smoked paprika mayonnaise, tagliatelle with roast garlic mushrooms, creamed leeks and stilton, gressingham duck breast with noodles, crispy seaweed and plum sauce, and veal chop with mustard butter or red wine jus. *Benchmark main dish: slow-cooked lamb shoulder with ratatouille £14.50. Two-course evening meal £20.45.*

Free house ~ Licensee Paul Dailey ~ Real ale ~ Bar food (12-2.30(3 Sun), 7-9.30 (9 Sun)) ~ Restaurant ~ (0118) 9884432 ~ Well behaved children welcome ~ Dogs allowed in bar ~ Open 12-11(10 Sun)

Recommended by Dr and Mrs R E S Tanner, Veryan Young

SWERFORD Oxfordshire   SP3830   Map 4

Masons Arms ☺ ♀

A361 Banbury—Chipping Norton; OX7 4AP

Attractive dining pub with imaginative food, a fair choice of drinks, a relaxed atmosphere, and country views from outside tables

As we went to press we heard that this popular dining pub had been taken over by new licensees, but early reader reports suggest that things are running as smoothly as ever. Many customers come here to enjoy the interesting food but they do keep Brakspears Bitter and Wychwood Hobgoblin on handpump, lots of wines by the glass, Weston's organic cider and home-made spicy tomato juice. The dining extension is light and airy and the bar has rugs on pale wooden floors, a carefully illuminated stone fireplace, thoughtful spotlighting, and beige and red armchairs around big circular wooden tables. Doors open on to a small terrace with a couple of stylish tables, while steps lead down into a cream-painted room with chunky tables and contemporary pictures. Round the other side of the bar is another roomy dining room with great views by day, candles at night and a civilised feel. Behind is a neat square lawn with picnic-sets and views over the Oxfordshire countryside.

Interesting food includes antipasti, vegetarian or seafood platters (to share), confit duck leg, puy lentils and fig jus, crab and leek fishcakes with caper mayonnaise, home-baked ham and duck egg, venison and juniper pie, gloucester old spot pork loin braised in milk, lemon, rosemary and sage, and mini shoulder of lamb pot-roasted in honey, soy, spring onions, chilli and garlic. *Benchmark main dish: changing scallop dish £18.00. Two-course evening meal £20.00.*

Free house ~ Licensees Jude and Vicky Kelly ~ Real ale ~ Bar food (12-2, 7-9; 12-6 Sun) ~ Restaurant ~ (01608) 683212 ~ Children welcome ~ Open 10-3, 6-11; 11-8(6 in winter) Sun

Recommended by Michael Dandy, George Atkinson, Sir Nigel Foulkes, David and Lexi Young, Charlie Mcgrath, P and J Shapley

---

Every entry includes a postcode for use in Sat Nav devices.

SWINBROOK Oxfordshire   SP2812   Map 4

Swan 🍴 ♀ 🛏

Back road a mile N of A40, 2 miles E of Burford; OX18 4DY

Rather smart old pub with handsome oak garden rooms, antique-filled bars, local beers and contemporary food; bedrooms

Handy for the A40, this civilised 17th-c pub is in a lovely spot by a bridge over the River Windrush and seats by the fuchsia hedge make the best of the view. It's owned by the Dowager Duchess of Devonshire (the last of the Mitford sisters who grew up in the village) and has lots of interesting old Mitford family photographs blown up on the walls. There's a little bar with simple antique furnishings, settles and benches, an open fire, and (in an alcove) a stuffed swan; locals do still drop in here for a pint and a chat. The small dining room to the right of the entrance opens into this room and there are two green oak garden rooms with high-backed beige and green dining chairs around pale wood tables, and views over the garden and orchard. Hook Norton Hooky Bitter and a couple of guests from breweries like Arkells and Sharps on handpump, several wines by the glass and Weston's organic cider. The bedrooms are in a smartly converted stone barn beside the pub.

🍴 Inventive food using beef from the family farm includes lunchtime sandwiches, foie gras and chicken liver parfait with quince jelly, chilli cheeseburger, smoked haddock, spinach, poached egg and hollandaise sauce, wild mushroom, leek and ricotta cannelloni, duck leg confit with thai noodle broth, and red mullet fillet with tagliatelle, artichokes, peas and brown shrimps. *Benchmark main dish: lamb chump with bubble and squeak, black pudding and red wine jus £17.50. Two-course evening meal £22.00.*

Free house ~ Licensees Archie and Nicola Orr-Ewing ~ Real ale ~ Bar food (12-2 (3 weekends), 7-9(9.30 Fri and Sat) ~ (01993) 823339 ~ Children welcome ~ Dogs allowed in bar ~ Open 11-11(10.30 Sun); 11-3, 6-11 in winter ~ Bedrooms: £70B/£120B

Recommended by Richard Tilbrook, MDN, Brian Glozier, Henry Midwinter, Myra Joyce, Malcolm and Jo Hart, Bruce and Sharon Eden, Anthony and Pam Stamer, Bernard Stradling, Mrs Blethyn Elliott, David Glynne-Jones, John and Enid Morris, Richard Wyld, Jeff and Wendy Williams, Richard Greaves, David and Lexi Young, Tim and Sue Halstead, Graham Oddey, Malcolm Greening

TADPOLE BRIDGE Oxfordshire   SP3200   Map 4

Trout ♀ 🛏

Back road Bampton—Buckland, 4 miles NE of Faringdon; SN7 8RF

Busy country inn by the River Thames with a fine choice of drinks, popular modern food, and seats in the waterside garden; bedrooms

This is a lovely place to stay and the refurbished bedrooms are extremely comfortable; breakfasts are plentiful and enjoyable, too. It's all very civilised and friendly and the L-shaped bar has attractive pink and cream checked chairs around a mix of nice wooden tables, some rugs on the flagstones, green paintwork behind a modern wooden bar counter, fresh flowers, two woodburning stoves and a large stuffed trout. The airy restaurant is appealingly candlelit in the evenings. Ramsbury Bitter, Wells & Youngs Bitter and a couple of guests like Loose Cannon Abingdon Bridge and White Horse Village Idiot on handpump, 14 wines by the glass from a wide-ranging and carefully chosen list, some fine sherries and several malt whiskies. This is a peaceful and picturesque spot by the

the Beautiful South

Thames and there are good quality teak chairs and tables under blue parasols in the pretty garden; it can get pretty packed on a fine day, so it's best to arrive early then. You can hire punts with champagne hampers and there are moorings for six boats – if you book in advance.

Enjoyable – if not cheap – food includes lunchtime sandwiches, ham hock terrine with rhubarb and red pepper salsa, yellowfin tuna tartare with ginger cucumber spaghetti, loin of wild rabbit with red lentils and coriander, slow-roasted suckling pig with braised apple and black pudding, and cutlet of rose veal with sweet potato gnocchi and cherry tomato confit. *Benchmark main dish: trout pie £12.95. Two-course evening meal £22.22.*

Free house ~ Licensees Gareth and Helen Pugh ~ Real ale ~ Bar food (not winter Sun evening) ~ Restaurant ~ (01367) 870382 ~ Children welcome ~ Dogs welcome ~ Open 11.30-3(4 Sat), 6-11; 12-4.30, 6.30-11 Sat; closed winter Sun evening ~ Bedrooms: $80B/$120B

Recommended by Mr and Mrs J C Cetti, Suzy Miller, Bob and Angela Brooks, Charles Gysin, Martin Cawley, Bruce and Sharon Eden, Bob and Margaret Holder, Glenwys and Alan Lawrence, Colin McKerrow, David and Diane Young, Eleanor Dandy, Tim Gray, Jennifer and Patrick O'Dell, Mary Rayner

THURSLEY Surrey   SU9039   Map 2

Three Horseshoes 🍴

Dye House Road, just off A3 SW of Godalming; GU8 6QD

SURREY DINING PUB OF THE YEAR

Civilised country village pub with a broad range of good food

For many readers this pretty tile-hung village pub ticks all the boxes. It's family run and is jointly owned by a consortium of villagers who rescued it from closure, and with its good food and drink, lovely staff and friendly clientele it has the feel of a gently upmarket country local. The convivial beamed front bar has a winter log fire, Hogs Back TEA and a guest such as Fullers London Pride on handpump, a farm cider and perry; piped music. Tables in the attractive two-acre garden take in pleasant views over Thursley Common and the 1,000-year-old Saxon church. The terrace has smart comfortable chairs around tables with parasols. A separate area has a big play fort, a barbecue and a charcoal spit-roast area which they use on bank holidays. It's well placed for heathland walks – ask at the bar for a walking map. Lucky visiting dogs and horses get a biscuit or carrot.

Great care goes into the food here, with breads, ice-creams, parsnip crisps and so forth all made in house. Bar food takes in chicken liver parfait, beetroot cured salmon, ploughman's, sausage and mash with cavolo nero, toad in the hole, confit duck leg with goose fat beans, and steak and kidney pudding. In the evening there might be fried squid with guacamole, tempura soft shell crab, roast butternut ravioli, and beef cheeks braised in red wine; Sunday roast. *Benchmark main dish: sausages and mash £9.50. Two-course evening meal £16.40.*

Free house ~ Licensees David Alders and Sandra Proni ~ Real ale ~ Bar food (12.30-2.15, 7-9.15; 12-3 Sun; not Sun evening) ~ Restaurant ~ (01252) 703268 ~ Children welcome ~ Dogs allowed in bar ~ Open 12-3, 5.30-11; 12-11 Sat; 12-10.30 Sun

Recommended by Ian Herdman, Conor McGaughey, Tony and Jill Radnor, Ellie Weld, David London, Richard Williams, Arthur Snell, Hunter and Christine Wright, John Branston, Martin and Karen Wake, Kate Funnell

TUNBRIDGE WELLS Kent   TQ5839   Map 3

Sankeys 🍴 🍷 🍺

Mount Ephraim (A26 just N of junction with A267); TN4 8AA

Pubby street-level bar, informal downstairs brasserie, real ales and good wines, chatty atmosphere, and super fish dishes

The street level bar at this laid-back Tunbridge Wells institution is light and airy with comfortably worn, informal leather sofas and pews around all sorts of tables on bare wooden boards. The walls are covered with a fine collection of rare enamel signs and antique brewery mirrors as well as old prints, framed cigarette cards and lots of old wine bottles and soda siphons. They keep a couple of beers from Goachers and Westerham Brewery on handpump, fruit beers, american and british craft beers and several wines by the glass from a good list; big flat-screen TV for sports (not football) and piped music. Steps by the entrance take you down to the flagstoned restaurant which enjoys a fine reputation for its fresh fish and has an oyster bar and lobster tank on display. As in the bar, the atmosphere is chatty and informal. Unfussy décor includes big mirrors on rustic stripped-brick walls, pews or chairs around sturdy tables. French windows open on to an inviting suntrap deck with wicker and chrome chairs and wooden tables. More reports please.

Very good value pubby food at lunchtime in the upstairs bar includes sandwiches, filo prawns, fish and chips, sausage and mash, pie of the day, greek salad and thai beef salad. Downstairs, the emphasis is on fish: oysters, pickled cockles, fresh anchovies, potted shrimps, local lemon sole, plaice, john dory, black bream, lobster and huge cornish cock crabs. Sunday roasts and summer barbecues. *Benchmark main dish: dressed cornish crab £16.95. Two-course evening meal £22.00.*

Free house ~ Licensee Matthew Sankey ~ Real ale ~ Bar food (12-3, 6-11) ~ Restaurant ~ (01892) 511422 ~ Children welcome in restaurant and till 6pm in bar ~ Dogs allowed in bar ~ Open 12-1am (3am Sat)
Recommended by Bob and Margaret Holder, Conor McGaughey, Laurence Smith, Alan Franck, Gerry and Rosemary Dobson

ULCOMBE Kent   TQ8550   Map 3

Pepper Box £

Fairbourne Heath; signposted from A20 in Harrietsham, or follow Ulcombe signpost from A20, then turn left at crossroads with sign to pub, then right at next minor crossroads; ME17 1LP

Friendly country pub with lovely log fire, well liked food, fair choice of drinks, and seats in a pretty garden

This rural pub is very well run by friendly licensees. The homely bar has standing timbers and a few low beams (some hung with hops), copper kettles and pans on window sills and two leather sofas by the splendid inglenook fireplace (nice horsebrasses on the bressumer beam) with its lovely log fire. A side area, more functionally furnished for eating, extends into the opened-up beamed dining room with a range in another inglenook and more horsebrasses. Shepherd Neame Master Brew, Spitfire and a seasonal beer are on handpump, with local apple juice and several wines by the glass; piped music. The two cats are called Murphy and Jim. There's a hop-covered terrace and a garden with shrubs has delightful

the Beautiful South

views of the Weald. The name of the pub refers to the pepperbox pistol – an early type of revolver with numerous barrels; the village church is worth a look and the Greensand Way footpath runs close by.

As well as lunchtime sandwiches, filled baguettes and ploughman's, the well liked bar food could include tiger prawns, sautéed lambs liver and chorizo with sherry glaze, chilli, scampi, roast duck breast with honey and chinese spices, slow-roasted pork belly with cider, apples and thyme, beef stroganoff, and walnut and gorgonzola cannelloni with spinach and provençale sauce. *Benchmark main dish: steak and kidney pudding £11.00. Two-course evening meal £19.00.*

Shepherd Neame ~ Tenant Sarah Pemble ~ Real ale ~ Bar food (12-2.15(3 Sun), 6.30-9.30) ~ Restaurant ~ (01622) 842558 ~ Dogs allowed in bar ~ Open 11-3, 6-midnight; 11-11 Sat; 12-5 Sun; closed Sun evening and Sat afternoon in winter

Recommended by Philip and Cheryl Hill, Michael Tack, Nick Lawless, N R White, Alec and Joan Laurence, Malcolm and Barbara Southwell, Kevin Thomas, Nina Randall

UPPER BASILDON Berkshire   SU5976 Map 2

Red Lion 🍴 🍷 🍺

Off A329 NW of Pangbourne; Aldworth Road; RG8 8NG

Laid-back country pub with friendly family atmosphere, inventive food, and a good choice of drinks

Although many customers come to this well run and friendly country pub for the interesting food, this by no means dominates and there is still a relaxed and informal atmosphere and plenty of chatty drinkers (and maybe their dogs, too). There are chapel chairs, a few pews and miscellaneous stripped tables on the bare boards, a green leather chesterfield and armchair, and pale blue-grey paintwork throughout – even on the beams, ceiling and some of the top-stripped tables. Beyond a double-sided woodburning stove, a pitched-ceiling area has much the same furniture on cord carpet, but a big cut-glass chandelier and large mirror give it a slightly more formal dining feel. Brakspears Bitter, Otter Bitter, West Berkshire Good Old Boy and a weekly changing guest on handpump and an extensive wine list; the *Independent* and *Racing Post* are available, occasional piped music and regular live music – usually jazz-related. There are sturdy picnic-sets in the sizeable enclosed garden, where they have summer barbecues and hog roasts.

Enjoyable food, using local produce, includes sandwiches, a tapas plate, pork terrine with piccalilli, home-cooked ham and free-range duck egg, home-made burger with bacon and cheese, mozzarella, mascarpone and parmesan risotto with confit tomatoes and basil oil, thyme and lemon chicken with aioli, and halibut fillet with prawn and caper butter. *Benchmark main dish: cornish seafood pasta £14.50. Two-course evening meal £17.50.*

Enterprise ~ Lease Alison Green ~ Real ale ~ Bar food (12-2.30, 6-9.30; 12-3, 6-9 Sun) ~ Restaurant ~ (01491) 671234 ~ Children welcome ~ Dogs allowed in bar ~ Open 11-3, 5-11; all day weekends

Recommended by Julia and Richard Tredgett, I H G Busby, Gene and Kitty Rankin, Ian Herdman

---

The price we give for a two-course evening meal in the featured top pub entries is the mean (average of cheapest and most expensive) price of a starter and a main course – no drinks.

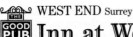

WEST END Surrey   SU9461   Map 2

Inn at West End 🍴 ⚲

Just under 2.5 miles from M3 junction 3; A322 S, on right; GU24 9PW

Clean-cut dining pub, with prompt friendly service; excellent food and wines, and terrace

The licensee at this immaculately run place is passionate about wine. He holds regular tastings and has recently opened a wine shop here. Needless to say, the wine list is fabulous, with around 20 by the glass – sensibly in a good range of sizes – and includes several sherries and dessert wines, with many from Spain and Portugal. Polished to a shine and well organised, the pub is open-plan and café-like, with bare boards, attractive modern prints on canary-yellow walls above a red dado, and a line of dining tables with crisp white linen over pale yellow tablecloths on the left. The bar counter, with Fullers London Pride and a guest such as Exmoor Ale on handpump, and over 25 malts, is straight ahead as you come in, and is quite a focus, with chatting regulars perched on the comfortable bar stools. The area on the right has a pleasant relaxed atmosphere, with blue-cushioned wall benches and dining chairs around solid pale wood tables, broadsheet daily papers, magazines and a row of reference books on the brick chimneybreast above an open fire. This opens into a garden room, which in turn leads to a grape and clematis pergola-covered terrace and very pleasant garden; boules.

Skilfully prepared using carefully sourced ingredients (some of the herbs and vegetables are grown here), they pluck their own game and use organic meat, the not cheap but very good bar food might include smoked pigeon pâté with beetroot relish, crispy mackerel with sorrel and sweet chilli and passion-fruit sauce, chicken caesar salad, sausage and mash, quails' eggs, onion and broccoli tartlet with tomato sauce, guinea fowl in puff pastry with thyme mousseline, sesame crusted bream with honey and soy and pak choi, and well hung steak; they also do lunchtime sandwiches. *Benchmark main dish: kedgeree £13.95. Two-course evening meal £26.80.*

Enterprise ~ Lease Gerry and Ann Price ~ Real ale ~ Bar food (12-2.30, 6-9.30; 12-3, 6-9 Sun) ~ Restaurant ~ (01276) 858652 ~ Children over 5 welcome if seated and dining ~ Dogs allowed in bar ~ Open 12-3, 5-11; 12-11 Sat; 12-10.30 Sun

Recommended by David M Smith, Edward Mirzoeff, Sheila Topham, Ellie Weld, David London, David and Cathrine Whiting, Ian Phillips, Alan Bowker, Ian Herdman, Rosemary and Mike Fielder, Gerald and Gabrielle Culliford, Sarah May-Miller

WEST HANNEY Oxfordshire   SU4092   Map 2

Plough £

Just off A338 N of Wantage; Church Street; OX12 0LN

Thatched village pub with good choice of drinks, decent food, and plenty of seats outside

Popular locally, this early 16th-c village pub is pretty and neatly thatched. The comfortable simply furnished bar has horsebrasses on beams, some bar stools, wheelback chairs around wooden tables, a log fire in the stone fireplace and lots of photographs of the pub on the walls; there are three pub cats. Loddon Ferryman's Gold, Sharps Doom Bar, Vale Best Bitter and West Berkshire Mr Chubb's Lunchtime Bitter on handpump, several wines by the glass and two farm ciders; separate dining room. There are seats and tables on the back terrace overlooking

the Beautiful South

the walled garden, with plenty of picnic-sets on the grass; aunt sally and a trampoline. Good walks start with a village path right by the pub. More reports please.

🍴 Using local farm produce, the bar food includes sandwiches, chicken liver pâté, aberdeen angus burgers with cheese and bacon, toad in the hole, vegetable risotto, and specials like crab claws and battered cod. *Benchmark main dish: lamb Hanney £13.95. Two-course evening meal £14.50.*

Free house ~ Licensee Trevor Cooper ~ Real ale ~ Bar food (12-2, 6-9) ~ Restaurant ~ (01235) 868674 ~ Children welcome ~ Dogs welcome ~ Open 12-3, 6-11; 12-11(7 Sun) Sat

Recommended by Bob and Angela Brooks

WEST HOATHLY Sussex   TQ3632 Map 3

Cat 🍴 🛏

SOUTH EAST PUB OF THE YEAR

Village signposted from A22 and B2028 S of East Grinstead; North Lane; RH19 4PP

Popular 16th-c inn with old-fashioned bar, airy dining rooms, real ales, good food, and seats outside; lovely bedrooms

With hands-on licensees, a genuinely warm welcome for all and highly thought-of food, it's not surprising that so many of our readers like to come back again and again to this bustling 16th-c tile-hung inn. There's a lovely old bar with beams, proper pubby tables and chairs on the old wooden floor, a fine log fire in the inglenook fireplace, Harveys Best and Old and Larkins Traditional Ale on handpump and several wines by the glass; look out for a glass cover over the 75-foot-deep well. The dining rooms are light and airy with a nice mix of wooden dining chairs and tables on the pale wood-strip flooring and throughout there are hops, china platters, brass and copper ornaments and a gently upmarket atmosphere. The contemporary-style garden room has glass doors that open on to a terrace with teak furniture. This is a comfortable and enjoyable place to stay (some of the rooms overlook the church) and the breakfasts are very good. The Bluebell Railway is nearby.

🍴 Cooked by one of the landlords, the enjoyable food includes lunchtime sandwiches, vietnamese rare roast beef rolls with coriander and mint salad, smoked chicken and ham hock terrine with celeriac rémoulade, beer-battered fish and chips, root vegetable and parmesan cheese crumble, anchovy-marinated local lamb rump with minted crushed new potatoes, and specials like scallops with soft

---

WELCOME TO THE ROYAL BOROUGH OF WINDSOR & MAIDENHEAD

This beautiful and historic part of England teems with top visitor attractions, from Windsor Castle, Eton College, the Savill Garden and Windsor Great Park, to River Thames cruises, guided walking tours, the Stanley Spencer Gallery, the Theatre Royal and more.

There are many great pubs here too – whether you prefer a traditional, historic or modern setting, you're sure to find some fine ales, great food and a lively atmosphere.

Seventy-nine years after the closure of Windsor's last brewery, Windsor & Eton Brewery are delighted to have brought craft brewing back to the heart of the area. In their first year they launched four ales: Guardsman Best, Knight of the Garter Golden Ale, Conqueror Black IPA and the Windsor Knot Royal Wedding Ale. Look out for these when you visit!

Contact the Royal Windsor Information Centre: (01753) 743900,
email **Windsor.tic@rbwm.gov.uk** or visit **www.windsor.gov.uk**

black pudding and pancetta, and chicken and oyster mushroom suet pudding. *Benchmark main dish: beer-battered fish and chips £12.50. Two-course evening meal £20.00.*

Free house ~ Licensees Ian Huxley and Andrew Russell ~ Real ale ~ Bar food (12-2(2.30 Fri-Sun), 6-9(9.30 Fri and Sat); not Sun evening) ~ (01342) 810369 ~ Children welcome if over 7 ~ Dogs allowed in bar ~ Open 12-3.30, 6-11.30; 12-4 Sun; closed Sun evening ~ Bedrooms: £85B/£100B

Recommended by Peter Meister, Terry Buckland, Nick Lawless, Colin and Louise English, Laurence Evans, Scott Kerr, Chris Bell, Simon and Mandy King

WHITE WALTHAM Berkshire   SU8477   Map 2

Beehive

Waltham Road (B3024 W of Maidenhead); SL6 3SH

Enjoyable bar food and welcoming staff at a traditional village pub

This is the sort of pub that once discovered, you tend to come back to again and again. It's a well run country local opposite the village cricket field and you can be sure of a warm welcome from the landlord and his staff. To the right, several comfortably spacious areas have leather chairs around sturdy tables and there's an airy conservatory. The neat bar to the left is brightened up by cheerful scatter cushions on its comfortable built-in wall seats and captain's chairs. Brakspears Bitter, Fullers London Pride, Greene King Abbot and a changing guest from Loddon on handpump, with a good choice of soft drinks; piped music, board games and a quiz evening on the last Thursday of the month. Picnic-sets and teak seats out in front on the terrace take in the pub's rather fine topiary, and there are more seats on a good-sized sheltered back lawn; disabled access and facilities.

Reliably good food includes sandwiches, scallops and shrimps with chorizo, home-baked ham and egg, battered fresh cod, a pie of the day, home-made burgers with cheese, pork tenderloin on puy lentils and red cabbage, and calves liver and bacon with champ and red wine jus. *Benchmark main dish: smoked haddock with spinach and poached egg £12.95. Two-course evening meal £19.90.*

Enterprise ~ Lease Guy Martin ~ Real ale ~ Bar food (12-2.30, 5-9.30; 12-9.30(8.30 Sun) Sat) ~ Restaurant ~ (01628) 822877 ~ Well behaved children welcome ~ Dogs allowed in bar ~ Quiz night last Thurs of month ~ Open 10.30-3, 5-11; 10.30am-midnight Sat; 12-10.30 Sun

Recommended by June and Robin Savage, A Hawkes, J D Franklin, Richard and Liz Thorne, Dr and Mrs A K Clarke, John Pritchard, Roy Hoing

WHITSTABLE Kent   TR1066   Map 3

Pearsons Arms

 Seawall off Oxford Street, after road splits into one-way system; public parking on left as road divides; CT5 1BT

Seaside pub with an emphasis on interesting food, but serves several ales and has a good mix of customers

Overlooking the pebble beach and with a good mix of both locals and visitors, this weatherboarded pub is doing particularly well under its new landlord. The two front bars are divided by a central chimney and have cushioned settles, captain's chairs and leather armchairs on the stripped-wood floor, driftwood walls and big modern flower

the Beautiful South

arrangements on the bar counter where they serve Ramsgate Gadds No 5, St Austell Tribute, Sharps Doom Bar and Timothy Taylors Landlord on handpump; piped music. A cosy lower room has trompe l'oeil bookshelves and a couple of big chesterfields and dining chairs around plain tables on the stone floor. Up a couple of flights of stairs, the restaurant has sea views, mushroom paintwork, contemporary wallpaper, more driftwood, and church chairs and pine tables on nice wide floorboards.

Quite a choice of interesting food using locally sourced produce might include ham hock ballottine with piccalilli and toasted sour dough, diver-caught scallops with ginger cream sauce, wild boar and apple sausages with caramelised onion gravy, beer-battered cod, steak in ale pie, and slow-roasted pork belly with black pudding and grain mustard sauce. *Benchmark main dish: fish and chips £14.50. Two-course evening meal £21.45.*

Free house ~ Licensee Richard Phillips ~ Real ale ~ Bar food (12-3.30, 6.30-10; not Mon) ~ Restaurant ~ (01227) 272005 ~ Children welcome ~ Dogs welcome ~ Open 12-midnight

Recommended by Mary McSweeney, Richard Mason

 WINCHESTER Hampshire   SU4829   Map 2

Wykeham Arms ♀

Kingsgate Street (Kingsgate Arch and College Street are now closed to traffic; there is access via Canon Street); SO23 9PE

Tucked-away pub with lots to look at, several real ales and lots of wines by the glass; no children inside

The series of bustling rooms in this tucked-away old pub have all sorts of interesting collections dotted about and three log fires. Also,19th-c oak desks retired from nearby Winchester College, a redundant pew from the same source, kitchen chairs and candlelit deal tables and big windows with swagged curtains. A snug room at the back, known as the Jameson Room (after the late landlord Graeme Jameson), is decorated with a set of Ronald Searle 'Winespeak' prints and a second one is panelled. Fullers London Pride, Seafarers and Gales HSB and a couple of guest beers like Flowerpots Goodens Gold and Perridge Pale on handpump, lots of wines by the glass and several malt whiskies. There are tables on a covered back terrace with more on a small courtyard.

Good, if not cheap, the food includes sandwiches, corn-fed chicken and foie gras terrine with spiced pear purée, crab cake with a caper, tomato, red onion and lemon salsa, mushroom risotto with a poached egg and parmesan, roast lamb rump with sweetbreads and trompette mushrooms, and pork tenderloin with black pudding hash and grain mustard jus. *Benchmark main dish: beer-battered haddock £12.50. Two-course evening meal £20.50.*

Fullers ~ Manager Jon Howard ~ Real ale ~ Bar food (12-3, 6-9.30) ~ Restaurant ~ (01962) 853834 ~ Children over 10 allowed in restaurant, younger children at landlord's discretion ~ Dogs allowed in bar and bedrooms ~ Open 11-11(10.30 Sun) ~ Bedrooms: £72S/£135S(£145B)

Recommended by Mrs C Roe, David Bangert, Martin and Karen Wake, Chris Glasson, the Didler, Franzi Florack, Ann and Colin Hunt

---

Virtually all pubs in the *Good Pub Guide* sell wine by the glass. We mention wines if they are a cut above the average.

WINEHAM Sussex   TQ2320   Map 3

Royal Oak

Village signposted from A272 and B2116; BN5 9AY

Splendidly old-fashioned local with interesting bric-a-brac in simple rooms, attentive staff, real ales, and well liked food

This is an unspoilt, traditional local and popular with both regulars (and their dogs) and visitors. As well as a blazing log fire in an enormous inglenook fireplace with its cast-iron Royal Oak fireback, there's a collection of cigarette boxes, a stuffed stoat and crocodile and some jugs and ancient corkscrews on the very low beams above the serving counter. Other bits of bric-a-brac too, views of quiet countryside from the back parlour and a bearded collie called Bella. Harveys Best and a couple of guests such as Dark Star Hophead and Old Chestnut tapped from the cask in a still room and quite a few wines by the glass. There are some picnic-sets outside.

Good, seasonally changing food includes good value sandwiches, soup, soft herring roes on toast, asparagus, peas and broad bean risotto, breaded veal escalope with lemon and rocket, cottage pie, local sausages with cider and onion gravy, and rump of lamb with wild mushrooms and red wine jus. *Benchmark main dish: home-made pie £10.00. Two-course evening meal £18.00.*

Punch ~ Managers Sharon and Michael Bailey ~ Real ale ~ Bar food (12-2.30, 7-9; not Sun evening) ~ (01444) 881252 ~ Children welcome away from bar area ~ Dogs welcome ~ Open 11-3(4 Sat), 5.30(6 Sat)-11; 12-4, 7-10.30 Sun; closed evenings 25 and 26 Dec and 1 Jan
Recommended by David and Pam Wilcox, Conor McGaughey, the Didler, Terry Buckland, John Redfern, N R White, Kevin and Maggie Balchin

WINTERBOURNE Berkshire   SU4572   Map 2

Winterbourne Arms ♀

3.7 miles from M4 junction 13; at A34 turn into Chieveley Services and follow Donnington signs to Arlington Lane, then follow Winterbourne signs; RG20 8BB

Bustling village pub with quite a choice of bar food, real ales, lots of wines by the glass, and a large landscaped garden

Handy for the M4, this is a pretty black and white village pub. The traditionally furnished bars have stools along the counter, a mix of pine dining chairs and tables, a collection of old irons around the big fireplace and early prints and old photographs of the village on the pale washed or exposed stone walls; piped music. Big windows take in peaceful views over rolling fields. Ramsbury Gold and a beer brewed by them for the pub called Winterbourne Whistle Wetter on handpump and 20 wines by the glass including sparkling and sweet wines. There are seats outside in the large landscaped side garden and pretty flowering tubs and hanging baskets. The surrounding countryside here is lovely, with nearby walks to Snelsmore Common and Donnington Castle.

As well as sandwiches, the varied bar food includes filled baguettes, duckling rillettes with red onion marmalade, a pie of the week, deep-fried fish and chips, mixed mushroom risotto, free-range pork chop on bubble and squeak with a grain mustard sauce, and calves liver and bacon with onion gravy. *Benchmark main dish: sirloin steak £17.95. Two-course evening meal £21.90.*

Free house ~ Licensee Frank Adams ~ Real ale ~ Bar food (12-2.30, 6-10; 12-3, 6-9 Sun)

~ Restaurant ~ (01635) 248200 ~ Children welcome ~ Dogs allowed in bar ~ Open 12-3, 6-11; 12-10.30 Sun

Recommended by Tracey and Stephen Groves, Angela Crum Ewing, Adele Summers, Alan Black, Phyl and Jack Street, Peter Meister, Rob and Catherine Dunster, Dr and Mrs A K Clarke, George and Maureen Roby, N R White, George Atkinson, Mike and Mary Carter, John Pritchard, Pat and Roger Davies

WOOBURN COMMON Buckinghamshire SU9187 Map 2

Chequers

From A4094 N of Maidenhead at junction with A4155 Marlow road keep on A4094 for another 0.75 miles, then at roundabout turn off right towards Wooburn Common and into Kiln Lane; if you find yourself in Honey Hill, Hedsor, turn left into Kiln Lane at the top of the hill; OS Sheet 175 map reference 910870; HP10 0JQ

Busy and friendly hotel with a bustling bar and smart restaurant; comfortable bedrooms

Although this is a bustling hotel, its heart is still in the friendly main bar which continues to thrive as a welcoming local. It feels nicely pubby with low beams, standing timbers and alcoves, characterful rickety furniture and comfortably lived-in sofas on bare boards, a bright log-effect gas fire, pictures, plates, a two-man saw and tankards. In contrast, the bar to the left, with its dark brown leather sofas at low tables on wooden floors, feels plain and modern. They have a good sizeable wine list (with a dozen by the glass), a fair range of malt whiskies and brandies and Greene King IPA and Old Speckled Hen and Rebellion Smuggler on handpump; piped music. The spacious garden, set away from the road, has seats around cast-iron tables and summer barbecues.

As well as sandwiches, the wide choice of popular food might include chicken liver parfait with onion marmalade, salmon, haddock and prawn fishcakes, home-made burger, mushroom risotto, cumberland sausages, corn-fed chicken with stewed tomato, polenta, olives and basil pesto, and navarin of lamb with saffron potatoes and buttered baby vegetables. *Benchmark main dish: fish and chips £10.95. Two-course evening meal £25.00.*

Free house ~ Licensee Peter Roehrig ~ Real ale ~ Bar food (12-2.30, 6-9.30(10 Fri); 12-10(9.30 Sun) Sat) ~ Restaurant ~ (01628) 529575 ~ Children welcome ~ Open 11am-midnight ~ Bedrooms: £99.50B/£107.50B

Recommended by Simon Collett-Jones, Peter and Giff Bennett, D and M T Ayres-Regan

WOODSTOCK Oxfordshire SP4416 Map 4

Kings Arms £ 🛏

Market Street/Park Lane (A44); OX20 1SU

Stylish hotel in centre of attractive town, well liked food, enjoyable atmosphere, and a wide choice of drinks; comfortable bedrooms

Quieter at lunchtime but lively in the evening, the simple and unfussy bar in this stylish town-centre hotel has quite a mix of customers creating a relaxed and informal atmosphere. There are brown leather furnishings on the stripped-wood floor, smart blinds and black and white photographs throughout and at the front, an old wooden settle and interesting little woodburner. In the room leading to the brasserie-style dining room, there's an unusual stained-glass structure used for newspapers and magazines; the restaurant is attractive, with its hanging lights and fine old fireplace. Brakspears Bitter and Oxford Gold on handpump, good coffees, 14 wines plus champagne by the glass and 20 malt whiskies; piped music. Comfortable bedrooms and good breakfasts (available from 7.30-midday for non-residents, too). There are seats and tables on the street outside.

🍴 Fair value lunchtime bar food includes sandwiches, honey and mustard baked ham and free-range eggs, leek, pea and cheese tart and organic beefburger with blue cheese and bacon, with more pricey evening choices like guinea fowl terrine with red onion marmalade, free-range chicken breast with mushroom mousse, braised leeks and tarragon butter sauce, and bass fillet with fennel and spinach and a crab and tomato cream sauce. *Benchmark main dish: pork belly with celeriac purée, caramelised apple and cider sauce £15.50. Two-course evening meal £22.00.*

Free house ~ Licensees David and Sara Sykes ~ Real ale ~ Bar food (12-2.30(3 Sat), 6.30-9(9.30 Sat); all day Sun) ~ Restaurant ~ (01993) 813636 ~ Children welcome in bar and restaurant but no under-12s in bedrooms ~ Open 11-11 ~ Bedrooms: £75S/£140S(£150B)

Recommended by Derek and Sylvia Stephenson, Michael Dandy, Rob and Catherine Dunster, Dave and Jenny Hughes, Martin and Pauline Jennings, John and Sharon Hancock, Pippa Manley, Paul and Mary Walmsley, David and Judy Robison, Graham Oddey

LONDON

CENTRAL LONDON   Map 13

Bountiful Cow

Eagle Street; ⊖ *Holborn; WC1R 4AP*

Bustling and informal place popular with those wanting either a chat at the bar or a meat-related meal

Although there is a basement dining room by the open kitchen with red-painted walls and cow prints, most customers prefer the informal street-level bar in this part pub/part grill house. The chrome and white leather bar stools are grabbed quickly by those wanting a chat and a pint of Adnams or Dark Star on handpump and there are quite a few tables – though there may be a short wait for a free one at peak times. The raised area by the windows has booth seating and the smallish main room has red wicker dining chairs around wooden tables on the stripped floorboards, beef-related prints and posters on the painted brick walls and a mixture of happy chat and piped jazz. Service is quick and friendly, and the licensees also run the Seven Stars in Carey Street.

🍴 As well as their range of terrific steaks, popular food includes duck rillettes, smoked salmon, charcuterie, couscous with roast vegetables, club sandwich, dill cured herring with potato salad, and grilled chicken breast with pancetta and mashed potatoes. *Benchmark main dish: bountyburger £12.80. Two-course evening meal £23.00.*

Free house ~ Licensee Roxy Beaujolais ~ Real ale ~ Bar food (11-10.30) ~ (020) 7404 0200 ~ Children welcome ~ Open 11-11; closed Sun

Recommended by Richard Gibbs

the Beautiful South

CENTRAL LONDON   Map 13

Harp ◀

47 Chandos Place; ⊖ ⇌ Charing Cross, Leicester Square; WC2N 4HS

Narrow little pub with eight real ales, friendly service, a cheerful atmosphere, and nice sausage baguettes

You can really tell that the cheerful long-serving landlady and her friendly staff take delight in welcoming their customers and running this busy little pub. Even with just a few customers there is a chatty atmosphere and in the early evening it hums with customers spilling out into the back alley. It pretty much consists of one long narrow, very traditional bar, with lots of high bar stools along the wall counter and around elbow tables, big mirrors on the red walls, some lovely front stained glass and loads of interesting quirkily executed celebrity portraits. If it's not too busy, you may be able to get one of the prized seats looking out through the front windows. A little room upstairs is much quieter, with comfortable furniture and a window looking over the road below. The eight real ales on handpump are particularly well kept and quickly changing. There's usually three from Dark Star, one from Harveys, two from Sambrooks and one or two widely sourced guests – maybe from Ascot or Twickenham; five farm ciders and three perries and quite a few malt whiskies.

🍴 Bar food consists of good changing sausages such as boar and apple, pork, port and stilton, venison and redcurrant, lamb and mint and so forth, served in baps with lots of fried onions. These are served until they run out. *Benchmark main dish: sausage baguette £2.50.*

Free house ~ Licensee Bridget Walsh ~ Real ale ~ Bar food (12-4; not Sun) ~ (020) 7836 0291 ~ Open 10.30am-11pm(midnight Fri, Sat); 12-10.30 Sun

Recommended by Tim Maddison, Roger and Donna Huggins, Mike Gorton, Barbarrick, Joe Green, Tracey and Stephen Groves, Peter F Marshall, LM, Taff Thomas, Matt and Vikki Wharton, Phil Bryant, the Didler, Mike and Sue Loseby

CENTRAL LONDON   Map 13

Old Bank of England ♀

Fleet Street; ⊖ Chancery Lane (not Sundays), Temple (not Sundays) ⇌ Blackfriars; EC4A 2LT

Dramatically converted former bank building, with gleaming chandeliers in impressive, soaring bar, well kept Fullers beers and good pies

Well worth including in a tour of London, this former subsidiary branch of the Bank of England has a quite astounding interior. The italianate building itself is rather austere but its sternness stops here. The soaring, spacious bar has three gleaming chandeliers hanging from the exquisitely plastered ceiling, high above an unusually tall island bar counter, crowned with a clock. The end wall has huge paintings and murals that look like 18th-c depictions of Justice, but in fact feature members of the Fuller, Smith and Turner families, who run the brewery that owns the pub. There are well polished dark wooden furnishings, luxurious curtains swagging massive windows, plenty of framed prints, and, despite the grandeur, some surprisingly cosy corners, with screens between some of the tables creating an unexpectedly intimate feel. Tables in a quieter galleried section upstairs offer a bird's-eye view of the

the Beautiful South

action, and some smaller rooms (used mainly for functions) open off. Seven Fullers beers are on handpump alongside a good choice of malt whiskies and a dozen wines by the glass. At lunchtimes the piped music is generally classical or easy listening; it's louder and livelier in the evenings. There's also a garden with seats (one of the few pubs in the area to have one).

🍴 Pies have a long if rather dubious pedigree in this area: it was in the vaults and tunnels below the Old Bank and the surrounding buildings that Sweeney Todd butchered the clients destined to provide the fillings in his mistress Mrs Lovett's nearby pie shop. Well, somehow or other, good home-made pies have become a speciality on the menu here, too: maybe steak in ale, fish, beef and venison and stilton, mushroom and red pepper. Other dishes include sandwiches, ploughman's, summer salads, sausages and mash, proper burgers, and fish and chips. *Benchmark main dish: pie of the day £9.75. Two-course evening meal £15.00.*

Fullers ~ Manager Jo Farquhar ~ Real ale ~ Bar food (12-9) ~ (020) 7430 2255 ~ Children welcome till 7pm ~ Open 11-11; closed weekends and bank holidays
Recommended by Michael Dandy, Peter Dandy, Barry Collett, the Didler, Chris and Jeanne Downing, Tom and Ruth Rees, Andy and Claire Barker

CENTRAL LONDON Map 13
Olde Mitre 🍺 £

Ely Place; the easiest way to find it is from the narrow passageway beside 8 Hatton Garden; ⊖ Chancery Lane (not Sundays); EC1N 6SJ

Hard to find but well worth it – an unspoilt old pub with lovely atmosphere, unusual guest beers and bargain toasted sandwiches

You need to be in the know to find this hidden gem that's tucked away down a tiny alley. These days, it's all too rare in London to find proper hands-on licensees who genuinely care for their pub and their customers – but Mr and Mrs Scott do just that and our readers love it. The cosy small rooms have lots of dark panelling as well as antique settles and – particularly in the popular back room, where there are more seats – old local pictures and so forth. It gets good-naturedly packed with the city suited and booted between 12.30 and 2.15, filling up again in the early evening, but in the early afternoons and by around 9pm becomes a good deal more tranquil. An upstairs room, mainly used for functions, may double as an overflow at peak periods. Adnams Broadside, Caledonian Deuchars IPA, Fullers London Pride and Gales Seafarer and guests like BrewDog Trashy Blonde and Titanic White Star on handpump, and they hold three beer festivals a year. No music, TV or machines – the only games here are board games. There's some space for outside drinking by the pot plants and jasmine in the narrow yard between the pub and St Ethelreda's church (which is worth a look). Note the pub doesn't open weekends. The iron gates that guard one entrance to Ely Place are a reminder of the days when the law in this district was administered by the Bishops of Ely. The best approach is from Hatton Garden, walking up the right-hand side away from Chancery Lane; an easily missed sign on a lamp post points the way down a narrow alley. No children.

🍴 Served all day, bar snacks are limited to scotch eggs, pork pies and sausage rolls, and really good value toasted sandwiches with cheese, ham, pickle or tomato. *Benchmark main dish: toasted sandwich £1.95.*

Fullers ~ Managers Eamon and Kathy Scott ~ Real ale ~ Bar food (11.30-9) ~ (020) 7405 4751 ~ Open 11-11; closed weekends and bank holidays

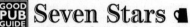

Recommended by Jim Frame, Richard Endacott, Tracey and Stephen Groves, Ross Balaam, John and Gloria Isaacs, Ian Phillips, N R White, Lawrence R Cotter, Anthony Longden, Barbarrick, the Didler, Tom McLean, Chris and Jeanne Downing, Andy and Claire Barker, Matt and Vikki Wharton, Taff Thomas

CENTRAL LONDON   Map 13

Seven Stars ◖

Carey Street; ✛ *Temple (not Sundays), Chancery Lane (not Sundays), Holborn; WC2A 2JB*

Quirky pub with cheerful staff, an interesting mix of customers and good choice of drinks and food

There's a genuinely timeless atmosphere at this unchanging, characterful little pub, which the licensees tell us was first established in 1602. There's always a good mix of customers – though as it faces the back of the Law Courts, it's a favourite with lawyers and court reporters; there are plenty of caricatures of barristers and judges on the red-painted walls of the two main rooms. There are also posters of legal-themed british films, big ceiling fans and a relaxed, intimate atmosphere; checked tablecloths add a quirky, almost continental touch. A third area is in what was formerly a legal wig shop next door – it still retains the original frontage, with a neat display of wigs in the window. It's worth getting here early as they don't take bookings and tables get snapped up quickly. Adnams Best and Broadside and a couple of guests such as Dark Star Hophead and Sambrooks Wandle are on handpump, and they do a particularly good dry Martini. On busy evenings there's an overflow of customers on to the quiet road in front; things generally quieten down after 8pm and there can be a nice, sleepy atmosphere some afternoons. The Elizabethan stairs up to the lavatories are rather steep, but there's a good strong handrail. Tom Paine, the large and somewhat po-faced pub cat, still remains very much a centre of attention. The licensees have a second pub, the Bountiful Cow, on Eagle Street, near Holborn tube station, which specialises in beef. No children.

🍴 Good, interesting food chosen and cooked according to the landlady's fancy and what's freshly available might include bruschetta with different toppings, a swedish dish of potato, anchovy, cream and dill, napoli sausage with mash, linguine with duxelle of mushrooms and truffle oil, vegetarian chinese stir fry, home-made meat pies, a large hamburger with trimmings, roast guinea fowl in lemony jus, chargrilled fish of the day, and posh ice-cream. *Benchmark main dish: goose pie £11.00. Two-course evening meal £15.00.*

Free house ~ Licensee Roxy Beaujolais ~ Real ale ~ Bar food (all day) ~ (020) 7242 8521 ~ Open 11(12 Sat, Sun)-11(10.30 Sun); closed some bank holidays

Recommended by LM, Tim Maddison, Eddie Edwards, Ian Martin, N R White, the Didler, Tracey and Stephen Groves, Andy and Claire Barker

EAST LONDON

Map 12

Grapes

Narrow Street; ✆ ⇄*Limehouse (or Westferry on the DLR); the Limehouse link has made it hard to find by car – turn off Commercial Road at signs for Rotherhithe Tunnel, then from the Tunnel Approach slip road, fork left leading into Branch Road, turn left and then left again into Narrow Street; E14 8BP*

Relaxed waterside pub with timeless London feel, particularly appealing cosy back room, helpful friendly staff, well liked Sunday roasts, and good upstairs fish restaurant

You get a lovely sense of history if you catch the Canary Wharf ferry to this 16th-c riverside pub and enter via the steps that lead up from the foreshore. Though much brushed up, it remains almost exactly as it was when Charles Dickens used it as a model for his Six Jolly Fellowship Porters in *Our Mutual Friend* – all the more remarkable considering the ultra-modern buildings that now surround it. It has bags of atmosphere, a good mix of customers and friendly service. The chatty, partly panelled bar has lots of prints, mainly of actors, and old local maps, as well as some elaborately etched windows, plates along a shelf, and newspapers to read; the cosy back part has a winter open fire. Adnams Best, Marstons Pedigree, Timothy Taylors Landlord and a guest on handpump, and Addlestone's cider, are served from the long thin bar; board games. The upstairs fish restaurant, with fine views of the river, is highly thought of. The pub was a favourite with James Whistler, who used it as the viewpoint for his river paintings. In summer, the small balcony at the back is a fine spot for a sheltered waterside drink, with easterly views towards Canary Wharf. No children, but they do have a bowl of water for dogs.

Reasonably priced and generously served bar food includes sandwiches, soup, a tankard of whitebait, sausage and mash with onion gravy, very good fish and chips, home-made fishcake with caper sauce, and puddings like apple crumble and bread and butter pudding; Sunday roast is highly regarded (no other meals then). The fish restaurant is pricier. *Benchmark main dish: fish and chips £8.75. Two-course evening meal £23.45.*

Free house ~ Licensee Barbara Haigh ~ Real ale ~ Bar food (12-2.30, 6.30-9.30; 12-4 Sun; not Sun evening) ~ Restaurant ~ (020) 7987 4396 ~ Dogs welcome ~ Open 12-3, 5.30-11; 12-11 Thurs, Fri; 12-10.30 Sun

Recommended by Barry and Anne, N R White, Mike Gorton, John Saville, Andy and Claire Barker, Claes Mauroy

EAST LONDON

Map 12

Gun 🍴 ♟

27 Coldharbour; ✆ *Blackwall on the DLR is probably closest, although the slightly longer walk from Canary Wharf has splendid Dockland views; E14 9NS*

LONDON DINING PUB OF THE YEAR

Top-notch gastropub, pricey but worth it, great views from the riverside terrace, plenty of character and history, well chosen wines

There is a terrific long narrow terrace behind this busy riverside pub, with uninterrupted views of the Dome across a broad sweep of the Thames. Heaters and huge umbrellas make it welcoming even on cooler days. Inside, crisp white walls and smart white tablecloths and napkins on tables at one end of the front bar contrast strikingly with dark wood floors and the black wood counter and back bar with its row of red stools. Towards the terrace is a busy flagstoned bar for drinkers, with antique guns on the wall, and no tables, just a large barrel in the centre of the room. It shares a warm log fire in winter with a cosy red-painted room next door, which has comfy leather sofas and armchairs, a stuffed boar's head, some modern prints, well stocked bookshelves and views on to the terrace. Friendly aproned staff serve three real ales such as Adnams, Fullers London Pride and Greene King Abbot and a good choice of wines. There's a relaxed chatty atmosphere throughout. On summer days, they open up another terrace as a portuguese barbecue; piped music. They may occasionally close the pub on Saturdays for weddings, and will keep your credit card if you are sitting on the terrace and want to run a tab.

You can eat from both the bar and restaurant menu in the bar so there is a good choice of dishes, starting with oysters, devilled whitebait, steak or fish finger sandwich, macaroni cheese and shepherd's pie from the bar menu, moving up to braised beef and ox tongue soup with roast marrow bone, crispy pork belly with snails, garlic and peppered chicory, mushroom and spinach pasty, smoked haddock and salmon fishcake with poached egg and chive butter sauce, braised sweetbreads with morels and veal jus, and well hung black angus rib-eye steak with béarnaise sauce from the restaurant menu. *Benchmark main dish: shin of beefburger £13.50. Two-course evening meal £30.00.*

Free house ~ Licensees Ed and Tom Martin ~ Real ale ~ Bar food (12-3(4 Sat, Sun), 6-10.30(9.30 Sun)) ~ Restaurant ~ (020) 7515 5222 ~ Children welcome ~ Quiz Mon evening ~ Open 11am-midnight(11pm Sun)
Recommended by LM, W T Selwood, Andy and Claire Barker

 NORTH LONDON   Map 13

Drapers Arms 🍴 ♀

Far west end of Barnsbury Street; ⊖ ⇌ *Highbury & Islington; N1 1ER*

Streamlined place with good mix of drinkers and diners, thoughtful choice of beers, wines and imaginative modern food, and seats in the attractive back garden

The spreading bar at this simply refurbished but stylish Georgian townhouse has a mix of elegant dark wooden tables and dining chairs on bare boards, an arresting bright green-painted counter contrasting with soft duck-egg walls, gilt mirrors over smart fireplaces, a sofa and some comfortable chairs. Harveys Best and a couple of guests such as Dark Star Hophead on handpump, and carefully chosen wines by the glass (about 20), carafe or bottle. The stylish upstairs dining room has similar tables and chairs on a striking chequerboard-painted wood floor; piped music and board games. The back terrace is most attractive with white or green benches and chairs around zinc-topped tables, flagstones and large parasols; more reports please.

Good modern cooking might include sandwiches, ploughman's, smoked haddock and bacon chowder, grilled razor clams with red onions, garlic and thyme, pork, pigeon and foie gras terrine, rump of lamb with courgettes, saffron and garlic, steak and oyster pie (for two or three), and puddings such as buttermilk pudding with rhubarb, chocolate pot and chocolate chip cookie. *Benchmark main dish: onglet steak £14.50. Two-course evening meal £20.50.*

Free house ~ Licensee Nick Gibson ~ Real ale ~ Bar food (12-3(4 Sun), 6-10.30(9.30

Sun)) ~ Restaurant ~ (020) 7619 0348 ~ Children welcome, but after 6pm must be
seated and eating ~ Dogs allowed in bar ~ Open 10-midnight(11 Sun)

Recommended by Richard Gibbs

 SOUTH LONDON   Map 13

Royal Oak ◀
Tabard Street/Nebraska Street; ❷ ⇄ Borough, London Bridge; SE1 4JU

**Old-fashioned Harveys corner house with all their beers excellently
kept; good, honest food too**

This enjoyable corner house is slightly off the beaten track, in rather
unprepossessing surroundings, and is the only London pub belonging
to Sussex brewer Harveys – needless to say, they stock the full range as
well as a guest such as Gales HSB. The brewery transformed the pub
when they took over, painstakingly re-creating the look and feel of a
traditional London alehouse – you'd never imagine it wasn't like this all
along. Filled with the sounds of happy chat, two busy little L-shaped
rooms meander around the central wooden servery, which has a fine old
clock in the middle. They're done out in a cosy, traditional style with
patterned rugs on the wooden floors, plates running along a delft shelf,
black and white scenes or period sheet music on the red-painted walls,
and an assortment of wooden tables and chairs; disabled ramp available
on the Nebraska Street entrance.

A reasonable range of bar food includes impressive doorstep sandwiches, and
generously served daily specials such as cod and chips, vegetable and stilton
and steak and ale pies, rabbit in mustard sauce, poached salmon salad, and roast
duck; Sunday roasts. *Benchmark main dish: ham, egg and chips £7.95. Two-course
evening meal £15.00.*

Harveys ~ Tenants John Porteous, Frank Taylor ~ Real ale ~ Bar food (12-2.30, 5-9.30;
12-7.30 Sun) ~ (020) 7357 7173 ~ Children welcome ~ Dogs allowed in bar ~ Open 11-11;
12-9 Sun; closed bank holidays

*Recommended by Mayur Shah, Andy Lickfold, Mike and Sue Loseby, Susan and John Douglas,
John Saville, R Anderson, Jeremy King, Comus and Sarah Elliott, the Didler*

 SOUTH LONDON   Map 12

Telegraph ◀
Telegraph Road; ⇄ Putney ❷ East Putney, Southfields but quite a walk;
SW15 3TU

**A good summer pub, with plenty of outdoor seats and a rural feel; nicely
reworked inside too, with excellent choice of beers, reliable food, and
good live blues on Fridays**

So verdant is this oasis it's hard to believe you're in London. The
outdoor space is the main appeal here, and on fine weekends it can
get very busy with families and dogs a big part of the mix. Tables are
nicely sheltered under big trees and a pergola, and there are a couple of
quirky cow-print sofas under a little verandah by the entrance. The two
modernised rooms inside have lots of leather armchairs and sofas and
framed period prints and advertisements. The long main bar on the left
also has quite a variety of wooden furnishings, including some unusually
high tables and stools, and a rather grand dining table at one end; there's
a TV for sport, rugs on the polished wooden floor, and an appealing little

alcove rather like a private lounge, with a fireplace and a table of newspapers; piped music, TV, board games and occasional quiz and blues nights. The beer range is enterprising – as well as Weltons Semaphore, five regularly changing real ales might be from brewers such as Hammerpots, Sambrooks, St Austell and Tintagel. There's a good wine list too, with about 18 by the glass. The pub is named after the Admiralty telegraph station that used to stand nearby, one of a chain of ten between Chelsea and Portsmouth (on a clear day, a message could be sent between the two in 15 minutes).

As well as sharing platters, bar food includes mushroom and rocket risotto, chicken, chorizo and halloumi skewers, fish and chips, pie of the day, asian duck salad, burgers, lemon pepper chicken schnitzel, provençale rabbit stew and braised lamb shank with rosemary jus, and daily specials such as bass fillet with thyme jus, and fried salmon with tagliatelle and roast pepper and orange sauce; Sunday roast. *Benchmark main dish: braised lamb shank £15.95. Two-course evening meal £21.00.*

Free house ~ Licensee Jay Cearns ~ Real ale ~ Bar food (12-9(10 Fri, Sat)) ~ Restaurant ~ (020) 8788 2011 ~ Children welcome ~ Dogs welcome ~ Open 12(11 Sat)-11(12 Sat,10.30 Sun)

Recommended by Michael Dandy, Peter Dandy, George Wallace, Colin McKerrow, Tracey and Stephen Groves, Sophie Holborow

WEST LONDON   Map 12

Havelock Tavern ❶ ♀
Masbro Road; ⊖ ⇄ Kensington(Olympia); W14 0LS

Friendly, often vibrant, atmosphere, very good food and well chosen wines

Though it looks pretty ordinary, this blue-tiled corner house is a well regarded gastropub that's very popular for its classy food and laid-back atmosphere. Until 1932 the building was two separate shops and it still has huge shop-front windows. The light and airy L-shaped bar is plain and unfussy with bare boards and long wooden tables that you may end up sharing. A second little room with pews leads to a small paved terrace with benches, a tree and wall climbers. Friendly staff serve Sambrooks Wandle, Sharps Doom Bar and a couple of guests beers like Purity Pure UBU on handpump from the elegant modern bar counter, as well as a good range of well chosen wines with around 19 by the glass; mulled wine in winter and maybe home-made lemonade in summer; board games. More reports please. If you run a tab, they may ask to keep your credit card in a secure box.

The imaginative menu here changes twice a day and everything, from the mayonnaise to ice-cream is home-made. Interesting modern dishes might include pork, duck, prune and pistachio terrine, creamed mushrooms on toast with parmesan and poached egg, warm broccoli, spinach and gorgonzola tart, leg of lamb steak with butternut purée, fillet of bass with mussels, saffron, leek and tomato broth, roast chicken breast with roast garlic, shallot and green peppercorn butter, and smoked ham hock and gruyère with spicy tomato sauce. *Benchmark main dish: bavette steak and chips £14.00. Two-course evening meal £20.00.*

Free house ~ Licensee Andrew Solley ~ Real ale ~ Bar food (12.30-2.30(3 Sun), 7-10(9.30 Sun)) ~ (020) 7603 5374 ~ Children welcome ~ Dogs welcome ~ Open 11-11; 12-10.30 Sun

Recommended by Derek Thomas, Martin and Karen Wake

 OUTER LONDON   TQ1769 Map 12

Bishop Out of Residence £

Bishop's Hall, down alley off Thames Street; ⇄ *Hampton Wick, Kingston KT1 1PY*

Contemporary pub in a fine Thames spot with plenty of chairs on waterside terrace, lots of space inside, modern décor, real ale and fair-priced food

In fine weather, the many seats on the terrace overlooking the Thames and with views of Kingston Bridge are a real bonus. Inside, the open-plan contemporary bar is split up into more cosy areas with all manner of seating from comfortable sofas facing each other across a chest table, to groups of armchairs beside small circular tables, and yet more tables lining a long curved red wall banquette. There are dark red walls and ornate wallpaper hung with lots of gilt-framed pictures, standard lamps and modern ceiling lights. The upstairs lounge has windows overlooking the water, lots of dining chairs and another long wall banquette by tables on bare boards and trompe l'oeil bookshelves, and a fireplace beside sofas and a chaise longue. Wells & Youngs Bombardier, IPA, Special and a guest on handpump, 27 wines by the glass and various cocktails.

Good modern british cooking includes sandwiches and stone-baked pizzas as well as a weekend brunch, sharing boards, gressingham duck and root vegetable terrine with spiced apple chutney, salmon and haddock fishcake with thyme and lemon butter sauce, bangers and mash with onion gravy, and mushroom, spinach, chestnut and pine nut risotto; prices are fair for the London area. *Benchmark main dish: home-made burger £10.00. Two-course evening meal £15.00.*

Youngs ~ Manager Tanya Tozer ~ Real ale ~ Bar food (12-9.30; 10-10 Sat; 10-9 Sun) ~ (0208) 546 4965 ~ Children and dogs welcome away from upstairs lounge bar ~ Open 11-11(midnight Fri); 10(11 in winter)-midnight Sat; 10(11 in winter)-10.30 Sun
Recommended by Richard Gibbs

 OUTER LONDON   TQ0490 Map 3

Old Orchard 🍴 �

Off Park Lane; Harefield UB9 6HJ

Wonderful views from the garden in front of this Edwardian house, a good choice of drinks, friendly staff and well liked, interesting food

The stunning view from teak tables and chairs on the terrace in front of this former country house are much prized, so it's best to arrive early if you want to bag one. You look down over the longboats on the canal and on to the lakes that make up a conservation area known as the Colne Valley Regional Park; it's a haven for wildlife. Seats from the gazebo and picnic-sets in the garden have the same amazing view. Inside, the knocked-through open-plan rooms have an attractive mix of cushioned dining chairs around all size and shape of dark wooden tables, lots of prints, maps and pictures covering the walls, books on shelves, old glass bottles on window sills and rugs on wood or parquet flooring. One room is hung with a sizeable rug and some tapestry. There are daily papers to read, three cosy coal fires, big pot plants and fresh flowers. Half a dozen real ales on handpump include Fullers London Pride, Phoenix Brunning & Price, Tring Side Pocket for a Toad, alongside guests from brewers such as Adnams, St Austell and Windsor & Eton; also about two dozen

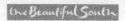

wines by the glass and over 100 whiskies; friendly, helpful staff. The atmosphere is civilised and easy-going.

Popular brasserie-type food (the orders are sent to the kitchen along an unusual vacuum tube) includes interesting sandwiches, light meals and dishes such as roquefort, chestnut and fig tart with caramelised onion salad, spiced cauliflower, sweet potato and coriander bhaji with red pepper and cucumber relish, charcuterie to share, kedgeree with spinach and poached egg, malaysian fish stew, battered haddock, cauliflower, chickpea and almond tagine with apricot and date couscous, chicken, ham and leek pie, and rump steak with watercress and horseradish butter. *Benchmark main dish: sausage and mash £9.95. Two-course evening meal £18.95.*

Brunning & Price ~ Manager Dan Redfern ~ Real ale ~ Bar food (12-10(9.30 Sun)) ~ (01895) 822631 ~ Children welcome ~ Dogs allowed in bar ~ Open 11.30-11; 12-10.30 Sun
Recommended by Richard Gibbs

ALSO WORTH A VISIT IN BERKSHIRE

Besides the region's top pubs, we recommend the following. Do tell us what you think of them: **feedback@goodguides.com**

ALDWORTH SU5579   RG8 9SE
☆ **Bell**
A329 Reading—Wallingford; left on to B4009 at Streatley

Unspoilt and unchanging (in same family for over 250 years), simply furnished, panelled rooms, beams in ochre ceiling, ancient one-handed clock, woodburner, glass-panelled hatch serving Arkells, West Berkshire and a monthly guest, Upton cider, good house wines, maybe winter mulled wine, good value rolls, ploughman's and winter soup, traditional pub games, no mobile phones, credit cards, piped music or machines; can get busy at weekends; well behaved children and dogs welcome, seats in quiet, cottagey garden by village cricket ground, animals in paddock behind pub, maybe Christmas mummers and summer morris men, closed Mon (open lunchtime bank holidays).
Recommended by Richard Endacott, Henry Midwinter, Dick and Madeleine Brown, the Didler, Mr and Mrs H J Langley, Guy Vowles and others

ASHMORE GREEN SU4969   RG18 9HF
☆ **Sun in the Wood**
B4009 (Shaw Road) off A339, right to Kiln Road, left to Stoney Lane

Cheery family pub with enthusiastic owners, genuine mix of loyal customers, comfortable unimposing high-beamed front bar, mix of nice old chairs, padded dining chairs and stripped pews around sturdy tables, big back dining area with candles on tables, some interesting touches like stripped bank of apothecary's drawers, small conservatory sitting area by side entrance, Wadworths ales and a guest, several wines by the glass, good popular food; seats under parasols on heated decked terrace, picnic-sets in big woodside garden, small child-free area, nine-hole woodland crazy golf pitch, closed Mon, Sun evening. *Recommended by Douglas and Ann Hare, Ian Herdman, R T and J C Moggridge, Dave Braisted, Paul Humphreys*

ASTON SU7884   RG9 3DG
☆ **Flower Pot**
Off A4130 Henley—Maidenhead at top of Remenham Hill

Roomy popular country pub with nice local feel, roaring log fire, array of stuffed fish and fishing prints on dark green walls of attractively done airy country dining area, enjoyable food from baguettes to fish and game, Brakspears, Hook Norton and Wychwood ales, quick friendly service, snug traditional bar with more fishing memorabilia; very busy with walkers and families at weekends; lots of picnic-sets giving quiet country views from nice big dog-friendly orchard garden, side field with poultry, crocodile on roof, Thames nearby, bedrooms. *Recommended by Roy Hoing, Susan and John Douglas, Mike and Mary Carter, Mark Hanley*

BEEDON SU4976   RG20 8SD
Coach & Horses
3 miles N of M4 junction 13, via A34

Modernised pub/restaurant with good food from pub staples and pizzas to more enterprising cooking, lunchtime set deals too, real ales and plenty of wines by the glass including champagne, friendly attentive service. *Recommended by Sharon Oldham*

BINFIELD SU8471   RG42 5PH
Jack o' Newbury
Terrace Road North

Friendly family-run Victorian pub, good choice of well kept local ales such as West Berkshire, good value pubby food including vegetarian choices, skittle alley; children welcome, seats out at front and in garden. *Recommended by Jez*

BRACKNELL SU8566   RG12 7PB
Golden Retriever
Nine Mile Ride (junction A3095/B3430)

Vintage Inn pastiche of olde-worlde beamed, tiled and thatched pub, comfortable farmhouse-style décor in maze of linked rooms, Caledonian Deuchars IPA, Fullers London Pride and Sharps Doom Bar, plenty of wines by the glass, good choice of decent food all day, friendly service, log fires, daily papers; ample seating outside. *Recommended by Jeremy Stephens, Rosemary and Mike Fielder, Mike and Jayne Bastin*

BURCHETTS GREEN SU8381   SL6 6QZ
Crown
Side road from A4 after Knowl Green on left, linking to A404

Popular dining pub under newish management, good interesting country cooking such as braised pig's cheek with crab apple purée, own bread and home-cured salami, good wines from small producers, compact bar for drinkers with well kept Greene King ales, other areas set for eating, rustic furniture and stripped-back décor; picnic-sets out at front, garden with vegetable patch, open all day (no food Sun evening). *Recommended by Susan and John Douglas, Paul Humphreys*

CHIEVELEY SU4773   RG20 8XB
☆ Olde Red Lion
Handy for M4 junction 13 via A34 N-bound; Green Lane

Attractive red-brick village pub, friendly landlord and helpful staff, well kept Arkells, nice varied choice of generously served food from good sandwiches and baguettes up, low-beamed carpeted L-shaped bar with panelling and hunting prints, log fire, extended back restaurant; piped music, games machine, TV; wheelchair accessible throughout, small garden, bedrooms in separate old building. *Recommended by Chris and Angela Buckell, Ian Herdman*

COOKHAM SU8985   SL6 9SQ
☆ Bel & the Dragon
High Street (B4447)

Smart old dining pub with panelling and heavy Tudor beams, log fires, bare boards and simple country furnishings in two-room front bar and dining area, hand-painted cartoons on pastel walls, more formal back restaurant, helpful friendly staff, interesting well presented food (at prices you might expect for the area), Greene King ales, good choice of wines; children welcome, well kept garden with terrace tables, Stanley Spencer Gallery almost opposite, open all day. *Recommended by N R White, David and Sue Atkinson*

COOKHAM SU8985   SL6 9SN
Ferry
Sutton Road

Splendidly placed riverside pub with relaxing contemporary décor, Rebellion IPA and Timothy Taylors Landlord, some interesting lagers and good wine range, all-day food including fixed-price menu (Mon-Thurs 12-6), light and airy Thames-view dining areas upstairs and down, sofas and coffee tables by fireplace, small servery in beamed core; piped music; children welcome, extensive decking overlooking river. *Recommended by Mrs Ann Gray, David and Sue Atkinson*

COOKHAM SU8985   SL6 9SJ
Kings Arms
High Street

Modernised linked areas behind old façade, most for dining but also comfortably furnished part for drinkers, good range of pubby and more elaborate food at fair prices, ales such as Adnams and Rebellion IPA, good cheerful service; pleasant back garden, open all day. *Recommended by Clive and Fran Dutson, David and Sue Atkinson, Robert Bell*

COOKHAM DEAN SU8785   SL6 9BQ
☆ ## Chequers
Dean Lane; follow signpost Cookham Dean, Marlow

Restauranty dining pub with good interesting food and professional helpful staff, compact beamed bar with comfortable old sofas on flagstones, fresh flowers on dining tables and crisp white linen, area on left with open stove in big brick fireplace, conservatory, Adnams Bitter, Marlow Rebellion IPA and St Austell Tribute, several wines by the glass, ten infused vodkas, single malt whiskies, good coffees and teas; may be piped music; children welcome, picnic-sets on front terrace and in garden behind, closed Sun evening. *Recommended by Hugh Roberts, P Waterman, Angela Crum Ewing, Paul Humphreys, Alan Sutton, Paul Goldman*

COOKHAM DEAN SU8785   SL6 9NT
Uncle Toms Cabin
Off A308 Maidenhead—Marlow; Hills Lane, towards Cookham Rise and Cookham

Welcoming small-roomed local doing well under present licensees, good pubby food from sandwiches and baguettes up, low beams, wood floors and half panelling, open fire; children in eating areas, sheltered sloping back garden. *Recommended by Paul Humphreys*

CRAZIES HILL SU7980   RG10 8LY
Horns
Warren Row Road off A4 towards Cockpole Green, then follow Crazies Hill signs

Comfortable and individual beamed pub, enjoyable generously served food including bargain OAP lunches (Tues-Sat), well kept Brakspears, good wines by the glass, friendly helpful service, stripped furniture and open fires, raftered barn dining room; children welcome, seats in big informal garden with ponies, rabbits and guinea pigs, closed Sun evening, Mon. *Recommended by Paul Humphreys, Roy and Jean Russell and others*

EASTBURY SU3477   RG17 7JN
Plough
Centre of village by stream

Large lively locals' bar, quieter lounge and contemporary restaurant, well kept changing ales, friendly staff, good value enjoyable food from lunchtime snacks and midweek bargains to more ambitious dishes, log fire; children welcome, dogs in public bar, closed Sun evening. *Recommended by Mark and Ruth Brock, Alex Hickson*

Post Office address codings confusingly give the impression that some pubs are in Berkshire, when they're really in Buckinghamshire, Oxfordshire or Hampshire (which is where we list them).

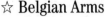

HARE HATCH SU8078
RG10 9TA
Queen Victoria
Blakes Lane; just N of A4 Reading—Maidenhead

Cheerful new landlady doing enjoyable good value food from baguettes up, well kept Brakspears, two low-beamed and panelled bars, conservatory; dogs welcome, some tables outside. *Recommended by Paul Humphreys, Tom Chambers*

HOLYPORT SU8977
SL6 2JR
☆ # Belgian Arms
1.5 miles from M4 junction 8/9 via A308(M), A330; in village turn left on to big green, then left again at war memorial

Bustling village-green pub, well kept Brakspears and Oxford Gold, several wines by the glass, enjoyable food and good friendly service, low-ceilinged bar with well spaced tables on stripped wood, interesting cricketing memorabilia, hot woodburner, old cellar dining area; piped music, TV; children welcome, dogs in bar, terrace overlooking pond, open all day Fri-Sun. *Recommended by Ian Barker, KC*

HOLYPORT SU8977
SL6 2JL
George
1.5 miles from M4 junction 8/9, via A308(M)/A330; The Green

Attractive old pub with colourful history, open-plan low-beamed interior with nice fireplace, good choice of enjoyable food (some quite expensive), Adnams, Courage Best and Fullers London Pride, friendly helpful service; picnic-sets on attractive terrace, lovely village green. *Recommended by A Hawkes, J D Franklin*

HUNGERFORD SU3468
RG17 0ED
Downgate
Down View, Park Street

Prettily placed and relaxing old country local with friendly licensees, decent well priced food including good Sun roast, well kept Arkells, two compact linked areas overlooking common, small lower room with open fire, coin/currency collection, model aircraft overhead, old tankards; difficult for wheelchairs, picnic-sets out at front. *Recommended by Phil Bryant*

HURLEY SU8281
SL6 6RB
Dew Drop
Small yellow sign to pub off A4130 just W

Flint and brick pub tucked away in nice rustic setting, enjoyable traditional food from sandwiches up, well kept Brakspears, friendly staff; children and dogs welcome, french windows to terrace, landscaped back garden with views, good walks, open all day Sat, closed Sun evening, Mon lunchtime. *Recommended by Paul Humphreys, DHV*

HURLEY SU8283
SL6 5LX
☆ # Olde Bell
High Street; off A4130

Handsome hotel with small old-fashioned bar, massive beams, simple seats and rustic tables on quarry tiles, rocking chair and tall farmhouse chairs by log fire, Rebellion IPA, malt whiskies, bistro-style food, dignified communicating lounge with chintz armchairs and sofas, various nooks and crannies; children and dogs welcome, large back terrace with sturdy oak furniture and barbecue, meadow garden with flower-arbour walk, heated dining tent, attractive Thames-side village, bedrooms, open all day. *Recommended by Susan and John Douglas*

HURST SU8074
RG10 0BP
Green Man
Off A321 just outside village

Partly 17th-c pub now run by former head chef, fairly standard menu from sharing plates

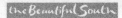

to steaks, takeaway fish and chips, well kept Brakspears, friendly uniformed staff, old-fashioned bar with dark beams and standing timbers, cosy alcoves, cushioned wall seats and built-in settles, hot little fire in one fireplace, old iron stove in another, dining area with modern sturdy wooden tables and high-backed chairs on solid oak floor; children welcome, sheltered terrace, picnic-sets under big oak trees in large garden with play area, open all day weekends (food all day then, too). *Recommended by Paul Humphreys, DHV*

KINTBURY SU3866   RG17 9UT
☆ **Dundas Arms**
Station Road

Fine summer pub, with tables out on deck above Kennet & Avon Canal and pleasant walks; well kept Adnams, Ramsbury, West Berkshire and a guest ale, good coffee and wines by the glass, good reasonably priced home-made pub food (not Sun), evening restaurant; they may ask to keep your credit card while you eat outside; children welcome, wheelchair accessible (helpful staff), comfortable bedrooms with own secluded waterside terrace, good breakfast, closed Sun evening. *Recommended by J C Burgis, Jeff and Wendy Williams*

KNOWL HILL SU8178   RG10 9UP
☆ **Bird in Hand**
A4, handy for M4 junction 8/9

Relaxed, civilised and roomy, with cosy alcoves, heavy beams, panelling and splendid log fire in tartan-carpeted main area with leather chairs, wide choice of popular home-made food even Sun evenings, well kept Brakspears and guests such as Ascot, Binghams and West Berkshire, good choice of other drinks, attentive prompt service, much older side bar, smart restaurant; soft piped music; tables on front terrace and neat garden, Sun summer barbecues, 15 tidy modern bedrooms. *Recommended by Richard Endacott, Susan and John Douglas*

KNOWL HILL SU8279   RG10 9UU
☆ **Old Devil**
Bath Road (A4)

Roomy and popular beamed roadhouse, leather sofas and chairs in bar, well spaced tables with fresh flowers in dining areas each side, chintzy feel, wide choice of generously served food, Fullers London Pride, good range of wines by the glass, friendly well organised service; pleasant verandah above attractive lawn. *Recommended by Paul Humphreys, A Hawkes, J D Franklin, Andy Beveridge*

LAMBOURN SU3180   RG17 8QN
Malt Shovel
Upper Lambourn

Décor and customers reflecting race-stables surroundings, traditional locals' bar, enjoyable home-made food in smart modern dining extension including good Sun carvery, good choice of wines by the glass, well kept ales, friendly helpful staff; racing TV. *Recommended by Michael Sargent*

LITTLEWICK GREEN SU8379   SL6 3RA
Cricketers
Not far from M4 junction 9; A404(M) then left on to A4 – village signed on left; Coronation Road

Proper old-fashioned welcoming country pub, well kept Badger and Wells & Youngs ales, good choice of wines by the glass, enjoyable reasonably priced food from lunchtime ciabattas to blackboard specials, huge clock above brick fireplace; piped music, can get crowded; charming spot opposite cricket green, bedrooms, open all day weekends. *Recommended by Paul Humphreys, Richard Endacott, Roger and Anne Newbury, Ian Barker and others*

☆ **Robin Hood**

MAIDENHEAD SU8682   SL6 6PR

Furze Platt Road, Pinkneys Green (A308N)

Well run Greene King dining pub with their ales and good choice of wines by the glass, extensive series of well divided and varied eating areas off oak-boarded bar, enjoyable good value food from sandwiches up, you can pick your own fish/meat (including kangaroo and ostrich) from counter, friendly helpful service, feature fireplace; piped music; round picnic-sets on big front terrace and lawn, sheltered bower with awning, open all day. *Recommended by Ron Clementson, Paul Humphreys, DHV, June and Robin Savage*

☆ **Coach & Horses**

MIDGHAM SU5566   RG7 5UX

Bath Road (N side)

Comfortable main-road pub with wide choice of good value generous food, cheerful helpful service even when busy, Fullers and West Berkshire ales; garden behind, closed Mon. *Recommended by Penny Royle*

☆ **Royal Oak**

PALEY STREET SU8676   SL6 3JN

B3024 W

Attractively modernised and stylish 17th-c restauranty pub owned by Sir Michael Parkinson and son Nick, good british cooking (not cheap) and helpful service, Fullers London Pride, wide choice of wines by the glass including champagne, smallish informal beamed bar with open fire, leather sofas and cricketing prints, dining room split by brick pillars and timbering with mix of well spaced wooden tables and leather dining chairs on bare boards or flagstones; piped jazz; children welcome but no pushchairs in restaurant, closed Sun evening. *Recommended by David and Sue Smith, Colin Holdsworth, Ray Carter, I D Barnett*

Allied Arms

READING SU7272   RG1 2LG

St Mary's Butts

Cosy old local with two rooms opening off little cobbled passageway, beams and dark wood, well kept Fullers London Pride, Loddon Hullabaloo and interesting guests, no food, juke box; nice garden, closed Sun and Mon lunchtime, otherwise open all day. *Recommended by Daniel Rooms, the Didler*

☆ **Fishermans Cottage**

READING SU7273   RG1 3DW

Kennet Side – easiest to walk from Orts Road, off Kings Road

Nice spot by canal lock and towpath, good value lunches especially sandwiches (very busy then but service quick and friendly), full Fullers beer range, small choice of wines, modern furnishings, pleasant stone snug behind woodburning range, light and airy conservatory, small darts room; influx of regulars in evenings, Sky TV; dogs allowed (not in garden), waterside tables, lovely big back garden. *Recommended by the Didler, Susan and John Douglas*

Griffin

READING SU7174   RG4 7AD

Church Road, Caversham

Popular roomy Chef & Brewer in beautiful Thames-side spot overlooking swan sanctuary, separate areas with log fires, four well kept ales including Wells & Youngs, good value generously served food all day, cafetière coffee, friendly efficient young staff; soft piped music and some live jazz; children welcome, tables in attractive heated courtyard, open all day. *Recommended by Tony Hobden, Chris Coleman*

We say if we know a pub has piped music.

READING SU7174 RG1 8BB
Moderation
Caversham Road

Modernised airy Victorian pub with some eastern influences, enjoyable reasonably priced food including thai/indonesian dishes, Greene King IPA and two other well kept ales; enclosed garden behind. *Recommended by Nigel and Sue Foster*

READING SU7073 RG1 7XD
Nags Head
Russell Street

Friendly local with good mix of customers, a dozen well kept changing ales, weekday lunchtime baguettes and bargain early evening meal (lunchtime food weekends only including Sun roasts), open fire, darts and cribbage, live music Sun; sports TV; garden with hops, open all day. *Recommended by the Didler, Jason Mackriell*

READING SU7173 RG1 7RD
☆ Sweeney & Todd
Castle Street

Pie shop with popular pub/restaurant behind, warren of private little period-feel alcoves and other areas on various levels, good home-made food all day including wide choice of pies such as venison and wild boar, cheery knowledgeable service, small bar with four well kept ales including Wadworths 6X, Weston's cider, good wines, children welcome in restaurant area, open all day (closed Sun and bank holidays). *Recommended by Ewan and Moira McCall, the Didler, Paul Humphreys, Susan and John Douglas, John Pritchard, Chris Coleman and others*

SHEFFORD WOODLANDS SU3673 RG17 7AA
☆ Pheasant
Under 0.5 miles from M4 junction 4 – A338 towards Wantage, first left on B4000

Tucked-away white-painted tile-hung pub with four neat communicating room areas, Loddon and Wadworths 6X, decent wines, enjoyable food, friendly attentive service, cut-away cask seats, wall pews and other chairs on carpeting or stone floors, racehorse prints, log fires, separate dining room, pub games; attractive views from garden, bedrooms. *Recommended by Mrs C Roe, Guy Vowles, John and Gloria Isaacs, Phil Bysh*

SHINFIELD SU7367 RG2 9EA
☆ Magpie & Parrot
2.6 miles from M4 junction 11, via B3270; A327 just SE of Shinfield on Arborfield Road

Unusual homely little roadside cottage with warm fire, lots of bric-a-brac (miniature and historic bottles, stuffed birds, dozens of model cars, veteran AA badges and automotive instruments), individualistic seats in two cosy spic-and-span bars, Fullers London Pride and Timothy Taylors from small corner counter, weekday lunchtime snacks and evening fish and chips (Thurs, Fri), hospitable landlady; no credit cards; dogs welcome, seats on back terrace and marquee on immaculate lawn, open 12-7.30, closed Sun evening. *Recommended by the Didler, Dr and Mrs A K Clarke, Simon Collett-Jones*

SHINFIELD SU7367 RG2 9EE
Royal Oak
School Green

Small straightforward pub with three well kept ales including Green King Abbot, short choice of good value traditional food from generously filled rolls/baguettes up, friendly service. *Recommended by John Pritchard*

SINDLESHAM SU7769 RG41 5BP
Walter Arms
Signed from B3349 or B3030

Victorian red-brick gabled dining pub, small modern bar with log fire, comfortable sofas

and low cushioned stools, eating areas with modern furniture on terracotta tiles or carpet, varied choice of good popular food (all day weekends) including pizzas, well kept real ales, efficient service and warm atmosphere; children welcome, parasoled picnic-sets at front and in side garden with arbour, open all day. *Recommended by David and Sue Smith*

SUNNINGHILL SU9367   SL5 7AQ
Dog & Partridge
Upper Village Road

Modern feel under hard-working owners with emphasis on good reasonably priced home-made food, friendly helpful staff, real ales, good range of wines; piped music; children and dogs welcome, disabled facilities, sunny garden with play area, closed Mon and lunchtimes Tues-Thurs, open all day weekends. *Recommended by Mary McSweeney, Paul Nickson, Ray Carter*

☆ THEALE SU6471   RG7 4BE
Fox & Hounds
2 miles from M4 junction 12; best to bypass restricted-access town centre – take first left at town-edge roundabout, then at railway turn right into Brunel Road, then left past station on Station Road; keep on over narrow canal bridge to Sheffield Bottom S of town

Large neatly kept dining pub, friendly and relaxed, with enjoyable well priced food (all day Fri-Sat, not Sun evening) from baguettes up, good service, several Wadworths ales, Weston's cider, decent wines and coffee, L-shaped bar with dividers, traditional mix of furniture on carpet or bare boards including area with modern sofas and low tables, two open fires, daily papers, pool and darts, Sun quiz; children and dogs welcome, outside seating at front and sides, lakeside bird reserve opposite, open all day Fri-Sun. *Recommended by Phil Bryant, John Pritchard*

THEALE SU6168   RG7 5JB
Winning Hand
A4 W, opposite Sulhamstead turn; handy for M4 junction 12

Good choice of bar and more pricey restaurant food, friendly efficient service, two changing real ales, varied wine list, dining room with stripped-pine furniture and church candles on wrought-iron stands, new restaurant with modern furniture on light wood floor and contemporary artwork; quiet piped music, no dogs; children welcome, front and back terrace tables, some picnic-sets on lawned area, three bedrooms, closed Sun evening, Mon. *Recommended by John Pritchard*

THREE MILE CROSS SU7167   RG7 1AT
Swan
A33 just S of M4 junction 11; Basingstoke Road

Built in the 17th c and later a posting house, genuine friendly welcome, reliable home-made pubby food including good sandwiches, up to five well kept ales, beams, feature fireplace with hanging black pots, old prints and some impressive stuffed fish; good outside seating, near Madejski Stadium (busy on match days), open all day weekdays, closed Sun evening. *Recommended by John Pritchard, Marita Lowry*

☆ WALTHAM ST LAWRENCE SU8376   RG10 0JJ
Bell
B3024 E of Twyford; The Street

Heavy-beamed and timbered 15th-c village local with cheerful landlord and chatty regulars, good log fires, efficient service, good home-made food (not Sun evening) from bar snacks to local game (may ask to keep your credit card while you eat), five well kept changing local ales such as Binghams, Loddon and West Berkshire (summer beer festival), real cider, plenty of malt whiskies and good wine, compact panelled lounge, daily papers; children and dogs welcome, tables in back garden with extended terrace, open all day weekends. *Recommended by Paul Humphreys*

WASH COMMON SU4563   RG20 0LU
Woodpeckers
Just off A343 S of Newbury, signposted to East Woodhay

Old beamed village pub spruced up under new management, Arkells ales, enjoyable well priced pub food, modern back dining area. *Recommended by Mr and Mrs H J Langley*

WEST ILSLEY SU4782   RG20 7AR
Harrow
Signed off A34 at E Ilsley slip road

Appealing family-run country pub in peaceful spot overlooking cricket pitch and pond, Victorian prints in deep-coloured knocked-through bar, some antique furnishings, log fire, enjoyable pub food including deals, well kept Greene King ales, good choice of wines by the glass; children in eating areas, dogs allowed in bar, picnic-sets in big garden, more seats on pleasant terrace, closed Sun evening. *Recommended by Helen and Brian Edgeley, Dave Snowden*

WINDSOR SU9676   SL4 1PB
☆ Carpenters Arms
Market Street

Town pub ambling around central servery with ales such as Everards, Fullers, Harveys, Pilgrim and Sharps Doom Bar, good value pubby food all day from sandwiches up including range of pies, friendly helpful service, good choice of wines by the glass (and bargain bottles), sturdy pub furnishings and Victorian-style décor with two pretty fireplaces, family areas up a few steps, also downstairs beside former tunnel entrance with suits of armour; piped music, no nearby parking, no dogs; tables out on cobbled pedestrian alley opposite castle, handy for Legoland bus stop, open all day. *Recommended by Terry Buckland, David and Sue Atkinson*

WOOLHAMPTON SU5766   RG7 5SH
Rowbarge
Station Road

Extended 18th-c canalside pub doing good fresh food all day, helpful friendly service, well kept West Berkshire and changing guests, plenty of wines by the glass, two woodburners in neatly modernised beamed bar, panelled side room, large water-view restaurant; light piped music; dogs and children welcome, tables out by water and in roomy garden, handy for A4, open all day. *Recommended by Ian Herdman, John Pritchard*

YATTENDON SU5574   RG18 0UG
☆ Royal Oak
The Square; B4009 NE from Newbury; right at Hampstead Norreys, village signed on left

Handsome brick-built old inn with charming rooms, beams and panelling, appealing choice of wooden dining chairs around interesting tables, some half-panelled wall seating, rugs on quarry tiles or bare boards, plenty of prints on brick, cream or red walls, lovely flower arrangements, four log fires, West Berkshire ales and well chosen wines by the glass, good modern food and friendly service; wicker armchairs under trellising in nice walled garden, some picnic-sets in front; attractive bedrooms. *Recommended by the Didler, Ray Carter, Phil Bysh*

A very few pubs try to make you leave a credit card at the bar, as a sort of deposit if you order food. They are not entitled to do this. The credit card firms and banks that issue them warn you not to let your card out of your sight. If someone behind the counter used your card fraudulently, the card company or bank could in theory hold you liable, because of your negligence in letting a stranger hang on to your card. Suggest instead that if they feel the need for security, they 'swipe' your card and give it back to you. And do name and shame the pub to us.

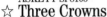

ALSO WORTH A VISIT IN BUCKINGHAMSHIRE

Besides the region's top pubs, we recommend the following. Do tell us
what you think of them: **feedback@goodguides.com**

AMERSHAM SU9597   HP7 0DY
Eagle
High Street

Rambling low-beamed pub, Adnams and Fullers London Pride, good choice of wines by
the glass, standard food, friendly helpful staff, simple décor with a few old prints, log fire,
pub games; pleasant streamside walled back garden, hanging baskets. *Recommended by
Peter and Giff Bennett*

ASKETT SP8105   HP27 9LT
☆ ## Three Crowns
W off A4010 into Letter Box Lane

Handsome, well run pub in small hamlet among Chiltern Hills; main emphasis on
particularly good, interesting food but also real ales from herringbone brick counter, two
contemporary-styled beamed dining rooms with mix of high-backed pale wood or black
leather dining chairs around dark wood tables on light flooring, minimal décor; some
picnic-sets under parasols outside and pretty front flower beds and baskets. *Recommended
by Doug Kennedy, Peter and Jan Humphreys, Mel Smith*

ASTON CLINTON SP8712   HP22 5EU
Oak
Green End Street

Cosy and attractive part-thatched pub under welcoming new licensees, well kept Fullers
ales and an interesting guest, good inexpensive food cooked to order (all day Sat, not Sun
evening), beams and inglenook log fire; garden with plenty of room for kids, open all day.
Recommended by Brian and Barbara Brown, Sean Hayward

AYLESBURY SP8213   HP20 1TX
Bell
Market Square

Newly opened Wetherspoons with linked beamed rooms; children welcome, open all day.
Recommended by Tim and Ann Newell

AYLESBURY SP7510   HP17 8TY
Bottle & Glass
A418 some miles towards Thame, beyond Stone

Rambling low-beamed pub completely renovated after 2003 fire, nice modern layout and
décor, enjoyable food from sandwiches up using local supplies, well kept beer, friendly
efficient staff. *Recommended by Joyce and Norman Bailey*

AYLESBURY SP8114   HP19 9AZ
Hop Pole
Bicester Road

Friendly open-plan pub tied to Vale, their ales and guests, good value food; open all day.
Recommended by Kevin Brown

AYLESBURY SP8113   HP20 2RW
☆ ## Kings Head
*Kings Head Passage (off Bourbon Street), also entrance off Temple Street; no nearby
parking except for disabled*

Handsome town-centre pub owned by National Trust, some beautiful early Tudor windows and stunning 15th-c stained glass in former Great Hall and three timeless carefully restored rooms – stripped boards, cream walls with little decoration, upholidaystered sofas and armchairs, high-backed cushioned settles and some simple modern furniture, all nicely low-key but civilised, Chiltern ales and guests, enjoyable bar food (not Sun-Tues evenings), friendly helpful service; disabled facilities, teak seats in atmospheric medieval cobbled courtyard shared with arts and crafts shop, open all day. *Recommended by Doug Kennedy, Clive and Fran Dutson, Paul Humphreys*

BEACONSFIELD SU9490   HP9 2JH
Royal Saracens
1 mile from M40 junction 2; London End (A40)

Striking timbered façade (former coaching inn), well updated open-plan layout, comfortable chairs around light wood tables, massive beams and timbers in one corner, log fires, welcoming efficient young staff, wide choice of enjoyable food including shared dishes and fixed-price weekday menu (busy weekends when best to book), well kept ales such as Fullers London Pride and Sharps Doom Bar, quite a few wines by the glass, large back restaurant; attractive sheltered courtyard. *Recommended by Neil Hardwick*

BENNETT END SU7897   HP14 4EB
☆ Three Horseshoes
Horseshoe Road; from Radnage on unclassified road towards Princes Risborough, left into Bennett End Road, then right into Horseshoe Road

Nicely converted country pub in lovely quiet spot – seemingly off the beaten track but close to M40; Rebellion IPA and a guest, several wines by the glass, decent choice of food including some traditional things (not cheap and service charge added), smartly uniformed staff, flagstoned softly lit snug bar with log fire in raised fireplace, original brickwork and bread oven, two further sitting areas, one with long winged settle, the other enclosed by standing timbers, stone floor dining room with big windows overlooking garden, red telephone box half submerged in duck pond and unspoilt valley beyond; children welcome till 9pm, dogs in bar, six bedrooms, closed Sun evening, Mon lunchtime. *Recommended by Di and Mike Gillam, Roy Hoing, Simon and Mandy King, Tracey and Stephen Groves, Brian and Anna Marsden, Anthony Lord and others*

BRADENHAM SU8297   HP14 4HF
☆ Red Lion
A4010, by Walters Ash turn-off

Charming, with friendly landlord, well kept Brakspears, enjoyable pubby food from good choice of baguettes up, small simple carpeted bar, good-sized smarter low-beamed dining room; picnic-sets on terrace and neat lawn, pretty village green nearby, closed Sun evening, Mon lunchtime. *Recommended by anon*

BRILL SP6514   HP18 9TG
☆ Pheasant
Windmill Street; off B4011 Bicester—Long Crendon;

More or less open-plan with some beams, chatty bar with smart chairs by counter, leather tub chairs in front of woodburner, Vale BB and a guest, well liked food, dining areas with high-backed leather or dark wooden chairs, attractively framed prints, books on shelves; piped music; children welcome, dogs in bar, seats on decked area and in garden, fine views over post windmill (one of the oldest in working order), bedrooms, open all day. *Recommended by Doug Kennedy, Jeremy Simmonds*

BUTLERS CROSS SP8407   HP17 0TS
Russell Arms
Off A4010 S of Aylesbury, at Nash Lee roundabout; or off A413 in Wendover, passing station; Chalkshire Road

Civilised pub with wide choice of good food in beamed and flagstoned bar and separate modern light and roomy restaurant, real ales, two open fires; small sheltered garden, well placed for Chilterns walks. *Recommended by Sean Hayward*

CADMORE END SU7793 · HP14 3PF
Tree
B482 towards Stokenchurch

Stylishly refurbished but keeping beamed rustic character, wide choice of enjoyable good value food including authentic indian and thai dishes, OAP deal Mon, Brakspears, linked rooms with nice mix of old furniture, restaurant, live jazz third Weds of month; some motorway noise; children welcome, modern hotel part with 16 bedrooms, open all day from 8am. *Recommended by Susan and John Douglas, D and M T Ayres-Regan*

CADSDEN SP8204 · HP27 0NB
Plough
Cadsden Road

Extended and refurbished former coaching inn with airy open-plan bar/dining area, well spaced tables on flagstones, exposed brick and some faux beams, very popular with families and Chilterns ramblers, good choice of real ales and of hearty home-made food (not Sun evening), cherry pie festival (first Sun in Aug), friendly efficient service; lots of tables in delightful quiet front and back garden, pretty spot on Ridgeway Path, bedrooms, open all day weekends. *Recommended by Doug Kennedy, Roy Hoing, C Galloway, Charles Gysin, N R White*

☆ CHALFONT ST GILES SU9895 · HP8 4RS
Ivy House
A413 S

Old brick-and-flint beamed coaching inn tied to Fullers, their ales, good food including some interesting choices, good wines by the glass, espresso coffee, friendly young staff, comfortable fireside armchairs in carefully lit and elegantly cosy L-shaped tiled bar, lighter flagstoned dining extension; dogs allowed in bar, pleasant terrace and sloping garden (can be traffic noise), five bedrooms. *Recommended by Mrs Ann Gray, Jonathan Holloway*

CHALFONT ST GILES SU9893 · HP8 4LP
White Hart
Three Households, Main Street

Spacious and airy with emphasis on the enjoyable food from interesting sandwiches up including fixed-price menu (Mon-Thurs), good service, well kept Greene King ales, lots of wines by the glass, smart modern furnishings in bar and bare-boards dining room, newspapers; soft piped music; children welcome, picnic-sets on sheltered back terrace and in garden beyond, 11 refurbished bedrooms, open all day. *Recommended by Karen Eliot, Revd R P Tickle*

CHALFONT ST PETER TQ0090 · SL9 9RA
Greyhound
High Street

Spacious beamed inn dating from 15th c but opened up in modern style, flagstoned bar with log fire, comfortable restaurant with light wood floor and painted panelling, enjoyable food (some quite pricey) from pubby things up, well kept Fullers London Pride and Greene King Old Speckled Hen, plenty of wines by the glass including champagne, friendly young staff; piped music, TV; small pleasant garden, 12 well equipped bedrooms, open all day. *Recommended by Mark Daniel, Antonia Doggart*

CHALFONT ST PETER SU9990 · SL9 9HH
Village Hall
Gold Hill W

Spacious and comfortable with separate bar and restaurant sides, friendly welcome, Fullers London Pride, Timothy Taylors Landlord and a local guest, enjoyable all-day food from pub standards and grills up, lunchtime deals (Mon-Weds) and themed evening menus; Tues quiz, Sat live music, sports TV; children welcome, tables out on decking. *Recommended by D Crook*

CHENIES TQ0198   WD3 6EQ
Bedford Arms
Signed from A404

Country-house hotel with two bars (one doing good pubby food) and more formal oak-panelled restaurant, three ales including Courage Directors and Wells & Youngs Bombardier, efficient service; tables in attractive garden, 18 bedrooms. *Recommended by Ian Phillips*

CHESHAM SP9501   HP5 1JD
Queens Head
Church Street

Welcoming red-brick Fullers corner pub, traditional interior with scrubbed tables, their ales kept well, good authentic thai food plus lunchtime bar snacks, open fires; sports TV; children welcome, tables in small courtyard popular with smokers, next to little River Chess, open all day. *Recommended by Brian Glozier, Chris Hall, N R White*

COLNBROOK TQ0277   SL3 0JZ
Ostrich
1.25 miles from M4 junction 5 via A4/B3378, then 'village only' road; High Street

Spectacular timbered Elizabethan building (with even longer gruesome history) given contemporary makeover, comfortable sofas on stripped wood and a startling red plastic and stainless steel bar counter, blazing log fires, well kept changing ales such as Hogs Back, Hook Norton and Windsor & Eton, good choice of wines by the glass including champagne, enjoyable food from pub favourites up, efficient friendly service, attractive restaurant; soft piped music, comedy and live music nights upstairs; children welcome, open all day Sun. *Recommended by Sally Norman, Terry Buckland, Peter Eyles, Ian Phillips*

CUDDINGTON SP7311   HP18 0BB
☆ # Crown
Spurt Street; off A418 Thame—Aylesbury

Convivial thatched cottage with good chatty mix of customers, comfortable pubby furnishings including cushioned settles in two low-beamed linked rooms, log fire in big inglenook, Fullers ales and maybe a guest such as Adnams, around 20 wines by the glass, well liked bar food (not Sun evening), carpeted two-room back area with dark red walls and country-kitchen chairs around nice mix of tables; children welcome; neat side terrace with modern garden furniture and planters, picnic-sets in front. *Recommended by Ian Herdman, Doug Kennedy, Dennis and Doreen Haward, Roy Hoing, Ian Kennedy and others*

DINTON SP7610   HP17 8UL
Seven Stars
signed off A418 Aylesbury—Thame, near Gibraltar turn-off; Stars Lane

Pretty 17th-c family-run pub with inglenook bar, beamed lounge and refurbished dining room, three well kept ales such as Black Sheep, Fullers and Timothy Taylors Landlord, several wines by the glass, good choice of enjoyable home-made food at realistic prices including carvery (Sun till 7pm, Weds evening), friendly service; tables under cocktail parasols in sheltered garden with terrace, pleasant village, open all day weekends. *Recommended by Garth Rodgers*

DORNEY SU9279   SL4 6QW
Palmer Arms
2.7 miles from M4 junction 7, via B3026; Village Road

Modernised extended dining pub in attractive conservation village, popular all-day food from pub favourites up, lots of wines by the glass, Greene King ales, open fires, daily papers, civilised front bar, back dining room; piped music; children welcome, dogs in certain areas, disabled facilities, terrace overlooking mediterranean-feel garden, enclosed play area, good riverside walks nearby, open all day. *Recommended by Simon Collett-Jones, Nigel and Sue Foster, I D Barnett, Susan and John Douglas, Roy and Jean Russell*

DORNEY SU9279   SL4 6QS
☆ **Pineapple**
Lake End Road: 2.4 miles from M4 junction 7; left on A4 then left on B3026

Nicely old-fashioned pub, shiny low Anaglypta ceilings, black-panelled dados, leather
chairs around sturdy country tables (one very long, another in big bow window),
woodburner and pretty little fireplace, china pineapples and other decorations on shelves
in one of three cottagey carpeted linked rooms on left, Black Sheep Bitter, Fullers
London Pride and Marstons Pedigree, up to 1,000 varieties of sandwiches in five different
fresh breads; piped music, games machine; children and dogs welcome, rustic seats on
roadside verandah, round picnic-sets in garden, fairy-lit decking under oak tree, some
motorway noise, open all day. *Recommended by Charles Harvey, Steve and Claire Harvey, Peter Price*

EMBERTON SP8849   MK46 5DH
Bell & Bear
Off A509 Olney—Newport Pagnell; High Street

Old family-run stone-built village pub, good value interesting home-made food (not Mon),
all locally sourced including own bread, well kept ales such as Hopping Mad, Isle of
Purbeck, Silverstone and Vale, farm cider, friendly efficient staff, public bar with fire,
darts, skittles, sports TV and quiz machine; children welcome, garden tables, open all day
Fri, closed Sun evening, Mon lunchtime. *Recommended by Christopher Middleton, Peter Martin*

EVERSHOLT SP9832   MK17 9DU
Green Man
Church End

Contemporary refurbishment of early Victorian country pub with emphasis on eating
(but keeping local feel), stone floor bar and adjacent restaurant, enjoyable food (not
Sun evening) including pub favourites and blackboard specials, Fullers London Pride,
St Austell Tribute and Sharps Doom Bar, friendly service, May Day beer/sausage festival;
piped music; children and dogs welcome, big terrace, picturesque village, open all day
weekends, closed Mon lunchtime. *Recommended by Michael Dandy*

FINGEST SU7791   RG9 6QD
☆ **Chequers**
Off B482 Marlow—Stokenchurch

15th-c pub under new welcoming family, unspoilt public bar with country charm, several
traditional rooms with big open fires, horsebrasses and pewter tankards, Brakspears,
Marstons and maybe a seasonal ale from Ringwood, several wines by the glass, enjoyable
home-made food, smart back dining extension; children and dogs welcome, terrace
picnic-sets, big garden with Hambleden Valley views, good walks, opposite interesting
church with twin-roofed Norman tower, has been closed Sun evening. *Recommended by*
Susan and John Douglas, Nick Massey, Roy Hoing

FORD SP7709   HP17 8XH
☆ **Dinton Hermit**
SW of Aylesbury

Carefully extended 16th-c stone inn in quiet hamlet; bar with scrubbed tables and
comfortable wicker-backed mahogany-look chairs on old black and red tiled floor, white-
painted plaster on thick uneven stone walls, old print of John Bigg (supposed executioner
of King Charles I and later known as the Dinton Hermit), huge inglenook fireplace, back
dining area with similar furniture on quarry tiles, church candles, hundreds of wine
bottles decorating walls and thick oak bar counter, Adnams, Batemans and Brakspears,
decent choice of wines, fair range of bar food; well behaved children allowed, lots of
garden picnic sets, bedrooms, open all day. *Recommended by J A Snell*

Post Office address codings confusingly give the impression that some pubs are in
Buckinghamshire, when they're really in Bedfordshire or Berkshire
(which is where we list them).

FRIETH SU7990   RG9 6PY
Prince Albert
Off B482 SW of High Wycombe

Friendly cottagey Chilterns local with low black beams and joists, high-backed settles, big black stove in inglenook, log fire in larger area on the right, decent food (mainly lunchtime) from sandwiches up, well kept Brakspears and Marstons; children and dogs welcome, nicely planted informal side garden with views of woods and fields, good walks, open all day. *Recommended by Tracey and Stephen Groves, Peter Dandy, the Didler*

GREAT HAMPDEN SP8401   HP16 9RQ
☆ Hampden Arms
W off A4128

Friendly village pub opposite cricket pitch, good mix of locals and visitors, comfortably furnished front and back rooms (back one more rustic with big woodburner). Adnams, Hook Norton and a guest from Vale, several wines by the glass and maybe Addlestone's cider from small corner bar, good pubby food, cheerful efficient service; children and dogs welcome, seats in tree-sheltered garden, good Hampden Common walks.
Recommended by Roy Hoing, Ross Balaam, Paul Humphreys

GREAT KINGSHILL SU8798   HP15 6EB
☆ Red Lion
A4128 N of High Wycombe

Carefully refurbished pub with contemporary décor, interesting, popular brasserie-style food, local beers, good wine list, plenty of space in 'lobby' plus cosy little bar with brown leather sofas and tub armchairs, low tables, log fire, spacious candlelit dining room on left with flagstones and modern paintings, relaxed atmosphere; well behaved children welcome, closed Sun evening, Mon. *Recommended by Tracey and Stephen Groves*

GREAT MISSENDEN SP8901   HP16 0AU
☆ Cross Keys
High Street

Relaxed and friendly village pub, unspoilt beamed bar divided by standing timbers, traditional furnishings including high-backed settle, log-effect gas fire in huge fireplace, well kept Fullers ales and often an unusual guest, decent food from sandwiches up including Sun roasts, cheerful helpful staff, spacious beamed restaurant; children and dogs welcome, back terrace with picnic sets, open all day. *Recommended by Mrs Ann Gray, Roy Hoing, Tracey and Stephen Groves, Paul Humphreys, Mel Smith*

HAMBLEDEN SU7886   RG9 6RP
☆ Stag & Huntsman
Off A4155 Henley—Marlow

Handsome brick and flint pub in pretty Chilterns village, congenial old-fashioned front public bar with masses of beer mats, big fireplace in low-ceilinged partly panelled lounge bar, Loddon Hoppit, Rebellion IPA, Sharps Doom Bar and a guest beer, farm cider and good wines, friendly efficient staff, good reasonably priced pubby food (not Sun evening), secluded dining room; darts, TV, piped music; children and dogs welcome, good garden with some raised areas and decking, summer Sun barbecues, nice walks, three bedrooms, open all day Fri-Sun; refurbishments planned as we went to press, when there will be a limited service. *Recommended by Roy Hoing, Simon Collett-Jones, Tracey and Stephen Groves, DHV*

HAWRIDGE SP9505   HP5 2UG
☆ Rose & Crown
Signed from A416 N of Chesham; The Vale

Roomy open-plan pub dating from 18th c, enjoyable home-made traditional food (not Sun evening, Mon) from snacks up, well kept local beers, good cider and perry, big log fire, peaceful country views from upper restaurant area; children and dogs welcome, pretty hanging baskets, broad terrace with lawn dropping down beyond, play area, open all day Thurs-Sun, closed Mon lunchtime. *Recommended by Taff Thomas*

HAWRIDGE COMMON SP9406 HP5 2UH
☆ **Full Moon**
Hawridge Common; left fork off A416 N of Chesham, follow for 3.5 miles towards Cholesbury

18th-c pub with low-beamed little bar, ancient flagstones and chequered floor tiles, built-in floor-to-ceiling oak settles, hunting prints and inglenook fireplace, Adnams, Bass, Fullers London Pride, Timothy Taylors Landlord and a guest, several wines by the glass, well liked bar food from sandwiches up; piped music; seats in pleasant garden or on heated covered terrace with views over fields and windmill beyond, paddock for hitching horses, walks on common. *Recommended by Ross Balaam, Roy Hoing, John and Victoria Fairley, Susan and John Douglas, John Branston, Peter and Giff Bennett and others*

HUGHENDEN VALLEY SU8697 HP14 4LX
☆ **Harrow**
Warrendene Road, off A4128 N of High Wycombe

Small brick and flint roadside cottage at start of Chilterns valley walks, pubby tiled-floor bar with black beams and joists, wall benches and plush stools round straightforward tables, old country engravings, big fireplace with pewter mugs on high mantelbeam, larger right-hand bar similarly furnished with sizeable dining tables on brick floor, Fullers London Pride, Rebellion and Wells & Youngs, decent pubby food, friendly staff; children welcome, picnic-sets out in front, more on back lawn with swings and slide, side terrace with modern wood and chrome furniture. *Recommended by Tracey and Stephen Groves, Mike and Eleanor Anderson*

ICKFORD SP6407 HP18 9JD
Rising Sun
E of Thame; Worminghall Road

Pretty thatched local with cosy low-beamed bar, friendly staff and regulars, four real ales including Adnams and Black Sheep, good range of simple reasonably priced home-made food with occasional game. *Recommended by David Lamb*

IVINGHOE ASTON SP9518 LU7 9DP
Village Swan
Aston; signed from B489 NE of Ivinghoe

Friendly village-owned pub, enjoyable home-made pubby food including Sun carvery, good choice of real ales; handy for Ivinghoe Beacon and Icknield Way. *Recommended by Ed Sturmer, Jeff and Joan Ward*

LACEY GREEN SP8200 HP27 0QU
Black Horse
Main Road

Friendly mix of customers in this little beamed country local, popular good value home-made food (not Sun evening, Mon), four real ales, good choice of wines by the glass, big open fire; sports TV; picnic-sets in garden with play area, closed Mon lunchtime, open all day Thurs-Sun. *Recommended by Graham Middleton, D and M T Ayres-Regan, Mel Smith*

LACEY GREEN SP8201 HP27 0RJ
☆ **Pink & Lily**
A4010 High Wycombe—Princes Risborough follow Loosley sign, then Great Hampden, Great Missenden one

Modernised dining pub with good mix of customers, reasonably priced generous food from sandwiches up, Brakspears Bitter, Red Squirrel RSB and Tring Royal Poacher, several wines by the glass, airy main bar with pubby furniture, open fire, cosier side areas and conservatory-style extension with big arches, small tap room with built-in wall benches on red tiles, old wooden ham rack hanging from ceiling, broad inglenook with low mantelpiece, framed Rupert Brooke poem (there's a room dedicated to him, too) that begins with a mention of the pub; piped music; children and dogs welcome, lots of tables and pretty hanging baskets in big garden, open all day, till 8pm Sun (4pm winter).

Recommended by Ryta Lyndley, Tim and Ann Newell, Doug Kennedy, the Didler, Roy Hoing, Edward Mirzoeff and others

LACEY GREEN SP8100 HP27 0PG
Whip
Pink Road

Cheery and attractive local welcoming walkers, mix of simple traditional furnishings in smallish front bar and larger downstairs dining area, usual food from sandwiches up, good choice of interesting well kept/priced ales including local Chiltern, Oct beer festival with jazz, friendly service; fruit machine, TV; tables in sheltered garden looking up to windmill. *Recommended by Brian and Anna Marsden*

LANE END SU8091 HP14 3JG
Grouse & Ale
High Street

Comfortable and welcoming with enjoyable food from standards up, great range of wines by the glass including champagne, well kept changing ales, helpful staff, fresh flowers, newspapers, log fires; soft piped music; children welcome (toys provided), seats outside. *Recommended by Simon Collett-Jones, Mrs Margo Finlay, Jörg Kasprowski*

LITTLE MARLOW SU8788 SL7 3RZ
☆ Kings Head
Church Road; A4155 about 2 miles E of Marlow

Long, flower-covered pub with friendly landlord, open-plan bar with low beams, captain's chairs and other traditional seating around dark wooden tables, cricketing memorabilia, log fire, Adnams, Fullers and Timothy Taylors, enjoyable food from baguettes up, gingham-clothed tables in attractive dining room; modern tables and chairs on terrace in big walled garden. *Recommended by Paul Humphreys, Doug Kennedy, Roy Hoing and others*

LITTLE MISSENDEN SU9298 HP7 0QZ
☆ Red Lion
Off A413 Amersham—Great Missenden

Unchanging pretty 15th-c cottage, small black-beamed bar, plain seats around elm pub tables, piano squashed into big inglenook beside black kitchen range packed with copper pots, kettles and rack of old guns, even smaller country dining room with pheasant décor, well kept Greene King IPA, Marstons Pedigree and Wadworths 6X, fair-priced wines, good coffee, inexpensive pubby food, good friendly service, live music Tues and Sat; children welcome, dogs in bar (there's a friendly pub dog), picnic-sets out in front and on grass behind little wall, more in sheltered back garden by pond with fancy waterfowl, aviaries with more foreign birds in meadow, open all day Fri, Sat. *Recommended by Roy Hoing, Susan and John Douglas, LM, Michael and Deborah Ethier*

LUDGERSHALL SP6617 HP18 9NZ
☆ Bull & Butcher
Off A41 Aylesbury—Bicester; bear left to The Green

Nicely old-fashioned country pub facing village green, bar with low beams in ochre ceiling, wall bench and simple pub furniture on dark tiles or flagstones, inglenook log fire, back dining room, decent bar food, Greene King IPA and Vale VPA, aunt sally and domino teams, quiz (second Sun of month); children welcome, picnic-sets on pleasant front terrace, play area, closed Mon. *Recommended by David Lamb*

MARLOW SU8486 SL7 1BA
Chequers
High Street

Attractive bar/restaurant reopened under the Tailor Made Steaks brand, contemporary styling mixing with bare boards and heavy beams, food from pubby things to more expensive restaurant food, counter where you can choose your own steak, ales such as Brakspears and Wychwood Hobgoblin tapped from the cask, good choice of wines by the glass, friendly service, three dining areas including more formal half-panelled grill room with view through to kitchen; piped music; children welcome, pavement tables, open all day (till late Fri, Sat). *Recommended by D and M T Ayres-Regan*

MARLOW BOTTOM SU8588   SL7 3RA
Three Horseshoes
Signed from Handy Cross roundabout, off M40 junction 4

Much-extended beamed pub tied to nearby Rebellion, usually their full range kept well, brewery photographs, knowledgeable helpful staff, extensive choice of popular blackboard food (not Sun evening), good value wines by the glass; open all day Fri-Sat. *Recommended by Tracey and Stephen Groves, Susan and John Douglas*

☆ ## MARSWORTH SP9114   HP23 4LU
Red Lion
Vicarage Road; off B489 Dunstable—Aylesbury;

Low-beamed partly thatched 18th-c pub close to impressive flight of locks on Grand Union Canal, main quarry-tiled bar with pews and open fire, front snug, steps up to lounge and dining area, Fullers London Pride with guests like Rebellion and Vale, well liked pubby food, cheerful, efficient staff, games room with bar billiards, darts and juke box; children and dogs welcome, picnic-sets in small sheltered back garden with heated smokers' gazebo, more seats at front facing quiet lane. *Recommended by Ross Balaam, Tracey and Stephen Groves, Roy Hoing, Susan and John Douglas*

MEDMENHAM SU8084   SL7 2HE
Dog & Badger
Bockmer (A4155)

Spacious low-beamed pub, nice décor with good mix of old furniture on polished boards, open fire, enjoyable food in bar and restaurant, charming service, Rebellion ales, resident golden retriever; piped and some live music; children welcome, terrace tables, open all day. *Recommended by T A R Curran, Paul Humphreys*

☆ ## OAKLEY SP6312   HP18 9QB
Chandos Arms
The Turnpike; brown sign to pub off B4011 Thame—Bicester

Friendly 16th-c thatched village local with warmly inclusive atmosphere, two smallish rooms, one for locals and one for diners, low black beams some stripped stone, padded country kitchen chairs on patterned carpet, inglenook housing big basket of books, Courage Best, Greene King IPA and Sharps Doom Bar, sensibly priced pubby food, helpful service, darts; games machine, maybe quiet radio, TV; picnic-sets on terrace and aunt sally. *Recommended by Malcolm Lock, Sharon Oldham, David Lamb, Andy and Maureen Pickering and others*

OLNEY SP8851   MK46 4EA
Bull
Market Place /High Street

Former 18th-c coaching inn smartened up by present licensees, sofas and other seats in three smallish front rooms, big airy eating area on the right, popular food (not Sun evening) from bar snacks up including mussels done in six ways and interesting vegetarian choices, pleasant efficient service, well kept Wells & Youngs and guests (Aug bank holiday beer festival), good coffee, open and log-effect gas fires; children welcome, seats in courtyard and big back garden (no dogs) with climbing frame; start of the famous Shrove Tuesday pancake race; open all day from 10am. *Recommended by George Atkinson*

☆ ## OLNEY SP8851   MK46 4AA
Swan
High Street S

Friendly beamed and timbered linked rooms, wide choice of enjoyable sensibly priced food (not Mon) from sandwiches up, well kept ales such as Shepherd Neame and

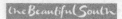

Wadworths 6X, good choice of wines by the glass, quick helpful service, daily papers, attractive flowers, rather close-set pine tables, log fires, small back bistro dining room (booking advised for this); back courtyard tables, some cover. *Recommended by Gerry and Rosemary Dobson, Michael Sargent, Michael Dandy*

OVING SP7821   HP22 4HN
☆ **Black Boy**
Off A413 N of Aylesbury

Extended 16th-c timbered pub near church, low heavy beams, log fire in enormous inglenook, steps up to snug stripped-stone area, well kept ales such as Batemans, Brakspears and Rebellion, lots of wines by the glass, pubby bar food and more elaborate restaurant menu, modern dining room with good-sized pine tables and picture windows, prompt friendly service; piped music; children and dogs welcome, tables on spacious sloping lawns and terrace (music here on Sun in summer), expansive Vale of Aylesbury views, closed Sun evening, Mon. *Recommended by Dick Vardy, Andy Dobbing, J A Snell, Malcolm Ward*

PENN STREET SU9295   HP7 0PX
☆ **Hit or Miss**
Off A404 SW of Amersham, keep on towards Winchmore Hill

Traditional pub with friendly licensees, heavily-beamed main bar with leather sofas and armchairs on parquet flooring, open fire, two carpeted rooms with interesting cricket and chair-making memorabilia, more sofas, wheelback and other dining chairs around pine tables, Badger ales (summer beer festivals), interesting if not cheap food; piped music; children welcome, dogs in bar, picnic-sets on terrace overlooking pub's cricket pitch, open all day. *Recommended by H Wainman, Tracey and Stephen Groves, D and M T Ayres-Regan, Mrs Ann Gray, LM and others*

PENN STREET SU9295   HP7 0PX
Squirrel
Off A404 SW of Amersham, opposite the Common

Family-friendly sister pub to nearby Hit or Miss, open-plan bar with flagstones, log fire, comfortable sofas as well as tables and chairs, good value home-made traditional food from baguettes up (not Sun evening), good children's meals, well kept changing ales, free coffee refills, bric-a-brac and cricketing memorabilia, darts; big garden with good play area and village cricket view, lovely walks, open all day weekends. *Recommended by David Lamb, C and R Bromage, Tracey and Stephen Groves*

PRINCES RISBOROUGH SP8104   HP27 0LL
Red Lion
Whiteleaf, off A4010; OS Sheet 165 map reference 817043

Simple comfortably worn-in village pub with welcoming landlady, good generous food at reasonable prices (freshly cooked so can take a while), well kept Greene King Gangly Ghoul and Sharps Doom Bar, log fire, traditional games; garden tables, charming village, good Chilterns walks. *Recommended by Peter Donaghy, Roy Hoing, Brian and Anna Marsden, David Lamb*

QUAINTON SP7420   HP22 4AR
George & Dragon
The Green

Traditional flower-decked pub on village green, well kept Hook Norton, Shepherd Neame, Wells & Youngs and guests, good choice of enjoyable home-made food (not Sun evening, Mon lunchtime), friendly efficient staff, split level bar, post office facility Weds afternoon; tables outside, good view of windmill, open all day in summer. *Recommended by Peter Lee, Tony and Wendy Hobden*

SEER GREEN   HP9 2YG
Jolly Cricketers
Chalfont Road, opposite the church

Refurbished 19th-c red-brick dining pub doing well under present management, good original modern cooking featuring fresh fish and game (no food Sun evening, Mon), four local ales, lots of wines by the glass, cricketing odds and ends, woodburner, live jazz and beer festivals; children and dogs welcome, picnic-sets in compact garden, good walks, open all day. *Recommended by anon*

SHERINGTON SP8946   MK16 9PE
White Hart
Off A509; Gun Lane

Good changing ales such as Archers, Greene King, Purity and Rebellion, helpful landlord and friendly staff, good pub food (not Sun evening) from sandwiches and tapas up, bright fire, two-room bar, contemporary flagstoned dining room; children and dogs welcome, picnic-sets in garden with terrace, pretty hanging baskets, bedrooms in adjacent building. *Recommended by Mrs C Roe, Gerry and Rosemary Dobson*

ST LEONARDS SP9107   HP23 6NW
White Lion
Jenkins Lane, by Buckland Common; off A4011 Wendover—Tring

Neat open-plan pub, highest in the Chilterns, with old black beams and inglenook, well kept ales such as Batemans, Greene King and Tring, good value pub food, friendly service; children and dogs welcome, attractive sheltered garden, good walks. *Recommended by Roy Hoing, Susan and John Douglas, David Lamb*

STOKE GOLDINGTON SP8348   MK16 8NR
☆ Lamb
High Street (B526 Newport Pagnell—Northampton)

Chatty village pub with friendly helpful licensees, up to four interesting changing ales, Weston's farm cider, good range of wines and soft drinks, good generous home-made food (all day Sat, not Sun evening) from baguettes to bargain Sun roasts, public bar with table skittles, quiet lounge with log fire and sheep decorations, two small pleasant dining rooms; may be soft piped music, TV; dogs welcome, terrace and sheltered garden behind, open all day weekends. *Recommended by JJW, CMW and others*

STONE SP7912   HP17 8QP
Bugle Horn
Oxford Road, Hartwell (A418 SW of Aylesbury)

Long 17th-c stone-built Vintage Inn (former farmhouse), friendly and comfortable linked rooms with mix of furniture, good choice of modestly priced food all day, friendly service, ales from Fullers, Wadworths and Wells & Youngs, lots of wines by the glass, log fires, conservatory; children welcome, attractive terrace, lovely trees in big garden with pastures beyond, open all day. *Recommended by Tim and Ann Newell, Phil and Jane Hodson*

SWANBOURNE SP8027   MK17 0SH
Betsy Wynne
Mursley Road

Popular new pub (part of the Swanbourne Estate) built in traditional timbered style, enjoyable freshly cooked food from landlord/chef using estate and other local produce, good choice of real ales, welcoming efficient staff, spacious layout with plenty of exposed oak beams including raftered dining room, wood or terracotta-tiled floors, woodburner in central brick fireplace; children and dogs welcome, tables on terrace and lawn, play house and old tractor, open all day. *Recommended by Brian Glozier*

We say if we know a pub allows dogs.

TAPLOW SU9182   SL6 0ET

Oak & Saw
Rectory Road

Open-plan bare-boards local opposite attractive village green, clean and unpretentious, with well kept Brakspears, Fullers and guests, plenty of wines by the glass, good choice of reasonably priced decent pubby food (not Sun or Mon evenings), efficient friendly service, interesting pictures; TV; children welcome, terrace and garden tables.
Recommended by Peter Scott

THE LEE SP8904   HP16 9LZ

☆ Cock & Rabbit
Back roads 2.5 miles N of Great Missenden, E of A413

Stylish place run for 25 years by same friendly italian family, although much emphasis on the good italian cooking they do keep Flowers and a guest ale and are happy to provide lunchtime baps, carefully decorated plush-seated lounge, cosy dining room and larger restaurant; seats outside on verandah, terraces and lawn. *Recommended by Paul Humphreys, Roy Hoing, David Lamb and others*

THE LEE SP8904   HP16 9NU

☆ Old Swan
Swan Bottom, back Road 0.75 miles N of The Lee

Welcoming tucked-away 16th-c dining pub, three attractively furnished linked rooms, low beams and flagstones, cooking-range log fire in inglenook, good choice of enjoyable food, Brakspears; big back garden with play area, good walks. *Recommended by Doug Kennedy, Paul Humphreys*

TURVILLE SU7691   RG9 6QU

☆ Bull & Butcher
Valley road off A4155 Henley—Marlow at Mill End, past Hambleden and Skirmett

Black and white pub in pretty village (famous as film and TV setting), two traditional low-beamed rooms with inglenooks, wall settles in tiled-floor bar, deep well incorporated into glass-topped table, well kept Brakspears and decent wines by the glass, enjoyable if pricey food, friendly welcoming service; piped and monthly live music, TV; children (away from bar) and dogs welcome, seats by fruit trees in attractive garden, good walks, open all day. *Recommended by Simon Collett-Jones, Doug Kennedy, Dr Kevan Tucker, John Saville, Peter Dandy, Stuart and Jasmine Kelly and others*

WEST WYCOMBE SU8394   HP14 3AB

George & Dragon
High Street; A40 W of High Wycombe

Popular rambling hotel bar in preserved Tudor village, massive beams and sloping walls, dim lighting, big log fire, Courage Best, Brakspears, St Austell Tribute and a guest, fairly priced food from sandwiches and baguettes up, good friendly staff, small family dining room; dogs welcome, grassed area with picnic-sets and fenced play area, character bedrooms (magnificent oak staircase), handy for West Wycombe Park, open all day weekends. *Recommended by Doug Kennedy, Paul Humphreys, Edward Mirzoeff, Mel Smith*

WING SP8822   LU7 0NS

Queens Head
High Street

Welcoming 16th-c pub with good freshly cooked food in bar and restaurant, well kept Courage Directors, Wells & Youngs and a guest like Slaters Queen Bee, decent wines, afternoon tea with home-made scones, log fires; children welcome, disabled facilities, garden picnic-sets, open all day. *Recommended by Peter Kirby, Trevor Brown, David and Diane Young*

WOOBURN MOOR SU9189   HP10 0NA
Falcon
Old Moor Lane; SE edge of Loudwater

Unpretentious little low-beamed local with friendly relaxing atmosphere, three well kept changing ales, freshly cooked pubby food including Sun roasts, homely lived-in linked rooms with bare boards, evening candles and coal fires, board games, paperback library, open-mike and quiz nights; garden. *Recommended by Susan and John Douglas*

ALSO WORTH A VISIT IN HAMPSHIRE

Besides the region's top pubs, we recommend the following. Do tell us what you think of them: **feedback@goodguides.com**

ALRESFORD SU5832   SO24 9AT
Bell
West Street

Comfortable and welcoming Georgian coaching inn (originally the Market Inn), good popular food including weekday fixed-price menu, efficient service, well kept local beer and good choice of wines, spic-and-span interior with bare boards, scrubbed tables, bric-a-brac and log fire, daily papers, smallish dining room, may be jazz on Sun in summer; attractive back courtyard, six bedrooms, open all day, closed Sun evening. *Recommended by Leon Wise, Ann and Colin Hunt, Val and Alan Green, Phyl and Jack Street*

ALRESFORD SU5831   SO24 9LW
Cricketers
Jacklyns Lane

Large comfortable and friendly local with popular food including good value set deals, real ales, good service, cottagey eating area down steps; children welcome, sizeable garden with covered terrace and good play area. *Recommended by Tony and Jill Radnor*

ALRESFORD SU5832   SO24 9AD
Swan
West Street

Long narrow oak-panelled red-carpeted bar in 18th-c hotel (former coaching inn), three ales including Courage Best, decent wines, tea and coffee, good choice of popular reasonably priced food plus good Sun carvery, two dining rooms; children welcome, 23 bedrooms. *Recommended by Val and Alan Green, Gordon Neighbour, Ann and Colin Hunt*

ALTON SU7138   GU34 1RT
French Horn
The Butts (A339 S of centre, by railway bridge)

Popular and cheery catslide-roof local with well kept Butcombe, Ringwood, Sharps, Triple fff, Wells & Youngs and a guest, plenty of wines by the glass, wide choice of enjoyable food including blackboard specials, nice coffee, good service, tankards and whisky-water jugs on beams, bowler hats and french horn above inglenook log fire, newspapers, partly stripped-brick dining room, separate skittle alley; piped music; children welcome, covered heated smokers' terrace, picnic-sets in two garden areas, play area, bedrooms in adjacent building, next to Watercress Line with occasional steam trains, open all day. *Recommended by LM, Phil and Sally Gorton*

If we know a pub has an outdoor play area for children, we mention it.

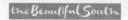

☆ **White Horse**

AMPFIELD SU4023   SO51 9BQ

A3090 Winchester—Romsey

Snug low-beamed front bar with candles and soft lighting, inglenook log fire and comfortable country furnishings, far-spreading beamed dining area behind, well kept Greene King ales and guests, good choice of enjoyable food including all-day snacks, several wines by the glass, efficient friendly service, locals' bar with another inglenook; piped music; children and dogs welcome, high-hedged garden with plenty of picnic-sets, cricket green beyond, good walks in Ampfield Woods, handy for Hillier Gardens, open all day. *Recommended by Phyl and Jack Street, Matt Cutting*

BALL HILL SU4263   RG20 0NQ
Furze Bush
Leaving Newbury on A343 turn right towards East Woodhay

Clean airy décor, pews and pine tables, log fire, wide choice of good generous food promptly served by friendly staff, several well kept ales including Fullers London Pride, decent wines, reasonable prices, restaurant; children welcome, tables on terrace by good-sized sheltered lawn with fenced play area. *Recommended by Mr and Mrs H J Langley, Ian Herdman, J V Dadswell*

BARTON STACEY SU4341   SO21 3RL
Swan
Village signed off A303

Warm friendly atmosphere in beamed former coaching inn, enjoyable food from pubby things up, well kept ales such as Bowman, Fullers and Otter, good choice of wines, little lounge area between front log-fire bar and cosy dining part, back restaurant; piped music; children and dogs welcome, tables on front lawn and back terrace, open all day Fri, Sat, closed Sun evening. *Recommended by Russell Traynor, Sarah Flynn*

☆ **Millstone**

BASING SU6653   RG24 8AE

Bartons Lane, Old Basing; follow brown signs to Basing House

Well run busy pub with lots of picnic-sets out by River Loddon (ducks and swans) looking across to former viaduct through scrubland, enjoyable freshly cooked food, full Wadworths range kept well, Weston's farm cider, good choice of wines by the glass, dark panelling, old prints and etchings, sturdy pub furnishings; may be faint piped jazz; children and dogs welcome, by ruins of Basing House, open all day. *Recommended by Douglas and Ann Hare, Karen Sloan*

BEAUWORTH SU5624   SO24 0PB
Milbury's
Off A272 Winchester/Petersfield

Attractive old tile-hung pub, beams, panelling and stripped stone, massive 17th-c treadmill for much older incredibly deep well, galleried area, good choice of real ales, straightforward reasonably priced food, good service, skittle alley; children in eating areas, garden with fine downland views, good walks. *Recommended by the Didler, Ann and Colin Hunt, Michael and Maggie Betton, Steve Frampton*

BISHOP'S WALTHAM SU5517   SO32 1AJ
Barleycorn
Lower Basingwell Street

Buoyant 18th-c two-bar local, enjoyable good value generous pub food, friendly efficient service, well kept Greene King ales and a guest, decent wine, beams and some low ceiling panelling, open fires; children and dogs welcome, large garden with back smokers' area, open all day. *Recommended by Robert Lorimer, Henry Fryer, Ann and Colin Hunt, Stephen and Jean Curtis and others*

BISHOP'S WALTHAM SU5517 SO32 1AD
☆ Bunch of Grapes
St Peter's Street – just along from entrance to central car park

Neat civilised little pub in quiet medieval street, smartly furnished keeping individuality and unspoilt feel (run by same family for a century), good chatty landlord and regulars, Courage Best, Goddards and a guest tapped from the cask, no food; charming back terrace garden with own bar, opening times may vary. *Recommended by Henry Fryer, the Didler, Stephen and Jean Curtis, Phil and Jane Villiers*

BOLDRE SZ3198 SO41 8NE
☆ Red Lion
Off A337 N of Lymington

Attractive black-beamed rooms with entertaining collection of bygones, pews and other seats, log fires, attentive friendly staff coping well at busy times, popular food including specials board, well kept Ringwood ales and a guest, great choice of wines by the glass, decent coffee; children and dogs welcome, tables in nice back garden, open all day. *Recommended by Phyl and Jack Street, Mr and Mrs W W Burke, Ann and Colin Hunt, Steve Kent and others*

BRAISHFIELD SU3724 SO51 0QE
Wheatsheaf
Village signposted off A3090 on NW edge of Romsey

Smartened up by newish management (the bric-a-brac collection has gone), well kept Flack Manor, Timothy Taylors Landlord and a guest, huge choice of wines by the glass including champagne, enjoyable seasonal food from sensibly short menu, log fire; piped music; children and dogs welcome, garden with good views, boules, woodland walks nearby, close to Hillier Gardens, open all day Fri-Sun. *Recommended by John Chambers*

BRAMBRIDGE SU4721 SO50 6HZ
☆ Dog & Crook
Near M3 junction 12, via B3335

Cheerful bustling 18th-c pub, traditional home-made food including plenty of fresh fish, cosy dining room, beamed bar with friendly drinking end, Fullers and Ringwood ales, lots of wines by the glass, neat efficient staff; piped music, TV, regular events and summer music nights; dogs welcome, garden with heated decking and arbour, Itchen Way walks nearby. *Recommended by Phyl and Jack Street, Ann and Colin Hunt, Mr and Mrs D G Waller*

BRAMDEAN SU6127 SO24 0LP
☆ Fox
A272 Winchester—Petersfield

Pleasant 17th-c weatherboarded dining pub with long-serving owners, loyal regulars in old-fashioned open-plan bar, black beams, cushioned wall pews and wheelbacks, tall stools with backrests at counter, Greene King Morland Original, standard bar food (not Sun evening) including good crab sandwiches; piped music, no children; dogs in bar if not busy, walled-in terraced area and neatly kept spacious lawn under fruit trees, good surrounding walks, closed Sun evening. *Recommended by Mr and Mrs W W Burke, Colin McKerrow*

BRANSGORE SZ1897 BH23 8AA
Crown
Ringwood Road; off A35 N of Christchurch

Rambling, traditionally done Vintage Inn, popular food from usual pub dishes to venison and guinea fowl, Fullers London Pride, Ringwood and a guest, lots of wines by the glass, log fire; children welcome, picnic-sets in big garden, open all day. *Recommended by Sue and Mike Todd*

If you have to cancel a reservation for a bedroom or restaurant, please telephone or write to warn them. You may lose your deposit if you've paid one.

BROOK SU2714   SO43 7HE
Bell
B3079/B3078, handy for M27 junction 1

Really a hotel with golf club and plush restaurant, but has neatly kept bar with lovely inglenook fire, good choice of well kept ales including Ringwood and good bar food from sandwiches to steak, helpful friendly uniformed staff; big garden, delightful village, 25 comfortable bedrooms. *Recommended by Phyl and Jack Street*

BROOK SU2713   SO43 7HE
☆ Green Dragon
B3078 NW of Cadnam, just off M27 junction 1

Immaculate thatched New Forest dining pub dating from 15th c, good welcoming service even when busy, enjoyable fresh food including plenty of seasonal game and fish as well as pubby favourites, well kept Fullers and Ringwood, daily papers, bright linked areas with stripped pine and other pubby furnishings; attractive small terrace, garden with paddocks beyond, picturesque village, self-catering apartment. *Recommended by Bob and Angela Brooks, R and M Thomas, PL, Howard G Allen, Mr and Mrs P D Titcomb and others*

BUCKLERS HARD SU4000   SO42 7XB
☆ Master Builders House
M27 junction 2 follow signs to Beaulieu, turn left onto B3056, then left to Bucklers Hard

Smart sizeable hotel with riverside garden (waterside walks) in charming village, two-level bar with heavy beams, mullioned windows, rugs on wood floor and log fire in old brick fireplace, bar stools on quarry tiles by counter serving Marstons and Ringwood, varied bar food; children and dogs welcome, front terrace, bedrooms, open all day. *Recommended by Mrs Ann Gray, Mr and Mrs D Hammond, Steven King and Barbara Cameron, Martin and Karen Wake*

BURGHCLERE SU4660   RG20 9JY
Carpenters Arms
Harts Lane, off A34

Small unpretentious pub under newish local management, well kept Arkells and an occasional guest, sensibly priced home-made food (not Sun evening), helpful staff, good country views from dining extension and terrace picnic-sets, log fire; piped music; children and dogs welcome, handy for Sandham Memorial Chapel (NT) and Highclere Castle, six comfortable annexe bedrooms, open all day. *Recommended by John Quinn, Sean Dunn, Mr and Mrs H J Langley*

BURITON SU7320   GU31 5RX
☆ Five Bells
Off A3 S of Petersfield

Low-beamed 17th-c pub, pleasant staff, fresh pubby food from baguettes up, Badger beers, good wines by the glass, big log fire, daily papers, flowers and church candles, some ancient stripped masonry and woodburner on public side; piped music; children and dogs welcome, nice garden and sheltered terraces, pretty village, good walks, self-catering in converted stables, open all day. *Recommended by W A Evershed, Terry and Eileen Stott*

BURLEY SU2202   BH24 4AZ
White Buck
Bisterne Close; 0.7 miles E, OS Sheet 195 map reference 223028

Popular 19th-c mock-Tudor hotel now owned by Fullers, their ales and a guest in long comfortably divided bar, lots of pictures, log fires each end, pleasant dining room with tables out on decking; children and dogs welcome, front terrace and spacious lawn, lovely New Forest setting, superb walks towards Burley itself and over Mill Lawn, seven bedrooms, open all day. *Recommended by Mrs Joy Griffiths, John and Joan Calvert, Mr and Mrs D Hammond, Sara Fulton, Roger Baker*

BURSLEDON SU4809   SO31 8DE

☆ **Fox & Hounds**

Hungerford Bottom; 2 miles from M27 junction 8

Popular rambling 16th-c Chef & Brewer of unusual character, ancient beams, flagstones and big log fires, linked by pleasant family conservatory area to ancient back barn with buoyant rustic atmosphere, lantern-lit side stalls, lots of interesting farm equipment, well kept ales such as Adnams and Ringwood, good choice of wines, decent coffee, enjoyable reasonably priced food from sandwiches up including vegetarian choices, cheerful obliging staff, daily papers; children allowed, tables outside. *Recommended by Phyl and Jack Street, Ann and Colin Hunt, Phil and Jane Villiers*

BURSLEDON SU4909   SO31 8DN

☆ **Jolly Sailor**

Off A27 towards Bursledon Station, Lands End Road; handy for M27 junction 8

Busy efficiently run Badger dining pub in prime spot overlooking yachting inlet, good fairly priced food cooked to order, their usual ales and good wine choice, log fires; open all day. *Recommended by the Didler, Ann and Colin Hunt, Louisa Fleming*

CADNAM SU2913   SO40 2NP

☆ **Sir John Barleycorn**

Old Romsey Road; by M27 junction 1

Wide choice of good up-to-date food in picturesque low-slung thatched pub extended from cosy beamed and timbered medieval core, good service, Ringwood and a guest ale, two log fires, modern décor and stripped wood flooring; suntrap benches in front and out in colourful garden, open all day. *Recommended by Bob and Angela Brooks, Phyl and Jack Street*

CHALTON SU7316   PO8 0BG

☆ **Red Lion**

Off A3 Petersfield—Horndean

Largely extended thatched all-day dining pub with interesting 16th-c core around ancient inglenook fireplace, wide range of popular food from good sandwiches up, well kept Fullers/Gales ales and lots of country wines, decent coffee, helpful smart staff, well spaced tables; children and dogs allowed, good disabled access and facilities, nice views from neat rows of picnic-sets on rectangular lawn by large car park, good walks, handy for Queen Elizabeth Country Park, open all day. *Recommended by David M Smith, Ann and Colin Hunt, Conor McGaughey*

CHARTER ALLEY SU5957   RG26 5QA

White Hart

White Hart Lane, off A340 N of Basingstoke

Handsome beamed pub with Bowman, Palmers and Triple fff, continental beers, summer farm cider, decent wines including country ones, good choice of generous well presented food (not Sun evening) from baguettes up, comfortable lounge bar with woodburner in big fireplace, dining area, simple public bar with skittle alley; small garden and water-feature terrace, nine bedrooms, open all day Sun. *Recommended by J V Dadswell, Joan and Michel Hooper-Immins*

CHAWTON SU7037   GU34 1SB

☆ **Greyfriar**

Off A31/A32 S of Alton; Winchester Road

Popular flower-decked beamed dining pub opposite Jane Austen's house, enjoyable if pricey food (not Sun evening) from good baguettes and sandwiches up, Sun roasts, Fullers ales, decent wines by the glass, good coffees, welcoming relaxed atmosphere and quite a few older midweek lunchers, comfortable seating and sturdy pine tables in neat linked areas, open fire in restaurant end; piped music; dogs in bar, children till 9pm, tables on terrace in small garden, good nearby walks, open all day. *Recommended by Ann and Colin Hunt, Maureen and Keith Gimson, B and F A Hannam, B M Eldridge*

CHERITON SU5828   SO24 0QQ

☆ **Flower Pots**

Off B3046 towards Beauworth and Winchester; OS Sheet 185 map reference 581282

Unspoilt country local in same family for over 40 years, own-brewed good value beers (brewery tours by arrangement) along with Flowerpots ales tapped from casks, standard food (not Sun evening or bank holiday evenings, and possible restrictions during busy times), popular curry night Weds, extended plain public bar with covered well, another straightforward but homely room with country pictures on striped wallpaper and ornaments over small log fire; no credit cards or children; dogs welcome, seats on pretty front and back lawns, summer marquee, bedrooms. *Recommended by Paul J Robinshaw, Klaus and Elizabeth Leist, Tony and Jill Radnor, N R White, the Didler, Ann and Colin Hunt and others*

CHILWORTH SU4118   SO16 7JZ

☆ **Chilworth Arms**

Chilworth Road (A27 Southampton—Romsey)

Stylish well run modern dining pub, popular food with some italian-influences from home-made pizzas to more adventurous things, fixed-price lunch/early evening menu Mon-Thurs, good wine choice, ales such as Greene King, Sharps and Wells & Youngs, neat efficient young staff, chunky furniture including quite a lot of leather, log fires, conservatory-style back restaurant, chattier areas too; piped music; children welcome, disabled facilities, large neat garden with terrace, open all day. *Recommended by Phyl and Jack Street, Howard G Allen, Dr and Mrs A K Clarke and others*

COLDEN COMMON SU4821   SO50 7HG

☆ **Fishers Pond**

Junction B3354/B2177 (Main Road), at Fishers Pond just S

Big Vintage Inn in appealing position by peaceful woodside lake, various different areas and alcoves making the most of waterside views, some painted brickwork, carpet or rugs on aged terracotta, dark leather built-in banquettes, heavy beams and log fires, brighter modern end section, popular all-day bar food, ales such as Ringwood and Sharps Doom Bar; piped music, machines; children welcome, solid teak furniture on heated partly covered lakeside terrace, handy for Marwell Zoo. *Recommended by Joan and Michel Hooper-Immins, Jim Metcalfe, Ann and Colin Hunt, Phyl and Jack Street and others*

CRAWLEY SU4234   SO21 2PR

☆ **Fox & Hounds**

Village signed from A272 and B3420 NW of Wincludinghester

Mock-Tudor building with jutting upper storeys, pegged structural timbers in neat brickwork and elaborately carved steep gable-ends; civilised neatly kept linked rooms with mix of attractive furniture on polished floors, built-in wall seats in traditional little bar, log fires, reasonably priced popular bar food, Ringwood, Wadworths and Wychwood, friendly licensees and efficient young staff; children welcome, gardens with picnic-sets and play equipment, picturesque village, bedrooms in converted outbuildings, closed Sun evening. *Recommended by Phyl and Jack Street, Brian Johnson and others*

CRONDALL SU7948   GU10 5NT

Plume of Feathers

The Borough

Attractive smallish 15th-c village pub popular for good range of home-made food from standards to more innovative dishes, friendly helpful staff, well kept Greene King and some unusual guests, good wines by the glass, beams and dark wood, prints on cream walls, restaurant with log fire in big brick fireplace (not usually lit lunchtimes); children welcome, picturesque village. *Recommended by KC*

If you stay overnight in an inn or hotel, they are allowed to serve you an alcoholic drink at any hour of the day or night.

CROOKHAM SU7952   GU51 5SU
Exchequer
Crondall Road

Welcoming refurbished pub doing enjoyable home-made food (not Sun evening) in bar
and restaurant, three local ales tapped from the cask, bar games and quiz nights; piped
music; near Basingstoke Canal and popular with walkers, open all day Sun till 7.30pm,
closed Mon evening. *Recommended by Jessica Courtney*

CURDRIDGE SU5314   SO32 2BH
Cricketers
Curdridge Lane, off B3035 just under a mile NE of A334 junction

Open-plan low-ceilinged Victorian village pub, sensibly priced food, cheerful efficient
staff, Greene King ales, banquettes in lounge area, traditional public area, rather smart
dining part; soft piped music; tables on front lawn, pleasant walks. *Recommended by
Henry Fryer*

DAMERHAM SU1016   SP6 3HQ
☆ Compasses
Signed off B3078 in Fordingbridge, or off A354 via Martin; East End

Appealing old country inn, well kept ales including Ringwood, good choice of wines by the
glass, lots of malt whiskies, good food from sandwiches up, small neat lounge bar divided
by log fire from pleasant dining area with booth seating, pale wood tables and kitchen
chairs, conservatory, separate bar with pool, friendly locals and dogs; children welcome,
long pretty garden by attractive village's cricket ground, high downland walks, nice
bedrooms. *Recommended by N R White, Susanne House*

DENMEAD SU6211   PO7 4QX
Chairmakers Arms
Forest Road

Roomy country pub surrounded by paddocks and farmland, good value quickly served
food from bar snacks up, Sun carvery, Fullers ales, log fires; can get busy; tables in
spacious garden with pergola, nice walks. *Recommended by W A Evershed*

DIBDEN PURLIEU SU4106   SO45 4PU
Heath
Beaulieu Road; B3054/A326 roundabout

Comfortable and welcoming family dining pub, popular and spacious, with bright clean
contemporary linked areas, good choice of enjoyable food all day, friendly efficient young
staff, beers such as Ringwood, Shepherd Neame Spitfire and Wadworths 6X. *Recommended
by Phyl and Jack Street and others*

DROXFORD SU6018   SO32 3PA
☆ Bakers Arms
High Street; A32 5 miles N of Wickham

Attractively opened-up pub with dark beams and exposed brickwork, well spaced mix of
tables on carpet or neat bare boards, leather chesterfields, log fire, good changing choice
of interesting home-made food including popular Sun roasts, home-baked bread, Bowman
Swift One and Wallops Wood, Weston's cider, attached post office; children and dogs
welcome, picnic-sets outside, closed Sun evening and Mon. *Recommended by Jenny Bolton,
Phyl and Jack Street, D and J Ashdown, Ann and Colin Hunt and others*

DUMMER SU5846   RG25 2AD
Queen
Under a mile from M3 junction 7; take Dummer slip road

Comfortable beamed pub well divided with lots of softly lit alcoves, Courage Best, Fullers
London Pride, John Smiths and a guest, decent choice of wines by the glass, popular food
from lunchtime sandwiches and light dishes up, friendly service, big log fire, Queen and

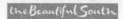

steeplechase prints, no mobile phones, restaurant allowing children; piped music; picnic-sets under parasols on terrace and in extended back garden, attractive village with ancient church. *Recommended by Mrs Ann Gray, Michael and Margaret Cross*

DUNBRIDGE SU3126   SO51 0LF

☆ **Mill Arms**
Barley Hill

Much extended 18th-c coaching inn opposite railway station, friendly informal atmosphere in spacious high-ceilinged rooms, scrubbed pine tables and farmhouse chairs on oak or flagstone floors, several sofas, two log fires, Ringwood Best and guests, good bistro-style food (all day weekends), dinning conservatory, two skittle alleys; piped music; children welcome, dogs in bar, big pretty garden, plenty of walks in surrounding Test Valley, bright comfortable bedrooms, open all day weekends (till 4pm winter Sun).
Recommended by Phyl and Jack Street, Ann and Colin Hunt, Dave Braisted, Martin and Karen Wake, Glenwys and Alan Lawrence and others

DUNDRIDGE SU5718   SO32 1GD

☆ **Hampshire Bowman**
Off B3035 towards Droxford, Swanmore, then right at Bishops W signpost

Good chatty mix at this friendly relaxed country tavern, five well kept local ales tapped from casks, summer farm cider, well liked food (all day Fri-Sun) from hearty pub dishes to specials using local produce including own herbs and vegetables, smart stable bar sitting comfortably alongside cosy and unassuming original one, some colourful paintings, Archie the pub dog, no mobile phones (£1 fine in charity box); children (under-14s in stable bar) and dogs welcome, hitching post for horses, heated terrace, peaceful lawn, play equipment, open all day. *Recommended by Robert Lorimer, Henry Fryer, Ann and Colin Hunt, the Didler, Stephen and Jean Curtis, Howard and Margaret Buchanan and others*

DURLEY SU5116   SO32 2BT

Farmers Home
B3354 and B2177; Heathen Street/Curdridge Road

Helpful long-serving landlord in comfortable beamed pub with two-bay dining area and big restaurant, generous reasonably priced food including fresh fish and lovely puddings, good friendly service, well kept Fullers/Gales and Ringwood BB, decent wine, log fire; children welcome, big garden with good play area, nice walks. *Recommended by Phyl and Jack Street, Ann and Colin Hunt*

DURLEY SU5217   SO32 2AA

Robin Hood
Durley Street, just off B2177 Bishops Waltham—Winchester – brown signs to pub

Open-plan beamed pub under newish enthusiastic landlord, Greene King ales and a guest, enjoyable food from varied blackboard menu (order at bar), friendly staff, log fire and leather sofas in bare-boards bar, dining area with stone floors and mix of old pine tables and chairs, bookcase door to lavatories; piped music; children and dogs welcome, disabled facilities, decked terrace with barbecue, garden with play area and nice country views, open all day Sun. *Recommended by Graham, Phyl and Jack Street*

EAST MEON SU6822   GU32 1NH

☆ **Olde George**
Church Street; signed off A272 W of Petersfield, and off A32 in West Meon

Relaxing heavy-beamed rustic pub, enjoyable if not cheap bar and restaurant food from sandwiches up including set lunch, good smartly dressed staff, well kept Badger ales, cosy areas around central bar counter, inglenook log fires; children and dogs welcome, nice back terrace, five comfortable bedrooms, pretty village with fine church, good walks, open all day Sun. *Recommended by E Clark, W A Evershed, Ann and Colin Hunt*

Tipping is not normal for bar meals, and not usually expected.

EAST TYTHERLEY SU2927   SO51 0LW

☆ **Star**

B3084 N of Romsey; turn off by railway crossing opposite Mill Arms, Dundridge

Pretty country inn with comfortable sofas and tub chairs mixing with traditional pubby furniture, rich red walls, bookcase to one side of log fire, ales from Andwell, Cottage and Itchen Valley, reasonably priced food cooked by licensees' son, formally set restaurant; piped music – live music Fri evening; children welcome, dogs in bar, tables out at front and on back terrace by giant chessboard, bedrooms overlooking cricket pitch, good breakfast, nearby walks, closed Sun evening, Mon. *Recommended by Christopher and Elise Way, Ann and Colin Hunt, T A R Curran, Phyl and Jack Street, P J Checksfield, JES and others*

EASTON SU5132   SO21 1EJ

Cricketers

Off B3047

Pleasantly smartened-up traditional local, home-made food with some modern touches in bar and smallish restaurant, good friendly service, Marstons-related ales including Ringwood, good choice of wines by the glass, dark tables and chairs on carpet, bare-boards area with darts, shove-ha'penny and other games; piped and some live music, sports TV; children and dogs welcome, front terrace with heated smokers' shelter, handy for Itchen Way walks, three bedrooms, open all day summer. *Recommended by Mrs Margaret Weir, Ann and Colin Hunt, Tony and Jill Radnor*

ELLISFIELD SU6345   RG25 2QW

☆ **Fox**

Green Lane; S of village off Northgate Lane

Simple tucked-away place under new ownership; mixed collection of stripped tables, country chairs and cushioned wall benches on bare boards and old floor tiles, some stripped masonry, open fires in plain brick fireplaces, Sharps Doom Bar, Fullers London Pride and a guest or two, home-made food; outside gents'; children and dogs welcome, picnic-sets in nice garden, good walking country near snowdrop and bluebell woods, open all day. *Recommended by anon*

EMERY DOWN SU2808   SO43 7DY

☆ **New Forest**

Village signed off A35 just W of Lyndhurst

In one of the best bits of the Forest for walking, well run and popular, with good reasonably priced food (all day weekends) including local venison, friendly attentive uniformed staff, ales such as Fullers, Ringwood and Shepherd Neame, real cider, good choice of wines by the glass, coffee and tea all day, attractive softly lit separate areas on varying levels, each with its own character, hunting prints, two log fires; piped music; children and dogs welcome, covered heated terrace, small pleasant three-level garden, bedrooms, open all day. *Recommended by Mr and Mrs D Hammond, Stephen Moss, Laurie Scott*

EVERSLEY SU7861   RG27 0NB

☆ **Golden Pot**

B3272

Small attractive creeper-covered dining pub with good food from traditional choices up (small helpings available), well kept changing ales such as Crondall, West Berkshire and Windsor & Eton, several wines by the glass, friendly landlord and staff, neatly refurbished linked areas, log fire; piped music – live Mon; children welcome, dogs in bar, tables out among colourful flowers, closed Sun evening. *Recommended by Joan and Tony Walker, Mrs Pam Mattinson, KC, G Ridgway, Caz Brant and others*

EVERTON SZ2994   SO41 0JJ

Crown

Old Christchurch Road; pub signed just off A337 W of Lymington

Quietly set New Forest-edge restaurant/pub with enjoyable varied food, good service, Ringwood and guests, reliable wine choice, two attractive dining rooms off tiled-floor bar,

log fires; picnic-sets on front terrace and in garden behind. *Recommended by Phyl and Jack Street, Steve Green, David Sizer*

EXTON SU6120   SO32 3NT
☆ **Shoe**
Village signposted from A32 NE of Bishop's Waltham

Newish licensees for pleasant brick-built country pub on South Downs Way, three linked rooms with log fires (not always lit), good food from traditional favourites to more imaginative restaurant-style dishes using own produce, Wadworths ales and a seasonal guest; children and dogs welcome, disabled facilities, seats under parasols at front, more in garden across lane overlooking River Meon. *Recommended by Henry Fryer, Glenwys and Alan Lawrence, Geoff and Linda Payne*

FACCOMBE SU3958   SP11 0DS
☆ **Jack Russell**
Signed from A343 Newbury—Andover

Light and airy creeper-covered pub in village-green setting opposite pond by flint church, enjoyable fairly priced traditional food (not Sun evening) from snacks to Sun roasts, well kept ales including Greene King IPA and one brewed for the pub, good service, carpeted bar with some old farming tools and other bric-a-brac, log fire, darts, conservatory restaurant (children welcome here); piped music; disabled facilities, lawn by beech trees, three bedrooms, good walks. *Recommended by Mr and Mrs H J Langley, David and Judy Robison*

FAIR OAK SU4919   SO50 7HB
Fox
Winchester Road (A3051)

Popular smartly refurbished pub with enjoyable food (all day Weds-Sun), ales such as Fullers London Pride and Ringwood, nice wines, welcoming bright young staff, clean modern décor in lounge, restaurant, coffee room and conservatory; children welcome, big garden, path to nearby Bishopstoke woods, open all day. *Recommended by Phyl and Jack Street and others*

FAREHAM SU5806   PO16 7AE
Golden Lion
High Street

Clean friendly Fullers pub, their ales and enjoyable food from nice baguettes up; open all day (till 9pm Mon, closed Sun evening). *Recommended by Val and Alan Green*

FARNBOROUGH SU8756   GU14 8AL
☆ **Prince of Wales**
Rectory Road, near station

Up to ten good changing ales in friendly Victorian local, exposed brickwork, carpet or wood floors, open fire, antiquey touches in its three small linked areas, popular lunchtime pubby food (not Sun) including sandwiches, good friendly service; smokers' gazebo, open all day Fri-Sun. *Recommended by Dr Martin Owton, Thurstan Johnston, Joan and Michel Hooper-Immins, Tim Gallagher*

FARRINGDON SU7135   GU34 3ED
☆ **Rose & Crown**
Off A32 S of Alton; Crows Lane – follow Church, Selborne, Liss signpost

Airy 19th-c village pub with L-shaped log-fire bar, comfortable and well run, several well kept ales including Adnams, good reasonably priced food (all day Sun) with some interesting choices and vegetarian options, efficient friendly young staff, formal back dining room, jazz nights (last Mon of month); well behaved children and dogs welcome, wide views from attractive back garden, open all day weekends. *Recommended by Ann and Colin Hunt, Tony and Jill Radnor, Simon Collett-Jones*

FAWLEY SU4603   SO45 1DT
Jolly Sailor
Ashlett Creek

Cottagey waterside pub near small boatyard and sailing club, straightforward good value bar food, Marstons Pedigree and Ringwood Best, cheerful service, raised log fire, mixed pubby furnishings on bare boards, second bar with darts and pool; children welcome, tables outside looking past creek's yachts and boats to busy shipping channel, handy for Rothschild rhododendron gardens at Exbury. *Recommended by Ann and Colin Hunt*

FINCLUDINGHDEAN SU7312   PO8 0AU
George
Centre of village

Red-brick pub dating from the 18th c, beamed front bar, separate dining area with conservatory, food (all day weekends) from good value bar menu up, efficient staff, well kept ales such as Fullers, Sharps and Wells & Youngs, live music; children welcome, dogs in bar, garden tables, good nearby walks, open all day weekends. *Recommended by Ann and Colin Hunt, W A Evershed*

FRITHAM SU2314   SO43 7HJ
☆ ## Royal Oak
Village signed from M27 junction1

Bustling country tavern in rural New Forest and part of working farm (ponies and pigs out on green), three straightforward but characterful black-beamed rooms, panelling, antique chairs at solid tables on oak floors, pictures of local characters, two log fires, up to seven real ales tapped from casks (September beer festival), simple but tasty lunchtime food, friendly chatty staff; no credit cards; children and dogs welcome, marquee and pétanque in big neatly kept garden, open all day (closed winter weekday lunchtimes). *Recommended by Mr and Mrs W W Burke, Simon Watkins, N R White, the Didler, Mr and Mrs D Hammond, Richard, Anne and Kate Ansell and others*

FROGHAM SU1712   SP6 2JA
☆ ## Foresters Arms
Abbotswell Road

Friendly chatty New Forest pub, chef/landlord doing good value blackboard food from sandwiches to very popular Sun lunch (compact dining room fills quickly – they ask to keep a credit card while you eat), welcoming attentive young staff, well kept Wadworths ales, good wines by the glass, cosy rustic refurbishment with frog-theme bar; children and dogs welcome, pleasant garden with pretty front verandah and good play area, small campsite adjacent, nearby ponies, deer and good walks, closed Tues. *Recommended by John and Joan Calvert, J Buckby*

GOODWORTH CLATFORD SU3642   SP11 7QY
Royal Oak
Longstock Road

Comfortably modern L-shaped bar with welcoming landlord and obliging staff, good carefully sourced food from pub staples up, well kept local ales, good choice of wines by the glass; sheltered and very pretty dell-like garden, large and neatly kept, attractive Test Valley village, good River Anton walks, closed Sun evening. *Recommended by Phyl and Jack Street*

GOSPORT SU6101   PO12 4LQ
☆ ## Jolly Roger
Priory Road, Hardway

Popular old beamed harbour-view pub with enjoyable fairly priced food, real ales such as Adnams, Greene King and Shepherd Neame, decent house wines, lots of bric-a-brac, log fire, attractive eating area including new conservatory; open all day. *Recommended by Ann and Colin Hunt*

GOSPORT SZ6100   PO12 1LG
Queens
Queens Road

Classic bare-boards local, long-serving landlady keeps Ringwood Fortyniner, Roosters, Wells & Youngs Special and two guests in top condition, beer festivals, quick service, three areas off bar with good log fire in interesting carved fireplace, sensibly placed darts, pub dog called Stanley; TV room – children welcome here daytime; closed lunchtimes Mon-Thurs, open all day Sat. *Recommended by Ann and Colin Hunt*

GREYWELL SU7151   RG29 1BY
Fox & Goose
Near M3 junction 5; A287 towards Odiham then first right to village

Traditional two-bar village pub popular with locals and walkers, country-kitchen furniture, home-made food from good lunchtime sandwiches up, well kept Courage Best and a couple of guests, friendly helpful service; dogs welcome, good-sized garden behind, attractive village, Basingstoke Canal walks, open all day Sun (can get very busy lunchtime then). *Recommended by Ann and Colin Hunt, Peter Farman*

HAMBLE SU4806   SO31 4HA
☆ Bugle
3 miles from M27 junction 8

Chatty and bustling little 16th-c village pub by River Hamble, beamed and timbered rooms with flagstones and polished boards, church chairs, woodburner in fine brick fireplace, bar stools along herringbone-brick and timbered counter, Bowman Swift One and Ringwood Best, popular food (all day weekends); piped music, TV; children welcome, dogs in bar, seats on the terrace from which you can see the boats), open all day. *Recommended by Bob and Angela Brooks, Phyl and Jack Street*

HAMBLEDON SU6716   PO8 0UB
☆ Bat & Ball
Broadhalfpenny Down; about 2 miles E towards Clanfield

Extended dining pub opposite cricket's first-ever pitch (matches most summer Sundays), plenty of cricketing memorabilia, log fires and comfortable modern furnishings in three linked rooms, Fullers ales, enjoyable food from well priced snacks up, good friendly service, panelled restaurant; children welcome, tables on front terrace, garden behind with lovely downs views, good walks, open all day. *Recommended by W A Evershed, N R White*

HANNINGTON SU5455   RG26 5TX
Vine
Signposted off A339

Spacious 19th-c village pub with light bright décor, comfy leather sofas and woodburner, real ales such as Black Sheep, good wines, fairly priced food using home-grown produce, friendly service, back dining conservatory; children and dogs welcome, big garden with terrace, nice spot up on downs, good walks, closed Sun evening and Mon in winter. *Recommended by Ann and Colin Hunt, N R White*

HAWKLEY SU7429   GU33 6NE
Hawkley Inn
Off B3006 near A3 junction; Pococks Lane

Small pubby village local with splendid range of well kept ales from central bar, farm ciders, too, including a blackberry one, good mix of customers, open fires, bare boards, flagstones and well used carpet, old pine tables and assorted chairs; piped music; children and dogs welcome, terrace tables and nice garden, useful for walkers (on Hangers Way), bedrooms, open all day weekends. *Recommended by the Didler, Tim Maddison, Ann and Colin Hunt, Geoff and Linda Payne*

HAYLING ISLAND SU7201   PO11 0PS
Maypole
Havant Road

Sizeable two-bar roadside local well run by friendly couple, parquet floors and polished panelling, plenty of good seating, well kept Fullers/Gales beers, good choice of generous reasonably priced pub food including fish on Fri; garden. *Recommended by Terry and Nickie Williams, Val and Alan Green, Ann and Colin Hunt, Dave Jennings*

HECKFIELD SU7260   RG27 0LE
New Inn
B3349 Hook—Reading (former A32)

Well run rambling open-plan dining pub, good welcoming service, enjoyable food including good light lunch selection, well kept Badger ales, good choice of wines by the glass, attractive layout with some traditional furniture in original core, two log fires; restaurant; good-sized heated terrace, bedrooms in comfortable and well equipped extension. *Recommended by Peter Sampson*

HERRIARD SS6744   RG25 2PN
Fur & Feathers
Pub signed just off A339 Basingstoke—Alton

Refurbished Victorian pub under newish ownership, three changing ales such as Ballards, Bowmans and Hogs Back, popular home-made blackboard food, friendly helpful service, smallish bar area with stools along counter, dining areas either side, pine furniture on stripped-wood flooring, painted half-panelling, old photographs and farm tools, log fire in big brick fireplace; piped music; garden behind, open Fri and Sat, closed Sun evening, Mon. *Recommended by Martin and Karen Wake*

HIGHCLERE SU4359   RG20 9PU
Red House
Andover Road (A343)

Traditional building given fresh contemporary revamp, spacious bar and separate restaurant, food from pub staples up, Timothy Taylors Landlord and West Berkshire ales, good choice of wines by the glass, pleasant service; children welcome away from bar, dogs away from eating areas, open all day Fri, closed Sun evening, Mon. *Recommended by John Redfern*

HIGHCLERE SU4358   RG20 9SE
Yew Tree
Hollington Cross

Smartly reworked country inn (Marco Pierre White is a major shareholder), good food (not too expensive) in nicely furnished comfortable low-beamed eating areas, relaxed civilised atmosphere, serious wine list, welcoming efficient staff, stylish contemporary bar, big inglenook log fire, attractive lighting and pictures; picnic-sets under cocktail parasols on pleasant terrace, six good bedrooms. *Recommended by Hunter and Christine Wright*

HOOK SU7354   RG27 9EH
Crooked Billet
A30 about a mile towards London

Comfortably extended and welcoming roadside pub with large dining area, wide choice of enjoyable food including interesting specials and plenty of fish, swift helpful service, well kept Courage Best and Directors with guests like Bath and Sharps, reasonably priced wines, good range of soft drinks, daily papers in area with sofa and log fire; soft piped music; children welcome, attractive smallish garden by stream with trout and ducks. *Recommended by Mike and Monnie Jefferies, Ian Herdman*

We include some hotels with a good bar that offers facilities comparable to those of a pub.

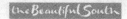

☆ **Mill at Gordleton**
HORDLE SZ2996   SO41 6DJ
Silver Street

Charming tucked-away country inn with very special waterside gardens, small relaxed panelled bar with leather armchairs, Victorian-style mahogany dining chairs, feature stove and pretty corner china cupboard, cosy lounge overflow and roomy second bar by sizeable beamed restaurant extension, good food – all home-made including breads and preserves, Dorset Piddle Cocky Hop and Ringwood Best, nice wines by the glass, daily papers; comfortable, individual bedrooms, excellent breakfasts, good walks. *Recommended by N R White*

☆ **Boot**
HOUGHTON SU3432   SO20 6LH
Village signposted off A30 in Stockbridge

Bustling country local with lots of stuffed creatures in cheery log-fire bar, good local Andwell ales, food from well filled baguettes up, friendly service, roomy more decorous lounge/dining room; well behaved children and dogs welcome, spacious tranquil garden with half a dozen picnic-sets down by lovely (unfenced) stretch of River Test, where they have fishing; good walks, and opposite Test Way cycle path. *Recommended by Edward Mirzoeff, Ann and Colin Hunt, N R White*

Kings Head
HURSLEY SU4225   SO21 2JW
A3090 Winchester—Romsey

Substantial early 19th-c coaching inn, good local home-made food, five well kept changing ales such as Ringwood and Sharps Doom Bar, good choice of ciders, friendly staff, restaurant, skittle alley; children and dogs welcome, garden tables, eight comfortable bedrooms, open all day. *Recommended by Chris and Jeanne Downing, Terry Buckland*

☆ **Gun**
KEYHAVEN SZ3091   SO41 0TP
Keyhaven Road

Busy rambling 17th-c pub looking over boatyard and sea to Isle of Wight, low-beamed bar with nautical bric-a-brac and plenty of character (less in family rooms and conservatory), good reasonably priced local food including crab, well kept beers tapped from the cask such as Flowers, Ringwood, Shepherd Neame and Wychwood, Weston's cider, lots of malt whiskies, helpful young staff, bar billiards; piped music; tables out in front and in big back garden with swings and fish pond; you can stroll down to small harbour and walk to Hurst Castle. *Recommended by Norma and David Hardy, N R White, Joshua Fancett*

Crown
KING'S SOMBORNE SU3531   SO20 6PW
Romsey Road (A3057)

Long low thatched pub opposite village church, friendly relaxed local atmosphere, good simple well priced home-made food, well kept ales such as Ringwood and Wychwood Hobgoblin, local cider, good wines and coffee, several linked rooms, comfortable sofas, fresh flowers; seats out at front and in garden behind, Test Way and Clarendon Way footpaths nearby. *Recommended by Ian and Rose Lock, Mr and Mrs H J Langley, David and Judy Robison, Mike*

Swan
KINGSCLERE SU5258   RG20 5PP
Swan Street

Old-fashioned 15th-c village inn, lots of beams, welcoming landlord and friendly helpful staff, Theakstons XB and three guests, enjoyable reasonably priced home-made food (not Sun evening); dogs welcome, tables outside, good walks, nine comfortable clean bedrooms. *Recommended by Ann and Colin Hunt, Steven Paine*

LANGSTONE SU7104   PO9 1RY
☆ **Royal Oak**
Off A3023 just before Hayling Island bridge; Langstone High Street

Charmingly placed waterside dining pub overlooking tidal inlet and ancient wadeway to Hayling Island, boats at high tide, wading birds when it goes out; four real ales including Greene King, good choice of wines by the glass, reasonably priced food with all-day sandwiches and snacks, smart friendly staff, spacious flagstoned bar and linked dining areas, log fire; children in eating areas, nice garden, good coastal paths nearby, open all day. *Recommended by W A Evershed*

LANGSTONE SU7104   PO9 1RD
Ship
A3023

Busy waterside 18th-c former grain store, lovely views to Hayling Island from roomy softly lit nautical bar with upper deck dining room, Fullers ales, good choice of wines by the glass, log fire, wide range of generous reasonably priced food including local fish and venison; children welcome, plenty of tables on heated terrace by quiet quay, good coast walks, open all day. *Recommended by Andy West, W A Evershed, Glen and Nola Armstrong*

LINWOOD SU1910   BH24 3QY
High Corner
Signed from A338 via Moyles Court, and from A31; keep on

Big rambling pub very popular for its splendid New Forest position up a track, with extensive neatly kept wooded garden and lots for children to do; some character in original upper bar with log fire, big back extensions for the summer crowds, nicely partitioned restaurant, verandah lounge, interesting family rooms, wide choice of generous bar snacks and restaurant-style food, well kept Wadworths; welcomes dogs and horses (stables and paddock available), seven bedrooms, open all day weekends. *Recommended by Dennis and Doreen Haward, J Buckby*

LINWOOD SU1809   BH24 3QT
Red Shoot
Signed from A338 via Moyles Court, and from A31; go on up heath to junction with Toms Lane

Edwardian pub in nice New Forest setting, big picture-window bar with attractive old tables, mixed chairs and rugs on bare boards, country pictures on puce walls, log fire, large back dining area, generous honest good value food (all day weekends), friendly helpful staff, well kept Wadworths and two or three ales brewed at the pub including Muddy Boot (beer festivals Apr and Oct); children, dogs and muddy boots welcome, some disabled access, sheltered side terrace, open all day summer – very touristy then (by big campsite and caravan park). *Recommended by S Harris, Carey Tyler*

LITTLETON SU4532   SO22 6QS
☆ **Running Horse**
Main Road; village signed off B3049 NW of Winchester

Popular dining pub refurbished in up-to-date style, enjoyable food from pubby to more elaborate dishes including two-course weekday lunch, good service, cushioned metal and wicker chairs at modern tables on polished boards, also some deep leather chairs, good colour photographs of Hampshire scenes, Andwell Resolute and Bowman Wallops Wood from marble and hardwood counter with swish bar stools, log fire, flagstoned back restaurant; piped music; children welcome, dogs in bar, good disabled facilities, nice front and back terraces and garden, bedrooms, open all day. *Recommended by Phyl and Jack Street, Karen Eliot, Mrs Ann Adams and others*

Half pints: by law, a pub should not charge more for half a pint than half the price of a full pint, unless it shows that half-pint price on its price list.

LOCKERLEY SU3025   SO51 0JF
Kings Arms
The Street

Fully refurbished under new management, enjoyable food from bar snacks to restaurant dishes, interesting wine list, well kept ales, good service and thriving local atmosphere. *Recommended by John Chambers*

LOCKS HEATH SU5006   SO31 9JH
☆ Jolly Farmer
Fleet End Road, not far from M27 junction 9

Popular flower-decked pub with relaxing series of softly lit linked rooms, nice old scrubbed tables and masses of interesting bric-a-brac and prints, emphasis on wide choice of enjoyable food (all day weekends) including good value Sun lunch (two-sittings), interesting long-serving landlord and good friendly service, Fullers/Gales ales, decent wines including country ones, coal-effect gas fires; two sheltered terraces (one with play area and children's lavatories), dogs allowed in public bar, nearby walks, five nice bedrooms, good breakfast, open all day. *Recommended by Phyl and Jack Street, Ann and Colin Hunt, David and Gill Carrington*

LONG SUTTON SU7447   RG29 1TA
☆ Four Horseshoes
Signed off B3349 S of Hook

Welcoming open-plan black-beamed country local with two log fires, long-serving landlord cooking bargain pubby food, friendly landlady serving good range of changing ales such as Palmers, decent wines and country wine, no piped music or machines, small glazed-in verandah; disabled access, picnic-sets on grass over road, boules and play area, three good value bedrooms (bunk beds available for cyclist/walkers). *Recommended by Tony and Jill Radnor*

LONGPARISH SU4344   SP11 6PZ
Cricketers
B3048, off A303 just E of Andover

Cheerful homely village pub with good chatty landlady, connecting rooms and cosy corners, woodburner, wide choice of carefully cooked food from light snacks to popular Sun lunch, prompt service, good range of real ales; sizeable back garden; closed Mon. *Recommended by Phyl and Jack Street, Mr and Mrs A Curry*

LONGPARISH SU4244   SP11 6PB
☆ Plough
B3048, off A303 just E of Andover

Bustling open-plan country pub with welcoming staff and comfortably upmarket feel; beams, standing timbers, flagstone and oak floors, contemporary paintwork, high-backed wooden or black leather dining chairs, working fireplaces (one with woodburner), good bar food (all day summer, till 4pm winter), Itchen Valley, Otter and Ringwood; children and dogs welcome, chickens, rabbits and tortoise in garden with plenty of seats on decking, open all day (till 9pm Sun). *Recommended by Edward Mirzoeff, Neil and Karen Dignan, Michael and Jenny Back, Evelyn and Derek Walter and others*

LYMINGTON SZ3295   SO41 3AY
☆ Ship
Quay Road

Lively well run pub with popular quayside deck overlooking harbour, light modern interior with lots of nautical bric-a-brac, including huge flags, blue gingham and leather sofas, raised log fire, Adnams Broadside, Fullers London Pride and Hook Norton Old Hooky (plenty of standing room by counter), enjoyable fair value interesting food (all day), attractive wall-planked restaurant with blue and cream paintwork and driftwood decorations; children and dogs welcome, showers for visiting sailors. *Recommended by John Voos*

LYMINGTON SZ3395   SO41 5SB
Wagon & Horses
Undershore Road; road to IOW ferry

Well run comfortable Wadworths pub, friendly staff, some interesting food, beamed
restaurant with leaded windows, games room; terrace tables, handy for IOW ferry.
Recommended by Joan and Michel Hooper-Immins

LYNDHURST SU2908   SO43 7BG
Fox & Hounds
High Street

Big busy low-beamed Chef & Brewer, comfortable and much-modernised, with good range
of food all day including blackboard specials, obliging cheerful staff, Ringwood and
several other ales, decent wines, exposed brickwork and standing timbers, back 19th-c
barn (moved here from Winchester); children welcome, disabled facilities, outside
picnic-sets, bedrooms. *Recommended by John Robertson, Phyl and Jack Street*

MAPLEDURWELL SU6851   RG25 2LU
Gamekeepers
Off A30, not far from M3 junction 6

Dark-beamed dining pub with good upmarket food (not cheap) from interesting
baguettes up, welcoming landlord, well kept Badger ales, good coffee, a few sofas by
flagstoned and panelled core, well spaced tables in large dining room; piped music, TV;
children welcome, terrace and garden, lovely thatched village with duck pond, good
walks, open all day. *Recommended by Edward Mirzoeff*

MARCHWOOD SU3809   SO40 4WU
Pilgrim
Hythe Road, off A326 at Twiggs Lane

Popular picturesque thatched pub (originally three cottages), good choice of enjoyable
sensibly priced food, efficient friendly service even at busy times, well kept Fullers ales,
decent wine, open fires; tree-lined garden with round picnic-sets, 14 stylish bedrooms in
building across car park, open all day. *Recommended by Phyl and Jack Street, Ian and Rose Lock
and others*

MICHELDEVER SU5142   SO21 3AU
Dove
Micheldever Station, off A33 or A303

Large square pub with several well refurbished interconnecting rooms around central
bar, enjoyable food from pub favourites up, Ringwood BB, obliging friendly service,
beams, exposed brickwork, woodburner; small side terrace, bedrooms. *Recommended by
Edward Mirzoeff, Diana Brumfit*

MINLEY MANOR SU8357   GU17 9UA
Crown & Cushion
A327, just N of M3 junction 4A

Attractive little traditional pub with enjoyable fairly priced food including some unusual
choices, well kept Shepherd Neame ales, coal-effect gas fire; big separate raftered and
flagstoned rustic 'meade hall' behind, very popular weekends (evenings more a young
people's meeting place), with huge log fire, friendly staff cope well when busy; children
in eating area, heated terrace overlooking own cricket pitch. *Recommended by David and
Sue Smith*

MINSTEAD SU2810   SO43 7FY
Trusty Servant
Just off A31, not far from M27 junction 1

Attractive 19th-c building in pretty New Forest hamlet with interesting church,
wandering cattle and ponies, and plenty of easy walks; bright and simple mildly upscale

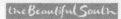

refurbishment, two-room bar and big dining room, real ales, food from sandwiches up; big sloping garden, open all day. *Recommended by Bob and Angela Brooks, Henry Fryer, John Redfern*

MONXTON SU3144   SP11 8AW
Black Swan
High Street

Friendly 17th-c rambling pub, enjoyable food including Sun carvery and takeaway fish and chips, well kept real ales, log fire; car park down street; children welcome, lovely sheltered garden by stream with ducks, open all day. *Recommended by Chris and Meredith Owen*

☆ NEW CHERITON SU5827   SO24 0NH
Hinton Arms
A272 near B3046 junction

Neatly kept popular country pub with cheerful accommodating landlord, three or four real ales including Bowman Wallops Wood and one brewed for the pub by Hampshire, decent wines by the glass, generous food including game specials, sporting pictures and memorabilia, relaxing atmosphere; TV lounge; terrace, big garden, very handy for Hinton Ampner House (NT). *Recommended by Phil and Jane Villiers, Ann and Colin Hunt, P J Checksfield*

NEWTOWN SU4763   RG20 9BH
Swan
A339 2 miles S of Newbury, by junction with old A34

Ancient black and white pub refitted in modern style, good nicely presented food, well kept Badger ales, friendly young staff, flagstones and open fires; children welcome, terrace and lovely streamside garden. *Recommended by Keith and Margaret Kettell*

NEWTOWN SU6112   PO17 6LL
Travellers Rest
Off A32 N of Wickham

Friendly lived-in country pub gently enlarged but still cosy, one chatty local bar, two further rooms mainly for food, four well kept ales including Bowman, open fires and traditional furnishings; children welcome, pretty back garden, caravan park. *Recommended by Val and Alan Green, Ann and Colin Hunt*

ODIHAM SU7450   RG29 1LY
Bell
The Bury

Simple unspoilt two-bar local in pretty square opposite church and stocks, three well kept changing ales, good value straightforward food, log fire; plenty of seats outside. *Recommended by Ann and Colin Hunt, Peter Farman*

ODIHAM SU7451   RG29 1AL
Water Witch
Colt Hill – quiet no through road signed off main street

Olde-worlde décor in nicely kept Chef & Brewer near picturesque stretch of Basingstoke Canal, big but cosily divided, wide choice of food, friendly staff, real ales; no dogs inside; disabled access, big garden with children's facilities. *Recommended by Chris and Jeanne Downing, Jim and Frances Gowers*

OTTERBOURNE SU4623   SO21 2EE
Old Forge
Main Road

Popular old bistro-style chain pub, welcoming and comfortable, with wide choice of enjoyable food all day, friendly well organised staff, ales such as Everards, Sharps and Timothy Taylors, good choice of wines by the glass, tables spread through linked rooms, cosy nooks and rather individual décor, log fires; children welcome. *Recommended by PL, Henry Fryer, Phyl and Jack Street, Mr and Mrs J J A Davis and others*

OTTERBOURNE SU4522   SO21 2HW
Otter
Boyatt Lane, off Winchester Road

Unpretentious dining pub opposite village green, enjoyable food from sandwiches and snacks up, Ringwood ales and Otter, good service, three-sided bar (one side set for dining), dark oak tables and chairs, banquettes; seats in garden. *Recommended by Mrs Joy Griffiths, M and GR, Val and Alan Green*

OVERTON SU5149   RG25 3HQ
Red Lion
High Street

Smartly refurbished old village pub with emphasis on good imaginative food, well kept ales such as Flowerpots and Triple fff, enthusiastic landlord and friendly efficient staff, wood floors including some parquet, open fires, skittle alley; piped music; terrace and garden, closed Sun evening. *Recommended by Bruce Bird*

PETERSFIELD SU7423   GU31 4AE
Red Lion
College Street

Newly refurbished Wetherspoons in former coaching inn, usual good value food and beers; open all day from 7am. *Recommended by Dom Humphries, Val and Alan Green*

PORTSMOUTH SZ6399   PO1 2JA
abarbistro
White Hart Road

Modern airy bar/restaurant (was the American Bar) with mural of beach huts and deckchair-stripe banquettes giving seaside feel, decent choice of food all day including some pubby things, special diets catered for, well kept ales such as Fullers London Pride, good choice of wines by the glass, friendly staff; terrace and secluded garden, handy for IOW ferry. *Recommended by Ann and Colin Hunt*

PORTSMOUTH SZ6399   PO1 2JJ
Bridge Tavern
East Street, Camber Dock

Flagstones, bare boards and lots of dark wood, comfortable furnishings, maritime theme with good harbour views, Fullers ales, plenty of fish dishes; nice waterside terrace. *Recommended by Ann and Colin Hunt, W A Evershed*

PORTSMOUTH SU6402   PO2 9AA
Fountain
London Road, North End

Unchanging tiled pub with large bar and family room off, nicely polished brass, interesting pictures of local pubs, mirrors each end, unusual ceiling lights, well kept beer including Gales HSB, no food; seats outside. *Recommended by Ann and Colin Hunt*

PORTSMOUTH SZ6399   PO1 3TY
☆ # Old Customs House
Vernon Buildings, Gunwharf Quays; follow brown signs to Gunwharf Quays car park

Handsome late 18th-c red-brick building (former customs house) in waterfront development, big-windowed high-ceilinged rooms with bare boards, nautical prints and photographs on pastel walls, coal-effect gas fires, good range of Fullers/Gales ales, well liked good value food all day (breakfast from 9am), good prompt service, stairs up to carpeted more restauranty floor with similar décor; piped music, machines and can get very busy; children allowed until 8pm (welcome upstairs after that), disabled facilities, picnic-sets out by water. *Recommended by Dave Braisted, Maureen Wood, Ann and Colin Hunt, Phil Bryant*

PORTSMOUTH SZ6399   PO1 2NR
Pembroke
Pembroke Road

Buoyant atmosphere in comfortable well run traditional local, unspoilt under long-serving landlord, Bass and Fullers/Gales, fresh rolls, real fire; open all day. *Recommended by Ann and Colin Hunt*

PORTSMOUTH SZ6299   PO1 2JL
Still & West
Bath Square, Old Portsmouth

Great location with superb views of narrow harbour mouth and across to Isle of Wight, especially from glazed-in panoramic upper family area and waterfront terrace with lots of picnic-sets; nautical bar with fireside sofas and cosy colour scheme, Fullers ales, good choice of wines by the glass, food all day including signature fish and chips; piped music may be loud, nearby pay & display; children welcome, handy for Historic Dockyard. *Recommended by Andy West, Ann and Colin Hunt, W A Evershed, J A Snell, B M Eldridge*

ROCKFORD SU1608   BH24 3NA
Alice Lisle
Follow sign on village green

Big well laid-out open-plan family dining pub (a former school) attractively placed on green by New Forest (can get very busy), large conservatory-style eating area, enjoyable varied choice of food (all day weekends) from sandwiches up, Fullers ales, good choice of wines by the glass, good service; baby-changing facilities, dogs welcome, big garden overlooking lake with ponies wandering nearby, play area, handy for Moyles Court, open all day. *Recommended by Mrs J Plante Cleall*

☆ ROMSEY SU3523   SO51 0HB
Dukes Head
A3057 out towards Stockbridge

Attractive 16th-c dining pub with good landlady and friendly staff, small comfortable spic-and-span linked rooms, big log fire, good range of enjoyable food, well kept Ringwood and guests, decent wines and coffee; children welcome, colourful hanging baskets, sheltered back terrace and pleasant garden, open all day. *Recommended by Phyl and Jack Street, J V Dadswell, Ann and Colin Hunt*

ROMSEY SU3520   SO51 8HL
Three Tuns
Middlebridge Street (but car park signed straight off A27 bypass)

Old bow-windowed beamed pub reopened after refurbishment by new owners, well kept ales such as Bath, traditional pub food; children welcome. *Recommended by John Evans*

☆ ROWLAND'S CASTLE SU7310   PO9 6DA
Castle Inn
Off B2148/B2149 N of Havant; Finchdean Road

Cheerful proper country pub with friendly hands-on tenants, comfortable bar with enormous log fire and good choice of Fullers/Gales ales, nice coffee, neat staff, two appealing little dining rooms on left, attractively priced pubby food with more exotic evening choices; children and dogs welcome, pony paddock by good-sized garden, good disabled facilities, open all day. *Recommended by Andy West, Ann and Colin Hunt, W A Evershed*

ROWLAND'S CASTLE SU7310   PO9 6AB
Robin Hood
The Green

Nicely refurbished pub on village green, light and airy bar, good choice of enjoyable food, Badger ales and a guest, efficient service, restaurant; children and dogs welcome, disabled facilities, picnic-sets on front terrace, six bedrooms, good breakfast, open all day. *Recommended by Tony and Gill Powell*

SARISBURY SU5008   SO31 7EL
Bold Forester
Handy for M27 junction 9; Bridge Road (A27), Sarisbury Green

Roomy and well run with good choice of popular food from baguettes and sharing plates up, friendly attentive staff, four real ales including Ringwood, pictures of this increasingly built-up area in its strawberry-fields days; children welcome, pretty hanging baskets and tubs in front, large recently redone garden behind, open all day. *Recommended by Christine Whitehead*

SELBORNE SU7433   GU34 3JJ
Queens
High Street

Comfortably refurbished under new licensee, interesting local memorabilia, open fires, well kept Hogs Back TEA and Triple fff Alton Pride, food (not Sun evening) from sandwiches and pubby things to french country dishes, cream teas, cheerful smartly dressed staff, occasional jazz; children and dogs welcome, garden picnic-sets, eight bedrooms, very handy for Gilbert White's house, open all day. *Recommended by Ann and Colin Hunt*

SHALDEN SU7043   GU34 4DJ
Golden Pot
B3349 Odiham Road N of Alton

Refurbished and under newish management, emphasis on dining but drinkers welcome, modern airy décor with sage-green walls, bare boards and log fires, enjoyable food including tapas, friendly service, good choice of wines by the glass, beers such as Andwell and Otter; tables outside. *Recommended by N R White, Martin and Karen Wake*

SHEDFIELD SU5513   SO32 2JG
Wheatsheaf
A334 Wickham—Botley

Busy friendly no-fuss local, Flowerpots ales tapped from the cask, farm cider, short sensible choice of bargain bar lunches (evening food Tues-Thurs); dogs welcome, garden, handy for Wickham Vineyard, open all day. *Recommended by Jenny and Peter Lowater, Val and Alan Green, Ann and Colin Hunt, Joan and Michel Hooper-Immins*

SHERFIELD ENGLISH SU3022   SO51 6FP
Hatchet
Romsey Road

Beamed and panelled 18th-c pub under new licensees, popular fairly priced generous food including good steaks and fish, Fullers London Pride, Ringwood and guests, good wine choice, friendly hard-working staff, long bar with cosy area down steps, woodburner, steps up to second bar with darts, TV, juke box and machines; children and dogs welcome, outside seating on two levels, garden play area, open all day weekends. *Recommended by Phyl and Jack Street, Steve Cogdell*

SHIRRELL HEATH SU5714   SO32 2JN
Prince of Wales
High Street (B2177)

Refurbished smallish front bar with restaurant behind, good well presented/priced food, real ales, welcoming staff; back garden with terrace and play area. *Recommended by Samuel Fancett, Ann and Colin Hunt, Jenny and Peter Lowater*

SOPLEY SZ1596   BH23 7AX
☆ ## Woolpack
B3347 N of Christchurch

Pretty thatched dining pub with rambling open-plan low-beamed bar, welcoming helpful staff, good generous traditional food, real ales such as Ringwood Best and Fortyniner, good choice of wines by the glass, modern dining conservatory; they ask to keep a credit

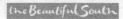

card if you're running a tab; children in eating areas, dogs in certain areas, terrace and charming garden with weeping willows, duck stream and footbridges, open all day. *Recommended by Hans Becker, Sue and Mike Todd, Jo Hankins, David Cannings*

☆ SOUTHAMPTON SU4111   SO14 2AH

Duke of Wellington
Bugle Street (or walk along city wall from Bar Gate)

Striking ancient timber-framed building dating from 14th c, cellars even older, heavy beams, great log fire, well kept ales such as Ringwood and Wadworths, good choice of wines by the glass, good value traditional pub food (not Sun) from baguettes to nursery puddings, friendly helpful service; piped music in cheery front bar, staider back area welcoming children; handy for Tudor House Museum, sunny streetside picnic-sets, open all day. *Recommended by Val and Alan Green*

SOUTHAMPTON SU4211   SO14 2DF

Standing Order
High Street

Big busy Wetherspoons with up to ten well kept ales, low-priced food, helpful efficient young staff, cosy corners (strange and interesting collection of books in one), civilised atmosphere; open all day. *Recommended by Val and Alan Green*

SOUTHSEA SZ6499   PO5 4BS

Eldon Arms
Eldon Street/Norfolk Street

Rambling backstreet tavern under newish management, Fullers London Pride and four changing guests, Thatcher's cider, simple cheap lunchtime food (not Mon), Sun carvery, flowers on tables, old pictures and advertisements, attractive mirrors, bric-a-brac and shelves of books; piped music, sensibly placed darts, bar billiards, pool, games machine; dogs on leads and children welcome, tables in back garden, open all day. *Recommended by Ann and Colin Hunt*

☆ SOUTHSEA SZ6499   PO5 3BY

Hole in the Wall
Great Southsea Street

Small friendly unspoilt local in old part of town, up to six good changing ales such as Dark Star, Hammerpot, Oakleaf and Tom Woods, Wheal Maiden alcoholic ginger beer, Thatcher's cider, simple good value food including speciality local sausages and meat puddings, nicely worn boards, dark pews and panelling, old photographs and prints, over 700 pump clips on ceiling, little snug behind the bar, daily papers, quiz night Thurs, Oct beer festival; small outside tiled area at front with benches, side garden, closed till 4pm weekdays, open all day Fri-Sun. *Recommended by Andy West, Joan and Michel Hooper-Immins, Ann and Colin Hunt*

SOUTHSEA SZ6499   PO5 4EH

King Street Tavern
King Street

Sympathetically refurbished corner pub in attractive conservation area, spectacular Victorian tiled façade, bare boards and original fittings, four well kept Wadworths ales and guests, real ciders, straightforward home-made food; piped and live music including fortnightly Sat jazz; courtyard tables, closed lunchtimes apart from Sun. *Recommended by Ann and Colin Hunt, Nick Birtley*

STOCKBRIDGE SU3535   SO20 6HB

Three Cups
High Street

Lovely low-beamed building dating from 1500, more restaurant than pub now, lots of smartly set pine tables but still some high-backed settles, country bric-a-brac and four well kept ales such as Ringwood; food can be very good including local trout fishcakes, amiable service, good wines by the glass; children and dogs welcome, vine-covered verandah and charming cottage garden with streamside terrace, bedrooms, open all day. *Recommended by Geoffrey Kemp*

STOCKBRIDGE SU3535   SO20 6HF
☆ White Hart
High Street; A272/A3057 roundabout

Thriving divided beamed bar, attractive décor with antique prints, oak pews and other seats, friendly helpful staff, enjoyable food from snacks to substantial daily specials, well kept Fullers/Gales beers, comfortable restaurant with blazing log fire (children allowed); dogs in bar, disabled facilities, terrace tables and nice garden, 14 good bedrooms, open all day. *Recommended by Phyl and Jack Street, Edward Mirzoeff, Dr and Mrs A K Clarke, Ann and Colin Hunt, Helen and Brian Edgeley and others*

STUBBINGTON SU5402   PO14 3QF
Crofton
Crofton Lane

Modern two-bar estate local, neat and airy, with friendly efficient staff, well kept Sharps Doom Bar and changing guests, good value wines, enjoyable nicely varied food including well liked weekday OAP deals; children and dogs welcome. *Recommended by Sally Matson*

SWANMORE SU5716   SO32 2PA
Brickmakers

Popular family-friendly pub smartly refurbished by current owners, four real ales including Bowman and Otter, good wines, enjoyable reasonably priced fresh food, armchairs and log fire; garden with raised deck. *Recommended by Val and Alan Green*

SWANMORE SU5815   SO32 2PS
☆ Rising Sun
Droxford Road; signed off A32 N of Wickham (and B2177 S of Bishops Waltham), at Hillpound E of village centre

Proper country pub (busy Sun) with friendly homely atmosphere, unpretentious furnishings and good log fire in low-beamed carpeted bar, stripped-brick barrel vaulting in one area of pleasant dining area, Adnams, Courage, Otter and Ringwood, well liked bar food including smaller helpings and weekday two-course set menu; piped music; children and dogs welcome, garden with play area, handy for Kings Way long-distance path. *Recommended by Ann and Colin Hunt, Martin and Karen Wake, Howard and Margaret Buchanan, Phyl and Jack Street*

THRUXTON SU2945   SP11 8EE
White Horse
Mullens Pond, just off A303 eastbound

Attractive old thatched pub tucked below A303 embankment, comfortably modernised, with emphasis on fresh food, good friendly service, plenty of wines by the glass, well kept ales such as Greene King, woodburner, a couple of sofas, very low beams, separate dining area; good-sized garden and terrace, four bedrooms, closed Sun evening, Mon. *Recommended by B J Harding*

TICHBORNE SU5730   SO24 0NA
☆ Tichborne Arms
Signed off B3047

Traditional thatched pub with latticed windows, panelling, antiques and stuffed animals, interesting changing ales tapped from the cask, food (not Sun evening) from baguettes up, locals bar, darts, board games and shove-ha'penny; children and dogs welcome, big garden in rolling countryside, Wayfarers Walk and Itchen Way pass close by, closed Sun evening. *Recommended by Conor McGaughey, Tony and Jill Radnor, Martin and Karen Wake, Tony and Wendy Hobden, the Didler and others*

☆ **TIMSBURY** SU3325   SO51 0LB
Bear & Ragged Staff
A3057 towards Stockbridge; pub marked on OS Sheet 185 map reference 334254

Reliable roadside dining pub with wide blackboard choice of popular food all day, friendly efficient service, lots of wines by the glass, Greene King IPA, log fire, good-sized beamed interior; children welcome in eating part, tables in extended garden with play area, handy for Mottisfont, good walks. *Recommended by Andrew Shore, Rich Best, Phil and Jane Villiers, Phyl and Jack Street*

TITCHFIELD SU5305   PO14 4AF
Bugle
The Square, off A27 near Fareham

Roomy and comfortable 18th-c coaching inn, popular good value food from light meals up in bar or old barn restaurant behind, friendly attentive service, four well kept ales including Timothy Taylors Landlord, log fires; no dogs; children welcome, attractive village handy for Titchfield Haven nature reserve, fine walk by former canal to coast, eight bedrooms. *Recommended by Val and Alan Green*

☆ **TITCHFIELD** SU5406   PO15 5RA
Fishermans Rest
Mill Lane, off A27 at Titchfield Mill pub

Open-plan pub/restaurant with wide choice of good value fresh food including deals, informal tables throughout, well kept Greene King ales and Ringwood, smartly dressed staff, two log fires, daily papers, trout-theme décor, some cosy nooks; fine riverside position opposite Titchfield Abbey, tables out behind overlooking water, open all day. *Recommended by Ann and Colin Hunt, Phyl and Jack Street*

TOTFORD SU5737   SO24 9TJ
Woolpack
B3046 Basingstoke—Alresford

Nicely refurbished roadside inn, clean and comfortable, with good food from bar snacks to restaurant dishes, Palmers, an ale brewed for the pub and a guest such as Bowman, several wines by the glass including champagne, nice italian coffee, efficient service, raised open fire in bar, smart split-level dining room; pool; round picnic-sets outside on gravel, lovely setting in good walking country, seven bedrooms, open all day. *Recommended by Janet Whittaker, Caroline Mackenzie*

TURGIS GREEN SU6959   RG27 0AX
Jekyll & Hyde
A33 Reading—Basingstoke

Bustling rambling pub with nice mix of furniture and village atmosphere in black-beamed and flagstoned bar, blazing fire, some interesting prints and pithy sayings dotted about, larger stepped-up three-room dining area, Badger ales, enjoyable sensibly priced pubby food all day including children's choices, attentive cheerful service; piped music; dogs welcome, disabled facilities, lots of picnic-sets in good sheltered garden (some traffic noise) with terrace, play area, open all day. *Recommended by Pat and Roger Davies*

☆ **TWYFORD** SU4824   SO21 1QT
Bugle
B3355/Park Lane

Nicely done modern pub with contemporary furniture, lots of leather, carpet or dark flagstones, good enterprising food, attentive friendly service, well kept ales from Bowman, Flowerpots and Upham, woodburner, highly coloured landscape photographs; piped music; attractive verandah seating area, good walks nearby, open all day. *Recommended by B J Harding, Phyl and Jack Street, Tony Hobden, Henry Fryer*

UPHAM SU5320   SO32 1JJ
☆ **Brushmakers Arms**
Shoe Lane; village signed from Winchester—Bishops Waltham downs road, and from
B2177

Plenty of regulars and weekend dog walkers at this cheery low-beamed village pub,
L-shaped bar divided by central woodburner, cushioned settles and chairs around mix of
tables, lots of brushes and related paraphernalia, little back snug with games machine
and piped music, enjoyable bar food, Fullers, Ringwood and a guest, decent coffee, pub
cats (Luna and Baxter); children and dogs welcome, big garden with picnic-sets on
sheltered terrace and tree-shaded lawn, open all day Sun. *Recommended by Val and*
Alan Green, Tony and Jill Radnor, Ann and Colin Hunt, Bruce and Penny Wilkie and others

WALHAMPTON SZ3396   SO41 5RE
Walhampton Arms
B3054 NE of Lymington; aka Walhampton Inn

Large comfortable Georgian-style family roadhouse with popular food including good
value carvery in raftered former stables and two adjoining areas, pleasant lounge,
Ringwood ales, cheerful helpful staff; attractive courtyard, good walks, open all day.
Recommended by Phyl and Jack Street and others

WALTHAM CHASE SU5614   SO32 2LX
Black Dog
Winchester Road

Low-ceilinged two-bar pub covered with lovely hanging baskets, good reasonably priced
food including vegetarian choices and weekday lunchtime deals from new french
chef/landlord, three well kept Greene King ales, wide choice of wines by the glass, smart
interior with big back restaurant extension; no dogs inside; children welcome, tables in
good-sized neatly kept garden, open all day weekends. *Recommended by Ann and Colin Hunt*

WELL SU7646   RG29 1TL
Chequers
Off A287 via Crondall, or A31 via Froyle and Lower Froyle

Appealing low-beamed and panelled country pub with welcoming landlord, enjoyable food
including popular Sun lunch, well kept Badger ales, decent wines by the glass, pews and
brocaded stools, 18th-c country-life prints and old sepia photographs, a few GWR carriage
lamps, log fire (not always lit); picnic-sets on vine-covered terrace and in spacious back
garden. *Recommended by Trish Bellamy, Sally Garside, Tony and Jill Radnor*

WEST END SU4514   SO18 3HW
White Swan
Mansbridge Road

Pleasantly refurbished family food pub in nice spot, Itchen Valley and Wells & Youngs
ales, busy carvery restaurant, conservatory; attractive terrace by River Itchen (so liable to
flooding). *Recommended by Phyl and Jack Street and others*

WEST MEON SU6424   GU32 1LN
☆ **Thomas Lord**
High Street

Friendly bustling village pub named for founder of Lord's cricket ground, individual rustic
style with interesting mix of chairs around candlelit wooden tables, old leather sofa,
stuffed animals in display cabinets, bare boards and log fires, back room lined with books
for sale, imaginative if not cheap food, cask-tapped ales such as Bowman, Ringwood and
Upham, farm cider; children and dogs welcome, attractive formal garden with outdoor
bar, wood-fired pizza oven, chicken run and neat vegetable patch, open all day weekends,
closed Mon except bank holidays. *Recommended by Val and Alan Green, Henry Fryer, Darryl and*
Lindy Hemsley, Phyl and Jack Street, Edward Bradley and others

WEST TYTHERLEY SU2730   SP5 1NF
Black Horse
North Lane

Compact unspoilt village local, welcoming licensees and chatty regulars, traditional bar with a couple of long tables and big fireplace, nicely set dining area off, three real ales, enjoyable reasonably priced food including good Sun roasts, takeaway fish and chips Thurs, skittle alley; dogs welcome. *Recommended by Phyl and Jack Street, Graham Horder, Ann and Colin Hunt*

WHERWELL SU3839   SO20 6AX
☆ Mayfly
Testcombe (over by Fullerton, and not in Wherwell itself); A3057 SE of Andover, between B3420 turn-off and Leckford where road crosses River Test; OS Sheet 185 map reference 382390

Well run busy pub with decking and conservatory overlooking River Test, spacious beamed and carpeted bar with fishing paraphernalia, rustic pub furnishings and woodburner, Adnams Best, Gales HSB, Hop Back Summer Lightning, Palmers Gold and Wadworths 6X, lots of wines by the glass, wide range of popular reasonably priced bar food all day (order from separate counter), good, courteous service; piped music; well behaved children and dogs on leads welcome. *Recommended by Ian Herdman, Terry and Nickie Williams, Betsy and Peter Little, Edward Mirzoeff, Mr and Mrs A Curry, Michael and Jenny Back and others*

WHERWELL SU3840   SP11 7JF
White Lion
B3420

Refurbished early 17th-c multi-level beamed village inn, emphasis on dining with good choice of enjoyable food, Harveys, Hop Back, Ringwood Best and guest such as Sharps Doom Bar, several wines by the glass, open fire, comfy leather armchairs, dining rooms either side of bar; piped music; dogs on leads and well behaved children welcome, new garden area with good quality furniture, Test Way walks, four bedrooms, open all day from 7.30am (breakfast for non-residents). *Recommended by B J Harding, Phyl and Jack Street, Stephen Pacey, Michael and Jenny Back and others*

WICKHAM SU5711   PO17 5JQ
☆ Greens
The Square, at junction with A334

Civilised dining place with clean-cut modern furnishings and décor, small bar with leather sofa and armchairs as well as bar stools, wide wine choice, Bowmans Swift One and another ale, efficient considerate young staff, step down to split-level balustraded dining areas, enjoyable food from typical bar lunches to imaginative specials; pleasant lawn overlooking water meadows, closed Sun evening and Mon. *Recommended by Darryl and Lindy Hemsley, Mrs Joy Griffiths, Phyl and Jack Street*

WICKHAM SU5711   PO17 5JN
Kings Head
The Square

Bustling refurbished village local, open-plan bar with big windows and open fires, well kept Fullers/Gales ales, enjoyable reasonably priced food from sandwiches up including tapas, back dining area up some steps; piped music; tables out on square and in garden behind (former coach yard). *Recommended by Ann and Colin Hunt, Val and Alan Green, Sally Matson*

WINCHESTER SU4828   SO23 9NQ
☆ Black Boy
B3403 off M3 junction 10 towards city then left into Wharf Hill; no nearby daytime parking – 220 metres from car park on B3403

Splendidly eccentric decor at this chatty old-fashioned pub, floor-to-ceiling books, lots of big clocks, mobiles made of wine bottles or spectacles, stuffed animals including a baboon and dachshund, two log fires, orange-painted room with big oriental rugs on red floorboards, barn room with open hayloft, half a dozen often local beers, straightforward food (not Sun evening, Mon, Tues lunchtime), service can be slow, table football and board games; piped music; supervised children and dogs welcome, slate tables out in front and seats on attractive secluded terrace, open all day. *Recommended by Val and Alan Green, Henry Fryer, Ann and Colin Hunt, MJVK and others*

WINCHESTER SU4829   SO23 9EX
☆ **Eclipse**
The Square, between High Street and cathedral

Chatty licensees in picturesque unspoilt 14th-c local with massive beams and timbers in its two small cheerful rooms, chilled ales including Fullers London Pride and Ringwood, decent choice of wines by the glass, good value lunchtime food from ciabattas to popular Sun roasts, open fire, oak settles, friendly burmese cat; children in back area, seats outside, very handy for cathedral. *Recommended by Ann and Colin Hunt*

WINCHESTER SU4829   SO23 8RZ
Old Gaol House
Jewry Street

Traditional Wetherspoons attracting good mix of customers, ten real ales, decent sensibly priced food all day, nice coffee, walls of books; children welcome. *Recommended by Ann and Colin Hunt, Val and Alan Green*

WINCHESTER SU4829   SO23 9HA
☆ **Old Vine**
Great Minster Street

Lively big-windowed town bar with well kept ales such as Bowman Swift One, Flowerpots, Ringwood Best and Timothy Taylors Landlord, efficient friendly staff, high beams, worn oak boards, smarter and larger dining side with good up-to-date seasonal food; faint piped music; by cathedral, with sheltered terrace, partly covered and heated, charming bedrooms, open all day. *Recommended by Alastair and Rebecca Lockwood, Glenwys and Alan Lawrence, David and Judy Robison, Richard Mason*

WINCHESTER SU4829   SO23 9EX
William Walker
The Square

Pleasantly refurbished rambling corner pub in Cathedral Close, decent range of food from sandwiches and baguettes up, Ringwood BB and Sharps Doom Bar, quick friendly service. *Recommended by Phil and Jane Villiers, Val and Alan Green, Dave Braisted*

WINCHESTER SU4829   SO23 8QX
☆ **Willow Tree**
Durngate Terrace; no adjacent weekday daytime parking, but Durngate car park is around corner in North Walls; a mile from M3 junction 9, by Easton Lane into city

Warmly welcoming and snug, landlord/chef using much local produce for often unusual and enjoyable food (gives cookery lessons, too), big perhaps even over-generous helpings, cheerful efficient young staff, well kept Greene King beers, good wines; long pleasant riverside garden. *Recommended by Ann and Colin Hunt, Geoff and Linda Payne*

WOODLANDS SU3211   SO40 7GH
Gamekeeper
Woodlands Road, just N of A336 Totton—Cadnam

Unspoilt traditional village local by New Forest, friendly landlord, reasonably priced food and beers including Wadworths 6X and one brewed for the pub, good coffee, dining room with conservatory; terrace tables. *Recommended by Phil and Jane Villiers*

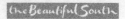

ALSO WORTH A VISIT ON THE ISLE OF WIGHT

Besides the region's top pubs, we recommend the following. Do tell us
what you think of them: **feedback@goodguides.com**

BEMBRIDGE SZ6488   PO35 5NN
Pilot Boat
Station Road/Kings Road

Small harbourside pub reworked in style of a ship, good food from sandwiches to local
seafood, decent choice of ales; tables out overlooking water or in pleasant courtyard
behind, well placed for coast walks, open all day. *Recommended by William Goodhart, George and
Linda Ozols*

BINSTEAD SZ5792   PO33 3RD
Fleming Arms

Welcoming with wide choice of good reasonably priced food, Ringwood Best and Flowers,
attentive service; children and dogs welcome, garden. *Recommended by Keith Widdowson,
Paul Baines*

BONCHURCH SZ5778   PO38 1NU
☆ Bonchurch Inn
*Bonchurch Shute; from A3055 E of Ventnor turn down to Old Bonchurch; opposite
Leconfield Hotel*

Quirky former stables with restaurant, owned by Italians, fairly basic family room and
congenial bar with narrow-planked ship's decking and old-fashioned steamer-style seats,
Courage ales tapped from the cask, bar food and good italian dishes, charming helpful
staff, darts, shove-ha'penny and other games; piped music; dogs welcome, delightful
continental-feeling central courtyard (parking here can be tricky), holiday flat.
*Recommended by J L and J A Johnston, Geoff and Linda Payne, George and Linda Ozols, Guy Vowles,
Mr and Mrs P D Titcomb, Mark Seymour, Jackie Roberts and others*

CARISBROOKE SZ4687   PO30 5SS
☆ Blacksmiths Arms
B3401 1.5 miles W

Quiet hillside pub with friendly landlord and staff, Fullers, Shepherd Neame and Yates,
decent wines and cider, food can be good including fresh fish, scrubbed tables in neat
beamed and flagstoned front bars, superb Solent views from airy bare-boards family
dining extension; dogs and walkers welcome, terrace tables and smallish back garden
with same view, play area, open all day. *Recommended by Penny and Peter Keevil, Peter Meister*

COWES SZ5092   PO32 6NB
☆ Folly
Folly Lane signed off A3021 just S of Whippingham

Glorious Medina estuary views from bar and waterside terrace of this cheery laid-back
place, timbered ship-like interior with simple wood furnishings, wide range of sensibly
priced hearty food from breakfast on, Greene King Old Speckled Hen, Goddards and
possibly a guest; piped and live music, TV, games machine and pool – can get very lively
at weekends; children and dogs welcome, showers, long-term parking and weather
forecasts for sailors, water taxi, open all day. *Recommended by Quentin and Carol Williamson,
George Atkinson, Simon Collett-Jones, Bruce and Sharon Eden, George and Linda Ozols, Terry and
Nickie Williams and others*

We checked prices with the pubs as we went to press in summer 2011.
They should hold until around spring 2012.

FRESHWATER SZ3485   PO40 9QX
Sandpipers
Coastguard Lane

Victorian hotel's refurbished bar, well kept ales such as Courage Best, Fullers ESB, Island Yachtsman's and Red Rat Crazy Dog Stout, enjoyable reasonably priced bar food, comfortable lounge areas with sofas, games room, dining conservatory, weekend music; children welcome, tables outside, bedrooms (some with sea views). *Recommended by Joan and Michel Hooper-Immins*

GODSHILL SZ5281   PO38 3HZ
☆ ## Taverners
High Street

Welcoming 17th-c pub with landlord/chef doing good seasonal food with emphasis on fresh local produce, children's menu and Sun roasts too, very popular at weekends when booking advised, well kept Fullers London Pride, a house beer from Yates and a guest, good friendly service, spacious bar and two front dining areas, beams, bare boards and slate floors, woodburner; dogs welcome, garden with terrace and play area, own shop, limited parking, open all day, closed Sun evening except bank/school summer holidays. *Recommended by C and R Bromage, George Atkinson, George and Linda Ozols, Alan Clark, Andy Hogben, the Farmers*

HULVERSTONE SZ3984   PO30 4EH
☆ ## Sun
B3399

Picture-book thatched country pub in charming peaceful setting with terrific views over the Channel, low-ceilinged bar with ales such as Adnams, Goddards, Ringwood and Timothy Taylors, nice mix of old furniture on flagstones and floorboards, brick and stone walls, horsebrasses and ironwork around fireplace, large windows in traditionally decorated newer dining area, all-day pubby food including local meat, darts and board games; piped music – live music Sat evening; children welcome away from bar area, dogs in bar, secluded split-level cottagey garden, open all day. *Recommended by Stuart Paulley, Simon Watkins, Paul Humphreys, Peter Meister, Geraldine and James Fradgley and others*

NEWCHURCH SZ5685   PO36 0NN
☆ ## Pointer
High Street

Popular two-room pub under newish management, generous good value food using local produce including good deli boards, well kept Fullers and a guest ale, friendly service; children and dogs welcome, pleasant back garden, boules. *Recommended by Guy Vowles*

NINGWOOD SZ3989   PO30 4NW
☆ ## Horse & Groom
A3054 Newport—Yarmouth, a mile W of Shalfleet

Possibly changing hands but has been roomy friendly pub liked by families; thoughtfully laid-out interior with comfortable leather sofas grouped around low tables, nice mix of sturdy tables and chairs, pale pink walls and old flagstones, Greene King, Goddards and Ringwood, good value standard bar food; piped music, games machine; ample tables in garden with terrific play area – bouncy castle, crazy golf, tyre trails and more. *Recommended by anon*

NITON SZ5075   PO38 2NE
☆ ## Buddle
St Catherine's Road, Undercliff; off A3055 just S of village, towards St Catherine's Point

Old smugglers haunt with views from clifftop sloping lawn and stone terraces, handy for coast path, charmingly timeless heavily black-beamed bar with massive oak mantelbeam over broad stone fireplace, captain's chairs and solid wood tables on big flagstones, pewter mugs, six real ales including local brews, tasty imaginative food, bar billiards and

darts; piped music; children in Old Barn, dogs welcome, open all day. *Recommended by David Glynne-Jones, J L and J A Johnston, Geoff and Linda Payne, Bruce and Sharon Eden, George and Linda Ozols*

NORTHWOOD SZ4983   PO31 8LS
Travellers Joy
Off B3325 S of Cowes

Friendly real-ale pub with eight well kept beers including local ones (tasters offered), enjoyable reasonably priced pubby food from sandwiches up, long bar with over 200 pump clips on the walls, conservatory, old pinball machine in games room, Sun quiz; piped radio; children and dogs welcome, garden with pétanque and play area, open all day Fri, Sat. *Recommended by Joan and Michel Hooper-Immins*

SEAVIEW SZ6291   PO34 5EX
☆ Seaview Hotel
High Street; off B3330 Ryde—Bembridge

Small gently civilised but relaxed hotel, traditional wood furnishings, seafaring paraphernalia and log fire in pubby bare-boards bar, comfortable more refined front bar with good soft furnishings, Goddards, Yates and a guest, good wine list including some local ones, well presented generous pub food and more elaborate restaurant menu using produce from their farm; they may ask for a credit card if you run a tab, piped music, TV; children welcome, dogs in bar, sea glimpses from tables on tiny front terrace, nice bedrooms (some with sea views), open all day. *Recommended by Thomas Moore, David Glynne-Jones, George Atkinson, Paul Humphreys, Mr and Mrs P D Titcomb, Karen Eliot and others*

VENTNOR SZ5677   PO38 1JX
☆ Spyglass
Esplanade, SW end; road down is very steep and twisty, and parking nearby can be difficult – best to use the pay-and-display (free in winter) about 100 yards up the road

Perched above the beach with a fascinating jumble of seafaring bric-a-brac in snug quarry-tiled interior, well kept Ringwood and a couple of guests, generously served food including good crab sandwiches, friendly helpful staff; piped music – live most evenings and Sun lunchtime, can get very busy; children welcome, dogs in bar, terrace tables with lovely sea views, coast walk towards Botanic Garden, heftier hikes on to St Boniface Down and towards the eerie shell of Appuldurcombe House, bedrooms, open all day. *Recommended by Penny and Peter Keevil, Dennis and Doreen Haward, George Atkinson, Tony and Maggie Harwood*

WHITWELL SZ5277   PO38 2PY
☆ White Horse
High Street

Popular sympathetically restored old thatched pub, extensive range of good value generous food from pub staples to more innovative dishes and good Sun roasts, several well kept ales including Goddards, good friendly service, large cheery high-ceilinged family dining area with small beamed bar and second area off; may be piped music; picnic-sets in big garden. *Recommended by Terry and Nickie Williams*

If a pub tries to make you leave a credit card behind the bar, be on your guard. The credit card firms and banks that issue them condemn this practice. After all, the publican who asks you to do this is in effect saying: 'I don't trust you'. Have you any more reason to trust his staff? If your card is used fraudulently while you have let it be kept out of your sight, the card company could say you've been negligent yourself – and refuse to make good your losses. So say that they can 'swipe' your card instead, but must hand it back to you. Please let us know if a pub does try to keep your card.

ALSO WORTH A VISIT IN KENT

Besides the region's top pubs, we recommend the following. Do tell us
what you think of them: **feedback@goodguides.com**

ADDINGTON TQ6559   ME19 5BB
Angel
Just off M20 junction 4; Addington Green

14th-c pub in classic village-green setting, olde-worlde décor with beams, scrubbed tables
and big fireplaces, enjoyable food from sandwiches/wraps and traditional things up
including weekday set menus, fair choice of beers from barrel-fronted counter, lots of
wines by the glass, good friendly service, stables restaurant, live music (Weds, Fri); tables
out at front and back, two bedrooms. *Recommended by A N Bance, Gill and Keith Croxton*

APPLEDORE TQ9529   TN26 2BU
Black Lion
The Street

Compact 1930s village pub with bustling atmosphere, very welcoming helpful staff, good
generous food all day from simple sandwiches to imaginative dishes, lamb from Romney
Marsh and local fish, three or four well kept changing ales, Biddenden farm cider, log
fire, partitioned back eating area; piped music; tables out on green, attractive village,
good Military Canal walks. *Recommended by Colin and Louise English, Peter Meister*

APPLEDORE TQ9729   TN26 2DF
Railway Hotel
Station Road (B2080 E)

Friendly refurbished red-brick Victorian hotel with rail memorabilia and open fire in big
bar, Shepherd Neame master brew and a guest, daily papers, bar billiards, darts and
other pub games, interesting food using local and organic ingredients in separate
restaurant (closed Mon, Tues); dogs welcome, garden tables, seven bedrooms, open all
day. *Recommended by Peter and Jean Hoare*

BEARSTED TQ8055   ME14 4EJ
Oak on the Green
The Street

Two hop-festooned bar areas with bare boards and half-panelling, bustling and friendly,
with wide choice of home-made food all day including children's menu, well kept regularly
changing ales, restaurant; disabled access, seats out at front under big umbrellas.
Recommended by Michael Tack

BEKESBOURNE TR1856   CT4 5ED
☆ ## Unicorn
Bekesbourne Hill, off Station Road; village E of Canterbury

Small, friendly pub with just a few scrubbed old pine tables on worn floorboards in simply
furnished bars, ales such as Ramsgate Gadds No. 5, Shepherd Neame Early Bird and
Westerham Grasshopper, Biddenden cider, traditional food (not Sun evening, limited
Mon); piped music, live folk music/acoustic on Sun; children welcome and dogs (not
during food times), prettily planted side terrace, garden with bat and trap, large back car
park reached from small track at end of adjacent terrace of cottages, open all day
weekends, closed Mon in winter. *Recommended by anon*

BENENDEN TQ8032   TN17 4DE
☆ ## Bull
The Street; by village green

Relaxed informal atmosphere in bare-boards or dark terracotta tiled rooms, pleasing mix
of furniture, church candles on tables, hops, fire in brick inglenook, friendly hands-on

licensees, Dark Star Hophead, Harveys Best, Larkins Traditional and a guest from carved wooden counter, local cider too, smarter dining room with burgundy brocade dining chairs, enjoyable home-made food (not Sun evening) including OAP menu and popular Sun roasts, live music most Sun afternoons; piped jazz, unobtrusive TV; children welcome, dogs in bar, picnic sets by road, open all day except Mon lunchtime. *Recommended by Conor McGaughey, Kevin Thomas, Nina Randall*

BIRLING TQ6860   ME19 5JW
Nevill Bull
Near M20 junction 4

Under welcoming newish licensees, generous well liked food, Kent Brewery ales, decent wines, friendly attentive service, cheery fires in beamed bar and dining room. *Recommended by John Mitchell*

BODSHAM TR1045   TN25 5JQ
☆ ## Timber Batts
Following Bodsham, Wye sign off B2068 keep right at unsigned fork after about 1.5 miles

Charming french owner in cottagey country pub, traditional carpeted bar with Adnams Bitter, Woodfordes Wherry and a guest, good french wines by the glass (some from Mr Gross's cousin's vineyard), informally rustic beamed dining area with happy mix of stripped-pine tables, pews, dark tables and dining chairs on carpet, delicious french food (not Sun evening, booking advised) cooked by landlord's son using local produce, three-course lunch menu, some pubby dishes too; children and dogs welcome (pub labrador called Bounty), lovely views over wide-spreading valley from back garden. *Recommended by Jill and Julian Tasker, John and Enid Morris, Derek Thomas, Peter Heaton, Justin and Emma King, Heather and Dick Martin and others*

BOXLEY TQ7758   ME14 3DR
Kings Arms
1.75 miles from M20 junction 7; opposite church

Cosy country dining pub under welcoming newish landlord, largely 16th/17th-c, low beams, red chesterfield by huge fireplace, well kept Greene King IPA, Harveys Best, Fullers London Pride, Gales HSB and guests, good choice of food (not Sun evening) from sandwiches and traditional things up; piped music, some live; children and dogs welcome, new furniture in appealing garden, pretty village, pleasant walks, open all day. *Recommended by Harry Ramsden*

BOYDEN GATE TR2265   CT3 4EB
☆ ## Gate Inn
Off A299 Herne Bay—Ramsgate – follow Chislet, Upstreet sign opposite Roman Gallery; Chislet also signed off A28 Canterbury—Margate at Upstreet – after turning right into Chislet main street keep right on to Boyden

The long-serving landlord at this delightfully unpretentious rustic pub has retired, but new licensee intends to keep things the same; comfortably worn traditional quarry-tiled rooms, flowery-cushioned pews around tables of considerable character, hop-hung beams, attractively etched windows, inglenook log fire, Shepherd Neame Master Brew, Spitfire and a couple of guests from tap room casks, interesting bottled beers, pubby food (now lunchtime and evening); children and dogs welcome, sheltered garden bounded by two streams with tame ducks and geese. *Recommended by Kevin Thorpe, N R White, Colin and Louise English*

BRABOURNE LEES TR0740   TN25 6QB
Plough
Lees Road

Welcoming beamed 18th-c village local (changed hands 2010), well kept Shepherd Neame, enjoyable home-made food including good Sun roasts, inglenook log fire, pool, board games, some live music; garden with bat & trap, nice country views, open all day. *Recommended by James Powell*

BRENCHLEY TQ6841   TN12 7AX
Halfway House
Horsmonden Road

Beamed 18th-c coaching inn with attractive olde-worlde mix of rustic and traditional furnishings on bare boards, old farm tools, two log fires, particularly friendly landlord and efficient staff, enjoyable home-made food including good fish and popular Sun roasts, good range of well kept changing ales tapped from the cask such as Goachers, two tranquil eating areas; children and dogs welcome, picnic-sets and play area in big garden, summer barbecues and beer festivals, bedrooms, open all day. *Recommended by Jamie and Sue May, N R White, Alan Franck, Peter Meister*

BROADSTAIRS TR3967   CT10 1AN
Royal Albion
Albion Street

Smartly refurbished 18th-c seafront hotel reputedly used by Dickens; Shepherd Neame ales, reasonably priced quickly served food from sandwiches up, pleasant conservatory-style area with modern wicker-backed dining chairs and lovely sea views, restaurant; stepped mediterranean-theme front terrace, 21 bedrooms, open all day from 8am. *Recommended by John Wooll*

BURMARSH TR1032   TN29 0JJ
Shepherd & Crook
Shear Way

Friendly two-bar traditional 16th-c marshside local with smuggling history, well kept Adnams and a guest beer, Biddenden cider, good straightforward home-made food at low prices, prompt service, interesting photographs and blow lamp collection, log fire; dogs welcome, open all day Fri-Sun. *Recommended by N R White*

CANTERBURY TR1458   CT1 2AA
Dolphin
St Radigund's Street

Modernised dining pub with enjoyable home-made pubby food from baguettes up, Sharps Doom Bar, Timothy Taylors Landlord and a couple of guests such as Gadds and Old Dairy, country wines, friendly staff, bric-a-brac on delft shelf, board games, flagstoned conservatory, pianist Sun evening, quiz night first Mon of month; no dogs; children welcome, disabled access, good-sized back garden with heaters, open all day. *Recommended by Rob and Catherine Dunster, John Baker*

CHIDDINGSTONE TQ5045   TN8 7AH
Castle Inn
Off B2027 Tonbridge—Edenbridge

Rambling old pub in pretty NT village, handsome beamed bar, settles and sturdy wall benches, attractive mullioned window seat, woodburners, brick-floor snug, Harveys Best and local Larkins including winter Porter (brewed in village), good choice of food with blackboard specials, friendly staff; children and dogs welcome, tables out in front and in nice secluded garden with own bar, circular walks from village, open all day. *Recommended by LM*

CHIDDINGSTONE CAUSEWAY TQ5146   TN11 8JJ
Little Brown Jug
B2027

Open-plan Whiting & Hammond pub next to Penshurst station, comfortable bar and big dining extension, enjoyable food at sensible prices from sandwiches and deli plates to full meals, well kept Greene King ales, good wine list, friendly efficient service, log fires; attractive garden with play area, beer and music festivals, open all day weekends. *Recommended by Gerry and Rosemary Dobson, Christian Mole*

☆ **White Horse**
CHILHAM TR0653   CT4 8BY
The Square

Popular 15th-c pub in picturesque village square, fresh modern décor, handsomely carved ceiling beams and massive fireplace with Lancastrian rose carved on mantelbeam, chunky light oak furniture on pale wooden flooring and more traditional pubby furniture on quarry tiles, bright paintings, horsebrasses and a couple of stained-glass panels, well kept changing ales, good popular freshly cooked food (not Sun evening) using local organic produce, home-made cakes and coffee all day; piped music and TV; children welcome, dogs in bar, handy for the castle, open all day. *Recommended by I A and D J Mullins*

Woolpack
CHILHAM TR0753   CT4 8DL
Off A28/A252; The Street

Friendly old inn dating from 15th c, traditional beamed bar with pews and good inglenook, well kept Shepherd Neame ales, enjoyable food including weekday set menu, bay-windowed red-carpeted restaurant; children welcome, courtyard tables, delightful village, 14 bedrooms, open all day. *Recommended by John Baker, I A and D J Mullins*

☆ **Griffins Head**
CHILLENDEN TR2653   CT3 1PS
SE end of village; 2 miles E of Aylesham

Attractive beamed, timbered and flagstoned 14th-c pub with two bar rooms and back flagstoned dining room, gently upscale local atmosphere, big log fire, full range of Shepherd Neame ales, good choice of enjoyable home-made food, good wine list, friendly attentive service; dogs welcome in some parts, pleasant garden surrounded by wild roses, Sun barbecues, attractive countryside. *Recommended by Philip and Cheryl Hill, Stephen Burke*

Bricklayers Arms
CHIPSTEAD TQ4956   TN13 2RZ
Chevening Road

Attractive pub overlooking lake and green, popular good value food (not Sun evening) served by cheerful helpful staff, full range of Harveys beers kept well and tapped from casks behind long counter, relaxed chatty atmosphere, heavily beamed bar with open fire and fine racehorse painting, unpretentious larger back restaurant; seats out front. *Recommended by Alan Cowell, N R White*

☆ **George & Dragon**
CHIPSTEAD TQ5056   TN13 2RW
Near M25 junction 5

Attractive country dining pub under same owners as the George and Dragon at Speldhurst; heavy black beams and standing timbers, grey-green panelling, old tables and chapel chairs on bare boards, log fires, good changing food all day using organic local produce, Westerham ales including Georges Marvellous Medicine brewed for the pub, good choice of wines by the glass, good service, upstairs restaurant; piped music; children and dogs welcome, terrace and garden with veg/herbs, play area, open all day. *Recommended by Sophie Broster, Derek Thomas, John Evans*

Fountain
COWDEN TQ4640   TN8 7JG
Off A264 and B2026; High Street

Good sensibly priced blackboard food in attractive tile-hung beamed village pub, steep steps up to unpretentious dark-panelled corner bar, well kept Harveys, decent wines, old photographs on cream walls, good log fire, mix of tables in adjoining room, woodburner in small back dining room with one big table; piped music; walkers and dogs welcome, picnic-sets on small terrace and lawn, pretty village. *Recommended by LM, Gwyn Jones, R and S Bentley*

CROCKHAM HILL TQ4450   TN8 6RD
Royal Oak
Main Road

Cosy old village pub revamped by Westerham brewery, their ales kept well, popular good value home-made food, friendly helpful staff, mix of furniture including leather sofas on stripped-wood floor, original Tottering-by-Gently cartoons, old local photographs, quiz nights and live folk; dogs and walkers welcome, small garden, handy for Chartwell (NT), open all day Sat. *Recommended by Gwyn Jones, Stephen Bennett*

DEAL TR3751   CT14 7EQ
Berry
Canada Road

Small no frills local opposite old Royal Marine barracks, welcoming enthusiastic landlord, L-shaped carpeted bar, well kept Harveys Best and several changing microbrews (tasting notes on slates, beer festivals), farm cider and perry, no food, coal fire, newspapers, quiz and darts teams, pool, live music Thurs; small vine-covered terrace, open all day weekends, closed Tues-Thurs lunchtimes. *Recommended by Kevin Thorpe, Dr Kevan Tucker, N R White*

DEAL TR3753   CT14 6JZ
Ship
Middle Street

Dimly lit local in historic maritime quarter, five well kept changing ales including Ramsgate Gadds, friendly landlord, lots of dark woodwork, stripped brick and local ship and wreck pictures, piano and woodburner in side bar; dogs welcome, small pretty walled garden, open all day. *Recommended by N R White, Dr Kevan Tucker*

DENTON TR2147   CT4 6QZ
Jackdaw
A260 Canterbury—Folkestone

Imposing old brick-and-flint open-plan pub, welcoming service, enjoyable family food all day, half a dozen well kept ales, friendly young staff, RAF memorabilia in front area, large back restaurant; quiet piped music; children welcome, good-sized charming garden, picturesque village, open all day. *Recommended by Michael and Judy Buckley*

DUNKS GREEN TQ6152   TN11 9RU
☆ Kentish Rifleman
Dunks Green Road

Tudor pub restored in modern rustic style, welcoming helpful staff, well kept ales such as Harveys and Westerham, enjoyable reasonably priced food (not Sun evening), bar and two dining areas, rifles on low beams, cosy log fire; children and dogs welcome, tables in pretty garden with well, good walks, open all day weekends. *Recommended by Mark Sowery, Nigel and Jean Eames, Bob and Margaret Holder, Conor McGaughey, B and M Kendall and others*

DUNTON GREEN TQ5156   TN13 2DR
☆ Bullfinch
London Road, Riverhead

Huge spreading place with modern décor in linked rooms, pubbier part to left with contemporary built-in wall benches, dining chairs and wooden tables, bare-boards area with sofas and brick fireplace, dining rooms with two-way log fire in glass enclosure, upholidaystered banquettes and wide mix of tables and chairs, popular slightly upmarket traditional food, pleasant staff, well kept McMullens ales, good choice of wines, newspapers; TV, fruit machine; children welcome, attractive garden with heated terrace, open all day weekends. *Recommended by Revd R P Tickle, Derek Thomas*

It's very helpful if you let us know up-to-date food prices when you report on pubs.

FARNINGHAM TQ5467   DA4 0DT
Chequers
High Street/Dartford Road, just off A20

Traditional one-bar corner local with good choice of real ales including Fullers and Timothy Taylors Landlord, unpretentious lunchtime food (not Sun), friendly staff; benches outside, picturesque village. *Recommended by N R White*

FAVERSHAM TR0161   ME13 7BP
Anchor
Abbey Street

Friendly two-bar character pub, good reasonably priced food from baguettes up, well kept Shepherd Neame range, simple dimly lit bare-boards bar with log fire, ancient beams and dark panelling, frosted windows, boat pictures and models, small side room with pub games and books, restaurant; some live music; dogs welcome, tables in pretty enclosed garden with bat and trap, attractive 17th-c street near historic quay, open all day.
Recommended by Quentin and Carol Williamson, the Didler, Nick Lawless

FAVERSHAM TR0161   ME13 7BH
Phoenix
Abbey Street

Historic town pub with heavy low beams and stripped stone, well kept beers such as Greene King, Harveys and Wells & Youngs, good choice of food (all day Fri and Sat, not Sun evening) from snacks up, afternoon teas, good friendly service, leather chesterfields by open fire, restaurant, various events including live music and poetry reading; some pavement tables, open all day. *Recommended by LM*

FAVERSHAM TR0161   ME13 7JE
Sun
West Street

Rambling old-world 15th-c pub in pedestrianised street, good unpretentious atmosphere with small low-ceilinged partly panelled rooms, big inglenook, well kept Shepherd Neame beers from nearby brewery, enjoyable bar food including OAP deals, smart restaurant attached, friendly efficient staff; unobtrusive piped music; wheelchair access possible (small step), pleasant back courtyard, eight bedrooms, open all day. *Recommended by the Didler, LM, Neil Hardwick*

FRITTENDEN TQ8141   TN17 2EJ
Bell & Jorrocks
Corner of Biddenden Road/The Street

Welcoming simple 18th-c tile-hung and beamed local includingorporating village post office, well kept Adnams, Harveys, Woodfords and guests, Weston's and Thatcher's ciders, good traditional home-made food (not Sun evening, lunchtimes Mon, Tues), open fire with propeller from crashed plane above, kentish darts; sports TV; children welcome, open all day. *Recommended by N R White, Donald Bremner*

GOODNESTONE TR2554   CT3 1PJ
Fitzwalter Arms
The Street; NB this is in East Kent NOT the other Goodnestone

Old dimly lit beamed village local with two little rustic bars, Shepherd Neame ales, good locally sourced food including seasonal game, friendly chatty service, small dining room, log fires; lovely church next door. *Recommended by N R White, Dr Kevan Tucker*

GOODHURST TQ7037   TN17 1HA
☆ ## Green Cross
Station Road (A262 W)

Good generous food with emphasis on fish and seafood, friendly helpful service, well kept Harveys Best, good wines and own sloe gin, two-room dark-wood bar with country prints and photographs, large stuffed fish above one fireplace, hop-strewn roomy back restaurant with stripped-wood floor and timbered walls, flowers on tables, paintings for sale, log fire; piped music; no dogs; terrace tables, light and airy good value bedrooms. *Recommended by David S Allen, Anthony Longden*

☆ **GROOMBRIDGE** TQ5337   TN3 9QH
Crown
B2110

Charming tile-hung wealden inn with snug low-beamed bar, old tables on worn flagstones, panelling, bric-a-brac, fire in sizeable brick inglenook, Harveys, Larkins and a guest, traditional food (not Sun evening), roughly plastered dining area with dark wood pubby tables; children welcome, dogs in bar, narrow old brick terrace overlooking steep green, bedrooms, open all day summer Fri-Sun, closed winter Sun evening. *Recommended by Ann and Colin Hunt, Mrs B Forster, Alan Franck*

HARBLEDOWN TR1358   CT2 9AB
Old Coach & Horses
Church Hill

Modern split-level two-room bistro/bar, airy yet cosy, with log fire in two-way fireplace, farmhouse chairs around pine tables, cabinet of toy vans and classic-car cigarette cards; more pubby part with curved cushioned pews, stone flagons and daily newspapers, interesting well liked food, upstairs restaurant with modern pine furniture, sitting room with black leather seating; garden picnic-sets, good views, parking on hill (no car park). *Recommended by Andy Towse*

☆ **HAWKHURST** TQ7531   TN18 5EJ
Great House
Gills Green; pub signed off A229 N

Busy stylish white-weatherboarded dining pub, popular food (not cheap, all day weekends), Harveys Best and a seasonal brew from marble counter, sofas, armchairs and bright scatter cushions in chatty bar, moving into dark wood dining tables and smartly upholidaystered chairs on slate floor, gilt-framed pictures on red or green walls, steps down to light airy dining room with big picture windows, colourful cushions on carved built-in shabby chic seating, plenty of modern art; piped music, TV; children welcome, dogs in bar, modern blue furniture on side terrace, open all day, closed Mon in Jan and Feb. *Recommended by Peter Veness*

HEADCORN TQ8344   TN27 9NL
George & Dragon
High Street

Good atmosphere and service, welcoming landlady, wide range of enjoyable home-made food, local ales and cider, extensive wine list, open fires, separate dining room. *Recommended by Bill Adie, Alec and Joan Laurence, Anna Smith*

HEAVERHAM TQ5758   TN15 6NP
Chequers
Watery Lane

Attractive 16th-c beamed pub with friendly locals' bar, decent food (not Sun evening or Mon), Shepherd Neame ales, dining room with inglenook, raftered barn restaurant with resident ghost; children welcome, big pretty garden, open all day, closed Mon. *Recommended by Gordon and Margaret Ormondroyd, Mark Waters*

HERNE BAY TR1768   CT6 5HT
Old Ship
Central Parade

Old white weatherboarded pub with window tables looking across road to sea, well kept beers including Bass, food (cheaper lunchtime menu) including Sun roasts; children welcome till 6pm, sea-view deck. *Recommended by John Wooll*

the Beautiful South

HEVER TQ4743   TN8 7LJ
Greyhound
Uckfield Lane

Well laid-out beamed bar with quiet corners, benches and chairs around scrubbed tables, friendly landlord and staff, reasonably priced bar food from sandwiches up, well kept ales such as Timothy Taylors Landlord, more formal restaurant; no dogs inside; tables on front decking and in garden behind, bedrooms, handy for Hever Castle. *Recommended by R and S Bentley*

HEVER TQ4744   TN8 7NH
Henry VIII
By gates of Hever Castle

Partly 14th-c pub, some fine oak panelling, wide floorboards and heavy beams, inglenook fireplace, Henry VIII décor, well kept Shepherd Neame ales, food from well filled baguettes up, small dining room, friendly efficient staff; no dogs even in garden; tables out on terrace and pondside lawn, bedrooms. *Recommended by Ann and Colin Hunt, LM*

HODSOLL STREET TQ6263   TN15 7LE
☆ # Green Man
Signed off A227 S of Meopham; turn right in village

Bustling village pub with neatly arranged traditional furnishings in big airy carpeted rooms, friendly atmosphere, Greene King Old Speckled Hen, Harveys Best, Timothy Taylors Landlord and a guest, well liked pubby food (all day Sun) including good baguettes and popular two-course weekday lunch; piped music – live music second Thurs of month, quiz Mon; children and dogs welcome, tables and climbing frame on well tended lawn, open all day Fri-Sun. *Recommended by Jeremy Hancock, Dr Jennifer Sansom, Gwyn Jones, Jan and Rod Poulter, D P and M A Miles, A N Bance and others*

HOLLINGBOURNE TQ8354   ME17 1TR
☆ # Windmill
M20 junction 8: A20 towards Ashford then left into B2163 – Eyhorne Street village

Old coaching inn with pleasant old-world feel and small pubby core but mainly set for dining, several smallish mostly carpeted areas with heavy low black beams, solid pub tables with padded country or library chairs, shelves of books, log fire in huge inglenook, Fullers London Pride, Harveys Best and Shepherd Neame Master Brew, traditional food (all day weekends) including good value two-course menu Mon-Thurs; piped music; children must remain seated in bar, dogs welcome, picnic-sets and play area in neatly kept sunny garden. *Recommended by Michael Doswell, Roger and Pauline Pearce, Charles and Pauline Stride, N R White*

IDE HILL TQ4851   TN14 6JN
Cock
Off B2042 SW of Sevenoaks

Pretty village-green local dating from the 15th c, chatty and friendly with long serving landlord, two dimly lit bars with steps between, Greene King ales, enjoyable traditional food including game (not Sun or Mon evenings, snacks Sun lunchtime), cosy in winter with good inglenook log fire; well behaved children and dogs welcome, picnic-sets out at front, handy for Chartwell (NT) and nearby walks. *Recommended by N R White, Heather and Dick Martin*

IDE HILL TQ4952   TN14 6BU
Woodman
Whitley Row, Goathurst Common; B2042 N

Large roadside pub with good choice of enjoyable food all day including dishes from South Africa (landlord's homeland), well kept beer, decent wine, young well trained staff; piped music and live jazz; nice garden, good walks. *Recommended by Tina and David Woods-Taylor*

IDEN GREEN TQ7437   TN17 2PB
Peacock
A262 E of Goudhurst

Tudor, with blazing inglenook log fire in low-beamed main bar, quarry tiles and old sepia photographs, well priced enjoyable pubby food (all day Sat, not Sun evening) from sandwiches up, very helpful service, well kept Shepherd Neame ales, pastel dining room with cork-studded walls, public bar; TV; well behaved dogs welcome, no muddy boots, good-sized garden, closed Sun evening. *Recommended by Conrad Freezer, Nigel and Jean Eames*

IDEN GREEN TQ8031   TN17 4HT
☆ Woodcock
Not the Iden Green near Goudhurst; village signed off A268 E of Hawkhurst and B2086 at W edge of Benenden; in village follow Standen Street sign, then fork left into Woodcock Lane

Informal friendly little local with a couple of big standing timbers supporting very low-ceilings, chatty regulars on high stools near corner counter, comfortable squashy sofa and low table by inglenook woodburner, concrete floor, brick walls hung with horsebrasses, Greene King Abbot, IPA, Morlands Original and XX Mild, well liked pubby food (not Sun evening), small panelled dining area with pine tables and chairs; children welcome, dogs in bar, back garden, open all day, closed Mon (except bank holidays). *Recommended by A and H Piper, Steve Coates, V Brogden, Gordon and Margaret Ormondroyd*

IGHTHAM TQ5956   TN15 9HH
☆ George & Dragon
A227

Stylishly refurbished ancient timbered pub, good reasonably priced food from generous snacks up (all day till 6.30pm, not Sun), plenty of friendly smartly dressed staff, well kept Shepherd Neame ales, decent wines, sofas among other furnishings in long sociable main bar, heavy-beamed end room, woodburner and open fires, restaurant; children and dogs welcome, back terrace, handy for Ightham Mote (NT), good walks, open all day.
Recommended by Bob and Margaret Holder, Gavin Markwick, Gordon and Margaret Ormondroyd

IVY HATCH TQ5854   TN15 0NL
☆ Plough
High Cross Road; village signed off A227 N of Tonbridge

Tile-hung 18th-c dining pub, light wood floors with mix of cushioned chairs around wooden tables, large plants, leather chesterfields by open fire, Harveys and a guest ale, local fruit juice, interesting if not cheap food (not Sun evening) using local produce including some home-grown, conservatory restaurant, may be own chutneys and eggs for sale; piped music; children welcome, seats in landscaped garden surrounded by cob trees, handy for Ightham Mote (NT), open all day Sat, closed winter Sun evening.
Recommended by Bob and Margaret Holder, Mr and Mrs J M Sennett, LM, Gordon and Margaret Ormondroyd and others

LITTLE CHART TQ9446   TN27 0QB
Swan
The Street

Comfortable and substantial 17th-c village local with lots of beams, open fires in simple unspoilt front bar and interesting smarter bar, good-sized dining area, enjoyable straightforward food, real ales and decent wines, friendly staff; dogs welcome, nice riverside garden. *Recommended by Richard Mason*

LOWER HARDRES TR1453   CT4 7AL
☆ Granville
Faussett Hill, Street End; B2068 S of Canterbury

Spacious airy interior with contemporary furnishings, unusual central fire with large conical hood and glimpses of kitchen, proper public bar with farmhouse chairs, settles and woodburner, deservedly popular food (not Sun evening, Mon – booking advised), fine choice of wines from blackboard, Shepherd Neame Master Brew and a seasonal beer, good service, daily papers; piped music; children and dogs welcome, french windows to garden with large spreading tree and small sunny terrace, open all day Sun. *Recommended by Barry and Patricia Wooding, Dr Kevan Tucker*

☆ **Cock**
LUDDESDOWN TQ6667   DA13 0XB

Henley Street, N of village – OS Sheet 177 map reference 664672; off A227 in Meopham, or A228 in Cuxton

Early 18th-c country pub, friendly long-serving no-nonsense landlord, at least six ales including Adnams, Goachers, Harveys and Shepherd Neame, sensibly priced all-day pubby food (not Sun evening) from wide choice of sandwiches up, rugs on polished boards in pleasant bay-windowed lounge bar, quarry-tiled locals' bar, woodburners, pews and other miscellaneous furnishings, aircraft pictures, masses of beer mats and bric-a-brac like stuffed animals, model cars and beer can collections, bar billiards and darts, back dining conservatory; no children in bar or part-covered heated back terrace; dogs welcome, big secure garden, good walks, open all day. *Recommended by A N Bance, N R White*

Cricketers
MEOPHAM TQ6364   DA13 0QA

Wrotham Road (A227)

Recently refurbished Whiting & Hammond pub (was the Long Hop) in nice spot overlooking cricket green, popular food, friendly staff; garden behind. *Recommended by Geoff Deaves, Christian Mole*

Farriers Arms
MERSHAM TR0438   TN25 6NU

The Forstal/Flood Street

Large community-run beamed pub owned by village and reopened in 2009 after refurbishment, good value fresh food, friendly staff, microbrewery, restaurant; streamside garden behind, pleasant country views. *Recommended by Simon Good*

☆ **George**
NEWNHAM TQ9557   ME9 0LL

The Street; village signed from A2 W of Ospringe, outside Faversham

Old-world village pub under new licensees, series of spreading open-plan rooms, hop-strung beams, stripped brickwork, polished floorboards, candles and lamps on handsome tables, two inglenooks one with woodburner, Shepherd Neame Master Brew and a seasonal beer, locally sourced food (not Sun evening) from lunchtime snacks up; piped and some live music, no dogs inside; children welcome, picnic-sets in spacious tree-sheltered garden, open all day Sun. *Recommended by anon*

Hare & Hounds
NORTHBOURNE TR3352   CT14 0LG

Off A256 or A258 near Dover; The Street

Chatty village pub with several well kept ales including Harveys, good choice of generous popular food (lamb from nearby farm), friendly efficient service, spacious modernised brick and wood interior, log fires; dogs welcome, terrace tables. *Recommended by N R White*

☆ **Shipwrights Arms**
OARE TR0163   ME13 7TU

S shore of Oare Creek, E of village; signed from Oare Road/Ham Road junction in Faversham

Remote and ancient marshland tavern with plenty of character, up to five kentish beers tapped from the cask (pewter tankards over counter), basic food (not Sun evening or Mon), three dark simple little bars separated by standing timbers, wood partitions and narrow door arches, medley of seats from tapestry-cushioned stools to black panelled built-in settles forming booths, flags or boating pennants on ceiling, wind gauge above main door (takes reading from chimney); piped local radio; children welcome away from bar area, dogs in bar, large garden, path along Oare Creek to Swale estuary, lots of surrounding bird life, closed Mon. *Recommended by Conor McGaughey, Colin McKerrow, Tony Brace, N R White, the Didler and others*

OARE TR0063   ME13 0QA
Three Mariners
Church Road

Comfortable simply restored old pub with good reputation for food including fresh fish, Tues-Fri lunch deals, Shepherd Neame ales, log fire; attractive garden overlooking Faversham Creek, open all day Sat, closed Sun evening, Mon (operates then as mid-morning post office). *Recommended by Warren Marsh, Alistair Jones, Ken and Lynda Taylor*

OLD ROMNEY TR0325   TN29 9SQ
Rose & Crown
A259 opposite church

Simple friendly village pub with good value standard food from sandwiches up, well kept Courage, Greene King, Rother Valley and guests, Biddenden cider, helpful staff, old local photographs, dining conservatory; TV; children welcome, pretty garden with boules, chalet bedrooms, open all day. *Recommended by Julia and Richard Tredgett, Colin McKerrow*

PENSHURST TQ5243   TN11 8BT
Leicester Arms
High Street

Country hotel feel with comfortable old bars and meadowland-view dining room up steps, well kept Fullers London Pride, Harveys and Greene King Old Speckled Hen, enjoyable food all day from bar and main menus, friendly polite service; lavatories down steps (disabled one in car park opposite); children and dogs welcome, pretty back garden, seven bedrooms. *Recommended by Peter Meister, Ann and Colin Hunt, Paul Rampton, Julie Harding*

PENSHURST TQ4943   TN8 7BS
☆ ## Rock
Hoath Corner, Chiddingstone Hoath, on back road Chiddingstone—Cowden; OS Sheet 188 map reference 497431

Tiny welcoming cottage with undulating brick floor, simple furnishings and woodburner in fine brick inglenook, well kept Larkins ales, enjoyable pub food from good sandwiches up, friendly young staff, large stuffed bull's head for ring the bull, up a step to smaller room with long wooden settle by nice table; dogs welcome (may be a biscuit), picnic-sets in front and on back lawn. *Recommended by Tina and David Woods-Taylor, LM, Grahame Brooks, Anthony Bradbury*

PENSHURST TQ5241   TN11 8EP
☆ ## Spotted Dog
Smarts Hill, off B2188 S

Quaint old weatherboarded pub under welcoming newish family, heavy low beams and timbers, attractive moulded panelling, rugs and tiles, antique settles, inglenook log fire, Harveys, Larkins and two guests, local cider, good mostly traditional food (all day weekends) including weekday lunch deals, smart staff; children and dogs welcome, tiered back terrace (they may ask to keep your credit card while you eat here), open all day. *Recommended by John Redfern, Andy Surman, Alan Franck, Heather and Dick Martin*

PETTERIDGE TQ6640   TN12 7NE
Hopbine
Petteridge Lane; NE of village

Small unspoilt cottage in quiet little hamlet, two small rooms with open fire between, traditional pubby furniture on red-patterned carpet, hops and horsebrasses, well kept Badger ales, enjoyable good value home-made food, friendly staff, steps up to simple back part with piano and darts, flagons in brick fireplace; seats in side garden. *Recommended by anon*

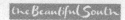

PLAXTOL TQ6054   TN15 0PT
☆ Golding Hop
Sheet Hill (0.5 miles S of Ightham, between A25 and A227)

Secluded traditional country local, simple dimly lit two-level bar with hands-on landlord
who can be very welcoming, cask-tapped Adnams, and guests kept well, local farm ciders
(sometimes their own), short choice of basic good value bar food (not Mon or Tues
evenings), old photographs of the pub, woodburners, bar billiards; portable TV for big
sports events; no children inside; suntrap streamside lawn and well fenced play area over
lane, good walks, open all day Sat. *Recommended by N R White, Bob and Margaret Holder,
Conor McGaughey, the Didler and others*

RYARSH TQ6759   ME19 5LS
Duke of Wellington
Birling Road; not far from M20 junction 4, via Leybourne and Birling

Appealing Tudor bar and bar/restaurant, good blackboard food including weekday deals,
several well kept real ales, live jazz Thurs evening; garden with pétanque. *Recommended by
David Jackman*

SANDWICH TR3358   CT13 9EF
Bell
Upper Strand Street

Comfortable nicely done Edwardian hotel opposite river, enjoyable bar food including
good value lunchtime set menu, well kept Greene King IPA, restaurant; children
welcome, seats outside, 34 bedrooms. *Recommended by MDN, John Wooll*

SEASALTER TR0864   CT5 4BP
☆ Sportsman
Faversham Road, off B2040

Restauranty dining pub just inside seawall and rather unprepossessing from outside; good
imaginative contemporary cooking with plenty of seafood (not Sun evening or Mon, must
book and not cheap), home-baked breads, good wine choice including english, well kept
Shepherd Neame ales, friendly staff; two plain linked rooms and long conservatory,
wooden floor, pine tables, wheelback and basket-weave dining chairs, big film star
photographs; plastic glasses for outside; children welcome, open all day Sun. *Recommended
by Colin McKerrow, Prof and Mrs J Fletcher, V Brogden, N R White*

SELLING TR0455   ME13 9RY
☆ Rose & Crown
Follow Perry Wood signs

Tucked-away 16th-c country pub, hops strung from beams, two inglenook log fires,
friendly service, well kept Adnams and Harveys, several ciders, generous food from
sandwiches up; piped music; children welcome, dogs on leads in bar, cottagey back
garden with play area, closed Sun evening. *Recommended by N R White, the Didler, Jenny Titford*

SELLING TR0356   ME13 9RQ
☆ White Lion
Off A251 S of Faversham (or exit roundabout, M2 junction 7); The Street

Comfortable 17th-c pub with well kept Shepherd Neame ales from unusual semicircular
bar counter, decent wines, friendly helpful staff, wide blackboard choice of good home-
made food, hop-hung main bar, paintings for sale, log fire with working spit, another fire
in small lower lounge with comfortable sofas, back restaurant; quiz nights; children
welcome, tables out at front and in attractive garden, colourful hanging baskets.
Recommended by Mike Trainer, John Roots, Peter Meister

All *Guide* inspections are anonymous. Anyone claiming to be a *Good Pub Guide*
inspector is a fraud. Please let us know.

SHIPBOURNE TQ5952   TN11 9PE

☆ **Chaser**

Stumble Hill (A227 N of Tonbridge)

Comfortably opened-up with civilised linked rooms converging on large central island, stripped-wood floors, frame-to-frame pictures on deep red and cream walls, pine wainscoting, candles on mix of old solid wood tables, shelves of books, open fires, Greene King ales, good wine and malt whisky choice, good popular food all day (breakfast Thurs, Sat and Sun), dark panelling and high timber-vaulted ceiling in striking chapel-like restaurant; piped music; children welcome, dogs in bar, courtyard and small side garden, Thurs morning farmers' market, open all day. *Recommended by Christian Mole, Tony Brace, Tina and David Woods-Taylor, N R White, David and Sally Cullen and others*

SHOREHAM TQ5162   TN14 7TJ

Crown

High Street

Friendly old-fashioned three-bar village pub, good value food including enjoyable Sun roasts, well kept ales such as Greene King and Westerham, open fires; walkers and dogs welcome. *Recommended by Chris and Carol Kendall*

SHOREHAM TQ5161   TN14 7SJ

Kings Arms

Church Street

Cosy old place serving good honest food and well kept beers, friendly staff, plates and brasses, restaurant; picnic-sets outside, quaint unspoilt village on River Darent, good walks. *Recommended by Richard Mason*

SHOREHAM TQ5261   TN14 7RY

Olde George

Church Street

Refurbished 16th-c pub with low beams, uneven floors and a cosy fire, friendly staff, changing real ales, dining area; children and dogs welcome, picnic sets by road with view of church, picturesque village. *Recommended by N R White*

SHOREHAM TQ5161   TN14 7TD

Two Brewers

High Street

Two softly lit smartly refurbished beamed bars, main emphasis on the popular food but drinkers welcome too, real ales including Adnams, friendly helpful staff; open all day Sun, closed Mon. *Recommended by N R White*

SNARGATE TQ9928   TN29 9UQ

☆ **Red Lion**

B2080 Appledore—Brenzett

Little changed since 1890 and in the same family for over 100 years, simple old-fashioned charm in three timeless little rooms with original cream wall panelling, heavy beams in sagging ceilings, dark pine Victorian farmhouse chairs on bare boards, an old piano stacked with books, coal fire, local cider and four or five ales including Goachers tapped from casks behind unusual free-standing marble-topped counter, no food, traditional games like toad in the hole, nine men's morris and table skittles; children in family room, dogs in bar, outdoor lavatories, cottage garden. *Recommended by Andrea Rampley, Tim Maddison, the Didler, Phil and Sally Gorton, B and M Kendall and others*

SPELDHURST TQ5541   TN3 0NN

☆ **George & Dragon**

Village signed from A264 W of Tunbridge Wells

Fine half-timbered building based around medieval manorial hall, main half-panelled bar to right has log fire in huge sandstone fireplace, heavy beams, wheelbacks and other dining chairs around tables on flagstones, horsebrasses, Harveys, Larkins and Westerham ales, several wines by the glass, second similarly furnished dining room with another inglenook, room to left of entrance hall used more for drinking with woodburner, high-winged settles and other seats, enjoyable if not cheap food (not Sun evening), upstairs restaurant; children welcome, dogs in bar, seats in front on nicely planted gravel terrace, more in back covered area and lower terrace (300-year-old yew tree and modern sculpturing), open all day. *Recommended by Simon and Helen Barnes, Derek Thomas, John Redfern, Christian Mole*

STAPLEHURST TQ7846   TN12 0DE
☆ **Lord Raglan**
About 1.5 miles from town centre towards Maidstone, turn right off A229 into Chart Hill Road opposite Chart Cars; OS Sheet 188 map reference 785472

Well run country pub, cosy chatty area around narrow bar counter, hop-covered low beams, big winter log fire, mixed comfortably worn dark wood furniture, enjoyable food from sandwiches up, Goachers, Harveys and a guest, farm cider and perry, good wine list; children and dogs welcome, reasonable wheelchair access, high-hedged terrace, picnic-sets in side orchard, closed Sun. *Recommended by Joan and Alec Lawrence, Malcolm and Barbara Southwell*

STODMARSH TR2160   CT3 4BA
☆ **Red Lion**
High Street; off A257 just E of Canterbury

Cheerfully quirky country pub with chatty landlord, all manner of bric-a-brac from life-size Tintin and Snowy to a tiger's head in hop-hung rooms, one wall covered in sheet music, empty wine bottles everywhere, green-painted, cushioned mate's chairs around nice pine tables, candles, big log fire, good interesting food using prime local meat and seasonal produce, Greene King IPA and Harveys Best tapped from casks, nice wine, good summer Pimms and winter mulled wine/cider, dining conservatory; piped jazz; children welcome, dogs in bar, pretty garden with roaming chickens and ducks, bat and trap, handy for Stodmarsh National Nature Reserve, bedrooms (not ensuite). *Recommended by Tony and Jill Radnor, N R White, Andy Towse, Mr D Matharu and others*

STONE IN OXNEY TQ9327   TN30 7JN
☆ **Crown**
Off B2082 Iden—Tenterden

Smart country pub with friendly landlord and staff, well kept Shepherd Neame and a guest like Larkins tapped from the cask, very good food from landlady/chef including some imaginative cooking, also wood-fired pizzas (takeaways available), light airy open feel with lots of wood, red walls, and big inglenook log fire; no under-12s after 7.30pm, rustic furniture on terrace, two bedrooms. *Recommended by Peter Meister*

STONE IN OXNEY TQ9428   TN30 7JY
☆ **Ferry**
Appledore Road; N of Stone-cum-Ebony

Attractive 17th-c smugglers' haunt, consistently good popular food including local fish (Rye scallops), welcoming landlord and friendly efficient staff, changing guest ales and a beer brewed for them by Westerham, small plain bar with woodburner and inglenook, bare boards, hops and old maps, steps up to pleasant dining area, games room; seats in garden and sunny front courtyard, lovely setting by marshes. *Recommended by Alec and Joan Laurence, Colin and Louise English, Peter Meister and others*

THURNHAM TQ8057   ME14 3LD
☆ **Black Horse**
Not far from M20 junction 7; off A249 at Detling

Large olde-worlde dining pub with enjoyable food all day, children's menu, well kept changing ales such as Sharps Doom Bar and Westerham Grasshopper, farm ciders and country wines, friendly efficient uniformed service, bare boards and log fires; dogs and walkers welcome, pleasant garden with partly covered back terrace, nice views, by Pilgrims Way, comfortable modern bedroom block, good breakfast. *Recommended by Brian and Anna Marsden, Alec and Joan Laurence*

☆ **TOYS HILL** TQ4752   TN16 1QG
Fox & Hounds
Off A25 in Brasted, via Brasted Chart and The Chart

Traditional country pub with plain tables and chairs on dark boards, leather sofa and easy chair by log fire, hunting prints, plates, old photographs, pewter mugs and copper jugs, modern carpeted dining extension with big windows overlooking tree-sheltered garden, enjoyable well presented home-made food (not Sun evening) including some interesting choices, well kept Greene King ales, several wines by the glass, traditional games, no mobile phones; piped music; children and dogs welcome, roadside verandah used by smokers, good local walks and views, handy for Chartwell and Emmetts Garden (both NT), open all day summer, closed Mon evening (and from 8pm Sun in winter). *Recommended by Tina and David Woods-Taylor, N R White, Cathryn and Richard Hicks, LM, C and R Bromage and others*

☆ **TUDELEY** TQ6145   TN11 0PH
Poacher
Hartlake Road

Smart modern bar and restaurant, light and airy, with wide range of good food including daily specials, ales such as Sharps, Shepherd Neame and one brewed for the pub by Kings, good choice of wines by the glass, friendly attentive staff, live music Thurs evening; terrace tables, near interesting church with Chagall stained glass. *Recommended by Nigel and Jean Eames, Peter Eyles, Kellie Williams*

TUNBRIDGE WELLS TQ5638   TN3 9JH
Beacon
Tea Garden Lane, Rusthall Common

Cheery and airy Victorian pub with Harveys Best, Larkins and Timothy Taylors Landlord, lots of wines by the glass, good coffee, fireside sofas, stripped panelling, bare boards and ornate wall units, linked dining areas; children welcome, decking tables with fine view, paths between lakes and springs, three bedrooms, open all day. *Recommended by Alan Franck*

TUNBRIDGE WELLS TQ5839   TN1 1RZ
Black Pig
Grove Hill Road

Refurbished pub under same ownership as George & Dragon at Speldhurst, good food (all day weekends) using local and organic supplies, home-baked bread, Harveys Best, interesting wine list, long narrow front bar, big leather sofas by woodburner, balustraded raised area, elegant mix of dining chairs, decorative fireplace, fresh flowers, Hogarth-style prints, olive-painted panelling, back dining room, open all day. *Recommended by Derek Thomas, Steve and Liz Tilley*

TUNBRIDGE WELLS TQ5837   TN2 5LH
Bull
Frant Road

Friendly refurbished local with two linked areas, neatly set dining part with well spaced pine tables and chunky chairs on stripped wood, similar bar area, corner black sofa, well kept Shepherd Neame ales, decent wine and food, daily papers; piped pop, TV, pool; dogs allowed. *Recommended by Tony Hobden, Steve Halsall, Imogen Cust*

TUNBRIDGE WELLS TQ5941   TN4 9BQ
High Brooms
High Brooms Road

Eccentric local crammed with bric-a-brac and home to the High Brooms Ukulele Group (alternate Mon nights). *Recommended by anon*

TUNBRIDGE WELLS TQ5839   TN1 2BJ
Last Post
Goods Station Road

Former Dog & Duck, reopened late 2010 under new licensees, aiming for relaxed atmosphere in wine-bar environment; no under-30s. *Recommended by anon*

TUNBRIDGE WELLS TQ5739   TN4 8BX
Mount Edgcumbe Hotel
The Common

Nicely updated tile-hung and weatherboarded 18th-c hotel, well kept Harveys Best, Weston's cider, bar and brasserie food including good steaks, unusual grotto-like snug cut into rock, live music Sun evening; children and dogs welcome, tables out under big heated umbrellas, pleasant setting with Common views, barbecues, five refurbished bedrooms, open all day. *Recommended by Tilly Hunt*

☆ **WINGHAM** TR2457   CT3 1BB
Dog
Canterbury Road

Pub/restaurant in Grade II* listed medieval building, log fires, uneven walls, heavy beams, old brickwork and panelling, leather sofas and armchairs on wood floors, conservatory restaurant, enjoyable food including good value set lunch, well kept Courage, Ramsgate and Shepherd Neame, good wines by the glass. *Recommended by Gavin Markwick, Julie and Bill Ryan*

☆ **WORTH** TR3356   CT14 0DF
St Crispin
Signed off A258 S of Sandwich

Dating from 16th c with low beams, stripped brickwork and bare boards, welcoming landlady and friendly attentive staff, popular generous home-made food from good baguettes to some imaginative dishes in bar, restaurant and back conservatory, three changing real ales, belgian beers, local farm cider, well chosen wines, central log fire; good bedrooms (including motel-style extension), charming big garden behind with terrace and barbecue, lovely village position. *Recommended by Dr Kevan Tucker*

WROTHAM TQ6258   TN15 7RR
Moat
London Road

Well refurbished Badger family dining pub in Tudor-style building, flagstones, beams and stripped masonry, wide range of good value food, their usual ales kept well, friendly efficient staff; garden tables, great playground, open all day. *Recommended by Gordon and Margaret Ormondroyd, Christian Mole*

☆ **YALDING** TQ6950   ME18 6JB
Walnut Tree
B2010 SW of Maidstone

Timbered village pub with split-level main bar, fine old settles, a long cushioned mahogany bench and mix of dining chairs on brick or worn carpeted floors, chunky wooden tables with church candles, interesting old photographs on mustard walls, hops, big inglenook, Harveys Best, Sharps Doom Bar and Wychwood Hobgoblin, good bar food and more inventive restaurant menu, attractive raftered dining room with high-backed leather dining chairs on parquet flooring, lots of local events (pumpkin carving and guess the weight on our visit); piped and occasional live music, TV; a few picnic-sets out at front by road, bedrooms. *Recommended by Steve and Claire Harvey*

Though we don't usually mention it in the text, most pubs now provide
coffee or tea – so it's always worth asking.

ALSO WORTH A VISIT IN OXFORDSHIRE

Besides the region's top pubs, we recommend the following. Do tell us
what you think of them: **feedback@goodguides.com**

ADDERBURY SP4735   OX17 3NG
☆ Red Lion
The Green; off A4260 S of Banbury

Attractive and congenial 17th-c coaching inn, good choice of enjoyable well priced food
(all day weekends), helpful friendly staff, Greene King ales and a guest, good wine range
and coffee, three linked bar rooms, big inglenook log fire, panelling, high stripped beams
and stonework, old books and Victorian/Edwardian pictures, daily papers, games area on
left; piped music; children in eating area, picnic-sets out on roadside terrace,
12 character bedrooms, good breakfast, open all day summer. *Recommended by Ian Herdman,
George Atkinson*

ALVESCOT SP2704   OX18 2PU
☆ Plough
B4020 Carterton—Clanfield, SW of Witney

Comfortable neatly kept bar with aircraft prints and cottagey pictures, china ornaments,
big antique case of birds of prey and sundry bric-a-brac, woodburner, Wadworths ales and
Weston's cider, straightforward food including good ploughman's, prompt service, proper
public bar with TV and darts, skittle alley, pub cats; piped music; children welcome,
picnic sets on back terrace (nice hanging baskets), aunt sally and children's play area in
garden (and perhaps ornamental pheasants and japanese quail), open all day.
Recommended by Tina and David Woods-Taylor, KN-R, R K Phillips, Guy Vowles

ASHBURY SU2685   SN6 8NA
Rose & Crown
B4507/B4000; High Street

Roomy open-plan beamed bistro bar, good choice of enjoyable food from pub favourites
up, well kept Arkells 2B and 3B, good range of wines by the glass, polished woodwork,
traditional pictures, chesterfields and pews, raised section with further oak tables and
chairs, games area with pool and darts, separate roomy restaurant; children welcome,
disabled facilities, tables out in front and behind, lovely view down pretty village street
of thatched cottages, handy for Ridgeway walks, bedrooms. *Recommended by Neil and
Karen Dignan*

ASTON TIRROLD SU5586   OX11 9EN
☆ Sweet Olive
aka Chequers; Fullers Road; village signed off A417 Streatley—Wantage

Has atmosphere of rustic french restaurant rather than village pub; main room with wall
settles, mate's chairs, a few sturdy tables, grass matting over quarry tiles, small fireplace,
good well liked food, nice french wines by the glass (wine box ends decorate the back of
the servery), Brakspears and Fullers beers, smaller room more formally set as restaurant
with restrained décor; piped music; children welcome, dogs in bar, picnic-sets under
parasols in small cottagey garden, aunt sally, closed Sun evening, Weds, all Feb and two
weeks in July. *Recommended by Neil and Karen Dignan, Dave Snowden*

BANBURY SP4540   OX16 5NA
☆ Olde Reindeer
Parsons Street, off Market Place

Interesting town pub always full of regulars and shoppers, welcoming front bar with
16th-c beams, broad polished oak boards, traditional solid furnishing and magnificent
carved overmantel for one of the two roaring log fires, Hook Norton ales and guests,
country wines, winter mulled wine, straightforward reasonably priced lunchtime food

including OAP weekday deals, worth looking at the handsomely proportioned Globe Room (used by Cromwell during the Civil War) with its fine 17th-c carved oak panelling, restaurant; children allowed in one area, dogs welcome in bar, seats under parasols in small back courtyard with aunt sally and pretty flowering baskets, open all day, closed Sun. *Recommended by Mick and Cathy Couchman, the Didler, Andy Lickfold, George Atkinson*

BECKLEY SP5611   OX3 9UU

☆ **Abingdon Arms**

Signed off B4027; High Street

Old dining pub in attractive unspoilt village, comfortably modernised simple lounge, smaller public bar with antique carved settles, open fires, well kept Brakspears and guests, fair range of wines, good choice of enjoyable home-made food including two-course deals (Mon–Thurs) and Sun roasts, good friendly service; piped and some live music; children and dogs welcome, big garden dropping away from floodlit terrace to trees, summer house, superb views over RSPB Otmoor reserve – good walks, open all day weekends. *Recommended by Canon Michael Bourdeaux, Colin McKerrow, Martin and Pauline Jennings, Melanie Court*

BLEWBURY SU5385   OX11 9PQ

Red Lion

Nottingham Fee – narrow turning N from A417

Attractive and popular downland village pub, enjoyable honest food, well kept Brakspears and a guest, good service, beams, tiled floor and big log fire, restaurant; children welcome, terrace tables in back garden, pretty surroundings. *Recommended by Tim and Sue Halstead*

BLOXHAM SP4235   OX15 4LY

☆ **Joiners Arms**

Old Bridge Road, off A361

Golden stone inn with some refurbishment in rambling rooms, plenty of exposed stone, white dining chairs around pale tables on wood floor, open fires, Courage and Theakstons beers, enjoyable traditional food, exposed well in raftered room off bar; children and dogs welcome, pretty window boxes, seats out under parasols on various levels – most popular down steps by stream (play house there, too), open all day. *Recommended by Mr and Mrs John Taylor*

BLOXHAM SP4631   OX15 0SJ

Red Lion

High Street (A361)

Comfortable beamed two-bar pub with open fire, good choice of food and friendly service, Fullers ales, nice coffee; TV; children welcome, sizeable back garden on lower level. *Recommended by Michael Dandy*

BRIGHTWELL SU5890   OX10 0RT

Red Lion

Signed off A4130 2 miles W of Wallingford

Welcoming community-spirited village pub, five well kept local ales, wines from nearby vineyard, enjoyable good value home-made food, two-part bar with snug seating by log fire, unobtrusive dining extension; dogs welcome, tables outside. *Recommended by Anne Worsnop, John Pritchard*

BROUGHTON SP4238   OX15 5ED

☆ **Saye & Sele Arms**

B4035 SW of Banbury

16th-c pub split into three distinct areas, dining room at one end with over 200 colourful water jugs hanging from beams, tiled area by bar counter with cushioned window seats, a few brasses and dark wooden furnishings, and a carpeted room with red walls and big fireplace, good food cooked by landlord, up to four well kept ales, several wines by the glass, friendly service; children allowed if dining, a mix of seats on terrace and lawn, pergola and smokers' shelter, herb garden, aunt sally, handy for Broughton Castle, closed Sun evening. *Recommended by Carolyn Drew, Rob and Catherine Dunster, Kevin Thomas, Nina Randall, Jane Hudson, Clive and Fran Dutson, R K Phillips and others*

BUCKLAND SU3497   SN7 8QN

☆ **Lamb**
Off A420 NE of Faringdon

Smart 18th-c stone-built dining pub with popular food (not Mon) from lunchtime special deals to grander and more expensive evening menus, several ales including local ones, good choice of wines by the glass, lamb motif everywhere, formal restaurant; piped music; children welcome, pleasant tree-shaded garden, good walks nearby, comfortable bedrooms, closed Sun evening and over Christmas and New Year. *Recommended by Graham and Toni Sanders, Henry Midwinter, the Didler, Jennifer and Patrick O'Dell*

BUCKNELL SP5525   OX27 7NE

☆ **Trigger Pond**
Handy for M40 junction 10; Bicester Road

Neatly kept and welcoming stone-built beamed pub opposite the pond, wide choice of good sensibly priced food from baguettes up (must book Sun lunch), helpful friendly service, Wadworths ales including seasonal, good value wines, small bar with dining areas either side, inglenook woodburner, conservatory; colourful terrace and garden.
Recommended by Mr and Mrs R Green, George Atkinson, David Lamb, Lucien Perring

BURFORD SP2512   OX18 4SN

☆ **Angel**
Witney Street

Long heavy-beamed dining pub in attractive ancient building, warmly welcoming with good reasonably priced brasserie food, good range of drinks; big secluded garden, three comfortable bedrooms, closed Sun evening, Mon. *Recommended by Leslie and Barbara Owen, David Glynne-Jones, Jennifer and Patrick O'Dell*

BURFORD SP2512   OX18 4LW

Bay Tree
Sheep Street

Attractive old village inn with smart yet informal and comfortable beamed bar, big log fires, cosy armchairs and leaded lights in small front room, second room with tartan seating, polished boards and sets of antlers, Brakspears, good choice of bar food from sandwiches up, friendly helpful staff, more formal restaurant; charming small walled terraced garden, bedrooms. *Recommended by Michael Dandy, N R White*

BURFORD SP2512   OX18 4QA

Golden Pheasant
High Street

Small early 18th-c hotel's flagstoned split-level bar, civilised yet relaxed and pubby, sofas, armchairs, well spaced tables and woodburner, enjoyable food from baguettes to steaks, well kept Greene King ales, good house wines, friendly helpful service, back dining room down steps; children welcome, pleasant terrace behind, bedrooms, open all day.
Recommended by Tim and Joan Wright, Michael Dandy, Malcolm Greening

BURFORD SP2512   OX18 4RG

☆ **Highway**
High Street (A361)

Comfortable 15th-c inn with notable windows in bar (each made up of several dozen panes of old float glass); you can sit at long cushioned window seat and look out on High Street, ancient stripped stone mixing with filigree black and pale blue wallpaper, other interesting touches such as stag candlesticks and Cecil Aldin hunting prints, log fire in attractively simple fireplace with old station clock above, second bar with another big

window seat, cellar restaurant, Hook Norton and a guest beer, lots of wines by the glass, mixed food reports recently; piped music; children welcome, dogs allowed in bar (resident springers Cassie and Oscar), picnic-sets standing above pavement, bedrooms, open all day, closed first two weeks in Jan. *Recommended by Nigel and Sue Foster, N R White, Graham Oddey*

BURFORD SP2512   OX18 4QF
☆ **Mermaid**
High Street

Handsome jettied Tudor dining pub with beams, flagstones, panelling, stripped stone and nice log fire, good food at sensible prices including local free-range meat and fresh fish, friendly efficient service, well kept Greene King ales and a guest, bay seating around row of tables on the left, further airy back dining room and upstairs restaurant; piped music (live Fri); children welcome, tables out at front and in courtyard behind, open all day. *Recommended by Michael Dandy, Mike Horgan, Di Wright*

BURFORD SP2512   OX18 4SN
☆ **Royal Oak**
Witney Street

Relaxed homely 17th-c stripped-stone local, an oasis in this smart village, with long-serving friendly landlord, Wadworths ales and an occasional guest from central servery, simple generous good value food using local produce from filled rolls up, good service, over a thousand beer mugs, steins and jugs hanging from beams, antlers over big log fire (underfloor heating, too), light wood tables, chairs and benches on flagstones, more in carpeted back room with bar billiards; well behaved children and dogs welcome, terrace tables, sensibly priced bedrooms by garden behind, good breakfast, open all day Sat, closed Tues lunchtime. *Recommended by Mr and Mrs W W Burke, Michael Dandy, Pam Service*

CHARLBURY SP3519   OX7 3PP
Bell
Church Street

Attractive two-room bar in small imaginatively refurbished 18th-c hotel, flagstones, stripped stonework and huge inglenook log fire, food from sandwiches up, Greene King and a guest ale, friendly welcoming service, restaurant, back family area including children's playroom; dogs welcome, suntrap terrace and pleasant garden down to stream, quiet refurbished bedrooms, open all day. *Recommended by Jon Carpenter, Mrs C A Murphy, Richard Greaves*

CHAZEY HEATH SU6979   RG4 7UG
Pack Horse
Just off A4074 Reading—Wallingford by B4526

Attractive 17th-c beamed pub (part of the Home Counties chain), good choice of enjoyable fairly priced food all day, real ales and lots of wines by the glass, friendly staff, polished tables on wood floors, built-in leatherette banquettes, big log fire in raised hearth; dogs welcome in main bar, disabled facilities, back garden. *Recommended by Sharon Dooley*

CHECKENDON SU6684   RG8 0TE
☆ **Black Horse**
Village signed off A4074 Reading—Wallingford

This charmingly old-fashioned country tavern (tucked into woodland away from main village) has been kept by the same family for 106 years; relaxing and unchanging series of rooms, back one with Hook Norton and West Berkshire tapped from the cask, one with bar counter has some tent pegs above fireplace (a reminder they used to be made here), homely side lounge with some splendidly unfashionable 1950s-look armchairs and another room beyond that, only filled rolls and pickled eggs; no credit cards; children allowed but must be well behaved, seats on verandah and in garden, popular with walkers and cyclists. *Recommended by the Didler*

CHURCH ENSTONE SP3725 OX7 4NN
☆ Crown
Mill Lane; from A44 take B4030 turn-off at Enstone

Pleasant uncluttered bar in beamed country pub, straightforward furniture, country pictures on stone walls, some horsebrasses, log fire in large fireplace, Fullers and Hook Norton beers, decent food, red-walled carpeted dining room, slate-floored conservatory with farmhouse furniture; children welcome, dogs in bar, white metal tables and chairs on front terrace overlooking lane, picnic-sets in sheltered back garden, closed Sun evening. *Recommended by Phil and Jane Hodson, Derek and Sylvia Stephenson, Barry Collett, Chris Glasson, Andy and Jill Kassube, JJW, CMW and others*

CHURCHILL SP2824 OX7 6NJ
☆ Chequers
Church Road; B4450 Chipping Norton—Stow-on-the-Wold (and village signed off A361 Chipping Norton—Burford)

Great welcome from licensees Assumpta and Peter Golding at this spic and span golden-stone village pub, front bar with modern oak furnishings on light flagstoned floor, some old timbers and country prints, exposed stone walls around big inglenook log fire, Hook Norton and up to three guests, decent wines, popular bar food, big back extension with soaring rafters and cosy upstairs dining area; children welcome, impressive church opposite, open all day. *Recommended by P and J Shapley, Martin and Pauline Jennings, Henry Midwinter, George Atkinson, Myra Joyce, Bernard Stradling and others*

CLANFIELD SP2802 OX18 2RG
☆ Clanfield Tavern
Bampton Road (A4095 S of Witney)

New licensees at this pleasantly extended pub and emphasis on traditional food; opened-up beamed interior keeping feel of separate areas, mostly carpeted with mix of pubby furniture including some old settles (built-in one by log fire), smallish bar with sofas in snug flagstoned area by woodburner, Banks's and a couple of guest ales, attractive dining conservatory; piped music; children welcome, dogs in bar, picnic-sets on small flower-bordered lawn looking across to village green, open all day weekends. *Recommended by anon*

CLIFTON SP4931 OX15 0PE
☆ Duke of Cumberlands Head
B4031 Deddington—Aynho

Warmly welcoming thatch and stone pub with big low-beamed lounge, good log fire in vast fireplace and simple furnishings, some emphasis on food from good reasonably priced bar snacks up (own pigs), friendly service, well kept Hook Norton and guests, good wine and whisky choice, cosy stripped-stone dining room, live music (classical/jazz) Sat night; children and dogs welcome, garden with barbecue, ten minutes' walk from canal, six bedrooms. *Recommended by Mrs Pat Parkin-Moore, Roy Hoing, Maurice Ricketts, David Jackman*

COLESHILL SU2393 SN6 7PR
☆ Radnor Arms
B4019 Faringdon—Highworth; village signposted off A417 in Faringdon and A361 in Highworth

Pub and village owned by NT, bar with cushioned settles, plush carver chairs and woodburner, back alcove with more tables, steps down to main dining area, once a blacksmith's forge with lofty beamed ceiling, log fire, dozens of tools and smith's gear on walls, Old Forge ales (brewed on site) and local Halfpenny, shortish choice of good well priced home-made food (not Sun evening), friendly efficient service; children and dogs welcome, garden with aunt sally and play area, open all day. *Recommended by Anne Morris, Graham Oddey, Jennifer and Patrick O'Dell, Simon Garfuncle*

Every entry includes a postcode for use in Sat Nav devices.

☆ **CRAWLEY** SP3412   OX29 9TW
Lamb
Steep Hill; just NW of Witney

Refurbished 18th-c stone-built dining pub, simple beamed bar with polished boards and lovely fireplace, steps to candlelit dining room, good food from nice sandwiches and pubby dishes to more enterprising things, set menu deals Tues and Weds, good choice of wines by the glass, well kept Brakspears, helpful friendly service; piped music; children welcome, dogs in bar, views from tables on back terrace and lawn, pretty village, good walks – on Palladian Way, closed Sun evening. *Recommended by Ian Phillips, Alan Perry*

CRAYS POND SU6380   RG8 7SH
White Lion
Goring Road (B471 near junction with B4526, about 3 miles E of Goring)

Recently refurbished old green-shuttered country pub/restaurant, enjoyable interesting choice of food (not Sun evening) including good value set lunchtime menu, Greene King ales, friendly staff, traditional beamed interior with contemporary touches, log fires, dining conservatory; children welcome, big garden with play area, lovely countryside, open all day. *Recommended by Anne Pickering*

CROPREDY SP4646   OX17 1PB
Red Lion
Off A423 N of Banbury

Popular rambling 15th-c thatch-and-stone pub charmingly placed opposite pretty village's churchyard, good food and service, Hook Norton and a couple of guests, low beams, inglenook log fire, high-backed settles, brass, plates and pictures, unusual dining room murals, games room; piped music, limited parking; children allowed in dining part, picnic-sets on part-covered terrace, near Oxford Canal (Bridge 152). *Recommended by George Atkinson, Clive and Fran Dutson, Dr Kevan Tucker*

☆ **CUMNOR** SP4503   OX2 9QH
Bear & Ragged Staff
Signed from A420; Appleton Road

Extensive restaurant/pub dating from 16th c, clean contemporary décor in linked rooms with wood floors, leather-backed dining chairs and mix of tables, low lighting, good food from shared charcuterie and meze plates to pub standards and up, weekday lunch deals, good friendly service, flagstoned bar with log fire, well kept Green King ales, good wine choice, leather sofas and armchairs in airy garden room; children welcome, decked terrace, fenced play area, new bedrooms, open all day. *Recommended by Joan and Tony Walker, Bob and Angela Brooks, Richard Greaves, Jan and Roger Ferris*

☆ **CUXHAM** SU6695   OX49 5NF
Half Moon
4 miles from M40 junction 6; S on B4009, then right on B480 at Watlington

Lovely 17th-c restaurant/pub under new french landlord, freshly prepared french food using produce from own kitchen garden as well as french suppliers, two main eating areas with beams, cushioned settles, mirrors and prints, little fireplace in small tiled bar, Brakspears ales, house wines by the glass or pichet (460ml bottle); children and dogs welcome, seats in good-sized garden, sleepy village surrounded by fine countryside, open all day Sat, closed Sun evening, Mon. *Recommended by anon*

☆ **DEDDINGTON** SP4631   OX15 0SH
Deddington Arms
Off A4260 (B4031) Banbury—Oxford; Horse Fair

Beamed and timbered hotel with emphasis on sizeable contemporary back dining room doing very good food, comfortable bar with mullioned windows, flagstones and log fire, good food here, too, Adnams, Black Sheep and a guest, plenty of wines by the glass, attentive friendly service; unobtrusive piped music; attractive village with lots of antiques shops and good farmers' market fourth Sat of month, nice walks, comfortable chalet bedrooms around courtyard, good breakfast, open all day. *Recommended by Phyl and Jack Street, Michael Dandy, John Taylor*

DEDDINGTON SP4631   OX15 0SE
☆ **Unicorn**
Market Place

Welcoming recently refurbished 17th-c inn, beamed L-shaped bar, cosy snug with inglenook log fire, candlelit restaurant, good sensibly priced home-made food from snacks and pub favourites up (not Mon), well kept Hook Norton and Wells & Youngs, good choice of wines by the glass, proper coffee, daily papers and pub games; piped music; well behaved children welcome, cobbled courtyard leading to long walled back garden, good bedrooms and breakfast, open all day weekends (from 9am for good farmers' market – last Sat of month). *Recommended by MP, Roxanne Chamberlain*

DENCHWORTH SU3891   OX12 0DX
Fox
Off A338 or A417 N of Wantage; Hyde Road

Comfortable 17th-c thatched and beamed pub in pretty village, good choice of sensibly priced generous food including good Sun carvery (best to book), friendly efficient staff, well kept Greene King Old Speckled Hen, good house wines, two good log fires and plush seats in low-ceilinged connecting areas, old prints and paintings, airy dining extension; children welcome, tables under umbrellas in pleasant sheltered garden, peaceful village. *Recommended by D C T and E A Frewer*

DORCHESTER SU5794   OX10 7HH
George
Just off A4074 Maidenhead—Oxford; High Street

Handsome timbered hotel in lovely village, roaring log fire and charming furnishings in smart beamed bar, enjoyable food including OAP deals, ales such as Adnams, Brakspears and Wadworths, cheerful efficient service; piped music; children welcome, bedrooms, open all day. *Recommended by Jonnie Supper, John and Helen Rushton*

EAST HENDRED SU4688   OX12 8JN
Wheatsheaf
Signed off A417; Chapel Square

Attractive 16th-c black and white timbered village pub with big inglenook log fire in carpeted bar, other cosy rooms off, three well kept ales, good choice of wines, enjoyable food from pub standards up, restaurant; dogs allowed in bar, some tables out in front, more in pleasant garden behind, barbecues, open all day weekends. *Recommended by Russell Traynor*

FIFIELD SP2318   OX7 6HR
Merrymouth
A424 Burford—Stow

Simple but comfortable stone inn dating to 13th c, L-shaped bar, bay-window seats, flagstones, low beams, some walls stripped back to old masonry, warm stove, quite dark in some areas, good sensibly priced generous food including blackboard fish choice, Hook Norton and a couple of other ales, decent wine choice, cheery landlord and friendly staff; piped music; children and dogs welcome, tables on terrace and in back garden, nine stable-block bedrooms. *Recommended by Noel Grundy, P M Newsome, Stanley and Annie Matthews, Chris Glasson, Colin McKerrow*

FINSTOCK SP3616   OX7 3BY
☆ **Plough**
Just off B4022 N of Witney; High Street

Thatched low-beamed village pub nicely split up by partitions and alcoves, long rambling bar with leather sofas by massive stone inglenook, some unusual horsebrasses and historical documents to do with the pub, roomy dining room with candles and fresh

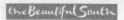

flowers on stripped-pine tables, good food cooked by landlord, Adnams Broadside, Butts Organic Jester and a guest, traditional cider, several wines by the glass and 20 malt whiskies, bar billiards, board games; children at discretion of licensees, dogs allowed in bar (pub has two cats), seats in neatly kept garden, aunt sally, walks among local woodland and along River Evenlode, open all day Sat, closed Sun evening, Mon and maybe two weeks in Feb. *Recommended by Jon Carpenter, Mr and Mrs J C Cetti, George and Linda Ozols, D R Ellis, Ian and Helen Stafford*

FOREST HILL SP5807   OX33 1EH
White Horse
Wheatley Road (B4027)

Small friendly stone-built beamed village pub, two real ales, a dozen wines by the glass, good fairly priced thai food, other food including children's, central log fire in restaurant; handy for Oxfordshire Way; closed Mon. *Recommended by JJW, CMW*

FRILFORD SU4497   OX13 6QJ
Dog House
Faringdon Road

Comfortable hotel with beamed open-plan log-fire bar, restaurant and conservatory, enjoyable good value traditional food from sandwiches to specials, Greene King ales, friendly attentive young staff; children welcome, garden with heated terrace, 20 bedrooms. *Recommended by Ian Herdman*

FYFIELD SU4298   OX13 5LW
☆ ## White Hart
Main Road; off A420 8 miles SW of Oxford

Grand medieval hall with soaring eaves, huge stone-flanked window embrasures and minstrel's gallery, contrasting cosy low-beamed side bar with large inglenook, fresh flowers and evening candles throughout, civilised friendly atmosphere and full of history, good imaginative modern food (best to book) cooked by licensee using home-grown produce, Hook Norton, Loddon, Rebellion and Sharps Doom Bar (festivals during May and Aug bank holidays), around 16 wines by the glass (including champagne), several malt whiskies and home-made summer elderflower pressé; piped music; children welcome if well behaved, elegant furniture under smart umbrellas on spacious heated terrace, lovely gardens, good Thames-side walks, open all day weekends, closed Mon. *Recommended by Rochelle Seifas, David and Sue Atkinson, Graham and Toni Sanders, Malcolm Ward, Ewan Shearer and others*

GODSTOW SP4809   OX2 8PN
☆ ## Trout
Off A40/A44 roundabout via Wolvercote

Pretty 17th-c M&B dining pub in lovely riverside location (gets packed in fine weather), good bistro-style food all day (booking essential at busy times), four beamed linked rooms with contemporary furnishings, flagstones and bare boards, log fires in three huge hearths, Adnams and Timothy Taylors Landlord, several wines by the glass; piped music; children welcome till 7pm, plenty of terrace seats under big parasols (dogs allowed here), footbridge to island (may be closed), abbey ruins opposite, open all day. *Recommended by Robert Lorimer, A R Mascall, Ros Lawler, Tina and David Woods-Taylor, Andrea Rampley, Martin and Pauline Jennings and others*

GOZZARD'S FORD SU4698   OX13 6JH
☆ ## Black Horse
Off B4017 NW of Abingdon; N of A415 by Marcham—Cothill Road

Ancient traditional pub in tiny hamlet, sensibly short choice of good generous food (all day Sun) especially fish and seafood, well kept Greene King ales, decent wines, cheerful efficient service, carpeted beamed main bar partly divided by stout timbers and low steps, end woodburner, separate plainer public bar with darts and pool; nice garden, open all day. *Recommended by William Goodhart, John Pritchard*

GREAT TEW SP3929   OX7 4DB
☆ **Falkland Arms**
The Green; off B4022 about 5 miles E of Chipping Norton

Golden-stone thatched cottage in lovely village, unspoilt partly panelled bar with high-backed settles, diversity of stools and plain tables on flagstones or bare boards, one-, two- and three-handled mugs hanging from beam-and-boards ceiling, dim converted oil lamps, shutters for stone-mullioned latticed windows and open fire in fine inglenook, Wadworths and guests, Weston's cider, 30 malt whiskies, country wines, enjoyable bar food, snuff for sale, live folk Sun evening; children and dogs welcome, tables out at front and under parasols in back garden, small fair value bedrooms (no under-16s), open all day.
Recommended by Tich Critchlow, the Didler, George Atkinson, Andy and Jill Kassube, David Heath, Mr and Mrs P R Thomas and others

HAILEY SP3414   OX29 9XP
Bird in Hand
Whiteoak Green; B4022 Witney—Charlbury

Attractive 17th-c extended stone inn, interesting food from shortish menu, helpful friendly service, well kept ales such as Ramsbury, beams and timbers, some stripped stone, comfortable armchairs on polished boards, large log fire, cosy corners in carpeted restaurant, lovely Cotswold views; parasol-shaded terrace tables, bedrooms, good breakfast, open all day. *Recommended by Nigel and Sue Foster, David Heath*

HAILEY SU6485   OX10 6AD
☆ **King William IV**
The Hailey near Ipsden, off A4074 or A4130 SE of Wallingford

Fine old pub in lovely countryside, beamed bar with good sturdy furniture on tiles in front of big log fire, three other cosy seating areas opening off (children allowed in two), enjoyable food including some interesting specials, Brakspears, friendly staff, miniature traffic lights on bar (red means bar closed, orange last orders, green open); dogs welcome, terrace and large garden enjoying wide-ranging peaceful views, may be red kites overhead, you can tether your horse in car park, Ridgeway National Trail nearby.
Recommended by Richard Endacott, Ray Carter, the Didler, Paul Humphreys

HAMPTON POYLE SP5015   OX5 2QD
☆ **Bell**
Off A34 S, take Kidlington turn and village signed from roundabout; from A34 N, take Kidlington turn, then A4260 to roundabout, third turning signed for Superstore (Bicester Road); village signed from roundabout

Front bar with three snug rooms, lots of big black and white photoprints, sturdy simple furnishings, scatter cushions and window seats, a stove flanked by bookshelves one end, large fireplace stacked with logs the other, biggish inner room made lively by open kitchen with its wood-fired pizza oven, a couple of fireside leather armchairs, spreading dining room with plenty of tables on pale limestone flagstones, inventive food, good choice of wines by the glass, Fullers London Pride and Hook Norton Old Hooky, good service by uniformed staff, cheerful informal atmosphere; piped jazz; children welcome, dogs in bar, modern seats on sunny front terrace by quiet village lane, bedrooms, open all day. *Recommended by Rob Hubbard*

HANWELL SP4343   OX17 1HN
Moon & Sixpence
Main Street

Good food from pub favourites up in clean comfortable bar and dining area, friendly staff, well kept Hook Norton and decent wines by the glass; pretty garden, nice village setting.
Recommended by Graham and Nicky Westwood, Martin and Sue Radcliffe

---

Post Office address codings confusingly give the impression that some pubs are in Oxfordshire, when they're really in Berkshire, Buckinghamshire, Gloucestershire or Warwickshire (which is where we list them).

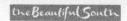

HARWELL SU4988   OX11 0LZ
☆ Kingswell
A417; Reading Road

Substantial hotel with dependably good imaginative bar food as well as restaurant meals, plenty of choice, helpful staff; comfortable bedrooms. *Recommended by Henry Midwinter*

HENLEY SU7682   RG9 1BH
Angel on the Bridge
Thames-side, by the bridge

Worth knowing for prime spot by Thames, with nice waterside deck (plastic glasses for this), small front bar with log fire, back bar and adjacent restaurant, Brakspears ales, good choice of wines by the glass, food from sandwiches and pubby things up, well organised staff; moorings for two boats, open all day at least in summer. *Recommended by David and Sue Atkinson*

HENLEY SU7582   RG9 2AA
Argyll
Market Place

Smartly comfortable and well run, with pleasant efficient service, enjoyable fairly priced pub food all day from sandwiches up, Greene King ales, decent wines by the glass, soft lighting, dark panelling; piped music; nice terrace garden behind, useful parking. *Recommended by Paul Humphreys*

HENLEY SU7882   RG9 2ED
Row Barge
West Street

Brakspears local under newish management, cosy low-beamed bar dropping down the hill in steps, their ales kept well, tasty good value well presented pubby food, good helpful service; sizable garden. *Recommended by Paul Humphreys*

HIGHMOOR SU7084   RG9 5DL
☆ Dog & Duck
B481

Appealing unspoilt 17th-c country pub, enjoyable food (not Sun evening) from nice baguettes up, also good vegetarian options, Brakspears ales, decent choice of wines, friendly efficient staff, log fires in small cosily furnished beamed bar and not much larger flagstoned dining room with old pictures and prints, family room off; dogs welcome (friendly pub labrador called Della), attractive long garden with some play equipment and small sheep paddock, surrounding walks, open all day in summer, closed lunchtimes in winter apart from Sun, may close Sun evening. *Recommended by Paul Humphreys, the Didler, John Pritchard, David Lamb*

HOOK NORTON SP3534   OX15 5DF
☆ Gate Hangs High
N towards Sibford, at Banbury—Rollright crossroads

Snug tucked-away family-run pub, low-ceilinged bar with traditional furniture on bare boards, attractive inglenook, good reasonably priced home-made food from bar snacks up, well kept Hook Norton ales and a guest, decent wines, friendly helpful service, slightly chintzy side dining extension (booking advised Sat evening and Sun); piped music; pretty courtyard and country garden, four good value bedrooms, good breakfast, quite near Rollright Stones. *Recommended by Colin McKerrow, George Atkinson*

HOOK NORTON SP3533   OX15 5NU
Pear Tree
Scotland End

Take-us-as-you-find-us village pub with engaging landlord and character locals, full Hook Norton range kept well from nearby brewery, country wines, enjoyable bar food (not Sun evening) from doorstep sandwiches to bargain Sun roast, knocked-together bar area with country-kitchen furniture, good log fire, daily papers; occasional live music Tues, TV; children and dogs welcome, attractive garden with play area, bedrooms, open all day. *Recommended by Steve Nye, Gene and Kitty Rankin, Jennifer and Patrick O'Dell, Barry Collett*

KELMSCOTT SU2499   GL7 3HG
Plough
NW of Faringdon, off B4449 between A417 and A4095

Refurbished interior with ancient flagstones, stripped stone and log fire, wide choice of food (more restauranty in evenings), beers such as local Halfpenny, Wye Valley and Wychwood, farm cider; children, dogs and booted walkers welcome, tables out in covered area and garden, lovely spot near upper Thames (good moorings a few minutes' walk away), eight bedrooms, open all day weekends. *Recommended by Meg and Colin Hamilton, Jennifer and Patrick O'Dell, R K Phillips*

KIDMORE END SU6979   RG4 9AU
New Inn
Chalkhouse Green Road; signed from B481 in Sonning Common

Newish licensees at this attractive black and white pub by church; beams and big fire, enjoyable freshly made food including good value weekday set lunch, pleasant restaurant; tables in large sheltered garden with pond, bedrooms. *Recommended by Bruce and Trish Field, Paul Humphreys*

LAUNTON SP6022   OX26 5DQ
Bull
Just E of Bicester

Partly thatched modernised 17th-c village pub, welcoming and well managed, with enjoyable food (not Sun evening) including OAP weekday lunch deals, three well kept Greene King ales and a guest, Sun quiz; piped music; children allowed away from bar, dogs on leads, wheelchair access from car park, disabled facilities, garden with terrace, open all day. *Recommended by Bill Hawkins, Meg and Colin Hamilton*

LEWKNOR SU7197   OX49 5TH
☆ ## Olde Leathern Bottel
Under a mile from M40 junction 6; off B4009 towards Watlington

A popular place and useful for motorway, two heavy beamed bars, low ceilings, understated décor and rustic furnishings, open fires, Brakspears, Marstons and Wychwood, several wines by the glass, pubby bar food, family room separated by standing timbers; dogs welcome, splendid garden with plenty of picnic-sets under parasols, play area and boules, handy for walks on Chiltern escarpment. *Recommended by Roger and Anne Newbury, Tina and David Woods-Taylor, Paul Humphreys, D and M T Ayres-Regan, Andy and Jill Kassube and others*

LONG WITTENHAM SU5493   OX14 4QH
Plough
High Street

Friendly chatty local with low beams, inglenook fires and lots of brass, well kept ales including Butcombe, good value wines by the glass, wide choice of generous well priced food (all day weekends), good friendly service, dining room, games in public bar; dogs welcome, Thames moorings at bottom of nice spacious garden with aunt sally, bedrooms. *Recommended by David Lamb*

MAIDENSGROVE SU7288   RG9 6EX
Five Horseshoes
Off B480 and B481, W of village

16th-c dining pub set high in the Chilterns, rambling bar with low ceiling and log fire, enjoyable food including salmon smoked by landlord and local game, friendly attentive service, well kept Brakspears, good choice of wines by the glass, airy conservatory

restaurant; children and dogs welcome, plenty of garden tables and lovely views, wood-fired pizzas on summer weekends (open all day then), good walks, closed Mon evening. *Recommended by Henry Midwinter, Philip Kingsbury, Tracey and Stephen Groves*

MILTON SP4535   OX15 4HH
☆ Black Boy
Off Bloxham Road; the one near Adderbury

Neatly refurbished dining pub with good comfortable furnishings, but still plenty of oak beams, exposed stonework, flagstones and a lovely big inglenook, good choice of enjoyable home-made food, friendly licensees, good service, ales such as Hook Norton; piped music; children and dogs welcome, narrow front terrace with heaters, tables across road in spacious garden beyond car park, play area. *Recommended by Martin and Pauline Jennings*

MURCOTT SP5815   OX5 2RE
☆ Nut Tree
Off B4027 NE of Oxford, via Islip and Charlton-on-Otmoor

Refurbished beamed and thatched 15th-c dining pub, imaginative if not cheap food using own produce including home-reared pigs, Hook Norton and a couple of guests, carefully chosen wines, neat friendly staff; children welcome, dogs allowed in bar, pretty garden, unusual gargoyles (modelled loosely on local characters) on front wall, ducks on village pond, closed winter Sun evening, all day Mon. *Recommended by William Goodhart, Laurence Smith, Paul Baxter*

NORTH MORETON SU5689   OX11 9AT
Bear at Home
Off A4130 Didcot—Wallingford; High Street

Dating from the 15th c with traditional beamed bar, cosy fireside areas and dining part with stripped-pine furniture, enjoyable reasonably priced food from baguettes up, friendly service, Timothy Taylors, a guest ale and a beer brewed for the pub (July beer festival), Weston's cider, several wines by the glass; attractive garden overlooking cricket pitch, pretty village, open all day Sat. *Recommended by Roy Hoing*

OXFORD SP5007   OX2 6TT
Anchor
Hayfield Road

Chef/landlord at this 1930s pub producing good quality interesting food using local supplies, friendly efficient service, good value house wine, well kept Wadworths beers, period furnishings, log fire, separate dining area; near Bridge 240 (Aristotle) on Oxford Canal. *Recommended by David Gunn, Dr Kevan Tucker*

OXFORD SP5106   OX1 4DH
Chequers
Off High Street

Narrow 16th-c courtyard pub with several areas on three floors, interesting architectural features, beams, panelling and stained glass, wide choice of rotating ales and of well priced pubby food (sausage specialities), quick friendly service, games room with balcony; walled garden. *Recommended by George Atkinson, Peter Lee*

OXFORD SP5106   OX1 3HB
Crown
In alley near MacDonalds, more or less opposite Boots

Refurbished Nicholson's pub with long narrowish rooms, popular food including speciality pies, eight or so real ales, friendly attentive staff; courtyard seats. *Recommended by George Atkinson*

> It's very helpful if you let us know up-to-date food prices when you report on pubs.

OXFORD SP5106 OX1 3LU

☆ **Eagle & Child**
St Giles

Nicholson's pub with two charmingly old-fashioned panelled front rooms, well kept Brakspears, Hook Norton and interesting guests, wide range of food all day from sandwiches to Sun roasts, stripped-brick back dining extension and conservatory, Tolkien and CS Lewis connections; games machine; children allowed in back till 8pm. *Recommended by Tim and Ann Newell, G Jennings, Susan and Nigel Brookes, MP, the Didler, Clive and Fran Dutson and others*

OXFORD SP5105 OX1 4LB

Head of the River
Folly Bridge; between St Aldates and Christchurch Meadow

Civilised well renovated pub by river, boats for hire and nearby walks; spacious split-level downstairs bar with dividing brick arches, flagstones and bare boards, Fullers/Gales beers, good choice of wines by the glass, popular pubby food from sandwiches up, good service, daily papers; piped music; tables on stepped heated waterside terrace, 12 bedrooms. *Recommended by Michael Dandy*

OXFORD SP5106 OX1 3SP

☆ **Kings Arms**
Holywell Street

Dating from early 17th c, convivial, relaxed and popular with locals and students, quick helpful service, well kept Wells & Youngs range and four guests, fine choice of wines by the glass, eating area with counter servery doing good variety of reasonably priced food all day, cosy comfortably worn-in partly panelled side and back rooms, interesting pictures and posters, daily papers; a few tables outside, open from 10.30am. *Recommended by Colin and Louise English, Andrea Rampley, the Didler, Tim and Ann Newell, Mr and Mrs M J Girdler, Revd R P Tickle and others*

OXFORD SP5106 OX1 3JS

Lamb & Flag
St Giles/Banbury Road

Old pub owned by nearby college, modern airy front room with light wood panelling and big windows over street, more atmosphere in back rooms with stripped stonework and low-boarded ceilings, a beer by Palmers for the pub (L&F Gold), Shepherd Neame Spitfire, Skinners Betty Stogs and guests, some lunchtime food including sandwiches and tasty home-made pies. *Recommended by Michael Dandy, the Didler, D W Stokes*

OXFORD SP5006 OX1 2EW

Oxford Retreat
Hythe Bridge Street

Civilised waterside pub with well kept Fullers London Pride, good choice of wines by the glass and cocktails, enjoyable well served food from pubby things up, restaurant with chunky tables and leather chairs overlooking river, attentive staff, log fire; garden with decking, open all day and till 3am Fri, Sat. *Recommended by Pippa Manley, Martin and Karen Wake*

OXFORD SP5106 OX1 3BB

☆ **White Horse**
Broad Street

Bustling and studenty, squeezed between bits of Blackwells bookshop, small narrow bar with snug one-table raised back alcove, low beams and timbers, ochre ceiling, beautiful view of the Clarendon building and Sheldonian, good choice of ales including Brakspears, St Austell, Timothy Taylors and White Horse, friendly staff, good value simple lunchtime food (the few tables reserved for this); open all day. *Recommended by Andrea Rampley, Terry and Nickie Williams, the Didler, Paul Humphreys, Nigel and Jean Eames and others*

the Beautiful South

PISHILL SU7190 RG9 6HH
☆ **Crown**
B480 Nettlebed—Watlington

Mainly 15th-c red-brick and flint pub, beamed bars with old local photographs and maps on part-panelled walls, nice old chairs around mix of wooden tables, lots of candles, three log fires, attractively presented food from sandwiches up, Brakspears and a couple of guests, cafetière coffee, friendly service, knocked-through back area with standing timbers, fine thatched 16th-c barn used for functions; dogs allowed in bar, picnic-sets under blue parasols in pretty garden, lots of nearby walks, bedrooms and self-contained cottage. *Recommended by Paul Humphreys, Penny and Peter Keevil, the Didler, Susan and John Douglas, Mrs Margaret Watson and others*

PLAY HATCH SU7477 RG4 9QU
Shoulder of Mutton
W of Henley Road (A4155) roundabout

Dining pub with low-ceilinged log-fire bar and large conservatory restaurant, good choice of enjoyable food including signature mutton dishes, well kept Greene King and guests such as Loddon; children welcome, picnic-sets in well tended walled garden with well, closed Sun evening. *Recommended by Paul Humphreys*

SATWELL SU7083 RG9 4QZ
☆ **Lamb**
2 miles S of Nettlebed; follow Shepherds Green signpost

16th-c country pub (originally two cottages) with low-beamed bar, nice pubby furniture on tiles, old photographs, agricultural and antique knick-knacks, inglenook log fire, Black Sheep, Loddon and Timothy Taylors, several wines by the glass, separate cosy dining room and often interesting food (all day weekends); piped music; children welcome, dogs in bar, seats on lawn in large garden with chickens, boules and maybe summer barbecues, plenty of surrounding walks. *Recommended by Susan and John Douglas, Mr and Mrs P R Thomas, John Pritchard, Jeremy Whitehorn*

SHENINGTON SP3742 OX15 6NQ
☆ **Bell**
Off A422 NW of Banbury

Good wholesome home cooking in hospitable 17th-c two-room pub, nice sandwiches too, well kept Flowers and Hook Norton, good wine choice, fair prices, friendly informal service and long-serving licensees, relaxed atmosphere, heavy beams, some flagstones, stripped stone and pine panelling, coal fire, amiable dogs, cribbage, dominoes; children in eating areas, tables out in front, small attractive back garden, charming quiet village, good walks, simple comfortable bedrooms, generous breakfast, closed Sun evening, Mon. *Recommended by Graham and Nicky Westwood, George Atkinson, Sir Nigel Foulkes*

SHIPLAKE SU7476 RG4 9RB
Flowing Spring
A4155 towards Play Hatch and Reading

Newish licensees for this roadside pub (built on bank, all on first floor with slight slope front to back), open fires in small two-room bar, various bric-a-brac, good value home-made food (not Sun or Mon evenings) from sandwiches, wraps and pizzas up, special diets catered for, Fullers ales, Aspall's cider, modern dining room with floor-to-ceiling windows, tables out on covered balcony, various events including astronomy nights and occasional live music; children and dogs welcome, lawned garden bordered by streams, summer marquee and barbecues, open all day. *Recommended by Paul Humphreys*

SHIPTON-UNDER-WYCHWOOD SP2717 OX7 6DQ
☆ **Lamb**
High Street; off A361 to Burford

Mother and son team at this handsome stone inn, beamed bar with oak-panelled settle, farmhouse chairs and polished tables on wood-block flooring, stripped-stone walls, church candles, log fire, three changing beers and quite a few wines by the glass, well liked food, restaurant area; children welcome, dogs allowed in bar (there are two pub dogs), garden with contemporary furniture on terrace, bedrooms, open all day. *Recommended by Lawrence R Cotter, R K Phillips, Simon Collett-Jones*

SIBFORD GOWER SP3537   OX15 5RX
☆ ## Wykham Arms
Signed off B4035 Banbury—Shipston on Stour; Temple Mill Road

Cottagey 17th-c thatched and flagstoned dining pub, good food from light lunchtime menu up, friendly attentive staff, two changing well kept ales, plenty of wines by the glass, comfortable open-plan interior with low-beams and stripped-stone, glass-covered well, inglenook; children and dogs welcome, country views from big garden, lovely manor house opp, open all day Sun, closed Mon. *Recommended by John Levell, Edward Mirzoeff*

SOULDERN SP5231   OX27 7JW
Fox
Off B4100; Fox Lane

Pretty pub with good choice of enjoyable fairly priced food including the Fox Sandwich (roast beef between two yorkshire puddings), well kept Hook Norton and two guests (beer festivals), good choice of wines by the glass, comfortable open-plan beamed layout, big log fire, settles and chairs around oak tables, quiz nights; delightful village, garden and terrace tables, aunt sally, four bedrooms. *Recommended by David Lamb, Andy and Jill Kassube*

SOUTH NEWINGTON SP4033   OX15 4JE
Duck on the Pond
A361

Dining pub with tidy modern-rustic décor in small flagstoned bar and linked carpeted eating areas up a step, enjoyable food from wraps, melts and other light dishes to steak and family Sun lunch, changing ales such as Purity and Wye Valley, range of coffees, neat friendly young staff, woodburner; piped music; spacious grounds with tables on deck and lawn, aunt sally, pond with waterfowl, walk down to River Swere, open all day weekends. *Recommended by George Atkinson, Lucien Perring*

SPARSHOLT SU3487   OX12 9PL
Star
Watery Lane

Compact 16th-c country pub, comfortable beamed bar with eating area to one side, generous blackboard food, usually three real ales, quick friendly service; may be piped music; back garden, pretty village – snowdrops fill churchyard in spring. *Recommended by David Lamb, D C T and E A Frewer*

STANDLAKE SP3902   OX29 7RH
Black Horse
High Street

Three-room pub with low ceilings and old brick fireplaces, wide choice of enjoyable food including bargain lunchtime fixed-price menu and Sun carvery, well kept Hook Norton ales, decent wines; garden picnic-sets, open all day weekends. *Recommended by Eddie Edwards, DHV, Miss Teresa Evans*

STANTON ST JOHN SP5709   OX33 1EX
☆ ## Star
Pub signed off B4027; village signed off A40 E of Oxford

Pleasant old Wadworths pub tucked away at end of village; two small low-beamed rooms, one with ancient brick floor, other with close-set tables, up stairs to attractive extension (on same level as car park) with old-fashioned dining chairs around dark oak or elm tables, rugs on flagstones, shelves of good pewter, bookshelves either side of inglenook log fire, also family room and conservatory; piped music; children and dogs welcome, seats

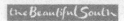

among flowerbeds in walled garden, some play equipment. *Recommended by John Robertson, Dennis and Doreen Haward, David Lamb, Dave Braisted*

☆ STEEPLE ASTON SP4725   OX25 4RY
Red Lion
Off A4260 12 miles N of Oxford

Welcoming village pub with plenty of cheerful customers, partly panelled neatly kept bar with beams, antique settle and other good furnishings, three real ales and decent wines, enjoyable popular bar food, helpful friendly service, back conservatory-style dining extension; well behaved children welcome lunchtime and until 7pm, dogs in bar, suntrap front garden with lovely flowers and shrubs, closed Sun evening. *Recommended by Brian Glozier, Ron and Sheila Corbett, Robert Watt, William Goodhart and others*

☆ STOKE ROW SU6884   RG9 5QA
Cherry Tree
Off B481 at Highmoor

Contemporary upscale pub/restaurant with particularly good and very popular food, Sun lunch till 5pm, attentive staff, well kept Brakspears ales, good choice of wines by the glass, minimalist décor and solid country furniture in four linked rooms with stripped wood, heavy low beams and some flagstones; TV in bar; seats in attractive garden, nearby walks, five good bedrooms in converted barn, open all day except Sun evening. *Recommended by Bob and Margaret Holder, Richard Endacott*

SUTTON COURTENAY SU5094   OX14 4NQ
Fish
Appleford Road

Civilised well run restaurant rather than pub, small front bar opening into attractive three-part dining room, good freshly cooked food with some emphasis on fish, also bar snacks and good value fixed-price menu, nice wines by the glass, Greene King Morland Original, competent service from french staff, back conservatory; children welcome, tables out in terrace arbour and on lawn, closed Sun evening, Mon. *Recommended by John and Helen Rushton*

SWINFORD SP4308   OX29 4BT
Talbot
B4044 just S of Eynsham

Roomy and comfortable 17th-c beamed pub, wide changing choice of generous fresh food, well kept Arkells ales direct from the cask, good choice of wines and soft drinks, friendly landlord and staff, long attractive bar with some stripped stone, cheerful log-effect gas fire, newspapers, some live jazz; may be piped music; children and dogs welcome, garden with decked area overlooking Wharf Stream, pleasant walk along lovely stretch of the Thames towpath, moorings quite nearby, eight good bedrooms. *Recommended by Meg and Colin Hamilton, Alistair and Joy Hamilton*

SYDENHAM SP7201   OX39 4NB
Crown
Off B4445 Chinnor—Thame

Friendly low-beamed pub in picturesque village, good reasonably priced food cooked by landlord, local ales, nice wines, open fires in long narrow bar; children welcome, small garden, views of lovely church. *Recommended by Mr and Mrs E Hughes*

THAME SP7105   OX9 3HP
Cross Keys
Park Street/East Street

One-bar 19th-c local continuing well under present landlord, six ales including own good Thame beers such as Mrs Tipples Ghost and Mr Splodges Mild, nice atmosphere; courtyard garden. *Recommended by Tim and Ann Newell, Doug Kennedy*

THAME SP7006 OX9 2AD
Six Bells
High Street

Recently refurbished 16th-c black-beamed Fullers pub, friendly relaxed atmosphere with cycling theme, interestingly varied menu (not Sun evening), good coffee, open fire; children and dogs welcome, large terrace, open all day. *Recommended by Tim and Ann Newell*

THRUPP SP4815 OX5 1JY
☆ ## Boat
Brown sign to pub off A4260 just N of Kidlington

Attractive 16th-c stone building, low ceilings, old coal stove, bare boards or ancient flooring tiles, good home-made food from panini and snacks to more upscale things, own bread and ice-creams too, friendly landlord and efficient service, Greene King ales, decent wine, restaurant; gets busy in summer; children and dogs welcome, fenced garden behind with plenty of tables, nearby Oxford Canal moorings. *Recommended by Ian B, Meg and Colin Hamilton, Phil Lowther*

UFFINGTON SU3089 SN7 7RP
Fox & Hounds
High Street

Traditional beamed village pub under newish ownership, enjoyable reasonably priced pubby food (not Sun evening), changing real ales; children and dogs welcome, garden picnic-sets, near Tom Brown's Museum and handy for White Horse Hill, open all day. *Recommended by R K Phillips*

WALLINGFORD SU6089 OX10 0BS
George
High Street

Handsome extended 16th-c coaching inn, decent food in bistro, restaurant or beamed bar with splendid log fireplace, good range of drinks, friendly service; tables in spacious central courtyard, 39 bedrooms. *Recommended by David and Sue Atkinson*

WANTAGE SU3988 OX12 9AB
Lamb
Mill Street, past square and Bell; down hill then bend to left

Popular comfortable pub with low beams, log fire and cosy corners, well kept Fullers London Pride and Greene King, wide choice of good generous food; children welcome, disabled facilities, garden tables. *Recommended by anon*

WEST HENDRED SU4489 OX12 8RH
Hare
A417 Reading Road, outside village

Big welcoming open-plan village pub popular for its generous mainly traditional food (not Sun evening), Greene King and a guest, efficient friendly staff, low-ceilinged main bar with bare boards and terracotta tiles, timber dividers, comfortable parquet-floor dining area; piped music; children welcome, colonnaded verandah, picnic-sets in side garden with covered deck, open all day. *Recommended by D C T and E A Frewer*

WESTON-ON-THE-GREEN SP5318 OX25 3RA
Ben Jonson
B430 near M40 junction 9

Ancient stone-and-thatch country pub, beamed bar with oak furniture, woodburner, well kept changing local ales, enjoyable food, newish dining room; children and dogs welcome. *Recommended by Laura Jones, Jane Sauyd*

You can send reports directly to us at **feedback@goodguides.com**

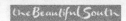

WESTON-ON-THE-GREEN SP5318
OX25 3QH

Chequers
Handy for M40 junction 9, via A34; Northampton Road (B430)

Extended thatched pub, homely and welcoming, with three areas off large semicircular raftered bar, popular interesting food including game and some lovely puddings, well kept Fullers and a guest, good wines by the glass; tables under parasols in attractive garden. *Recommended by Val and Alan Green, Martin and Alison Stainsby*

WHITCHURCH SU6377
RG8 7EL

Greyhound
High Street, just over toll bridge from Pangbourne

Pretty former ferryman's cottage taken over recently by friendly enthusiastic licensees, cosy low-beamed bar with fire, real ales including Hook Norton; small sheltered back garden, attractive village on Thames Path, open all day weekends. *Recommended by N R White*

WHITCHURCH HILL SU6378
RG8 7PG

Sun
Hill Bottom; signed from B471

Friendly unassuming brick-built pub in sleepy village, L-shaped bar with carpet and bare boards, white textured walls, dark woodwork, plush chairs and wall benches, enjoyable reasonably priced food including vegetarian choices, Brakspears, Hook Norton and Marstons ales; children welcome, couple of picnic-sets out at front, small side terrace, back lawn with play area. *Recommended by Phil Bryant*

WITNEY SP3509
OX28 4AZ

Fleece
Church Green

Smart civilised town pub on green, popular for its wide choice of good food including deli boards, friendly attentive service, Greene King ales, leather armchairs on wood floors, daily papers, restaurant; piped music; children welcome, tables out at front, ten bedrooms, open all day. *Recommended by Nigel and Sue Foster, R K Phillips*

WITNEY SP3510
OX28 6BS

☆ Three Horseshoes
Corn Street, junction with Holloway Road

Welcoming and accommodating staff in attractive 16th-c modernised stone-built pub, wide choice of good home-made food from pubby lunchtime things to more imaginative restaurant dishes, well kept Greene King ales and a guest, decent house wines, heavy beams, flagstones, well polished comfortable old furniture, log fires, separate dining room; back terrace. *Recommended by Nigel and Sue Foster, Sally Simon, Peter Lee*

WOLVERCOTE SP4909
OX2 8AH

Plough
First Turn/Wolvercote Green

Comfortably well worn-in pubby linked areas, friendly helpful service, bustling atmosphere, armchairs and Victorian-style carpeted bays in main lounge, well kept Greene King ales, farm cider, decent wines, enjoyable good value usual food in flagstoned former stables dining room and library (children allowed here), traditional snug, woodburner; picnic-sets on front terrace looking over rough meadow to canal and woods. *Recommended by Tony and Jill Radnor, Paul Humphreys*

WOOLSTONE SU2987
SN7 7QL

White Horse
Off B4507

Appealing old partly thatched pub with Victorian gables and latticed windows, plush furnishings, spacious beamed and part-panelled bar, two big open fires, Arkells ales, enjoyable good value food, restaurant; well behaved children allowed, plenty of seats in front and back gardens, secluded interesting village handy for White Horse and Ridgeway, bedrooms, open all day. *Recommended by Martin and Karen Wake, David Knowles, Jim and Frances Gowers, Jennifer and Patrick O'Dell*

ALSO WORTH A VISIT IN SURREY

Besides the region's top pubs, we recommend the following. Do tell us what you think of them: **feedback@goodguides.com**

ABINGER COMMON TQ1146   RH5 6HZ
Abinger Hatch
Off A25 W of Dorking, towards Abinger Hammer

Modernised dining pub in beautiful woodland spot, popular food (not Sun evening) from light dishes up, Fullers London Pride, Ringwood and Surrey Hills, heavy beams and flagstones, log fires, pews forming booths around oak tables in carpeted side area, plenty of space (very busy weekends when service can be slow); piped music, plain family extension; dogs welcome, some disabled access, tables in nice garden, near pretty church and pond, summer barbecues, open all day. *Recommended by CP, Ian Phillips*

ALBURY TQ0447   GU5 9AG
Drummond Arms
Off A248 SE of Guildford; The Street

Attractive recently refurbished country pub, Adnams, Courage, Fullers and Surrey Hills ales, good choice of wines, food from sandwiches and light dishes up, good service, opened-up bar with leather chesterfields, parquet-floored dining room, conservatory; pretty streamside back garden with new furniture, duck island, summer barbecues and hog roasts, pretty village with pleasant walks nearby, nine good bedrooms, open all day weekends. *Recommended by Ian Phillips, John and Verna Aspinall*

ALFOLD TQ0435   GU6 8JE
Alfold Barn
Horsham Road

Beautifully preserved 16th-c building with bar and restaurant, good food including bargain lunchtime deal, good service, a changing well kept ale, beams and rafters, mixed furniture on flagstones or carpet, log fires; garden with play area, closed Sun evening, Mon. *Recommended by Shirley Mackenzie, George James*

BANSTEAD TQ2559   SM7 2NZ
Woolpack
High Street

Well run and busy open-plan dining pub, well kept changing ales such as Sharps Doom Bar, pleasant service; open all day. *Recommended by C and R Bromage*

BETCHWORTH TQ1950   RH3 7HB
Arkle Manor
Reigate Road

Smart M&B dining pub with enjoyable gently upscale food, attractive rambling layout with easy chairs and so forth, real ales, good choice of wines by the glass, good service. *Recommended by C and R Bromage*

BETCHWORTH TQ2149   RH3 7DW
Dolphin
Off A25 W of Reigate; The Street

16th-c village pub on Greensand Way, plain tables on ancient flagstones in neat front bar,

smaller bar, panelled restaurant/bar with blazing fire and chiming grandfather clock, nice old local photographs, well kept Wells & Youngs ales, blackboard food, service can struggle at times; children and dogs welcome, small front courtyard, weekend summer barbecues in back garden, picturesque village (fine pre-Raphaelite pulpit in church), open all day. *Recommended by Geoffrey Kemp, J R Osborne, LM, C and R Bromage*

BETCHWORTH TQ2150   RH3 7DS
Red Lion
Old Road, Buckland

Comfortable dining pub with good sensibly priced home-made food, friendly helpful staff, Adnams, Fullers London Pride and Sharps Doom Bar, rather old-fashioned carpeted bar with dark wood furniture, restaurant; children welcome, picnic-sets on lawn with cricket ground beyond, dining terrace, good bedrooms in separate modern block, open all day. *Recommended by Phil Bryant*

BLETCHINGLEY TQ3250   RH1 4NU
Red Lion
Castle Street (A25), Redhill side

Old beamed village dining pub with fresh modern décor, well spaced tables, lots of racing prints, good reasonably priced mainly traditional food all day, friendly staff, well kept Greene King ales, good choice of wines by the glass, monthly quiz and some live music; no children after 6pm, tables under umbrellas on heated terrace, secret garden. *Recommended by John Atkins, Geoffrey Kemp, John Branston*

BUCKLAND TQ2250   RH3 7BG
☆ ## Jolly Farmers
Reigate Road (A25 W of Reigate)

Unusual place part pub/part restaurant/part deli, most customers come for the enjoyable all-day food using meticulously sourced local produce, but they do keep Harveys and Dark Star, local wines and home-made cordials, informal beamed and flagstoned bar with hops, smart leather sofas and armchairs, brick fireplace separating small dining room, three-room shop sells fresh vegetables, deli meats, cheeses, cakes and own range of produce, food market (Sat 9am-3pm); children welcome, tables on back terrace overlooking car park, open all day from 9.15am (breakfast served weekends). *Recommended by Derek and Maggie Washington, Derek Thomas, Colin and Louise English, Cathryn and Richard Hicks, LM, M G Hart and others*

BYFLEET TQ0661   KT14 7QT
Plough
High Road

Small pub with good range of changing ales, usually simple food from sandwiches to three or four bargain hot dishes lunchtime and Weds evening, friendly service, two log fires, rustic furnishings, farm tools, brass and copper, dominoes, more modern back area, sociable cat, no mobiles; terrace and small shady back garden. *Recommended by Ian Phillips*

CHARLWOOD TQ2441   RH6 0DS
Half Moon
The Street

Old pub next to churchyard, good-sized L-shaped bar with pubby furniture and a couple of sofas, front part open to original upstairs windows, good food from baguettes to substantial specials and enjoyable Sun lunch, friendly service, well kept ales such as Harveys and Wells & Youngs Bombardier, formal back dining room; piped music; tables out at front and in attractive courtyard area, nice village handy for Gatwick Airport. *Recommended by John Michelson, Phil Bryant, Barry Moses*

CHILWORTH TQ0347   GU4 8NP
Percy Arms
Dorking Road

Refurbished partly 18th-c pub with south african influences in décor and food, good choice of wines by the glass, Greene King IPA and Abbot, front bar and lounge with steps down to dining area, efficient service despite being busy; children welcome, garden tables with pretty views over Vale of Chilworth to St Martha's Hill, good walks. *Recommended by Phil Bryant*

CHIPSTEAD TQ2757   CR5 3NP
Ramblers Rest
Outwood Lane (B2032)

M&B country dining pub with contemporary furnishings and cocktail-bar décor in partly 14th-c rambling building, panelling, flagstones, low beams and log fires, enjoyable up-to-date and more traditional food including popular Sun lunch, real ales, good value wines by the glass, young friendly staff, daily papers; children welcome, big pleasant garden with terrace, attractive views, good walks, open all day. *Recommended by Maureen and Keith Gimson, John Branston, C and R Bromage, Grmbj*

CHIPSTEAD TQ2757   CR5 3QW
White Hart
Hazelwood Lane

Refurbished L-shaped bar, tasty if not cheap food, half a dozen real ales, helpful staff; walled garden. *Recommended by C and R Bromage*

CLAYGATE TQ1663   KT10 0HW
Griffin
Common Road

Properly old-fashioned Victorian village local with well kept ales including Fullers London Pride, some interesting dishes as well as usual pub food freshly cooked and reasonably priced. *Recommended by Gordon Stevenson*

CLAYGATE TQ1563   KT10 0JL
Hare & Hounds
The Green

Renovated flower-decked Victorian/Edwardian village pub with small restaurant, good sensibly priced french food, fine wine choice, competent service; outside seating at front and in small back garden. *Recommended by Tom and Ruth Rees, Nick Stafford*

COBHAM TQ1058   KT11 3NX
☆ ## Cricketers
Downside Common; 3.75 miles from M25 junction 10; A3 towards Cobham, first right on to A245, right at Downside signpost into Downside Bridge Road, follow road into its right fork – away from Cobham Park – at second turn after bridge, then eventually turn into the pub's own lane, immediately before Common crossroads

Worth visiting for idyllic terrace views across village green; open-plan room areas much in need of redecoration, though lots of character with crooked standing timbers, low oak beams (some with crash-pads), wide oak ceiling boards and ancient plastering laths, log fire, Fullers, Greene King and a guest, bar food; piped music; children and dogs welcome, neatly kept garden, pretty hanging baskets, open all day. *Recommended by Conor McGaughey, Michael Cross, C and R Bromage, Ian Wilson, Ron and Sheila Corbett, Ian Phillips and others*

COBHAM TQ1059   KT11 3DX
Old Bear
Riverhill

Part of Wildwood restaurant chain and no longer pubby; enjoyable bistro-style food in various smartly refurbished contemporary dining rooms, beige plush button-back sofas, pale oak cushioned dining chairs and nice old farmhouse seats on light flooring, shelves

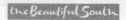

of italian olive oil, pasta and flour, silver candelabra, large modern lamps (a huge movie one too), comfortable sitting room; seats out on raised terrace. *Recommended by Geoffrey Kemp*

COBHAM TQ1159   KT11 3EZ
Running Mare
Tilt Road

Attractive old pub overlooking the green, popular for its good food (very busy Sun lunchtime), well kept Fullers, Hogs Back and Wells & Youngs ales, good friendly service, two timbered bars and restaurant; children very welcome, a few tables out at front and on back rose-covered terrace. *Recommended by Colin McKerrow*

COLDHARBOUR TQ1544   RH5 6HD
Plough
Village signposted in the network of small roads around Leith Hill

Cosy two-bar pub with own-brewed Leith Hill ales and guests, Biddenden cider, several wines by the glass, pleasant service, open fires, light beams and timbering, snug games room (darts, board games and cards), food in bar and evening restaurant (Tues-Sat) specialising in steaks (not cheap); piped music, TV; children welcome if eating, dogs in bar, front terrace and quiet back garden overlooking fields, bedrooms (ones over bar noisy), open all day. *Recommended by Sara Fulton, Roger Baker, N R White*

COMPTON SU9646   GU3 1JA
☆ ## Withies
Withies Lane; pub signed from B3000

Carefully altered 16th-c pub, charmingly civilised and gently old-fashioned, with low-beamed bar, some 17th-c carved panels between windows, splendid art nouveau settle amongst old sewing-machine tables, log fire in massive inglenook, Adnams, Greene King and a guest, popular (not cheap) bar food served by efficient, helpful, bow-tied staff; children welcome, seats on terrace, under apple trees and creeper-hung arbour, flower-edged neat front lawn, on edge of Loseley Park and close to Watts Gallery, closed Sun evening. *Recommended by B and M Kendall, Ellie Weld, David London, LM, Helen and Brian Edgeley, Gerald and Gabrielle Culliford, Ian Herdman*

DORMANSLAND TQ4042   RH7 6PS
Plough
Plough Road, off B2028 NE

Hard-working licensees and friendly staff in traditional old pub in quiet village, well kept Fullers, Harveys and Sharps, Weston's cider, decent wines, good choice of enjoyable bar food including specials board, thai restaurant, log fires and original features; children welcome, disabled facilities, good-sized garden, barbecues. *Recommended by Richard Redgrove, David Clarke*

EAST CLANDON TQ0551   GU4 7RY
☆ ## Queens Head
Just off A246 Guildford—Leatherhead; The Street

Rambling dining pub in same small group as Duke of Cambridge at Tilford and Stag in Eashing, enjoyable food from light dishes up including set deals (Mon-Thurs), good friendly service, well kept ales such as Shepherd Neame Spitfire and Surrey Hills Shere Drop from fine old elm bar counter, comfortable linked rooms, big inglenook log-effect fire; children welcome, picnic-sets on pretty front terrace and in quiet side garden, handy for two NT properties, open all day Sat and till 9pm Sun. *Recommended by Geoffrey Kemp, Ian Phillips, Richard Tilbrook*

Bedroom prices include full english breakfast, VAT and any
inclusive service charge that we know of.

EFFINGHAM TQ1153 KT24 5SW
☆ **Plough**
Orestan Lane

Popular Youngs pub with consistently well kept ales from traditional bar, good choice of enjoyable if a little pricey food including Sun roasts, plenty of wines by the glass, nice staff, two coal-effect gas fires, beamery, panelling, old plates and brassware in long lounge, carpeted floors; plenty of tables on forecourt and in attractive garden, disabled parking, handy for Polesden Lacey (NT). *Recommended by Shirley Mackenzie*

ELLENS GREEN TQ0936 RH12 3AS
Wheatsheaf
B2128 N of Rudgwick

Family-run dining pub with good home-made food from lunchtime sandwiches up, good service, Badger ales and decent wines by the glass, tiled-floor bar with large fireplace, dining areas either side; dogs welcome, some seats in front, more on back terrace, open all day. *Recommended by Shirley Mackenzie*

ENGLEFIELD GREEN SU9771 TW20 0UF
Sun
Wick Lane, Bishopsgate

Well used, beamed local, Courage Best, Greene King Abbot and Wells & Youngs Bombardier and Bitter kept well, good blackboard wine choice, generous inexpensive pubby food from sandwiches up, friendly service, small wooden tables with banquettes and low stools, lots of pub bric-a-brac including interesting beer bottle collection, colourful photographs, open fire, conservatory; soft piped music; children welcome, biscuits and water for dogs, a few tables out at front, quiet garden with aviary, handy for Savill Garden and Windsor Park. *Recommended by LM, Ian Phillips*

EPSOM TQ2158 KT18 5LE
Derby Arms
Downs Road, Epsom Downs

Comfortably reworked M&B dining pub, their usual popular food, good range of wines by the glass, two real ales, open contemporary feel in bar and restaurant with horseracing theme, two-way log fire; picnic-sets outside, good views – opposite racecourse grandstand, open all day. *Recommended by John Branston, Miss Amy Jones*

EPSOM TQ2158 KT18 5LJ
Rubbing House
Langley Vale Road (on Epsom racecourse)

Popular restauranty dining pub with attractive modern décor, good value food promptly served even when busy, tables perhaps a little close together, Fullers London Pride and Greene King IPA, serious wine list, fantastic racecourse views, upper balcony; piped music; tables outside. *Recommended by Maureen and Keith Gimson, DWAJ, Ian Wilson*

ESHER TQ1364 KT10 9RQ
Bear
High Street

Thriving Youngs pub with their full range kept well, good choice of wines by the glass, prompt friendly service, popular reasonably priced food in bar and dining end, two landmark life-size bears behind roof parapet; big-screen sports TV; outside seating with awnings, comfortable bedrooms, open all day. *Recommended by Tom and Ruth Rees, Michael Dandy, Ian Phillips*

FARNHAM SU8547 GU9 9JB
Shepherd & Flock
Moor Park Lane, on A31/A324/A325 roundabout

Flower-decked pub on Europe's largest inhabited roundabout, welcoming landlord, eight

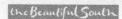

interesting changing well kept ales, enjoyable food from baguettes up, simple up-to-date décor; they may try to keep your credit card while you eat; picnic-sets out in front and in pleasant enclosed back garden with barbecue, open all day weekends. *Recommended by Rosemary and Mike Fielder*

FARNHAM SU8545
GU10 3QT
Spotted Cow
Bourne Grove, Lower Bourne (towards Tilford)

Pleasant pastel-décor dining pub on edge of town in nice wooded setting, good choice of enjoyable food from pub standards to specials, friendly helpful staff, changing ales, several wines by the glass; children and dogs welcome, big garden, open all day weekends. *Recommended by Martin and Karen Wake*

FICKLESHOLE TQ3960
CR6 9PH
White Bear
Featherbed Lane/Fairchildes Lane; off A2022 Purley Road just S of A212 roundabout

16th-c country dining pub popular for its good value generous food (all day Fri and Sat, best to book weekends), lots of small rooms, beams, flagstones and open fires, friendly prompt service, four well kept changing ales; children welcome, picnic-sets on front terrace with stone bear, sizeable back garden, open all day. *Recommended by J M and R J Hope, John Branston, Lois Kench, Grahame Brooks*

FOREST GREEN TQ1241
RH5 5RZ
 ## Parrot
B2127 just W of junction with B2126, SW of Dorking

Genuinely aged village pub with cheerful atmosphere, heavy beams, timbers, flagstones and nooks and crannies hidden away behind inglenook, generous helpings of well liked food (not Sun evening) using produce from own farm, five well kept changing ales including Ringwood, 16 wines by the glass, local juice, efficient service; shop selling own meat, cheeses, cured hams, pies and so forth; dogs allowed in bar, attractive gardens with lovely country views, good walks nearby, open all day (till midnight Sat). *Recommended by Tom and Ruth Rees, Colin and Louise English, D M Jack, C and R Bromage, LM, John Branston and others*

FRIDAY STREET TQ1245
RH5 6JR
Stephan Langton
Off B2126

Prettily placed 1930s pub in tucked-away hamlet, new owners since 2009, enjoyable well presented food (not cheap – service charge added), ales including Fullers and Surrey Hills, log fire in bar, woodburner in large modern dining area; children and dogs have been welcome, smart seating at front, wooded setting with pond, good nearby walks. *Recommended by Ian Phillips, N R White, Jill Hurley*

GODSTONE TQ3551
RH9 8DX
Bell
Under a mile from M25 junction 6, via B2236

Good up-to-date and more traditional food in refurbished open-plan M&B family dining pub, good service, comfortably modern furnishings and lighting in handsome old building, separate bar with well kept Timothy Taylors Landlord, three open fires; back terrace and garden. *Recommended by David and Diane Young, Grahame Brooks, Mr and Mrs A Curry, Keith Sangster*

GOMSHALL TQ0847
GU5 9LA
Compasses
A25

Plain bar (open all day) and much bigger, neat and comfortable dining area, popular good value home-made food, real ales such as Surrey Hills Shere Drop, decent wines by the glass, friendly service; may be piped music; children welcome, pretty garden sloping down to roadside mill stream, open all day. *Recommended by DWAJ, Alan and Shirley Sawden*

GUILDFORD SU9949   GU1 3SA
Albany
Sydenham Road

Refurbished pub tucked away behind top of high street, Caledonian Deuchars IPA,
Wadworths 6X and Wychwood Hobgoblin from original ornate counter, 20 wines by the
glass, good varied choice of promptly served food including well priced lunchtime menu,
leather tub chairs and sofas, bare boards, some striking wallpaper, raised dining area;
tables on small front terrace and in secluded garden, four bedrooms. *Recommended by*
Phil Bryant

GUILDFORD SU9949   GU2 4BL
Keystone
Portsmouth Road

Good choice of food (not Fri-Sun evenings) including deals, Black Sheep, Wadworths 6X
and two guests, friendly helpful young staff, bistro atmosphere with simple décor and
furnishings including a couple of settles and leather sofas; tables on heated back terrace
(dogs allowed here only), open all day, closed Sun evening. *Recommended by John and*
Joan Nash, Tracey and Stephen Groves, Tony Hobden, Robin Bowen

HAMBLEDON SU9639   GU8 4DR
Merry Harriers
Off A283; just N of village

Popular beamed country local with huge inglenook log fire and pine tables on bare
boards, ales such as Hop Back, Palmers, Surrey Hills and Triple fff, decent wines,
enjoyable generous pub food from sandwiches up, friendly staff, beer festivals and live
music; children welcome, big garden with boules, llamas and wandering chickens,
campsite, attractive walking countryside near Greensand Way. *Recommended by Phil Bryant*

HORLEY TQ2844   RH6 9LJ
Farmhouse
Langshott

17th-c former farmhouse, a pub since 1985, with linked beamed rooms, well kept ales
such as Greene King Old Speckled Hen, pubby food all day including late-night pizzas; big
child-friendly back garden, front smokers' shelter. *Recommended by John Branston*

HORSELL SU9959   GU21 4JL
Plough
Off South Road; Cheapside

Small friendly local overlooking wooded heath, relaxed atmosphere, well kept changing
ales such as Hogs Back TEA and St Austell Tribute, good choice of wines by the glass and
of malt whiskies, good value fresh food (all day Sat, not Sun evening) including fine range
of home-made pies and vegetarian options, quiet dining area one side of L, games
machines and TV the other; children and dogs welcome, tables in pretty garden with play
area, open all day. *Recommended by Ian Phillips, David M Smith*

HORSELL COMMON TQ0160   GU21 5NL
☆ Sands at Bleak House
Chertsey Road, The Anthonys; A320 Woking—Ottershaw

Smart contemporary restauranty pub, grey split sandstone for floor and face of bar
counter, brown leather sofas and cushioned stools, two dining rooms with dark wood
furniture, good if not cheap food, Hogs Back TEA, Surrey Hills Shere Drop and a guest,
fresh juices, friendly attentive uniformed staff, woodburners, daily newspapers; piped
jazz, TV, lively acoustics; smokers' marquee in courtyard with picnic-sets, good shortish
walks to sandpits which inspired H G Wells's *War of the Worlds*, seven bedrooms, open
all day, till 8pm Sun. *Recommended by Ian Phillips*

We say if we know a pub has piped music.

the Beautiful South

IRONS BOTTOM TQ2546   RH2 8PT
Three Horseshoes
Sidlow Bridge, off A217

Welcoming renovated local, enjoyable good value home-made food, seven well kept ales such as Fullers, Harveys and Surrey Hills, darts; tables outside, summer barbecues. *Recommended by C and R Bromage*

LEATHERHEAD TQ1656   KT22 8AW
Edmund Tylney
High Street

Cosy Wetherspoons with standard good value food and wide choice of real ales, friendly service, big fire in upstairs library-style dining room; open all day. *Recommended by R C Vincent*

LIMPSFIELD TQ4053   RH8 0DR
Bull
High Street

Friendly village local dating from the 16th c, shortish choice of tasty reasonably priced food, good value wines, Adnams and Marstons Pedigree, helpful service, darts; sports TVs, juke box; children welcome, terrace tables. *Recommended by Simon Good, Grahame Brooks, Judy Brua, Christine and Neil Townend*

LINGFIELD TQ3844   RH7 6BZ
☆ # Hare & Hounds
Turn off B2029 N at the Crowhurst/Edenbridge signpost

Smallish open-plan bar, bare boards and flagstones, mixed seating including button-back leather chesterfield, dining area, good wide-ranging food from french landlord, friendly efficient service, well kept ales such as Fullers London Pride and Harveys; children and dogs welcome, tables in pleasant split-level garden with decking, good walking country near Haxted Mill – leave boots in porch, open all day, closed Sun evening. *Recommended by Tony and Shirley Albert, Simon and Helen Barnes, Steven and Yvonne Parker, Derek Thomas, Melanie Alcock, Cathryn and Richard Hicks and others*

MERSHAM TQ3051   RH1 4EU
Inn on the Pond
Nutfield Marsh Road, off A25 W of Godstone

Popular dining pub doing enjoyable interesting food (all day Sun) including children's meals, well kept ales from Hogs Back, Kings and Sharps, Weston's cider, good choice of wines by the glass including champagne, comfortable casually contemporary dining room, back conservatory; sheltered terrace behind, views over pond and nearby cricket ground to North Downs. *Recommended by Fleur Perkie, John Branston, Peter Eyles, R K Phillips*

MICKLEHAM TQ1753   RH5 6EL
King William IV
Just off A24 Leatherhead—Dorking; Byttom Hill

Steps up to small nicely placed country pub, well kept Hogs Back TEA, Surrey Hills Shere Drop and Triple fff Alton's Pride, wide choice of food including blackboard specials, friendly service, pleasant outlook from snug plank-panelled front bar; piped music, outside gents'; children welcome, plenty of tables (some in heated open-sided timber shelters) in lovely terraced garden with great valley views, closed evenings Sun and Mon. *Recommended by LM, Phil Bryant*

Post Office address codings confusingly give the impression that some pubs are in Surrey when they're really in Hampshire or London (which is where we list them). And there's further confusion from the way the Post Office still talks about Middlesex – which disappeared in local government reorganisation nearly 50 years ago.

MICKLEHAM TQ1753   RH5 6DU

☆ **Running Horses**

Old London Road (B2209)

Upmarket all-rounder with genuinely wide mix of customers (and dogs) and easy-going
atmosphere, neatly kept open-plan bar with hunting pictures, racing cartoons and
Hogarth prints, lots of race tickets hanging from beams, straightforward pubby furniture,
inglenook with summer fresh flowers or winter fire, Fullers, Wells & Youngs and guests,
wines by the glass from a serious list, good (not cheap) food from pubby meals to more
elaborate choices, big formal restaurant with crisp white cloths and candles, competent
service; children over 10 welcome, disabled facilities, busy front terrace with lovely tubs
and hanging baskets, peaceful view of old church with stubby steeple, bedrooms, open all
day, get there early for a seat or parking space. *Recommended by Conor McGaughey,
Sheila Topham, Brian and Anna Marsden, Tony and Jill Radnor and others*

NEWDIGATE TQ2043   RH5 5DZ

☆ **Surrey Oaks**

Off A24 S of Dorking, via Beare Green; Parkgate Road

Cheery village pub with friendly landlord, well kept Harveys, Surrey Hills and three guests
from smaller breweries (beer festivals May and Aug), bottled continental beers and farm
cider/perry, well liked reasonably priced bar food (not Sun or Mon evenings), pubby
interior divided into four areas, older part has locals by the open fire in a snug beamed
room, standing area with unusually large flagstones and woodburner in inglenook, rustic
tables in light and airy main lounge, separate games room with pool, skittle alley; piped
classical music, TV and machines; children and dogs welcome, pleasingly complicated
garden has terrace, rockery with pools and waterfall, play area and two boules pitches,
open all day Sun. *Recommended by C and R Bromage, Roger and Donna Huggins, Pam and John Smith,
Peter Dandy, the Didler and others*

OCKLEY TQ1440   RH5 5TD

Inn on the Green

Billingshurst Road (A29)

Welcoming former 17th-c coaching inn on the green of a charming village, good fresh
traditional food, well kept Greene King and a guest like Kings Horsham, friendly attentive
service, slightly dated décor with usual pubby furniture, steps up to quiet eating area and
dining conservatory; tables in secluded garden, six comfortable bedrooms, good
breakfast. *Recommended by Phil Bryant*

OCKLEY TQ1439   RH5 5TH

☆ **Old School House**

Stane Street

Primarily a fish restaurant, but has thriving pubby eating area around small bar counter
with well kept Fullers ales, good wines by the glass including champagne, wonderful log
fire, buoyant atmosphere, prompt attentive young staff, good bar food from sandwiches
up; picnic-sets under cocktail parasols on sunny terrace with flowers around car park.
Recommended by Karen Eliot

OCKLEY TQ1337   RH5 5PU

☆ **Punchbowl**

Oakwood Hill, signed off A29 S

Attractive 16th-c tile-hung country pub with Horsham slab roof, welcoming relaxed
atmosphere, wide food choice (all day weekends) from sandwiches up, Badger ales,
central bar with huge inglenook, polished flagstones and low beams, restaurant area to
left and another bar to right with a couple of sofas, daily papers; children welcome away
from bar, picnic-sets in pretty garden, smokers' awning, quiet spot with good walks
including Sussex Border Path. *Recommended by Phil Bryant*

OTTERSHAW TQ0263   KT16 0LW

☆ **Castle**

Brox Road, off A320 not far from M25 junction 11

Friendly two-bar early Victorian local with big crackling log fires, country paraphernalia on black ceiling joists and walls, half a dozen well kept ales such as Harveys, Sharps, Surrey Hills and Timothy Taylors, Addlestone's cider, enjoyable bar food (not Sun evening); TV, piped music; children welcome in conservatory till 7pm, dogs in bar, tables on terrace and grass, open all day weekends. *Recommended by Ian Phillips*

OUTWOOD TQ3246   RH1 5PN

☆ **Bell**

Outwood Common, just E of village; off A23 S of Redhill

Attractive extended 17th-c country pub/restaurant, smartly rustic beamed bar with oak and elm tables and chairs (some in Jacobean style), low beams and vast stone inglenook, Fullers ales, decent wines by the glass, large range of liqueurs, enjoyable food including plenty of fish (all day Sun); piped music, Tues quiz; children and dogs welcome, neat garden with play area, seats on sheltered lawn, nice country views, handy for windmill, open all day. *Recommended by Phil Bryant, John Atkins, M G Hart*

OUTWOOD TQ3146   RH1 5QU

Dog & Duck

Princludinge of Wales Road; turn off A23 at station sign in Salfords, S of Redhill – OS Sheet 187 map reference 312460

Unhurried beamed country pub with good home-made food in bar or restaurant, welcoming service, well kept Badger ales, decent wines, warm winter fires, some live music; children welcome, garden with duck pond and play area. *Recommended by Sally Cullen, Richard Tilbrook*

OXTED TQ4048   RH8 0RR

Royal Oak

Caterfield Lane, Staffhurst Wood, S of town

Popular well managed pub, cheerful and comfortable, with good range of beers including Adnams, Harveys and Larkins, Biddenden cider, good value house wines, enjoyable locally sourced food including some imaginative dishes, back dining room; dogs welcome, nice garden with lovely views across fields, open all day weekends. *Recommended by John Branston, William Ruxton, N R White*

PYRFORD LOCK TQ0559   GU23 6QW

☆ **Anchor**

3 miles from M25 junction 10 – S on A3, then take Wisley slip road and go on past RHS garden

Light and airy Badger family dining pub (can get very busy), food all day (small helpings available), lunchtime sandwiches too, good value wines, cheerful service, simple tables on bare boards, quieter more comfortable panelled back area, narrow-boat memorabilia, pleasant conservatory, daily papers; dogs allowed in part, splendid terrace in lovely spot by bridge and locks on River Wey Navigation (handy for RHS Wisley), fenced-off play area, open all day. *Recommended by John Saville, Peter Rozée, D Crook*

REIGATE HEATH TQ2349   RH2 8RL

Skimmington Castle

Off A25 Reigate—Dorking via Flanchford Road and Bonny's Road

Nicely located small country pub, emphasis on enjoyable home-made food, ales such as Adnams and St Austell, panelled beamed rooms, big working fireplace; children and dogs welcome. *Recommended by John Michelson, Gaynor Lawson, Phil Bryant, C and R Bromage*

If we know a pub has an outdoor play area for children, we mention it.

RIPLEY TQ0456
Seven Stars
Newark Lane (B367)

GU23 6DL

Neat family-run traditional 1930s pub popular lunchtimes for enjoyable food from sandwiches to plenty of seafood, Brakspears, Fullers London Pride, Hook Norton Old Hooky and Shepherd Neame Spitfire, good wines and coffee, gleaming brasses, open fire; quiet piped music; picnic-sets in large tidy garden, river and canalside walks.
Recommended by Ian Phillips, Barrie and Mary Crees

SEND TQ0156
New Inn
Send Road, Cartbridge

GU23 7EN

Well placed old pub by River Wey Navigation, long bar decorated to suit, Adnams, Greene King Abbot and one or two unusual guests, friendly landlord, good value food from sandwiches up, log-effect gas fires; large waterside garden with moorings and smokers' shelter. *Recommended by Ian Phillips*

SEND MARSH TQ0455
☆ ## Saddlers Arms
Send Marsh Road

GU23 6JQ

Genial and attentive licensees in unpretentious low-beamed local, homely and warm, with Fullers London Pride, Hogs Back TEA, Shepherd Neame Spitfire and Wychwood Hobgoblin, good value generous home-made food (all day Sun) from sandwiches to pizzas and pubby favourites, roaring log fire, sparkling brassware, toby jugs, etc; dogs welcome, picnic-sets out front and back. *Recommended by Ian Phillips, Shirley Mackenzie, DWAJ*

SHALFORD SU9946
Parrot
Broadford Road

GU4 8DW

Big warmly welcoming pub with wide range of enjoyable fairly priced food from good snacks up, Fullers London Pride, Hogs Back TEA and Surrey Hills Shere Drop, friendly attentive staff, rows of neat pine dining tables, some easy chairs around low tables, pleasant conservatory; children welcome till 8pm, attractive garden, five bedrooms, handy for Loseley Park. *Recommended by C and R Bromage*

SHALFORD TQ0047
☆ ## Seahorse
A281 S of Guildford; The Street

GU4 8BU

Gently upmarket M&B dining pub with wide choice of food from simple to more sophisticated things, popular fixed-priced menu (weekday lunchtimes, early evenings), friendly well trained young staff, Hogs Back TEA, good choice of wines and other drinks, good contemporary furniture and artwork, smart dining room, comfortable part near entrance with sofas and huge window; picnic-sets in big lawned garden, covered terrace, open all day. *Recommended by MDN, Malcolm and Carole Lomax*

SHERE TQ0747
William Bray
Shere Lane

GU5 9HS

Major refurbishment and emphasis on good well presented locally sourced food, ales such as Hogs Back, Sharps and Surrey Hills, good choice of wines, attentive service, roomy contemporary bar with stone floor and woodburner, more formal airy restaurant with comfortable leather chairs and large F1 racing photographs (owner was driver for Tyrell and Lotus); very busy weekends; dogs welcome, tables on front split-level terrace, pretty landscaped garden. *Recommended by Martin Stafford, J D Derry, N R White, Ian Phillips, Tracey and Stephen Groves, Terry Buckland*

SOUTH GODSTONE TQ3549   RH9 8LY
Fox & Hounds
Tilburstow Hill Road/Harts Lane, off A22

Pleasant old tile-hung country pub with woodburner in low-beamed bar, welcoming staff, enjoyable good value food from pubby staples up, well kept Greene King ales from tiny bar counter, restaurant with inglenook; open all day. *Recommended by Conor McGaughey, C and R Bromage*

SUTTON GREEN TQ0054   GU4 7QD
☆ **Olive Tree**
Sutton Green Road

Big rambling dining pub in quiet countryside, good honest fresh food (not Sun, Mon evenings), cheaper bar menu including sandwiches, fireside leather sofas, relaxing back dining room, bare boards and clean-cut pastel décor, well kept Fullers London Pride, Ringwood and Timothy Taylors Landlord, good choice of wines by the glass, pleasant helpful staff; terrace tables. *Recommended by LM, Paddy and Annabelle Cribb, Katherine Tonks, Ian Phillips*

THAMES DITTON TQ1567   KT7 0QY
Albany
Queens Road, signed off Summer Road

M&B bar-with-restaurant in lovely Thames-side position, light airy modern feel, with good variety of food from sharing plates and pizzas to more upscale dishes, weekday fixed-price menu lunchtime and early evening, good choice of wines by the glass, cocktails, a couple of beers such as Sharps Doom Bar and Timothy Taylors Landlord, log fire, river pictures, daily papers; nice balconies and river-view terrace, moorings, open all day. *Recommended by Tom and Ruth Rees, Katherine Tonks, Jennie George*

THAMES DITTON TQ1666   KT7 0XY
Ferry
Portsmouth Road

Welcoming and relaxed bistro-style dining pub with good reasonably priced food from chef/landlord, well kept ales; some tables out at front. *Recommended by Tom and Ruth Rees, Lauren Bennett, Tim Grey*

TILFORD SU8743   GU10 2BU
Barley Mow
The Green, off B3001 SE of Farnham; also signed off A287

Opposite pretty cricket green, with woodburner in snug little low-ceilinged traditional bar, nice scrubbed tables in two small rooms set for food on left, interesting cricketing prints and old photographs, well kept ales such as Courage Best, Greene King Abbot, Hook Norton and Sharps Doom Bar, imaginative wine list, pubby food, weekend afternoon teas; darts and table skittles, no children except in back coach house; narrow front terrace, picnic-sets in back garden fenced off from Wey tributary, open all day Sun and, in summer, Sat. *Recommended by Phil Bryant, Rosemary and Mike Fielder*

TILFORD SU8742   GU10 2DD
Duke of Cambridge
Tilford Road

Civilised smartly done pub in same small local group as Stag at Eashing and Queens Head at East Clandon, enjoyable food with emphasis on local ingredients from standard fare to more imaginative things, children's menu, good choice of wines, Hogs Back TEA and Surrey Hills Shere Drop, efficient helpful service; terrace and garden with picnic-sets, good play area, open all day weekends. *Recommended by Canon George Farran, Martin and Karen Wake*

There are report forms at the back of the book.

VIRGINIA WATER TQ9768 GU25 4QF
Wheatsheaf
London Road; A30

Several linked areas in large 18th-c inn (Chef & Brewer), reasonably priced food, real ales; children welcome, garden tables (traffic noise), by wooded entry to lake area, bedrooms, open all day. *Recommended by Rosemary and Mike Fielder*

WALTON-ON-THAMES TQ1065 KT12 1JP
Ashley Park
Station Approach/Ashley Park Road

Comfortable well run Ember Inn with good reasonably priced food, interesting choice of well kept ales, competent friendly service, good atmosphere; open all day, bedrooms in adjoining Innkeepers Lodge. *Recommended by Ron and Sheila Corbett, Ian Phillips*

WEST CLANDON TQ0451 GU4 7ST
☆ Bulls Head
A247 SE of Woking

Comfortable, spotless and unchanging, based on 1540s timbered hall house, popular especially with older people lunchtime for good value hearty food from sandwiches up including home-made proper pies (no food Sun evening), friendly helpful staff, Surrey Hills Shere Drop, good coffee, small lantern-lit beamed front bar with open fire and some stripped brick, old local prints and bric-a-brac, simple raised back inglenook dining area, games room with darts and pool; no credit cards; children and dogs on leads welcome, disabled access, good play area in neat garden, handy for Clandon Park, good walks. *Recommended by David Lowe, DWAJ, Phil Bryant*

WEST HORSLEY TQ0853 KT24 6HR
☆ Barley Mow
Off A246 Leatherhead—Guildford at Bell & Colvill garage roundabout; The Street

Welcoming tree-shaded traditional pub, low beams, mix of flagstones, bare boards and carpet, leather sofas, two log fires, well kept ales such as Fullers London Pride, Greene King IPA and Shepherd Neame Spitfire, decent wines, good value food (not Sun evening) including nice lunchtime sandwiches, daily papers, vintage and classic car pictures (may be an AC Cobra or Jaguar XK outside), comfortable softly lit barn-like dining room; unobtrusive piped music, TV; dogs and children welcome, picnic-sets in good-sized garden, open all day. *Recommended by Ian Phillips, David Lowe, Brian Dawes, David M Smith and others*

WEST HORSLEY TQ0752 KT24 6BG
King William IV
The Street

Comfortable and welcoming early 19th-c pub with very low-beamed open-plan rambling bar, enjoyable food from baguettes up here and in conservatory restaurant, decent choice of wines by the glass, well kept Courage and a guest, good coffee, log fire, board games; piped music; children and dogs welcome, good disabled access, small sunny garden with decking and lovely hanging baskets. *Recommended by Ian Phillips, John Branston*

WEYBRIDGE TQ0864 KT13 9BN
Jolly Farmer
Princes Road

Attractive little low-beamed local opposite picturesque cricket ground, friendly efficient service, good value pubby food from sandwiches up, well kept ales such as Gales, Ringwood, St Austell and Sharps, good choice of wines by the glass, toby jugs and interesting old photographs; may be loud live music weekends; front terrace and nice back garden. *Recommended by Ian Phillips, Hunter and Christine Wright*

Oatlands Chaser
WEYBRIDGE TQ0965   KT13 9RW
Oatlands Chase

Big attractively modernised building in quiet residential road, rambling bar with stylish modern décor, pastels and unusual wallpaper, glazed panels, flagstones and painted boards, feature central fireplace, carefully mismatched furnishings mainly laid out for the wide range of enjoyable all-day food including bargain set menu, Sun roasts and proper children's meals, good service, three well kept changing ales, good wine choice, newspapers; disabled access, lots of tables out at front (some under trees), 19 immaculate bedrooms, open all day. *Recommended by Katherine Tonks, Minda and Stanley Alexander, Ian Phillips*

☆ **Old Crown**
WEYBRIDGE TQ0765   KT13 8LP
Thames Street

Comfortably old-fashioned three-bar pub dating from the 16th c, good value traditional food (not Sun-Tues evenings) from sandwiches to fresh fish, well kept Courage, Greene King and Wells & Youngs, good choice of wines by the glass, friendly efficient service, family lounge and conservatory, coal-effect gas fire; may be sports TV in back bar with Lions RFC photographs, silent fruit machine; children welcome, secluded terrace, smokers' shelter, steps down to suntrap garden overlooking Wey/Thames confluence, mooring for small boats. *Recommended by DWAJ, Jeremy King, Ian Phillips, LM and others*

☆ **Prince of Wales**
WEYBRIDGE TQ0865   KT13 9NX
Cross Road/Anderson Road off Oatlands Drive

Civilised and attractively restored flower-decked pub, good value generous pubby food from baguettes up, Sun roasts, beers from Adnams, Fullers, Wells & Youngs and one brewed for the pub, ten wines by the glass, relaxed lunchtime atmosphere, friendly service, daily papers, log-effect fire, tribal mask collection, stripped-pine dining room down a couple of steps; big-screen TVs for major sports events; well behaved children welcome, small pretty garden at side and back. *Recommended by Jeremy King, Ian Phillips*

Bee
WINDLESHAM SU9264   GU20 6PD
School Road

Stylishly refurbished with emphasis on eating, enjoyable if pricey upscale food but good value weekday set lunches, morning coffee and pastries, Sun roasts, good choice of wines by the glass, four well kept real ales; picnic-sets on small front terrace and in nice back garden with play area. *Recommended by Rosemary and Mike Fielder*

☆ **Half Moon**
WINDLESHAM SU9363   GU20 6BN
Church Road

Enjoyable if not cheap pub, much extended and mainly laid for pubby food from sandwiches up, well kept ales such as Fullers London Pride, Hogs Back TEA, Ringwood Fortyniner, Timothy Taylors Landlord and Theakstons Old Peculier, Weston's farm cider, decent wines, plenty of children's drinks, cheerful enthusiastic young staff, log fires, World War II pictures and modern furnishings, attractive barn restaurant out along covered flagstoned walkway; piped music, silenced games machine; big tidy garden with two terraces and play area. *Recommended by Guy Consterdine, Ian Phillips, Dr Martin Owton, Bertil Nygren*

White Hart
WITLEY SU9439   GU8 5PH
Petworth Road

Picture-book beamed Tudor local now owned by Wells & Youngs, their ales kept well, friendly helpful staff, enjoyable home-made food, log fire in cosy panelled inglenook snug

where George Eliot drank, bar and restaurant; tables on cobbled terrace and in garden, open all day Fri and Sat (Sun 12-6pm). *Recommended by Richard Williams*

WORPLESDON SU9854   GU3 3RN
☆ **Jolly Farmer**
Burdenshott Road, off A320 Guildford—Woking, not in village

Old pub in pleasant country setting, dark-beamed carpeted bar with small log fire, Fullers and Gales beers, stripped-brick dining extension with rugs on bare boards, generous traditional food (not cheap and they may ask to swipe your credit if running a tab); piped music; children and dogs welcome, garden tables under parasols, open all day.
Recommended by Mrs Ann Gray, Gerry and Rosemary Dobson, Ian Phillips

---

ALSO WORTH A VISIT IN SUSSEX

Besides the region's top pubs, we recommend the following. Do tell us what you think of them: **feedback@goodguides.com**

ALFRISTON TQ5203   BN26 5UE
☆ **Olde Smugglers**
Waterloo Square

Charming 14th-c inn, low beams and panelling, brick floor, sofas by huge inglenook, masses of bric-a-brac and smuggling mementoes, various nooks and crannies, welcoming licensees, wide range of good value bar food from sandwiches to imaginative specials, well kept Dark Star, Harveys and a guest like Sharps Doom Bar, real cider, good choice of wines by the glass; piped music, can get crowded – lovely village draws many visitors; children in eating area and conservatory, dogs welcome, tables on well planted back suntrap terrace and lawn, three bedrooms, open all day. *Recommended by Bruce Bird, MP, John Beeken, Phil and Jane Villiers, N R White*

AMBERLEY SO0313   BN18 9NL
☆ **Black Horse**
Off B2139

Pretty pub with character main bar (dogs allowed), plenty of pictures, high-backed settles on flagstones, beams over serving counter festooned with sheep bells and shepherds' tools, lounge with many antiques and artefacts, log fires in both bars and restaurant, straightforward bar food (all day Sun) from sandwiches up, well kept Greene King and Harveys, friendly service; piped music, children must be well behaved, nice sheltered raised garden, open all day. *Recommended by Bea Games, Michael and Deborah Ethier*

AMBERLEY TQ0211   BN18 9LR
Bridge
B2139

Popular open-plan dining pub, comfortable and relaxed even when busy, with welcoming staff, pleasant bar and separate two-room dining area, decent range of reasonably priced food from good sandwiches up, well kept ales including Harveys; children and dogs welcome, seats out in front, more tables in side garden, handy for station, open all day.
Recommended by N R White

AMBERLEY TQ0313   BN18 9NR
☆ **Sportsmans**
Crossgates; Rackham Road, off B2139

Warmly welcoming licensees and friendly efficient young staff, good fairly priced food including popular Sun roasts, well kept Dark Star, Harveys and other local ales (Aug festival), three bars including a brick-floored one with darts, great views over Amberley

Wild Brooks from pretty back conservatory restaurant and tables outside; dogs welcome, good walks, neat up-to-date bedrooms. *Recommended by LM, Miss Hazel Orchard, N R White, Bruce Bird, PL*

ANGMERING TQ0704   BN16 4AW
☆ Spotted Cow
High Street

Generally well liked food from sandwiches up and good friendly service, ales such as Fullers, Greene King, Harveys, Sharps and Timothy Taylors kept well, decent wines by the glass, smallish bar on left, long dining extension with large conservatory on right, two fires, sporting caricatures, smuggling history; children welcome, disabled access, big garden with boules and play area, lovely walk to Highdown hill fort, open all day Sun (afternoon jazz, sometimes, then). *Recommended by CP, Pam Adsley, Terry Buckland, Tony and Wendy Hobden, PL*

ARDINGLY TQ3430   RH17 6TJ
☆ Gardeners Arms
B2028 2 miles N

Reliable reasonably priced pub food in olde-worlde linked rooms, Badger beers, pleasant efficient service, standing timbers and inglenooks, scrubbed pine on flagstones and broad boards, old local photographs, mural in back part, nice relaxed atmosphere; children and dogs welcome, disabled facilities, attractive wooden furniture on pretty terrace, lots of picnic-sets in side garden, opposite South of England show ground and handy for Borde Hill and Wakehurst Place, open all day. *Recommended by Colin and Louise English, Chris Bell, C and R Bromage*

ARLINGTON TQ5507   BN26 6SJ
☆ Old Oak
Caneheath; off A22 or A27 NW of Polegate

17th-c former almshouse with open-plan L-shaped bar, beams, log fires and comfortable seating, Harveys and a guest tapped from the cask, traditional bar food (all day weekends), toad in the hole played here; piped music; children and dogs welcome, seats in quiet garden, walks in nearby Abbot's Wood nature reserve, open all day. *Recommended by anon*

ARLINGTON TQ5407   BN26 6RX
Yew Tree
Off A22 near Hailsham, or A27 W of Polegate

Neatly modernised Victorian village pub popular for its wide range of good value generous home-made food (booking advised), well kept Harveys Best and decent wines, prompt friendly service even when busy, log fires, hop-covered beams and old local photographs, darts in thriving bare-boards bar, plush lounge, comfortable conservatory; children welcome, nice big garden with play area, paddock with farm animals, good walks. *Recommended by John Beeken, Pam Adsley, Della Heath*

ARUNDEL TQ0208   BN18 9PB
☆ Black Rabbit
Mill Road, Offham; keep on and don't give up!

Comfortably refurbished riverside pub well organised for families and can get very busy, lovely spot near wildfowl reserve with timeless views of water meadows and castle; long bar with eating areas at either end, enjoyable fairly priced food all day from baguettes up, mixed recent reports on service, well kept Badger ales, several decent wines by the glass, log fires, newspapers; piped music; dogs welcome, covered tables and pretty hanging baskets out at front, terrace across road overlooking river, play area, boat trips and good walks, open all day. *Recommended by John Beeken, Colin McKerrow, N R White, David H T Dimock, Ann and Colin Hunt, Michael Butler and others*

ARUNDEL TQ0107 BN18 9AG

 ☆ **Swan**

High Street

Smart but comfortably relaxed open-plan L-shaped bar with attractive woodwork and matching fittings, friendly efficient young staff, well kept Fullers ales, good tea and coffee, good value enjoyable food from baguettes up, sporting bric-a-brac and old photographs, beaten brass former inn sign on wall, fire, restaurant, live jazz (third Sun of month from 5pm); 15 bedrooms, no car park, open all day. *Recommended by Tony and Wendy Hobden, Jestyn Phillips, Ann and Colin Hunt, Phil and Jane Villiers*

ARUNDEL TQ0107 BN18 9JG

White Hart

Queen Street

Old tile-hung inn with several roomy linked areas, wood floors and stripped-pine tables, some contemporary touches, well kept Harveys ales, pubby food from short chalked menu, chatty landlord; covered terrace tables at back, bedrooms. *Recommended by Joan and Michel Hooper-Immins*

ASHURST TQ1816 BN44 3AP

☆ **Fountain**

B2135 S of Partridge Green

Attractive well run 16th-c country local with fine old flagstones, rustic tap room on right with some antique polished trestle tables and housekeeper's chairs by inglenook log fire, second inglenook in opened-up heavy-beamed snug, good well priced food including pub staples, Fullers, Harveys and two guests, folk music (second Weds of month), regular vintage car club meetings; no under-10s; dogs welcome, pretty garden with duck pond (pay ahead if you eat out here), open all day. *Recommended by John Redfern*

BALCOMBE TQ3033 RH17 6QD

Cowdray Arms

London Road (B2036/B2110 N of village)

Bright and airy main-road pub with good blackboard food using local suppliers, well kept Greene King and a guest, good value wines by the glass, comfortable settees in L-shaped bar, darts, conservatory restaurant; children and dogs welcome, large garden. *Recommended by David Zackheim*

BALLS CROSS SU9826 GU28 9JP

 ☆ **Stag**

Village signed off A283 at N edge of Petworth

Unchanging and cheery 17th-c country pub with friendly staff, fishing rods and country knick-knacks, tiny flagstoned bar with log fire in huge inglenook, a few seats and bar stools, Badger beers, summer cider and several wines by the glass, second tiny room and appealing old-fashioned restaurant with horsey pictures, pubby food (not Sun evening), bar skittles, darts and board games in separate carpeted room; veteran outside lavatories; well behaved children allowed away from main bar, dogs welcome, seats in front under parasols, more in good-sized back garden divided by shrubbery, bedrooms. *Recommended by John Robertson, Gerry and Rosemary Dobson, the Didler, N R White*

BARNS GREEN TQ1227 RH13 0PS

Queens Head

Chapel Road

Traditional welcoming village pub, decent choice of home-made pub food from baguettes up and some good local real ales, reasonable prices; children welcome, tables out at front, garden behind with play area. *Recommended by Peter Martin*

There are report forms at the back of the book.

BEPTON SU8620   GU29 0LR
Country Inn
Severals Road

Old-fashioned friendly country local, well kept Banks's, Fullers and Wells & Youngs, good value food, heavy beams, stripped brickwork and log fire, darts-playing regulars; children welcome, tables out at front and in big garden with shady trees and play area, quiet spot. *Recommended by John Beeken, Tony and Wendy Hobden*

BERWICK TQ5105   BN26 6SP
☆ Cricketers Arms
Lower Road, S of A27

Charming local with three small unpretentious bars, huge supporting beam in each low ceiling, simple country furnishings on quarry tiles, cricketing pastels and bats, two log fires, well kept Harveys tapped from the cask, country wines, good coffee, tasty bar food (all day weekends and summer weekdays), old Sussex coin game – toad in the hole; children in family room only, dogs welcome, delightful cottagey front garden with picnic-sets amongst small brick paths, more seats behind, Bloomsbury Group wall paintings in nearby church, good South Downs walks, open all day in summer. *Recommended by Nick Lawless, Tony and Shirley Albert, Andrea Rampley, Conor McGaughey, the Didler, Michael and Margaret Cross and others*

BEXHILL TQ7208   TN39 4JE
Denbigh
Little Common Road (A259 towards Polegate)

Friendly local with enjoyable reasonably priced fresh food, well kept Harveys Best, decent wine, cheery efficient service; enclosed side garden. *Recommended by MP, Christopher Turner, Sue Addison*

BLACKBOYS TQ5220   TN22 5LG
☆ Blackboys Inn
B2192, S edge of village

Attractive old weatherboarded pub with bustling beamed locals' bar, lots of bric-a-brac here and in main parquet-floored bar on right with beams, timbers and old photos on red walls, log fire, similarly furnished restaurant; Harveys and guests, several wines by the glass, good choice of food (all day weekends) using some own-grown produce, board games; piped music; children and dogs welcome, contemporary furniture on terrace, more seats under cover by sizeable pond, pretty gazebo on side lawn, Vanguard Way passes pub and Wealdway is close by, Woodland Trust opposite, bedrooms, open all day (till 1am Fri, Sat). *Recommended by Dr Martin Owton, John Atkins, the Didler*

BODLE STREET GREEN TQ6514   BN27 4RE
White Horse
Off A271 at Windmill Hill

Roomy country pub with friendly landlord, enjoyable homely food at varnished tables, well kept Harveys, open fires; some tables outside. *Recommended by R and S Bentley, Merul Patel*

BOLNEY TQ2623   RH17 5RL
Bolney Stage
London Road, off old A23 just N of A272

Sizeable well refurbished 16th-c timbered dining pub, enjoyable varied food all day including sandwiches, ales such as Dark Star, Fullers and Harveys, good choice of wines by the glass, low beams and polished flagstones, nice mix of old furniture, woodburner and big two-way log fire; children welcome, dogs in main bar, disabled facilities, tables on terrace and lawn, play area, handy for Sheffield Park and Bluebell Railway. *Recommended by John Redfern*

We accept no free drinks or meals and inspections are anonymous.

BOLNEY TQ2622 · RH17 5QW
Eight Bells
The Street

Welcoming village pub with wide food choice from ciabattas and light dishes to enjoyable specials, bargain OAP lunch Tues, Weds, well kept Harveys, Hop Back Summer Lightning and an ale brewed for the pub, local wines from Bookers vineyard, brick-floor bar with eight handbells suspended from ceiling, good log fire, timbered dining extension, exemplary lavatories; tables under big umbrellas on outside decking with neatly lit steps, bedrooms. *Recommended by Tony and Wendy Hobden, John Beeken*

BOSHAM SU8003 · PO18 8LS
☆ Anchor Bleu
High Street

Waterside inn overlooking Chichester Harbour, two simple bars with some beams in low ochre ceilings, worn flagstones and exposed timbered brickwork, lots of nautical bric-a-brac, robust, simple furniture, up to six real ales and popular bar food; children and dogs welcome, seats on back terrace looking out over ducks and boats on sheltered inlet, massive wheel-operated bulkhead door wards off high tides, church up lane figures in Bayeux Tapestry, village and shore are worth exploring, open all day in summer.
Recommended by Terry and Nickie Williams, Val and Alan Green, Ann and Colin Hunt, Pam Adsley, Maureen and Keith Gimson and others

BREDE TQ8218 · TN31 6EJ
Red Lion
A28 opposite church

Relaxed beamed village pub with plain tables and chairs on bare boards, candles, inglenook log fire, tasty reasonably priced food including local fish, changing ales such as Edge, Old Dairy and Wells & Youngs, friendly helpful staff, pub sheepdog called Billy; a few picnic-sets out at front, garden behind, narrow entrance to car park, open all day weekends. *Recommended by Mick B, Carol Wells, Peter Meister*

BRIGHTON TQ3104 · BN1 4AD
☆ Basketmakers Arms
Gloucester Road – the E end, near Cheltenham Place; off Marlborough Place (A23) via Gloucester Street

Cheerful bustling backstreet local with eight changing ales, decent wines by the glass, over 100 malt whiskies and quite a choice of spirits, enjoyable very good value bar food all day (till 6pm weekends), two small low-ceilinged rooms, lots of interesting old tins, cigarette cards on one beam, whisky labels on another, and beermats, old advertisements, photographs and posters; piped music; children welcome till 8pm, dogs on leads, a few pavement tables, open all day (till midnight Fri, Sat). *Recommended by Conor McGaughey, Jeremy King, S T W Norton, the Didler, Colin Gooch, Peter Meister and others*

BRIGHTON TQ3104 · BN1 1UF
Colonnade
New Road, off North Street; by Theatre Royal

Small richly restored Edwardian bar, with red plush banquettes, velvet swags, shining brass and mahogany, gleaming mirrors, interesting pre-war playbills and signed theatrical photographs, well kept Fullers London Pride and Harveys Best, lots of lagers, bar snacks, daily papers; tiny front terrace overlooking Pavilion gardens. *Recommended by Val and Alan Green, Jeremy King*

BRIGHTON TQ3104 · BN1 1ND
☆ Cricketers
Black Lion Street

Cheerful and genuine town pub, friendly bustle at busy times, good relaxed atmosphere when quieter, cosy and darkly Victorian with lots of interesting bric-a-brac – even a stuffed bear; attentive service, well kept Fullers, Greene King, Harveys and Sharps tapped

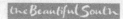

from the cask, good coffee, well priced pubby food (till 7.30pm weekends) from sandwiches up in covered former stables courtyard and upstairs bar, restaurant (where children allowed); piped and some live music; tall tables out in front, open all day. *Recommended by Dr and Mrs A K Clarke, Michael Butler, Ann and Colin Hunt, Nigel and Jean Eames*

BRIGHTON TQ3104   BN1 1HJ
Druids Head
Brighton Place

Brick and flint pub dating from the 16th c with smuggling history, well kept Harveys and guests, wide choice of enjoyable good value food; children welcome till 6pm, seats out in front under hanging baskets, open all day. *Recommended by Colin Gooch*

☆ BRIGHTON TQ3004   BN1 3PB
Evening Star
Surrey Street

Popular chatty drinkers' pub with up to four good Dark Star ales (originally brewed here), lots of changing guest beers including continentals (in bottles too), farm ciders and perries, country wines, lunchtime baguettes, friendly staff coping well when busy, simple pale wood furniture on bare boards, nice mix of customers; unobtrusive piped music, some live; pavement tables, open all day. *Recommended by the Didler, N R White, Peter Meister, Paul Davis*

☆ BRIGHTON TQ3105   BN2 9UA
Greys
Southover Street, off A270 Lewes Road opposite The Level (public park)

Certainly not a standard pub but does have basic simple furnishings on bare boards and flagstones, some wood panelling and a flame-effect stove, bar on right liked by regulars, dining side on left with flowers and candles on tables, Harveys and Timothy Taylors Landlord, several belgian bottled beers, carefully chosen wines, good food (not Sun evening, Mon or Fri) using local ingredients, live music Mon evening (tickets only), posters and flyers from previous performers on stair wall; no children; dogs in bar, seats under parasols on heated terrace, almost no parking on this steep lane or in nearby streets, open from 4pm, all day weekends. *Recommended by anon*

BRIGHTON TQ3103   BN2 1JN
Hand in Hand
Upper St James's Street, Kemptown

Brighton's smallest pub (can get crowded) brewing its own unusual Kemptown ales, also five weekly changing guests, plenty of bottled beers and Weston's cider, hot pies and sausage rolls, cockles and mussels Fri, cheerful service, dim-lit bar with tie collection and newspaper pages all over walls, photographs including Victorian nudes on ceiling, colourful mix of customers; veteran fruit machine, interesting piped music, live jazz Sun; open all day. *Recommended by Eddie Edwards*

BRIGHTON TQ3004   BN1 1AD
Pub du Vin
Ship Street

Next to Hotel du Vin, long and narrow with comfortable wall seating one end, soft lighting, local photographs, stripped boards, five well kept ales including Dark Star and Harveys from ornate pewter bar counter, good choice of wines by the glass, friendly helpful staff, enjoyable pubby food, modern grey leather-seated bar chairs and light oak tables, flame-effect fire, small cosy coir-carpeted room opposite with squashy black armchairs and sofas; marvellous original marble urinals worth a look; 11 comfortable bedrooms. *Recommended by Dr and Mrs A K Clarke, M E and F J Thomasson, Jeremy King*

We can always use photos of pubs on our website – do email one to us:
feedback@thegoodpubguide.co.uk

BRIGHTON TQ3004   BN1 1AH
Victory
Duke Street

Bustling Lanes' corner local with lovely green-tiled façade and etched windows, long
benches and medley of chairs and tables on bare boards, open fire in cosy snug, upstairs
area, local ales such as Dark Star, real cider, generous food including some unusual
things like zebra, live music, free wi-fi; children till 8pm, some pavement and courtyard
tables, open all day (till 2am Fri, Sat). *Recommended by Val and Alan Green*

BURPHAM TQ0308   BN18 9RR
☆ George & Dragon
Off A27 near Warningcamp

Main emphasis in this busy 17th-c dining pub is on interesting modern food and the front
part is restaurant, small area for drinkers, Arundel and Sharps ales, efficient service;
children welcome, dogs in bar, some picnic-sets out in front, hilltop village and short walk
from pub gives splendid views down to Arundel Castle and river. *Recommended by Karen Eliot,
CP, Guy Vowles, Di and Mike Gillam, Tony Middis, Ben Samways and others*

BYWORTH SU9821   GU28 0HL
☆ Black Horse
Off A283

Popular and chatty country pub with smart simply furnished bar, pews and scrubbed
tables on bare boards, pictures and old photographs, daily papers and open fires, ales
such as Dark Star, Flowerpots, Langham and Wells & Youngs, well liked food (not winter
Sun evening) from light lunchtime dishes up, children's menu, nooks and crannies in
back restaurant, spiral staircase to a heavily beamed function room, games room with
pool; dogs allowed in bar, attractive garden with tables on steep grassy terraces, lovely
Downs' views, open all day. *Recommended by Bruce Bird, the Didler, Tony and Wendy Hobden, Ann
and Colin Hunt*

CHAILEY TQ3919   BN8 4DA
☆ Five Bells
A275, 9 miles N of Lewes

Attractive rambling roadside pub, spacious and interesting, with enjoyable food putting
unusual touches to good local and organic ingredients, well kept Harveys and Timothy
Taylors Landlord, decent wine choice, young helpful staff, lots of different rooms and
alcoves leading from low-beamed central bar with fine old brick floor, brick walls,
inglenook, leather sofas and settles, live jazz Fri; piped music; pretty garden front and
side with picnic-sets, closed Mon. *Recommended by John Beeken*

CHAILEY TQ3919   BN8 4BD
Horns Lodge
A275

Traditional former coaching inn, heavily timbered inside, with settles, horsebrasses and
rural prints, log fires at each end of longish front bar, well kept Harveys and guests such
as Dark Star and Dorking, good range of fairly priced bar food (not Tues) from
sandwiches up, obliging staff, brick-floored restaurant, games room with darts and bar
billiards, cribbage, dominoes and board games, too; piped music; children and dogs
welcome, tables in garden with sandpit, bedrooms, open all day weekends. *Recommended by
John Beeken, Tony and Wendy Hobden*

CHICHESTER SU8604   PO19 1LP
Old Cross
North Street

Refurbished open-plan pub in partly 16th-c building, bargain pubby food including pre-
theatre weekday evening deals, friendly helpful staff, Ringwood Best and Wells & Youngs
Bombardier from island bar, log fires. *Recommended by Alec Summers, Ann and Colin Hunt*

CHIDDINGLY TQ5414   BN8 6HE
☆ **Six Bells**
Village signed off A22 Uckfield—Hailsham

Cheerful unpretentious village local with long-serving licensees and plenty of loyal
regulars, bars with shabby charm, simple seats, bric-a-brac, posters and pictures, log
fires, more space in sensitive extension, well kept Courage, Harveys and a guest beer, well
liked low-priced bar food (all day Fri-Sun), weekend live music; seats at back beyond
goldfish pond, boules, monthly vintage car meetings, church opposite with interesting
Jefferay monument, pleasant area for walks, open all day weekends. *Recommended by*
John Beeken, Mike Horgan, Di Wright, B and M Kendall, Nick Lawless, Tom Wexler

CHILGROVE SU8116   PO18 9JZ
☆ **Royal Oak**
Off B2141 Petersfield—Chichester, signed Hooksway

Chatty long-serving licensee at this unchanging old country pub, popular with walkers
and locals; two simple cosy bars, plain kitchen tables and chairs, log fires, Exmoor, Gales,
Sharps and a guest beer, simple affordable food, cottagey dining room with woodburner,
straightforward family room, shut the box; piped music, but live music second and last
Fri of month; dogs welcome in bar, plenty of picnic-sets in big pretty garden, near South
Downs Way, closed Sun evening, Mon and possibly from mid-Oct to mid-Nov. *Recommended*
by Ann and Colin Hunt, J A Snell

CLIMPING SU9902   BN17 5RU
Oystercatcher
A259/B2233

Roomy part-thatched popular Vintage Inn dining pub, olde-worlde décor, friendly well
trained young staff, wide choice of reasonably priced traditional food all day from
sandwiches and starters doubling as light dishes up, good value set menu too, well kept
Harveys Best, Shepherd Neame Spitfire and Timothy Taylors Landlord, good wines by the
glass, nicely served coffee, log fires; disabled lavatories, picnic-sets in pleasant front
garden (some traffic noise). *Recommended by David H T Dimock, N J Roberts, Graham Lewis*

COLEMANS HATCH TQ4533   TN7 4EJ
☆ **Hatch**
Signed off B2026, or off B2110 opposite church

Quaint and attractive little weatherboarded Ashdown Forest pub dating from 1430, big
log fire in quickly filling beamed bar, small back dining room with another fire, very wide
choice of good generous home-made food, well kept Harveys, Larkins and one or two
guest beers, friendly quick young staff, good mix of customers including families and
dogs; not much parking so get there early; picnic-sets on front terrace and in beautifully
kept big garden, open all day Sat, Sun. *Recommended by Vernon Rowe, the Didler, Laurence Smith,*
Christian Mole, Bruce Bird

COMPTON SU7714   PO18 9HA
Coach & Horses
B2146 S of Petersfield

Welcoming 17th-c two-bar local in pleasant village not far from Uppark (NT), pine
shutters and panelling, woodburner, three or four interesting changing ales, enjoyable
food from landlord/chef including two-for-one steak night Weds, bar billiards; children
and dogs welcome, tables out by village square, good surrounding walks. *Recommended by*
Geoff and Linda Payne

COOLHAM TQ1423   RH13 8GE
☆ **George & Dragon**
Dragons Green, Dragons Lane; pub signed off A272

Tile-hung cottage with cosy chatty bar, massive unusually low black beams (see if you can
decide whether the date cut into one is 1677 or 1577), timbered walls, simple chairs and
rustic stools, roaring log fire in big inglenook, Badger beers and decent pub food served

by friendly staff, smaller back bar, separate restaurant; piped music – live music last Sun of month; children and dogs welcome, picnic-sets in pretty orchard garden, open all day weekends (till 8pm Sun). *Recommended by Philip and Cheryl Hill, Mrs J Ekins-Daukes, Ian Phillips*

COWBEECH TQ6114   BN27 4JQ
☆ Merrie Harriers
Off A271

White clapboarded village local, beamed public bar with inglenook log fire, high-backed settle and mixed tables and chairs, old local photographs, carpeted dining lounge, well kept Harveys Best and a guest, good food from nice bar snacks up, friendly service, brick-walled back restaurant; a few picnic-sets out in front, rustic seats in terraced garden with country views. *Recommended by Laurence Smith, Peter Meister, Tobias Sheppard, Gary Neate*

CROWBOROUGH TQ5130   TN6 1BB
Blue Anchor
Beacon Road (A26)

Improved and continuing well under brother licensees, well kept Shepherd Neame ales, enjoyable fairly priced home-made food using local suppliers, friendly service; children welcome, dogs in bar, big garden with terrace and play area, open all day. *Recommended by Peter Meister, SRK*

CROWBOROUGH TQ5329   TN6 2NF
Wheatsheaf
Off Mount Pleasant

Friendly three-room 18th-c Harveys pub with their full range, reasonably priced home-made food (not Fri-Sun evenings or Mon), open fires, beer and music festivals, other events like leek and dog shows; side garden with seats under large tree, bedrooms in adjacent cottage, open all day. *Recommended by Scott Walters*

CUCKFIELD TQ3025   RH17 5BS
Rose & Crown
London Road

17th-c beamed and panelled pub under new ownership, comfortably refurbished with emphasis on spanish tapas, decent wines, well kept Harveys; children welcome, tables out in front and in garden behind, open all day, closed Sun evening. *Recommended by Terry Buckland, Mitch Clarke*

CUCKFIELD TQ3024   RH17 5JX
Talbot
High Street

Thriving under new management, light airy feel, imaginative food in bar and upstairs restaurant, real ales, good service. *Recommended by Terry Buckland*

DALLINGTON TQ6619   TN21 9LB
☆ Swan
Woods Corner, B2096 E

Popular local with cheerful chatty atmosphere, well kept Harveys, decent wines by the glass, enjoyable pubby food including deals, takeaway fish and chips (Tues), efficient service, bare-boards bar divided by standing timbers, woodburner, mixed furniture including cushioned settle and high-backed pew, candles in bottles and fresh flowers, simple back restaurant with far-reaching views to the coast; piped music; steps down to lavatories and smallish back garden. *Recommended by N R White, Mike and Eleanor Anderson*

DELL QUAY SU8302   PO20 7EE
Crown & Anchor
Off A286 S of Chichester – look out for small sign

Modernised 19th/20th-c beamed pub in splendid spot overlooking Chichester Harbour – best at high tide and quiet times, can be packed on sunny days; comfortable bow-

windowed lounge bar, panelled public bar (dogs welcome), two log fires, lots of wines by the glass, well kept Wells & Youngs ales and a guest such as Butcombe, enjoyable food all day, friendly service; large terrace, nice walks. *Recommended by Ann and Colin Hunt, Jim and Frances Gowers, Miss A E Dare, N J Roberts, J A Snell, Martin and Karen Wake*

DENTON TQ4502   BN9 0QB
☆ Flying Fish
Denton Road

Attractive 17th-c flint village pub by South Downs Way, floor tiles throughout, simple main bar, tiny end room with facing sofas, nice middle room with little log fire by built-in wall seats, long cushioned pews and mixed dining chairs, modern paintings, high-ceilinged end dining room, Shepherd Neame ales, decent wines by the glass, fish and game and more pubby food cooked well by french chef/landlord, reasonable prices, friendly service; picnic-sets in front and on long back decking looking up to sloping garden, good bedrooms. *Recommended by John Beeken, the Didler, Michael Rugman*

DEVILS DYKE TQ2511   BN1 8YJ
Devils Dyke
Devils Dyke Road

Vintage Inn set alone on Downs above Brighton and worth visiting for the spectacular views night and day, their usual food, ales such as Harveys Best, Shepherd Neame Spitfire and Timothy Taylors Landlord; children welcome, tables outside, NT pay car park, open all day. *Recommended by Colin Gooch*

DITCHLING TQ3215   BN6 8TA
☆ Bull
High Street (B2112)

Handsome rambling old building, beams, old wooden furniture on bare boards, fire, well kept Harveys, Timothy Taylors Landlord and two guests, home-made food from sandwiches up including good Sun roasts, nicely furnished dining rooms with mellow décor and candles, snug area with chesterfields; piped music – live folk music last Sun of month; children welcome, dogs in bar, disabled access, attractive big garden and suntrap terrace, barbecue, four nice bedrooms, good breakfast, open all day. *Recommended by Nick Lawless*

EAST DEAN SU9012   PO18 0JG
☆ Star & Garter
Village signed with Charlton off A286 in Singleton; also signed off A285

Emphasis very much on good fresh seafood (other choices too) in this well run airy dining pub, attractively furnished bar and restaurant with stripped panelling, exposed brickwork and oak floors, furnishings from sturdy stripped tables and country kitchen chairs through chunky modern to some antique carved settles, Arundel and guests tapped from the cask, several wines by the glass, friendly young staff, daily papers; piped music; children welcome, dogs in bar, teak furniture on heated terrace, smokers' shelter, steps down to walled lawn with picnic-sets, peaceful village green position and near South Downs Way, bedrooms, open all day weekends (food all day then too).
Recommended by Nick Lawless, CP, Maureen and Keith Gimson, Henry Midwinter, Graeme Manson, Christopher Turner and others

EAST GRINSTEAD TQ3936   RH19 4AT
☆ Old Mill
Dunnings Road, S towards Saint Hill

Interesting 16th-c mill cottage over stream reworked as spacious informal Whiting & Hammond dining pub; lots of panelling, old photographs and pictures, carpeted main dining area with mix of old tables (each with church candle), steps down to ancient very low-ceilinged part with fine timbers and inglenook woodburner, sizeable bar with long curved counter and bright plush stools, library dining area off, enjoyable hearty fresh food (all day), good choice of wines by the glass, Harveys ales including seasonal ones, friendly efficient service; piped music; children welcome, picnic-sets in front garden, covered decking next to working waterwheel, handy for Standen (NT). *Recommended by N J Roberts, Andrew Hughes, Laurence Evans*

EAST HOATHLY TQ5216   BN8 6DR
☆ **Kings Head**
High Street/Mill Lane

Well kept 1648 ales (brewed here) and Harveys Best in long comfortably worn-in open-plan bar, some dark panelling and stripped brick, upholidaystered settles, old local photographs, log fire, wide choice of enjoyable sensibly priced hearty food, friendly helpful service, daily papers, restaurant; TV; garden up steps behind. *Recommended by John Beeken*

EAST LAVANT SU8608   PO18 0AX
☆ **Royal Oak**
Pook Lane, off A286

Restauranty dining pub in pretty Georgian house, really good imaginative food, home-baked breads, good wine list, low beams and crooked timbers, stripped brickwork, scrubbed tables and church candles, log fires, small drinking area with wall seats and sofas, ales such as Sharps and Skinners tapped from the cask; no dogs; tables on flagstoned front terrace with far-reaching views, comfortable bedrooms and self-catering cottages, open all day. *Recommended by Miss A E Dare, R and M Thomas, John Chambers*

EAST PRESTON TQ0701   BN16 1PD
Sea View
Sea Road

Hidden-away comfortable seaside pub, enjoyable good value home-made food (not Sun, Mon evenings), children's menu and OAP lunches (Mon, Tues), well kept ales including Arundel Castle, neat friendly staff; nice garden, limited parking, bedrooms. *Recommended by Tony and Wendy Hobden*

EASTBOURNE TV6199   BN22 7NE
Marine
Seaside Road (A259)

Spacious comfortable pub near seafront run by welcoming long-serving licensees, panelled bar, lounge with sofas and tub chairs, log fire, well kept ales such as Fullers London Pride and Wychwood Hobgoblin, good choice of wines and brandies, enjoyable pubby food from sandwiches up, back conservatory; children welcome. *Recommended by John Atkins, John Walker, Jon Baker, Matt Colson*

EASTERGATE SU9405   PO20 3UT
Wilkes Head
Just off A29 Fontwell—Bognor; Church Lane

Small friendly two-bar local with dining extension, flagstones and inglenook log fire, enjoyable reasonably priced food from sandwiches up, real ales such as Castle Rock Harvest Pale and Hop Back Summer Lightning, pleasant service, darts; tables in big garden with covered smokers' area, open all day weekends. *Recommended by Tony and Wendy Hobden*

ELSTED SU8320   GU29 0JT
Elsted Inn
Elsted Marsh

New welcoming licensees at this attractive country pub, enjoyable food from shortish menu, real ales such as Ballards, Otter and Sharps, two log fires, nice country furniture, old Goodwood racing photos (both horses and cars), dining area at back; plenty of seating in lovely enclosed Downs-view garden with big terrace, bedrooms, has been open all day weekends. *Recommended by Geoff and Linda Payne*

☆ **Three Horseshoes**
ELSTED SU8119   GU29 0JY

Village signed from B2141 Chichester—Petersfield; from A272 about 2 miles W of Midhurst, turn left heading W

A congenial bustle at this pretty white-painted old pub, beamed rooms, log fires and candlelight, ancient flooring, antique furnishings, fresh flowers and attractive prints and photographs, four changing ales tapped from the cask, summer cider, often interesting bar food including lovely puddings; well behaved children allowed, dogs in bar, delightful flowering garden with plenty of seats and fine views of South Downs, good surrounding walks. *Recommended by Tony and Jill Radnor, Karen Eliot, Henry Midwinter, D and J Ashdown, John Beeken and others*

☆ **Huntsman**
ERIDGE STATION TQ5434   TN3 9LE

Signed off A26 S of Eridge Green

Country local with two opened-up rooms, pubby furniture on bare boards, hunting pictures, ales from Badger and Gribble, over two dozen wines by the glass, popular bar food (not Sun evening, Mon) using some own-grown produce, friendly staff; children and dogs welcome, picnic-sets and heaters on decking, outside bar, more seats on lawn among weeping willows, parking can be difficult weekdays (lots of commuters cars), open all day weekends, closed Mon lunchtime. *Recommended by Heather and Dick Martin, Mrs J Ekins-Daukes, B J Harding, Peter Meister, N R White, Alan Franck and others*

Foresters Arms
FAIRWARP TQ4626   TN22 3BP

B2026

Chatty Ashdown Forest local handy for Vanguard Way and Weald Way, comfortable lounge bar, wide choice of enjoyable well priced food, friendly staff, Badger ales, farm cider, woodburner; piped music; children and dogs welcome, tables out on terrace and in garden, play area on small village green opposite. *Recommended by Mrs Diana Courtney*

Red Lion
FERNHURST SU9028   GU27 3HY

The Green, off A286 via Church Lane

Friendly wisteria-covered 16th-c pub tucked quietly away by green and cricket pitch near church, heavy beams and timbers, attractive furnishings, food from interesting sandwiches and snacks up, well kept Fullers ales and a guest, good wines, cheerful helpful service, restaurant; children welcome, pretty gardens front and back, open all day Sun. *Recommended by Chris Harrington, Ann and Colin Hunt*

Henty Arms
FERRING TQ0903   BN12 6QY

Ferring Lane

Six well kept changing ales (often an unusual one like Sadlers Wee Shimmy), generous attractively priced food (can get busy so best to book), breakfast from 9am Tues-Fri, neat friendly staff, opened-up lounge/dining area, log fire, separate bar with games and TV; garden tables. *Recommended by Tony and Wendy Hobden*

Gun
FINDON TQ1208   BN14 0TA

High Street

Low-beamed pub with friendly atmosphere, good fairly priced food (not Sun evening, Mon), well kept beers; children welcome, sheltered garden, pretty village below Cissbury Ring. *Recommended by Gerald and Gabrielle Culliford*

We say if we know a pub allows dogs.

FINDON TQ1208   BN14 0TE
Village House
High Street; off A24 N of Worthing

Attractive converted 16th-c coach house, panelling, pictures and big open fire in large L-shaped bar, restaurant beyond, enjoyable fresh pubby food (not Sun evening) including blackboard specials and bargains for two, Arundel Gold, Gales HSB, Fullers London Pride and Harveys Best, fortnightly jazz, monthly quiz; small attractive walled garden, six comfortable bedrooms, handy for Cissbury Ring and downland walks. *Recommended by Trish McManus, Tony and Wendy Hobden*

FIRLE TQ4607   BN8 6NS
☆ ## Ram
Village signed off A27 Lewes—Polegate

Refurbished 16th-c village pub geared for dining but welcoming drinkers, popular if not particulary cheap restauranty food including good Sun roasts, well kept Harveys with guests such as Dark Star and Sharps, real cider, friendly staff, three main areas with log fires, rustic furniture on wood floors, soft lighting; children and dogs welcome, picnic-sets out in front, big walled garden behind with fruit trees, play area, good walks, four stylish bedrooms, open all day. *Recommended by J A Snell, Alan Franck, N R White*

FISHBOURNE SU8304   PO19 3JP
☆ ## Bulls Head
Fishbourne Road (A259 Chichester—Emsworth)

Thoroughly traditional, with friendly staff, well kept Fullers/Gales ales, popular good value food (not Sun evening) changing daily, copper pans on black beams, some stripped brick and panelling, good log fire, daily papers, exemplary lavatories; unobtrusive piped music; children welcome, tables on heated covered deck, four bedrooms in former skittles alley. *Recommended by Terry and Nickie Williams, John Beeken, David H T Dimock, Miss A E Dare*

FLETCHING TQ4223   TN22 3ST
Rose & Crown
High Street

Well run 16th-c beamed village pub, inglenook log fire and comfortable wall banquettes in carpeted bar, wide range of enjoyable fairly priced home-made food from baguettes to generous Sun roasts, small restaurant, good attentive service, Harveys and guests; dogs welcome, tables in pretty garden, three bedrooms, open all day. *Recommended by C and R Bromage, Jason Bunce*

FULKING TQ2411   BN5 9LU
Shepherd & Dog
Off A281 N of Brighton, via Poynings

Old bay-windowed pub in beautiful spot below Downs, beams, panelling and inglenook, ales such as Dark Star, food from baguettes up; terrace and pretty streamside garden with well used picnic-sets, straightforward climb to Devils Dyke. *Recommended by Tim Loryman, John Redfern, Martin and Karen Wake*

FUNTINGTON SU7908   PO18 9LL
Fox & Hounds
Common Road (B2146)

Welcoming beamed family pub with cottagey rooms and huge log fire, wide choice of enjoyable food including popular Sun carvery (best to book weekends), good service, well kept Badger ales, reasonably priced wines and nice coffee, comfortable dining extension; garden behind, pair of inn signs – one a pack of hounds, the other a family of foxes. *Recommended by Terry and Nickie Williams, Ann and Colin Hunt*

GLYNDE TQ4508   BN8 6SS
☆ **Trevor Arms**
Over railway bridge S of village

Brick and flint village pub, impressive dining room with mix of high-backed settles, pews and cushioned dining chairs around mixed tables, carpeted middle room with Glyndebourne pictures leading to snug bar with small fireplace and fine downland views, reasonably priced food including OAP weekday lunch deals, well kept Harveys ales, friendly service, locals' bar with parquet flooring, panelled dado, old photographs of the pub, darts and toad in the hole; big garden with rows of picnic-sets and Downs backdrop, popular with walkers, railway station next door, open all day. *Recommended by John Beeken*

HAMMERPOT TQ0605   BN16 4EU
☆ **Woodmans Arms**
On N (eastbound) side of A27

Well kept pretty thatched pub rebuilt after 2004 fire, beams and timbers, good choice of enjoyable food from sandwiches up (smaller helpings available), Fullers/Gales and a guest beer, neat polite staff, woodburner in inglenook; no dogs inside; children welcome if eating, garden tables, open all day, closed Sun evening. *Recommended by Jo Connelly, Ann and Colin Hunt, Tony and Wendy Hobden*

HEATHFIELD TQ5920   TN21 9AH
☆ **Star**
Church Street, Old Heathfield, off A265/B2096 E

Good mix of locals and visitors in this characterful country pub by village church, two main bar rooms (one more set up for eating) with heavy beams, built-in settles and window seats, panelling, inglenook log fire in one, woodburner in other, well kept Harveys, Shepherd Neame and a guest, decent wines by the glass, good choice of enjoyable blackboard food, upstairs dining room; piped music, pleasant helpful staff; children welcome in eating areas, dogs in bar, prettily planted garden with rustic seats under parasols and lovely view over rolling countryside (Turner thought it fine enough to paint), open all day. *Recommended by Laurence Smith, Mike Gorton*

HENFIELD TQ2116   BN5 9HP
White Hart
High Street (A281)

Friendly 17th-c village pub (former coaching inn), Badger beers and enjoyable locally sourced food including good value weekday set menu, decent wines, comfortable L-shaped lounge, log fire in stone fireplace, dark beams and panelling, pine furniture on parquet floor, chess and draughts, large civilised dining area; children welcome, picnic-sets in small pleasant courtyard garden, open all day weekends (food all day then, too). *Recommended by Dr and Mrs M Davies, Martin Šayers*

HENLEY SU8925   GU27 3HQ
☆ **Duke of Cumberland Arms**
Off A286 S of Fernhurst

Wisteria-covered 15th-c stone-built pub with log fires in two small rooms, low ceilings, scrubbed oak furniture on brick or flagstoned floors, rustic decorations, well kept Harveys and a couple of guests tapped from the cask, popular often interesting bar food (not Sun evening), separate restaurant, friendly attentive staff; well behaved children and dogs welcome, seats on terrace, lovely hill views, charming sloping garden and trout ponds, open all day. *Recommended by Bruce Bird, Richard Follett, Henry Midwinter, the Didler, Chris Harrison, Miss A E Dare and others*

HOUGHTON TQ0111   BN18 9LW
George & Dragon
B2139 W of Storrington

Elizabethan beams and timbers, attractive old-world bar rambling up and down steps,

Arun Valley views from back extension, reasonably priced generous food (all day weekends), friendly service, Marstons-related ales and decent wines, note the elephant photograph above the fireplace; piped music; children welcome, charming well organised sloping garden, good walks. *Recommended by Michael and Deborah Ethier*

HURSTPIERPOINT TQ2816   BN6 9RQ
☆ New Inn
High Street

Popular 16th-c beamed pub under same management as Bull in Ditchling, well kept ales including Harveys, good wines by the glass, enjoyable food with plenty for vegetarians, good friendly young staff, contrasting linked areas including oak-panelled dim-lit back part with bric-a-brac and open fire, and a smart apple-green dining room; sports TV; children and dogs welcome, garden tables, open all day. *Recommended by Terry Buckland, Tim Loryman*

ICKLESHAM TQ8716   TN36 4BL
☆ Queens Head
Off A259 Rye—Hastings

Friendly well run country pub, extremely popular locally (and at weekends with cyclists and walkers), open-plan areas around big serving counter with high beamed walls, vaulted roof, shelves of bottles, plenty of farming implements and animal traps, pubby furniture on brown pattered carpet, other areas with inglenooks and a back room with old bicycle memorabilia, Greene King, Harveys and a couple of guests, local cider, several wines by the glass, straightforward reasonably priced bar food (all day weekends); piped jazz or blues, live 4-6pm Sun; well behaved children allowed away from bar till 8.30pm, dogs welcome in bar, picnic-sets, boules and play area in peaceful garden with fine Brede Valley views, you can walk to Winchelsea, open all day. *Recommended by V Brogden, Robert Kibble, Peter Meister, Tom and Jill Jones, N R White, Colin and Louise English and others*

ICKLESHAM TQ8716   TN36 4BD
☆ Robin Hood
Main Road

Friendly no-frills beamed pub with enthusiastic landlord and cheerful attentive staff, great local atmosphere, good value unpretentious home-made food including blackboard specials, six well kept changing ales (many from small breweries), hops overhead, lots of copper bric-a-brac, log fire, games area with pool, back dining extension; big garden with Brede Valley views. *Recommended by Tom and Jill Jones, Bruce Bird, Conrad Freezer, Peter Meister*

ISFIELD TQ4417   TN22 5XB
Laughing Fish
Station Road

Opened-up Victorian local, jovial landlord and friendly staff, good value home-made pubby food (not Sun evening), Greene King and guests, extensive wine list, open fire, traditional games, events including entertaining beer race Easter bank holiday Mon; children and dogs welcome, disabled access, small pleasantly shaded walled garden with enclosed play area, right by Lavender Line, open all day. *Recommended by John Beeken*

JEVINGTON TQ5601   BN26 5QB
Eight Bells
Jevington Road, N of East Dean

Village pub with simple furnishings, heavy beams, panelling, parquet floor and inglenook flame-effect fire, good choice of popular home-made food (all day Sun – best to book weekends) from sandwiches up, nice puddings, Adnams Broadside, Flowers Original and Harveys Best; piped music; dogs welcome, front terrace, secluded Downs-view garden with some sturdy tables under cover, adjacent cricket field, good walking country, open all day. *Recommended by Pam Adsley*

KINGSFOLD TQ1635   RH12 3SA
Wise Old Owl
Dorking Road (A24 Dorking—Horsham, near A29 junction)

Nicely rambling olde-worlde reworking of 1930s pub, standing timbers dividing seating areas, Dark Star and Hepworth from long planked counter, good choice of wines by the glass, enjoyable well priced food from sandwiches up including popular Sun lunch, cream teas, good friendly service, contemporary restaurant with high-backed wicker chairs and mixed tables on coir or wood flooring, some modern art, church candles and fresh flowers, log fires, deli/farm shop; piped music, sports TV, games machines in bar alcove, upstairs lavatories; children welcome, picnic-tables on fenced-off gravel areas, open all day from 9.30am. *Recommended by Ian Phillips*

KINGSTON TQ3908   BN7 3NT
☆ # Juggs
Village signed off A27 by roundabout W of Lewes

Popular rose-covered village pub, heavy 15th-c beams and very low front door, lots of neatly stripped masonry, sturdy wooden furniture on bare boards and stone slabs, smaller eating areas including a family room, wide choice of enjoyable food including plenty of fish and good vegetarian options, well kept Shepherd Neame and a beer brewed for the pub, good coffee and wine list, friendly helpful staff, log fires; piped music; children and dogs welcome, disabled facilities, nice covered area outside with heaters, lots of hanging baskets, play area, good walks, open all day. *Recommended by John Beeken, Ann and Colin Hunt, Evelyn and Derek Walter, Mr and Mrs John Taylor, PL and others*

LEWES TQ4210   BN7 2RD
Dorset
Malling Street

Light, airy and comfortable with large mellow area around central bar, smaller snug, lots of bare wood, welcoming competent staff, good varied choice of fairly priced food, well kept Harveys, smart restaurant; large back terrace, six bedrooms. *Recommended by Ann and Colin Hunt*

LEWES TQ4210   BN7 2AN
Gardeners Arms
Cliffe High Street

Warmly welcoming, unpretentious small local opposite brewery, light and airy, with plain scrubbed tables on bare boards around three narrow sides of bar, well kept Harveys and interesting changing guests, farm ciders, some lunchtime food including good pies, Sun bar nibbles, newspapers and magazines, toad in the hole played here; open all day. *Recommended by Mike and Eleanor Anderson, the Didler, N Wiseman, Ann and Colin Hunt*

LEWES TQ4210   BN7 2AN
John Harvey
Bear Yard, just off Cliffe High Street

No-nonsense tap for nearby Harveys brewery, all their beers including seasonals kept perfectly, some tapped from the cask, good well priced food from huge lunchtime sandwiches, baked potatoes and ciabattas up, friendly efficient young staff, basic dark flagstoned bar with one great vat halved to make two towering 'snugs' for several people, lighter room on left; piped music and machines; a few tables outside, open all day, breakfast from 10am. *Recommended by Gene and Kitty Rankin, Ben Williams, Ann and Colin Hunt and others*

LEWES TQ4110   BN7 1YH
☆ # Lewes Arms
Castle Ditch Lane/Mount Place – tucked behind castle ruins

Cheerful unpretentious little local with half a dozen real ales, 30 malt whiskies and good choice of wines by the glass, really good reasonably priced bar food (all day Sat, not Sun

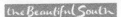 **SUSSEX** | **429**

evening), tiny front bar on right with stools along nicely curved counter and bench window seats, two other simple rooms hung with photographs and information about the famous Lewes bonfire night, beer mats pinned over doorways, poetry and folk evenings; children (not in front bar) and dogs welcome, picnic-sets on attractive two-level back terrace, open all day (till midnight Fri, Sat). *Recommended by the Didler, Ann and Colin Hunt, John Beeken, Mike and Eleanor Anderson and others*

LEWES TQ4210   BN7 2BU
Snowdrop
South Street

Tucked below the cliffs and doing well under present owners, narrowboat theme with brightly painted bar front and colourful jugs, lanterns etc hanging from planked ceiling, well kept Dark Star, Harveys, Hogs Back and Rectory, hearty helpings of enjoyable good value local food including good vegetarian choice, friendly efficient service, live jazz Mon; they may ask to keep your credit card while running a tab; dogs very welcome (even a menu for them), small garden and terrace, open all day. *Recommended by John Beeken, Ann and Colin Hunt*

LITTLEHAMPTON TQ0202   BN17 5DD
☆ ## Arun View
Wharf Road; W towards Chichester

Airy attractive 18th-c pub in lovely harbour spot with busy waterway directly below windows, very popular lunchtimes with older people (younger crowd in evenings) for its enjoyable interesting food (all day Sun) from sandwiches to good fresh fish, well kept Arundel ASB, Fullers London Pride and Ringwood Best, 20 wines by the glass, cheerful helpful service, lots of drawings, caricatures and nautical collectables, flagstoned and panelled back bar with banquettes and dark wood tables, large waterside conservatory; piped and some live music, two TVs, pool; disabled facilities, flower-filled terrace, summer barbecues, interesting waterside walkway to coast, four redone bedrooms, open all day. *Recommended by Trevor and Sheila Sharman, Roger Laker*

LITTLEHAMPTON TQ0202   BN17 5EG
Crown
High Street

No-frills town-centre pub with six changing ales including own Anchor Springs, good value pubby food. *Recommended by Tony and Wendy Hobden*

LODSWORTH SU9223   GU28 9BZ
☆ ## Hollist Arms
Off A272 Midhurst—Petworth

200-year-old village pub under new management, small snug room on right with tables by open fire, public bar on left with stools against pale counter, comfortable window seat and a few tables, well kept Kings, Langhams and Timothy Taylors Landlord, enjoyable bar food, L-shaped dining room with sofas by inglenook, elegant dining chairs and wheelbacks on wood-strip floor, interesting prints and paintings; children and dogs welcome, up steps to pretty cottagey back garden, picnic-sets on terrace or you can sit under a huge horse chestnut on the green, good walks nearby, open all day. *Recommended by Neil Ivens, Tony and Wendy Hobden, Martin and Karen Wake*

LOWFIELD HEATH TQ2539   RH11 0QA
Flight
Charlwood Road

Pictures and models of aircraft, friendly helpful staff, well kept beers, enjoyable generously served food including home-made cakes and scones; caters well for children in conservatory, with view of planes taking off from Gatwick, plenty of tables outside, too. *Recommended by R C Vincent*

Onslow Arms
LOXWOOD TQ0331   RH14 0RD

B2133 NW of Billingshurst

Comfortable and welcoming with popular food from doorstep sandwiches up, Badger ales, good house wines, coffees and teas, daily papers and lovely log fires; dogs welcome, picnic-sets in good-sized garden sloping to river and nearby restored Wey & Arun Canal, good walks and boat trips. *Recommended by Terry and Nickie Williams, Ian Phillips*

Six Bells
LYMINSTER TQ0204   BN17 7PS

Lyminster Road (A284), Wick

Unassuming flint pub, enjoyable elegantly presented food from weekday soups and sandwiches and daily roast bargains to some interesting specials, helpful staff, well kept Fullers London Pride and Greene King Abbot, good house wine, low black beams and big inglenook, pubby furnishings, friendly welcoming service; terrace and garden seating. *Recommended by Tony and Wendy Hobden*

Chequers
MARESFIELD TQ4623   TN22 2EH

High Street

Imposing three-floor Georgian coaching inn stylishly reworked under the Marco Pierre White Wheeler's of St James brand, good food including cheaper set menus in various linen-clothed dining areas – one with high-raftered ceiling, another with collection of Jak's cartoons on white-panelled walls, well kept Harveys in bare-boards oyster bar with beams and open fire; two decked areas in walled garden, ten refurbished bedrooms. *Recommended by Michael Butler*

Middle House
MAYFIELD TQ5826   TN20 6AB

High Street

Handsome 16th-c timbered inn, L-shaped beamed bar with massive fireplace, several well kept ales including Harveys, local cider, decent wines, quiet lounge area with leather chesterfields around log fire in ornate carved fireplace, good choice of food, panelled restaurant; piped music; children welcome, terraced back garden with lovely views, five bedrooms, open all day. *Recommended by Steve Godfrey*

☆ Rose & Crown
MAYFIELD TQ5927   TN20 6TE

Fletching Street

Pretty 16th-c weatherboarded cottage with two cosy front character bars, low ceiling boards (coins stuck in paintwork), bench seats built into partly panelled walls, stripped floorboards and inglenook log fire, small room behind servery and larger lower room (less character), Harveys and a guest, ten wines by the glass, bar food all day; children welcome and dogs (resident chocolate labrador called Bob), picnic-sets under parasols on front terrace, open all day (till midnight Sat). *Recommended by Ingrid and Peter Terry*

Earl of March
MID LAVANT SU8508   PO18 0BQ

A286

Refurbished and extended with emphasis on eating but seats for drinkers in the flagstoned log-fire bar serving ales such as Ballards, Harveys and Hop Back, good if pricey food, much sourced locally, in plush dining area and conservatory with seafood bar, polite efficient staff; nice view up to Goodwood from neatly kept garden with good furniture, local walks. *Recommended by Miss A E Dare, Tracey and Stephen Groves*

For those of you who use Sat Nav devices, we include a postcode for
every entry in the *Guide*.

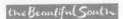

MIDHURST SU8821   GU29 9BX
Wheatsheaf
Wool Lane/A272

Cosy low-beamed and timbered pub dating from the 16th c, friendly local atmosphere, good range of enjoyable reasonably priced food, well kept local ales, restaurant.
Recommended by Geoff and Linda Payne

MILTON STREET TQ5304   BN26 5RL
☆ Sussex Ox
Off A27 just under a mile E of Alfriston roundabout

Extended country pub (originally a 1900s slaughterhouse) with magnificent Downs views – particularly popular at weekends; bar area with a couple of high tables and chairs on bare boards, old local photographs, Dark Star and Harveys, good choice of wines by the glass, lower brick-floored room with farmhouse furniture and woodburner, similarly furnished hop-draped dining room (children allowed here), further two-room front dining area with high-backed rush-seated chairs, bistro-style bar food, friendly service; dogs welcome in bar, teak seating on raised back deck taking in the view, picnic-sets in garden below and more under parasols at front, closed Sun evening in winter and between Christmas and New Year. *Recommended by Helen Greatorex, Jeremy Christey, Laurence Smith*

NUTBOURNE TQ0718   RH20 2HE
Rising Sun
Off A283 E of Pulborough; The Street

Unspoilt creeper-clad village pub dating partly from the 16th c, beams, bare boards and scrubbed tables, friendly helpful licensees (same family ownership for 30 years), well kept Fullers London Pride and guests such as Hogs Back and Langham, good range of bar food and blackboard specials, big log fire, daily papers, enamel signs and 1920s fashion and dance posters, cosy snug, attractive back family room, some live music; dogs welcome, garden with small back terrace under apple tree, smokers' shelter, listed outside lavatory. *Recommended by John Beeken*

OFFHAM TQ3912   BN7 3QD
☆ Blacksmiths Arms
A275 N of Lewes

Civilised and comfortable open-plan dining pub with chef/owner doing wide choice of good food including bargain two-course specials and nice vegetarian choices, well kept Harveys Best and a seasonal beer, good friendly uniformed staff, huge end inglenook; french windows to terrace with picnic-sets, four bedrooms. *Recommended by Ann and Colin Hunt, Tom and Ruth Rees*

OFFHAM TQ4011   BN7 3QF
☆ Chalk Pit
Offham Road (A275 N of Lewes)

Former late 18th-c chalk pit office building on three levels, well kept Harveys and a guest ale, decent wines by the glass, good choice of popular home-made food including OAP bargains, attentive cheerful staff, neat restaurant extension, skittle alley, toad in the hole played Mon nights; children welcome, garden with terrace seating, smokers' shelter with pool table, three bedrooms, open all day Fri-Sun (usually food all day then, too).
Recommended by Ann and Colin Hunt, PL, John Beeken

OVING SU9005   PO20 2BP
☆ Gribble Inn
Between A27 and A259 E of Chichester

16th-c thatched pub with own-brewed beers and guests, chatty bar with lots of heavy beams and timbering, old country-kitchen furnishings and pews, other linked rooms with cottagey feel, huge winter log fires, home-made food (not Sun evening) using own ale in some dishes, skittle alley with bar, live jazz (first Tues of month); children in family room, dogs allowed in bar, seats outside under covered area, more in pretty garden, open all day

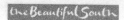

weekends. *Recommended by Ian and Barbara Rankin, Guy Vowles, Susan and John Douglas, the Didler, David H T Dimock and others*

PARTRIDGE GREEN TQ1819
☆ ## Green Man
RH13 8JT

Off A24 just under a mile S of A272 junction – take B2135 at West Grinstead signpost; pub at Jolesfield, N of Partridge Green

Relaxed gently upmarket dining pub with enterprising food, several champagnes by the glass and other good wines, Dark Star and Harveys Best, truly helpful service; unassuming front area by counter with bentwood bar chairs, stools and library chairs around one or two low tables, old curved high-back settle, main eating area widens into another area with pretty enamelled stove and a pitched ceiling on left, more self-contained room on right with stag's head, minimal decoration but plenty of atmosphere; cast-iron seats and picnic-sets under cocktail parasols in neat back garden. *Recommended by David Cosham, Terry Buckland, Ron and Sheila Corbett, Philip Stott*

PETT TQ8613
Two Sawyers
TN35 4HB

Pett Road; off A259

Family run with meandering low-beamed rooms including bare-boards bar with stripped tables, tiny snug, passage sloping down to restaurant allowing children, enjoyable good value freshly made food, friendly service, well kept Harveys with guests like Dark Star and Ringwood, local farm cider and perry, wide range of wines; piped music; dogs allowed in bar, suntrap front brick courtyard, back garden with shady trees and well spaced tables, three bedrooms, open all day. *Recommended by Peter Meister, Ellie Weld, David London, Kevin Booker, Julia Atkins*

PETWORTH SU9721
Star
GU28 0AH

Market Square

Airy open-plan pub in centre, Fullers ales, decent wine, enjoyable reasonably priced food, good coffee, leather armchairs and sofa by open fire, friendly atmosphere. *Recommended by Lindsey Hedges, Richard Griffiths, Ann and Colin Hunt*

PETWORTH SU9921
☆ ## Welldiggers Arms
GU28 0HG

Low Heath; A283 E

Unassuming L-shaped bar, low beams, log fire, pictures askew on shiny ochre walls, long rustic settles with tables to match, some stripped tables laid for eating, side room, no music or machines, enjoyable food (not always cheap), Wells & Youngs, decent wines, friendly landlord; children (in family area) and dogs welcome, plenty of tables on attractive lawns and terrace, nice views, closed Mon, also evenings Tues, Weds, Sun. *Recommended by Mrs Blethyn Elliott, Richard Tilbrook*

PLUMPTON TQ3613
Half Moon
BN7 3AF

Ditchling Road (B2116)

Enlarged beamed and timbered dining pub with interesting home-made food using local produce, children's menu, Sun roasts, local ales and wines (even an organic Sussex lager), good service, log fire with unusual flint chimneybreast; piped music – live music Thurs; dogs welcome, tables in wisteria-clad front courtyard and on new back terrace, big Downs-view garden with picnic area, summer family days (last Sun of July and Aug) with face painting and bouncy castle, good walks, open all day. *Recommended by Dominic and Claire Williams*

Places with gardens or terraces usually let children sit there – we note in the text the very few exceptions that don't.

RINGMER TQ4415   BN8 5RP
Old Ship
Uckfield Road (A26 Lewes—Uckfield, outside village S of Isfield turn-off)

Sizeable low-beamed roadside pub with emphasis on dining, wide choice of enjoyable home-made food all day from sandwiches and baked potatoes to steaks and fresh fish, children's menu, friendly service, Harveys Best, Biddenden cider, nautical pictures and memorabilia; dogs welcome, good-sized attractive garden with play area, open all day. *Recommended by Nigel and Jean Eames, Ian Forbes*

ROBERTSBRIDGE TQ7323   TN32 5AW
☆ George
High Street

Attractive contemporary dining pub, armchairs and sofa by inglenook log fire on right, friendly helpful licensees, Adnams, Harveys, Hop Back and Rother Valley, good wines by the glass, enjoyable locally sourced food from tasty baguettes to some enterprising main dishes, bustling chatty atmosphere; piped music – live music lunchtime (last Sun of month); children welcome and dogs (they have one called Stanley), back courtyard, four bedrooms. *Recommended by Simon Tayler, David and Sally Cullen, Mrs A S Crisp, Nigel and Jean Eames*

ROGATE SU8023   GU31 5EA
☆ White Horse
East Street; A272 Midhurst—Petersfield

Rambling heavy-beamed local in front of village cricket field, civilised and friendly, with Harveys full range kept particularly well, relaxed atmosphere, flagstones, stripped stone, timbers and big log fire, attractive candlelit sunken dining area, good range of enjoyable reasonably priced food (not Sun evening), friendly helpful staff, traditional games (and quite a collection of trophy cups), no piped music or machines; quiz and folk nights; some tables on back terrace, open all day Sun. *Recommended by D and J Ashdown, Geoff and Linda Payne*

ROWHOOK TQ1234   RH12 3PY
☆ Chequers
Off A29 NW of Horsham

Attractive welcoming 16th-c pub, relaxing beamed and flagstoned front bar with portraits and inglenook fire, step up to low-beamed lounge, well kept Fullers London Pride, Harveys and guests such as Weltons, decent wines by the glass, good coffee, good food from ciabattas up, separate restaurant; piped music; children and dogs welcome, tables out on front terraces and in pretty garden behind with good play area, attractive surroundings. *Recommended by Steve and Hilary Nelson, Ian Phillips, Ian and Rose Lock*

RUDGWICK TQ0934   RH12 3EB
Kings Head
Off A281; Church Street (B2128)

Beamed 13th-c pub by fine old church in pretty village, well kept Fullers, Shepherd Neame and Harveys, good italian cooking including lots of seafood, reasonable prices; flower-decked seating area at front, more seats behind. *Recommended by John Beeken*

RUSHLAKE GREEN TQ6218   TN21 9QE
☆ Horse & Groom
Off B2096 Heathfield—Battle

Cheerful village-green local, little L-shaped low-beamed bar with brick fireplace and local pictures, small room down a step with horsey décor, simple beamed restaurant, enjoyable home-made food, Shepherd Neame ales, decent wines by the glass; children and dogs welcome, attractive cottagey garden with pretty country views, nice walks. *Recommended by Chris Saunders*

RUSPER TQ1836   RH12 4QA
☆ **Royal Oak**
*Friday Street, towards Warnham – back road N of Horsham, E of A24 (OS Sheet 187
map reference 185369)*

Old-fashioned and well worn-in tile-hung pub in very rural spot on Sussex Border Path,
small carpeted top bar with leather sofas and armchairs, log fire, steps down to long
beamed main bar with plush wall seats, pine tables and chairs and homely knick-knacks,
well kept Surrey Hills Ranmore and six changing guests, farm ciders and perries, short
choice of enjoyable home-made lunchtime food (evenings and Sun lunch by
prearrangement), local farm produce for sale, plain games/family room with darts; a few
picnic-sets on grass by road and in streamside garden beyond car park, roaming chickens,
open all day Sat, till 9pm Sun. *Recommended by Bruce Bird, Conor McGaughey, the Didler and others*

RYE TQ9220   TN31 7JT
George
High Street

Sizeable hotel with lively up-to-date feel in bar and adjoining dining area, beams, bare
boards and log fire, leather sofa and armchairs, a couple of quirky sculptures, Adnams,
Greene King Old Speckled Hen and Harveys Best, continental beers on tap too, enjoyable
interesting food, popular afternoon tea, pleasant courteous staff (some french); soft
piped jazz; good bedrooms, open all day. *Recommended by Colin and Louise English, John Atkins*

RYE TQ9220   TN31 7EY
☆ **Mermaid**
Mermaid Street

Lovely old timbered hotel on famous cobbled street with civilised antiques-filled bar,
Victorian gothick carved chairs, older but plainer oak seats, huge working inglenook with
massive bressumer beam, Fullers, Greene King and Harveys, good selection of wines and
malt whiskies, short bar menu, more elaborate restaurant choices; piped music; children
welcome, seats on small back terrace, bedrooms, open all day. *Recommended by
Terry Buckland, the Didler, Colin and Louise English, N J Roberts, Richard Mason, Meg and Colin Hamilton
and others*

RYE TQ9220   TN31 7LH
Queens Head
Landgate

Friendly old pub refurbished under newish licensees, good selection of changing ales and
ciders (regular festivals), short choice of enjoyable low-priced home-made food, live
music; small area out at back for smokers, bedrooms. *Recommended by Peter Meister, Mike and
Eleanor Anderson*

RYE TQ9220   TN31 7HH
☆ **Ypres Castle**
Gun Garden; steps up from A259, or down past Ypres Tower

Traditional pub perched above river, bustling bars with various old tables and chairs,
local artwork and log fire, informal almost scruffy feel which adds to character,
straightforward promptly served bar food (all day Sat, not Sun evening), well kept
Fullers, Harveys and Timothy Taylors Landlord; piped and some live music, no dogs
inside; children welcome lunchtime, seats in sheltered garden, boules, open all day, Sun
till 8pm (6pm winter). *Recommended by Robert Kibble, Sue and Mike Todd, Sue Callard, Barry Collett,
Richard Mason, Tony and Wendy Hobden and others*

SELSFIELD COMMON TQ3433   RH19 4RA
White Hart
B2028 N of Haywards Heath, near West Hoathly

14th-c century cottage restaurant and large attached Sussex barn (bar here), welcoming
staff, well kept Harveys, Shepherd Neame and Wells & Youngs Bombardier, Weston's cider,
several wines by the glass, traditional bar food, more upmarket dishes in restaurant with

inglenook log fire; piped music in barn – live music Fri; garden picnic-sets, handy for Wakehurst Place, open all day, closed Sun evening. *Recommended by M Vingoe, C and R Bromage, Terry Buckland*

SHOREHAM-BY-SEA TQ2105 BN43 5TE
Red Lion
Upper Shoreham Road

Modest dimly lit low-beamed and timbered 16th-c pub with settles in snug alcoves, wide choice of good value pubby food including speciality pies, half a dozen well kept changing ales such as Adur, Arundel and Hepworths (Easter beer festival), farm cider, decent wines, friendly efficient staff, log fire in unusual fireplace, another open fire in dining room, further bar with covered terrace; pretty sheltered garden behind, old bridge and lovely Norman church opposite, good Downs views and walks. *Recommended by Tim Loryman, Tony and Wendy Hobden, Bruce Bird*

SIDLESHAM SZ8697 PO20 7NB
☆ Crab & Lobster
Mill Lane; off B2145 S of Chichester

Restaurant-with-rooms rather than pub but walkers and bird-watchers welcome in small flagstoned bar for a light meal, Harveys and Sharps, 17 wines by the glass including champagne, stylish upmarket restaurant with good imaginative (and pricey) food including local fish, friendly efficient staff; piped music; children welcome, tables on back terrace overlooking marshes, smart bedrooms, self-catering cottage, open all day (food all day weekends). *Recommended by Graeme Manson, Peter La Farge, Peggy and Alec Ward, Susan and John Douglas, Richard Tilbrook, N R White and others*

SLINDON SU9708 BN18 0NE
Spur
Slindon Common; A29 towards Bognor

Civilised, roomy and attractive 17th-c pub, good choice of upmarket but good value food changing daily, well kept Courage Directors, cheerful efficient staff, welcoming atmosphere, two big log fires, pine tables, large elegant restaurant, games room with darts and pool, friendly dogs; children welcome, pretty garden (traffic noise). *Recommended by David H T Dimock*

SMALL DOLE TQ2112 BN5 9XE
Fox
Henfield Road

Popular open-plan village local on busy road, good choice of reasonably priced bar food from sandwiches up, well kept Harveys Best and Wells & Youngs Bombardier, friendly staff coping well at busy times, raised dining areas; piped music; tables on small front terrace, handy for downland walks. *Recommended by John Beeken*

SOMPTING TQ1605 BN15 0AR
Gardeners Arms
West Street

Smartened up by friendly licensees, just off main coast road (the famous Saxon church is unfortunately on the far side of the dual carriageway), good choice of tasty food all day including some bargains (the railway-carriage restaurant is not currently in use), well kept Bass, Harveys, Sharps Doom Bar and a guest, log fire; piped music; dogs welcome, smokers' terrace. *Recommended by Bruce Bird, Tony and Wendy Hobden*

SOUTHWATER TQ1528 RH13 0LA
Bax Castle
Two Mile Ash, a mile or so NW

Popular early 19th-c flagstoned country pub pleasantly extended with former barn restaurant, big log fire in back room, Ringwood, Jennings and Wychwood ales, good value generous home-made food including good Sun lunch (best to book); some piped music;

children and dogs welcome, picnic-sets on two pleasant lawns, play area, near Downs Link Way on former rail track. *Recommended by Tony and Wendy Hobden, Ian Phillips*

ST LEONARDS TQ8008   TN38 0EB
Horse & Groom
Mercatoria

Friendly traditional town local in old Maze Hill area, carved horseshoe bar serving front and back rooms, Adnams, Greene King, Harveys and guests, interesting pictures, no food but connecting restaurant next door; small garden. *Recommended by Steve Long*

STAPLEFIELD TQ2728   RH17 6EF
Jolly Tanners
Handcross Road, just off A23

Neatly kept split-level local by cricket green, welcoming landlord and pub dogs, two good log fires, padded settles, lots of china, brasses and old photographs, well kept Fullers London Pride, Harveys and guests (always a mild; three beer festivals), real ciders, pubby food, chatty atmosphere; piped music, jazz Sun evening, quiz Thurs; children welcome and dogs (may be a treat), attractive suntrap garden with plenty of space for kids, quite handy for Nymans (NT). *Recommended by Sheila Topham, Mike and Eleanor Anderson*

STEYNING TQ1711   BN44 3RE
Chequer
High Street

Rambling low-beamed Tudor coaching inn, five or so well kept ales such as Cottage, Dark Star, Gales, Harveys and Timothy Taylors, good choice of wines, enjoyable well priced usual food (not Sun evening) from sandwiches up including breakfast from 10am, log fire, antique snooker table, large painting featuring locals, some live music; smokers' shelter, bedrooms, open all day. *Recommended by Bruce Bird, Greta and Christopher Wells, Richard Wilkie, Tony and Wendy Hobden*

STEYNING TQ1711   BN44 3YE
White Horse
High Street

Smart contemporary bar in creeper-covered former coaching inn, enjoyable interesting food, good choice of wines by the glass, Greene King ales, good courteous uniformed service; children welcome, spacious terrace. *Recommended by John Redfern*

STOUGHTON SU8011   PO18 9JQ
Hare & Hounds
Signed off B2146 Petersfield—Emsworth

Airy pine-clad country dining pub with simple contemporary décor, good reasonably priced fresh food including doorstep sandwiches and Sun roasts (till 4pm), four well kept changing ales, real cider, good helpful service, big open fires, public bar with darts, quiz nights; children in eating areas, dogs welcome, tables on pretty front terrace and on grass behind, lovely setting near Saxon church, good local walks. *Recommended by Rodney and Mary Milne-Day, Martin and Karen Wake, Paul Smurthwaite, R and R Goodenough*

SUTTON SU9715   RH20 1PS
☆ ## White Horse
The Street

Opened-up country inn with minimalist contemporary décor, island servery separating bar from two-room barrel-vaulted dining area with modern hardwood chairs and tables on coir, church candles and several open fires, ales such as Harveys and Sharps, decent wines by the glass, bar food with bistro touches; children and dogs welcome, steps up to garden with plenty of picnic-sets, walks in lovely surrounding countryside right from the door (packed lunches on request), Bignor Roman villa close by, bedrooms, closed Sun and Mon evenings. *Recommended by A N Bance, Nick Lawless, J A Snell*

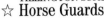

THAKEHAM TQ1017   RH20 3EP
White Lion
Off B2139 N of Storrington; The Street

Tile-hung 16th-c two-bar village local, good robust home-made food (not Sun-Weds evenings) from open kitchen, friendly informal service, real ales such as Arundel, Fullers, Harveys and St Austell, good choice of wines by the glass, heavy beams, panelling, bare boards and traditional furnishings including settles, pleasant dining room with inglenook woodburner, fresh flowers; dogs welcome, sunny terrace tables, more on small lawn, wendy house and rabbits, small pretty village, open all day. *Recommended by Mike and Eleanor Anderson*

TILLINGTON SU9621   GU28 9AF
☆ Horse Guards
Off A272 Midhurst—Petworth

Prettily set dining pub converted from three cottages, some traditional dishes as well as fancier pricier things, home-baked bread, Harveys and a guest, good choice of wines by the glass, friendly helpful service, log fire and country furniture in neat low-beamed front bar, lovely views from bow window, simple pine tables in dining room with fire, own and local produce for sale; children welcome, terrace tables and sheltered garden behind, attractive ancient church opposite, three bedrooms, good breakfast. *Recommended by Richard Tilbrook, Colin McKerrow, Barry Steele-Perkins, Martin Walker, Ann and Colin Hunt*

TROTTON SU8322   GU31 5ER
☆ Keepers Arms
A272 Midhurst—Petersfield

Pretty cottage above River Rother with beamed and timbered L-shaped bar, comfortable sofas and old winged-back leather armchairs around big log fire, simple rustic tables on oak flooring, other interesting old furniture, two dining rooms, one with woodburner, tasty bar food, Ballards, Dark Star and a guest ale; children welcome (no babies or toddlers in evening), dogs allowed in bar, seats on south-facing terrace, closed Sun evenings in Jan and Feb. *Recommended by Angus Wilson, John Branston*

TURNERS HILL TQ3435   RH10 4NU
☆ Red Lion
Lion Lane, just off B2028

Old-fashioned and unpretentious country local with snug, curtained, parquet-floored bar, plush wall benches, homely memorabilia and small open fire, steps up to carpeted area with inglenook log fire, cushioned pews and settles forming booths, Harveys ales, generous home cooking, friendly staff, daily papers; piped music (some live music in summer), games machine; children (away from bar) and dogs welcome, picnic-sets on side grass overlooking village, open all day, Sun till 10pm (8pm in winter). *Recommended by Terry Buckland, John Branston, Nick Lawless, N J Roberts, Colin and Louise English and others*

UPPER BEEDING TQ1910   BN44 3HZ
Kings Head
High Street

Old pub opened up but keeping some intimate seating areas, more formal dining area at one end, well kept Fullers London Pride and Harveys Best, decent pubby food, good service, warming log fire; children, dogs and walkers welcome, attractive back garden with beautiful downland views, play area and access to River Adur. *Recommended by Tim Loryman, Tony and Wendy Hobden*

UPPER BEEDING TQ1910   BN44 3TN
Rising Sun
Shoreham Road (A2037)

Friendly old pub (just off South Downs Way) smartened up by newish landlord, enjoyable home-made food, well kept Fullers London Pride, Harveys and guests, good welcoming service, cosy rooms, small dining conservatory; big garden with downland views. *Recommended by Bruce Bird*

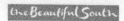

VINES CROSS TQ5917   TN21 9EN
Brewers Arms
Vines Cross Road off B2203, then left at T junction; 1 mile E of Horam

Victorian country pub redecorated under new management; sizeable public bar, stools by counter, quite a mix of dining chairs, benches and settles around wooden tables on stripped boards, three similarly furnished connecting rooms, one with open fire, another with woodburner, Greene King and guests, several wines by the glass, good food from pubby dishes up, helpful staff; children and dogs welcome, some picnic-sets in front and to the side, open all day. *Recommended by anon*

WADHURST TQ6131   TN5 6JH
Best Beech
Mayfield Lane (B2100 a mile W)

Dining pub taken over by twin brothers and reopened in 2010 after fresh contemporary refurbishment, good well priced food from traditional choices up, fixed-price menus including Sun lunch, Shepherd Neame ales and several wines by the glass, friendly service; children welcome, garden, six comfortably updated bedrooms, open all day Sat, closed Sun evening. *Recommended by Steven Tait*

WALDERTON SU7910   PO18 9ED
Barley Mow
Stoughton Road, just off B2146 Chichester—Petersfield

Country pub with good value generous food from lunchtime sandwiches up including Sun carvery, well kept ales such as Arundel, Harveys and Ringwood, good wine choice, friendly service even on busy weekends, two log fires and rustic bric-a-brac in U-shaped bar with roomy dining areas, live jazz suppers (third Tues of month), popular skittle alley; children welcome, big pleasant streamside back garden, good walks, handy for Stansted House. *Recommended by J A Snell, R and R Goodenough*

WALDRON TQ5419   TN21 0RA
Star
Blackboys—Horam side road

Big inglenook log fire in candlelit, beamed and panelled bar, padded window seat and nice mix of furniture including small settle on bare boards and quarry tiles, old prints and photographs, snug off to left, well kept Harveys and a guest such as 1648 or Bass, reliable food from good lunchtime sandwiches up, friendly prompt service, separate back dining room; picnic-sets in pleasant garden, a couple more at front overlooking pretty village. *Recommended by PL*

☆ WARNINGLID TQ2425   RH17 5TR
Half Moon
B2115 off A23 S of Handcross or off B2110 Handcross—Lower Beeding

Good modern cooking (not Sun evening) in this informal simply furnished brick and stone dining pub, Harveys, a changing guest and decent wines by the glass, bustling bare-boards locals' bar with small fireplace, room off with 18th-c beams and flagstones, steps down to unpretentious main bar, panelling, bare brick and photos of the village, down again to smaller carpeted area with big paintings; no children inside; dogs allowed in bar, picnic-sets on lawn in sizeable garden with spectacular avenue of trees, open all day weekends. *Recommended by Brian Dawes, Pat and John Carter, Terry Buckland, Ian Wilson and others*

☆ WARTLING TQ6509   BN27 1RY
Lamb
Village signed with Herstmonceux Castle off A271 Herstmonceux—Battle

Family-run country pub with three log fires, small entrance bar leading through to beamed and timbered snug with comfortable leather sofas, Harveys and Sharps, several wines by the glass, enjoyable food served by friendly staff, separate restaurant; children welcome away from bar, dogs away from restaurant, up steps to flower-filled back terrace, closed Sun evening, Mon. *Recommended by John Atkins, N J Roberts*

WEST ASHLING SU8007 PO18 8EA
Richmond Arms
Just off B2146; Mill Road

Newly refurbished village dining pub in quiet pretty setting near big mill pond with ducks and geese, good food from bar snacks up, Harveys ales; no dogs; children welcome, two smart bedrooms, closed Sun evening, Mon and Tues. *Recommended by Bill Oliver*

WEST WITTERING SZ8099 PO20 8QA
Lamb
Chichester Road; B2179/A286 towards Birdham

Welcoming 18th-c tile-hung country pub doing well under present landlord, good choice of enjoyable food from light meals to giant fish and chips, Badger ales, good service even during busy summer months, rugs on tiles, blazing fire; children and dogs welcome, tables out in front and in small sheltered back garden. *Recommended by David H T Dimock, Tony and Wendy Hobden*

WEST WITTERING SZ7798 PO20 8AD
Old House At Home
Cakeham Road

Roomy and cheerfully brightened up with three bar areas on two levels, wood floors and modern décor, well kept ales including Fullers London Pride, enjoyable if a little pricey food, friendly staff, log fires; children and dogs welcome, garden with play area, three bedrooms. *Recommended by John Whitney, Michael Butler*

WILMINGTON TQ5404 BN26 5SQ
☆ ## Giants Rest
Just off A27

Busy country pub with affable long-serving landlord, long wood-floored bar, adjacent open areas with simple furniture, log fire, well kept Harveys, Hop Back and Timothy Taylors, quite a choice of bar food (all day weekends), wooden puzzles and board games; piped music; children and dogs welcome, lots of seats in front garden, surrounded by South Downs walks and village famous for chalk-carved Long Man, bedrooms. *Recommended by Evelyn and Derek Walter, John Beeken, Mark Jiskoot*

WINCHELSEA TQ9017 TN36 4EN
New Inn
German Street; just off A259

Attractive pub with L-shaped front bar mainly laid for dining – new owners concentrating on good, fair value food, some slate flagstones and log fire, well kept Greene King ales, friendly helpful staff, separate back bar with darts and TV; piped music; children welcome, pleasant walled garden, delightful setting opposite church – Spike Milligan buried here, comfortable bedrooms, good breakfast. *Recommended by Michael Butler, Mr and Mrs Price*

WITHYHAM TQ4935 TN7 4BD
☆ ## Dorset Arms
B2110

Unpretentious 16th-c pub handy for Forest Way walks, friendly service, well kept Harveys ales, decent wines including local ones, good choice of fairly priced food, sturdy tables and simple country seats on wide oak boards, good log fire in Tudor fireplace, darts, dominoes, shove-ha'penny, cribbage, carpeted restaurant; piped music; dogs welcome, white tables on brick terrace by small green, closed Mon. *Recommended by Peter Meister, the Didler*

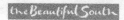

WORTHING TQ1204
North Star
Littlehampton Road (A259)

BN13 1QY

Comfortable Ember Inn with competitively priced food from noon to 8pm, real ales such as Greene King, Harveys, Purity and Shepherd Neame, good choice of wines by the glass, friendly service. *Recommended by Tony and Wendy Hobden*

WORTHING TQ1502
Selden Arms
Lyndhurst Road, between Waitrose and hospital

BN11 2DB

Friendly chatty local with welcoming long-serving licensees, well kept Dark Star Hophead and several changing guests, belgian beers and farm cider, bargain lunchtime food (not Sun) including doorstep sandwiches, log fire, lots of old pub photographs, occasional live music; dogs welcome, open all day. *Recommended by Tony and Wendy Hobden*

WORTHING TQ1502
Swan
High Street

BN11 1DN

Villagey atmosphere with good mix of customers in big open-plan pub, welcoming long-serving licensee, reasonably priced pubby lunchtime food and specials, several well kept ales including Harveys and Hop Back, old-fashioned interior with beams and some stained glass, regular entertainment from folk nights to quizzes; handy for hospital. *Recommended by Bruce Bird*

ALSO WORTH A VISIT IN LONDON

Besides the region's top pubs, we recommend the following. Do tell us what you think of them: **feedback@goodguides.com**

CENTRAL LONDON

EC1
☆ Bishops Finger
West Smithfield

EC1A 9JR

Smartly civilised little pub close to Smithfield Market, friendly welcoming atmosphere, well laid-out bar with cushioned chairs on polished boards, framed market prints on cream walls, big windows, fresh flowers, Shepherd Neame and seasonal ales, a fine range of sausages (other dishes too), efficient service, upstairs restaurant; children welcome, seats outside, closed weekends and bank holidays, otherwise open all day. *Recommended by Mayur Shah, Ian Phillips, Michael Dandy, Peter Dandy, Colin and Louise English, Derek Thomas*

Butchers Hook & Cleaver
West Smithfield

EC1A 9DY

Fullers bank conversion with their full range kept well, all-day pubby food including good choice of pies, breakfast from 7.30am, friendly helpful staff, daily papers, relaxed atmosphere, nice mix of chairs including some button-back leather armchairs, wrought-iron spiral stairs to pleasant mezzanine; piped music, big-screen sports TV; open all day, closed weekends. *Recommended by DC, Peter Dandy, Michael Dandy, Colin and Louise English*

☆ Eagle
Farringdon Road

EC1R 3AL

Original gastropub and still popular – you must arrive early as dishes run out or change quickly; open-plan room dominated by a giant range and all too busy, noisy and scruffy for some, basic well worn school chairs, assortment of tables, a couple of sofas on bare boards, modern art (gallery upstairs too), Wells & Youngs, good wines by the glass, decent

coffee; piped music sometimes loud, not ideal for a quiet dinner (weekends quieter); children and dogs welcome, closed Sun evening, bank holidays and for a week at Christmas, otherwise open all day. *Recommended by Dr and Mrs A K Clarke*

Gunmakers EC1R 5ET
Eyre Street Hill

Two-room Victorian pub with four well kept changing ales, friendly knowledgeable staff, enjoyable traditional food with a few twists; dogs welcome, open all day weekdays, closed weekends. *Recommended by Barbarrick, John and Gloria Isaacs*

☆ Jerusalem Tavern EC1M 5UQ
Britton Street

Convincing and atmospheric re-creation of a dark 18th-c tavern (1720 merchant's house with shopfront added 1810), tiny dimly lit bar, simple wood furnishings on bare boards, some remarkable old wall tiles, coal fires and candlelight, stairs to a precarious-feeling (though perfectly secure) balcony, plainer back room, full range of St Peters beers tapped from casks, good lunchtime food, friendly attentive young staff; can get very crowded at peak times, no children; dogs welcome, seats out on pavement, open all day during the week, closed weekends, bank holidays, 24 Dec-2 Jan. *Recommended by Dominic McGonigal, Mayur Shah, Peter Dandy, Anthony Longden, Giles and Annie Francis, the Didler and others*

Peasant EC1V 4PH
St John Street

Good imaginative food in strikingly furnished upstairs restaurant with a more traditional menu in welcoming downstairs bar, well kept ales and some reminders of its days as a more traditional corner house including a tiled picture of St George and the Dragon, mosaic floor and open fire. *Recommended by Andrew Bosi*

Viaduct EC1A 7AA
Newgate Street

Opposite Old Bailey on site of Newgate Prison (a couple of cells surviving below), big copper lanterns outside, fine ornate high-ceilinged Victorian interior, three or four snug areas, Fullers ales from horseshoe bar, food from sandwiches up, friendly service; popular with after-work drinkers; open all day, closed Sun. *Recommended by N R White*

EC2

☆ Dirty Dicks EC2M 4NR
Bishopsgate

Busy re-creation of traditional City tavern, fun for foreign visitors, booths, barrel tables, low beams, interesting old prints, Wells & Youngs ales, enjoyable well priced food from sandwiches up, pleasant service, calmer cellar wine bar with wine racks overhead in brick barrel-vaulted ceiling, further upstairs area too; piped music, games machines and TV; closed weekends. *Recommended by the Didler, Michael Dandy*

☆ Hamilton Hall EC2M 7PY
Bishopsgate; also entrance from Liverpool Street Station

Showpiece Wetherspoons with flamboyant Victorian baroque décor, plaster nudes and fruit mouldings, chandeliers, mirrors, good-sized comfortable mezzanine, reliable food all day, lots of real ales including interesting guests, decent wines and coffee, good prices; silenced machines, can get very crowded after work; good disabled access, tables outside, open all day. *Recommended by Ian Phillips, Jeremy King*

Lord Aberconway EC2M 1QT
Old Broad Street

Victorian feel with dark panelling and furniture, real ales such as Fullers, Sharps, Timothy Taylors and Woodlands Midnight Stout, reasonably priced food from sandwiches up, wrought-iron railed upper dining gallery; handy for Liverpool Street Station. *Recommended by Michael Dandy, Ian Phillips*

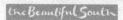

Railway Tavern

EC2M 7NX

Liverpool Street

Light and airy, with high ceilings and vast front windows, Greene King ales and several wines by the glass from a long bar, fairly priced pubby food from sandwiches up including sharing boards, second room upstairs; TVs and machines; pavement tables.
Recommended by Jeremy King, Michael Dandy

EC3

Chamberlain

EC3N 1NU

Minories

Comfortable high-ceilinged bar in substantial hotel, Fullers ales, sensibly priced bar food from sandwiches up, helpful prompt service, smart back restaurant; handy for the Tower of London, 64 bedrooms. *Recommended by Richard Tilbrook*

East India Arms

EC3M 4BR

Fenchurch Street

Standing-room Victorian pub refurbished by Shepherd Neame, their ales kept well, good service, old local photographs and brewery mirrors, hops; unobtrusive TV; closed weekends. *Recommended by Barbarrick*

Simpsons Tavern

EC3V 9DR

Just off Cornhill

Pleasingly old-fashioned place founded in 1757, rather clubby small panelled bar serving Bass, Harveys and a couple of guests, stairs down to another bar with snacks, traditional chophouse with upright stall seating (expect to share a table) and similar upstairs restaurant, good value food such as braised oxtail stew, steak and kidney pie and lancashire hotpot; open weekday lunchtimes and from 8am Tues-Fri for breakfast.
Recommended by Barbarrick

Walrus & Carpenter

EC3R 8BU

Monument Street/Lovat Lane

Nicholsons pub with good choice of well kept changing ales, food from sandwiches and pub favourites up; open all day weekdays, closed Sat evening, Sun. *Recommended by anon*

EC4

☆ Black Friar

EC4V 4EG

Queen Victoria Street

An architectural gem (some of the best Edwardian bronze and marble art nouveau work to be found anywhere) and built on the site of a 13th-c Dominican Priory; inner back room (the Grotto) with low vaulted mosaic ceiling, big bas-relief friezes of jolly monks set into richly coloured florentine marble walls, gleaming mirrors, seats built into golden marble recesses, and an opulent pillared inglenook, tongue-in-cheek verbal embellishments such as Silence is Golden and Finery is Foolish, and try to spot the opium-smoking hints modelled into the front room's fireplace, Fullers, Sharps and Timothy Taylors, plenty of wines by the glass, traditional food (all day) including speciality pies, friendly efficient service despite crowds; children welcome if quiet, smart furniture and plenty of standing room on wide forecourt. *Recommended by Dr and Mrs A K Clarke, Dave Braisted, N R White, Barry Collett, the Didler and others*

Old Bell

EC4Y 1DH

Fleet Street, near Ludgate Circus

Dimly lit 17th-c tavern backing on to St Bride's, heavy black beams, flagstones, stained-glass bow window, brass-topped tables, good changing choice of ales from island servery (can try before you buy), friendly efficient young foreign staff, usual food, coal fire, cheerful atmosphere; piped music; covered heated outside area. *Recommended by N R White, the Didler*

We include some hotels with a good bar that offers facilities comparable to those of a pub.

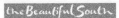

☆ Olde Cheshire Cheese
EC4A 2BU
Wine Office Court, off 145 Fleet Street

Best to visit this 17th-c former chophouse outside peak times (early evening especially) when packed and staff can struggle; soaked in history with warmly old-fashioned unpretentious rooms, high beams, bare boards, old built-in black benches, Victorian paintings on dark brown walls, big open fires, tiny snug and steep stone steps down to unexpected series of cosy areas and secluded alcoves, Sam Smiths, all-day pubby food; look out for the famous parrot (now stuffed) who entertained princes and other distinguished guests for over 40 years; children allowed in eating area lunchtime only, closed Sun evening. *Recommended by N R White, John Wooll, Jeremy King, Peter Dandy and others*

SE1

Rake
SE1 9AG
Winchester Walk

Tiny, discreetly modern bar with amazing bottled beer range in wall-wide cooler as well as half a dozen continental lagers on tap and perhaps a couple of rare real ales, good friendly service; fair-sized terrace with decking and heated marquee. *Recommended by Mike and Sue Loseby, Andrew Hobbs, the Didler*

SW1

☆ Buckingham Arms
SW1H 9EU
Petty France

Welcoming and relaxed bow-windowed 18th-c local, good value pubby food from back open kitchen, Wells & Youngs ales and guests from long curved bar, good wines by the glass, elegant mirrors and woodwork, unusual side corridor fitted out with elbow ledge for drinkers; TVs; dogs welcome, handy for Buckingham Palace, Westminster Abbey and St James's Park, open all day, till 6pm weekends. *Recommended by the Didler, N R White*

Cask
SW1V 2EE
Charlwood Street/Tachbrook Street

Modern and spacious with simple comfortable furnishings, Dark Star and great choice of other ales from far and wide, continental beers, decent wine range too, enjoyable generous food served by friendly helpful staff, chatty atmosphere – can get packed in evenings. *Recommended by N R White, David Sizer*

Clarence
SW1A 2HP
Whitehall

Civilised olde-worlde beamed corner pub now taken over by Geronimo (Youngs), well spaced tables and varied seating including tub chairs and banquettes, decent wines by the glass, friendly chatty landlord, popular food all day from snacks up, upstairs dining area; pavement tables. *Recommended by Ian Phillips*

☆ Grenadier
SW1X 7NR
Wilton Row; the turning off Wilton Crescent looks prohibitive, but the barrier and watchman are there to keep out cars

Steps up to cosy old mews pub with lots of character and military history, but not much space (avoid 5-7pm); simple unfussy bar, stools and wooden benches, changing ales such as Fullers, Hook Norton, Timothy Taylors and Wells & Youngs from rare pewter-topped counter, famous bloody marys, may be bar food, intimate back restaurant (best to book), no mobiles or photography; children (over 8) and dogs allowed, sentry box and single table outside, open all day. *Recommended by Lawrence R Cotter, Mike and Sue Loseby, N R White, LM*

Jugged Hare
SW1V 1DX
Vauxhall Bridge Road/Rochester Row

Popular Fullers Ale & Pie pub in former colonnaded bank, pillars, dark wood, balustraded balcony, large chandelier, busts and old London photographs, back dining room, reasonably priced food from sandwiches up including pie range, good friendly service;

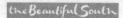

piped music, TVs, silent fruit machine; open all day. *Recommended by N R White, the Didler,*
Peter Roberts, Roger and Donna Huggins, Jeremy King

☆ Loose Box
Horseferry Road

SW1P 2AA

Modern bar-cum-restaurant named after horse-drawn ferry that crossed the Thames, dark
tables and chairs on wood flooring, fresh flowers and large plants, relaxed area with
comfortable squashy sofas, lots of cartoons on the walls, enjoyable food from breakfast
through coffee and pastries to good contemporary dishes, real ales and decent wines by
the glass, friendly helpful staff, buzzy atmosphere; TV, seats on front terrace by pavement,
open all day. *Recommended by Colin McKerrow*

☆ Lord Moon of the Mall
Whitehall

SW1A 2DY

Wetherspoons bank conversion with elegant main room, big arched windows looking over
Whitehall, old prints and a large painting of Tim Martin (founder of the chain), through
an arch the style is more recognisably Wetherspoons with neatly tiled areas, bookshelves
opposite long bar, up to nine real ales and their good value food; silenced fruit machines,
cash machine; children allowed if eating, dogs welcome, open all day from 9am (till
midnight Fri, Sat). *Recommended by Ian Phillips, Katrin Schmidt, Jeremy King, Andy Lickfold,*
Michael Dandy

☆ Morpeth Arms
Millbank

SW1P 4RW

Sparkling clean Victorian pub facing Thames, roomy and comfortable, some etched and
cut glass, old books and prints, photographs, earthenware jars and bottles, well kept
Wells & Youngs and a guest, decent choice of wines and of enjoyable good value food (all
day), welcoming service even at busy lunchtimes, upstairs room with fine view across
river; games machine, may be unobtrusive sports TV (there's also a monitor to check for
cellar ghosts), young evening crowd; seats outside (a lot of traffic), handy for Tate Britain
and Thames Path walkers, open all day. *Recommended by Ros Lawler, N R White, the Didler,*
Robert Pattison, Pete Coxon

Orange
Pimlico Road

SW1W 8NE

Refurbished gastropub with good choice of enjoyable food including wood-fired pizzas,
friendly attentive staff, real ales such as Adnams, linked light and airy rooms with rustic
furniture and relaxed weathered feel; children welcome, four bedrooms, open all day
from 8am. *Recommended by Miss Jennifer Harvey, Mr Stuart Brown, Richard Tilbrook*

Red Lion
Parliament Street

SW1A 2NH

Congenial pub by Houses of Parliament, used by Foreign Office staff and MPs, soft
lighting, parliamentary cartoons and prints, Fullers/Gales beers and decent wines from
long bar, good range of food, efficient staff, also cellar bar and small narrow upstairs
dining room, outside seating. *Recommended by Michael Dandy, David Pulford*

☆ Red Lion
Duke of York Street

SW1Y 6JP

Pretty little Victorian pub, remarkably preserved and packed with customers often
spilling out on to pavement by mass of foliage and flowers; series of small rooms with lots
of polished mahogany, a gleaming profusion of mirrors, cut and etched windows and
chandeliers, striking ornamental plaster ceiling, Fullers/Gales beers, simple bar food
(all day weekdays, snacks in evening, diners have priority over a few of the front tables);
no children; dogs welcome, open all day, closed Sun and bank holidays. *Recommended by*
N R White, Val and Alan Green, Michael Dandy, Andrea Rampley, the Didler and others

Speaker
Great Peter Street

SW1P 2HA

Pleasant chatty atmosphere in unpretentious smallish corner pub, well kept Shepherd
Neame Spitfire, Wells & Youngs and quickly changing guests, lots of whiskies, limited

simple food including good sandwiches, friendly helpful staff, panelling, political cartoons and prints, no mobiles or piped music; open all day, closed Sat, Sun evening.
Recommended by N R White

☆ Star

SW1X 8HT

Belgrave Mews West, behind the German Embassy, off Belgrave Square

Bustling recently smartened up local with astonishing array of summer hanging baskets and flowering tubs, restful bar, main seating area with polished tables and chairs, Fullers ales, upstairs dining room (no food weekends), good service; children and dogs welcome, the Great Train Robbery is said to have been planned here, open all day. *Recommended by Mike Tucker, Tracey and Stephen Groves, N R White, Lawrence R Cotter, the Didler and others*

Thomas Cubitt

SW1W 9PA

Elizabeth Street

Popular tastefully refurbished dining pub with floor-to-ceiling french doors opening to street, oak floors, panelling and open fires, enjoyable food in bar or upstairs dining room, decent wines, good mix of customers. *Recommended by Derek Thomas, Peter Loader*

White Swan

SW1V 2SA

Vauxhall Bridge Road

Roomy corner pub handy for Tate Britain, lots of dark dining tables on three levels in long room, good value pubby food from sandwiches up, ales such as Adnams Broadside and Timothy Taylors Landlord, decent wines by the glass, quick helpful uniformed staff; piped music; open all day. *Recommended by John Wooll*

SW3

Builders Arms

SW3 3TY

Britten Street

Trendy place, relaxed, comfortable and chatty, with good food, ales such as St Austell Tribute from long counter, good choice of wines; pavement tables under awnings, attractive street. *Recommended by anon*

☆ Coopers Arms

SW3 5TB

Flood Street

Newly refurbished and useful bolthole for King's Road shoppers, dark-walled open-plan bar with mix of good-sized tables on floorboards, pre-war sideboard and dresser, railway clock, moose head, Wells & Youngs ales, decent all-day bar food; well behaved children till 7pm, dogs in bar, seats in courtyard garden. *Recommended by anon*

☆ Cross Keys

SW3 5NB

Lawrence Street

Bustling civilised 18th-c pub with roomy high-ceilinged bar, sofas around low tables, settles and dining chairs on flagstones, two open fires, light and airy conservatory-style back restaurant with fully retractable roof, interesting modern bar food, Courage, Sharps and a guest, quite a choice of wines by the glass, attentive young staff; piped music; children welcome, dogs in bar, open all day till midnight, closed bank holidays.
Recommended by LM

Hour Glass

SW3 2DY

Brompton Road

Small welcoming pub handy for the V&A and other nearby museums, well kept Fullers London Pride and a guest, good value pubby food (not Sun evening); sports TV; pavement benches. *Recommended by LM*

W1

☆ Argyll Arms

W1F 7TP

Argyll Street

Popular and unexpectedly individual pub, three interesting little front cubicle rooms (essentially unchanged since 1860s) with wooden partitions and impressive frosted and engraved glass, mirrored corridor to spacious back room, well liked bar food (all day), Fullers, Greene King, Timothy Taylors and up to four guests, quieter upstairs bar (children welcome here) overlooking pedestrianised street, theatrical photographs, newspapers; piped music, machines; open all day (till midnight Fri, Sat). *Recommended by Peter Dandy, Ian Phillips, Michael Dandy, Barry Collett, Mike and Sue Loseby, Joe Green and others*

☆ Audley
W1K 2RX
Mount Street

Classic late-Victorian Mayfair pub, opulent red plush, mahogany panelling and engraved glass, chandelier and clock hanging in lovely carved wood bracket from ornately corniced ceiling, Fullers London Pride, Greene King IPA, Wells & Youngs Bombardier and guests from long polished bar, good choice of all-day pub food (reasonably priced for the area), friendly efficient service, upstairs panelled dining room; quiet piped music, TV, pool; children till 6pm, pavement tables. *Recommended by Nigel and Jean Eames*

☆ Dog & Duck
W1D 3AJ
Bateman Street/Frith Street

Tiny Soho pub squeezing in bags of character, unusual old tiles and mosaics (the dog with tongue hanging out in hot pursuit of a duck is notable), heavy old advertising mirrors, open fire, cosy upstairs bar/restaurant, four well kept ales including Fullers from unusual little counter, several wines by the glass, food all day, friendly staff, very busy evenings when people spill on to street; piped music; children allowed in dining room, dogs in bar. *Recommended by Richard Endacott, Jeremy King, LM, Lawrence R Cotter, Mike Gorton, Simon Collett-Jones and others*

☆ Grapes
W1J 7QQ
Shepherd Market

Genuinely old-fashioned pub with dimly lit bar, plenty of well worn plush red furnishings, stuffed birds and fish in display cases, wood floors, panelling, coal fire and snug back alcove, Fullers, Sharps and up to four guests, huge choice of thai food (not Sun evening) cooked by thai chefs, lots of customers (especially early evening) often spilling out on to square; children till 6pm weekdays (anytime weekends), open all day. *Recommended by Tracey and Stephen Groves, Ian Phillips, N R White, Lawrence R Cotter, the Didler, Mike Gorton and others*

☆ Guinea
W1J 6NL
Bruton Place

Lovely hanging baskets and chatty customers outside this tiny 17th-c mews pub, standing room only at peak times, appealingly simple with a few cushioned wooden seats and tables tucked to left of entrance, more in snug back area (most people prop themselves against the little side shelf), bare boards, old-fashioned prints, red planked ceiling with raj fans, famous steak and kidney pie, some sandwiches (no food weekends), Wells & Youngs and seasonal brews from striking counter; very easy to walk into the smart Guinea Grill (uniformed doormen will politely redirect you); no children; closed Sat lunchtime, Sun and bank holidays. *Recommended by Michael Dandy, the Didler*

Newman Arms
W1T 1NG
Rathbone Street/Newman Passage

18th-c pub in the same family for three generations, small panelled bar with particularly well kept Fullers London Pride and guests, traditionally redecorated upstairs dining room serving range of home-made pies and suet puddings, pictures and prints reflecting pub's association with George Orwell and director Michael Powell, good friendly staff and old-school character landlord; open all day, closed weekends. *Recommended by Tracey and Stephen Groves*

Running Horse
W1K 5JE
Corner of Davies Street/Davies Mews

Busy 18th-c oak-panelled Mayfair pub, enjoyable food from sandwiches up (highish prices), good service, small fire in tiled fireplace, newspapers, smart upstairs restaurant with linen tablecloths; pavement tables, colourful hanging baskets, open all day, closed Sun. *Recommended by Barry and Anne*

W2
Mad Bishop & Bear
W2 1HB

Paddington Station

Up escalators from concourse, full Fullers range kept well and a guest beer, good wine choice, reasonably priced standard food quickly served including breakfast from 8am (10am Sun), ornate plasterwork, etched mirrors and fancy lamps, parquet, tiles and carpet, booths with leather banquettes, lots of wood and prints, train departures' screen; piped music, TVs, games machine; tables out overlooking concourse, open all day till 11pm (10.30pm Sun). *Recommended by Dr and Mrs A K Clarke, Roger and Donna Huggins, Giles and Annie Francis, Susan and Nigel Wilson, Taff Thomas*

☆ # Victoria
W2 2NH

Strathearn Place

Well run pub with lots of Victorian pictures and memorabilia, cast-iron fireplaces, gilded mirrors and mahogany panelling, brass mock-gas lamps above attractive horseshoe bar, bare boards and banquettes, relaxed chatty atmosphere, good friendly service, full Fullers range kept well, good choice of wines by the glass, well priced food counter; upstairs has leather club chairs in small library/snug, and (mostly for private functions now) replica of Gaiety Theatre bar, all gilt and red plush; quiet piped music, TV; pavement picnic-sets, open all day. *Recommended by Ian Herdman, N R White, Dr and Mrs A K Clarke*

WC1
☆ # Cittie of Yorke
WC1V 6BN

High Holborn

Splendid back bar rather like a baronial hall with extraordinarily extended bar counter, 1,000-gallon wine vats resting above gantry, big bulbous lights hanging from soaring raftered roof, intimate ornately carved booths, triangular fireplace with grates on all three sides, smaller comfortable panelled room with lots of little prints of York, cheap Sam Smiths, bar food, lots of students, lawyers and City types but plenty of space to absorb crowds; fruit machine; children welcome, open all day, closed Sun. *Recommended by Ian Phillips, Jeremy King, N R White, Barry Collett, Michael Dandy, Anthony Longden and others*

☆ # Lamb
WC1N 3LZ

Lamb's Conduit Street

Famously unspoilt and unchanging Victorian pub, plenty of character and lots to look at especially the cut-glass swivelling snob-screens, traditional furnishings, sepia photographs of 1890s actresses on ochre panelled walls, snug little back room, up to seven real ales, good choice of whiskies, pubby bar food; children in dining area only till 5pm, seats in small courtyard, Foundling Museum nearby, pub (like street) named after William Lamb who brought fresh water to Holborn in 1577, open all day, till midnight Thurs-Sat. *Recommended by John and Gloria Isaacs, Dr and Mrs A K Clarke, Eddie Edwards, Roy Hoing, the Didler and others*

Mabels
WC1H 9AZ

Mabledon Place, just off Euston Road

Neat open-plan pub on two levels, well kept Shepherd Neame ales, good wine choice, decent reasonably priced pubby food, friendly welcoming staff, bright décor; big-screen TV; pavement tables, open all day. *Recommended by Ross Balaam*

Museum Tavern
WC1B 3BA

Museum Street/Great Russell Street

Traditional high-ceilinged ornate Victorian pub facing British Museum, busy lunchtime and early evening, but can be quite peaceful other times, good choice of well kept beers including some unusual ones, several wines by the glass, good hot drinks, straightforward food from end servery, friendly helpful staff; one or two tables out under gas lamps, open all day. *Recommended by Michael Butler, Pete Coxon, David and Sue Atkinson*

Penderels Oak

WC1V 7HJ

High Holborn

Vast Wetherspoons with attractive décor and woodwork, lots of books, pew seating around central tables, their usual well priced food and huge choice of good value real ales, efficient charming staff; open all day. *Recommended by Tracey and Stephen Groves*

☆ Princess Louise

WC1V 7EP

High Holborn

Splendid Victorian gin palace with extravagant décor – even the gents' has its own preservation order; gloriously opulent main bar with wood and glass partitions, fine etched and gilt mirrors, brightly coloured and fruity-shaped tiles, slender Portland stone columns soaring towards the lofty and deeply moulded plaster ceiling, open fire, cheap Sam Smiths from long counter, pubby bar food (not Fri-Sun); gets crowded early weekday evenings, no children; open all day. *Recommended by Tim Maddison, Mayur Shah, Ian Phillips, Barry Collett, Eleanor Dandy, Mr and Mrs C F Turner and others*

☆ Skinners Arms

WC1H 9NT

Judd Street

Richly decorated, with glorious woodwork, marble pillars, high ceilings and ornate windows, lots of London prints, interesting layout including comfortable back seating area, well kept Greene King ales and guests from attractive long bar, efficient staff, bar food; unobtrusive piped music, muted corner TV; pavement picnic-sets, interesting tiled frontage, handy for British Library, open all day, closed Sun. *Recommended by Tracey and Stephen Groves, N R White*

WC2

☆ Chandos

WC2N 4ER

St Martins Lane

Busy bare-boards bar with snug cubicles, lots of theatre memorabilia on stairs up to smarter more comfortable lounge with opera photographs, low wooden tables, panelling, leather sofas, coloured windows; cheap Sam Smiths OBB, prompt cheerful service, bargain food, air conditioning, darts; can get packed early evening, piped music and games machines; note the automaton on the roof (working 10-2 and 4-9); children upstairs till 6pm, open all day from 9am (for breakfast). *Recommended by Ian Phillips, Bruce Bird, Susan and Nigel Wilson, Taff Thomas*

☆ Cross Keys

WC2H 9EB

Endell Street/Betterton Street

Relaxed and friendly, quick service even at busy times, good lunchtime sandwiches and a few bargain hot dishes, Courage Best and Wells & Youngs ales kept well, decent wines by the glass, masses of photographs and posters including Beatles memorabilia, brassware and tasteful bric-a-brac; games machine, gents' downstairs; sheltered picnic-sets out on cobbles, pretty flower tubs, open all day. *Recommended by the Didler, John and Gloria Isaacs*

Edgar Wallace

WC2R 3JE

Essex Street

Simple spacious open-plan pub dating from the 18th c, half a dozen well kept ales including some unusual ones and a beer brewed for them by Nethergate, friendly efficient service, good value all-day food including doorstep sandwiches, half-panelled walls and red ceilings, interesting old London and Edgar Wallace memorabilia (pub renamed 1975 to mark his centenary), friendly chatty atmosphere; a few high tables in side alleyway, open all day, closed weekends. *Recommended by N R White, LM*

George

WC2R 1AP

Strand

Timbered pub near law courts, long narrow bare-boards bar, good choice of changing ales, several wines by the glass including champagne, lunchtime food from open sandwiches and ciabattas to weekday carvery in upstairs bar, separate evening menu, comedy club Fri, Sat nights, open all day. *Recommended by Pete Coxon, Dr Martin Owton*

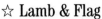

☆ Lamb & Flag
WC2E 9EB
Rose Street, off Garrick Street

This basic unpretentious tavern is usually packed, spartan front room leading to cosy low-ceilinged bar with open fire and high-backed black settles, half a dozen ales, decent malt whiskies, short choice of simple lunchtime food, friendly efficient service, upstairs Dryden Room often less crowded (children welcome here lunchtime), jazz Sun evening; lots of lively well documented history including Regency bare-knuckle prize-fights when known as the Bucket of Blood, open all day. *Recommended by Roger and Donna Huggins, Anthony Longden, Mike and Sue Loseby, Bruce Bird, the Didler and others*

Lyceum
WC2R 0HS
Strand

Panelling and pleasantly simple furnishings downstairs, several small discreet booths, steps up to a bigger alcove with darts, food in much bigger upstairs panelled lounge with deep button-back leather settees and armchairs, low-priced Sam Smiths beer, civilised atmosphere and efficient service. *Recommended by Mike and Eleanor Anderson, Taff Thomas, Susan and Nigel Wilson*

Marquess of Anglesey
WC2E 7AU
Bow Street/Russell Street

Light and airy, with Wells & Youngs and a guest beer, decent food including interesting specials, friendly staff, a couple of big sofas, more room upstairs. *Recommended by Michael Dandy, Taff Thomas*

☆ Porterhouse
WC2E 7NA
Maiden Lane

Good daytime pub (can be packed in evenings), London outpost of Dublin's Porterhouse microbrewery, their interesting if pricey draught beers including Porter and two Stouts (comprehensive tasting tray), also their TSB real ale and a guest, lots of bottled imports, good choice of wines by the glass, reasonably priced food from soup and open sandwiches up, with some emphasis on rock oysters, shiny three-level labyrinth of stairs (lifts for disabled), galleries and copper ducting and piping, some nice design touches, sonorous openwork clock, neatly cased bottled beer displays; piped music, irish live music, big-screen sports TV (repeated in gents'); tables on front terrace, open all day. *Recommended by Jeremy King, Taff Thomas*

☆ Salisbury
WC2N 4AP
St Martins Lane

Gleaming Victorian pub surviving unchanged in the heart of the West End with enthusiastic landlord, a wealth of cut glass and mahogany, curved upholstered wall seat creating impression of several distinct areas, wonderfully ornate bronze light fittings, lots of mirrors, back room popular with diners and separate small side room, some interesting photographs including Dylan Thomas enjoying a drink here in 1941, lots of theatre posters, up to six well kept ales, hot toddies, summer Pimms, good bar food all day, coffees and helpful staff; children allowed till 5pm, fine details on building exterior, seats in pedestrianised side alley, open till midnight Fri, Sat. *Recommended by Tracey and Stephen Groves, Jeremy King, David and Sue Smith, Roger and Donna Huggins, Mike Gorton, Joe Green and others*

White Lion
WC2E 8NS
James Street

Panelling and bare boards, Fullers London Pride, Timothy Taylors Landlord and guest ales, Nicholsons menu, dining room upstairs; open all day. *Recommended by Michael Dandy*

Most pubs with any outside space now have some kind of smokers' shelter. There are regulations about these – for instance, they have to be substantially open to the outside air. The best have heating and lighting and are really quite comfortable.

EAST LONDON

E1

☆ # Prospect of Whitby

Wapping Wall

E1W 3SH

Claims to be oldest pub on the Thames dating back to 1520, with a colourful history (Pepys and Dickens used it regularly and Turner came for weeks at a time to study the river views) – tourists love it; L-shaped bar has plenty of beams, bare boards, flagstones and panelling, ales including Fullers, Sharps and Wells & Youngs from 400-year-old pewter counter, good choice of wines by the glass, bar food from sandwiches up, more formal restaurant upstairs; children welcome (only if eating after 5.30pm), unbeatable views towards Docklands from tables on waterfront courtyard, open all day. *Recommended by Bill Adie, Barry and Anne, the Didler, Paul Rampton, Julie Harding and others*

Town of Ramsgate

Wapping High Street

E1W 2PN

Interesting old London Thames-side setting, with restricted but evocative river view from small back floodlit terrace with mock gallows (hanging dock was nearby), long narrow chatty bar with squared oak panelling, ales such as Fullers London Pride and Sharps Doom Bar, friendly helpful service, good choice of generous standard food and daily specials; piped music, Mon quiz; open all day. *Recommended by Bill Adie, N R White*

E3

☆ # Crown

Grove Road/Old Ford Road

E3 5SN

Stylish dining pub with relaxed welcoming bar, faux animal hide stools and chunky pine tables on polished boards, big bay window with comfortable scatter-cushion seating area, books and objects on open shelves, well kept Adnams Broadside, Redemption Pale Ale and Sharps Doom Bar, good choice of wines by the glass, friendly chatty young staff, three individually decorated upstairs dining areas overlooking Victoria Park, imaginative food (all day Sun); piped music; children and dogs welcome, open all day. *Recommended by Andy and Claire Barker, Georgina Tacagni*

Eleanor Arms

Old Ford Road

E3 5JP

Traditional two-room Shepherd Neame corner pub, four of their ales kept well, chatty landlord and friendly atmosphere, no food, live jazz Sun, pool and darts in back bar; dogs welcome, open all day. *Recommended by Mick O'Rorke, Tony Hobden*

Palm Tree

Haverfield Road

E3 5BH

Lone survivor of blitzed East End terrace, by Regent's Canal and beside windmill and ecology centre in futuristic-looking Mile End Park; two Edwardian bars around oval servery, a couple of well kept changing ales, lunchtime sandwiches, long serving landlord and good local atmosphere, live music weekends. *Recommended by Tony Hobden*

E11

Birkbeck Tavern

Langthorne Road

E11 4HL

Down-to-earth high-ceilinged two-room local, stained glass and worn-in furnishings, three or four well kept often unusual ales, good value snacks; TV, fruit machine, pool and darts; children allowed in nice garden with plenty of tables. *Recommended by Jeremy King, Andrew Bosi*

E14

☆ # Narrow

Narrow Street

E14 8DJ

Popular stylish dining pub with good Thames views from window seats and terrace, simple but smart bar with white walls and dark blue doors, mosaic-tiled fireplaces and colourfully striped armchairs, Adnams, Greene King and a guest, good wines, food from bar snacks to pricier restaurant meals, dining room also white with matching furnishings, local maps and prints, and a boat complete with oars; piped music; children welcome, open all day. *Recommended by John Saville, Andy and Claire Barker, Mike Owen, Ian Phillips*

North Pole
E14 8LG
Manilla Street

Good honest traditional Victorian pub surviving in the high-rise shadow of Canary Wharf, friendly welcome, bargain home-made pub food, well kept Fullers London Pride, Timothy Taylors Landlord and a guest such as Sharps or Wychwood, darts; closed weekends. *Recommended by Barbarrick*

E15

King Edward VII
E15 4BQ
Broadway

Nicely old-fashioned with dark woodwork and etched-glass screens in traditional bar, small lounge area, back dining room with well lit prints above panelled dado, decent food and four changing real ales, daily papers, open fires; piped music, live music Thurs, Sun quiz. *Recommended by Karen Sloan*

NORTH LONDON

N1

Albion
N1 1HW
Thornhill Road

Front bar and spacious dining area, interesting choice of mid-priced home-made food, well kept Black Sheep and Greene King Abbot, prompt cheerful service, Victorian gents'; tables out at front and on back terrace. *Recommended by Nigel and Sue Foster*

Charles Lamb
N1 8DE
Elia Street

Small friendly backstreet pub with well kept Fullers Chiswick, Timothy Taylors Landlord and a guest, some interesting imports on tap or bottled, good choice of wines by the glass, good blackboard food, big windows, polished boards and simple traditional furniture; piped jazz; tables outside. *Recommended by Kevin Booker, Julia Atkins, Jim Slattery*

Compton Arms
N1 2XD
Compton Avenue, off Canonbury Road

Tiny villagey local again under new management, simply furnished unpretentious low-ceilinged rooms, Greene King and guests; sports TV, can be busy Arsenal match days; dogs welcome, tables under big sycamore tree and glass-covered area, open all day. *Recommended by Tim Maddison*

Crown
N1 0EB
Cloudesley Road

Good food and bustling atmosphere in Victorian Fullers pub, their ales from impressive island bar with snob-screens, scrubbed boards, plenty of light oak panelling and cut and etched glass, helpful friendly staff; tables out on small railed front terrace. *Recommended by Jim Slattery*

☆ Duke of Cambridge
N1 8JT
St Peters Street

London's first organic pub and a landlady passionate about the environment; organic real ales, lagers, ciders, wines and spirits and interesting bar food using seasonal produce, big busy main room with good mix of customers, chunky wooden tables, pews and benches on bare boards, a couple of big metal vases with colourful flowers, daily papers, corridor past open kitchen to smaller candlelit rooms set for eating, conservatory; children and dogs welcome, open all day. *Recommended by anon*

Fellow
N1 9AA
York Way

Contemporary pub/restaurant, popular and relaxed, with enjoyable unusual food (not cheap and they add a service charge), real ales and good choice of wines, friendly staff coping at busy times, upstairs cocktail bar (DJ nights Thurs, Fri); piped music; roof terrace. *Recommended by Adam Madai, Graham Coult*

Hemingford Arms
N1 1DF
Hemingford Road

Invitingly dark Capital pub filled with bric-a-brac, good choice of real ales from central servery, traditional food alongside good evening thai menu, open fire, upstairs bar, live music and Weds quiz night; sports TV; picnic-sets outside. *Recommended by Immanuel von Bennigsen*

 ## Marquess Tavern
N1 2TB
Canonbury Street/Marquess Road

Surprisingly traditional and fairly plain bar in imposing Victorian building, bare boards, a mix of wooden tables around big, horseshoe servery, old leather sofa and faded pictures, a couple of fireplaces, Wells & Youngs beers, around 30 malt whiskies, traditional food in bar or back dining room; piped music; children and dogs welcome, some picnic-sets out behind front railings, open all day weekends, closed weekday lunchtimes. *Recommended by anon*

N4

White Lion of Mortimer
N4 3PX
Stroud Green Road

One of the earliest Wetherspoons, good choice of changing ales kept well, good value food, back conservatory, some character regulars; TVs. *Recommended by Giles and Annie Francis*

N14

Cherry Tree
N14 6EN
The Green

Roomy beamed Vintage Inn (former coaching inn) with good value food all day from breakfast on, wide choice of wines by the glass and reasonably priced beers, good service, mix of big tables, some leather chesterfields; children welcome, tables out behind, bedrooms in adjacent Innkeepers Lodge, open all day. *Recommended by Colin Moore, Darren Shea, David Jackson*

N16

Jolly Butchers
N16 7HU
Stoke Newington High Street

Good range of changing real ales and ciders, bustling atmosphere. *Recommended by Tony and Gill Powell*

NW1

Betjeman Arms
NW1 2QL
St Pancras Station

On upper concourse with outside seating area facing Eurostar trains, good all-rounder with enjoyable food, well kept Sambrooks and a house beer from Sharps, friendly efficient service, modern décor. *Recommended by Derek Thomas, N R White*

Bree Louise
NW1 2HH
Cobourg Street/Euston Street

Partly divided open-plan bar with half a dozen or more interesting real ales, food emphasising pies (Mon-Thurs bargains), basic décor with prints, UK flags, mixed used furnishings; can get very busy early evening; open all day. *Recommended by Joe Green, Jake Lingwood, Jeremy King*

☆ **Chapel** NW1 5DP
Chapel Street

Usually busy evenings (quieter during the day), this dining pub attracts an equal share of drinkers, spacious cream-painted rooms dominated by open kitchen, smart but simple furnishings, sofas at lounge end by big fireplace, Adnams and Greene King ales, good choice of wines by the glass, several coffees and teas, food usually good; children and dogs welcome, picnic-sets in sizeable back garden, more seats on decking under heated parasols, open all day. *Recommended by Phil and Jane Hodson, Kevin Thomas, Nina Randall, Bruce and Sharon Eden*

☆ **Doric Arch** NW1 2DN
Eversholt Street

Virtually part of Euston Station, upstairs from bus terminus with raised back part overlooking it, two well kept Fullers ales and a guest, Weston's cider, friendly prompt service (even when busy), enjoyable well priced pubby food lunchtime and from 4pm weekdays (12-5pm weekends), pleasantly nostalgic atmosphere and some quiet corners, intriguing train and other transport memorabilia including big clock at entrance, downstairs restaurant; discreet sports TV, machines, lavatories on combination lock; open all day. *Recommended by Ian and Helen Stafford, Joe Green, the Didler, Dennis Jones, Dr and Mrs A K Clarke, Jeremy King and others*

☆ **Engineer** NW1 8JH
Gloucester Avenue

Mix of foodies and drinkers in big informal L-shaped bar, lively and popular, with good interesting food (not cheap), St Peters Organic and Wells & Youngs Bombardier, enterprising wine list, good range of spirits, handsome original woodwork and rather unusual décor, individual more ornate candlelit rooms upstairs (may need to book); piped and live music; children welcome, attractive garden, handy for Primrose Hill, open all day from 9am. *Recommended by Jeremy King, Stephen Ogden*

Euston Flyer NW1 2RA
Euston Road, opposite British Library

Big welcoming open-plan pub, Fullers/Gales beers, good choice of standard food all day, relaxed lunchtime atmosphere, plenty of light wood, mix of furniture on carpet or boarded floors, mirrors, photographs of old London, smaller raised areas and private corners, big doors open to street in warm weather; piped music, Sky TV, silent games machine, can get packed evenings; open all day, till 8.30pm Sun. *Recommended by Jeremy King, the Didler, N R White, Brian and Janet Ainscough*

Metropolitan NW1 5LA
Baker Street tube station, Marylebone Road

Wetherspoons in impressively ornate Victorian hall, large with lots of tables on one side, very long bar the other, leather sofas and some elbow tables, good range of well priced ales, good coffee, their usual inexpensive food; silent fruit machine; family area, open all day. *Recommended by Tony Hobden, Jeremy King*

NW3

☆ **Flask** NW3 1HE
Flask Walk

Bustling local (popular haunt of Hampstead artists, actors and local characters), unassuming old-fashioned bar, unique Victorian screen dividing it from cosy lounge with smart banquettes, panelling, lots of little prints and attractive fireplace, Wells & Youngs ales, 30 wines by the glass, well liked bar food (all day Fri-Sun); piped music, TV; children (till 8pm) and dogs welcome, seats and tables in alley, open all day, till midnight Fri, Sat. *Recommended by Tracey and Stephen Groves, John and Gloria Isaacs, the Didler, Stephen Ogden, N R White*

☆ **Holly Bush** NW3 6SG
Holly Mount

Timeless old favourite tucked away in villagey streets, bare-boards bar with dark sagging ceiling, brown and cream panelled walls, old advertisements and hanging plates, partly glazed partitions forming secretive bays, open fires, cosy back room with lots of small prints, panelled and etched-glass alcoves, three Fullers ales and a couple of guests including Harveys, lots of wines by the glass and malt whiskies, food from traditional choices up (all day weekends), upstairs dining room; children (till 7pm) and dogs welcome, pavement benches, open all day. *Recommended by John Wooll, Barry Collett, the Didler, Stephen Ogden, N R White and others*

☆ ## Spaniards Inn
NW3 7JJ
Spaniards Lane

Busy 16th-c pub right next to Hampstead Heath with charming big garden split up into areas by careful planting, flagstoned walk amongst roses, side arbour with climbing plants and plenty of seats on crazy-paved terrace (arrive early weekends as popular with dog walkers and families); attractive and characterful low-ceilinged rooms with oak-panelling, antique winged settles, snug alcoves and open fires, half a dozen real ales, two ciders, continental draught lagers and several wines by the glass, enjoyable unfussy food (all day); car park fills fast and nearby parking difficult; children and dogs welcome. *Recommended by Karen Eliot, John Wooll, David Jackson, Mike and Lynn Robinson, Nick Lawless*

NW4

Greyhound
NW4 4JT
Church End

Friendly three-bar Youngs pub with their ales and a guest kept well, decent bar lunches including home-made pizzas (evening meals Thurs, Fri only), plaque commemorating first greyhound track meeting, some live jazz; dogs welcome, open all day (till 1am Fri, Sat). *Recommended by Ross Balaam*

NW5

☆ ## Bull & Last
NW5 1QS
Highgate Road

Traditional décor with a stylish twist and liked by customers of all ages; single room with big windows, colonial-style fans in planked ceiling, collection of tankards, faded map of London, stuffed bulls' heads and pheasants, four changing ales, good wines and own sloe gin, imaginative if not cheap food, takeaway tubs of home-made ice-cream and picnic hampers for Hampstead Heath, friendly staff; quiz Sun evening; children (away from bar) and dogs welcome, hanging baskets and picnic-sets by street, open all day. *Recommended by Richard Greaves*

Junction Tavern
NW5 1AG
Fortess Road

Victorian corner pub with good fresh food including some enterprising dishes in bar and dining room (service charge added), well kept Caledonian Deuchars IPA and three other well kept ales (beer festivals), good choice of wines by the glass, back conservatory; piped music; no children after 7pm, garden tables, open all day Fri-Sun. *Recommended by Nick Angel*

SOUTH LONDON

SE1

Anchor
SE1 9EF
Bankside

In great spot near Thames with river views from upper floors and roof terrace, extensively refurbished with beams, stripped brickwork and old-world corners, well kept Fullers London Pride and Greene King IPA, good choice of wines by the glass, popular fish and chip bar including takeaways, other good value all-day food as well as breakfast and tearoom; piped music; provision for children, disabled access, more tables under big parasols on raised riverside terrace, bedrooms in friendly quiet Premier Inn behind, open all day. *Recommended by Phil and Jane Hodson, Mike and Sue Loseby, Paul Humphreys, Eleanor Dandy, Pete Coxon*

Anchor & Hope
The Cut SE1 8LP

Busy informal bare-boards gastropub, contrasting reports on food ranging from excellent to rough and ready, prices can be high and service erratic, well kept Wells & Youngs and guests, wine by tumbler or carafe, plain bar with big windows and mix of furniture including elbow tables, curtained-off dining part with small open kitchen, tight-packed scrubbed tables and contemporary art on purple walls; children and dogs welcome, closed Sun evening and Mon lunchtime, otherwise open all day. *Recommended by Ian Phillips, Eleanor Dandy, Mike and Sue Loseby, Susan and John Douglas, Phil Bryant*

Barrow Boy & Banker
Borough High Street, by London Bridge Station SE1 9QQ

Comfortable civilised bank conversion with roomy upper gallery, full Fullers beer range kept well, decent wines, efficient young staff, no-nonsense food including good pies, music-free; right by Southwark Cathedral. *Recommended by Fergus McDonald, Phil and Jane Villiers*

☆ Fire Station
Waterloo Road SE1 8SB

Unusual fire station conversion, busy and noisy, with two huge knocked-through tiled rooms, lots of wooden tables and mix of chairs, pews and worn leather armchairs, distinctive box-shaped floral lampshades, sizeable plants, back bar with red fire buckets on shelf, smarter dining room, good modern all-day food including breakfast from 9am, Fullers, Marstons and a guest, good choice of wines and spirits; children welcome, tables out in front, picnic-sets in scruffy side alley, handy for Old Vic theatre, open till midnight. *Recommended by Ian Phillips, Eleanor Dandy, Rob and Catherine Dunster, Tom and Ruth Rees and others*

☆ Founders Arms
Hopton Street SE1 9JH

Modern building with glass walls in superb location – outstanding terrace views along the Thames and handy for South Bank attractions; plenty of customers (city types, tourists, theatre and gallery goers) spilling on to pavement and river walls, Wells & Youngs and a guest, lots of wines by the glass, good bar food all day (weekend breakfasts from 9am), cheerful service; piped music; children welcome away from bar, open till midnight Fri, Sat. *Recommended by N R White, Jeremy King, John Wooll, Kevin Thomas, Nina Randall, Mike and Sue Loseby and others*

☆ George
Off 77 Borough High Street SE1 1NH

Tucked-away 16th-c coaching inn (mentioned in *Little Dorrit*), now owned by the National Trust and beautifully preserved; lots of tables in bustling cobbled courtyard with views of the tiered exterior galleries, series of no-frills ground-floor rooms with black beams, square-latticed windows and some panelling, plain oak or elm tables on bare boards, old-fashioned built-in settles, dimpled-glass lanterns and a 1797 Act of Parliament clock, impressive central staircase up to series of dining-rooms and balcony, well kept Greene King ales plus a beer brewed for the pub, good value traditional food all day (not Sun evening), friendly staff; children welcome away from bar, open all day. *Recommended by Mayur Shah, Mike and Sue Loseby, the Didler, Rob and Catherine Dunster, Andy and Claire Barker and others*

Goldsmith
Southwark Bridge Road SE1 0EF

Pub/dining room with well kept Adnams Best, Wadworths 6X and a guest, imaginative wine list with many by the glass, enjoyable sensibly priced food, friendly service. *Recommended by Mike and Sue Loseby, Oliver Ward*

☆ Hole in the Wall
Mepham Street SE1 8SQ

Quirky no-frills hideaway in railway arch virtually underneath Waterloo, rumbles and shakes with the trains, fine range of well kept ales, basic bargain food all day, plush red banquettes in small quieter front bar, well worn mix of tables set well back from long bar in larger back room; big-screen sports TV, machines; open all day, closed weekend afternoons. *Recommended by Jason Pound, Ian Phillips*

☆ Horniman
Hays Galleria, off Battlebridge Lane

SE1 2HD

Spacious, bright and airy Thames-side drinking hall with lots of polished wood, comfortable seating including a few sofas, upstairs seating, several real ales with unusual guests (may offer tasters), teas and coffees at good prices, lunchtime bar food from soup and big sandwiches up, snacks other times, efficient service coping with large numbers after work; unobtrusive piped music; fine river views from picnic-sets outside, open all day. *Recommended by Phil and Jane Villiers*

☆ Kings Arms
Roupell Street

SE1 8TB

Proper corner local, bustling and friendly, with curved servery dividing traditional bar and lounge, bare boards and attractive local prints, well kept changing ales, good wine and malt whisky choice, welcoming efficient service, enjoyable food from thai dishes to Sun roasts, big back extension with conservatory/courtyard dining area; piped music; open all day. *Recommended by Colin and Louise English, Peter Dandy, Eleanor Dandy*

☆ Market Porter
Stoney Street

SE1 9AA

Properly pubby no-frills place opening at 6am weekdays for workers at neighbouring market, up to ten unusual real ales (over 60 guests a week) often from far-flung brewers, a handful of good value pubby dishes, particularly helpful, friendly service, main part of bar is pretty straightforward with bare boards and open fire, beams with beer barrels balanced on them, simple furnishings, it gets more old-fashioned the further you venture in; piped music; children allowed weekends till 7pm, dogs welcome, drinkers spill out on to street, open all day. *Recommended by Jeremy King, Mayur Shah, Peter Dandy, N R White, Mike Gorton, Mike and Sue Loseby and others*

White Hart
Cornwall Road/Whittlesey Street

SE1 8TJ

Vibrant corner local in upcoming area, friendly bustle, comfortable sofas, stripped boards and so forth, ales such as Brakspears, Fullers London Pride, Purity and Sharps Doom Bar, several belgian beers, good range of ciders and wines, sensibly priced up-to-date blackboard food including pub standards, helpful efficient staff; piped music. *Recommended by Peter Dandy, Eleanor Dandy*

SE8

Dog & Bell
Prince Street

SE8 3JD

Friendly old-fashioned tucked-away local on Thames Path, wood benches around bright cheerfully decorated L-shaped bar, half a dozen well kept changing ales, bottled belgian beers, prompt friendly service, reasonably priced pub food including good sandwiches, dining room; TV; tables in yard, open all day. *Recommended by N R White*

SE9

Park Tavern
Passey Place

SE9 5DA

Traditional Victorian corner pub off Eltham High Street, up to eight well kept ales, log fire, friendly easy-going atmosphere; soft piped music. *Recommended by Michael and Deborah Ethier*

With the iPhone Good Pub Guide App, you can use the iPhone's camera to send us pictures of pubs you visit – outside or inside.

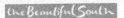

SE10

☆ Cutty Sark

SE10 9PD

Ballast Quay, off Lassell Street

Smashing Thames views from early 19th-c tavern, genuinely unspoilt old-fashioned bar, dark flagstones, simple furnishings, open fires, narrow openings to tiny side snugs, upstairs room (reached by winding staircase) with ship-deck-feel and prized seat in big bow window, up to four changing ales, organic wines, malt whiskies, all-day bar food; piped music; children and dogs welcome, busy riverside terrace across narrow cobbled lane, limited parking (but free if you get a space). *Recommended by John Saville, Susan and John Douglas, the Didler*

☆ Greenwich Union

SE10 8RT

Royal Hill

Friendly, nicely renovated pub with ales from local Meantime and guests, some unusual bottled beers too, long narrow flagstoned room (feels more bar than pub) with simple front area, woodburner, newspapers, other area with brown leather cushioned pews and armchairs under framed editions of *Picture Post*, modern-feeling conservatory, bar food (all day weekends); piped music, TV; children and dogs welcome, appealing terrace with green picnic-sets and fencing painted to resemble poppy or wheat fields, seats in front overlooking street, open all day. *Recommended by D Crook, N R White, Dave Allister, the Didler, Mrs B Billington*

Kings Arms

SE10 9JH

King William Walk

Well placed dark-panelled open-plan pub, shortish choice of enjoyable good value food, Greene King ales, friendly attentive staff; piped music; pleasant shady back terrace. *Recommended by George Atkinson*

☆ Richard I

SE10 8RT

Royal Hill

Friendly refurbished two-bar Youngs local, popular food including enjoyable Sun lunch, carpets and panelling; children welcome, picnic-sets out in front, lots more in pleasant paved back garden with weekend barbecues – busy summer weekends and evenings. *Recommended by the Didler, D Crook, N R White*

SE11

Prince of Wales

SE11 4EA

Cleaver Square

Comfortably traditional little Edwardian pub in smart quiet Georgian square, well kept Shepherd Neame ales, bar food from good sandwiches up, friendly landlord and staff, arch to small saloon; pavement seats, boules available to play in the square. *Recommended by Tim Maddison*

SE16

☆ Mayflower

SE16 4NF

Rotherhithe Street

Unchanging, cosy, old riverside pub in unusual street with lovely early 18th-c church, wide choice of enjoyable generous food all day, black beams, panelling, nautical bric-a-brac, high-backed settles and coal fires, good Thames views from upstairs restaurant (closed Sat lunchtime), Greene King ales, good coffee and good value wines, friendly service; piped music; children welcome, nice jetty/terrace over water, open all day. *Recommended by the Didler, N R White*

SE21

☆ Crown & Greyhound

SE21 7BJ

Dulwich Village

Big, busy (especially evenings), Victorian pub with cosy period interior, traditional

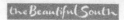

upholstered settles and stripped kitchen tables on bare boards, big back dining room, conservatory, Fullers London Pride, Harveys and a couple of guests (Easter beer festival and summer cider festival), just under two dozen wines by the glass, straightforward bar food (all day), popular Sun carvery; piped music; children and dogs welcome, summer barbecues in pleasant back garden, open all day. *Recommended by Bill Adie, Tracey and Stephen Groves, John Saville, Giles and Annie Francis*

SE22

Herne Tavern
Forest Hill Road
SE22 0RR

Smart traditional panelled pub with well kept ales, enjoyable food in separate dining area; children welcome, big garden with play area, open all day. *Recommended by Giles and Annie Francis*

SE24

Florence
Dulwich Road
SE24 0NG

Handsome Victorian pub visibly brewing its own Weasel ale, farm cider, enjoyable food including Sun roasts, friendly busy atmosphere, glossy bar and appealing contemporary décor, comfortable booth seating, open fire, dining conservatory; children welcome, good terrace tables. *Recommended by Greg Bailey, Mark Stafferton*

SE26

☆ Dulwich Wood House
Sydenham Hill
SE26 6RS

Extended well refurbished Youngs pub in Victorian lodge gatehouse complete with turret, nice local atmosphere, friendly service, decent food cooked to order; steps up to entrance (and stiff walk up from station); children welcome, big pleasant back garden with old-fashioned street lamps, summer barbecues, handy for Dulwich Wood. *Recommended by B J Harding, Jake Lingwood*

SW4

Bread & Roses
Clapham Manor Street
SW4 6DZ

Contemporary café-style with two real ales and some unusual continental beers, good wines by the glass, imaginative well priced food; piped music. *Recommended by Tracey and Stephen Groves*

Windmill
Clapham Common South Side
SW4 9DE

Big bustling pub by Clapham Common, contemporary front bar, quite a few original Victorian features, pillared dining room leading through to conservatory-style eating area, good varied choice of food all day, Wells & Youngs ales and decent wines by the glass, piped music; outside satay bar, tables under red umbrellas along front, also seats in side garden area, good bedrooms. *Recommended by anon*

SW8

Canton Arms
South Lambeth Road
SW8 1XP

Large airy corner pub doing well under newish management, good food from huge sharing plates up, good choice of wines. *Recommended by KJ*

SW11

Eagle
Chatham Road
SW11 6HG

Attractive unpretentious backstreet local, good choice of changing ales including southern brewers like Harveys, Surrey Hills and Westerham, welcoming prompt service, worn leather chesterfield in fireside corner of L-shaped bar; big-screen sports TV; dogs welcome, back terrace with heated marquee, small front terrace too. *Recommended by Mitchell Humphreys*

Falcon   SW11 1RU
St Johns Hill

Restored Victorian pub with good choice of well kept beers from remarkably long light oak counter, bargain pub food, friendly service, lively front bar, period partitions, cut glass and mirrors, subdued lighting, quieter back dining area, daily papers; big-screen TV; handy for Clapham Junction station. *Recommended by Tim Loryman, Mike Gorton, Barbarrick*

☆ # Fox & Hounds   SW11 2JU
Latchmere Road

Big Victorian local with particularly good mediterranean cooking (all day Sun, not Mon-Thurs lunchtimes), Fullers, Harveys and a guest, several wines by glass, spacious straightforward bar with big windows overlooking street, bare boards, mismatched tables and chairs, photographs on walls, fresh flowers, daily papers, view of kitchen behind, two rooms off; piped music, TV; children (till 7pm) and dogs welcome, garden seats under big parasols, open all day Fri-Sun, closed Mon lunchtime. *Recommended by anon*

SW13

Bridge   SW13 9DW
Castelnau Gardens

Edwardian corner pub fitted out in relaxed bistro-style, raised booth seating at front overlooking road, original bar behind with Adnams and Fullers London Pride, light and airy back part, good variety of moderately priced food with some creative touches from open kitchen; children welcome, tables on decking in back garden, open all day – handy for Thames Path. *Recommended by Simon and Mandy King*

Brown Dog   SW13 0AP
Cross Street

Well renovated with warm relaxed atmosphere, gastropub menu (not cheap), good choice of wines, well kept Sambrooks and Twickenham, friendly helpful staff, subtle lighting and open fires, daily papers; children and dogs welcome (resident labrador called Willow), garden tables, open all day. *Recommended by Jim Jolliffe, C Cooper*

SW14

Victoria   SW14 7RT
West Temple Sheen

Contemporary styling with emphasis on conservatory restaurant, well kept Fullers London Pride and Timothy Taylors Landlord in small wood-floored bar with leather sofas and woodburning stoves, food can be good if not cheap including breakfast Sat and all day Sun, friendly service; piped music; dogs welcome, children's play area in nice garden, comfortable bedrooms, open all day. *Recommended by Noel Ferrin, Richard Morris*

SW15

Dukes Head   SW15 1JN
Lower Richmond Road, near Putney Bridge

Smartly modernised and expanded Victorian pub, comfortable furnishings in knocked-together front bars and trendy downstairs cocktail bar in disused skittle alley (very popular weekends), good range of well presented pubby food all day including sharing platters and snacks, Wells & Youngs ales, lots of wines by the glass, light and airy back dining room with great river views, friendly service; plastic glasses for outside terrace or riverside pavement; children welcome (high chairs and smaller helpings), open all day. *Recommended by Peter Dandy, N R White*

the Beautiful South

Green Man
SW15 3NG
Wildcroft Road, Putney Heath

Small friendly old local by Putney Heath, nicely redecorated rooms and alcoves, good choice of enjoyable food, well kept Wells & Youngs ales with a guest such as St Austell; TV; attractive good-sized back garden with decking, also some seats out at front near road, open all day. *Recommended by Peter Dandy*

SW16

Earl Ferrers
SW16 6JF
Ellora Road

Opened-up Streatham corner local, Sambrooks and several other well kept ales like Ascot, Pilgrim and Twickenham (tasters offered), some interesting food as well as pub favourites and Sun roasts, good informal service, mixed tables and chairs, sofas, old photographs; piped music – live music every other Sun, quiz night Weds, pool and darts; children welcome, some tables outside with tractor-seat stools, open all day weekends, from 4pm weekdays. *Recommended by Richard Warrick, LM, Kevin Chamberlain*

SW18

Ship
SW18 1TB
Jews Row

Popular riverside pub by Wandsworth Bridge with light and airy conservatory-style décor, pleasant mix of furnishings on bare boards, basic public bar, well kept Wells & Youngs ales and Caledonian Deuchars IPA, freshly cooked interesting bistro food in extended restaurant with own garden, attractive good-sized terrace with barbecue and outside bar; children and dogs welcome, open all day. *Recommended by Peter Dandy, Mike Bell*

SW19

Fox & Grapes
SW19 4UN
Camp Road

18th-c dining pub by Wimbledon Common recently refurbished under new french chef/owner, modern bistro feel but keeping some original features in the two dining areas (steps between), good adventurous cooking alongside more traditional dishes, cheaper set menus, well chosen wines by the glass, ales such as Hogs Back and Sharps Doom Bar from central servery, relaxed atmosphere; children and dogs welcome, three bedrooms.
Recommended by Paul Bonner, Susan and John Douglas

WEST LONDON
SW6

☆ Atlas
SW6 1RX
Seagrave Road

Busy tucked-away pub with long, simple, knocked-together bar, plenty of panelling and dark wall benches, school chairs and tables, brick fireplaces, enjoyable bar food (all day Sun), Fullers, St Austell, Sharps and a guest, lots of wines by the glass, big mugs of coffee, friendly service; piped music and they may ask to keep a credit card while you run a tab; children (till 7pm) and dogs welcome, seats under awning on heated and attractively planted side terrace, open all day. *Recommended by Nigel and Sue Foster, Evelyn and Derek Walter, Alistair Forsyth, Nick and Elaine Hall*

Harwood Arms
SW6 1QP
Walham Grove

Interesting bare-boards gastropub, good bar snacks as well as enterprising pricey full meals (oyster fritters, pheasant kiev), friendly caring staff, separate eating area, well kept ales such as Fullers London Pride and St Austell Tribute in proper bar area with leather sofas, young lively atmosphere; closed Mon lunchtime. *Recommended by Antony O'Brien, Katharine Cowherd, Richard Tilbrook*

Sands End
SW6 2PR

Stephendale Road

Enterprising seasonal food, real ales such as Black Sheep, Greene King Old Speckled Hen and Hook Norton, simple country furnishings and open fire. *Recommended by Sam West*

☆ White Horse
SW6 4UL

Parsons Green

Busy pub with stylishly modernised U-shaped bar, huge windows with wooden blinds, coal and log fires, plenty of sofas and wooden tables, half a dozen changing ales and many more draught continentals, 120 bottled beers, a perry and good interesting wines, imaginative bar food all day from 9.30am, quick friendly service, regular beer festivals; children and dogs welcome, plenty of seats on heated front terrace (popular barbecues), open till midnight Thurs-Sat. *Recommended by Tracey and Stephen Groves, N R White, the Didler, B and M Kendall, C Cooper and others*

SW7

☆ Anglesea Arms
SW7 3QG

Selwood Terrace

Very busy Victorian pub run well by friendly landlady, mix of cast-iron tables on wood-strip floor, central elbow tables, panelling and heavy portraits, large brass chandeliers hanging from dark ceilings, big windows with swagged curtains, several booths at one end with partly glazed screens, half a dozen ales including Adnams, Fullers London Pride and Sambrooks, around 20 malt whiskies and 30 wines by the glass, interesting bar food, steps down to refurbished dining room; children welcome, dogs in bar, heated front terrace, open all day. *Recommended by Barry and Anne, the Didler, Stephen Ogden*

Queens Arms
SW7 5QL

Queens Gate Mews

Victorian corner pub with open-plan bare-boards bar, enjoyable good value home-made pubby food, good wines by the glass, ales including Adnams and Fullers; disabled facilities, handy for the Albert Hall, open all day. *Recommended by LM, Megan and Jen*

W4

☆ Bell & Crown
W4 3PF

Strand on the Green

Well run Fullers local, good friendly staff, enjoyable sensibly priced food, panelling and log fire, great Thames views from back bar and conservatory, lots of atmosphere; dogs welcome, terrace and towpath area, good walks, open all day. *Recommended by Bob and Angela Brooks, N R White*

☆ Bulls Head
W4 3PQ

Strand on the Green

Recently renovated old Thames-side pub (served as Cromwell's HQ during Civil War), seats by windows overlooking the water in beamed rooms, steps up and down, ales such as Fullers and Wells & Youngs, several wines by the glass, decent all-day pubby food, friendly helpful service; piped music, games machine; seats outside by river, pretty hanging baskets, part of Chef & Brewer chain. *Recommended by N R White, Tracey and Stephen Groves*

☆ Duke of Sussex
W4 5LF

South Parade

Big bonus for this Victorian local is the large back garden with lots of tables and careful planting; smartly refurbished but simple bar with huge windows, some original etched glass, well kept Fullers and a couple of guests from big horseshoe counter with fresh flowers, enjoyable food (not Mon lunchtime) including some spanish influences, helpful efficient service, nicely restored dining room with wooden furnishings, little booths and splendid skylight framed by colourfully painted cherubs, lots of black and white photographs; well behaved children and dogs welcome, open all day. *Recommended by B and M Kendall, Tracey and Stephen Groves*

Swan
W4 5HH
Evershed Walk, Acton Lane

Cosy, well supported local, enjoyable food including some interesting dishes, friendly staff, good range of wines by the glass, three real ales; dogs very welcome, children till 7.30pm, good spacious garden. *Recommended by Catherine Woodman, Antony O'Brien, Seb Royce*

W6

☆ Anglesea Arms
W6 0UR
Wingate Road

Good interesting food including weekday set lunches in homely bustling pub, welcoming staff, good choice of wines by the glass and of real ales, close-set tables in dining room facing kitchen, roaring fire in simply decorated panelled bar; children welcome, tables out by quiet street, open all day. *Recommended by David Gunn, the Didler, Robert Del Maestro, C Cooper*

Brook
W6 0XF
Goldhawk Road/Stamford Brook Road (formerly Queen of England)

Handsome brick pub with spacious high-ceilinged rooms, Fullers ales, enjoyable modern food, bustling bar with comfortable squashy sofas, leather tub chairs and mix of dining chairs around pine tables on stripped boards, airy dining room with leather wall seats and white-clothed (or plain wood) tables, fresh flowers, helpful, cheerful young staff; terrace. *Recommended by anon*

☆ Dove
W6 9TA
Upper Mall

Lots of history at this 17th-c riverside pub (framed list of writers, actors and artists who have been here), also in *Guinness World Records* book for smallest bar room – front snug is a mere 4ft 2ins by 7ft 10ins with traditional black panelling, red leatherette built-in wall settles and stools around dimpled copper tables, bigger similarly furnished room with old framed advertisements and photographs of the pub, Fullers ales, 20 wines by the glass including champagne, pubby food (all day weekends), live band once a month; dogs welcome, terrace with seats on flagstoned area and on verandah overlooking Thames Reach (much prized so get there early), tiny exclusive area up spiral staircase too (prime spot for watching rowing crews), open all day. *Recommended by Peter Dandy, Dominic McGonigal, the Didler*

Thatched House
W6 0ET
Dalling Road

Traditional open-plan Victorian corner pub – Youngs, their ales and guests from large wooden servery, mixed furniture including leather chesterfields on bare boards, old books and photographs, station clocks, stained-glass windows, open fire, good choice of food and wine, efficient friendly service, back conservatory; two-tier garden, open all day weekends. *Recommended by Dan Stratton*

W7

Viaduct
W7 3TD
Uxbridge Road

Well maintained Fullers pub with railway memorabilia and old photographs of nearby viaduct, decent food from fairly extensive menu, helpful charming service; sports TV in public bar; open all day. *Recommended by Sue and Mike Todd*

W8

☆ Churchill Arms
W8 7LN
Kensington Church Street

Character irish landlord at this bustling old local, welcoming even when crowds spill on to the street, eclectic interior dense with bric-a-brac including Churchill memorabilia, butterfly prints/books (one of the landlord's passions), foxgloves grown in pots, well kept Fullers ales, two dozen wines by the glass, good reasonably priced thai food (all day) and

traditional dishes at lunchtime in spacious and plant-filled dining conservatory, good value Sunday roast; children and dogs welcome, chrome tables and chairs outside, stunning display of window boxes and hanging baskets, open all day. *Recommended by LM and others*

☆ **Scarsdale**   W8 6HE
Edwardes Square

Busy Georgian pub in lovely leafy square, stripped-wood floors, good coal-effect gas fires, various knick-knacks, well kept Fullers/Gales ales from ornate counter, enjoyable good value pubby food, friendly helpful service; nice tree-shaded front courtyard, open all day. *Recommended by Barbarrick, Jill Bickerton*

☆ **Uxbridge Arms**   W8 7TQ
Uxbridge Street

Friendly and cottagey backstreet local with three brightly furnished linked areas, well kept Fullers and a guest such as Harveys, good choice of bottled beers, china, prints and photographs; sports TV; open all day. *Recommended by the Didler, Giles and Annie Francis*

☆ **Windsor Castle**   W8 7AR
Campden Hill Road

One of the city's best pub gardens with high ivy-sheltered walls, summer bar, winter heaters and lots of seats on flagstones; plenty of inside character in three tiny unspoilt rooms (fun trying to navigate the minuscule doors between them), a wealth of dark oak furnishings, high-backed sturdy built-in elm benches, time-smoked ceilings and coal-effect fire, cosy pre-war-style dining room, fair-priced enjoyable food (all day Fri-Sun), Fullers, Timothy Taylors and three guests, summer Pimms and winter mulled wine, friendly staff; children (till 7pm) and dogs welcome, open all day. *Recommended by Tich Critchlow, the Didler, LM, Giles and Annie Francis*

W9

☆ **Warrington**   W9 1EH
Warrington Crescent

Most are here for the short choice of interesting modern bar food (not Mon-Weds lunchtimes), but it's also worth exploring this carefully refurbished Victorian gin palace with its opulent art nouveau interior, elaborately patterned tiles, ceilings and stained glass, two exquisitely tiled pillars, drawings of nubile young women, small coal fire, four changing real ales from a splendid marble and mahogany bar counter, unusual bottled beers, several wines by the glass; children welcome till 7pm, open all day (till midnight Fri, Sat). *Recommended by Peter Dandy, LM*

W11

☆ **Portobello Gold**   W11 2QB
Middle of Portobello Road

Cheerful informal atmosphere at this engaging combination of pub, hotel and restaurant; smallish front bar with cushioned banquettes and nice old fireplace, exotic dining room with big tropical plants and sliding roof, impressive wall-to-wall mirror, vocal canaries, wide choice of enjoyable food all day (also cream teas and Sun roasts), Fullers London Pride, Harveys Best and several draught belgian beers, good selection of bottled imports, particularly good wine list with just under two dozen by the glass, cigar menu, board games, monthly art and photographic exhibition; piped music (live music Sun evening), sports TV, internet café; children welcome, street tables, bedrooms and spacious apartment with rooftop terrace and putting green, open all day. *Recommended by Jeremy King, Dave Braisted*

W12

☆ **Princess Victoria**   W12 9DH
217 Uxbridge Road

Imposing Victorian gin palace with carefully restored rather grand bar, oil paintings on

slate-coloured walls, a couple of stuffed animal heads, comfortable leather wall seats, parquet flooring, small fireplace, Fullers and Timothy Taylors, 36 wines by the glass and lots of spirits from handsome marble-topped horseshoe counter, imaginative modern bar food, large dining room with plenty of original features and more paintings, wine and cigar shop; children allowed if eating, dogs in bar, white wrought-iron furniture on pretty terrace, popular Sat artisan market in front, open all day. *Recommended by Sophie Harrowes, Antony O'Brien*

W13
Duke of Kent
W13 8DL
Scotch Common

Large open-plan pub with discrete areas, coal fires and interesting photos of old Ealing, Fullers ales with guests such as Adnams, food from sandwiches up, newspaper and games. *Recommended by Revd R P Tickle*

W14
☆ Colton Arms
W14 9SD
Greyhound Road

Long-serving landlord at this unspoilt and unchanging little pub, U-shaped main bar with log fire, fine collection of carved antique oak furniture, hunting crops and hunting-scene plates, polished brasses, two small back rooms with tiny serving counter (ring bell for service), Fullers, Sharps and a guest, weekday lunchtime sandwiches only; no credit cards – note the old-fashioned brass-bound till; children welcome till 7pm, dogs in bar, charming back terrace, next to Queen's Club tennis courts. *Recommended by Giles and Annie Francis, Barbarrick, Susan and John Douglas, N R White*

OUTER LONDON

BECKENHAM TQ3769
BR3 6NR
Jolly Woodman
Chancery Lane

Welcoming old-fashioned local in conservation area, cosy chatty atmosphere in small bar with larger room off, woodburner, five or so good changing ales such as Harveys and Timothy Taylors Landlord, good value home-made weekday lunchtime food including sandwiches; flower-filled backyard and pavement tables, open all day, closed Mon lunchtime. *Recommended by N R White*

BIGGIN HILL TQ4359
TN16 3AX
☆ Old Jail
Jail Lane; (E off A233 S of airport and industrial estate, towards Berry's Hill and Cudham)

Big family garden with picnic-sets, substantial trees and good play area at this busy country pub (close to the city); traditional beamed and low-ceilinged rooms with RAF memorabilia, two cosy small areas to right divided by timbers, one with big inglenook, the other with cabinet of Battle of Britain plates, Fullers, Harveys and Shepherd Neame, standard fairly priced food (not Sun evening) from sandwiches up, step up to dining room with more wartime prints/plates and small open fire; discreet piped music; dogs welcome, nice hanging baskets, open all day weekends. *Recommended by B and M Kendall*

BROMLEY TQ4069
BR1 3LG
Red Lion
North Road

Chatty well managed backstreet local in conservation area, traditional dimly lit interior with wood floor, tiling, green velvet drapes and shelves of books, well kept Greene King, Harveys and guests, good service; tables out in front, open all day. *Recommended by N R White*

CARSHALTON TQ2764   SM5 3PE

☆ # Greyhound
High Street

18th-c coaching inn opposite duck ponds in picturesque outer London 'village', comfortable panelled front lounge bar with log fire, dining areas, friendly service, Youngs ales, wide choice of enjoyable food from interesting sandwiches and ciabattas up; TV in large public bar; picnic-sets out by road, bedrooms. *Recommended by Mierion Perring*

CHELSFIELD TQ4864   BR6 7RE

Five Bells
Church Road; just off A224 Orpington bypass

Ancient chatty village local with two separate bars and dining area, friendly staff, well kept ales such as Cottage, Courage and Sharps Doom Bar, well priced food from snacks up (evening food Thurs-Sat only), live music including jazz, Tues quiz; children welcome, picnic-sets among flowers out in front, open all day. *Recommended by Tony Hobden*

HAMPTON TQ1370   TW12 2EA

Bell
Thames Street

Extensive refurbishment under new owners with focus on food (all day weekends), good service; across road from the Thames, open all day. *Recommended by John Soones*

ISLEWORTH TQ1576   TW7 6QJ

Red Lion
Linkfield Road

Friendly unspoilt backstreet local with nine real ales, three ciders and good choice of belgian beers, home-made food (not Sun evening, Mon, Tues) including popular Sun lunch, four annual beer festivals, theatre company, live music including Mon jazz; children and dogs welcome, picnic-sets out at front, garden with smokers' shelter. *Recommended by C Cooper*

KEW TQ1977   TW9 3BH

Coach & Horses
Kew Green

Modernised former coaching inn overlooking green, decent Wells & Youngs ales and a guest, good coffees, fairly standard bar food from sandwiches up, young friendly staff, relaxed open-plan interior with armchairs, sofas and log fire, small restaurant; piped music, sports TV; teak tables on front terrace, nice setting handy for Kew Gardens and the National Archive, 30 refurbished bedrooms. *Recommended by N R White, Geof Cox, Jeremy King*

KEW TQ1976   TW9 3PZ

Railway
Station Parade

Appealing former station buffet, real ales including Adnams, draught ciders and a decent choice of wines by the glass, reasonably priced generous food, mix of comfortable sofas, tall and more regular tables, newspapers; TVs; large covered and heated area outside. *Recommended by David M Smith*

KINGSTON TQ1869   KT2 5AU

Boaters
Canbury Gardens (park in Lower Ham Road if you can)

Family-friendly pub by the Thames, half a dozen real ales, variety of good value food including vegetarian (some themed evenings), efficient staff, comfortable banquettes in quiet charming bar, newspapers, Sun jazz; smart riverside terrace, in small park, ideal for children in summer, open all day. *Recommended by Ian Phillips, David and Sally Frost*

the Beautiful South

KINGSTON TQ1869   KT2 6LQ
Canbury Arms
Canbury Park Road

Big-windowed bare-boards open-plan pub with simple fresh contemporary décor, relaxed friendly atmosphere, good up-to-date food including breakfast from 9am (10pm Sun), two-for-one deal Tues evening, five well kept ales such as Harveys, Sharps and Timothy Taylors, good wine choice (bargains Mon night), nice coffee, attentive young staff, stone floor in side conservatory, frequent events; children and dogs welcome, tables out at front iunder parasols, open all day. *Recommended by Keith M Long, Charlotte Salaman, Louis Jones*

LONGFORD TQ0576   UB7 0EE
White Horse
Bath Road, off A3044 (and A4)

Brasses on low 17th-c black beams, fireplace between the two spotless areas, comfortable seats, cosy and friendly with pot plants in windows and rustic decorations such as antique rifles and equestrian bronzes, popular food from hearty traditional things to curries and thai dishes (booking advised), good service, three well kept ales; piped music, games machine; flower tubs and picnic-sets outside, one in a little barn, surprisingly villagey surroundings despite the parking meters, open all day. *Recommended by Andy and Jill Kassube, M J Winterton*

ORPINGTON TQ4963   BR6 7QL
☆ ## Bo-Peep
Hewitts Road, Chelsfield; 1.7 miles from M25 junction 4

Useful M25 country-feel dining pub, old low beams and enormous inglenook in carpeted bar, two cosy candlelit dining rooms, airy side room overlooking lane, Adnams, Courage and Harveys, cheerful service, pubby food (not Sun evening) as well as some more interesting choices, miniature english bull terrier called Milo; piped music; children welcome, dogs in bar, picnic-sets on big brick terrace, open all day. *Recommended by Guy Vowles, N R White, Tony Brace*

OSTERLEY TQ1578   TW7 5PR
☆ ## Hare & Hounds
Windmill Lane (B454, off A4 – called Syon Lane at that point)

Roomy suburban Fullers dining pub, wide choice of enjoyable food from sandwiches to hearty reasonably priced main dishes, prompt friendly service, pleasant dining extension, local wartime photographs; disabled facilities, spacious terrace and big floodlit mature garden, nice setting opposite beautiful Osterley Park. *Recommended by Ellie Weld, David London, Revd R P Tickle*

RICHMOND TQ1875   TW9 2NQ
Orange Tree
Kew Road

Big open-plan Youngs pub with lots of sofas and other seating, their ales and often a guest, good reasonably priced wine list including some unusual choices, decent pubby food using good quality ingredients, more formal dining part at back, upstairs area (jazz Weds); tables out in front, small covered terrace behind, open all day. *Recommended by Sue and Mike Todd*

RICHMOND TQ1774   TW9 1LX
Princes Head
The Green

Large unspoilt open-plan pub overlooking cricket green near theatre, clean and well run, with low-ceilinged panelled areas off big island bar, full Fullers range in top condition, popular imaginative food, friendly young staff and chatty locals, coal-effect fire; over-21s only, seats outside – fine spot. *Recommended by Ian Phillips, Richard and Sissel Harris, N R White*

RICHMOND TQ1774   TW9 1TJ
Watermans Arms
Water Lane

Friendly old-fashioned Youngs local, well kept beer, open fire, traditional layout, pub games, enjoyable thai food; handy for the Thames. *Recommended by N R White, Claes Mauroy*

RICHMOND TQ1874   TW9 1TH
☆ # White Cross
Water Lane

Very pleasant garden with terrific Thames views, seats on paved area, outside bar and boats to Kingston and Hampton Court; two chatty main rooms with hotel feel (which it was), local prints and photographs, three log fires (one unusually below a window), Wells & Youngs and guests from old-fashioned island servery, a dozen wines by the glass, decent bar food all day, bright and airy upstairs room (children welcome here till 6pm) with pretty cast-iron balcony for splendid river view, good mix of customers; piped music, TV; dogs welcome. *Recommended by Thurstan Johnston, Ian Phillips, the Didler, Paul Humphreys, Michael Dandy and others*

RICHMOND TQ1774   TW9 1PG
White Swan
Old Palace Lane

Small cottagey pub, civilised and relaxed, with rustic dark-beamed open-plan bar, good friendly service, well kept ales such as Fullers London Pride, St Austell Tribute and Timothy Taylors Landlord, fresh wholesome bar lunches, coal-effect fires, popular upstairs restaurant; piped music; children allowed in back conservatory, some seats on narrow paved area at front, more in pretty walled back terrace below railway. *Recommended by LM, Jennifer Banks, N R White*

RICHMOND TQ1873   TW10 6RN
Roebuck
Richmond Hill

Comfortable and attractive 18th-c bay-windowed pub with friendly helpful staff, well kept changing ales, enjoyable food including vegetarian choices, stripped-brick alcoves, some substantial bygones, old Thames photographs and prints; children and dogs welcome, terrace over road with fine views of meadows and river, open all day. *Recommended by Jennifer Banks*

TEDDINGTON TQ1671   TW11 9NN
Tide End Cottage
Broom Road/Ferry Road, near bridge at Teddington Lock

Low-ceilinged pub in Victorian cottage terrace next to Teddington Studios, two rooms united by big log-effect gas fire, well kept Greene King ales and a guest, decent low-priced bar food to numbered tables from sandwiches up, lots of river, fishing and rowing memorabilia and photographs, interesting Dunkirk evacuation link, back dining extension; piped music, TV, minimal parking; children (till 7.30pm) and dogs welcome, small terraces front and back, open all day. *Recommended by Clare Carter, Chris Evans, LM*

We mention bottled beers and spirits only if there is something unusual about them – imported belgian real ales, say, or dozens of malt whiskies; so do please let us know about them in your reports.

The East of England

Bedfordshire

Cambridgeshire

Essex

Hertfordshire

Norfolk

Suffolk

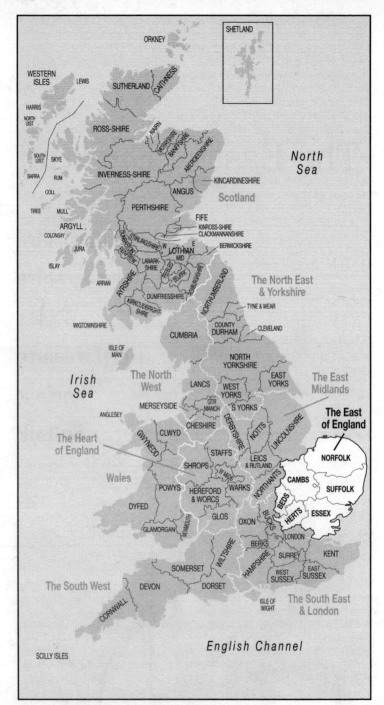

ORKNEY

SHETLAND

WESTERN
ISLES   LEWIS

HARRIS

NORTH
UIST   SUTHERLAND   CAITHNESS

SOUTH
UIST   SKYE   ROSS-SHIRE   NAIRN

BARRA   RUM   MORAYSHIRE   BANFFSHIRE

COLL   INVERNESS-SHIRE   ABERDEENSHIRE

TIREE   MULL   KINCARDINESHIRE

ARGYLL   ANGUS   Scotland

COLONSAY   PERTHSHIRE

JURA   FIFE

ISLAY   KINROSS-SHIRE
                                CLACKMANNANSHIRE

                        DUNBARTONSHIRE   W E   BERWICKSHIRE
                        RENFREW   LOTHIAN
ARRAN   LANARK-   MID
                        SHIRE
                        AYRSHIRE   PEEBLES   SELKIRK

                                   DUMFRIESSHIRE   ROXBURGHSHIRE

                        KIRKCUDBRIGHT-
                        SHIRE   NORTHUMBERLAND

WIGTOWNSHIRE   TYNE & WEAR

                        CUMBRIA   COUNTY
                                       DURHAM   CLEVELAND

ISLE OF
MAN   NORTH
                                   YORKSHIRE

Irish   The North   EAST
Sea   West   LANCS   WEST   YORKS
                                    YORKS

                        MERSEYSIDE   GTR   S YORKS   The East
                                      MANCH   Midlands

ANGLESEY   CHESHIRE   The East
                                             NOTTS   of England

GWYNEDD   CLWYD   DERBYSHIRE LINCOLNSHIRE

The Heart   STAFFS   NORFOLK
of England   LEICS
                        SHROPS   & RUTLAND   CAMBS   SUFFOLK
                              W MIDS
Wales   POWYS   WARKS   NORTHANTS   ESSEX
                        HEREFORD   BEDS
            DYFED   & WORCS   HERTS

                        GLOS   OXON   BUCKS
            GLAMORGAN   MONMOUTH   LONDON

                                         BERKS
                                 WILTSHIRE   SURREY   KENT

            The South West SOMERSET   HAMPSHIRE
                                              WEST   EAST
            DEVON   DORSET   SUSSEX SUSSEX

CORNWALL   ISLE OF   The South East
                                      WIGHT   & London

SCILLY ISLES   English Channel

North
Sea

Scotland

The North East
& Yorkshire

EDITORS' FAVOURITES
THE EAST OF ENGLAND

The region's top pub for 2012 is the Rose & Crown in Snettisham in **Norfolk** (a top all-rounder, **Norfolk Dining Pub of the Year** and the **East of England Pub of the Year**). Other special pubs here include the Dabbling Duck at Great Massingham (friendly, busy and with some real character), Kings Head in Letheringsett (carefully converted manor house, bistro-type food), Fat Cat in Norwich (fantastic choice of real ales and always lively), Hare Arms at Stow Bardolph (particularly well run by long-serving owners) and the Orange Tree in Thornham (new to us and highly enjoyable). Also worth a visit are the Chequers at Binham, Buckinghamshire Arms in Blickling, White Horse at Brancaster Staithe, Lord Nelson in Burnham Thorpe, Jolly Farmers in North Creake, Sculthorpe Mill at Sculthorpe, Vernon Arms in Southrepps and Three Horseshoes at Warham.

Two pubs doing particularly well in **Bedfordshire** are the Bedford Arms at Souldrop (pubby, great value food) and the Horse & Jockey at Ravensden (spic and span and **Bedfordshire Dining Pub of the Year**). Also worth a visit are the Falcon in Bletsoe, Plough in Bolnhurst, Cock at Broom and the Bedford Arms in Oakley

Our top picks for **Cambridgeshire** are the Free Press in Cambridge (super little pub for a quiet drink), Blue Ball in Helpston (professional, hands-on landlord), Cock at Hemingford Grey (part pub, part restaurant and **Cambridgeshire Dining Pub of the Year**), Red Lion in Hinxton (especially well run by first-class landlord) and Old Bridge Hotel at Huntingdon (proper pubby bar in smart hotel). Also worth a visit are the Red Lion in Histon, Pheasant in Keyston, Queens Head in Newton, Eagle and the Old Spring – both in Cambridge – and Anchor at Sutton Gault.

Essex is a surprisingly good bet for good value food with many pubs here qualifying for our new Value Award. The Crown at Little Walden (warm and homely), White Harte at Burnham-on-Crouch (timeless, down-to-earth and by the water), the waterside Queens Head in Fyfield and the Bell at Horndon-on-the-Hill (which is both pubby and civilised and **Essex Dining Pub of the Year**). Also worth a visit are the Alma in Chelmsford, Sun at Dedham, Square & Compasses in Fuller Street, Thatchers Arms in Mount Bures and Prince of Wales in Stow Maries.

Pubs doing well in **Hertfordshire** include the traditional Fullers-owned White Horse in Hertford (ten real ales), the Holly Bush in Potters Crouch (neatly kept and with sensibly priced food), the Bricklayers Arms in Flaunden (carefully prepared inventive food), the Alford Arms in Frithsden (lively atmosphere and **Hertfordshire Dining Pub of the Year**), and the Red Lion in Preston (simple, pubby and with interesting beers). Also worth a visit are the Cricketers at Sarratt and the Kings Arms at Tring.

Smashing pubs in **Suffolk** are the Old Cannon in Bury St Edmunds (own-brew beers and interesting food), Ship in Dunwich (super little place for a drink, a meal or overnight stay), Red Rose at Lindsey Tye (full of contented customers), White Horse in Sibton (lovely food and **Suffolk Dining Pub of the Year**), Lord Nelson in Southwold (seafront pub, good value food) and the White Horse in Whepstead (friendly, civilised and well run). Also worth a visit are the Nutshell in Bury St Edmunds, Fox & Goose at Fressingfield, Fat Cat in Ipswich, Kings Head in Laxfield, St Peters Brewery at South Elmham and the Fountain at Tuddenham.

ALDEBURGH Suffolk   TM4656   Map 5

Cross Keys

Crabbe Street; IP15 5BN

Seats outside this 16th-c pub near the beach, chatty atmosphere, friendly licensee, and local beer; bedrooms

At any time of the year, this cheerful old pub is a favourite with many of our readers. It's warm and cosy in winter with roaring open fires and being by the seafront is a big draw in summer. The friendly licensees create a bustling, buoyant atmosphere and the low-ceilinged interconnecting bars have antique and other pubby furniture, the landlord's collection of oils and Victorian watercolours, paintings by local artists and two inglenook fireplaces. Adnams Bitter, Broadside and Explorer on handpump, Aspall's cider, decent wines by the glass and several malt whiskies; piped music, games machine and board games. The bedrooms are attractively furnished. The terrace behind is sheltered by two walls and has views across the promenade and shingle to the sea.

Traditional bar food includes sandwiches, pâté with toast, moules and chips, popular local cod, vegetable lasagne, and steak and kidney pie. *Benchmark main dish: beer-battered cod and chips £8.95. Two-course evening meal £15.00.*

Adnams ~ Tenants Mike and Janet Clement ~ Real ale ~ Bar food (12-2(3.30 Sat, Sun), 7-9) ~ (01728) 452637 ~ Children welcome ~ Dogs welcome ~ Open 11am(midday Sun)-midnight ~ Bedrooms: £55B/£89.50S(£85B)

Recommended by Charles and Pauline Stride, S T W Norton, Barry Collett, Dr D J and Mrs S C Walker, Terry Mizen, Geoff and Linda Payne, Mike and Sue Loseby

AMPTHILL Bedfordshire   TL0338   Map 5

Prince of Wales

Bedford Street (B540 N from central crossroads); MK45 2NB

Civilised with contemporary décor and menu; bedrooms

The neatly modernised interior of this open-plan bar-brasserie is on two levels, with big leather deco-style armchairs and sofas at low tables on wood-strip flooring as you come in. It then angles around past a slightly sunken flagstoned bit, with an exposed brick fireplace, to a partly ply-panelled dining area with comfortable dark leather dining chairs set around a mixed batch of sturdy tables. Modern prints decorate the mainly cream walls (dark green and maroon accents at either end) and it's all nicely lit; piped music. They have Wells & Youngs Bombardier and Eagle on handpump, good coffee, and service is brisk and helpful. There are picnic-sets out on a nicely planted two-level lawn, and a terrace by the car park.

 As well as lunchtime snacks such as tortilla wraps and filled baguettes, bar food might include toad in the hole, chilli, steak and kidney pudding, lamb shank with rosemary and red wine reduction, moroccan-style stuffed peppers, and teriyaki salmon. Roasts only on Sunday and a two- or three-course set menu only on Monday evenings. *Benchmark main dish: cod and chips £10.25. Two-course evening meal £23.50.*

Charles Wells ~ Lease Richard and Neia Heathorn ~ Real ale ~ Bar food (12-2.30(3 Sun), 6.30(7 Fri, Sat)-9.30) ~ Restaurant ~ (01525) 840504 ~ Children welcome ~ Dogs allowed in bar ~ Open 12-3, 6-11 (12-midnight Fri, Sat); 12-5 Sun; closed Sun evening ~ Bedrooms: £55S/£70S

Recommended by Michael Dandy, Dave Hollins, David and Diane Young, Libby Spinks, Sheila Allcock

ARKESDEN Essex   TL4834   Map 5

Axe & Compasses ♀

Off B1038; CB11 4EX

Comfortably traditional pub with Greene King beers and decent food

Newly thatched this year, this enjoyable village pub dates back to the 17th c. The oldest part is the traditionally carpeted lounge bar which has low-slung ceilings, polished upholstered oak and elm seats, plush easy chairs, a blazing fire and gleaming brasses. A smaller quirky public bar is uncarpeted, with built-in settles and darts. The atmosphere is relaxed and welcoming with friendly service from the pleasant staff and licensee. You'll find a very good wine list (with 15 wines by the glass) and around two dozen malt whiskies, along with Greene King Abbot, IPA and Old Speckled Hen and perhaps Ruddles County served under a light blanket pressure on handpump. There are seats out on a side terrace with pretty hanging baskets; parking at the back.

 They grow their own herbs on a farm in the village. The tasty bar food includes lunchtime sandwiches, chicken liver pâté, whitebait, crunchy squid with lime and chilli mayonnaise, grilled or battered haddock, good breaded scampi, pork loin with stilton, mushroom and cream sauce, fish pie and sirloin steak, and there is a more elaborate pricier restaurant menu. *Benchmark main dish: steak, mushroom and kidney pie £12.95. Two-course evening meal £20.00.*

Greene King ~ Tenants Themis and Diane Christou ~ Real ale ~ Bar food ~ Restaurant ~ (01799) 550272 ~ Children welcome ~ Open 12-2.30, 6-11; 12-3, 7-10.30 Sun

Recommended by Mr and Mrs B Watt, Ian Wilson, David Jackson

ASHWELL Hertfordshire   TL2739   Map 5

Three Tuns

Off A505 NE of Baldock; High Street; SG7 5NL

Comfortable gently old-fashioned hotel bars, generous helpings of tasty food and a substantial garden

Wood panelling, dark green walls, relaxing chairs, big family tables, lots of pictures, stuffed pheasants and fish, piped light classical music and antiques lend an air of Victorian opulence to the cosy lounge at this red brick inn. The public bar is more modern, with leather sofas on reclaimed oak flooring; cribbage, dominoes, games machine and TV. They stock a good choice of wines as well as Greene King IPA, St Edmunds and three or four guests from brewers such as Holts and Thwaites on handpump. A big terrace has metal tables and chairs, while a large garden has picnic-sets and boules under the shade of apple trees. The charming village is full of pleasant corners and is popular with walkers as the landscape around rolls enough to be rewarding.

Sensibly priced bar food includes filled baguettes, breaded whitebait, chilli tiger prawns, sausages and mash, liver and bacon, fish and chips, chicken caesar salad, risotto of the day, and lamb chops; Sunday roast. *Benchmark main dish: steak and kidney pie £10.75. Two-course evening meal £16.40.*

Greene King ~ Lease Bill Pennell ~ Real ale ~ Bar food (12-2, 7-9; 12-9.30 Sat, Sun) ~ Restaurant ~ (01462) 742107 ~ Children welcome ~ Dogs welcome ~ Open 11(12 Sun)-11.30(12.30 Sat) ~ Bedrooms: £39(£53B)/£59(£69B)
Recommended by Eithne Dandy, Mike and Lynn Robinson

BALSHAM Cambridgeshire   TL5850 Map 5

Black Bull

Village signposted off A11 SW of Newmarket, and off A1307 in Linton;
High Street; CB21 4DJ

Pretty thatched pub with bedroom extension – a good all-rounder and recently reopened

Set well back from the village road, this handsome black and white timbered building has just been extensively and sympathetically overhauled inside, its beamed bar now spreading around a central servery with well kept Adnams Bitter, Greene King IPA, Woodfordes Wherry and a guest beer on handpump, and a good choice of wines by the glass. Part dividers and standing timbers break up the space, which has an open fire, low black beams in the front part, and seating on the new board flooring running from small leatherette-seated dining chairs to red plush banquettes. A restaurant extension, with pitched rafters and timbered ochre walls, has simple pale wood country furnishings. The front terrace has round picnic-sets by a long pleasantly old-fashioned verandah; there are more in a small sheltered back garden. We have not yet heard from readers staying in the neat single-storey bedroom extension. This pub is under the same good ownership as the Red Lion at Hinxton.

Good bar food includes sandwiches, home-smoked duck with celeriac rémoulade, chicory, sun-dried tomatoes and red wine dressing, fresh crab tian with a pomegranate dressing, goats cheese, tomato and asparagus tart, slow-cooked pork belly with leek mash, caramelised apple and sage jus, and rack of lamb with ratatouille, parmentier potatoes, red wine and rosemary jus. *Benchmark main dish: steak in Guinness pie £10.00. Two-course evening meal £18.00.*

Free house ~ Licensee Alex Clarke ~ Real ale ~ Bar food (12-2.30, 7-9.30; not Sun evening) ~ Restaurant ~ (01223) 893844 ~ Well behaved children welcome ~ Dogs welcome ~ Open 11-3.30, 6-11.30; 11-11.30 Sat; 12-4.30, 7-10.30 Sun ~ Bedrooms: £79B/£99B
Recommended by Jerry Brown

We checked prices with the pubs as we went to press in summer 2011.
They should hold until around spring 2012.

 BATFORD Hertfordshire   TL1415   Map 5

Gibraltar Castle

Lower Luton Road; B653, S of B652 junction; AL5 5AH

Pleasantly traditional pub with interesting militaria displays, some emphasis on food (booking advised); pretty terrace

The quite traditional long carpeted bar at this neatly kept, welcoming pub is decked out with an impressive collection of military memorabilia – everything from rifles to swords, medals, uniforms and bullets (with plenty of captions to read) and pictures depicting various moments in Gibraltar's history. In one area the low beams give way to soaring rafters and there are comfortably cushioned wall benches, and a couple of snugly intimate window alcoves, one with a fine old clock, several board games are piled on top of the piano and a pleasant old fireplace. Fullers London Pride and ESB and a Fullers guest are on handpump; piped music. Outside, there are tables on a front terrace overlooking a nature reserve, on a large pretty decked area with lots of flowers at the back and in a tree-lined garden to one side.

Bar food includes a good range of lunchtime sandwiches, ploughman's, duck and port pâté with rhubarb chutney, risotto of the day, fish and chips, steak and kidney pudding, chicken pie, and daily specials such as fried sailfish with beetroot and dill sauce, and lamb wellington stuffed with goats cheese and wrapped with parma ham with red wine jus. *Benchmark main dish: lamb shank with rosemary jus £12.95. Two-course evening meal £16.90.*

Fullers ~ Tenant Hamish Miller ~ Real ale ~ Bar food (12-2.30(6 Sun), 6-9) ~ Restaurant ~ (01582) 460005 ~ Children welcome ~ Dogs allowed in bar ~ Open 11.30-11(12 Fri, Sat); 12-10.30 Sun

Recommended by David and Ruth Shillitoe

BIRCHANGER Essex   TL5122   Map 5

Three Willows

Under a mile from M11 junction 8: A120 towards Bishop's Stortford, then almost immediately right to Birchanger Village; don't be waylaid earlier by the Birchanger Services signpost; CM23 5QR

Full of cricketing memorabilia, a happy civilised place serving good food

Just a few minutes from the motorway but nevertheless feeling nicely tucked away, this creamy yellow dining pub makes a very handy break from the M11. With the friendly landlord much in evidence and its cheery warm service, it's a reliable place for a good meal. It's worth booking ahead or arriving early as it is popular with an older set at lunchtime and a more varied crowd in the evening. The spacious carpeted main bar has a cricket theme, with lots of cricketing prints, photographs, cartoons and other memorabilia, and Greene King Abbot and IPA and a guest on handpump and decent house wines. There's a well furnished small lounge bar. Though children are not welcome inside, there is plenty for them outside including a sturdy climbing frame, swings and a basketball hoop. There are picnic-sets out on a terrace (with heaters) and on the lawn behind (you can hear the motorway and Stansted Airport out here).

Besides a wide range of generously served pubby standards such as sandwiches, filled baked potatoes and ploughman's (lunchtime only), steak and ale pie, steaks and vegetable curry, they serve quite a lot of fresh fish dishes –

maybe cod, tuna steak, crab salad and lemon sole. They don't offer starters.
Benchmark main dish: cod and chips £11.95.

Greene King ~ Tenants Paul and David Tucker ~ Real ale ~ Bar food (12-2, 6-9) ~
(01279) 815913 ~ Dogs allowed in bar ~ Open 11.30-3, 6-11; 12-3 Sun; closed Sun evening

*Recommended by Mrs Margo Finlay, Jörg Kasprowski, Grahame and Myra Williams, Terry and
Nickie Williams, Ian, Keith and Sandra Ross*

 BLAKENEY Norfolk   TG0243   Map 8

White Horse

Off A149 W of Sheringham; High Street; NR25 7AL

**Cheerful small hotel with popular dining conservatory, interesting food
and drinks and helpful staff; bedrooms**

Just a stroll from the small tidal harbour, this is an enjoyable place with
a bustling and friendly main bar. It's a former coaching inn and
although many customers are here for the popular food, those just
wanting a drink and a chat do pop in. Adnams Bitter and Broadside,
Woodfordes Wherry and Yetmans Red on handpump and a huge choice of
40 wines by the glass. The informal long bar is cream-coloured above a
pale green dado (two end walls have tartan wallpaper) and has high-
backed suede dining and other chairs around light oak tables on the
green-patterned carpet, contemporary window blinds and watercolours
by a local artist (for sale). There's also an airy conservatory and smarter
restaurant. The suntrap courtyard and pleasant paved garden both have
plenty of tables. This area is a haven for bird-watchers and sailors.

As well as making their own bread and using local seasonal produce, the well
liked food includes lunchtime sandwiches, tequila- and lime-cured trout
gravadlax with ginger crème fraîche, chargrilled courgette and goats cheese tart,
smoked collar of bacon with fried duck eggs, lamb three ways (rump, cutlet and
sweetbread with chorizo), and halibut with dill beurre blanc. *Benchmark main
dish: fresh local mussels £12.95. Two-course evening meal £20.00.*

Free house ~ Licensee Dan Goff ~ Real ale ~ Bar food (12-2.15, 6-9) ~ Restaurant ~
(01263) 740574 ~ Children allowed away from bar ~ Dogs allowed in bar ~ Open 11-11 ~
Bedrooms: £70S/£100S

*Recommended by MDN, David Carr, Tracey and Stephen Groves, Michael and Maggie Betton,
Sandy Butcher*

 BRANCASTER Norfolk   TF7743   Map 8

Ship

A149; PE31 8AP

**Carefully renovated inn with contemporary but comfortable bars, real
ales, modern cooking and friendly staff; stylish bedrooms**

Newly opened and carefully refurbished in line with the other pubs in
this growing small group of Flying Kiwi Inns, this 18th-c inn is in a
traditional fishing village close to the salt marshes, dunes and beaches.
The elegant bar has contemporary paintwork, built-in cushioned and
planked wall seats and attractive stools around a mix of tables, and this
leads into a dining area with a woodburning stove at one end, a few pale
settles and a nice variety of wooden dining chairs around all manner of
tables, and rugs on bare boards. The restaurant has unusual Norfolk map

wallpapering, plates on a dresser, lots of differing chairs and tables, and logs stacked up in the fireplace. There are bookcases, shipping memorabilia and lots of prints on the pale walls, their own JoC's Norfolk Ale and Adnams Bitter on handpump and good wines by the glass; piped music, TV, daily papers to read and nice coffee. There are seats outside. The bedrooms are well equipped and attractively furnished and breakfasts are enjoyable.

Good modern food includes lunchtime sandwiches, pigeon terrine with pickled red cabbage and mustard dressing, natural, tempura or grilled local oysters, beer-battered haddock, butternut squash, rocket and goats cheese pasta, lambs liver, smoked bacon and mash, and slow-cooked pork belly with sage mash and cider syrup. *Benchmark main dish: bass fillet with crab mash and asparagus and shallot dressing £18.45. Two-course evening meal £19.70.*

Flying Kiwi Inns ~ Licensee Chris Coubrough ~ Bar food (12-2.30, 6.30-9.30) ~ Restaurant ~ (01485) 210333 ~ Children welcome ~ Dogs welcome ~ Open 11am-11.30pm ~ Bedrooms: £70B/£90B

Recommended by Tracey and Stephen Groves, R C Vincent

BURNHAM MARKET Norfolk   TF8342   Map 8

Hoste Arms 🍴 ♟ 🛏

The Green (B1155); PE31 8HD

Civilised and stylish with excellent food and drinks, a proper bar plus several lounge areas and dining rooms, and a lovely garden; elaborately decorated bedrooms

This is a smart 17th-c coaching inn in a lovely village of Georgian houses and although many customers are here to enjoy the thriving, professionally run restaurant and hotel side, there is a proper front bar with a cheerful mix of chatty drinkers. This room is panelled, with a log fire, a series of watercolours showing scenes from local walks and Greene King Abbot and Woodfordes Nelsons Revenge and Wherry on handpump. The extensive and carefully chosen wine list has helpful notes and around 18 (including champagne and sparkling wine) by the glass; lots of whiskies and liqueurs. There's a conservatory with leather armchairs and sofas, a lounge for afternoon tea and several restaurants (for which it's best to book to be sure of a table). The lovely walled garden has plenty of seats and a big awning covers the moroccan-style dining area.

As well as lunchtime sandwiches, the first-class food includes truffled chicken liver parfait with date and apple chutney, vanilla, vodka, dill and goji berry cured salmon with celeriac rémouade, wild mushroom, rocket and mascarpone risotto with a poached egg, cajun chicken with sweetcorn fritters and a tomato and avocado salsa, beer-battered cod, steak burger with bacon and cheese, and herb-crusted rack of lamb with roasted root vegetables. *Benchmark main dish: steak and kidney pudding £13.75. Two-course evening meal £22.00.*

Free house ~ Licensee Emma Tagg ~ Real ale ~ Bar food ~ Restaurant ~ (01328) 738777 ~ Children welcome ~ Dogs allowed in bar and bedrooms ~ Open 11-11(10.30 Sun) ~ Bedrooms: £122S/£149B

Recommended by Mike Proctor, Kay and Alistair Butler, Michael Dandy, Mr and Mrs W W Burke, Walter and Susan Rinaldi-Butcher, David Carr, George and Linda Ozols, Derek Thomas, Roy Hoing, Mike and Sue Loseby, John and Victoria Fairley, Jeremy and Ruth Preston-Hoar, Peter and Giff Bennett, Sandy Butcher

BURNHAM-ON-CROUCH Essex   TQ9495 Map 5

White Harte
The Quay; CM0 8AS

Lovely waterside position, with an aptly nautical theme to the décor, and waterside tables

---

There's a timeless down-to-earth charm to this comfortably old-fashioned hotel. Its relaxed partly carpeted bars are filled with assorted nautical bric-a-brac and hardware – anything from models of Royal Navy ships to a compass set in the hearth. Other traditionally furnished high-ceilinged rooms have sea pictures on brown panelled or stripped-brick walls, with cushioned seats around oak tables, and an enormous log fire making it cosy in winter. In summer they open the doors and windows, giving the place a nice airy feel. Charming staff serve Adnams and Crouch Vale from handpump. Just across the road there are some picnic-sets spaced out on a small jetty by the River Crouch – a lovely spot to sit and watch the lazy yachts go by.

Bar food includes lunchtime sandwiches, steak and kidney pie, a choice of three local fish such as cod, plaice and skate, and specials such as lasagne, chicken madras and cottage pie. *Benchmark main dish: steak and ale pie £8.20. Two-course evening meal £19.50.*

Free house ~ Licensee G John Lewis ~ Real ale ~ Bar food ~ Restaurant ~ (01621) 782106 ~ Dogs allowed in bar and bedrooms ~ Open 11-11; 12-10.30 Sun ~ Bedrooms: £28(£57B)/£50(£89B)

Recommended by LM

BURSTON Norfolk   TM1383 Map 8

Crown ◀
Village signposted off A140 N of Scole; Mill Road; IP22 5TW

Friendly, relaxed village pub usefully open all day, with a warm welcome, real ales and well liked bar food

---

There's always something going on at this bustling village pub and you can be sure of a warm welcome from the friendly staff. Locals tend to gather in an area by the bar counter, with its high bar chairs, where they serve Adnams Bitter, Greene King Abbot and guests such as Elgoods Pageant Ale and Elmtree Mad Maudie on handpump, two farm ciders and several wines by the glass. In cold weather, the best place to sit in this heavy-beamed, quarry-tiled room is on the comfortably cushioned sofas in front of the big log fire in its huge brick fireplace, and there are also some stools by the low chunky wooden table and newspapers and magazines to read. The public bar on the left has a nice long table and panelled settle on an old brick floor in one alcove, another sofa, straightforward tables and chairs on the carpet by the pool table, games machine and juke box, and up a step, more tables and chairs. Both of these cream-painted rooms are hung with cheerful naive local character paintings; piped music and board games. The simply furnished, beamed dining room has another big brick fireplace. Outside, there's a smokers' shelter, a couple of picnic-sets in front of the old brick building and more seats in a hedged-off area with a barbecue.

Using local produce, the well liked bar food includes sandwiches, chicken liver and spiced rum parfait, spinach and cream cheese pancakes, beer-battered hake, oriental stir-fried chicken, steak and kidney pie, honey roast duck with a port and rhubarb sauce, and griddled tuna loin with niçoise salad. *Benchmark main dish: duck confit with garlic puy lentils £13.50. Two-course evening meal £19.50.*

Free house ~ Licensees Bev and Steve Kembery and Jonathan Piers-Hall ~ Real ale ~ Bar food (12-2(4 Sun), 6.30-9; not Sun evening) ~ Restaurant ~ (01379) 741257 ~ Children welcome ~ Dogs allowed in bar ~ Live music Thurs evening and every other Sun at 5pm ~ Open 12-11(10.30 Sun); closed evenings 25 and 26 Dec and evening 1 Jan
Recommended by R C Vincent

 BURY ST EDMUNDS Suffolk   TL8564   Map 5

Old Cannon

Cannon Street, just off A134/A1101 roundabout at N end of town; IP33 1JR

Busy own-brew town pub with local drinks and good bar food

Their own-brewed real ales and popular bar food make it fairly essential to book a table in advance at this Victorian town house. The bar is dominated by two huge gleaming stainless-steel brewing vessels and has views up to a steel balustraded open-plan malt floor above the counter where they serve Old Cannon Best, Black Pig, Gunner's Daughter and Hornblower and guests like Adnams Bitter and Timothy Taylors Landlord on handpump. A row of chunky old bar stools line the ochre-painted counter (which also serves Aspall's cider and apple juice, a local lager, continental beers, 16 wines by the glass and around 25 malt whiskies) and there's a happy mix of old and new chairs and tables and upholstered banquettes on well worn bare boards; piped music. Behind, through the old side coach arch, is a good-sized cobbled courtyard with hanging baskets and stylish metal tables and chairs. The bedrooms are in what was the old brewhouse across the courtyard.

Under the new landlord, the interesting food includes lunchtime filled baguettes, local moules marinière, sausages with colcannon, onion gravy and a beer-batter pudding, local sardines with a bacon and radish salad, lamb breast with local sheeps cheese, mint and apricot stuffing and rosemary gravy, and pork and mango curry; there's a thai feast on the first Tuesday of each month. *Benchmark main dish: fresh cod and chips £10.75. Two-course evening meal £16.50.*

Free house ~ Licensee Mark Jones ~ Real ale ~ Bar food (12-2(3 weekends), 6-9.15; not Sun or Mon evenings) ~ Restaurant ~ (01284) 768769 ~ Children in restaurant only ~ Open 12-3, 5-11; 12-11 Sat and Sun ~ Bedrooms: £70S/£90S
Recommended by Jeremy King, John Saville, John and Sharon Hancock

 CAMBRIDGE Cambridgeshire   TL4558   Map 5

Free Press £

Prospect Row; CB1 1DU

Quiet and unspoilt with interesting local décor, up to six real ales, and good value food

Tucked away in a narrow street, this is a reliably enjoyable little pub – just the place to enjoy a pint and a newspaper by a warm log fire; the unspoilt atmosphere is undisturbed by mobile phones, piped music or games machines. In a nod to the building's history as home to a local newspaper, the walls of the characterful bare-boarded rooms are hung with old newspaper pages and printing memorabilia, as well as old printing trays that local customers are encouraged to top up with little items. Greene King IPA, Abbot and Mild and regularly changing guests such as Copper Dragon Scotts, Holts Fifth Sense and Okells Olde Skipper on handpump, 25 malt whiskies, a dozen wines by the glass, and lots of rums, gins and vodkas; assorted board games. There are seats in the suntrap sheltered and paved garden and perhaps summer morris men. Wheelchair access.

Robust food at fair prices includes lunchtime sandwiches and a full english breakfast, smoked haddock with a poached egg on horseradish mash, spaghetti with a spicy tomato and italian sausage sauce, lamb or black bean curry, and barbary duck with spring onion mash and redcurrant sauce. *Benchmark main dish: platter of scotch egg, pork pie, cheese and pickles £6.50. Two-course evening meal £14.45.*

Greene King ~ Lease Craig Bickley ~ Real ale ~ Bar food (12-2(2.30 Sat and Sun), 6(7 Sun)-9) ~ (01223) 368337 ~ Children welcome ~ Dogs welcome ~ Open 12-2.30, 6(4.30 Fri)-11; 12-11 Sat; 12-3, 7-10.30 Sun

Recommended by R T and J C Moggridge, John Wooll, the Didler, David and Gill Carrington, Ralph Holland, Barry and Anne

CHELMONDISTON Suffolk   TM2037   Map 5

Butt & Oyster

Pin Mill – signposted from B1456 SE of Ipswich; IP9 1JW

Chatty old riverside pub with pleasant views, decent food and drink and seats on the terrace

To make the most of the splendid views and goings-on by the River Orwell, you must get to this staunchly simple old bargemen's pub early to bag a window seat; tables and chairs on the terrace also overlook the water. The half-panelled timeless little smoke room is pleasantly worn and unfussy and has model sailing ships around the walls and high-backed and other old-fashioned settles on the tiled floor. There's also a two-level dining room with country-kitchen furniture on bare boards and pictures and artefacts to do with boats and the water on the walls above the blue dado. Adnams Best, Broadside and Explorer on handpump or tapped from the cask, several wines by the glass and local cider; board games. The annual Thames Barge Race (end June/beginning July) is fun. The car park can fill up pretty quickly.

Tasty bar food includes sandwiches, baked stuffed mushrooms, scallops and bacon with a pea and mint purée, ham and free-range egg, wild mushroom risotto, burger with home-made relish, chicken breast with mushroom and bacon sauce, and skate wing with lemon and caper dressing. *Benchmark main dish: fresh cod and chips £10.95. Two-course evening meal £16.95.*

Adnams ~ Lease Steve Lomas ~ Real ale ~ Bar food (12-9.30) ~ Restaurant ~ (01473) 780764 ~ Children welcome ~ Dogs allowed in bar ~ Folk music Sun evenings monthly ~ Open 11-11

Recommended by Pat and Tony Martin, N R White, the Didler, Alistair Mackie, Nicholas Rust, J F M and M West, Jeremy King

The price we give for a two-course evening meal in the featured top pub entries is the mean (average of cheapest and most expensive) price of a starter and a main course – no drinks.

CLAVERING Essex   TL4832 Map 5

Cricketers ♀ 🛏

B1038 Newport—Buntingford CB11 4QT

Busy dining pub with inventive food, real ales, a carefully chosen wine list and a friendly welcome; individually decorated bedrooms

Run by the parents of celebrity chef Jamie Oliver, this bustling dining pub places much emphasis on the well presented, imaginative food – but there's always a warm welcome if it's just a pint and a chat that you want. The main area has bays of deep purple button-backed banquettes and neat, padded leather dining chairs on dark floorboards, very low beams (the padding is a necessity, not a gimmick), and a big open fireplace. Back on the left is more obviously an eating part – two fairly compact carpeted areas, a step between them. The right side is similar but set more formally for dining, and has some big copper and brass pans on its dark beams and timbers. Adnams Bitter, Nethergate Lemon Head and a beer named for the pub on handpump, Aspall's cider, over a dozen wines by the glass and a good choice of soft drinks; piped music. Signed books by son Jamie are on sale. The attractive front terrace has wicker-look seats around teak tables among colourful flowering shrubs. The pub is handy for Stansted Airport.

They make their own bread and pasta and use properly hung meat, as well as produce supplied by their son's nearby organic garden: sandwiches, an antipasti plate, ham and pork terrine with home-made piccalilli, five-spice duck salad, lemony crab and pea fusilli, their much-loved sausage bolognese, aubergine and goats cheese gratin, a pie of the day, rump of lamb with a rich jus of mint, olives balsamic, well hung sirloin steak with wholegrain mustard mash and tomato salsa, and daily fresh fish dishes. *Benchmark main dish: steak in ale pie £14.50. Two-course evening meal £22.00.*

Free house ~ Licensee Trevor Oliver ~ Real ale ~ Bar food (12-2(2.30 Sun), 6.30-9.30; home-made cakes and tea all afternoon) ~ Restaurant ~ (01799) 550442 ~ Children welcome ~ Open 7am-11pm ~ Bedrooms: £67.50B/£95B

Recommended by Christopher and Elise Way, Peter Rozée, Mrs Margo Finlay, Jörg Kasprowski, Tina and David Woods-Taylor, Richard Cole, David Glynne-Jones and others

CLEY NEXT THE SEA Norfolk   TG0443 Map 8

George ♀ 🛏

Off A149 W of Sheringham; High Street; NR25 7RN

Pubby bar and two dining rooms in sizeable inn, real ales, super choice of wines and bar and restaurant food; bedrooms

This bustling inn is just a stroll away from the salt marshes and fantastic bird life and there are seats in the garden across the small lane. Inside, there are two dining rooms – although those wanting just a drink and a chat head for the little public bar. As well as Adnams Broadside, Woodfordes Wherry and Yetmans Red on handpump and up to 30 wines by the glass, there are photographs of Norfolk wherries and other local scenes on the cream walls, a long leather settle and sturdy dark wooden chairs by a couple of green-topped tables on the carpet, a huge candle in a big glass jar on one window sill, a table of newspapers and a stained-glass window showing St George and the dragon. The dining rooms are similarly furnished with pale wooden cushioned dining chairs around a mix of tables; the end room has prints of Leonardo drawings on the fleur-de-lys wallpaper, brown blinds on the windows, an ornamental woodburning stove in the end room with nightlights along the mantelbeam and some rather nice old-fashioned glass wall lamps.

Tasty bar food includes sandwiches, spicy crab cakes, ham and eggs, lasagne, pork belly with mustard mash and pak choi, mushroom stroganoff, chicken, chickpea and chorizo casserole, and bass with a red onion, fennel and potato salad. *Benchmark main dish: beer-battered haddock and chips £12.95. Two-course evening meal £18.00.*

Free house ~ Licensee Daniel Goff ~ Real ale ~ Bar food ~ Restaurant ~ (01263) 740652 ~ Children welcome ~ Dogs allowed in bar and bedrooms ~ Live music monthly in winter ~ Open 10am-11pm ~ Bedrooms: /£90S

Recommended by John and Victoria Fairley, Tracey and Stephen Groves, Jim Farmer, MDN, David Carr

COLKIRK Norfolk   TF9226 Map 8

THE GOOD PUB GUIDE Crown ♀

Village signposted off B1146 S of Fakenham, and off A1065; Crown Road; NR21 7AA

Neatly kept, bustling local with cheerful landlord, splendid wines, tasty food, and a pleasant garden

The buzz of cheerful conversation flows through this unpretentious and friendly red brick building and although you'll find a good few people eating, it's still very much a traditional village pub. If it's just a chat and a drink you want, head for the bar on the right – those eating, head for the left-hand room. Both rooms are comfortable and cosy and kept spotless with solid country furniture on the rugs and flooring tiles, interesting things to look at and open fires. Greene King IPA and Abbot and a guest beer on handpump and a splendid range of wines, many by the glass; quick service even when busy. There's also a separate dining room. Outside, the suntrap terrace and pleasant garden have plenty of picnic-sets.

Popular bar food includes lunchtime sandwiches, a changing pâté, coconut prawns with a chilli dip, anchovy and bacon salad, pork fillet in madeira sauce, and quite a few fishy choices like bass, black bream and salmon. *Benchmark main dish: steak in ale pie £10.95. Two-course evening meal £15.00.*

Greene King ~ Tenant Roger Savell ~ Real ale ~ Bar food (12-1.45(2 Sun), 6-8.30 (8 Sun)) ~ Restaurant ~ (01328) 862172 ~ Children welcome ~ Dogs allowed in bar ~ Open 11-2.30, 6-10.30(11 Sat, 10 Sun)

Recommended by Mr and Mrs T B Staples, R A P Cross, D M Jack, Gillian Grist, Jim Farmer, Anthony Barnes, John Cook

DUNWICH Suffolk   TM4770 Map 5

THE GOOD PUB GUIDE Ship ◀

St James Street; IP17 3DT

Pleasantly traditional pub in a coastal village, tasty bar food and local ales and cider; bedrooms

Our readers have very much enjoyed their visits over the last year to this well run old brick pub. It's a comfortable place to stay, the food is honest, the beers well kept and you can be sure of a friendly welcome. The traditionally furnished main bar has benches, pews, captain's chairs and wooden tables on its tiled floor, a woodburning stove (left open in cold weather) and lots of sea prints. From the handsomely panelled bar counter they serve Adnams Bitter and Broadside, Grainstore IPA, Green Jack Lurcher Stout and Humpty Dumpty Little Sharpie from antique handpumps, Aspall's cider, a local lager and several wines by the glass; board games. A simple conservatory looks on to a back terrace, and the large garden is very pleasant, with its well spaced picnic-sets, two large anchors and enormous fig tree, and they may have Shakespeare performances in August. The RSPB reserve at Minsmere and nearby Dunwich Museum are certainly worth visiting and there are some of Suffolk's best coastal walks nearby.

Listing their local suppliers, the highly thought of food includes chicken liver pâté with fig pickle, spinach and ricotta flan with roast endive, ham and free-range eggs, their famous fish and chips, and a pie of the day. *Benchmark main dish: pork chop with caramelised apple gravy £10.50. Two-course evening meal £15.75.*

Free house ~ Licensee Matt Goodwin ~ Real ale ~ Bar food (12-3, 6-9) ~ Restaurant (evening only) ~ (01728) 648219 ~ Children welcome away from bar ~ Dogs allowed in bar and bedrooms ~ Open 11(midday Sun)-11 ~ Bedrooms: £65B/£95B

Recommended by M and GR, Trevor Swindells, RS, ES, Colin and Ruth Munro, Charles and Pauline Stride, Revd R P Tickle, MJVK, Edward Mirzoeff, DHV, Phil and Jane Hodson, Anthony Longden, Norma and Noel Thomas, Geoff and Linda Payne, Sara Fulton, Roger Baker

EARL SOHAM Suffolk   TM2263   Map 5

Victoria ♣ £

A1120 Yoxford—Stowmarket; IP13 7RL

Nice beers from brewery across the road in this friendly, informal local

The beers from the Earl Soham brewery across the road are the main attraction to this easy-going and unmodernised local. On handpump, these include Albert Ale, Brandeston Gold, Sir Roger's Porter and Victoria Bitter; also, Aspall's cider. Fairly basic and definitely well worn, the bar is sparsely furnished with kitchen chairs and pews, plank-topped trestle sewing-machine tables and other simple scrubbed pine country tables, and there's stripped panelling, tiled or board floors, an interesting range of pictures of Queen Victoria and her reign, and open fires; board games. There are seats on a raised back lawn, with more out in front. The pub is quite close to a wild fritillary meadow at Framlingham and a working windmill at Saxtead.

Bar food includes sandwiches, beef casserole, curries, salads, and fish specials. *Benchmark main dish: beef casserole £9.95. Two-course evening meal £15.00.*

Earl Soham ~ Licensee Paul Hooper ~ Real ale ~ Bar food (12-2, 7-10) ~ (01728) 685758 ~ Children welcome ~ Dogs welcome ~ Open 11.30-3, 6-11; 12-3, 7-10.30 Sun

Recommended by Derek and Sylvia Stephenson, WAH, John Saville, Ian and Nita Cooper

---

If a service charge is mentioned prominently on a menu or accommodation terms, you must pay it if service was satisfactory. If service is really bad, you are legally entitled to refuse to pay some or all of the service charge as compensation for not getting the service you might reasonably have expected.

EAST RUDHAM Norfolk   TF8228   Map 8

Crown 🍴 ♟ ⇌

A148 W of Fakenham; The Green; PE31 8RD

Stylish open-plan seating areas, cosy back sitting room, first-class contemporary cooking, and a friendly atmosphere; bedrooms

Beside the village green, this is a neatly kept and rather civilised place with friendly staff. The contemporary open-plan bar has several distinct seating areas with brown leather and wood dining chairs around a mix of tables (including a huge round one), a log fire in a modern brick fireplace (with a grandfather clock and bookshelves on either side) and rugs on the stripped floorboards. High bar chairs beside the handsomely slate-topped counter are popular and they keep their own-brewed JoC's Norfolk Ale plus Adnams Bitter and Broadside on handpump and several wines by the glass. The other end of the room is slightly more informal with a mix of leather-seated dining chairs around all sorts of tables, a couple of built-in wall seats, another bookshelf beside a second fireplace and 1950s and 1960s actor prints in Shakespearean costume on the walls. There's also more of a pubby part with planked and cushioned white-painted built-in seats and nice photographs on the pink walls, and a cosy lower area to the back of the building with comfortable leather sofas and armchairs and a flatscreen TV; newspapers to read. Upstairs is yet another dining room with a high-pitched ceiling. There are neat picnic-sets under parasols on the front gravel. This pub is in the growing Flying Kiwi Inns group.

Imaginative modern food includes sandwiches, pork rillettes with red onion marmalade, smoked mackerel, saffron potato and beetroot terrine with vanilla aioli, open lasagne of pepper, aubergine caviar and herb béchamel, keralan spiced pollack en papillote with orange and sultanas and lime pickle, and seared calves liver with sage mash and onion purée. *Benchmark main dish: confit pork belly, mustard mash, carrot purée, apple sauce and crackling £14.25. Two-course evening meal £21.20.*

Flying Kiwi Inns ~ Licensee Chris Coubrough ~ Real ale ~ Bar food (12-2.30, 6.30-9.30) ~ (01485) 528530 ~ Children welcome ~ Dogs allowed in bar and bedrooms ~ Open 11am-11.30pm ~ Bedrooms: £90B/£100B

Recommended by Christopher and Elise Way, Anthony Barnes, John Wooll, George and Linda Ozols, David and Sue Atkinson, R L Borthwick, Mr and Mrs Roberts, Jeff and Wendy Williams, Mike and Margaret Banks

ELTON Cambridgeshire   TL0894   Map 5

Crown 🍴 ♟ ⇌

Off B671 S of Wansford (A1/A47), and village signposted off A605 Peterborough—Oundle; Duck Street; PE8 6RQ

Lovely thatched inn in charming village, interesting food, several real ales, well chosen wines, and a friendly atmosphere; stylish bedrooms

This lovely thatched stone inn is run by a hard-working young chef/landlord and his wife. The food is very good but they also keep a fair range of real ales and many customers do drop in for a pint and chat. The layout is most attractive and the softly lit beamed bar has an open fire in the stone fireplace, good pictures and pubby ornaments on pastel walls, and cushioned settles and chunky farmhouse furniture on the tartan carpet. The beamed main dining area has fresh flowers and candles and similar tables and chairs on stripped boards; a more formal, circular, conservatory-style restaurant is open at weekends. Golden Crown (brewed for them by Tydd Steam), Greene King IPA and a guest beer on handpump, well chosen wines by the glass and farm cider. There are tables outside on the front terrace. Elton Mill and Lock are a short walk away.

Good enjoyable food includes sandwiches, terrine of ham hock and wild mushrooms with beetroot relish, spring onion and smoked haddock fishcake with a poached egg and grain mustard sauce, vegetable cottage pie, cajun chicken burger, home-cooked mustard and sugar-glazed ham with a duck egg, vegetable cottage pie, and roasted lamb rump with rosemary sauce. *Benchmark main dish: slow-cooked pork belly with apple and pork samosa £13.95. Two-course evening meal £16.45.*

Free house ~ Licensee Marcus Lamb ~ Real ale ~ Bar food (12-2(3 Sun), 6.30-9; not Sun evening, Mon) ~ Restaurant ~ (01832) 280232 ~ Children welcome ~ Dogs allowed in bar ~ Open 12-11 (Mon 5-11); closed Mon lunchtime ~ Bedrooms: £65B/£95B
Recommended by Ian and Helen Stafford

EPPING GREEN Hertfordshire   TL2906 Map 5

Beehive

Off B158 SW of Hertford, via Little Berkhamsted; back road towards Newgate Street and Cheshunt; SG13 8NB

Cheerful bustling country pub, popular for its good value food

This weatherboarded pub is well liked for its generous helpings of good value food and its relaxed atmosphere. The traditional and slightly old-fashioned bar has low ceilings, wheelback chairs and brocaded benches around tables on a patterned carpet. During the winter months, a woodburning stove in a panelled corner keeps it cosy and warm. Greene King IPA, London Glory and Old Speckled Hen on handpump alongside a good range of wines by the glass; service is prompt and pleasant; piped music. Between the low building and quiet country road is a neat lawn and a decked area with plenty of tables to take in the summer sunshine; good woodland walks nearby.

Fresh fish is delivered daily from Billingsgate, and main courses might include baked cod with bacon, baked skate with caper butter, scampi, calamari, mushroom and thyme sauce, steak, mushroom and ale pudding, and snacks such as sandwiches, ploughman's, crab and mango salad, tuna and mozzarella fishcake, and vegetable, cranberry and goats cheese nut roast. *Benchmark main dish: fish and chips £10.95. Two-course evening meal £15.90.*

Free house ~ Licensee Martin Squirrell ~ Real ale ~ Bar food (12-2.30(4 Sun), 6-9.30 (8.30 Sun)) ~ Restaurant ~ (01707) 875959 ~ Children welcome ~ Dogs welcome ~ Open 11.30-3, 5.30-11; 12-10.30 Sun
Recommended by Mike and Lynn Robinson, Jestyn Phillips, Grahame and Myra Williams

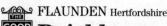 FLAUNDEN Hertfordshire   TL0101 Map 5

Bricklayers Arms ⑪ ♀

4 miles from M25 junction 18; village signposted off A41 – from village centre follow Boxmoor, Bovingdon road and turn right at Belsize, Watford signpost into Hogpits Bottom; HP3 0PH

Cosy country restaurant with fairly elaborate food; very good wine list

The emphasis at this neatly kept virginia creeper-covered dining pub is very much on the upmarket intricately presented food (with prices to match) and its calmly civilised atmosphere – it's not the place for a quick cheap lunch. It's fairly open-plan with stubs of knocked-through oak-timbered wall indicating the layout of the original rooms here. The well refurbished low-beamed bar is snug and comfortable, with a roaring log fire in winter. The extensive wine list includes about 20 by the glass, and they've Fullers London Pride and two or three guests from brewers such as Tring and Rebellion on handpump. This is a lovely peaceful spot in summer, when the terrace and beautifully kept old-fashioned garden with its foxgloves against sheltering hedges comes into its own. Just up the Belsize road there's a path on the left which goes through delightful woods to a forested area around Hollow Hedge.

They smoke their own meat and fish, and attractively presented dishes might include goose rillettes with red onion jam, haddock and mullet mousse with citrus cream, lamb shank with rosemary jus, pea risotto with leek, mozzarella and tomato coulis, fried bass with dill and shallot cream, chicken breast with poppyseed and whole grain mustard crust, sausage and chive mash, and well hung steak. *Benchmark main dish: game pie £16.45. Two-course evening meal £24.60.*

Free house ~ Licensee Alvin Michaels ~ Real ale ~ Bar food (12-2.30(3.30 Sun); 6.30-9.30(8.30 Sun)) ~ Restaurant ~ (01442) 833322 ~ No children under 4 ~ Dogs allowed in bar ~ Open 12-11.30(12.30 Sat, 10.30 Sun)

Recommended by Eleanor Dandy, Rob Harris, Peter and Giff Bennett, Chris Woodhead, John and Victoria Fairley, N J Roberts

 FLITTON Bedfordshire   TL0535 Map 5

White Hart

Brook Lane; MK45 5EJ

Simply furnished and friendly village pub with bar and dining area, real ales, enterprising food, and seats in garden

This is a friendly village pub run by helpful licensees. The minimally decorated front bar has some dark leather tub chairs around low tables, contemporary leather and chrome seats by pedestal tables, boldly patterned wallpaper, B & T Two Brewers and Youngs on handpump and a good choice of wines by the glass; TV. Steps lead down to a good-sized, simply furnished back dining area with red plush seats and banquettes on dark wooden floorboards. Outside, there are teak seats and tables on a terrace shaded by cedars and weeping willows, and a fair-sized garden has neat shrub borders. The pub is nicely set between Flitton Moor and the 13th-c church.

As well as sandwiches, the often enterprising bar food might include crayfish and apple cocktail, poached pear, stilton and walnut salad, ham, egg and chips, grilled bass, chicken breast with creamed leek and bacon sauce, and a range of aberdeen angus steaks. The menu is purposely kept short for freshness and they make all their own puddings. *Benchmark main dish: steak £13.25. Two-course evening meal £20.80.*

Free house ~ Licensees Phil and Clare Hale ~ Real ale ~ Bar food (12-2(2.30 Sun), 6.30-9(9.30 Fri, Sat)) ~ Restaurant ~ (01525) 862022 ~ Children welcome ~ Dogs allowed in bar ~ Open 12-3(4.30 Sun), 6-11(midnight Sat); closed Sun evening, Mon

Recommended by Eithne Dandy, Michael Dandy

 FRITHSDEN Hertfordshire   TL0109   Map 5

Alford Arms 🍴 🍷

From Berkhamsted take unmarked road towards Potten End, pass Potten End turn on right, then take next left towards Ashridge College; HP1 3DD

HERTFORDSHIRE DINING PUB OF THE YEAR

Thriving dining pub with a chic interior, good food from imaginative menu, and a thoughtful wine list

You do need to book a table at this pretty Victorian pub as it's usually full to the brim with cheerful diners – though you might still find a few locals (and perhaps a jack russell perched on a stool) chatting at the bar. The fashionably elegant but understated interior has simple prints on pale cream walls, with blocks picked out in rich Victorian green or dark red, and an appealing mix of good antique furniture (from Georgian chairs to old commode stands) on bare boards and patterned quarry tiles. It's all pulled together by luxuriously opulent curtains; darts and piped jazz. All the wines on their list are european, with most of them available by the glass, and they've Sharps Doom Bar, Rebellion IPA and a guest brewer such as Tring on handpump. The pub stands by a village green and is surrounded by lovely National Trust woodland. There are plenty of tables outside.

The seasonally changing menu might include rabbit and hazelnut terrine with onion jam, smoked mackerel and horseradish pâté, blue cheese and herb fritters with pea hummus, slow-cooked lamb shoulder with rosemary dumplings and tomato jus, parmesan and chorizo crusted whiting with shallot butter, roast bream on pearl barley, courgettes and fennel with broad bean salad with a lemon and chilli dressing, and well hung steak. *Benchmark main dish: pork suet pudding with puy lentils and mustard jus £13.75. Two-course evening meal £24.00.*

Salisbury Pubs ~ Lease Darren Johnston ~ Real ale ~ Bar food (12-2.30(3 Sat, 4 Sun), 6.30(7 Sun)-9.30(10 Sat)) ~ Restaurant ~ (01442) 864480 ~ Children welcome ~ Dogs allowed in bar ~ Open 11-11; 12-10.30 Sun

Recommended by Kevin Thomas, Nina Randall, Peter and Giff Bennett, John Picken, John and Joyce Snell

 FYFIELD Essex   TL5706   Map 5

Queens Head 🍷

Corner of B184 and Queen Street; CM5 0RY

Very friendly 16th-c pub with a good wine list and the accent on elaborate food (booking advised at weekends)

Readers particularly enjoy dining in the prettily planted little back garden with its weeping willows trailing in the sleepy River Roding behind this spotless 16th-c pub. The main focus is the very good food, but a pubby balance is maintained by their good range of half a dozen real ales: Adnams Southwold and Broadside and a couple of guests from brewers such as Crouch Vale and Timothy Taylors. They've also Weston's Old Rosie farm cider, over a dozen wines by the glass (including champagne) and some very decent malts. The low-beamed, compact L-shaped bar has some exposed timbers in cream and mocha walls, fresh flowers and pretty lamps on nice sturdy elm tables, and comfortable seating, from button-back wall banquettes to attractive and unusual high-backed chairs, some in a snug little side booth. In summer, two facing fireplaces have lighted church candles instead of a fire; piped music. The same menu is offered throughout the pub, but you can go for a more intricate white linen experience upstairs in the smart restaurant.

Besides good lunchtime sandwiches, ploughman's and filled huffers, dishes from the daily changing, though by no means cheap, menu might include seared pigeon breast with butternut glazed plums and five spice jus, crisp pork belly with scallops, apple purée, pea foam and pancetta, honey and soy roast salmon with thai-style vegetables and crab consommé and fried parmesan gnocchi with confit tomatoes, wilted spinach and balsamic and beurre noisette; reasonably priced set menus, and Sunday roasts. *Benchmark main dish: roast rump of lamb £20.50. Two-course evening meal £28.35.*

Free house ~ Licensee Daniel Lamprecht ~ Real ale ~ Bar food (12-2.30, 7-9.30; 12-4, 6.30-9.30 Sat; 12-6 Sun) ~ Restaurant ~ (01277) 899231 ~ Children welcome ~ Open 11-3.30, 6-11.30; 11-11.30 Sat; 12-10.30 Sun

Recommended by Mr and Mrs C F Turner, Mrs Margo Finlay, Jörg Kasprowski

GOSFIELD Essex   TL7829   Map 5

Kings Head £

The Street (A1017 Braintree—Halstead); CO9 1TP

Comfortable dining pub with proper public bar and good value food

Bright splashes of warm contemporary colour brighten the modernised interior of this ancient pub. The softly lit beamed main bar, with red panelled dado and ceiling, has neat modern black leather armchairs, bucket chairs and a sofa, as well as sturdy pale wood dining chairs and tables on dark boards, and a log fire in a handsome old brick fireplace with big bellows. Black timbers mark off a red carpeted and walled dining area with red furnishings that opens into a carpeted conservatory; piped music. They have Adnams Bitter, Timothy Taylors Landlord and a guest such as Mauldons Silver Adder on handpump, around a dozen wines by the glass and over 60 internationally sourced whiskies (their well supported whisky club meets for tastings four times a year); daily papers. The good-sized quite separate public bar, with a purple pool table, games machine, darts and TV, has its own partly covered terrace; the main terrace has round picnic-sets.

Neat black-clad young staff serve very fairly priced food such as filled baguettes, chicken, pine nut and apricot pâté, beef carpaccio with redcurrant dressing, lancashire hotpot, roast pork belly with green pea stew, fried dover sole with caper butter, duck breast in black bean sauce with stir-fried vegetables and noodles, marrow filled with raisin and walnut rice with tomato sauce; Sunday roast, including table joints, for which they need four days' notice. *Benchmark main dish: pork belly with cider jus £8.95. Two-course evening meal £17.00.*

Enterprise ~ Manager Mark Bloorfield ~ Real ale ~ Bar food (12-2.30, 6-9.30; 12-6 Sun)
~ Restaurant ~ (01787) 474016 ~ Children welcome ~ Dogs allowed in bar ~ Open
12-11(1am Sat)
Recommended by R T and J C Moggridge, Nick Gadd, Justin and Emma King

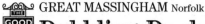 GREAT MASSINGHAM Norfolk   TF7922   Map 8

Dabbling Duck

Off A148 King's Lynn—Fakenham; Abbey Road; PE32 2HN

**Unassuming from the outside but with a friendly atmosphere,
traditional furnishings, warm coal fires, real ales and interesting food**

Our readers very much enjoy their visits here, whether for just a pint
and a chat or for a meal – and you can be sure of a cheerful welcome
from the friendly young staff. The bar to the right of the door is nicely
informal with a very high-backed settle, some comfortable armchairs and
a leather and brass-button settle facing each other across a pine table in
front of a coal fire in the huge raised fireplace. Further in, there are
beams and standing timbers, an attractive mix of wooden dining chairs
and tables, reproduction prints of 18th- and 19th-c cartoons on pale grey
walls, rugs on the stripped-wood floor and another fireplace with shelves
of books to one side. At the back of the pub is a room just right for a
private group and to the left there's more of a drinking bar with library
chairs and leather easy chairs on bare boards, darts, another coal fire,
and country prints above a tall grey dado. Adnams Broadside, Beestons
Worth the Wait, Greene King IPA, Woodfordes Wherry and a guest beer
on handpump from a bar counter made of great slabs of polished tree
trunk; daily papers on a rod and a pile of interesting old journals. There
are tables and chairs on a front terrace looking over the sizeable village
green with its big duck ponds.

Good, highly thought-of food includes sandwiches, chicken liver pâté, a fish
platter for two, sausage and mash with onion gravy, mackerel fillet with serrano
ham, wild mushrooms, spinach and a horseradish cream, lemon chicken with caesar
salad, cherry tomato and wild mushroom gnocchi, and cockle and clam linguine.
Benchmark main dish: duck pie £10.95. Two-course evening meal £17.00.

Free house ~ Licensee Dominic Symington ~ Real ale ~ Bar food (12-2.30(3 Sun), 6.30-9;
not Sun evening) ~ Restaurant ~ (01485) 520827 ~ Children welcome ~ Dogs allowed in
bar ~ Open 12-11(10.30 Sun) ~ Bedrooms: /£80B
*Recommended by Christopher and Elise Way, Graham and Carol Uren, DC, Gillian Grist, John Cook,
R C Vincent, Tracey and Stephen Groves, Philip and Susan Philcox, John Wooll*

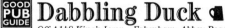 GREAT WILBRAHAM Cambridgeshire   TL5558   Map 5

Carpenters Arms ⑪ ♀ ◀ £

*Off A14 or A11 SW of Newmarket, following The Wilbrahams signposts; High
Street; CB21 5JD*

**Inviting village pub with traditional bar, good food here and in back
restaurant; nice garden**

Reopened in 2010 under welcoming new owners who used to run a
restaurant in France, this has a properly pubby low-ceilinged village
bar on the right, with well kept ales such as Brandon Rusty Bucket,
Cambridge Moonshine CB1 and Greene King IPA on handpump, a
carefully chosen wine list (strong on the Roussillon region where their

restaurant was), bar billiards, a sturdy settle by the big inglenook with its woodburning stove, copper pots and iron tools, and cushioned pews and simple seats around the solid pub tables on the flooring tiles. Service is spot on: thoughtful, helpful and cheerful. On the left, a chintzy carpeted sitting room with easy chairs, another big stone fireplace, overflowing bookshelves and plenty of magazines, leads through to the light and airy extended dining room, with country-kitchen chairs around chunky tables. A huge honeysuckle swathes the tree in the pretty back courtyard, and beyond an attractive homely garden, with fruit and vegetables, has round picnic-sets shaded by tall trees.

Top quality french-style food (the Value Award is for lunchtime dishes) using local and own-grown produce might include sandwiches, upside-down apple tart with foie gras and port sauce, tomato stuffed with mediterranean vegetables, various lunchtime platters, sausages and mash with onion gravy, ratatouille, pesto, mozzarella and ricotta lasagne, pork braised in cider and apples, and papillote of mixed fish and seafood in saffron sauce. *Benchmark main dish: chicken forestière £14.95. Two-course evening meal £21.90.*

Free house~ Licensee Rick and Heather Hurley ~ Real ale ~ Bar food (12-2.30(3 Sun), 7-9; not Tues and Sun evenings) ~ Restaurant ~ (01223) 882093 ~ Children welcome ~ Open 11.30-3, 6.30-11; closed Sun evening

Recommended by M and GR, Jacki Grant

HATFIELD BROAD OAK Essex   TL5416 Map 5

Dukes Head ♀

B183 Hatfield Heath—Takeley; High Street; CM22 7HH

Relaxed well run dining pub with enjoyable food, attractive layout of nicely linked separate areas

Thanks to the L-shaped layout of the building itself, its various seating areas ramble pleasantly around the central feature log fire and side servery with its big bunch of lilies, all in touch yet keeping enough sense of separation for a feeling of intimacy. Seating is mainly good solid wooden dining chairs around a variety of more or less chunky stripped and sealed tables, with a comfortable group of armchairs and sofa down one end, and a slightly more formal area at the back on the right. Cheerful prints on the walls, and occasional magenta panels in the mainly cream décor, make for quite a buoyant mood, as does the lively attitude of the friendly helpful staff; well kept Greene King IPA, Shepherd Neame Spitfire and St Austell Tribute on handpump and over two dozen wines by the glass from a good list. There may be somewhat muffled piped pop music. Sam the dog welcomes other dogs and there are always dog biscuits behind the bar. The back garden, with a sheltered terrace and an end wendy house, has comfortable chairs around teak tables under cocktail parasols; there are also some picnic-sets in the front angle of the building, which has some nice pargeting.

Good bar food might include mussels, potted crab and duck salad, a tender lamb hotpot with red cabbage, venison suet pudding, crispy pork belly with seared scallops and thyme jus, king prawn spaghetti, mushroom, asparagus, goats cheese and pepper open lasagne, and well hung steaks. *Benchmark main dish: bubble and squeak £11.75. Two-course evening meal £22.85.*

Enterprise ~ Lease Liz Flodman ~ Real ale ~ Restaurant ~ (01279) 718598 ~ Children welcome ~ Dogs allowed in bar ~ Open 12-3, 6-11.30; 12-11.30 Sat; 12-11 Sun

Recommended by Mrs Margo Finlay, Jörg Kasprowski, David Kenny, Brian Adams, Tony Adams, Grahame Brooks

HELPSTON Cambridgeshire   TF1205   Map 5

Blue Bell ◧ £
Woodgate; off B1443; PE6 7ED

Bustling pub with friendly landlord and cheerful staff, quickly changing beers and good value, tasty food

Exceptionally popular locally, this is a busy, friendly and well run pub with a professional hands-on landlord and cheerful, helpful staff; it's best to book in advance to be sure of a table. The lounge, parlour and snug have comfortable cushioned chairs and settles, plenty of pictures, ornaments, mementoes and cartwheel displays, and a homely atmosphere. The dining extension is light and airy with a sloping glass roof. Grainstore John Clare (exclusive to this pub) and quickly changing guests such as Adnams Bitter and Fullers London Porter on handpump, and summer scrumpy cider; they hold a July beer festival with live music. They may have marmalade and jam for sale; piped music and TV. A sheltered and heated terrace has cafe-style chairs and tables, an awning and pretty hanging baskets; wheelchair access. The poet John Clare lived in the cottage next door which is open to the public.

Fairly priced and generously served, the good traditional food includes sandwiches, duck pâté, prawn cocktail, lasagne, stilton and vegetable crumble, liver and bacon hotpot, gammon with egg or pineapple, and luxury fish pie. *Benchmark main dish: steak in ale pie £8.45. Two-course evening meal £13.00.*

Free house ~ Licensee Aubrey Sinclair Ball ~ Real ale ~ Bar food (not Sun evening or all Mon) ~ Restaurant ~ (01733) 252394 ~ Children welcome away from bar ~ Dogs allowed in bar ~ Open 11.30-2.30(3 Sat), 5(6 Sat)-11(midnight Sat); 12-6 Sun; closed Sun evening
Recommended by Michael and Jenny Back, George Atkinson

HEMINGFORD GREY Cambridgeshire   TL2970   Map 5

Cock ⊕ ♟ ◧
Village signposted off A14 eastbound, and (via A1096 St Ives road) westbound; High Street; PE28 9BJ

CAMBRIDGESHIRE DINING PUB OF THE YEAR

Imaginative food in pretty pub, extensive wine list, plus four interesting beers, a bustling atmosphere, and a smart restaurant

Cleverly, this well run place manages to be a pub as well as a restaurant – and you can be sure of a genuinely friendly welcome wherever you choose to sit and whether you are dining or just popping in for a drink. The bar rooms have dark or white-painted beams, lots of contemporary pale yellow and cream paintwork, artwork here and there, fresh flowers and church candles, and throughout a really attractive mix of old wooden dining chairs, settles and tables. They've sensibly kept the traditional public bar on the left for drinkers only: an open woodburning stove on the raised hearth, bar stools, wall seats and a carver, steps that lead down to more seating, Brewsters Hophead, Great Oakley Wagtail, Nethergate IPA and Tydd Steam Barn Ale on handpump, 17 wines by the glass and local farm cider. In marked contrast, the stylishly simple spotless restaurant on the right – you must book to be sure of a table – is set for dining with flowers on each table, pale wooden floorboards and another woodburning stove. There are seats and tables among stone troughs and flowers in the neat garden and lovely hanging baskets.

🍴 As well as a two- and three-course set lunch menu (not Sunday), the excellent food might include lunchtime sandwiches, celeriac, potato and chive rösti with marinated mushrooms, spinach and a poached egg, duck parcel with sweet and sour cucumber, cauliflower and chestnut toad in the hole with braised onions and stilton, pork cheeks with lamb sweetbreads, parsnip purée and ale gravy, and chicken breast with jerusalem artichoke and herb gratin, crème fraîche and truffle oil. *Benchmark main dish: bass fillets with potato hash and butter sauce £15.00. Two-course evening meal £20.00.*

Free house ~ Licensees Oliver Thain and Richard Bradley ~ Real ale ~ Bar food (12-2.30 (3 Sun), 6.30-9(6-9.30 Fri and Sat; 6.30-8.30 Sun)) ~ Restaurant ~ (01480) 463609 ~ Children allowed lunchtime only ~ Dogs allowed in bar ~ Open 11.30-3, 6-11; 11.30-11 summer Sat; 12-10.30 summer Sun; closed between 3 and 6 Sat in winter and between 4 and 6.30 Sun in winter

Recommended by Moira and John Cole, Howard and Margaret Buchanan, Gordon and Margaret Ormondroyd, Jeff and Wendy Williams, M Mossman, Jane Hudson, Sarah Flynn, George and Maureen Roby, Michael Sargent, Rob and Catherine Dunster, John Pritchard, Don and Carole Wellings, Malcolm and Barbara Southwell, R Anderson, Derek Thomas

HERTFORD Hertfordshire   TL3212   Map 5

White Horse 🍺 £

Castle Street; SG14 1HH

Up to nine real ales at traditional town-centre local

Always kept in tip-top condition, the terrific range of about eight Fullers beers and possibly a guest or two such as Adnams (with more during their May and August bank holiday beer festivals) are served from handpump at this chattily unpretentious little pub; also a dozen country wines. Tucked away in a side road, parts of this timber-framed building date from the 14th c and you can still see Tudor brickwork in the three quietly cosy upstairs family rooms. The two downstairs rooms are small and homely, the one on the left being more basic, with bare boards, some brewery memorabilia and a few rather well worn tables, stools and chairs. A warming open fire separates it from the more comfortable beamed right-hand bar, which has a winged leather armchair, some old local photographs and a red-tiled floor; bar billiards. Two simple benches out on the pavement face the castle, and there are tables and chairs on a back terrace with hanging baskets and window boxes.

🍴 Inexpensive pubby food includes sandwiches, baguettes, ploughman's, chilli, lasagne, sausages, Sunday roast, and on summer Thursday evenings they may cook sirloin steak and chicken. *Benchmark main dish: rib-eye steak £9.95. Two-course evening meal £16.50.*

Fullers ~ Lease Chris van der Heever ~ Real ale ~ Bar food (12-2) ~ Restaurant ~ (01992) 503911 ~ Children welcome ~ Dogs welcome ~ Open 12-midnight(10.30 Sun)
Recommended by Pat and Tony Martin

> 'Children welcome' means the pub says it lets children inside without any special restriction. If it allows them in, but to restricted areas such as an eating area or family room, we specify this. Places with separate restaurants often let children use them, and hotels usually let them into public areas such as lounges. Some pubs impose an evening time limit – let us know if you find one earlier than 9pm.

HINGHAM Norfolk   TG0202   Map 5

White Hart 🍽 �

Market Place, just off B1108 W of Norwich; NR9 4AF

Carefully and interestingly refurbished town pub with thoughtful furnishings, a good choice of drinks, and imaginative modern cooking

In a market square of attractive Georgian houses, this handsome, civilised place has been completely refurbished recently. It's another pub in the successful small group of Flying Kiwi Inns, all of which are much enjoyed by our readers. The rooms here are arranged over two floors and have a great deal of character. There are stripped floorboards throughout, a few oriental and other colourful rugs, an attractive variety of chairs and tables (some rather fine), a few beams and standing timbers, lots of prints and photographs and a few objects such as antique hanging scales on walls painted in mushroom and cream, several woodburning stoves, and quiet corners with comfortable sofas. Lighting is good from ceiling spots to interesting lanterns and even – in one rather grand room with a barrel-vaulted ceiling – antler chandeliers. The galleried long room up steps from the main bar with its egyptian frieze is just right for a sizeable party. Adnams Bitter, Grain Harvest Moon, Woodfordes Nelsons Revenge and their own JoC's Norfolk Ale on handpump, 20 wines by the glass and a wide choice of spirits. There are some modern benches and seats in the gravelled courtyard.

Well presented and extremely good, the modern food includes lunchtime sandwiches, ham hock terrine with piccalilli, tempura of red mullet and tiger prawn with a hot and sour thai salad, pork belly and fillet with chorizo and butternut squash risotto, pollack fillet with a brown shrimp sauce and asparagus, and lamb cutlets with basil mash, lamb beignet and ratatouille. *Benchmark main dish: pork belly with butternut squash risotto £14.95. Two-course evening meal £21.90.*

Flying Kiwi Inns ~ Manager Ben Gibbins ~ Real ale ~ Bar food (12-2.30, 6.30-9.30) ~ (01953) 850214 ~ Children welcome ~ Dogs allowed in bar ~ Open 11-11(midnight Sat)
Recommended by Richard Gibbs

HINXTON Cambridgeshire   TL4945   Map 5

Red Lion ♀

2 miles off M11 junction 9 northbound; take first exit off A11, A1301 N, then left turn into village – High Street; a little further from junction 10, via A505 E and A1301 S; CB10 1QY

Pink-washed old pub, handy for the Imperial War Museum at Duxford, with friendly staff, interesting bar food, real ales, and a big landscaped garden; bedrooms

The low-beamed bar in this extended pink-washed 16th-c inn has been refurbished this year and now has new oak chairs and tables on oak floors, two leather chesterfield sofas, an open fire in the dark green fireplace, an old wall clock and a relaxed, friendly atmosphere. Adnams Bitter, Greene King IPA, Woodfordes Wherry and a guest such as Brandon Rusty Bucket on handpump, 17 wines by the glass, a dozen malt whiskies and first-class service. An informal dining area has high-backed settles and the smart dry-pegged oak-raftered restaurant is decorated with various pictures and assorted clocks. The neatly kept big garden has a pleasant terrace with teak tables and chairs, picnic-sets on grass, a dovecote and views of the village church. The bedrooms are in a separate flint and brick building. They also own the Black Bull in Balsham just up the road (a new entry in this year's *Guide*).

🍴 Top-notch and very popular – if not particularly cheap – food might include sandwiches, confit duck leg with saffron and baby fennel risotto, scottish salmon fishcake with sweet chilli dressing, ham and free-range eggs, roast butternut squash curry with a filo basket, aubergine caviar and lime pickle, steak in ale suet pudding, and bass and scallops with orange butter sauce and lemon grass foam. *Benchmark main dish: steak in ale pie £12.00. Two-course evening meal £22.00.*

Free house ~ Licensee Alex Clarke ~ Real ale ~ Bar food (12-2(2.30 Fri and Sat), 7-9 (6.45-9.30 Fri and Sat)) ~ Restaurant ~ (01799) 530601 ~ Well behaved children welcome ~ Dogs allowed in bar ~ Open 11-11; 12-5, 7-10.30 Sun ~ Bedrooms: £85B/£120S(£109B)

Recommended by Gordon Stevenson, Jenny and Brian Seller, Jerry Brown, Adele Summers, Alan Black, Peter and Heather Elliott, Dave Braisted, Phil and Jane Hodson, Edward Mirzoeff, Gerry and Rosemary Dobson

 HORNDON-ON-THE-HILL Essex   TQ6783   Map 3

Bell

M25 junction 30 into A13, then left into B1007 after 7 miles, village signposted from here; SS17 8LD

ESSEX DINING PUB OF THE YEAR

Lovely old historic pub with great food and a very good range of drinks, and attractive bedrooms

You get the feeling you are enjoying the best of all worlds at this beautiful Tudor inn, particularly as the heavily beamed bar maintains a strongly pubby appearance and stocks a great range of drinks, though in fact the jolly good imaginative food does take some precedence. It's furnished with lovely high-backed antique settles and benches, with rugs on the flagstones and highly polished oak floorboards. Look out for the curious collection of ossified hot cross buns hanging along a beam in the saloon bar. The first was put there some 90 years ago to mark the day (it was a Good Friday) that Jack Turnell became licensee. The hanging tradition continues to this day, but now the oldest person in the village (or available on the day) hangs the bun. During the war, privations demanded that they hang a concrete bun. The impressive range of drinks includes Bass (tapped straight from the cask), Crouch Vale Brewers Gold, Greene King IPA and guests such as Greene King Morland Original and Sharps Doom Bar, and over a hundred well chosen wines (16 by the glass). You do need to get here early or book, as tables are often all taken soon after opening time. Two giant umbrellas cover the courtyard which is very pretty is summer with hanging baskets.

🍴 They offer a handful of pubby dishes such as open sandwiches, battered haddock with balsamic mayonnaise, game suet pudding with caramelised onions and grilled gammon and fried egg, as well as daily changing specials such as roast butternut soup with tarragon crème fraîche, devilled quail egg with ham hock and fine bean salad, venison won ton with shallot jam, rocket and parmesan, grilled pork cutlet on roast sage and butternut with cheddar rarebit, confit and roast duck with bean sprouts and sweet and sour cabbage, grilled hake with salsify cream, sautéed samphire and wild garlic sauce, and well hung steak with aioli, buttered spinach and fried egg. *Benchmark main dish: suckling pig with creamed corn and redcurrant jus £18.95. Two-course evening meal £25.80.*

Free house ~ Licensee John Vereker ~ Real ale ~ Bar food (12-2, 6.30-9.45) ~ Restaurant ~ (01375) 642463 ~ Children welcome in restaurant and eating area of bar ~ Dogs allowed in bar and bedrooms ~ Open 11-2.30, 5.30-11; 11-3, 6-11 Sat; 12-4, 7-10.30 Sun ~ Bedrooms: £54.50B/£69B

Recommended by John and Enid Morris, Clifford Blakemore, Steve Moore, J V Dadswell, Steve Aluzzi, Phil Clarke, Roxanne Chamberlain, Bob and Tanya Ekers

 HUNTINGDON Cambridgeshire   TL2471   Map 5

Old Bridge Hotel

1 High Street; ring road just off B1044 entering from easternmost A14 slip road; PE29 3TQ

Georgian hotel with smartly pubby bar, splendid range of drinks, first-class service and excellent food; lovely bedrooms

A marvellous refuge from the dreaded A14, this civilised Georgian hotel remains much enjoyed by a very wide range of customers. The hotel side of things clearly dominates but not at the expense of the more traditional pubby bar, which has a log fire, comfortable sofas and low wooden tables on polished floorboards and Adnams Bitter and Broadside and City of Cambridge Hobson's Choice on handpump; service is first class. They also have an exceptional wine list (up to 40 by the glass in the bar) and a wine shop where you can taste a selection of the wines before you buy them. You can eat in the big airy Terrace (an indoor room, but with beautifully painted verdant murals suggesting the open air) or in the slightly more formal panelled restaurant. There are seats on the terrace by the Great Ouse. This is a very nice place to stay and some bedrooms overlook the river.

Inventive and delicious, the food includes all-day sandwiches and light meals as well as terrine of confit duck and caramelised shallots with beetroot relish, linguine with crab, garlic and chilli, fish and chips with pease pudding, wild boar and apple sausages with grain mustard sauce, saddle of lamb with lamb rösti, baby turnips, girolle mushrooms and madeira and thyme sauce, and wild bass fillet with roast squash and fennel and thai lobster sauce; they also offer a set two- and three-course lunchtime menu (not Sunday when they offer it as an evening alternative). *Benchmark main dish: cod fillet and chips £13.95. Two-course evening meal £21.00.*

Huntsbridge ~ Licensee John Hoskins ~ Real ale ~ Bar food (12-2, 6.30-10; snacks all day) ~ Restaurant ~ (01480) 424300 ~ Children welcome ~ Dogs welcome ~ Open 11-11 ~ Bedrooms: £99B/£150B

Recommended by Dr A B Clayton, Michael Dandy, Martin and Pauline Jennings, Michael Sargent, R Anderson

 ICKLINGHAM Suffolk   TL7872   Map 5

Red Lion

A1101 Mildenhall—Bury St Edmunds; IP28 6PS

16th-c thatched pub with a relaxed atmosphere, good food and local beers

With interesting local beers, good food and friendly staff, this old thatched pub is extremely popular with our readers. The most striking part is the beamed bar with its cavernous inglenook fireplace and attractive furnishings including a nice mixture of wooden chairs and oriental rugs on the polished floorboards; board games, cribbage, darts and piped music. The carpeted and candlelit dining area is behind a knocked-through fireplace. Earl Soham Albert Ale and Victoria Bitter and Humpty Dumpty Bad Egg and Railway Sleeper on handpump, nine wines by the glass plus pudding wines, and quite a choice of coffees. There are seats on the back terrace overlooking surrounding fields; boules. West Stow Country Park and the Anglo-Saxon Village are close by.

Using local seasonal produce, the inventive bar food includes filled baguettes, pork, apricot, cured ham and pine nut pâté, crab, prawn and crayfish cocktail, ham and eggs, portabello mushroom, spinach and goats cheese risotto, chicken, tiger prawn, coconut and cream goan curry with mango, pawpaw and orange chutney, and slow-cooked lamb with redcurrant and red wine gravy, yorkshire pudding and rosemary and sea salted roast potatoes; they offer two- and three-course choices, too. *Benchmark main dish: slow-cooked pork belly, black pudding, root vegetable mash and a cider and mustard sauce £11.95. Two-course evening meal £16.95.*

Free house ~ Licensees Ed Lockwood and Aileen Towns ~ Real ale ~ Bar food (12-2.30, 6-8.30) ~ Restaurant ~ (01638) 711698 ~ Children welcome if well behaved ~ Dogs allowed in bar ~ Open 12-3(2.30 winter weekdays), 6-11; 12-4(3 in winter) Sun; closed Sun evening, Mon (except bank holidays)

Recommended by Tim and Rosemary Wells, Jeremy King, George Atkinson

KIMBOLTON Cambridgeshire   TL0967   Map 5

New Sun ⑪ ♀

High Street; PE28 0HA

Interesting bars and rooms, tapas menu plus other good food, and a pleasant back garden

There's always a friendly crowd of customers in this interesting old place and all get quickly served by the efficient, welcoming staff. The cosiest room is perhaps the low-beamed front lounge with a couple of comfortable armchairs and a sofa beside the log fire, standing timbers and exposed brickwork, and books, pottery and brasses. This leads into a narrower locals' bar with Wells & Youngs Bombardier and Eagle and a weekly changing guest on handpump, and 15 wines by the glass (including champagne and pudding wines); piped music and quiz machine. The traditionally furnished dining room opens off here. The airy conservatory with high-backed wicker dining chairs has doors leading to the terrace where there are smart seats and tables under giant umbrellas. Do note that some of the nearby parking spaces have a 30-minute limit. This high street is lovely.

Interesting and highly thought-of, the food includes lunchtime sandwiches, a range of tapas, kiln roast salmon with celeriac and chilli rémoulade, pork belly nuggets with watercress and quince purée, popular caesar salads, oyster mushroom, parmesan and truffle oil risotto, smoked haddock fishcake with a poached egg and grain mustard sauce, and a proper beef stroganoff. *Benchmark main dish: steak and kidney pudding £10.50. Two-course evening meal £17.85.*

Charles Wells ~ Lease Stephen and Elaine Rogers ~ Real ale ~ Bar food (12-2.15(2.30 Sun), 7-9.30; not Sun or Mon evenings) ~ Restaurant ~ (01480) 860052 ~ Children allowed but not in main bar ~ Dogs allowed in bar ~ Open 11.30-2.30, 6(6.30 Sat)-11; 12-10.30 Sun

Recommended by Mrs C Roe, JCW, Jeremy King, Ryta Lyndley, Susan and Jeremy Arthern, Rob and Catherine Dunster, Dr A B Clayton, John Picken, Michael Dandy, John Cook

 **LARLING** Norfolk TL9889 Map 5

Angel

From A11 Thetford—Attleborough, take B1111 turn-off and follow pub signs; NR16 2QU

Good-natured chatty atmosphere in busy pub, several real ales and tasty bar food; bedrooms

With interesting nearby attractions like Peter Beale's old-fashioned rose nursery and St George's (England's only whisky distillery), this well run and genuinely friendly pub makes a fine base for an enjoyable drink or lunch. The comfortable 1930s-style lounge on the right has a good mix of customers, cushioned wheelback chairs, a nice long cushioned and panelled corner settle, some good solid tables for eating and squared panelling; also, a collection of whisky-water jugs on the delft shelf over the big brick fireplace, a woodburning stove, a couple of copper kettles and some hunting prints. Adnams Bitter and four guests from breweries such as Crouch Vale, Elmtree, Hop Back and Orkney on handpump, 100 malt whiskies and ten wines by the glass. They hold an August beer festival with over 70 real ales and ciders, live music and barbecues. The quarry-tiled black-beamed public bar has a good local feel with darts, juke box (a rarity nowadays), a games machine, board games and piped music. A neat grass area behind the car park has picnic-sets around a big fairy-lit apple tree and there's a safely fenced play area. They also have a four-acre meadow and offer caravan and camping sites from March to October.

As well as sandwiches and toasties, the good, traditional food includes chicken liver pâté, sweet pepper lasagne, ham and egg, smoked haddock mornay, chicken and mushroom stroganoff, and prawn red thai curry. *Benchmark main dish: fresh cod and chips £9.95. Two-course evening meal £16.45.*

Free house ~ Licensee Andrew Stammers ~ Real ale ~ Bar food (all day) ~ Restaurant ~ (01953) 717963 ~ Children welcome ~ Open 10am-midnight ~ Bedrooms: £45B/£80S
Recommended by Michael Mellers, Rita Scarratt, Adrian Johnson, John Cook, Dave Braisted

LETHERINGSETT Norfolk TG0638 Map 8

Kings Head

A148 (Holt Road) W of Holt; NR25 7AR

Comfortably contemporary areas in neat country house, friendly young staff, real ales, good wines by the glass, bistro-type food, and plenty of outside seating

None of the carefully refurbished pubs in this small group, Flying Kiwi Inns, feels in the least bit contrived and they all have real character and interest. This one looks more like a small country house than a straightforward pub but there's equal emphasis on both drinks and the imaginative food, and the atmosphere is informal and civilised. To the right of the main door, a small room has dining chairs around scrubbed wooden tables, bookshelves beside a black fireplace, a flatscreen TV and apple-green paintwork. The main bar, to the left, is comfortable with daily papers and an open fire, big leather armchairs and sofas, stools and various dining chairs, reproduction hunting and coaching prints on the mushroom paintwork, rugs on quarry tiles and their own-brewed JoC's Norfolk Ale, Adnams Best and a couple of guest beers on handpump; quite a choice of wines by the glass and good coffee. The partly skylit dining room has built-in white-painted planked wall seating with maroon cushions and a mix of dining chairs around wooden tables, rugs on stripped floorboards, and a few farm tools and cabinets of taps and spiles on the cream-painted flint and cob walls. A back area under a partly pitched ceiling with painted rafters has more comfortable leather sofas and armchairs in front of another big flatscreen TV; Scrabble and piped music. Outside, there are lots of picnic-sets under parasols on the front gravel with many more on a grass side lawn (where there's also a play fort under tenting).

Good – if not cheap – bistro-style food includes lunchtime filled sandwiches, ham hock, pistachio and grain mustard terrine with piccalilli, chicken livers with tagliatelle, peas and sage, aubergine cannelloni with pearl barley and hazelnut risotto, rack and slow-braised shoulder of lamb with spinach purée and rosemary jus, and duck cassoulet with vegetable crisps. *Benchmark main dish: beer-battered haddock £13.95. Two-course evening meal £21.75.*

Flying Kiwi Inns ~ Licensee Chris Coubrough ~ Real ale ~ Bar food (12-2.30, 6.30-9.30) ~ (01263) 712691 ~ Children welcome ~ Dogs allowed in bar ~ Open 11-11
Recommended by R C Vincent, David Carr, Charles Gysin, Derek Field, Tracey and Stephen Groves

LEVINGTON Suffolk   TM2339   Map 5

Ship

Gun Hill; from A14/A12 Bucklesham roundabout take A1156 exit, then first sharp left into Felixstowe Road, then after nearly a mile turn right into Bridge Road at Levington signpost, bearing left into Church Lane; IP10 0LQ

Plenty of nautical trappings and character, in a lovely rural position

Surrounded by lovely countryside (with good nearby walks), this pub is attractively placed by a little lime-washed church and has views (if a little obscured) over the River Orwell estuary. The theme inside tends towards the nautical, with lots of ship prints and photographs of sailing barges, a marine compass under the serving counter in the middle room and a fishing net slung overhead. Along with benches built into the walls, there are comfortably upholstered small settles (some of them grouped round tables as booths) and a big black round stove. The flagstoned dining room has more nautical bric-a-brac and beams taken from an old barn. Adnams Bitter, Broadside and Explorer on handpump or tapped from the cask, several wines by the glass and Aspall's cider.

It's worth noting that they don't take bookings for fewer than six people for food which includes a charcuterie plate, tomato, red onion jam and goats cheese tarte tatin with pesto dressing, cod with spinach, shrimp and caper butter, pork fillet and chorizo brochette with sour cream, and parmesan-breaded chicken with sautéed potatoes. *Benchmark main dish: liver and bacon with madeira jus £9.95. Two-course evening meal £18.45.*

Adnams ~ Lease Adrian and Susan Searing ~ Real ale ~ Bar food (12-2.30(3 Sun), 6.30-9) ~ Restaurant ~ (01473) 659573 ~ Children welcome but no high chairs or special menu ~ Dogs allowed in bar ~ Open 11.30-3, 6-11; 11.30-11 Sat; 12-10.30 Sun
Recommended by J F M and M West, Ian and Nita Cooper

The price we give for a two-course evening meal in the featured top pub entries is the mean (average of cheapest and most expensive) price of a starter and a main course – no drinks.

LINDSEY TYE Suffolk   TL9846   Map 5

Red Rose

Village signposted off A1141 NW of Hadleigh; IP7 6PP

Carefully kept 15th-c Hall House with a couple of neat bars, enjoyable food, real ales, and plenty of outside seating

This is a well run pub with friendly, helpful staff and a warm and inviting atmosphere – it's not surprising that there are always plenty of contented chatty customers. The main bar has low beams and some standing timbers, a mix of wooden tables and chairs, red-painted walls and dried teasels in glass jugs on the window sills. In front of a splendid log fire in its old brick fireplace are a couple of comfortable red leather squashy sofas, a low table and some brass measuring jugs. A second room is furnished exactly the same and has a second big brick fireplace but is much simpler in feel, and perhaps quieter; piped music. Adnams Bitter, Hellhound Dirty Blond and Mauldons Moletrap Bitter on handpump and ten wines by the glass. It has a neat gravelled car park, flowering tubs and a few picnic-sets in front, and more picnic-sets at the back – where there's also a children's play area, football pitch and a new animal pen with chickens, rabbits and sheep.

Popular food includes lunchtime baguettes, pigeon and blue cheese salad with hazelnut and apple dressing, chicken liver parfait with home-made chutney, beer-battered haddock, chicken stuffed with mozzarella and sun-dried tomatoes, and pork escalope with wholegrain mustard sauce. *Benchmark main dish: rare-breed burger £12.95. Two-course evening meal £17.00.*

Free house ~ Licensee Peter Miller ~ Real ale ~ Bar food (12-2.30(3 Sun), 6.30-9.30 (7-9 Sun)) ~ (01449) 741424 ~ Children welcome ~ Dogs welcome ~ Open 11-3, 5.30-11; 11-11 Sun

Recommended by Pat and Tony Martin, David and Gill Carrington, Mrs Margo Finlay, Jörg Kasprowski, John Prescott, MDN, Jeremy King

LITTLE WALDEN Essex   TL5441   Map 5

Crown ✦ £

B1052 N of Saffron Walden; CB10 1XA

Bustling 18th-c cottage with a warming log fire, hearty food, and bedrooms

It's the particularly warm and cheery welcome from the licensees and their staff that make this homely low-ceilinged local so appealing, plus they serve tasty food and a good pint, too. Four changing beers are tapped straight from casks racked up behind the bar – normally Adnams Best and Broadside, Greene King IPA and Woodfordes Wherry. The interior is traditional, with bookroom-red walls, floral curtains, bare boards, navy carpeting, cosy warm fires and an unusual walk-through fireplace. A higgledy-piggledy mix of chairs ranges from high-backed pews to little cushioned armchairs spaced around a good variety of closely arranged tables, mostly big, some stripped. The small red-tiled room on the right has two little tables; piped light music; disabled access. Tables out on the terrace take in views of surrounding tranquil countryside.

The traditional bar food is good value and popular, so you may need to book at weekends: sandwiches, including a delicious hot pork baguette (not Sunday), devilled whitebait, crayfish cocktail, scampi, caribbean king prawn curry, steak and mushroom pie, lasagne, nut loaf, pork fillet in cajun sauce, and steak. *Benchmark main dish: steak and mushroom pie £9.95. Two-course evening meal £16.35.*

Free house ~ Licensee Colin Hayling ~ Real ale ~ Bar food (not Sun, Mon evenings) ~ Restaurant ~ (01799) 522475 ~ Children welcome ~ Dogs welcome ~ Trad jazz Weds evening ~ Open 11.30-3, 6-12; 12-11 Sun ~ Bedrooms: £65S/£70S

Recommended by John Wooll, Simon Watkins, the Didler, Marion and Bill Cross, Alec and Joan Laurence

---

MARGARETTING TYE Essex   TL6801   Map 5

White Hart ◖ £

From B1002 (just S of A12/A414 junction) follow Maldon Road for 1.3 miles, then turn right immediately after river bridge, into Swan Lane, keeping on for 0.7 miles; The Tye; CM4 9JX

Fine choice of ales tapped from the cask in cheery country pub with good family garden

Fresh, airy and clean, the open-plan yet cottagey interior of this cream-painted weatherboarded pub has walls and wainscoting painted in chalky traditional colours, dark old timbers and a mix of old wooden chairs and tables, mostly ready for diners to arrive. A stuffed deer head is mounted on the chimneybreast above the woodburning stove. A neat carpeted back conservatory is similar in style, and the front lobby has a charity paperback table; darts, quiz machine, skittles, board games and piped music. Their impressive range of eight real ales are all tapped straight from the cask. Besides Adnams Best and Broadside and Mighty Oak IPA and Oscar Wilde and Red Fox Hunters Gold, they bring on a constant stream of nationwide guest beers. They do takeaways and have interesting bottled beers, too, and during their popular June and October beer festivals might have up to 60 beers a day; winter mulled wine. There are plenty of picnic-sets out on grass and terracing around the pub, with a sturdy play area, a safely fenced duck pond, an aviary with noisy cockatiels (they don't quite drown the larks), and pens of rabbits, guinea-pigs and a pygmy goat.

Bar food includes an italian meat platter, grilled mushroom topped with goats cheese and sun-dried tomatoes, lambs liver and bacon casserole, chicken and ham pie, smoked fishcakes, battered catch of the day, nut roast with tomato and red pepper sauce and goats cheese, with specials such as dressed crab and king prawn salad, venison hotpot, and baked bass. *Benchmark main dish: steak and ale pie £9.20. Two-course evening meal £15.20.*

Free house ~ Licensee Elizabeth Haines ~ Real ale ~ Bar food (12-2, 6-9; 12-2.30, 6-9.30 Sat; 12-5, 6.30-8.30 Sun, 12-5 bank holidays; not Mon evening) ~ (01277) 840478 ~ Children under 14 in conservatory ~ Dogs allowed in bar ~ Open 11.30-3, 6-midnight; 11.30-1am Sat; 12-midnight Sun ~ Bedrooms: /£80B

Recommended by N R White, Roxanne Chamberlain

Real ale to us means beer that has matured naturally in its cask – not pressurised or filtered. We name all real ales stocked. We usually name ales preserved under a light blanket of carbon dioxide too, though purists – pointing out that this stops the natural yeasts developing – would disagree (most people, including us, can't tell the difference!).

  MIDDLETON Suffolk   TM4267   Map 5

Bell ◖ £

Off A12 in Yoxford via B1122 towards Leiston, also signposted off B1125
Leiston—Westleton; The Street; IP17 3NN

Thatch and low beams, friendly chef/landlord, good beer, good value food – a peaceful spot

Well placed for walks on the coast or at RSPB Minsmere bird reserve, this pub occupies a quiet village spot overlooked by the church's grand flint tower. It's a pretty cream-washed building, with picnic-sets under cocktail parasols out in front, and camping available in the broad meadow behind. The traditional bar on the left has a log fire in a big hearth, old local photographs, a low plank-panelling ceiling, bar stools and pew seating, well kept Adnams Bitter, Broadside, Explorer and seasonal ales tapped from the cask, and darts. The landlord's warmth and courtesy make for a really relaxed and contented atmosphere. On the right, an informal two-room carpeted lounge/dining area has padded mate's and library chairs around the dark tables below its low black beams, with pews by a big woodburning stove, and cheery modern brewery seaside prints. Dogs are welcomed with treats and a bowl of water.

Using carefully sourced local produce, the well liked and fairly priced food includes lunchtime sandwiches, chicken and duck liver paté with home-made relish, sausage and wholegrain mustard mash, bubble and squeak on buttered spinach with stilton cream and a poached egg, lambs liver and bacon with onion gravy, beer-battered fish and chips, and daily specials such as pork fillet wrapped in smoked bacon with home-made black pudding and a pork and leek breadcrumbed sausage, and dover sole with a caper, lemon and red onion salsa. *Benchmark main dish: pork belly rolled and stuffed with sausagemeat, apricots and raisins £10.50. Two-course evening meal £17.00.*

Adnams ~ Tenant Nicholas Musgrove ~ Real ale ~ Bar food (12-2.15, 6-9.15; 12-5 Sun; not Mon except bank holidays) ~ Restaurant ~ (01728) 648286 ~ Children welcome ~ Dogs allowed in bar ~ Open 12-3, 6-11; 12-12(11 Sun) Sat; closed Mon lunchtime
Recommended by Charles and Pauline Stride, Giles and Annie Francis

  MILL GREEN Essex   TL6401   Map 5

Viper ◖ £

The Common; from Fryerning (which is signposted off NE-bound A12
Ingatestone bypass) follow Writtle signposts; CM4 0PT

Delightfully unpretentious with local ales, simple pub food and no modern intrusions

Morris men sometimes dance outside this charmingly unspoilt old local. The timeless feel continues into its cosy little lounge rooms that have spindleback and armed country kitchen chairs and tapestried wall seats around neat little old tables, and there's a log fire. Booted walkers, dogs and children are directed towards the fairly basic parquet-floored tap room, which is more simply furnished with shiny wooden traditional wall seats and a coal fire. Beyond, another room has country kitchen chairs and sensibly placed darts, also dominoes and cribbage; the pub cat is Millie and the west highland terrier is Jimmy. They have Nethergate Viper, Mighty Oak Jake the Snake (both produced for the pub) and Oscar Wilde, and a couple of quickly changing guests from brewers such as Batemans and Tring on handpump and Old Rosie farm cider. Live bands play during their Easter and August beer festivals. Tables on the lawn overlook a beautifully tended cottage garden – a dazzling mass of colour in summer, further enhanced at the front by overflowing hanging baskets and window boxes

🍴 Simple but tasty lunchtime bar snacks might include sandwiches, pâtés, ploughman's, steak and ale pie, sausage and mash, curry and lasagne; Sunday roasts. The tasty bread comes from a local baker a mile or so down the road. *Benchmark main dish: steak and ale pie £6.95.*

Free house ~ Licensees Peter White and Donna Torris ~ Real ale ~ Bar food (12-2(3 Sat, Sun); not evenings) ~ No credit cards ~ (01277) 352010 ~ Children and dogs in public bar ~ Open 12-3, 6-11; 12-11(10.30 Sun) Sat

Recommended by LM, the Didler, John Saville, Roxanne Chamberlain

---

 NORWICH Norfolk   TG2309   Map 5

Adam & Eve £

Bishopgate; follow Palace Street from Tombland, N of cathedral; NR3 1RZ

A good mix of customers in busy old pub with four ales, fair value food, and seats by a fantastic array of hanging baskets and tubs

There's a bustling atmosphere in this ancient pub and an interesting mix of customers from choristers, regulars and those off on a Ghost Walk (which starts from here May-October; the pub offers a 'spooky meal' plus the walk for £10). The building is thought to date back to at least 1249 (when it was used by workmen building the cathedral) and even has a Saxon well beneath the lower bar floor; the striking dutch gables were added in the 14th and 15th centuries. The little old-fashioned bars have antique high-backed settles, cushioned benches built into partly panelled walls and tiled or parquet floors. Adnams Bitter, Theakstons Old Peculier, Wells & Youngs Bombardier and a guest such as Mauldons Mole Trap on handpump, over 40 malt whiskies, 11 wines by the glass and Aspall's cider; piped music. There are picnic-sets by the award-winning colourful tubs and hanging baskets.

🍴 Very reasonably priced pubby food includes sandwiches, chilli con carne, vegetable cannelloni, steak and mushroom pie, beer-battered cod, and specials like chicken in mushroom and maderia sauce, and rack of ribs with chips. *Benchmark main dish: steak and mushroom pie £8.95.*

Unique (Enterprise) ~ Lease Rita McCluskey ~ Real ale ~ Bar food (12-7; 12-5 Sun; not evenings) ~ (01603) 667423 ~ Children in snug until 7pm ~ Open 11-11; 12-10.30 Sun; closed 25 and 26 Dec, 1 Jan

Recommended by Lawrence Pearse, Colin and Ruth Munro, David Carr, Barry Collett, N R White, the Didler, Ralph Holland, John Cook, Mike and Eleanor Anderson, Jane and Alan Bush

---

A very few pubs try to make you leave a credit card at the bar, as a sort of deposit if you order food. They are not entitled to do this. The credit card firms and banks that issue them warn you not to let your card out of your sight. If someone behind the counter used your card fraudulently, the card company or bank could in theory hold you liable, because of your negligence in letting a stranger hang on to your card. Suggest instead that if they feel the need for security, they 'swipe' your card and give it back to you. And do name and shame the pub to us.

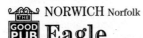 **NORWICH** Norfolk TG2207 Map 5

Eagle

Newmarket Road (A11, between A140 and A147 ring roads); NR2 2HN

Well run pub with a variety of seating areas for both drinking and dining, real ales, lots of coffees, wines by the glass, and quite a choice of fairly priced food

Handily open all day, this sizeable place spreads around both downstairs and upstairs, giving plenty of different seating areas. There are comfortable sofas and armchairs by the open fire in its ornate fireplace, white-painted chairs around pine tables on tiled or stripped-wood flooring, cream paintwork above a red dado and more sofas and straightforward pubby seating in a cosy end room. There's also a low-ceilinged dining room and a spiral staircase in the bar leading to another dining room with high-backed brown leather chairs around various tables on pale floorboards. Greene King IPA and a house beer from Bass called Eagles Nest on handpump and decent wines; piped music. A 'conservatory' with chrome and bentwood chairs and wooden tables leads on to a sunny terrace with picnic-sets and a smart barbecue and there are more seats on grass.

Popular food includes sandwiches, spiced lamb terrine with mango purée, thick ham and a duck egg, caramelised onion and blue cheese tart, salmon and haddock fishcakes with lemon mayonnaise, chicken breast wrapped in parma ham with a saffron cream sauce, and monkfish and prawn curry. *Benchmark main dish: pork belly on apple and thyme mash with creamy cider sauce £11.25. Two-course evening meal £15.50.*

Free house ~ Licensee Nigel Booty ~ Real ale ~ Bar food (12-2.30, 6-9.30) ~ Restaurant ~ (01603) 624173 ~ Children welcome ~ Dogs allowed in bar ~ Open 11am-11.30pm
Recommended by David Carr

 **NORWICH** Norfolk TG2109 Map 5

Fat Cat

West End Street; NR2 4NA

A place of pilgrimage for beer lovers, and open all day

There's always the most extraordinary choice of up to 32 real ales quickly served by knowledgeable staff in this hugely popular, friendly pub. On handpump or tapped from the cask in a stillroom behind the bar – big windows reveal all – there are their own beers The Fat Cat Brewery Tap Bitter, Cougar, Honey Ale, Marmalade Cat and Wild Cat, as well as Adnams Bitter, Batemans Salem Porter, Burton Bridge Stairway to Heaven, Dark Star American Pale, Felinfoel Double Dragon, Fox Heacham Gold, Fullers ESB, Greene King Abbot, Hop Back Summer Lightning, Kelham Island Pale Rider, Oakham Bishops Farewell, Potbelly Beijing Black, Spectrum Trip Hazard, Timothy Taylors Landlord, Tipples Moonrocket, Winters Bitter and Woodfordes Wherry. You'll also find imported draught beers and lagers, over 50 bottled beers from around the world plus ciders and perries. There's a lively bustling atmosphere at busy times, with maybe tranquil lulls in the middle of the afternoon, and a good mix of cheerful customers. The no-nonsense furnishings include plain scrubbed pine tables and simple solid seats, lots of brewery memorabilia, bric-a-brac and stained glass. There are tables outside.

Bar food consists of freshly made filled rolls and good pies at lunchtime (not Sunday). *Filled rolls £0.60.*

Free house ~ Licensee Colin Keatley ~ Real ale ~ Bar food (filled rolls available until sold out; not Sun) ~ No credit cards ~ (01603) 624364 ~ Children allowed until 6pm ~ Dogs allowed in bar ~ Open 12-11; 11-midnight Sat

Recommended by David Carr, the Didler, Ralph Holland, Andy and Claire Barker

 OLD BUCKENHAM Norfolk   TM0691   Map 5

Gamekeeper

B1077 S of Attleborough; The Green; NR17 1RE

Pretty pub with nicely refurbished bars, friendly service, interesting food, real ales and seats on the terrace

This pretty 16th-c pub has an appealing layout suiting both drinkers and diners. The civilised beamed bar, with two main areas, has leather armchairs and a sofa in front of the big open woodburning stove in the capacious inglenook fireplace, a pleasant variety of nice old wooden seats and tables on the fine old flagstones or wooden flooring, and local watercolours on the walls; there's an unusual interior bow window. Adnams Bitter and Woodfordes Wherry on handpump, quite a few wines by the glass and several malt whiskies. Besides the comfortable main back dining area, there's a small separate room used for private dining. The back terrace has seats and tables, and there are picnic-sets on the grass beyond.

 Popular bar food includes sandwiches, mussels with wine, cream, thyme and garlic, duck leg braised in orange, tomato and cinnamon, burger with cheese, bacon and tomato relish, battered hake with minted mushy peas, puy lentil, butternut squash and chestnut bake with goats cheese and potato topping, and griddled rosemary chicken with dijon mustard sauce and a gnocchi, chorizo and bean salad. *Benchmark main dish: rib-eye steak £15.95. Two-course evening meal £18.00.*

Enterprise ~ Lease David Francis ~ Real ale ~ Bar food (not Sun evening) ~ Restaurant ~ (01953) 860397 ~ Children allowed away from bar ~ Dogs allowed in bar ~ Open 11.30-3, 6-11; 12-5 Sun; closed Sun evening

Recommended by Sheila Topham, Julia Mann, Michael Mellers, Nicola Eaton, Noreen Collin, John Cook, Helena Reis

 OLD WARDEN Bedfordshire   TL1343   Map 5

Hare & Hounds

Village signposted off A600 S of Bedford and B658 W of Biggleswade; SG18 9HQ

Comfortably elegant dining pub with emphasis on good food served by welcoming well turned-out staff; lovely gardens

This carefully run dining pub is part of the swiss-styled Shuttleworth Estate, and the glorious sloping garden (with tables on a terrace) which stretches up to pine woods behind the pub dates back to the same period and was designed in the same style. Inside, four beautifully kept beamed rooms, with dark standing timbers, work their way around the central servery. Cleverly blending contemporary styling with the attractive old structure, décor is in cosy reds and creams, with upholstered armchairs and sofas and coffee tables on stripped flooring, light wood tables, a woodburning stove in an inglenook fireplace and fresh flowers on the bar. Prints and photographs depict historic aircraft in the famous Shuttleworth Collection just up the road. Wells & Youngs Eagle IPA and Youngs Bitter are on handpump, with a dozen or so wines by the glass including some from a local vineyard; piped music. Though there's an ample car park, you may need to use the village hall parking as an overflow. There are some substantial walks nearby.

Food here is thoughtfully prepared and presented. Breads and ice-cream are home-made and they make an effort to use local and organic ingredients. The changing menus might include chicken liver parfait, tempura king prawns and squid with soy, lime and chilli dressing, chickpea, tomato and potato curry, roast bass with grilled courgettes, aubergine, red pepper and fennel, ploughman's, pie of the day, rump burger, thai green curry, and well hung steak. *Benchmark main dish: home-made pies £10.95. Two-course evening meal £20.00.*

Charles Wells ~ Lease Jane and Jago Hurt ~ Real ale ~ Bar food (till 3.30 Sun, not Sun evening) ~ Restaurant ~ (01767) 627225 ~ Children welcome ~ Dogs allowed in bar ~ Open 12-3, 6-11; 12-10.30 Sun; closed Mon (except bank holiday lunchtime)
Recommended by Robert Turnham, R T and J C Moggridge, Michael Dandy, Michael Sargent

ORFORD Suffolk   TM4249   Map 5

Jolly Sailor
Quay Street; IP12 2NU

Lovely old pub with views from the garden, plenty of boating memorabilia; camping and bedrooms

A good base for walkers, fishermen and bird-watchers, this is a friendly, happy pub. Built mainly from wrecked ships' timbers, several snug rooms have lots of exposed brickwork, boating pictures and shipping charts celebrating the river, and are served from counters and hatches in an old-fashioned central cubicle. There's an unusual spiral staircase in the corner of the flagstoned main bar – which also has horsebrasses, local photographs, two cushioned pews and a long antique stripped deal table, and an open woodburning stove in the big brick fireplace (with nice horsebrasses above it). Four Adnams beers are on handpump. Picnic-sets on grass at the back have views over the marshes, there's a play tower and camping in the orchard.

Tasty bar food includes filled baguettes, ham and free-range eggs, lunchtime omelettes, crayfish linguine, cumberland sausage ring with onion gravy, and rack of lamb with a port and redcurrant sauce. *Benchmark main dish: cod and chips £12.25. Two-course evening meal £17.95.*

Adnams ~ Tenants Gordon and Judy Williams ~ Real ale ~ Bar food (12-3, 6-9) ~ (01394) 450243 ~ Children welcome ~ Dogs welcome ~ Open 11-11; may close afternoons in winter ~ Bedrooms: /£80B
Recommended by Mrs M E Mills, Neil Powell, Charles and Pauline Stride, Maria Taylor, Philip Smith, Terry Mizen, David Field

ORFORD Suffolk   TM4249   Map 5

Kings Head 🛏

Front Street; IP12 2LW

Nicely pubby local with tasty food and Adnams beers

Parts of this likeable old place date back 700 years and there's plenty of authentic atmosphere. It's got the character of a traditional harbourside pub and the snug main bar has heavy low beams, straightforward furniture on red carpeting, Adnams Bitter, Broadside and Oyster Stout, several wines by the glass and Aspall's cider. The candlelit dining room has nice old stripped brick walls and rugs on the ancient bare boards; occasional piped music, board games, magazines and cards.

🍴 Well liked bar food includes sandwiches, chicken liver pâté with pear chutney, sausages and mash with onion gravy, parmesan-breaded baked chicken caesar salad, liver and bacon, fish or steak in ale pies, and lamb cutlets with creamed celeriac and thyme jus. *Benchmark main dish: beer-battered cod and chips £10.95. Two-course evening meal £16.50.*

Adnams ~ Lease Adrian and Susan Searing ~ Real ale ~ Bar food (12-2.30(3 Sun), 6.30-9) ~ Restaurant ~ (01394) 450271 ~ Children welcome ~ Dogs welcome ~ Open 11.30-3, 6-11.30; 11.30-11.30 Sat; 12-10.30 Sun ~ Bedrooms: $65S/$85S

Recommended by Martin and Alison Stainsby, Derek and Sylvia Stephenson, Trevor Swindells, Dr Peter Andrews, Barry Collett, Norma and Noel Thomas, Edward Mirzoeff

PAMPISFORD Cambridgeshire   TL4948   Map 5

Chequers 🍺 £

2.6 miles from M11 junction 10: A505 E, then village and pub signed off; Town Lane; CB2 4ER

Cosy and civilised traditional pub with good value food – a nice find so close to the motorway

With a relaxed atmosphere and friendly, hard-working licensees, this is a traditional, neatly kept old place and very much the heart of the community. There are comfortably pubby old-fashioned furnishings under the low beams in the ochre ceiling, booth seating on the pale ceramic tiles of the cream-walled main area and a low step down to a floorboarded part with dark pink walls (and a TV). Greene King IPA, Timothy Taylors Landlord, and Woodfordes Wherry on handpump, several wines by the glass and nicely served coffee. The prettily planted simple garden has picnic-sets and is lit by traditional black streetlamps; the resident collie is called Snoopy.

🍴 Reasonably priced and well liked, the food might include sandwiches, chicken liver pâté with onion marmalade, filo prawns with a sweet chilli dip, cajun-spiced burger with barbecue sauce, moroccan lamb tagine, yellow prawn thai curry, flaked ham hock in a horseradish cream sauce, and poached salmon in a fresh herb and citrus butter; they also offer two-course set menus. *Benchmark main dish: steak in Guinness pie £9.90. Two-course evening meal £15.50.*

~ Manager Maureen Hutton ~ Real ale ~ Bar food (all day – restricted menu between 2-6); 12-2.30 Sun; not Sun evening) ~ (01223) 833220 ~ Children welcome ~ Dogs welcome ~ Open 11-11(4 Sun)

Recommended by D and M T Ayres-Regan, James Morrell, Jerry Brown, JPR, Charles Gysin, Roy Hoing

POTTERS CROUCH Hertfordshire   TL1105   Map 5

Holly Bush ◖ £

2.25 miles from M25 junction 21A: A405 towards St Albans, then first left, then after a mile turn left (ie away from Chiswell Green), then at T junction turn right into Blunts Lane; can also be reached fairly quickly, with a good map or Sat Nav, from M1 exits 6 and 8 (and even M10); AL2 3NN

Well tended cottage with gleaming furniture, fresh flowers and china, well kept Fullers beers, good value food, and an attractive garden

New licensees at this beautifully kept pub have freshened it up with a lick of paint and have brought under control the enormous wisteria that threatened to swamp it. The interior is cleverly partitioned and has something of the feel of a smart country house. There are quite a few antique dressers (several filled with plates), a number of comfortably cushioned settles, a fox's mask, some antlers, a fine old clock with a lovely chime, daily papers, and on the right as you go in, a big fireplace. In the evening, neatly placed candles cast glimmering light over darkly varnished tables, all sporting fresh flowers. The long, stepped bar has particularly well kept Fullers Chiswick, ESB, London Pride and a Fullers seasonal beer on handpump. Service is calm, friendly and sincere, even when they're busy. Behind the pub, the very pleasant fenced-off garden has a nice lawn, handsome trees and sturdy picnic-sets. Though the pub seems to stand alone on a quiet little road, it's only a few minutes' drive from the centre of St Albans (or a pleasant 45-minute walk). Children are welcome in the garden.

As well as a good choice of sandwiches and burgers, the very fairly priced, seasonally changing menu might include a fish platter, half a pint of prawns, cornish pasty, salmon, cumberland sausage and spring onion mash, sweet potato and coriander fishcakes, warm duck salad, and lamb cutlets with onion confit. *Benchmark main dish: chilli con carne £7.40. Two-course evening meal £16.75.*

Fullers ~ Tenants Steven and Vanessa Williams ~ Real ale ~ Bar food (12-2(2.30 Sun), 6-9; not Sun-Tues evenings) ~ (01727) 851792 ~ Open 12-2.30, 6-11(7-10 Sun)
Recommended by Tina and David Woods-Taylor, Peter and Giff Bennett, Chris and Jeanne Downing, Jo Wilson, David Uren

PRESTON Hertfordshire   TL1824   Map 5

Red Lion ◖

Village signposted off B656 S of Hitchin; The Green; SG4 7UD

Homely village local with changing beers and neat colourful garden

One of the first community-owned pubs in the country, this welcoming place offers three regularly changing interesting guests from brewers such as Brewsters, Marston Moor and Red Squirrel, as well as Fullers London Pride and Wells & Youngs. They also tap farm cider from the cask, have several wines by the glass (including an english house wine), a perry and mulled wine in winter. Pubbily simple but cheery, the grey wainscoted main room on the left has sturdy well varnished pub furnishings including padded country-kitchen chairs and cast-iron-framed tables on a patterned carpet, a generous window seat, a log fire in a brick fireplace and foxhunting prints. The somewhat smaller room on the right has steeplechasing prints, some varnished plank panelling, and brocaded bar stools on flagstones around the servery; darts and dominoes. A few picnic-sets out on the front grass face lime trees on a peaceful village green. At the back, a pergola-covered terrace gives way to many more picnic-sets (with some shade from a tall ash tree) and a neatly kept colourful herbaceous border in a good-sized sheltered garden beyond.

🍴 Reasonably priced bar food might include sandwiches and ploughman's, fish pie, chilli, chicken curry, ham, egg and chips, grilled plaice with caper butter, and steaks. *Benchmark main dish: steak and ale pie £8.95. Two-course evening meal £11.90.*

Free house ~ Licensee Raymond Lamb ~ Real ale ~ Bar food (12-2, 7-8.30; not Sun evening or Tues) ~ (01462) 459585 ~ Children welcome ~ Dogs welcome ~ Open 12-2.30(3.30 Sat), 5.30-11(12 Sat); 12-3.30, 7-10.30 Sun

Recommended by Andy Lickfold, Stuart Gideon, Mrs Catherine Simmonds, Simon and Mandy King

 RAVENSDEN Bedfordshire   TL0754   Map 5

Horse & Jockey 🍴 ♟

Village signed off B660 N of Bedford; pub at Church End, off village road; MK44 2RR

BEDFORDSHIRE DINING PUB OF THE YEAR

Contemporary comfort, with old-fashioned virtues on the food and drinks side

They really take the trouble to get things right at this comfortably refurbished pub. Careful lighting, hardwood venetian blinds, modern leather easy chairs in the bar, the quiet colour scheme of olive greys and dark red, the meticulous layout of one wall of old local photographs, and the pleasing chunky tables and high-backed seats in the bright dining room, with its well lit prints and contemporary etched glass screen – all suggest quality. Service is charming, they have a good choice of wines by the glass, guest ales from brewers such as Hopping Mad and Wells & Youngs on handpump, 20 wines by the glass, nicely served coffee, and a rack of recent *Country Life* issues as well as daily papers; piped music and board games. The dining room overlooks a sheltered terrace with smart modern tables and chairs under cocktail parasols, with a few picnic-sets on the grass beside, and the handsome medieval church in its churchyard just beyond; there's a heated smokers' shelter.

🍴 Enjoyable food might include chestnut mushroom and garlic crêpe, smoked fish florentine, lemon and thyme poussin, beetroot risotto with rocket and tomato salad, steak and kidney pudding, lamb curry with sweet dumpling, red onion salad and naan bread, and baked goats cheese tart with tomato jam. *Benchmark main dish: roast pork belly with red wine jus £14.95. Two-course evening meal £21.70.*

Free house ~ Licensees Darron and Sarah Smith ~ Real ale ~ Bar food (12-2, 6-9; 12-6.30 Sun) ~ Restaurant ~ (01234) 772319 ~ Children welcome ~ Dogs allowed in bar ~ Open 12-3, 6-11; 12-midnight Sat; 12-11 Sun; 12-3, 6-12 Sat in winter; closed Mon, Tues in Jan

Recommended by Michael Dandy, Michael Sargent, D C Poulton

'Children welcome' means the pub says it lets children inside without any special restriction. If it allows them in, but to restricted areas such as an eating area or family room, we specify this. Places with separate restaurants often let children use them, and hotels usually let them into public areas such as lounges. Some pubs impose an evening time limit – let us know if you find one earlier than 9pm.

REACH Cambridgeshire

TL5666 Map 5

Dyke's End ◀

From B1102 follow signpost to Swaffham Prior and Upware; village signposted; CB5 0JD

Candlelit rooms in former farmhouse, enjoyable food and own-brewed beer

Next to the church and the charming village green, this 17th-c former farmhouse is proud of its old-fashioned values – no piped music, games machines or food sachets. A high-backed winged settle screens off the door and the simply decorated ochre-walled bar has stripped heavy pine tables and pale kitchen chairs on dark boards and one or two rugs. In a panelled section on the left are a few rather smarter dining tables, and on the right there's a step down to a red-carpeted part with the small red-walled servery and sensibly placed darts at the back; board games. All the tables have lighted candles and there may be a big bowl of lilies to brighten up the serving counter. As well as their own-brewed Devils Dyke Bitter, they keep guests such as Adnams Bitter, St Austell Tribute and Thwaites Wainwright on handpump alongside a decent wine list, and Old Rosie cider. There are picnic-sets under parasols on the front grass and the pub dachshund is called Banger.

Good bar food includes sandwiches, moules marinière, ham and egg, local sausages with onion gravy, vegetable pie, chicken wrapped in parma ham with herb butter, and slow-cooked leg and roasted breast of duck with citrus sauce. *Benchmark main dish: steak frites £12.95. Two-course evening meal £18.00.*

Free house ~ Licensee Simon Owers ~ Real ale ~ Bar food (12-2(3 Sun), 7-9; not Sun evening, not Mon) ~ Restaurant ~ (01638) 743816 ~ Children allowed but must be well behaved ~ Dogs welcome ~ Quiz night last Sun of month ~ Open 12-2.30, 6-11; 12-11(10.30 Sun) Sat; closed Mon lunchtime
Recommended by John Saville, M and GR

REDBOURN Hertfordshire

TL1011 Map 5

Cricketers ◀

3.2 miles from M1 junction 9; A5183 towards St Albans, bear right on to B487, first right into Chequer Lane, then third right into East Common; AL3 7ND

Good food and beer in a nicely placed attractively updated pub

The front bar at this refurbished place (knocked into quite an unusual shape during restyling of the building) is snugly civilised with leather tub armchairs, plush banquettes and some leather cube stools on its pale carpet. It leads back into an attractive and comfortably modern dining room, also gaining from its oddly wiggly shape. Four thoughtfully sourced guests alongside Greene King IPA might be from brewers such as Ossett, Tring, Sharps and York. They also serve local Millwhite's Rum Cask cider and about 17 wines by the glass and decent coffees. Staff are friendly and helpful; well reproduced piped music. An upper restaurant overlooks the cricket pitch and common, which has gentle interesting walks (shown on a map board by the next-door local museum). There are picnic-sets out on the side grass and sheltered benches by the front door.

As well as simpler lunchtime snacks such as sandwiches and sausage and mash, the fairly involved menu might include seared scallops with cauliflower purée and crispy pancetta, crayfish risotto, potted beef brisket with poached pear and pickle cucumber, celeriac and chestnut strudel with truffle and chive risotto, braised guinea fowl breast with butterbean, chickpea and tomato broth and guinea fowl and bacon dumplings, and yellowfin tuna with water chestnuts, radish and broad bean salad. *Benchmark main dish: rack of lamb £16.75. Two-course evening meal £19.45.*

Free house ~ Licensees Colin Baxter and Andy Stuart ~ Real ale ~ Bar food (12-3, 6-9 (10 Fri, Sat); 12-5 Sun; not Sun evening) ~ Restaurant ~ (01582) 620612 ~ Dogs allowed in bar ~ Open 12-11(midnight Sat, 10.30 Sun)

Recommended by David M Smith, Alex Balance, John Picken, Anthony and Marie Lewis

SARRATT Hertfordshire   TQ0498   Map 5

Cock

Church End: a very pretty approach is via North Hill, a lane N off A404, just under a mile W of A405; WD3 6HH

Plush pub popular with older dining set at lunchtime and families outside during summer weekends; Badger beers

During the early evenings and at lunchtimes you're likely to find an older set making the most of the good value OAP meals on offer at this comfortably traditional place. The latched front door opens straight into the homely tiled snug with a cluster of bar stools, vaulted ceiling and original bread oven. Through an archway, the partly oak-panelled cream-walled lounge has a lovely log fire in an inglenook, pretty Liberty-style curtains, red plush chairs at dark oak tables, lots of interesting artefacts, and several namesake pictures of cockerels. Badger Best, Sussex, Tanglefoot and a seasonal Badger guest are on handpump; piped music. The restaurant is in a nicely converted barn. In summer, children can play on the bouncy castle and play area, leaving parents to take in the open country views from picnic-sets on the pretty, sheltered lawn and terrace. There are more picnic-sets in front that look out across a quiet lane towards the churchyard.

Pubby food includes sandwiches, ploughman's, whitebait, cheese and broccoli tagliatelle, chicken caesar salad, battered cod, steak and ale pie, and rib-eye steak. *Benchmark main dish: steak and ale pie £10.95. Two-course evening meal £16.00.*

Badger ~ Tenants Brian and Marion Eccles ~ Real ale ~ Bar food (12-2.30, 6.30-9; 12-7 Sun; not Mon, Sun evenings) ~ Restaurant ~ (01923) 282908 ~ Children welcome ~ Dogs allowed in bar ~ Open 12-11(12 Sat, 9 Sun)

Recommended by Barry and Anne, Tracey and Stephen Groves, Peter and Giff Bennett, Roy Hoing, David Jackson, LM, N J Roberts

SIBTON Suffolk   TM3570   Map 5

White Horse

Halesworth Road; IP17 2JJ

SUFFOLK DINING PUB OF THE YEAR

Particularly well run inn, nicely old-fashioned bar, good mix of customers, real ales and imaginative food; comfortable bedrooms

They've cleverly struck a balance between village pub and first-class restaurant in this 16th-c inn – and you can be sure of a genuinely warm welcome from the hard-working licensees, too. The comfortable bar has horsebrasses and tack on the walls, old settles and pews, and a large inglenook fireplace with a roaring log fire. Adnams Bitter, Brandon Rusty Bucket, Green Jack Trawlerboys Best Bitter and Woodfordes Wherry on handpump, several wines by the glass and a dozen malt whiskies are served from the old oak-panelled counter, and there's a viewing panel showing the working cellar and its Roman floor. Steps take you up past an ancient partly knocked-through timbered wall into a carpeted gallery and there's a smart dining room, too. The big garden has plenty of seats, and the comfortable bedrooms are in a converted outbuilding; delicious breakfasts.

Using vegetables from their own kitchen garden and their own eggs and other local produce, the excellent food includes sandwiches, free-range pork terrine with apple, sultana and apricot chutney, honey and mustard home-roasted ham with fried duck eggs, venison burger with fennel mayonnaise, wild mushroom and goats cheese risotto with herb oil, gressingham duck breast with morello cherry jus, and line-caught wild bass with spring onion mash and sauce vierge. *Benchmark main dish: rare-breed sirloin steak £17.50. Two-course evening meal £20.00.*

Free house ~ Licensees Neil and Gill Mason ~ Real ale ~ Bar food ~ Restaurant ~ (01728) 660337 ~ Well behaved children welcome but must be over 13 for accommodation ~ Dogs allowed in bar ~ Quiz night every Mon (not bank holidays) ~ Open 12-2.30, 6.30-11; 12-3.30, 7-10.30 Sun ~ Bedrooms: £70S/£90B

Recommended by Bruce and Sharon Eden, S T W Norton, Ian and Nita Cooper, Charles and Pauline Stride, David Rule, Peter Hulland, David Field, Jane and Alan Bush

SNAPE Suffolk   TM4058   Map 5
Golden Key
Priory Lane; IP17 1SA

New licensees for traditionally furnished village pub with Adnams beers and changing bar food

Friendly new licensees have taken over this 16th-c pub and have opened up letting bedrooms. The traditional low-beamed lounge bar has an old-fashioned settle curving around a couple of venerable stripped tables on the chequerboard tiled floor, a winter open fire and a mix of pubby tables and chairs; there's also a small snug. The two dining rooms have open fireplaces and are furnished with settles and scrubbed pine tables. Adnams Bitter, Broadside and Explorer on handpump with seasonal beers tapped from the cask, 14 wines by the glass, local cider, good coffee and home-made soft drinks. Outside are two terraces (one for the morning and a suntrap evening one), both with pretty hanging baskets and seats under large parasols.

Using some home-grown vegetables, the food now includes lunchtime sandwiches, pork and chicken liver pâté with home-made red onion marmalade, asparagus, leek and blue cheese tart, local sausages and mash, gammon steak with a bantam egg, and sole with jersey royals and courgettes. *Benchmark main dish: seasonal pie £13.50. Two-course evening meal £19.00.*

Adnams ~ Tenant Inga Haselmann ~ Real ale ~ Bar food (12-3, 6(7 Sun)-9) ~ Restaurant ~ (01728) 688510 ~ Children welcome ~ Dogs welcome ~ Open 12-3, 6(7 Sun)-11 ~ Bedrooms: /£95S

Recommended by Edward Mirzoeff, John and Eleanor Holdsworth, Charles and Pauline Stride, Roger and Lesley Everett, R L Borthwick, Stephen Funnell, Simon Cottrell, Roger White, S T W Norton, John and Sharon Hancock, Adrian and Dawn Collinge, Kay and Alistair Butler, Evelyn and Derek Walter, Norma and Noel Thomas

SNAPE Suffolk   TM3957 Map 5

Plough & Sail

The Maltings, Snape Bridge (B1069 S); IP17 1SR

Nicely placed dining pub extended airily around an older bar, real ales, food all day weekends, and seats outside

Bright and airy and with plenty of room, this pink-washed pub is part of the Snape Maltings complex. It's mostly open-plan and is a clever blend of the traditional and modern with wicker and café-style furnishings – as well as having an older heart with a woodburning stove, high bar chairs by the serving counter and rustic pine dining chairs and tables on terracotta tiling; another cosy little room has comfortable blue sofas and low coffee tables. Most diners head for the simply furnished bar hall and spacious airy dining room with blue-cushioned dining chairs around straightforward tables on the light, woodstrip flooring and high ceilings with A-frame beams; motifs illustrating the history of the Maltings decorate the walls. Another restaurant upstairs has similar furnishings; piped music and darts. Adnams Bitter, Woodfordes Wherry and a couple of guest beers on handpump and several wines by the glass. The flower-filled terrace has plenty of teak chairs and tables and there are some picnic-sets at the front. The shops and other buildings in the attractive complex are interesting to wander through.

Popular food includes lunchtime sandwiches, chicken liver pâté, filo-wrapped tiger prawns with sweet chilli dip, mixed bean casserole, steak in ale pudding, smoked haddock with a chive cream sauce, tomatoes and mozzarella, and slow-roasted lamb shank with garlic mash and red wine and rosemary gravy. *Benchmark main dish: cod and chips £9.95. Two-course evening meal £16.40.*

Deben Inns ~ Lease Steve and Louise Lomas ~ Real ale ~ Bar food (12-2.30, 6-9.30; all day weekends) ~ Restaurant ~ (01728) 688413 ~ Children welcome ~ Dogs allowed in bar ~ Open 11-11

Recommended by RS, ES, Tracey and Stephen Groves, Adrian and Dawn Collinge

SNETTISHAM Norfolk   TF6834 Map 8

Rose & Crown

EAST OF ENGLAND PUB OF THE YEAR

Village signposted from A149 King's Lynn—Hunstanton just N of Sandringham; coming in on the B1440 from the roundabout just N of village, take first left turn into Old Church Road; PE31 7LX

NORFOLK DINING PUB OF THE YEAR

Particularly well run old pub, log fires and interesting furnishings, imaginative food, a fine range of drinks, and stylish seating on heated terrace; well equipped bedrooms

The neatly dressed, courteous staff in this well run and pretty cottage offer a genuinely warm welcome to all – children and dogs, too. The smallest of the three bars is a pale grey colour with coir flooring and old prints of King's Lynn and Sandringham. Each of the other two bars has a separate character: an old-fashioned beamed front bar with black settles on its tiled floor and a big log fire, and a back bar with another large log fire and the landlord's sporting trophies and old sports equipment (which are being slowly edged out to make way for the pub cricket team photos). There's also the Garden Room with inviting wicker-based wooden chairs, careful lighting and a quote by Dr Johnson in old-fashioned rolling script on a huge wall board, and a residents' lounge (liked by non-residents, too) with squashy armchairs and sofas, rugs on the floor, newspapers, magazines, jigsaws and board games. Adnams Bitter and Broadside, Black Sheep Ruddy Ram and Woodfordes Wherry on handpump, nine wines by the glass and cider and perry. In the garden, there are stylish café-style blue chairs and tables under cream parasols on the terrace, outdoor heaters and colourful herbaceous borders; there's a new wooden galleon-shaped climbing fort. Two of the comfortable bedrooms are downstairs and there are disabled lavatories and wheelchair ramps. The Bank House in King's Lynn is under the same management and also worth a visit.

Excellent food using carefully sourced produce includes sandwiches, seared pigeon breast, pine nut and pancetta salad, parsnip and wild mushroom risotto with truffle butter, bangers and mash with onion gravy, poussin with champ, honey-roast parsnips and confit garlic, steak frites, and salmon with chorizo-spiced couscous, coriander and spring onion salad. *Benchmark main dish: steak burger with bacon and cheese £10.95. Two-course evening meal £18.45.*

Free house ~ Licensee Anthony Goodrich ~ Real ale ~ Bar food (12-2(2.30 weekends), 6.30-9(9.30 Fri and Sat) ~ Restaurant ~ (01485) 541382 ~ Children welcome ~ Dogs welcome ~ Open 11-11(10.30 Sun) ~ Bedrooms: £75B/£95B

Recommended by John Saville, Michael Dandy, Eithne Dandy, DF, NF, John Wooll, Tracey and Stephen Groves, R L Borthwick, Jeff and Wendy Williams, Henry Fryer, J F M and M West, Peter and Lesley Barrett, Mark, Amanda, Luke and Jake Sheard

SOULDROP Bedfordshire   SP9861   Map 4

Bedford Arms ◖ £

Village signposted off A6 Rushden—Bedford; High Street; MK44 1EY

Proper country tavern with good value food in cottagey dining area

This cosy relaxed place is given real heart by its lively welcoming licensees, and with its few chatty regulars settled into the bar chairs by the counter (which has Black Sheep, Greene King IPA and Phipps Red Star on handpump alongside a guest such as Hopping Mad Brainstorm and several wines by the glass) there's no doubting its pubbiness. There are just a few more seats in this small low-beamed area, including a couple of tables in one very low-ceilinged snug hutch of an alcove. The cottagey dining area has more low beams (one way through is potentially a real head-cracker) and a central fireplace – and, like the rest of the pub, broad floorboards, shelves of china, and original artwork (for sale). In the evenings and at weekends, the roomy mansard-ceilinged public area (once a brew house) perks into life, with well placed hood skittles, darts and board games; it has a big inglenook fireplace, and opens on to a neat garden with pretty flower borders. The landlady is fond of her pets – look out for Poky the cat and, out in the garden, JD, Gin and Tonic the rabbits.

Straightforward bar food includes sandwiches, baguettes and ciabattas, battered king prawns, blue cheese and walnut soufflé, quorn cottage pie, salmon and monkfish kebabs, curries, battered cod, and mixed grill. You need to book weekend evenings and Sunday lunchtime. *Benchmark main dish: steak and ale pie £9.25. Two-course evening meal £15.10.*

Free house ~ Licensees Sally Rushworth and Fred and Caroline Rich ~ Real ale ~ Bar food (12-2, 6.30-9; 12-4 Sun; not Sun evening) ~ Restaurant ~ (01234) 781384 ~ Children

welcome ~ Dogs allowed in bar ~ Open 12-3, 6-11; 12-midnight Fri, Sat; 12-11 Sun; closed
Mon except bank holidays

Recommended by D C Poulton, S Holder

SOUTH HANNINGFIELD Essex TQ7497 Map 5

Old Windmill ♀

Off A130 S of Chelmsford; CM3 8HT

**Extensive but invitingly converted Brunning & Price pub with
interesting food and good range of drinks**

A seeming maze of stripped standing timbers at this rambling knocked-
through place, makes it feel at once open-plan and intimate, too.
Décor is comfortably inviting with all sorts of highly polished old tables
and chairs, frame to frame pictures on cream walls, woodburning stoves
and homely pot plants. Deep green or dark red dado and one or two old
rugs dotted on the glowing wood floors provide splashes of colour; other
areas are more subdued with beige carpeting. Adnams, Black Sheep,
Phoenix Brunning & Price Original and up to three guests from brewers
such as Crouch Vale and Mighty Oak are on handpump, with 20 wines by
the glass, farm cider, 70 malts and a good range of spirits. A back terrace
has tables and chairs and there are picnic sets on the lawn here and a few
out in front.

As well as interesting sandwiches, bar food might include split pea and ham
soup, seared spiced lamb with apricot couscous and aubergine relish, fried
scallops and chorizo with butternut purée, crab linguine, poached chicken, fennel
and orange salad, ham, egg and chips, fish pie, roast duck leg with Toulouse sausage
and red wine dressing, battered haddock, steak mushroom and ale pie, aubergine,
lentil and mushroom moussaka, and grilled hake with mussel, bacon, potato and
saffron chowder with corn fritters. *Benchmark main dish: steak and ale pie £10.95.
Two-course evening meal £18.40.*

Brunning & Price ~ Manager Tom Wortley ~ Real ale ~ Bar food (12-10(9.30 Sun)) ~
(01268) 712280 ~ Well behaved children welcome ~ Dogs allowed in bar ~
Open 11.30-11; 12-10.30 Sun

Recommended by Richard Gibbs

DISCOVER ESSEX – A COUNTY OF MANY TREASURES

Between London and the sea lies the ancient Saxon county of Essex. Traces of medieval
times can be found in delightful small towns such as Saffron Walden, Coggeshall and
Thaxted. The Normans left their mark with castles at Colchester, Castle Hedingham and
Stansted, while the Romans made Colchester their capital.

The Essex Discovery Coast boasts a real maritime flavour. Vibrant seaside towns merge with
isolated beaches, tidal inlets and estuaries rich in wildlife. While Southend and Clacton,
and the other 'Sunshine Coast Resorts', offer family entertainment, quieter ports such as
Harwich and Maldon have enormous character, and coastal towns like Burnham-on-Crouch
and Brightlingsea come alive with yachts during the boating season.

Inland, ancient woodlands such as Epping and Hatfield Forest add interest to a landscape
characterised by thatched cottages, timber-framed farmhouses and windmills. Lovely
country houses include Audley End House, Ingatestone Hall and Layer Marney. Essex
remains a rural county, perfect for an interesting day out or short break away.

Find out more at **www.visitessex.com**

SOUTHWOLD Suffolk   TM5076   Map 5

Crown 🍴 🍺 🛏
High Street; IP18 6DP

Comfortable hotel with relaxed bars, a fine choice of drinks, papers to read, imaginative food and seats outside; bedrooms

Civilised and warmly welcoming, this smart hotel remains much loved by our readers. It's extremely well run by courteous staff and is just as enjoyable if you drop in for a drink and a chat or stay overnight in the restful bedrooms. At the back, there's a cosy oak-panelled locals' bar (reserved for drinkers) which has a proper pubby atmosphere, red leatherette wall benches on red carpeting, Adnams Bitter, Broadside, Explorer and a seasonal guest on handpump, 20 wines by the glass from a splendid list and quite a few malt whiskies. The elegant beamed front bar has a relaxed, informal atmosphere, a stripped curved high-backed settle and other dark varnished settles, kitchen chairs and some bar stools, and a carefully restored rather fine carved wooden fireplace; maybe newspapers to read. The tables out in a sunny sheltered corner are very pleasant.

 Tables are still on a first-come first-served basis so you do need to arrive early for the inventive – if not cheap – food: sandwiches, vodka-cured salmon with bloody mary jelly and fennel salad, braised pig's cheek with black pudding, caramelised leeks and wholegrain mustard jus, dressed crab with chilli mayonnaise, pork belly cooked in hay with apple and thyme sauce, and cod with wild mushrooms, roasted leeks and celeriac and pancetta lardons. *Benchmark main dish: roasted local cod fillet £16.50. Two-course evening meal £22.45.*

Adnams ~ Manager Francis Guildea ~ Real ale ~ Bar food (12-2.30, 6.30(6 Sat)-9) ~ (01502) 722275 ~ Children welcome ~ Dogs allowed in bar ~ Open 11-11; 12-10.30 Sun ~ Bedrooms: £105B/£173.50B

Recommended by Tony and Shirley Albert, Stephen Funnell, Mike and Sue Loseby, MJVK, M and GR, Michael Dandy, Martin Smith, Alan and Jill Bull, Ann and Colin Hunt, Mrs Margo Finlay, Jörg Kasprowski, David Rule, Peter and Giff Bennett, David Carr, J F M and M West

---

SOUTHWOLD Suffolk   TM5076   Map 5

Lord Nelson 🍺 £
East Street, off High Street (A1095); IP18 6EJ

Bow-windowed town pub with long-serving owners, well liked pubby food and a good choice of drinks; seats outside

This is the sort of pub that customers return to again and again. It's very well run, has a friendly bustling atmosphere, good-natured staff and is just a step or two away from the seafront. The partly panelled traditional bar and its two small side rooms are kept spotless, with good lighting, a small but extremely hot coal fire, light wood furniture on the tiled floor, lamps in nice nooks and corners, and some interesting Nelson memorabilia, including attractive nautical prints and a fine model of HMS *Victory*. They serve all the seasonal range of Adnams beers alongside Aspall's cider and several good wines by the glass; daily papers and board games. There are seats out in front with a sidelong view down to the sea and more in a sheltered (and heated) back garden, with the brewery in sight (and often the appetising fragrance of brewing in progress). Disabled access is not perfect but is possible.

🍴 Fair value traditional bar food includes sandwiches, spicy chicken wings with sour cream, stuffed roasted red pepper with goats cheese, ham with pineapple and chips, free-range chicken burger in beer batter, prawn thai green curry, and smoked haddock and cod in a cream, tomato and tarragon sauce topped with cheese. *Benchmark main dish: beer-battered fish and chips £9.75. Two-course evening meal £17.20.*

Adnams ~ Tenants David and Gemma Sanchez ~ Real ale ~ Bar food ~ (01502) 722079 ~ Children welcome in side rooms ~ Dogs welcome ~ Open 10.30am-11pm; 12-10.30 Sun

Recommended by Robert Lorimer, Pat and Tony Martin, Tracey and Stephen Groves, Stephen Funnell, Michael Dandy, Charles and Pauline Stride, Derek Field, S T W Norton, Dr D J and Mrs S C Walker, Mike and Sue Loseby, the Didler, Rob and Catherine Dunster, Giles and Annie Francis, Martin Smith, DHV, Ann and Colin Hunt, Terry Mizen, Peter and Giff Bennett, David Carr, David Field

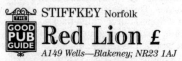

STIFFKEY Norfolk   TF9643   Map 8

Red Lion £

A149 Wells—Blakeney; NR23 1AJ

Traditional pub with bustling atmosphere, attractive layout, tasty food and real ales; bedrooms

Always bustling and friendly, this is a traditional pub with a good mix of customers. The oldest parts of the unpretentious bars have a few beams, aged flooring tiles or bare floorboards and big open fires. There's also a mix of pews, small settles and a couple of stripped high-backed settles, a nice old long deal table among quite a few others, Greene King St Edmunds, Woodfordes Nelsons Revenge and Wherry and a guest beer on handpump and 25 malt whiskies; board games. A back gravel terrace has proper tables and seats, with more on grass further up beyond; there are some pleasant walks nearby. The bedrooms are eco-friendly.

🍴 Hearty bar food at fair prices includes sandwiches, chicken liver pâté with onion jam, beer-battered cod, lamb and pearl barley casserole with root mash, wild mushroom and white wine risotto, sausages with red wine and onion gravy, and smoked salmon and dill linguine. *Benchmark main dish: battered cod and chips £9.95. Two-course evening meal £15.50.*

Free house ~ Licensee Stephen Franklin ~ Real ale ~ Bar food (12-2.30, 6-9; all day Sun) ~ (01328) 830552 ~ Children welcome ~ Dogs welcome ~ Open 11am-midnight ~ Bedrooms: £90B/£110B

Recommended by Mike Proctor, Mike and Shelley Woodroffe, Derek Field, Chris Johnson, the Didler, A Kirk, Roy Hoing, Jeremy and Ruth Preston-Hoar, Anthony Longden, Peter and Giff Bennett, David Carr, Neil Shaw, Sandy Butcher

STILTON Cambridgeshire   TL1689   Map 5

Bell 🍷 🛏

High Street; village signposted from A1 S of Peterborough; PE7 3RA

Fine coaching inn with several civilised rooms including a residents' bar, bar food using the famous cheese, and seats in the very pretty courtyard; bedrooms

The two neatly kept right-hand bars in this lovely example of a 17th-c coaching inn have the most character here and are where most of our readers head for. There are bow windows, sturdy upright wooden seats on flagstone floors as well as plush button-back built-in banquettes and a good big log fire in one handsome stone fireplace; one bar has a large cheese press. The partly stripped walls have big prints of sailing and winter coaching scenes and there's a giant pair of blacksmith's bellows hanging in the middle of the front bar. Digfield Fools Nook, Greene King IPA and Old Speckled Hen, Oakham Bishops Farewell and Inferno on handpump, a dozen malt whiskies and 20 wines by the glass. Other rooms include a residents' bar, a bistro and a restaurant. Through the fine coach arch is a very pretty sheltered courtyard with tables and a well which dates back to Roman times.

As well as their famous soup, the bistro-style food includes sandwiches, stilton pâté with pineapple and chilli jam, pasta with broad beans and a lemon and oregano-infused sauce, home-made burger with cheese and smoked bacon, chicken suprême with bubble and squeak and red wine jus, and beef goulash with potato pancakes and sour cream. *Benchmark main dish: stilton soup £4.95. Two-course evening meal £20.00.*

Free house ~ Licensee Liam McGivern ~ Real ale ~ Bar food (12-2(2.30 Sat), 6-9.30; all day Sun) ~ Restaurant ~ (01733) 241066 ~ Children allowed away from bar areas ~ Open 12-2.30, 6-11; 12-midnight(11 Sun) Sat; 12-11 Sun ~ Bedrooms: £73.50B/£100.50B

Recommended by Phil and Jane Hodson, Jeremy King, Jeff and Wendy Williams, Simon Collett-Jones

STOCK Essex

TQ6999   Map 5

Hoop £

B1007; from A12 Chelmsford bypass take Galleywood, Billericay turn-off; CM4 9BD

Happy weatherboarded pub with interesting beers and a large garden

They put on over 200 real ales and 80 ciders and perries, and open all day for the eight days of their beer festival (which is held around the late May bank holiday) at this old weatherboarded pub. The rest of the time Adnams is kept alongside three guests from brewers such as Crouch Vale and Wells & Youngs. Simple wood fixtures and fittings, including stripped floors, wooden tables and brocaded wooden settles, keep the interior feeling appropriately down-to-earth and pubby – just the right setting for the cheery locals and visitors enjoying the happy bustle here. Standing timbers and beams in the open-plan bar hint at the building's great age and its original layout as a row of three weavers' cottages and, in winter, a warm fire burns in a big brick-walled fireplace. A restaurant up in the timbered eaves (very different in style, with a separate à la carte menu) is light and airy with pale timbers set in white walls and more wood flooring. Prettily bordered with flowers, the large sheltered back garden has picnic-sets and a covered seating area. Parking is limited, so it is worth getting here early.

Pubby food includes sandwiches, chicken liver parfait with onion chutney, prawn and crayfish cocktail, liver and bacon, battered fish of the day, beef and ale pie, mushroom risotto and well rung steak; they may ask to hold your credit card in a personal locked box if you run a tab. *Benchmark main dish: roast pork belly £11.50. Two-course evening meal £18.95.*

Free house ~ Licensee Michelle Corrigan ~ Real ale ~ Bar food (12-2.30(5 Sun), 6-9.30; not Sun evening) ~ Restaurant ~ (01277) 841137 ~ Children welcome in one area ~ Dogs allowed in bar ~ Open 11-11; 12-10.30 Sun

Recommended by LM, John and Enid Morris, Jim and Frances Gowers

STOKE-BY-NAYLAND Suffolk   TL9836   Map 5

Crown ★

Park Street (B1068); CO6 4SE

Smart dining pub with attractive modern furnishings, imaginative food, real ales and a fantastic wine choice; bedrooms

They are serious about their wine here with 38 by the glass from a list of around 200 kept in an unusual glass-walled wine 'cellar' in one corner (you can go and choose your wine to drink here or take away) and they helpfully suggest a wine for each dish on the menu. It's a civilised inn with quite an emphasis on the comfortable bedrooms and excellent food but drinkers do pop in for a drink and a chat. Most of the place is open to the three-sided bar servery, but there are two or three cosy tucked-away areas, too. The main part, with a big woodburning stove, has quite a few closely spaced tables in a variety of shapes, styles and sizes; elsewhere, several smaller areas have just three or four tables each. Seating varies from deep armchairs and sofas to elegant dining chairs and comfortable high-backed woven rush seats – and there are plenty of bar stools. Some of the low ceilings are heavily beamed and there are cheerful wildlife and landscape paintings, quite a few attractive tables and floors varying from old tiles through broad boards or dark new flagstones to beige carpet; daily papers. Adnams Bitter, Crouch Vale Brewers Gold, Woodfordes Wherry and a guest such as Mersea Island Yo Boy Bitter on handpump and Aspall's cider. A sheltered back terrace, with cushioned teak chairs and tables under big canvas parasols, looks out over a neat lawn to a landscaped shrubbery, and there are many more picnic-sets out on the front terrace. Breakfasts are first class, disabled access is good and the car park is big.

Enterprising modern food might include smoked haddock and horseradish pâté, beef and marjoram cheeseburger with smoked bacon, leek and pea risotto with deep-fried poached egg, buttermilk chicken with apple and fennel coleslaw, rump of salt marsh lamb with spring onion and wild garlic mash, and maple-roasted pork chop with a black pudding lollipop. *Benchmark main dish: beer-battered haddock £11.95. Two-course evening meal £22.25.*

Free house ~ Licensee Richard Sunderland ~ Real ale ~ Bar food (12-2.30, 6-9.30(10 Fri and Sat); all day Sun) ~ (01206) 262001 ~ Children welcome ~ Dogs allowed in bar ~ Open 11-11; 12-10.30 Sun ~ Bedrooms: £80S(£95B)/£110S(£135B)

Recommended by Mrs Margo Finlay, Jörg Kasprowski, Bruce and Sharon Eden, Jeremy King, Marcus Mann, MDN, John and Enid Morris, Alan and Jill Bull, John Prescott, J F M and M West

STOW BARDOLPH Norfolk   TF6205   Map 5

Hare Arms ♀

Just off A10 N of Downham Market; PE34 3HT

Long-serving licensees in this bustling village pub, real ales, good mix of customers, tasty bar food, and a big back garden

Very much enjoyed by our readers, this is a neatly kept and very well run village pub with friendly, helpful staff. The bar has some interesting bric-a-brac such as old advertising signs and golf clubs suspended from the ceiling, as well as dark pubby furniture and comfortable built-in wall seats, a good log fire and a cheerful, bustling atmosphere. There's also a well planted conservatory where families are allowed. From the central bar they serve Greene King IPA, Abbot and Old Speckled Hen, Holdens

Golden Glow and Holts Fifth Sense on handpump, quite a few wines by the glass and several malt whiskies. There are plenty of seats in the large garden behind, with more in the pretty front garden; there might be a peacock or two, some chickens wandering around and perhaps the plump, elderly pub cat. Church Farm Rare Breeds Centre is a five-minute walk away and is open all year.

Using their own eggs and other local produce, the popular bar food includes lunchtime sandwiches, tempura-battered haddock with a chive, onion, lemon and caper dressing, a curry of the day, nut cutlets with a spicy chilli dip, sausages with horseradish mash and red onion gravy, hickory chicken breast, and seared tuna with raisin and coriander couscous and a tomato and aubergine chutney; there's also a set price menu Monday-Thursday. *Benchmark main dish: steak in creamy peppercorn and brandy sauce pie £11.00. Two-course evening meal £16.75.*

Greene King ~ Lease David and Trish McManus ~ Real ale ~ Bar food (12-2, 6-10; all day Sun) ~ Restaurant ~ (01366) 382229 ~ Children allowed away from main bar ~ Open 11-2.30, 6-11; 12-10.30 Sun; closed 25 and 26 Dec

Recommended by Mike Proctor, Moira and John Cole, Ian Phillips, John Saville, Henry Fryer, Peter and Lesley Barrett, Phil and Jane Hodson, John Wooll, Malcolm and Barbara Southwell, R C Vincent, Tracey and Stephen Groves

SWANTON MORLEY Norfolk   TG0217   Map 8

Darbys

B1147 NE of Dereham; NR20 4NY

Unspoilt country local with six real ales, plenty of farming knick-knacks, tasty bar food, and children's play area

With half a dozen changing real ales and well liked food, this friendly pub is as busy as ever. The long bare-boarded country-style bar has a comfortable lived-in feel with big stripped-pine tables and chairs, lots of gin traps and farming memorabilia, a good log fire (with the original bread oven alongside) and tractor seats with folded sacks lining the long, attractive serving counter. Adnams Bitter and Broadside, Beeston Afternoon Delight, Woodfordes Wherry and two guests on handpump, several wines by the glass and quite a few coffees; good, efficient service. A step up through a little doorway by the fireplace takes you through to the attractive dining room with neat, dark tables and chairs on the wooden floor; the children's room has a toy box and a glassed-over well, floodlit from inside. Piped music, TV and board games. There are picnic-sets and a children's play area in the back garden. Plenty to do locally (B&B is available in carefully converted farm buildings a few minutes away) as the family also own the adjoining 720-acre estate. They also have a well equipped camping site.

Tasty bar food includes sandwiches, smoked salmon pâté, chicken, mozzarella and bacon melt, pork tenderloin in a creamy mushroom and mustard sauce, popular burgers (vegetarian, cajun chicken, lamb and classic), and lamb shank with a cranberry orange and mint jus. *Benchmark main dish: steak in ale pie £10.75. Two-course evening meal £17.00.*

Free house ~ Licensees John Carrick and Louise Battle ~ Real ale ~ Bar food (12-2.15, 6-9.45; all day weekends) ~ Restaurant ~ (01362) 637647 ~ Children welcome ~ Dogs allowed in bar ~ Open 11.30-3, 6-11; 11.30-11 Fri and Sat; 12-10.30 Sun ~ Bedrooms: £35S(£40B)/£60(£70S)(£75B)

Recommended by S T W Norton, R C Vincent

THORNHAM Norfolk   TF7343 Map 8

Orange Tree
Church Street/A149; PE36 6LY

Nice combination of friendly bar and good contemporary dining

Stripped beams, a log fire, low ceiling, comfortable leather and basket-weave chairs on the tiled floor, Adnams and Woodfordes Wherry on handpump, 24 wines by the glass, good courteous service – add the warmly chatty and informal atmosphere, and you have all the right ingredients for a really nice country bar, complete with visiting dogs; their own labrador is called Poppy. Much the same relaxed feel runs through the more extensive two-part dining area, which is cheerfully modern in style, partly carpeted, with colourful neat modern seating around plain tables, and contemporary artworks above its dark grey dado; this part may have piped pop music. The main garden, shaded by tall sycamores, has picnic-sets under white canvas parasols, and a round smokers' shelter in one discreet corner; a second area has safely enclosed play things. We have not yet heard from readers using the courtyard bedrooms, but would expect this to be a good base for this lovely north Norfolk coast.

Enjoyable food using local seafood and seasonal produce might include sandwiches, duck foie gras terrine with port jelly, roasted apples and wild mushrooms, smoked haddock fishcakes with a soft boiled egg, herb salad and saffron butter sauce, moroccan preserved lemon and chickpea burger with yoghurt dressing, chicken, prawn or vegetable tikka jalfrezi, and crab and tiger prawn spaghetti with chilli, lemon oil and parsley. *Benchmark main dish: rare breed chargrilled burger £11.50. Two-course evening meal £18.00.*

Punch ~ Lease Mark Goode ~ Real ale ~ Bar food (12-3, 6-9.30; 12-5, 6-9 Sun) ~ Restaurant ~ (01485) 512213 ~ Children welcome ~ Dogs allowed in bar and bedrooms ~ Open 11-11(midnight Sat); 12-10.30 Sun ~ Bedrooms: /£85B

Recommended by Meriel Packman, Emma Beacham, Tracey and Stephen Groves

THORPENESS Suffolk   TM4759 Map 5

Dolphin
Just off B1353; village signposted from Aldeburgh; IP16 4NB

Neatly kept light and airy extended pub in an interesting village, popular food, local ales, and plenty of outside seating; bedrooms

With interesting views over the almshouses in this unusual village (a fascinating early 20th-c curio, built as a small-scale upmarket holiday resort) and a five-minute walk to the bracing shingle beach, this airy, well run pub is just the place for drink or a meal. The main bar is a light room with an almost scandinavian feel: little candles in glass vases on each of the well spaced, pale wooden tables and a nice mix of old chairs on broad modern quarry tiles, a built-in cushioned seat in the sizeable bay window, a winter log fire in its brick fireplace, and fresh flowers on the wooden bar counter where they keep Adnams Bitter and Broadside, Woodfordes Wherry and a couple of guests such as Green Jack Trawler Boys and St Peters Golden Ale on handpump, 18 wines by the glass and Aspall's cider; darts, TV, piped music and board games. The public bar to the left of the door is more traditional with a mix of pubby furniture on the stripped wooden floor, built-in cushioned wall seats with open 'windows' to the bar and fine old photographs of long-ago sporting teams, villagers and local scenes on the bottle-green planked walls; there's also a small area with a few high bar stools. The sizeable dining room has lots of windows hung with cheerful curtains, wide strips of coir matting on light wooden flooring, similar wooden furniture and seaside prints. French windows lead on to a terrace with teak tables and chairs, and beyond that, there are picnic-sets on an extensive stretch of grass; you can hire electric bikes from here. The pub also runs the village stores.

 Enjoyable food using local produce might include sandwiches, baked field mushrooms with grilled goats cheese and walnuts, roast pepper and courgette galette with feta and pesto, whole sole with buttered leeks and edamame beans, pork belly with mustard mash and red wine gravy, and chicken breast with chorizo. *Benchmark main dish: local fish and chips £10.50. Two-course evening meal £18.00.*

Free house ~ Licensee David James ~ Real ale ~ Bar food (12-2.30(3 Sun), 6.30-9; not Sun evening) ~ Restaurant ~ (01728) 454994 ~ Children welcome ~ Dogs allowed in bar and bedrooms ~ Open 11-11(10 Sun); closed winter Mon ~ Bedrooms: £65B/£95B

Recommended by Trevor Swindells, Bruce and Sharon Eden, K Hunt, M Smith, Rob and Catherine Dunster, Paul Humphreys, Terry Buckland, Phil and Jane Hodson, Sophie Roberts

THRIPLOW Cambridgeshire   TL4346   Map 5

Green Man

3 miles from M11 junction 10; A505 towards Royston, then first right; Lower Street; SG8 7RJ

Comfortable and cheery with pubby food and changing ales

If you like well kept ales and home-cooked food in a bustling atmosphere, then this cheerfully run village pub is just the place to head for. There are always plenty of customers and it's all comfortably laid out with modern tables and attractive high-backed dining chairs and pews; there are beer mats on the ceiling and champagne bottles on high shelves and two arches lead through to a restaurant on the left. The regularly changing real ales might be from breweries such as Buntingford, Milton, Nethergate, Oakham, St Peters and Woodfordes. There are tables in the pleasant garden and the vivid blue paintwork makes an excellent backdrop for the floral displays.

Well liked bar food includes filled baguettes, sausages with whole-grain mustard mash and onion gravy, beer-battered cod and chips, seared tuna with salsa verde, slow-roast pork belly, paprika beef, and chicken with bacon, cheese and mustard sauce. *Benchmark main dish: chicken with bacon, cheese and mustard sauce £9.50. Two-course evening meal £17.50.*

Free house ~ Licensee Mary Lindgren ~ Real ale ~ Bar food (not Sun evening or Mon) ~ (01763) 208855 ~ Children welcome ~ Dogs allowed in bar ~ Open 12-3, 7-11; closed Sun evening, all day Mon, Christmas week, Easter weekend

Recommended by Simon Watkins, LM

TRING Hertfordshire   SP9211   Map 5

Robin Hood  £

Brook Street (B486); HP23 5ED

Really welcoming pub with good beer and popular pubby food

We're delighted to be able to give this pleasingly traditional pub a Value Award this year for its reasonably priced food. It's the sort of place where diners who are in for a good value meal happily co-exist with regulars on stools along the counter enjoying the half a dozen Fullers ales. It's a carefully run place with a homely atmosphere and genial service in its several immaculately kept smallish linked areas. The main bar has banquettes and standard pub chairs on spotless bare boards or carpets. Towards the back, you'll find a conservatory with a vaulted ceiling and woodburner. The licensees' two little yorkshire terriers are called Buddy and Sugar; piped music. There are tables out on the small pleasant back terrace.

Enjoyable food includes sandwiches, filled baguettes, ploughman's, breaded whitebait, sausage and mash, steak and kidney pudding, fish and chips, scampi, burgers, and vegetable curry. They do sausage specials on Tuesday and Thursday night, and Sunday roast. *Benchmark main dish: ham, egg and chips £9.35. Two-course evening meal £14.60.*

Fullers ~ Tenants Terry Johnson and Stewart Canham ~ Real ale ~ Bar food (12-2.15, 6-9.15; not Sun evening) ~ (01442) 824912 ~ Children welcome ~ Dogs welcome ~ Open 11.30-3.30, 5.30-11(11.30 Fri); 12-11.30 Sat; 12-11 Sun
Recommended by John Branston, D and M T Ayres-Regan, Taff Thomas

 WALDRINGFIELD Suffolk   TM2844   Map 5

Maybush £
Off A12 S of Martlesham; The Quay, Cliff Road; IP12 4QL

Busy pub with tables outside by the riverbank; nautical décor and a fair choice of drinks and bar food

Carefully refurbished recently, this busy family pub is in a beautiful spot by the bird-haunted River Deben; lots of outside tables make the most of this. The knocked-through spacious bar is divided into separate areas by fireplaces or steps. There's a nautical theme, with an elaborate ship's model in a glass case and a few more in a light, high-ceilinged extension – as well as lots of old lanterns, pistols and aerial photographs. Piped music, cards, dominoes and board games. Adnams Bitter, Gun Hill and a changing guest on handpump and a fair choice of wines by the glass. There are river cruises available nearby but you have to pre-book.

Fair value, traditional food includes sandwiches, breaded garlic mushrooms, ham and free-range eggs, smoked haddock and salmon fishcakes, vegetable lasagne, steak in Guinness pie, barbecue chicken, and a mixed grill. *Benchmark main dish: fresh cod and chips £10.95. Two-course evening meal £15.90.*

Adnams ~ Lease Steve and Louise Lomas ~ Real ale ~ Bar food (12-9.30) ~ Restaurant ~ (01473) 736215 ~ Children welcome ~ Dogs allowed in bar ~ Open 11(12 Sun)-11
Recommended by K Hunt, M Smith, Jim and Frances Gowers, Alistair Mackie, Neil Brightwell

 **WELLS-NEXT-THE-SEA** Norfolk   TF9143   Map 8

Crown
The Buttlands; NR23 1EX

Smart coaching inn with a friendly informal bar, local ales, good modern food and elegant restaurant; well equipped bedrooms

Overlooking a tree-lined green, this is a rather smart old coaching inn with a good mix of both drinkers and diners. The rambling bar is on several levels with beams and the odd standing timber and the contemporary décor includes burnt-orange walls hung with local photographs, grey-painted planked wall seats with orange cushions and high-backed dark brown leather dining chairs around wooden-topped tables on the stripped-wood floors; newspapers to read, an open fire, their own JoC's Norfolk Ale, Adnams Bitter and Woodfordes Nelsons Revenge on handpump, quite a few wines by the glass and several whiskies and brandies; helpful staff and piped music. There's an airy dining room with bookshelves and cushioned, grey-painted farmhouse chairs and tables on wide floorboards and an elegant, more formal restaurant, too. This is part of the growing group of Flying Kiwi Inns.

Good, modern food includes sandwiches, crab and fennel linguine with lemon dressing, quail, chicken and lentil terrine with pepper chutney, herb polenta topped with grilled chicory and blue cheese glaze, poached salmon with beetroot rösti and a cockle and horseradish dressing, and venison with roast vegetable purée and chestnut jus. *Benchmark main dish: thai fish and watermelon curry £10.95. Two-course evening meal £19.00.*

Flying Kiwi Inns ~ Licensee Chris Coubrough ~ Real ale ~ Bar food (12-2.30, 6.30-9.30) ~ Restaurant ~ (01328) 710209 ~ Children welcome ~ Dogs allowed in bar and bedrooms ~ Open 11-11 ~ Bedrooms: £70B/£90B

Recommended by David Carr, DF, NF, R C Vincent, John Wooll, Jeremy King

WESTLETON Suffolk   TM4469 Map 5

Crown 🍴 ♇ 🛏

B1125 Blythburgh—Leiston; IP17 3AD

Bustling old inn with a cosy chatty bar, plenty of dining areas, carefully chosen drinks and interesting food; comfortable modern bedrooms

There's an attractive little bar at the heart of this comfortably stylish old coaching inn with a lovely log fire and plenty of original features. Many customers are here to stay or to enjoy a meal but locals do drop into this bar and they keep Adnams Bitter and Nethergate Suffolk County on handpump and a thoughtfully chosen wine list; piped music and board games. There's also a parlour, a dining room and conservatory, a happy mix of wooden dining chairs and tables, and old photographs on some fine old bare-brick walls. The charming terraced garden has plenty of seats and the airy, comfortable bedrooms are either in the main inn (some are up steep stairs) or in converted stables and cottages.

Under the new licensee, the good modern – if not cheap – food includes lunchtime sandwiches, potted chicken liver and black truffle pâté with onion chutney, slow-cooked chicken, mushroom and tarragon suet pudding, tempura of seasonal vegetables with garlic aioli and sweet chilli sauce, steamed lemon sole fillet with ratatouille and roast fish sauce, and rack of lamb with fennel risotto and honey-roast garlic. *Benchmark main dish: fish and chips £13.25. Two-course evening meal £20.50.*

Free house ~ Licensee Gareth Clarke ~ Real ale ~ Bar food (12-2.30, 6.30-9.30) ~ Restaurant ~ (01728) 648777 ~ Children welcome ~ Dogs allowed in bar and bedrooms ~ Open 11-11(10.30 Sun) ~ Bedrooms: £90B/£120B

Recommended by Simon and Mandy King, M V Burke, George and Beverley Tucker, John and Enid Morris, Keith and Margaret Kettell, George Wallace, John and Sharon Hancock, Kay and Alistair Butler, Phil and Jane Hodson, Anthony Longden

Tipping is not normal for bar meals, and not usually expected.

WHEPSTEAD Suffolk   TL8258   Map 5

White Horse 🍴 ♀

Off B1066 S of Bury; Rede Road; IP29 4SS

Imaginative food and relaxed civilised atmosphere in charmingly reworked country pub

The friendly, professional licensees are sure to make you feel at home straight away in this warmly welcoming pub. The dark-beamed bar has a winter log fire in its big 17th-c fireplace (a cluster of lighted church candles in summer). Linked rooms off give more choice of where to sit, mainly at sturdy, country kitchen tables on beige carpet or antique floor tiles, with some attractively cushioned traditional wall seats. Landscape paintings (for sale) and old prints decorate walls painted in soft canary or sage; the bookshelves have books that are actually worth reading. Adnams Bitter and Broadside on handpump and eight wines by the glass. The resident westie is called Skye. A neat sheltered back terrace is brightened up by colourful oilcloth tablecloths, and at the picnic-sets out on the grass, birdsong emphasises what a peaceful spot this is.

Enjoyable, interesting food includes smooth chicken liver and basil parfait, crispy fried rabbit with garlic mayonnaise, warm rocket and blue cheese tart, venison burger with tomato chilli jam, moroccan-style lamb with sultanas, oregano and couscous, and seared tuna with a tomato and celery confit. *Benchmark main dish: rib-eye steak £14.95. Two-course evening meal £17.45.*

Free house ~ Licensees Gary and Di Kingshott ~ Real ale ~ Bar food ~ Restaurant ~ (01284) 735760 ~ Children welcome ~ Dogs welcome ~ Open 11.30-3, 7-11; closed Sun evening

Recommended by Dr G and Mrs J Kelvin, Adele Summers, Alan Black, Geoffrey Baber, John Saville, Marianne and Peter Stevens, Jenny Smith, M and GR

WOODBASTWICK Norfolk   TG3214   Map 8

Fur & Feather 🍺

Off B1140 E of Norwich; NR13 6HQ

Full range of first-class beers from next-door Woodfordes brewery, friendly service, and popular bar food

The Woodfordes brewery is right next door to this thatched cottagey pub so the full range of their beers is in tip-top condition and tapped from the cask by friendly, efficient staff: Admirals Reserve, Headcracker, Mardlers Mild, Nelsons Revenge, Norfolk Nip, Norfolk Nog, Once Bittern, Sundew and Wherry. You can also visit the brewery shop. A dozen wines by the glass and around a dozen malt whiskies. The style and atmosphere are not what you'd expect of a brewery tap as it's set out more like a comfortable and roomy dining pub; piped music. There are seats and tables out in a pleasant garden. This is a lovely estate village.

As well as serving breakfast from 10am, the well liked bar food includes sandwiches, salmon, chilli and cucumber terrine, honey-roast ham and egg, steak and kidney pudding, popular burgers such as lamb with red onion relish, and venison pie with red wine and thyme gravy. *Benchmark main dish: steak and kidney pudding £11.95. Two-course evening meal £17.70.*

There are report forms at the back of the book.

Woodfordes ~ Tenant Tim Ridley ~ Real ale ~ Bar food (10am-9pm) ~ Restaurant ~
(01603) 720003 ~ Children welcome but must be well behaved ~ Open 10am-
10.30pm(11pm Sat); 10am-10pm Sun-Thurs in winter

*Recommended by Mike Proctor, JDM, KM, Fred and Lorraine Gill, the Shiread family, R C Vincent,
the Didler, Roy Hoing, John and Victoria Fairley, Tracey and Stephen Groves, Ralph Holland,
Andy and Claire Barker, David Carr*

ALSO WORTH A VISIT IN BEDFORDSHIRE

Besides the region's top pubs, we recommend the following. Do tell us
what you think of them: **feedback@goodguides.com**

BEDFORD TL0549   MK40 3PD
Embankment
The Embankment

Airy L-shaped bar in refurbished mock-Tudor hotel adjacent to the river, mix of modern
furniture on wood floor, Wells & Youngs ales, several wines by the glass, good choice of
food all day including deli boards and daily roast, nice coffee, cheerful helpful service,
back restaurant; piped music; seats out at front, 20 bedrooms (best ones with river views),
good breakfast. *Recommended by Michael Dandy, Eithne Dandy, Martin and Clare Warne, Ian Legge*

BEDFORD TL0550   MK40 2PF
Park
Park Avenue/Kimbolton Road

Large comfortably modernised pub with mix of furnishings including leather sofas in
partly flagstoned linked areas, enjoyable food from good sandwiches up, good friendly
service, well kept Wells & Youngs and guests, decent wines and coffee, daily papers,
conservatory eating area (best to book Sun lunch); piped music; courtyard garden with
tables on decking, open all day. *Recommended by Eithne Dandy, Andy Lickfold, Revd R P Tickle*

BEDFORD TL0650   MK41 9PX
White Horse
Newnham Avenue

Welcoming landlord and staff, large open-plan dining area and bar, wide choice of
enjoyable sensibly priced pub food, well kept Wells & Youngs and a guest in good
condition, beer festivals and other well organised events; garden. *Recommended by S Holder,
Sarah Flynn*

BIDDENHAM TL0249   MK40 4BD
Three Tuns
Off A428

Refurbished part-thatched village dining pub under new chef/owner, good seasonal food
(not Sun evening, Mon) from traditional favourites to some imaginatively presented
modern cooking, extensive wine list, well kept Greene King ales, good service; spacious
garden with picnic-sets, more contemporary furniture on terrace and decked area, open
all day. *Recommended by John Saville, Sandra Nash, Stephenie Staples, Carol Gould*

BLETSOE TL0157   MK44 1QN
 ### Falcon
Rushden Road (A6 N of Bedford)

17th-c building with comfortable welcoming bar, low beams and joists, seating from
cushioned wall/window seats to high-backed settles, winter open fires (look out for wild-
tongued gargoyles around the one by the front door), side snug with sofas and skittles,
panelled dining room, some interesting food alongside more traditional pub dishes, Wells

& Youngs ales and a guest like Everards Tiger, decent choice of wines by the glass, good coffee, daily papers; unobtrusive piped music; sheltered terrace and lovely big garden down to the River Ouse. *Recommended by Michael Dandy, O K Smyth, Dennis and Doreen Haward, Bruce and Sharon Eden, Ryta Lyndley, D C Poulton and others*

BOLNHURST TL0858   MK44 2EX
☆ **Plough**
Kimbolton Road

Stylish conversion of ancient building with a thriving atmosphere, charming staff, top-notch food, real ales such as local Potton Village Bike and a couple of guests, good carefully annotated wine list (including organic vintages) with well over a dozen by the glass, home-made summer lemonade and tomato juice, new airy dining extension; children welcome, dogs in bar, attractive tree-shaded garden overlooking pond, remains of old moat, closed Sun evening, Mon, first two weeks in Jan. *Recommended by Ryta Lyndley, Michael Sargent, G Jennings, R T and J C Moggridge and others*

BROMHAM TL0050   MK43 8LS
Swan
Bridge End; near A428, 2 miles W of Bedford

Popular refurbished beamed pub in quiet village, wide food choice including meal deals, good separate restaurant menu, quick friendly service, well kept Greene King ales and a guest, good choice of wines by the glass, log fire, lots of pictures, locals' bar, quiz nights; children welcome, disabled access, picnic-sets out by car park. *Recommended by Peter Wiser, Howard Galloway, Michael Tack*

BROOM TL1743   SG18 9NA
☆ **Cock**
High Street; from A1 opposite Biggleswade turn-off, follow Old Warden 3, Aerodrome 2 signpost, and take first left signed Broom

Friendly village-green pub with tasty straightforward good value food, Greene King ales tapped from casks by cellar steps off central corridor (no counter), original latch doors linking one quietly cosy little room to the next (four in all), low ochre ceilings, stripped panelling, farmhouse tables and chairs on antique tiles, warming winter fires, darts, bar skittles and board games; piped (perhaps classical) music; children and dogs welcome, picnic-sets on terrace by back lawn; caravanning and camping facilities, closed Sun evening. *Recommended by the Didler, Robert Turnham*

BROOM TL1742   SG18 9NN
White Horse
Southill Road

Comfortable country pub with rooms off small front bar, Greene King ales, enjoyable reasonably priced straightforward food from sandwiches up, friendly staff; picnic-sets in big back garden, campsite. *Recommended by Geoff and Carol Thorp, Michael Dandy, Richdamico*

CARDINGTON TL0847   MK44 3SP
☆ **Kings Arms**
The Green; off A603 E of Bedford

Comfortably refurbished M&B village dining pub with contemporary rustic feel, well cooked food including standard and more enterprising dishes, good choice of wines by the glass, good coffee, well kept Fullers London Pride, Greene King IPA and Timothy Taylors Landlord, helpful friendly staff, attractive linked areas with nice mix of varying-sized tables on bare boards and coir matting, log fire, interesting local airship photographs; well behaved children and dogs welcome, disabled facilities, good tables and chairs out on peaceful front terrace. *Recommended by Michael Dandy, Eithne Dandy*

You can send reports directly to us at **feedback@goodguides.com**

CLOPHILL TL0837   MK45 4AD
Flying Horse
2 The Green

Refurbished dining pub with good choice of food including fixed-price menu (Mon-Fri till 7pm), ales such as Timothy Taylors Landlord and Wells & Youngs Bombardier, several wines by the glass, split-level bar with mix of contemporary furniture on wood and stone floors, beams and inglenook log fire, spacious dining areas including raftered room; open all day. *Recommended by Michael Dandy*

CLOPHILL TL0838   MK45 4BY
Stone Jug
N on A6 from A507 roundabout, after 200 yards, second turn on right into Back Street

Secluded stone-built local, cosy and welcoming, with enjoyable bargain pubby lunchtime food from sandwiches up, good service, good choice of well kept ales, pleasantly unpretentious comfortable bar with family area and darts in small games extension; piped music; small pretty back terrace, roadside picnic-sets. *Recommended by Howard Galloway, Ross Balaam, Geoff and Carol Thorp*

FELMERSHAM SP9957   MK43 7EU
Sun
Grange Road

Cosy old-fashioned thatched village pub, low ceilings and open fire, well kept Wells & Youngs, good value home-made food (not Sun evening) from bar snacks up, raftered restaurant (closed Mon, Tues) with woodburner and own bar, quiz night (first Thurs of month); picnic-sets in front, more in garden area, open all day. *Recommended by Peter Martin*

GREAT BARFORD TL1351   MK44 3LF
Anchor
High Street; off A421

Open-plan bar with ales such as Badger, Courage and Wells & Youngs, usual food from sandwiches up, back restaurant; piped music, no under-14s; picnic-sets overlooking River Ouse by medieval bridge and church, bedrooms. *Recommended by Michael Dandy, David and Gill Carrington, Marion and Bill Cross*

HENLOW TL1738   SG16 6BS
Crown
High Street

Small inviting pub with good choice of popular food all day, several wines by the glass, well kept Adnams Broadside and Greene King IPA, good coffee, nice log fire, daily papers; piped music, games machine; terrace and small garden. *Recommended by Michael and Deborah Ethier, David Gunn*

HENLOW TL1738   SG16 6AA
☆ Engineers Arms
A6001 S of Biggleswade; High Street

Traditional, spic and span village pub, up to ten ales including Caledonian Deuchars IPA and Oakham, five ciders and a perry, bottled belgian beers, decent wines by the glass, helpful knowledgeable staff, limited range of good value snacks, comfortable carpeted front room with old local photographs on green fleur-de-lys wallpaper, bric-a-brac collections, traditional cushioned wall seats, armchair-style bar stools, daily papers, good log fire, small tiled inner area and another comfortable carpeted one, occasional live music, beer festivals; TVs, juke box, silenced fruit machine, board games; dogs allowed in bar, heated no-smoking back terrace (smokers' area in front), open all day. *Recommended by Michael and Deborah Ethier, Howard Galloway, Andy Lickfold*

IRELAND TL1341   SG17 5QL
☆ **Black Horse**
Off A600 Shefford—Bedford

Contemporary décor in cottagey dining pub, popular imaginative food served by attentive friendly staff, well kept Adnams, Fullers London Pride and a dozen wines by the glass from long black counter, mix of modern banquettes, bucket chairs and low tables on wood-strip or stone floors, simple ornaments and lamps, pleasant spacious feel; children welcome, lovely garden with attractive terraces and mature topiary, play area, bedrooms, closed Sun evening. *Recommended by Michael Dandy, Howard Galloway, Michael Sargent, Robert Turnham, Gordon Smale and others*

KEMPSTON TL0347   MK43 8RS
Slaters Arms
Box End Road (A5134, off A4218 W of Bedford)

Refurbished country pub under newish friendly licensees, good value food, Greene King ales and a guest, good service; piped music; children welcome, picnic-sets in big back tree-shaded garden with fenced-off play area, has been open all day. *Recommended by Michael Dandy, S Holder*

KEYSOE TL0763   MK44 2HR
☆ **Chequers**
Pertenhall Road, Brook End (B660)

Good value tasty home-made food from sandwiches to blackboard specials in down-to-earth village local with friendly long-serving licensees, two homely, comfortably worn-in beamed rooms divided by stone-pillared fireplace, changing real ales, Weston's cider, reasonably priced wines; piped music/radio, no credit cards; children welcome, wheelchair access through side door, seats on front lawn and on terrace behind, play area, closed Mon evening, Tues. *Recommended by Michael and Jenny Back and others*

MAULDEN TL0538   MK45 2AD
☆ **Dog & Badger**
Clophill Road E of village, towards A6/A507 junction

Attractive neatly kept bow-windowed cottage, family run, with good generous well priced bar food including set weekday lunches (booking advised weekends), Wells & Youngs and guests served by friendly staff, beams and exposed brickwork, high stools on bare boards by carved wooden counter, mix of dining chairs including high-backed leather ones around wooden tables, two-way fireplace, steps down to two carpeted areas and restaurant; piped music; children welcome, tables and smokers' shelter in front, back garden with sturdy play area, open all day weekends. *Recommended by Michael Dandy, Paul Goldman, Dudley and Moira Cockroft, Dawn Butler, Michelle Dodson-Finn*

NORTHILL TL1446   SG18 9AA
☆ **Crown**
Ickwell Road; off B658 W of Biggleswade

Prettily situated village pub refurbished under new management, cosy bar with copper-topped counter, heavy low beams and bay window seats, big open fire, modern tables and chairs on wood floor in dining room, brasserie-style food (not Sun evening), Greene King ales and a guest; piped music; no dogs inside; children welcome, tables out at front and on sheltered side terrace, more in big back garden with good play area, open all day. *Recommended by Mrs Margo Finlay, Jörg Kasprowski, Robert Turnham, Michael Dandy, M and GR, Andy Lickfold, Simon and Mandy King and others*

Post Office address codings confusingly give the impression that some pubs are in Bedfordshire, when they're really in Buckinghamshire or Cambridgeshire (which is where we list them).

OAKLEY TL0053 MK43 7RH

 ## Bedford Arms
High Street

Large refurbished 16th-c village pub under relatively new family management, pleasant contemporary feel, well kept Wells & Youngs ales, good food (not Sun evening) especially fish in various dining areas including conservatory, attentive friendly service, log fire; garden tables, open all day. *Recommended by Peter Martin, Mrs C Roe, S Holder*

ODELL SP9657 MK43 7AS
Bell
Off A6 S of Rushden, via Sharnbrook; High Street

Popular thatched village pub with several low-beamed rooms around central servery, mix of old settles and neat modern furniture, log or coal fires, good service under friendly licensees, Greene King ales, good choice of generous usual food (not Sun evening) from sandwiches and baked potatoes up, children welcome away from counter, delightful big garden backing on to River Ouse, handy for Harrold-Odell country park. *Recommended by Ross Balaam, Anthony Barnes, D C Poulton*

PEGSDON TL1130 SG5 3JX
☆ Live & Let Live
B655 W of Hitchin

Neatly kept dining pub on edge of the Chilterns with snug traditional tiled and panelled core, wide choice of enjoyable generous food including bargain weekday lunch (popular with older diners), friendly service, Adnams, Fullers London Pride, Greene King IPA and Marstons Pedigree, fair choice of wines; piped music; nice terrace and garden below Deacon Hill, tables under parasols and a great show of hanging baskets and tubs, handy for Luton Airport (offers a park and ride service), open all day. *Recommended by Michael Dandy, David and Ruth Shillitoe*

RISELEY TL0462 MK44 1DT
☆ Fox & Hounds
High Street; off A6 and B660 N of Bedford

Cheery traditional old pub with timber uprights under heavy low beams, clubby lounge area with comfortable leather chesterfields, low tables, wing chairs, Wells & Youngs Eagle and Bombardier and a guest, bin-end wines, speciality steaks cooked on open grill and other pubby food; unobtrusive piped classical or big band music; children welcome, dogs in bar, attractive garden with pergola and heated decked terrace. *Recommended by Michael Dandy, Susan and Jeremy Arthern, Michael Sargent, Sarah Flynn*

SHEFFORD TL1438 SG17 5JA
Woolpack
Hitchin Road

Good old-fashioned untied local with welcoming landlady, no food. *Recommended by Sarah Flynn*

SOUTHILL TL1441 SG18 9LD
White Horse
Off B658 SW of Biggleswade

Comfortable well run country pub with extensive eating area, wide range of generous pubby food from baguettes up, friendly staff, well kept changing ales, good wine choice; piped music; children welcome, lots of tables in big neatly kept garden with play area. *Recommended by Michael Dandy, Richdamico*

STUDHAM TL0215 LU6 2QA
Red Lion
Church Road

Open-plan pub in attractive setting below grassy common, bright and cheerful décor in bare-boards front bar, roaring fire, back carpeted dining area, well kept Adnams, Fullers London Pride, Greene King IPA and a guest ale, decent wines, enjoyable pubby food from sandwiches to steaks, friendly service, darts in small side area; quiet piped music; some garden tables, handy for Whipsnade. *Recommended by David Gurr, Ross Balaam, Fiona McDougal*

THURLEIGH TL0558 MK44 2DB
Jackal
High Street

Friendly quiet village pub with easy chairs and good fire in tiled-floor bar (where dogs allowed), another in comfortable carpeted dining lounge, good home-made food and service, well kept Wells & Youngs ales; piped music; seats out by road, more in nice rambling garden behind. *Recommended by D C Poulton*

☆ TODDINGTON TL0028 LU5 6AA
Sow & Pigs
A mile from M1 junction 12; A5120 (Church Square)

Greene King and guest ales in traditional town-style bar with mixed furnishings from ecclesiastical-looking chairs to button-backed leather on worn tiles and boards, lots of breweriana, bar food including pizzas and Sun roasts, chatty landlord, two log fires, upstairs restaurant; children welcome, picnic-sets in small garden, smokers' shelter, open all day weekends, closed weekday lunchtimes. *Recommended by Conor McGaughey*

TURVEY SP9352 MK43 8ER
Three Fyshes
A428 NW of Bedford; Bridge Street, W end of village

Refurbished early 17th-c beamed pub, big inglenook with woodburner, mix of easy and upright chairs around tables on tiles or ancient flagstones, enjoyable interesting home-made food (all day weekends), good friendly service, Adnams, Greene King and Oldershaws, decent choice of wines, daily papers, extended restaurant; piped music; dogs welcome, children in eating areas, decking and canopy in charming garden overlooking bridge and mill on Great Ouse, open all day. *Recommended by Susan and Jeremy Arthern, George Atkinson, Eithne Dandy, Howard Galloway*

WOBURN SP9433 MK17 9QJ
Bell
Bedford Street

Small beamed bar area, longer bare-boards dining lounge up steps, pleasant décor and furnishings, decent all-day good value food from sandwiches to some interesting dishes, friendly helpful service, Greene King ales, good choice of wines by the glass, good coffee; piped music; games; children welcome at lunchtime, back terrace, hotel part across busy road, handy for Woburn Park. *Recommended by George Atkinson*

☆ WOBURN SP9433 MK17 9HX
Birch
3.5 miles from M1 junction 13; follow Woburn signs via A507 and A4012, right in village then A5130 (Newport Road)

Well run neatly kept dining pub with modern furnishings in extensive linked areas, good nicely presented food from lunchtime sandwiches and light dishes up, interesting wines by the glass, well kept Adnams and Fullers London Pride from contemporary bar counter, friendly accommodating staff, brown leather dining chairs, sofas on dark hardwood flooring, modern prints on deep red or cream walls, a continental-feel back conservatory, daily papers; unobtrusive piped music; children welcome, tables out on sheltered deck, closed Sun evening. *Recommended by Eithne Dandy, Michael Sargent, John Saville, Michael Butler, George Atkinson, Ian and Rose Lock and others*

WOBURN SP9433   MK17 9PX
Inn at Woburn
George Street

Attractive Georgian hotel with sofas and high-backed leather seats in beamed bar, Wells
& Youngs Bombardier and Eagle, good service, up-to-date all-day bar food and good
reasonably priced set lunches, good choice of wines by the glass; 50 bedrooms.
Recommended by Michael Dandy

WOOTTON TL0045   MK43 9HP
Chequers
Hall End Road

Pretty black-beamed 15th-c pub, cosy and well kept, with open fire and woodburner in
inglenooks, enjoyable home-made food (not Sun evening) including good value set menu
Mon-Thurs, Wells & Youngs Eagle IPA and changing guests, friendly efficient staff,
restaurant; attractive hamlet, open all day Fri-Sun. *Recommended by Joanne Douglas,
Gwynneth Poole*

ALSO WORTH A VISIT IN CAMBRIDGESHIRE

Besides the region's top pubs, we recommend the following. Do tell us
what you think of them: **feedback@goodguides.com**

ABINGTON PIGOTTS TL3044   SG8 0SD
Pig & Abbot
High Street

Spotless Queen Anne local with two small traditional bars and restaurant, good choice of
enjoyable well priced food, friendly attentive staff, well kept Adnams, Fullers London
Pride and guests, log fires, quiz night second Weds of month; back terrace, pretty village
with good walks, open all day weekends. *Recommended by David Billings, Lucien Perring,
Steve Nye, David Harris*

ARRINGTON TL3250   SG8 0AH
☆ # Hardwicke Arms
Ermine Way (A1198)

Handsome 18th-c coaching inn with 13th-c origins and 1792 work by Sir John Soane,
enjoyable food from sandwiches and pub favourites up including bargain weekday lunch
and Sun carvery, Greene King IPA and two or three interesting guests, good friendly
service, dark-panelled dining room, huge central fireplace, daily papers; piped music;
12 bedrooms, handy for Wimpole Hall, open all day. *Recommended by Michael Dandy,
Margaret Haworth*

BABRAHAM TL5150   CB22 3AG
George
High Street; just off A1307

Beamed and timbered dining pub under newish management, good well presented food
from sandwiches and pub favourites to lots of fresh fish, Greene King ales and a guest,
bar area with comfortable seating, refurbished dining room, efficient service; children
welcome, tables in garden with heated terrace, nice setting on quiet road, open all day
Fri-Sun. *Recommended by Jeremy King, Jeremy Hebblethwaite*

BARNACK TF0704   PE9 3ET
Millstone
Off B1443 SE of Stamford; Millstone Lane

Timbered bar in stone-built pub with clean contemporary feel, open fires, cosy corner, well kept Adnams, Greene King Old Speckled Hen and Everards Tiger, several well priced wines by the glass, good home-made food (not Sun evening, Mon, Tues), friendly service; piped music; children welcome, sheltered courtyard, pretty village near Burghley House. *Recommended by Susan and Nigel Brookes, Sarah Manley*

BARRINGTON TL3849   CB22 7RZ
Royal Oak
Turn off A10 about 3.7 miles SW of M11 junction 11, in Foxton; West Green

Rambling thatched Tudor pub with tables out overlooking a classic village green, heavy low beams and timbers, mixed furnishings, beers from Adnams, Potton and Wells & Youngs, Aspall's cider, enjoyable if not particularly cheap food, good friendly service, airy dining conservatory; piped music; children welcome. *Recommended by Michael Dandy, DC, Chris Smith, Kay and Alistair Butler*

BOURN TL3256   CB23 2SQ
Willow Tree
High Street

Modernised dining pub with fresh contemporary feel, good choice of imaginative well presented food, friendly efficient staff, well kept Woodfordes, log fires, some live jazz and acoustic music; heated decked terrace under retractable cover, purple deckchairs in garden with fruit trees and big weeping willow, summer garden menu. *Recommended by John Saville*

BOXWORTH TL3464   CB3 8LY
Golden Ball
High Street

Attractive partly thatched building under newish management, comfortable open-plan contemporary bar with scrubbed-pine tables, three-part restaurant in original core, friendly helpful staff, enjoyable food from baguettes up, well kept Wells & Youngs ales; children welcome, nice garden and heated terrace, pastures behind, 11 quiet bedrooms in adjacent block, open all day. *Recommended by Simon Watkins, R Anderson*

BRANDON CREEK TL6091   PE38 0PP
Ship
A10 Ely—Downham Market

Lovely spot on Norfolk border at confluence of Great and Little Ouse, plenty of tables out by the moorings; welcoming helpful staff, good choice of enjoyable pub food including specials, ales such as Adnams, St Austell, Shepherd Neame Spitfire and seasonal beers, spacious tastefully modernised bar with massive stone masonry in sunken former forge area, big log fire one end, woodburner the other, interesting old photographs and prints, evening restaurant; bedrooms. *Recommended by Marion and Bill Cross*

BUCKDEN TL1967   PE19 5XA
George
High Street

Handsome and stylish Georgian-faced hotel with bustling, informal bar, fine fan beamwork, leather and chrome chairs, log fire, Adnams Best and a changing guest from chrome-topped counter, lots of wines including champagne by the glass, good choice of teas and coffees, friendly well trained staff, good modern food in popular brasserie with smart cream dining chairs around carefully polished tables; piped music; children and dogs welcome, tables under large parasols on pretty sheltered terrace with box hedging, charming bedrooms, open all day. *Recommended by Ryta Lyndley, Michael Dandy, Michael Sargent and others*

BUCKDEN TL1967
☆ Lion
High Street

PE19 5XA

Partly 15th-c coaching inn, black beams and big inglenook log fire in airy and civilised bow-windowed entrance bar with plush bucket seats, wing armchairs and sofas, good food from lunchtime sandwiches up, fine choice of wines, Adnams Bitter and a guest, prompt friendly staff, no music or machines, panelled back restaurant beyond latticed window partition; children welcome, newly done back courtyard, bedrooms. *Recommended by Lois Dyer, Gerry and Rosemary Dobson, Michael Dandy*

CAMBRIDGE TL4558
Burleigh Arms
Newmarket Road

CB5 8EG

Two bars, enjoyable reasonably priced food, prompt service, good wines by the glass. *Recommended by Ralph Holland*

CAMBRIDGE TL4658
☆ Cambridge Blue
85 Gwydir Street

CB1 2LG

Smashing little backstreet local, knowledgeable landlord and a dozen interesting ales (some tapped from the cask – festival Feb and Jun), bottled beers, traditional bar food, small, attractive conservatory and two simply decorated peaceful rooms with lots of breweriana, bare-boards-style furnishings, board games; can get busy weekends; children and dogs welcome, seats in surprisingly rural-feeling back garden, open all day. *Recommended by Geoff Reynolds, Jerry Brown, the Didler, Lawrence R Cotter, Ralph Holland, John Saville and others*

CAMBRIDGE TL4459
Castle
Castle Street

CB3 0AJ

Full Adnams beer range and several interesting guests in big airy bare-boards bar, several pleasantly simple rooms, wide range of good value quick pubby food from sandwiches up, quick friendly staff, peaceful upstairs (downstairs can be louder, with piped music – live jazz Sun night); picnic-sets in good walled back courtyard. *Recommended by the Didler, Ralph Holland, R Anderson, Pete Coxon*

CAMBRIDGE TL4658
Champion of the Thames
King Street

CB1 1LN

Small traditional two-room local with welcoming knowledgeable landlord, well kept Greene King and guests, unspoilt interior with low ceilings, lots of woodwork, padded seating and coal fires. *Recommended by Simon and Amanda Southwell*

CAMBRIDGE TL4658
Clarendon Arms
Clarendon Street

CB1 1JX

Partly flagstoned backstreet local under newish landlord, L-shaped bar with interesting wall hangings, Greene King and guest ales, traditional reasonably priced food, carpeted dining area, books and daily papers, darts; piped music, sports TV, Thurs quiz; children and dogs welcome, small back terrace, one bedroom, open all day. *Recommended by P and D Carpenter*

CAMBRIDGE TL4657
Devonshire Arms
Devonshire Road

CB1 2BH

Popular light and airy Milton-tied pub with two linked bare-boards bars, their ales plus guests, local Cassels cider, good choice of wines by the glass, a dozen malts, enjoyable food from sandwiches and snacks up, cheerful chatty staff, architectural prints and steam engine pictures; disabled access. *Recommended by MP, Chris and Angela Buckell, Phil Randall*

CAMBRIDGE TL4458   CB2 3QN
☆ # Eagle
Bene't Street

Go for the original architectural features (once the city's most important coaching inn); rambling rooms with two medieval mullioned windows and remains of two possibly medieval wall paintings, two fireplaces dating to around 1600, lovely worn wooden floors and plenty of pine panelling, dark red ceiling left unpainted since World War II to preserve signatures of British and American airmen worked in with Zippo lighters, candle smoke and lipstick, Greene King and two guests; children welcome, heavy wooden seats in attractive cobbled and galleried courtyard, open all day and can get very busy. *Recommended by David and Sue Atkinson, Simon Watkins, David and Gill Carrington, the Didler, Michael Dandy, Chris and Angela Buckell and others*

CAMBRIDGE TL4457   CB3 9EX
Granta
Newnham Terrace

Early 19th-c pub with balcony and heated terrace taking full advantage of view over mill-pond, ducks and weeping-willow meadow, inexpensive pub food from sandwiches up, Greene King ales and a guest, helpful attentive service, nice lively atmosphere; children welcome, punt hire. *Recommended by John Wooll, Frank Dowsland*

CAMBRIDGE TL4659   CB4 1NZ
Green Dragon
Water Street, Chesterton

Attractive late medieval beamed and timber-framed building with comfortable linked areas and huge inglenook fireplace, Greene King and changing guests, usual food; dogs welcome, waterside green. *Recommended by Steve Turner*

CAMBRIDGE TL4657   CB1 2NU
☆ # Kingston Arms
Kingston Street

Well kept interesting changing ales from a dozen or so handpumps, good fresh lunchtime food including bargains, companionably big plain tables and basic seating, thriving chatty largely studenty atmosphere, good choice of wines by the glass, friendly service, no music or children inside, two internet points; small pretty backyard, torch-lit, heated and partly covered, open all day Fri-Sun. *Recommended by David Miles-Dinham, Jerry Brown, Ralph Holland*

CAMBRIDGE TL4557   CB1 2EA
Live & Let Live
Mawson Road

Popular backstreet alehouse, friendly and relaxed, with well kept Everards Tiger, Nethergate Umbel Magna and six changing guests tapped from the cask, lots of bottled belgian beers, local ciders, good value bar food, heavily timbered brickwork rooms with sturdy varnished pine tables on bare boards, country bric-a-brac and some steam railway and brewery memorabilia, gas lighting (not always lit), cribbage and dominoes; children and dogs welcome, disabled access. *Recommended by R T and J C Moggridge, Ralph Holland, Revd R P Tickle*

Post Office address codings confusingly give the impression that some pubs are in Cambridgeshire, when they're really in Bedfordshire, Lincolnshire, Norfolk or Northamptonshire (which is where we list them).

CAMBRIDGE TL4458   CB2 1UF
Mitre
Bridge Street, opposite St John's College

Welcoming M&B pub close to the river, rambling bar on several levels with soft lighting and old-fashioned tavern décor, bargain food all day including speciality fish and chips, good friendly service, several well kept mainly mainstream ales, farm cider, well priced wines by the glass, log-effect fire; piped music can be intrusive; disabled access.
Recommended by Michael Dandy, D W Stokes, Chris and Angela Buckell

CAMBRIDGE TL4559   CB4 1HB
Old Spring
Ferry Path; car park on Chesterton Road

Extended Victorian pub, roomy and airy, with smartly old-fashioned scrubbed-wood décor, bare boards, lots of old pictures, enjoyable well priced home-made food including enterprising dishes and Sun roasts, efficient welcoming service, well kept Greene King IPA, Abbot and three guests, good coffee and choice of wines by the glass, two log fires, long back conservatory; piped music, no under-21s evenings, dogs outside only; disabled facilities, large heated well planted terrace, open all day. *Recommended by P and D Carpenter, Andrew Watson, J Cameron, Raith Overhill*

CAMBRIDGE TL4459   CB3 0AF
Pickerel
Magdalene Street

Nicely old-fashioned multi-roomed coaching inn, popular with locals and students (can get crowded in evenings), bars front and back, low beams and some dark panelling, well kept Oakham, Theakstons and Woodfordes, good choice of wines by the glass, good value food till 8pm, helpful staff; wheelchair access with help, heated courtyard. *Recommended by Chris and Angela Buckell*

CAMBRIDGE TL4459   CB3 0AE
Punter
Pound Hill

Attractive dining pub (former coaching house) with good interesting food from varied menu including bargain lunch offers, prompt friendly service, decent wines by the glass, Adnams and Wells & Youngs Bombardier, continental lagers, Addlestone's cider, leather sofas, log fire, several areas including an adjoining barn; children and dogs welcome, sunny courtyard. *Recommended by John Wooll, Colin Woodward*

CASTOR TL1298   PE5 7AL
Prince of Wales Feathers
Off A47

Friendly stone-built local with well kept local Castor, Woodfordes and interesting guests, farm cider and perry, landlady doing good value food (not weekend evenings) including Sun roasts, side dining area; Sky TV, games machines, pool (free Thurs), Sat live music, Sun quiz; children and dogs welcome (they have a friendly setter), attractive front terrace, back one with shelters, open all day, till late weekends. *Recommended by Ian and Helen Stafford, Phil and Jane Hodson*

CLAYHITHE TL5064   CB5 9HZ
☆ Bridge Hotel
Clayhithe Road

Popular Chef & Brewer with good choice of enjoyable reasonably priced food, plenty of tables inside and out, friendly chatty staff, small bar area, well kept ales, beams and timbers; picturesque spot by River Cam with pretty waterside garden, moorings.
Recommended by M and GR, Phil and Jane Hodson

COTON TL4158 CB23 7PL

Plough

Just off M11 junction 13; High Street

Most come here for the popular well presented food from tapas to full meals, prompt helpful service, Greene King IPA, Woodfordes Wherry and a guest, airy clean-cut contemporary décor with pale wood, pastel colours, sofas and log fires; no dogs inside; children welcome, sizeable garden, open all day. *Recommended by John Saville, P and D Carpenter*

CROYDON TL3149 SG8 0DN

☆ Queen Adelaide

Off A1198 or B1042; High Street

Spreading open-plan carpeted local with wide range of enjoyable food including Mon-Weds OAP lunches, friendly prompt service, ales such as Greene King and Potton, several wines by the glass, lots of spirits, big low-beamed main area with standing timbers dividing off part with sofas, banquettes and stools, games area with pool, conservatory extension, daily papers; piped music (even in gents' – a shrine to Marilyn Monroe), TV, machines; heated terrace with smokers' shelter, lawn with play area, bedrooms, open all day Fri-Sun. *Recommended by Simon Watkins, Michael Dandy, David Harris, P and D Carpenter and others*

DUXFORD TL4746 CB2 4PP

☆ John Barleycorn

Handy for M11 junction 10; right at first roundabout, then left at main village junction

Charming thatched village pub with character low-beamed log-fire bar, old floor tiles, eclectic mix of seating and bric-a-brac, hops, lots of pictures on blue or pale yellow walls, welcoming landlord and staff, good popular food, Greene King, Hook Norton and a changing guest, also a beer named after the pub, large wine list; piped music; children welcome, blue-painted picnic-sets on pretty front terrace and in back garden, comfortable bedrooms in converted barn, good breakfast, open all day. *Recommended by Caroline and Michael Abbey, Mr and Mrs T B Staples, John Pritchard, Mrs Margo Finlay, Jörg Kasprowski, Dave Braisted*

ELSWORTH TL3163 CB3 8JQ

☆ George & Dragon

Off A14 NW of Cambridge, via Boxworth, or off A428

Busy brick-built dining pub with neatly kept fishy-themed panelled main bar, slightly elevated dining area, woodburner, steps down to garden room overlooking attractive terraces, more formal restaurant, enjoyable popular food including good value weekday set menu, Greene King ales and a guest, friendly polite staff; children welcome, dogs in bar, attractive village. *Recommended by Michael and Jenny Back, Peter Martin, Simon Watkins and others*

ELSWORTH TL3163 CB23 4JS

Poacher

Brockley Road

Welcoming 17th-c thatched and beamed local under newish management, Shepherd Neame Spitfire, Woodfordes Wherry and Wychwood Hobgoblin, good value fresh food; children and dogs welcome, tables in back garden, good walks, open all day. *Recommended by Dennis and Doreen Haward*

ELTISLEY TL2759 PE19 6TG

Eltisley

Signed off A428; The Green

Attractive dining areas including stylish barn room, flagstoned bar with beams, timbering, some zinc-topped cast-iron tables and big log fire, good carefully sourced home-made food, friendly service, Wells & Youngs ales and guests like Hop Back Summer Lightning, good choice of wines by the glass; piped music and live jazz (first Sun of month); children welcome, dogs in bar, nice garden behind, six good value bedrooms, closed Sun evening, Mon. *Recommended by Michael Dandy, Michael Sargent, Eithne Dandy, D C Poulton*

ELTON TL0893 PE8 6RU
☆ Black Horse
Overend; B671 off A605 W of Peterborough and A1(M)

Newish licensee and redecoration for this handsome honey-stone dining pub, beams and log fires, some ornaments and bric-a-brac including old-fashioned telephone on one wall, parquet-floored dining areas at each end of bar, stripped- stone back lounge with interesting fireplace, separate restaurant, food has been well liked, several real ales; children and dogs welcome, terrace and garden with views across to Elton Hall park and village church, open all day. *Recommended by Gordon and Margaret Ormondroyd, Clive Flynn*

ELY TL5479 CB7 4BN
☆ Cutter
Annesdale, off Station Road (or walk S along Riverside Walk from Maltings)

Beautifully placed contemporary riverside pub with carpeted dining bar and smart restaurant, enjoyable promptly served food from sandwiches up including good value Sun roasts, well kept Shepherd Neame and Woodfordes, nice wines by the glass, decent coffee, good views from window seats and front terrace. *Recommended by Mr and Mrs T B Staples, John Saville, Michael Butler, Ryta Lyndley, D Goodger and others*

ELY TL5380 CB6 3AY
West End House
West End, off Cambridge Road

Popular old corner local with beams, some stripped brickwork and open fires, mixed furniture including leather armchairs, pews and plush banquettes, assorted pictures and pub bric-a-brac, well kept Adnams, Shepherd Neame and two guests, lunchtime sandwiches and light snacks (no food evenings or Sun); no dogs; children welcome, courtyard garden with pergola, open all day Fri, Sat. *Recommended by Andy Wilkinson*

FEN DRAYTON TL3468 CB4 5SJ
☆ Three Tuns
Off A14 NW of Cambridge at Fenstanton; High Street

Friendly well preserved thatched pub in charming village, heavy Tudor beams and timbers, inglenook fireplaces, tiled-floor bar, comfortable settles and other seats, well laid out dining end (children welcome), Greene King ales, enjoyable good value standard food (not Sun evening) from lunchtime sandwiches to steaks, sensibly placed darts; piped music; tables on covered terrace and neat back lawn, good play area, open all day. *Recommended by Celia Jones, Barry and Anne, Chris Smith*

FOWLMERE TL4245 SG8 7SR
☆ Chequers
B1368

Civilised 16th-c coaching inn with two comfortable downstairs rooms, long cushioned wall seats, dining chairs around dark tables, open log fire, good imaginative modern food, real ales and several wines by the glass, smart upstairs beamed and timbered dining room with interesting moulded plasterwork above one fireplace, spacious conservatory (children here only); terrace and garden with lots of tables under green parasols. *Recommended by Roy Hoing, M R D Foot*

GODMANCHESTER TL2470 PE29 2HZ
Exhibition
London Road

Big flagstones and traditional furnishings, enjoyable well priced food, well kept Greene King IPA, decent choice of wines by the glass; picnic-sets on back lawn (a couple in front, too), open all day. *Recommended by John Saville*

☆ **Blue Ball**

GRANTCHESTER TL4355   CB3 9NQ

Broadway

Particularly well kept Adnams and a guest ale in character bare-boards village local, said to be the area's oldest, proper hands-on landlord, good log fire, Aspall's cider, cards and traditional games including shut the box and ring the bull, lots of books; dogs welcome, tables on small terrace with lovely views to Grantchester meadows, nice village.
Recommended by Simon Watkins, Jerry Brown, Stuart Gideon, Mrs Catherine Simmonds

GRANTCHESTER TL4355   CB3 9NF
Red Lion
High Street

Comfortable and spacious thatched pub, wide choice of enjoyable food including plenty of fish dishes and bargain weekday specials, children's menu, good friendly service, Greene King ales, four modernised open areas with beams, timbers and panelling; piped music; sheltered terrace, good-sized lawn, play area, easy walk to river, open all day. *Recommended by Rod Weston*

GREAT CHISHILL TL4239   SG8 8SR
☆ **Pheasant**
Follow Heydon signpost from B1039 in village

Good freshly made food using local produce in popular split-level flagstoned pub with beams, open fires, timbering and some elaborately carved though modern seats and settles, welcoming friendly staff, ales such as Adnams, Courage and Theakstons, good choice of wines by the glass, small dining room (best to book), darts, cribbage, dominoes; children welcome, charming secluded back garden with small play area. *Recommended by Nick Wooder, Oliver Thain, Paul Elkington, R Anderson*

HARDWICK TL3758   CB23 7QU
Blue Lion
Signed off A428 (was A45) W of Cambridge; Main Street

Attractive old pub smartened up under newish licensees, beams and timbers, leather armchairs by copper-canopied inglenook, good food from landlord/chef in bar and extended dining area with conservatory, friendly young uniformed staff, Greene King and guest ales; pretty roadside front garden, handy for Wimpole Way walkers, open all day.
Recommended by David and Gill Carrington, Phil and Jane Hodson

HARSTON TL4251   CB22 7NH
Queens Head
Royston Road (A10, near M11 junction 11)

Greene King pub under newish management, enjoyable well priced pubby food including OAP lunch deals, good friendly service, charity quiz (second Sat of month); children welcome, garden tables, open all day Fri and Sun, closed Sun evening. *Recommended by Sidney and Jean Gould*

HEMINGFORD ABBOTS TL2870   PE28 9AH
Axe & Compass
High Street

Appealing 15th-c two-bar thatched and beamed pub with flagstones and inglenook, friendly helpful staff, ales such as Adnams, Greene King IPA and Timothy Taylors Landlord, plenty of wines by the glass, good value above-average traditional food, contemporary extension dining areas; piped and live music, Tues quiz, TV, pool, darts; children and dogs welcome, disabled facilities, café-style furniture in garden with play equipment, nearby walks, quiet pretty village, one bedroom, open all day. *Recommended by Lyn Thorne*

HEYDON TL4339   SG8 8PW
☆ **King William IV**
Off A505 W of M11 junction 10

Rambling rooms with fascinating rustic jumble (ploughshares, yokes, iron tools, cowbells and so forth) and china in nooks and crannies, log fire, Fullers, Greene King and Timothy Taylors Landlord, good varied choice of food, helpful staff; piped music; children welcome, dogs in bar area, teak furniture on heated terrace and in pretty garden, open all day weekends. *Recommended by Anthony Barnes, Mrs Margo Finlay, Jörg Kasprowski*

HISTON TL4363   CB4 9JD
☆ **Red Lion**
High Street, off Station Road: 3.7 miles from M11 junction 1; signposted off A14 E via B1049

A shrine to real ale; ceiling joists in L-shaped main bar packed with hundreds of beer mats and pump clips among hop bines and whisky-water jugs, fine collection of old brewery advertisements and rack of real ale campaign literature, impressive choice of beers such as Everards, Grainstore, Mighty Oak, Oakham, Stonehenge, Theakstons and Tring, Pickled Pig farm cider and Weston's perry, splendid range of bottled beers too, spring and early autumn festivals, limited lunchtime food (not on Sun), cheerful efficient service, comfortable brocaded wall seats, matching mate's chairs and pubby tables, log fires, nice antique one-arm bandit, bar on left with darts, TV and huge collection of beer bottles; no credit cards; well behaved children allowed in one part only, picnic-sets in neat garden, play area, limited parking, open all day. *Recommended by Jerry Brown, Phil and Jane Hodson, Stuart Gideon, Mrs Catherine Simmonds, Kevin McPheat*

HOLYWELL TL3370   PE27 4TG
Old Ferry Boat
Signed off A1123

Welcoming partly thatched Greene King pub in lovely peaceful setting, low beams, open fires and interesting side areas, window seats overlooking the Great Ouse, well kept beer, good coffee, but mixed reports on food and they may ask for a credit card if you run a tab; quiet piped music, machines; children welcome, plenty of tables and cocktail parasols on front terrace and riverside lawn, moorings, seven good bedrooms, open all day weekends. *Recommended by David and Sue Atkinson*

HORSEHEATH TL6147   CB21 4QF
Old Red Lion
Linton Road

Neatly kept Greene King pub, good value food, efficient staff; 12 bedroom cabins. *Recommended by Mr and Mrs T B Staples, Simon Watkins*

HUNTINGDON TL2371   PE29 3AB
☆ **George**
George Street

Relaxed, friendly and comfortable hotel lounge bar, generous reasonably priced sandwiches and bar and brasserie meals, Greene King IPA and Abbot, several wines by the glass, good coffee (or tea and pastries); piped music; magnificent galleried central courtyard, comfortable bedrooms. *Recommended by Michael Dandy*

KEYSTON TL0475   PE28 0RE
☆ **Pheasant**
Just off A14 SE of Thrapston; village loop road, off B663

Attractive, long, low, thatched dining pub, spacious oak-beamed bar with civilised atmosphere, open fires, country paintings on pale walls, three distinct dining areas, well kept ales such as Digfield, Grainstore and Potbelly, 17 wines by the glass including champagne from extensive list, good restaurant-style food (not Sun evening, best to book weekends), helpful competent service, weekend bakery; children and dogs welcome, seats out at front and on back terrace, open all day. *Recommended by David Gunn, Ryta Lyndley, Mike Penny, Sarah Garelick, George Atkinson*

LITTLE SHELFORD TL4551
CB2 5ES
Navigator
2.5 miles from M11 junction 11: A10 towards Royston, then left at Hauxton, The Shelfords signpost

Attractive 16th-c village local with beams, pine panelling, pews and a hot coal fire, good authentic thai food (not Sat lunchtime or Sun evening, offers Mon-Weds), Greene King and a guest ale, Aspall's cider, decent wines, quick obliging service; children welcome, some picnic-sets outside. *Recommended by Jerry Brown, Nathan Ward*

LITTLE WILBRAHAM TL5458
CB1 5JY
☆ # Hole in the Wall
High Street; A1303 Newmarket Road to Stow cum Quy off A14, then left at The Wilbrahams signpost, then right at Little Wilbraham signpost

Charming tucked-away dining pub with new licensees starting as we went to press – reports please; right-hand bar with log fire in big fireplace, 15th-c beams and timbers, snug little window seats and other mixed seating around scrubbed kitchen tables, similar middle room with fire in open range, plusher main dining room (yet another fire), has served Old Cannon, Woodfordes and a guest ale; seats on verandah and in neat side garden, quiet hamlet with interesting walk to nearby unspoilt Little Wilbraham Fen, has closed Sun evening, Mon. *Recommended by anon*

MADINGLEY TL3960
CB23 8AB
☆ # Three Horseshoes
High Street; off A1303 W of Cambridge

Civilised thatched restauranty pub and most customers come here for the imaginative if not cheap italian food; there is, though, a small pleasantly relaxed bar, with simple wooden furniture on bare boards and open fire (can be a bit of a crush at peak times), Adnams and Jennings Cumberland, outstanding wine list with 23 by the glass, efficient friendly service, pretty dining conservatory; children welcome, picnic-sets under parasols in sunny garden. *Recommended by Peter and Eleanor Kenyon, Tony Middis, Tom and Ruth Rees, Gordon and Margaret Ormondroyd, Mike and Hilary Doupe, Ian Willis*

MILTON TL4762
CB24 6AJ
White Horse
High Street

Large white-painted old brick pub, reasonably priced pubby food, changing real ales, huge collection of beer mats. *Recommended by Phil and Jane Hodson*

NEWTON TL4349
CB2 5PG
☆ # Queens Head
2.5 miles from M11 junction 11; A10 towards Royston, then left on to B1368

Lovely traditional unchanging pub run by same welcoming family for many years, lots of loyal customers, peaceful bow-windowed main bar with crooked beams in low ceiling, bare wooden benches and seats built into cream walls, curved high-backed settle, paintings, big log fire, Adnams ales tapped from the cask, farm cider, hearty simple food, small carpeted saloon, pubby games including table skittles, shove-ha'penny and nine men's morris; no credit cards; children on best behaviour allowed in games room only, dogs welcome, seats out in front by vine trellis. *Recommended by Simon Watkins, Jerry Brown, John Walker, Prof James Stevens Curl and others*

OFFORD D'ARCY TL2166
PE19 5RH
Horseshoes
High Street

Extended former 17th-c farmhouse, emphasis on enjoyable food from sandwiches and pub favourites to local game, popular Sun lunch (must book), changing real ales, two bars and restaurant, beams and log fires; children welcome, garden with play area, open all day Sun. *Recommended by Phil and Jane Hodson*

OVER TL3769   CB24 5PS
Exhibition
2 King Street

Friendly local with oak-beamed bar and two eating areas, generous bar food from good baguettes up. *Recommended by David and Sharon Collison*

PETERBOROUGH TL1899   PE1 2AA
 ## Brewery Tap
Opposite Queensgate car park

Striking conversion of old labour exchange with own-brewed Oakham beers and up to eight guests, well liked good value thai food, easy-going relaxed feel in open-plan contemporary interior with expanse of light wood and stone floors (vast glass wall divides bar and brewery), blue-painted iron pillars supporting steel-corded mezzanine, stylish lighting, long sculpted light wood counter backed by impressive display of bottles, comfortable downstairs area, regular live bands and comedy nights; piped music, big-screen sports TV, games machines, gets packed evenings; children welcome during food times only, dogs allowed in bar, same owners as Charters (see below), open all day. *Recommended by Ian and Helen Stafford, the Didler, David Warren, Mike and Sue Loseby, P Dawn*

PETERBOROUGH TL1998   PE1 1FP
 ## Charters
Town Bridge, S side

Remarkable conversion of dutch grain barge with impressive range of local ales and good value pan-asian food, sizeable timbered bar on lower deck, restaurant above, lots of wooden tables and pews, regular beer festivals, live bands (some Fri and Sat after 11pm); piped music, games machines; children welcome, dogs in bar, huge riverside garden (gets packed in fine weather), open all day. *Recommended by R T and J C Moggridge, Barry Collett, the Didler, Steve Nye, P Dawn, Andy and Jill Kassube*

PETERBOROUGH TL1898   PE1 1LZ
Drapers Arms
Cowgate

Roomy relaxed open-plan Wetherspoons in sympathetically converted draper's, fine ale range, bargain food all day; can get very busy Fri, Sat evenings; children welcome, open all day from 9am. *Recommended by JPR, Ian and Helen Stafford*

PETERBOROUGH TL1897   PE2 9PA
Palmerston Arms
Oundle Road

Open-plan stone pub, partly 17th-c, with Batemans and up to nine changing guests poured from tap room behind bar, bottled continental beers, real ciders and over 40 malt whiskies, welcoming staff, large jug collection, no food but can bring your own – plates and cutlery provided; well behaved children and dogs welcome, picnic-sets in backyard with mosaic of licensees and regulars, open all day Sat, from 3pm other days – new licensees taking over as we went to press. *Recommended by the Didler, Theocsbrian*

ST NEOTS TL1859   PE19 2TA
☆ ## Chequers
St Mary's Street (B1043 S of centre)

Friendly 16th-c village pub with small carpeted beamed bar, appealing mix of furniture including an unusual rocking chair, log fire in big inglenook, changing real ales, good choice of food from baguettes up including vegetarian options, attractive back restaurant with rugs on brick floor; piped music; children allowed in restaurant, tables on terrace and in sheltered garden behind, closed Sun evening, Mon. *Recommended by John Watson*

ST NEOTS TL1761   PE19 7DB
Eaton Oak
A1

Now under same ownership as the George & Dragon at Elsworth and Rose at Stapleford, wide choice of enjoyable food including fresh fish and good value set menus, Wells & Youngs ales, good service, spacious dining area, conservatory; tables outside under parasols, nine bedrooms, open all day (breakfast for non-residents). *Recommended by Michael and Jenny Back*

STAPLEFORD TL4651   CB22 5DG
☆ Rose
London Road

Comfortable sister pub to George & Dragon at Elsworth, and Eaton Oak, St Neots (see above), with an emphasis on dining and can get very busy, good choice of well cooked reasonably priced food (10 per cent discount for NHS members), pleasant uniformed staff, well kept Greene King IPA, St Austell Tribute and Woodfordes Wherry, small low-ceilinged lounge with inglenook woodburner, roomy dining area; faint piped music; picnic-sets on back grass. *Recommended by Gordon and Margaret Ormondroyd, Phil and Jane Hodson*

STILTON TL1689   PE7 3RP
Stilton Cheese
Signed off A1; North Street

Former coaching inn with wide range of good food from sandwiches up including lots of fish, a couple of real ales, decent wines, welcoming staff, old interior with roaring log fire in unpretentious central bar, good tables in two rooms off, separate two-room restaurant; no dogs; tables out in back garden with sheltered decking, bedrooms. *Recommended by Gordon and Margaret Ormondroyd*

STOW CUM QUY TL5260   CB25 9AB
White Swan
Off A14 E of Cambridge, via B1102

Cosy beamed village local, several well kept ales such as Adnams and Woodfordes Wherry, enjoyable reasonably priced pubby food from snacks up, various bric-a-brac, big fireplace; children allowed in dining room, terrace picnic-sets, handy for Anglesey Abbey (NT), closed Mon. *Recommended by Phil and Jane Hodson*

SUTTON GAULT TL4279   CB6 2BD
☆ Anchor
Bury Lane, off High Street (B1381)

Most emphasis is on interesting food at this friendly tucked-away dining inn, but also well kept City of Cambridge and Old Cannon ales and good wines by the glass including champagne, four heavily timbered rooms with antique settles and old pine tables, good lithographs and big prints, two log fires (not always lit); children welcome, seats outside and you can walk along the high embankment – good bird-watching, bedrooms. *Recommended by M and GR, David and Sharon Collison, Michael Butler, R T and J C Moggridge, Graeme Manson and others*

UFFORD TF0904   PE9 3BH
☆ White Hart
Main Street; S on to Ufford Road off B1443 at Bainton, then right

17th-c village pub with good food all day using local organic supplies including own meat and free-range eggs, good Ufford ales (brewed here) and guests, nice wines by the glass and good coffee, friendly staff, comfortable seating, log fire and railway/farming memorabilia in busy stripped-stone and flagstoned bar, rustic back dining area, orangery with modern tables and chairs; children welcome, nice big garden with terrace and play area, bedroom block, open all day. *Recommended by Max Williams, Phil and Jane Hodson, Jeff and Wendy Williams, Bruce and Sharon Eden*

WANSFORD TL0799   PE8 6JB
Paper Mills
London Road

Attractively refurbished old pub doing well under present licensees, buzzy atmosphere and good friendly service, ales such as Adnams, Everards, Greene King and Marstons, popular modestly priced food, flagstoned bar with fireplaces either side, conservatory; dogs welcome, tables in well tended garden. *Recommended by Mr and Mrs D Gipson, Clive Flynn, Maurice and Janet Thorpe*

WARESLEY TL2454   SG19 3BS
Duncombe Arms
Eltisley Road (B1040, 5 miles S of A428)

Comfortable welcoming old pub, long main bar with fire at one end, good value wholesome food cooked to order, well kept Greene King ales, friendly service, back room and restaurant; occasional live music; picnic-sets in small shrub-sheltered garden. *Recommended by D C Poulton, Michael Dandy*

WHITTLESFORD TL4648   CB2 4NZ
Bees in the Wall
North Road; handy for M11 junction 10

Comfortably worn-in split-level timbered lounge with flowers on polished tables and country prints, small tiled public bar with old wall settles, darts, decent good value food (not Sun or Mon evenings) from sandwiches up including good fish and chips, well kept Fullers London Pride, Timothy Taylors Landlord and a guest beer, open fires; may be piped classical music, games machine, no dogs; picnic-sets in big paddock-style garden with terrace, bees' nest visible in wall, handy for Duxford air museum, open all day weekends. *Recommended by Noel Young, Ruth Whitehead, David and Gill Carrington, Nigel Dawson, Chris Smith*

WICKEN TL5670   CB7 5XR
Maids Head
High Street

Thatched dining pub with good food (not Sun evening) from bar snacks up, friendly informal atmosphere, up to four local ales, fair-priced house wines, unpretentious bar with pool and darts, restaurant, two open fires, events including quiz night (last Sun of month); children welcome in restaurant, dogs in bar, tables outside, village-green setting, handy for Wicken Fen nature reserve (NT), open all day weekends (till 1am Sat). *Recommended by Rita Scarratt, David Edge, Keith and Margaret Evans*

WISBECH TF4707   PE14 0DD
Elm Tree
Elm Low Road

Newly reopened and refurbished to a high standard; roomy bar and restaurant, enjoyable food from varied affordable menu, Greene King ales, welcoming helpful service; summer barbecues in garden. *Recommended by Mrs Lorna Walsingham, Mr and Mrs P Dorrington*

WOODDITTON TL6558   CB8 9SQ
Three Blackbirds
Signed off B1063 at Cheveley

Sympathetically restored two-bar thatched pub reopened after a long closure, low 17th-c beams, mix of old country furniture on bare boards, pictures and knick-knacks, open fires, some enterprising food together with pub favourites and lunchtime sandwiches, Adnams, Timothy Taylors and changing local guests, restaurant; children welcome, garden, closed Sun evening and Mon (except bank holidays). *Recommended by Rupert Clark*

If we know a pub has an outdoor play area for children, we mention it.

ALSO WORTH A VISIT IN ESSEX

Besides the region's top pubs, we recommend the following. Do tell us
what you think of them: **feedback@goodguides.com**

AYTHORPE RODING TL5915   CM6 1PP
☆ ## Axe & Compasses
B184 S of Dunmow

Nice balance between dining and drinking at this neatly kept roadside pub, exposed
masonry, beams and dark pubby furniture on pale boards or patterned carpet, interesting
well presented food (all day Sun), Nethergate IPA and guests racked behind bar in
temperature-stabilised casks, Weston's ciders, friendly atmosphere; piped music; children
welcome, dogs in bar, stylish tables and chairs in small garden, open all day. *Recommended
by M and GR, George Atkinson, Mrs Lorna Walsingham*

BANNISTER GREEN TL6920   CM6 3ND
Three Horseshoes
Off B1417 near Felsted

Small 15th-c beamed country local under new licensees, good food, Adnams and Fullers
London Pride, compact restaurant; children welcome, tables out on broad village green
(has play area) and in garden with nice views. *Recommended by David and Gill Carrington,
J A Snell*

BELCHAMP ST PAUL TL7942   CO10 7DP
Half Moon
Cole Green

Thatched 16th-c pub overlooking green, well kept Adnams, Earl Soham and Greene King,
enjoyable good value home-made food (not Sun evening, Mon), hospitable staff, snug
beamed lounge, log fire, cheerful locals' bar, restaurant, Aug beer/music festival, small
shop; children welcome, tables out in front and in back garden, closed Mon lunchtime.
Recommended by Jeremy King, Mr and Mrs T B Staples

BRENTWOOD TQ5993   CM14 5ND
Nags Head
A1023, just off M25 junction 28

Popular open-plan dining pub with good food and wine choice, several real ales, Aspall's
cider, prompt friendly service; pleasant garden, open all day. *Recommended by John Saville*

BRIGHTLINGSEA TM0916   CO7 0EH
Rosebud
Hurst Green

Warmly welcoming village pub with good reasonably priced food including local seafood
and game, well kept changing ales; children welcome, good outside seating, nice views.
Recommended by Fiona Pleasant, Don and Carole Wellings

BULMER TYE TL8438   CO10 7EB
☆ ## Bulmer Fox
A131 S of Sudbury

Thriving dining pub with enjoyable fairly priced food, neatly laid tables with forms on
which to write your order (or order at the bar), Adnams and Greene King IPA, help-
yourself water fountain, friendly service from bustling staff, pastel colours and lively
acoustics, bare boards (look out for one or two 'rugs' painted on them), quieter side room
and intimate central snug; sheltered back terrace with arbour, children welcome.
Recommended by John Prescott

CASTLE HEDINGHAM TL7835   CO9 3EJ
Bell
B1058

Beamed and timbered three-bar pub dating from the 15th c, unpretentious and unspoilt (run by same family for over 40 years), with Adnams, Mighty Oak and guests (July beer festival), pubby food including specials; piped and some live music (lunchtime jazz last Sun of month); dogs welcome, children away from public bar, garden, handy for Hedingham Castle, open all day Fri-Sun. *Recommended by Ian Wilson, Peter Meister, Peter Thornton, Eddie Edwards, Charles Gysin, Roderic Martin*

CHAPPEL TL8928   CO6 2DD
Swan
Wakes Colne; off A1124 Colchester—Halstead

Ancient oak-beamed dining pub with restauranty atmosphere but welcoming drinkers, enjoyable food including good value Sun lunch, well kept Adnams and local ales, friendly attentive service, cosy rustic-style refurbishment, soft lighting, inglenook log fire; cobbled courtyard, view of Victorian viaduct from spreading garden by the River Colne, open all day weekends. *Recommended by Colin and Penny Smith*

CHELMSFORD TL7107   CM1 7RG
☆ Alma
Arbour Lane, off B1137

Upscale pub/restaurant with well liked food from lunchtime sandwiches and good value set menu up, friendly service, leather sofas, contemporary artwork and attractive tiling in stylish bar, real ales such as Adnams Broadside and Greene King IPA, good choice of wines by the glass, smart dining area with big open fire; piped music, live music some evenings; children welcome in restaurant, pretty terraces, comfortable smokers' shelter. *Recommended by Mrs Margo Finlay, Jörg Kasprowski, Michael Holdsworth*

CHELMSFORD TL7006   CM2 0AS
Orange Tree
Lower Anchor Street

Bargain lunchtime bar food in spacious local with good cheerful service, well kept Mighty Oak, Sharps Doom Bar and up to half a dozen changing guests (some tapped from the cask), Tues quiz, live music; back terrace. *Recommended by Tony Hobden, Andrew Bosi*

CHELMSFORD TL7006   CM2 0AS
☆ Queens Head
Lower Anchor Street

Lively well run Victorian side-street local with very well kept Crouch Vale ales and interesting guests, summer farm cider, good value wines, friendly staff, winter log fires, bargain lunchtime food from doorstep sandwiches up (not Sun); children welcome, colourful courtyard, open all day. *Recommended by Justin and Emma King, the Didler, Andrew Bosi*

CHRISHALL TL4439   SG8 8RN
Red Cow
High Street; off B1039 Wendens Ambo—Great Chishill

Popular refurbished 14th-c thatched pub with lots of atmosphere, timbers, low beams, wood floors and log fires, one half laid for dining, decent choice of food from simple bar meals up including good value weekday set lunch, well kept beers and interesting wine list; children welcome, nice garden, handy for Icknield Way walkers, open all day weekends, closed Mon. *Recommended by Mrs Margo Finlay, Jörg Kasprowski*

Most pubs with any outside space now have some kind of smokers' shelter. There are regulations about these – for instance, they have to be substantially open to the outside air. The best have heating and lighting and are really quite comfortable.

COGGESHALL TL8224   CM77 8BG
☆ **Compasses**
Pattiswick, signed off A120 W

Attractively reworked as more country restaurant than pub, good choice of enjoyable well presented food using local produce, also cheaper weekday set menu and children's meals, well kept Adnams and Woodfordes Wherry, good wine choice, cheerful attentive staff, neatly comfortable spacious beamed bars, barn restaurant; plenty of lawn and orchard tables, rolling farmland beyond. *Recommended by RS, ES*

COLCHESTER TM9824   CO3 3HA
Hospital Arms
Crouch Street (opposite hospital)

Friendly pub with several small linked areas, wide range of well kept Adnams ales, enjoyable inexpensive food from sandwiches and panini to pies and spicy sausage casserole, quick cheerful service, home of Colchester RFC; games machines. *Recommended by Pat and Tony Martin*

COLNE ENGAINE TL8530   CO6 2HY
Five Bells
Signed off A1124 (was A604) in Earls Colne; Mill Lane

Welcoming and popular traditional village pub, good home-made food (all day weekends) using local produce including some modern bistro-style dishes, well kept changing ales, friendly efficient service, woodburner and old photographs in lounge/dining room, public bar, some live music; attractive front terrace with gentle views, open all day Thurs-Sun. *Recommended by Helen Sherfield, Mrs Margo Finlay, Jörg Kasprowski*

COOPERSALE STREET TL4701   CM16 7QJ
☆ **Theydon Oak**
Off B172 E of Theydon Bois; or follow Hobbs Cross Open Farm brown sign off B1393 at N end of Epping

Attractive old weatherboarded dining pub, very popular especially with older lunchers for ample straightforward food (all day Sun) from sandwiches up including good value specials, Sun roasts and puddings' cabinet, Courage Best, Greene King IPA and John Smiths, friendly prompt service, beams and masses of brass, copper and old brewery mirrors, two woodburners; piped music, no dogs; children welcome, tables on side terrace and in fenced garden with small stream, lots of hanging baskets, separate play area, open all day. *Recommended by LM*

DANBURY TL7704   CM3 4ED
Cricketers Arms
Penny Royal Road

Welcoming beamed country local overlooking common, good value home-made food from baguettes to blackboard specials, well kept Shepherd Neame Master Brew, woodburner; good walks. *Recommended by Tina and David Woods-Taylor*

DEDHAM TM0533   CO7 6DF
☆ **Sun**
High Street (B2109)

Stylish old Tudor coaching inn with good italian food (not cheap but with an emphasis on seasonal produce using local suppliers), impressive wine selection (lots of bin ends, 20 by the glass), Adnams, Crouch Vale and a couple of guests, friendly efficient service, historic panelled interior with high carved beams, handsome furnishings and big log fires in splendid fireplaces, fruit and vegetable shop; piped music, TV; children welcome, dogs in bar, picnic-sets on quiet back lawn with mature trees, characterful panelled bedrooms, good Flatford Mill walk, open all day. *Recommended by Marcus Mann, Tom and Ruth Rees, Simon Cottrell, Hugh Roberts, Trevor Swindells, Patrick Harrington and others*

ELMDON TL4639 CB11 4NH

☆ **Elmdon Dial**

Village signposted off B1039 Royston—Saffron Walden; Heydon Lane

Partly timbered bar with oriental rugs on bare boards, carefully collected furniture including a beautifully carved early 18th-c pew said to come from Norwich Cathedral, framed *Flying* covers (landlord is ex-RAF), bar skittles and board games, smarter brightly up-to-date lounge in cheerful orange and pinks with leather tub chairs, modern tables and a decanter collection on the handsome mantelpiece, Adnams, Mighty Oak and Timothy Taylors Landlord, appealing bar food (not Sun evening) from good baguettes up, charming efficient service, back dining room in modern extension with pitched ceiling; big-screen sports TV; children welcome, dogs in bar, neat terrace with picnic-sets under parasols, more on peaceful lawn with big weeping willow, and chimes from the church clock opposite (its unusual stained-glass sundial gives the pub its name), open all day Sun, closed Mon. *Recommended by Mrs Margo Finlay, Jörg Kasprowski, Martyn Postle*

FINCHINGFIELD TL6832 CM7 4JX

Fox

The Green

Splendidly pargeted old building with spacious beamed bar, exposed brickwork and central fireplace, ales from Adnams, Nethergate and Woodfordes, good choice of wines by the glass, traditional home-made food including Sun roasts, evening takeaway fish and chips, tea and coffee; piped music – live music monthly; children and dogs welcome, picnic-sets in front overlooking the village duck pond, open all day. *Recommended by George Atkinson*

FINGRINGHOE TM0220 CO5 7BG

Whalebone

Off A134 just S of Colchester centre, or B1025

Old pub geared for dining, airy country-chic rooms with cream-painted tables on oak floors, above-average local food (not Sun evening) with some interesting choices (freshly cooked so can be a wait), good sandwiches too, well kept beers, friendly chatty staff, barn function room; piped music; children welcome, charming back garden with peaceful valley view, front terrace, handy for Fingringhoe nature reserve, open all day weekends. *Recommended by Ryta Lyndley, N R White, Stephanie Gray*

FULLER STREET TL7416 CM3 2BB

☆ **Square & Compasses**

Back road Great Leighs—Hatfield Peverel

Small well looked after traditional country pub, welcoming and popular, with wide choice of good fresh food from sandwiches to specials, ales tapped from the cask and several wines by the glass, big log fire in L-shaped beamed bar, attention to detail such as linen napkins; soft piped music; gentle country views from tables outside. *Recommended by Michelle Donnelly, Mrs Margo Finlay, Jörg Kasprowski, David Jackson*

GESTINGTHORPE TL8138 CO9 3AU

Pheasant

Off B1058

Enjoyable seasonal food including local game and home-grown produce, they also smoke their own fish, friendly service, Adnams, a house beer brewed by Mauldons and a guest, good value wines by the glass, neat simple décor, log fires; children welcome, picnic-sets in garden with far-reaching Stour Valley views, five new bedrooms, open all day. *Recommended by anon*

GOLDHANGER TL9008 CM9 8AS

☆ **Chequers**

Church Street; off B1026 E of Heybridge

Six rambling miscellaneously furnished rooms including a spacious lounge bar with dark beams, black panelling and a huge sash window overlooking the church and graveyard, functional games room with bar billiards, traditional dining room, carpets and bare boards, real fires and woodburner, up to nine real ales (beer festivals), extensive choice of popular fairly priced blackboard food (not evenings Sun and bank holiday Mon) including fresh fish on Fri, friendly staff; piped music, TV; children welcome (except in tap room), dogs in bar, picnic sets and grapevine in little courtyard, open all day. *Recommended by David Jackson, Marion and Bill Cross, Evelyn and Derek Walter, N R White*

GREAT CHESTERFORD TL5142   CB10 1PL
Crown & Thistle
1.5 miles from M11 junction 9A; pub signposted off B184, in High Street

Substantial old pub with good fire in 16th-c inglenook, attractive decorative plasterwork and lovely old curved wooden benches, three changing ales such as Adnams, Buntingford and Fullers, mainly pubby food (not Sun evening), friendly helpful service, long handsomely proportioned dining room with striking photographic mural of the village; they may ask to keep a credit card while you eat; children welcome, dogs in bar, picnic-sets in suntrap back courtyard, toddlers' slide on side grass. *Recommended by anon*

GREAT STAMBRIDGE TQ8991   SS4 2AX
Royal Oak
Stambridge Road

Pleasant well cared for country pub, wide choice of good generous food in bar and separate restaurant, Greene King IPA, several wines by the glass, friendly staff; nice views from big garden, nearby walk to river, open all day. *Recommended by Tina and David Woods-Taylor, Rosanna Luke, Matt Curzon, Mrs Margo Finlay, Jörg Kasprowski*

HASTINGWOOD TL4807   CM17 9JX
☆ Rainbow & Dove
0.5 miles from M11 junction 7

Pleasantly traditional 16th-c pub with three low-beamed homely rooms, stripped stone, golfing memorabilia, woodburner, Adnams Broadside and guests, popular reasonably priced pubby food in generous helpings, friendly service; piped music; children welcome, covered picnic-sets on stretch of grass hedged off from car park, closed Sun evening. *Recommended by Grahame and Myra Williams, Jerry Brown, Paul Humphreys, Jeremy King, Ed Hayden*

HEMPSTEAD TL6337   CB10 2PD
Bluebell
B1054 E of Saffron Walden

Comfortable and attractive beamed bar with two rooms off and a restaurant, enjoyable generous food including popular Sun roasts, Adnams, Woodfordes and guests, Aspall's cider, friendly service, log fires, folk music Tues evening, classic car meetings (first Sat of month); children welcome, terrace and garden seating, play area. *Recommended by Mrs Margo Finlay, Jörg Kasprowski*

HENHAM TL5428   CM22 6AN
Cock
Church End

Welcoming old timbered pub striking good balance between community local and dining venue, wide choice of good value home-made food from local suppliers, ales including Adnams and Saffron (brewed in the village), decent wines, good open fires, restaurant with leather-backed chairs on wood floor, sports TV in snug, live music last Sun of month; children welcome, dogs in bar, seats out at front and in tree-shaded garden. *Recommended by Charles Gysin*

LEIGH-ON-SEA TQ8385   SS9 2EP
☆ Crooked Billet
High Street

Homely old pub with waterfront views from big bay windows, packed on busy summer days when service can be frantic but friendly, well kept Adnams, Fullers London Pride and changing guests including seasonal ales, enjoyable basic pub food (some bargain prices), log fires, beams, panelled dado and bare boards, local fishing pictures and bric-a-brac; piped music, winter jazz Fri nights, no under-21s after 6pm; side garden and terrace, seawall seating over road shared with Osborne's good shellfish stall (plastic glasses for outside drinking), pay-and-display parking by flyover, open all day. *Recommended by David Jackson, George Atkinson, LM*

LITTLE BRAXTED TL8413   CM8 3LB

☆ ## Green Man
Kelvedon Road; signed off B1389; OS Sheet 168 map reference 848133

Homely place with cottagey feel, windsor chairs on patterned carpets, mugs hanging from beams and some 200 horsebrasses, open fire in traditional little lounge, tiled public bar with darts and cribbage, Greene King ales and a guest, good sensibly priced food, friendly helpful staff and nice chatty atmosphere; children till 8pm, dogs in bar, picnic-sets in pleasant sheltered garden, closed Sun evening. *Recommended by Tina and David Woods-Taylor, Maria Taylor, Philip Smith, N R White*

LITTLEY GREEN TL6917   CM3 1BU

Compasses
Off A130 and B1417 SE of Felsted

Unpretentiously quaint and old-fashioned country pub, isolated but thriving, with Adnams and guest ales tapped from cellar casks, farm cider and perry, good range of whiskies, basic wholesome food (they may ask to keep a credit card while you eat), roaring log fire; tables in big back garden, benches at front, good walks, open all day Thurs-Sun. *Recommended by the Didler, Dave Lowe, Mitchell Humphreys*

MALDON TL8407   CM9 4QE

☆ ## Blue Boar
Silver Street; car park round behind

Quirky cross between coaching inn and antiques or auction showroom, most showy in the main building's lounge and dining room, interesting antique furnishings and pictures also in the separate smallish dark-timbered bar and its spectacular raftered upper room, good Farmers ales brewed at the back, Adnams and Crouch Vale too, enjoyable bar food including daily specials, friendly helpful staff; tables outside, bedrooms (some with four-posters), good breakfast, open all day. *Recommended by Ian Scott-Thompson*

MISTLEY TM1131   CO11 1HE

☆ ## Thorn
High Street (B1352 E of Manningtree)

American chef/landlady's good food (especially seafood) is central here, but there's also a friendly all-day welcome if you just want a drink or a good coffee; high black beams give a clue to the building's age (Matthew Hopkins, the notorious 17th-c witchfinder general, based himself here), décor, though, is crisply up to date – comfortable basket-weave chairs and mixed dining tables on terracotta tiles around the horseshoe bar, cream walls above a sage dado, colourful modern artwork, end brick fireplace with woodburner, good range of wines by the glass, newspapers and magazines, cookery classes; front terrace tables look across to Robert Adam's swan fountain, interesting waterside village, seven comfortable bedrooms. *Recommended by anon*

MONK STREET TL6128   CM6 2NR

Farmhouse
Just off B184 S of Thaxted

Partly 16th-c country pub, good value food in carpeted bar and restaurant, Mighty Oak ales; good-sized attractive garden with terrace and play area, 11 bedrooms. *Recommended by N R White*

We say if we know a pub allows dogs.

MORETON TL5307   CM5 0LF
White Hart
Off B184, just N of A414

Traditional old village pub, spacious bar with leather sofas by woodburner, two other
areas, well kept Adnams Bitter and Broadside and a guest (bank holiday weekend beer
festivals), decent house wines, popular enjoyable food from bar snacks up including good
value weekday set lunch, attractive small timbered dining room, quiz night (first Weds of
month); piped music; children and dogs welcome, picnic-sets on smart decked terrace,
garden, six newly refurbished bedrooms, open all day. *Recommended by Mrs Margo Finlay,*
Jörg Kasprowski

MOUNT BURES TL9031   CO8 5AT
☆ ## Thatchers Arms
Off B1508

Well run modernised pub with good local food (freshly prepared so may be a wait), mid-
week meal deals, well kept interesting ales (occasional beer festivals), friendly young
staff and dog (visiting ones welcome); plenty of picnic-sets out behind, peaceful Stour
Valley views, open all day weekends, closed Mon. *Recommended by David and Lesley Elliott,*
John Prescott, James Cracknell

MOUNTNESSING TQ6297   CM15 0TZ
George & Dragon
Roman Road (B1002)

Contemporary refurbishment blending with old beams and timbers, good choice of food
all day including some mediterranean influences, weekday lunchtime and early evening
fixed-price menu, plenty of wines by the glass including champagne, real ales, friendly
landlord, colourful armchairs and stools on polished wood floors, newspapers, open fires;
open all day. *Recommended by John Saville*

NEWNEY GREEN TL6506   CM1 3SF
☆ ## Duck
W of Chelmsford

Tucked-away old pub with attractive rambling dining bar, dark beams and timbering,
panelling, interesting bric-a-brac, comfortable furnishings and nice log fire, enjoyable
good value food, well kept ales such as Batemans, decent wines by the glass, friendly
service; pleasant terrace, open all day, closed Mon. *Recommended by Andrew Davids,*
Trevor Humphreys

NORTH SHOEBURY TQ9286   SS3 8UD
Angel
Parsons Corner

Conversion of timbered and partly thatched former post office, Greene King ales, popular
usual food including Sun roasts, courteous friendly service, panelling and exposed
brickwork, open fire, restaurant; piped music. *Recommended by George Atkinson*

PAGLESHAM TQ9293   SS4 2DP
☆ ## Punchbowl
Church End

16th-c former sailmaker's loft with low beams and stripped brickwork, pews, barrel chairs
and lots of brass, lower room laid for dining, Adnams Bitter and changing guests,
straightforward fairly priced food including good OAP menu, prompt friendly service,
cribbage and darts; piped music (mostly 60s and 70s); children usually welcome but
check first, lovely rural view from sunny front garden. *Recommended by Pat and Tony Martin,*
George Atkinson, Bob and Tanya Ekers

We accept no free drinks or meals and inspections are anonymous.

PELDON TM0015 CO5 7QJ

☆ **Rose**

B1025 Colchester—Mersea (do not turn left to Peldon village)

Attractive dining pub with elegant interior, dark bowed 17th-c beams, standing timbers, little leaded-light windows, gothic-arched brick fireplace, good antique furniture, spacious modern conservatory (disabled access), good sensibly priced changing food (all day Sun in summer, booking advised), good wines from wine merchant owners Lay & Wheeler including many by the glass, Adnams, Greene King and interesting guests, friendly efficient service; children welcome away from bar, teak furniture in sizeable garden with duck pond, bedrooms (one over kitchen can be noisy), open all day, closed Sun evening in winter. *Recommended by Marcus Mann, Ryta Lyndley, Bill Adie, Jeff and Wendy Williams*

PLESHEY TL6614 CM3 1HA

☆ **White Horse**

The Street

Refurbished 15th-c beamed pub under newish management, four bar areas, nooks and knick-knacks, open fires, big back extension with two dining rooms, traditional home-made blackboard food from huffers up including good fish choice, meal deals, Adnams and two changing local guests, theme nights; piped music; no dogs; children welcome, tables on terrace and in good-sized garden, pretty village with ruined castle, open all day Sun. *Recommended by George Atkinson, Marion and Bill Cross*

RIDGEWELL TL7340 CO9 4SG

White Horse

Mill Road (A1017 Haverhill—Halstead)

Comfortable low-beamed village pub with good range of well kept ales tapped from the cask, farm ciders, good generous food (changing bar and restaurant menus), friendly service, fireside sofa; no dogs; terrace tables, bedroom block with good disabled access, open all day. *Recommended by Simon Watkins*

STAPLEFORD TAWNEY TL5001 CM16 7PU

☆ **Mole Trap**

Tawney Common; signed off A113 N of M25 overpass – keep on; OS Sheet 167 map reference 500013

Popular unpretentious little country pub, carpeted beamed bar (mind your head as you go in) with brocaded wall seats and plain pub tables, steps down to similar area, warming fires, well kept Fullers London Pride and changing guests, pubby food (not Sun or Mon evenings); no credit cards, quiet piped radio; plastic tables and chairs outside along with various animals from rabbits and hens to goats and horses. *Recommended by Simon and Sally Small, Grahame and Myra Williams, the Didler, Mrs Ann Gray, David Jackson and others*

STEEPLE TL9302 CM0 7RH

Sun & Anchor

The Street

Village local set back from road with cream and brown 50s décor, well kept ales such as Greene King IPA, Mighty Oak Maldon Gold and Sharps Doom Bar tapped from side room casks, well priced food from good thick-cut sandwiches to generous Sun roasts, friendly efficient staff; disabled facilities, smartened-up garden with painted picnic-sets and two smokers' tents. *Recommended by LM*

STOW MARIES TQ8399 CM3 6SA

☆ **Prince of Wales**

B1012 between South Woodham Ferrers and Cold Norton Posters

Cheery atmosphere in several little low-ceilinged unspoilt rooms, bare boards and log fires, conservatory dining area, half a dozen widely sourced beers, bottled and draught belgian beers including fruit beers, tasty bar food (all day Sun), home-made pizzas (Thurs) from Victorian baker's oven, live jazz (third Fri of month); children in family room, terrace and garden, summer Sun barbecues, bedrooms, open all day. *Recommended by Peter Meister, Roger and Pauline Pearce, David Warren, David Jackson*

TENDRING TM1523   CO16 9AP
Cherry Tree
Crow Lane, E of village centre

Extended old red-brick pub doing well under newish management, good nicely presented food (not Sun evening, Mon) from traditional to more imaginative things including good value set lunch, well kept ales such as Sharps Doom Bar, reasonably priced wines by the glass, decent coffee, friendly helpful service, oak beams, bare boards and open fires, restaurant, friendly tabby cat; disabled facilities, seats out by road and in good-sized garden behind. *Recommended by Ryta Lyndley and others*

 THAXTED TL6031   CM6 2PL
Swan
Bull Ring

Attractively renovated dark-beamed Tudor inn, Adnams and Greene King, good choice of whiskies and of enjoyable food, friendly staff, plenty of well spaced tables in long open bar, leather sofas and log fire, restaurant; roadside picnic-sets overlooking lovely church (Holst was organist here), windmill nearby, 20 bedrooms (back ones quieter), open all day. *Recommended by Giles and Annie Francis*

THEYDON BOIS TQ4599   CM16 7ES
Queen Victoria
Coppice Row (B172)

Cosy beamed and carpeted traditional lounge, roaring log fire, local pictures, mug collection, two further bars, popular good value food including children's menu, friendly efficient staff, McMullens ales and decent house wines, end restaurant; piped music; dogs welcome, picnic-sets on well laid out front terrace, open all day. *Recommended by Robert Lester, N R White and others*

 WENDENS AMBO TL5136   CB11 4JY
Bell
B1039 W of village

Small cottagey local well run by cheery landlady, brasses on ancient timbers in low-ceilinged pubby rooms, wheelback chairs at neat tables, open fire, Adnams, Woodfordes Wherry and three changing guests (Aug bank holiday beer/music festival), tasty pubby food (not Sun evening, Mon) including good Sun lunch; piped music; children and dogs welcome, big tree-sheltered lawn with timber play area, open all day (closed Mon lunchtime in winter). *Recommended by Roxanne Chamberlain, Jerry Brown, David Jackson*

WEST BERGHOLT TL9528   CO6 3DD
White Hart
2 miles from Colchester on Sudbury Road

Welcoming old village pub, former coaching inn, with good choice of reasonably priced food including plenty of fish, set lunch deals and children's menu, three ales including Adnams, comfortable dining area; big garden, four bedrooms, closed Sun evening. *Recommended by Marion and Bill Cross*

☆ WICKHAM ST PAUL TL8336   CO9 2PT
Victory
SW of Sudbury; The Green

Attractive and spacious old dining pub, interesting choice of good fresh food, friendly efficient service, Adnams and Woodfordes Wherry, beams and timbers, leather sofas and armchairs, inglenook woodburner; piped music; children welcome, neat garden overlooking village cricket green, open all day, closed Mon. *Recommended by Mrs J Kendrick*

WIDDINGTON TL5331   CB11 3SG
☆ **Fleur de Lys**
Signed off B1383 N of Stansted

Welcoming unpretentious low-beamed and timbered village local, well cooked food (not Mon) in bar and restaurant including good Sun roasts, children's helpings, well kept Adnams, Hook Norton and guests, decent wines, dim lighting and inglenook log fire, games in back bar including pool, friendly black labrador; picnic-sets in pretty garden, handy for Mole Hall wildlife park, open all day Fri-Sun. *Recommended by N R White*

WOODHAM MORTIMER TL8004   CM9 6TJ
Royal Oak
Chelmsford Road (A414 Danbury—Maldon)

Two cleanly modernised bars, emphasis on enjoyable well presented pubby food, prompt friendly service, sturdy tables and high-backed chairs on wood flooring, Greene King IPA; small side terrace and garden behind. *Recommended by Paul Rampton, Julie Harding*

ALSO WORTH A VISIT IN HERTFORDSHIRE

Besides the region's top pubs, we recommend the following. Do tell us what you think of them: **feedback@goodguides.com**

ALDBURY SP9612   HP23 5RT
☆ **Greyhound**
Stocks Road; village signed from A4251 Tring—Berkhamsted, and from B4506

Picturesque village pub with some signs of real age inside, copper-hooded inglenook in cosy traditional beamed bar, more contemporary area with leather chairs, airy oak-floored back restaurant with wicker chairs at big new tables, Badger ales, traditional food (all day weekends) from sandwiches up; children welcome, dogs in bar, front benches facing green with whipping post, stocks and duck pond, suntrap gravel courtyard, bedrooms, open all day. *Recommended by Peter and Giff Bennett, N R White, Taff Thomas*

ALDBURY SP9612   HP23 5RW
☆ **Valiant Trooper**
Trooper Road; (towards Aldbury Common); off B4506 N of Berkhamsted

Cheery traditional all-rounder with series of unspoilt beamed rooms, attractive country furniture, some exposed brickwork, inglenook and woodburner, Brakspears, Fullers London Pride, Tring and guests, local Millwhite's cider, generous quickly served pubby food (all day Sat, not Sun or Mon evenings), back barn restaurant where children welcome; dogs in bar, wooden adventure playground in enclosed garden, well placed for Ashridge Estate (NT) beech woods, open all day. *Recommended by Kevin Thomas, Nina Randall, Peter and Giff Bennett, Steve and Sue Griffiths*

ALDENHAM TQ1498   WD25 8BG
Round Bush
Roundbush Lane

Cheery 19th-c village pub with plenty of atmosphere, two front rooms and back restaurant, popular generously served food, ales such as Black Sheep and St Austell in very good condition, friendly efficient staff; big garden. *Recommended by Jack and Sandra Clarfelt, David M Smith*

We say if we know a pub has piped music.

AYOT GREEN TL2213   AL6 9AA
Waggoners
Off B197 S of Welwyn

Refurbished former 17th-c coaching inn doing well under french owners, food in cosy low-beamed bar, more upmarket french cooking in comfortable good-sized restaurant extension, friendly attentive staff, good wine list, real ales; attractive and spacious suntrap back garden with sheltered terrace (some A1(M) noise), wooded walks nearby. *Recommended by Mrs Ann Adams, Hans Liesner, Huw Thomas*

BARKWAY TL3834   SG8 8EX
☆ # Tally Ho
London Road (B1368)

Quirky little local with inviting old sofa, armchairs, horsebrasses and log fire in cottagey bar, extraordinary range of drinks including 48 wines by the glass, 136 malt whiskies, over 200 different spirits, Buntingford Highwayman and a couple of guests (apparently tapped from big casks behind bar, but actually gently pumped), Aspall's farm cider, fresh flowers and silver candelabra, old-fashioned prints on brown ply panelling, another log fire in old-world dining area serving traditional food; children welcome, dogs in bar, well spaced picnic-sets, weeping willow and fruit trees in garden behind car park, open all day (closed Sun evening). *Recommended by M R D Foot*

BERKHAMSTED SP9907   HP4 2NB
Old Mill
A4251, Hemel end

Huge rambling dining pub, attractive layout, extensive choice of enjoyable food all day, three well kept ales including Greene King, friendly staff, two good fires; tables outside, some overlooking unspectacular stretch of Grand Union Canal. *Recommended by Kevin Thomas, Nina Randall, John Branston*

BISHOP'S STORTFORD TL4821   CM23 2LD
Half Moon
North Street

Well kept changing real ales, Weston's farm cider and lots of country wines, friendly staff, lovely old building with bare-boards rooms of different sizes and levels, décor tastefully in keeping; piped and live music; open all day. *Recommended by Nic Courtman, Mark Crossley*

BISHOP'S STORTFORD TL5021   CM23 5HP
Nags Head
Dunmow Road

Fully refurbished 1930s art deco pub (Grade II listed) reopened after long closure by McMullens, their ales from island servery and plenty of wines by the glass, wide choice of pubby food, good service; children welcome, open all day. *Recommended by Charles Gysin*

BOURNE END TL0206   HP1 2RZ
☆ # Three Horseshoes
Winkwell; just off A4251 Hemel—Berkhamsted

Renovated 16th-c pub in charming setting by unusual swing bridge over Grand Union Canal, low-beamed three-room core with inglenooks, traditional furniture including settles, a few sofas, three well kept changing ales, straightforward reasonably priced food all day (they may ask to keep a credit card while you eat), efficient uniformed staff, bay-windowed extension overlooking canal; comedy and quiz nights; children welcome, picnic-sets out by water. *Recommended by Clive and Fran Dutson, Gill and Keith Croxton, Peter Martin, Dennis Jones*

With the iPhone Good Pub Guide App, you can use the iPhone's camera to send us pictures of pubs you visit – outside or inside.

BRAMFIELD TL2915 SG14 2QJ
Grandiston Arms
Main Road

Neat comfortably refurbished dining pub reopened after long closure, enjoyable food including some pub standards, Woodfordes Wherry and three guests, good choice of wines; garden tables, farm shop/deli next door, charming village, open all day. *Recommended by Mick Hitchman*

BRAUGHING TL3925 SG11 2QR
Axe & Compass
Just off B1368; The Street

Pleasant country local in pretty village with ford, enjoyable food and well kept ales, friendly service, modern décor and mix of furnishings in two roomy bars, restaurant; well behaved children and dogs welcome. *Recommended by Simon Watkins, Kevin McPheat*

BRAUGHING TL3925 SG11 2PE
Golden Fleece
Green End (B1368)

Dining pub improved under current licensee, good varied choice of freshly made food, Adnams and guests, several wines by the glass including champagne, cheerful service, bare-boards bar and two dining rooms, beams and timbers, open fire; back garden with metal furniture on paved terrace, round picnic-sets out at front. *Recommended by Charles Gysin*

CHANDLERS CROSS TQ0698 WD3 4LU
☆ Clarendon
M25 junction 20; A41 towards Watford, right at first traffic lights signed Sarratt, then into Redhall Lane

Stylish modern bar with tall swivelling chrome and leather chairs at long high dark wood counter, colourful contemporary artwork, side area with log fire and leather chesterfields, dining part with open kitchen, grand upstairs restaurant, cheerful well drilled young staff, Tring ales, good choice of wines by the glass, elaborate food from 10am onwards (not between 5-6 and 4-6 Sun); piped music; children welcome, square-cut metal benches and tables on neatly landscaped terrace, open fire in substantial brick-built smokers' shelter, open all day. *Recommended by C Galloway, Peter and Giff Bennett*

CHAPMORE END TL3216 SG12 0HF
☆ Woodman
Off B158 Wadesmill—Bengeo; pub signed 300 yards W of A602 roundabout; OS Sheet 166 map reference 328164

Peaceful early Victorian country local, plain seats around stripped pub tables, floor tiles or broad bare boards, working period fireplaces, well kept Greene King beers poured from the cask, minimal lunchtime food (also a winter Sun roast and summer barbecues), backgammon, shove ha'penny and cribbage; dogs welcome, children till 8pm, picnic-sets out in front under a couple of walnut trees, bigger back garden with fenced play area and boules, open all day Sat, closed Mon lunchtime. *Recommended by Thomas Lane*

CHIPPERFIELD SP0401 WD4 9BH
Royal Oak
The Street

Two immaculate small bars, enjoyable freshly made food (evenings by arrangement, not Sun) from sandwiches to crab and venison (nothing fried), well kept Adnams Broadside, Fullers London Pride, Wells & Youngs Bitter and an occasional guest, friendly relaxed atmosphere, copper-top tables, log fire, vintage car photographs (regular car club meetings in function room); children welcome at lunchtime, dogs in one bar, back terrace with cover. *Recommended by Jack and Sandra Clarfelt*

CHORLEYWOOD TQ0395   WD3 5EG
☆ **Black Horse**
Dog Kennel Lane, the Common

Welcoming old country pub popular for its good value generous food (smaller helpings available) from good sandwiches up, OAP lunch some days, well kept ales including Wadworths and Wells & Youngs, decent wines, tea and coffee, good cheery service even when busy, low dark beams and two log fires in thoroughly traditional rambling bar, daily papers; big-screen TV; children, walkers and dogs welcome, picnic-sets overlooking common, open all day. *Recommended by LM, Peter and Giff Bennett, Roy Hoing, Peter Collins and others*

CHORLEYWOOD TQ0294   WD3 5BS
☆ **Land of Liberty Peace & Plenty**
Long Lane, Heronsgate, just off M25 junction 17

Well kept local Red Squirrel, Tring and interesting guest beers, Millwhite's and Weston's ciders and perry, bottled belgian beers, decent coffee, enjoyable lunches with some imaginative dishes, all-day snacks, good friendly service, simple traditional layout, darts, skittles and board games; TV, no children inside; dogs welcome, covered decking, more picnic-sets in garden, open all day. *Recommended by LM*

DATCHWORTH TL2618   SG3 6TB
Tilbury
Watton Road; off A602 SE of Stevenage

Civilised and attractively timbered two-room dining pub, imaginative seasonal food including cheaper set-menu choices, lots of wines by the glass; big garden, closed Sun evening. *Recommended by J Marques*

GREAT HORMEAD TL4030   SG9 0NT
Three Tuns
B1038/Horseshoe Hill

Proper old timbered country pub with warm welcome, good home-made food from baguettes up (just roasts on Sun), Greene King ales, small linked areas, huge inglenook with another great hearth behind, big back conservatory extension; lovely surroundings. *Recommended by Paul Sollohub*

HARPENDEN TL1116   AL5 3QE
Fox
Luton Road, Kinsbourne Green; 2.2 miles from M1 junction 10; A1081 towards town

Contemporary dining pub, tiled floor, usual leather armchairs and sofas, lots of modern dining tables in alcoves, enjoyably up-to-date pubby food, friendly helpful service, interesting wines by the glass, well kept Timothy Taylors Landlord, open fire; piped music; terrace tables. *Recommended by Clifford Blakemore, Michael Dandy*

HARPENDEN TL1312   AL5 2JP
☆ **White Horse**
Redbourn Lane, Hatching Green (B487 just W of A1081 roundabout)

This smart dining pub has reopened under Peach Pub Co after short closure – news please. *Recommended by anon*

HEMEL HEMPSTEAD TL0411   HP2 6EY
☆ **Crown & Sceptre**
Bridens Camp; leaving on A4146, right at Flamstead/Markyate sign opposite Red Lion

Traditional neatly refurbished rambling pub, welcoming and relaxed, with well kept Greene King and six guests, good generous reasonably priced pubby food (not Sun evening), friendly efficient staff, dining room with woodburner, quiz nights and beer festivals; children and dogs welcome, picnic-sets out at front and in pleasant garden, good walks, open all day weekends. *Recommended by Ross Balaam, Peter and Jan Humphreys, Val and Alan Green*

HEMEL HEMPSTEAD TL0508   HP1 3AT
Marchmont Arms
By roundabout on new northerly route of A4147

Spacious 18th-c pub/brasserie with good choice of interesting modern food including weekday fixed-price menu, lots of wines by the glass, Adnams and Sharps Doom Bar, friendly efficient uniformed staff, long split-level bar with stylish contemporary décor, elegant restaurant with chunky pine furniture on wood floor, log fires, dining conservatory, heated covered balcony; children welcome, picnic-sets in pleasant sloping garden, open all day. *Recommended by Val and Alan Green, Dennis Jones*

HERTFORD HEATH TL3510   SG13 7PW
College Arms
B1197

Recently reopened village pub/restaurant under new management, enjoyable varied choice of food including good value fixed-price menu, friendly service; children welcome. *Recommended by J Marques*

HEXTON TL1030   SG5 3JB
Raven
Signed off B655

Part of attractive mock-Tudor estate village, very popular for wide range of good value food from baguettes up, children's meals, friendly efficient service, ales such as Everards, Greene King and Timothy Taylors Landlord, good choice of wines by the glass, open fire, plenty of dining tables in four linked areas, paintings (some for sale); piped music; big garden with heated terrace, barbecue and play area. *Recommended by Michael Dandy*

HIGH WYCH TL4714   CM21 0AY
Hand & Crown
Signed off A1184 Harlow—Sawbridgeworth

Nice interior with some interesting features including huge central fireplace dividing off restaurant area, good reasonably priced and generously served food (popular so best to book), well kept Adnams and Greene King, plenty of whiskies, attentive service; piped music. *Recommended by Grahame and Myra Williams, Terry Walsh*

HITCHIN TL1828   SG4 9TZ
Half Moon
Queen Street

Tucked-away open-plan local, friendly and welcoming, with well kept Adnams, Youngs Special and four interesting guests, real cider and perry, good choice of wines by the glass, traditional food; open all day Fri-Sat. *Recommended by Stuart Gideon, Mrs Catherine Simmonds*

HITCHIN TL1929   SG4 9ST
Radcliffe Arms
Walsworth Road

Busy modernised pub/restaurant with enjoyable freshly made food, local Buntingford ales, extensive wine list – many by the glass, decent coffee, friendly staff; children welcome, terrace tables, open all day from 8am for breakfast. *Recommended by Stuart Gideon, Mrs Catherine Simmonds*

LITTLE GADDESDEN SP9913   HP4 1PD
Bridgewater Arms
Nettleden Road, off B4506

Pleasant well cared-for 19th-c stone dining pub, good value food including enjoyable set lunches, well kept Greene King IPA and Abbot, good wine choice by the glass, decent coffee, friendly attentive service, daily papers, carpeted bar and smart high-ceiling restaurant, a couple of fires (one log-effect gas), games in small bare-boards public area;

garden tables, good walks from the door. *Recommended by Mike and Jennifer Marsh, Malcolm and Sue Scott, Taff Thomas*

MUCH HADHAM TL4219   SG10 6BU

 ## Bull
High Street

Neatly kept dining pub with good home-made food changing daily, good choice of wines by the glass including champagne, well kept Hancocks HB, cheerful efficient service even when busy, inglenook log fire in unspoilt bar, attractive pastel décor in roomy civilised dining lounge and back dining room; children welcome, good-sized garden. *Recommended by Ross Balaam, Simon Watkins, Steve and Sue Griffiths, James Hill, MDN*

NUTHAMPSTEAD TL4134   SG8 8NB

☆ ## Woodman
Off B1368 S of Barkway

Tucked-away thatched and weatherboarded village pub, welcoming and well run, with comfortable unspoilt core, worn tiled floor, nice inglenook log fire, another fire opposite and 17th-c low beams/timbers, plainer extension, enjoyable home-made traditional food (not Sun evening), home-baked bread, well kept McMullens, efficient friendly service, interesting USAF memorabilia and memorial outside (nearby World War II airfield); benches out overlooking tranquil lane, comfortable bedrooms, open all day Sat, Mon 5-8pm. *Recommended by Simon Watkins, John Walker, M R D Foot, Steve Nye, Marion and Bill Cross and others*

PERRY GREEN TL4317   SG10 6EF

Hoops
Off B1004 Widford—Much Hadham

Recently refurbished 19th-c pub/restaurant in grounds of the Henry Moore Foundation (the sculptor in evidence through posters, photographs, prints and even the cushion covers), airy open-plan interior with beams and standing timbers, spindleback chairs around painted tables on tiled floor, green banquettes, inglenook woodburner, good reasonably priced locally sourced food from new landlord/chef, Adnams Best; no dogs inside; children welcome, garden with large covered terrace, open all day summer, till 6pm Sun, closed Mon. *Recommended by Mrs Margo Finlay, Jörg Kasprowski*

REED TL3636   SG8 8AH

☆ ## Cabinet
Off A10; High Street

Friendly 16th-c weatherboarded pub-restaurant, good food from upscale pricey things to cheaper set-lunch deals and bar food, Fullers London Pride and two guests in compact bar with inglenook log fire, fine choice of wines by the glass, brick-floor snug with darts, smart dining room, ghost called Stan; children and dogs welcome, charming big garden with pond, open all day weekends, closed Mon. *Recommended by M R D Foot, Tom and Ruth Rees*

RICKMANSWORTH TQ0594   WD3 1DJ

Feathers
Church Street

Quietly set off the high street, civilised and smart, with beams, panelling and soft lighting, well kept Adnams, Fullers London Pride and interesting guests, good wine list, varied choice of freshly prepared food (all day weekends) from sandwiches up including lunchtime deals, good friendly young staff coping well when busy; children till 5pm, picnic-sets out behind, open all day. *Recommended by Tracey and Stephen Groves, Brian Glozier*

ROYSTON TL3540   SG8 9AW

Old Bull
High Street

Chatty and relaxed bow-fronted Georgian coaching inn with roomy high-beamed bar, exposed timbers, handsome fireplaces, big pictures, fine flooring, easy chairs and a leather sofa, papers and magazines, dining area with cheerfully served good value food including Sun carvery, Adnams and Greene King, several decent wines by the glass; piped music; children welcome, dogs in bar, suntrap courtyard, 11 bedrooms, open all day. *Recommended by John Wooll*

SARRATT TQ0499   WD3 6BL
Boot
The Green

Refurbished early 18th-c tiled pub under newish management and now geared for dining, young friendly staff, selection of real ales, rambling bar with unusual inglenook, more modern dining room; good-sized garden, pleasant spot facing green, handy for Chess Valley walks. *Recommended by N R White*

SARRATT TQ0499   WD3 6AS
☆ Cricketers
The Green

Big bustling beamed dining pub in row of old buildings, refurbished linked rooms with cricket theme, interesting variety of good fresh food all day, well priced wine list, four changing ales, enthusiastic helpful young staff, central open fire; children welcome, dogs in main bar area, disabled facilities, tables out at front overlooking large green with pond, more in small garden behind with terrace and pergola, open all day weekends. *Recommended by Peter and Giff Bennett, Peter and Jan Humphreys, Jeff Quilter, Martin and Karen Wake*

SPELLBROOK TL4817   CM22 7SE
Three Horseshoes
Spellbrook Lane E

Spacious Chef & Brewer dining pub largely extended from thatched and very low-beamed core, usual food from largish menu including offers, pleasant young staff (service may be a little slow when busy), Adnams Broadside and Courage Directors, good choice of wines by the glass; children welcome, dogs in garden only, disabled facilities, lots of tables on lawns and terrace, bridge from streamside car park. *Recommended by George Atkinson*

ST ALBANS TL1407   AL3 4PT
Farriers Arms
Lower Dagnall Street

Plain friendly two-bar backstreet local, McMullens and guests, bar food weekdays, lots of old pictures of the pub (Campaign for Real Ale started here in the early 1970s). *Recommended by the Didler, P Dawn*

ST ALBANS TL1406   AL1 1RL
Hare & Hounds
Sopwell Lane

Traditional pub with ales such as Timothy Taylors Landlord, Sharps Doom Bar and Woodfordes Wherry, enjoyable good value local food including good Sun lunch, friendly staff, sofa by nice open fire; sports TV; seats outside. *Recommended by P Dawn, Mike Cook*

ST ALBANS TL1407   AL3 4RX
Lower Red Lion
Fishpool Street

Hospitable beamed local dating from the 17th c (right-hand bar has most character), up to eight or so well kept changing ales including local Alehouse (regular beer festivals), imported beers, enjoyable inexpensive lunchtime food including sandwiches, speciality sausages and popular Sun roast, red plush seats and carpet, board games; no nearby parking; tables in good-sized back garden, bedrooms (some sharing bath), open all day Fri-Sun. *Recommended by the Didler, P Dawn*

ST ALBANS TL1307 AL3 4SG
Rose & Crown
St Michael's Street

16th-c, with low beams, timbers and panelling, good speciality lunchtime sandwiches and a few hot dishes, Adnams, Fullers London Pride and Shepherd Neame Spitfire, welcoming service, big log fire, small snug; piped music and some live; children and dogs welcome, lots of tables and benches outside, pretty floral and ivy-hung backyard, handy for Verulamium Musem. *Recommended by Mike and Jennifer Marsh*

ST ALBANS TL1307 AL3 4SH
☆ Six Bells
St Michael's Street

Well cared-for rambling old pub popular for its good generous reasonably priced food, cheerful attentive service, beers such as Fullers, Oakham, Timothy Taylors and York kept well, low beams and timbers, log fire, quieter panelled dining room; children welcome, occasional barbecues in small back garden, handy for Verulamium Museum, open all day. *Recommended by David and Ruth Shillitoe, Maria Thomas, Mrs M G Uglow, Mike and Jennifer Marsh, LM*

STAPLEFORD TL3017 SG14 3NW
Woodhall Arms
High Road

Well kept Greene King, Wells & Youngs and guests, good bar food (not Sat evening), Sun roasts, separate spacious restaurant; ten comfortable bedrooms, good breakfast. *Recommended by Mike and Lynn Robinson*

TRING SP9211 HP23 6BE
☆ Kings Arms
King Street; by junction with Queen Street (which is off B4635 Western Road – continuation of High Street)

Widely appealing spic-and-span backstreet pub with cheerful relaxed atmosphere, well kept Wadworths 6X and four quickly changing guests, Weston's cider, good value food including several spicy dishes, cushioned pews and bentwood chairs around cast-iron tables on carpet, old brewery advertisements on green walls, some pine panelling and two little fireplaces; dogs welcome, children till 8.30pm, tables and heaters in attractive side wagon yard. *Recommended by Tracey and Stephen Groves, David M Smith, Taff Thomas, Roy Hoing*

WATER END TL0410 HP1 3BD
Red Lion
Leighton Buzzard Road (A4146)

Large pub extended from 18th-c core, beams and timbers, enjoyable food with an italian slant, friendly service, real ales from attractive carved bar; garden and terrace tables. *Recommended by David Gurr, Simon Scott*

WATTON-AT-STONE TL3019 SG14 3TA
☆ George & Dragon
High Street (B1001)

Appealing candlelit country dining pub under new licensees, good food from sandwiches up using local produce (gluten-free diets catered for), good service, Greene King IPA and Abbot plus guest beers, interesting mix of antique and modern prints on partly timbered walls, big inglenook fireplace, daily papers; no dogs; children in eating areas, pretty shrub-screened garden with heaters, boules, open all day. *Recommended by Mrs Margo Finlay, Jörg Kasprowski*

Post Office address codings confusingly give the impression that some pubs are in Hertfordshire, when they're really in Bedfordshire, Buckinghamshire or Cambridgeshire (which is where we list them).

WELWYN TL2316   AL6 9EE

Wellington
High Street, old village – not the Garden City

Restaurant-with-rooms rather than pub, smartly restored after 2009 fire; good choice of popular food (all day weekends) from lunchtime sandwiches up, Greene King ales, some interesting wines by the glass with emphasis on australian, cheerful attentive young staff, open fires; no dogs; children welcome, extended heated terrace, six contemporary bedrooms, open all day. *Recommended by Jane Plaza*

WHEATHAMPSTEAD TL1712   AL4 8EL

☆ ## Wicked Lady
Nomansland Common; B651 0.5 miles S

Unpretentious chain dining pub with clean contemporary décor, wide range of good well presented food including some unusual dishes, well kept Adnams, Fullers London Pride and Timothy Taylors Landlord, plenty of wines by the glass, reasonable prices, friendly attentive young staff, various rooms and alcoves, low beams and log fires, lots of stainless steel, conservatory; garden with nice terrace. *Recommended by Eleanor Dandy, Michael Dandy, Eithne Dandy, Andy Lickfold, Mike and Jennifer Marsh*

WILLIAN TL2230   SG6 2AE

☆ ## Fox
A1(M) junction 9; A6141 W towards Letchworth then first left

Restauranty dining pub with fresh contemporary décor, light wood furniture on stripped boards or big ceramic tiles, modern pictures on white and pastel walls, pale blue-fronted counter with modern bar stools, Adnams, Brancaster, Fullers, Woodfordes and a guest, good wine list with over a dozen by the glass, creative food (not cheap) from changing menu (not Sun evening, service added automatically), helpful young uniformed staff; piped music, TV; children welcome, dogs in bar, disabled access and parking, smart tables on side terrace, picnic-sets in good-sized garden below handsome 14th-c church, open all day. *Recommended by David and Ruth Shillitoe, A and H Piper, Mr and Mrs T B Staples, D M Jack, Stuart Gideon, Mrs Catherine Simmonds*

ALSO WORTH A VISIT IN NORFOLK

Besides the region's top pubs, we recommend the following. Do tell us what you think of them: **feedback@goodguides.com**

AYLSHAM TG1926   NR11 6EH

☆ ## Black Boys
Market Place; off B1145

Small hotel with imposing Georgian façade and informal open-plan bar, good value food (all day) from snacks up, Adnams and guests such as Timothy Taylors Landlord, Woodfordes Wherry and Wychwood Hobgoblin, decent wines in three glass sizes, comfortable seats and plenty of tables, high beams, part carpet, part bare boards, helpful young uniformed staff; children and dogs welcome, modern seats in front by market place, bedrooms, open all day. *Recommended by John Wooll, Lawrence Pearse, D and M T Ayres-Regan, John Cook and others*

BAWBURGH TG1508   NR9 3LS

☆ ## Kings Head
Harts Lane; A47 just W of Norwich then B1108

Bustling 17th-c pub with small low-beamed rooms, leather sofas and nice mix of old tables on wood-strip floors, knocked through open fire and woodburners, interesting food (not Sun evening, winter Mon) from listed suppliers, Adnams, Woodfordes Wherry and a guest, 16 wines by the glass, helpful, friendly staff; piped music; children welcome, dogs in bar, garden tables, little green opposite, open all day. *Recommended by John Robertson, Tina and David Woods-Taylor*

BINHAM TF9839   NR21 0AL
☆ Chequers
B1388 SW of Blakeney

Long low-beamed 17th-c local with welcoming friendly atmosphere, coal fires at each end, sturdy plush seats, nice old local prints, own-brewed Front Street beers and changing guests, lots of bottled imports, decent house wines, enjoyable pubby food; children welcome, picnic-sets in front and on back grass, interesting village with huge priory church. *Recommended by Mike Proctor, Chris Johnson, R C Vincent, Steve Nye and others*

BLICKLING TG1728   NR11 6NF
☆ Buckinghamshire Arms
B1354 NW of Aylsham

Handsome well run Jacobean inn much visited for its enviable spot by gates to Blickling Hall (NT), small and appealing proper unpretentious bar, lounge set for eating with woodburner, smarter more formal dining room with another woodburner, enjoyable fairly priced food, ales such as Adnams, Fullers, Wolf and Woodfordes kept well, good choice of wines by the glass, attentive cheery young staff; children welcome, lots of lawn tables, lovely walks nearby, bedrooms. *Recommended by Mike Proctor, Dr and Mrs R G J Telfer, Christopher and Elise Way, JDM, KM, Mr and Mrs W W Burke, Margaret and Peter Staples and others*

BRANCASTER STAITHE TF7944   PE31 8BJ
☆ Jolly Sailors
Main Road (A149)

Bustling village pub with own-brewed Brancaster beers (brewery not on site) and guests like Adnams and Woodfordes, main bar has traditional pubby furniture on red quarry tiles, stripped-stone walls and log fire in brick fireplace, two further snugs with local books and harbour views, comfortably old-fashioned dining lounge, straightforward food (all day in summer), friendly staff, pool room with TV; children welcome, dogs in bar, serving hatch to terrace, play area, open all day in summer, all day Fri-Sun in winter. *Recommended by Michael Dandy, Henry Pursehouse-Tranter, Tracey and Stephen Groves, John and Victoria Fairley, Terry and Elizabeth Tyrrell, Chris Johnson and others*

BRANCASTER STAITHE TF8044   PE31 8BY
☆ White Horse
A149 E of Hunstanton

Very popular well run place – not a pub but does have proper informal front locals' bar, three Brancaster ales and Woodfordes, lots of wines by the glass, good photographs, bar billiards; middle area with comfortable sofas and newspapers, big airy dining conservatory overlooking tidal marshes, enjoyable bar and restaurant food including plenty of fish; children welcome, dogs in bar, seats on sun deck with fine views, more under cover on heated terrace, nicely seasidey bedrooms, coast path at bottom of garden, open all day. *Recommended by Michael Dandy, John Ainscough, Peter and Josie Fawcett, Henry Pursehouse-Tranter, George and Beverley Tucker, Jenny and Brian Seller and others*

BROOME TM3591   NR35 2NZ
Artichoke
Yarmouth Road

Eight well kept ales including Adnams and Elgoods, belgian fruit beers and good range of whiskies in properly unpretentious split-level roadside pub, enjoyable traditional home-made food in bar or dining room, friendly helpful staff, wood or flagstone floors, inglenook log fire; dogs welcome, garden picnic-sets, smokers' shelter, open all day except closed Mon. *Recommended by Martin Crisp*

BURNHAM THORPE TF8541   PE31 8HL

 Lord Nelson

Off B1155 or B1355, near Burnham Market

Neatly kept 17th-c pub with lots of Nelson memorabilia (he was born in this sleepy village), antique high-backed settles on worn red tiles in small bar, smoke ovens in original fireplace, little snug leading off, two dining rooms one with flagstones and open fire, good bar food, Greene King, Woodfordes and a guest tapped from the cask, several wines by the glass, secret rum-based recipes (Nelson's Blood and Lady Hamilton's Nip); children and dogs welcome, good-sized play area and pétanque in big garden, open all day in summer, closed Mon evening (except school/bank holidays). *Recommended by Mike Proctor, Ian Phillips, Henry Pursehouse-Tranter, Walter and Susan Rinaldi-Butcher, David Carr, Tracey and Stephen Groves and others*

CASTLE ACRE TF8115   PE32 2AE

☆ **Ostrich**

Stocks Green

16th-c inn with some nice original features (masonry, trusses and beams) overlooking tree-lined green, L-shaped two-level bar with woodburner in big fireplace (log fire in upper part), pubby furniture on wood-strip floor, gold patterned wallpaper, Greene King and a guest, several wines including sparkling by the glass, separate dining room with another fire and fair choice of decent food (not Sun evening); children and dogs welcome, picnic-sets under parasols in sheltered garden, remains of Norman castle in the village as well as a Cluniac monastery, bedrooms, open all day (till 12.30am Sat). *Recommended by Dr and Mrs R G J Telfer, Tom and Sally Millest, Brian Glozier, Debby Horsman, Charles Gysin, John Baxter and others*

CATFIELD TG3821   NR29 5AA

Crown

The Street

Immaculate archetypal village inn with warmly welcoming landlady, good choice of changing ales, real ciders, enjoyable food from italian chef/landlord; bedrooms, not far from Hickling Broad, closed Mon (except bank holidays when closed Tues). *Recommended by Roy Hoing*

CAWSTON TG1422   NR10 4HA

Ratcatchers

Off B1145; Eastgate, S of village

Popular beamed dining pub with old chairs and fine mix of walnut, beech, elm and oak tables, quieter candlelit dining room on right, nice food, Adnams and Woodfordes, quite a few malt whiskies, conservatory; piped music, no dogs; children welcome, heated terrace, open all day Sun. *Recommended by A Kirk, Dr and Mrs R G J Telfer, David Carr*

COLTISHALL TG2719   NR12 7EA

 Kings Head

Wroxham Road (B1354)

Welcoming reliable dining pub close to river, good imaginative food especially fish, generous bar snacks and good value lunch deals, friendly helpful service, well kept Adnams, nice wines by the glass, open fire, fishing nets and stuffed fish including monster pike (personable chef/landlord a keen fisherman); piped music; reasonably priced bedrooms, decent breakfast, moorings nearby. *Recommended by Roger and Lesley Everett, Julie and Bill Ryan*

COLTON TG1009   NR9 5DG

Ugly Bug

Well signed once off A47

Comfortable country pub with plenty of beamery, plush banquettes and some old enamel signs in extensive carpeted bar, enthusiastic friendly staff, enjoyable food including changing blackboard choice in bar and restaurant, ales from Humpty Dumpty and

Theakstons, good value wines, friendly pub dog called Alfie, jazz nights; terrace and big garden with koi carp lake, eight bedrooms, closed Tues lunchtime. *Recommended by Julia and Richard Tredgett, Peter Hallinan*

CROMER TG2242   NR27 9HD
Red Lion
Off A149; Tucker Street/Brook Street

Substantial refurbished Victorian hotel with elevated sea views, original features including panelling and open fires, well kept ales such as Woodfordes in bare-boards, flint-walled bar, enjoyable food from sandwiches and ciabattas up, good service, restaurant and conservatory; piped music; children welcome, disabled facilities, back courtyard tables, 12 bedrooms, open all day. *Recommended by Fred and Lorraine Gill, Lawrence Pearse, David Carr, Tony Middis*

DOWNHAM MARKET TF6103   PE38 9HF
Castle
High Street

Black and white painted market-town inn, friendly and comfortable, with interesting local photographs, cartoons and cuttings in small cosy bar, tasty fairly priced food (separate restaurant menu), Greene King IPA, efficient service; piped music; children welcome, pavement tables, 11 bedrooms. *Recommended by John Wooll*

DOWNHAM MARKET TF6103   PE38 9DH
Crown
Bridge Street

Popular rambling 17th-c coaching inn, all steps, nooks and crannies, with good log fire in oak-panelled bar, 635 Pathfinder bomber squadron photographs, Adnams, Greene King and guests, reasonably priced food from snacks to specials; seats in coachyard, bedrooms. *Recommended by John Wooll, David and Sue Atkinson*

DOWNHAM MARKET TF6003   PE38 9EN
Railway Arms
At railway station, Railway Road

Small station bar with tiny adjoining rooms, one with glowing coal fire, another with second-hand bookshop, real ales, tea and coffee, model train sometimes running around; best to check opening times. *Recommended by David and Sue Atkinson, John Wooll*

DRAYTON TG1813   NR8 6AE
Cock
Drayton High Road

Popular pub with plenty of loyal regulars, good choice of well kept Marstons-related ales, good value food including bargain Sun lunch served at well spaced tables, friendly efficient staff. *Recommended by R C Vincent*

EAST BARSHAM TF9133   NR21 0LH
White Horse
B1105 3 miles N of Fakenham

Extended pub with big log fire in long beamed main bar, steps to other areas, well kept Adnams, decent wine and good coffee, pleasant swift service, good choice of enjoyable home-made food including bargain OAP lunches, two small attractive dining rooms; piped music, darts; children welcome, three well priced bedrooms. *Recommended by R C Vincent, Roger and Lesley Everett*

☆ EDGEFIELD TG0934   NR24 2RL
Pigs
Norwich Road; B1149 S of Holt

Friendly bustling pub with carpeted bar, Adnams, Woodfordes and guests tapped from casks, arches through to simply furnished area with mixed chairs and pews on broad pine boards, airy dining extension in similar style split into stall areas by standing timbers and low brick walls, good interesting food (all day Sun), games room with bar billiards, also children's playroom; piped music; dogs allowed in bar, good wheelchair access, rustic seats and tables on big covered terrace, adventure playground, boules, bedrooms, open all day Sun. *Recommended by Dr and Mrs R G J Telfer, Tracey and Stephen Groves, Amanda Stark, David Carr, Muriel and John Hobbs, Annette Tress and others*

ERPINGHAM TG1732   NR11 7LZ
☆ **Saracens Head**
Wolterton; Erpingham signed off A140 N of Aylsham, on through Calthorpe

Gently refurbished and freshened up but still civilised and relaxed; two-room bar remains simple and stylish with high ceilings, light terracotta walls, nice mix of seating from built-in wall seats to wicker fireside chairs, tall windows with elegant drapes, fresh flowers, pretty little parlour with big log fire, Woodfordes ales, several wines by the glass, enjoyable food; well behaved children allowed, dogs in bar, seats in charming old-fashioned gravel stableyard, bedrooms, good breakfast, closed Mon and lunchtime Tues, otherwise open all day. *Recommended by Philip and Susan Philcox, R C Vincent, John and Victoria Fairley, Sue Demont, Tim Barrow, Canon Michael Bourdeaux and others*

GAYTON TF7219   PE32 1PA
Crown
Lynn Road (B1145/B1153)

Low-beamed country pub with plenty of character, unusual old features and charming snug as well as three main areas, good choice of popular sensibly priced food from sandwiches up, Greene King ales, friendly service, sofas and good log fire, games room; tables in attractive sheltered garden. *Recommended by John Wooll*

GELDESTON TM3990   NR34 0HW
☆ **Locks**
Off A143/A146 NW of Beccles; off Station Road S of village, obscurely signed down long rough track

Remote candlelit pub at navigable head of River Waveney, ancient tiled-floor core with beams and big log fire, Green Jack and guest ales tapped from casks, good choice of enjoyable food including vegetarian, large extension for summer crowds, weekend music nights; riverside garden, moorings, open all day weekends and in summer; in winter closed Mon, Tues and lunchtimes Weds-Fri. *Recommended by Robert Lorimer, the Didler, Richard Martin*

GREAT BIRCHAM TF7632   PE31 6RJ
☆ **Kings Head**
B1155, S end of village (called and signed Bircham locally)

More hotel/restaurant than pub, yet with plenty of regulars and four real ales in small attractively contemporary bar with log fire and comfortable sofas, good innovative food including deals in light and airy modern restaurant, friendly helpful staff; TV in bar; tables and chairs out front and back with rustic view, 12 comfortable bedrooms, good breakfast. *Recommended by Tracey and Stephen Groves, R C Vincent*

GREAT CRESSINGHAM TF8401   IP25 6NN
☆ **Windmill**
Village signed off A1065 S of Swaffham; Water End

Interesting pictures and bric-a-brac in warren of rambling linked rooms, plenty of cosy corners, good value fresh bar food from baguettes to steak, Sun roasts, good changing beer range including Windy Miller Quixote (brewed for the pub), good coffee, decent wines, plenty of malt whiskies, cheery staff, well lit pool room, pub games; piped music, big sports TV in side snug; children and dogs welcome, picnic-sets and good play area in big garden, caravan parking, bedroom extension. *Recommended by Gordon Smale*

HAINFORD TG2219   NR10 3AY
Chequers
Stratton Road

Comfortable thatched and beamed dining pub in charming setting, wide choice of popular food from baguettes up, four or five well kept ales including Woodfordes and Greene King, polite service; children welcome, well arranged gardens with play area. *Recommended by R C Vincent, C Galloway*

HARLESTON TM2483   IP20 9AD
J D Young
Market Place

Refurbished hotel/pub, convivial bar with three local ales, comfortable spacious library-feel dining room with lamps on well spaced tables, open fire, enjoyable good value fresh food all day from 7am, friendly efficient staff; bedrooms. *Recommended by Martin and Pauline Jennings*

HEACHAM TF6737   PE31 7EX
Fox & Hounds
Station Road

Unpretentious open-plan pub brewing its own good Fox Heacham Gold, also well kept guest beers and Saxon farm cider (regular beer festivals), cheery chatty service, good generous home-made food (not Sun evening) in comfortable bar and spotless light and airy dining area; pool; small garden, open all day. *Recommended by Alan Weedon, Tracey and Stephen Groves*

HICKLING TG4123   NR12 0YA
Greyhound
The Green

Small busy pub with welcoming open fire, enjoyable food including nice crab salad and good Sun roasts in bar and neat restaurant, well kept Woodfordes Wherry, friendly long-serving landlord; well behaved children welcome, pretty garden with terrace tables, bedroom annexe. *Recommended by Rosemary Willett, J F M and M West, Roy Hoing*

HOLKHAM TF8943   NR23 1RG
☆ Victoria
A149 near Holkham Hall

Upmarket but informal small hotel (owned by Holkham Estate), eclectic mix of furnishings including deep low sofas, lighted candles in heavy sticks, big log fire, well kept Adnams Bitter, Woodfordes Wherry and a guest, nice wines and coffee, good local seasonal food, friendly if not speedy service, anglo-indian décor in linked dining rooms (best to book); piped music; children welcome, dogs in bar, sheltered courtyard with retractable awning, walks to nature-reserve salt marshes and sea, ten stylish bedrooms, open all day. *Recommended by Michael Dandy, George Atkinson, Mike and Sue Loseby, Tony Middis, David Carr, Tracey and Stephen Groves and others*

HOLME NEXT THE SEA TF7043   PE36 6LH
White Horse
Kirkgate Street

Attractive old-fashioned place, cosy and rambling, with warm log fire, ample choice of good generous food including local fish and Sun roasts, reasonable prices, friendly helpful service, Adnams beers and decent wine, two friendly pub dogs and cat; children welcome, small back garden, seats out in front and on lawn opposite. *Recommended by John Wooll, Tracey and Stephen Groves, Linda Miller and Derek Greentree and others*

Bedroom prices include full english breakfast, VAT and any
inclusive service charge that we know of.

HOLT TG0738
Feathers
Market Place

NR25 6BW

Unpretentious hotel with popular locals' bar comfortably extended around original panelled area, open fire, antiques in attractive entrance/reception area, good choice of enjoyable fairly priced food, quick friendly service, Greene King ales and decent wines, good coffee, restaurant and dining conservatory; piped music, no dogs; children welcome, 15 comfortable bedrooms, open all day. *Recommended by David Carr, D and M T Ayres-Regan*

HOLT TG0738
Kings Head
High Street/Bull Street

NR25 6BN

Reworked inn under newish ownership, enjoyable food including charcoal grilled steaks, prompt friendly service, beers such as Adnams, Humpty Dumpty and Woodfordes, fair choice of wines, bustling rustic public bar, two roomy back bars and conservatory; some live music, sports TV, pool; children welcome, back terrace with heated smokers' shelter, good-sized garden, three stylish bedrooms, open all day. *Recommended by Gerry and Rosemary Dobson, Derek Field, Tracey and Stephen Groves, Jeremy King*

HUNSTANTON TF6740
Waterside
Beach Terrace Road

PE36 5BQ

Former station buffet just above prom, now bar/restaurant with great sea views from conservatory (children welcome here), Adnams and Greene King Abbot, good value wines, inexpensive straightforward food all day from sandwiches up, quick service by friendly uniformed staff, Fri quiz; dogs on leads allowed. *Recommended by John Wooll*

HUNWORTH TG0735
 ☆ ## Hunny Bell
Signed off B roads S of Holt

NR24 2AA

Welcoming carefully furnished 18th-c pub, neat bar with nice mix of cushioned dining chairs around wooden tables, stone floor and woodburner, cosy snug with homely furniture on old tiles, some original stripped-brick walls throughout, another woodburner in high-raftered dining room, good variety of popular well presented food, Adnams Bitter, Greene King Abbot, Woodfordes Wherry and a guest; children and dogs welcome, picnic-sets on terrace overlooking village green, more seats in garden among fruit trees. *Recommended by Philip and Susan Philcox, Tracey and Stephen Groves, D and M T Ayres-Regan, Roger and Lesley Everett, Jeremy King*

INGHAM TG3926
☆ ## Swan
Off A149 SE of North Walsham; signed from Stalham

NR12 9AB

Smart 14th-c thatched dining pub nicely placed for Broads and coast; rustic main area divided by massive chimneybreast with woodburner on each side, low beams and hefty standing timbers, bare boards or parquet, some old farm tools, quieter small brick-floored part with leather sofas, good well presented restaurant-style food including cheaper lunchtime set menu, home-baked bread, Woodfordes ales and local cider; children welcome, picnic-sets on sunny back terrace, more at side, five bedrooms in converted stables, good breakfast. *Recommended by Peter Sutton, Richard Ball, Roy Hoing, Tony Middis, Sandy Butcher, Sue Kinder and others*

ITTERINGHAM TG1430
Walpole Arms
Village signposted off B1354 NW of Aylsham

NR11 7AR

Unpretentious 18th-c brick pub close to Blickling Hall, sizeable open-plan beamed bar with stripped-brick walls and mix of dining tables, quietly chatty atmosphere, well kept Adnams Bitter and Broadside, Woodfordes Wherry and guest on handpump, good wines by the glass, ambitious and generally very well liked food, light airy dining room with beamery; children welcome, dogs in bar, two-acre landscaped garden with vine-covered terrace, closed Sun evening. *Recommended by R C Vincent, Julie and Bill Ryan, Tracey and Stephen Groves*

KING'S LYNN TF6119   PE30 1RD
☆ ## Bank House
Kings Staithe Square

Attractive and civilised big-windowed bar/brasserie under same management as Rose & Crown at Snettisham; contemporary conversion of handsome Georgian building in splendid quiet quayside spot, sofas, armchairs and pastel colours, Fullers London Pride and Greene King Abbot, enjoyable food from sandwiches to steaks including light dishes all day, may be weekday lunch deals too, pleasant efficient service, daily papers; children welcome, 11 good bedrooms. *Recommended by John Wooll, Sophie de Winton*

KING'S LYNN TF6119   PE30 5DT
Bradleys
South Quay

Stylishly simple bar/restaurant with good sensibly priced food, good choice of wines by the glass, Adnams, more expensive upstairs restaurant with river views, ornate mirrors, elegant curtains and plenty of flowers, pleasant helpful service; quayside tables and small courtyard garden, open all day. *Recommended by John Wooll*

KING'S LYNN TF6120   PE30 1LJ
Crown & Mitre
Ferry Street

Old-fashioned pub in great riverside spot, lots of interesting Naval and nautical memorabilia, well kept Tom Woods and changing guests such as local Tydd Steam, own brews still planned by no-nonsense landlord, good value straightforward home-made food, river-view back conservatory; no credit cards; well behaved children and dogs welcome, quayside tables, barbecue. *Recommended by R C Vincent, John Wooll*

KING'S LYNN TF6120   PE30 1JS
Dukes Head
Tuesday Market Place

Imposing refurbished early 18th-c hotel, small cosy bar and popular dining room, good value tasty food including set deals, Adnams, good choice of wines, cheerful attentive service, back lounge and more formal restaurant; bedrooms. *Recommended by John Wooll, George Atkinson*

KING'S LYNN TF6220   PE30 1EG
Lattice House
Corner of Market Lane, off Tuesday Market Place

Old beamed and raftered Wetherspoons with good choice of ales, well priced food and friendly speedy service; children welcome, open all day. *Recommended by R C Vincent*

MORSTON TG0043   NR2 7AA
☆ ## Anchor
A149 Salthouse—Stiffkey; The Street

Three traditional rooms with pubby furniture on original wood floors, coal fires and woodburner, local 1950s beach photographs, prints and bric-a-brac, Greene King IPA, Winters Golden and Woodfordes Wherry, several wines by the glass, contemporary airy extension with deep leather sofas around low tables, grey-painted country dining furniture, enjoyable straightforward food all day; children and dogs welcome, tables and benches out in front, wonderful bird-watching/walking, you can book seal-spotting trips from here, open all day from 9am. *Recommended by Terry Devine, Derek Field, Adrian Johnson, Robert Fuge, Dave Braisted and others*

NORTH CREAKE TF8538   NR21 9JW
☆ **Jolly Farmers**
Burnham Road

Welcoming village local with three cosy rooms, main bar with large open fire, farmhouse
and high-backed leather dining chairs around pine tables on quarry tiles, cabinet of
model cars, smaller bar with woodburner, another in red-walled dining room, Woodfordes
tapped from the cask and a couple of guests, several wines by the glass, good well
presented food served by friendly staff; piped music; children and dogs welcome, seats on
terrace and in garden; charming flintstone village, closed Mon, Tues. *Recommended by*
R L Borthwick, Tracey and Stephen Groves, Linda Miller and Derek Greentree, Revd John E Cooper

NORTHREPPS TG2439   NR27 0AA
Foundry Arms
Church Street

Welcoming village pub with enjoyable traditional food including bargain Sun lunch, well
kept Adnams and Woodfordes, decent choice of wines, woodburner; children and dogs
welcome, garden picnic-sets, open all day. *Recommended by Karen Bell, Conrad Freezer*

NORWICH TG2408   NR1 1BA
Coach & Horses
Thorpe Road

Light and airy tap for Chalk Hill brewery, friendly staff, generous inexpensive home-made
food 12-9 (8 Sun) including all-day breakfast, bare-boards L-shaped bar with open fire,
dark wood, posters and prints, pleasant back dining area; sports TVs, gets very busy on
home match days; disabled access possible (not to lavatories), front terrace, open all day.
Recommended by David Carr, the Didler, Jeremy King

NORWICH TG2309   NR3 1JE
☆ **Kings Head**
Magdalen Street

Well run traditional Victorian local, friendly licensees and good atmosphere in two bare-
boards bars, ten or so very well kept changing regional ales, good choice of imported
beers, local ciders, no food except pork pies, bar billiards; open all day. *Recommended by*
David Carr, the Didler, Ralph Holland, Mike and Eleanor Anderson and others

NORWICH TG2108   NR2 3LD
☆ **Mad Moose**
Warwick Street/Dover Street, off A140 ring road via Unthank Road

Comfortable historic hotel high on the moors, pubby bar food (all day) and more
elaborate restaurant menu, ancient-feeling long narrow stone barrel-vaulted crypt bar
with plush stools down either side on aged flagstones, Black Sheep Best, Theakstons Best
and a guest from Hadrian & Border on handpump, flatscreen TV, smarter reception rooms
have low beams, old settles and sepia photographs and a massive 13th-c fireplace, lovely
walled garden in former cloisters; children and dogs welcome. *Recommended by anon*

NORWICH TG2208   NR2 4AR
Plough
St Benedict's Street

Taken over and refurbished by Grain, their ales and guests kept well, good wines,
knowledgeable staff, comfortable seating and open fire; good garden. *Recommended by*
Ralph Holland

NORWICH TG2308   NR3 1HY
Ribs of Beef
Wensum Street, S side of Fye Bridge

Welcoming and comfortable with good range of real ales including local brews, farm
cider, good wine choice, deep leather sofas and small tables upstairs, attractive smaller

downstairs room with river view, generous low-priced food (till 5pm Sun), quick cheerful service, Tues quiz; tables out on narrow waterside walkway. *Recommended by John Wooll, David Carr, the Didler*

NORWICH TG2207   NR2 2DR
Unthank Arms
Newmarket Street

Relaxed Victorian corner pub, spaciously refurbished, with enjoyable sensibly priced food (all day Sun), good choice of wines by the glass, real ales, friendly service, open fires, upstairs dining room and lounge, annual comedy festival; children welcome, garden behind with covered area, summer barbecues, open all day. *Recommended by Robert Watt, Anthony Barnes*

NORWICH TG2308   NR3 3AQ
White Lion
Oak Street

Small traditional pub with well kept ales including Milton, belgian bottled beers, enjoyable generous home-made food (all day Fri and Sat), reasonable prices, pub games including bar billiards, friendly atmosphere, open all day Fri-Sun. *Recommended by Steve Nye, D Williams, Adam Oxbury, Keith Denton, Wayne Martin*

OVERSTRAND TG2440   NR27 0AB
White Horse
High Street

Light fresh refurbishment, comfortable and stylish, with good choice of enjoyable food in bar, dining room or barn restaurant, at least three well kept local ales, friendly staff, pool room; prominent piped music, silent sports TV; children and dogs welcome, terrace and garden tables, play equipment, eight bedrooms, open all day from 8am. *Recommended by MDN, Jeremy King*

OXBOROUGH TF7401   PE33 9PS
Bedingfeld Arms
Opposite church

Peaceful setting opposite NT Oxburgh Hall, enjoyable generous food, friendly staff; tables in big garden, popular with cyclists, bedrooms. *Recommended by Nigel Lambert, Julia and Richard Tredgett*

☆ RINGSTEAD TF7040   PE36 5JU
Gin Trap
Village signed off A149 near Hunstanton; OS Sheet 132 map reference 707403

Attractive well run 17th-c coaching inn with friendly helpful licensees, two bar areas, original part with beams, woodburner and pubby furniture, Adnams and Woodfordes ales, enjoyable if not particularly cheap food, airy dining conservatory; piped music; children welcome, dogs in bar, garden tables, art gallery next door, Peddar's Way walks, bedrooms, open all day in summer. *Recommended by Michael Dandy, M V Burke, Mrs Margo Finlay, Jörg Kasprowski, John Wooll, Roy Hoing and others*

SCULTHORPE TF8930   NR21 9QD
Hourglass
The Street

Long open room combining light modern style with beams and bare boards, good choice of enjoyable well priced food at well spaced tables, Wells & Youngs Bombardier and Woodfordes Wherry, quick friendly service. *Recommended by John Wooll, M and J White*

It's very helpful if you let us know up-to-date food prices when you report on pubs.

SCULTHORPE TF8930   NR21 9QG
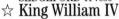 **Sculthorpe Mill**
Inn signed off A148 W of Fakenham, opposite village

Welcoming dining pub in rebuilt 18th-c mill, appealing riverside setting, seats out under weeping willows and in attractive garden behind; light, airy and relaxed with leather sofas and sturdy tables in bar/dining area, good reliable well priced food from sandwiches up, may have excellent fresh crab, prompt friendly service, well kept Greene King ales, nice house wines, upstairs restaurant; piped music; six comfortable bedrooms, good breakfast, open all day weekends and in summer. *Recommended by John Wooll, Mark, Amanda, Luke and Jake Sheard and others*

SEDGEFORD TF7036   PE36 5LU
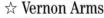 **King William IV**
B1454, off A149 Kings Lynn—Hunstanton

Extended and refurbished inn with homely bar, several intimate dining areas with high-backed dark leather chairs around pine tables on slate tiles, log fires, good choice of food from baguettes and pubby things up, Adnams, Greene King, Woodfordes and a guest, good wines by the glass, friendly obliging staff; children allowed till 6.30pm, seats on terrace, picnic-sets under parasols on grass, attractive covered dining area, comfortable bedrooms, good breakfast, closed Mon lunchtime except bank holidays. *Recommended by Tracey and Stephen Groves, Stuart and Joan Bloomer, Amanda Stark*

SHERINGHAM TG1543   NR26 8BA
Windham Arms
Wyndham Street

Well kept Woodfordes and other ales in cheerful local, enjoyable sensibly priced food with greek influences (chef is greek), friendly efficient service, woodburner in carpeted beamed lounge, tightly packed dining tables, separate public bar with pool; picnic-sets outside, sizeable car park (useful here), open all day. *Recommended by Brian Glozier*

SKEYTON TG2524   NR10 5DH
Goat
Off A140 N of Aylsham; Long Road

Extended thatched and low-beamed food pub, well kept ales, efficient service, long dark-raftered dining area and small restaurant; pleasant terrace and tables under trees by pub's neat playing field – very quiet spot. *Recommended by Dr and Mrs R G J Telfer*

SOUTH WOOTTON TF6622   PE30 3HQ
Farmers Arms
Part of Knights Hill Hotel, Grimston Road (off A148/A149)

Hotel complex's olde-worlde barn and stables conversion, food all day including bargain weekday lunchtime carvery, Adnams and guests, good wines and abundant coffee, friendly service, stripped brick and timbers, quiet snugs and corners, hayloft restaurant; piped music; tables and play area outside, 79 comfortable bedrooms, open all day. *Recommended by John Wooll, R C Vincent*

SOUTHREPPS TG2536   NR11 8NP
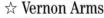 **Vernon Arms**
Church Street

Popular old-fashioned village pub, welcoming and relaxed, with good food (not Mon evening) running up to steaks and well priced crab and lobster specials (must book weekend evenings), friendly helpful young staff, real ales such as Adnams, Black Sheep, Timothy Taylors and Wells & Youngs, good choice of wines and malt whiskies, log fire; children, dogs and muddy walkers welcome. *Recommended by Conrad Freezer, Judith and David Salter, M J Winterton, Jim Farmer and others*

SPOONER ROW TM0997   NR18 9LL

Boars

Just off A11 SW of Wymondham

1920s pub/restaurant in tiny village, well kept Adnams, good range of wines (three glass sizes), enjoyable locally sourced food from light choices to more expensive things, friendly service, amazing collection of food/wine books; tables in well tended garden. *Recommended by Evelyn and Derek Walter, Noreen Collin, Darrell Bethell*

SPORLE TF8411   PE32 2DR

Squirrels Drey

The Street

Smallish pub with log-fire bar, refurbished restaurant and little conservatory, good interesting food (not Sun evening) from short menu, also good value weekday set choice, Adnams, Greene King IPA and a guest like Woodfordes Wherry, Aspall's cider, decent house wine, quick friendly service; children and dogs welcome (resident jack russell called Jake), garden with play area, closed Mon. *Recommended by Martin Hickey, John Wooll*

STANHOE TF8037   PE31 8QD

☆ Duck

B1155 Docking—Burnham Market

Recently transformed gastropub (former Crown) – original bar area now two-part dining room, and new extension houses, side bar with skylights; Elgoods Pageant from fine slab-topped counter, banquettes around unusual glass display table showing all sorts of stones, simpler furnishings on new black slate flooring, seaside and fish prints, motley collection of old books, wicker hurdling (resembling draped fishing nets) screens off bare-boards dining area with stripped or white-painted chairs around kitchen tables, good fairly priced food (not Sun evening, Mon) with emphasis on fish, efficient black-clad staff; well behaved children allowed, dogs in bar, elegant smokers' shelter and circular picnic-sets in side garden, two well appointed bedrooms and site for caravans. *Recommended by Tracey and Stephen Groves*

STOKE HOLY CROSS TG2302   NR14 8QJ

☆ Wildebeest Arms

Village signposted off A140 S of Norwich; turn left in village

More restaurant than pub with all tables set for diners, but several bar stools by sleek bar for just a drink; long room with understated african theme, carefully placed carvings and hangings on dark sandy walls, unusual dark leather chairs grouped around striking tables, neatly dressed staff, good contemporary food including fixed-price menus, fine range of wines by the glass, Woodfordes Wherry; children welcome, subtly lit front terrace with comfortable wicker armchairs or cushioned benches around glass-topped tables, garden behind. *Recommended by Nicola Eaton*

TACOLNESTON TM1495   NR16 1AL

Pelican

Norwich Road

Rambling pub with dark-beamed and flagstoned log-fire bar and modern restaurant, new chef doing good choice of food from pub favourites up, four local ales including one brewed for them, 32 malt whiskies, shop selling local produce and bottled Norfolk/Suffolk ales; bedrooms, closed Sun evening. *Recommended by Anthony Barnes*

THORNHAM TF7343   PE36 6LT

☆ Lifeboat

A149 by Kings Head, then first left

In administration as we go to press but hopefully all will settle; characterful inn facing coastal sea flats, several interesting bars, pews, window seats, carved oak tables, masses of guns, swords, reed-slashers and other antique farm tools, lighting by antique paraffin lamps, pubby food, Adnams, Greene King and Woodfordes ales; children welcome, dogs in bar, back terrace with play area, lots of surrounding walks, bedrooms, has been open all day. *Recommended by John Saville, Mike Proctor, Michael Dandy, George Atkinson, David and Ruth Hollands, David and Sue Atkinson and others*

WALSINGHAM TF9336 NR22 6BP
Bull
Common Place/Shire Hall Plain

Unpretentious rather quirky pub in pilgrimage village; bar's darkly ancient walls covered with clerical visiting cards and pictures of archbishops, various odds and ends including a half-size statue of Charlie Chaplin, welcoming landlord and good-humoured staff, well kept Adnams, Clarks and Woodfordes, lunchtime food from good value sandwiches up, log fire, pool room, old-fashioned cash register in gents'; dovecote above entrance stuffed with plastic lobsters and crabs, picnic-sets out in courtyard and on attractive flowery terrace by village square, open all day. *Recommended by David Carr, Pam and John Smith, Giles Smith and Sandra Kiely*

WARHAM TF9441 NR23 1NL
☆ Three Horseshoes
Warham All Saints; village signed from A149 Wells-next-the-Sea—Blakeney, and from B1105 S of Wells

Old-fashioned pub with gas lighting in simple rooms looking unchanged since the 1920s (parts date back to 1720); stripped-deal or mahogany tables (one marked for shove-ha'penny) on stone floor, red leatherette settles built around partly panelled walls of public bar, royalist photographs, old working American one-arm bandit, big longcase clock with clear piping strike, twister on ceiling to point out who gets next round, open fires in Victorian fireplaces, Humpty Dumpty and Woodfordes ales, local cider, generous helpings of pubby food, gramophone museum opened on request; no credit cards; children (away from bar area) and dogs welcome, seats in courtyard garden with flower tubs and well, bedrooms. *Recommended by Henry Pursehouse-Tranter, David Carr, Muriel and John Hobbs, Chris Johnson, Barry Collett and others*

WEASENHAM ST PETER TF8522 PE32 2TD
Fox & Hounds
A1065 Fakenham—Swaffham; The Green

Traditional 18th-c beamed local with bar and two dining areas, spotless and well run by friendly family, three Tom Woods ales, good honest home-made food at reasonable prices (including breakfast and Sun roasts), lots of military prints; children welcome, big well kept garden and terrace. *Recommended by D and M T Ayres-Regan, Tony Middis*

WELLS-NEXT-THE-SEA TF9143 NR23 1AE
Edinburgh
Station Road/Church Street

Traditional pub near main shopping area, good affordable home-made pubby food, well kept Bass, Woodfordes and a guest, open fire, local photographs for sale, sizeable restaurant (check winter opening times); piped and occasional live music, sports TV, no credit cards (bank next door); children and dogs welcome, disabled access, courtyard with heated smokers' shelter, three bedrooms, open all day. *Recommended by David Carr*

WELLS-NEXT-THE-SEA TF9143 NR23 1EU
☆ Globe
The Buttlands

Handsome Georgian inn with opened-up rooms spreading spaciously back from front bar with its comfortable sofas and armchairs, three big bow windows, tables on oak boards, contemporary décor, enjoyable food using seasonal local ingredients, Adnams and Woodfordes ales, thoughtful wine selection, good coffee; piped music – live evening jazz (second Sun of month), TV; children and dogs welcome, green cast-iron furniture on heated back terrace, colourful hanging baskets, short walk from quay, seven bedrooms, open all day. *Recommended by Henry Pursehouse-Tranter, David Carr, DF, NF, Jeremy and Ruth Preston-Hoar*

WEST BECKHAM TG1439

NR25 6NX

☆ **Wheatsheaf**

Church Road; off A148 Holt—Cromer

Brick-built pub with bars mainly set for dining, beams and standing timbers, cottagey doors and traditional pubby furnishings, horsebrasses and old photographs, log fires, Greene King, Woodfordes and a guest, several wines by the glass, enjoyable food (best to book weekends); piped music; children welcome, dogs in bar, charming ramshackle garden with covered terrace (they may ask to keep a credit card while you eat out here), play area, closed Sun evening (and Mon in winter). *Recommended by Fred and Lorraine Gill, Philip and Susan Philcox, David Carr, Derek Field and others*

WEYBOURNE TG1143

NR25 7SZ

Ship

A149 W of Sheringham; The Street

Popular village pub with half a dozen local ales such as Buffys, Grain, Humpty Dumpty and Winters, big straightforward bar with pubby furniture and woodburner, two dining rooms, good reasonably priced food, pleasant service; piped music; well behaved children welcome, dogs in bar, nice garden and pretty hanging baskets, handy for Muckleburgh Military Vehicle Museum, open all day in summer. *Recommended by Derek Field, Tom Ambrose, David Field, Alan Sutton*

WIGHTON TF9439

NR23 1PF

☆ **Carpenters Arms**

High Street; off main road, past church

Unusual décor with mix of brightly painted tables and chairs on wood floor, bric-a-brac on shelves, vintage Holkham pottery, assorted artwork, leather sofas, and a mulberry dining room; warm welcome, good generous local food (not Mon lunchtime in winter) from pub favourites to more individual dishes, charming service, well kept Adnams, Woodfordes and a local beer bottled for them; picnic-sets in informal back garden, open all day weekends and bank holidays. *Recommended by Tracey and Stephen Groves*

WIVETON TG0442

NR25 7TL

☆ **Bell**

Blakeney Road

Enjoyable modern food in very popular dining pub (a couple of tables left for drinkers), mainly open-plan with beams, nice mix of dining chairs and wooden tables on stripped-wood floor, good log fire, sizeable conservatory with smart beige dining chairs on coir, Wolf, Woodfordes and Yetmans ales; children welcome, dogs in bar, picnic-sets on front grass looking across to church, stylish wicker furniture on decked areas behind, comfortable realistically priced bedrooms, self-catering cottage, open all day. *Recommended by George Cowie, Frances Gosnell, Michael and Maggie Betton, Peter and Giff Bennett, Phil Revell, David Carr, Sandy Butcher and others*

WYMONDHAM TG1001

NR18 0PH

☆ **Green Dragon**

Church Street

Picturesque heavily timbered 14th-c inn, simple beamed and timbered back bar, log fire under Tudor mantelpiece, interesting pictures, bigger dining area (children allowed), friendly helpful staff, four well kept ales including Adnams; children and dogs welcome, modest bedrooms, near glorious 12th-c abbey church. *Recommended by Mr and Mrs W W Burke, the Didler*

Post Office address codings confusingly give the impression that some pubs are in Norfolk, when they're really in Cambridgeshire or Suffolk (which is where we list them).

ALSO WORTH A VISIT IN SUFFOLK

Besides the region's top pubs, we recommend the following. Do tell us
what you think of them: **feedback@goodguides.com**

BARHAM TM1251   IP6 0PG
Sorrel Horse
Old Norwich Road

Open-plan country inn with good log fire in central chimneybreast, dark beams and
timbers, well kept real ales and popular food; children welcome, picnic-sets on side grass
with big play area, bedrooms in converted barn, open all day Weds-Sun. *Recommended by
Nicholas Rust*

BARNBY TM4789   NR34 7QF
Swan
Off A146 Beccles—Lowestoft; Swan Lane

Plush 17th-c beamed dining pub with Lowestoft connections giving excellent choice of
good fresh fish, Adnams and Greene King, good house wines, helpful friendly young staff,
large bar with raised eating area, pleasant good-sized dining room, fishing décor; seats
outside among flowering tubs and hanging baskets. *Recommended by Judith and David Salter*

BARTON MILLS TL72173   IP28 6AA
Olde Bull
Just S of Mildenhall; The Street

Attractive rambling bars and restaurant, reasonable choice of home-made food all day
from lunchtime sandwiches up, Sun roasts, big log fire, Adnams, Greene King and a local
guest, decent wine list and coffee; piped and some live music; well behaved children
welcome, central courtyard, 14 bedrooms, open all day. *Recommended by Jeremy King*

BLAXHALL TM3656   IP12 2DY
Ship
Off B1069 S of Snape; can be reached from A12 via Little Glemham

Popular low-beamed 18th-c pub, good traditional home-made food in bar and restaurant,
well kept Adnams Bitter, Woodfordes Wherry and guests, some live music; children in
eating areas, dogs in bar, eight chalet bedrooms, good breakfast, attractive country
setting; open all day Sun. *Recommended by Alistair Bacon, Ken Anderson*

BLYTHBURGH TM4575   IP19 9LQ
White Hart
A12

Open-plan roadside family dining pub, a former courthouse dating to the 16th c, with fine
ancient beams, woodwork and staircase, full Adnams range kept well, Aspall's cider and
good choice of wines, good coffee, enjoyable food from huge sandwiches up, friendly
service, inglenook log fire; children in eating areas, back terrace and spacious lawns
looking down on tidal bird marshes, magnificent church over road, four bedrooms, open
all day. *Recommended by Bruce and Sharon Eden, Charles and Pauline Stride, Barry Collett,
Giles and Annie Francis, DHV*

 BRAMFIELD TM3973   IP19 9HT
☆ Queens Head
The Street; A144 S of Halesworth

High-raftered lounge with scrubbed pine tables, impressive fireplace and some old farm
tools, side room with comfortable fireside seats, well kept Adnams, Aspall's cider, decent
wines by the glass, seasonal home-made elderflower cordial, good reasonably priced food
(emphasis on local organic), home-made bread and ice-creams, friendly service, monthly
live music (Fri); children (away from bar) and dogs welcome, cheerful blue-painted

picnic-sets in pretty garden with dome-shaped willow bower, nice church next door. *Recommended by R L Borthwick, M and GR, S T W Norton, Neil Powell*

BROCKLEY GREEN TL7247   CO10 8DT

☆ **Plough**

Hundon Road

Friendly neatly kept knocked-through bar, beams, timbers and stripped brick, scrubbed tables and open fire, good food from lunchtime sandwiches to some enterprising dishes and nice puddings, Tues steak night, cheerful efficient staff, Greene King IPA, Woodfordes Wherry and a guest, good choice of wines by the glass and malt whiskies, restaurant; children and dogs welcome, extensive attractive grounds with good tables and terrace, peaceful country views, refurbished bedrooms. *Recommended by A Black, Muriel Farnden*

BURY ST EDMUNDS TL8463   IP33 3JU

Dove

Hospital Road

19th-c alehouse with rustic bare-boards bar and separate parlour, half a dozen or more well kept beers, no food, some folk and blues nights; closed weekday lunchtimes. *Recommended by Julia Mann, Mo Uchegbu*

BURY ST EDMUNDS TL8564   IP33 1BJ

☆ **Nutshell**

The Traverse, central pedestrian link off Abbeygate Street

Tiny simple local with timeless interior (can be quite a crush at busy times), lots of interest such as a mummified cat (found walled up here) hanging from dark brown ceiling (seems to have a companion rat, too), bits of a skeleton, vintage bank notes, cigarette packets, military and other badges, spears and a great metal halberd, one short wooden bench along shop-front corner windows, a cut-down sewing-machine table and an elbow rest running along a rather battered counter, Greene King ales, no food; piped music, steep narrow stairs up to lavatories; children (till 7pm) and dogs welcome, open all day. *Recommended by Danny Savage, the Didler, Barry Collett*

BURY ST EDMUNDS TL8563   IP33 1NP

☆ **Rose & Crown**

Whiting Street

Cheerful black-beamed corner local with affable helpful landlord, bargain simple lunchtime home cooking (not Sun), particularly well kept Greene King ales (including Mild) and guests, pleasant lounge with lots of piggy pictures and bric-a-brac, good games-oriented public bar, rare separate off-sales counter; piped radio, no credit cards; pretty back courtyard, open all day. *Recommended by Julia Mann, Jeremy King*

BUXHALL TM9957   IP14 3DW

☆ **Crown**

Off B1115 W of Stowmarket; Mill Road

Warm welcome from enthusiastic landlord, cosy low-beamed inglenook bar with leather chairs and pews, airy dining room, well kept Greene King ales, good choice of wines by the glass, enjoyable blackboard food including good value set menu; children and dogs welcome, plenty of tables on heated terrace, pretty enclosed garden, nice country views, closed Sun evening, Mon. *Recommended by Dr G and Mrs J Kelvin, Jeremy King, J F M and M West*

CAVENDISH TL8046   CO10 8BA

☆ **George**

The Green

Attractively laid out as more restaurant than pub, good interesting food including set deals, nice atmosphere and friendly efficient service, beamed and bow-windowed front part, further good-sized eating area, well priced wines; tables out in garden behind, lovely village, good bedrooms up rather steep staircase. *Recommended by Sarah Flynn, Penny Lang, Marianne and Peter Stevens, Adele Summers, Alan Black, Neil and Brenda Skidmore*

CHELSWORTH TL9848   IP7 7HU
Peacock
B1115 Sudbury—Needham Market

New management at this attractive and prettily set old dining pub with lots of Tudor brickwork and exposed beams, separate pubby bar with big inglenook log fire, real ales and fairly standard food, friendly service; attractive small garden and village. *Recommended by MDN*

DENNINGTON TM2867   IP13 8AB
Queens Head
A1120; The Square

Well refurbished beamed and timbered Tudor pub prettily placed by church, L-shaped main bar, Adnams and maybe a guest, local cider, enjoyable food (best to book weekends) including some unusual choices and creative children's menu, friendly service; piped music; children in family room, side lawn by grand lime trees, pond at back with ducks and carp, backs on to Dennington Park with swings etc. *Recommended by Simon Cottrell, MDN, Ian and Nita Cooper, Jeremy Hebblethwaite and others*

EASTBRIDGE TM4566   IP16 4SN
☆ Eels Foot
Off B1122 N of Leiston

Hospitable country local bordered by freshwater marshes, split-level bar with light modern furnishings on stripped-wood floors, warming fire, well kept Adnams and several wines by the glass, Aspall's cider, neat back dining room with good value blackboard food, friendly helpful staff, folk evenings Thurs and last Sun of month; children and dogs welcome, seats on terrace and in lovely back garden, handy for Minsmere bird reserve, bridleway to the sea, cycle hire, six bedrooms (one adapted for wheelchairs) in newish building, open all day. *Recommended by Charles and Pauline Stride, Revd R P Tickle, Lois Dyer, Roy Hoing, Tim Maddison, Norma and Noel Thomas and others*

EASTON TM2858   IP13 0ED
☆ White Horse
N of Wickham Market on back road to Earl Soham and Framlingham

Pretty pink-rendered 16th-c pub, neatly kept, with two smartly simple rooms, country kitchen chairs, good small settles, cushioned stripped pews and stools, open fires, Adnams and a local guest, 30 wines by the glass, good seasonally changing bar food using own produce including home-reared meat, friendly helpful landlord, separate games room, table tennis in barn; piped music; children and dogs welcome, seats in rustic garden, croquet, closed Weds lunchtime and Sun evening. *Recommended by Peter Webb, M Ross-Thomas*

EDWARDSTONE TL9542   CO10 5PX
☆ White Horse
Mill Green, just E; village signed off A1071 in Boxford

Unpretentious local with eight beers from own Mill Green brewery, local farm cider and organic fruit juices, hearty pub food (not Sun evening, Mon), several varying-sized bar rooms with bare boards, rustic prints and photographs, second-hand tables and chairs including old steamer bench and panelled settle, piano, woodburner and open fire, bar billiards, ring the bull and quoits; piped music – open mike night Weds, live bands last Sat of month; children (till 8pm) and dogs welcome, sturdy teak seats on end terrace, attractive smokers' shelter and makeshift picnic-sets on grass, scandinavian-style self-catering, campsite, open all day Fri-Sun, closed Mon-Thurs lunchtime in winter. *Recommended by MDN*

FELIXSTOWE FERRY TM3237   IP11 9RZ
Ferry Boat
Off Ferry Road, on the green

Much modernised 17th-c pub tucked between golf links and dunes near harbour, Martello tower and summer rowing-boat ferry; good value generous food from snacks to fresh fish, Adnams and Greene King, friendly efficient service, good log fire; piped music, busy on summer weekends, and they may ask to keep a credit card while you eat; dogs welcome, tables out in front, on green opposite and in fenced garden, good coast walks. *Recommended by WAH, Ryta Lyndley*

FLIXTON TM3187   NR35 1NZ
Buck
The Street

Friendly and welcoming with several bars and big restaurant, good range of beers, enjoyable reasonably priced food including Sun carvery; quiet spot, handy for Aviation Museum. *Recommended by Christine Evans*

FORWARD GREEN TM0959   IP14 5HN
☆ # Shepherd & Dog
A1120 E of Stowmarket

Smart dining pub with attractive pastel décor, comfortable dining tables and some sofas, good interesting food in contemporary bar and restaurant including upmarket burgers from local wagyu herd, well kept Greene King IPA and Fullers London Pride, good wines by the glass and coffee, helpful young staff; disabled access, terrace tables, closed Sun evening, Mon. *Recommended by Conrad Freezer, Ian and Nita Cooper, J F M and M West*

FRAMLINGHAM TM2863   IP13 9BP
Castle Inn
Castle Street

Small single-storey building next to the castle, short blackboard choice of fairly priced food (not evenings), cream teas and good coffee, Adnams beers, Aspall's cider, light wood furniture on stripped boards; quiet piped music; children and dogs welcome, front picnic-sets overlooking duck pond, more in pretty back courtyard, open all day. *Recommended by Paul Humphreys, Jeremy King*

FRESSINGFIELD TM2677   IP21 5PB
☆ # Fox & Goose
Church Street; B1116 N of Framlingham

Relaxed dining pub in beautifully timbered 16th-c building next to church, very good food in cosy informal heavy-beamed rooms with log fire, upstairs restaurant, friendly attentive service, good wines by the glass, Adnams and a guest tapped from the cask in side bar; faint piped music; children welcome, downstairs disabled facilities, tables out by duck pond, closed Mon. *Recommended by John and Enid Morris, Dr Ian S Morley, Paul Humphreys*

FRISTON TM4160   IP17 1NP
Old Chequers
Just off A1094 Aldeburgh—Snape

Improved under friendly new licensees, sofas in L-shaped bar with cosy log fire, enjoyable food, well kept Adnams Bitter and interesting guests, live music; nice circular walks to Aldeburgh and Snape. *Recommended by Mark Farrington*

GREAT GLEMHAM TM3461   IP17 2DA
Crown
Between A12 Wickham Market—Saxmundham and B1119 Saxmundham—Framlingham

Big entrance hall with sofas on rush matting, civilised open-plan beamed lounge with wooden pews and captain's chairs around stripped and waxed kitchen tables, log fires in two big fireplaces, Adnams and guests from old brass handpumps, bar food; children and dogs welcome, disabled access, garden tables, smokers' shelter, closed Mon. *Recommended by John and Eleanor Holdsworth, Charles Gysin, Terry Buckland*

GRUNDISBURGH TM2250   IP13 6TA
 ## Dog
The Green; off A12 via B1079 from Woodbridge bypass

Civilised, convivial and popular pub run by two brothers, villagey public bar with dark carvers around mixed tables on tiled floor, oak settles and log fire, comfortable carpeted lounge with antique engravings on raspberry walls, bare-boards dining room, particularly enjoyable good value food using local farm produce, up to ten well kept changing ales, real cider, half a dozen wines by the glass, good coffee; TV; children and dogs welcome in certain parts (resident jack russell called Poppy), picnic-sets in front by flowering tubs, fenced back garden with play area, open all day Fri-Sun, closed Mon. *Recommended by Tom Gondris, Charles and Pauline Stride, Jeremy King, J F M and M West, S T W Norton*

HAUGHLEY TM0262   IP14 3NT
Kings Arms
Off A45/B1113 N of Stowmarket; Old Street

New management at this 16th-c extended timbered pub, horsebrasses and other bits and pieces, big brick fireplace with woodburner, decent good value pub food, well kept Greene King ales and a guest, busy public bar with TV and pool; piped music, no dogs inside; children welcome, tables in back garden with play area, nice village, open all day weekends. *Recommended by Jeremy King*

HAWKEDON TL7953   IP29 4NN
Queens Head
Between A143 and B1066

Charming unpretentious 17th-c village pub, half a dozen well kept changing regional ales, friendly helpful staff, good generous sensibly priced food, cosy beamed bar with big log fire, pretty dining room; dogs welcome, tables out in front and in large garden behind, closed weekday lunchtimes, open all day weekends. *Recommended by Gill Janzen*

HESSETT TL9361   IP30 9AX
Five Bells
Off A14 E of Bury; The Street

Refurbished low-ceilinged open-plan pub near spectacular Norman church, well kept Greene King ales, enjoyable food (choose your own steak or seafood from display counter), caring staff, big log fire; children welcome, large sheltered garden with terrace, closed Mon, Tues lunchtime. *Recommended by Jim Dew*

HOXNE TM1877   IP21 5AS
Swan
Low Street; off B1118, signed off A140 S of Diss

Timber-framed 15th-c building with pubby bar, two solid oak counters, broad oak floorboards and deep-set inglenook, Adnams, Woodfordes and a guest tapped from the cask (beer festivals May and Nov), Aspall's cider and several wines by the glass, enjoyable well presented bar food, restaurant; children and dogs welcome, seats under parasols on two sheltered terraces or in spacious garden extending to stream, boules; nearby is tree to which King Edmund was tied at his execution; open all day Sun. *Recommended by Tina and David Woods-Taylor, Jeremy King, D and J Ashdown, Nicola Eaton*

ICKLINGHAM TL7772   IP28 6PL
Plough
The Street

Cosy bar area with settles and adjacent good-sized restaurant, wide choice of enjoyable blackboard food, six ales including Greene King IPA and Hook Norton, champagne and good choice of wines by the glass, no mobile phones; children welcome at lunchtime, big garden, six bedrooms. *Recommended by Tony Middis, Simon Watkins, M and G R*

IPSWICH TM1644 IP4 2LA
Dove Street
76 St Helen's Street

Over 20 well kept quickly changing ales, farm ciders, bottled beers and whiskies, cheap hot drinks, friendly staff, bargain basic food, regular beer festivals; dogs welcome. *Recommended by Joanna Oldham, Richard Fearn*

IPSWICH TM1844 IP4 5NL
☆ Fat Cat
Spring Road, opposite junction with Nelson Road (best bet for parking up there)

Staggering choice of up to 22 quickly changing real ales (most cask tapped) in this busy well run town pub, also bottled belgian beers, local lager and fruit wines, bare-boarded bars with café and bar stools, unpadded wall benches and cushioned seats around cast-iron and wooden pub tables, lots of enamel brewery signs and posters on canary-yellow walls, spacious back conservatory, scotch eggs, pasties and pies, pub cat called Dave and the sausage dog is Stanley; picnic-sets on terrace and lawn, little parking nearby, open all day (till 1am Sat). *Recommended by Danny Savage, N R White, the Didler*

IPSWICH TM1645 IP1 3SE
Greyhound
Henley Road/Anglesea Road

Popular 19th-c pub with aged tables in cosy front bar, corridor to larger lounge, five well kept Adnams ales and a couple of guests, good substantial home cooking including bargain weekday lunch, quick service by well trained young staff; outside lavatories; children welcome, picnic-sets under parasols on quiet back terrace, open all day weekends (breakfast Sun from 10am). *Recommended by the Didler, Alex Hayton, Jeremy King*

LAVENHAM TL9149 CO10 9QZ
☆ Angel
Market Place

Handsome Tudor inn now owned by Marco Pierre White (Horatio Inns) and some refurbishment underway as we went to press – reports please; light and airy long bar area with big inglenook log fire under heavy mantelbeam, further beamed dining part towards the back, Adnams, Greene King, Hellhound and Lees (worth asking if they've time to show you interesting Tudor cellar), good choice of wines by the glass, early 17th-c ceiling plasterwork in residents' upstairs sitting room; children and dogs welcome, tables in sizeable back garden, nine bedrooms, open all day. *Recommended by Mike and Shelley Woodroffe*

LAXFIELD TM2972 IP13 8DW
☆ Kings Head
Gorams Mill Lane, behind church

Unspoilt thatched pub with no bar counter – instead, Adnams and three guests poured from casks in tap room; interesting little chequer-tiled front room dominated by a three-sided booth of high-backed settles in front of old range fire, two other equally unspoilt rooms with pews, old seats and scrubbed deal tables, well liked tasty bar food served by friendly helpful staff; children and dogs welcome, neatly kept garden with colourful borders, arbour covered with hops and grape vine, small pavilion for cooler evenings, boules, bedrooms and self-catering apartment, open all day summer. *Recommended by Simon and Mandy King, S T W Norton, Dr D J and Mrs S C Walker, the Didler, Ian and Nita Cooper, Tim Maddison and others*

LIDGATE TL7257 CB8 9PP
☆ Star
B1063 SE of Newmarket

Snug old pink-washed pub with handsome moulded beams in main room, big log fire, candles in iron candelabra on polished oak or stripped-pine tables, some antique catalan plates over bar, second similar room on right and cosy little dining room, Greene King ales, tasty food (not Sun evening and not cheap) including some spanish dishes (landlady is spanish); piped jazz; children welcome, dogs in bar, tables on raised front lawn and in rustic back garden, closed Mon. *Recommended by Mrs Margo Finlay, Jörg Kasprowski, R T and J C Moggridge, M and GR*

LONG MELFORD TL8646   CO10 9DN

☆ **Black Lion**

Church Walk

Hotel in striking village street, bar rooms either side of oak servery, one decorated in ochre with deeply cushioned sofas, leather wing armchairs and antique settles, the other in shades of terracotta with leather dining chairs around handsome set tables, well presented modern food, friendly helpful uniformed staff, Adnams ales, local cider, several wines by the glass and some good whiskies, open fires in both rooms, large racehorse portraits and big windows overlooking green; piped music; children welcome, dogs in drinking side, seats under parasols on terrace and in appealing Victorian walled garden, bedrooms, open all day. *Recommended by Andy Lickfold, John and Enid Morris, Ian Wilson, Bob and Tanya Ekers*

LONG MELFORD TL8645   CO10 9JG

☆ **Bull**

Hall Street (B1064)

Small 15th-c hotel full of character, beautifully carved beams in old-fashioned timbered front lounge, antique furnishings, log fire in huge fireplace, more spacious back bar with sporting prints, well kept Greene King ales, decent wines, reasonably priced standard Old English Inns menu, cheerful helpful staff, daily papers, restaurant; children welcome, tables in attractive courtyard, comfortable bedrooms, open all day weekends. *Recommended by R C Vincent, Paul and Marion Watts, Mrs Margo Finlay, Jörg Kasprowski*

LONG MELFORD TL8645   CO10 9JL

Crown

Hall Street

Friendly partly 17th-c inn, real ales such as Adnams and Nethergate from central servery with unusual bar chairs, log fire, some stripped brickwork and nicely placed furnishings, good choice of food, restaurant; attractive terrace with big awnings, 12 well equipped bedrooms. *Recommended by Ian Wilson*

LOWESTOFT TM5593   NR32 1QA

Triangle

St Peter's Street

Popular two-bar tap for Green Jack ales, guest beers, too, and real cider, regular beer festivals, breweriana, open fire; pool and TV in back bar, live music Fri; open all day (till 1am Fri, Sat). *Recommended by Mike Mason*

MONKS ELEIGH TL9647   IP7 7AU

☆ **Swan**

B1115 Sudbury—Stowmarket

Gently upmarket dining pub but has informal side, too; long pleasantly bright bar room with high-backed leather-seated dining chairs around light wood tables on pale oak floor, red walls hung with Jack Vetriano prints and framed UK special edition stamps, good imaginative food, quietly efficient service, open fire in small brick fireplace in high-ceilinged end room, fresh flowers on cream-painted wooden-topped bar counter, Adnams and a guest, good choice of wines by the glass; children welcome, village post office in car park, closed Sun evening, winter Mon and two weeks in school holidays (best to ring). *Recommended by Jeremy King, MDN, Mr and Mrs C Prentis, Alan and Jill Bull, M and GR*

NAYLAND TL9734   CO6 4JL

☆ **Anchor**

Court Street; just off A134 – turn off S of signposted B1087 main village turn

Bare-boards bar in dining pub with interesting old photographs of village characters, farmhouse tables and chairs, open fires, Adnams and Greene King, several wines by the glass (some from own vineyard), another room behind with similar furniture and fire, small carpeted sun room, upstairs restaurant, bar food can be interesting using home-smoked and home-grown produce; piped music; children welcome, seats on terrace overlooking River Stour, adjacent farmland worked by suffolk punch horses – visitors welcome to watch, open all day summer. *Recommended by MDN, David and Sue Medcalf, Paul Humphreys, John Prescott, Ian Wilson*

NEWBOURNE TM2743   IP12 4NY

 Fox

Off A12 at roundabout 1.7 miles N of A14 junction; The Street

Pink-washed 16th-c pub, low-beamed bar with slabby elm and other dark tables on tiled floor, stuffed fox in inglenook, comfortable carpeted dining room with modern artwork and antique mirrors, Adnams, Greene King and two guests, decent wines by the glass, good variety of enjoyable generously served food (all day weekends) including reasonably priced Sun roasts; piped music; children welcome, dogs in bar, attractive grounds with rose garden and pond, open all day. *Recommended by K Hunt, M Smith, Neil Brightwell, Alistair Mackie*

NEWTON TL9140   CO10 0QJ

Saracens Head

A134 4 miles E Sudbury

Refurbished roadside pub, nice and light with good modern furniture, some older features too, Adnams ales, decent food; garden overlooking village green. *Recommended by John Prescott*

PETTISTREE TM2954   IP13 0HP

☆ **Greyhound**

The Street; brown sign to pub off B1438 S of Wickham Market, 0.5 miles N of A12

Two smallish well maintained traditional rooms with polished dark tables on green carpet, matching padding for chairs and heavy settles, pale sage dado, rather low dark brown beams and open fires, Crouch Vale, Earl Soham, Woodfordes and a guest, several wines by the glass, enjoyable bar and restaurant food, friendly service; children welcome in dining part, picnic-sets in side garden with more in front gravel car park. *Recommended by Mr and Mrs A Curry, Simon Cottrell, Charles and Pauline Stride, MDN*

POLSTEAD TL9938   CO6 5AL

Cock

Signed off B1068 and A1071 E of Sudbury, then pub signed; Polstead Green

Beamed and timbered local with unassuming bar, woodburner and open fire, well kept Adnams, Greene King IPA and a guest, good choice of wines and malt whiskies, nice coffee, good home-made food from fresh lunchtime baguettes up, smarter light and airy barn restaurant; piped music; children and dogs welcome, disabled facilities, picnic-sets out overlooking attractive village's quiet green, side play area, closed Mon. *Recommended by Martin and Alison Stainsby, John Prescott, David and Gill Carrington, Eddie Edwards*

RAMSHOLT TM3041   IP12 3AB

☆ **Ramsholt Arms**

Signed off B1083; Dock Road

Lovely isolated spot overlooking River Deben, welcoming open-plan nautical bar busy on summer weekends and handy for bird walks and Sutton Hoo; wide choice of good value quickly served food including seafood and game, two sittings for Sun lunch, Adnams and a guest ale, decent wines by the glass, winter mulled wine, good log fire; dogs (pub has two) and children welcome, plenty of tables outside with summer afternoon terrace bar (not Sun), roomy bedrooms with stunning view, open all day. *Recommended by Tim Elliot, Tom Gondris, David Field*

RATTLESDEN TL9758   IP30 0RJ

☆ **Brewers Arms**

Lower Road; off B1115 via Buxhall or A45 via Woolpit, W of Stowmarket

New licensees for this 16th-c beamed village pub; traditionally furnished bar on right, lounge on left winding back through standing timbers to restaurant area – partly flint-walled with magnificent old bread oven, Greene King and guests, freshly made daily-changing food from landlord/chef including lunchtime sandwiches, pub favourites and some more ambitious choices; piped music, open mike second Tues of month; walled garden with table tennis, children welcome, dogs in bar, open all day from 10am. *Recommended by Jeremy King*

REDE TL8055   IP29 4BE

☆ **Plough**

Village signposted off A143 Bury St Edmunds—Haverhill

Pretty thatched pub in tucked-away village, traditional low-beamed bar with comfortable seating, solid fuel stove in brick fireplace, Fullers London Pride, Ringwood Best and Timothy Taylors Landlord, popular food (not Sun evening) from quickly changing menu; children welcome till 8pm, picnic-sets in sheltered cottage garden and in front near village green. *Recommended by Peter and Jean Hoare, Simon Watkins, Gill Janzen*

RENDHAM TM3564   IP17 2AF

White Horse

B1119 Framlingham—Saxmundham

Partly divided open-plan pub with good reasonably priced home-made food using local suppliers, Earl Soham, Mauldons, Timothy Taylors and a guest, two open fires; garden tables, lovely spot opposite 14th-c church, good local walks. *Recommended by Martin Smith*

REYDON TM4977   IP18 6PZ

☆ **Randolph**

Wangford Road (B1126 just NW of Southwold)

Stylish inn with quite an emphasis on dining and bedroom side; bar with high-backed leather dining chairs around chunky wooden tables on parquet floor, sofa and a couple of comfortable armchairs, prints of pub from 1910 and photographs of Southwold beach, Adnams beers, dining room with more high-backed chairs on red carpet, pretty little Victorian fireplace filled with candles, nicely varied reasonably priced menu, pleasant staff; piped music, TV, games machine; children welcome, dogs in little back bar, wheelchair access, picnic-sets on decked area and grass, ten bedrooms, good breakfast, open all day. *Recommended by Ann and Colin Hunt, Phil and Jane Hodson*

ROUGHAM TL9063   IP30 9JA

☆ **Ravenwood Hall**

Off A14 E of Bury St Edmunds

Country-house hotel with two compact bar rooms, tall ceilings, patterned wallpaper and big heavily draped windows overlooking sweeping lawn with stately cedar, back area set for eating with upholstered settles and dining chairs, sporting prints and log fire, interesting well presented bar food (own smoked meats and fish), well kept Adnams, good choice of wines and malts, comfortable lounge area with horse pictures, a few moulded beams and good-sized fragment of early Tudor wall decoration above big inglenook, separate more formal restaurant; piped music; children and dogs welcome, teak furniture in garden, swimming pool, geese and pygmy goats in big enclosures, croquet, 14 bedrooms, open 9am-midnight. *Recommended by J F M and M West, Rob and Catherine Dunster, Keith and Margaret Kettell, Derek Field, Martin Smith and others*

SAXTEAD GREEN TM2564   IP13 9QE

Old Mill House

B1119; The Green

Roomy dining pub across green from windmill, beamed carpeted bar, neat country-look flagstoned restaurant extension, wooden tables and chairs, good choice of generous well priced fresh food (all day Sun) including daily carvery, good friendly service, well kept Greene King, decent wines; discreet piped music; children very welcome, attractive sizeable garden with terrace and good play area. *Recommended by Ian and Nita Cooper, Jeremy King*

SHOTTISHAM TM3244   IP12 3HD

Sorrel Horse
Hollesley Road

Charming two-bar 15th-c thatched local, attentive helpful staff, Adnams, Woodfordes and guests tapped from the cask, decent choice of home-made food including deals, good log fire in tiled-floor bar with games area (bar billiards), attractive dining room with woodburner; piped music; children and dogs welcome, tables out on sloping front lawn and in small garden behind, open all day summer weekends, closed Mon. *Recommended by the Didler, Pat and Tony Martin*

SNAPE TM3958   IP17 1SL

Crown
Bridge Road (B1069)

Small cheery beamed 15th-c pub with brick floors, inglenook log fire and fine double Suffolk settle, well kept Adnams ales, enjoyable fresh food using local ingredients including own veg and meat (reared behind the pub), folk night last Thurs of month, darts; children and dogs welcome, garden. *Recommended by Tom and Ruth Rees, WAH, John and Eleanor Holdsworth*

SOUTH ELMHAM TM3385   NR35 1NQ

☆ St Peters Brewery
St Peter South Elmham; off B1062 SW of Bungay

Beautifully but simply furnished manor dating back to the 13th c (much extended in 1539) with own St Peter's draught ales and bottled beers, bar and dining hall with dramatic high-ceiling, imposing chandelier, elaborate woodwork and flagstoned floor, antique tapestries, candles and fresh flowers on crisp white-clothed tables, two further rooms reached up steepish stairs, pubby lunch dishes and more elaborate evening food; children welcome, outside tables overlooking original moat, open all day Sat, closed Sun evening, Mon. *Recommended by MDN, Jenny Clarke, the Didler*

SOUTHWOLD TM4975   IP18 6TA

☆ Harbour Inn
Blackshore, by the boats; from A1095, turn right at the Kings Head, and keep on past the golf course and water tower

Waterside pub by Blyth estuary now run by licensee from the Golden Key at Snape; lots of nautical character, seafaring bric-a-brac, tiny low-beamed tiled and panelled front bar with antique settles, cushioned wooden benches built into stripped panelling, good value traditional food, Adnams ales and Aspall's cider, live folk music; children and dogs welcome, tables outside with great views, open all day. *Recommended by Norma and Noel Thomas, Theocsbrian, Mike and Sue Loseby, M and GR*

SOUTHWOLD TM5076   IP18 6ET

☆ Red Lion
South Green

Nice atmosphere and warm friendly service, good reasonably priced food from sandwiches up, well kept Adnams, big windows looking over green to sea, pale panelling, ship pictures, lots of brassware and copper, pub games, separate back dining room; children and dogs welcome, lots of tables outside, right by the Adnams retail shop. *Recommended by Charles and Pauline Stride, Mike and Sue Loseby, Michael Dandy, Martin Smith, DHV, Ann and Colin Hunt and others*

Post Office address codings confusingly give the impression that some pubs are in Suffolk, when they're really in Cambridgeshire, Essex or Norfolk (which is where we list them).

SOUTHWOLD TM5076
IP18 6JN
Sole Bay
East Green

Airy refurbished pub near Adnams Brewery, their full range kept well and good wine choice, cheerful efficient staff, enjoyable simple food from doorstep sandwiches up, well spaced tables, conservatory; sports TV; children and dogs welcome, disabled facilities, picnic-sets outside, moments from sea and lighthouse, open all day. *Recommended by MDN, Michael Dandy, Giles and Annie Francis, Pat and Tony Martin, Mike and Sue Loseby*

SOUTHWOLD TM5076
IP18 6EG
 ## Swan
Market Place

Relaxed comfortable back bar in smart Adnams-owned hotel, their full range and bottled beers, fine wines and malt whiskies, good bar food including early evening deals, competent staff, coffee and teas in luxurious chintzy front lounge, restaurant; nice garden, 42 bedrooms including separate block where (by arrangement) dogs can stay too, good breakfast. *Recommended by MDN, Michael Dandy*

STOKE-BY-NAYLAND TL9836
CO6 4SA
Angel
B1068 Sudbury—East Bergholt

Refurbished 16th-c beamed dining pub under new ownership; two large areas around bar with smaller rooms off, stripped brickwork, timbers and big log fire, well kept Adnams and guests, wide choice of wines by the glass, modern food, takeaway fish and chips too; piped music; dogs (in some areas) and children welcome, terrace with big umbrella, six comfortable bedrooms, open all day from 8am (breakfast for non-residents). *Recommended by Jeremy King*

STONHAM ASPAL TM1359
IP14 6AF
Ten Bells
The Street

Modernised early 17th-c timbered village pub with inglenook in extended beamed main bar, small lounge bar with dining area beyond, enjoyable good value home-made food (all day Sun, not Weds) including specials, well kept Greene King IPA, Wells & Youngs Bombardier and a guest such as Adnams, cheerful relaxed atmosphere; TV, pool; disabled facilities, some tables out by car park, shuts 9.30pm Mon. *Recommended by Jeremy King*

TOSTOCK TL9563
IP30 9PA
Gardeners Arms
Off A14 or A1088

Low-beamed village pub popular under current licensees, enjoyable well priced food generously served, Weds curry night, Greene King and a guest ale, log fire, games in tiled separate bar; sheltered garden. *Recommended by Pat and Tony Martin*

TUDDENHAM TM1948
IP6 9BT
☆ ## Fountain
The Street; village signed off B1077 N of Ipswich

Buzzy well run dining pub in nice village, several linked café-style rooms (minimal décor) with heavy beams and timbering, stripped floors, wooden dining chairs around light tables, open fire, lots of prints (including some by Giles who spent time here after World War II), good choice of food (not Sun evening) with set menus, Adnams, decent coffee, pleasant helpful service; piped music; no under-10s in bar after 6.30pm, wicker and metal chairs on covered heated terrace, more seats under huge parasols on sizeable lawn, closed Sun evening, first week in Jan. *Recommended by Charles and Pauline Stride, Ryta Lyndley, Beckie Harvey, Dickie and Alex Brooks*

WALBERSWICK TM4974   IP18 6UA

☆ **Anchor**

The Street (B1387); village signed off A12

More restaurant with bar than pub, food generally well liked; simply furnished front bar divided into snug halves by two-way open fire, big windows, heavy stripped tables on original oak flooring, sturdy built-in green leather wall seats and nicely framed black and white photographs of fishermen on colourwashed panelling, Adnams and Meantime, lots of bottled beers, 25 wines by the glass, extensive dining area stretching back from small more modern-feeling lounge; young children (not in bar) and dogs welcome, garden bar serving flagstoned terrace, coast path and pleasant walk across to Southwold – may be summer pedestrian ferry, renovated bedrooms, open all day. *Recommended by Simon and Mandy King, Tom and Ruth Rees, Robert Lorimer, John Ainscough, George and Beverley Tucker, K Hunt, M Smith and others*

WALBERSWICK TM4974   IP18 6TN

Bell

Just off B1387

Fine setting near beach, plenty of original features, 400-year-old brick floors, uneven flagstones, wonky steps and oak beams, traditional main bar with high-backed settles and woodburner, second bar with large open fire, up to seven Adnams beers, food from sandwiches up, darts and board games; piped and maybe some live music (since change of management); children and dogs welcome, tables on sheltered lawn, bedrooms overlooking sea or river. *Recommended by Mike and Sue Loseby, Norma and Noel Thomas*

WOODBRIDGE TM2648   IP12 4AG

Cherry Tree

Opposite Notcutts Nursery, off A12; Cumberland Street

Comfortably worn-in open-plan pub, well kept Adnams and guest ales helpfully described (beer festival), good wines by the glass, welcoming helpful staff, good value pubby food including breakfast, beams and two log fires, pine furniture, old local photographs and aircraft prints; children welcome, garden with play area, three good bedrooms in adjoining barn conversion, open all day weekends. *Recommended by MDN*

WOODBRIDGE TM2749   IP12 4LP

Kings Head

Market Hill

Handsome Elizabethan beams, flagstones and timbering in nicely opened-up town bar, log fire in massive central chimneybreast, fairly priced food in bar and dining room down a couple of steps, Adnams ales, some nice local pictures; piped music; disabled facilities, picnic-sets outside. *Recommended by Pat and Tony Martin*

WOODBRIDGE TM2749   IP12 1DZ

Olde Bell & Steelyard

New Street, off Market Square

Ancient and unpretentious timber-framed pub with welcoming helpful licensees, two smallish beamed bars and compact dining room, lots of brassware, log fire, Greene King ales and guests from canopied servery, real ciders, food from bar snacks to short varied choice of substantial main dishes, takeaway service too, traditional games including bar billiards, live music; well behaved children and dogs welcome (two pub dogs and a cat), back terrace, steelyard still overhanging street, open till late Fri and Sat. *Recommended by Dr D J and Mrs S C Walker, Phil and Jane Hodson, BT*

WOOLPIT TL9762   IP30 9QN

Swan

The Street

Old coaching inn pleasantly situated in village square, heavy beams and painted panelling, mixed tables and chairs on carpet, roaring log fire one end, promptly served bar food, Adnams ales from slate-top bar, lots of wines by the glass; soft piped music; walled garden behind, four bedrooms in converted stables. *Recommended by D and J Ashdown, Jeremy King*

The East Midlands

Derbyshire

Leicestershire

Lincolnshire

Northamptonshire

Nottinghamshire

Rutland

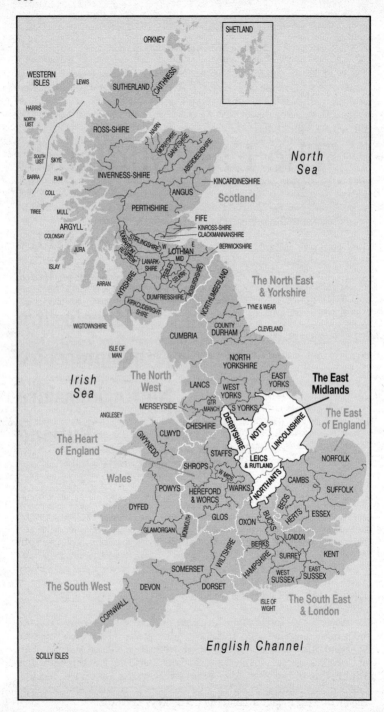

EDITORS' FAVOURITES
THE EAST MIDLANDS

The region's top pub for 2012 is the characterful Bear at Alderwasley in **Derbyshire** (a terrific all-rounder, **Derbyshire Dining Pub of the Year** and **East Midlands Pub of the Year**). Food in this county is often good value. Of the half a dozen with a Value Award, readers particularly like the cheery Church inn at Chelmorton, cosy Coach & Horses in Fenny Bentley, the pubby Cheshire Cheese in Hope and Red Lion at Litton (a homely all-rounder). The Devonshire Arms at Pisley (new this year) has a Stay, Wine and Beer Award, the Plough at Hathersage (lovely grounds and three awards, too) is doing well. Also worth a visit are Eyre Arms in Hassop, Red Lion in Hognaston, Barley Mow in Kirk Ireton, Anglers Rest in Millers Dale, Monsal Head Hotel in Monsal Head, Cock & Pullet in Sheldon and Three Stags Heads in Wardlow.

The Marquess of Exeter in Lyddington (friendly with excellent food) is the **Leicestershire & Rutland Dining Pub of the Year**. You can also get great food at the Three Horse Shoes at Breedon on the Hill (imaginative if not cheap) and Olive Branch in Clipsham (bustling all-rounder). The Grainstore in Oakham (down-to-earth and friendly brewery tap) supplies beer to many pubs in Leicestershire, and the Wheatsheaf in Woodhouse Eaves (great county pub) is doing well. Also worth a visit are the Wheel at Branston, Fox & Hounds at Exton, Nevill Arms in Medbourne and Bakers Arms in Thorpe Langton.

The Chequers in Woolsthorpe (great all-rounder with terrific food) is **Lincolnshire Dining Pub of the Year**. Two enjoyable new top pubs here are the Plough at Great Casterton (carefully prepared imaginative food) and Tobie Norris in Stamford (ancient place with own-brew beers). Also worth a visit are the Blue Bell at Belchford, Willys at Cleethorpes, Wheatsheaf at Dry Doddington, Brownlow Arms at Hough-on-the-Hill, Victoria in Lincoln and the Ship at Surfleet Seas End.

There's good value food in **Northamptonshire** – almost half the top pubs in this county have a Value Award. Of these, the Red Lion at Crick (friendly and unpretentious) is doing particularly well. For a great meal choose the upmarket Falcon at Fotheringhay (exceptional service and **Northamptonshire Dining Pub of the Year**), for a pubby experience the Althorp Coaching Inn at Great Brington (eight real ales) stands out, and the cheery Kings Head at Wadenhoe is in a fabulous location. Also worth a visit are the Cartwright at Aynho, George at Great Oxendon, George in Kilsby, Cromwell Cottage in Kislingbury and the Snooty Fox at Lowick.

Two top pubs in **Nottinghamshire** are equally terrific and represent both sides of the pubbing coin. The Black Horse at Caythorpe brews its own beer and offers jolly good value food, while the civilised Martins Arms at Colston Bassett is lovely for a meal out and is the **Nottinghamshire Dining Pub of the Year**. Also worth a visit are the Victoria at Beeston, Dovecote at Laxton, Olde Trip to Jerusalem in Nottingham, Stratford Haven in West Bridgford and the Cross Keys at Upton.

ALDERWASLEY Derbyshire SK3153 Map 7

Bear ★ ♀ ◖

EAST MIDLANDS PUB OF THE YEAR

Left off A6 at Ambergate onto Holly Lane (turns into Jackass Lane) then right at end (staggered crossroads); DE56 2RD

DERBYSHIRE DINING PUB OF THE YEAR

Unspoilt country inn with low-beamed cottagey rooms, good range of real ales, and a peaceful garden; bedrooms

Readers can't heap enough praise on this terrific all-rounder. Justifiably popular, this happy characterful tavern has lovely dark low-beamed rooms with warming open fires and a cheerful miscellany of antique furniture including high-backed settles and locally made antique oak chairs with derbyshire motifs. One little room is filled right to its built-in wall seats by a single vast table. Other décor includes staffordshire china ornaments, old paintings and engravings. There's no obvious front door – you get in through the plain back entrance by the car park, and as it can get busy you may need to book. Bass, Derby Blue Bear, Hartington IPA, Thornbridge Jaipur and Timothy Taylors Landlord are on handpump alongside a guest or two, and they do several wines by the glass from a decent list, as well as malt whiskies. Well spaced picnic-sets out on the side grass have peaceful country views.

As well as sandwiches and home-made crusty rolls (afternoons only), bar food might include smoked haddock fishcakes with citrus mayonnaise, whitebait, chicken breast with tomato, onion and chorizo, pork medallions with wholegrain mustard and cider sauce, duck breast with orange and brandy sauce, scallops on warm pancetta and black pudding salad, battered haddock, spinach and ricotta tortellini, and steaks. *Benchmark main dish: steak and ale pie £9.95. Two-course evening meal £18.45.*

Free house ~ Licensee Pete Buller ~ Real ale ~ Bar food (12-3, 6-9; 12-9 Fri-Sun) ~ Restaurant ~ (01629) 822585 ~ Children welcome ~ Dogs allowed in bar ~ Open 12-11(10.30 Sun) ~ Bedrooms: /£75B

Recommended by Richard Cole, Peter F Marshall, Pam and John Smith, Don Mitchell, John and Enid Morris, the Didler, Brian and Jean Hepworth, Bruce and Sharon Eden, Simon Le Fort, Terry Davis, David and Sue Atkinson, Lindsey White

ASHFORD IN THE WATER Derbyshire SK1969 Map 7

Bulls Head

Off A6 NW of Bakewell; Church Street (B6465, off A6020); DE45 1QB

Cheerfully civilised village pub with enjoyable food, in lovely Peak District village

Run by the same welcoming family for the last 50 years, this attractive 17th-c stone coaching inn has a nicely traditional two-room beamed and turkey-carpeted bar. It's warm and cosy with a blazing log and coal fire, daily papers, one or two character gothic seats as well as the usual spindleback and wheelback chairs around cast-iron-framed tables, and local photographs and country prints on cream walls. Robinsons Unicorn and Old Stockport are on handpump, and service is friendly and efficient; may be unobtrusive piped jazz. There are hardwood tables and benches both out in front and in the good-sized garden behind which also has boules and garden Jenga; they have overshoes for walkers.

As well as lunchtime sandwiches, bar food might include mulligatawny soup, warm mackerel salad with sweet and sour onions, duck liver parfait, spicy three-bean casserole, baked halibut on potatoes, red onions, tomatoes, red peppers and olives, fennel and smoked cheese tart, and chicken breast with mushroom and brandy cream sauce. *Benchmark main dish: steak and ale pie £11.00. Two-course evening meal £18.50.*

Robinsons ~ Tenant Debbie Shaw ~ Real ale ~ Bar food (12-2, 6.30-9; 12-2.30, 7-9 Sun; not Thurs evening in winter) ~ (01629) 812931 ~ Children welcome in some areas ~ Dogs allowed in bar ~ Open 12(11 Sat)-3, 6-11; 12-3.30, 7-10.30 Sun

Recommended by Peter F Marshall, Bruce and Sharon Eden, P J and R D Greaves, Neil and Brenda Skidmore, Sue Tucker

 BARNOLDBY LE BECK Lincolnshire   TA2303   Map 8

Ship ♀

Village signposted off A18 Louth—Grimsby; DN37 0BG

Very good fish menu (and other choices) at tranquil plush dining pub

Most customers visit this calmly sedate place to enjoy the first-class fish dishes, but drinkers do pop in, too – helpful staff serve Black Sheep and Tom Woods from handpump, up to a dozen malt whiskies and they've a good wine list. The rather charming collection of Edwardian and Victorian bric-a-brac here makes it feel just that little bit different and demure. The neatly kept bar houses stand-up telephones, violins, a horn gramophone, bowler and top hats, old racquets, crops and hockey sticks. Heavy dark-ringed drapes swathe the windows, with plants in ornate china bowls on the sills. Furnishings include comfortable dark green plush wall benches with lots of pretty propped-up cushions, and heavily stuffed green plush Victorian-looking chairs on a green fleur de lys carpet; piped music. A fenced-off sunny area behind has hanging baskets and a few picnic-sets under parasols.

 Using top quality fish, good food includes seared scallops with lemon, ginger and coriander, fried crispy beef salad with hoisin, plum and chilli sauce, beef and ale pie, pork loin medallions with cider and sage jus, chicken breast filled with cheese and spring onion with tomato and basil sauce, vegetable madras, good fish pie, herb-crusted halibut, and skate wing with caper butter. *Benchmark main dish: fish and chips £9.50. Two-course evening meal £18.55.*

Free house ~ Licensee Michele Hancock ~ Real ale ~ Bar food (12-2, 6-9) ~ Restaurant ~ (01472) 822308 ~ Children welcome ~ Open 12-2, 6-11; 12-5 Sun; closed Sun evening

Recommended by Newbury family, P Pywell, David and Jenny Reed, C A Hall

 **BEELEY** Derbyshire   SK2667   Map 7

Devonshire Arms ⑪ ♀ 🍷 🛏

B6012, off A6 Matlock—Bakewell; DE4 2NR

Contemporary twist to lovely old interior; local beers, good wine list, interesting carefully sourced food, attractive comfortable bedrooms

This handsome stone-built village inn (converted from cottages back in 1741) is almost more restaurant-with-rooms, offering a slightly more formal dining experience, though it does give a nod to pubbyness at lunchtime. Contemporary colours contrast with the attractive traditional interior features: between black beams, flagstones, stripped stone, traditional settles and cheerful log fires, you'll find bright candy coloured modern furnishings, prints and floral arrangements. Despite the accent on dining, they keep up to six changing real ales, most likely including Buxton Blonde and Kinder Sunset, Peak Ales Chatsworth Gold, Thornbridge Jaipur and Whim Hartington, and they've several wines by the glass from a well chosen list and a good range of malt whiskies, as well as local mineral water. The inn stands in an attractive village in the Peak District on the fringes of the Chatsworth Estate and you can walk to Chatsworth House itself from here (though you might not feel completely at ease in the pub in walking gear). Note that although dogs are allowed to stay in the stylishly comfortable bedrooms, they are not allowed in the bar.

Sourcing what ingredients they can from the Chatsworth Estate, the imaginative food (with restaurant prices) is cooked to order so there might be a wait at busy times. The short but well balanced changing menu could include crab scotch egg with coleslaw, spiced chickpea fritter with pineapple chaat and paneer, whole dressed crab, herb crumbed pollack with truffle mash, shallot sauce and garlic butter, goosnargh gold cheese, spinach and olive tart, steak and kidney pudding, and beef fillet with morel and madeira sauce and stilton croûton. *Benchmark main dish: sausage and mash £13.95. Two-course evening meal £26.50.*

Free house ~ Licensee Alan Hill ~ Real ale ~ Bar food (12-3, 6-9.30) ~ Restaurant ~ (01629) 733259 ~ Children welcome ~ Dogs allowed in bedrooms ~ Open 12-11 ~ Bedrooms: £114B/£134B

Recommended by Marian and Andrew Ruston, Margaret and Jeff Graham, M G Hart, S P Watkin, P A Taylor, Ann and Colin Hunt, Richard Cole, Richard and Mary Bailey

BREEDON ON THE HILL Leicestershire   SK4022 Map 7

Three Horse Shoes ▯
Main Street (A453); DE73 8AN

Comfortable pub with friendly licensees and popular food

Much emphasis is placed on the popular often interesting food served at this agreeable 18th-c pub. It's been nicely restored to reveal its attractive structure and there are heavy worn flagstones, a log fire, pubby tables, a dark wood counter and green walls and ceilings that give a stylishly simple feel to the clean-cut central bar: Marstons Pedigree on handpump, 30 malt whiskies and decent house wines. Beyond here, a further eating room has maroon walls, dark pews and cherry-stained tables. The two-room dining area on the right has a comfortably civilised chatty feel with big quite close-set antique tables on seagrass matting and colourful modern country prints and antique engravings on canary walls. Even at lunchtime there are lighted candles in elegant modern holders.

Enjoyable – if not cheap – food includes sandwiches, ploughman's, fish and spinach pancake with cheese, rabbit terrine with cumberland sauce, creamy pork and cider casserole, beef and mushroom pudding, duck breast with cabbage and whisky, salmon with sweet potato curry, mushroom stroganoff, sausage and mash, and steaks; Sunday roast. *Benchmark main dish: fish and chips £10.75. Two-course evening meal £27.00.*

Free house ~ Licensees Ian Davison, Jennie Ison, Stuart Marson ~ Real ale ~ Bar food ~ Restaurant ~ (01332) 695129 ~ Children welcome ~ Dogs allowed in bar ~ Open 11.30-2, 5.30-11; 12-3 Sun; closed Sun evening

Recommended by Steve Cocking, Theocsbrian

BUCKMINSTER Leicestershire   SK8822 Map 7

Tollemache Arms ⓨ

B676 Colsterworth—Melton Mowbray; Main Street; NG33 5SA

Emphasis on good food in stylishly updated pub recently reopened by two enthusiastic young couples

The two men run the kitchen here, while their wives look after the customers – service is quick and attentive. The stone and brick building is surprisingly stately for a village pub, and the refurbishment suits it well. One rather elegant corner room has comfortable easy chairs around its log fire, and quite a library of books. The series of other linked areas includes a dark leather chesterfield by a low table of magazines and papers in another fireside corner, and otherwise a mix of wheelback, dining or stripped kitchen chairs, and some rather nice specially made small pews, around the tables on the floorboards; table lamps and standard lamps, big bunches of flowers, and a shelf of board games add a homely touch, and they don't turn up their noses at dogs or muddy boots. They have a good choice of wines by the glass and changing ales such as Belvoir Golden Flash and Grainstore Cooking on handpump, good nibbles such as pickled eggs and onions, and perhaps discreet nostalgic piped music. There are teak tables out on the back grass, by quite a clump of sycamores; beyond is a small herb and salad garden, and a swing.

Besides some excellent lunchtime sandwiches (not weekends), such as cured beef with beetroot and horseradish, bar food might include starters like potted shrimps and sorrel on toast and whitebait with spiced mayonnaise, and main courses such as tagliatelle with peashoots, radicchio and balsamic, roast rack of lamb, fillet of bream with samphire and basil and lobster bisque sauce, and rib-eye steak with tarragon butter. *Benchmark main dish: fish and chips £9.95. Two-course evening meal £18.50.*

Free house ~ Licensees Matt and Amanda Wrisdale, Paul and Matilda Adams ~ Real ale ~ Bar food (12-2 (3 Sun), 6.30-9) ~ Restaurant ~ (01476) 860477 ~ Children welcome ~ Dogs welcome ~ Open 12-3, 5-11; 12-4 Sun; closed Sun evening

Recommended by Pat and Stewart Gordon

CAYTHORPE Nottinghamshire   SK6845 Map 7

Black Horse ◖ £

Turn off A6097 0.25 miles SE of roundabout junction with A612, NE of Nottingham; into Gunthorpe Road, then right into Caythorpe Road and keep on; NG14 7ED

Quaintly old-fashioned little pub brewing its own beer, simple interior and homely enjoyable food; no children or credit cards

The uncluttered carpeted bar at this timeless 300-year-old country local has just five tables. There are decorative plates on a delft shelf and a few horsebrasses on the ceiling joists, brocaded wall banquettes and settles, and a warm woodburning stove. Cheerful regulars might occupy the few bar stools to enjoy the two tasty Caythorpe beers that are brewed by the friendly licensee family in outbuildings here and are served alongside Caythorpe Dover Beck and a couple of guests from Bass, Adams or Greene King Abbot. Off the front corridor is a partly panelled inner room with a wall bench running right the way around three unusual long copper-topped tables, and there are quite a few old local photographs; darts and board games. Down on the left, an end room has just one huge round table. There are some plastic tables outside, and the River Trent is fairly close for waterside walks.

🍴 The good value meals attract an older lunchtime set so you will need to book. Simple freshly cooked traditional food from a shortish menu includes sandwiches, celery and blue cheese soup, cod roe on toast, steak and kidney pie, seafood salad, and sausage and mash. *Benchmark main dish: fried cod fillet with parsley sauce £9.00. Two-course evening meal £13.00.*

Own brew ~ Licensee Sharron Andrews ~ Real ale ~ Bar food (not Sat evening or Sun) ~ Restaurant ~ No credit cards ~ (0115) 966 3520 ~ Dogs allowed in bar ~ Open 12-2.30, 6-11.30; 12-5, 8-11.30 Sun; closed Mon except bank holidays and Tues lunchtime after the third Mon monthly

Recommended by the Didler, P Dawn, David Eberlin, Chris Johnson

CHELMORTON Derbyshire   SK1170   Map 7

Church Inn 🍺 £

Village signposted off A5270, between A6 and A515 SE of Buxton; keep on up through village towards church; SK17 9SL

Cosy, convivial traditional inn beautifully set in High Peak walking country – good value

The warm can-do hospitable greeting from the licensees and staff really sets the tone at this welcoming village pub. The chatty low-ceilinged tiled bar has a warming fire and is traditionally furnished with cushioned built-in benches and simple chairs around polished cast-iron-framed tables – one or two still with their squeaky sewing treadles. Shelves of readable books, Tiffany-style lamps and house plants in the curtained windows, atmospheric Dales photographs and prints, and a coal-effect stove in the stripped-stone end wall all add a cosy feel. Adnams, Marstons Bitter and Pedigree and a couple of guests such as Burton Blonde and Wincle Sir Philip are on handpump; darts and pool in a tiled-floor games area on the left; TV, piped music and board games. The pub is in a quiet spot at the end of the road up to the moors, opposite a largely 18th-c church and prettily tucked into woodland. It has fine views over the village and the hills beyond from good teak tables on its two-level terrace.

🍴 Sensibly priced food includes sandwiches, whitebait, creamy garlic mushrooms on garlic toast, chicken balti, chilli, stuffed vegetable crêpe with cheese and tomato sauce, steak and kidney pie, and daily specials such as shank of lamb with red wine and rosemary sauce, fie pie, battered haddock, and mushroom stroganoff. *Benchmark main dish: rabbit pie with suet crust £11.25. Two-course evening meal £12.85.*

Free house ~ Licensees Julie and Justin Satur ~ Real ale ~ Bar food (12-2.30, 6-9; 12-9 Sat, 12-8 Sun) ~ (01298) 85319 ~ Children welcome ~ Dogs allowed in bar ~ Open 12-3, 6-midnight; 12-midnight Sat; 12-10.30 Sun; 12-3, 7-midnight weekdays in winter ~ Bedrooms: /£75S

Recommended by J and E Dakin, Bruce and Sharon Eden, Peter F Marshall, Mr and Mrs A Woolstone, Edward Leetham, Mike Proctor, Pat and Stewart Gordon, Barry Collett

---

The price we give for a two-course evening meal in the featured top pub entries is the mean (average of cheapest and most expensive) price of a starter and a main course – no drinks.

CLIPSHAM Rutland   SK9716   Map 8

Olive Branch ★ ⑪ ♈ ◖ ⇥

Take B668/Stretton exit off A1 N of Stamford; Clipsham signposted E from exit roundabout; LE15 7SH

A special place for an exceptional meal in comfortable surroundings, fine choice of drinks, and luxury bedrooms

This is a great place to make a weekend of it. Their bedrooms (just opposite in Beech House with delicious breakfasts) are lovely, the food is first class and the range of drinks exceptional. It can get pretty busy at peak times, so if you're not staying it's worth getting here early for a good peaceful table. The various small but charmingly attractive bars have a relaxed country cottage atmosphere, with dark joists and beams, rustic furniture, an interesting mix of pictures (some by local artists), candles on tables, and a cosy log fire in the stone inglenook fireplace. Many of the books dotted around were bought at antiques fairs by one of the partners and are sometimes for sale; piped music. A carefully chosen range of drinks includes Grainstore Olive Ale and a local guest beer on handpump, an enticing wine list (with a dozen by the glass), a fine choice of malt whiskies, armagnacs and cognacs, and quite a few different british and continental bottled beers. Outside, there are tables, chairs and big plant pots on a pretty little terrace, with more on the neat lawn, sheltered in the L of its two low buildings.

 Extremely highly thought-of (if not cheap) food might include sandwiches, a smashing tapas board, smoked salmon and pea chowder, tempura battered tiger prawns with sweet chilli sauce, coronation guinea fowl terrine with mango salsa, loin of rabbit with hazelnut and pickled carrot salad, baked bass with chickpea and chorizo caponata, and roast duck breast with confit duck pasty and glazed beetroot. *Benchmark main dish: fish and chips £14.50. Two-course evening meal £29.50.*

Free house ~ Licensees Sean Hope and Ben Jones ~ Real ale ~ Bar food (12-2(3 Sun), 7-9.30(9 Sun); 12-2, 2.30-5.30, 7-9.30 Sat) ~ Restaurant ~ (01780) 410355 ~ Children welcome ~ Dogs allowed in bar and bedrooms ~ Open 12-3, 6-11; 12-11(10.30 Sun) Sat; may close first week in Jan ~ Bedrooms: £112.50S(£130B)/£130S(£160B)

Recommended by Peter and Josie Fawcett, D M Jack, Jill and Julian Tasker, Graeme Manson, Barry Collett, Bruce and Sharon Eden, Howard and Margaret Buchanan, Mike and Sue Loseby, P Dawn, P and J Shapley, Pam and John Smith, Pat and Stewart Gordon, Roy Bromell, Di and Mike Gillam, Sandy Butcher, David and Ruth Shillitoe, Tony and Maggie Harwood, Bob and Tanya Ekers

COLEORTON Leicestershire   SK4117   Map 7

George

Loughborough Road (A512 E); LE67 8HF

Attractively traditional civilised proper pub with big garden

The friendly couple who run this comfortable pub are very much at the heart of its homely welcoming atmosphere. The carpeted bar on the right is nicely laid out to give a comfortable feel of varied and fairly small separate areas: dark leather sofa and tub chairs by a woodburning stove in front, scatter-cushioned pew and mixed chairs below shelves of books in one corner, and other mixed seating elsewhere. This room has lots of local photographs on its ochre or dove-grey walls, black beams and joists, and a dark-panelled dado. A bigger room on the left, broadly similar and again with plenty to look at, has another woodburning stove, and more of a dining-room feel. Greene King Abbot and Old Speckled Hen and Marstons Pedigree are on handpump. The spreading garden behind has sturdy wooden furniture among sizeable trees, and a play area.

🍴 Honest pub food prepared using local produce includes lunchtime filled panini, mustard chicken and orange salad, thai spiced crab cakes, lasagne, beef and ale pie, scampi, liver and bacon, roast butternut with griddled mediterranean vegetables and goats cheese, and rib-eye steak with welsh rarebit. *Benchmark main dish: battered cod and chips £10.25. Two-course evening meal £15.75.*

Free house ~ Licensees Mark and Jan Wilkinson ~ Real ale ~ Bar food (12-2.30(3 Sun), 6-9(9.30 Fri, Sat)) ~ (01530) 834639 ~ Well behaved children allowed away from bar areas till 8.30 ~ Dogs allowed in bar ~ Open 12-11(5 Sun); closed Sun evening, Mon

Recommended by Paul J Robinshaw, Dave and Jenny Hughes, Comus and Sarah Elliott, Henry Paulinski, Rod Weston

COLSTON BASSETT Nottinghamshire   SK6933   Map 7

Martins Arms 🏮 ⏛ ◀

Village signposted off A46 E of Nottingham; School Lane, near market cross in village centre; NG12 3FD

NOTTINGHAMSHIRE DINING PUB OF THE YEAR

Smart dining pub with imaginative food, good range of drinks including six real ales and attractive grounds

This lovely country pub is smartly decorated with period fabrics and colourings, antique furniture and hunting prints. There are warm log fires in Jacobean fireplaces and the atmosphere is comfortably civilised. If you are dining in the elegant restaurant, you may be welcomed by Salvatore, the friendly front of house man, and neatly uniformed staff serve Bass, Greene King IPA, Marstons Pedigree, Timothy Taylors Landlord and a couple of guests from brewers such as Castle Rock and Greene King, as well as Belvoir organic ginger beer, a good range of malt whiskies and cognacs and an interesting wine list; cribbage, dominoes and board games.The sizeable lawned garden (summer croquet here) backs on to National Trust parkland and readers recommend visiting the church opposite and Colston Bassett Dairy, which sells its own stilton cheese, and is just outside the village.

🍴 They use seasonal carefully sourced ingredients so the menu changes frequently but might include crab and edamame cocktail, rabbit and black pudding terrine, tempura scallops with cockles and pancetta salad, ploughman's, mushroom, stilton and tomato tart, pork belly with black pudding and cider jus, fish and chips, roast monkfish with thyme cream, braised venison with parsnip mash, and well hung steaks. Bread and chutneys are home-made. *Benchmark main dish: sirloin steak £19.95. Two-course evening meal £25.50.*

Free house ~ Licensees Lynne Strafford Bryan and Salvatore Inguanta ~ Real ale ~ Bar food (12-2(3 Sun), 6-9.30; not Sun evening) ~ Restaurant ~ (01949) 81361 ~ Children welcome in dining room and snug ~ Open 12-3, 6-11; 12-4, 7-11 Sun

Recommended by the Didler, P Dawn, Dennis and Doreen Haward, David Glynne-Jones

---

If we know a featured top pub does sandwiches, we always say so – if they're not mentioned, you'll have to assume you can't get one.

CRICK Northamptonshire   SP5872   Map 4

Red Lion £

1 mile from M1 junction 18; in centre of village off A428; NN6 7TX

Nicely worn-in friendly coaching inn off M1 with straightforward lunchtime food and pricier more detailed evening menu

One reader tells us that the landlord at this old stone thatched pub 'is just the type of jovial chap you want to see behind a bar'. He goes on to say that 'the beer is well kept, the prices are reasonable and the food is tasty but not pretentious'. We couldn't have put it better ourselves. Popular with locals, the traditional low-ceilinged bar has lots of comfortable seating, some rare old horsebrasses, pictures of the pub in the days before it was surrounded by industrial estates and a tiny log stove in a big inglenook. Four well kept beers on handpump include Caledonian Deuchars IPA, Greene King Old Speckled Hen, Wells & Youngs Bombardier and a guest. There are a few picnic-sets under parasols on a terrace by the car park, and in summer you can eat out in the old coachyard which is sheltered by a perspex roof and decorated with lots of pretty hanging baskets.

Generous helpings of bar food (they don't do starters) includes sandwiches and ploughman's, chicken and mushroom or steak pie, tuna pasta bake, breaded plaice, and vegetable pancake rolls. Prices go up a little in the evening when they offer a wider range of dishes that might include stuffed salmon fillet, lamb shank, half a roast duck, and sirloin steak; bargain-price Sunday roast. *Benchmark main dish: steak pie £4.80.*

Wellington ~ Lease Tom and Paul Marks ~ Real ale ~ Bar food (not Sun evening) ~ (01788) 822342 ~ Children under 12 lunchtimes only ~ Dogs welcome ~ Open 11-2.30, 6.15-11; 12-3, 7-10.30 Sun

Recommended by Dr D J and Mrs S C Walker, Margaret and Peter Staples, Edward Mirzoeff, George Atkinson, John and Joyce Snell, Roger and Pauline Pearce, Stuart and Jasmine Kelly, Gerard Dyson

EAST HADDON Northamptonshire   SP6668   Map 4

Red Lion

High Street; village signposted off A428 (turn right in village) and off A50 N of Northampton; NN6 8BU

Appealing old hotel with pleasant grounds and good food

The neatly set out dining areas at this elegantly substantial golden stone inn are light and airy with contemporary wallpaper and long curtains at elegant floor to ceiling windows. Walls are painted in warmer pastel shades and floors are from reclaimed wood and stone. A small amount of carefully chosen and arranged bric-a-brac, a pleasant mix of farmhouse and black leather tub chairs and a woodburning stove add a homely touch. French windows open to a walled side garden which is pretty with lilac, fruit trees, roses and neat flowerbeds and leads back to the bigger lawn. A small side terrace has more tables under parasols, and a big copper beech shades the gravel car park. Knowledgeable staff serve Wells & Youngs Bombardier, Bitter and Eagle and ten wines by the glass; piped music.

Attractively presented bar food might include scotch egg with caper mayonnaise, roast red pepper soup with goats cheese fritter, grilled sardines on toasted brioche with tomato dressing, penne with tomato sauce, globe artichokes and blue cheese, grilled mackerel with grilled new potatoes, crispy shallot rings and tomato and courgette relish, roast chump of lamb with garlic cream potatoes and mint jelly, and well hung steaks. *Benchmark main dish: pork belly with sage mash £15.00. Two-course evening meal £22.40.*

Charles Wells ~ Lease Nick Bonner ~ Real ale ~ Bar food (12-2.30, 6-10; 12-4 Sun) ~ Restaurant ~ (01604) 770223 ~ Children welcome ~ Open 12-2.30, 6-11; 12-4 Sun; closed Sun evening ~ Bedrooms: £80S/£95S

Recommended by John and Susan Miln, Ryta Lyndley, R W Allen, Michael Dandy, Alan Sutton, George Atkinson, Mrs J Plante Cleall

 FARTHINGHOE Northamptonshire   SP5339   Map 4

Fox
Just off A422 Brackley—Banbury; Baker Street; NN13 5PH

Sprucely refurbished, with enjoyable food and well kept ales

Well restored, this lichened golden stone building has small landscapes, old country photographs and framed old advertisements well spaced on its pastel walls, and a striking bigger triptych of a prowling fox. Seating ranges from dark leather tub chairs, green-padded seats, wall banquettes and neatly built-in traditional wall seats to the well cushioned ladder-back and other dining chairs of the eating area, which has quite a low plank-panelled ceiling in one part. The dark-beamed front bar has a log fire in a great stripped-stone fireplace with a side salt cupboard. Lighting is sympathetic, and good new flooring includes some attractively coloured slate tiling. They have Wells & Youngs Bitter, Bombardier and Courage Directors on handpump, and service is friendly and efficient; there may be piped music. Behind is a sheltered terrace with teak tables, with picnic-sets under cocktail parasols in the neatly kept garden beyond. We have not yet heard from readers using the newish bedrooms in the adjoining barn conversion, which do look comfortable.

Besides lunchtime sandwiches, starters, generous sharing plates and pubby favourites like home-baked ham and eggs, burgers and sausage and mash, well prepared food using fresh local supplies runs to such things as salmon coulibiac, ratatouille and brie in a filo basket, and dry-aged aberdeen angus steak; they do summer barbecues. *Benchmark main dish: fish and chips £10.00. Two-course evening meal £17.80.*

Charles Wells ~ Lease Mark Higgs ~ Real ale ~ Bar food (12-2(2.30 Sat), 6.30(6 Sat)-9.30;12-4, 6-8 Sun) ~ Restaurant ~ (01295) 713965 ~ Children welcome ~ Open 12-3, 6-11; 12-11 Sat, Sun ~ Bedrooms: /£60S

Recommended by David and Lexi Young, P and J Shapley

 FENNY BENTLEY Derbyshire   SK1750   Map 7

Coach & Horses £
A515 N of Ashbourne; DE6 1LB

Cosy former coaching inn with pretty country furnishings, roaring open fires, and food all day

This popular 17th-c coaching inn is quite traditional, with a welcoming atmosphere and a good mix of customers. Its homely interior has flagstone floors, black beams hung with horsebrasses and wagon-wheels, hand-made pine furniture that includes flowery-cushioned wall settles, warm winter fires on exposed brick hearths and pewter mugs. There's also a conservatory dining room; quiet piped music. Marstons Pedigree and a guest such as Blue Monkey BG Sips are on handpump, and the landlord is knowledgeable about malt whiskies – he stocks just over two dozen. There are views across fields from tables in the side garden by an elder tree, and modern tables and chairs under cocktail parasols on the front terrace. The pub is within a few minutes' walk of the popular Tissington Trail (which follows a former railway line) and is best joined at the nearby picture-book village of Tissington.

As well as lunchtime and afternoon sandwiches, tasty bar food includes crayfish tail and prawn cocktail, goats cheese wrapped in filo with red onion chutney, salmon fillet with cream wine and crabmeat sauce, roast duck with ginger sauce, roast vegetable nut loaf with cream, wine and leek sauce, and lamb casserole with dumplings. *Benchmark main dish: bacon steak and egg £9.95. Two-course evening meal £15.75.*

Free house ~ Licensees John and Matthew Dawson ~ Real ale ~ Bar food (12-9) ~ Restaurant ~ (01335) 350246 ~ Children welcome ~ Open 11-11; 12-10.30 Sun

Recommended by John and Enid Morris, Bob and Pauline Fletcher, Jeremy and Ruth Preston-Hoar, the Didler, Bernard Stradling, Jill and Julian Tasker, John and Sharon Hancock, Neil Ingoe, John Wooll, Jon Porter, Ken and Barbara Turner

FOOLOW Derbyshire   SK2078   Map 7

Barrel

Bretton, N of village; S32 5QD

Remote dining pub with traditional decor and friendly staff

High up on the lonely Eyam Ridge, this magnificently placed stone-roofed turnpike inn can have sweeping views over five counties. Seats out on the front terrace by the road and a courtyard garden are nicely sheltered from the inevitable breeze at this height. The peacefully cosy dark oak-beamed bar looks very traditional with its gleaming copper, warming fire, patterned carpet, studded doors in low doorways and stools lined up at the counter, which has Greene King IPA, Old Speckled Hen and Hardys & Hanson Olde Trip on handpump, and tankards hanging above. Stubs of massive knocked-through stone walls divide it into several areas; piped radio.

Bar food might include thai marinated chicken skewers, ham hock and black pudding terrine, beef, pork and chicken pie, tomato and mozzarella salad with pesto and ciabatta, duck breast with shallot and garlic confit and madeira sauce, grilled cod loin with tiger prawns and garlic and parsley butter, fisherman's crumble, and rib-eye steak. *Benchmark main dish: fish and chips £10.95. Two-course evening meal £18.75.*

Free house ~ Licensee Philip Cone ~ Real ale ~ Bar food (12-2, 6-9; 12-9 Sun) ~ (01433) 630856 ~ Well behaved children welcome ~ Dogs allowed in bar ~ Open 11-11; 11-3, 6-11 Mon-Fri Oct-March ~ Bedrooms: £45S/£65B

Recommended by Peter F Marshall, Ann and Tony Bennett-Hughes

Please let us know what you think of a pub's bedrooms: feedback@goodguides.com or (no stamp needed) The Good Pub Guide, FREEPOST TN1569, Wadhurst, E Sussex TN5 7BR.

FOTHERINGHAY Northamptonshire   TL0593 Map 5

Falcon 🍴 ♀

Village signposted off A605 on Peterborough side of Oundle; PE8 5HZ

NORTHAMPTONSHIRE DINING PUB OF THE YEAR

Upmarket dining pub, good range of drinks and food from snacks up, and attractive garden

Staff at this neatly kept civilised pub are exceptionally friendly and polite, creating a delightful atmosphere for the good inventive food they serve. Everything is neatly kept, with fresh flower arrangements and sedate cushioned slatback arm and bucket chairs, and good winter log fires in stone fireplaces. Surprisingly, given the emphasis on dining here, it does have a thriving little locals' tap bar and a darts team. The very good range of drinks includes three changing beers from brewers such as Digfield, Fullers and Nethergate on handpump, good wines (over a dozen by the glass), Weston's organic cider, organic cordials and fresh orange juice. There's a pretty conservatory restaurant and terrace which have lovely views of the vast church behind, and an attractively planted garden. The village is lovely, and the ruins of Fotheringhay Castle, where Mary Queen of Scots was executed, are not far away.

🍴 As well as imaginative sandwiches, thoughtful bar food might include smoked duck breast with blood oranges, crab salad with curry mayonnaise, ham hock terrine with piccalilli, mushroom and leek fricassée with tagliatelle, tarragon and parmesan cream, seabream fillet with crayfish and saffron risotto, braised pork belly with rösti potato, parsnip purée and thyme jus, and they do a snackier bar menu and two- and three-course meal deals. *Benchmark main dish: salmon, crab and dill fishcakes £9.50. Two-course evening meal £21.95.*

Free house ~ Licensee Sally Facer ~ Real ale ~ Bar food (12.15-2.15(3 Sun), 6.15-9.15(8.30 Sun)) ~ Restaurant ~ (01832) 226254 ~ Children welcome ~ Dogs allowed in bar ~ Open 12-11(10.30 Sun)

Recommended by O K Smyth, P and J Shapley, Michael Doswell, Alan Sutton, Robert Wivell, Michael Sargent, Clive Flynn

GREAT BRINGTON Northamptonshire   SP6664 Map 4

Althorp Coaching Inn ◀

Off A428 NW of Northampton, near Althorp Hall; until recently known as the Fox & Hounds; NN7 4JA

Friendly golden stone thatched pub with great choice of real ales, tasty food, and sheltered garden

There's quite a lot of the archetypal old English pub about this lovely old coaching inn, not to mention the fact that they serve eight real ales. The ancient bar has all the traditional features you'd wish for, from a dog or two sprawled out by the huge log fire, to old beams, saggy joists and an attractive mix of country chairs and tables (maybe with fresh flowers) on its broad flagstones and bare boards. There are plenty of snug alcoves and nooks and crannies with some stripped-pine shutters and panelling, two fine log fires and an eclectic medley of bric-a-brac from farming implements to an old clocking-in machine and country pictures. Cheery staff serve the splendid range of real ales that include Fullers London Pride, Greene King IPA and Abbot, St Austell Tribute and thoughtfully sourced, often local, guests from brewers such as Cottage,

Nobbys, Purity and Tring. The extended dining area gives views of the 30 or so casks racked in the cellar. Also eight wines by the glass and a decent range of malt whiskies. One of the old coaching bars is used for pub games and an old garden cottage adjoins the lovely little paved courtyard (also accessible by the old coaching entrance) which has sheltered tables and tubs of flowers; more seating in the side garden.

🍴 Food here is popular so it's advisable to book. As well as sandwiches, dishes might include seared scallops with sherry and chilli dressing, mushrooms and smoked bacon with stilton sauce, penne with scallops and crayfish tails with tarragon sauce, braised beef and Guinness casserole, lasagne, leek and macaroni cheese and chestnut-stuffed chicken breast wrapped in smoked bacon with mushroom cream sauce. *Benchmark main dish: pork fillet stuffed with apricot and sage with pear cider sauce £13.25. Two-course evening meal £18.60.*

Free house ~ Licensee Michael Krempels ~ Real ale ~ Bar food (12-3(5 Sun), 6.30-9.30(10 Fri, Sat); 6-8 Sun) ~ Restaurant ~ (01604) 770651 ~ Dogs allowed in bar ~ Live music Tues evening ~ Open 11-11.30; 12-10.30 Sun

Recommended by John and Susan Miln, Gerry and Rosemary Dobson, George Atkinson, Tim and Ann Newell

---

GREAT CASTERTON Lincolnshire   SK9909   Map 8

Plough 🍴

B1081, just off A1 N of Stamford (coming from the S or returning to A1 southbound, use A606 junction instead); Main Street; PE9 4AA

Cheerful atmosphere and good food in well run comfortably modernised pub, handy for A1

Very hands-on, the landlady keeps a kindly eye on everything here, so as well as good service the little details work well, too: good coffee, for instance, and unusual bar nibbles such as warmed chorizo, as well as a good choice of wines by the glass and the well kept Bass and Greene King IPA on handpump – from a counter with comfortable leather-and-chrome bar stools. The unassuming carpeted bar on the left is small and quite brightly decorated – light and welcoming, with colourful scatter cushions on seats built into the wall and big bow window. There may be unobtrusive piped music (Peggy Lee and the like), and board games. The main lounge bar, also carpeted, has a mix of dark pub tables and some banquette seating as well as dining chairs. The good-sized garden, like the pub itself kept very neatly, has well spaced picnic-sets by a big weeping willow, with swings and a rabbit hutch; there are also tables on a small wood-screened terrace.

🍴 Besides a good choice of sandwiches, starters or light dishes such as twice-baked roquefort soufflé, and familiar but carefully done things (they make their own bread, too) like home-made burgers and lasagne, the interesting food might include rewarding main courses such as a butternut squash, goats cheese and leek pie, lightly spiced plaice fillets with sagaloo and onion bhajee, or seared scallops with pork belly and black pudding. *Benchmark main dish: roast pork belly with haggis mash £13.95. Two-course evening meal £17.40.*

Punch ~ Lease Peter Lane and Amy Thompson ~ Real ale ~ Bar food (12-2.30(3 Sun), 6-9.30) ~ Restaurant ~ (01780) 762178 ~ Children welcome ~ Dogs allowed in bar ~ Open 12-2.30(3 Sat, 3.30 Sun), 6-11.30; closed Sun evening, Mon, one week in Jan

Recommended by Marlene and Jim Godfrey

GREAT LONGSTONE Derbyshire   SK1971 Map 7

Crispin £
Main Street; DE45 1TZ

Spotless traditional pub with emphasis on good value pubby food; good drinks choice, too

---

Décor at this family-run pub is thoroughly traditional, running from decorative plates, some brass or copper implements, a collage of regulars' snapshots, horsebrasses on the beams in the red ceiling to padded built-in wall benches and upholstered chairs and stools around polished tables on green carpet, and a coal-effect fire. A corner area is snugly partitioned off, and on the right is a separate more formal dining room; darts, board games and may be faint piped music. Welcoming and obliging staff serve a good choice of wines and whiskies as well as four Robinsons beers on handpump. There are picnic-sets out in front, set well back above the quiet lane (one under a heated canopy), with more in the garden behind.

Using eggs from their own hens, the good value food includes sandwiches, hot baguettes, fried camembert with warm cranberry, battered cod, red pepper and spinach lasagne, gammon steak with pineapple, a hefty mixed grill, and daily specials such as derbyshire oatcakes with spinach, brie and walnuts, and aberdeen angus burger with stilton; set menus and OAP lunches are also deservedly popular here. *Benchmark main dish: steak, kidney and Guinness pie £9.95. Two-course evening meal £14.20.*

Robinsons ~ Tenant Paul Rowlinson ~ Real ale ~ Bar food (12-2.30, 6.30-9) ~ Restaurant ~ (01629) 640237 ~ Children welcome ~ Dogs welcome ~ Quiz night Fri ~ Open 12-3, 6-midnight; 12-midnight Sat, Sun

Recommended by Peter F Marshall, John and Jackie Rippon, Derek and Sylvia Stephenson

---

HATHERSAGE Derbyshire   SK2380 Map 7

Plough 🍽 ♀ 🛏
Leadmill; B6001 towards Bakewell, OS Sheet 110 map reference 235805; S32 1BA

Comfortable dining pub usefully placed for exploring the Peak District, with good food, beer and wine, waterside garden, and bedrooms

---

One of the most appealing things about this 16th-c inn are its nine acre grounds in a lovely spot on the banks of the River Derwent. The pretty garden slopes right down to the water and there's a lovely suntrap courtyard. Recently smartened up but still fairly traditional, the immaculately kept interior is neat and tidy with rows of dark wood tables (with cruets giving away the emphasis on dining) and a long banquette running almost the length of one wall on bright tartan and turkey patterned carpets. There's a big log fire and a woodburning stove, decorative plates are displayed on terracotta walls and pewter tankards hang from a dark beam; quiet piped music. They've a good wine list (with a dozen by the glass), 25 malt whiskies, and Black Sheep, Timothy Taylors and a guest such as Adnams on handpump.

Bar food includes sardine fillets with wild garlic risotto, spinach and chilli oil, leek and gruyère risotto, beef carpaccio with horseradish aioli, sausage and mash with red wine jus, battered cod, lemon sole with dauphinoise potato, asparagus and langoustine cream, oriental spiced roast duck leg with vegetable stir fry, and pheasant breast with puy lentils and mushrooms. *Benchmark main dish: chicken breast with couscous, smoked aubergine and chermoula dressing £13.00. Two-course evening meal £17.00.*

Free house ~ Licensees Bob, Cynthia and Elliott Emery ~ Real ale ~ Bar food (11-9; 12-8.30 Sun) ~ Restaurant ~ (01433) 650319 ~ Children welcome ~ Dogs allowed in bar ~ Open 11-11; 12-10.30 Sun ~ Bedrooms: £70B/£95B

Recommended by Marian and Andrew Ruston, P A Rowe, DC, John and Enid Morris, Barry and Anne, Alun Jones, Rochelle Seifas, Jill and Julian Tasker, Karen Eliot, Ann and Colin Hunt, Mr and Mrs M Hargrave, John Branston, Richard Cole, Colin and Pat Honey

 HAYFIELD Derbyshire   SK0388   Map 7

Lantern Pike
Glossop Road (A624 N) at Little Hayfield, just N of Hayfield; SK22 2NG

Friendly retreat from the surrounding moors of Kinder Scout, with reasonably priced food; bedrooms

The traditional red plush bar at this homely place proudly displays photos of the original *Coronation Street* cast, many of whom were regulars here, along with Tony Warren, one of its earlier script writers, and Arthur Lowe of *Dad's Army* fame. It's quite possible that the interior you'll find hasn't changed much since those days – with its warm fire, brass platters in numbers, china and toby jugs, fresh flowers on the tables and counter lined with red plush stools (Thornbridge Lord Marples, Timothy Taylors Landlord and a guest such as Whim Hartington on handpump); TV and piped music. Lying as it does within the bounds of the Peak District National Park, this is a great place to come down to if you've been walking on the windswept moors, and tables on a stone-walled terrace look over a big-windowed weaver's house towards Lantern Pike. Dogs may be allowed in at the licensees' discretion and if clean.

Served in generous helpings, bar food includes sandwiches, haddock and spring onion fishcakes, cajun breaded chicken, stilton vegetable bake, thai-style lamb on tagliatelle, steak and ale pie, and steaks. *Benchmark main dish: steak and kidney pie £9.95. Two-course evening meal £14.00.*

Enterprise ~ Lease Stella and Tom Cunliffe ~ Real ale ~ Bar food (12-2.30, 5-8.30 (8 Mon); 12-8.30 Sat, 12-8 Sun) ~ Restaurant ~ (01663) 747590 ~ Children welcome ~ Open 12-3, 5-11; 12-11 Sat, Sun; closed Mon lunchtime ~ Bedrooms: £40B/£56B

Recommended by Dean Johnson, Dennis Jones

 HOPE Derbyshire   SK1783   Map 7

Cheshire Cheese ● £ ⇔
Off A6187, towards Edale; S33 6ZF

Cosy up-and-down old stone pub, with good real ales, in attractive Peak District village; bedrooms

The two very snug oak-beamed rooms at this popular honey-coloured 16th-c inn are arranged on different levels, each with its own warming fire, carpets or stone floors, traditional dark wood furnishings and gleaming brasses. It's a well liked place and often fills to capacity with locals as well as tourists, all welcomed equally by the friendly barman and staff. Bradfield Blonde, Peak Ales Swift Nick, Whim Hartington and a local guest are on handpump and they've a dozen malts. There's a glorious range of local walks near here, taking in the summits of Lose Hill and Win Hill, or the cave district of the Castleton area, and the village of Hope itself is worth a stroll; parking is limited. The bedrooms were being refurbished as we went to press so prices may change.

 As well as lunchtime snacks such as sandwiches and salads, food includes daily changing dishes such as steak and kidney pudding, lasagne, yorkshire pudding and sausage, smoked haddock and spring onion fishcake, gammon steak, chicken and asparagus pie, and nut roast; pie night Wednesday. *Benchmark main dish: beer-battered haddock £9.95. Two-course evening meal £13.00.*

Enterprise ~ Lease Craig and Laura Lockwood ~ Real ale ~ Bar food (12-2(4 Sat, 8 Sun)) ~ Restaurant ~ (01433) 620381 ~ Children welcome ~ Dogs allowed in bar ~ Open 12-3, 6-12; 12-midnight Sat, Sun; closed Mon except bank holidays ~ Bedrooms: £30B/£60B

Recommended by Peter F Marshall, John Fiander, Peter La Farge, the Didler, Ann and Colin Hunt, Stuart and Jasmine Kelly

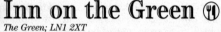

INGHAM Lincolnshire   SK9483   Map 8

Inn on the Green ⑪
The Green; LN1 2XT

Nicely modernised place serving thoughtfully prepared food; chatty atmosphere

Although most tables at this friendly dining pub are occupied by people here for the good popular food, it does still have quite a pubby feel (particularly in the locals' bar). Its beamed and timbered dining room is spread over two floors with lots of exposed brickwork, a mix of brasses and copper, local prints, bric-a-brac and a warm winter fire. The brick bar counter has home-made jams, marmalade and chutney for sale alongside Black Sheep, a couple of guests such as Adnams and Charles Wells Bombardier and nine wines by the glass. Opposite is a comfortably laid-back area with two red leather sofas; piped music; good service; more reports please.

 Using some home-grown produce, good food might include sandwiches, a pint of prawns, battered squid, venison and pigeon terrine, fishcakes with sweet chilli jam, battered haddock and chips, moroccan spiced monkfish with lemon couscous, roast duck leg with beetroot and orange, butternut risotto, and grilled plaice with clams and chives. *Benchmark main dish: rabbit and mustard stew £10.50. Two-course evening meal £17.70.*

Free house ~ Licensees Andrew Cafferkey and Sarah Sharpe ~ Real ale ~ Bar food (12-2(4.45 Sun), 6.30(5 Sat)-9; not Tues lunchtime, Sun evening) ~ Restaurant ~ (01522) 730354 ~ Children welcome ~ Open 11.30-3, 6(5 Fri)-11; 11.30-11 Sat; 12-10.30 Sun; closed Mon

Recommended by Bill Bartlett

INGLEBY Derbyshire   SK3427   Map 7

John Thompson ◖ £ 🛏
NW of Melbourne; turn off A514 at Swarkestone Bridge or in Stanton by Bridge; can also be reached from Ticknall (or from Repton on B5008); DE73 7HW

Own-brew pub that strikes the right balance between attentive service, roomy comfort, and good value lunchtime food

Things tick along in a perfectly relaxed way at this nicely pubby place, with plenty of readers enthusing about the quality of the beer brewed out back, the tasty good value food and the friendly staff. Simple but comfortable and beautifully kept, the big modernised lounge has ceiling joists, some old oak settles, button-back leather seats, sturdy oak tables, antique prints and paintings and a log-effect gas fire; piped music. A couple of smaller cosier rooms open off; piano, games machine, board games, darts, TV, and pool in the conservatory. They usually serve three of their own beers but may supplement a guest such as Black Sheep. Surrounded by pretty countryside and near the River Trent, there are lots of tables by flower beds on the neat lawns, or you can sit on the partly covered terrace. Breakfast is left in the fridge for you if you stay in one of their self-catering detached chalet lodges in the grounds. The pub takes its name from the licensee's father.

The short lunchtime menu includes sandwiches, baked potatoes, salads, mediterranean vegetable risotto and a roast beef carvery, with puddings such as fruit crumble and Mrs Thompson's famous bread and butter pudding – a speciality of the pub for the past 40 years. *Benchmark main dish: roast beef carvery £7.45.*

Own brew ~ Licensee Nick Thompson ~ Real ale ~ Bar food (12-2) ~ (01332) 862469 ~ Dogs welcome ~ Open 11-2.30, 6-11; 11-11 Sat; 12-10.30 Sun; closed Mon lunchtime ~ Bedrooms: /£60S

Recommended by Pam and John Smith, Richard Stanfield, Mr and Mrs H Franklin, Phil and Jane Hodson, David and Gill Carrington, the Didler, Simon Donan, Jill and Julian Tasker, Theo, Anne and Jane Gaskin

 KIRKBY LA THORPE Lincolnshire   TF0945 Map 8

Queens Head
Village and pub signposted off A17, just E of Sleaford, then turn right into Boston Road cul-de-sac; NG34 9NU

Reliable dining pub very popular for its enjoyable food and good service

This extended pub is well organised, with plenty of neat dark-waistcoated staff, open woodburning stoves, huge elaborate flower arrangements and carefully folded table napkins. You can choose almost any degree of formality (and fresh air), from the teak tables and chairs in a lantern-lit back arbour with a glazed canopy, through a sizeable brightly carpeted bar with button-back banquettes and sofas and dining chairs around its shiny dark tables, to a light and airy conservatory with informal dining tables, or – beyond heavily swagged curtains – a smartly linen-set beamed restaurant area. Nice decorative touches take in thoughtful lighting, big prints and five handsome longcase clocks (it's quite something when they all go off at midday). Batemans XB and a guest such as Bass are on handpump and in summer they serve home-made lemonade; easy disabled access and piped music

You can eat from the bar or restaurant menu, though the full choice does make rather daunting reading. As well as sandwiches, there might be chicken caesar salad, sausage and mash, salmon and coriander fishcakes with thai sweet chilli jam, blue cheese filo tart with smoked cherry tomatoes and pesto, honey and mustard roast pork fillet with apple mash and calvados and cider sauce, seafood platter, and steaks. *Benchmark main dish: steak and kidney pudding £13.95. Two-course evening meal £23.00.*

Free house ~ Licensee John Clark ~ Real ale ~ Bar food (12-2.30, 6-9.30(10 Sat) 12-8.30 Sun) ~ Restaurant ~ (01529) 305743 ~ Children welcome till 7pm ~ Open 12-3, 6-11; 12-10.30 Sun

Recommended by Maurice and Janet Thorpe

LITTON Derbyshire

SK1675 Map 7

Red Lion ▰ £

*Village signposted off A623, between B6465 and B6049 junctions; also
signposted off B6049; SK17 8QU*

**Convivial all-rounder with reasonably priced food and unspoilt charm,
prettily placed by the village green**

One reader tells us that this happy place is 'surely one of the very best
pubs in the Peak District' – we put it all down to the hard-working
and ever-cheerful landlady. Two homely linked front rooms are nicely
traditional with low beams, some panelling and blazing log fires. There's a
bigger back room with good-sized tables and large antique prints on its
stripped-stone walls. Featuring local beers, the small bar counter has
Abbeydale Absolution, Oakwell Barnsley and a couple of guests such as
Buxton SPA and Blue Monkey 99 Red Baboons, a good choice of decent
wines and several malt whiskies (all spirits are available as doubles for
an extra £1); darts, shove-ha'penny, bagatelle, board games and piped
music (evenings only). It does get very full at times, so do book if you
want to eat here. Outdoor seating is on the pretty village green, which is
covered in daffodils in early spring. A particularly interesting time to visit
this village is during the annual well-dressing carnival (usually the last
week in June), when locals create a picture from flower petals, moss and
other natural materials.

Well liked good value bar food includes sandwiches, crayfish tail salad, lambs
liver and bacon with horseradish mash, chicken leek and bacon casserole, fish
and chips, spicy vegetable curry and salmon fillet with lemon dill butter, and daily
specials such as smoked haddock chowder, and beef and chorizo in red wine.
Unusually, there's an entire gluten-free menu too; Sunday roast all day. *Benchmark
main dish: steak and kidney pie £8.95. Two-course evening meal £9.80.*

Enterprise ~ Lease Suzy Turner ~ Real ale ~ Bar food (12-8(8.30 Thurs-Sun)) ~
Restaurant ~ (01298) 871458 ~ Children over 6 welcome ~ Dogs allowed in bar ~
Open 12-11(midnight Fri, Sat, 10.30 Sun)

*Recommended by Greta and Guy Pratt, John and Enid Morris, Peter F Marshall, the Didler,
Barry Collett, Michelle and Graeme Voss, Ann and Tony Bennett-Hughes, Gene and Kitty Rankin,
M G Hart, Dennis Jones, Robin Constable*

LYDDINGTON Rutland

SP8797 Map 4

Marquess of Exeter ▯

Main Street; LE15 9LT

LEICESTERSHIRE & RUTLAND DINING PUB OF THE YEAR

**Stone inn with contemporary décor, real ales, and excellent food cooked
by the landlord**

Readers speak of the particularly friendly and accommodating service
at this rather handsome inn. The refurbished beamed bars are simple
yet stylish with some stripped-stone walls and some painted pale grey or
yellow chairs upholstered in a striking navy print dotted between leather
sofas and tub chairs, wooden wall settles and all manner of tables on the
wood-strip or flagstoned floors, pine chests and old barrels, fresh flowers
and several open fires (one has heraldic shields above it). Marstons
Pedigree and a guest like Brakspears Bitter are on handpump and they
offer several wines by the glass. There are seats out on the terrace and on
the lawns. The pub is named after the Burghley family, who have long

owned this charming village (Burghley House is about 15 miles away).

Excellent food (you must book ahead to be sure of a table) includes sandwiches, grilled squid with red pepper chilli salsa, goats cheese crostini, roast lamb rump with pesto, mushroom and goats cheese tart, game terrine with pickled walnut salsa, grilled chicken breast with creamy mushrooms, fried gurnard fillet with tomato and chorizo stew, confit duck leg with butter bean, tomato and spinach stew and parsnip purée, and osso bucco with saffron mash. *Benchmark main dish: steak with café de paris butter £13.25. Two-course evening meal £22.20.*

Marstons ~ Lease Brian Baker ~ Real ale ~ Bar food (12-2.30 (3 Sun), 6.30-10(6-9 Sun)) ~ Restaurant ~ (01572) 822477 ~ Children welcome but must be supervised by parents ~ Dogs allowed in bar and bedrooms ~ Open 12-11(10.30 Sun) ~ Bedrooms: £69.50B/£89.50B

Recommended by Roy Bromell, Mike and Margaret Banks, Jeff and Wendy Williams, Mike and Sue Loseby, Robin Constable, Michael Goodden, Malcolm Lee, R L Borthwick

MOWSLEY Leicestershire   SP6488   Map 4

Staff of Life ⚓ 🍴 ♟

Village signposted off A5199 S of Leicester; Main Street; LE17 6NT

Neat, high-gabled pub popular for a good meal out; seats in back garden

The roomy bar at this well run little village pub is spotlessly kept and quite traditional with a panelled ceiling, warming woodburning stove, high-backed settles on flagstones, wicker chairs on shiny wood floors and stools lined up along the unusual circular counter. Friendly staff serve Banks's Bitter and a couple of guests such as Langton Hop On and Inclined Plane from handpump, and they've up to 20 wines (and champagne and fizz) in three different-sized glasses; piped music. There are some seats out in front of the building with more on a delightful little deck shaded by leafy foliage.

Well liked bar food might include fried pigeon breast wrapped in smoked bacon on parsnip purée with madeira sauce, seared scallops on tarragon black pudding with black bean sauce, peking duck with all the trimmings, sausage and mash, penne with pesto, roast vegetables and pine nuts, poached smoked haddock with poached egg and parsley cream sauce, and beef shin with parsnip crisps, port jus and wholegrain mustard sauce. *Benchmark main dish: roast pork belly with sage, onion and garlic and tomato port jus £13.50. Two-course evening meal £21.20.*

Free house ~ Licensee Spencer Farrell ~ Real ale ~ Bar food (12-2.30(3.30 Sun), 6-9.15; not Sun evening) ~ Restaurant ~ (0116) 240 2359 ~ Children welcome ~ Open 12-3, 6-11; 12-10.30 Sun; closed Mon lunchtime (except bank holidays) and Tues lunchtime

Recommended by Duncan Cloud, Leslie and Barbara Owen, Michael Butler, Michael Sargent, Mike and Margaret Banks, Veronica Brown

NETHER HEYFORD Northamptonshire   SP6658   Map 4

Olde Sun 🍴 £

1.75 miles from M1 junction 16: village signposted left off A45 westbound – Middle Street; NN7 3LL

Unpretentious place handy for M1 with diverting bric-a-brac, reasonably priced food, and garden with play area

The first thing that will catch your eye when you arrive at this tucked-away 18th-c golden stone pub is a row of bright blue-painted grain kibblers along the edge of the fairy-lit front terrace (with picnic-sets), though these are by no means the last of the bric-a-brac you'll find here. All manner of it hangs from the ceiling and is packed into nooks and crannies in the several small linked rooms. There's brassware (one fireplace is a grotto of large brass animals), colourful relief plates, 1930s cigarette cards, railway memorabilia and advertising signs, World War II posters and rope fancywork. The nice old cash till on one of the two counters where they serve the well kept Banks's, Greene King Ruddles, Hoggleys and Marstons Pedigree is wishfully stuck at one and a ha'penny. Furnishings are mostly properly pubby, with the odd easy chair. There are beams and low ceilings (one painted with a fine sunburst), partly glazed dividing panels, steps between some areas, rugs on parquet, red tiles or flagstones, a big inglenook log fire, and up on the left a room with full-sized hood skittles, a games machine, darts, Sky TV, cribbage and dominoes; piped music. In the garden you'll find other antiquated hand-operated farm machines, some with plants in their hoppers.

A short choice of snacky meals includes tasty sandwiches, prawn cocktail, spicy chicken goujons, fish and chips, haddock fishcakes, steak pie, lamb shank in red wine and rosemary gravy, thai green curry, mediterranean vegetable risotto, and sirloin steak. *Benchmark main dish: ham, egg and chips £6.95. Two-course evening meal £16.00.*

Free house ~ Licensees P Yates and A Ford ~ Real ale ~ Bar food (not Sun evening) ~ Restaurant ~ (01327) 340164 ~ Children welcome ~ Dogs welcome ~ Open 12-2.30, 5-11; 12-11 Sat, Sun

Recommended by Dr D J and Mrs S C Walker, R T and J C Moggridge, Brian and Anna Marsden, David and Sue Atkinson, George Atkinson

NORTHAMPTON Northamptonshire SP7559 Map 4
Malt Shovel ◾ £

Bridge Street (approach road from M1 junction 15); no nearby street parking; best to park in Morrisons central car park, far end – passage past Europcar straight to back entrance; NN1 1QF

Friendly well run real ale pub with bargain lunches and over a dozen beers

Even when they don't have one of their beer festivals on, 13 real ales are served from a formidable battery of handpumps lined up on the long counter at this pubby place. As well as the brewer-landlord's three Great Oakley house beers and their regular Frog Island Natterjack and Fullers London Pride, they run through a quickly changing guest list taking in interesting brewers such as Brown Cow, Elland, Frog Island, Hoggleys, Oakham and Vale. They also have belgian draft and bottled beers, over 40 malt whiskies, english country wines and Rich's farm cider. This is home to quite an extensive collection of breweriana including quite a few things from Phipps Northampton Brewery Company which was across the road – the site is now occupied by Carlsberg Brewery. Look out for the rare Phipps Northampton Brewery Company star, mounted outside the pub, and some high-mounted ancient beer engines from the Carlsberg Brewery. Staff are cheery and helpful; darts, daily papers, disabled facilities, may be piped music. The secluded back yard has picnic-sets, a smokers' shelter and occasional barbecues.

Bargain lunchtime food includes baguettes, wraps, baked potatoes, ploughman's, spinach and ricotta cannelloni, and daily specials such as plaice goujons, gammon, egg and chips, and sausage casserole. *Benchmark main dish: prawn rogan josh £5.95. Two-course evening meal £9.00.*

Free house ~ Licensee Mike Evans ~ Real ale ~ Bar food (12-2) ~ (01604) 234212 ~ Well behaved children welcome ~ Dogs allowed in bar ~ Blues music Weds evening ~ Open 11.30-3, 5-11.30; 11.30-11 Sat; 12-3, 7-10.30 Sun

Recommended by D and K, JJW, CMW, Maria Scotland, the Didler, Joanna Oldham, George Atkinson, Dr J Barrie Jones

 OAKHAM Rutland   SK8509   Map 4

Grainstore ◖ £
Station Road, off A606; LE15 6RE

Super own-brewed beers in a converted railway grain warehouse, friendly staff, cheerful customers, and pubby food

As per the traditional tower system of production, the beer at this interesting place is brewed on upper floors of the building, directly above the down-to-earth bar. During work hours you'll hear all the busy noises of the brewery workings rumbling above your head. They produce ten beers which are served traditionally at the left end of the bar counter and through swan necks with sparklers on the right. The atmosphere is always genial and the friendly staff will happily let you taste a sample or two. This was once a three-storey Victorian grain warehouse and the décor is plain and functional with wide well worn bare floorboards, bare ceiling boards above massive joists supported by red metal pillars, a long brick-built bar counter with cast-iron bar stools, tall cask tables and simple elm chairs; games machine, darts, board games, giant Jenga and bottle-walking. In summer they pull back the huge glass doors, opening the bar up to a terrace with picnic-sets, often stacked with barrels. You can tour the brewery by arrangement, they do takeaways, and hold a real ale festival with over 80 real ales and live music during the August bank holiday weekend; disabled access.

Wholesome unfussy food includes panini, baked potatoes, mussels prepared in three ways, good sharing platters, burgers, sausage and mash, and chicken curry. *Benchmark main dish: ale sausages and stilton mash £6.50. Two-course evening meal £11.00.*

Own brew ~ Licensee Peter Atkinson ~ Real ale ~ Bar food (11-3; not Sun) ~ (01572) 770065 ~ Children welcome till 8pm ~ Dogs welcome ~ Open 11-11(midnight Fri, Sat)

Recommended by Tony and Maggie Harwood, Barry Collett, the Didler, Andy Lickfold, Ian and Helen Stafford, P Dawn, Ryta Lyndley, Dr J Barrie Jones

 OUNDLE Northamptonshire   TL0388   Map 5

Ship ◖ £
West Street; PE8 4EF

Bustling down-to-earth town pub with interesting beers and good value pubby food

The heavily beamed lounge bar (watch your head if you're tall) at this proper, enjoyable local is made up of three cosy areas that lead off the central corridor. Up by the street there's a mix of leather and other seats, with sturdy tables and a warming log fire in a stone inglenook, and down one end a charming little panelled snug has button-back leather seats built in around its walls. The wood-floored public side has a TV, games machine and board games, and you can play poker here on Wednesdays; piped music. Friendly staff serve Brewsters Hophead, Oakham Bishops Farewell, Phipps IPA and a guest such as Digfield Shackle Bush, and they've a good range of malt whiskies. Midnight, the sleepy black and white pub cat, seems oblivious to all the cheery chatter and bustle here. The wooden tables and chairs out on the series of small sunny, covered terraces are lit at night.

🍴 Enjoyable bar food served in generous helpings includes sandwiches, breaded whitebait, chilli, sausage and mash, chicken nuggets, and specials such as thai chicken curry, and spicy tomato and red pepper spaghetti. *Benchmark main dish: ham, egg and chips £9.00. Two-course evening meal £14.20.*

Free house ~ Licensees Andrew and Robert Langridge ~ Real ale ~ Bar food (12-3, 6-9; 12-9 Sat, Sun) ~ (01832) 273918 ~ Children welcome ~ Dogs allowed in bar ~ Folk music second Mon of month ~ Open 11-11.45(midnight Fri, Sat); 12-11.45 Sun ~ Bedrooms: £30(£39S)/£69B

Recommended by John Robertson, the Didler, Barry Collett, Ryta Lyndley

PEGGS GREEN Leicestershire   SK4117   Map 7

New Inn £

Signposted off A512 Ashby—Shepshed at roundabout, then turn immediately left down Zion Hill towards Newbold; pub is 100 yards down on the right, with car park on opposite side of road; LE67 8JE

Intriguing bric-a-brac in unspoilt pub, friendly welcome, good value food and drinks; cottagey garden

One reader tells us this is 'probably the most friendly pub we've ever been in' – it's the sort of comment we are used to hearing about this simple and unspoilt little pub with its genial irish licensees and chatty locals. Quirky and quite unique-feeling, the two cosy tiled front rooms are each filled with a diverting collection of old bric-a-brac which covers almost every inch of the walls and ceilings. The little room on the left, a bit like an old kitchen parlour (they call it the Cabin), has china on the mantelpiece, lots of prints and photographs, and little collections of this and that, three old cast-iron tables, wooden stools and a small stripped kitchen table. The room to the right has nice stripped panelling and more appealing bric-a-brac. The small back Best room, with a stripped-wood floor, has a touching display of old local photographs including some colliery ones. Bass, Marstons Pedigree and Theakstons Best on handpump; piped music and board games. There are plenty of seats in front of the pub, with more in the peaceful back garden.

🍴 Unbelievably cheap food includes filled rolls and baked potatoes, soup, ham and eggs, corned beef hash, sausages in onion gravy, and a few daily specials. When they are not serving food, you can order in takeaways, and on summer evenings and Sunday lunchtimes you can bring your own picnic and they will provide rugs. *Benchmark main dish: steak and Guinness pie £5.25. Two-course evening meal £6.75.*

Enterprise ~ Lease Maria Christina Kell ~ Real ale ~ Bar food (12-2, Mon, Fri and Sat, 6-8 Mon; filled rolls might be available at other times) ~ (01530) 222293 ~ Well supervised children welcome ~ Dogs welcome ~ Open 12-2.30, 5.30-11; 12-3, 6.30-11 Sat; 12-3, 7-10.30 Sun; closed Tues-Thurs lunchtimes

Recommended by the Didler, Richard and Jean Green

PILSLEY Derbyshire   SK2371 Map 7

Devonshire Arms ♀ ▪ ⇔

Village signposted off A619 W of Baslow, and pub just below B6048; High Street; DE45 1UL

Charming country inn freshly reworked, simple yet stylish, good all round; nice place to stay

Owned by the Duke and Duchess of Devonshire and reopened in 2010, this puts a neatly contemporary slant on what is essentially a civilised and traditional small country inn, with a relaxed and chatty atmosphere. The flagstoned bar has well kept ales such as Peak Chatsworth Gold (brewed nearby, using honey) and Swift Nick, Thornbridge Jaipur and Whim Hartington on handpump, and a good choice of wines by the glass. Several fairly compact, mainly carpeted areas open off, each with a distinct character: stripped stone here, soft grey paintwork there, rather sumptuous crimson and gold wallpaper in one part, soft heather curtains and big modern paintings, log fires in stone fireplaces, comfortable seating in leather or fabric, and thick new wooden table-tops on either sturdy modern metal columns or old cast-iron bases – at least one still with its old sewing-machine treadle. Service is polite and efficient. There are some tables outside, and the renowned Chatsworth farm shop is just up at the top of the lane.

The enjoyable traditional food takes centre stage here, largely using produce from the Chatsworth Estate: whitebait and lemon mayonnaise, gammon, egg and chips, crab and chilli fishcake, thai green curry, dressed crab, pepper stuffed with butternut risotto, and rib-eye steak with peppercorn sauce. *Benchmark main dish: steak and kidney pudding £10.95. Two-course evening meal £16.40.*

Free house ~ Licensee Alan Hill ~ Real ale ~ Bar food (12-2.30, 5-9) ~ (01246) 583258 ~ Children welcome ~ Open 11-11(10.30 Sun) ~ Bedrooms: /£110.50B
Recommended by Peter F Marshall, Derek and Sylvia Stephenson

SILEBY Leicestershire   SK6015 Map 7

White Swan £

Off A6 or A607 N of Leicester; in centre turn into King Street (opposite church), then after mini-roundabout turn right at Post Office signpost into Swan Street; LE12 7NW

Exemplary town local, a boon to its chatty regulars, its good honest home cooking luring others from further afield

Although at first glance unassuming in appearance, this solidly built red-brick pub has all the touches that marked the best of between-wars estate pub design, such as its deco-tiled lobby, the polychrome-tiled fireplaces, the shiny red anaglypta ceiling and the comfortable layout of linked but separate areas including a small restaurant (now lined with books). It's packed with bric-a-brac from bizarre hats to decorative plates and lots of prints, and quickly draws you in with its bright and cheerful feeling of genuine welcome, and this, with its food and the can-do attitude of its helpful staff, is what sets it above the thousands of other good locals. Fullers London Pride is on handpump, and they stock good value house wines.

Very popular, homely bar food includes filled rolls (they bake their own bread), fried scallops with ginger, chilli, garlic and bacon, baked mushrooms with stilton sauce, roast pork belly with sage and onion mash, crab, prawn and leek pancake with cheese sauce, beef, ale and mushroom pie, and chicken, leek and bacon pasta; they offer OAP lunches and good Sunday roasts. *Benchmark main dish: baked chicken breast with parmesan sauce and parma ham £10.95. Two-course evening meal £14.50.*

Free house ~ Licensee Theresa Miller ~ Real ale ~ Bar food (12-1.30, 7-8.30) ~ (01509) 814832 ~ Children welcome ~ Open 12-2, 7-11; 7-11 Sat; 12-3 Sun; closed Sat lunchtime, Sun evening and Mon, and 1-7 Jan

Recommended by GNI

STAMFORD Lincolnshire   TF0306   Map 8

George of Stamford ★ ⑪ ♀ 🛏

High Street, St Martins (B1081 S of centre, not the quite different central pedestrianised High Street); PE9 2LB

Handsome coaching inn, beautifully relaxed and civilised, with very good (though pricey) food and wines, and lovely courtyard and garden; bedrooms

This carefully preserved and rather grand old coaching inn is an exceptional place on all counts. Very civilised but not in the least stuffy, its various lovely areas are furnished with all manner of seats from leather, cane and antique wicker to soft sofas and easy chairs – there's a room to suit all occasions. The central lounge is particularly striking with sturdy timbers, broad flagstones, heavy beams and massive stonework. Though the York Bar is surprisingly pubby with a relaxed, local feel, you might not feel comfortable turning up in walking gear. There's an oak-panelled restaurant (jacket or tie required) and a less formal Garden Restaurant which has well spaced furniture on herringbone glazed bricks around a central tropical grove. The staff are professional and friendly, with waiter drinks' service in the charming cobbled courtyard at the back: comfortable chairs and tables among attractive plant tubs and colourful hanging baskets on the ancient stone buildings. A fine range of drinks includes Adnams Broadside, Grainstore Triple B and Greene King Ruddles County on handpump, an excellent choice of wines (many of which are italian, with about 17 by the glass), and freshly squeezed orange juice. The immaculately kept walled garden is beautifully planted and there's a sunken lawn where croquet is often played.

Quality as high as this does come at a price. The simplest option is the York Bar snacks which include sandwiches and toasties, ploughman's and chicken liver pâté with cumberland sauce. In the restaurants (you may need to book), there might be prawn and crab cocktail, fish and chips, roast cod fillet on chorizo and tomato risotto, spaghetti with half a lobster, tomato and chilli, lamb shank braised in middle eastern spices, pea and basil risotto, and a seafood platter. Their morning coffee and afternoon teas are popular. *Benchmark main dish: steak, onion, mushroom and tomato sandwich £9.95. Two-course evening meal £29.00.*

Free house ~ Licensees Chris Pitman and Ivo Vannocci ~ Real ale ~ Bar food (12-11) ~ Restaurant ~ (01780) 750750 ~ Children must be over 10 in restaurant ~ Dogs allowed in bar ~ Open 11(12 Sun)-11 ~ Bedrooms: £95B/£150B

Recommended by Mrs P Bishop, Marcus Mann, Ian Phillips, Michael Dandy, Clive Watkin, J Woodgate, the Didler, John and Sylvia Harrop, Andy Lickfold, Roy Hoing, Mike and Sue Loseby, J F M and M West, Alan and Jill Bull, Val and Alan Green, Roy Bromell, Graham Oddey ,C Cooper, Clifford Blakemore, Pete Coxon

STAMFORD Lincolnshire   TF0307 Map 8

Tobie Norris ★ ♀ ◗

St Pauls Street; PE9 2BE

Great period atmosphere in a warren of ancient rooms, splendid drinks' choice, nice pub food, pleasant courtyard

Very special, this is one of those pubs which makes you grin with delight at its sheer character the moment you step inside – then goes on to reveal more and more pleasures. It's many centuries old, beautifully restored so as to make the most of its age – worn flagstones, meticulously stripped stonework, huge hearth for one room's woodburning stove, steeply pitched rafters in one of the two upstairs rooms. Furnishings run from pews and heavy leatherette wall settles to comfortable armchairs, with flickering church candles, and abundant books and antique prints. Downstairs, several linked rooms include a handsomely panelled shrine to Nelson and Trafalgar on the left. These open off a spinal corridor, glass-roofed at the far end, to make a snug conservatory which opens to a narrow but sunny two-level courtyard with cast-iron tables, hanging baskets and plant tubs. Add careful attention by friendly staff, a fine changing range of wines, well kept Adnams and (from the owner's microbrewery) Ufford White Hart on handpump, three guest beers including ones from Adnams and Ufford, and Weston's organic farm cider, and you get a most enjoyable, relaxed and easy-going atmosphere – particularly liked by the two labradoodles Fraggle and Sprucket. The lavatories are up rather steep stairs.

Besides their much-admired 'compile your own' pizzas (and their signature peking duck pizza) which are prepared in a stone pizza oven, a useful menu includes goats cheese and chorizo salad, roast bass with sesame and soy sauce on crushed mango and potato with pak choi, an indian burger, and penne pomodoro. *Benchmark main dish: home-made pizza £11.00. Two-course evening meal £15.45.*

Free house ~ Licensee William Fry ~ Real ale ~ Bar food (12-2.30, 6-9) ~ (01780) 753800 ~ Children over 10 at lunchtimes, over 21 in evenings ~ Dogs welcome ~ Open 11-11 (midnight Fri, Sat); 12-10.30 Sun

Recommended by Peter and Pam Watkins, Simon and Amanda Southwell, Dr J Barrie Jones, Tony and Maggie Harwood

STATHERN Leicestershire   SK7731 Map 7

Red Lion ♀ ◗

Off A52 W of Grantham via the brown-signed Belvoir road (keep on towards Harby—Stathern signposted on left); or off A606 Nottingham—Melton Mowbray via Long Clawson and Harby; LE14 4HS

Fine range of drinks and popular food in country-style dining pub with open fires and good garden with a play area; own shop, too

This rather civilised dining pub is decorated in a charming rustic style and the atmosphere throughout is relaxed and informal. The yellow room on the right, with its collection of wooden spoons and lambing chairs, has a simple country-pub feel. The lounge bar has sofas, an open fire and a big table with books, newspapers and magazines. It leads off the smaller, more traditional flagstoned bar with terracotta walls, another fireplace with a pile of logs beside it, and lots of beams and hops. A little room with tables set for eating leads to the long, narrow, main dining room, and out to a nicely arranged suntrap with good hardwood furnishings spread over its lawn and terrace; piped music. Red Lion Ale (from Grainstore) and a couple of guests such as Brewsters Decadence and Fullers London Pride are on handpump, with draught belgian and continental bottled beers, several ciders and a varied wine list (several by the glass). There's an unusually big play area behind the car park with swings, climbing frames and so on. This is under the same ownership as the Olive Branch in Clipsham. More reports please.

As well as a popular two- and three-course set lunch, the often imaginative food includes sandwiches, potted prawns, whitebait with lemon mayonnaise, ham hock terrine with piccalilli, fish or steak and ale pie, sausage and mustard mash, roast chicken with tarragon mash and smoked bacon and mushroom sauce, vegetable curry, and roast brisket with rösti potatoes and creamy cabbage. *Benchmark main dish: fish and chips £9.95. Two-course evening meal £19.10.*

Free house ~ Licensees Sean Hope and Ben Jones ~ Real ale ~ Bar food (12-2(3 Sun), 7-9) ~ Restaurant ~ (01949) 860868 ~ Children welcome ~ Dogs allowed in bar ~ Open 12-3, 6-11; 12-11 Sat; 12-6 Sun; closed Sun evening

Recommended by Jeff and Wendy Williams, Leslie and Barbara Owen, David Glynne-Jones, P Dawn, Gwyn and Anne Wake, Derek and Sylvia Stephenson, Bruce and Sharon Eden

STRETTON Rutland   SK9415 Map 8

Jackson Stops

Rookery Lane; a mile or less off A1, at B668 (Oakham) exit; follow village sign, turning off Clipsham Road into Manor Road, pub on left; LE15 7RA

Attractive former farmhouse with good food, just off A1

This is a beautiful old stone building with plenty of lovely period features in its meandering interior. The black-beamed country bar down on the left has some wall timbering, a couple of bar stools, a cushioned wall pew and an elderly settle on the worn tile and brick floor, and a coal fire in one corner. A beer from local Grainstore and a changing guest are on handpump alongside several wines by the glass. The smarter main room on the right is light and airy with a nice mix of ancient and modern tables on dark blue carpeting, and another coal fire in a stone corner fireplace. Right, along past the bar, is the dining room with stripped-stone walls, a tiled floor and an old open cooking range, and there's a second smaller dining room, too; piped music.

Bar food includes sandwiches, timbale of prawn, smoked salmon and crayfish, duck breast, wild boar sausage and ham hock terrine with redcurrant and apple chutney, steak and mushroom pie, rump of lamb with mint jus and red onion, and butternut, spinach and goats cheese tart; good value two-course menus. The new licensees hadn't long settled in when we went to press so we look forward to hearing from you about your meal here. *Benchmark main dish: salmon fillet on spring vegetable risotto £11.95. Two-course evening meal £17.90.*

Free house ~ Licensee Robert Reid ~ Real ale ~ Bar food (12-2.30, 6.30-9) ~ Restaurant ~ (01780) 410237 ~ Children welcome ~ Dogs allowed in bar ~ Open 11-3, 6-midnight; closed Sun evening and Mon except bank holidays

Recommended by Roxanne Chamberlain, Derek and Sylvia Stephenson, John and Eleanor Holdsworth, John Wooll, Leslie and Barbara Owen, Alison Ball, Ian Walton, Ken and Lynda Taylor, John Prescott, Maurice and Janet Thorpe, Tony and Glenys Dyer, John Cooper, Barry Collett, Arthur Pickering, Ian Prince

We include some hotels with a good bar that offers facilities comparable to those of a pub.

SWITHLAND Leicestershire   SK5512   Map 7

Griffin

Main Street; between A6 and B5330, between Loughborough and Leicester; LE12 8TJ

A good mix of cheerful customers, well liked food in a bustling pub

This comfortable three-room local is in a tucked-away village in the heart of Charnwood Forest and is handy for Bradgate Country Park and walks in Swithland Woods. Its tidy streamside garden has seats overlooking open fields. Inside, the beamed communicating rooms have some panelling and a nice mix of wooden tables, chairs and bar stools. Everards Original and Adnams are on handpump alongside a guest such as Greene King Abbot, several malt whiskies and wines by the glass from a good list; piped music and skittle alley.

Well liked bar food includes ploughman's, burger, lamb tagine, baked stuffed peppers with cheddar cheese, mushroom and parmesan risotto, fried lambs liver with red wine and onion gravy, battered haddock, and fried bass with sauce vierge. *Benchmark main dish: sausage and mash £9.50. Two-course evening meal £16.85.*

Everards ~ Tenant John Cooledge ~ Real ale ~ Bar food (12-2, 6-9) ~ Restaurant ~ (01509) 890535 ~ Children welcome, not in bar area evenings ~ Open 10am(9am Sat, Sun)-11pm(10.30pm Sun)

Recommended by Duncan Cloud, Kevin and Maggie Balchin, Rob and Catherine Dunster, Gwyn and Anne Wake

WADENHOE Northamptonshire   TL0183   Map 5

Kings Head

Church Street; village signposted (in small print) off A605 S of Oundle; PE8 5ST

Country pub in idyllic riverside spot; decent range of beers, pubby food

One of the main attractions at this cheery stone-built 16th-c inn is the idyllically sited garden. In summer you can relax at picnic-sets among willows and aspens on grass leading right down to the River Nene – you can even arrive by boat and moor here. Inside, there's an uncluttered simplicity (maybe too much so for some) to the very welcoming partly stripped-stone main bar, which has pleasant old worn quarry tiles, solid pale pine furniture with a couple of cushioned wall seats, and a leather-upholstered chair by the woodburning stove in the fine inglenook. The bare-boards public bar has similar furnishings and another fire; steps lead up to a games room with darts, dominoes and table skittles, and there's more of the pale pine furniture in an attractive little beamed dining room. They keep three beers from local Digfield and usually have around three changing guests from brewers such as Daleside, Marstons and Phipps, and about a dozen wines by the glass.

Pubby food includes sandwiches, ploughman's, burger, chicken liver pâté, potted crab, tomato, basil and goats cheese quiche, lamb breast with redcurrant reduction, and seared tuna on a niçoise-style salad. *Benchmark main dish: battered haddock £10.95. Two-course evening meal £15.20.*

Free house ~ Licensee Aletha Ainsworth ~ Real ale ~ Bar food (12-3, 6-9; 12-9 Sat) ~ Restaurant ~ (01832) 720024 ~ Children welcome ~ Dogs welcome ~ Open 11-11; 12-11 Sat, Sun; closed Sun evening in winter

WING Rutland   SK8902   Map 4

Kings Arms 🍽 ♀ 🛏

Village signposted off A6003 S of Oakham; Top Street; LE15 8SE

Nicely kept old pub, big log fires, super choice of wines by the glass and good modern cooking

Most customers at this civilised 17th-c inn are here to enjoy the good modern food, though they do keep an interesting range of drinks. You need to book and readers tell us that service can slow down at peak times. The neatly kept and attractive bar has various nooks and crannies, nice old low beams and stripped stone, two large log fires (one in a copper-canopied central hearth) and flagstoned or wood-strip floors. Friendly, helpful staff serve over 20 wines by the glass, as well as Grainstore Cooking and Rutland Beast, Marstons Pedigree and possibly a guest on handpump, several grappas and malt whiskies and a local cider; board games. There are seats out in front, and more in the sunny yew-sheltered garden; the car park has plenty of space. There's a medieval turf maze just up the road, and we are told that the pub is just a couple of miles away from one of England's two osprey hot-spots.

As well as their own smokehouse producing everything from charcuterie to smoked nuts, they cook with some unusual ingredients such as squirrel and bake their own bread and biscuits. The changing menu might include filled cobs, smoked eel with tomato and calvados scrambled egg, oysters, veal chop with mushrooms and marsala reduction, herb-baked cod with lemon hollandaise, and butternut, leek and thyme risotto with goats cheese and sunflower seeds. *Benchmark main dish: various pies £12.00. Two-course evening meal £23.25.*

Free house ~ Licensee David Goss ~ Real ale ~ Bar food (12-2(2.30 Sat, Sun), 6.30-8.30 (9 Fri, Sat)) ~ Restaurant ~ (01572) 737634 ~ Well behaved children welcome but must be over 8 in evening ~ Dogs allowed in bar ~ Open 12-3, 6.30-11; closed Sun evening, Mon lunchtime (except bank holidays), all day Mon and Tues lunchtime in winter ~ Bedrooms: £77.50S/£100S

WOODHOUSE EAVES Leicestershire   SK5313   Map 7

Wheatsheaf 🛏

Brand Hill; turn right into Main Street, off B591 S of Loughborough; LE12 8SS

Bustling and friendly country pub, interesting things to look at, good bistro-type food and a fair choice of drinks; well equipped bedrooms

Nicely maintaining a genuinely pubby atmosphere, there's an easy balance between the good food, beers and accommodation at this rather smart country inn. The beamed bar areas are traditionally furnished (with wooden pews, log fires, daily papers and the like) and are full of interesting motor-racing and family RAF and flying memorabilia. A cosy dining area called The Mess even has an RAF Hurricane propeller. The atmosphere is cheerful and chatty and the service helpful and welcoming, even when pushed. Adnams Broadside, Greene King IPA, Marstons Pedigree and Timothy Taylors Landlord are on handpump, with about 17 wines, including champagne, by the glass, from a thoughtfully compiled list. The floodlit, heated terrace has plenty of seating.

 Interesting bar food includes sandwiches, dressed crab salad, ploughman's, chicken caesar salad, spaghetti and meatballs, vegetarian moussaka, salmon and prawn fishcake, fish and chips, roast cod fillet on chorizo and sun-dried tomato risotto, venison casserole, ham, egg and chips, and sirloin steak. *Benchmark main dish: pie of the day £11.95. Two-course evening meal £17.00.*

Free house ~ Licensees Richard and Bridget Dimblebee ~ Real ale ~ Bar food (12-2(2.30 Sat, 4 Sun), 6.30-9.15) ~ Restaurant ~ (01509) 890320 ~ Children welcome ~ Dogs allowed in bar and bedrooms ~ Open 11.30-3, 6-11; 12-11 Sat; 12-5 Sun; 12-3, 6-11 Sat in winter; closed Sun evening ~ Bedrooms: £60S/£80B

Recommended by DF, NF, the Didler, Chris and Jeanne Downing, Jim Farmer, Michael and Maggie Betton, Rob and Catherine Dunster, Tim and Joan Wright, Sandy Butcher, Andy and Jill Kassube, Ken Marshall, Dennis and Doreen Haward

WOOLLEY MOOR Derbyshire SK3661 Map 7

White Horse

Badger Lane, off B6014 Matlock—Clay Cross; DE55 6FG

Attractive old dining pub in pretty countryside

The interior of this smart old inn is uncluttered, with neatly arranged furniture (including a leather sofa on new stone floors or wooden boards), boldy patterned curtains and blinds, little to distract on the cream walls and uniform lamps on window sills. There's a buoyantly chatty feel to the tap room, with three local beers from Bradfield and Peak Ales on handpump and a dozen wines by the glass from the newly built brick counter; conservatory; piped music. The garden has a boules pitch, picnic-sets and a children's play area with a wooden train, boat, climbing frame and swings. This is in a charming rural spot with Ogston Reservoir just a couple of minutes' drive from here.

Good bar food includes sandwiches, ploughman's, smoked mackerel pâté, warm chicken and bacon salad, battered cod, scampi in lemonade batter, stilton glazed pork fillet with spring onion mash and red wine sauce, roast monkfish tail with chive sauce, and venison steak with rosemary jus. *Benchmark main dish: chicken breast with smoked bacon mash and white wine and leek sauce £12.95. Two-course evening meal £19.25.*

Free house ~ Licensees David and Melanie Boulby ~ Real ale ~ Bar food (12-1.45(2.30 Sun), 6-8.45) ~ Restaurant ~ (01246) 590319 ~ Children welcome ~ Open 12-2.30, 5.30-11; 12-3 Sun; closed Sun evening, first three weeks of Jan

Recommended by Steve Wigham, Andrew and Mary Ransom, Peter F Marshall

'Children welcome' means the pub says it lets children inside without any special restriction. If it allows them in, but to restricted areas such as an eating area or family room, we specify this. Places with separate restaurants often let children use them, and hotels usually let them into public areas such as lounges. Some pubs impose an evening time limit – let us know if you find one earlier than 9pm.

WOOLSTHORPE Lincolnshire SK8334 Map 8

Chequers 🍴 🍷

The one near Belvoir, signposted off A52 or A607 W of Grantham; NG32 1LU

LINCOLNSHIRE DINING PUB OF THE YEAR

Interesting food at comfortably relaxed inn with good drinks and appealing castle views from outside tables

Emphasis at this 17th-c coaching inn tends to be on the food, so it is worth booking. It's run with great care by friendly licensees and service is cheery and welcoming. The heavy-beamed main bar has two big tables (one a massive oak construction), a comfortable mix of seating including some handsome leather chairs and leather banquettes, and a huge boar's head above a good log fire in the big brick fireplace. Among cartoons on the wall are some of the illustrated claret bottle labels from the series commissioned from famous artists, initiated by the late Baron Philippe de Rothschild. The lounge on the right has a deep red colour scheme, leather sofas and a big plasma TV, and on the left, there are more leather seats in a dining area in what was once the village bakery. A corridor leads off to the light and airy main restaurant, with contemporary pictures and another bar; piped music and board games. Greene King IPA and Old Speckled Hen and a guest such as Everards Tiger are on handpump, with around 35 wines by the glass, 50 malt whiskies and local fruit pressé. There are good quality teak tables, chairs and benches outside and, beyond these, some picnic-sets on the edge of the pub's cricket field, with views of Belvoir Castle. If you stay here, please do let us know how you find the recently refurbished bedrooms.

Good, often interesting bar food might include sandwiches, potted duck and orange rillettes, seared scallops and pancetta salad with sweetcorn cream, tempura prawns with sweet chilli sauce, bream fillet with garlic and basil cream, leek and stilton tart, sausage and mash, battered haddock, and rib of beef for two with garlic, mushroom and peppercorn sauce. *Benchmark main dish: rib-eye steak with peppercorn sauce £18.50. Two-course evening meal £22.00.*

Free house ~ Licensee Justin Chad ~ Real ale ~ Bar food (12-2.30(4 Sun), 6-9.30(8.30 Sun)) ~ Restaurant ~ (01476) 870701 ~ Children welcome ~ Dogs allowed in bar and bedrooms ~ Open 12-3, 5.30-11; 12-midnight Sat; 12-10.30 Sun ~ Bedrooms: £50B/£70S

Recommended by Ellie Weld, David London, Peter and Josie Fawcett, D Goodger, Bob and Angela Brooks, Richard and Jean Green, Alan and Jill Bull, Simon Hatton

WYMONDHAM Leicestershire SK8518 Map 7

Berkeley Arms

Main Street; LE14 2AG

Pleasant village pub with interesting food and sunny terrace

Homely touches from magazines to table lamps, knick-knacks dotted around and cushions in window seats at this attractive golden stone 16th-c inn lend a welcoming relaxed feel. At one end two wing chairs on the patterned carpet are set beside a low coffee table and a log fire. The red tiled dining area has light wood tables and red-cushioned chunky chairs under stripped beams and standing timbers. A smarter dining area has dark leather chairs. Real ales include Greene King IPA, Marstons Pedigree and a guest such as Ruddles County, and they keep a local cider. Outside in front, on small terraces either side of the entrance, picnic-sets benefit from the sun nearly all day and there are more tables in a garden at the back.

🍴 Bar food, in quite busy presentations, might include celery and almond soup, battered prawns with sweet chilli dipping sauce, crayfish and avocado cocktail, battered whiting with mushy peas, steak and ale pie, pork belly with apple cider sauce, duck breast with orange and ginger sauce, bass with fennel salad, roast chorizo and cherry tomatoes, and fillet steak with stilton butter. *Benchmark main dish: fish and chips £10.50. Two-course evening meal £18.95.*

Free house ~ Licensee Louise Hitchen ~ Real ale ~ Bar food (12-2(3 Sun), 6.30-9.30) ~ Restaurant ~ (01572) 787587 ~ Children welcome if eating ~ Dogs allowed in bar ~ Open 12-3(5 Sun), 6-11; closed Sun evening, Mon lunchtime, 2-17 Jan
Recommended by Andy Miksza

ALSO WORTH A VISIT IN DERBYSHIRE

Besides the region's top pubs, we recommend the following. Do tell us what you think of them: **feedback@goodguides.com**

ASHBOURNE SK1846   DE6 1GH
Green Man Royal Hotel
St John Street

17th-c coaching inn with gallows sign spanning road, tap for Leatherbritches (brewery at back) with their full range kept well and five guests (Aug bank holiday beer festival), summer farm ciders, reasonably priced straightforward food, cosy traditional oak-panelled bar with leather sofas and open fires, modern bar with sports TVs, pool and music, lively cheerful atmosphere; children and dogs welcome, 18 refurbished bedrooms, open all day, till late Fri and Sat. *Recommended by Pam and John Smith, the Didler, John Wooll*

ASHFORD IN THE WATER sk1969   DE45 1QB
☆ Ashford Arms
Church Street

Attractive 18th-c inn, good choice of enjoyable reasonably priced food (not Sun evening) including good Weds steak night, well kept ales such as Peak, friendly staff, restaurant and dining conservatory; children welcome, plenty of tables outside, eight bedrooms, pretty village. *Recommended by Revd John E Cooper*

ASHOVER SK3462   S45 0EW
☆ Old Poets Corner
Butts Road (B6036, off A632 Matlock—Chesterfield)

Enthusiastic owners and plenty of local customers (and dogs) in simple laid-back village pub, ten real ales (some from own Ashover microbrewery), six farm ciders plus perries, fruit wines, belgian beers, reasonably priced honest food, lived-in bar with lots of knick-knacks, hops over counter, old photographs, board games and open fire, small room with second fire, newspapers, vintage comics and french door to tiny balcony, simple dining room; piped and live music including open mike nights Sun and Tues, quiz night Weds; children allowed away from bar till 9pm, bedrooms and holiday cottage, open all day.
Recommended by John and Enid Morris, Andrew and Mary Ransom, John and Susan Miln, John and Sarah Perry, the Didler, Derek and Sylvia Stephenson and others

---

Post Office address codings confusingly give the impression that some pubs are in Derbyshire, when they're really in Cheshire (which is where we list them).

BAKEWELL SK2168   DE45 1DU
Castle Inn
Bridge Street

Bay-windowed Georgian-fronted 17th-c pub, well kept Greene King ales and good value food, daily papers, three candlelit rooms with two open fires, flagstones, stripped stone and lots of pictures; dogs welcome, tables outside, four bedrooms. *Recommended by David Carr, Derek and Sylvia Stephenson*

BARLOW SK3474   S18 7TD
Old Pump
B6051 (Hackney Lane)

Villagey dining pub with long narrow beamed bar and tiny alcove, book-ended by dining room and two comfortably traditional little rooms, two changing ales, enjoyable food including good value Sun lunch, competent young staff; children welcome, some tables out at front and in sheltered side garden, bedrooms, open all day Sun. *Recommended by Jeremy and Ruth Preston-Hoar, C and R Bromage*

BELPER SK3547   DE56 1FZ
Cross Keys
Market Place

Friendly pub with well kept Bass, Batemans (including a house beer) and one or two guests, straightforward food, coal fire and bar billiards in lounge, pool and TV in bar, regular beer festivals; open all day. *Recommended by the Didler*

BELPER SK3549   DE56 2JF
Fishermans Rest
Broadholme Lane

Four-square gritstone Marstons pub with their well kept ales, enjoyable reasonably priced hearty food including warming casseroles and hotpots, friendly attentive service, L-shaped lounge bar, restaurant, pleasant relaxed atmosphere (can be quiet weekday lunchtimes); children and dogs welcome, garden with play area, nice surroundings. *Recommended by Jack Melkins, Michael Mellers, Richard and Jean Green*

BIRCHOVER SK2362   DE4 2BL
Druid
Off B5056; Main Street

Two-storey dining pub with four spacious areas, good varied food including some unusual choices, friendly willing service, three well kept local beers; children welcome, picnic-sets out in front, good area for walks, open all day Sat, closed Sun evening. *Recommended by Stephen Fountain, Tich Critchlow, Steve and Sue Griffiths, Trevor and Sylvia Millum, Derek and Sylvia Stephenson*

BIRCHOVER SK2362   DE4 2BN
Red Lion
Main Street

Friendly early 18th-c stone-built pub with two refurbished rooms, popular good value home-made food with italian influences (landlord is from Sardinia), well kept ales – up to five in summer, glass covered well inside, woodburners; nice rural views from outside seats, popular with walkers, open all day weekends, closed Mon. *Recommended by S P Watkin, P A Taylor, the Didler*

☆ BONSALL SK2758   DE4 2AY
Barley Mow
Off A5012 W of Cromford; The Dale

Basic one-room stone-built local, friendly colourful atmosphere, beams, character furnishings and coal fire, pictures and bric-a-brac, well kept Greene King, Whim and guests, decent straightforward food, live music Fri and Sat including UFO-enthusiast landlord playing his accordion; short walk out to lavatories; dogs welcome, nice little front terrace, events such as hen racing and marrow dressing, walks organised from the pub, open all day weekends, closed Mon. *Recommended by Adrian Johnson, the Didler, Tony Harrison, Rob Garrett, Reg Fowle, Helen Rickwood*

BRACKENFIELD SK3658   DE55 6DD
Plough
A615 Matlock—Alfreton, about a mile NW of Wessington

Much modernised oak-beamed stone-built 16th-c former farmhouse in lovely setting, tidy and welcoming three-level bar, cheerful log-effect gas fire, well kept ales including interesting local brews, plenty of wines by the glass, good value fresh food (not Sun evening) plus two-course lunchtime deal (Mon-Sat), appealing stone-built lower-level restaurant extension; large neatly kept gardens with terrace, open all day. *Recommended by Steve Godfrey*

BRADWELL SK1781   S33 9JQ
Bowling Green
Smalldale, off B6049 at Gore Lane/Townend

Lovely views from terrace of attractive 16th-c stone-built local, modernised bar, dining room and garden room extension, good choice of simple food (not Sun evening) including winter Sun carvery, four well kept ales, open fires, friendly welcoming atmosphere; six bedrooms in separate building. *Recommended by Ann and Tony Bennett-Hughes*

BRASSINGTON SK2354   DE4 4HJ
☆ Olde Gate
Village signed off B5056 and B5035 NE of Ashbourne

Unspoilt listed building close to Carsington Water, attractive period features from mullioned windows to Georgian panelling, fine furnishings including ancient oak settle, gleaming copper pots on 17th-c kitchen range, pewter mugs hanging from beam, side shelf with embossed Doulton stoneware flagons, log fires, small hatch-served lobby with another cosy beamed room on left, Brakspears, Marstons and a guest, several malt whiskies, fair-priced bar food with more evening choice (no food Sun evening), pub games; children and dogs welcome, benches in small front yard, more seats in nice garden looking over pastures, closed Mon, Tues lunchtime. *Recommended by Susan Lang, John and Enid Morris, the Didler, Peter F Marshall and others*

BUXTON SK1266   SK17 9QQ
☆ Bull i' th' Thorn
Ashbourne Road (A515), 6 miles S of Buxton, near Flagg and Hurdlow

Fascinating medieval hall doubling as straightforward roadside dining pub, handsome panelling, old flagstones and big log fire, armour, longcase clocks and all sorts of antique features, decent choice of enjoyable good value food all day including vegetarian options, Sun carvery, well kept Robinsons ales, jovial landlord, plain games room and family room; dogs welcome, terrace and big lawn, rare breeds farm behind, good walks, bedrooms, big breakfast, camping, open all day from 9.30am, may be closed Mon. *Recommended by the Didler, Barry Collett, Gene and Kitty Rankin*

BUXTON SK0573   SK17 6BD
Old Hall
The Square, almost opposite Opera House

Large usefully placed hotel with two bars, a wine bar doing good value enjoyable food (all day weekends), various lounges and a more formal restaurant, well kept Buxton, Timothy Taylors and Whim, good choice of wines by the glass; 38 bedrooms, open all day. *Recommended by Derek and Sylvia Stephenson*

When you report on a pub, please tell us any lunchtimes or evenings when it doesn't serve bar food.

☆ **Old Sun**
BUXTON SK0573 SK17 6HA
High Street

Charming old building with several cosy and interesting traditional linked areas, well kept Marstons-related ales, good choice of wines by the glass, bargain home-made food from good sandwiches up, low beams, bare boards or tiles, soft lighting, old local photographs, open fire; piped music and some live acoustic evenings, Sun quiz, no dogs; children till 7pm, roadside garden, open all day. *Recommended by the Didler, Barry Collett, Ann and Tony Bennett-Hughes*

Navigation
BUXWORTH SK0282 SK23 7NE
S of village towards Silkhill, off B6062

Popular inn by restored canal basin, five well kept ales including Timothy Taylors Landlord, pubby food from sandwiches up, cheery young staff, linked low-ceilinged rooms, canalia, brassware and old photographs, open fires, games room with pool and darts, Thurs quiz night; piped music; children allowed away from main bar, dogs in some areas, disabled access, tables on sunken flagstoned terrace, play area, bedrooms, breakfast 8-11am (non residents welcome), open all day. *Recommended by Dennis Jones, Ben Williams*

Derwentwater Arms
CALVER SK2374 S32 3XQ
In centre, bear left from Main Street into Folds Head; Low Side

Largely bright and modern inside, big windows looking down from village-centre knoll, friendly hard-working licensees, good value food from varied menu (best to book), well kept Theakstons and guests; children and dogs welcome, terraces on slopes below (disabled access), boules, open all day Sun. *Recommended by Susan Lee, G Wordsworth, Robert Dudgeon*

☆ **Bulls Head**
CASTLETON SK1582 S33 8WH
Cross Street (A6187)

Imposing building spreading through several attractive linked areas, handsome panelling and pictures, appealing mix of comfortable seating including sofas and easy chairs, heavy drapes, good reasonably priced food from ciabattas up, helpful friendly service, well kept Robinsons Dragons Fire and Unicorn, coal fires; fairly unobtrusive piped music, may be live jazz; some roadside picnic-sets, five bedrooms. *Recommended by anon*

☆ **Castle Hotel**
CASTLETON SK1482 S33 8WG
High Street/Castle Street

Roomy and welcoming Vintage Inn with extensive choice of good well priced food all day from sizeable sandwiches up, good selection of real ales and of wines by the glass, decent coffee, friendly efficient staff even at busy times, log fires, stripped-stone walls, beams and some ancient flagstones; piped music; children welcome, heated terrace, comfortable bedrooms and good breakfast, open all day. *Recommended by Bruce and Sharon Eden, Gene and Kitty Rankin, M G Hart, B M Eldridge*

☆ **George**
CASTLETON SK1482 S33 8WG
Castle Street

Busy but relaxed old pub with flagstoned bar and restaurant, well kept ales such as Courage and Wells & Youngs, good choice of malts, enjoyable home-made food at reasonable prices, friendly staff, ancient beams and stripped stone, copper and brass, log fires; children and dogs welcome, tables out at front and back, castle views, good walks, bedrooms, open all day. *Recommended by Mike and Lynn Robinson, Ann and Colin Hunt, Roger and Pauline Pearce*

CASTLETON SK1583   S33 8WJ
Olde Cheshire Cheese
How Lane

17th-c inn with two linked beamed and carpeted areas, cosy and spotless, with well kept
ales such as Acorn, Bradfield and Peak, good range of enjoyable reasonably priced food
all day, good house wine, quick friendly service, two gas woodburners, lots of
photographs, toby jugs and brassware, back dining room; piped music, TV, and they may
swipe your credit card before running a tab; children welcome in restaurant, dogs in bar,
ten bedrooms, open all day. *Recommended by Keith Rochell, Mike and Lynn Robinson, David and
Gill Carrington, Gene and Kitty Rankin*

CASTLETON SK1582   S33 8WH
 ## Olde Nags Head
Cross Street (A6187)

Small solidly built and recently refurbished hotel dating from the 17th c, interesting
antique oak furniture and coal fire in civilised beamed and flagstone bar with nice
pictures, beers such as Black Sheep and Timothy Taylors, good coffee, helpful staff, good
locally sourced food (including meat from rare breeds) in bars and bistro, well priced
Sun carvery (second helpings encouraged); attractive village, comfortable bedrooms,
good breakfast choice, open all day till late. *Recommended by Mike and Lynn Robinson,
Mike Proctor*

CHESTERFIELD SK3871   S41 7PH
Chesterfield Arms
Newbold Road (B6051)

Carefully restored and doing well under beer-enthusiast landlord, ten changing ales
including Everards and Leatherbritches, six ciders and good choice of wines, enjoyable
straightforward home-made food (Thurs curry night), open fire, oak panelling and
stripped wood/flagstoned floors, weekend back barn room, beer festivals, some live music;
outside tables on decking, open all day. *Recommended by the Didler*

CHESTERFIELD SK3670   S40 2QT
Rose & Crown
Old Road (A619)

Owned by Brampton Brewery with their full range plus Everards and two changing
guests, Weston's cider, enjoyable home-made food, spacious traditional refurbishment
with leather banquettes, panelling, carpet or wood floors, cast-iron Victorian fireplace,
cosy snug area, Tues quiz; tables outside; open all day. *Recommended by the Didler*

CHESTERFIELD SK3871   S40 1XL
Rutland
Stephenson Place

Uncomplicated pub next to crooked-spire church, welcoming and thriving, with well kept
Badger Best, Timothy Taylors Landlord, local Brampton and five interesting changing
guests, Weston's cider, low-priced pub food all day from sandwiches up, friendly polite
service even when very busy, rugs and assorted wooden furniture on bare boards, old
photographs, darts; piped music; children welcome, open all day. *Recommended by the Didler,
Alan Johnson, Roxanne Chamberlain*

CODNOR SK4249   DE5 9QY
Poet & Castle
Alfreton Road

Friendly pub with well kept Ashover ales and interesting guests, farm cider and fruit
wines, simple wholesome food (not Mon) including popular Sun lunch, good service,
comfortable low-ceilinged bar/lounge, upstairs restaurant, music nights; open all day.
Recommended by the Didler, Derek and Sylvia Stephenson

COMBS SK0378   SK23 9UT
☆ **Beehive**
Village signposted off B5470 W of Chapel-en-le-Frith

Roomy, neat and comfortable, with emphasis on good freshly made food (all day Sun)
from baguettes to steaks and interesting specials, also very good value weekday set menu,
well kept ales such as Copper Dragon Golden Pippin and Courage Directors, good choice
of wines by the glass, friendly service, log fire, heavy beams and copperware; piped music,
TV, Tues quiz; plenty of tables out in front, by lovely valley tucked away from main road,
good walks, one bed holiday cottage next door, open all day. *Recommended by Rita and
Keith Pollard, Brian and Anna Marsden*

CRICH SK3454   DE4 5DP
Cliff
Cromford Road, Town End

Traditional little two-room local with well kept Black Sheep, Greene King IPA and usually
three guests, reliable straightforward food, welcoming landlady and friendly regulars,
open fire; children welcome, great views and walks, handy for National Tramway Museum.
Recommended by the Didler

DENBY SK4047   DE5 8PW
☆ **Bulls Head**
Denby Common, between A609 and A6007 S of Ripley

Clean-cut modern dining pub serving baguettes and grill-style food all day, Bass and
Greene King, pleasant uniformed staff, real mix of traditional and contemporary
furnishings, stoves in two-way fireplace, smaller bar with flagstones and woodburner, live
jazz Mon evening; piped music, games machine; children and dogs welcome, disabled
facilities, picnic-sets under big front canopy and in garden behind, handy for Denby
Pottery visitor centre, open all day. *Recommended by Phil and Jane Hodson*

DERBY SK3538   DE22 1DX
☆ **Abbey Inn**
Darley Street, Darley Abbey

A treasure, former abbey gatehouse opposite Derwent-side park (pleasant riverside walk
from centre), massive 15th-c or older stonework remnants, brick floor, studded oak doors,
coal fire in big stone inglenook, stone spiral stair to upper bar (open Sun afternoon) with
oak rafters and tapestries, bargain Sam Smiths and lunchtime bar food, pleasant service;
the lavatories with their beams, stonework and tiles are worth a look, too; piped music;
children welcome, open all day weekends. *Recommended by the Didler*

DERBY SK3635   DE1 2QE
Alexandra
Siddals Road

Imposing Victorian pub freshened up by new enthusiastic couple, two simple rooms, good
heavy traditional furnishings on bare boards or carpet, breweriana and railway
prints/memorabilia, Castle Rock ales and quickly changing guests, lots of continental
bottled beers and more on tap, snack food such as pork pies and rolls; piped music;
children and dogs welcome, nicely planted backyard, four updated bedrooms, open all
day. *Recommended by the Didler*

DERBY SK3535   DE1 1TA
Babington Arms
Babington Lane

Large well run open-plan Wetherspoons with up to 18 real ales, regulars including Derby,
Falstaff, Greene King Abbot and Marstons Pedigree, good welcoming service, well priced
food, comfortable seating with steps up to relaxed back area; attractive verandah, open
all day from 7am for breakfast. *Recommended by the Didler, Brian and Jean Hepworth*

DERBY SK3635   DE1 2RU

☆ **Brunswick**

Railway Terrace; close to Derby Midland Station

One of Britain's oldest railwaymen's pubs with fantastic range of 16 ales tapped from casks or on handpump (seven from own microbrewery), cheap traditional lunchtime food (not Sun), welcoming high-ceilinged panelled bar with whisky-water jugs, another room with little old-fashioned prints and high-backed wall settle by coal fire, chatty family parlour, wall displays showing history and restoration of building, interesting old train photographs, darts, jazz Thurs evening upstairs; TV, games machines, no credit cards; dogs welcome, two outdoor seating areas, open all day. *Recommended by the Didler, Brian and Jean Hepworth, Andy Lickfold*

DERBY SK3534   DE23 6UJ

Falstaff

Silver Hill Road, off Normanton Road

Basic unsmart local, aka the Folly, brewing its own good value ales, guest beers too, left-hand bar with games, coal fire in quieter lounge, some brewery memorabilia; open all day. *Recommended by the Didler*

DERBY SK3436   DE22 3AD

Mr Grundys Tavern

Georgian House; Ashbourne Road

Hotel bar serving own Mr Grundys ales (brewed here) and plenty of guests, two inviting dimly lit rooms, coal fires, panelling, old bench seating, superb collection of hats, a wall of classic film star pictures, lots of breweriana and an old red telephone box, decent food (not Sun evening); garden picnic-sets, 18 bedrooms, open all day. *Recommended by the Didler*

DERBY SK3536   DE1 3AF

Old Silk Mill

Full Street

Refurbished keeping traditional feel, cosy inside with two open fires, eight changing ales from main bar including a house beer from Blue Monkey, second hop-adorned bar (open Thurs-Fri evenings, Sat, Sun lunchtime) with usually four cask-tapped beers, friendly service, live music; open all day. *Recommended by the Didler*

DERBY SK3536   DE1 3DL

Olde Dolphin

Queen Street

Quaint 16th-c timber-framed pub just below cathedral, four small dark unpretentious rooms including appealing snug, big bowed black beams, shiny panelling, opaque leaded windows, lantern lights and coal fires, half a dozen predominantly mainstream ales (good July beer festival), cheap simple food all day, upstairs steak bar (not always open); no under-14s inside; sizeable outside area for drinkers/smokers, open all day. *Recommended by Jeremy King, the Didler*

DERBY SK3335   DE22 3LL

Rowditch

Uttoxeter New Road (A516)

Popular character local with own microbrewery, well kept Marstons Pedigree and guests too, country wines, friendly landlord, attractive small snug on right, coal fire, pianist third Sat of month; no children or dogs; pleasant back garden, closed weekday lunchtimes. *Recommended by the Didler, Malc Newton*

DERBY SK3536   DE1 2BH

☆ **Smithfield**

Meadow Road

Friendly bow-fronted local, well kept Bass, Durham, Oakham, Phoenix, Whim and guests, hearty bar lunches, back lounge with traditional settles, old prints, curios and breweriana, coal fires, daily papers; piped music, good games room (children welcome here), quiz and band nights; riverside terrace with weekend barbecues, open all day. *Recommended by the Didler*

DERBY SK3436   DE1 3GL
☆ Standing Order
Irongate

Spacious Wetherspoons in grand and lofty-domed former bank, main part with large island bar, booths down each side, handsome plasterwork, pseudo-classical torsos, high portraits of mainly local notables; good range of ales including some unusual ones, standard popular food all day, reasonable prices, daily papers, quick service even when very busy; good disabled facilities. *Recommended by Jeremy King, the Didler, Brian and Jean Hepworth, Dave Braisted*

DRONFIELD SK3479   S18 2GD
Coach & Horses
Sheffield Road (B6057)

Well managed comfortable tap for Thornbridges interesting beers, friendly knowledgeable staff, good home-made food (not Sun evening, Mon), decent wines by the glass; next to Sheffield FC ground, open all day Fri-Sun, closed Mon lunchtime. *Recommended by the Didler*

EARL STERNDALE SK0966   SK17 0BU
☆ Quiet Woman
Village signed off B5053 S of Buxton

Old-fashioned unchanging country local in lovely Peak District countryside, simple beamed interior with plain furniture on quarry tiles, china ornaments and coal fire, well kept Marstons Pedigree and guests, own-label bottled beers (available in gift packs), good pork pies, family room with pool, skittles and darts; picnic-sets out in front along with budgies, hens, turkeys, ducks and donkeys, you can buy free-range eggs, local poetry books and even hay; good hikes across nearby Dove Valley towards Longnor and Hollinsclough, small campsite next door, caravan for hire. *Recommended by Malc Newton, the Didler, Barry Collett, Ann and Tony Bennett-Hughes*

EDALE SK1285   S33 7ZD
Old Nags Head
Off A625 E of Chapel-en-le-Frith; Grindsbrook Booth

Relaxed well used traditional pub at start of Pennine Way, good friendly staff coping well, generous pubby food, good local ales, log fire, flagstoned area for booted walkers, airy back family room with board games; TV, can get very busy weekends; front terrace and garden, open all day, closed Mon and Tues lunchtimes out of season. *Recommended by T G Sunderland, Ann and Colin Hunt*

ELMTON SK5073   S80 4LS
Elm Tree
Off B6417 S of Clowne

Softly lit and popular country pub with good value unpretentious bar food all day, children's menu, up to seven well kept ales including Black Sheep and Wells & Youngs, wide choice of wines, quick friendly service, stripped stone and panelling, back barn restaurant (Fri/Sat evenings and for good Sun lunch); children welcome, garden tables, play area. *Recommended by Derek and Sylvia Stephenson*

ELTON SK2260   DE4 2BW
☆ Duke of York
Village signed off B5056 W of Matlock; Main Street

Unspoilt local kept spotless by very long-serving amiable landlady, bargain Adnams and Marstons, lovely little quarry-tiled back tap room with coal fire in massive fireplace, glazed bar and hatch to flagstoned corridor, nice prints and more fires in the two front rooms – one like a private parlour with piano and big table, the other with pool, darts, dominoes, friendly chatty locals; outside lavatories; in charming village, open 8.30pm-11pm plus Sun lunchtime. *Recommended by the Didler, Tich Critchlow*

FOOLOW SK1976   S32 5QR
 ☆ **Bulls Head**
Village signposted off A623 Baslow—Tideswell

Friendly pub by green in pretty upland village, simply furnished flagstoned bar with interesting collection of photographs including risqué Edwardian ones, Adnams, Black Sheep, Peak and a guest, over two dozen malts, good food with more elaborate evening choices, step down into former stables with high ceiling joists, stripped stone and woodburner, sedate partly panelled dining room with plates on delft shelves; piped music, live music Fri evening; children and dogs welcome (resident westies are Holly and Jack), side picnic-sets with nice views, paths from here out over rolling pasture enclosed by drystone walls, bedrooms, closed Mon. *Recommended by Greta and Guy Pratt, Derek and Sylvia Stephenson, Michelle and Graeme Voss, Ann and Tony Bennett-Hughes, Gail Elliman, Beth Woodhouse and others*

FROGGATT EDGE SK2476   S32 3ZJ
 ☆ **Chequers**
A625, off A623 N of Bakewell

Smart well run dining pub with good food (all day weekends), solid country furnishings in civilised and cosily attractive dining bar with woodburner, antique prints and longcase clock, good choice of wines by the glass, three well kept changing ales, friendly staff; unobtrusive piped music; children welcome, peaceful back garden with Froggatt Edge just up through the woods behind, comfortable clean bedrooms (quarry lorries use the road from 6am weekdays), very good breakfast, open all day weekends. *Recommended by P A Rowe, Ian Malone, Dennis Jones*

FROGGATT EDGE SK2577   S11 7TZ
Grouse
Longshaw, off B6054 NE of Froggatt

Plush front bar, log fire and wooden benches in back bar, big dining room, enjoyable honest home-made food from nice sandwiches to blackboard specials, well kept Banks's, Caledonian Deuchars IPA, Greene King Abbot and Marstons Pedigree, friendly prompt service, handsome views; dogs welcome, verandah and terrace, good moorland walking country, open all day. *Recommended by Barry and Anne, DC, Robert Dudgeon, Geoff Schrecker*

GLOSSOP SK0294   SK13 8HJ
Globe
High Street W

Own microbrews including a good rich porter, local guest ales, bottled beers and farm cider, bargain food, good vegetarian dishes, friendly licensees, comfortable relaxed atmosphere, old fittings and photographs, Sat live music upstairs (busy then), Mon folk music, occasional beer festivals; walled back garden, closed lunchtime and Tues, open till early hours and all day Sun. *Recommended by the Didler, Frank Blanchard*

GLOSSOP SK0394   SK13 7DD
Star
Howard Street

Unpretentious alehouse opposite station with Black Sheep and six well priced changing ales, farm cider, friendly helpful staff, no food (you can bring your own), interesting layout including flagstoned tap room with hatch service, old local photographs; piped music; bedrooms, open all day from 2pm (4pm Mon and Tues, noon Sun). *Recommended by Dennis Jones, the Didler*

GREAT HUCKLOW SK1777   SK17 8RF
Queen Anne
Main Street

Comfortably refurbished 17th-c stone-built pub, good choice of enjoyable food from baguettes up including two-course lunchtime deals, takeaway pizzas too, well kept ales such as Copper Dragon, Jennings and Tetleys, low beams, big log fire, gleaming brass and copper, walkers' bar, pub games; no dogs; french windows to small back terrace and charming garden with picnic-sets and lovely views, two quiet bedrooms, closed Mon, open all day Fri-Sun. *Recommended by G Wordsworth, Peter F Marshall, the Didler, Ann and Tony Bennett-Hughes*

HARDWICK HALL SK4663   S44 5QJ
Hardwick Inn
Quite handy for M1 junction 29; Doe Lea

Golden stone building dating from the 15th c at the south gate of Hardwick Park, several busy linked rooms including proper bar, open fires, fine range of some 220 malt whiskies and plenty of wines by the glass, well kept Black Sheep, Greene King, Theakstons and Wells & Youngs, popular well priced bar food served all day, carvery restaurant, long-serving landlord and efficient staff; unobtrusive piped music; children allowed, pleasant back garden, more tables out in front. *Recommended by Bob and Angela Brooks, Martin and Anne Muers, the Didler, Terry Davis, Peter Kay*

HARTINGTON SK1260   SK17 0AL
Charles Cotton
Market Place

Popular four-square stone-built hotel in attractive village centre, large comfortable carpeted bar with open fire, simple dining room off, tearoom too, good straightforward generous home-made food all day, five ales including two from Whim, bottled beers and real cider, good wines, cafetière coffee, friendly helpful service; nostalgic piped music; dogs welcome in bar, bedrooms, open all day. *Recommended by Richard and Jean Green, the Didler, David and Sue Atkinson and others*

HARTINGTON SK1260   SK17 0AL
Devonshire Arms
Market Place

Traditional unpretentious two-bar pub in attractive village, welcoming landlord, Marstons Pedigree, Jennings Cumberland and Wells & Youngs Bombardier, generous home-made food (all day weekends), log fires; may be piped music; children and dogs welcome, tables out in front facing duck pond, more in small garden, good walks, open all day weekends. *Recommended by Michael Butler, John Wooll, Steve and Sue Griffiths, Jill and Julian Tasker, Mike Proctor, Alan Johnson*

HASSOP SK2272   DE45 1NS

☆ Eyre Arms
B6001 N of Bakewell

Neatly kept 17th-c ivy-clad pub, low-beamed log-fire rooms, settles and comfortable plush chairs, lots of copper and brass, grandfather clock, good choice of enjoyable food including children's menu, Black Sheep, Marstons and Peak ales, several wines by the glass, public bar with teapot collection; piped classical music; fine Peak views from garden with gurgling fountain, good nearby walks, closed Mon evenings Nov-Easter. *Recommended by DC, Derek and Sylvia Stephenson, Ann and Tony Bennett-Hughes, Mrs B Billington*

HATHERSAGE SK2680   S11 7TY
Fox House
A6187/A625 3 miles towards Sheffield – just over Yorkshire border

Popular well run 18th-c stone-built Vintage Inn with several linked rooms on different levels, oak-framed open fireplaces, wide range of good value food from sandwiches up, well kept ales such as Black Sheep, Greene King IPA and Timothy Taylors Landlord, good wine choice, quick friendly service; nice moorland location, good views from back terrace, bedrooms, open all day. *Recommended by Ann and Colin Hunt*

HATHERSAGE SK2381   S32 1DA
Millstone
Sheffield Road (A6187 E)

Reasonably priced traditional food including Sun carvery in carpeted half-panelled bar and side dining room, friendly staff, well kept Black Sheep, Timothy Taylors Landlord and four local ales, lots of knick-knacks, open fire in central stone fireplace; children welcome, tables outside with excellent Hope Valley views, eight well appointed bedrooms, good breakfast. *Recommended by Ann and Colin Hunt, David Heath*

HATHERSAGE SK2381   S32 1BZ
☆ Scotsmans Pack
School Lane, off A6187

Cosy relaxed inn equally popular with drinkers and diners; area on left with fireplace, lots of brasses and stuffed animal heads, elsewhere plenty of dark panelling, hanging tankards, plates on delft shelving and other knick-knacks, Jennings, Marstons and guests under light blanket pressure, popular food (all day Fri-Sun in summer) from pubby standards to more elaborate blackboard specials, board games and darts; piped music, games machine, TV; children welcome, pleasant terrace by trout stream, bedrooms, open all day (closed weekday lunchtimes in winter). *Recommended by Peter F Marshall, David Carr, Barry and Anne and others*

HAYFIELD SK0387   SK22 2EP
☆ Pack Horse
Off A624 Glossop—Chapel-en-le-Frith; Market Street

Smartly modernised dining pub with good well presented food all day at reasonable prices, from baguettes to some interesting main dishes and Sun roasts, four real ales, good choice of wines and spirits, friendly efficient service, nice chatty atmosphere, cosier areas near door; piped music; walkers welcome, open all day. *Recommended by Trevor and Sheila Sharman*

HAYFIELD SK0387   SK22 2EP
☆ Royal
Market Street

18th-c stone-built hotel in former vicarage, separate pubby areas with open fires, well kept Hydes and six interesting guests (beer festival first weekend Oct), straightforward homely food including weekday deals, good friendly service, dark oak panelling, brasses, house plants, daily papers; piped music; children and dogs welcome, seats on sunny front terrace, spotless bedrooms, good breakfast, open all day. *Recommended by John Wilmott, the Didler, Malcolm Shoreditch*

HAYFIELD SK0486   SK22 2LE
☆ Sportsman
Off A624 Chapel-en-le-Frith—Buxton; Kinder Road, up past the Royal, off Market Street

Wide choice of enjoyable good value food in roomy and neatly kept traditional pub, good friendly staff, well kept Thwaites, decent wines, lots of malt whiskies, two coal fires; children and dogs welcome, lovely location (handy for Kinder Scout walks), bedrooms. *Recommended by John and Sylvia Harrop, Mike Proctor, Jim Collins*

HEANOR SK4445   DE75 7NJ
Queens Head
Breach Road, Marlpool

Nicely refurbished five-room Victorian alehouse, traditional clean interior with tiled floors, cast-iron tables, padded stools around old barrel tables, two open fires and woodburner, up to 20 well kept beers including Castle Rock, Oakham and Thornbridge (many served from cellar where customers welcome), 28 ciders, half a dozen perries, good range of wines and spirits too, some snacky food (you can bring your own), daily papers; children and dogs welcome, back terrace with open-fronted log-fire room, beer garden, open all day. *Recommended by Yvonne and Rob Warhurst, the Didler*

HEATH SK4467   S44 5SE
Elm Tree
Just off M1 junction 29; A6175 towards Clay Cross, then first right

Roadside pub with half-panelled lounge/dining areas, good choice of enjoyable well priced blackboard food (all day weekends) including generous Sun carvery, friendly efficient service, three Jennings ales and a guest, wide choice of wines, mix of traditional wooden furniture and leather armchairs on wood and stone floors, woodburner in stone fireplace, darts in smallish bar; soft piped music; children and dogs welcome, some picnic-sets out at front, attractive garden with play area and lovely views to Bolsover and beyond (but traffic noise). *Recommended by Derek and Sylvia Stephenson, Robert Thornberry, Krish Kumar*

HOGNASTON SK2350   DE6 1PR
 # Red Lion
Off B5035 Ashbourne—Wirksworth

Traditional 17th-c inn with open-plan beamed bar, three open fires, attractive mix of old tables, curved settles and other seats on ancient flagstones, friendly licensees, good well presented home-made food from shortish menu in bar and conservatory restaurant, nice wines by the glass, Marstons Pedigree and guests; piped music; picnic-sets in field behind, boules, handy for Carsington Water, three good bedrooms, big breakfast. *Recommended by Rob and Catherine Dunster, Cathryn and Richard Hicks, Trevor and Sylvia Millum, John Beeken, Derek and Sylvia Stephenson*

HOLBROOK SK3645   DE56 0TQ
☆ # Dead Poets
Chapel Street; village signed off A6 S of Belper

Reassuringly pubby and unchanging drinkers' local with nine real ales (some served from jugs), farm cider, country wines, filled cobs and good value weekday bar food, simple cottagey décor with beams, stripped-stone walls and broad flagstones, high-backed settles forming booths, big log fire, plenty of tucked-away corners, woodburner in snug, children allowed in back conservatory till 8pm; piped music, no credit cards; dogs welcome, seats in heated verandah room, more in yard, open all day Fri-Sun. *Recommended by Richard Stanfield, the Didler*

HOLYMOORSIDE SK3369   S42 7EU
Lamb
Loads Road, just off Holymoor Road

Small spotless village pub with half a dozen particularly well kept ales such as Adnams, Black Sheep, Daleside Blonde, Fullers London Pride and Timothy Taylors Landlord, charming comfortable lounge, coal fire in cosy bar, friendly locals, pub games; tables outside, leafy spot, closed weekday lunchtimes. *Recommended by the Didler*

HORSLEY WOODHOUSE SK3944   DE7 6AW
Old Oak
Main Street (A609 Belper—Ilkeston)

Busy roadside local linked to nearby Bottle Brook and Leadmill microbreweries, their ales and weekend back bar with another half-dozen well priced guests tapped from the cask, farm ciders, good basic snacks, beamed rooms with blazing coal fires, chatty friendly atmosphere, occasional live music; children and dogs welcome, hatch to covered courtyard tables, nice views, closed weekday lunchtimes, open all day weekends. *Recommended by the Didler*

ILKESTON SK4742   DE7 5TE
Dewdrop
Station Street, Ilkeston Junction, off A6096

Large Victorian corner local in old industrial area, not strong on bar comfort but popular
for its half-dozen good ales including Castle Rock, Nottingham and Oakham, simple bar
snacks, back lounge with fire and piano, connecting lobby to front public bar with pool,
darts and TV, some Barnes Wallis memorabilia; sheltered outside seating at back,
bedrooms, walks by former Nottingham Canal, open all day. *Recommended by MP, Yvonne and
Rob Warhurst, the Didler*

ILKESTON SK4742   DE7 5LJ
Good Old Days
Station Road

Welcoming half-timbered one-room pub with downstairs family room, good choice of well
kept interesting ales, simple food, darts, dominoes and pool; piped music, TV; children
and dogs welcome, tables in canalside garden, own moorings, open all day Fri-Sun.
Recommended by the Didler, Dave Wildey

ILKESTON SK4641   DE7 5QJ
Spanish Bar
South Street

Busy café-bar with well kept and well priced changing ales, bottled belgian beers,
friendly efficient staff, evening overspill room with woodburner, Tues quiz night, popular
Sun lunchtime card games with free nibbles; small garden, skittle alley, open all day.
Recommended by the Didler

KIRK IRETON SK2650   DE6 3JP
☆ Barley Mow
Village signed off B5023 S of Wirksworth

Unaltered and unchanging Jacobean house with particularly kind landlady (here for 30
years); pubby-feeling small main bar with antique settles on tiles or built into panelling,
shuttered mullioned windows, coal fire, another room with low beams, built-in cushioned
pews, oak parquet, landscape prints and small woodburner, five usually local beers, farm
cider, cheap filled rolls and simple evening meals; no credit cards; children and dogs
welcome, couple of benches out in front, good sized garden, stable shop, pretty hilltop
village (you can walk to Carsington Water from here), bedrooms, nice breakfasts in
flagstoned kitchen. *Recommended by Pam and John Smith, Steve Kirby, Andrew and Mary Ransom,
Eddie Edwards, the Didler, Tich Critchlow and others*

LADYBOWER RESERVOIR SK1986   S33 0AX
☆ Ladybower Inn
A57 Sheffield—Glossop, just E of junction with A6013

Quiet old-fashioned hotel above reservoir in good walking country; linked bays in long
carpeted bar, four changing beers (mostly local), all-day bar food, straightforwardly
pubby furnishings, Lancaster bomber pictures recalling the Dambusters' practice runs on
reservoir, two fires; piped music; children welcome, circular picnic-sets out in front,
parking across fast road, bedrooms. *Recommended by Fiona Pleasant, Ann and Colin Hunt*

LADYBOWER RESERVOIR SK2084   S33 0AZ
☆ Yorkshire Bridge
A6013 N of Bamford

Pleasant hotel in useful stopping point in dramatic Upper Derwent Valley; one plush area
with patterned carpets, floral wallpaper and staffordshire dogs and toby jugs above big
stone fireplace, another extensive lighter area with second fire, good big black and white
photographs and lots of polished brass and decorative plates, bridge room (yet another
fire) and garden room with valley views. Peak Ales, Chatsworth, Kelham Island and a
guest ale, straightforward bar food (all day Sun); piped music; children welcome,

disabled facilities, bedrooms, open all day. *Recommended by Bruce and Sharon Eden, John and Enid Morris, Richard and Julie Hay, Maurice Ricketts, Hilary Forrest*

LITTLE LONGSTONE SK1971 DE45 1NN
Packhorse
Off A6 NW of Bakewell via Monsal Dale

Three comfortable linked beamed rooms, pine tables on flagstones, well kept Thornbridge and usually Theakstons Bitter, good choice of wines by the glass, popular good value substantial food (Sat breakfast from 8.30am), good service, coal fires; hikers welcome (on Monsal Trail), terrace in steep little back garden. *Recommended by Derek and Sylvia Stephenson*

LULLINGTON SK2513 DE12 8EG
☆ # Colvile Arms
Off A444 S of Burton; Main Street

Popular neatly preserved 18th-c village pub with high-backed settles in simple panelled bar, cosy comfortable beamed lounge, pleasant atmosphere and friendly staff, four well kept ales including Bass, Marstons Pedigree and a mild, enjoyable good value food; may be piped music; picnic-sets on small sheltered back lawn overlooking bowling green, closed weekday lunchtimes. *Recommended by the Didler*

MAKENEY SK3544 DE56 0RX
☆ # Holly Bush
From A6 heading N after Duffield, take first right after crossing River Derwent, then first left

Down-to-earth two-bar village pub (former farmhouse) with three blazing coal fires (one in old-fashioned range by snug's curved high-backed settle), flagstones, beams, black panelling and tiled floors, lots of brewing advertisements, half a dozen or so well kept changing ales (some brought from cellar in jugs), real cider, cheap food including rolls and pork pies, may be local cheeses for sale, games lobby with hatch service (children allowed here), regular beer festivals; picnic-sets outside, dogs welcome, open all day Fri-Sun. *Recommended by Richard Stanfield, the Didler*

MARSTON MONTGOMERY SK1338 DE6 2FF
Crown
On corner of Thurvaston Road and Barway

Welcoming beamed pub with friendly landlord and staff, at least three changing ales such as Leatherbritches and Marstons, good food from sandwiches to steaks, leather sofas and armchairs on tiled floor, woodburner in brick fireplace, restaurant; terrace tables, nice village, seven comfortable bedrooms. *Recommended by Mrs C D Westwood, Derek King*

MILFORD SK3545 DE56 0RR
William IV
Milford Bridge

Friendly and relaxing stone-built riverside pub, long room with low beams, bare boards, quarry tiles, old settles and a blazing coal fire, well kept Bass, Marstons Pedigree, Timothy Taylors Landlord and guests, simple food; bedrooms, closed lunchtime weekdays, open all day weekends. *Recommended by the Didler*

MILLERS DALE SK1473 SK17 8SN
☆ # Anglers Rest
Just down Litton Lane; pub is PH on OS Sheet 119 map reference 142734

Spotless ivy-clad pub in lovely quiet riverside setting on Monsal Trail, two bars and dining room, log fires, good simple home-made food (Thurs pie night), well kept changing ales, cheery helpful service, reasonable prices; darts, pool and muddy walkers in public bar; children welcome, wonderful gorge views and river walks. *Recommended by Peter F Marshall, the Didler, Terry Davis, Dennis Jones, Derek and Sylvia Stephenson*

MILLTOWN SK3562   S45 0ES
Nettle
Fallgate, Littlemoor

Interesting 16th-c family-run pub with small traditional bar and linked areas behind, well kept ales such as Bradfield and Peak, good range of enjoyable food from bar snacks up, beams, stone walls, tartan carpets and log fires, restaurant; children and dogs welcome, tables outside, bedrooms open all day Sun. *Recommended by the Didler, Hilton White*

MONSAL HEAD SK1871   DE45 1NL
 ## Monsal Head Hotel
B6465

Popular inn in outstanding hilltop location, cosy stables bar with stripped timber horse-stalls, harness and brassware, cushioned oak pews on flagstones, big open fire, local ales such as Buxton and Whim, german bottled beers, several wines by the glass, locally sourced food from lunchtime sandwiches up (they may ask to keep your credit card while you eat); children (over 3), well behaved dogs and muddy walkers welcome, big garden, stunning views of Monsal Dale with its huge viaduct, seven bedrooms, open all day till midnight. *Recommended by S P Watkin, P A Taylor, Peter F Marshall, Mike Proctor, Ann and Colin Hunt, Andy and Jill Kassube*

MONYASH SK1566   DE45 1JH
☆ ## Bulls Head
B5055 W of Bakewell

Friendly high-ceilinged beamed local with simple furnishings and log fire, four well kept changing ales, enjoyable fairly traditional food (all day weekends) from sandwiches and baked potatoes up, more contemporary dining room, small back bar with pool, darts and board games; piped music; well behaved children and dogs welcome, gate from garden to village play area, open all day Fri-Sun. *Recommended by Malc Newton, David and Sue Atkinson, Dennis Jones*

NEW MILLS SJ9886   SK22 3AY
Fox
Brookbottom; OS Sheet 109 map reference 985864

Tucked-away unmodernised country local at end of single-track road, a nice summer family outing, friendly long-serving landlord, particularly well kept Robinsons, good value basic food (not Tues evening) including good sandwiches, log fire, darts and pool; lots of tables outside, good walking area, open all day Fri-Sun. *Recommended by Bob Broadhurst, the Didler, David Hoult, John Fiander, Ann and Tony Bennett-Hughes and others*

OAKERTHORPE SK3856   DE55 7LL
Amber
Furnace

Charming old-fashioned village local with friendly landlady, straightforward food, well kept Abbeydale, Fullers London Pride, Timothy Taylors Landlord and guests, blazing winter fires, lots of antiques including piano, well worn seating; good views from the back terrace, walks. *Recommended by the Didler*

OCKBROOK SK4236   DE72 3SE
Royal Oak
Off B6096 just outside Spondon; Green Lane

Quiet 18th-c village local run by same friendly family for half a century, bargain honest food (not Sat or Sun evenings) from super lunchtime cobs to steaks, Sun lunch and OAP meals, Bass and interesting guest beers, good soft drinks' choice, tile-floor tap room, carpeted snug, inner bar with Victorian prints, larger and lighter side room, nice old settle in entrance corridor, open fires, darts and dominoes; children welcome, sheltered cottage garden and cobbled front courtyard, separate play area. *Recommended by the Didler*

OSMASTON SK1943   DE6 1LW
Shoulder of Mutton
Off A52 SE of Ashbourne

Down-to-earth red-brick pub with enjoyable generous home-made food, quick friendly service, three well kept ales including Marstons Pedigree; attractive garden, farmland views, peaceful pretty village with thatched cottages, duck pond and good walks. *Recommended by Robert Pickard, C and R Bromage*

OVER HADDON SK2066   DE45 1JE
☆ ## Lathkil
Signed from B5055 SW of Bakewell

Traditional inn with glorious views over Lathkil Dale; airy beamed bar with eclectic mix of tables and chairs, upholstered settles and open fire, up to five well kept ales such as Abbeydale, Blue Monkey, Everards, Peak and Whim, good value buffet-style lunch menu, more elaborate evening food, spacious refurbished dining room; piped music, can get very busy with day trippers/walkers (leave muddy boots in lobby); dogs and children welcome (no under-14s in bar), walled garden, four bedrooms, open all day except Mon, Weds and Thurs in winter. *Recommended by Hugh Roberts, Peter F Marshall, S P Watkin, P A Taylor, the Didler and others*

PARWICH SK1854   DE6 1QL
☆ ## Sycamore
By church

Chatty old country pub well run by cheerful welcoming young landlady, generous wholesome food lunchtimes and most Weds-Sat evenings, Robinsons ales such as Unicorn and Ginger Tom, super log fire in neat traditional back bar, pool in small front hatch-served games room, another room serving as proper village shop; tables in front courtyard, picnic-sets on neat side grass, good walks. *Recommended by the Didler, Brian and Anna Marsden*

PEAK FOREST SK1179   SK17 8EJ
Devonshire Arms
Hernstone Lane (A623)

Fresh contemporary refurbishment, light wood floor, dark leather furniture, woodburner with logs stacked beside, three real ales including Wells & Youngs Bombardier, reasonably priced traditional food with some modern touches (all day Sun), attentive chatty staff; children welcome, bedrooms. *Recommended by Matthew Lidbury*

PENTRICH SK3852   DE5 3RE
☆ ## Dog
Main Road (B6016 N of Ripley)

Extended pub popular for its enjoyable all-day food, well kept ales such as Bass, Dodgem Funfair and Hook Norton from carved church-look bar counter, nice wines by the glass, woodburner, pubby bar furniture, smarter modern dining area beyond part with leather sofas etc; piped music; well behaved children allowed if eating, extensive garden behind, nice views, good walks. *Recommended by the Didler, Derek and Sylvia Stephenson*

RENISHAW SK4578   S21 3WF
Sitwell Arms
A616, 2 miles from M1 junction 30

Extended 18th-c stone-built hotel set in six-acre grounds, comfortable lounge bar with real ales and good value enjoyable pubby food, more expensive restaurant menu, reasonably priced wines including a local white, good friendly service, civilised dining room; sports TV, Thurs quiz night; children welcome, large terrace, play equipment, 30 bedrooms, handy for Renishaw Hall (gardens and Sitwell family memorabilia), open all day weekends. *Recommended by John and Sylvia Harrop*

RIPLEY SK3950   DE5 3LT
Talbot Taphouse
Butterley Hill

Full range of local Amber ales and changing guests kept well by knowledgeable landlord, farm ciders and bottled beers too, long narrow panelled room with new bar counter, comfy chairs, brick fireplace; friendly staff; open all day Fri-Sun, from 5pm Mon-Thurs. *Recommended by Michael Mellers, the Didler*

ROWARTH SK0189   SK22 1EB
Little Mill
Signed well locally; off A626 in Marple Bridge at Mellor sign, sharp left at Rowarth sign

Beautifully tucked-away 18th-c pub with welcoming landlord, well kept Banks's, Marstons and guests, good value generous food all-day (till 7pm Sun) including weekend carvery, roomy open-plan bar and upstairs restaurant, big log fire, unusual features like working waterwheel and vintage Pullman-carriage bedrooms; piped music – live Fri evenings; children and dogs welcome, disabled access, verandah with terrace below, pretty garden dell across stream, good play area, picnic-sets on decking, open all day. *Recommended by John Fiander, Dennis Jones, Brian and Anna Marsden*

ROWSLEY SK2565   DE4 2EB
Grouse & Claret
A6 Bakewell—Matlock

Attractive family dining pub in old stone building, spacious, clean and comfortable, with welcoming licensees and friendly staff, enjoyable low-priced food (all day weekends) from sandwiches up, well kept Jennings Cumberland and Marstons Pedigree, decent wines, open fires, tap room popular with walkers; tables outside, good value bedrooms. *Recommended by Guy and Caroline Howard, Brian and Jacky Wilson, Derek and Sylvia Stephenson, David Carr*

SHARDLOW SK4430   DE72 2HG
☆ # Malt Shovel
3.5 miles from M1 junction 24, via A6 towards Derby; The Wharf

Busy old-world beamed pub in 18th-c former maltings, interesting odd-angled layout with cosy corners, Marstons-related ales, bargain home-made food (not Sat evening) from baguettes up, quick friendly service, good central open fire, black panelling, farm tools and bric-a-brac; lots of terrace tables by Trent & Mersey Canal, pretty hanging baskets. *Recommended by the Didler*

SHARDLOW SK4330   DE72 2HG
New Inn
The Wharf

Popular unpretentious canalside pub, two large rooms with central bar, well kept Ringwood and decent house wine, wide range of good generous food including several vegetarian dishes, nice coffee, prompt pleasant service. *Recommended by Richard and Jean Green, Ross Coxon*

SHARDLOW SK4429   DE72 2HL
Old Crown
Off A50 just W of M1 junction 24; Cavendish Bridge, E of village

Good value pub with great range of Marstons-related ales and guests all kept well, nice choice of malt whiskies, pubby food (not Fri or Sun evenings) from sandwiches and baguettes up, beams with masses of jugs and mugs, walls covered with other bric-a-brac and breweriana, big inglenook; children and dogs welcome, simple bedrooms, good breakfast, open all day. *Recommended by the Didler*

SHELDON SK1768 DE45 1QS

☆ **Cock & Pullet**

Village signed off A6 just W of Ashford

Charming village pub with friendly courteous licensees and plenty of locals; low beams, exposed stonework, flagstones and open fire, cheerfully mismatching furnishings, 30 clocks, various representations of poultry (including some stuffed), well kept Hartington, Timothy Taylors and a guest, good traditional food from shortish menu, pool and TV in plainer public bar; quiet piped music, no credit cards; children and dogs welcome, seats and water feature on pleasant back terrace, pretty village just off Limestone Way and popular all year with walkers, bedrooms, open all day. *Recommended by DC, J and E Dakin, A J Liles, Peter F Marshall, S P Watkin, P A Taylor and others*

SHIRLEY SK2141 DE6 3AS

Saracens Head

Church Lane

Nicely modernised late 18th-c dining pub in attractive village; good range of interesting well presented food from pubby things to more expensive restaurant dishes, four Greene King ales, speciality coffees, simple country-style dining furniture, two pretty little working art nouveau fireplaces; piped music; children welcome, dogs in bar area, picnic-sets under parasols on front and back terraces, self-catering cottage, open all day Sun. *Recommended by A J Liles*

SMISBY SK3419 LE65 2UA

Smisby Arms

Nelsons Square

Ancient low-beamed village local with good range of enjoyable reasonably priced mainstream food, friendly efficient service, well kept Marstons Pedigree and a changing guest, decent coffee, bright little dining extension down steps; no dogs; children welcome, a few tables out in front. *Recommended by Richard and Jean Green, Roger and Anne Newbury*

SNAKE PASS SK1489 S33 0BJ

Snake Pass Inn

A57 E of Glossop

Remote well presented inn with good-sized bar and separate restaurant, Theakstons Black Bull and BB, reasonably priced traditional food (not Mon or evenings Sun and Tues), friendly staff, open fire; good stopping-place for walkers, cyclists and motorists at 1100 feet halfway up the pass (often snowed up in winter), bedrooms and holiday apartments. *Recommended by Malcolm and Pauline Pellatt*

SOUTH WINGFIELD SK3755 DE55 7NH

Old Yew Tree

B5035 W of Alfreton; Manor Road

Atmospheric village pub, friendly and well run, with good choice of changing ales and modestly priced home-made food (not Sun evening), good value wines, log fire, panelling, kettles and pans hanging from beams, separate restaurant area, folk music night (first Weds of month), Sun quiz night; children welcome, open all day Sun, closed Mon lunchtime. *Recommended by John and Susan Miln, A J Liles*

SPARKLOW SK1265 SK17 9QJ

Royal Oak

Monyash—Longnor Road, just off A515 S of Buxton

Relaxed country atmosphere in open-plan beamed pub, wide choice of generous fairly priced local food all day, friendly helpful service, three well kept ales including Whim Hartington, good wine choice, small bar, split-level lounge/dining room, log fire; children and dogs welcome, on Tissington Trail, overnight stabling, self-catering barn with bunk bedrooms, campsite. *Recommended by Richard Stanfield, Mike Proctor, Beth Garrard, Ivan Neary*

SPONDON SK3935
DE21 7LH

☆ **Malt Shovel**

Off A6096 on edge of Derby, via Church Hill into Potter Street

Homely traditional pub with several well kept mainly Marstons-related ales in tiny bar or from hatch in tiled corridor, various other little rooms, old-fashioned décor and a huge inglenook, decent inexpensive bar lunches, friendly helpful staff, steps down to big games bar with darts and pool; lots of picnic-sets, some under cover, in large back garden with good play area, open all day Fri-Sun. *Recommended by the Didler, Peter Kay*

STANTON IN PEAK SK2364
DE4 2LW

☆ **Flying Childers**

Main Road; village signed off B5056

Unspoilt warm-hearted local named after unbeatable 18th-c racehorse; snug little right-hand bar with dark beam-and-plank ceiling, wall settles and a single pew, blazing fire, interesting real ales chosen by friendly landlord, simple lunchtime food, bigger similarly plain lounge bar (children allowed here), acoustic music first Thurs of month and quiz night fourth Thurs of month; piped music; dogs welcome, picnic-sets out at front, lovely stone village overlooking rich green valley, good walks, closed Mon, Tues lunchtime. *Recommended by the Didler, Dennis Jones, Mike Proctor*

STRETTON EN LE FIELD SK2913
DE12 8AP

Cricketts

Burton Road

Stylishly modernised 19th-c pub with enjoyable good value food including some interesting specials, Sun carvery, good friendly service; children welcome, garden with play area, open all day. *Recommended by Deryn Mitchell, Elizabeth Devey Smith*

SUTTON CUM DUCKMANTON SK4371
S44 5JG

Arkwright Arms

A632 Bolsover—Chesterfield

Friendly mock-Tudor pub with bar, pool room (dogs allowed here) and dining room, all with real fires, good choice of well priced food at lunch and in evening till 7.30pm (not weekend evenings), up to nine changing ales including local Raw, ten real ciders and two perries (beer/cider festivals on bank holidays); TV, games machine; no children in bar, picnic-sets out at front and in side garden with play equipment, attractive hanging baskets, open all day. *Recommended by JJW, CMW, Ian Prince and others*

TANSLEY SK3159
DE4 5FY

Royal Oak

A615 Matlock—Mansfield

Pleasant village pub with wide choice of good food cooked to order including vegetarian options, two dining rooms (one upstairs) with well spaced tables, friendly efficient service, Bass and Worthington; popular, good value and best to book. *Recommended by Emma Morley, A J Liles*

TICKNALL SK3523
DE73 7JZ

☆ **Wheel**

Main Street (A514)

Stylish contemporary décor in bar and restaurant, enjoyable interesting home-made food (all day weekends), friendly staff, well kept Marstons Pedigree and a guest; children welcome, nice outside area with café tables on raised deck, near entrance to Calke Abbey. *Recommended by Kay Brough*

TINTWISTLE SK0297
SK13 1JY

Bulls Head

Old Road (off A628, N side)

Low-beamed Tudor pub tucked away in pretty stone-built village, good home-made food served by friendly staff, well kept ales such as Howard Town and Timothy Taylors, big log fire, plenty of character and furnishings to suit its age; children, dogs and walking groups welcome, handy for Woodhead Pass. *Recommended by Nancy Jackson*

TUPTON SK3966   S42 6XP
Britannia
Ward Street, New Tupton

Tap for Spire brewery (can arrange tours), four of theirs kept well and up to four guests too, good bottled range, farm cider, chatty licensees, lively bar with sports TV, quieter lounge; open from 4pm Mon-Fri, from 3pm Sat, all day Sun. *Recommended by the Didler*

WARDLOW SK1875   SK17 8RW
☆ Three Stags Heads
Wardlow Mires; A623/B6465

Basic farm pub of great individuality, flagstoned floors (often muddied by boots and dogs in winter), old country furniture, heating from cast-iron kitchen ranges, old photographs, plain-talking landlord and locals in favourite corners, well kept Abbeydale ales including Black Lurcher (brewed for the pub at a hefty 8% ABV), lots of bottled beers, hearty seasonal food on hardy home-made plates (licensees are potters), may be free roast chestnuts, perhaps folk music; no credit cards; children and dogs welcome, hill views from front terrace, closed lunchtimes, open all day weekends. *Recommended by the Didler, Dennis Jones, Steve Sharples, Ann and Tony Bennett-Hughes, Mike Proctor and others*

WHITTINGTON MOOR SK3873   S41 8LS
☆ Derby Tup
Sheffield Road; B6057 just S of A61 roundabout

Spotless no-frills Castle Rock local with up to a dozen well kept interesting changing ales from long line of gleaming handpumps, farm cider, irish whiskeys, pleasant service, simple furniture, coal fire and lots of standing room as well as two small side rooms (children allowed here), daily papers, good value basic bar lunches (not Mon); can get very busy weekend evenings; dogs welcome, open all day at least Fri-Sun. *Recommended by Peter F Marshall, the Didler, Jeremy King*

WINDLEY SK3244   DE56 4AQ
Puss in Boots
S on B5023

Former mill nicely situated above the Ecclesbourne in wooded countryside, two character rooms with open fires, low beams and oak panelling, lots of plates and brass, well kept Bass and Marstons Pedigree, popular home-made lunchtime food from good farm ham sandwiches up, well run place with friendly regulars; swings in pleasant garden, good walks. *Recommended by the Didler*

WINSTER SK2460   DE4 2DS
☆ Bowling Green
East Bank, by NT Market House

Traditional old stone pub with good chatty atmosphere, character landlord and welcoming staff, enjoyable reasonably priced food, at least three well kept changing local ales, good selection of whiskies, end log fire, dining area and family conservatory, quiz nights and singalongs; nice village, good walks, closed Mon, Tues and lunchtimes Weds to Fri, open all day Sun. *Recommended by Trevor and Sylvia Millum, Reg Fowle, Helen Rickwood*

WINSTER SK2360   DE4 2DR
Miners Standard
Bank Top (B5056 above village)

Simply furnished 17th-c stone local, relaxed at lunchtime, livelier in evenings, well kept ales such as Black Sheep, Flowers IPA and Marstons Pedigree, good value generous pubby food including huge pies, big woodburner, lead-mining photographs and minerals, lots of brass, backwards clock, ancient well, snug and restaurant; piped music; children allowed away from bar, attractive view from garden, campsite next door, interesting stone-built village below, open all day weekends. *Recommended by Dennis Jones, Trevor and Sylvia Millum, Reg Fowle, Helen Rickwood*

YEAVELEY SK1840   DE6 2DT
Yeaveley Arms
On byroads S of Ashbourne

Under new management; comfortable modern open-plan interior with bar, lounge and big airy restaurant, enjoyable food from pub favourites up, friendly efficient service, Marstons Pedigree and three guests; no dogs inside; children welcome, seats out at front and on back terrace with smokers' shelter, closed Sun evenings, Mon. *Recommended by Paul and Margaret Baker*

YOULGREAVE SK2164   DE45 1WN
George
Alport Lane/Church Street

Handsome 17th-c stone-built inn opposite Norman church, comfortably worn inside, with friendly service, wide range of good value home-made food (all day) in huge helpings, well kept John Smiths, Theakstons Mild and a local guest, banquettes running around three sides of main bar, flagstoned tap room (walkers and dogs welcome), games room; roadside tables, attractive village handy for Lathkill Dale and Haddon Hall, simple bedrooms. *Recommended by David and Gill Carrington, Dennis Jones*

ALSO WORTH A VISIT IN
LEICESTERSHIRE & RUTLAND

Besides the region's top pubs, we recommend the following. Do tell us what you think of them: **feedback@goodguides.com**

AB KETTLEBY SK7519   LE14 3JB
Sugar Loaf
Nottingham Road (A606 NW of Melton)

Beamed pub with comfortably modernised open-plan carpeted bar, country prints and big photographs of Shipstones brewery dray horses, bare-boards end with coal-effect gas fire, reasonably priced all-day food, well kept Bass, Marstons Pedigree and guests, decent coffee, friendly attentive staff, dining conservatory; quiet juke box, games machine; children welcome if eating, picnic-sets out by road and car park, open all day. *Recommended by George Atkinson*

BARKBY SK6309   LE7 3QG
Malt Shovel
Main Street

Popular well run old village pub, enjoyable good value food including bargain steak night Mon, four or five real ales such as Caledonian Deuchars IPA, Courage and Marstons, good choice of wines by the glass, charming service, U-shaped open-plan bar, small dining room (was the local jail); garden with partly covered heated terrace. *Recommended by Phil and Jane Hodson, Jim Farmer*

BARROW UPON SOAR SK5716   LE12 8LQ
Navigation
Off South Street (B5328)

Extended split-level canalside pub based on former barge-horse stabling, friendly bustling atmosphere, good value freshly made food, five well kept changing ales from unusual bar top made from old pennies, central open fire, old local photographs, darts and skittle alley, family room; piped music, TV; tables under umbrellas by water, canopied smokers' shelter with red leather sofa, moorings, open all day. *Recommended by Richard and Jean Green*

BARROWDEN SK9400   LE15 8EQ

☆ **Exeter Arms**

Main Street, just off A47 Uppingham—Peterborough

Former coaching inn popular with locals, open-plan bar with beams, stripped stone and open fire, own-brewed ales plus a couple of guests from long central counter, enjoyable pubby food and specials, collection of pump clips, beer mats and brewery posters, darts; piped music; children and dogs welcome, picnic sets on narrow front terrace with lovely views over village green and Welland Valley, big informal garden behind with boules, red kites in nearby Fineshades woods and nice walks, bedrooms, closed Sun evening, Mon lunchtime. *Recommended by Duncan Cloud, Barry Collett, the Didler, Andy Kendal, Jim Farmer, Becky Randall*

BILLESDON SK7102   LE7 9AE

Queens Head

Church Street

Beamed and thatched pub near village square, friendly landlord and staff, well kept Everards and good choice of wines by the glass, generous reasonably priced food, carpeted lounge bar with log fire, bare-boards public bar with stripped-pine tables, small conservatory; children welcome, pretty stone village. *Recommended by Barry Collett*

BOTCHESTON SK4804   LE9 9FF

Greyhound

Main Street, off B5380 E of Desford

Beamed village pub popular for its freshly cooked generous food including some unusual dishes (should book), bargain OAP weekday lunch and other deals, pine tables in two light and airy dining rooms, three well kept changing ales, friendly service; children welcome, garden with play area. *Recommended by Duncan Cloud, SAB and MJW*

BRANSTON SK8129   NG32 1RU

☆ **Wheel**

Main Street

18th-c stone-built beamed village pub with stylishly simple décor, friendly attentive landlady and smartly dressed staff, chef/landlord doing good country food such as pheasant, bacon and prune pie, and some quite out of the ordinary things like stilton ice-cream, three changing ales from central servery (could be Batemans, Clarks and Derventio), log fires; attractive garden, next to church, splendid countryside near Belvoir Castle, closed Mon. *Recommended by Phil and Jane Hodson, Richard and Jean Green*

BRAUNSTON SK8306   LE15 8QS

Blue Ball

Off A606 in Oakham; Cedar Street

Pretty thatched and beamed dining pub gaining good reputation for food under present licensees, well kept Marstons-related ales, decent wines, log fire, leather furniture and country pine in quiet linked rooms including small conservatory; children welcome, tables outside, attractive village. *Recommended by R L Borthwick, Barry Collett, Gerry and Rosemary Dobson*

BRAUNSTON SK8306   LE15 8QT

Old Plough

Off A606 in Oakham; Church Street

Comfortably opened-up black-beamed village local, big helpings of enjoyable food, Adnams, Fullers London Pride and a guest, pleasant attentive service, log fire, back dining conservatory; tables in small sheltered garden, open all day weekends. *Recommended by Barry Collett*

BRUNTINGTHORPE SP6089   LE17 5QH

 ## Joiners Arms
Off A5199 S of Leicester: Church Walk/Cross Street

More restaurant than pub with most of the two beamed rooms set for eating, drinkers have area by small light-oak bar with open fire, an ale such as Greene King or Sharps, plenty of wines (including champagne) by the glass, first-class imaginative food, friendly efficient staff, candles on tables, elegant dining chairs, big flower arrangements, civilised but relaxed atmosphere; picnic-sets in front, closed Sun evening, Mon. *Recommended by Jeff and Wendy Williams, Henry Paulinski, Rob and Catherine Dunster, V Masharani*

CALDECOTT SP8693   LE16 8RS

Plough
Main Street

Welcoming pub in attractive ironstone village, carpeted bar with banquettes and small tables leading to spacious eating area, well kept Langton and a guest like Wychwood Hobgoblin, wide range of enjoyable inexpensive food; children welcome, back garden. *Recommended by Barry Collett, Simon Collins, Ian Roberts and family*

CASTLE DONINGTON SK4427   DE74 2NH

Jolly Potters
Hillside

Genuine unspoilt town local, basic and friendly, with pews on flagstones, hanging tankards and jugs, framed beer mats, good coal fire, well kept Bass, Fullers, Marstons, Timothy Taylors and guests, back room with darts and juke box; open all day. *Recommended by the Didler*

COLEORTON SK4016   LE67 8GB

Angel
The Moor

Friendly modernised old pub with good range of enjoyable reasonably priced home-made food including Sun carvery, well kept beers such as Marstons Pedigree and Wychwood Hobgoblin, hospitable attentive staff, character landlord (in shorts whatever the weather), beams and coal fires; tables outside. *Recommended by Gill and Keith Croxton, David Barnes*

COTTESMORE SK9013   LE15 7DH

☆ ## Sun
B668 NE of Oakham

17th-c thatched stone-built village pub with good atmosphere and pleasant staff, good choice of wines by the glass, Adnams Best, Everards Tiger and guest, good coffee, wide choice of good reasonably priced bar food from lunchtime sandwiches up, stripped pine on flagstones, inglenook fire, lots of pictures and ornaments, carpeted back restaurant; piped music; dogs and children welcome, terrace tables, open all day weekends. *Recommended by Jeremy Hancock, Richard and Jean Green, Pam and John Smith*

EAST LANGTON SP7292   LE16 7TW

Bell
Off B6047; Main Street

Appealing creeper-clad beamed country inn buzzing with locals and families, well kept Brewsters, Greene King and local Langton, nice wine, good interesting food including popular Sun carvery, good service, long low-ceilinged stripped-stone bar, spacious restaurant, modern pine furniture, log fires; picnic-sets on sloping front lawn, bedrooms. *Recommended by Duncan Cloud, R L Borthwick, Jim Farmer*

Post Office address codings confusingly give the impression that some pubs are in Leicestershire, when they're really in Cambridgeshire (which is where we list them).

☆ **EXTON** SK9211   LE15 8AP
Fox & Hounds
The Green; signed off A606 Stamford—Oakham

Handsome old coaching inn handy for Rutland Water and Barnsdale Gardens, traditionally civilised and comfortable high-ceilinged lounge bar with plush seats and pine tables, maps and hunting prints, log fire, Grainstore, Greene King and a guest, enjoyable italian influenced food cooked by landlord (not Sun evening, booking advised), good value set menu, friendly welcoming staff; piped music, TV; children welcome, dogs in bar, seats among rose beds in sheltered walled garden overlooking paddocks, charming bedrooms, good breakfast, closed Mon. *Recommended by Susan and Nigel Brookes, Roy Bromell, Howard and Margaret Buchanan, Mark Farrington, Leslie and Barbara Owen, Barry Collett and others*

☆ **FOXTON** SP6989   LE16 7RA
Foxton Locks
Foxton Locks, off A6 3 miles NW of Market Harborough (park by bridge 60/62 and walk)

Nice setting at foot of long flight of canal locks, large comfortably reworked L-shaped bar, popular well priced food including winter fixed-price menu, converted boathouse does snacks, friendly service, half a dozen well kept ales such as Caledonian Deuchars IPA, Fullers London Pride and Theakstons; children welcome, large raised terrace and covered decking, steps down to fenced waterside lawn, good walks. *Recommended by Duncan Cloud, Margaret and Peter Staples, Martin Smith, Gerry and Rosemary Dobson*

GILMORTON SP5787   LE17 5PN
Grey Goose
Lutterworth Road

Refurbished bar/restaurant with good range of enjoyable freshly made food from lunchtime sandwiches up, Sun carvery, Sharps Doom Bar and Wells & Youngs Bombardier, several wines by the glass including champagne, good friendly service, light contemporary décor, stylish wood and metal bar stools mixing with comfortable sofas and armchairs, woodburner in stripped-brick fireplace with logs stacked up beside; modern furniture on terrace. *Recommended by R L Borthwick*

GREETHAM SK9214   LE15 7NJ
Plough
B668 Stretton—Cottesmore

Friendly popular village local tied to Grainstore, their beers kept well, good wine selection, wide choice of enjoyable home-made food from substantial sandwiches up, coal-effect gas fire dividing cosy lounge from eating area, pub games; tables out behind (with quoits), handy for Rutland Water, open all day Fri-Sun. *Recommended by Pierre Richterich, Pat and Stewart Gordon*

GREETHAM SK9314   LE15 7NP
Wheatsheaf
B668 Stretton—Cottesmore

Attractive old stone-built pub with linked L-shaped rooms, popular well prepared food from regularly changing menu including good sandwiches (home-baked bread) and nice steaks, home-made ice-cream too, friendly welcoming service, well kept ales such as Great Oakley, Greene King and Oldershaws, good choice of wines, log fire and blazing open stove; soft piped music, games room with darts, pool and sports TV; children welcome, dogs in bar (pub labradoodle called Mia), wheelchair access using ramp, front lawn, back terrace by pretty stream with duck house, open all day weekends, closed Mon, no food first two weeks of Jan. *Recommended by Michael and Jenny Back and others*

Every entry includes a postcode for use in Sat Nav devices.

GRIMSTON SK6821   LE14 3BZ
Black Horse
Off A6006 W of Melton Mowbray; Main Street

Popular village-green pub with interesting interior, welcoming licensees and friendly locals, well kept ales, fairly priced wholesome food, darts; attractive village with stocks and 13th-c church. *Recommended by Phil and Jane Hodson*

GUMLEY SP6890   LE16 7RU
Bell
NW of Market Harborough; Main Street

Neatly kept beamed village pub with wide choice of good value food (not Sun or Mon evenings) including bargain OAP lunches (Tues-Sat), Black Sheep, Fullers, Greene King and Timothy Taylors kept well, traditional country décor, lots of hunting prints, small fire, darts, cribbage and dominoes, separate dining room, border collie called Bailey; no mobile phones, muddy boots or children under 10; pond in pretty terrace garden (not for children or dogs), open all day, closed Sun evening. *Recommended by Ken and Barbara Turner, Jim Farmer, Gerry and Rosemary Dobson*

HALLATON SP7896   LE16 8UB
Bewicke Arms
On Eastgate, opposite village sign

Attractive thatched pub dating from the 16th c, Greene King IPA, local Langton and Timothy Taylors Landlord, two bar dining areas, restaurant of small linked areas, two log fires, scrubbed pine tables, memorabilia of ancient local Easter Monday inter-village bottle-kicking match, darts; piped music; children in eating areas, dogs allowed on leads, disabled facilities, big terrace overlooking paddock and lake with play area, stables tearoom/gift shop, three bedrooms in yard, open all day Sun. *Recommended by Jim Farmer*

HALLATON SP7996   LE16 8UJ
Fox
North End

Good value home-cooked food including some interesting light meals, Timothy Taylors Landlord and Woodfordes Wherry, welcoming friendly staff, beamed bar with log fire, restaurant; sizeable garden by duck pond. *Recommended by R L Borthwick*

HATHERN SK5021   LE12 5HY
Dew Drop
Loughborough Road (A6)

Unspoilt two-room beamed local, welcoming landlord, well kept Greene King and guests, lots of malts, coal fire, good lunchtime cobs, darts and dominoes; tables outside. *Recommended by the Didler*

HEMINGTON SK4527   DE74 2RB
Jolly Sailor
Main Street

Picturesque three-room village pub, eight real ales (Greene King and guests), food in bar and separate restaurant, log fire, big country pictures, bric-a-brac on heavy beams and shelves, daily papers; children and dogs welcome, picnic-sets out in front, open all day Fri-Sun. *Recommended by MP, the Didler*

HOSE SK7329   LE14 4JE
Rose & Crown
Bolton Lane

Friendly simply refurbished village local, well kept beer, enjoyable food served promptly, small raised dining area and steps up to intimate restaurant; tables out on back decking. *Recommended by Phil and Jane Hodson*

HOTON SK5722   LE12 5SJ
Packe Arms
A60

Spacious beamed Vintage Inn, good choice of enjoyable well priced food, well kept ales such as Batemans, Black Sheep and Everards, cheerful service; tables outside.
Recommended by Maurice and Janet Thorpe

HOUGHTON ON THE HILL SK6703   LE7 9GD
Old Black Horse
Main Street (just off A47 Leicester—Uppingham)

Lively and comfortable, with above-average home-made food (no hot food Mon lunchtime), welcoming helpful staff, Everards and a guest beer, good wines by the glass, reasonable prices, bare-boards dining area with lots of panelling; piped music; big attractive garden. *Recommended by Jim Farmer*

HUNGARTON SK6907   LE7 9JR
Black Boy
Main Street

Large open-plan partly divided restauranty bar, good well priced food cooked to order (weekend booking advised), changing ales such as Adnams, Greene King and Fullers, friendly service, minimal decoration, open fire; piped music; picnic-sets out on deck, closed Sun evening, Mon. *Recommended by R L Borthwick, Jim Farmer*

ILLSTON ON THE HILL SP7099   LE7 9EG
☆ ## Fox & Goose
Main Street, off B6047 Market Harborough—Melton Mowbray

Individual two-bar local, plain, comfortable and friendly, with interesting pictures and assorted oddments, good coal fire, long-serving landlord, well kept Everards and guests, quick service, some food (Weds-Sat); closed Mon lunchtime. *Recommended by the Didler, Jim Farmer*

KEGWORTH SK4826   DE74 2FF
☆ ## Cap & Stocking
Handy for M1 junction 24, via A6; Borough Street

Nicely old-fashioned unchanging three-room pub, brown paint, etched glass, coal fires, big cases of stuffed birds and locally caught fish, Bass (from the jug) and well kept guests such as Jennings and Wells & Youngs, home-made food (not Weds evening) from fresh sandwiches to bargain Sun lunch, dominoes, back room opening to secluded garden with decking; piped music/radio, no credit cards; children welcome. *Recommended by the Didler, Roger and Donna Huggins*

KIBWORTH BEAUCHAMP SP6894   LE8 0NN
Coach & Horses
A6 S of Leicester

Friendly and snug 16th-c carpeted local with mugs on beams and candlelit restaurant, wide choice of home-made food including good value OAP lunches and popular all-day Sun roasts, well kept Bass, Fullers London Pride, Greene King IPA and Wadworths 6X, regular events; piped music, TVs; children welcome, dogs in bar, disabled access, some outside seating at front and on side terrace, open all day weekends, closed Mon lunchtime. *Recommended by Duncan Cloud, Henry Paulinski*

KIRBY MUXLOE SK5104   LE9 2AN
Royal Oak
Main Street

Comfortable modernish pub (don't be put off by the plain exterior) doing good food from sandwiches and snacks through pub favourites to more inventive things, early-bird deals, pleasant prompt service, Everards ales, good wine choice, sizeable restaurant, some live jazz, Mon quiz night; disabled facilities, picnic-sets outside, nearby 15th-c castle ruins. *Recommended by Ian and Joan Blackwell*

LEICESTER SK5804   LE1 1RE
Ale Wagon
Rutland Street/Charles Street

Basic 1930s two-room local with great beer choice including own Hoskins ales, Weston's cider and perry, coal fire, events such as comedy nights; juke box, sports TV; handy for station, open all day (Sun afternoon break). *Recommended by the Didler, Dave Braisted*

LEICESTER SK5804   LE2 3TT
Cradock Arms
Knighton Road/Newmarket Street

New management and major refurbishment for this substantial beamed and partly thatched Everards pub, good choice of enjoyable well priced food (all day – till 4pm Sun) from open kitchen including two-for-one weekday lunch deal, Tues quiz night; children welcome, disabled facilities, beer garden with new terrace, open all day. *Recommended by Veronica Brown*

LEICESTER SK5804   LE1 5JN
Criterion
Millstone Lane

Modern building with dark wood and burgundy décor in carpeted main room, Oakham ales and up to ten guests at weekends, 100 bottled beers, decent wines by the glass, good value stone-baked pizzas, tapas and more traditional pub food (not Sun evening, Mon), relaxed room on left with games, old-fashioned juke box, music, comedy and quiz nights; wheelchair access (small front step), picnic-sets outside, open all day. *Recommended by the Didler, John Martin, Jim Farmer*

LEICESTER SK5804   LE1 5EU
☆ Globe
Silver Street

Lots of woodwork in cheerfully well worn partitioned areas off central bar, mirrors and wrought-iron gas lamps, five Everards ales and four guests, friendly staff, bargain straightforward food 12-7pm (5pm Sun) from snacks up including a good vegetarian choice, charming more peaceful upstairs dining/function room; piped music (not in snug) and live music (very popular with young people) weekend evenings; children welcome, open all day. *Recommended by the Didler*

LEICESTER SK5804   LE1 5JN
☆ Rutland & Derby Arms
Millstone Lane; nearby metered parking

Smartly renovated old pub with clean-cut modern bar/brasserie décor, friendly staff, interesting well priced food using local organic meat including bargain two-course Sun lunch, home-baked sourdough bread, Everards and guest ales, wide choice of lagers, spirits and juices; well reproduced piped music; terrace tables at back. *Recommended by Jeremy King, Dave Braisted*

LEICESTER SK5804   LE1 5SH
Shakespeares Head
Southgates

Welcoming chatty local with good low-priced Oakwell Barnsley and Old Tom Mild, well filled cobs Fri and Sat, popular Sun roasts, basic bar, lounge popular with older regulars; open all day. *Recommended by the Didler*

If we know a pub has an outdoor play area for children, we mention it.

☆ ## Swan & Rushes
LEICESTER SK5803   LE1 5WR
Oxford Street/Infirmary Square

Triangular-shaped pub with nine well kept ales including Batemans and Oakham, bottled beers, farm cider, welcoming staff and thriving atmosphere in two rooms with big oak tables, enjoyable home-made lunchtime food (not Sun) like stone-baked pizzas, fish and chips Fri evening, live music Sat; open all day Fri-Sun. *Recommended by the Didler*

☆ ## Swan in the Rushes
LOUGHBOROUGH SK5319   LE11 5BE
The Rushes (A6)

Bare-boards town local with three smallish high-ceilinged rooms, open fire, good value Castle Rock and interesting changing ales, foreign bottled beers, farm cider, well priced chip-free food (not Sat or Sun evenings), good service, daily papers, traditional games; good juke box – live music nights Thurs-Sat; children welcome in eating areas, tables outside, four bedrooms, open all day. *Recommended by the Didler, Andy Lickfold, Steven Paine, Frank Swann*

Tap & Mallet
LOUGHBOROUGH SK5319   LE11 1EU
Nottingham Road

Basic friendly pub with well kept Jennings, Marstons and five changing guests including microbrews, foreign beers, farm cider and perry, nice cobs, coal fire, pool, juke box; walled back garden with play area and pets corner, open all day. *Recommended by the Didler*

Ferrers Arms
LOUNT SK3819   LE65 1SD
A453 NE of Ashby de la Zouch

Much extended red-brick dining pub, open-plan interior separated by low dividing walls, reliable good value food including deals, friendly efficient young staff, Marstons-related ales from central bar, decent fairly priced wines; children welcome, outside tables and play area, open all day. *Recommended by Richard and Jean Green*

☆ ## Old White Hart
LYDDINGTON SP8796   LE15 9LR
Village signed off A6003 N of Corby

Popular welcoming old pub, softly lit front bar with heavy beams in low ceiling, just a few tables, glass-shielded log fire, Greene King and Timothy Taylors Landlord, good food (not winter Sun evening) including own sausages and cured meats (landlord is a butcher), attractive restaurant, further tiled-floor room with rugs, lots of fine hunting prints and woodburner; children welcome, seats by heaters in pretty walled garden, eight floodlit boules pitches, handy for Bede House and good nearby walks, bedrooms. *Recommended by Mike and Sue Loseby, Jeff and Wendy Williams, Roy Bromell, John Robertson, Rochelle Seifas, Anthony Barnes and others*

Horse & Jockey
MANTON SK8704   LE15 8SU
St Mary's Road

Welcoming early 19th-c refurbished stone pub, well kept Grainstore ales and a guest, decent inexpensive food (all day weekends) from baguettes to blackboard specials, good service, low beams, stone or wood floors, woodburner; piped music; children and dogs welcome, pretty terrace, nice location – on Rutland Water cycle route (bike racks provided), open all day summer, all day Fri-Sun winter. *Recommended by Comus and Sarah Elliott, Adam Freckingham, Gill and Keith Croxton, R L Borthwick*

There are report forms at the back of the book.

MARKET HARBOROUGH SP7387   LE16 7AF
Angel
High Street

Popular former coaching inn with good range of reasonably priced food in bar and restaurant including fixed-price menu, friendly efficient uniformed staff, well kept Marstons and a guest, good coffee, daily papers; discreet sports TV; 24 bedrooms. *Recommended by Gerry and Rosemary Dobson, Michael Dandy*

MARKET HARBOROUGH SP7387   LE16 7NJ
Sugar Loaf
High Street

Popular Wetherspoons, smaller than many, with half a dozen sensibly priced real ales (frequent beer festivals), good value food all day; children welcome. *Recommended by Gerry and Rosemary Dobson*

MARKET HARBOROUGH SP7387   LE16 7NJ
☆ # Three Swans
High Street

Comfortable banquettes and plush-cushioned library chairs in traditional bay-windowed front bar of Best Western conference hotel, local ales such as Grainstore and Langton, good spread of enjoyable well presented pubby food from sandwiches up including set deals, decent wines, friendly uniformed staff, flame-effect fires (one in grand coaching-era inglenook), flagstoned back area, corridor to popular conservatory bistro (evenings Mon-Sat), more formal upstairs restaurant; piped music; attractive suntrap courtyard, useful parking, good bedrooms. *Recommended by George Atkinson, Gerry and Rosemary Dobson*

MARKET OVERTON SK8816   LE15 7PW
Black Bull
Off B668 in Cottesmore

Attractive thatched and low-beamed stone-built pub in pretty village well placed for Rutland Water, welcoming landlord and staff, good interesting home-made food in long red-carpeted bar and two separate dining areas, four well kept ales including Theakstons and Wells & Youngs, banquettes and sofas, newspapers; some piped and live music; children welcome, tables out in front by small carp pool, bedrooms, open all day Fri-Sun. *Recommended by Barry Collett, Mike and Ann Pepper*

MEDBOURNE SP7992   LE16 8EE
☆ # Nevill Arms
B664 Market Harborough—Uppingham

Handsome stone-built Victorian inn nicely located by stream and footbridge, wide range of good bar and restaurant food including Sun roasts, pleasant helpful staff, well kept Bass, Fullers London Pride and Greene King IPA, beams and mullion windows, log fires, modern artwork, stylish restaurant; no dogs; back terrace with stable-conversion café (8am-4pm), streamside picnic-sets, 11 refurbished bedrooms, good breakfast, open all day. *Recommended by Duncan Cloud, Barry Collett, Nigel and Sue Foster, Mike and Sue Loseby, Richard and Jean Green, Jim Farmer and others*

MOUNTSORREL SK5715   LE12 7AT
Swan
Loughborough Road, off A6

Log fires, old flagstones and stripped stone, friendly staff and locals, enjoyable well priced food from baguettes and light dishes to generous full meals, Theakstons and guest ales, good choice of wines, pine tables and gingham cloths in neat dining area and restaurant; pretty walled back garden down to canalised River Soar, self-contained accommodation, open all day Sat. *Recommended by Mick and Moira Brummell*

NETHER BROUGHTON SK6925   LE14 3HB
Red House
A606 N of Melton Mowbray

Substantial and elegant extended Georgian roadside inn, emphasis on good popular restaurant, also more reasonably priced bar food including sandwiches and light dishes, good service, an ale from local Belvoir, comfortable lounge bar with red leather fireside sofas and armchairs, another bar on right with TV; children welcome, dogs in bar, courtyard and garden with picnic-sets, eight well equipped stylish bedrooms, open all day Fri and Sat, closed Sun evenings. *Recommended by Alex Boyles*

NEWTON BURGOLAND SK3709   LE67 2SE
☆ ## Belper Arms
Off B4116 S of Ashby

Ancient rambling pub said to date from the 13th c, roomy lounge with low-beamed areas off, changing floor levels, stripped brick, some good antique furniture and plenty to look at including framed story of pub's ghost, nice log fire, Greene King and Theakstons ales, Weston's cider, many wines by the glass, several malt whiskies, cheerful helpful service, restaurant; some piped music; children and dogs welcome, big garden with terrace, open all day. *Recommended by Duncan Cloud, Richard and Jean Green, Alan Thwaite, the Didler*

OADBY SK6202   LE2 2FB
☆ ## Cow & Plough
Gartree Road (B667 N of centre)

Former farm and dairy (converted about 20 years ago), fantastic collection of brewery memorabilia (interesting enamel signs and mirrors), up to eight real ales including local Steamin' Billy, six ciders, bar food (not Sun evening) from sandwiches up, a couple of individual original rooms, long front extension and conservatory with real mix of furniture, hop-draped beams, darts; TV, piped music, Booze & Blues festival May; children and dogs welcome, picnic-set in yard, open all day. *Recommended by Barry Collett, the Didler, Tony and Wendy Hobden, Jim Farmer, Rob and Catherine Dunster and others*

OADBY SP6399   LE2 4RH
Grange Farm
Off Glen Road (A6)

Popular roomy Vintage Inn based on early 19th-c farmhouse, smart welcoming young staff, wide choice of generous reasonably priced food, Batemans, Black Sheep and Everards, good range of wines and spirits, log fires, old local photographs, daily papers; no dogs; well behaved children welcome, tables out in front, open all day. *Recommended by Phil and Jane Hodson*

OAKHAM SK8508   LE15 6AS
Admiral Hornblower
High Street

Former 17th-c farmhouse with several differently decorated areas from panelling and tradition to fresher informality, warm and inviting with three log fires, food from pubby things up including Sun carvery, well kept ales, conservatory; country-feel garden, ten comfortable bedrooms. *Recommended by John Robertson, P Dawn*

OAKHAM SK8508   LE15 6LE
Horseshoe
Braunston Road

Change of management at this 1960s pub; well kept Everards and guests, enjoyable pubby food, comfortable lounge bar leading to games room with pool, dining room; front picnic-sets, garden behind. *Recommended by Barry Collett*

OAKHAM SK8508   LE15 6QS

Wheatsheaf
Northgate

Attractive 17th-c local near church, friendly helpful staff, well kept Adnams, Everards and guests, good lunchtime pub food, a couple of rocking chairs by open fire, plenty of bric-a-brac, books and posters, cheerful bar, comfortable quieter lounge and conservatory (children welcome here); pretty suntrap back courtyard with entertaining installation.
Recommended by Barry Collett, Tony and Maggie Harwood

OAKTHORPE SK3212   DE12 7QT

Shoulder of Mutton
Chapel Street

Friendly 18th-c black and white beamed village pub, good range of ales, reasonably priced restaurant (no food Sun evenings, Mon), folk club Sun night; disabled facilities, terrace. *Recommended by B M Eldridge*

OLD DALBY SK6723   LE14 3LF

Crown
Debdale Hill

Creeper-clad with intimate farmhouse rooms up and down steps, black beams, antique oak settles among other seats, rustic prints, open fires, several well kept ales including Belvoir and Castle Rock from expanded bar area, plenty of wines by the glass, good up-to-date fresh local food (not Sun evening, Mon) from bar menu or more expensive evening one, good service, extended dining room opening on to terrace; children and dogs welcome, disabled facilities, attractive garden with boules, closed Mon lunchtime.
Recommended by Comus and Sarah Elliott, Adrian Johnson, the Didler, P Dawn

ROTHLEY SK5812   LE7 7PD

Woodmans Stroke
Church Street

Immaculate family-run pub with good value weekday lunchtime bar food from sandwiches up, well kept changing ales, good wines by the glass including champagne, friendly service, beams and settles in front rooms, open fire, lots of rugby and cricket memorabilia; sports TV; pretty front hanging baskets, cast-iron tables in attractive garden with heaters, open all day. *Recommended by John Martin*

SHEARSBY SP6290   LE17 6PL

Chandlers Arms
Fenny Lane, off A50 Leicester—Northampton

Comfortable old creeper-clad village pub, four well kept ales, good choice of food including some lunchtime bargains, wall seats and wheelback chairs; piped music, pool, Weds quiz night; tables in secluded raised garden, nice hanging baskets, attractive village. *Recommended by JJW, CMW, Jim Farmer*

SIBSON SK3500   CV13 6LB

Cock
A444 N of Nuneaton; Twycross Road

Picturesque old black and white thatched pub with Dick Turpin connection, Bass and Hook Norton, a dozen wines by the glass, decent if pricey food, cheerful quick service, low doorways, heavy black beams and genuine latticed windows, immense inglenook; piped music, games machine; children welcome, tables in courtyard and small garden, handy for Bosworth Field. *Recommended by Joan and Tony Walker*

Please tell us if any pub deserves to be included or upgraded to a featured top pub – and why: **feedback@goodguides.com**, or (no stamp needed) The Good Pub Guide, FREEPOST TN1569, Wadhurst, E Sussex TN5 7BR.

SOMERBY SK7710   LE14 2QB
☆ **Stilton Cheese**
High Street; off A606 Oakham—Melton Mowbray, via Cold Overton, or Leesthorpe and Pickwell

Friendly staff in enjoyable ironstone pub with comfortable beamed and hop-strung bar/lounge, comfortable furnishings on red patterned carpets, country prints, copper pots and a stuffed badger, Grainstore, Marstons, Tetleys and guests, 30 malt whiskies, reasonably priced pubby food and some interesting daily specials, restaurant; children welcome, seats on terrace, peaceful setting on edge of pretty village, bedrooms.
Recommended by Phil and Jane Hodson, Duncan Cloud, Ken and Barbara Turner, Mike and Margaret Banks, Jim Farmer, George Atkinson

SOUTH LUFFENHAM SK9401   LE15 8NT
☆ **Coach House**
Stamford Road (A6121)

Nicely reworked old inn with flagstoned bar, stripped stone or terracotta walls, bright scatter cushions on small pews, church candles, log fire, Adnams, Greene King and Timothy Taylors, decent wines by the glass, good food using some own-grown produce, friendly staff, neat built-in seating in separate red-walled snug, smarter more modern feeling back dining room with brown suede seating; children welcome, dogs in bar, small deck behind, bedrooms, closed Sun evening, Mon lunchtime. *Recommended by Marcus Mann, Sandy Butcher*

SPROXTON SK8524   LE14 4QB
Crown
Coston Road

Friendly 19th-c stone-built inn with spotless well laid-out interior, good reasonably priced food from bar snacks to restaurant dishes like partridge and rack of lamb, well kept Greene King ales, good wines and coffee, light airy bar with woodburner, restaurant with big glassed-off wine store; children welcome, dogs in bar, lovely sunny courtyard, attractive village and nice local walks, three bedrooms, closed Sun evening, Mon.
Recommended by Phil and Jane Hodson, Howard and Margaret Buchanan

STRETTON SK9415   LE15 7QX
☆ **Ram Jam Inn**
Just off A1 by B668 Oakham turn-off

Useful A1 stop, this bustling dining place serves food from 7am, big open-plan bar/dining area with bucket chairs, sofas and mix of tables, two back rooms one with fire, daily papers, changing beer, good house wines and coffee; children welcome away from bar, garden tables, comfortable bedrooms, open all day. *Recommended by John Coatsworth*

THORPE LANGTON SP7492   LE16 7TS
☆ **Bakers Arms**
Off B6047 N of Market Harboro

Civilised restaurant with bar rather than pub, very good regularly changing imaginative food in cottagey beamed linked areas (must book), stylishly simple country décor, well kept local Langton ale, good choice of wines by the glass, friendly efficient staff, maybe a pianist; no under-12s; garden picnic-sets, closed weekday lunchtimes, Sun evening and Mon. *Recommended by Duncan Cloud, Gerry and Rosemary Dobson, John and Sylvia Harrop, R L Borthwick, Jim Farmer and others*

TUR LANGTON SP7194   LE8 0PJ
Crown
Off B6047; Main Street (follow Kibworth signpost from centre)

Attractive pub with enjoyable competitively priced food from standards up, prompt friendly service, well kept ales including Caledonian Deuchars IPA and Timothy Taylors Landlord, bar with central log fire, side room, back restaurant with own bar; terrace tables. *Recommended by Jim Farmer*

UPPER HAMBLETON SK8907   LE15 8TL
☆ **Finchs Arms**
Off A606; Oakham Road

17th-c stone inn with outstanding views over Rutland Water, four log fires, beamed and
flagstoned bar, Black Sheep, Timothy Taylors Landlord and a guest, several wines by the
glass including champagne, afternoon teas, elegant restaurant with decorative bay trees
and modern seating, second newly built dining room, generally well liked food and set
menus; no dogs; children welcome, suntrap hillside terrace, good surrounding walks, ten
bedrooms, open all day. *Recommended by Maurice and Janet Thorpe, John Robertson, Michael Doswell,
Marcus Mann, Pat and Stewart Gordon, Clive Watkin and others*

WALTHAM ON THE WOLDS SK8024   LE14 4AH
Marquis of Granby
High Street

Friendly stone-built country local with popular good value pubby food, quick service, four
well kept Everards ales and a guest, decent wines by the glass, upper games area with
pool and darts, skittle alley; children welcome, tables out on decking, closed Mon.
Recommended by Phil and Jane Hodson

WESTON BY WELLAND SP7791   LE16 8HZ
Wheel & Compass
Valley Road

Old stone-built pub with wide choice of enjoyable generous food at attractive prices,
Bass, Marstons Pedigree and three changing guests, friendly staff, good wine and soft
drinks choice, comfortable bar, good-sized back dining area and restaurant; children
welcome, open all day. *Recommended by Jim Farmer*

WHITWELL SK9208   LE15 8BW
Noel at Whitwell
Main Road (A606)

Smart spacious bistro/pub handy for Rutland Water, wide choice of food including good
value set lunches, friendly young staff, local real ales, decent wines by the glass, good
coffee, live music; children welcome, suntrap tables outside, play area, bedrooms.
Recommended by Roy Bromell

WHITWICK SK4316   LE67 5GN
Three Horseshoes
Leicester Road

Unpretentious unchanging two-room local with tiny snug; long quarry-tiled bar with old
wooden benches and open fires, well kept Bass and Marstons Pedigree, piano, darts,
dominoes and cards, newspapers, no food (but fish and chip shop below); outdoor
lavatories, no proper pub sign so easy to miss. *Recommended by the Didler*

WILSON SK4024   DE73 8AE
Bulls Head
Side road Melbourne—Breedon on the Hill

Small, welcoming and well cared-for village pub, low-beams and cosy alcoves, enjoyable
reasonably priced traditional food including sandwiches till 7pm, well kept Marstons
Pedigree and Timothy Taylors Landlord, friendly staff, log fire, quiz nights; children and
dogs welcome, tables out on decking. *Recommended by Nick Humphreys*

WOODHOUSE EAVES SK5214   LE12 8QZ
Curzon Arms
Maplewell Road

Welcoming old beamed pub with enjoyable food (not Sun evening) from lunchtime
sandwiches and pub favourites up, also good value weekday set menu, Adnams Bitter,
Marstons EPA, Sharps Doom Bar and a guest, good service, attractive up-to-date décor,

interesting collection of wall clocks, carpeted dining room; piped music; children and dogs welcome, ramp for disabled access, good-sized front lawn and terrace, open all day weekends. *Recommended by R L Borthwick, Ken and Barbara Turner*

WOODHOUSE EAVES SK5214   LE12 8RZ
Old Bulls Head
Main Street

Large open-plan contemporary dining pub, good choice of interesting food including fixed-price menu (lunchtime till 7pm weekdays), good wine list, well kept ales such as Timothy Taylors Landlord, friendly staff in black; well behaved children welcome, outside tables, nice village setting, open all day. *Recommended by Mrs Joy Griffiths, Peter and Josie Fawcett*

WYMESWOLD SK6023   LE12 6TZ
Three Crowns
Far Street (A6006)

Snug chatty 18th-c local in attractive village, good friendly staff, four real ales such as Adnams, Bass and Belvoir, good soft drinks choice, reasonably priced pubby food, pleasant character furnishings in beamed bar and lounge, lots of atmosphere; picnic-sets out on decking. *Recommended by Comus and Sarah Elliott, the Didler, P Dawn*

ALSO WORTH A VISIT IN LINCOLNSHIRE

Besides the region's top pubs, we recommend the following. Do tell us
what you think of them: **feedback@goodguides.com**

ALLINGTON SK8540   NG32 2EA
☆ Welby Arms
The Green; off A1 at N end of Grantham bypass

Friendly well run inn with helpful staff, large simply furnished bar divided by stone archway, beams and joists, log fires (one in an attractive arched brick fireplace), comfortable plush wall banquettes and stools, six changing ales, over 20 wines by the glass and good malt whisky choice, popular bar food in civilised back dining lounge; piped music; children welcome, tables in walled courtyard with pretty flower baskets, picnic-sets on front lawn, bedrooms, open all day Sun. *Recommended by John R Ringrose, Michael and Jenny Back, Gordon and Margaret Ormondroyd, John and Angie Millar, Janet and Peter Race, D Goodger and others*

ASLACKBY TF0830   NG34 0HL
Robin Hood & Little John
A15 Bourne—Sleaford

Timbered village pub reopened and revamped after long closure, emphasis on food with separate restaurant, ales such as Greene King, Batemans and Oldershaws. *Recommended by Andy Leighton*

BELCHFORD TF2975   LN9 6LQ
☆ Blue Bell
Village signed off A153 Horncastle—Louth

Smart 18th-c dining pub with cosy comfortable bar, relaxing pastel décor, mix of chairs and armchairs, Black Sheep and Greene King ales, fair priced lunchtime dishes with more inventive (and pricier) restaurant choices, efficient friendly service; children welcome, picnic-sets in neat terraced back garden, good base for Wolds walks and Viking Way (remove muddy boots), closed Sun evening, Mon and second and third weeks in Jan. *Recommended by Ian Robinson, Richard and Mary Bailey, Mrs Denise Dowd*

BILLINGBOROUGH TF1134   NG34 0QB

☆ **Fortescue Arms**

B1177, off A52 Grantham—Boston

Popular country local with old stonework, exposed brick, wood panelling, beams and big
see-through fireplace in carpeted rooms, well kept Adnams, Everards, Greene King and
Timothy Taylors, pubby food (all day Sun), good friendly service, Victorian prints, brass
and copper, stuffed badger and pheasant, fresh flowers and pot plants, attractive
flagstoned dining rooms each end and another open fire; children welcome, picnic-sets
on side lawn, more in sheltered courtyard with flowering tubs, open all day weekends.
Recommended by Dr and Mrs R G J Telfer, Ian and Helen Stafford

BRANDY WHARF TF0196   DN21 4RU

☆ **Cider Centre**

B1205 SE of Scunthorpe (off A15 about 16 miles N of Lincoln)

Up to 15 draught ciders, many more in bottles etc, also country wines and meads; plain
take-us-as-you-find-us bright main bar and dimmer lounge with lots of cider memorabilia
and jokey bric-a-brac, reasonably priced straightforward food (all day Sun); piped music;
children in eating area, simple glazed verandah, tables in meadows or by river with
moorings and slipway, play area, closed Mon-Weds in winter. *Recommended by the Didler,
Mike and Lynn Robinson*

BURTON COGGLES SK9725   NG33 4JS

Cholmeley Arms

Village Street

Well kept ales such as Fullers London Pride, Greene King Abbot and Grainstore in small
pubby bar with warm fire, enjoyable reasonably priced simple food, good friendly service,
restaurant; handy for A1. *Recommended by G Jennings, Angela Nicholson, Maurice and Janet Thorpe*

CLEETHORPES TA3009   DN35 8AX

No 2 Refreshment Room

Station Approach

Comfortably refurbished, carpeted platform bar, friendly staff, well kept Greene King,
Worthington and guests, no food, Thurs quiz; tables out under heaters, open all day from
9am. *Recommended by the Didler, P Dawn*

CLEETHORPES TA3108   DN35 8RQ

☆ **Willys**

Highcliff Road; south promenade

Popular open-plan bistro-style seafront pub with panoramic Humber views, café tables,
tiled floor and painted brick walls; visibly brews its own good ales, also changing guests
and belgian beers, good home-made bargain bar lunches (evening food Mon, Tues and
Thurs), friendly fast service, nice mix of customers from young and trendy to weather-
beaten fishermen; quiet juke box; a few tables out on the promenade, open all day.
Recommended by the Didler, Pat and Tony Martin, P Dawn, Chris Johnson

COWBIT TF26178   PE12 6AL

Olde Dun Cow

Barrier Bank; A1073 S of Spalding

Friendly old pub in bypassed village, beamed split-level bar and restaurant, good choice
of freshly made food from landlord/chef, ales such as Batemans, Black Sheep and
Everards Tiger, Thatcher's cider, lots of knick-knacks, african grey parrot called Chiku;
disabled facilities, garden. *Recommended by Michael and Jenny Back*

Anyone claiming to arrange or prevent inclusion of a pub in the *Guide* is a fraud.
Pubs are included only if recommended by genuine readers and if our own anonymous
inspection confirms that they are suitable.

DENTON SK8632   NG32 1LG
Welby Arms
Church Street

Welcoming local, clean and comfortable, with well cooked attractively served food at
reasonable prices; pretty village nestling in Vale of Belvoir. *Recommended by Mrs B H Adams*

DRY DODDINGTON SK8546   NG23 5HU
☆ ## Wheatsheaf
Main Street; 1.5 miles off A1 N of Grantham

Popular 16th-c colourwashed village pub with enthusiastic young owners, front bar
(basically two rooms) with woodburner, seats in windows facing the green and lovely
14th-c church, Greene King, Timothy Taylors, Tom Woods and a guest, comfortable
extended carpeted dining room (once a cow byre and maybe dating to the 13th c), good
food cooked by landlord using own vegetables and herbs and local rare-breed meat; piped
music; children and dogs welcome, disabled access at side, seats under parasols on front
terrace, open all day weekends, closed Mon, Tues lunchtime. *Recommended by
Tom and Ruth Rees, Michael and Jenny Back and others*

DYKE TF1022   PE10 0AF
Wishing Well
Village signed off A15 N of Bourne; Main Street

Long heavily beamed stripped-stone front bar with huge fireplace, friendly helpful staff,
Greene King Abbot, Shepherd Neame Spitfire and three guests, enjoyable reasonably
priced food from sandwiches to steaks, big restaurant, small conservatory, darts, pool, TV
and so forth in public bar, live music and quiz nights; children welcome, garden with
tables and play area, 12 bedrooms, caravan park, open all day. *Recommended by
Mr and Mrs M Norris*

GAINSBOROUGH SK8189   DN21 2DW
Eight Jolly Brewers
Ship Court, Silver Street

Small comfortable real ale pub with up to eight including regulars Abbeydale, Castle
Rock and Glentworth, low prices, also farm cider and country wines, simple lunchtime
food (not Sun), friendly staff and locals, beams, bare bricks and brewery posters, quieter
areas upstairs, live folk music; terrace, open all day weekends. *Recommended by the Didler*

GRANTHAM SK9136   NG31 6RQ
☆ ## Blue Pig
Vine Street

Cosy three-bar Tudor pub with enjoyable home-made pubby food including OAP bargains,
well kept Caledonian Deuchars IPA, Timothy Taylors Landlord and changing guests, good
choice of wines, quick cheerful service, low beams, panelling, stripped stone and
flagstones, open fire, daily papers, lots of pig ornaments, prints and bric-a-brac; piped
music, juke box, games machines, no children or dogs; tables out behind, open all day.
Recommended by the Didler, Ian and Nita Cooper

HACONBY TF1025   PE10 0UZ
Hare & Hounds
Off A15 N of Bourne; West Road

Warmly welcoming village pub doing enjoyable well priced traditional food, weekday OAP
and early-bird deals too, Marstons-related ales, live folk music, darts; no dogs inside;
children welcome in restaurant and snug, enclosed garden, open all day weekends.
Recommended by Mr and Mrs M Norris

Post Office address codings confusingly give the impression that some pubs are in
Lincolnshire, when they're really in Cambridgeshire (which is where we list them).

HEIGHINGTON TF0369　　　　　　　　　　　　　　　　　　LN4 1JS

☆ **Butcher & Beast**
High Street

Welcoming recently refurbished Batemans pub, their ales and three local guests kept well
(beer festivals), bottled continental beers, enjoyable hearty bar food (not Sun evening,
Weds) using local suppliers, two small cosy front rooms, log fire, dining area; quiz nights;
dogs allowed in bar, garden down to stream, pretty village. *Recommended by Chris Johnson*

HOUGH-ON-THE-HILL SK9246　　　　　　　　　　　　　　NG32 2AZ

☆ **Brownlow Arms**
High Road

Smart 16th-c restaurant-with-rooms, comfortable beamed bar cleverly designed to give
impression of cosy separate areas, local prints on exposed brick walls, panelling, stylish
slightly mismatched furniture, log fire, good if not cheap food, Marstons and Timothy
Taylors, several wines by the glass and malt whiskies, friendly courteous staff; piped
music; children over 12 allowed, bedrooms, hearty breakfast, closed Sun evening, Mon
and lunchtimes (except Sun). *Recommended by P and J Shapley, Alan Clark*

KIRKBY ON BAIN TF2462　　　　　　　　　　　　　　　　LN10 6YT

Ebrington Arms
Main Street

Popular good value generous food (booking advised), five or more well kept changing ales
such as Batemans and Black Sheep (festivals Easter and Aug bank holidays), prompt
friendly service, low 16th-c beams, two open fires, nicely set out dining areas each side,
copper-topped tables, banquettes, jet fighter and racing car pictures, daily papers, games
area with darts, back restaurant; may be piped music; children welcome, wheelchair
access, tables out in front, swings on side lawn, campsite behind, open all day.
Recommended by Kay and Alistair Butler, Andy Beveridge

LINCOLN SK9871　　　　　　　　　　　　　　　　　　　LN2 4AW

Morning Star
Greetwell Gate

Friendly traditional local handy for the cathedral, enjoyable good value lunches, well kept
reasonably priced ales, helpful service, two bar areas and comfortable snug, aircraft
paintings, coal fire, some live music (piano often played); nice covered outside area, open
all day. *Recommended by the Didler*

LINCOLN SK9771　　　　　　　　　　　　　　　　　　　LN1 3BG

Strugglers
Westgate

Cosily worn-in beer lovers' haunt, well kept ales such as Bass, Black Sheep, Greene King,
Oldershaws, Northumberland, Rudgate and Timothy Taylors Landlord, bargain pub
lunches (from 10.30am, not Sun), coal-effect fire in back snug, some live music; no
children inside; dogs welcome after 3pm, steps down to back courtyard with heated back
canopy, open all day (till 1am Thurs-Sat). *Recommended by Peter and Josie Fawcett, the Didler*

LINCOLN SK9771　　　　　　　　　　　　　　　　　　　LN1 1ES

Tap & Spile
Hungate

Friendly lived-in pub with several well kept changing ales, farm cider and country wines,
small choice of reasonably priced pubby food, central bar, linked areas with flagstones,
bare boards and brickwork, breweriana; open all day. *Recommended by Chris Johnson*

LINCOLN SK9770　　　　　　　　　　　　　　　　　　　LN5 7AF

Treaty of Commerce
High Street

Warmly welcoming, lively and simple pub in beamed Tudor building, fine stained glass, panelling, etchings, good value bar lunches from baguettes up, well kept Batemans and guests, darts; open all day. *Recommended by the Didler, Malc Newton*

☆ Victoria
LINCOLN SK9771   LN1 3BJ

Union Road

Main draw to this old-fashioned backstreet local are the eight changing real ales, foreign draught and bottled beers and farm cider (beer festivals end Jun, Aug bank holiday and Halloween); simply furnished tiled front lounge with pictures of Queen Victoria, coal fire, basic lunchtime food, friendly staff and good mix of customers (gets especially busy lunchtime and later in evening); children and dogs welcome, small conservatory and seats on heated terrace, castle views, open all day till midnight (1am Fri, Sat). *Recommended by Adam Jackson, Chris Johnson, the Didler, P Dawn, Colin Bettany and others*

Widow Cullens Well
LINCOLN SK9771   LN2 1LU

Steep Hill

Ancient revamped building on two floors, cheap Sam Smiths beers and bar food, chatty mix of customers, good service; back terrace. *Recommended by David Toulson, Chris Johnson, Malc Newton, Susan and Nigel Brookes, Pete Coxon*

☆ Wig & Mitre
LINCOLN SK9771   LN2 1LU

Steep Hill; just below cathedral

Civilised café-style dining pub with plenty of character and attractive period features over two floors; big-windowed downstairs bar, beams and exposed stone walls, pews and gothic furniture on oak boards, comfortable sofas in carpeted back area, quieter upstairs dining room with views of castle walls and cathedral, antique prints and caricatures of lawyers/clerics, all-day food from breakfast on including good value set menus and some interesting seasonal dishes, extensive choice of wines by the glass from good list, Batemans XB, Black Sheep and a guest; children and dogs welcome, open 8am-midnight. *Recommended by Dave Braisted, Adam Jackson, Mike and Lynn Robinson, Pam and John Smith, Simon Pyle and others*

Black Horse
LUDFORD TF1989   LN8 6AJ

A631 Market Rasen—Louth

Old-fashioned dining pub undergoing refurbishment as we went to press; welcoming and relaxed, with good, imaginative, locally sourced food, good local beers too, log fire in old raised hearth; closed Sun evening. *Recommended by Newbury family, Rick Steele, Vee Ridgley*

New Inn
NORTH THORESBY TF2998   DN36 5QS

Station Road

Popular and friendly with good reliable pub food, well kept Marstons Pedigree, Theakstons and guests, nice fire in bar, roomy restaurant; disabled facilities, terrace. *Recommended by Steven King and Barbara Cameron*

Houblon Arms
OASBY TF0039   NG32 3NB

Village signed off A52

Large rambling 17th-c inn with lots of low beams, panelling, stonework and good open fire, Black Sheep, Everards Tiger, Timothy Taylors Landlord and a guest, Aspall's and Weston's ciders, good choice of home-made food, cheerful service; garden area behind with small tables on gravel, boules, four comfortable bedrooms, closed Mon lunchtime. *Recommended by Alun and Jennifer Evans*

PINCHBECK TF2326   PE11 3SE
Ship
Northgate

Old thatched and beamed riverside pub with tables set for dining in bar and extended back dining area, good value pubby food including lunchtime deals (popular with older diners) and Fri night, Sun carvery, two or three real ales, friendly staff, nostalgic odds and ends; children welcome, terrace tables, garden with play equipment, open all day Fri-Sun, closed Mon. *Recommended by T A Green, Phil and Jane Hodson*

POTTERHANWORTH TF0565   LN4 2DS
Chequers
Cross Street, off Main Road

Recently refurbished village pub, good food at moderate prices, welcoming attentive service. *Recommended by Sue Kinder*

REDBOURNE SK9799   DN21 4QR
Red Lion
Main Road (B1206 SE of Scunthorpe)

Welcoming and comfortable 17th-c coaching inn with thriving atmosphere, good food (fish in particular) from lunchtime sandwiches up, helpful staff, three or four real ales, open fire, flagstones and polished panelling, darts end, garden room restaurant; dogs welcome, attractive village, 11 bedrooms, open all day. *Recommended by Kay and Alistair Butler*

SOUTH ORMSBY TF3675   LN11 8QS
☆ ## Massingberd Arms
Off A16 S of Louth

Small brick-built village local with unusual arched windows, welcoming landlord, three well kept changing ales, short choice of good fresh food including nice Sun lunch, restaurant; no credit cards or dogs; pleasant garden, good Wolds walks, open all day Weds-Sun, closed Mon lunchtime. *Recommended by the Didler*

STAMFORD TF0207   PE9 2PP
Jolly Brewer
Foundry Road

Welcoming old stone-built pub with at least five well kept ales and up to three ciders/perries, good range of wines, reasonably priced food including lunchtime baguettes, nice open fire, regular beer festivals; sports TV. *Recommended by Dave Robbo, Simon and Amanda Southwell*

STAMFORD TF0303   PE9 1EL
Mama Liz's
9a North Street

New Orleans themed bar in former warehouse, real ales and US bottled beers, cocktails, upstairs cajun/creole restaurant (other food available too), regular live music in Voodoo Lounge cellar bar; decked terrace, closed Tues, otherwise open all day. *Recommended by Tony and Maggie Harwood*

STOW SK8881   LN1 2DD
☆ ## Cross Keys
Stow Park Road; B1241 NW of Lincoln

Cosy carpeted bar in traditional pub with big woodburner, straightforward furnishings, some wood panelling, decorative china and country prints, Batemans, Theakstons and a couple of guests, quite a range of bar food in neatly laid dining areas; piped music; children welcome, open all day Sun till 8.30pm, closed Mon lunchtime, near interesting Saxon minster church. *Recommended by Janet and Peter Race, Kay and Alistair Butler*

SURFLEET SEAS END TF2729   PE11 4DH
☆ **Ship**
Reservoir Road; off A16 N of Spalding

Immaculately rebuilt pub just below seawall, woodburner, chesterfields and handsomely
made seating in good-sized civilised bar with old scrubbed tables in open bays, enjoyable
reasonably priced food including OAP and early-bird deals, changing well kept ales such
as Batemans, Marstons and Slaters, good helpful service, upstairs overflow restaurant;
tables on front terrace, boating-view benching and picnic-sets on embankment across
lane, good value bedrooms. *Recommended by Margaret and Peter Staples, Ian Hill, F and M Pryor*

TATTERSHALL THORPE TF2159   LN4 4PE
Blue Bell
Thorpe Road; B1192 Coningsby—Woodhall Spa

Attractive very low-beamed pub said to date from the 13th c and used by the Dambusters,
RAF memorabilia and appropriate real ales such as Tom Woods Bomber County, well
priced pubby bar food, log fires, small dining room; garden tables, bedrooms. *Recommended
by the Didler*

THEDDLETHORPE ALL SAINTS TF4787   LN12 1PB
☆ **Kings Head**
Pub signposted off A1031 N of Maplethorpe; Mill Road

Remote 15th-c thatched pub doing well under good licensees, small low-beamed front bar
with easy chairs by open fire, neatly furnished main bar with plush wall banquettes,
sturdy rustic furniture in dining room, carpets throughout, well above-average fresh local
food including plenty of fish, lunchtime deals, Batemans XB and a guest; pretty side
garden, open all day, closed Mon. *Recommended by Robert Vevers*

THREEKINGHAM TF0836   NG34 0AU
Three Kings
Just off A52 12 miles E of Grantham; Saltersway

Big entrance hall (former coaching inn), beamed and dark panelled bar with coal fire,
pubby furniture including banquettes, compact dining room, good choice of enjoyable
home-made food from baguettes up, Greene King Old Speckled Hen and Timothy Taylors
Landlord, friendly staff; terrace with covered smokers' area, closed Mon. *Recommended by
Maurice and Janet Thorpe, D H Bennett*

WAINFLEET TF5058   PE24 4JE
☆ **Batemans Brewery**
Mill Lane, off A52 via B1195

Circular bar in brewery's ivy-covered windmill tower, Batemans ales in top condition,
czech and belgian beers on tap, ground-floor dining area with cheap food including
baguettes and a few pubby dishes, plenty of old pub games (more outside), lots of
brewery memorabilia and plenty for families to enjoy; entertaining brewery tours and
shop, tables out on terrace and grass, opens 11.30am-3.30pm. *Recommended by the Didler*

WOODHALL SPA TF1963   LN10 6UJ
Village Limits
Stixwould Road

Landlord/chef doing good choice of reasonably priced local food including well liked Sun
lunch, ales such as Batemans, Poachers and Tom Woods in good condition, obliging
service, smallish bar with plush banquettes and aeroplane prints; nine courtyard
bedrooms. *Recommended by Peter and Eleanor Kenyon*

We mention bottled beers and spirits only if there is something unusual about them –
imported belgian real ales, say, or dozens of malt whiskies; so do please let us
know about them in your reports.

ALSO WORTH A VISIT IN NORTHAMPTONSHIRE

Besides the region's top pubs, we recommend the following. Do tell us
what you think of them: **feedback@goodguides.com**

ABTHORPE SP6446 NN12 8QR
☆ New Inn
Signed from A43 at first roundabout S of A5; Silver Street

Traditional partly thatched country local run by cheery farming family, fairly basic
rambling bar with four well kept Hook Norton beers and Stowford Press cider, good pubby
food (not Sun evening) using their own meat and home-grown herbs, beams, stripped
stone and inglenook log fire, darts and table skittles; juke box, TV; children and dogs
welcome, garden tables, bedrooms in converted barn (short walk across fields), open all
day Sun, closed Mon, Tues lunchtime. *Recommended by Peter and Pam Watkins, Christopher Hayle,
Alan Sutton, George Atkinson, David Uren and others*

ARTHINGWORTH SP7581 LE16 8JZ
Bulls Head
Kelmarsh Road, just above A14 by A508 junction; pub signed from A14

Much extended pub with woodburner in big beamed L-shaped bar, popular good value
food from sandwiches to steaks and specials, Thwaites and two guests, cheery attentive
service, dining room, darts and skittles; piped music; disabled access, terrace picnic-sets,
eight bedrooms in separate block, handy for Kelmarsh Hall, open all day Sun and perhaps
in summer. *Recommended by George Atkinson*

ASHBY ST LEDGERS SP5768 CV23 8UN
☆ Olde Coach House
*Main Street; 4 miles from M1 junction 18; A5 S to Kilsby, then A361 S towards
Daventry; village also signed off A5 N of Weedon*

Handsome creeper-clad stone inn, modernised but retaining some original character,
several dining areas, paintwork ranging from white and light beige to purple, flooring
from stripped boards and carpet to red and white tiles, high-backed leather dining chairs,
comfortable sofas and armchairs, hunting pictures, large mirrors, log fire and old stove,
Everards and Wells & Youngs Bombardier, decent wines, pubby food (all day Sun)
including bargain weekday set lunch, friendly relaxed atmosphere; piped music, TV;
children and dogs welcome, picnic-sets in back garden, modern seating in front under
hanging baskets, boules, interesting church nearby, bedrooms, open all day weekends.
Recommended by Rob and Catherine Dunster, P M Newsome, George Atkinson, Mary McSweeney and others

AYNHO SP5133 OX17 3BE
☆ Cartwright
Croughton Road (B4100)

Carefully refurbished 16th-c coaching inn, linked areas with smart contemporary
furniture on wood or tiled floors, cream, maroon and exposed stone walls, well chosen
artwork, leather sofas by big log fire in small bar, Black Sheep and Adnams, nice wines
and coffee, very good food including set deals, competent service from friendly uniformed
staff, daily papers; piped music, TV; children welcome, a few seats in pretty corner of
former coachyard, pleasant village with apricot trees growing against old cottage walls,
bedrooms, good breakfast, open all day. *Recommended by Michael Dandy, David and Anne,
Andy and Jill Kassube, Lois Dyer, Susan and John Douglas, C and R Bromage and others*

AYNHO SP4932 OX17 3BP
☆ Great Western Arms
Aynho Wharf, Station Road; off B4031 W

Attractive old pub with series of linked cosy rooms, fine solid country tables on broad
flagstones, golden stripped-stone walls, warm cream and deep red plasterwork, fresh
flowers and candles, log fires, Hook Norton ales, good wines by the glass, enjoyable pubby

food all day, attentive service, elegant dining area on right, daily papers and magazines, extensive GWR collection including lots of steam locomotive photographs, pool, skittle alley; piped music; children and dogs welcome, white cast-iron furniture in back former stable courtyard, moorings on Oxford Canal and nearby marina, bedrooms (may ask for payment on arrival). *Recommended by Phil and Jane Hodson, Robert Watt, Eithne Dandy, Michael Dandy, George Atkinson, Meg and Colin Hamilton and others*

BADBY SP5659   NN11 3AF
Maltsters
The Green

Stone-built pub refurbished under newish management, long beamed carpeted room with a fire at each end, pine tables and chairs, good choice of enjoyable well priced food from lunchtime ciabattas up, well kept ales such as Black Sheep, Greene King, St Austell and Wells & Youngs, friendly service; a couple of picnic-sets out at front, more in side garden and courtyard, well placed for walks on nearby Knightley Way, bedrooms, open all day. *Recommended by George Atkinson, Laurence Smith, Brian and Anna Marsden, M Walker*

BADBY SP5558   NN11 3AN
Windmill
Village signposted off A361 Daventry—Banbury

Attractive thatched and beamed pub revamped under new licensee; brightened-up bar area with new furniture on re-laid flagstone floor, huge inglenook, modern restaurant, four ales such as Bass, Hoggleys, St Austell and Timothy Taylors, enjoyable varied choice of good value food from lunchtime sandwiches up, friendly welcoming staff; terrace out by attractive village green, nice walks, bedrooms. *Recommended by Roger and Kathy Elkin, George Atkinson, M Walker*

BARNWELL TL0584   PE8 5PH
Montagu Arms
Off A605 S of Oundle, then fork right at Thurning, Hemington sign

Attractive stone-built pub with Adnams, Digfield (brewed in village) and guests, decent ciders, good range of well priced food, cheerful staff, log fire, low beams, flagstones or tile and brick floors, back dining room and conservatory; children welcome, big garden with good play area, pleasant streamside village, nice walks. *Recommended by J Buckby*

BRACKLEY SP5836   NN13 7DP
Crown
Market Place

Smartly refurbished Georgian inn with open fire and some stripped masonry in comfortable carpeted bar overlooking the market square, lots of motor-racing memorabilia, ales such as Bass and Hook Norton, attentive staff, reasonably priced food including some bargain offers, more formal dining room and small lounge; children welcome, dogs in bar (not at eating times), back courtyard leading to popular antiques centre, 26 bedrooms, open all day. *Recommended by George Atkinson*

BRACKLEY HATCH SP6441   NN13 5TX
Green Man
A43 NE of Brackley (tricky exit)

Big Chef & Brewer dining pub on busy dual carriageway near Silverstone, comfortable old-look beamed lounge area, conservatory overlooking road, big family restaurant, wide range of all-day food generously served, changing ales such as Adnams, Greene King and Wadworths, good wines and coffee, cheerful staff, daily papers, log fire; pervasive piped music, games; tables on lawn, bedrooms in Premier Lodge behind, open all day. *Recommended by R C Vincent, Michael Dandy, Hilary Thorpe, George Atkinson*

You can send reports directly to us at **feedback@goodguides.com**

BUCKBY WHARF SP6066   NN6 7PW
☆ New Inn
A5 N of Weedon

Good range of tasty quickly served pubby food from good baguettes to popular 'Desperate Dan Pie', friendly staff, well kept Frog Island, Hook Norton and guests, good short choice of wines, several rooms radiating from central servery including a small dining room with nice fire, games area with table skittles; TVs, games machine; children welcome, dogs outside only, pleasant terrace with heated smokers' area, by busy Grand Union Canal lock, popular with boaters, open all day. *Recommended by George Atkinson*

BUGBROOKE SP6756   NN7 3QB
Wharf Inn
The Wharf; off A5 S of Weedon

Super spot by Grand Union Canal, plenty of tables on big lawn with moorings, large water-view restaurant, bar/lounge with small informal raised eating area either side, lots of stripped brickwork, good food using local organic produce including Sun roasts, prompt cheerful service, well kept local Frog Island and Greene King IPA, lots of wines by the glass, woodburner; piped music; children welcome, dogs in garden only, disabled facilities, heated smokers' shelter, open all day. *Recommended by Mary McSweeney, George Atkinson, Gerry and Rosemary Dobson*

BULWICK SP9694   NN17 3DY
☆ Queens Head
Off A43 Kettering—Duddington

New licensees for this lovely 600-year-old stone cottage – news please; partly beamed two-room bar, small fire at each end, has had up to five changing ales and good food, spruced-up dining room; decked terrace, attractive village with interesting church. *Recommended by Mike and Sue Loseby*

CHACOMBE SP4943   OX17 2JR
George & Dragon
Handy for M40 junction 11, via A361; Silver Street

17th-c pub with beams, flagstones, panelling and bare stone walls, two inglenook woodburners, even a glass-covered well, good popular food (not Sun evening) from lunchtime sandwiches and traditional choices up including vegetarian options, Everards and a guest ale, several wines by the glass, decent coffee, good service, two restaurant areas, darts; piped music, no dogs; children welcome, terrace picnic-sets, pretty village with interesting church, open all day. *Recommended by William Ruxton, George Atkinson*

CHAPEL BRAMPTON SP7366   NN6 8BA
☆ Brampton Halt
Pitsford Road, off A5199 N of Northampton

Well laid out pub on Northampton & Lamport Railway (which is open at weekends), large restaurant, railway memorabilia and train theme throughout, wide choice of enjoyable generous food (smaller helpings available) from sandwiches up including Sun roasts, meal deals Mon-Thurs, well kept Adnams, Fullers London Pride, Sharps Doom Bar and a guest, good wine choice, cheerful service, games and TV in bar; piped music; children welcome, lots of tables in big garden with awnings and heaters, summer barbecues, pretty views over small lake, Nene Valley Way walks. *Recommended by Eithne Dandy, Michael Dandy, George Atkinson, Revd R P Tickle, Gerry and Rosemary Dobson*

CHAPEL BRAMPTON SP7366   NN6 8AE
Spencer Arms
Northampton Road

Comfortable Chef & Brewer family dining pub, plenty of stripped tables in long timber-divided L-shaped bar, good choice of sensibly priced food all day, Adnams, Fullers, Greene King and a guest ale, several wines by the glass, friendly service, beams, two log fires, knick-knacks, daily papers; soft piped music; tables outside, open all day. *Recommended by R L Mobbs, S Holder*

CHARLTON SP5235   OX17 3DP
Rose & Crown
Main Street

Cosy well run thatched pub in nice village, good choice of enjoyable local food (not Mon) from bar snacks up including lunchtime bargains (Tues-Sat), changing ales, friendly prompt service, stripped stone, well spaced pale wood tables and chairs, inglenook log fires, picnic-sets outside, wisteria arbour. *Recommended by Sir Nigel Foulkes, M J Winterton*

CLIPSTON SP7181   LE16 9RS
Old Red Lion
The Green

Unpretentious little village-green pub with locals' bar and log-fire lounge, well kept Wells & Youngs ales and a guest from the central servery, decent home-made bar food including sandwiches and snacks, small back dining room; children welcome. *Recommended by Gerry and Rosemary Dobson, R T and J C Moggridge*

COLLYWESTON SK9902   PE9 3PQ
☆ # Collyweston Slater
The Drove (A43)

Roomy main-road dining pub with enjoyable bar and restaurant food (not Sun evening), surprisingly contemporary with brown leather easy chairs and sofas, smart modern two-part formal dining room (with log fire) and two or three more informal areas, one with a raised stove in dividing wall, beams, stripped stone and mix of dark flagstones, bare boards and carpeting, Everards ales and decent wines, friendly service; piped music; children welcome, teak seats on flagstoned terrace, bedrooms, open all day; may be recent change of tenancy. *Recommended by Jeff and Wendy Williams, Phil and Jane Hodson, Roy Bromell, Jeremy King*

COSGROVE SP7942   MK19 7JD
Barley Mow
The Stocks

Old village pub by Grand Union Canal, up to four well kept Everards ales, good value pubby food and blackboard specials, cheerful service, lounge/dining area with dark furniture, small public bar, pool, table football and skittles; children welcome, tables on terrace and on lawn down to canal, open all day. *Recommended by Gerry and Rosemary Dobson*

COSGROVE SP7843   MK19 7BE
Navigation
Castlethorpe Road

Lovely canalside setting, attractive open-plan bar up steps with open fire, lots of canal prints and memorabilia, friendly helpful service, good choice of beers and wines, popular well presented food including some interesting choices and good value Sun roasts, live music Fri; can be very busy weekends and school holidays; children welcome, lots of tables out by water, moorings. *Recommended by Dennis and Doreen Haward*

EASTON ON THE HILL TF0104   PE9 3NS
Exeter Arms
Stamford Road

Renovated 18th-c pub reopened in 2010 after long closure; country-feel bar in pastel green with traditional furniture on stone floor, well kept Ufford ales and a guest from panelled bar, Aspall's cider, wide choice of good food (must book weekends) including pizzas and pub favourites, friendly service, restaurant and new orangery dining area; piped music; split-level terrace, paddock, six bedrooms, open all day, closed Sun evening. *Recommended by G Jennings, Michael and Jenny Back*

EYDON SP5450   NN11 3PG

☆ **Royal Oak**

Lime Avenue; village signed off A361 Daventry—Banbury, and from B4525

Interestingly laid-out 300-year-old ironstone inn, some lovely period features including fine flagstone floors and leaded windows, cosy snug on right with cushioned benches built into alcoves, seats in bow window, cottagey pictures and inglenook log fire, long corridor-like central bar linking three other small characterful rooms, Fullers, Hook Norton and a guest, pubby food (takeaway only Mon evening), lots of tapas, friendly staff, table skittles in old stable; piped music; children and dogs welcome, terrace seating (some under cover), closed Mon lunchtime. *Recommended by Christopher Hayle, Rob and Catherine Dunster, Alan Sutton, Jenny and Peter Lowater*

FARTHINGSTONE SP6155   NN12 8EZ

☆ **Kings Arms**

Off A5 SE of Daventry; village signed from Litchborough

Gargoyle-embellished 18th-c stone country pub with cosy flagstoned bar, homely sofas and armchairs near entrance, whisky-water jugs hanging from beams, lots of pictures and decorative plates, huge log fire, three changing beers, country wines, pubby food; no credit cards, note the interesting newspaper-influenced décor in the outside gents'; children and dogs welcome, lovely garden full of little nooks, seats on tranquil terrace with hanging baskets and plant-filled tractor tyres, picturesque village, good walks including Knightley Way, closed Mon and weekday lunchtimes. *Recommended by JJW, CMW, Adrian Johnson, Anne Edmonds*

GAYTON SP7054   NN7 3HD

Queen Victoria

High Street

Four comfortable neat areas off central bar, Wells & Youngs and occasional guests, good wine choice, enjoyable food (not Sun evening) from snacks to blackboard specials including good value Sun lunch, light panelling, beams, lots of pictures, books and shelves of china, inglenook woodburner; piped music, pool, games machines, Tues quiz night; bedrooms, closed Mon. *Recommended by Alan Sutton, Gerry and Rosemary Dobson*

GRAFTON REGIS SP7546   NN12 7SR

☆ **White Hart**

A508 S of Northampton

Good pubby food (not Sun evening) including fine range of baguettes and popular well priced Sun roasts in thatched dining pub with several linked rooms, Greene King ales, good wines by the glass, friendly helpful staff coping well when busy, african grey parrot (can be very vocal), restaurant with open fire and separate menu; piped music; good-sized garden (food not usually served there) with terrace tables, closed Mon. *Recommended by George Atkinson, Howard and Margaret Buchanan*

GREAT HOUGHTON SP7959   NN4 7AT

Old Cherry Tree

Cherry Tree Lane; No Through Road off A428 just before White Hart

Thatched village pub with low beams, stripped stone, panelling and open fires, enjoyable food from lunchtime snacks up, prompt friendly service, well kept Wells & Youngs and occasional guests, steps up to restaurant; garden tables. *Recommended by Gerry and Rosemary Dobson*

GREAT OXENDON SP7383   LE16 8NA

☆ **George**

A508 S of Market Harborough

Elegant 16th-c pub with emphasis on dining but with a convivial bar, well kept Adnams, Timothy Taylors and a guest, lots of wines by the glass, good often interesting bar food from sandwiches up including fixed-price menus, friendly efficient staff, green leatherette bucket chairs around small tables, brown panelled dado with wallpaper or dark painted walls above, big log fire, entrance lobby with easy chairs and former inn sign, carpeted conservatory; piped easy-listening music; children welcome, big shrub-sheltered garden, bedrooms, closed evenings on Sun and bank holidays. *Recommended by R T and J C Moggridge, O K Smyth, MDN, Rob and Catherine Dunster, Jeff and Wendy Williams, Nigel and Sue Foster and others*

GREENS NORTON SP6649   NN12 8BA
Butchers Arms
High Street

Comfortable welcoming village pub, four well kept changing ales, enjoyable straightforward food from sandwiches and pizzas up, reasonable prices, separate bar and games room with pool, darts and skittles; piped and some live music; children and dogs allowed, disabled access, picnic-sets outside, play area, pretty village near Grafton Way walks. *Recommended by Mark Semke, Ken Savage, George Atkinson, David Uren*

HACKLETON SP8054   NN7 2AD
White Hart
B526 SE of Northampton

Comfortably traditional 18th-c country pub, wide choice of enjoyable generous food (smaller helpings available) from sandwiches up including early evening bargains, good friendly staff, Fullers London Pride, Greene King IPA and a guest, decent choice of other drinks, good coffee, dining area up steps with flame-effect fire, stripped stone, beamery and brickwork, illuminated well, brasses and artefacts, split-level flagstoned bar with log fire, pool and hood skittles, curry/quiz night Tues; quiet piped music; children (not in bar after 5pm) and dogs welcome, disabled access, garden with picnic-sets and goal posts, open all day. *Recommended by Gerry and Rosemary Dobson*

HARRINGTON SP7780   NN6 9NU
Tollemache Arms
High Street; off A508 S of Market Harborough

Pretty thatched Tudor pub in lovely quiet ironstone village, very low ceilings in compact bar with log fire and in pleasant partly stripped-stone dining room, enjoyable food from generous sandwiches up, well kept ales such as Elgoods, Grainstore, Great Oakley and Wells & Youngs, friendly staff, table skittles; children welcome, nice back garden with country views. *Recommended by George Atkinson, Mark Eliot, R T and J C Moggridge, Eliot Cram*

HARRINGWORTH SP9197   NN17 3AF
☆ ## White Swan
Seaton Road; village SE of Uppingham, signed from A6003, A47 and A43

Handsome former coaching inn with imposing central gable, traditional furnishings, open fire dividing bar and two cosy dining areas, pictures of World War II aircraft at nearby Spanhoe Airfield, old village photos, nice hand-crafted oak counter (sweets in old-fashioned jars behind), Adnams and a couple of guests, enjoyable food, good smiling service, darts and board games; piped music; children welcome, tables on partly covered terrace, pretty hanging baskets, not far from magnificent 82-arch viaduct spanning the River Welland, bedrooms, closed Sun evening, Mon lunchtime. *Recommended by Brigette Lepora, Tracey and Stephen Groves*

KETTERING SP8778   NN16 0BU
Alexandra Arms
Victoria Street

Friendly real ale pub, with up to 14 changing quickly, hundreds each year, also Julian Church ales brewed in cellar, may be sandwiches, games bar with hood skittles; back terrace, open all day (from 2pm weekdays). *Recommended by the Didler, P Dawn*

If you know a pub's ever open all day, please tell us.

KETTERING SP8577   NN15 7RH
Trading Post
Off A14 junction 8; Bignal Court

Big modern Marstons pub with wide choice of good value food from snacks up including daily carvery, their ales (usually a mild) and plenty of wines by the glass, friendly helpful staff; children welcome, tables outside, play area, open all day. *Recommended by R C Vincent*

KILSBY SP5671   CV23 8YE
☆ George
2.5 miles from M1 junction 18: A428 towards Daventry, left on to A5 – pub off on right at roundabout

Popular pub, handy for motorway, with friendly hard-working landlady, proper old-fashioned public bar, wood-panelled lounge with plush banquettes and coal-effect gas stove opening into smarter area with solidly comfortable furnishings, four well kept ales, splendid range of malt whiskies, good value pubby food, speedy service; darts, free-play pool tables, TV, quiz nights; children welcome if dining, dogs in bar, garden picnic-sets, bedrooms. *Recommended by Rob and Catherine Dunster, R T and J C Moggridge, David and Sue Atkinson and others*

KISLINGBURY SP6959   NN7 4AG
☆ Cromwell Cottage
High Street

Sizeable low-ceilinged M&B family dining pub, informal lounge seating, open fire, separate smart bistro dining area with candles on tables, wide choice of good popular food including set choices and specials (booking advised), well kept Adnams, Black Sheep and Wells & Youngs Bombardier, good service from neat cheerful staff. *Recommended by D C T and E A Frewer, George Atkinson, Roger Braithwaite, Gerry and Rosemary Dobson, Alan Sutton*

KISLINGBURY SP6959   NN7 4AQ
Olde Red Lion
High Street, off A45 W of Northampton

Roomy renovated 19th-c stone-fronted pub, good freshly cooked bar and restaurant food, well kept Timothy Taylors ales and a guest, friendly helpful service, beams, woodburners and open fire, events including summer beer festival; piped music and some live, TV, no dogs; suntrap back terrace with marquee, barbecues, two bedrooms, closed all Sun, Mon and Tues lunchtime. *Recommended by Robin M Corlett, Michael Dandy, Rose Howell*

LITTLE BRINGTON SP6663   NN7 4HS
☆ Saracens Head
4.5 miles from M1 junction 16, first right off A45 to Daventry; also signed off A428; Main Street

Friendly old pub with enjoyable reasonably priced food from interesting baguettes and wraps up, well kept real ales such as Batemans, Greene King and Timothy Taylors, roomy U-shaped lounge with good log fire, flagstones, chesterfields and lots of old prints, book-lined dining room; plenty of tables in neat back garden, handy for Althorp House and Holdenby House. *Recommended by Rob and Catherine Dunster, George Atkinson, Gerry and Rosemary Dobson*

LITTLE HARROWDEN SP8671   NN9 5BH
Lamb
Orlingbury Road/Kings Lane – off A509 or A43 S of Kettering

Two-level lounge with log fire and brasses on 17th-c beams, dining area, good bargain food, well kept changing ales, short sensibly priced wine list, good coffee, games bar with darts, hood skittles and machines; piped music; children welcome, small raised terrace and garden, delightful village. *Recommended by Howard and Margaret Buchanan*

LITTLE HOUGHTON SP8059   NN7 1AB
Four Pears
Bedford Road, off A428 E of Northampton

Former Red Lion refurbished in contemporary style, three well kept changing ales, several wines by the glass, fresh coffee, enjoyable food (not Sun evening) from open ciabattas and light dishes up, good-sized bar, comfortable lounge with woodburner, separate restaurant; spacious outside area, open all day. *Recommended by Gerry and Rosemary Dobson*

LOWICK SP9780   NN14 3BH
☆ Snooty Fox
Off A6116 Corby—Raunds

Spacious and attractively reworked 16th-c stone-built pub, leather sofas and chairs, beams and stripped stonework, log fire in huge fireplace, good food from open kitchen, well kept ales, nice coffee, good friendly service, board games; piped music; children and dogs welcome, picnic-sets on front grass, play area, open all day. *Recommended by Ryta Lyndley, Mrs Joyce Smith, Michael Sargent, Alan Sutton, Cam Smith*

MAIDWELL SP7477   NN6 9JA
☆ Stags Head
Harborough Road (A508 N of Northampton)

Comfortable dining pub with log fire in pubby part by bar, extensive eating areas, enjoyable pubby food including OAP two-course lunch and other deals, helpful friendly staff and cheery locals, well kept ales such as Batemans, Black Sheep and Church End, good choice of other drinks; quiet piped music; disabled facilities, picnic-sets on back terrace (dogs on leads allowed here), good-sized sheltered sloping garden beyond, bedrooms, not far from splendid Palladian Kelmarsh Hall and park. *Recommended by Michael Tack, Mr and Mrs D J Nash, John Saul, Gerry and Rosemary Dobson, Jeff and Wendy Williams, George Atkinson and others*

NASSINGTON TL0696   PE8 6QB
Queens Head
Station Road

Smartly refurbished bar/bistro and separate restaurant, wide choice of enjoyable good value food using local ingredients, pleasant helpful uniformed staff, nice choice of wines by the glass, changing real ales, good coffee; pretty garden by River Nene, delightful village, nine chalet bedrooms. *Recommended by Phil and Jane Hodson*

RINGSTEAD SP9875   NN14 4DW
Axe & Compass
Carlow Road

Extended stone-built village pub with popular good value food including lunchtime deals, Marstons-related ales, open fire in lounge; garden. *Recommended by Ryta Lyndley*

RUSHDEN SP9566   NN10 0AW
Station Bar
Station Approach

Not a pub, part of station HQ of Rushden Historical Transport Society (non-members can sign in), restored in 1940s/60s style, with Fullers, Oakham and guests, tea and coffee, friendly staff, filled rolls (perhaps some hot dishes), gas lighting, enamel signs, old-fangled furnishings; authentic waiting room with piano, also museum and summer steam-ups; open all day Sat, closed weekday lunchtimes. *Recommended by the Didler, P Dawn*

> Though we don't usually mention it in the text, most pubs now provide
> coffee or tea – so it's always worth asking.

SLIPTON SP9579   NN14 3AR
☆ Samuel Pepys
Off A6116 at first roundabout N of A14 junction, towards Twywell and Slipton

Smartly reworked old stone pub, long gently modern bar with heavy low beams and log fire, great central pillar, area with squashy leather seats around low tables, six changing ales including local Digfield, interesting reasonably priced wines, enjoyable food from good value sandwiches up, friendly efficient service, dining room extending into roomy conservatory with country views; piped music; children welcome, dogs in bar, wheelchair access, well laid-out sheltered garden including heated terrace, open all day weekends.
Recommended by Michael and Jenny Back and others

STAVERTON SP5461   NN11 6JH
Countryman
Daventry Road (A425)

Beamed and carpeted dining pub under enthusiastic new landlord, wide choice of reasonably priced food from sandwiches and baguettes up, Fullers London Pride and two changing guests such as local Hoggleys, friendly attentive staff; piped music; children welcome, disabled access, some tables outside and in small garden. *Recommended by George Atkinson*

STOKE BRUERNE SP7449   NN12 7SB
Boat
3.5 miles from M1 junction 15 – A508 towards Stony Stratford, then signed on right; Bridge Road

Old-world flagstoned bar in picturesque canalside spot by restored lock, more modern central-pillared back bar and bistro, half a dozen Marstons-related ales and local Frog Island, fairly standard food from baguettes up, friendly efficient young staff, comfortable upstairs bookable restaurant with more upmarket menu, shop for boaters (nice ice-creams); piped music, can get busy in summer especially at weekends and parking nearby is difficult; welcomes dogs and children (local school in for lunch from midday), disabled facilities, tables out by towpath opposite British Waterways Museum, boat trips, open all day. *Recommended by Gerry and Rosemary Dobson, George Atkinson, Brian and Anna Marsden, Peter Lee*

STOKE BRUERNE SP7449   NN12 7SD
Navigation
E side of bridge

Large Marstons canalside pub with changing selection of their well kept beers, quite a few wines by the glass, wide choice of good fairly priced pubby food, friendly busy young staff, several levels and cosy corners, sturdy wood furniture, separate family room, pub games; piped music (outside too) and some live jazz; wheelchair access, plenty of tables out overlooking the water, big play area, open all day. *Recommended by Brian and Anna Marsden, Michael Tack, Ross Balaam*

STOKE DOYLE TL0286   PE8 5TG
☆ Shuckburgh Arms
Village signed (down Stoke Hill) from SW edge of Oundle

Attractively reworked 17th-c pub in quiet hamlet, four traditional rooms with some modern touches, low black beams in bowed ceiling, pictures on pastel walls, lots of pale tables on wood or carpeted floors, stylish art deco seats and elegant dining chairs, stove in inglenook, Digfield and Timothy Taylors from granite-top bar, enjoyable food; faint piped music; children welcome, garden with decked area and play frame, bedrooms in separate modern block, closed Sun evening. *Recommended by Robin M Corlett*

SULGRAVE SP5545   OX17 2SA
☆ Star
Manor Road; E of Banbury, signed off B4525

Creeper-covered farmhouse, small bar with pews, cushioned window seats and wall benches, flagstones by inglenook (red carpet elsewhere), Hook Norton ales, pubby food, separate dining room with motor-racing theme; children and dogs welcome, seats out at front and in back garden, short walk to Sulgrave Manor (ancestral home of George Washington), four bedrooms, open all day weekends. *Recommended by Nigel and Sue Foster, Malcolm and Jo Hart, Dennis and Doreen Haward, G Jennings, Peter Martin*

THORNBY SP6675   NN6 8SJ
Red Lion
Welford Road; A5199 Northampton—Leicester

Friendly old country pub with half a dozen well kept changing ales, good well priced home-made food (not Mon), beams and log fire, back dining area; children and dogs welcome, garden picnic-sets, open all day weekends when can be busy. *Recommended by Gerry and Rosemary Dobson*

THORPE MANDEVILLE SP5344   OX17 2EX
☆ **Three Conies**
Off B4525 E of Banbury

Attractive welcoming 17th-c pub with wide choice of food from good value sandwiches up, well kept Hook Norton ales including a bargain beer brewed for the pub (even cheaper Fri afternoon), beamed bare-boards bar with some stripped stone, mix of old dining tables, three good log fires, large dining room, pub cat called Pepper; piped music; children and dogs welcome, disabled facilities, tables out in front and behind on decking and lawn, open all day. *Recommended by Nigel and Sue Foster, George Atkinson*

THORPE WATERVILLE TL0281   NN14 3ED
Fox
A605 Thrapston—Oundle

Extended and redecorated stone-built pub, emphasis on chef/landlord's enjoyable food including Sun roasts, well kept Wells & Youngs ales from central bar, several wines by the glass, friendly attentive staff, nice fire, light modern dining area; piped music; children welcome, small garden with play area, open all day. *Recommended by George Atkinson, Iain Akhurst*

TURWESTON SP6037   NN13 5JX
Stratton Arms
E of crossroads in village; pub itself just inside Buckinghamshire

Friendly chatty local in picturesque village, five well kept ales, good choice of other drinks, enjoyable reasonably priced food (not Sun evening, Mon), low ceilings, log fires, restaurant; TV, games machine; children and dogs welcome, good-sized garden by the Great Ouse, barbecues and play area. *Recommended by Michael Tack, Nancy*

WALGRAVE SP8072   NN6 9PN
Royal Oak
Zion Hill, off A43 Northampton—Kettering

Welcoming old stone-built village local, up to five well kept changing ales, decent wines, good value food (not Sun evening) including some unusual choices and lunchtime deals, friendly efficient service, long three-part carpeted beamed bar, small lounge, restaurant extension behind; children welcome, small garden with play area, open all day Sun. *Recommended by Barry Collett, Gerry and Rosemary Dobson*

WOODNEWTON TL0394   PE8 5EB
White Swan
Main Street

Small village pub/restaurant under newish management, Digfield beers, good food with a mediterranean twist including competitively priced set lunch, pleasant service. *Recommended by Roy Bromell*

YARDLEY HASTINGS SP8656
Rose & Crown
Just off A428 Bedford—Northampton

NN7 1EX

Spacious 18th-c pub in pretty village, flagstones, beams, stripped stonework and quiet corners, step up to big comfortable family dining room, flowers on tables, enjoyable popular food, six real ales, decent range of wines and soft drinks, newspapers; piped and live music; dogs welcome, picnic-sets in small courtyard and good-sized garden, open from 5pm Mon-Thurs, all day Fri, Sat, closed Sun evening. *Recommended by JJW, CMW, James Meikle*

ALSO WORTH A VISIT IN NOTTINGHAMSHIRE

Besides the region's top pubs, we recommend the following. Do tell us what you think of them: **feedback@goodguides.com**

AWSWORTH SK4844
Gate
Main Street, via A6096 off A610 Nuthall—Eastwood bypass

NG16 2RN

Friendly three-room Victorian local taken over recently and now a free house, up to five well kept ales including Blue Monkey and Burton Bridge, cosy bar, coal fire in lounge, small pool room; tables out in front, skittle alley, near site of once-famous railway viaduct, open all day (till 1am Fri, Sat). *Recommended by the Didler, Yvonne and Rob Warhurst*

BAGTHORPE SK4751
Dixies Arms
A608 towards Eastwood off M1 junction 27, right on B600 via Sandhill Road, left into School Road; Lower Bagthorpe

NG16 5HF

Friendly unspoilt 18th-c beamed and tiled-floor local with D H Lawrence connections, well kept Greene King Abbot, Theakstons Best and a guest, no food, good fire in small part-panelled parlour's fine fireplace, entrance bar with tiny snug, longer narrow room with toby jugs, darts and dominoes, busy weekends with live music and Sun quiz; children and dogs (on leads) welcome, good big garden with play area and football pitch, own pigeon, gun and morris dancing clubs, open all day. *Recommended by the Didler*

BEESTON SK5236
Crown
Church Street

NG9 1FY

Bought and sensitively refurbished by Everards, real ale enthusiast landlord serving up to 14 (some keenly priced), also real ciders, perry and good choice of bottled beers (regular beer festivals), no hot food but fresh cobs and other snacks available; front snug and bar with quarry-tiled floor, carpeted parlour with padded wall seats, Victorian décor and new polished bar in lounge, beams, panelling, bric-a-brac, old red telephone box; terrace tables, open all day. *Recommended by the Didler, MP, Steve Bakewell*

BEESTON SK5336
 ### Victoria
Dovecote Lane, backing on to railway station

NG9 1JG

Genuine down-to-earth all-rounder attracting good mix of customers, up to 15 real ales (beer festivals Jan, Easter, end July, Oct), two farm ciders, 120 malt whiskies and 30 wines by the glass, good value food (half the menu is vegetarian), efficient service, three fairly simple unfussy rooms with original long narrow layout, solid furnishings, bare boards and stripped woodwork, stained-glass windows, open fires, newspapers and board games, live music (Sun, Mon evening Oct-May); children welcome till 8pm, dogs in bar, seats out on covered heated area overlooking railway platform (trains pass just a few feet away), limited parking, open all day. *Recommended by David Eberlin, John Read, Maurice Ricketts, the Didler, MP, Andy Lickfold and others*

BINGHAM SK7039   NG13 8AF
☆ Horse & Plough
Off A52; Long Acre

Former 1818 Methodist chapel with low beams, flagstones and stripped brick, prints and old brewery memorabilia, comfortable open-plan seating including pews, well kept Caledonian Deuchars IPA, Fullers London Pride, Theakstons XB and three guests (tasters offered), real cider, good wine choice, enjoyable reasonably priced home-made weekday bar food, popular upstairs grill room (Tues-Sat evenings and Sun lunch) with polished boards, hand-painted murals and open kitchen; piped music; children and dogs welcome, disabled facilities, open all day. *Recommended by the Didler, MP, P Dawn, Jack Matthew and others*

BRAMCOTE SK5037   NG9 3HH
White Lion
Just off A52 W of Nottingham; Town Street

Small homely open-plan pub with well kept Greene King ales from bar serving two split-level adjoining rooms, pubby food including bargain Sun roast, darts and dominoes; tables in attractive garden behind. *Recommended by MP*

BUNNY SK5829   NG11 6QT
☆ Rancliffe Arms
Loughborough Road (A60 S of Nottingham)

Substantial early 18th-c former coaching inn reworked with emphasis on linked dining areas, upscale food from enterprising sandwich range to adventurous dishes, popular carvery (Mon evening, Weds, Sat and Sun), friendly efficient service, chunky country chairs around mixed tables on flagstones or carpet, well kept Marstons ales in comfortable log-fire bar with sofas and armchairs; children welcome, decking outside, open all Fri-Sun. *Recommended by Gerry and Rosemary Dobson, John and Sylvia Harrop, Kay and Alistair Butler, P Dawn and others*

CAR COLSTON SK7242   NG13 8JE
Royal Oak
The Green, off Tenman Lane (off A46 not far from A6097 junction)

Helpful licensees doing good, well priced, traditional food (not Sun evening) in biggish 19th-c pub opposite one of England's largest village greens, three or more well kept Marstons-related ales, decent choice of wines by the glass, woodburner in lounge bar with tables set for eating, public bar with unusual barrel-vaulted brick ceiling, spotless housekeeping; children welcome, picnic-sets on spacious back lawn, heated smokers' den, camping, open all day weekends, closed Mon lunchtime. *Recommended by Phil and Jane Hodson, Alan Bowker, Sarah Greenway, Richard and Jean Green, David Glynne-Jones, P Dawn and others*

CAUNTON SK7459   NG23 6AE
☆ Caunton Beck
Newark Road

Cleverly reconstructed low-beamed dining pub made to look old using original timbers and reclaimed oak, scrubbed pine tables and country-kitchen chairs, rag-finished paintwork, some clever lighting, open fire, Batemans, Black Sheep and Marstons, over two dozen wines by the glass, good popular food from breakfast onwards, decent coffee and daily papers, helpful friendly staff; children welcome, dogs in bar, seats on flowery terrace, open all day from 8am. *Recommended by James Stretton, Jeremy King, Ian and Nita Cooper, Richard Cole, Pat and Stewart Gordon, John Prescott and others*

Tipping is not normal for bar meals, and not usually expected.

COLLINGHAM SK8361   NG23 7LA
Kings Head
High Street

Gently upscale modern pub/restaurant behind unpretentious Georgian façade, two well kept changing ales from long steel bar, courteous staff, food from baguettes to good restaurant dishes with unusual touches, light and airy dining area with pine furniture on polished boards; children welcome, no dogs, disabled access, garden tables, open all day Sun. *Recommended by David and Ruth Hollands*

COTGRAVE SK6435   NG12 3HQ
Rose & Crown
Main Road, off A46 SE of Nottingham

Friendly and comfortable village pub, good value generous food all day including mid-week and early evening bargains, more elaborate evening and weekend dishes, young helpful staff, three changing ales, good wine and soft drinks' choice, log fires, newspapers, back eating area with fresh flowers and candles; piped music, Sun quiz; children welcome, garden picnic-sets. *Recommended by JJW, CMW, P Dawn, David Glynne-Jones*

EASTWOOD SK4846   NG16 2DN
Foresters Arms
Main Street, Newthorpe

Friendly cosy local with well kept Greene King ales, darts, dominoes and table skittles, open fire, old local photographs, lounge with weekend organ sing-along; TV; nice garden. *Recommended by the Didler*

EDINGLEY SK6655   NG22 8BE
Old Reindeer
Off A617 Newark—Mansfield at Kirklington; Main Street

Refurbished roadside pub dating from the 18th- c, well liked food (all day weekends) including good fish and chips and bargain carvery, efficient service, well kept Jennings ales, front lounge bar with pool in side area, comfortable back restaurant; piped music; children and dogs welcome, attractive garden, four bedrooms, open all day. *Recommended by David Errington, D S Thrall*

EDWINSTOWE SK6266   NG21 9QA
Forest Lodge
Church Street

Friendly 17th-c inn with enjoyable home-made food in pubby bar or restaurant, good service, well kept ales from Crouch Vale, Kelham Island and others, log fire; children welcome, 13 comfortable bedrooms, handy for Sherwood Forest, open all day. *Recommended by Derek and Sylvia Stephenson*

ELKESLEY SK6875   DN22 8AJ
Robin Hood
Just off A1 Newark—Blyth; High Street

Neat dining pub with good food including mid-week deals, friendly efficient staff, Wells & Youngs Bitter, dark furnishings on patterned carpets, yellow walls; piped music, TV and pool in bar on left; children and dogs welcome, picnic-sets and play area, closed Sun evening, Mon lunchtime. *Recommended by Derek and Sylvia Stephenson, Gordon and Margaret Ormondroyd*

FARNDON SK7652   NG24 3SX
☆ Boathouse
Off A46 SW of Newark; keep on towards river – pub in North End, just past Britannia

Big-windowed contemporary bar-restaurant overlooking the River Trent, emphasis decidedly on food but with Caythorpe and Marstons ales from stylish counter, good choice of wines, main area indeed reminiscent of a boathouse with high ceiling trusses supporting bare ducting and scant modern decoration, second dining area broadly similar, modern cooking and some pubby dishes, too, served by neat young staff; piped and live music; children welcome, wicker chairs around teak tables on terrace, open all day. *Recommended by Michael and Maggie Betton*

GRANBY SK7436 NG13 9PN

☆ **Marquis of Granby**

Off A52 E of Nottingham; Dragon Street

Popular, stylish and friendly 18th-c pub in attractive Vale of Belvoir village, tap for Brewsters with their ales and interesting guests from chunky yew bar counter, decent home-made food Fri evening (fish and chips) to Sun lunchtime, two small comfortable rooms with broad flagstones, some low beams and striking wallpaper, open fire; children and dogs welcome, open from 4pm Mon-Fri, all day weekends. *Recommended by the Didler*

HALAM SK6754 NG22 8AE

Waggon & Horses

Off A612 in Southwell centre, via Halam Road

Under new management and now more pubby with less emphasis on food – news please; low-ceilinged open-plan interior with several cosy areas formed by layout of original 17th-c building, wood or tiled floors; a few roadside picnic-sets. *Recommended by anon*

HARBY SK8870 NG23 7EB

☆ **Bottle & Glass**

High Street; village signed off A57 W of Lincoln

Civilised dining pub with pair of bay-windowed front bars, attractive pubby furnishings, lots of bright cushions on built-in wall benches, arts-and-crafts chairs, dark flagstones and red walls, log fire, splendid range of wines (big vineyard map of Côte de Beaune in left-hand bar), Black Sheep and Titanic beers, good country cooking all day including a set menu, friendly attentive service, small area with squashy sofas and armchairs and more formal restaurant; children welcome, dogs allowed in bar, modern wrought-iron furniture on back terrace, picnic-sets on grass beyond. *Recommended by Peter and Eleanor Kenyon, David and Ruth Hollands, Adam Jackson, Sue Kinder*

HOVERINGHAM SK6946 NG14 7GR

☆ **Reindeer**

Main Street

Friendly beamed pub with intimate bar and busy restaurant (best to book), good home-made food from pubby things to enterprising dishes, lunchtime set deals and vegan choices too, Castle Rock, Caythorpe and guests, good wines by the glass, daily papers, open fires; children welcome, seats outside overlooking cricket pitch, open all day weekends, closed lunchtimes Mon and Tues. *Recommended by the Didler, Graham and Jan Pigott, David and Sue Atkinson*

JACKSDALE NG16 5HY

Corner Pin

Palmerston Street, Westwood; off B6016

Traditional old side-street local, two rooms with coal fires, old-fashioned simple furnishings, own-brew beers (microbrewery in former skittle alley) and six guests, real cider, pool and table skittles, friendly relaxed atmosphere; sports TV, not much street parking; open all day weekends, from 1pm Mon-Fri. *Recommended by the Didler*

KIMBERLEY SK4944 NG16 2NR

☆ **Nelson & Railway**

Station Road; handy for M1 junction 26 via A610

Comfortable beamed Victorian pub with well kept Greene King ales and guests, mix of Edwardian-looking furniture, brewery prints (was tap for defunct H&H Brewery) and railway signs, dining extension, traditional games including alley and table skittles; juke box, games machine; children and dogs allowed, nice front and back gardens, good value bedrooms, open all day. *Recommended by the Didler*

KIMBERLEY SK5044 NG16 2NB
Stag
Nottingham Road

Friendly 16th-c traditional local kept spotless by devoted landlady, two cosy rooms, small central counter and corridor, low beams, dark panelling and settles, vintage working slot machines, old Shipstones Brewery photographs, good range of ales including Adnams, Black Sheep, Marstons and Timothy Taylors (May beer festival), no food; attractive back garden with play area, opens 5pm (1.30 Sat, 12 Sun). *Recommended by the Didler*

LAMBLEY SK6345 NG4 4QB
Woodlark
Church Street

Welcoming and interestingly laid-out village local, neatly furnished bare-brick beamed bar, careful extension into next house giving comfortable lounge/dining area, popular good value freshly made food, downstairs steak bar (weekend evenings), well kept ales including Castle Rock, Copper Dragon, Courage Directors and Timothy Taylors Landlord, open fire; children and dogs welcome, tables on side terrace, open all day Fri, short afternoon break Sat and Sun. *Recommended by the Didler*

LAXTON SK7266 NG22 0NU
 ## Dovecote
Off A6075 E of Ollerton

Traditional village pub handy for A1, three traditionally furnished carpeted or wood-floored dining areas, coal-effect gas fire, tasty fair-priced food served by friendly staff, Batemans, Hawkshead and Springhead ales, farm cider, pool room; piped music – live music last Fri of month, no dogs; children welcome, seats on small front terrace and sloping garden with views of church, bedrooms, camping, open all day Sun. *Recommended by Terry Devine, Jenny and Peter Lowater, Keith and Chris O'Neill, Terry Davis*

LINBY SK5351 NG15 8AE
Horse & Groom
Main Street

Picturesque four-room village pub with welcoming enthusiastic landlord, Greene King, Theakstons, Wells & Youngs and changing guests, enjoyable well presented pub food (not Sun-Thurs evenings) from shortish menu, inglenook log fire, conservatory, no mobile phones; quiet piped music, big-screen TV, games machines in lobby; children welcome, tables outside, big play area, attractive village near Newstead Abbey, good walks, open all day. *Recommended by the Didler, P Dawn*

MANSFIELD SK5561 NG18 4AF
Il Rosso
Nottingham Road (A60)

Refurbished dining pub with enjoyable food including good fresh fish, pizza menu too, well kept changing ales such as Adnams, Blue Monkey, Bradfield and Timothy Taylors Landlord, good service. *Recommended by Derek and Sylvia Stephenson*

MANSFIELD SK5260 NG18 5EX
Nell Gwynne
Sutton Road (A38 W of centre)

Former gentlemen's club, chatty and welcoming with locals of all ages, two changing beers, no food, colliery plates and mementoes of old Mansfield pubs, open fire, games room; sports TV, piped music; open all day weekends and from 2pm Mon-Fri. *Recommended by the Didler*

Post Office address codings confusingly give the impression that some pubs are in Nottinghamshire, when they're really in Derbyshire (which is where we list them).

MANSFIELD SK5363   NG18 1EF
Railway Inn
Station Street; best approached by viaduct from near Market Place

Friendly traditional local with long-serving landlady, three changing ales, good bottled beer choice, bargain home-made lunchtime food (also mid-week evenings), bright front bar and cosier back room; small courtyard garden, handy for Robin Hood Line station, open all day, closed Sun evening. *Recommended by the Didler, P Dawn*

MANSFIELD WOODHOUSE SK5463   NG19 8BD
Greyhound
High Street

Friendly 17th-c village local with half a dozen well kept ales including Adnams, Caledonian Deuchars IPA and Theakstons Mild (beer festivals), cosy lounge, darts, dominoes and pool in busy bar, no food; open all day. *Recommended by the Didler, P Dawn*

☆ MAPLEBECK SK7160   NG22 0BS
Beehive
Signed down pretty country lanes from A616 Newark—Ollerton and from A617 Newark—Mansfield

Relaxing beamed country tavern in nice spot, chatty landlady, tiny front bar, slightly bigger side room, traditional furnishings and antiques, open fire, well kept Maypole and guests, no food; tables on small terrace with flower tubs and grassy bank running down to a stream, summer barbecues, play area, may be closed weekday lunchtimes in winter, very busy weekends and bank holidays. *Recommended by the Didler*

☆ MORTON SK7251   NG25 0UT
Full Moon
Pub and village signed off Bleasby—Fiskerton back road, SE of Southwell

Attractive village pub brought up to date with cream, green and brown colour scheme, eclectic mix of reclaimed furnishings and smart grey slate bar counter, Bass, Blue Monkey and three guests, short choice of good food using local produce, restaurant; piped music, TV; children and dogs welcome, picnic-sets on peaceful back terrace and sizeable lawn, sturdy play equipment, open all day weekends. *Recommended by David Glynne-Jones, the Didler, MP, Derek and Sylvia Stephenson, Dr and Mrs A K Clarke and others*

NEWARK SK7954   NG24 1AZ
Castle
Castle Gate

Spotless old low-ceilinged pub, five or so well kept ales including Sharps Doom Bar, bare-boards front room, long panelled and carpeted back room, old wooden furniture, lots of mirrors and prints; piped and live music; open all day. *Recommended by the Didler*

☆ NEWARK SK8053   NG24 1JY
Fox & Crown
Appleton Gate

Convivial bare-boards open-plan Castle Rock pub with their keenly priced ales and several interesting guests from a central servery, Stowford Press cider, dozens of whiskies, vodkas and other spirits, good tea, coffee and decent wines by the glass, friendly obliging staff, inexpensive simple food from rolls and baked potatoes up, several side areas; piped and weekly live music; children welcome in dining room, good wheelchair access, open all day. *Recommended by the Didler, Derek and Sylvia Stephenson, Simon Elvidge, Richard Martin, David and Ruth Hollands*

NEWARK SK7953   NG24 1BG
Just Beer
Swan & Salmon Yard, off Castle Gate (B6166)

Small welcoming one-room pub (opened in 2010) with six interesting microbrewery ales, bright airy minimalist décor, half a dozen tables on stone floor, brick-built bar, good mix of customers; open all day. *Recommended by the Didler*

NEWARK SK7953   NG24 1AW
Prince Rupert
Stodman Street, off Castlegate

Ancient timber-framed pub renovated after years of closure (was the Woolpack), several small rooms on two floors, beams, exposed brickwork and many original features (some previously covered up), nice old furniture including high-backed settles, conservatory, Ufford and guest ales, blackboard choice of wines by the glass, speciality pizzas with some unusual toppings and other imaginative food, friendly staff, maybe live jazz; courtyard, open all day (till 1am Fri, Sat). *Recommended by Mr and Mrs Beardsley, the Didler, Richard Martin, G Jennings, Jennie Roberts*

NEWSTEAD SK5252   NG15 0BZ
Station Hotel
Station Road

Basic down-to-earth red-brick village local opposite Robin Hood Line station, chatty welcoming landlady and character locals, well kept bargain Oakwell ales, no food except Thurs curry night, unmodernised rooms off central bar, panelling, fine steam railway photographs, two blazing coal fires, pub games; juke box, TV; a few tables out at front, beer garden. *Recommended by the Didler, P Dawn*

NOTTINGHAM SK5739   NG1 6DQ
Approach
Friar Lane

Big open-plan pub attracting younger crowd, wood floor with raised carpeted areas, purple walls and lighting, large modern art prints, leather sofas and mixed tables, Batemans, Mallards and Nottingham ales, good wine range, enjoyable food, comedy and music nights; piped music, silent fruit machine and sports TV; open all day. *Recommended by P Dawn*

NOTTINGHAM SK5739   NG1 6HL
 # Bell
Angel Row; off Market Square

Deceptively large pub with late Georgian frontage concealing two 500-year-old timber-framed buildings; front Tudor Bar with café feel in summer when french windows open to pavement tables, bright blue walls with glass panels protecting patches of 300-year-old wallpaper; larger low-beamed Elizabethan Bar with half-panelled walls, maple parquet flooring and upstairs Belfry with more heavy panelling and 15th-c crown post roof; up to a dozen real ales from remarkable deep sandstone cellar, ten wines by the glass, reasonably priced straightforward bar food, welcoming staff; piped and regular live music including trad jazz, TV, silent fruit machine; children welcome in some parts, open all day (till 1am Sat). *Recommended by Jeremy King, the Didler, Barry Collett, P Dawn and others*

NOTTINGHAM SK5843   NG3 5JL
Bread & Bitter
Woodthorpe Drive

In former suburban bakery still showing ovens, three bright and airy bare-boarded rooms, well kept Castle Rock and great choice of other beers, farm cider, decent wine choice, good value home-made food all day, defunct brewery memorabilia. *Recommended by the Didler, P Dawn*

NOTTINGHAM SK5739   NG1 7EH
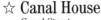 # Canal House
Canal Street

Converted wharf building, bridge over indoors canal spur complete with narrowboat, lots of bare brick and varnished wood, huge joists on steel beams, long bar with good choice of house wines, well kept Castle Rock and changing guests, lively efficient staff, sensibly priced pubby food (not Sun evening), lots of standing room; good upstairs restaurant and second bar, masses of tables out on attractive waterside terrace; piped music (live music Sun), busy with young people at night; open all day. *Recommended by the Didler, Jeremy King, P Dawn*

NOTTINGHAM SK5739   NG1 1HF
Cock & Hoop
High Pavement

Tiny carpeted front bar with fireside armchairs and flagstoned cellar bar attached to decent hotel, characterful décor, interesting food (all day Sun including good roasts), well kept ales such as Blue Monkey, Cumberland and Nottingham, attentive friendly service; piped music; children and dogs welcome, disabled facilities, smart bedrooms (ones by the street can be noisy at weekends), open all day. *Recommended by the Didler, George Atkinson, P Dawn*

NOTTINGHAM SK5739   NG1 2GJ
Cross Keys
Byard Lane

Victorian city-centre pub reopened after long closure, refurbished interior on two levels, lower carpeted part with leather banquettes, panelling and chandeliers, upper area with old wooden chairs and tables on polished boards, interesting prints and pictures and more chandeliers, Fullers London Pride, Mallards Duckling and guests, enjoyable home-made food from breakfast (8am) on, friendly service; seats outside, open all day till 12.30am. *Recommended by P Dawn, the Didler*

NOTTINGHAM SK5739   NG1 7EH
☆ ## Fellows Morton & Clayton
Canal Street (part of inner ring road)

Former canal warehouse with own good beers (finished by Nottingham) plus Black Sheep, Mallards, Sharps and Timothy Taylors, good value all-day pubby food (not Sun evening), softly lit bustling downstairs bar with red plush alcove seats, shiny wood floors and lots of exposed brickwork, two raised areas, photographs of old Nottingham, daily papers, restaurant; piped music – live music Fri, games machines, several big TVs, no dogs; well behaved children in eating areas, large canal-view deck, open all day, till late Fri, Sat. *Recommended by the Didler, Jeremy King, Michael Dandy*

NOTTINGHAM SK5542   NG6 0GA
Fox & Crown
Church Street/Lincoln Street, Old Basford

Good range of Alcazar beers brewed behind refurbished open-plan pub (window shows the brewery, tours Sat, next-door beer shop), also guest ales, continental beers and good choice of wines, enjoyable thai food; good piped music, games machines, big-screen sports TV; disabled access, terrace tables behind, open all day. *Recommended by the Didler, P Dawn*

NOTTINGHAM SK5642   NG5 2AW
Gladstone
Loscoe Road, Carrington

Welcoming backstreet local with well kept ales including Castle Rock, Courage Directors, Fullers London Pride, Greene King Abbot and Timothy Taylors Landlord, good range of malt whiskies, comfortable lounge with reading matter, basic bar with old sports equipment and darts; piped music, big-screen sports TV; upstairs folk club Weds, quiz Thurs; tables in yard with lots of hanging baskets, closed weekday lunchtimes, open all day weekends (from 3pm Fri). *Recommended by the Didler, P Dawn*

NOTTINGHAM SK5738 NG2 3BQ
Globe
London Road

Light and airy roadside pub with six well kept ales including Mallards and Nottingham, good value food, coal fire; sports TV; handy for cricket or football matches, open all day. *Recommended by P Dawn*

NOTTINGHAM SK5542 NG7 7EA
Horse & Groom
Radford Road, New Basford

Nine good changing ales in well run unpretentious open-plan local by former Shipstones Brewery, still with their name and other memorabilia, good value fresh straightforward food from sandwiches to Sun lunch, daily papers, nice snug; music and regular beer festivals in stable block behind, open all day. *Recommended by the Didler, P Dawn*

NOTTINGHAM SK5739 NG1 1QA
☆ Keans Head
St Mary's Gate

Cheery Tynemill pub in attractive Lace Market area; fairly functional single room with something of a continental bar atmosphere, simple wooden café furnishings on wooden boards, some exposed brickwork and red tiling, low sofa by big windows overlooking street, stools by wood counter and small fireplace, Castle Rock and three guests, draught belgian and interesting bottled beers, 20 wines by the glass, 39 malt whiskies and lots of teas/coffees, tasty traditional english and some italian food (not Sun, Mon evenings), friendly staff, daily papers; piped music; children welcome till 7pm, church next door worth a look, open all day. *Recommended by Jeremy King, the Didler, MP, P Dawn, Tony and Wendy Hobden*

NOTTINGHAM SK5539 NG2 4PB
King William IV
Manvers Street/Eyre Street, Sneinton

Two-room Victorian corner local, plenty of character, Oakham and several other well kept ales such as Black Sheep, Kelham Island and Newby Wyke from circular bar, Weston's Old Rosie cider, good fresh cobs, friendly staff, fine tankard collection, pool upstairs, irish music Thurs; silenced sports TV; heated smokers' shelter, handy for cricket, football and rugby grounds, open all day. *Recommended by the Didler, P Dawn*

NOTTINGHAM SK5838 NG2 6AJ
Larwood & Voce
Fox Road, West Bridgford

Well run open-plan dining pub mixing modern and traditional, good locally sourced home-made food all day from lunchtime bar meals to more extensive and imaginative evening menu, good choice of wines by the glass including champagne, nice cocktails, three real ales, cheerful staff; sports TV; children welcome away from bar, on the edge of the cricket ground and handy for Nottingham Forest FC, open all day, from 9am weekends for breakfast. *Recommended by David Glynne-Jones, P Dawn, Ajay Sethi*

NOTTINGHAM SK5740 NG1 3FR
☆ Lincolnshire Poacher
Mansfield Road; up hill from Victoria Centre

Impressive range of drinks at this popular down-to-earth pub (attracting younger crowd in the evening), ten or so real ales, continental draught and bottled beers, farm cider and over 70 malt whiskies, good value all-day bar food; big simple traditional front bar with wall settles, wooden tables and breweriana, plain but lively room on left and corridor to chatty panelled back snug with newspapers and board games, conservatory overlooking tables on large heated back area, live music Sun evening; children (till 8pm) and dogs welcome, open all day (till midnight Sat). *Recommended by Jeremy King, the Didler, MP, Derek and Sylvia Stephenson, P Dawn and others*

NOTTINGHAM SK5541   NG7 7FQ
☆ Lion
Lower Mosley Street, New Basford

Ten ales including regulars Batemans and Mallards from one of the city's deepest cellars (glass viewing panel – can be visited at quiet times), farm ciders, ten wines by the glass, good value home-made food all day including doorstep sandwiches; well fabricated feel of separate areas, bare bricks and polished dark oak boards, old brewery pictures and posters, open fires, daily papers, weekend live music including Sun lunchtime jazz, beer festivals; children welcome till 8pm, disabled facilities, garden with terrace and smokers' shelter, summer barbecues, open all day. *Recommended by the Didler, P Dawn*

NOTTINGHAM SK5739   NG1 7HB
News House
Canal Street

Friendly two-room Castle Rock pub with their ales and half a dozen changing guests, belgian and czech imports on tap, farm cider, good wine and hot drinks' choice, decent fresh lunchtime food including good value Sun lunch, mix of bare boards and carpet, local newspaper/radio memorabilia, darts, table skittles and bar billiards, Thurs quiz; big-screen sports TV; tables out at front, attractive blue exterior tiling, open all day. *Recommended by the Didler, P Dawn*

NOTTINGHAM SK5739   NG1 6AD
☆ Olde Trip to Jerusalem
Brewhouse Yard; from inner ring road follow The North, A6005 Long Eaton signpost until in Castle Boulevard, then right into Castle Road; pub is on the left

Unusual rambling pub seemingly clinging to sandstone rock face (and some rooms actually burrowed into it), largely 17th c and a former brewhouse supplying the hilltop castle; downstairs bar carved into the rock with leatherette-cushioned settles built into dark panelling, tables on flagstones, rocky alcoves, Greene King, Nottingham and guests, good value food all day, efficient staff dealing well with busy mix of customers; little tourist shop with panelled walls soaring up into a dark stone cleft, cellar tours (must book); children welcome till 7pm, seats in snug courtyard, open all day (till midnight Fri, Sat). *Recommended by Jeremy King, Bob and Angela Brooks, the Didler, Barry Collett, P Dawn and others*

NOTTINGHAM SK5540   NG7 3EN
☆ Plough
St Peter's Street, Radford

Friendly 19th-c local brewing its own good value Nottingham ales at the back, also guest beers and farm cider, decent cheap food including fresh cobs and popular Sun lunch, mosaic floors, old tables and chairs, two coal fires, traditional games, skittle alley, Thurs quiz; sports TV; covered smokers' area, open all day Fri-Sun. *Recommended by the Didler, P Dawn*

NOTTINGHAM SK5640   NG1 5BB
Rope Walk
Derby Road

Appealing, nicely divided open-plan layout, bare boards, comfortable chairs around low tables, good value food from snacks up, prompt service, decent beer choice, Sun quiz, open mike Weds; free wi-fi. *Recommended by P Dawn*

NOTTINGHAM SK5739   NG1 7AA
Salutation
Hounds Gate/Maid Marion Way

Proper pub, low beams, flagstones, ochre walls and cosy corners including two small quiet rooms in ancient lower back part, plusher modern front lounge, half a dozen real ales, quickly served food till 7pm, helpful staff; piped music; open all day. *Recommended by Barry Collett, P Dawn*

NOTTINGHAM SK5640
NG7 3GD
Sir John Borlase Warren
Ilkeston Road/Canning Circus (A52 towards Derby)

Roadside pub with four comfortable linked rooms, interesting Victorian decorations, enjoyable good value food all day, friendly staff, Everards, Greene King, Timothy Taylors and guests, art for sale, mix of customers including students; no children Fri or Sat evenings, tables in nicely lit back garden, open all day. *Recommended by the Didler, John Fredericks, Dominique*

NOTTINGHAM SK5744
NG5 3GG
Vale
Mansfield Road

Friendly 1930s local with original layout, panelling and woodwork, Black Sheep, Caledonian Deuchars IPA, Fullers London Pride and three guests, low-priced food, Sun quiz night; open all day. *Recommended by the Didler*

NOTTINGHAM SK5739
NG2 1NB
☆ Vat & Fiddle
Queens Bridge Road; alongside Sheriffs Way (near multi-storey car park)

Plain open-plan brick pub next to Castle Rock Brewery, unspoilt 1930s feel, varnished pine tables, bentwood chairs and stools on parquet or terrazzo flooring, some brewery memorabilia, interesting photographs of demolished local pubs, six real ales, bottled continental beers, farm ciders, 60 malt whiskies, cobs and a couple of pubby lunchtime weekday specials, nice chatty atmosphere; no credit cards; children and dogs welcome, picnic-sets out front by road, open all day (till midnight Fri, Sat). *Recommended by the Didler, P Dawn, MP*

ORSTON SK7741
NG13 9NS
Durham Ox
Church Street

Comfortable open-plan split-level village pub opposite church, four well kept mainstream ales and a guest, short choice of well presented food, old local photographs, small dining room with coal fire; piped music and some live music; children and dogs welcome, tables out at front and in big back garden with four heated summer houses, hitching rails for horses and ferrets, pleasant countryside, open all day weekends; all profits go to a charity (www.oliversarmy.org). *Recommended by the Didler, David Glynne-Jones*

RADCLIFFE ON TRENT SK6439
NG12 2AA
Manvers Arms
Main Road, opposite church

Newish management for this early 19th-c village pub opposite the church; enjoyable nicely presented food (till 7pm Sun) including set menus, prompt friendly service, good fairly priced wines, well kept ales such as Fullers, Jennings, St Austell, Wychwood and York, spotless opened-up interior keeping original fireplaces and other features, assorted pubby furniture, some cosy areas with banquettes, pictures and ornaments, chandeliers and potted palms, an old harmonium; mellow piped music – live jazz Thurs; well behaved children and dogs welcome, plenty of seats in large garden with trees and shrubs. *Recommended by David Glynne-Jones*

RADCLIFFE ON TRENT SK6439
NG12 2FD
Royal Oak
Main Road

Revamped and opened up by small local Mole Face chain; wide choice of enjoyable food from open kitchen including breakfast (till noon), sandwiches (home-baked bread) and bar/restaurant meals, good friendly service, plenty of wines by the glass including champagne, Castle Rock and two guests; children welcome, open all day from 10am. *Recommended by David Glynne-Jones*

RAVENSHEAD SK5554 NG15 9HJ
Hutt
A60 Nottingham—Mansfield

Chef & Brewer with characterful softly lit rooms, alcoves and intimate areas, good food and well kept ales including Adnams, Greene King and Harviestoun, efficient friendly service; open all day. *Recommended by Derek and Sylvia Stephenson*

ROLLESTON SK7452 NG23 5SG
Crown
Staythorpe Road

Smartly modernised and under newish management, good food including set lunch and early evening deals, real ales; small garden, five bedrooms, handy for Southwell Racecourse, open all day Sun till 9pm (food till 7pm). *Recommended by Maurice and Janet Thorpe*

RUDDINGTON SK5733 NG11 6LB
Three Crowns
Easthorpe Street

Open-plan village pub with well kept Fullers, Nottingham and guest ales, lunchtime bar food, interesting evening menu (not Sun, Mon) in refurbished back restaurant, Sun carvery, local art for sale, Jun beer festival; open all day weekends, closed Mon lunchtime. *Recommended by the Didler, P Dawn*

RUDDINGTON SK5733 NG11 6HD
White Horse
Church Street

Cheerful 1930s local with half a dozen ales including Black Sheep and Wells & Youngs Bombardier (Jun beer festival), enjoyable home-made food, comfortable lounge, old photographs, bar with darts, pool, juke box and TV, Thurs quiz; spacious sunny courtyard garden, barbecues, open all day. *Recommended by the Didler, P Dawn*

SELSTON SK4553 NG16 6FB
☆ ## Horse & Jockey
Handy for M1 junctions 27/28; Church Lane

Dating from the 17th c, intelligently renovated with interesting 18th- and 19th-c survivals and good carving, different levels, low heavy beams, dark flagstones, individual furnishings, good log fire in cast-iron range, friendly staff, mainstream ales such as Timothy Taylors Landlord (poured from jug) and some unusual guests, real cider, no food; games area with darts and pool; dogs welcome, terrace with very smart smokers' shelter, pleasant rolling country. *Recommended by the Didler, Derek and Sylvia Stephenson*

SOUTH LEVERTON SK7881 DN22 0BT
Plough
Town Street

Tiny village local doubling as a morning post office, basic trestle tables, benches and pews, log fire, helpful welcoming staff, Greene King and changing guests, traditional games; nice garden, open all day (from 2pm weekdays). *Recommended by the Didler*

SOUTHWELL SK7054 NG25 0ET
Final Whistle
Station Road

Former Newcastle Arms reopened after major revamp; ten ales including Blue Monkey, Everards and Leatherbritches (beer festivals), real ciders and perries, foreign bottled beers and good range of wines, snacky food, traditional opened-up bar area with tiled or wood floor, settles and armchairs in quieter carpeted room, corridor drinking area, two open fires, panelling, railway memorabilia and other odds and ends; some live music, Tues quiz; children and dogs welcome, back garden with wonderful mock-up of old station platform complete with track, open all day. *Recommended by the Didler*

SOUTHWELL SK7053   NG25 0HQ
☆ **Hearty Goodfellow**
Church Street (A612)

Traditional open-plan pub under friendly landlord, Everards Tiger and seven changing guests including Mallards, good range of house wines, good value lunchtime food from snacks up, lots of polished wood, two brick fireplaces; children and dogs welcome, nice big tree-shaded garden beyond car park, handy for Southwell Workhouse (NT) and Minster, open all day Fri-Sun, closed Mon lunchtime. *Recommended by the Didler, Steven Morris*

THURGARTON SK6949   NG14 7GP
Red Lion
Southwell Road (A612)

Cheery 16th-c pub with split-level beamed bars and restaurant, Black Sheep, Marstons and Springhead from dark panelled bar, food all day weekends and bank holidays, comfortable banquettes and other seating on patterned carpets, lots of nooks and crannies, grandfather clock, open fires, big windows to attractive, good-sized two-level back garden (dogs on leads allowed here); games machine, steepish walk back up to car park; children welcome. *Recommended by JJW, CMW*

UNDERWOOD SK4751   NG16 5HD
☆ **Red Lion**
Off A608/B600, near M1 junction 27; Church Lane, nearly in Bagthorpe

Welcoming 17th-c split-level beamed village pub, reliable sensibly priced food including set-lunch deals (Mon-Fri), other bargains and good fresh fish (best to book), interesting changing ales, good soft drinks' choice, pleasant service, open-plan quarry-tiled bar with dining area, some cushioned settles, open fire; piped music, games machine in lobby; no dogs; children till 7pm away from bar, good play area in big woodside garden with terrace and barbecues, good nearby walks, open all day Fri-Sun. *Recommended by Derek and Sylvia Stephenson*

UPTON SK7354   NG23 5SY
☆ **Cross Keys**
A612

Under good new licensees (previously at the Wagon & Horses in Halam), good fairly priced bistro-style food, well kept ales such as Blue Monkey BG Sips, Castle Rock Harvest Pale and Fullers London Pride, nice coffee, rambling heavy-beamed bar with lots of alcoves, central log fire, back extension with long carved pew, upstairs overspill/function room; occasional live folk music; children and dogs welcome, tables on decked terrace, opposite British Horological Institute, open all day weekends, closed Mon lunchtime. *Recommended by Derek and Sylvia Stephenson*

WATNALL CHAWORTH SK5046   NG16 1HT
☆ **Queens Head**
3 miles from M1 junction 26: A610 towards Nottingham, left on B600, then keep right; Main Road

Reasonably priced pubby food including good fish and chips (Fri night) in tastefully extended 18th-c roadside pub, well kept Adnams, Castle Rock, Everards, Greene King, Wells & Youngs and a guest, efficient staff, beams and stripped pine, old pictures and photographs, grandfather clock, coal fire, intimate snug, dining area; piped music; children welcome, flower baskets and tubs on small front terrace, picnic-sets on attractive back lawn with big play area, beer festivals and barbecues, open all day. *Recommended by the Didler, JJW, CMW*

Please tell us if any pub deserves to be included or upgraded to a featured top pub – and why: **feedback@goodguides.com**, or (no stamp needed) The Good Pub Guide, FREEPOST TN1569, Wadhurst, E Sussex TN5 7BR.

WATNALL CHAWORTH SK5046
Royal Oak
Main Road; B600 N of Kimberley

NG16 1HS

Friendly beamed village local, Greene King ales and a guest, good fresh cobs, interesting collection of plates and pictures, woodburner, back games area with pool, comfortable upstairs lounge open Fri-Sun, live music and beer festivals; sports TV; tables out front and back, open all day. *Recommended by the Didler*

WEST BRIDGFORD SK5837
☆ ### Stratford Haven
Stratford Road, Trent Bridge

NG2 6BA

Good Tynemill pub, bare-boards front bar leading to linked areas including airy skylit back part with relaxed local atmosphere, their well kept Castle Rock ales, plus Batemans, Everards and six changing guests (monthly brewery nights), exotic bottled beers, farm ciders, ample whiskies and wines, good value home-made food all day, fast friendly service, daily papers, some live music (nothing loud); dogs welcome, terrace, handy for cricket ground and Nottingham Forest FC (busy on match days), tables outside, open all day from 10.30am (midday Sun). *Recommended by MP, the Didler, P Dawn, Steve Holden and others*

WILFORD SK5637
Ferry
Off B679 S of Nottingham

NG11 7AA

Split-level Chef & Brewer partly dating from the 14th c, enjoyable reasonably priced food, Black Sheep, small rooms, low beams and bare boards, bays of banquettes, open fires, restaurant with pitched roof and imposing fireplace; piped music; children welcome, back terrace, garden with play area, view over River Trent to Nottingham Castle. *Recommended by Derek and Sylvia Stephenson*

WYSALL SK6027
Plough
Keyworth Road; off A60 at Costock, or A6006 at Wymeswold

NG12 5QQ

Attractive 17th-c beamed village local, popular good value food from shortish menu, cheerful staff, changing well kept ales, rooms either side of bar with nice mix of furnishings, soft lighting, big log fire; french doors to pretty terrace with flower tubs and baskets. *Recommended by M Mossman, Ajay Sethi*

If a pub tries to make you leave a credit card behind the bar, be on your guard. The credit card firms and banks that issue them condemn this practice. After all, the publican who asks you to do this is in effect saying: 'I don't trust you'. Have you any more reason to trust his staff? If your card is used fraudulently while you have let it be kept out of your sight, the card company could say you've been negligent yourself – and refuse to make good your losses. So say that they can 'swipe' your card instead, but must hand it back to you. Please let us know if a pub does try to keep your card.

The Heart of England

Gloucestershire

Herefordshire

Shropshire

Staffordshire

Warwickshire

West Midlands

Worcestershire

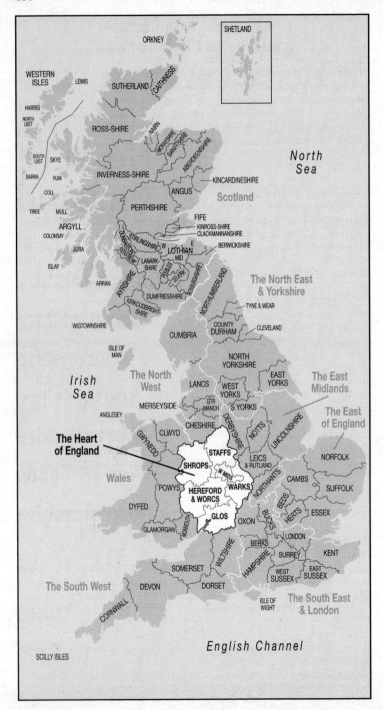

EDITORS' FAVOURITES
THE HEART OF ENGLAND

The region's top pub is the Bell & Cross in Holy Cross (a terrific all-rounder and **Worcestershire Dining Pub of the Year**). Other great **Worcestershire** pubs are the Jockey in Baughton (friendly and good value local dining), Fleece at Bretforton (charming historic interior), Crown & Trumpet in Broadway (genuinely hospitable welcome), Three Kings at Hanley Castle (unspoilt quirky country local), and Nags Head in Malvern (splendidly individual). Also worth a visit are the Marwood in Worcester and the Monkey House in Defford.

Special pubs in **Gloucestershire** are the Boat at Ashleworth Quay (in the same family for hundreds of years), Kings Head in Bledington (smashing food, comfortable bedrooms, lots of return visits from customers), Yew Tree in Clifford's Mesne (unusual pub with own wine shop and inventive food), Old Spot in Dursley (a firm favourite, fantastic real ales and friendly landlord), Ebrington Arms in Ebrington (delightful pub and a true all-rounder), Fossebridge Inn at Fossebridge (civilised place, bustling bar and super food), Ostrich at Newland (lovely landlady, lots of real ales and top-class food), Wheatsheaf in Northleach (excellent modern food and our **Gloucestershire Dining Pub of the Year** – but pubby, too), and the Bell at Sapperton (run with love and care by hands-on licensees, first-rate food, wide choice of drinks). Also worth a visit are the Black Horse in Amberley, Bear at Bisley, Horse & Groom at Bourton-on-the-Hill, Green Dragon at Cowley, Five Mile House in Duntisbourne Abbots, Wild Duck at Ewen, Hunters Hall in Kingscote, Fox at Lower Oddington, Queens Head in Stow-on-the-Wold, and the Ram at Woodchester.

Top pubs in **Herefordshire** are the Live & Let Live at Bringsty Common (plenty of character, good local ales), Cottage of Content in Carey (friendly old cottage, interesting food, tranquil bedrooms), Victory in Hereford (home of the Hereford Brewery and with amusing nautical décor), Three Horseshoes in Little Cowarne (smashing landlord and popular food cooked by landlady and her son), Stagg at Titley (quite exceptional food – but still a pub and **Herefordshire Dining Pub of the Year**), Carpenters Arms in Walterstone (in the same family for many years and quite unchanging) and Butchers Arms in Woolhope (professional landlord cooks the first-rate food). Also worth a visit are the Riverside Inn at Aymestrey, Wellington in Colwall, Stockton Cross Inn at Stockton Cross, and the Bell in Yarpole.

Great places to visit in **Shropshire** are the cheery White Horse at Clun (up to seven local beers), the lively Church Inn at Ludlow (eight local real ales) and the cosy, full of bric-a-brac George & Dragon at Much Wenlock. Both Brunning & Price pubs, the Fox at Chetwynd Aston (**Shropshire Dining Pub of the Year**) and Armoury at Shrewsbury offer terrific sensibly priced food. Also worth a visit are the Castle Hotel at Bishop's Castle, Crown at Munslow, Hundred House at Norton, Bottle & Glass in Picklescott, and the Queens Head at Queens Head.

Staffordshire has a charming range of pubs. Particularly worth visiting are the museum-like Yew Tree at Cauldon, the chocolate-box Holly Bush at Salt (extremely good value food) and the Hand & Trumpet at Wrinehill (**Staffordshire Dining Pub of the Year** and the best of all worlds). Also worth a visit are the Burton Bridge Inn at Burton Upon Trent, Blue Bell at Kidsgrove and Queens Head at Lichfield.

Pubs in **Warwickshire** serve terrific food, most notably the Bell in Alderminster (stylishly refurbished), Red Lion at Hunningham (wonderfully relaxing), Crabmill at Preston Bagot (super imaginative menu) and Bell at Welford-on-Avon (fabulous hands-on hospitality and **Warwickshire Dining Pub of the Year**). For the entire range of Fullers ales and good value food, find the Old Joint Stock in Birmingham (stunning building, too). Other good pubs worth a visit include the Case is Altered at Five Ways, the Fox & Hounds in Great Wolford, Howard Arms in Ilmington, Buck & Bell in Long Itchington and the Stag at Offchurch.

ALDERMINSTER Warwickshire   SP2348   Map 4

 Bell

A3400 Oxford—Stratford; CV37 8NY

Handsome coaching inn with contemporary décor mixing easily with original features, real ales, a good choice of wines, excellent modern cooking and helpful service; individually decorated bedrooms

This Georgian former coaching inn – now part of the Alscot Estate – has been refurbished in an attractive contemporary style. There's a small bustling bar with Alscot Ale (brewed for them by Warwickshire) and a guest beer, a good range of wines by the glass, proper cocktails (including a special bloody mary), newspapers to read, comfortable brown leather armchairs in front of the open fire and high bar chairs by the blue-painted counter. The open-plan layout gives an easy-going atmosphere and throughout there are beams, standing timbers, flagstones or wooden floors and fresh flowers. The restaurant has an eclectic mix of furniture such as painted dining chairs and tables, and leads into the conservatory which shares the same Stour Valley views as the modern chairs and tables in the pretty courtyard. The four boutique-style bedrooms are comfortable and individually decorated.

Using much Estate-grown (and their own) produce, the interesting food ranges from morning coffees, weekend brunches, sandwiches and filled baguettes to grazing platters and excellent restaurant meals. It might include crab, crayfish, chilli and coriander fishcakes, butternut and sage risotto, chicken with chorizo, linguine, maple syrup and spring onions, chicken fillets with cranberry and coriander salsa and chargrilled vegetables, seared bass with sesame pak choi with sweet red pepper sauce, sweet potato, cauliflower and chickpea thai curry, and grilled pork loin chop with niçoise salad and tapenade dressing. *Benchmark main dish: steak and kidney pudding £14.00. Two-course evening meal £20.00.*

Free house ~ Licensee Emma Holman-West ~ Real ale ~ Bar food ~ Restaurant ~ (01789) 450414 ~ Children welcome ~ Dogs allowed in bar ~ Open 9.30-3, 6.30-11; 9.30-11 Sat; closed Mon, Sun evenings in winter ~ Bedrooms: £100B/£135B

Recommended by David Gunn, Michael Dandy

 ASHLEWORTH Gloucestershire   SO8125   Map 4

Queens Arms

Village signposted off A417 at Hartpury; GL19 4HT

Neatly kept pub with civilised bar, highly thought-of food, thoughtful wines, and sunny courtyard

Now into their fourteenth year here, the friendly, hard-working south african licensees continue to welcome their customers, old and new. It's all spic and span throughout and the civilised main bar has a nice mix of farmhouse and brocaded dining chairs around big oak and mahogany tables on the green carpet, and faintly patterned wallpaper and washed red ochre walls; at night it is softly lit by fringed wall lamps and candles. Brains Rev James and guests like Sharps Doom Bar and Timothy Taylors Landlord on handpump, 15 wines by the glass including south african ones, 22 malt whiskies, winter mulled wine and summer home-made lemonade; piped music, board games and (on request) a skittle alley. The little black cat, Bonnie, does still entertain customers with her ping-pong ball, but now that she is 15 she is a bit less active. There are cast-iron chairs and tables in the sunny courtyard; two perfectly clipped mushroom-shaped yews dominate the front of the building.

Using top quality local produce, the reliably good, interesting food might include specials such as asparagus and crab tartlet with a saffron and chive beurre blanc, ostrich fillet with a brandy, green peppercorn and cream sauce, and loin of lamb stuffed with rosemary and garlic and topped with a lemon and honey butter, as well as pubby choices like pork and duck liver terrine with cumberland sauce, steak and kidney pie, home-cooked ham and eggs, and salmon fishcakes with a lemon and dill cream cheese. *Benchmark main dish: steak and kidney pie £11.60. Two-course evening meal £17.75.*

Free house ~ Licensees Tony and Gill Burreddu ~ Real ale ~ Bar food (not Sun evening) ~ Restaurant ~ (01452) 700395 ~ Well behaved children allowed ~ Open 12-3, 7-11; 12-3 Sun; closed Sun evening; 25 and 26 Dec, 1 Jan

Recommended by Kim Merrifield, Dave and Jackie Kenward, Bernard Stradling, J J Hatton, Mr Richard Sleep, Wayne Davis

 ASHLEWORTH QUAY Gloucestershire   SO8125   Map 4

Boat ★

Ashleworth signposted off A417 N of Gloucester; quay signed from village; GL19 4HZ

Delightful and unchanging Severn-side pub with swiftly changing beers – and in the same family for hundreds of years

This quaint and unpretentious alehouse is very much the kind of place where strangers soon start talking to each other and the charming licensees work hard at preserving the unique character. It's tiny and spotlessly clean and the little front parlour has a built-in settle by a long scrubbed-deal table that faces an old-fashioned open kitchen range with a side bread oven and a couple of elderly fireside chairs; there are rush mats on the scrubbed flagstones, house-plants in the window, fresh garden flowers and old magazines to read; cribbage and dominoes in the front room. Two antique settles face each other in the back room where swiftly changing beers such as Church End Gravedigger's Ale, Otley Boss, RCH Double Header, Stonehenge Pigswill and Wye Valley Dorothy Goodbody's Golden Ale are tapped from the cask, along with the full range of Weston's farm ciders. The front suntrap crazy-paved courtyard is bright with plant tubs in summer and there are a couple of picnic-sets under parasols; more seats and tables under cover at the sides.

Lunchtime filled rolls and ploughman's as well as cakes and ice-cream. *Benchmark main dish: ploughman's £4.50.*

Free house ~ Licensees Ron, Elisabeth and Louise Nicholls ~ Real ale ~ Bar food (lunchtime only; not Mon and Weds) ~ No credit cards ~ (01452) 700272 ~ Children welcome ~ Open 11.30-2.30(3 Sat), 6.30-11; 12-3, 7-10.30 Sun; evening opening 7pm in winter; closed all day Mon, Weds lunchtime

Recommended by Theocsbrian, Stuart Doughty, the Didler, Ken and Barbara Turner, MLR

BARFORD Warwickshire   SP2660   Map 4

Granville

1.7 miles from M40 junction 15; A429 S (Wellesbourne Road); CV35 8DS

Civilised, attractive respite from the motorway, for fireside comfort or a good meal (all day Sat)

This pleasing pub has a gently up-to-date feel with its sage-green paintwork, berber-pattern hangings on the end walls, and contemporary lighting. Soft leather deco sofas nestle by the fire in the angle of the L-shaped main bar. You can eat here, at newish pale wood tables and chairs on pale boards, or simple more mixed tables and chairs in a carpeted section, or you can head through to a more formally laid raftered and stripped-brick restaurant. They have Hook Norton Old Hooky and Purity Mad Goose and UBU on handpump, and decent wines by the glass; service is efficient; piped music and TV for major events. A floodlit back terrace has smart rattan chairs and loungers under huge retractable awnings, and the grass beyond rises artfully to a hedge of pampas grass and the like, which neatly closes the view, and there's a new tucked-away rustic play area; more reports please.

As well as lunchtime doorstep sandwiches, good bar food might include duck liver parfait with pear chutney, hot and cold smoked salmon roulade with citrus salad, ham hock terrine with piccalilli and walnut bread, chicken and leek pie, sun-dried tomato, globe artichoke, mozzarella and pesto tagliatelle, fried bass fillet with crab, chilli and ginger linguine, and roast pork belly with bramley apple. *Benchmark main dish: battered fish with crushed mint peas £10.95. Two-course evening meal £16.45.*

Enterprise ~ Lease Val Kersey ~ Real ale ~ Bar food (12-2.30, 6-9.30; 12-9.30 Sat; 12-5 Sun; not Sun evening) ~ Restaurant ~ (01926) 624236 ~ Children welcome ~ Dogs welcome ~ Open 12-3, 5-11(11.30 Fri); 12-11.30(Sat, Sun)

Recommended by Val and Alan Green, Clive and Fran Dutson, Andy Rose

We say if we know a pub allows dogs

BARNSLEY Gloucestershire   SP0705   Map 4

Village Pub 🍴 🍷 🛏

B4425 Cirencester—Burford; GL7 5EF

Enjoyable modern food in civilised communicating rooms, candles and open fires, good choice of drinks and seats in the back courtyard; bedrooms

The imaginative food in this smart and civilised country pub continues to draw customers in from far and wide, but this remains very much a local with regulars and their dogs still dropping in for a drink and a chat. The low-ceilinged communicating rooms have flagstones and oak floorboards, oil paintings, plush chairs, stools and window settles around polished candlelit tables, three open fireplaces and country magazines and newspapers to read. Butcombe Bitter and a couple of guest beers on handpump and an extensive wine list with several by the glass. The sheltered back courtyard has good solid wooden furniture under parasols, outdoor heaters and its own outside servery.

Under the new licensee, the interesting food might include potted brown shrimps, breaded goats cheese with waldorf salad and chutney, rough-cut pasta with greens and pesto, crispy duck salad with chilli and soy, braised lamb hotpot, slow-roasted pork belly with rhubarb and apple compote, and cod fillet with curried mussels and spinach. *Benchmark main dish: fish and chips £13.25. Two-course evening meal £20.25.*

Free house ~ Licensee Michael Mellor ~ Real ale ~ Bar food (12-2.30, 6-9.30(10 Fri and Sat); 12-4, 6-9 Sun) ~ (01285) 740421 ~ Children welcome ~ Dogs welcome ~ Open 12-11(10 Sun) ~ Bedrooms: £90B/£120B

Recommended by Anthony and Pam Stamer, Steve and Liz Tilley, Michael Sargent, Graham Oddey, John Holroyd

BAUGHTON Worcestershire   SO8742   Map 4

Jockey £

4 miles from M50 junction 1; A38 northwards, then right on to A4104 Upton—Pershore; WR8 9DQ

Thoughtfully run dining pub with an appealing layout

Readers enjoy the good value food and friendly welcome at this home-from-home local dining pub. The open-plan interior is nicely divided by stripped-brick half walls, some with open timbering to the ceiling. There's a mix of good-sized tables, a few horse-racing pictures on butter-coloured walls and a cream Rayburn in one brick inglenook; piped music. Drinks include Butty Bach, Courage Directors, Brains Rev James and a changing guest from a brewer such as Wye Valley, and they've farm cider and a rewarding choice of wines, with ten by the glass. There are picnic-sets out in front, amid a pleasing array of flowers.

As well as lunchtime sandwiches, baguettes and baked potatoes (not Sundays), bar food includes whitebait or king prawns in garlic butter, poached salmon fillet with oyster mushrooms in white wine sauce, turkey, ham and leek pie, sirloin or rib-eye steak, and specials such as mushroom stroganoff, poached salmon in tarragon sauce, and venison faggots; weekday lunchtime two-course menu £10. *Benchmark main dish: steak and kidney pie £9.95. Two-course evening meal £14.90.*

Free house ~ Licensee Colin Clarke ~ Real ale ~ Bar food (12-2(3 Sat), 6-9; 12-8.30 Sun) ~ (01684) 592153 ~ Children welcome ~ Open 12.30-3, 6-11; 12-11 Fri, Sat; 12-10.30 Sun

*Recommended by Bernard Stradling, Philip and Jan Medcalf, Jason Caulkin, Dave Braisted,
Dr A J and Mrs Tompsett, John Wooll*

BEWDLEY Worcestershire   SO7875 Map 4

Little Pack Horse

*High Street; no nearby parking – best to park in main car park, cross A4117
Cleobury road, and keep walking on down narrowing High Street; DY12 2DH*

Friendly town pub full of interesting paraphernalia; decent food

Cosy on a winter's evening with a warming woodburning stove and
cheerful chatty atmosphere, the time-honoured interior of this 450-
year-old place is much bigger than its unassuming exterior suggests. It
looks very much like the other houses in this tucked-away historic street,
with little pavement and no parking (see directions above). It's nicely
timbered with reclaimed oak panelling and floorboards, and there's an
eye-catching array of old advertisements, photos and other memorabilia.
Alongside Bewdley Worcestershire Way, they keep a couple of guests
from brewers such as Sharps and Timothy Taylors, a selection of bottled
ciders, perries and just under two dozen wines; piped music and TV. An
area outside has heaters.

Bar food includes smoked mackerel pâté, spiced potato skins, a range of pies,
roast chicken, fish and chips, tagliatelle provençale, and steaks. *Benchmark
main dish: beef and ale pie £9.99. Two-course evening meal £16.20.*

Punch ~ Tenant Mark Payne ~ Real ale ~ Bar food (12-2.15(4 Sat, Sun), 6-9.15(9.30
Sat); 5.30-8.15 Sun) ~ Restaurant ~ (01299) 403762 ~ Dogs allowed in bar ~ Open
12-2.30, 6-11; 12-midnight Sat; 12-11 Sun; closed Mon lunchtime
Recommended by Alan and Eve Harding, N R White

BIRMINGHAM   SP0686 Map 4

Old Joint Stock  £

Temple Row West; B2 5NY

**Big bustling Fullers pie-and-ale pub with impressive Victorian façade
and interior, and a small back terrace**

It's worth popping into this well run city-centre pub (formerly the City
Library and opposite the cathedral) just for a glimpse of its impressive
interior – though there's plenty more on offer here too. Chandeliers hang
from the soaring pink and gilt ceiling, gently illuminated busts line the top
of the ornately plastered walls, and there's a splendid, if well worn, cupola
above the centre of the room. Big portraits and smart long curtains create
an air of unexpected elegance. Around the walls are plenty of tables and
chairs, some in cosy corners, with more on a big dining balcony that
overlooks the bar and is reached by a grand staircase. A separate room,
with panelling and a fireplace, has a more intimate, clubby feel. It does get
busy, particularly with local office workers, but effortlessly absorbs what
seems like huge numbers of people, and service remains as friendly and
helpful as ever. As far as we know, this is the northernmost venue to be
owned by London-based brewer Fullers and they keep the full range of
Fullers beers on handpump alongside up to four local guests from perhaps
Aston Manor, Backyard, Purity and Warwickshire, a dozen wines by the
glass and a decent range of malt whiskies, all served from a handsome
dark wood island bar counter; daily papers, games machine, piped music

and board games. Most nights see something on in the smart purpose-built little theatre on the first floor, and a small back terrace has some cast-iron tables, chairs and wall-mounted heaters.

🍴 The very reasonably priced menu includes sandwiches, mushroom and tarragon pâté, artichoke, tomato and rocket quiche, ploughman's, salads, sausage and mash, fish and chips and a great choice of pies. Tasty daily specials might include herb-crusted salmon fillet, stilton, red pepper and chilli potato cake, and a steak sizzler with watercress butter. *Benchmark main dish: steak and ale pie £9.50. Two-course evening meal £14.50.*

Fullers ~ Manager Paul Bancroft ~ Real ale ~ Bar food (12-10(4 Sun)) ~ Restaurant ~ (0121) 200 1892 ~ Children welcome till 7pm away from main bar ~ Jazz in the bar monthly; theatre ~ Open 11-11; 12-5 Sun; closed Sun evening
Recommended by the Didler, Steve and Liz Tilley, Henry Pursehouse-Tranter, Ian and Nita Cooper, Martin Smith, Barry Collett, Theocsbrian, Jeremy King, Andy Dolan

BLAISDON Gloucestershire   SO7016 Map 4
Red Hart ◀
Village signposted off A4136 just SW of junction with A40 W of Gloucester; OS Sheet 162 map reference 703169; GL17 0AH

Busy pub with some interesting bric-a-brac in attractive rooms, popular bar food and several real ales

Always bustling and cheerful, this village inn has a good mix of chatty locals and visitors. The flagstoned main bar has cushioned wall and window seats, traditional pub tables, a big sailing-ship painting above the log fire, Hook Norton Bitter and guests from Exe Valley, Otter and RCH on handpump, several wines by the glass and local cider; piped music and board games. On the right, there's an attractive beamed restaurant with interesting prints and bric-a-brac, and on the left, you'll find additional dining space for families. There are some picnic-sets in the garden and a children's play area, and at the back of the building is a terrace for summer barbecues. The little church above the village is worth a visit.

🍴 Well liked bar food includes sandwiches, pork pâté with red onion chutney, deep-fried camembert with cranberry sauce, chicken breast with a stilton and cream sauce, lamb shank with red wine and rosemary, local trout with almonds, and slow-roasted pork belly with black pudding and celeriac mash. *Benchmark main dish: steak, mushroom and ale pie £10.95. Two-course evening meal £17.75.*

Free house ~ Licensee Guy Wilkins ~ Real ale ~ Bar food ~ Restaurant ~ (01452) 830477 ~ Well behaved children welcome ~ Dogs allowed in bar ~ Open 12-3, 6(7 Sun)-11
Recommended by Robert Turnham, Reg Fowle, Helen Rickwood, Theocsbrian, Ken and Barbara Turner, Lucien Perring

BLEDINGTON Gloucestershire   SP2422 Map 4
Kings Head ⑪ ♀ ◀ ⇦
B4450; OX7 6XQ

Beams and atmospheric furnishings in a civilised old inn, super wines by the glass, real ales and interesting food; bedrooms

Our readers tend to come back to this civilised old inn again and again – either for a meal or to stay overnight in the comfortable courtyard bedrooms. The main bar is full of ancient beams and other atmospheric furnishings (high-backed wooden settles, gateleg or pedestal tables) and there's a warming log fire in the stone inglenook where there are bellows and a big black kettle; sporting memorabilia of rugby, racing, cricket and hunting. To the left of the bar, a drinking area for locals has built-in wall benches, stools and dining chairs around wooden tables, rugs on bare boards and a woodburning stove. Hook Norton Best and guests from breweries such as Butts, Purity and Stroud on handpump, an excellent wine list with ten by the glass and 25 malt whiskies; piped music, board games and darts. There are seats in front of the inn with more in the back courtyard garden. This is a pretty setting, just back from the green, in a tranquil village.

Using meat from the family farm, game from the nearby estates and local vegetables, the appealing bar food might include lunchtime sandwiches, smoked chicken, ham hock and baby onion terrine with chutney, beer-battered fish and chips, braised leg of rabbit with thyme butter sauce, crab, chilli, garlic and parsley linguine, and roast loin of pork, slow-cooked suckling pork belly, spiced lentils, orange-glazed carrots and red wine jus; nice breakfasts. *Benchmark main dish: aberdeen angus steak £18.00. Two-course evening meal £19.00.*

Free house ~ Licensees Nicola and Archie Orr-Ewing ~ Real ale ~ Bar food ~ Restaurant ~ (01608) 658365 ~ Children welcome ~ Dogs allowed in bar ~ Open 11.30(12 Sun)-11; closed 25 and 26 Dec ~ Bedrooms: £75B/£90B

Recommended by John and Val Shand, Anthony and Pam Stamer, Jeff and Wendy Williams, Richard Greaves, John and Jackie Chalcraft, Bruce and Sharon Eden, M and J White, Christian Mole, Jamie and Sue May

BODENHAM Herefordshire   SO5454   Map 4

Englands Gate

On A417 at Bodenham turn-off, about 6 miles S of Leominster; HR1 3HU

Some fine original features in a comfortable 16th-c inn, four real ales and tasty food; pleasant garden

In an attractive area, this half-timbered 16th-c coaching inn has a rambling, open-plan interior that looks every year of its age. There are heavy brown beams and joists in low ochre ceilings around a vast central stone chimneypiece, well worn flagstones, sturdy timber props, one or two steps, and lantern-style lighting. One corner has a high-backed settle with scatter cushions, a cosy partly stripped-stone room has a long stripped table (just right for a party of eight) and a lighter upper area with flowers on its tables has winged settles painted a soft eau de nil. Hobsons Twisted Spire, Wye Valley Butty Bach and HPA and a guest such as Hereford Best on handpump, and the pub holds a beer and sausage festival in July; piped pop music, board games and TV. There are tables with sun umbrellas out in the garden and on the terrace. The smart, modern bedrooms and suites are in a converted coach house next door.

Well liked food includes lunchtime filled baguettes, beer-battered brie with a tomato and basil salsa, pork and leek sausages with mash and onion gravy, chicken stuffed with black pudding and sage on marsala sauce, meatballs in a spicy tomato sauce with pasta, creole prawns with chilli and lime yoghurt, and navarin of lamb in red wine and rosemary. *Benchmark main dish: steak in ale pie £15.00. Two-course evening meal £20.00.*

Free house ~ Licensee Evelyn McNeil ~ Real ale ~ Bar food (12-2.30, 6-9.30; 12-3, 6-8.30 Sun) ~ (01568) 797286 ~ Children welcome until 9pm ~ Dogs allowed in bar and bedrooms ~ Open 12-11(midnight Sat, 10 Sun) ~ Bedrooms: /£82S

Recommended by R T and J C Moggridge, Paul Humphreys

BRANSFORD Worcestershire   SO8052 Map 4

Bear & Ragged Staff ♀

Off A4103 SW of Worcester; Station Road; WR6 5JH

Cheerfully run dining pub with pleasant places to sit both inside and outside

You can choose between the formal restaurant (with its proper tablecloths and linen napkins) or the more relaxed bar at this friendly dining pub, as the menus are the same throughout. They've a good range of wines to choose from, with about a dozen by the glass, lots of malt whiskies, quite a few brandies and liqueurs, and Fullers London Pride and Hobsons Twisted Spire on handpump. In fine weather, the garden and terrace are enjoyable places to sit, with a pleasant backdrop of rolling country. Inside, the interconnecting rooms give fine views too, and in winter you'll find an open fire; piped music; good disabled access and facilities.

Prepared using carefully sourced produce and some vegetables from their own patch, bar food includes lunchtime sandwiches (not Sunday), terrine of pork belly and black pudding with fruity chutney, lemon grass and spring onion dressing, smoked salmon and sage tart, chicken breast stuffed with mushroom and tarragon with madeira sauce and parsnip crisp, seafood and leek risotto, curry of the day, aubergine, spinach, pine kernels, tomato and cream cheese pithiviers with tomato and basil garlic sauce, gammon, egg and chips, and steaks. *Benchmark main dish: fish and chips with mushy peas £12.50. Two-course evening meal £19.00.*

Free house ~ Real ale ~ Bar food (12-2(2.30 Sun), 6-9) ~ Restaurant ~ (01886) 833399 ~ Children welcome ~ Dogs allowed in bar ~ Open 11.30-2, 6-11; 12-2.30 Sun; closed Sun evening

Recommended by Dr and Mrs Michael Smith, Mrs J May, Alan and Eve Harding, Jeff and Wendy Williams

BRETFORTON Worcestershire   SP0943 Map 4

Fleece ◖ £

B4035 E of Evesham: turn S off this road into village; pub is in central square by church; there's a sizeable car park at one side of the church; WR11 7JE

Marvellously unspoilt medieval pub owned by the National Trust

Try and visit this lovely old farmhouse mid-week as its dimly lit museum-like interior is pretty famous these days and can draw a weekend crowd. Before becoming a pub in 1848, it was owned by the same family for nearly 500 years and many of the furnishings, such as the great oak dresser that holds a priceless 48-piece set of Stuart pewter, are heirlooms passed down generations of the family. Its traditional little rooms have massive beams, exposed timbers and marks scored on the worn and crazed flagstones to keep out demons. There are two fine grandfather clocks, ancient kitchen chairs, curved high-backed settles, a rocking chair and a rack of heavy pointed iron shafts (probably for spit roasting) in one of the huge inglenook fireplaces, and two more log fires. Plenty of oddities include a great cheese-press and set of cheese moulds, and a rare dough-proving table; a leaflet details the more bizarre items. Four or five real ales on handpump are from brewers such as Cannon Royall, Hook Norton, Purity, Uley and Woods, alongside two farm ciders (one made by the landlord), local apple juices, german wheat beer and fruit wines, and ten wines by the glass; darts, shove-ha'penny and various board games. As part of the Vale of Evesham Asparagus Festival, they hold an asparagus auction at the end of May and host the village fête on August bank holiday Monday; there's sometimes morris dancing and the village silver band plays here regularly, too. The lawn (with its fruit trees) around the beautifully restored thatched and timbered barn is a lovely place to sit, and there are more picnic-sets and a stone pump-trough in the front courtyard; they may want to keep your credit card if you run a tab outside.

Bar food includes sandwiches, filo wrapped brie with port and cranberry sauce, smoked salmon, dill and lemon terrine, chicken, bacon and chorizo salad, sausages and chive mash, roast butternut filled with cream cheese, red onion and leeks with melted cheddar, steak and kidney suet pudding, pork, cider and winter vegetable casserole, and fish and chips which they also do as a takeaway. *Benchmark main dish: faggots with chive mash and red wine gravy £8.50. Two-course evening meal £14.40.*

Free house ~ Licensee Nigel Smith ~ Real ale ~ Bar food (12-2.30(4 Sun), 6.30-9(8.30 Sun)) ~ Restaurant ~ (01386) 831173 ~ Children welcome ~ Folk session Thurs evening ~ Open 11-3, 6-11; 11-11 Weds-Sun ~ Bedrooms: /£97.50S

Recommended by Peter and Audrey Dowsett, Mike Proctor, Dennis and Doreen Haward, Andy Lickfold, Lawrence Pearse, John Wooll, Michael Dandy, Paul J Robinshaw, Roger and Ann King, N R White, Theocsbrian, Dr A J and Mrs Tompsett, Ian and Rose Lock

BRIDGNORTH Shropshire   SO7192 Map 4

Old Castle £

West Castle Street; WV16 4AB

Traditional pub, relaxed and friendly, with well kept ales and good-sized suntrap terrace

The low-beamed open-plan bar at this pretty little flower-bedecked pub is properly pubby, with tiles and bare boards, cushioned wall banquettes and settles around cast-iron-framed tables, and bar stools alongside the counter which serves well kept Greene King IPA, Hobsons Town Crier and a guest such as Sharps Doom Bar on handpump. A back conservatory extension has darts and pool; piped music, games machine and big-screen TV for sports events. A big plus here is the sunny back terrace, with shrub borders, big pots of flowers and children's playthings. The decking at the far end gives a high view over the west side of town. Do walk up the street to see the castle ruin, best seen before rather than after a drink: its 20-metre Norman tower tilts at such an extraordinary angle that it makes the leaning tower of Pisa look a model of rectitude.

Good value pubby food includes sandwiches and baguettes, rosemary and garlic crusted brie wedges, salads, vegetable tagine, chilli, battered haddock, fish pie, minted lamb shank, and steaks. *Benchmark main dish: steak and ale pie £6.95. Two-course evening meal £11.00.*

Punch ~ Tenants Bryn Charles Masterman and Kerry Senior ~ Real ale ~ Bar food (12-3, 6.30-8.30; not Sun evening) ~ (01746) 711420 ~ Children welcome ~ Dogs welcome ~ Open 11.30-11

Recommended by George Atkinson, Chris and Angela Buckell

The details at the end of each featured top pub start by saying whether the pub is a free house, or if it belongs to a brewery or pub group (which we name).

BRIMPSFIELD Gloucestershire   SO9413   Map 4

Golden Heart ◖

Nettleton Bottom (not shown on road maps, so we list the pub instead under the name of the nearby village); on A417 N of the Brimpsfield turning northbound; GL4 8LA

Nice old-fashioned furnishings in several cosy areas, big log fire, friendly licensees, and seats on the suntrap terrace; bedrooms

Handy after enjoying one of the nearby walks, this is a traditional inn with quite a lot of character. The main low-ceilinged bar is divided into five cosily distinct areas; there's a roaring log fire in the huge stone inglenook fireplace in one, well worn and traditional built-in settles and other old-fashioned furnishings throughout, quite a few brass items and typewriters, foreign banknotes, exposed stone walls and wood panelling; maybe newspapers to read. A comfortable parlour on the right has another decorative fireplace and leads into a further room that opens on to the terrace. Brakspears Bitter, Jennings Cumberland, Otter Bitter and Ringwood Best Bitter on handpump and several wines by the glass. From the tables and chairs under parasols on the suntrap terrace, there are pleasant views down over a valley.

Quite a choice of bar food includes sandwiches, deep-fried brie, garlic mushrooms, steak in ale pie, goats cheese and caramelised onion tart, lamb noisettes with mint gravy, ham hock with parsley sauce, and chicken stuffed with apple and cider and wrapped in bacon; many of their dishes are gluten free. *Benchmark main dish: steak in ale pie £11.25. Two-course evening meal £17.20.*

Free house ~ Licensee Catherine Stevens ~ Real ale ~ Bar food (12-3, 6-10) ~ (01242) 870261 ~ Children welcome ~ Dogs welcome ~ Open 11-3, 5.30-11; all day school holidays; 11(12 Sun)-11 Sat ~ Bedrooms: £35S/£55S

Recommended by Tom and Ruth Rees, Giles and Annie Francis, Gwyn and Anne Wake, Bob and Angela Brooks, Ken Marshall, Chris Flynn, Wendy Jones, Comus and Sarah Elliott, Andy and Claire Barker, Guy Vowles, Graham Oddey, Jeremy King

BRINGSTY COMMON Herefordshire   SO6954   Map 4

Live & Let Live ◖

Off A44 Knightwick—Bromyard 1.5 miles W of Whitbourne turn; take track southwards at black cat inn sign, bearing right at fork; WR6 5UW

Bustling country tavern surrounded by rolling, partly wooded common, with good drinks

Going from strength to strength, this carefully restored old timbered cottage has plenty of enjoyable character. The cosy bar has non-matching scrubbed or polished tables on its flagstones, a very high-backed traditional winged settle by the log fire in its cavernous stone fireplace, and a variety of seats from comfortably cushioned little chairs to a long stripped pew. Earthenware jugs hang from the low stripped beams, with more bygones on the mantelshelf. The landlady is usually behind the hop-hung bar counter (with old casks built into its facing) serving Ludlow Best, Malvern Hills Black Pear and Wye Valley Butty Bach on handpump, two local ciders and local apple juice. A pair of cottagey dining rooms are tucked up in upstairs under the steep rafters. Outside, a glass-topped well and big wooden hogshead have been pressed into service as tables for the flagstoned terrace. Picnic-sets give long peaceful views from the grassy former orchard, which blends into the common.

There are plenty of good surrounding walks. NT Brockhampton Estate is close by.

 Well liked food includes lunchtime sandwiches, black pudding and streaky bacon topped with a free-range egg, vegetable tagliatelle with a creamy garlic sauce, a trio of sausages with spring onion mash, steak and kidney pie, and bacon-wrapped chicken breast stuffed with onions and mushrooms with a mushroom sauce. *Benchmark main dish: beer-battered fresh fish £10.95. Two-course evening meal £16.00.*

Free house ~ Licensee Sue Dovey ~ Real ale ~ Bar food ~ Restaurant ~ No credit cards ~ (01886) 821462 ~ Children welcome ~ Dogs welcome ~ Open 12-11(10.30 Sun); closed 2.30-6 Tues-Thurs in winter; closed Mon (except bank holidays)

Recommended by the Didler, Chris Flynn, Wendy Jones, Mike and Mary Carter, Dave Braisted, Guy Vowles, Michael Dandy

 BROADWAY Worcestershire   SP0937 Map 4

Crown & Trumpet 🍺 £
Church Street; WR12 7AE

Unreconstructed honest local with good real ale and decent food

One happy reader wrote about his visit here that he was 'delighted to find such a genuine pub. There was a blazing fire and a folk group – really lovely', and that's just how we know this cheerfully bustling down-to-earth place. The relaxed beamed and timbered bar has antique dark high-backed settles, large solid tables and a blazing log fire. Seasonal beers (one for each season) are brewed for the pub by the local Stanway Brewery and served on handpump alongside Cotswold Spring Codrington Codger and Stroud Tom Long, local cider, hot toddies, mulled wine and a good range of soft drinks. They have an assortment of pub games, including darts, shove-ha'penny, cribbage, shut the box, dominoes and ring the bull as well as a quiz machine, TV and piped music. The hardwood tables and chairs outside, among flowers on a slightly raised front terrace, are popular with walkers – even in adverse weather.

 Straightforward bar food includes baguettes, fried whitebait, fried brie and cranberry sauce, ploughman's, vegetable lasagne, sausage and mash, battered haddock, steak and kidney pie, rib-eye steak, and Sunday roasts. *Benchmark main dish: home-made pies £8.75. Two-course evening meal £14.00.*

Laurel (Enterprise) ~ Lease Andrew Scott ~ Real ale ~ Bar food (12-2.30, 6-9.30; 12-9.30 Sat, Sun) ~ (01386) 853202 ~ Children welcome ~ Dogs allowed in bar ~ Live music Sat evening, jazz or blues Thurs ~ Open 11-3(2.30 weekdays in winter), 5-11; 11-midnight Fri, Sat; 11-11pm Sun ~ Bedrooms: £48S/£70S(£75B)

Recommended by Dennis Jones, Derek and Sylvia Stephenson, Theocsbrian, R T and J C Moggridge, Don Bryan, Tracey and Stephen Groves

BROADWELL Gloucestershire   SP2027 Map 4

Fox
Off A429 2 miles N of Stow-on-the-Wold; GL56 0UF

Attractive stone pub in a pretty village, with friendly staff, real ales, honest food and seats in the sizeable garden

This golden stone pub is set above the broad green in a Cotswold village and you can be sure of a warm welcome from the friendly staff. The bar has traditional pubby furnishings on flagstones, stripped-stone walls, beams hung with jugs, a log fire and Donnington BB and SBA on handpump; they also have a large number of rums and winter mulled wine. There are two carpeted dining areas, too. Piped music, darts and board games; the pub cat is called Molly. There are picnic-sets on gravel in the sizeable family-friendly back garden and summer aunt sally.

🍴 Honest pubby food includes lunchtime filled baguettes, garlic mushrooms, ham and eggs, lasagne, beer-battered cod, and a big mixed grill. *Benchmark main dish: braised lamb shank in rosemary and red wine £9.95. Two-course evening meal £16.00.*

Donnington ~ Managers Michael and Carol East ~ Real ale ~ Bar food (11.30(12 Sun)-2, 6.30-9; not Sun evening) ~ Restaurant ~ (01451) 870909 ~ Children welcome ~ Dogs allowed in bar ~ Open 11-2.30(3 Sat), 6-11.30; 12-3, 7-11 Sun
Recommended by Andy Dolan

BROCKHAMPTON Gloucestershire   SP0322   Map 4

Craven Arms ♀

Village signposted off A436 Andoversford—Naunton – look out for inn sign at head of lane in village; can also be reached from A40 Andoversford—Cheltenham via Whittington and Syreford; GL54 5XQ

Friendly village pub with tasty bar food, real ales, seats in a big garden and nice surrounding walks

Quite a long way down a country lane, this attractive 17th-c pub is in a lovely spot; the large garden has plenty of seats and lovely views, and there are fine surrounding walks. Inside, the bars have low beams, thick roughly coursed stone walls and some tiled flooring, and though much of it has been opened out to give a sizeable eating area off the smaller bar servery, it's been done well to give a feeling of several communicating rooms. The furniture is mainly pine with some comfortable leather sofas, wall settles and tub chairs, and there are gin traps and various stuffed animal trophies, and a warm log fire. Otter Bitter, Uley Bitter and a couple of changing guests on handpump and several wines by the glass; juke box and board games. The dog is called Max and the cat Polly.

🍴 Well liked bar food includes filled baguettes, soup, fig and goats cheese salad, moules marinière, spinach and ricotta cannelloni, fresh battered cod, ham and eggs, bass with samphire, and duck with cherry brandy sauce. *Benchmark main dish: steak in ale pie £10.95. Two-course evening meal £16.00.*

Free house ~ Licensees Barbara and Bob Price ~ Real ale ~ Bar food (not Sun evening or Mon) ~ Restaurant ~ (01242) 820410 ~ Children welcome ~ Dogs allowed in bar ~ Open 12-3, 6-11; 12-11 Sat; 12-6 Sun; closed Sun evening and all day Mon in winter
Recommended by Richard Tilbrook

CARDINGTON Shropshire   SO5095   Map 4

Royal Oak

Village signposted off B4371 Church Stretton—Much Wenlock, pub behind church; also reached via narrow lanes from A49; SY6 7JZ

Wonderful rural position, heaps of character inside, too

This beautifully positioned rural place is reputedly Shropshire's oldest continuously licensed pub. It dates from the 15th c, is packed with character and historical atmosphere, and one can imagine that little has changed inside since then – it's even a little frayed round the edges. Its rambling low-beamed bar has a roaring winter log fire, cauldron, black kettle and pewter jugs in its vast inglenook fireplace, the aged standing timbers of a knocked-through wall, and red and green tapestry seats solidly capped in elm; darts, shove-ha'penny and dominoes; Hobsons Best, Wychwood Hobgoblin and a couple of guests such as Three Tuns XXX and Woods Shropshire Lass are on handpump. A comfortable dining area has exposed old beams and studwork. This is glorious country for walks like the one to the summit of Caer Caradoc, a couple of miles to the west (ask for directions at the pub), and the front courtyard makes the most of the setting. Dogs are only allowed in the bar when food isn't being served and if you run a tab they may ask to keep your credit card.

Bar food includes lunchtime baguettes and ploughman's, red onion and cherry tomato tart, fish pie, lasagne, scampi, lamb shank, battered cod, grilled trout with almonds, and steaks. *Benchmark main dish: fidget pie £10.65. Two-course evening meal £14.50.*

Free house ~ Licensees Steve and Eira Oldham ~ Real ale ~ Bar food (12-2, 6.30-9 Tues-Sat; 12-2.30, 7-9 Sun) ~ Restaurant ~ (01694) 771266 ~ Children welcome ~ Open 12-2.30, 6.30-11(midnight Fri); 12-3.30; 7-midnight Sun; closed Mon except bank holiday lunchtimes

Recommended by MDN, Brian and Anna Marsden, R T and J C Moggridge, Maurice and Gill McMahon, David Edwards, Roger and Anne Newbury, Mike Proctor, Tracey and Stephen Groves

CAREY Herefordshire   SO5631   Map 4

Cottage of Content 🍴 🛏

Village signposted from good back road betweeen Ross-on-Wye and Hereford E of A49, through Hoarwithy; HR2 6NG

Country furnishings in a friendly rustic cottage, interesting food, real ales and seats on terraces; quiet bedrooms

Happily unchanging, this quietly positioned medieval cottage is much enjoyed by our readers – who tend to return on a regular basis. Originally three labourers' cottages with its own integral cider and ale parlour, the building has kept much of its old character, with a multitude of beams and country furnishings such as stripped-pine kitchen chairs, long pews by one big table and various old-fashioned tables on flagstones or bare boards. Hobsons Best and Wye Valley Butty Bach on handpump, and the friendly landlady serves a local cider during the summer months; piped music. There are picnic-sets on the flower-filled front terrace or in the rural-feeling garden at the back. This is a nice place to stay.

Highly thought-of food includes chicken liver and pork pâté with caramelised red cabbage and olive and herb toasts, smoked quail eggs with charred pepper salad and smoked paprika mayonnaise, fresh fish pie, vegetable wellington, pork medallions, confit belly and chorizo with black pudding crisp and crackling and a sage and apple sauce, and free-range chicken with pesto on wild mushroom risotto. *Benchmark main dish: local lamb and mint crumble £12.75. Two-course evening meal £18.00.*

Free house ~ Licensees Richard and Helen Moore ~ Real ale ~ Bar food (not Sun evening, Mon, Tues lunchtime in winter) ~ Restaurant ~ (01432) 840242 ~ Children welcome ~ Dogs allowed in bar ~ Live music first Weds of month ~ Open 12-2(2.30 Sat), 6.30-11; 12-3 Sun; closed Sun evening, all day Mon, Tues lunchtime in winter ~ Bedrooms: £55(£65B)/£65(£75B)

*Recommended by C R Cann, the Didler, Mrs A S Crisp, Mike and Mary Carter, Phil Bryant,
Dr and Mrs Michael Smith*

 CAULDON Staffordshire   SK0749   Map 7

Yew Tree ★★ £

*Village signposted from A523 and A52 about 8 miles W of Ashbourne;
ST10 3EJ*

**Treasure-trove of fascinating antiques and dusty bric-a-brac; very
eccentric**

This uniquely idiosyncratic place is not exactly what you'd call spic and
span (far from it) and in the past has been affectionately described as
a junk shop with a bar, but most readers love its unusual charm and for
many it's an institution. Over the years, the characterful landlord has
amassed a museum's worth of curiosities. The most impressive pieces are
perhaps the working polyphons and symphonions – 19th-c developments
of the musical box, often taller than a person, each with quite a repertoire
of tunes and elaborate sound-effects. But there are also two pairs of
Queen Victoria's stockings, ancient guns and pistols, several penny-
farthings, an old sit-and-stride boneshaker, a rocking horse, swordfish
blades, a little 800 BC greek vase, and even a fine marquetry cabinet
crammed with notable early staffordshire pottery. Soggily sprung sofas
mingle with 18th-c settles, plenty of little wooden tables and a four-
person oak church choir seat with carved heads which came from
St Mary's church in Stafford; above the bar is an odd iron dog-carrier. As
well as all this, there's a choir of fine tuneful longcase clocks in the
gallery just above the entrance, a collection of six pianolas (one of which
is played most nights) with an excellent repertoire of piano rolls, a
working vintage valve radio set, a crank-handle telephone, a sinuous
medieval wind instrument made of leather, and a Jacobean four-poster
which was once owned by Josiah Wedgwood and still has his original wig
hook on the headboard. Clearly, it would be almost an overwhelming task
to keep all this sprucely clean. The drinks here are very reasonably
priced, so no wonder it's popular with locals. You'll find well kept Bass,
Burton Bridge and Rudgate Ruby Mild on handpump or tapped from the
cask, along with about a dozen interesting malt whiskies; piped music
(probably Radio 2), darts, shove-ha'penny, table skittles, dominoes and
cribbage. When you arrive, don't be put off by the plain exterior, or the
fact that the pub is tucked unpromisingly between enormous cement
works and quarries and almost hidden by a towering yew tree.

Simple good value tasty snacks include pork, meat and potato, chicken and
mushroom and steak pies, hot big filled baps and sandwiches, quiche, smoked
mackerel or ham salad; no starters. *Benchmark main dish: pork pie £2.80.*

Free house ~ Licensee Alan East ~ Real ale ~ Bar food ~ No credit cards ~
(01538) 308348 ~ Children in polyphon room ~ Dogs welcome ~ Folk music first Tues
of month ~ Open 10-2.30(3 Sat), 6-midnight; 12-3, 7-midnight Sun
*Recommended by S J and C C Davidson, John Dwane, Mike Horgan, Di Wright, the Didler, Jill and
Julian Tasker, David Austin, Barry Collett, Mr & Mrs N Hall*

The price we give for a two-course evening meal in the featured top pub entries is
the mean (average of cheapest and most expensive) price of a starter
and a main course – no drinks.

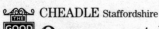 **CHEADLE** Staffordshire   SK0342 Map 7

 # Queens at Freehay £

1 mile SE of Cheadle; take Rakeway Road off A522 (via Park Avenue or Mills Road), then after 1 mile turn into Counslow Road; ST10 1RF

Enjoyable dining pub with a couple of local beers and a decent garden

The comfortable lounge bar at this agreeable 18th-c dining pub is gently modern but still has small country pictures and pretty curtains with matching cushions. It opens through an arch into a light and airy dining area, with neatly spaced tables. Pleasant welcoming staff serve Burton Bridge and Peakstones Rock Alton Abbey from handpump; piped music. The attractive little back garden with its mature shrubs and neatly arranged picnic-sets is kept in immaculate condition.

Fairly priced food is cooked carefully and nicely presented. As well as reasonably priced lunchtime oatcakes, sandwiches and salads, there might be black pudding topped with bacon and melted cheddar cheese, thai-style prawns, moroccan lamb tagine, fish and chips, fried duck breast with plum and hoi sin sauce, grilled cod loin with parsley hollandaise sauce, and steaks. *Benchmark main dish: beef and wine pie £10.95. Two-course evening meal £15.90.*

Free house ~ Licensee Adrian Rock ~ Real ale ~ Bar food (12-2(2.30 Sun), 6(6.30 Sun)-9.30) ~ Restaurant ~ (01538) 722383 ~ Children welcome ~ Open 12-3, 6-11(6.30-10.30 Sun)

Recommended by Meg and Colin Hamilton, Mr and Mrs M Plant

CHEDWORTH Gloucestershire   SP0512 Map 4

Seven Tuns ♀

Village signposted off A429 NE of Cirencester; then take second signposted right turn and bear left towards church; GL54 4AE

Bustling, enjoyable little pub with several open fires, lots of wines by the glass, popular bar food and plenty of outside seats

Always friendly and with a cheerful, bustling atmosphere, this is an enjoyable little 17th-c pub in a charming village. It's popular locally but has plenty of visitors, too, and the small snug lounge on the right has comfortable seats and decent tables, sizeable antique prints, tankards hanging from the beam over the serving bar, a partly boarded ceiling, and a good winter log fire in a big stone fireplace. Down a couple of steps, the public bar on the left has an open fire and this leads into a dining room with yet another open fire. Wells & Youngs Bitter and Special and a guest such as St Austell Tribute on handpump, up to 14 wines by the glass and 19 malt whiskies; piped music and skittle alley. One sunny terrace has a boules pitch and across the road there's another little walled, raised terrace with a waterwheel and a stream; plenty of tables and seats. There are nice walks through the valley. The famous Roman villa is nearby.

They bake their own bread and make their own pasta for the well presented food which might include lunchtime filled baguettes, scallops on beetroot and potato cakes with a champagne dressing, a burger with home-made relish and onion jam, garlic-roasted mediterranean vegetables with pesto and linguine, black pudding-stuffed pork loin with chorizo and an apple and cider jus, and gresham duck breast with a soy and teriyaki reduction. *Benchmark main dish: beer-battered fish and chips £11.95. Two-course evening meal £18.45.*

Youngs ~ Tenant Mr Davenport-Jones ~ Real ale ~ Bar food (12-2.30(3 Sat and Sun),

6.30-9.30(9 Sun)) ~ Restaurant ~ (01285) 720242 ~ Children welcome ~ Dogs allowed in bar ~ Open 12-3, 6-11; all day in July and Aug; 12-midnight(10.30 Sun) Sat
Recommended by Keith and Sue Ward, Richard Tilbrook, Guy Vowles, Ian and Nita Cooper, Ken and Barbara Turner

 CHELTENHAM Gloucestershire   SO9624   Map 4

Royal Oak ♀ ◨

Off B4348 just N; The Burgage, Prestbury; GL52 3DL

Bustling and friendly with quite a range of bar food, real ales and seats in the sheltered garden

Since it's the closest pub to Cheltenham racecourse, things can get pretty hectic on race days. At other times too, it's a popular place and there always seems to be something going on. The congenial low-beamed bar has fresh flowers and polished brasses, a comfortable mix of seating including chapel chairs on the parquet flooring, some interesting pictures on the ochre walls and a woodburning stove in the stone fireplace. Dark Star Hophead, Otter Bitter, Saltaire Cascade Pale and Timothy Taylors Landlord on handpump and several wines by the glass; they hold a beer and sausage festival over the late May bank holiday and a cider and cheese festival over the August bank holiday. Service is efficient and friendly. Dining room tables are nicely spaced so that you don't feel crowded and the skittle alley can also be used as a function room; piped music. There are seats and tables under canopies on the heated terrace and in a sheltered garden.

Well thought-of food includes lunchtime filled ciabattas, rare-breed pork terrine with fig compote, spicy squid stew with a tapenade croûton, asparagus and leek tart with tomato and garlic confit, braised lamb shoulder provençale style, and bass fillet with goan curry spiced vegetable and coconut milk sauce. *Benchmark main dish: pork belly with soy dressing £12.95. Two-course evening meal £19.00.*

Enterprise ~ Lease Simon and Kate Daws ~ Real ale ~ Bar food (all day Sun) ~ Restaurant ~ (01242) 522344 ~ Children welcome ~ Open 11.30-11; 12-10.30 Sun; 11-3, 5.30-11 Mon-Thurs in winter
Recommended by Michael Sargent, R T and J C Moggridge, Guy Vowles

 CHETWYND ASTON Shropshire   SJ7517   Map 7

Fox ⊕ ♀ ◨

Village signposted off A41 and A518 just S of Newport; TF10 9LQ

SHROPSHIRE DINING PUB OF THE YEAR

Civilised dining pub with generous food and a fine array of drinks served by ever-attentive staff

Although big, this handsome 1920s Brunning & Price pub is intimate and friendly, with its welcoming atmosphere very much helped along by its kindly capable staff. It was done up by a few years ago, and its style will be familiar to anyone who has tried other pubs in this successful little chain. A series of linked semi-separate areas, one with a broad arched ceiling, has plenty of tables in all shapes and sizes, some quite elegant, and a vaguely matching diversity of comfortable chairs, all laid out in a way that's fine for eating but serves equally well for just drinking and chatting. There are masses of attractive prints, three open fires and a few oriental rugs on polished parquet, boards or attractive floor tiling; big windows and careful lighting contribute to the relaxed effortless atmosphere; board games. The handsome bar counter, with a decent complement of bar stools, serves an excellent changing range of about 18 wines by the glass and 50 malt whiskies; Phoenix Brunning & Price Original, Three Tuns XXX, Woods Shropshire Lad and three guests from brewers such as Newmans, Slaters and Titanic are on handpump. Although they do provide highchairs, pushchairs and baby buggies are not allowed; good disabled access. The spreading garden is quite lovely, with a sunny terrace, picnic-sets tucked into the shade of mature trees and extensive views across quiet country fields.

As well as sandwiches, well liked food, served in generous helpings from a changing menu, might include spiced fried halloumi on fennel and red onion salad with poppyseed yoghurt, crisp breaded ox tongue with salsa vierge, charcuterie, sweet potato, leek and goats cheese dumplings with red pepper and courgette puy lentils, sun-dried tomato and basil dressing, roast duck with pomegranate couscous, good steak and kidney pie, sausage and mash, battered haddock, and rump steak with watercress and horseradish butter. *Benchmark main dish: steak burger £10.95. Two-course evening meal £17.00.*

Brunning & Price ~ Manager Samantha Forrest ~ Real ale ~ Bar food (12-10(9.30 Sun and bank holidays)) ~ (01952) 815940 ~ Children welcome ~ Dogs allowed in bar ~ Open 12-11(10.30 Sun)

Recommended by Liz Bell, Bruce and Sharon Eden, C A Bryson, Steve Whalley

CHIPPING CAMPDEN Gloucestershire   SP1539 Map 4

Eight Bells 🍽 🍺

Church Street (which is one way – entrance off B4035); GL55 6JG

Handsome inn with massive timbers and beams, log fires, interesting bar food, real ales and seats in the large terraced garden; handy for the Cotswold Way; bedrooms

There's always a buoyant atmosphere in this handsome old inn – and a good mix of both visitors and locals, too. The bars have heavy oak beams, massive timber supports and stripped-stone walls with cushioned pews, sofas and solid dark wood furniture on the broad flagstones and log fires in up to three restored stone fireplaces. Inset into the floor of the newly refurbished dining room is a glass panel showing part of the passage from the church by which Roman Catholic priests could escape from the Roundheads. Hook Norton Best, Goffs Jouster, Purity Mad Goose and a guest such as Wye Valley HPA on handpump from the fine oak bar counter, quite a few wines by the glass and Old Rosie cider. Piped music and board games. There's a large terraced garden with plenty of seats, and striking views of the almshouses and church. The pub is handy for the Cotswold Way walk which takes you to Bath.

Quite a choice of well presented food might include lunchtime sandwiches (not Sunday), lamb koftas on lime and coriander couscous, smoked trout pâté, pork and leek sausages with grain mustard sauce and home-battered onion rings, oriental-style vegetable and egg noodle stir fry, chicken breast topped with a tomato and olive sauce, mozzarella, pesto and pasta, and slow-braised lamb shank with rosemary jus; they also offer a two- and three-course set lunchtime menu. *Benchmark main dish: beer-battered fish and chips £12.50. Two-course evening meal £20.80.*

Free house ~ Licensee Neil Hargreaves ~ Real ale ~ Bar food (12-2(2.30 Fri-Sun), 6.30-9 (9.30 Fri and Sat, 8.45 Sun)) ~ Restaurant ~ (01386) 840371 ~ Well behaved children welcome but only in dining room after 6pm ~ Dogs allowed in bar ~ Open 12(11 Sat)-11(10.30 Sun) ~ Bedrooms: £65B/£85B

Recommended by Mike Proctor, MDN, George Atkinson, Paul Humphreys, Michael Dandy, Eithne Dandy, Eleanor Dandy, Mike and Sue Loseby, Martin and Pauline Jennings, Peter Smith and Judith Brown, Peter Dandy, M G Hart

CLIFFORD'S MESNE Gloucestershire SO6922 Map 4

Yew Tree 🍴 ♀ ◀

From A40 W of Huntley turn off at May Hill 1, Clifford's Mesne 2.5 signpost, then pub eventually signed up steep narrow lane on left; Clifford's Mesne also signposted off B4216 S of Newent, pub then signed on right; GL18 1JS

Unusual dining pub nicely tucked away on slopes of May Hill; wine bargains

For those interested in provincial french wines from small producers – just head for this friendly, well run pub. They have a seating area in their small informal wine shop making it a sort of wine bar with nibbles and if you buy a bottle with your meal, they charge just the shop price plus £6. So you end up paying, say, £11, for a wine which in another pub would typically cost £18, or £16 instead of over £30, or even £25 instead of around £60 – the better the wine, the bigger the bargain. But they also have Cotswold Spring Gloucestershire's Glory, Sharps Doom Bar and Wickwar BOB on handpump, local farm cider and good value winter mulled wine; service is prompt and genial. The smallish two-room beamed bar has an attractive mix of small settles, a pew and character chairs around interesting tables including antiques, rugs on an unusual stone floor, and a warm woodburning stove. You can eat more formally up a few steps, in a carpeted dining room beyond a sofa by a big log fire; daily papers and unobtrusive piped nostalgic pop music. Teak tables on a side terrace are best placed for the views and there are steps down to a sturdy play area. Plenty of nearby walks.

Using their own rare-breed pigs, home-grown vegetables and other seasonal local produce, the enjoyable food includes duck and chicken terrine with pistachios, goujons of pheasant with a redcurrant dip, beefsteak tomato, mozzarella and spring onion tart, sausages and mash, beefcake with rich gravy and mash, free-range chicken with rosemary and thyme-roasted vegetables, and seared duck breast on a rhubarb, ginger and balsamic compote. *Benchmark main dish: rare-breed pork loin steak with wild garlic and apricot butter £13.50. Two-course evening meal £19.50.*

Free house ~ Licensees Mr and Mrs Philip Todd ~ Real ale ~ Bar food (12-2, 6-9; 12-4 Sun; not Mon or Tues lunchtimes) ~ (01531) 820719 ~ Children welcome ~ Dogs allowed in bar ~ Live music monthly ~ Open 12-2.30, 6-11; 12-5 Sun; closed Sun evening, Mon and Tuesday lunchtimes

Recommended by Mike and Mary Carter, J E Shackleton, Bernard Stradling, Rod Stoneman, Chris and Val Ramstedt, Alistair Stanier, TB, Guy Vowles

---

'Children welcome' means the pub says it lets children inside without any special restriction. If it allows them in, but to restricted areas such as an eating area or family room, we specify this. Places with separate restaurants often let children use them, and hotels usually let them into public areas such as lounges. Some pubs impose an evening time limit – let us know if you find one earlier than 9pm.

CLUN Shropshire   SO3080 Map 6

White Horse ◀ £

The Square; SY7 8JA

Cheery village local with seven real ales and good value traditional food

The heart of this refurbished 18th-c village pub is the cheery low-beamed front bar, where drinkers and eaters mingle in a friendly atmosphere, warmed in winter by a cosy inglenook woodburning stove. From the bar, a door leads into a separate little dining room where you will see a rare plank and muntin screen. In the games room at the back, you'll find a TV, games machine, darts, pool, juke box and board games. Attentive staff serve up to seven, usually local, well kept changing ales from brewers such as Clun, Hobsons, Salopian, Stonehouse, Three Tuns and Wye Valley, as well as Weston's farm cider and a good range of bottled beers; small garden.

Traditional, good value pubby bar food, served in generous helpings, includes sandwiches, breaded brie with redcurrant jelly, ploughman's, cajun chicken, smoked mackerel salad, mushroom and bean chilli, scampi, suet pudding of the day, and quorn sausage, egg and chips. *Benchmark main dish: suet pudding £9.25. Two-course evening meal £13.00.*

Free house ~ Licensee Jack Limond ~ Real ale ~ Bar food (12-2, 6.30-8.30) ~ (01588) 640305 ~ Children welcome ~ Dogs allowed in bar and bedrooms ~ Live music Fri fortnightly ~ Open 12-12 ~ Bedrooms: £32.50S/£55S

Recommended by Ann and Colin Hunt, A N Bance, Dr D J and Mrs S C Walker, Malcolm and Jo Hart, MLR, Guy Vowles, Alan and Eve Harding

COATES Gloucestershire   SO9600 Map 4

Tunnel House ◀

Follow Tarlton signs (right then left) from village, pub up rough track on right after railway bridge; OS Sheet 163 map reference 965005; GL7 6PW

Friendly pub with interesting décor, lots of character, popular food and drink, and seats in the sizeable garden; guards derelict canal tunnel

The view from tables on the pleasant terrace in front of the eccentric bow-fronted stone house is pretty impressive and the big garden slopes down to the derelict entrance tunnel of the old Thames & Severn Canal (which is under slow restoration). Inside, there's a lively atmosphere and a cheerful mix of customers – it's especially popular with students from the Royal Agricultural College. The rambling rooms have beams, flagstones, a happy mix of furnishings including massive rustic benches and seats built into the sunny windows, lots of enamel advertising signs, racing tickets and air travel labels, a stuffed wild boar's head and stuffed owl, plenty of copper and brass and an upside-down card table complete with cards and drinks fixed to the beams; there's a nice log fire with sofas in front of it (but you have to arrive early to grab them). The more conventional dining extension and back conservatory fill up quickly at mealtimes. Braydon Pot Walloper, Sharps Doom Bar, Uley Bitter and a guest beer on handpump, several wines by the glass and two draught ciders; piped music. Good walks nearby; disabled lavatories.

Well liked bar food includes sandwiches, chicken liver and wild mushroom parfait with home-made chutney, moules marinière, beef or vegetarian burgers with cheese, gloucester old spot sausages with mash and red onion marmalade, crab and pesto linguine topped with fennel and parmesan, and lamb steak on ratatouille couscous. *Benchmark main dish: beer-battered cod and chips £10.75. Two-course evening meal £17.00.*

Free house ~ Licensee Michael Hughes ~ Real ale ~ Bar food (12-9.30) ~ Restaurant ~ (01285) 770280 ~ Children welcome ~ Dogs welcome ~ Open 12-midnight

Recommended by Suzy Miller, Roger and Donna Huggins, Mike and Lynn Robinson, Alan Bulley, Jean and Douglas Troup, Guy Vowles

DIDMARTON Gloucestershire   ST8187 Map 2

Kings Arms ♀ ⇚

A433 Tetbury road; GL9 1DT

Bustling pub with knocked-through rooms, several real ales, tasty bar food and pleasant back garden; bedrooms and self-catering cottages

Handy for Westonbirt Arboretum, this is a 17th-c former coaching inn with a friendly and efficient landlord. The several knocked-through beamed bar rooms work their way around a big central counter, with deep terracotta walls above a dark green dado in some rooms, yellow and cream paintwork in others, an attractive mix of wooden tables and chairs on bare boards, quarry tiles and carpet, fresh flowers, and a big stone fireplace. There's also a smart restaurant. Otter Ale, Exmoor Fox, Timothy Taylors Landlord and Uley Bitter on handpump and several wines by the glass; darts. There are seats out in the pleasant back garden and boules. As well as comfortable bedrooms they have self-catering cottages in a converted barn and stable block.

As well as lunchtime filled ciabattas, the bar food might include pork terrine with medlar jelly, chilli and garlic prawns, home-baked ham and eggs, burger with bacon and cheese, fish crumble, chicken confit with wild mushroom sauce, and calves liver with a blackberry dressing. *Benchmark main dish: venison casserole £12.95. Two-course evening meal £18.70.*

Free house ~ Licensees R A and S A Sadler ~ Real ale ~ Bar food (12-2, 7-9; 12-7.15 Sun) ~ Restaurant ~ (01454) 238245 ~ Children welcome ~ Dogs allowed in bar ~ Open 11-11; 12-10.30 Sun ~ Bedrooms: £65S/£85S

Recommended by Bob and Angela Brooks, John Chambers, Bruce and Sharon Eden, Heather and Dick Martin, Barry and Anne, KC, Phil and Gill Wass

DURSLEY Gloucestershire   ST7598 Map 4

Old Spot ◀ £

Hill Road; by bus station; GL11 4JQ

Unassuming and cheery town pub with up to ten real ales and regular beer festivals

For many of our readers, this very well run town local is an absolute favourite. It's run by a genuinely friendly landlord who keeps a fantastic range of up to ten real ales on handpump which might include Bath Ales Gem Bitter, Moles Tap Bitter, Otter Ale, Sawbridgeworth Dragons Blood, Severn Vale Severn Sins, Springhead Bees Knees, Uley Old Ric, Wickwar BOB and Wye Valley Dorothy Goodbody's Golden Ale; they also hold four annual beer festivals and stock quite a few malt whiskies, too. There are always plenty of good-humoured locals and the front door opens into a deep pink small room with stools on shiny quarry tiles along its pine-boarded bar counter and old enamel beer advertisements on the walls and ceiling; there's a profusion of porcine paraphernalia. A small room on the left leads off from here and the little dark wood-floored room to the right has a stone fireplace. A step takes you down to a cosy Victorian tiled snug and (to the right) the meeting room. There are seats in the heated and covered garden.

🍴 Good value lunchtime bar food (though they now offer food on Monday evenings) includes doorstep sandwiches, pork and apple burger, cauliflower cheese, ham and asparagus bake, steak in ale pie, and haddock and chive fishcakes. *Benchmark main dish: a grazing board of meats, cheeses, fish, olives and bread £9.95. Two-course evening meal £11.00*

Free house ~ Licensee Steve Herbert ~ Real ale ~ Bar food (12-3; no evening meals except Mon (6.30-9)) ~ (01453) 542870 ~ Children in family room only (best to book) ~ Dogs welcome ~ Open 11(12 Sun)-11

Recommended by Dr and Mrs A K Clarke, Julian Jewitt, PL, the Didler

---

EBRINGTON Gloucestershire   SP1839   Map 4

Ebrington Arms 🍴
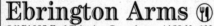
Off B4035 E of Chipping Campden or A429 N of Moreton-in-Marsh;
GL55 6NH

17th-c village inn with enthusiastic young licensees, good choice of real ales, wines by the glass and interesting food; bedrooms

In an attractive village surrounded by good walks, this 17th-c Cotswold-stone pub is a delightful place with friendly, hard-working licensees. There's plenty of character and charm and the beamed bar has lots of cheerful locals, ladder-back chairs around a mix of tables on the flagstoned floor, a fine inglenook fireplace and some seats built into the airy bow window. The beamed dining room is similarly furnished and has original iron work in its inglenook fireplace. A good choice of real ales only from Gloucestershire might include Severn Vale Ale, Stanway Stanney Bitter, Stroud Organic Ale, Uley Bitter and a changing guest on handpump, and several wines by the glass; they have two-pint takeaway beer cartons, too. Darts, a monthly quiz and maybe TV for sports. An arched stone wall shelters a terrace with picnic-sets under parasols and there are more on the lawn. The inn is handy for Hidcote and Kiftsgate gardens. Dogs must be kept on a lead.

🍴 Highly enjoyable food includes sandwiches, twice-baked smoked haddock and cheese soufflé with a rich crab bisque, hot smoked duck breast, liver pâté, olive croûtes and red onion jam, beer-battered fish and chips (which you can take away as well), spiced beef, coriander and grain mustard burger with avocado salsa and horseradish mayonnaise, home-made pork, apple and chestnut sausages with caramelised shallot gravy, and wild bass fillet with roasted fennel, chorizo-crushed new potatoes and shellfish cream sauce; they also serve afternoon tea. *Benchmark main dish: beer-battered fish and chips £11.00. Two-course evening meal £17.50.*

Free house ~ Licensees Clare and Jim Alexander ~ Real ale ~ Bar food (12-2.30, 6.30-9(9.30 Fri and Sat); afternoon tea 3.30-5.30) ~ (01386) 593223 ~ Children welcome ~ Dogs allowed in bar ~ Folk music first Mon of month ~ Open 12-11; closed Sun evening ~ Bedrooms: /£100B

Recommended by Keith and Sue Ward, Martin and Pauline Jennings, Eithne Dandy, Di and Mike Gillam, Guy Vowles, Tim Maddison, David Gunn

---

We say if we know a pub has piped music.

ELDERSFIELD Worcestershire SO8131 Map 4

Butchers Arms 🍴 🍺

Village signposted from B4211; Lime Street (coming from A417, go past the Eldersfield turn and take the next one), OS Sheet 150 map reference 815314; also signposted from B4208 N of Staunton; GL19 4NX

Booking required for good interesting cooking of prime ingredients in unspoilt country local's compact dining room

Kept deliberately simple and unspoilt, the little locals' bar at this pretty cottage has one or two high bar chairs, plain but individual wooden chairs and tables on bare oak boards, a big warming woodburner in quite a cavernous fireplace, black beams, clean cream paintwork and a traditional quoits board. The friendly landlady serves Dorothy Goodbody, St Austell Tribute and Wye Valley Bitter straight from the cask, a farm cider and a short but well chosen list of wines. Food is served in the little dining room, also simple, which has just three tables and seats only 12. You must reserve a table to eat at lunchtimes and it's advised in the evening. Don't leave it late as they do get booked up.

Using first-class ingredients from named local farms, including rare-breed meats, line-caught fresh fish and all sorts of freshly gathered wild mushrooms (something of a speciality here), James Winter keeps the choice short and seasonal, and changes it daily. The results are full of flavour and interest and beautifully presented. Starters might include home-smoked sea trout with beetroot relish and potato pancake, onion tart with melted brie and crab risotto with seared scallop, and main courses such as turbot fillet with truffle mash and cider-braised pork belly, and pork loin with cider-braised shoulder with lentils and bacon. *Benchmark main dish: middle white cheek with crackling and apple sauce £9.00. Two-course evening meal £27.50.*

Free house ~ Licensees James and Elizabeth Winter ~ Real ale ~ Restaurant ~ (01452) 840381 ~ Open 12-2.30, 7-11(10.30 Sun); closed Mon, Sun evening, ten days in Jan, ten days at end Aug
Recommended by John and Mary Ling, T Harrison

FORD Gloucestershire SP0829 Map 4

Plough

B4077 Stow—Alderton; GL54 5RU

16th-c inn opposite racehorse trainer's yard, with lots of horse talk, bustling atmosphere, good food and beer; bedrooms

This extremely well run pub is so popular that it's best to book a table in advance if you are hoping to eat – but no matter how busy they are, the friendly landlord and his staff remain efficient and helpful. There's a chatty atmosphere and the beamed and stripped-stone bar has racing prints and photos on the walls (many of the customers here are to do with racing as a well known racehorse trainer's yard is opposite), old settles and benches around the big tables on its uneven flagstones, oak tables in a snug alcove and open fires or woodburning stoves (a couple are the real thing). Darts, TV (for the races) and piped music. Donnington BB and SBA on handpump. There are some picnic-sets under parasols and pretty hanging baskets at the front of the stone building and a large back garden with a play fort for children. The Cotswold Farm Park is nearby. The comfortable bedrooms away from the pub are the quietest and there are views of the gallops. It does get pretty packed on race meeting days.

As well as race day breakfasts, the enjoyable food (using free-range meat and seasonal game) includes lunchtime filled baguettes, thai crab fishcakes with sweet chilli dipping sauce, baked field mushroom filled with goats cheese and creamed leeks, chicken, ham and asparagus pie, game casserole with dumplings, gammon with free-range eggs, and slow-roasted half shoulder of lamb with gravy and mint sauce. *Benchmark main dish: half crispy duck with bubble and squeak and orange sauce £16.95. Two-course evening meal £19.90.*

Donnington ~ Tenant Craig Brown ~ Real ale ~ Bar food (all day Fri-Sun) ~ Restaurant ~ (01386) 584215 ~ Children welcome ~ Dogs allowed in bar ~ Open 9am-11pm ~ Bedrooms: £60S/£80S

Recommended by D Goodger, Dr A Y Drummond, Anne and Jeff Peel, Simon Watkins, William Goodhart, the Didler, Michael Dandy, Chris and Val Ramstedt, Mrs Blethyn Elliott, Gerry and Rosemary Dobson, Peter Smith and Judith Brown, Terry Buckland, Giles and Annie Francis, Bob Jones, Ian Herdman, KC

 FOSSEBRIDGE Gloucestershire   SP0711 Map 4

Fossebridge Inn 🍴 ⇋
A429 Cirencester—Stow-on-the-Wold; GL54 3JS

Handsome old inn with a proper bar, a good mix of customers, real ales, interesting food and seats in four acres of grounds; smart bedrooms

Whatever the time of year, this handsome Georgian inn is such an enjoyable place to visit. There are winter log fires and lovely summer gardens and you can be sure of a friendly welcome from the staff whether you are a local or a visitor. At its heart is the bustling bar with a relaxed and informal atmosphere, plenty of chatty regulars, Bath Ales SPA and St Austell Proper Job and Tribute on handpump and several wines by the glass. The two rooms have beams and arches, stripped-stone walls and fine old flagstones, a happy mix of dining chairs, stools and wooden tables, copper implements, candles and fresh flowers. Two other dining rooms are rather grand. Outside, there are picnic-sets under parasols and four acres of lawned, riverside gardens with a lake. The bedrooms are comfortable and they have a self-catering cottage. The Roman villa at Chedworth is nearby.

Inventive and very good, the food includes pigeon and crispy pancetta with a sunblush tomato and watercress salad and a honey and mustard dressing, sautéed wild mushroom croûte and a poached egg with a creamy white wine and tarragon sauce, mediterranean vegetable lasagne, chargrilled burger, thai monkfish, mussel and tiger prawn curry, and specials such as steak and kidney in ale pie, and honey-glazed duck breast with sweet chilli broccoli, parsnip crisps and rosemary jus. *Benchmark main dish: saddle of lamb £17.50. Two-course evening meal £19.45.*

Free house ~ Licensee Samantha Jenkins ~ Real ale ~ Bar food (12-2.30(3 Sat, 3.30 Sun), 6-9) ~ Restaurant ~ (01285) 720721 ~ Children welcome ~ Dogs welcome ~ Open 12-11.30 ~ Bedrooms: £110B/£120B

Recommended by Keith and Sue Ward, Guy Vowles, Richard Tilbrook, Rob and Catherine Dunster, Mr and Mrs M J Girdler, Barry and Anne

 GAYDON Warwickshire   SP3654   Map 4

 Malt Shovel ◀

Under a mile from M40 junction 12; B4451 into village, then over roundabout and across B4100; Church Road; CV35 0ET

In a quiet village just off the M40; nice mix of pubby bar and smarter restaurant, tasty food and five real ales

The cheery licensees at this spotlessly kept and friendly pub serve particularly well kept Fullers London Pride, Greene King Abbot, Everards Tiger, Wadworths 6X, Wye Valley and possibly a guest such as Black Sheep, and most of their dozen or so wines are available by the glass. Mahogany-varnished boards link through to bright carpeting the entrance with the bar counter and its lined-up stools on the right and the blazing log fire on the left. The central area has a high-pitched ceiling, milk churns and earthenware containers in a loft above the bar. Three steps take you up to a little space with some comfortable sofas overlooked by a big stained-glass window and reproductions of classic posters. Dining is as important here as the beer, and at the other end is a busy eating area with fresh flowers on the mix of kitchen, pub and dining tables; piped music, darts and games machine. They will keep your credit card if you run a tab outside. The springer spaniel is called Rosie and the jack russell is Mollie.

Enjoyable food, cooked by the chef/landlord, includes good lunchtime sandwiches and panini, ploughman's, salads, duck with orange, lemon and honey, wild boar and apple sausages, battered haddock, four cheese ravioli, gammon, egg and chips, battered fish, and steaks. *Benchmark main dish: home-made pie £9.45. Two-course evening meal £15.70.*

Enterprise ~ Lease Richard and Debi Morisot ~ Real ale ~ Bar food (12-2, 6.30-9) ~ Restaurant ~ (01926) 641221 ~ Children welcome ~ Dogs allowed in bar ~ Open 11-3, 5-11, 11-11 Fri, Sat; 12-10.30 Sun

Recommended by Pam and John Smith, Tina and David Woods-Taylor, John and Judy Selby, Paul Goldman, Susan and John Douglas, Jean and Douglas Troup, George Atkinson, Ian and Jane Irving

GREAT RISSINGTON Gloucestershire   SP1917   Map 4

Lamb ♀ ⇐

Turn off A40 W of Burford to the Barringtons; keep straight on past Great Barrington until Great Rissington is signed on left; GL54 2LN

Busy inn with civilised bar, well liked bar food, changing real ales and seats in the sheltered garden; bedrooms

Overlooking the village and the surrounding hills, this partly 17th-c inn is smart and comfortable. The rather civilised two-roomed bar has heritage red- and stone-coloured walls, high-backed leather chairs grouped around polished tables, and a woodburning stove in the Cotswold-stone fireplace. Some interesting things to look out for are parts of a propeller, artefacts in display cases and pictures of the Canadian crew from the Wellington bomber that crashed in the garden in October 1943. The restaurant has another woodburning stove and various old agricultural tools on the walls. Brakspears Bitter, Wychwood Hobgoblin and a guest beer on handpump, quite a few wines by the glass from a comprehensive list and several malt whiskies; piped music, TV, board games and books for sale (the money goes towards guide dogs for the blind). You can sit outside on the front terrace or in the sheltered, well kept hillside garden. There's a local circular walk which takes in part of the idyllic village, church, River Windrush and stunning countryside surrounding the pub.

🍴 Well liked food includes sandwiches and paninis, duck liver and orange pâté with pear and cider chutney, whitebait, pasta with chestnut mushrooms, spinach, plum tomato and pesto, free-range chicken wrapped in parma ham with a goats cheese and basil sauce, baked whole bibury trout in a parsley and balsamic butter, and steak and kidney in ale pie. *Benchmark main dish: fresh haddock in cider and sesame seed batter £11.95. Two-course evening meal £17.90.*

Free house ~ Licensees Paul and Jacqueline Gabriel ~ Real ale ~ Bar food (12-2.30, 6.30-9) ~ Restaurant ~ (01451) 820388 ~ Children welcome ~ Dogs allowed in bar and bedrooms ~ Open 12-11.30(midnight Sat, 11 Sun) ~ Bedrooms: £55B/£80B

Recommended by George Atkinson, Steve and Sue Griffiths, Tim Maddison

---

GUITING POWER Gloucestershire   SP0924   Map 4

Hollow Bottom

Village signposted off B4068 SW of Stow-on-the-Wold (still called A436 on many maps); GL54 5UX

Popular old inn with lots of racing memorabilia and a good bustling atmosphere

There's always a really good mix of customers in this snug old stone cottage – all of whom are made to feel genuinely welcomed by the hard-working licensees and their staff. The comfortable beamed bar has plenty of atmosphere, lots of racing memorabilia including racing silks, tunics, photographs, race badges, framed newspaper cuttings and horseshoes (their local horse won the Gold Cup in 2010 and they have dedicated an area in the bar to him); there's a winter log fire in an unusual pillar-supported stone fireplace. The public bar has flagstones and stripped-stone masonry, and racing on TV; newspapers to read, darts, board games and piped music. Festival Gold, Donnington SBA and a beer named for the pub on handpump, several wines (including champagne) by the glass and 16 malt whiskies. From the pleasant garden behind the pub there are views towards the sloping fields; decent nearby walks.

🍴 As well as daily specials such as smoked mackerel pâté with a horseradish cream, spaghetti with wild mushroom sauce and local venison in a red wine and shallot sauce, the tasty food might include filled baguettes, home-made burger,

---

THE HEART OF ENGLAND'S TOP PUBS | 711

sausages with creamy mash and gravy, ham and free-range eggs, and a pie of the day. *Benchmark main dish: smoked haddock on mash £12.95. Two-course evening meal £15.40.*

Free house ~ Licensees Hugh Kelly and Charles Pettigrew ~ Real ale ~ Bar food (all day) ~ Restaurant ~ (01451) 850392 ~ Children welcome ~ Dogs allowed in bar ~ Live music first Sun evening of month ~ Open 9am-midnight ~ Bedrooms: £75B/£90B

Recommended by John Taylor, Keith and Sue Ward, Michael and Jenny Back, Michael Sargent, John and Val Shand, T Harrison, Ian Herdman, Tracey and Stephen Groves

HAMPTON IN ARDEN Warwickshire   SP2080   Map 4

White Lion

High Street; handy for M42 junction 6; B92 0AA

Useful village local, five real ales; bedrooms

Sympathetic redecorations seem to have brought back an appealingly pubby atmosphere at this former farmhouse. It's nice and relaxed, with a mix of furniture trimly laid out in the carpeted bar with its neatly curtained little windows, low-beamed ceilings and some local memorabilia on the fresh cream walls. Black Sheep, Everards M&B Brew XI, Purity Mad Goose, Sharps Doom Bar and St Austell Tribute are served on handpump from the timber-planked bar; piped music, TV and board games. The dining areas are fresh and airy with light wood and cane chairs on stripped boards. The pub is in an attractive village, oppposite a church mentioned in the Domesday Book, and is handy for the NEC.

Pubby bar food includes sandwiches, baguettes, chicken caesar salad, fish and chips, sausage and mash, vegetable risotto, and sirloin steak. *Benchmark main dish: fish and chips £9.75. Two-course evening meal £17.50.*

Punch ~ Tenant Chris Roach ~ Real ale ~ Bar food (12-2.30(4 Sun), 6.30-9.30; not Sun evening) ~ Restaurant ~ (01675) 442833 ~ Children welcome ~ Dogs welcome ~ Open 12-11(midnight Sat, 10.30 Sun) ~ Bedrooms: £65S/£75S

Recommended by Paul Humphreys, Lawrence R Cotter, Comus and Sarah Elliott, Peter and Heather Elliott, Gerard Dyson, Mark, Amanda, Luke and Jake Sheard, Mr and Mrs Graham Prevost, N R White

HANLEY CASTLE Worcestershire   SO8342   Map 4

Three Kings £

Church End, off B4211 N of Upton upon Severn; WR8 0BL

Timeless hospitable gem with five real ales and simple snacks

Genuinely locked in a time warp, this friendly unspoilt country local has been run by the same characterful family for over a hundred years now. It's the cheerful welcome, rather than the housekeeping, that counts in the eyes of readers who have had a great time here, so we've certainly no quibbles with their happy relaxed approach. A homely little tiled-floor tap room on the right is separated from the entrance corridor by the monumental built-in settle which faces its equally vast inglenook fireplace. A hatch serves very well kept Butcombe Bitter, Hobsons and three guests on handpump from smaller brewers such as Hereford, Mayfields and Three Tuns, with around 75 malt whiskies and farm cider. On the left, another room has darts, dominoes, cribbage and other board games. A separate entrance leads to the timbered lounge with another inglenook fireplace and a neatly blacked kitchen range, little leatherette armchairs and spindleback chairs around its tables, and another antique winged and high-backed settle. Bow windows in the three main rooms and old-fashioned wood-and-iron seats on the front terrace look across to the great cedar which shades the tiny green.

> ☗ Food is limited to sandwiches, toasties and ploughman's. *Benchmark main dish: toasted bacon sandwich £1.75.*

Free house ~ Licensee Sue Roberts ~ Real ale ~ Bar food (12-2; not weekends and evenings) ~ No credit cards ~ (01684) 592686 ~ Children welcome ~ Dogs welcome ~ Jam sessions Fri lunchtime, Sun evening ~ Open 12-3, 7-11(10.30 Sun)

Recommended by David and Gill Carrington, the Didler, P Dawn, Guy Vowles, Theocsbrian, MLR

HEREFORD Herefordshire   SO5139   Map 6
Victory ◖ £
St Owen Street, opposite fire station; HR1 2QD

Great fun, with humorous nautical décor, their own beers and a good range of ciders

Although this cheerful pub still brews its own real ales, the name of the brewery has changed to the Hereford Brewery (and if they're not too busy, they will show you round). They keep five of their own beers on handpump: Hereford Best Bitter, Celtic Gold, Dark, Original Bitter and Owd Bull. Also, three farm ciders and a perry; juke box, piped music, darts, games machine, TV, skittle alley, table skittles, cribbage, quoits, board games and a back pool table. The counter re-creates a miniature galleon complete with cannon poking out of its top, and down a companionway the long back room is amusingly decked out as the inside of a man o' war with dark wood, rigging and netting everywhere, benches along sides that curve towards a front fo'c'sle, stanchions and ropes forming an upper crow's nest, and appropriate lamps. The garden has a pagoda, climbing plants and some seats. We'd love to get more reports on this remarkable pub.

> ☗ Tuesday night is curry and quiz night and they also do Sunday roasts; no other food. *Benchmark main dish: Sunday roasts £7.95.*

Own brew ~ Licensee James Kenyon ~ Real ale ~ Bar food (12-5 Sun) ~ No credit cards ~ (01432) 342125 ~ Children welcome ~ Dogs welcome ~ Live band Sat ~ Open 3(1 Fri)-midnight; 11am-midnight Sat; 12-10.30 Sun; closed lunchtimes until 3pm except Fri

Recommended by Richard Gibbs

HOLY CROSS Worcestershire   SO9278   Map 4
Bell & Cross ★ ☗ ♀
HEART OF ENGLAND PUB OF THE YEAR
4 miles from M5 junction 4: A491 towards Stourbridge, then follow Clent signpost off on left; DY9 9QL
WORCESTERSHIRE DINING PUB OF THE YEAR

Super food, staff with a can-do attitude, delightful old interior, and pretty garden

This charmingly well kept place is clearly run with loving care and attention to detail. Service is friendly and attentive, with everything geared to ensure that you have a most enjoyable visit. Successful as a dining pub yet still extremely welcoming if you're just popping in for a drink, it's in an unspoilt early 19th-c layout with five beautifully decorated little rooms and a kitchen opening off a central corridor with a black-and-white tiled floor. Rooms offer a choice of carpet, bare boards, lino or nice old quarry tiles, and there's a variety of mood – from snug and chatty to bright and airy and with an individual décor in each: theatrical engravings on red walls here, nice sporting prints on pale green walls there, and racing and gundog pictures above the black panelled dado in another room. Two of the rooms have small serving bars, with Banks, Enville, Timothy Taylors Landlord and a guest such as St Austell Tribute on handpump, around 50 wines (with about a dozen by the glass), organic soft drinks and a range of coffees; daily papers, coal fires in most rooms with regulars sometimes playing cards in one of the front two; piped music. A spacious lawn has well maintained picnic sets, and you get pleasant views from the garden terrace.

As well as lunchtime sandwiches, panini and ploughman's, delicious dishes from a changing seasonal menu might include tomato, red pepper and cannellini bean salad with garlic ciabatta, fishcakes with prawn, chive and wine sauce, battered cod and chips, grilled bass fillet with roast tuscan vegetable salad and pesto rissole potatoes, pie of the day, yellow thai curry, and cannelloni of spinach gorgonzola with balsamic roasted vegetables. *Benchmark main dish: pot-roast pork belly with black pudding and cider jus £14.25. Two-course evening meal £20.50.*

Enterprise ~ Tenants Roger and Jo Narbett ~ Real ale ~ Bar food (12-2(7 Sun), 6.30-9(9.30 Fri, Sat); not Sun evening) ~ (01562) 730319 ~ Children welcome ~ Dogs allowed in bar ~ Open 12-3, 6-11; 12-10 Sun

Recommended by Clifford Blakemore, John and Gloria Isaacs, Philip and Jan Medcalf, Dr D J and Mrs S C Walker, John and Hilary Penny, Susan and John Douglas, Stephen H Johnston, Neil Kellett, Pat and Tony Martin, KC, Christine and Neil Townend, Brian and Ruth Young

HUNNINGHAM Warwickshire   SP3768   Map 4

Red Lion ⊕ ♀

Village signposted off B4453 Leamington—Rugby just E of Weston, and off B4455 Fosse Way 2.5 miles SW of A423 junction; CV33 9DY

Informal, airy and civilised, good individual food; fine riverside spot

The landlord at this spacious pub is an avid collector of vintage comic books and the dazzling collection of 320 brightly coloured comics framed and crammed on the white walls are likely to leave you with a lasting impression. He previously worked for Brunning & Price, and has brought many of that group's virtues here, from the relaxing atmosphere and positive staff attitudes to the open-plan yet cleverly sectioned layout. The white walls and red ceilings, mix of seating from varnished chapel chairs to a variety of dining chairs, various mainly stripped tables, the rugs on bare boards or even the chunkily old-fashioned radiators are all from the same pleasing school. Windows at one end take in views of the garden with a charmingly arched 14th-c bridge over the gurgling River Leam and a 1948 Massey Ferguson tractor that's been converted into a really enjoyable children's climbing frame; good coal fires, and the day's *Times*, piped music and board games. Drinks include an enterprising changing choice of about 30 wines by the glass, a good range of spirits including 40 single malts, Greene King IPA and Abbot and a guest such as Holts Fifth Sense on handpump, and home-made elderflower cordial.

Food here is good, fresh, generous and individual. As well as sandwiches, it might include home-cured salmon with cucumber and coriander yoghurt, veal carpaccio with rocket and parmesan crisps, antipasti platter, ploughman's, spinach and mushroom pie with goats cheese and garlic mash, smoked haddock and prawn fishcakes, and rib-eye steak. *Benchmark main dish: steak burger £10.95. Two-course evening meal £17.50.*

Greene King ~ Lease Sam Cornwall-Jones ~ Real ale ~ Bar food (12-9.30 Sun) ~ (01926) 632715 ~ Children welcome but no prams or pushchairs ~ Dogs welcome ~ Open 12-11(10.30 Sun)

Recommended by Clive and Fran Dutson, Terry Buckland, Ian and Nita Cooper, Ryta Lyndley, Rob and Catherine Dunster, Ian and Joan Blackwell, George Atkinson, Steve Green, Peter and Janet Astbury, Antony Townsend, Katie Carter, Andy Dolan

 KNIGHTWICK Worcestershire SO7355 Map 4

Talbot ♀ ◖ 🛏

Knightsford Bridge; B4197 just off A44 Worcester—Bromyard; WR6 5PH

Interesting old coaching inn with good beer from its own brewery, and riverside garden

The heavily beamed and extended traditional lounge bar at this rambling country hotel can be quite lively with locals warming up by the good log fire and enjoying the This, That, T'other and the seasonal ale that are brewed in the pub's own Teme Valley microbrewery using locally grown hops. These are served alongside Hobsons Bitter, a farm cider, a dozen wines by the glass and a number of malt whiskies. A variety of traditional seats runs from small carved or leatherette armchairs to winged settles by the windows, and a vast stove squats in the big central stone hearth. The bar opens on to a terrace and arbour with summer roses and clematis. The well furnished back public bar has pool on a raised side area, a TV, games machine, darts, juke box and cribbage. In contrast, the dining room is a sedate place for a quiet (if not cheap) meal. Across the lane, a lovely lawn has tables by the River Teme (they serve out here, too), or you can sit out in front on old-fashioned seats. A farmers' market takes place here on the second Sunday in the month; dogs may be allowed to stay in the bedrooms by prior arrangement.

The long-standing enthusiastic licensees here grow some of their own veg, prepare their own breads, pickles and jams and also rear their own pigs. The bar menu changes constantly but might include vegetable casserole, duck egg omelette, shepherd's pie, pint of prawns, lasagne, and fish pie. There's a pricier more elaborate restaurant menu. *Benchmark main dish: sausage, egg and chips £8.50. Two-course evening meal £17.50.*

Own brew ~ Licensee Annie Clift ~ Real ale ~ Bar food (12-2, 6.30-9) ~ Restaurant ~ (01886) 821235 ~ Children welcome ~ Dogs allowed in bar and bedrooms ~ Open 10am-11pm; 11am-10.30pm Sun ~ Bedrooms: £57.50S/£95B

Recommended by Jim and Frances Gowers, Gordon Tong, Guy Vowles, Dave Braisted, David Heath, Patrick and Daphne Darley, J R Simmons

 **LEDBURY** Herefordshire SO7137 Map 4

Feathers ⑪ ♀ 🛏

High Street (A417); HR8 1DS

Handsome old hotel with chatty relaxed bar, more decorous lounges, good food and friendly staff; comfortable bedrooms

Although this elegant 16th-c timbered place is by no means a pub, it does have a bar with a convivial atmosphere and plenty of chatty drinkers mixing happily with more formal diners. The beamed interior has restored brickwork, seats around oak tables on oak flooring, hop bines, some country antiques, 19th-c caricatures and fancy fowl prints on the stripped-brick chimneybreast (with a lovely winter fire), copper jam pots and fresh flowers on the tables – some very snug and cosy, in side bays. The civilised lounge is just right for afternoon teas, with high-sided armchairs and sofas in front of a big log fire, and newspapers to read. Fullers London Pride and a guest such as Ludlow Gold on handpump, several wines by the glass and 30 malt whiskies. In summer, the sheltered back terrace has abundant pots and hanging baskets.

As well as lunchtime sandwiches, the enjoyable food might include moules frites, beef and thyme burgers with home-made tomato relish, mushroom risotto with tarragon crème fraîche, calves liver with apple and bacon champ, bass fillet with crayfish butter and herb risotto, and slow-cooked pork belly with crispy onions. *Benchmark main dish: bass fillet done different ways £15.25. Two-course evening meal £20.25.*

Free house ~ Licensee David Elliston ~ Real ale ~ Bar food (12-2.30, 7-9.30(10 Fri, Sat); 12-2.30, 7-9 Sun) ~ Restaurant ~ (01531) 635266 ~ Children welcome ~ Dogs allowed in bar and bedrooms ~ Open 10am-11pm(10.30pm Sun) ~ Bedrooms: £89.50B/£137B

Recommended by Dave and Jenny Hughes, P J and R D Greaves, Chris and Val Ramstedt, Pete Coxon, Neil Kellett, Joan and Tony Walker

LITTLE COWARNE Herefordshire SO6050 Map 4

THE GOOD PUB GUIDE Three Horseshoes ♀

Pub signposted off A465 SW of Bromyard; towards Ullingswick; HR7 4RQ

Long-serving licensees and friendly staff in bustling country pub with well liked food using home-grown produce; bedrooms

This is a particularly well run and neatly kept pub and our readers enjoy their visits here very much. Mr and Mrs Whittall are warmly friendly licensees who genuinely care about all their customers – regulars or visitors – and there's always a good mix of chatty drinkers and those out for a special meal. The quarry-tiled L-shaped middle bar has leather-seated bar stools, upholstered settles and dark brown kitchen chairs around sturdy tables, old local photographs above the corner log fire and hop-draped beams. Opening off one side is a sun room with a sky light, wicker armchairs around more tables and at the other end, there's a games room with darts, pool, juke box, games machine and cribbage. Greene King Old Speckled Hen and Wye Valley Bitter and Butty Bach on handpump, local Oliver's cider and perry, a dozen wines by the glass and 12 malt whiskies. A popular Sunday lunchtime carvery is offered in the roomy and attractive, stripped-stone raftered restaurant extension. There are well sited tables and chairs on the terrace or on the neat, prettily planted lawn. They have disabled access.

Cooked by Mrs Whittall and son Philip using their own-grown and other local produce and local game, the highly thought-of food includes sandwiches, chicken liver pâté with home-made preserves, blue cheese, leek, celery, apple and walnut filo pastry parcel, steak in ale pie, breast of chicken in cider with mushroom sauce, bass fillet with confit of vegetables, spinach and capers, and braised lamb shoulder with red wine gravy. *Benchmark main dish: steak in ale pie £10.50. Two-course evening meal £18.75.*

Free house ~ Licensees Norman and Janet Whittall ~ Real ale ~ Bar food (not winter Sun evenings) ~ Restaurant ~ (01885) 400276 ~ Children welcome until 9pm ~ Open

11-3(3.30 Sat), 6.30-11(12.30 Sat); 12-4, 7-10.30 Sun; closed Sun evening in winter ~ Bedrooms: £40S/£70S

Recommended by John Robertson, Jeff and Wendy Williams, Alan and Eve Harding, Denys Gueroult, Guy Vowles, David and Stella Martin, Mike and Eileen Vokins

 LITTLE STRETTON Shropshire   SO4492   Map 6

 **Ragleth £**

Village signposted off A49 S of Church Stretton; Ludlow Road; SY6 6RB

Prettily placed and attractively renovated with tasty food, local beer, and fine hill walks nearby

One happy readers who'd visited this opened-up 17th-c brick-built dining pub told us they were 'charmed by the idyllic setting and the characterful interior'. It's located beneath the steep slopes of the Long Mynd, and is a particularly inviting place on a fine summer's day, with tables on a lawn shaded by a tulip tree looking across to a thatched and timbered church, and there's a good play area. Inside, the bay-windowed front bar is light and airy with fresh plaster and an eclectic mix of light wood old tables and chairs. Some of the original wall brick-and-timber work has been exposed and there's a cheery atmosphere with locals and their dogs, and a warming winter fire. The heavily beamed brick-and-tile-floored public bar has a huge inglenook; TV, darts, board games and piped music. Cheerful attentive owners and staff serve Hobsons, Three Tuns 1642, Wye Valley Butty Bach and possibly a guest such as Greene King Old Speckled Hen on handpump.

Good generously served and reasonably priced bar food might include baguettes, fried red mullet with mustard sauce, breaded brie wedges with cranberry sauce, steak and ale pie, lasagne, nut roast with madeira sauce, battered cod, and steaks. *Benchmark main dish: steak and ale pie £9.95. Two-course evening meal £16.00.*

Free house ~ Licensees Chris and Wendy Davis ~ Real ale ~ Bar food (12-2.15, 6.30-9.15) ~ Restaurant ~ (01694) 722711 ~ Children welcome ~ Dogs allowed in bar ~ Open 12-3, 6-midnight; 12-midnight Sat, Sun; 12-3, 6-11 Sat in winter

Recommended by Dan Bones, Richard Carter, MDN, Gerry and Rosemary Dobson, Dave Braisted, George and Maureen Roby, Simon and Mandy King, Alan and Eve Harding, Dr P Brown, Tracey and Stephen Groves

---

WITHIN WARWICKSHIRE

Warwickshire is England's England – appealing rural landscape and traditional, unspoilt pubs. Its four main towns each make great days out: Stratford-upon-Avon, Royal Leamington Spa, Warwick and Kenilworth. Explore the county's more rural attractions and you'll come across genuinely superb and surprising finds.

Shakespeare fans can trace the Bard's bucolic connections at Anne Hathaway's Cottage (Shottery), Mary Arden's House (Wilmcote) and the Bell Inn, Welford-on-Avon. Intriguing historic houses include Palladian Ragley Hall with its astonishing sculpture trail; Compton Verney, the Georgian mansion, now a world-class art gallery, National Trust Coughton Court and Baddesley Clinton for dramatic Gunpowder Plot tales. Meander the heritage trail around the 'sheep-wash-town' of Shipston-on-Stour, go boating in picturesque Bidford-on-Avon, discover Roman Alcester and the old world streetscapes of Henley-in-Arden.

Find more ideas for great days out, excellent pubs and places to stay at
www.withinwarwickshire.co.uk

 LONG COMPTON Warwickshire   SP2832 Map 4

Red Lion 🛏

A3400 S of Shipston-on-Stour; CV36 5JS

Traditional character and contemporary touches in comfortably refurbished coaching inn; bedrooms

This lovely old coaching inn has been beautifully refurbished with mindfulness for its original features. The roomy lounge bar is beamed with exposed stone and although airy, has some nice rambling corners with old-fashioned built-in settles among pleasantly assorted and comfortable seats and leather armchairs; there are tables on flagstones and carpets, and a warming woodburning stove. Well kept Hook Norton and a couple of guests such as Goffs Jouster and Vale VPA on handpump. The simple public bar has pool, a fruit machine, juke box and TV; piped music. There are tables out in the big back garden, with a play area.

 Bar food includes sandwiches, rare breed pork and chicken liver terrine with pickled vegetables, twice-baked mushroom and gruyère soufflé, fish and chips with mushy peas, parmesan and sage crumbled pork schnitzel with celeriac rémoulade, chicken casserole with pearl barley, baby vegetables, honey and herbs, and rib-eye steak with café de paris butter. *Benchmark main dish: steak and ale pie £12.95. Two-course evening meal £20.35.*

Free house ~ Licensee Lisa Phipps ~ Real ale ~ Bar food (12-2.30, 6-9; 12-9.30 Fri-Sun) ~ Restaurant ~ (01608) 684221 ~ Children welcome ~ Dogs welcome ~ Open 10-2.30, 6-11; 10-11 Fri-Sun ~ Bedrooms: £55B/£110B
Recommended by Chris Glasson, Eithne Dandy

LUDLOW Shropshire   SO5174 Map 4

Church Inn 🍺 £

Church Street, behind Butter Cross; SY8 1AW

Characterful town-centre inn with impressive range of real ales

Bustling with cheery customers, the ground floor at this lively pub is divided into three appealingly decorated areas, with hops hanging from the heavy beams, comfortable banquettes in cosy alcoves off the island counter (part of it is a pulpit), and pews and stripped stonework from the church. There are displays of old photographic equipment, plants on window sills and church prints in the side room. A long central area has a fine stone fireplace (good winter fires), and the more basic side bar has old black and white photos of the town; daily papers and piped music. Coming mostly from brewers of the region, eight real ales on handpump are likely to include a choice from Hobsons, Ludlow, Mayfield, Weetwood and Wye Valley – you can try three as part of their third of a pint taster. They also serve several malt whiskies and mulled cider. The civilised upstairs lounge bar has good views of the church and surrounding countryside, vaulted ceilings, a display case of glass, china and old bottles, and musical instruments on the walls. The bedrooms are simple but comfortable, breakfasts are good, and one reader told us their dog was welcomed with dog treats and a bowl of water.

Straightforward but wholesome tasty food includes sandwiches, battered brie wedges with cranberry sauce, cajun chicken, ploughman's, scampi, battered cod, lamb chops with mint gravy, ham and parsley sauce, several pies, and steaks. *Benchmark main dish: beef and ale pie £6.95. Two-course evening meal £12.00.*

Free house ~ Licensee Graham Willson-Lloyd ~ Real ale ~ Bar food (12-2.30, 6.30-9) ~ (01584) 872174 ~ Dogs allowed in bar and bedrooms ~ Open 10(11 Sun)-midnight (1am Sat) ~ Bedrooms: £50B/£80B

Recommended by Ann and Colin Hunt, Dr D J and Mrs S C Walker, Gerry and Rosemary Dobson, Alan and Eve Harding, Stuart Doughty, P J and R D Greaves, Mr and Mrs A H Young, Chris Flynn, Wendy Jones, Joe Green, P Dawn, Pete Coxon, Michael Dandy, Brian and Anna Marsden,Tracey and Stephen Groves, MLR

 MALVERN Worcestershire   SO7845   Map 4

Nags Head

Bottom end of Bank Street, steep turn down off A449; WR14 2JG

Remarkable range of real ales, delightfully eclectic layout and décor, and warmly welcoming atmosphere

Should you feel daunted by the astonishing range of 14 beers at this terrifically enjoyable little pub, the cheery staff will happily help you choose by offering you a taster. House beers are Banks's, Bathams, St Georges Charger, Friar Tuck and Dragons Blood, Sharps Doom Bar, Woods Shropshire Lad and Wychwood Hobgoblin, and they've changing guests (last year they got through over 1,000) from far-flung brewers such as Battledown, Cottage, Kinver and Three Tuns. They also keep two farm ciders and about two dozen malt whiskies. The superb range of well kept beers, tasty bar food, splendid individuality and easy-going chatty mood attract a good mix of jolly visitors and locals. A series of snug individually decorated rooms, with one or two steps between, gives plenty of options on where to sit. Each is characterfully filled with all sorts of chairs including leather armchairs, pews sometimes arranged as booths, a mix of tables with sturdy ones stained different colours, bare boards here, flagstones there, carpet elsewhere, and plenty of interesting pictures and homely touches such as house plants, shelves of well thumbed books and broadsheet newspapers, and there's a coal fire opposite the central servery; shove-ha'penny, cribbage and dominoes. There are picnic-sets and rustic tables and benches on the front terrace (with heaters and umbrellas) and in the garden.

Tasty lunchtime bar food, served in generous helpings, includes good sandwiches, soup, chicken and mushroom pie, stuffed mushrooms, and fish and chips. In the evenings meals are served in the barn extension dining room only and might include scallops with balsamic vinegar, chicken liver pâté, chicken breast with mushroom sauce and sweetcorn fritter, beef bourguignon, fish of the day, and steaks. *Benchmark main dish: ham, egg and chips £8.50. Two-course evening meal £19.25.*

Free house ~ Licensee Clare Willets ~ Real ale ~ Bar food (12-2, 6.30-8.30) ~ Restaurant ~ (01684) 574373 ~ Children welcome ~ Dogs welcome ~ Open 11-11.15(11.30 Fri, Sat); 12-11 Sun

Recommended by Chris Glasson, Barry Collett, David and Gill Carrington, Chris Flynn, Wendy Jones, P Dawn, Pat and Tony Martin, N R White, Mr and Mrs M J Girdler, Don Bryan, Amanda Kelly

---

Real ale to us means beer that has matured naturally in its cask – not pressurised or filtered. We name all real ales stocked. We usually name ales preserved under a light blanket of carbon dioxide too, though purists – pointing out that this stops the natural yeasts developing – would disagree (most people, including us, can't tell the difference!).

MUCH WENLOCK Shropshire   SO6299 Map 4

George & Dragon ♨ £
High Street (A458); TF13 6AA

Bustling, snugly atmospheric, plenty to look at, reasonably priced food, good beer selection, and usefully open all day

This cosy old place is filled with a thoroughly engaging collection of all sorts of pub paraphernalia. You'll find old brewery and cigarette advertisements, bottle labels, beer trays and George-and-the-Dragon pictures, as well as a plethora of 200 jugs hanging from the beams. The front door takes you straight into a beamed and quarry-tiled room with wooden chairs and tables and antique settles all the way around the walls, and there are a couple of attractive Victorian fireplaces (with coal-effect gas fires). At the back is a timbered dining room. As well as a very wide selection of wines by the glass and a dozen decent malts, five real ales on handpump feature Greene King Abbot, St Austell Tribute, Wadworths 6X and a couple of guests from brewers such as Hobsons and Hook Norton; they may do three third of a pint tasters; piped music, dominoes, cards, board games and daily papers.

Good value lunchtime food includes sandwiches, ploughman's, faggots and peas, pie of the day, vegetable lasagne, battered cod, daily specials such as lamb braised with rosemary, garlic and tomato and beef wellington, with a few additional evening dishes such as stilton and walnut pâté and duck breast with black cherry and port sauce. They have various special offers including pie and a pint on Tuesday, and two meals for £10 on Thursday and their Sunday lunch is particularly reasonable. *Benchmark main dish: beef in ale pie £7.95. Two-course evening meal £12.00.*

Punch ~ Lease James Scott ~ Real ale ~ Bar food (12-2.30, 6-9 (not Weds evenings all year or Sun evening Oct-Jun)) ~ Restaurant ~ (01952) 727312 ~ Children welcome in bar till 7pm, restaurant till 9pm ~ Dogs allowed in bar ~ Open 12-11(12 Sat)

Recommended by Les and Sandra Brown, Ann and Colin Hunt, Alistair Stanier, Reg Fowle, Helen Rickwood, Tim Maddison, Peter Salmon, Pat and Tony Martin, Pete Yearsley, Tracey and Stephen Groves

 NAILSWORTH Gloucestershire   ST8699 Map 4

Weighbridge ⑪ ♗
B4014 towards Tetbury; GL6 9AL

Super two-in-one pies served in cosy old-fashioned bar rooms, a fine choice of drinks, and a sheltered garden

Well run and neatly kept, this is a bustling pub that our readers enjoy very much. The relaxed bar has three cosily old-fashioned rooms with stripped-stone walls, antique settles and country chairs, window seats and open fires. The black beamed ceiling of the lounge bar is thickly festooned with black ironware – sheepshears, gin traps, lamps and a large collection of keys, many from the old Longfords Mill opposite the pub. Upstairs is a raftered hayloft with an engaging mix of rustic tables. No noisy games machines or piped music. Uley Old Spot and Wadworths 6X and a couple of guest beers like Bath Ales Gem Bitter and Palmers Tally Ho! on handpump, 16 wines (and champagne and prosecco) by the glass, Weston's cider and 14 malt whiskies; staff are welcoming and helpful. Behind the building is a sheltered landscaped garden with picnic-sets under umbrellas. Good disabled access and facilities.

🍽 The extremely popular two-in-one pies come in a large bowl – half of which contains the filling of your choice while the other is full of home-made cauliflower cheese (or broccoli mornay or root vegetables) and topped with pastry: root vegetables with various pulses in a spicy tomato sauce, chicken, ham and leek in a creamy tarragon sauce, and turkey and trimmings. Also, a burger with smoked cheddar and bacon, free-range omelettes, chicken roasted with garlic and rosemary, and lamb shank in a rich red wine jus. *Benchmark main dish: two-in-one pies £14.80. Two-course evening meal £18.40.*

Free house ~ Licensee Howard Parker ~ Real ale ~ Bar food (12-9.30) ~ Restaurant ~ (01453) 832520 ~ Children allowed away from the bars ~ Dogs welcome ~ Open 12-11 (10.30 Sun)

Recommended by John Taylor, Tom and Ruth Rees, Dr and Mrs C W Thomas, Howard Moorey

---

NEWLAND Gloucestershire   SO5509   Map 4

Ostrich 🍽 🍷 🍺

Off B4228 in Coleford; or can be reached from the A466 in Redbrook, by the turning off at the England/Wales border – keep bearing right; GL16 8NP

Liked by walkers and their dogs with a friendly feel in spacious bar, super choice of beers, open fire, daily papers, and smashing food

As well as a genuinely warm welcome from the landlady and her staff in this lovely old pub, there's a marvellous choice of real ales and a fine mix of locals, visitors and walkers. The atmosphere is chatty and relaxed and the low-ceilinged bar is spacious but cosily traditional with creaky floors, window shutters, candles in bottles on the tables, miners' lamps on the uneven walls and comfortable furnishings such as cushioned window seats, wall settles and rod-backed country-kitchen chairs. There's a fine big fireplace, newspapers to read, perhaps quiet piped jazz, and board games. Adnams Bitter, Kingstone Abbey Ale, Otter Ale, Sharps Doom Bar, Timothy Taylors Landlord, Wells & Youngs Bombardier and Wye Valley Butty Bach on handpump and several wines by the glass. The pub lurcher is called Alfie. There are picnic-sets in a walled garden behind and more out in front; the church, known as the Cathedral of the Forest, is well worth a visit, and this is a charmingly picturesque village.

🍽 Extremely good, interesting food includes goose rillettes with apricot chutney, smoked salmon and prawn terrine with pickled cucumber, steak in ale pie, fresh smoked haddock in cream, egg and horseradish topped with dauphinoise potatoes and mozzarella, taleggio, caramelised red onion, olive and basil tart with chilli jam, and lemon and parsley-breadcrumbed chicken with sunblush tomato sauce. *Benchmark main dish: salmon and spinach fishcakes in parsley sauce £10.50. Two-course evening meal £17.25.*

Free house ~ Licensee Kathryn Horton ~ Real ale ~ Bar food (12-2.30, 6.30(6 Sat)-9.30) ~ Restaurant ~ (01594) 833260 ~ Children welcome ~ Dogs allowed in bar ~ Open 12-3, 6.30-11; 12-3, 6-midnight Sat; 12-4, 6.30-10.30 Sun

Recommended by Dave and Jane Stirling, Peter Dearing, Peter J and Avril Hanson, LM, M G Hart, Peter and Celia Gregory, Steve Pepper, Paul J Robinshaw, Christine Shewell

---

The price we give for a two-course evening meal in the featured top pub entries is the mean (average of cheapest and most expensive) price of a starter and a main course – no drinks.

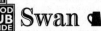 NEWLAND Worcestershire   SO7948   Map 4

Swan

Worcester Road (set well back from A449 just NW of Malvern); WR13 5AY

Attractive and interesting old creeper-clad pub, good all round

You get the immediate impression here that you're in a pub where everything has been really carefully thought out for the pleasure of its customers. It starts with the warmth of the welcome from the efficient young staff, then as you acclimatise to the dim lighting of the dark-beamed bar and look around, plenty of nice touches catch your eye. There's quite an overhead forest of whisky-water jugs, beakers and tankards, one or two tapestries on the walls, and several of the comfortable and clearly individually chosen seats are worth a close look for their carving. The end counter (also carved) has well kept Hobsons, St Georges Dragons Blood, Friar Tuck and Sharps Doom Bar and Wychwood Hobgoblin on handpump, with a couple of guests from brewers such as Ruddles County and Teme Valley. On the right is a broadly similar red-carpeted dining room, and beyond it an ultra-modern glass cube of a garden room. The garden itself is as individual as the pub, with a cluster of huge casks topped with flowers, even a piano doing flower-tub duty, and a set of stocks on the pretty front terrace.

Lunchtime food includes sandwiches, crispy whitebait, chicken caesar salad, battered cod and chips, lamb and vegetable pie, courgette and walnut moussaka and chicken tikka masala. In the evening there might be smoked salmon pâté with chive butter, pea, spinach and artichoke risotto, grilled swordfish steak with roast mediterranean vegetables and spicy tomato sauce, and fillet steak with mushroom and leek hash and oxford blue butter. *Benchmark main dish: beef and ale pie £12.50. Two-course evening meal £19.50.*

Free house ~ Licensee Nick Taylor ~ Real ale ~ Bar food (12-2.30, 6.30-9; 12-3, 7-9 Sun) ~ Restaurant ~ (01886) 832224 ~ Children welcome ~ Dogs welcome ~ Open 12-midnight
Recommended by Denys Gueroult

NORTH CERNEY Gloucestershire   SP0208   Map 4

Bathurst Arms

A435 Cirencester—Cheltenham; GL7 7BZ

Bustling inn with beamed bar, open fires, fine wines, real ales and changing bar food; comfortable bedrooms

There's a lot of genuine character in this handsome old inn and a friendly welcome for all. The original beamed and panelled bar has a fireplace at each end (one quite huge and housing an open woodburner), a good mix of old tables and nicely faded chairs and old-fashioned window seats. There are country tables in an oak-floored room off the bar, as well as winged high-backed settles forming a few booths around other tables; piped music and TV. The restaurant has leather sofas and another woodburning stove. Hook Norton Hooky Bitter and guests like Box Steam Golden Bolt, Cotswold Spring Mad March Hare and Whittington Cats Whiskers on handpump and they have a wine room where you can choose your own wines or one of the 30 by the glass; local soft drinks and juices, too. The pleasant riverside garden has picnic-sets sheltered by trees and shrubs, and plenty of surrounding walks. Cerney House Gardens are worth a visit.

🍴 Quite a choice of bar food might include sandwiches, chicken and grain mustard terrine, chargrilled burger with cheese and tomato relish, beer-battered cod with home-made tartare sauce, sweet potato, butternut squash and spicy bean casserole, and lamb cutlets with confit garlic mash and redcurrant sauce. *Benchmark main dish: beef in ale pie £11.95. Two-course evening meal £17.90.*

Free house ~ Licensee James Walker ~ Real ale ~ Bar food (12-2(2.30 Fri and Sat), 6-9(9.30 Fri and Sat); 12-2.30, 7-9 Sun) ~ Restaurant ~ (01285) 831281 ~ Children welcome ~ Dogs allowed in bar and bedrooms ~ Open 12-11 ~ Bedrooms: £65B/£85B

Recommended by Howard and Lorna Lambert, Evelyn and Derek Walter, David Skelding, Val Carter, Martin Stafford, R J Herd, Gary Dunstan, E McCall, T McLean, D Irving, Guy Vowles, Andy and Claire Barker, David Gunn, Comus and Sarah Elliott

NORTHLEACH Gloucestershire   SP1114   Map 4

Wheatsheaf 🍴 ▯ 🛏

West End; the inn is on your left as you come in following the sign off the A429, just SW of its junction with the A40; GL54 3EZ

GLOUCESTERSHIRE DINING PUB OF THE YEAR

17th-c stone inn with excellent contemporary food, real ales, candles and fresh flowers, and a relaxed atmosphere; stylish bedrooms

Smart and ivy-clad, this handsome old coaching inn manages effortlessly to be both a pub and a restaurant without letting either dominate – and it's now a free house. The big-windowed airy linked rooms have high ceilings, antique and contemporary artwork, lots of pictures, church candles and fresh flowers, an attractive mix of dining chairs and stools around wooden tables, flagstones in the central bar, wooden floors in the airy dining rooms and three open fires. Bath Ales Gem Bitter, Purity Pure UBU and Wye Valley HPA on handpump, several wines by the glass from a fantastic list of around 500 and farm cider, too. There are seats in the pretty back garden and they can arrange fishing on the River Coln. This is an attractive Cotswold town with a fine old market square. If you are staying, the breakfasts are excellent. Dogs are genuinely welcomed and they even keep a jar of pigs' ears behind the bar.

🍴 Impressive and very highly thought-of, the food might include a charcuterie plate, creamed ham hock with peas, tarragon and a poached egg on toast, devilled crab tagliatelle, chicken with braised celery, asparagus and peas, Loch Dart salmon with wild mushrooms, pancetta and spinach, rare roast venison with apple, hazelnuts and chard, and rump of lamb with tapenade and dauphinoise potatoes. *Benchmark main dish: devilled kidneys on toast £5.00. Two-course evening meal £20.00.*

Free house ~ Licensees Sam and Georgina Pearman ~ Real ale ~ Bar food (12-4, 6-10) ~ Restaurant ~ (01451) 860244 ~ Children welcome ~ Dogs welcome ~ Open 12(10 Sat and Sun)-11 ~ Bedrooms: /£120B

Recommended by Valerie Worthington, Katharine Cowherd, Chris Glasson, Roger Braithwaite, Charles Gysin, Richard Tilbrook, Peter Smith and Judith Brown, Guy Vowles, Andy and Claire Barker, R and S Bentley, Susan Lang, Graham Oddey

---

Most pubs with any outside space now have some kind of smokers' shelter. There are regulations about these – for instance, they have to be substantially open to the outside air. The best have heating and lighting and are really quite comfortable.

OLDBURY-ON-SEVERN Gloucestershire ST6092 Map 2

Anchor ♀ ◖ £

Village signposted from B4061; BS35 1QA

Friendly country pub with tasty bar food, a fine choice of drinks, and a pretty garden with hanging baskets

With prompt cheerful service and a bustling atmosphere, this friendly place always has a good mix of customers. The neatly kept lounge has modern beams and stonework, a variety of tables including an attractive oval oak gateleg, cushioned window seats, winged seats against the wall, oil paintings by a local artist and a big winter log fire; the bar has old photographs and farming and fishing bric-a-brac on the walls. Diners can eat in the lounge or bar area or in the dining room at the back of the building (good for larger groups) and the menu is the same in all rooms. Bass, Butcombe Bitter, Otter Bitter and a changing guest on handpump well priced for the area; 75 malt whiskies (the tasting notes are really helpful) and quite a few wines by the glass. In summer, you can eat in the pretty garden and the hanging baskets and window boxes are lovely then; boules. They have wheelchair access and a disabled lavatory. Plenty of walks to the River Severn and along the many footpaths and bridleways, and St Arilda's church nearby is interesting on its odd little knoll with wild flowers among the gravestones (the primroses and daffodils in spring are quite a show).

 Fair-priced, popular food includes ciabatta sandwiches, devilled kidneys and mushrooms on herb bread, home-baked ham and free-range eggs, spinach and ricotta ravioli, smoked haddock and salmon pie, beef curry, and duck breast with a port and plum sauce; they also offer a good value two-course set menu (Monday-Friday lunchtimes, Sunday-Thursday evenings). *Benchmark main dish: crisp pork belly and local black pudding £9.50. Two-course evening meal £15.95.*

Free house ~ Licensees Michael Dowdeswell and Mark Sorrell ~ Real ale ~ Bar food (12-2(2.30 Sat, 3 Sun), 6-9) ~ Restaurant ~ (01454) 413331 ~ Children in dining room only ~ Dogs allowed in bar ~ Open 11.30-3, 6-11.30; 11-11.30 Sat; 12-10.30 Sun
Recommended by Tom Evans, Chris and Angela Buckell, Bob and Angela Brooks, James Morrell, Peter Meister, John and Gloria Isaacs, Charles and Pauline Stride, Jim and Frances Gowers, Richard and Judy Winn, Dr and Mrs C W Thomas

 OMBERSLEY Worcestershire SO8463 Map 4

Cross Keys

Just off A449; Main Road (A4133, Kidderminster end); WR9 0DS

Enjoyable food cheerfully served in comfortably relaxed bar and smarter restaurant

The good easy-going atmosphere in the carpeted bar here is indicative that this simple white building is a proper pub. Archways open into several separate areas – perhaps the nicest on the left, with attractive Bob Lofthouse animal etchings, a big antique print of draught horses advertising Talbots mineral waters, and some horse tack on dark-varnished country panelling. The hops strung from beams and joists suggest that they're serious about their beers – well kept Timothy Taylors Landlord and a guest such as Wye Valley HPA on handpump; and they have good value wines by the glass, and good coffee. For extreme comfort, head to the back, where one gently lit room is filled with softly upholstered sofas and armchairs. Beyond is a comfortable back dining conservatory, looking out on a terrace with alloy furniture under a big heated canopy. Service is friendly and efficient; there may be unobtrusive piped pop music.

The generous menu includes nourishing country dishes such as chicken and leek or steak and kidney pies, salmon and spinach fishcakes and steaks, and an enterprising range of changing specials such as smoked duck breast with five spice sauce, cajun chicken salad, pasta carbonara, beef wellington, and lots of fresh fish from black bream to sea trout. At lunchtime (not Sunday), they also do baguettes and very good omelettes. *Benchmark main dish: teriyaki salmon with noodle stir fry £13.50. Two-course evening meal £19.75.*

Enterprise ~ Lease Valerie James ~ Real ale ~ Bar food (12-2.30, 6-9(9.30 Fri, Sat)) ~ Restaurant ~ (01905) 620588 ~ Children welcome if dining and not in bar ~ Open 12-3, 6-11(10.30 Sun)

Recommended by Paul Hanson, Bruce and Sharon Eden

OMBERSLEY Worcestershire   SO8463 Map 4

Kings Arms
Main Road (A4133); WR9 0EW

Inviting Tudor building with tasty food and attractive courtyard

Though under new licensees and much neatened-up since the last edition of the *Guide*, this rambling black and white timbered inn still retains tremendous historical character. Said to date from about the 1400s, its charming aged interior is dimly lit and cosy with various nooks and crannies, and three splendid fireplaces with good log fires. The low-ceilinged bar is tidily traditional with a latched door, dark wood pew and red leatherette stools around cast-iron-based tables on rosy red quarry tiles, and a few horsebrasses on its black beams. Three dining areas have gently contemporary new carpets and upholstery that work amazingly well with the age of the building. King Charles is said to have stopped here after fleeing the Battle of Worcester in 1651, and one room has his coat of arms moulded into its decorated plaster ceiling as a trophy of the visit. Jennings Cocker Hoop, Marstons Burton and a guest or two such as Jennings Cocky Blonde are on handpump; piped music. A tree-sheltered courtyard has tables under cocktail parasols and colourful hanging baskets and tubs in summer, and there's another terrace.

As well as lunchtime sandwiches, ploughman's and snacks such as sausage and mash and steak burger, bar food includes king prawn skewers with catalan salad, mushroom, tarragon and spinach risotto, mediterranean vegetable lasagne with pesto and parmesan cream, steak and ale suet pudding, roast duck breast with redcurrant and port jus, fried bass with lemon and caper butter, and braised blade of beef with red wine and mushroom jus and horseradish mash. *Benchmark main dish: fish and chips £12.00. Two-course evening meal £18.00.*

Banks's (Marstons) ~ Lease Nick Mossop ~ Real ale ~ Bar food (12-9.30(9 Sun)) ~ Restaurant ~ (01905) 620142 ~ Children welcome ~ Dogs allowed in bar ~ Open 10-11(10.30 Sun)

Recommended by Adele Summers, Alan Black, Bruce and Sharon Eden, Eric Thomas Yarwood

---

Cribbage is a card game where you use a block of wood with holes for matchsticks or special pins to score with; regulars in cribbage pubs are usually happy to teach strangers how to play.

PRESTON BAGOT Warwickshire SP1765 Map 4

Crabmill 🍴 ☖

A4189 Henley-in-Arden—Warwick; B95 5EE

Mill conversion with comfortable décor, relaxed atmosphere, and smart bar food

Still on terrific form, this rambling old cider mill gains particular praise for its enjoyable atmosphere, accommodating friendly service and delicious food. This is a lovely building that has been attractively decorated with contemporary furnishings and warm colour combinations that are easy on the eye. The smart two-level lounge area has comfortable sofas and chairs, low tables, big table lamps and one or two rugs on bare boards. The elegant and roomy low-beamed dining area has caramel leather banquettes and chairs at pine tables, and a beamed and flagstoned bar area has some stripped-pine country tables and chairs, snug corners and a gleaming metal bar serving Greene King Abbot and IPA and Purity Pure UBU on handpump, with ten wines by the glass from a mostly new world list. Piped music is well chosen and well reproduced. There are lots of tables (some of them under cover) out in a large, attractive, decked garden. Booking is advised, especially Sunday lunchtime when it's popular with families.

🍴 As well as their lunchtime snack menu which includes interestingly filled pitta, bagels and wraps and a couple of good value dishes such as bolognese with linguine, the imaginative menu might include chilli and fennel crumbed squid with spiced tomato pickle and aioli, crispy duck salad with asian vegetables, vermicelli noodles and sweet chilli sauce, lentil, potato and chickpea curry with fennel bhajis and chapati, moroccan-style bass with butternut, tomato, nuts and couscous, and pork tenderloin in parma ham with spring onion and herb potato cake and apple and apricot chutney. *Benchmark main dish: ostrich wrapped in parma ham with tomato salsa £18.25. Two-course evening meal £20.45.*

Free house ~ Licensee Sally Coll ~ Real ale ~ Bar food (12-3(5 Fri, Sat, 4 Sun), 6.30-9.30; not Sun evening) ~ Restaurant ~ (01926) 843342 ~ Children welcome ~ Dogs welcome ~ Open 11-11; 12-6 Sun; closed Sun evening

Recommended by Martin and Pauline Jennings, P and J Shapley, Mike and Mary Carter, Martin Smith, KC, Dr A B Clayton, Brendon Skinner, Simon and Mandy King, Clive and Fran Dutson, R L Borthwick

SALT Staffordshire SJ9527 Map 7

Holly Bush £

Village signposted off A51 S of Stone (and A518 NE of Stafford); ST18 0BX

Delightful medieval pub popular for mainly traditional all-day food

In summer, a mass of flowering tubs and baskets turn this charming white-painted 14th-c house into a truly delightful spectacle. It's lovely inside too, with several cosy areas spreading off from the standing-room serving section, with high-backed cushioned pews, old tables and more conventional seats. The oldest part has a heavy-beamed and planked ceiling (some of the beams are attractively carved), a woodburning stove, and a salt cupboard built into the big inglenook, with other nice old-fashioned touches such as an ancient pair of riding boots on the mantelpiece. A modern back extension, with beams, stripped brickwork and a small coal fire, blends in well. Adnams, Marstons Pedigree and a guest from a brewer such as Three Tuns are on handpump, alongside a dozen wines by the glass. The back of the pub is beautifully tended, with rustic picnic-sets on a big lawn. It can get busy so do arrive early for a table. They operate a locker system for credit cards, which they will ask to keep if you are running a tab.

Readers enjoy the good value generously served bar food which, as well as lunchtime sandwiches, might include staffordshire oatcake stuffed with spiced black pudding with herby tomato sauce, pears stuffed with blue cheese, greek lamb, venison casserole, braised ham hock with creamy horseradish sauce, battered cod, skate wing with prawns and capers, and steaks; they've a wood fired pizza oven in the beer garden. *Benchmark main dish: steak and kidney pudding £9.95. Two-course evening meal £13.90.*

Admiral Taverns ~ Licensees Geoffrey and Joseph Holland ~ Real ale ~ Bar food (12-9.30 (9 Sun)) ~ (01889) 508234 ~ Children allowed but must leave the bar by 8.30pm ~ Open 12-11 (10.30 Sun)

Recommended by Brian and Anna Marsden, Chris and Jo Parsons, S J and C C Davidson, Mike Horgan, Di Wright, Adrian Johnson, Brian and Jacky Wilson, Susan and Nigel Brookes, Charles and Pauline Stride, Paul Humphreys, N R White, R Anderson, Andy Dolan

SAPPERTON Gloucestershire ⬤⬤⬤ SO9403 Map 4

Bell ⓦ ♀ ◢

Village signposted from A419 Stroud—Cirencester; OS Sheet 163 map reference 948033; GL7 6LE

Super pub with beamed cosy rooms, a really good mix of customers, delicious food, local ales, and a very pretty courtyard

Carefully run with great thought for their wide mix of customers, the hard-working licensees of this smashing pub are as hands-on as ever. And although many people are here to enjoy the particularly good food, they do keep Bath Ales Gem, Otter Bitter, St Austell Tribute and Uley Old Spot on handpump, 20 wines by the glass and carafe from a large and diverse wine list with very helpful notes, 20 malt whiskies, two farm ciders and local soft drinks. Harry's Bar has big cushion-strewn sofas, benches and armchairs where you can read the daily papers with a pint in front of the woodburning stove – or simply have a pre-dinner drink. The two other cosy rooms have beams, a nice mix of wooden tables and chairs, country prints and modern art on stripped-stone walls, one or two attractive rugs on the flagstones, fresh flowers and open fires. The gents' has schoolboy humour cartoons on the walls. Their new young springer spaniel is called William. There are tables out on a small front lawn and in a partly covered and very pretty courtyard, for eating outside. Horses have their own tethering rail (and bucket of water).

Using rare-breed beef and pork and other carefully sourced local produce, the imaginative food includes lunchtime sandwiches, ham hock terrine with apple and thyme chutney, pigeon breast with a beetroot and orange salad, beer-battered pollack with home-made tartare sauce, caramelised red onion, spinach and tomato risotto, prime burger with smoked bacon, cheese and dill pickles, and free-range slow-roasted pork belly with wholegrain mustard sauce; Wednesdays are for curries. *Benchmark main dish: duck breast with confit leg, creamed cabbage and chorizo £17.95. Two-course evening meal £21.70.*

Free house ~ Licensees Paul Davidson and Pat LeJeune ~ Real ale ~ Bar food (12-2.15 (2.30 Sun), 7-9.30(9 Sun)) ~ (01285) 760298 ~ Children allowed but must be over 10

after 6.30pm ~ Dogs welcome ~ Open 11-2.30, 6.30-11; 11-11 Sat; 12-10.30 Sun; closed
Sun evening mid-Nov to mid-March

Recommended by Howard G Allen, Martin and Karen Wake, Dr A Y Drummond, Bernard Stradling,
Chris and Martin Taylor, Chris Flynn, Wendy Jones, Mike Buckingham, Peter and Audrey Dowsett,
R and S Bentley, Jennifer and Patrick O'Dell

 SHEEPSCOMBE Gloucestershire   SO8910   Map 4

Butchers Arms

Village signed off B4070 NE of Stroud; or A46 N of Painswick (but narrow
lanes); GL6 7RH

Bustling country pub with enjoyable bar food, real ales, friendly young
licensees, and fine views

Reached down narrow lanes, this 17th-c rural pub is popular with
walkers and cyclists (who can pre-book their food orders). The
lounge bar has a thriving atmosphere, beams, wheelback chairs,
cushioned stools and other comfortable seats around simple wooden
tables, built-in cushioned seats in the big bay windows, interesting
oddments like assorted blow lamps, irons and plates, and a woodburning
stove. The restaurant has an open log fire. Butcombe Gold, Otter Bitter
and a guest like St Austell Tribute on handpump, several wines by the
glass and Weston's cider; darts, chess, cribbage and draughts. The view
over the lovely surrounding steep beechwood valley is terrific and there
are seats outside to make the most of it. It is thought that this area was
once a royal hunting ground for Henry VIII.

Using as much local produce as possible, the well liked food might include
lunchtime sandwiches, chicken liver and port pâté, tomato, mixed pepper and
spring onion risotto, beer-battered fish and chips, chicken, broccoli and ham pie,
and specials like smoked bacon chop with a fried egg, braised leeks and a grain
mustard sauce and fresh tuna niçoise; they also offer a pie and a pint deal (weekday
lunchtimes and every evening except Saturday). *Benchmark main dish: home-made*
burger £8.95. Two-course evening meal £14.70.

Free house ~ Licensees Mark and Sharon Tallents ~ Real ale ~ Bar food (12-2.30, 6.30-
9.30; all day weekends; no food after 6pm Sun Jan, Feb) ~ Restaurant ~ (01452) 812113
~ Children welcome ~ Dogs allowed in bar ~ Open 11.30-3, 6.30-11; 11.30-11.30 Sat;
12-10.30 Sun; closed evenings 25, 26 and 31 Dec, evening 1 Jan

Recommended by Dr and Mrs A K Clarke, Martin and Pauline Jennings, Johnn and Jennifer Wright,
Guy Vowles, Ken and Barbara Turner, Mike and Mary Carter, Sue Wilson Roberts

 SHREWSBURY Shropshire   SJ4812   Map 6

Armoury 🍴 🍷 🍺

Victoria Quay, Victoria Avenue; SY1 1HH

Vibrant atmosphere in interestingly converted riverside warehouse,
enthusiastic young staff, good food all day, excellent drinks' selection

A terrific all-rounder, and a lot of fun too, this lively former warehouse
is light and fresh with an amazingly long run of big arched windows
giving views across the broad River Severn. The spacious open-plan
interior has a comfortable mix of eclectic décor and a nicely intimate
furniture layout, giving it all a personal feel despite the vast space. Mixed
wood tables and chairs are grouped on expanses of stripped-wood floors,
a display of floor-to-ceiling books dominates two huge walls, there's a

grand stone fireplace at one end and masses of old prints mounted edge to edge on the stripped-brick walls. Colonial-style fans whirr away on the ceilings, which are supported by occasional green-painted columns, and small wall-mounted glass cabinets displaying smoking pipes. The long bar counter has a terrific choice of drinks, with up to eight real ales from brewers such as Phoenix, Purple Moose, Salopian, Shires, Six Bells and Woods on handpump, a great wine list (with 16 by the glass), around 50 malt whiskies, a dozen different gins, lots of rums and vodkas, a variety of brandies, some unusual liqueurs and a great range of soft drinks. The massive uniform red brick exteriors are interspersed with hanging baskets and smart coach lights at the front; there may be queues at the weekend. The pub doesn't have its own parking, but there are plenty of places nearby.

🍽 As well as interesting sandwiches, tempting food, from a daily changing menu, could include ploughman's, mackerel and ginger pâté with pickled cucumber and celery salad, crab cakes with sweet chilli jam, butternut risotto with apple and rocket salad, grilled bass fillet with prawn, chilli and lime linguine with pak choi and spinach, battered haddock with mushy peas, fried venison with braised red cabbage, and steak burger topped with mozzarella. *Benchmark main dish: fishcakes £9.95. Two-course evening meal £17.40.*

Brunning & Price ~ Manager John Astle-Rowe ~ Real ale ~ Bar food (12-10(9.30 Sun)) ~ (01743) 340525 ~ Children welcome ~ Dogs allowed in bar ~ Open 12-11(10.30 Sun)

Recommended by Ann and Colin Hunt, Brian Brooks, Henry Pursehouse-Tranter, Rochelle Seifas, George and Maureen Roby, Andy and Jill Kassube, Joe Green, P Dawn, C A Bryson, Steve Whalley, Barry Collett, Geraldine and James Fradgley, Mike and Mary Carter, Bruce and Sharon Eden, Jane Woodhull

 SOUTHROP Gloucestershire   SP2003 Map 4

Swan 🍽 ♀

Off A361 Lechlade—Burford; GL7 3NU

Creeper-covered pub with proper village bar, two dining rooms, imaginative food, and a fine choice of drinks

Right on the green in a pretty village, this 17th-c creeper-covered inn is doing particularly well under its present licensees. The chatty public bar is very much for those wanting a pint and a natter: it's got stools against the counter, simple tables and chairs, Hook Norton Hooky Bitter, Severn Vale Dursley Steam Bitter, Sharps Doom Bar and a beer named for the pub on handpump, 16 wines by the glass from a carefully chosen list and daily non-alcoholic cocktails. The low-ceilinged front dining rooms have open fires, all manner of leather dining chairs around a nice mix of old tables, cushions on settles, rugs on flagstones, nightlights, candles and lots of fresh flowers. There's a skittle alley and tables in the sheltered back garden. They have self-catering cottages to let.

🍽 Using local, seasonal produce, the inventive food might include sandwiches, lamb sweetbread fritters with tartare sauce, stuffed globe artichoke with field mushrooms, a poached duck egg and hollandaise, linguine with shellfish, capers, chilli, wild garlic and tomatoes, fish and chips with mushy peas, lamb tagine, and braised shin of beef with horseradish dumplings, chestnuts, parsnip mash and bone marrow crostini. *Benchmark main dish: crisp confit pork belly with artichokes and mushrooms £15.75. Two-course evening meal £22.25.*

Free house ~ Licensees Sebastian and Lana Snow ~ Real ale ~ Bar food (12-3, 6-10; not Sun evening) ~ Restaurant ~ (01367) 850205 ~ Children welcome ~ Dogs

welcome ~ Open 12-3, 6-11; 12-11 Sat; 12-3 Sun; closed Sun evenings
Recommended by Guy Vowles, Graham Oddey, Stephanie Gray, Alan Bulley

STANTON Gloucestershire

SP0634   Map 4

Mount

*Village signposted off B4632 SW of Broadway; keep on past village on
no-through road up hill, bear left; WR12 7NE*

**Bustling pub in a lovely spot with fantastic views, keen, friendly young
licensees, and good food**

Just up the steep lane from a lovely golden-stone village, this 17th-c pub
is in a lovely spot with fantastic views over the Vale of Evesham and on
towards the welsh mountains. There are seats on the terrace that make
the most of this and more seats in the peaceful garden; they have a
boules pitch. The friendly bars have low ceilings, heavy beams and
flagstones and there's a big log fire in the inglenook fireplace. The
restaurant has large picture windows overlooking the village. Donnington
BB and SBA on handpump served by cheerful staff and a good choice of
wines by the glass; darts and board games, and they keep dog biscuits
behind the bar. The pub is on the Cotswold Way National Trail.

Good, popular food includes lunchtime filled baguettes, various tapas, free-
range chicken wings in a crispy curry crumb with mint yoghurt and mango
chutney, beer-battered haddock, pasta carbonara, beef suet pudding topped with an
oyster fritter with a rich thyme jus, vegetable crumble, and chicken breast on
creamy leeks with bacon; they also offer good value two- and three-course set
menus. *Benchmark main dish: slow-roast gloucester old spot belly pork on sage
mash with apple and garlic confit and baby onion jus £14.00. Two-course evening
meal £20.00.*

Donnington ~ Tenants Karl and Pip Baston ~ Real ale ~ Bar food (12-2, 6-9(8.30 Sun)) ~
Restaurant ~ (01386) 584316 ~ Children welcome ~ Dogs welcome ~ Open 12-3, 6-11
*Recommended by Keith and Sue Ward, Michael Neilan, Richard Tilbrook, Ewan and Moira McCall,
Julie and Bill Ryan, P M Newsome, Alan Bulley, M G Hart, Karl Baston, Phil and Helen Holt,
David and Jane Hill, Julia and Richard Tredgett, Dr A J and Mrs Tompsett*

SYMONDS YAT Herefordshire

SO5616   Map 4

Saracens Head

Symonds Yat E, by ferry, ie over on the Gloucestershire bank; HR9 6JL

**Lovely riverside spot with a fine range of drinks in friendly inn,
interesting food and seats on waterside terraces; comfortable bedrooms**

Even on a miserable winter's day, this friendly pub is packed out with
happy customers. But of course, one of the main draws in summer is
its stunning position at the epicentre of the most scenic stretch of the
Wye gorge, far below the celebrated Symonds Yat viewpoint; picnic-sets
out on the waterside terrace look across the river. Inside it's warm and
relaxed with cheerful staff who make you feel at home and the bustling
bar has a buoyant atmosphere. Kingstone Gold, Mayfields Copper Fox,
Theakstons Old Peculier, Wye Valley Butty Bach and HPA and a guest
beer on handpump, 14 wines by the glass and local cider. Pool, games
machine, TV and piped music. There's also a cosy lounge and a
modernised bare-boards dining room. As well as bedrooms in the main
building, there are two contemporary ones in the boathouse annexe. It's

well worth approaching this spot on foot: an entertaining riverside walk crosses the Wye a little downstream by an entertainingly bouncy wire bridge at the Biblins and recrosses at the pub by the long-extant hand-hauled chain ferry that one of the pub staff operates. Plenty of nearby walks.

As well as lunchtime sandwiches, the popular food includes duck and grand marnier terrine with kumquat jam, mussels with local cider and creamed leeks, spinach and goats cheese risotto with pesto, lemon and herb-roasted spatchcock chicken with lyonnaise potatoes, local venison and parsnip cobbler with herb dumplings, and specials such as goats cheese and honey filo parcels, and pork and leek sausages with roasted root vegetables and onion gravy. *Benchmark main dish: beer-battered fish and chips £12.95. Two-course evening meal £21.90.*

Free house ~ Licensees P K and C J Rollinson ~ Real ale ~ Bar food (12-2.30, 6.30-9) ~ Restaurant ~ (01600) 890435 ~ Children welcome but must be over 7 to stay overnight ~ Dogs allowed in bar ~ Open 11-11 ~ Bedrooms: £59B/£89B

Recommended by David Heath, Marcus Mann, Barry and Anne, Mike Horgan, Di Wright, N R White, Phil Bryant, MLR

 TETBURY Gloucestershire   ST8494   Map 4

Gumstool

Part of Calcot Manor Hotel; A4135 W of town, just E of junction with A46; GL8 8YJ

Civilised bar with relaxed atmosphere, super choice of drinks, and enjoyable food

Of course, this is more of a dining pub (being attached to the very smart Calcot Manor Hotel) but as a bar/brasserie it does have an informal and relaxed atmosphere and is a highly enjoyable place for a drink or meal. Butcombe Bitter and Mendip Spring Bitter and a guest beer on handpump, lots of interesting wines by the glass and quite a few malt whiskies. The stylish layout is well divided to give a feeling of intimacy without losing the overall sense of contented bustle: flagstones, elegant wooden dining chairs and tables, well chosen pictures and drawings on mushroom-coloured walls, and leather armchairs in front of the big log fire; piped music. Westonbirt Arboretum is not far away.

Prices are reasonable for such a civilised setting and the food is excellent: twice-baked Arbroath smokies and cheddar soufflé, devilled lambs kidneys with crisp puff pastry, duck confit salad with sweet and sour dressing, free-range sausages with onion gravy, crab and leek tart, organic steak and kidney pudding, and roast and confit free-range chicken with bread sauce, bacon and dauphinoise potatoes. *Benchmark main dish: beer-battered cod with tartare sauce £14.00. Two-course evening meal £21.45.*

Free house ~ Licensees Paul Sadler and Richard Ball ~ Real ale ~ Bar food (12-2(4 Sun), 5.30-9.30) ~ Restaurant ~ (01666) 890391 ~ Children welcome ~ Open 10am-11pm ~ Bedrooms: £234B/£260B

Recommended by Clifford Blakemore, Bernard Stradling, Mr and Mrs P R Thomas, Rod Stoneman, Roger and Donna Huggins, Dr and Mrs C W Thomas, Mrs P Sumner

---

Bedroom prices are for high summer. Even then you may get reductions for more than one night, or (outside tourist areas) at weekends. Winter special rates are common, and many inns cut bedroom prices if you have a full evening meal.

TITLEY Herefordshire

SO3359 Map 6

Stagg 🍴 ♀ 🛏

B4355 N of Kington; HR5 3RL

HEREFORDSHIRE DINING PUB OF THE YEAR

Terrific food using tip-top ingredients served in extensive dining rooms, real ales and a fine choice of other drinks, and two-acre garden; comfortable bedrooms

Obviously, the excellent food remains the main draw here (this is one of Britain's top dining pubs after all) but it's still very much a pub rather than a pure restaurant and the staff are genuinely welcoming and courteous. The little bar is comfortably hospitable with a civilised atmosphere, a fine collection of 200 jugs attached to the ceiling, Hobsons Best and Ludlow Gold on handpump, nine house wines by the glass (there's also a carefully chosen 100-bin list), local potato and apple vodkas, local gins, farm cider, and quite a choice of spirits. The two-acre garden has seats on the terrace and a croquet lawn. The accommodation is in bedrooms above the pub, as well as in the additional rooms within a Georgian vicarage four minutes' walk away; super breakfasts.

Using their own-grown vegetables (they keep free-range chickens as well), the excellent inventive food includes some pubby dishes (not Saturday evenings or Sunday lunch) such as open sandwiches, devilled kidneys, home-made pork sausage and mash, and smoked haddock risotto. The more elaborate menu might have local snails with home-made chorizo and parmentier potatoes, seared scallops on parsnip purée, chicken breast with truffled mushrooms, jerusalem artichoke and dauphinoise potatoes, monkfish with a roast tomato and basil risotto, and duck breast, confit of duck leg, rhubarb and cider potato fondant; there are vegetarian choices, an amazing cheeseboard, home-made crisps, and a three-course Sunday lunch menu (£19.30). *Benchmark main dish: fillet of local beef £21.50. Two-course evening meal £24.80.*

Free house ~ Licensees Steve and Nicola Reynolds ~ Real ale ~ Bar food (not Sun evening or Mon) ~ Restaurant ~ (01544) 230221 ~ Children welcome ~ Dogs allowed in bar and bedrooms ~ Open 11-3, 6.30-11; closed Sun evening, all day Mon, first two weeks in Nov and ten days in Jan-Feb ~ Bedrooms: £70B/£85B

Recommended by Richard Cole, Dr Kevan Tucker, M G Hart, P J and R D Greaves, Chris Flynn, Wendy Jones, Rod Stoneman, Karen Eliot, R and S Bentley, Guy Vowles, Gaynor Gregory

TODENHAM Gloucestershire

SP2436 Map 4

Farriers Arms ♀

Between A3400 and A429 N of Moreton-in-Marsh; GL56 9PF

Friendly country pub; interesting décor, good bar food, and fine views

This unspoilt old pub has a lovely welcoming atmosphere and our readers tend to come back again and again. The bar has exposed stone and old plastered walls, hop-hung beams, fine old polished flagstones by the stone bar counter and a woodburning stove in a huge inglenook fireplace. A cosy room off the bar (full of old books and photographs) can seat parties of ten people and the restaurant has been recently refurbished. Hook Norton Hooky Bitter and two regularly changing guests on handpump, ten wines by the glass and locally brewed lager; piped music, darts and board games. The pub has fine views over the surrounding countryside from the walled garden and a couple of tables on the terrace overlook the quiet village road and church; aunt sally. Good surrounding walks.

🍴 Good, nicely served food using local produce includes filled baguettes, three cheese and apple tart with a beetroot dressing, a duo of local sausages in grain mustard sauce, spiced chicken breast with sweet potato and parmesan, chive mash and a mango salsa, salmon and spinach wellington, pork wrapped in parma ham, and wild mushroom, spinach and ricotta cannelloni. *Benchmark main dish: braised steak in ale pie £10.95. Two-course evening meal £17.00.*

Free house ~ Licensees Nigel and Louise Kirkwood ~ Real ale ~ Bar food (12-2(2.30 Sun), 6-9) ~ Restaurant ~ (01608) 650901 ~ Children welcome ~ Dogs allowed in bar ~ Open 12-3, 6-11; evening opening 6.30 in winter

Recommended by Pat Crabb, Alun and Jennifer Evans, Michael Dandy, Trevor and Sheila Sharman, M G Hart, John Holroyd, M and GR

 UPPER ODDINGTON Gloucestershire   SP2225   Map 4

Horse & Groom

Village signposted from A436 E of Stow-on-the-Wold; GL56 0XH

Pretty 16th-c Cotswold inn with imaginative food, lots of wines by the glass, and local beers and other local drinks; bedrooms

You can be sure of a warm welcome from the charming licensees in this partly ivy-covered old stone pub. The bar has pale polished flagstones, a handsome antique oak box settle among other more modern seats, some nice armchairs at one end, oak beams in the ochre ceiling, stripped-stone walls and a log fire in the inglenook fireplace. Box Steam Chuffin Ale, Wickwar Long John Silver and Wye Valley Bitter on handpump, 30 wines (including champagne) by the glass, local apple juice and elderflower pressé, local cider and a locally brewed lager. There are seats and tables under green parasols on the terrace and in the pretty garden.

🍴 Popular food using top quality local produce includes lunchtime sandwiches, bacon, black pudding and croûton salad topped with a poached egg, beetroot-cured salmon gravadlax with horseradish crème fraîche, juniper and spiced gloucester old spot pork belly with slow-cooked white cabbage and bacon, and specials such as duck liver and brandy pâté with apple, raisin and shallot marmalade, free-range chicken breast wrapped in bacon with a light tarragon jus, and bass fillets with noodles and an oriental broth. *Benchmark main dish: pie of the day £11.75. Two-course evening meal £20.00.*

Free house ~ Licensees Simon and Sally Jackson ~ Real ale ~ Bar food ~ Restaurant ~ (01451) 830584 ~ Children welcome ~ Dogs allowed in bar ~ Open 12-3, 5.30-11; 12-3, 6-10.30 Sun ~ Bedrooms: £79S/£99S(£105B)

Recommended by Alun and Jennifer Evans, Phil Bryant, Julie and Bill Ryan, Richard Greaves, K H Frostick, Michael Doswell

WALFORD Herefordshire   SO5820   Map 4

Mill Race 🍴 �

B4234 Ross-on-Wye—Lydney; HR9 5QS

Contemporary furnishings in uncluttered rooms, emphasis on good quality food ingredients, attentive staff, terrace tables and nearby walks

Consistently well run, this is an airy, stylish dining pub with welcoming staff and a relaxed atmosphere. The décor is fresh and contemporary, there's a row of strikingly tall arched windows and comfortable leather armchairs and sofas on flagstones – as well as smaller chairs around broad pedestal tables. The granite-topped modern bar counter has Wye Valley Bitter and Butty Bach on handpump, four local ciders, fairly priced wines by the glass and several malt whiskies; opposite are a couple of tall, nicely clean-cut tables with matching chairs. The walls are mainly cream or dark pink, with photographs of the local countryside, and there's good unobtrusive lighting. One wall stripped back to the stonework has a woodburning stove, also open to the comfortable and compact dining area on the other side; piped music. There are tables out on the terrace with views towards Goodrich Castle, a newly redesigned garden with plenty of dining space, and an external kitchen. They offer leaflets detailing pleasant nearby walks of an hour or so.

The pub owns a 1,000-acre farm and woodland close by which supply them with game, rabbits, poultry, beef, fruit and vegetables: sandwiches, moules marinière, home-smoked mackerel with smoked ham and rocket cakes and dill crème fraîche, home-made burger with bacon and cheese, thai green chicken curry, a pie of the day, fresh tagliatelle with wild mushrooms, and venison haunch with red wine sauce and cassis jelly. *Benchmark main dish: beer-battered fish and chips £11.50. Two-course evening meal £18.70.*

Free house ~ Licensee Luke Freeman ~ Real ale ~ Bar food (12-2(2.30 Sat), 6-9.30; 12-9 Sun) ~ (01989) 562891 ~ Children welcome ~ Open 11-3, 5-11; 10am-11pm Sat; 12-11 Sun

Recommended by Mike and Mary Carter, Guy Vowles, Dr A J and Mrs Tompsett, Nick and Meriel Cox

WALTERSTONE Herefordshire   SO3424   Map 6

Carpenters Arms

Village signposted off A465 E of Abergavenny, beside Old Pandy Inn; follow village signs, and keep eyes skinned for sign to pub, off to right, by lane-side barn; HR2 0DX

Unchanging country tavern in the same family for many years

Thankfully, little has changed at this charming, old-fashioned pub and the landlady Vera – who has been here some seventy years – took over from her mother; Pauline her daughter helps out now. It's in a quiet out-of-the-way position and the traditional rooms have ancient settles against stripped-stone walls, some pieces of carpet on broad polished flagstones, a roaring log fire in a gleaming black range (complete with hot-water tap, bread oven and salt cupboard), and pewter mugs hanging from beams. Breconshire Golden Valley and Wadworths 6X tapped from the cask. The snug main dining room has mahogany tables and oak corner cupboards and maybe a big vase of flowers on the dresser. Another little dining area has old oak tables and church pews on flagstones. The outside lavatories are cold but in character.

Straightforward food such as sandwiches, soup, a vegetarian choice, gammon and egg, lamb cutlet with redcurrant and rosemary sauce, daily specials, and Sunday roasts. *Benchmark main dish: steak £13.00. Two-course evening meal £12.00.*

Free house ~ Licensee Vera Watkins ~ Real ale ~ Bar food ~ Restaurant ~ No credit cards ~ (01873) 890353 ~ Children welcome ~ Open 12-3, 6-11; 12-11 Sat and Sun

Recommended by Nick and Sandra Blaney, Stuart and Doreen Ritchie, Howard Deacon, Maurice and Gill McMahon, Terry Davis

 WELFORD-ON-AVON Warwickshire SP1452 Map 4

Bell

Off B439 W of Stratford; High Street; CV37 8EB

WARWICKSHIRE DINING PUB OF THE YEAR

Enjoyably civilised pub with appealing ancient interior, good carefully sourced food, and a great range of drinks including five real ales; terrace

The charming licensees are almost always on hand to give personal attention and you can see this reflected in the general high standards and warmth at this delightful 17th-c place. Over the last year, readers have really enjoyed their kind welcome, well kept beer and delicious food (most people come to dine so booking is advised). The attractive interior (full of signs of the building's venerable age) is divided into five comfortable areas, each with its own character, from the cosy terracotta-painted bar to a light and airy gallery room with its antique wood panelling, solid oak floor and contemporary Lloyd Loom chairs. Flagstoned floors, stripped or well polished antique or period-style furniture, and three good fires (one in an inglenook) add warmth and cosiness. Hobsons, Purity Pure Gold and UBU, and two or three guests such as Greene King Old Speckled Hen and Purity Mad Goose are on handpump, and they've a dozen or so wines including champagne and local ones by the glass; piped music. In summer, the creeper-covered exterior is hung with lots of colourful baskets, and there are tables and chairs on a vine-covered dining terrace. This riverside village has an appealing church and pretty thatched black and white cottages.

If you turn to the back of the menu you will see a list of the local food suppliers they use here – the licensees put a lot of effort into sourcing good produce. The menu includes a good choice of sandwiches, fried brie with ginger and apricot compote, crispy whitebait, ploughman's, faggots with sage and onion gravy, smoked salmon and crayfish tail salad, and sirloin steak. Daily specials might take in sardines in tempura batter on oriental and ginger salad, lamb burger on toasted focaccia with cucumber salad and mint and ginger yoghurt, cajun sweet potato and red pepper curry, and roast salmon on paella-style rice with chorizo; popular Sunday roast, fish and chips night Tuesday and Spice Night Friday. *Benchmark main dish: steak and ale pie £12.75. Two-course evening meal £19.90.*

Laurel (Enterprise) ~ Lease Colin and Teresa Ombler ~ Real ale ~ Bar food (11.45-2.30(3 Sat), 6-9.30(10 Fri, Sat); 11.45-9.30 Sun) ~ (01789) 750353 ~ Children welcome ~ Open 11.30-3, 6-11; 11.30-11.30 Sat; 11.45-10.30 Sun

Recommended by Keith and Sue Ward, Chris and Jeanne Downing, Mr and Mrs A Curry, Leslie and Barbara Owen, Allan Westbury, John and Sharon Hancock, Eithne Dandy, Rod Stoneman, Prof H G Allen, Michael Dandy, Roger Whittaker, Martin and Pauline Jennings, Mike and Mary Carter, Joan and Tony Walker, R J Herd, Mr and Mrs R L Ham

 WOOLHOPE Herefordshire · SO6135 Map 4

Butchers Arms ⚒ ♀ 🍺

Off B4224 in Fownhope; HR1 4RF

Pleasant country inn in peaceful setting with an inviting garden, excellent food, and a fine choice of real ales

Down a country lane in lovely countryside, this 16th-c timber-framed pub is surrounded by a pretty garden with picnic-sets beside a stream. Inside, the bar has very low beams (some draped with hops), built-in, red-cushioned wall seats, farmhouse chairs and red-topped stools around a mix of old tables (some set for dining) on the red patterned carpet, hunting and horse pictures on the cream walls and an open fire in the big fireplace; there's also a little beamed dining room, similarly furnished. Breconshire Golden Valley, a couple of changing beers from Tudor and Wye Valley Bitter and Butty Bach on handpump and a well-annotated wine list with several by the glass. To enjoy some of the best of the surroundings, turn left as you come out of the pub and take the tiny left-hand road at the end of the car park; this turns into a track and then into a path, and the view from the top of the hill is quite something.

Using rare-breed meat and other carefully sourced produce, the first-rate food cooked by the professional landlord includes sandwiches using home-made bread, potted crab with rollmop salad, hot sweetcorn pudding with crispy chorizo and parsley oil, oxtail pie, boiled collar of bacon with a potato cake and mustard sauce, fillet of pollack with brown shrimps, fondant potato and tarragon butter sauce, and roast breast of duck with a lime compote and rösti potato. *Benchmark main dish: beer-battered whiting with home-made tartare sauce £11.00. Two-course evening meal £19.75.*

Free house ~ Licensee Stephen Bull ~ Real ale ~ Bar food (not Sun evening or Mon) ~ Restaurant ~ (01432) 860281 ~ Children welcome ~ Dogs welcome ~ Open 12-2.30, 6.30-11(midnight Sat); 12-3, 7-10.30 Sun; closed Sun evening and Mon (except bank holiday lunchtimes)
Recommended by Tansy Spinks, Nick Rampley, John and Jennifer Spinks, K and B Barker

WRINEHILL Staffordshire · SJ7547 Map 7

Hand & Trumpet ⚒ ♀ 🍺

A531 Newcastle—Nantwich; CW3 9BJ

STAFFORDSHIRE DINING PUB OF THE YEAR

Big attractive dining pub with good food all day, professional service, nice range of real ales and wines; pleasant garden

With its easy-on-the-eye light and airy open-plan interior and friendly attentive staff, this substantial dining pub is a relaxing place for an enjoyable meal. At its heart is a long solidly built counter with Caledonian Deuchars IPA, Phoenix B&P Original, Salopian Oracle and guests from brewers such as Titanic and Wincle, as well as a fine range of about nine wines by the glass and 70 or so whiskies. It's done out in typical Brunning & Price style with a gentle mix of dining chairs and sturdy tables on polished tiles or stripped-oak boards and several big warming oriental rugs that soften the acoustics. There are lots of nicely lit prints on cream walls between mainly dark dado and deep red ceilings. Its original bow windows and in one area a big skylight keep it light and airy, and french windows open onto a spacious balustraded deck with teak tables and chairs looking down to ducks swimming on a big pond in the sizeable garden which has plenty of trees; good disabled access and facilities; board games.

🍴 Food is well prepared, and the menu ranges from good takes on traditional dishes to more imaginative ones. As well as interesting sandwiches and ploughman's, there might be pigeon and duck faggot with parsnip cake, seared scallops with minted pea purée and confit tomatoes, crab linguine, sausage and mash, thai chicken with ginger and coriander dumplings, braised lamb shoulder with celeriac dauphinoise, steak, mushroom and ale pie, and fried bass with chorizo, caper and lemon dressing. *Benchmark main dish: beer-battered haddock £11.95. Two-course evening meal £18.00.*

Brunning & Price ~ Manager John Unsworth ~ Real ale ~ Bar food (12-10(9.30 Sun)) ~ (01270) 820048 ~ Children welcome ~ Dogs allowed in bar ~ Open 11.30-11(10.30 Sun)

Recommended by Paul and Margaret Baker, Henry Pursehouse-Tranter, Dr and Mrs A K Clarke, C A Bryson, Brian and Anna Marsden, Glenwys and Alan Lawrence, Dave Webster, Sue Holland, Cath, Frank Blanchard

---

ALSO WORTH A VISIT IN GLOUCESTERSHIRE

Besides the region's top pubs, we recommend the following. Do tell us what you think of them: **feedback@goodguides.com**

ALDERTON SP9933   GL20 8NL
Gardeners Arms
Beckford Road, off B4077 Tewkesbury—Stow

Attractive thatched Tudor pub with snug bars and informal restaurant, wide choice of decent home-made food from filled baps and baked potatoes to bistro dishes, fresh fish (including takeaway fish and chips) and good Sun roast, well kept Greene King and guests, above-average wines, hospitable landlady and good service, log fire; may be piped music; dogs and children welcome, tables on sheltered terrace, good-sized well kept garden with boules. *Recommended by Pat and Graham Williamson, Theocsbrian, Dr A J and Mrs Tompsett*

ALMONDSBURY ST6084   BS32 4DT
☆ ## Bowl
Church Road; 1.25 miles from M5 junction 16; from A38 towards Thornbury, turn left signed Lower Almondsbury, then right down Sundays Hill, then right

Pretty setting by church and a popular M5 stop; Brains, Butcombe and Fullers, good choice of enjoyable straightforward food (all day Fri-Sun), long beamed front bar with traditional settles, cushioned stools and mate's chairs around elm tables, horsebrasses on bare-stone walls, log fire and woodburner, restaurant extension; piped music; children allowed during food times, seats in front and on the back terrace, parking (£1) refundable at bar, bedrooms, open all day. *Recommended by Moira and John Cole, Bob and Angela Brooks, James Morrell, Chris and Martin Taylor, Roger and Donna Huggins, David A Hammond and others*

AMBERLEY SO8401   GL5 5AL
☆ ## Black Horse
Off A46 Stroud—Nailsworth to Amberley; left after Amberley Inn, left at war memorial; Littleworth; best to park by war memorial and walk down

Relaxed local with spectacular valley views from conservatory and terrace, good choice of changing ales, Moles Black Rat cider, decent wines by the glass, enjoyable varied food from baguettes to specials, helpful staff, wood and flagstone floors, high-backed settles, woodburner, cheerful sporting pictures, brasses and bells, large family area, games room, live music; they keep your card in a locked box if you're running a tab, big TV; children, walkers and wet dogs welcome, plenty of tables outside, barbecue. *Recommended by E McCall, T McLean, D Irving, LM, Guy Vowles, Neil and Anita Christopher*

AMPNEY CRUCIS SP0701   GL7 5RS

 ## Crown of Crucis
A417 E of Cirencester

Bustling roadside food pub, good value and plenty of choice, real ales in restored bar, good house wines, efficient service, beams and log fires, split-level restaurant; children welcome, disabled facilities, lots of tables out on grass by car park, quiet modern bedrooms around courtyard, good breakfast, cricket pitch over stream, open all day. *Recommended by Steve Cocking, Jennifer and Patrick O'Dell*

AMPNEY ST PETER SP0801   GL7 5SL

☆ ## Red Lion
A417, E of village

This unspoilt and unchanging country pub has long been a monument to traditional hospitality under its welcoming veteran landlord – only the third in over a century; just two simple chatty little rooms, log fires, well kept Timothy Taylors Landlord and Golden Best and maybe Hook Norton from the hatch, no food, outside lavatories; currently open evenings Fri, Sat and Mon plus Sun lunchtime. *Recommended by Stephen Funnell, Giles and Annie Francis, Ewan and Moira McCall, Ray Carter, the Didler and others*

AUST ST5788   BS35 4AX

Boars Head
0.5 miles from M48 junction 1, off Avonmouth Road

Marstons pub handy for the 'old' Severn bridge, their ales and Bath Gem, good house wines, decent choice of well priced food from good sandwiches up including weekday meal deals, friendly service, linked rooms and alcoves, beams and some stripped stone, huge log fire; piped music; wheelchair access possible, children in eating area away from bar, dogs on leads in bar, pretty sheltered garden. *Recommended by Barry and Anne, Jim and Frances Gowers, Roger and Donna Huggins*

BIBURY SP1006   GL7 5ND

Catherine Wheel
Arlington; B4425 NE of Cirencester

Bright cheerful dining pub with enjoyable reasonably priced fresh food from sandwiches up, well kept ales including Hook Norton, helpful friendly service, open-plan main bar and smaller back rooms, low beams, stripped stone, log fires, raftered dining room; picnic-sets out behind in good-sized garden, famously beautiful village, handy for country and riverside walks, four bedrooms. *Recommended by Dominic Brockbank, Jo White, Mo and David Trudgill, Guy Vowles, R K Phillips, Robert Pattison*

BIRDLIP SO9316   GL4 8JY

Air Balloon
A417/A436 roundabout

Loftily placed busy chain dining pub, good range of food from sandwiches, wraps and baguettes up all day, meal deals, friendly helpful service, changing ales such as Hook Norton Old Hooky, good wine and soft drinks choice, many levels and alcoves including restaurant and brasserie, pubbier front corner with open fire, beams and stripped stone; unobtrusive piped music; tables, some covered, on heated terrace and in garden with play area, open all day. *Recommended by Caroline and Michael Abbey*

BISLEY SO9006   GL6 7BD

☆ ## Bear
Village signed off A419 E of Stroud

Elegantly gothic 16th-c inn with bustling L-shaped bar, old oak settles, brass and copper implements around extremely wide low stone fireplace, low ochre ceiling, St Austell

Tribute, Tetleys and Wells & Youngs Bombardier, enjoyable pubby food, separate stripped-stone family area; dogs welcome, small flagstoned courtyard, stone mounting blocks in garden across quiet road, bedrooms, open all day Sun. *Recommended by Dr and Mrs A K Clarke, Bernard Stradling, Myra Joyce, Nick and Meriel Cox*

BISLEY SO9006   GL6 7BL
Stirrup Cup
Cheltenham Road

Spacious opened-up local with roaring fire and friendly welcome, two or three well kept ales such as Sharps Doom Bar and Wickwar, Weston's cider, uncomplicated generous food at reasonable prices, themed evenings, OAP discount weekday lunchtime, good service; dogs and walkers welcome, interesting village. *Recommended by Guy Vowles, Neil and Anita Christopher*

BLOCKLEY SP1635   GL56 9DT
Great Western Arms
Station Road (B4479)

Nicely updated beamed pub in attractive village, welcoming landlady, well kept Hook Norton ales, good choice of wines, enjoyable simple home-made food, dining room and busy public bar (dogs very welcome here – pub has two retrievers) with pool, juke box and darts; terrace seating, lovely valley view, closed Mon lunchtime. *Recommended by Elizabeth Charnley, B M Eldridge*

BOURTON-ON-THE-HILL SP1732   GL56 9AQ
☆ Horse & Groom
A44 W of Moreton-in-Marsh

Plenty of original features in this handsome honey-stone Georgian inn, warm welcome from licensee brothers, good interesting modern food using local and home-grown produce (not Sun evening, booking advised), chatty regulars in airy stripped-stone pubby bar with nice mix of wooden furniture on bare boards, log fire, Goffs Jouster and guests, local lager, 14 wines by the glass and home-made summer cordials; children welcome, seats out under smart umbrellas, lovely country views from large back garden, handy for Batsford Arboretum, stylish bedrooms, closed Sun evening. *Recommended by Roger Braithwaite, Peter J and Avril Hanson, P Waterman, Chris Glasson, Richard Tilbrook, Anthony and Pam Stamer and others*

BOURTON-ON-THE-WATER SP1620   GL54 2BS
Kingsbridge Inn
Riverside

Roomy open-plan riverside pub, well kept Marstons-related ales, traditional food including children's choices, friendly service, refurbished interior with country-style furniture and nice log fire; can get packed with day-trippers; dogs welcome, pleasant village/river view from terrace tables, open all day. *Recommended by Ted George*

BOX SO8500   GL6 9AE
☆ Halfway House
By Minchinhampton Common

300-year-old dining pub with light airy open-plan areas around central servery, simple sturdy furniture on stripped-wood floors, downstairs restaurant, Butcombe and Sharps, decent wines by the glass; piped and some live music; children and dogs welcome, seats in landscaped garden, open all day Fri-Sun, closed Mon lunchtime. *Recommended by Jenny Huggins, J R Cason, E McCall, T McLean, D Irving, Tom and Ruth Rees*

BROAD CAMPDEN SP1537   GL55 6UR
☆ Bakers Arms
Village signed from B4081 in Chipping Campden

Good mix of locals and visitors at this friendly village pub with beams and stripped stone, tiny characterful bar with inglenook, Donnington, Stanway, Tetleys, Wells & Youngs and a guest from oak counter, standard food (all day in summer), dining room, walkers' groups welcome in back rooms, folk music third Tues of month; no credit cards; children allowed away from bar, seats on terraces and in back garden, open all day (closed Mon-Thurs afternoons in winter). *Recommended by John R Ringrose, Mike Proctor, Martin and Pauline Jennings, Simon Watkins, Paul Humphreys and others*

BROADOAK SO6912   GL14 1JB
White Hart
A48 Gloucester—Chepstow

Overlooking tidal Severn, plenty of tables out on high terrace by quay, sensibly priced pubby food from sandwiches up, Greene King ales, carpeted bar and dining area, low beams, nautical décor; piped music; wheelchair access. *Recommended by Dr A Y Drummond*

BROOKEND SO6801   GL13 9SF
Lammastide
New Brookend

Small friendly 1930s pub in quiet roadside spot inland from Sharpness, linked carpeted rooms with roughcast walls and panelling, usual pubby furniture, brass, earthenware, old maps and cartoons, raised bare-boards area in bay window with faux-leather sofas, good choice of enjoyable food from baguettes to some interesting specials, Bass, Marstons Pedigree, Wye Valley and a guest, decent wines from short list, newspapers; fruit machine; children and dogs welcome, wheelchair access using ramp, picnic-sets on raised terrace, good views to Forest of Dean, play area. *Recommended by Chris and Angela Buckell*

CAMBRIDGE SO7403   GL2 7AL
George
3 miles from M5 junction 13 – A38 towards Bristol

Two spacious dining areas serving enjoyable good value food from filled rolls to specials, bargain lunches and Tues steak night, well kept Butcombe and Moles, helpful well organised service, two woodburners back-to-back; piped music, no dogs inside; children welcome, picnic-sets in side garden with new play area, one bedroom, pleasant campsite, handy for Slimbridge wildfowl centre, open all day. *Recommended by Steve and Liz Tilley*

CERNEY WICK SU0796   GL7 5QH
Crown
Village signed from A419

Friendly old village inn with roomy modern lounge bar, comfortable conservatory dining extension, popular inexpensive food, well kept Wadworths 6X, Wells & Youngs Bombardier and a guest, coal-effect gas fires, games in public bar; children welcome, good-sized garden with swings, ten refurbished bedrooms in motel-style extension. *Recommended by Giles and Annie Francis, Ian Herdman*

CHELTENHAM SO9421   GL50 2EZ
Jolly Brewmaster
Painswick Road

Popular lively local with open-plan linked areas around big semicircular counter, good range of ales such as Archers, Caledonian Deuchars IPA, Donnington and Hook Norton, up to eight farm ciders, perhaps a perry, friendly obliging young staff, newspapers, log fires; dogs welcome, coachyard tables. *Recommended by Richard and Ruth Dean, Stuart Doughty, Theocsbrian*

CHELTENHAM SO9624   GL52 3BG
 # Plough
Mill Street, Prestbury

Good new management for this thatched village local opposite church, comfortable front lounge, service from corner corridor hatch in flagstoned back tap room, grandfather clock and big log fire, well kept Adnams Broadside, Wells & Youngs Bombardier and three guests tapped from the cask, real ciders and perry, good traditional home-made food including blackboard specials; lovely big flower-filled back garden (dogs on leads), some summer weekend barbecues, immaculate boules pitch, open all day. *Recommended by Stuart Doughty, B M Eldridge*

CHELTENHAM SO9321   GL50 2TT
Royal Union
Hatherley Street

Backstreet pub but with large bar and cosy snug up steps, good choice of well kept ales, reasonably priced wines, enjoyable well priced food – landlord cooks nice steaks, skittle alley; courtyard behind. *Recommended by Guy Vowles*

CHELTENHAM SO9420   GL53 0EH
Somerset Arms
Moorend Street

Cosy town local in narrow terraced street, friendly atmosphere with customers of all ages, fine choice of real ales including a house beer from Hook Norton, interesting knick-knacks, no food. *Recommended by Jane and Alan Bush*

CHELTENHAM SO9522   GL50 1EE
Strand
High Street

Bright and airy renovation with shop-window frontage, mix of old furniture on bare boards, some exposed brick, modern artwork, four well kept changing ales with tasting notes such as Brewdog Trashy Blonde and Festival Gold, simple well balanced menu, live music; children welcome, small decked terrace behind, open all day. *Recommended by Andy and Claire Barker*

CHIPPING CAMPDEN SP1539   GL55 6AW
☆ ## Kings
High Street

Fresh eclectic décor in 18th-c hotel's bar/brasserie and separate restaurant, cheery helpful service, good food from lunchtime sandwiches and baguettes to pubby dishes and more elaborate meals, Hook Norton and a guest, good choice of wines by the glass, nice log fire, daily papers; secluded back garden with picnic-sets and terrace tables, 12 comfortable bedrooms, open all day Sat. *Recommended by Michael Dandy, Eithne Dandy, Peter Dandy*

CHIPPING CAMPDEN SP1539   GL55 6HB
☆ ## Lygon Arms
High Street

Refurbished low-beamed bar in 16th-c coaching inn, ales such as Hook Norton, Wadworths 6X and Wye Valley, generous traditional food including daily roasts, good service, new furniture on stone floor, stripped-stone walls and open fires, small back restaurant; children welcome, tables in shady cobbled courtyard, comfortable beamed bedrooms, good breakfast, open all day weekends and summer. *Recommended by Michael Dandy*

CHIPPING CAMPDEN SP1539   GL55 6AT
Noel Arms
High Street

Handsome 16th-c inn with refurbished beamed and stripped-stone bar, modern furniture, open fire, decent food from sandwiches to steaks, Hook Norton and local guests, good choice of wines by the glass, austrian coffee lounge (7.30am-6pm), conservatory, restaurant; children and dogs welcome, sunny courtyard tables, 28 well appointed bedrooms, good breakfast, open all day. *Recommended by Eithne Dandy, Michael Dandy, Eleanor Dandy*

CLEEVE HILL SO9826
Rising Sun
B4632

GL52 3PX

Hotel with splendid view over Cheltenham to the Malvern Hills from conservatory, covered terrace and lawn; large carpeted bar with friendly efficient service, Greene King ales, decent wine choice, good value pubby food all-day, lower eating area, restaurant beyond; sports TV; pleasant affordable bedrooms, good breakfast. *Recommended by Derek and Sylvia Stephenson, Michael Dandy*

COMPTON ABDALE SP0717
 ## Puesdown Inn
A40 outside village

GL54 4DN

Spacious series of stylish bar areas, wide choice of good enterprising food (not Sun evening) from landlord/chef, stone-baked pizzas too, friendly helpful staff, well kept Hook Norton, good coffees and wines by the glass, log fire and woodburner, bare boards, bright rugs and rafter-effect ceilings, leather or brightly upholstered sofas and armchairs, big art posters and other interesting pictures, cream and dark red walls, mainly stripped stone in extensive eating areas, well reproduced piped music; dogs welcome in bar (they have chocolate labradors), nice garden behind, bedrooms, open all day Sat. *Recommended by Rod Stoneman, Ian Herdman*

COOMBE HILL SO8926
Gloucester Old Spot
Elmstone Hardwicke; A4019 near M5 junction 10

GL51 9SY

Now under the same ownership as the Royal Oak in Cheltenham, some restoration but keeping original rustic charm, linked areas and adjoining flagstoned dining barn with large portraits on stripped-brick walls and candles on farmhouse tables, inviting menu using locally sourced produce including rare-breed pork, set lunchtime deals and Sun roasts, prompt helpful service, well kept ales such as Otter, Purity and Timothy Taylors, farm ciders and perry, log fires; piped music; tables out at front and behind. *Recommended by Andy and Claire Barker, Guy Vowles, Mrs C G Powell-Tuck*

COOMBE HILL SO8827
Swan
A38/A4019

GL19 4BA

Light airy dining pub with several rooms, popular generous fresh food from sandwiches up including deals, good friendly service, Greene King Abbot, Uley Old Spot and a guest, decent house wine, polished boards and panelling, red leather chesterfields; piped music. *Recommended by Rod Stoneman, John and Gloria Isaacs*

COWLEY SO9714
☆ ## Green Dragon
Off A435 S of Cheltenham at Elkstone, Cockleford sign; OS Sheet 163 map reference 970142

GL53 9NW

Smart yet characterful dining pub with cosy genuinely old-fashioned feel, good food and friendly helpful service, well kept Butcombe, Courage Directors and Otter, furniture and bar counters made by Robert Thompson – the 'Mouse Man of Kilburn', big flagstones and bare floorboards, candlelit tables, log fires in two stone fireplaces, skittle alley; piped music; children welcome, dogs in bar, terrace seating, good walking area, comfortable bedrooms, open all day. *Recommended by Keith and Sue Ward, Guy Vowles, Mrs S Hayden, Mike and Mary Carter, Giles and Annie Francis and others*

CRANHAM SO8912
☆ ## Black Horse
Village signposted off A46 and B4070 N of Stroud

GL4 8HP

Newish licensees at this down-to-earth 17th-c local, cosy lounge, main bar with traditional furniture, window seats and log fire, well kept Hancocks HB, Sharps Doom Bar and a guest, real ciders, home-made blackboard food (not Sun evening – pub open from

8.30pm then), two upstairs dining rooms (one with log fire); well behaved children and dogs welcome, tables out in front and to the side, good country views and walks, closed **Mon.** *Recommended by Giles and Annie Francis, Andy and Claire Barker*

☆ DOYNTON ST7174   BS30 5TF
Cross House
High Street; signed off A420 Bristol—Chippenham E of Wick

Easy-going 18th-c village pub near fine walking country and Dyrham Park, convivial landlord and staff, honest reasonably priced food, Bass, Bath, Courage, Sharps and Timothy Taylors, around 18 wines by the glass, softly lit carpeted bar with beams, some stripped stone, simple pub furniture and woodburner, cottagey candlelit dining room; piped music, games machine, TV; children welcome, dogs in bar, picnic-sets out by the road, open all day Sun. *Recommended by Barry and Anne, Jim and Frances Gowers, Colin and Peggy Wilshire, Dr and Mrs C W Thomas*

☆ DUNTISBOURNE ABBOTS SO9709   GL7 7JR
Five Mile House
E of A417 on parallel old Main Road

Cheerful father and son team at this characterful village pub, nice old traditional rooms, roaring fire, popular well presented food (not Sun evening) including gourmet evenings, well kept changing ales, interesting wine list, newspapers, darts; children welcome, dogs in bar, garden with nice views and summer marquee. *Recommended by Ann and Colin Hunt, Dennis Jenkin, Neil and Anita Christopher, Guy Vowles, Ewan and Moira McCall and others*

☆ EASTLEACH TURVILLE SP1905   GL7 3NQ
Victoria
Off A361 S of Burford

Open-plan low-ceilinged rooms around central servery, attractive seats built in by log fire, unusual Queen Victoria pictures, Arkells ales, several good value wines by the glass, shortish choice of sensibly priced pub food (not winter Sun evening) including baguettes; piped music; children and dogs welcome, small pleasant front garden with picnic-sets overlooking picturesque village, good walks. *Recommended by Maurice Holt, Chris Glasson*

☆ EDGE SO8409   GL6 6ND
Edgemoor
Gloucester Road (A4173)

Tidy, modernised and spacious 19th-c dining pub with panoramic valley view across to Painswick from picture windows and pretty terrace, good food, friendly efficient service, well kept local ales such as Goffs Jouster, nice coffee, restaurant; children welcome, good walks nearby. *Recommended by M W Riddiford, Neil and Anita Christopher*

☆ ELKSTONE SO9610   GL53 9PL
Highwayman
Beechpike; A417 6 miles N of Cirencester

Interesting rambling 16th-c building, low beams, stripped stone, log fires, cosy alcoves, bric-a-brac, antique settles, armchairs and sofa among more usual furnishings, good value home-made food, friendly service, full Arkells range, good house wines, family room and big back eating area; disabled access, outside play area. *Recommended by the Didler, Guy Vowles, Mrs Y Ebdon*

☆ EWEN SU0097   GL7 6BY
Wild Duck
Off A429 S of Cirencester

Unchanging 16th-century inn with stylishly old-fashioned furnishings and pictures in high-beamed log-fire main bar, lounge with handsome Elizabethan fireplace and antique furnishings, some interesting if not cheap food, six real ales including Duck Pond brewed for the pub, very good choice of wines by the glass; piped music; children welcome, tables in neatly kept heated courtyard (if you eat here they may ask to keep your credit card behind the bar), garden, 12 bedrooms, open all day. *Recommended by Dr and Mrs A K Clarke, Stuart and Doreen Ritchie, D Crook, Andy and Claire Barker, Mr and Mrs A Curry, Jennifer and Patrick O'Dell and others*

FAIRFORD SP1501   GL7 4AA

 Bull

Market Place

Rather smart old timbered hotel with bustling, chatty atmosphere, comfortable pubby furnishings in relaxed bar including dark pews and settles, aircraft pictures and photographs of actors (previous guests) on ochre walls, coal-effect gas fire, Arkells 2B, 3B and Kingsdown, reasonably priced, traditional bar food, friendly service; children welcome, dogs in bar, disabled facilities, charming village and church with intact set of medieval stained-glass windows, bedrooms, open all day. *Recommended by Howard G Allen, Anthony Barnes, David and Gill Carrington, Jennifer and Patrick O'Dell*

FOREST OF DEAN SO6212   GL16 7EL
Speech House
B4226 nearly 1 mile E of junction with B4234

Superbly placed hotel in centre of Forest (former 17th-c hunting lodge), refurbished interior with oak panelling, huge log fire, all-day bar food from nice sandwiches up, real ales such as Wye Valley, afternoon teas, big conservatory, restaurant; comfortable bedrooms, tables outside. *Recommended by Mike and Mary Carter, E McCall, T McLean, D Irving, John and Gloria Isaacs*

FRAMPTON COTTERELL ST6681   BS36 2AB
Globe
Church Road

Large knocked-through bar/dining area with black beams and some stripped stone, usual furniture on parquet or carpet, woodburner in old fireplace, half a dozen well kept changing ales such as Butcombe, Sharps and Uley, real ciders, interesting wine list, enjoyable well presented pubby food, attentive friendly young staff, flowers on tables, newspapers; piped music; children welcome, wheelchair access via side door, garden with play area and smokers' gazebo. *Recommended by Chris and Angela Buckell*

FRAMPTON COTTERELL ST6681   BS36 2EF
Live & Let Live
Off A432; Clyde Road

Attractive pub refurbished by Bath Brewery, their ales, helpful staff, bargain food (not Sun evening) from sandwiches to popular Sun lunch, decent wines by the glass, daily papers, linked rooms with carpeted bar and bare-boards dining areas, pastel walls with panelled dado, darts; piped music, no dogs; children welcome, disabled facilities, picnic-sets in big garden, open all day. *Recommended by Chris and Angela Buckell*

FRAMPTON MANSELL SO9202   GL6 8JG
 Crown
Brown sign to pub off A491 Cirencester—Stroud

Welcoming licensees doing good choice of enjoyable home-made food from baguettes up at reasonable prices, well kept changing local ales including Stroud and Uley, efficient charming service, heavy 17th-c beams, stripped stone and rugs on bare boards, two log fires and woodburner, restaurant; children and dogs welcome (there's a friendly pub dog), disabled access, picnic-sets in sunny front garden, pretty outlook, 12 decent bedrooms in separate block, open all day from midday. *Recommended by Myra Joyce, Paul Humphreys, Mrs P Sumner*

FRAMPTON ON SEVERN SO7408   GL2 7EP
Bell
The Green (B4071, handy for M5 junction 13, via A38)

Handsome creeper-covered Georgian inn attractively opened up, enjoyable generous food in extensive all-day family dining area, local's bar with quarry tiles and flagstones, Bath Gem, Moles and Sharps Doom Bar, real cider, steps up to restaurant, rebuilt skittle alley; piped music; dogs welcome, plenty of seats outside (front and back), good play area and kids' farm, stabling, village cricket green opposite, open all day. *Recommended by W K Wood, Jo Rees, Chris and Angela Buckell, Dr A J and Mrs Tompsett*

GLASSHOUSE SO7121   GL17 0NN

 ## Glasshouse Inn
Off A40 just W of A4136

Much-extended red-brick beamed pub with appealing old-fashioned and antique furnishings, cavernous black hearth, big flagstoned conservatory, well kept ales including Butcombe tapped from the cask, Stowford Press cider, reasonably priced wines, decent home-made food from sandwiches and basket meals to interesting specials, good friendly service; piped music, no under-14s in bars, no bookings except Sun lunch, and they may try to keep your credit card while you eat; good disabled access, neat garden with rustic furniture, interesting topiary, flower-decked cider presses and lovely hanging baskets, nearby paths up wooded May Hill, closed Sun evening. *Recommended by Chris and Angela Buckell, the Didler, Neil and Anita Christopher*

GLOUCESTER SO8318   GL1 1TP

Café René
Southgate Street

Spacious cheerful place with plenty of character, beams and exposed brick, masses of empty wine bottles, belgian beer memorabilia, some cask tables, good value food all day from lunchtime sandwiches up including vegetarian choices, two or three changing ales, restaurant, cellar bar (DJ nights); piped and live music, big screen sports TV, silent fruit machine; seats outside, open all day (till 4am Fri, Sat – entrance fee after 11pm). *Recommended by Alan and Eve Harding, Jeremy King*

GLOUCESTER SO8318   GL1 2NW

Fountain
Westgate Street

Tucked-away 17th-c pub off pedestrianised street, well kept St Austell Tribute, Greene King Abbot and four mainly local guests, good choice of reasonably priced pubby food from sandwiches up, handsome stone fireplace, plush seats and built-in wall benches; piped music; children welcome, disabled access, flower-filled courtyard, handy for cathedral, open all day. *Recommended by the Didler, Joe Green, Theocsbrian*

GREAT BARRINGTON SP2013   OX18 4TB

Fox
Off A40 Burford—Northleach; pub towards Little Barrington

17th-c inn with stripped stone, simple country furnishings and low ceiling, Donnington BB and SBA, farm cider and good apple juice, wide choice of quickly served food (all day Sun and summer Sat, not Mon night winter) from sandwiches through oysters to local meats, big bare-boards river-view dining room with riverbank mural, traditional games, Aug 'Foxstock' folk festival; can get very busy, games machine, TV; children and dogs welcome, heated terraces by the Windrush (swans and private fishing), informal orchard with pond, four bedrooms, open all day. *Recommended by Martin and Pauline Jennings, the Didler, David Glynne-Jones*

GRETTON SP0130   GL54 5EP

Royal Oak
Off B4077 E of Tewkesbury

Popular lived-in country pub with linked bare-boarded or flagstoned rooms, friendly caring licensees and good service, straightforward generous food, well kept Goffs and a guest ale, decent wines, mix of furniture, beams hung with tankards and chamber-pots, interesting old motor-racing pictures, modern dining conservatory; children and dogs welcome, fine views from flower-filled terrace, big garden with play area and tennis, GWR private railway runs past, good nearby walks, open all day summer weekends. *Recommended by Gordon Briggs, Theocsbrian, Chris and Angela Buckell*

GUITING POWER SP0924   GL54 5TZ
☆ **Farmers Arms**
Fosseway (A429)

Stripped stone and flagstones, well kept cheap Donnington BB and SBA, wide blackboard range of enjoyable food cooked by landlord including good rabbit pie, welcoming prompt service, nice log fire, lots of pictures, carpeted back dining part, games area with darts, dominoes, cribbage and pool, skittle alley; piped music, games machine; children welcome, garden with quoits, lovely village, good walks, bedrooms. *Recommended by the Didler, Jo Rees, Mr and Mrs A J Hudson, Richard Tilbrook*

HAM ST6898   GL13 9QH
Salutation
On main road through village

Friendly local with good range of ales and simple well cooked food at bargain prices, good service. *Recommended by Barry Collett, John and Gloria Isaacs, Chris and Angela Buckell*

HAWKESBURY UPTON ST7786   GL9 1AU
☆ **Beaufort Arms**
High Street

Unpretentious 17th-c pub in historic village, welcoming landlord and friendly local atmosphere, well kept Wickwar ales and cider, guest beers, popular no-nonsense food (no starters, small helpings available), extended uncluttered dining lounge on right, darts in more spartan stripped-brick bare-boards bar, interesting local and brewery memorabilia, lots of pictures (some for sale), skittle alley; well behaved children allowed, dogs in bar, disabled access throughout and facilities, picnic-sets in smallish enclosed garden, on Cotswold Way, open all day. *Recommended by Chris and Angela Buckell, M G Hart, Neil and Anita Christopher, Jim and Frances Gowers, Dr and Mrs A K Clarke, Les Halpin*

HILLESLEY ST7689   GL12 7RD
Fleece
Hawkesbury Road/Chapel Lane

Attractive village pub under new management, popular traditional home-made food (not Sun evening, Mon) plus some south african specials from landlord/chef, reasonable prices and friendly service, well kept Butcombe, Fullers, Theakstons and a guest, good choice of wines by the glass, main bar with steps down to dining room, snug with books and games; children, dogs and walkers welcome, back garden with play area, small village in lovely countryside near Cotswold Way, closed Mon lunchtime, open all day weekends. *Recommended by Barry Collett*

HORSLEY ST8497   GL6 0QE
☆ **Tipputs**
Tiltups End; A46 2 miles S of Nailsworth

Enjoyable food all day from good value lunches to interesting evening meals, cheerful efficient service, Greene King ale, beams, stripped stone, big log fire and abstract art, comfortable leather seats in anteroom to galleried barn restaurant; nice chairs and tables in pretty garden with raised deck, lovely setting, open all day. *Recommended by Tom and Ruth Rees*

KEMBLE ST9899   GL7 6NZ
☆ **Thames Head**
A433 Cirencester—Tetbury

Stripped stone, timberwork, log fire, intriguing little front alcove, pews in cottagey back area with log-effect gas fire in big fireplace, country-look dining room with another big fire, wide choice of enjoyable food, good value wines, well kept ales such as Otter, friendly obliging staff, skittle alley; TV; children welcome, tables outside, good value four-poster bedrooms, good breakfast, walk to nearby Thames source. *Recommended by Neil and Anita Christopher, Mike Buckingham*

KEMPSFORD SU1596

GL7 4EQ

George
High Street

Well cared-for village pub with gleaming brasses, woodburners in roomy bare-boards dining area, carpeted bar, welcoming landlord, enjoyable good value traditional food, well kept Arkells; children welcome, big back play area. *Recommended by Stephen Funnell, Jennifer and Patrick O'Dell*

KINETON SP0926

GL54 5UG

Halfway House
Signed from B4068 and B4077 W of Stow-on-the-Wold

Simple 17th-c beamed village pub doing well under welcoming couple, good nicely presented food from sandwiches up, well kept Donnington BB and SBA, decent wines, farm cider, restaurant, log fire; pool; children welcome, sheltered back garden, good walks, bedrooms, open all day weekends. *Recommended by Mr and Mrs Adam Helliker, John and Helen Rushton, Michael Dandy, Eleanor Dandy and others*

KINGSCOTE ST8196

GL8 8XZ

☆ # Hunters Hall
A4135 Dursley—Tetbury

Tudor beams, stripped stone, big log fires and plenty of character in individually furnished spotless linked rooms, some sofas and easy chairs, wide choice of good food from lunchtime sandwiches up, well kept Greene King and Uley, friendly attentive service, flagstoned back bar with darts, pool and TV; children and dogs welcome, garden with good play area, 13 bedrooms, open all day. *Recommended by Brian Goodson, Nick and Meriel Cox, Roger and Donna Huggins, Laurence Davis*

LECHLADE SU2199

GL7 3AE

Crown
High Street

Friendly old pub brewing its own good Halfpenny ales (six on offer), bar with two open fires, back games room with pool and table football; children welcome, beer garden, three bedrooms in separate block, open all day. *Recommended by Graham Oddey, Simon Garfuncle*

LEIGHTERTON ST8290

GL8 8UN

Royal Oak
Off A46 S of Nailsworth

Welcoming stone-built pub recently refurbished by new owners; opened-up bar with beams, log fires, stripped stone/brick walls and mullioned windows, good sensibly priced food, well kept changing ales and decent wines, good friendly service; wheelchair access, nice garden, quiet village with good surrounding walks, quite handy for Westonbirt Arboretum. *Recommended by Chris and Angela Buckell, David Shaw, Les Halpin, David and Jill Wyatt, Devereaux Harry-Barnwell*

LITTLE BARRINGTON SP2012

OX18 4TN

Inn For All Seasons
A40 3 miles W of Burford

Handsome old coaching inn with attractive comfortable lounge bar, low beams, stripped stone and flagstones, old prints, log fire, Sharps Doom Bar and Wadworths 6X, lots of wines by the glass and malt whiskies, restaurant and conservatory, food and service can be good; piped music; dogs welcome, seats in garden, aunt sally, walks from door, bedrooms. *Recommended by Evelyn and Derek Walter, Anthony Longden, Graham Oddey, Mr and Mrs J Mandeville, Mark and Ruth Brock*

LITTLE WASHBOURNE SO9933   GL20 8NQ
Hobnails
B4077 Tewkesbury—Stow-on-the-Wold

Attractive traditional front core with 15th-c beams and log fire, comfortable and extensive eating areas around this, wide choice of enjoyable food including popular good value carvery, friendly prompt service, ales such as Fullers London Pride and Goffs Jouster, decent wines; children welcome, disabled facilities, terrace tables, play area, bedroom extension. *Recommended by Dr A J and Mrs Tompsett, Derek and Sylvia Stephenson*

LITTLETON-UPON-SEVERN ST5989   BS35 1NR
White Hart
3.5 miles from M48 junction 1

Former farmhouse with three main rooms, log fires, nice mix of country furnishings, loveseat in inglenook, flagstones at front, huge tiles at back, hops on beams, fine old White Hart Inn Simonds Ale sign, family room, back snug, Wells & Youngs ales and guests, bar food (all day Sun); dogs welcome, wheelchair access with help, picnic-sets on front lawn, cottagey flowerbeds, teak seating on brick terrace by big car park, walks from door, open all day. *Recommended by John and Gloria Isaacs, Bob and Angela Brooks, Chris and Angela Buckell*

LONGBOROUGH SP1729   GL56 0QU
Coach & Horses
Ganborough Road

Small friendly 17th-c stone-built local, Donnington ales, Weston's cider, enjoyable wholesome food (not Sun evening or Mon-Weds), friendly staff, leather armchairs on flagstones, inglenook stove, darts, dominoes and cribbage; some piped music; well behaved children and dogs welcome, tables out at front looking down on stone cross and village, two simple clean bedrooms. *Recommended by Michael Dandy, Liam and Sue McGreevy*

LOWER ODDINGTON SP2326   GL56 0UR
☆ Fox
Signed off A436

Smart 16th-c creeper-covered inn with good modern food served by efficient friendly staff, well kept Hook Norton, St Austell Tribute and a guest like Wickwar BOB, little country-style flagstoned rooms with mix of chairs around pine tables, fresh flowers, hunting figures and pictures, inglenook fireplace, elegant red-walled dining room; children welcome, dogs in bar, white tables and chairs on heated terrace in cottagey garden, pretty village, bedrooms. *Recommended by John Taylor, Keith and Sue Ward, Andrea Rampley, William Goodhart, Caroline and Michael Abbey and others*

MAYSHILL ST6882   BS36 2NT
☆ New Inn
Badminton Road (A432 Frampton Cotterell—Yate)

Good food (all day Sun) in popular largely 17th-c coaching inn with two comfortably carpeted bar rooms leading to restaurant, friendly staff, well kept changing ales such as Bristol Beer Factory and Cotswold Spring, Stowford Press cider, log fire; children and dogs welcome, garden with play area. *Recommended by Roger and Donna Huggins*

MINSTERWORTH SO7716   GL2 8JQ
Apple Tree
A48 S of Gloucester

Refurbished dining pub extended around oak-beamed 17th-c farmhouse, wide choice of well priced generous food including daily specials and Sun carvery, good service from friendly young staff, well kept ales, various eating areas including large barn-like room, inglenook log fires; children welcome, big garden with play area, lane beside pub leads down to the Severn. *Recommended by Eric Thomas Yarwood, Bernard Stradling, Neil and Anita Christopher, Christine and Neil Townend*

MINSTERWORTH SO7515   GL2 8JX
Severn Bore
A48 2 miles SW

In splendid Severn-side position and refurbished under present owners, spotlessly clean open layout with central fireplace, usual pubby furniture, welcoming staff, ales such as Wickwar Severn Bore, Ashton's and Weston's cider, pubby food, skittle alley with pool table and darts; fruit machine, TV; wheelchair access (low step into bar), big riverside garden with rustic furniture and superb views to the Cotswolds, play area, board giving times/heights of Severn Bore (open for breakfast on Bore days), handy for Westbury Court Gardens (NT). *Recommended by Chris and Angela Buckell*

MISERDEN SO9308   GL6 7JA
Carpenters Arms
Off B4070 NE of Stroud

Two open-plan bar areas with low beams, stripped-stone walls, bare boards, and two big log fires, friendly landlord, well kept Wye Valley ales, good wine list, enjoyable reasonably priced pub food using home-grown veg, meal deals, small dining room; garden tables, popular with walkers and handy for Miserden Park. *Recommended by Giles and Annie Francis, Dr A J and Mrs Tompsett*

MORETON-IN-MARSH SP2032   GL56 0AX
Black Bear
High Street

Unpretentious beamed and stripped-stone pub, well kept/priced local Donnington ales, good coffee, good value wholesome pub food, attentive landlord, large airy dining room, public bar with games and sports TV; tables outside, big bedrooms sharing bathrooms. *Recommended by Peter Smith and Judith Brown*

MORETON-IN-MARSH SP2032   GL56 0AW
☆ Redesdale Arms
High Street

Relaxed old coaching inn with prettily lit alcoves, sofas and big stone fireplace in solidly furnished comfortable panelled bar on right, darts in flagstoned public bar, log fires, stripped stone, Cotswold and Hook Norton ales, decent wines and coffee, enjoyable good value food, courteous helpful service, spacious back child-friendly brasserie and dining conservatory; piped music, TVs, games machine; heated floodlit courtyard decking, 24 comfortable bedrooms beyond, open all day from 8am. *Recommended by Keith and Sue Ward, Michael Dandy, George Atkinson, Lawrence R Cotter, Michael Sargent, Jason Caulkin and others*

MORETON-IN-MARSH SP2032   GL56 0BA
White Hart Royal
High Street

Refurbished partly 15th-c inn, cosy beamed quarry-tiled bar with fine inglenook, adjacent smarter panelled room with Georgian feel, separate lounge and restaurant, Hook Norton and North Cotswold ales, good choice of wines, food from interesting wraps and sandwiches up, cream teas, friendly attentive service from smart staff; piped music; courtyard tables, bedrooms. *Recommended by Michael Dandy, Eithne Dandy, George Atkinson*

NAILSWORTH ST8499   GL6 0AE
☆ Egypt Mill
Off A46; heading N towards Stroud, first right after roundabout, then left

Stylishly converted 16th-c stone-built mill on three-floors, millstream flowing through and good views of working waterwheels from brick-and-stone-floored split-level bar, emphasis on enjoyable all-day bar food, Nailsworth and Stroud ales, comfortable carpeted lounge with beams and hefty ironwork from the old machinery; piped music and TV; children welcome, floodlit terraced garden overlooking millpond, 28 bedrooms, open all day. *Recommended by Dr and Mrs A K Clarke, Bob and Angela Brooks, David A Hammond*

NAILSWORTH ST8499   GL6 0RF
George
Newmarket

Good valley views, attractive central bar with lounge/eating area one side, dining room the other, beams and flagstones, fresh food, up to four ales including Moles, friendly and comfortable. *Recommended by the Didler*

NAILSWORTH ST8499   GL6 0HH
Village Inn
Bath Road

Thriving pub with good value Nailsworth ales (brewed here) and guests, appealingly done series of rambling linked areas with steps down to back area for view of the process, woody décor with panelling, dividers and oak floors, log fire, pub food including good local pies, brewery tours; dogs welcome, open all day. *Recommended by Dave Irving, Jenny Huggins, J R Cason, the Didler, Dr and Mrs A K Clarke*

NAUNTON SP1123   GL54 3AD
 ## Black Horse
Off B4068 W of Stow-on-the-Wold

Friendly stripped-stone proper pub with well kept/priced Donnington BB and SBA, good fresh food from baguettes to good value Sun roasts (veg may come from local allotments), good service, plain tables, flagstones, black beams and log fire, darts, cribbage, dominoes, dining room; piped music; children and dogs welcome (resident labrador), some nice seating outside, charming village, fine Cotswold walks, bedrooms. *Recommended by John Taylor, Richard Tilbrook, Michael Dandy, Charlie Keitch, Dr A Y Drummond*

NETHER WESTCOTE SP2220   OX7 6SD
☆ ## Feathered Nest
Off A424 Burford—Stow-on-the-Wold

Former Westcote Inn fully refurbished by present licensees, welcoming and homely, with good food from bar snacks to enterprising restaurant dishes, well kept Hook Norton and two guests, good choice of wines, friendly efficient staff, events including live jazz, wine tasting and quiz nights; discreet sports TV; children welcome, terrace tables with lovely Evenlode Valley views, four bedrooms, closed Mon. *Recommended by Richard Greaves, Christian Mole*

NEWENT SO7225   GL18 1PU
George
Church Street

Redecorated former coaching inn, friendly locals, three or four well kept changing ales, decent home-made food, carpeted open-plan bar with log fire, evening restaurant; children and dogs welcome, nice location, bedrooms, open all day. *Recommended by MLR, TB*

NORTH NIBLEY ST7596   GL11 6EF
New Inn
E of village itself; Waterley Bottom

Former cider house in secluded rural setting popular with walkers, well kept ales such as Cotleigh, Goffs, Wickwar and Wye Valley from antique pumps, five ciders (plenty more in bottles), basic bar food including good ploughman's, lounge bar with cushioned windsor chairs and high-backed settles, partly stripped-stone walls, simple cosy public bar with darts, beer and cider festivals; children and dogs welcome, tables on lawn and covered decked area with pool table, good walks, bedrooms, open all day weekends, closed Mon lunchtime. *Recommended by Guy Vowles*

Post Office address codings confusingly give the impression that some pubs are in Gloucestershire, when they're really in Warwickshire (which is where we list them).

NORTHLEACH SP1114   GL54 3EJ
Red Lion
Market Place

Handsome renovated old pub with welcoming landlady and friendly locals, enjoyable home-made food, well kept changing ales and good choice of other drinks including organic wines and cider, nice log fire, restaurant; sunny garden behind, attractive village. *Recommended by Gene and Kitty Rankin*

NYMPSFIELD SO7900   GL10 3TU
Rose & Crown
The Cross; signed off B4066 Stroud—Dursley

Previously well liked 17th-c stone-built pub under new management – reports please; log fire in bare-boards beamed front bar with pine tables, pews and old settles, large back dining area; disabled access, picnic-sets in side yard and sheltered lawn with play area, handy for Cotswold walks and Woodchester (NT), bedrooms, has been open all day. *Recommended by anon*

OAKRIDGE LYNCH SO9103   GL6 7NZ
Butchers Arms
Off Eastcombe—Bisley Road E of Stroud

Welcoming beamed pub under newish management, enjoyable food (not Sun evening) from landlord/chef, well kept Wadworths ales, rambling partly stripped-stone bar with open fire and woodburner, dining room; children and dogs welcome, picnic-sets on lawn overlooking valley, good walks, closed Mon. *Recommended by Sue Kinder, David and Stella Martin*

OLD DOWN ST6187   BS32 4PR
☆ ## Fox
Off A38 Bristol—Thornbury; Inner Down

Fine range of real ales in popular low-beamed cottagey local, good reasonably priced hearty food with some interesting specials (best to book), friendly efficient staff, farm cider and good choice of wines by the glass, log fire, carpeted eating area, high-backed settles in family room; children welcome, disabled access, verandah with grapevine, garden play area. *Recommended by John Luckes, David Langford, James Morrell, Chris and Angela Buckell*

OLD SODBURY ST7581   BS37 6LZ
☆ ## Dog
3 miles from M4 junction 18, via A46 and A432; The Hill (a busy road)

Welcoming and popular two-level bar with low beams and stripped-stone, wide range of enjoyable food cooked to order (so can be a wait) including reasonably priced fish specials, friendly young staff, three well kept changing ales, good wine and soft drinks choice; games machine, juke box; children and dogs welcome, big garden with barbecue and good play area, bedrooms, open all day. *Recommended by JJW, CMW, Mr Rynap, Roy Hoing, Dr and Mrs A K Clarke, Jim and Frances Gowers, Jonathan Holloway and others*

PARKEND SO6308   GL15 4HN
Rising Sun
Off B4431

Perched on wooded hillside and approached by roughish single-track drive, popular with walkers and cyclists, open-plan carpeted bar with modern pub furniture, Butcombe and a guest, straightforward well priced generous food from sandwiches and baked potatoes up, friendly service, lounge/games area with pool and machines; children and dogs welcome, wheelchair access with help, balcony and terrace tables under umbrellas, big woodside garden with play area and pond, self-catering bedroom, open all day summer weekends. *Recommended by Peter Meister, Howard G Allen, Chris and Angela Buckell*

PARKEND SO6107   GL15 4JF
Woodman
Folly Road, Whitecroft

Roomy and relaxed stripped-stone carpeted bar, heavy beams, forest pictures and old tools, smaller back bar and dining room, stone fireplaces (one with woodburner), wide choice of enjoyable fresh food, ales such as Greene King, Fullers and Sharps, pleasant service; wheelchair access from car park, picnic-sets on front terrace facing green, sheltered back courtyard and garden, bedrooms, good Forest of Dean walks, open all day weekends. *Recommended by Mike Horgan, Di Wright, Chris and Angela Buckell*

PAXFORD SP1837   GL55 6XH
☆ Churchill Arms
B4479, SE of Chipping Campden

Smart dining pub with good reasonably priced food, friendly efficient service, Hook Norton Bitter, Sharps Doom Bar and Wadworths 6X, good blackboard wine list, low ceilings and some timbering, flagstones, log fire, dining extension; children welcome, seats outside, four bedrooms, good breakfast. *Recommended by DRH and KLH, Canon Michael Bourdeaux, Nick Wilson-Holt, Michael Dandy, John and Hilary Penny, Peter Smith and Judith Brown and others*

PILNING ST5684   BS35 4JJ
Plough
Handy for M5 junction 17 via B4055 and Station Road; Pilning Street

Thriving local atmosphere under hard-working licensees, flagstones and bare boards, some faux beams, plates, country prints and repro adverts on dark cream/red dado walls, sofas and armchairs in small lounge area, newspapers in public bar, Wadworths ales, good value bar food (something available all day), cheerful efficient staff; children welcome, disabled access to main areas, garden with play area overlooking open country. *Recommended by Chris and Angela Buckell*

POULTON SP1001   GL7 5HN
Falcon
London Road

Reopened under new management – early reports suggest good food from landlord/chef and well kept local ales such as Cotswold Spring; well behaved children welcome. *Recommended by Guy Vowles*

PURTON SO6904   GL13 9HU
Berkeley Arms
Just upstream from Sharpness village, Severn left bank

Basic rustic Severn-side local only a short walk from canal bridge, wonderful estuary view, flagstones, high-backed settles, open fire, well kept Uley, long-serving landlady; garden, closed Mon, Tues. *Recommended by Gerry Dawson, Giles and Annie Francis*

REDBROOK SO5309   NP25 4AJ
☆ Boat
Car park signed on A466 Chepstow—Monmouth, then 100-yard footbridge over Wye; or very narrow steep car access from Penallt in Wales

Beautifully set Wyeside pub with well kept Wye Valley and guests tapped from the cask, lots of ciders, perries and country wines, enjoyable good value simple food from baguettes and baked potatoes up (nothing fried), helpful staff, unchanging interior with stripped-stone walls, flagstones and roaring woodburner; children and dogs welcome, rough home-built seats in informal tiered suntrap garden with stream spilling down waterfall cliffs into duck pond, open all day. *Recommended by Bob and Margaret Holder, Michael Mellers, LM, B M Eldridge, MLR*

SAPPERTON SO9303   GL7 6LN
Daneway Inn
Daneway; off A419 Stroud—Cirencester

Quiet tucked-away local in charming wooded countryside, flagstones and bare boards, woodburner in amazing floor-to-ceiling carved oak dutch fireplace, sporting prints, well kept Wadworths ales, farm ciders, generous simple food from filled baps up, long-serving landlord and friendly staff, small family room, traditional games in inglenook public bar, folk night Tues; no dogs, tricky wheelchair access; terrace tables and lovely sloping lawn, camping possible, good walks by canal under restoration with tunnel to Coates.
Recommended by Giles and Annie Francis, Chris and Angela Buckell, Russell Blackaller

SHIPTON MOYNE ST8989   GL8 8PN
Cat & Custard Pot
Off B4040 Malmesbury—Bristol; The Street

Popular with good food from sandwiches to restaurant dishes (booking recommended), helpful friendly service even when busy, well kept Flowers, Timothy Taylors and Wadworths, Thatcher's cider, well priced wines, several dining areas, beams and bric-a-brac, hunting prints, cosy back snug, chatty locals; walkers and dogs welcome, wheelchair access, picturesque village. *Recommended by Chris and Angela Buckell, Guy Vowles, Penny and Peter Keevil, Alan Bulley*

SIDDINGTON SU0399   GL7 6HR
☆ Greyhound
Ashton Road; village signed from A419 roundabout at Tesco

Popular village local, two linked rooms with big log fires, enjoyable good value pubby food from landlord/chef, Sun carvery and Tues thai curry night (landlady is from Thailand), well kept Wadworths, darts and cribbage, Sun folk evening; piped music; children welcome, garden tables, open all day. *Recommended by E McCall, T McLean, D Irving, Roger and Donna Huggins, D Crook*

SLAD SO8707   GL6 7QA
Woolpack
B4070 Stroud—Birdlip

Friendly and unpretentiously old-fashioned hillside village local with lovely valley views, several linked rooms with Laurie Lee and other interesting photographs, some of his books for sale, log fire and nice tables, enjoyable pub food (not Sun evening) from sandwiches and baguettes up, home-baked bread, well kept Uley and guest ales, local farm ciders and perry, decent wines by the glass, good young staff, games and cards; children and dogs welcome, nice garden. *Recommended by Myra Joyce, Bob and Angela Brooks, Guy Vowles*

SLIMBRIDGE SO7204   GL2 7BP
Tudor Arms
Shepherds Patch; off A38 towards Wildfowl & Wetlands Trust

Welcoming and popular, with generous food (all day weekends) from baguettes up, half a dozen interesting changing ales, good wines by the glass, farm ciders and perries, linked areas with parquet floor, flagstones or carpet, some leather chairs and settles, comfortable dining room, conservatory, darts, pool and skittle alley; children and dogs welcome, disabled facilities, picnic-sets outside, canal boat trips, caravan site off car park, 12 refurbished bedrooms, open all day. *Recommended by Chris and Angela Buckell, Mrs P Sumner, Ewan and Moira McCall*

SOMERFORD KEYNES SU0195   GL7 6DN
☆ Bakers Arms
On main street through village

Pretty little 17th-c stone-built pub with catslide roof, four real ales including Butcombe and Stroud, Addlestone's cider, good house wine, enjoyable traditional food and specials, good friendly service even when busy, lots of pine tables in two linked stripped-stone areas, two log fires; children and dogs welcome, nice garden with play area, lovely village, handy for Cotswold Water Park. *Recommended by Stephen Funnell, Jo Rees, Mike Buckingham*

ST BRIAVELS SO5504   GL15 6TA

George
High Street

Comfortable Wadworths pub, their beers and wide choice of good sensibly priced food including OAP deals, friendly service, spotless rambling linked black-beamed rooms with attractive old-fashioned décor and big stone fireplace, restaurant; can get very busy weekends (booking advised Sun); children and dogs welcome, flagstoned terrace over former moat of neighbouring Norman fortress, four refurbished bedrooms. *Recommended by Bob and Margaret Holder, Bob and Angela Brooks, Edward Hutchings and others*

STOW-ON-THE-WOLD SP1729   GL56 0QZ

Coach & Horses
Ganborough (on A424 about 2.5 miles N)

Beamed and flagstoned country pub, bright and clean, with enjoyable reasonably priced local food from changing menu, friendly helpful service, well kept Donnington ales and farm cider, decent wines by the glass, log fire, step up to compact dining area with high-backed settles on wood floor, cat called Molly and black labrador called Pennell; children welcome, skittle alley, big garden. *Recommended by Rolsh Lake, Michael Dandy*

STOW-ON-THE-WOLD SP1925   GL54 1AF

Kings Arms
The Square

Refurbished coaching inn under newish management; black-beamed bar with wood floor, some blue-painted panelling and stripped stone, woodburner, Greene King ales, enjoyable food here or in upstairs oak-floored Chophouse restaurant; 11 bedrooms including three courtyard 'cottages', has been open all day. *Recommended by Michael Dandy*

STOW-ON-THE-WOLD SP1925   GL54 1AB

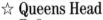 # Queens Head
The Square

Splendidly unpretentious for this upmarket town, well kept low-priced Donnington BB and SBA, good wines by the glass, good value sandwiches and basic pub meals (not Sun) including proper steak and kidney pudding, cheerful helpful service, bustling and chatty stripped-stone front lounge, heavily beamed and flagstoned back bar with high-backed settles, big log-effect fire, horse prints; quiet piped music; children and dogs welcome, tables in attractive sunny back courtyard, occasional jazz Sun lunchtime, open all day. *Recommended by Phil Bryant, the Didler, Gerry and Rosemary Dobson, Eleanor Dandy, R K Phillips and others*

STOW-ON-THE-WOLD SP1925   GL54 1BQ

 # Talbot
The Square

Light and airy modern décor, relaxed café-bar feel, food from sandwiches and baguettes up including some interesting blackboard specials, good friendly service even when busy, Wadworths ales, lots of good value wines by the glass, nice coffee, huge mirror over big log fire, plain tables and chairs on wood block floor, modern artwork, daily papers, upstairs room; no children inside, may be piped radio, lavatories upstairs; open all day. *Recommended by Michael Dandy, Dennis Jones, Martin and Pauline Jennings*

STOW-ON-THE-WOLD SP1925   GL54 1HQ

Unicorn
Sheep Street (A429 edge of centre)

Handsome hotel with comfortably traditional low-beamed upmarket bar, nice mix of tables, chairs and settles on wood or flagstones, some panelling, big log fire, Hook Norton and Wye Valley ales, good well presented food, attentive service from east european staff, formal modern restaurant; car park with barrier across busy road; 20 bedrooms. *Recommended by George Atkinson*

SWINEFORD ST6969   BS30 6LN
☆ **Swan**
A431, right on the Somerset border

Stone-built pub with well kept Bath Ales and a guest, decent ciders and carefully chosen wines, enjoyable food using locally raised meat from bar snacks and pub favourites up, helpful friendly staff, plain furniture on bare boards or tiles, pastel paintwork and panelled dado, big open fire; children welcome, wheelchair access, large garden with play area, open all day. *Recommended by Chris and Angela Buckell, Jim and Frances Gowers, Colin and Peggy Wilshire, Andy Cox*

TETBURY ST8893   GL8 8JJ
Priory
London Road

More civilised eating house than pub, with central log fire in comfortable if somewhat sombre high-raftered stone-built former stables, and strong emphasis on interesting local produce, even a local slant to their good wood-fired pizzas, cheerful service, Courage Best and Uley, decent wines by the glass; comfortable coffee lounge, live music Sun; children very welcome, wheelchair access (staff helpful), roadside terrace picnic-sets, 14 good bedrooms. *Recommended by Tom Price*

TETBURY ST8993   GL8 8DD
☆ **Snooty Fox**
Market Place

High-ceilinged stripped-stone hotel lounge, unstuffy with well kept ales such as Butcombe, Wadworths and Wickwar, good house wines, friendly young staff, enjoyable all-day bar food from sandwiches up, medieval-style chairs and cast-iron tables, elegant fireplace, brass ceiling fans and Ronald Searle pony-club cartoons, nice side room and anteroom, restaurant, gentle great dane called Fred; unobtrusive piped music, bar can get very busy weekend evenings; children and dogs welcome, large sheltered terrace, comfortable bedrooms. *Recommended by Jim and Frances Gowers, Dr and Mrs A K Clarke, A Green, Ian Herdman, Martin and Pauline Jennings*

TETBURY ST9195   GL8 8SG
Trouble House
A433 towards Cirencester, near Cherington turn

Pretty 17th-c pub under newish management; well liked food including good value weekday set lunch, Wadworths ales from small saggy-beamed middle room, pleasant staff, big log fire; picnic-sets in back gravel courtyard. *Recommended by A Helme, Graham Oddey, Mrs P Sumner*

TEWKESBURY SO8931   GL20 5SG
☆ **Gupshill Manor**
Gloucester Road (off A38 S edge of town)

Quaint old timbered building with Tardis-like series of lounge and dining areas, plenty of easy chairs and sofas on wood floors, beams and open fires, well priced food (all day Sun) from pubby dishes up including lunchtime deals, friendly efficient staff, three well kept Greene King ales and a guest, decent wine list, good coffees; piped music; children welcome, disabled access, teak tables on extensive heated terrace, open all day. *Recommended by Robert W Buckle, Alan and Eve Harding, Scott Mitchell, Jeremy King, J Chilver*

TEWKESBURY SO8933   GL20 5BJ
☆ **Olde Black Bear**
High Street

County's oldest pub (early 14th c), well worth a look for its intricately rambling rooms with ancient tiles, heavy timbering and low beams; up to five real ales, reasonably priced wines, cheap but decent pubby food, well worn furnishings, open fire, cheerful atmosphere; piped music; children welcome, terrace and play area in nice riverside garden, open all day. *Recommended by Roger and Donna Huggins, Dave Braisted, the Didler, P Dawn, Paul Goldman*

TEWKESBURY SO8932   GL20 5RT
Royal Hop Pole
Church Street

Wetherspoons conversion of old inn with original features, their usual value-minded all-day food and drink, good service; lovely garden leading down to river, bedrooms. *Recommended by Chris and Martin Taylor, Reg Fowle, Helen Rickwood, Theocsbrian*

TEWKESBURY SO8933   GL20 5BH
Tudor House
High Street

Comfortable Tudor hotel with enjoyable food and three or four real ales including Fullers and Greene King, good service; river-view garden behind, 25 nicely modernised old bedrooms. *Recommended by Derek and Sylvia Stephenson*

TODDINGTON SP0432   GL54 5DT
Pheasant
A46 Broadway—Winchcombe, junction with A438 and B4077

Extended stone-built roadside pub with emphasis on good choice of reasonably priced food, friendly helpful staff, well kept/priced Stanway (brewed nearby), lots of railway prints – handy for preserved Gloucestershire Warwickshire Railway Station; no dogs while food being served. *Recommended by Ewan and Moira McCall, Dr A J and Mrs Tompsett, Guy Vowles, Jo Rees, B M Eldridge*

TOLLDOWN ST7577   SN14 8HZ
Crown
1 mile from M4 junction 18 – A46 towards Bath

Heavy-beamed dining pub (most people are here to eat), cosy and friendly, with good interesting food from ciabattas up, Wadworths ales, plenty of wines by the glass, pine tables, bare stone walls and warm log fires; children welcome, disabled access, garden, open all day. *Recommended by Tom and Ruth Rees*

TWYNING SO9036   GL20 6DF
Village Inn
Twyning Green

Warmly welcoming whitewashed pub facing green, traditional low-beamed interior with open fire, good range of ales from local and more distant brewers such as Rudgate, Stowford Press cider, enjoyable generously served food, skittle alley; picnic-sets out at front, peaceful enclosed garden behind, small picturesque village. *Recommended by Roger and Marion Brown*

UPTON CHEYNEY ST6969   BS30 6LY
Upton Inn
Signed off A431 at Bitton

18th-c stone-built village pub, bar with old prints on stone and dark panelled walls, old tables and captain's chairs, step up to carpeted/bare-boards dining area with log fire and carvery, home-made food from sandwiches up, smaller helpings available, well kept Badger ales, modern opulent mock-regency restaurant with pictures of Bath, friendly helpful service; piped jazz or classical music; children and dogs welcome, wheelchair access, picnic-sets on terrace and in back garden, picturesque spot, with Avon Valley views. *Recommended by Tom and Ruth Rees, Guy Vowles*

Every entry includes a postcode for use in Sat Nav devices.

WESTBURY-ON-SEVERN SO7114   GL14 1PA
Red Lion
A48, corner of Bell Lane

Beamed and half-timbered traditional pub on busy road but by quiet lane past church down to river, cheerful obliging landlord, wide choice of enjoyable fairly priced local food, well kept ales such as Wye Valley, farm cider, decent wine, comfortable carpeted bar with wall seats, velvet curtains, open fire, snug off to the right, dining room to the left with log fire; children and dogs welcome, some seats out at front, more in back garden, three comfortable clean bedrooms, handy for Westbury Court Gardens (NT). *Recommended by Alun and Ann Keen, Mr and Mrs J R Shrimpton, T E Duncan, B M Eldridge*

WESTON SUBEDGE SP1241   GL55 6QH
Seagrave Arms
B4632

Nicely refurbished Georgian country inn/restaurant, small log-fire bar, two dining rooms with mix of furniture on wood floors, good imaginative seasonal food using local suppliers, Hook Norton and Purity UBU, Hogan's cider, friendly efficient staff; large seating area outside, six bedrooms, open all day weekends (food all day then, too). *Recommended by Michael Dandy, David Gunn*

WESTONBIRT ST8690   GL8 8QL
Hare & Hounds
A433 SW of Tetbury

Substantial roadside hotel with separate entrance for pub, enjoyable food from snacks up, Hook Norton and Wickwar, lots of wines by the glass, interesting malts and english vodka, flagstoned bar with another panelled one to the left, series of interconnecting rooms with polished wood or sisal floors, woodburner in two-way fireplace, some leather sofas and banquettes, more formal restaurant; wheelchair access, shaded tables out on paved area, pleasant gardens, 42 bedrooms including some in annexe, handy for Arboretum. *Recommended by Chris and Angela Buckell*

WHITECROFT SO6005   GL15 4PE
Miners Arms
B4234 N of Lydney

Friendly unpretentious local with up to five changing ales, farm ciders and perries, generous good value food including some greek dishes, attentive helpful service, two rooms on either side of bar, slate and parquet floors, pastel walls with old photographs, conservatory, skittle alley; piped and some live music; children and dogs welcome, disabled access, good gardens front and back, one with stream, quoits and boules, good local walks, handy for steam railway, self-catering accommodation, open all day. *Recommended by Robert Wivell, Theocsbrian, Mike Horgan, Di Wright, Chris and Angela Buckell*

WHITMINSTER SO7607   GL2 7PD
Fromebridge Mill
Fromebridge Lane (A38 near M5 junction 13)

Handy for M5, comfortable mill-based dining pub with interconnecting rooms, beams, bare brick walls, flagstone and carpeted floors, some tables overlooking river, well kept Greene King and guests, good choice of wines by the glass, reasonably priced food all day including popular lunchtime carvery (evenings too at weekends); can get very busy and service may suffer, no dogs inside; children welcome, wheelchair access, picnic-sets in big garden with play area, pretty waterside setting, footbridge from car park, open all day. *Recommended by Chris and Angela Buckell, Eric Thomas Yarwood, Dr and Mrs C W Thomas, Martin and Pauline Jennings*

If you stay overnight in an inn or hotel, they are allowed to serve you an alcoholic drink at any hour of the day or night.

WILLERSEY SP1039   WR12 7PJ

 Bell

B4632 Cheltenham—Stratford, near Broadway

Well run neatly modernised stone-built pub, comfortable front dining area with popular
home-made food, Aston Villa memorabilia and huge collection of model cars in back area
past big L-shaped bar counter, reasonably priced Flowers, Hook Norton and Wadworths
6X, relaxed atmosphere, quick friendly service, darts; children welcome, overlooks village
green and duck pond, lots of tables in big garden (dogs allowed here only), five bedrooms
in outbuildings. *Recommended by Keith and Margaret Kettell*

WINCHCOMBE SP0228   GL54 5LX
Old Corner Cupboard
Gloucester Street

Attractive old golden-stone pub improved under new landlord, generous fairly priced food
in nice back dining room, Fullers, Hook Norton and local Stanway ales, good range of
wines, comfortable stripped-stone lounge bar with heavy-beamed Tudor core, traditional
hatch-service lobby, small side room with woodburner in massive stone fireplace,
traditional games; children welcome, tables in back garden, open all day. *Recommended by
Dr A J and Mrs Tompsett*

WINCHCOMBE SP0228   GL54 5LJ
☆ **White Hart**
High Street (B4632)

16th-c inn with big windows looking out over village street, mix of chairs and small settles
around pine tables, bare boards, grey/green paintwork, cricket memorabilia, well kept
Goffs, Otter and Wickwar, wine shop at back (they add corkage if you buy to drink on the
premises), wide choice by the glass too, specialist sausage menu plus other enjoyable
food, separate restaurant; children welcome, dogs in bar and bedrooms, open all day from
9am (10am Sun). *Recommended by Julia and Richard Tredgett, Ellie Weld, David London, Derek and
Sylvia Stephenson, Steve Whalley, Dr A J and Mrs Tompsett*

WINTERBOURNE ST6678   BS36 1DP
Willy Wicket
Wick Wick Close, handy for M4 junction 19 via M32, A4174 E

Popular Vintage Inn family dining pub, good all-day food, ales such as Butcombe,
St Austell and Sharps, friendly courteous service, two eating areas off big central bar,
stripped stone, picture windows, two log fires; open all day. *Recommended by Peter Grant*

WOODCHESTER SO8403   GL5 5NB
☆ **Old Fleece**
Rooksmoor; A46 a mile S of Stroud

Old wisteria-clad roadside pub – part of the small Cotswold Food Club chain; good choice
of well presented interesting food, friendly efficient staff, well kept mostly local ale such
as Box Stream, Stroud and Great Western, good wines by the glass, bar, dining room and
snug, big windows and bare boards, panelling, stripped-stone or dark salmon pink walls,
modern paintings, large log fire, daily papers; children welcome, wheelchair access
(except dining area – you can also eat in bar), two front terraces, open all day.
Recommended by Tom and Ruth Rees, Chris and Angela Buckell

WOODCHESTER SO8302   GL5 5EL
☆ **Ram**
High Street, South Woodchester; off A46 S of Stroud

Bustling country pub with up to half a dozen interesting changing ales (tasting notes and
samples of three available in third-of-a-pint glasses), friendly helpful landlord, homely
bar food (not Sun) including small choice of bargain main courses, relaxed L-shaped
beamed bar with nice mix of traditional furnishings including several cushioned antique
panelled settles on bare boards, stripped stonework, open fires, live music; children and
dogs welcome, spectacular valley views from terrace, open-air theatre in summer, open

all day. *Recommended by John Taylor, J R Cason, Dr and Mrs A K Clarke, Steve and Claire Harvey, Chris and Angela Buckell and others*

YATE ST6983   BS37 7LQ
Cross Keys
Signed off B4059 Yate bypass at the Fox; North Road

Unpretentious two-bar beamed village local, good honest reasonably priced food (5-8pm and Sat lunchtime, not Sun, Mon) from sandwiches up including nice old-fashioned puddings, well kept Bass, Bristol Beer Factory, Courage Best, Sharps Doom Bar and a guest, cheerful chatty landlord, fires in both rooms, stripped stone and panelling, flagstones and carpet, mixed pubby furniture including pews and old dining tables, brasses and prints; fruit machine and darts in public bar, Weds quiz night; disabled access (perhaps a bit tricky for some wheelchairs), open all day Fri-Sun. *Recommended by Roger and Donna Huggins and others*

ALSO WORTH A VISIT IN HEREFORDSHIRE

Besides the region's top pubs, we recommend the following. Do tell us what you think of them: **feedback@goodguides.com**

AYMESTREY SO4265   HR6 9ST
☆ Riverside Inn
A4110, at N end of village, W of Leominster

Terrace and tree-sheltered garden making the most of lovely waterside spot by ancient stone bridge over the Lugg; cosy rambling beamed interior with some antique furniture alongside stripped country kitchen tables, fresh flowers, hops strung from a ceiling wagon-wheel, horse tack, open fires, chatty landlord, Hobsons, Wye Valley and a guest, local draft ciders, enjoyable lunchtime bar food and more expensive evening menu using local rare-breed meat and venison, own-grown fruit and veg; quiet piped music; children welcome, dogs in bar, bedrooms (fly-fishing for residents), closed Sun evening, Mon lunchtime (all day Mon winter). *Recommended by D R Grossmark, Mr and Mrs M Stratton, Jane Hudson, Ian and Helen Stafford, Paul J Robinshaw, Stanley and Annie Matthews and others*

BROMYARD DOWNS SO6755   HR7 4QP
☆ Royal Oak
Just NE of Bromyard; pub signed off A44

Beautifully placed 17th-c low-beamed open-plan pub with wide views, interesting bric-a-brac in carpeted bar, dining room with huge bay window, enjoyable good value food including some interesting dishes, well kept Spinning Dog ales, Weston's cider, friendly service; flagstoned bar with woodburner, pool, darts, juke box and TV, piped music; walkers welcome, picnic-sets on colourful front terrace, orchard, swings, open all day. *Recommended by P J and R D Greaves, R K Phillips*

COLWALL SO7440   WR13 6HW
☆ Wellington
A449 Malvern—Ledbury

Welcoming landlord and friendly staff, wide choice of generous food from good standards to more imaginative dishes, set price lunch weekdays, well kept ales such as Goffs, good wines by the glass, neat two-level beamed bar with nice fire, spacious relaxed dining area, newspapers and magazines; children welcome, closed Sun evening, Mon. *Recommended by J E Shackleton, Mrs B H Adams, Barry Standham, Revd Michael Vockins*

DINMORE SO5150
HR1 3JP
Railway Inn
Village and pub signed off A49

Recently reopened and refurbished, good home-made food, friendly service, good range of ales and wines; garden, splendid views to Malvern Hills. *Recommended by Dr A J and Mrs Tompsett*

DORSTONE SO3141
HR3 6AN
Pandy
Pub signed off B4348 E of Hay-on-Wye

Ancient timbered inn by village green, homely traditional rooms with low hop-strung beams, stout timbers, upright chairs on worn flagstones and in various alcoves, vast open fireplace, locals by bar with good range of beers including Wye Valley Butty Bach, summer farm cider, quite a few malts and irish whiskeys, pubby food from baguettes up and some interesting specials, friendly staff, board games; piped music; children welcome, dogs in bar (resident red setter is called Apache), neat side garden with picnic-sets and play area, bedrooms in purpose-built annexe, open all day Sat, closed Mon lunchtime (except summer and bank holidays). *Recommended by Guy Vowles, R T and J C Moggridge, the Didler, Jason Caulkin, Mike and Eileen Vokins*

EARDISLAND SO4258
HR6 9BW
Cross
A44

Friendly two-room local in lovely village, quick service, good value honest food (not Tues) from decent sandwiches up, Hobsons and Wye Valley ales; events including Thurs quiz night, TV; dogs welcome, open all day. *Recommended by Michael Butler, Paul Humphreys, MLR*

EARDISLEY SO3149
HR3 6PG
Tram
Corner of A4111 and Woodseaves Road

Welcoming old village pub with enjoyable home-made food, three well kept ales including Wye Valley, comfortable bar with woodburner, room to right mainly for eating; garden. *Recommended by Alistair Stanier, John and Bryony Coles, MLR*

FOWNHOPE SO5734
HR1 4PE
Green Man
B4224

New management and refurbishment for this striking 15th-c black and white inn, wall settles, window seats and leather chairs in one beamed bar, standing timbers dividing another, warm woodburners in old fireplaces, good food in bar and restaurant, three changing ales and Weston's cider, nice coffee; piped music, no dogs; children welcome, redesigned quiet garden, 11 revamped bedrooms, open all day. *Recommended by Trevor Swindells*

GORSLEY SO6726
HR9 7SW
Roadmaker
B4221, just off M50 junction 3

Popular 19th-c village pub run well by group of retired Gurkha soldiers, tasty pub food from baguettes up, also good nepalese curries (weekday takeaways), well kept Brains Rev James and Butcombe, large carpeted lounge bar with central log fire, evening restaurant (also Sun lunch), courteous service; no dogs; terrace with water feature, open all day. *Recommended by Neil and Anita Christopher, Joe Green, Gerry and Ruth Lowth*

Post Office address codings confusingly give the impression that a few pubs are in Herefordshire when they're really in Gloucestershire or even in Wales (which is where we list them).

HAREWOOD END SO5227   HR2 8JT
Harewood End Inn
A49 Hereford—Ross

Comfortable panelled dining lounge in interesting old building, good choice of enjoyable well priced food, helpful friendly staff, well kept ales such as Brains and Flowers, good sensibly priced wines; nice garden and walks, five bedrooms. *Recommended by Tony and Gill Powell, Dennis and Doreen Haward*

HEREFORD SO5139   HR1 2JQ
Barrels
St Owen Street

Friendly two-bar local with seven very well kept/priced Wye Valley ales from barrel-built counter (beer festival end Aug), several farm ciders, no food, cheerful efficient staff, basic furniture, lots of modern stained-glass, side pool room with games, juke box and big-screen sports TV; piped blues and rock, some live jazz; picnic-sets out on partly decked and covered area behind, open all day. *Recommended by Derek and Sylvia Stephenson, MLR, Reg Fowle, Helen Rickwood, the Didler, Rick Shallcross and others*

HEREFORD SO4940   HR4 0HH
Britannia
Cotterell Street

Victorian pub freshly refurbished and extended by Wye Valley, their full range and guest ales, no food; round picnic-sets on new terrace, open all day Fri-Sun, closed Mon lunchtime. *Recommended by Reg Fowle, Helen Rickwood*

HEREFORD SO5140   HR1 2BP
Kings Fee
Commercial Road

Big Wetherspoons with good value well kept ales including one brewed for it, good coffee, their usual food, cheerful attentive service, raised back section; terrace seats, open all day from breakfast on. *Recommended by George Atkinson*

HEREFORD SO5039   HR1 2LR
Lichfield Vaults
Church Street

Comfortable and roomy traditional pub in picturesque pedestrianised street near cathedral, charming greek landlord and friendly staff, well kept Adnams, Bass, Caledonian, Theakstons and a local guest from long bar, enjoyable food from sandwiches up including selection of greek dishes, good value Sun lunch, front and back bars with chunky olde-worlde décor, beams and dark panelling, wood and quarry-tiled floors, some exposed brickwork, inglenook fireplace; piped music, live blues/rock (last Sun of month), no dogs; children welcome, picnic-sets in pleasant back courtyard, open all day. *Recommended by Reg Fowle, Helen Rickwood, Dennis Jones, Martin Ferries, Michael Dandy*

HEREFORD SO5039   HR4 0BX
Stagecoach
West Street

16th-c black and white building, comfortable unpretentious lounge with dark oak panelling, well kept/priced Wye Valley ales and a guest, cheerful efficient service, bargain food including Sun carvery, low-beamed upstairs restaurant; machines and TV in bar; children welcome, open all day. *Recommended by Reg Fowle, Helen Rickwood, Alan and Eve Harding*

KILPECK SO4430   HR2 9DN
Kilpeck
Follow signs to church

Well refurbished village inn with beamed bar, sizeable L-shaped restaurant and small conservatory area, enjoyable good value locally sourced food from bar snacks up, ales such as Butcombe, Golden Valley, Mayfields and Wye Valley, Weston's cider, several wines by the glass, Sun quiz; seats outside, adjacent castle ruins and interesting romanesque church, four bedrooms, open all day Sun. *Recommended by Neil Hogg, Reg Fowle, Helen Rickwood, Martin and Pauline Jennings, Mr and Mrs M J Girdler*

KINGSLAND SO4461   HR6 9QS
Angel
B4360

Open-plan 17th-c traditional beamed and timbered dining pub, enjoyable locally sourced home-made food, well kept ales including one brewed for the pub, decent wines, helpful friendly staff, comfortable bar with big hot stove, neat restaurant extension, live music Fri, pool; picnic-sets on front grass, garden behind. *Recommended by Frankie Owens*

KINGSLAND SO4461   HR6 9RY
Corners Inn
B4360 NW of Leominster

Good reasonably priced food from pubby things up at this welcoming 16th-c black and white village inn, well kept Hobsons and a guest like Wye Valley, good wine choice, efficient cheerful service, beamed bar, restaurant in converted hay loft; no dogs; children welcome, no garden, ten bedrooms. *Recommended by Alan and Eve Harding, Paul Humphreys*

KINGTON SO3056   HR5 3BX
 ## Olde Tavern
Victoria Road, just off A44 opposite B4355 – follow sign to Town Centre, Hospital, Cattle Market; pub on right opposite Elizabeth Road, no inn sign but Estd 1767 notice

Gloriously old-fashioned with hatch-served side room opening off small plain parlour and public bar, plenty of dark brown woodwork, big windows, settles and other antique furniture on bare floors, gas fire, old local pictures, china, pewter and curios, well kept mainly local beers (they no longer brew Dunn Plowman ales), Weston's cider, beer festivals, no food – may sell rolls and chocolate bars, friendly atmosphere; children and dogs welcome, little yard at back, outside gents', closed weekday lunchtimes. *Recommended by the Didler, MLR, Mike and Eleanor Anderson*

KINGTON SO2956   HR5 3DR
Oxford Arms
Duke Street

Woodburners in main bar on left and dining area on right, smaller lounge with sofas and armchairs, well kept local ales such as Hereford Top Dog and Mayfields Copper Fox, enjoyable reasonably priced food, good friendly service; closed lunchtimes Mon, Tues. *Recommended by MLR, Alan and Eve Harding, Carol White*

LEA SO6621   HR9 7JZ
Crown
A40 Ross—Gloucester

Old rambling roadside pub with enjoyable food and well kept changing ales, attentive staff, original features, window seats, plenty of regulars around bar, traditional dining area; open all day. *Recommended by R K Phillips*

LEINTWARDINE SO4073   SY7 0LP
☆ ## Sun
Rosemary Lane, just off A4113

Fascinating time-warp continuing sympathetically under local consortium (after the long-serving landlady died in 2009); bare benches and farmhouse tables by coal fire in wallpapered brick-floored front bar (dogs welcome here), well kept Hobsons tapped from the cask and an occasional guest (Aug beer festival), another fire in snug carpeted parlour, no food unless prearranged, friendly staff; new pavilion-style building with bar and garden room, closed Mon lunchtime. *Recommended by Margaret Dickinson, Brian and Jacky Wilson, Reg Fowle, Helen Rickwood, the Didler*

LEOMINSTER SO4959   HR6 8AE

Bell
Etnam Street

Old pub under enthusiastic licensees, opened-up beamed interior with light décor, bare boards and big log fire, five well kept ales such as Hobsons, Malvern Hills and Wye Valley from central servery, good value pubby food (lunchtime only) from sandwiches up, good mix of customers, regular live music; tables in sheltered back courtyard, garden, open all day. *Recommended by MLR, Paul Humphreys, Reg Fowle, Helen Rickwood, Alan and Eve Harding*

LEOMINSTER SO4958   HR6 8AE

Chequers
Etnam Street

Attractive 15th-c beamed and timbered two-bar pub, well kept ales such as Box Steam, Hereford (Spinning Dog) and Wye Valley, good value food from sandwiches up, cheerful attentive service, cosy window seats, log fires, back two-level dining room; children and dogs welcome, courtyard, open all day. *Recommended by Alan and Eve Harding*

LETTON SO3346   HR3 6DH

Swan
A438 NW of Hereford

Friendly family-run roadside pub, good value home-made food all day including popular Sun carvery, two or three well kept local ales such as Golden Valley, accommodating service, large opened-up beamed bar, some comfy sofas at low tables, log fire, pool, darts and quoits, some live music and quiz nights; children and dogs welcome, garden with play area and pétanque, two bedrooms, camping. *Recommended by Reg Fowle, Helen Rickwood, MLR*

LINTON SO6525   HR9 7RY

Alma
On main road through village

Cheerful unspoilt local in small village, four well kept/priced changing ales such as Butcombe and Malvern Hills, no food (may be free Sun nibbles), homely carpeted front room with cats in front of good fire, small back room with pool, summer charity music festival; children very welcome, good-sized garden behind with nice view, closed weekday lunchtimes. *Recommended by TB*

LUGWARDINE SO5441   HR1 4AB

☆ Crown & Anchor
Just off A438 E of Hereford; Cotts Lane

Cottagey timbered pub with enjoyable food including plenty of lunchtime sandwiches and splendid smoked ham and eggs, well kept Butcombe, Timothy Taylors Landlord and guest beers, several wines by the glass, various smallish rooms, some interesting furnishings, fresh flowers, big log fires, daily papers, no piped music or machines; children welcome, pretty garden, open all day. *Recommended by Rochelle Seifas, Denys Gueroult*

MUCH DEWCHURCH SO4831   HR2 8DJ

Black Swan
B4348 Ross—Hay

Roomy and attractive beamed and timbered local, partly 14th-c, with log fires in cosy well worn bar and lounge with eating area, well kept Hook Norton ales, decent wines, inexpensive wholesome food, friendly atmosphere; pool room with darts, TV, juke box, no credit cards; dogs welcome. *Recommended by Bob and Margaret Holder, Alistair Stanier, A Helme*

MUCH MARCLE SO6634   HR8 2ND

Royal Oak
On A449 Ross-on-Wye—Ledbury

Superb rural spot with magnificent views, pleasant lounge with open fire, enjoyable reasonably priced food, efficient friendly service, well kept ales such as Jennings,

Marstons and Wye Valley, large back dining area; garden. *Recommended by Alan and Eve Harding, Dr A Y Drummond*

MUCH MARCLE SO6533   HR8 2NG
☆ **Slip Tavern**
Off A449 SW of Ledbury

Recently redecorated country pub with splendidly colourful gardens overlooking cider orchards (Weston's Cider Centre close by), welcoming landlady (from Trinidad) and friendly informal service, good food from pub standards to caribbean dishes, reasonable prices, Butcombe and two guests, log fire, conservatory restaurant, some live jazz and folk; children welcome, dogs on leads, open most of the day (short afternoon break). *Recommended by Andrew Gardner*

NORTON CANON SO3748   HR4 7BH
Three Horseshoes
A480 Yazor—Eccles Green

Basic two-bar rustic pub brewing its own good Shoes ales, including fearsomely strong Farriers, friendly long-serving landlord, woodburner and log fire, skittle alley with shooting gallery and pool; may be home-pickled eggs; children and dogs welcome, garden tables, lovely countryside near Davies Meadows wildflower reserve, closed lunchtimes except Weds and weekends. *Recommended by Reg Fowle, Helen Rickwood*

ORLETON SO4967   SY8 4HN
☆ **Boot**
Off B4362 W of Woofferton

Popular pub with beams, timbering, even some 16th-c wattle and daub, inglenook fireplace in charming cosy traditional bar, steps up to further bar area, good-sized two-room dining part (some internal alterations planned as we went to press), enjoyable interesting food, friendly service, Hobsons, Wye Valley and a local guest, real ciders; children and dogs welcome, seats in garden under huge ash tree, barbecue, fenced-in play area, open all day weekends. *Recommended by J Martin, Dr P Brown, Alistair Stanier, Michael and Jenny Back*

PEMBRIDGE SO3958   HR6 9DZ
New Inn
Market Square (A44)

Timeless ancient inn overlooking small black and white town's church, unpretentious lived-in three-room bar with antique settles, beams, worn flagstones and impressive inglenook log fire, one room with sofas, pine furniture, books and family photographs, several well kept changing ales (usually a local one), farm cider, big helpings of enjoyable good value plain food (booking advised), friendly service, traditional games, quiet little family dining room; downstairs lavatories; simple bedrooms. *Recommended by Allan Westbury, MLR, Alistair Stanier, Phil Bryant, Simon Velate, Steve Whalley*

ROSS-ON-WYE SO5924   HR9 5HL
☆ **Kings Head**
High Street

Comfortable, warm and friendly hotel bar, beams, panelling and log-effect fire, lots of old pictures and some cosy armchairs, good generous sensibly priced food, efficient service, Wye Valley and a guest beer, front restaurant, back dining conservatory; dogs welcome in bar, 15 bedrooms, good breakfast, open all day. *Recommended by George Atkinson, Mrs P Sumner, Pete Coxon, Lucien Perring*

ROSS-ON-WYE SO5922   HR9 5RS
Vine Tree
Walford Road (B4234), Tudorville

Small pub on edge of town, well kept Wye Valley and a guest ale, enjoyable home-made pub food in refurbished dining room, friendly service, skittle alley; popular with walkers. *Recommended by Lucien Perring*

☆ **Lough Pool**
SELLACK SO5526   HR9 6LX
Off A49

This character-laden black and white cottage closed in Dec 2010; new owners intend to restore and reopen it – news please.

☆ **Bateman Arms**
SHOBDON SO4061   HR6 9LX
B4362 NE of village

Striking 18th-c inn with enjoyable good value food freshly made from local supplies, Sun roasts, well kept Wychwood and a guest ale, good wines by the glass, cheerful service, inglenook woodburner in smallish comfortable beamed bar with relaxed local feel, well decorated restaurant, games room with pool and darts; children welcome, resident dogs (ask before bringing yours), picnic-sets on small lawn behind, nine bedrooms, good walks, open all day. *Recommended by Alistair Stanier, Phil Bryant*

New Inn
ST OWEN'S CROSS SO5424   HR2 8LQ
Junction A4137 and B4521, W of Ross-on-Wye

Newish licensees for half-timbered 16th-c dining pub; huge inglenook fireplaces, dark beams and timbers, various nooks and crannies, old pews and mix of tables and chairs, Marstons, Wychwood and a guest, several malt whiskies and wines by glass, food all day including thai dishes in bar and restaurant, service can be slow; piped music; children welcome, dogs in bar, spacious sheltered garden with play things, views to Black Mountains, open all day. *Recommended by Dave Braisted*

Oak
STAPLOW SO6941   HR8 1NP
Bromyard Road (B4214)

Popular roadside village pub improved under current licensees, friendly bustle in comfortable beamed bar, restaurant with open kitchen producing enjoyable good value food, real ales, reasonably priced wines, cheerful attentive service; bedrooms planned. *Recommended by Dave and Jenny Hughes, John and Elizabeth Allman, John and Mary Ling, Mel Poole*

Red Lion
STIFFORDS BRIDGE SO7348   WR13 5NN
A4103 3 miles W of Great Malvern

Beamed roadside pub refurbished after flood damage, wide choice of enjoyable good value home-made food, Greene King and some interesting guest ales, farm ciders; children and dogs welcome, tables in nicely kept garden. *Recommended by Denis Kavanagh, Tim and Joan Wright, Reg Fowle, Helen Rickwood, Jim Jones*

☆ **Stockton Cross Inn**
STOCKTON CROSS SO5161   HR6 0HD
Kimbolton; A4112, off A49 just N of Leominster

Cosy half-timbered coaching inn with heavily beamed spotless interior, huge log fire, woodburner, handsome antique settle, old leather chairs and brocaded stools, cast-iron-framed tables, old-time prints, copper and brass, Wye Valley ales and a guest, Robinson's Flagon cider, reasonably priced tasty food, friendly efficient service; piped music, open mike night (second Weds of month); children welcome, pretty garden, handy for Berrington Hall (NT), closed Sun evening, Mon (except bank holidays). *Recommended by D R Grossmark, John Fredericks, Paul Humphreys, Ian and Rose Lock, Mike and Mary Carter and others*

Golden Cross
SUTTON ST NICHOLAS SO5345   HR1 3AZ
On corner of Ridgeway Road

Doing well under hard-working landlord, well presented locally sourced food including meal deals, weekly changing ales (perhaps locals such as Golden Valley or Mayfields), good service, clean décor, some breweriana, upstairs weekend restaurant, pool and darts, live music Fri; dogs welcome, pretty village and good walks. *Recommended by Reg Fowle, Helen Rickwood*

UPPER COLWALL SO7643
Chase
WR13 6DJ

Chase Road, off B4218 Malvern—Colwall, first left after hilltop on bend going W

Cheerful staff in welcoming buoyant two-bar pub, plenty of tables for enjoyable reasonably priced food from sandwiches to good Sun lunch, good range of well kept ales and several wines by the glass; dogs and walkers welcome, small neat garden, lovely sweeping views, open all day. *Recommended by Dr A J and Mrs Tompsett, Tim and Joan Wright*

WELLINGTON SO4948
☆ **Wellington**
HR4 8AT

Village signed off A49 N of Hereford

Welcoming red-brick Victorian pub with comfortably civilised atmosphere, big high-backed settles, antique farm and garden tools, historical photographs of the village, log fire in brick fireplace, Hobsons, Wye Valley and a guest (July beer festival), good pubby bar food and more elaborate (not cheap) restaurant menu, charming candlelit stable dining room and conservatory; piped music; children welcome, dogs in bar, pleasant back garden, closed Sun evening, Mon lunchtime; for sale as we went to press. *Recommended by J E Shackleton, MLR, Dr A J and Mrs Tompsett*

WESTON-UNDER-PENYARD SO6323
Weston Cross Inn
HR9 7NU

A40 E of Ross

Substantial creeper-covered stone-built pub overlooking picturesque village, good value food, Bass, Boddingtons and Brains, Stowford Press cider, efficient service, comfortably worn-in beamed dining lounge, separate public bar; children and walkers welcome (they have a walks map), good-sized garden with plenty of picnic-sets and play area. *Recommended by Guy Vowles*

WHITNEY-ON-WYE SO2647
Boat
HR3 6EH

Pub signed off A438

Spacious, quiet and neatly kept red-brick pub with big windows and picnic-sets in pleasant garden for lovely views (possibly riverside otters); wide blackboard choice of good food, courteous helpful service, real ale and farm cider, comfortable L-shaped lounge with dining area, games room with pool; children welcome, bedrooms, campsite. *Recommended by Mary Lawrence*

WHITNEY-ON-WYE SO2447
☆ **Rhydspence**
HR3 6EU

A438 Hereford—Brecon

Splendid half-timbered inn on the border with Wales, rambling rooms with heavy beams and timbers, attractive old-fashioned furnishings, log fire in fine big stone fireplace in central bar, a beer from Golden Valley, no food (except breakfast for residents); no dogs inside; children welcome, garden with Wye valley views, six bedrooms. *Recommended by Alistair Stanier, the Didler, John Mikadoson*

WOOLHOPE SO6135
☆ **Crown**
HR1 4QP

Village signposted off B4224 in Fownhope

Tucked-away but busy village local with impressive range of 18 local ciders and perries, Wye Valley and a changing guest (regular festivals), well liked food, cheerful service, straightforward bar with traditional dark pubby furniture and built-in banquettes on patterned carpets, standing timbers, woodburners; piped music, sports TV; fine views from big garden with own bar (open in cricket season), comfortable smokers' shelter. *Recommended by Caroline and Michael Abbey, Dr and Mrs Michael Smith, Dave and Jenny Hughes, Adrian Johnson, Tim and Joan Wright*

☆ YARPOLE SO4664   HR6 0BD
Bell
Just off B4361 N of Leominster

Pleasant old black and white pub with basic tap room, comfortable beamed lounge with log fire, traditional furniture and some modern art, brass taps embedded into the stone counter serving Hook Norton Old Hooky, Timothy Taylors Landlord and a guest, large high-raftered restaurant in former cider mill (the press and wheel remain), good food from pub standards to more enterprising dishes; piped music; children welcome, dogs in bar, picnic-sets under green parasols in pretty gardens, handy for Croft Castle, closed Sun evening, Mon. *Recommended by Michael Butler, Alan and Eve Harding, J E Shackleton, M G Hart, Neil Kellett, P J and R D Greaves and others*

ALSO WORTH A VISIT IN SHROPSHIRE

Besides the region's top pubs, we recommend the following. Do tell us what you think of them: **feedback@goodguides.com**

BISHOP'S CASTLE SO3288   SY9 5AE
Boars Head
Church Street

Comfortable beamed and stripped-stone bar with well made wall benches around pleasant tables, big log fire, welcoming efficient young staff, well kept ales such as Courage, Salopian and Theakstons, enjoyable good value pubby food (all day in summer); four good roomy high-raftered bedrooms in converted barn. *Recommended by Alan and Eve Harding*

☆ BISHOP'S CASTLE SO3288   SY9 5BN
Castle Hotel
Market Square, just off B4385

Imposing early 18th-c panelled coaching inn with three neatly kept bar areas, fire in each, warm welcome, good food including lunchtime meal deal, more restaurant evening menu, well kept Hobsons and Six Bells, decent wines and malt whiskies, bar billiards and other games; children and dogs welcome, disabled access, tables in front and in back garden with nice views, seven bedrooms, good breakfast, closed bank holiday Mon. *Recommended by Ann and Colin Hunt, Brian and Anna Marsden, the Didler, P J and R D Greaves, Theocsbrian, Pat and Tony Martin and others*

☆ BISHOP'S CASTLE SO3288   SY9 5AA
Six Bells
Church Street

17th-c pub with own-brew beers the main draw – you can tour brewery, July beer festival; smallish no-frills bar with mix of well worn furniture, old local photographs and prints, bigger room with stripped-stone walls, benches around plain tables on bare boards and inglenook woodburner, country wines and summer farm cider, mixed reports on food (not Sun, Mon, Tues evenings); no credit cards; children and dogs welcome, open all day Sat, closed Mon lunchtime. *Recommended by Brian and Anna Marsden, Mike and Lynn Robinson, the Didler, Alan Cowell, Guy Vowles, Theocsbrian and others*

BISHOP'S CASTLE SO3288   SY9 5BW

☆ **Three Tuns**

Salop Street

Extended and updated old pub adjacent to unique four-storey Victorian brewhouse (a brewery said to have existed here since 1642), busy chatty atmosphere in public, lounge and snug bars, Three Tuns beers (including 1642) from old-fashioned handpumps, several wines by the glass, tasty generous food (not Sun evening), modernised dining room done out in smart oak and glass; lots going on including film club, live jazz, local rugby club events, July beer festival, may be morris dancers or a brass band in the garden; children and dogs welcome, open all day. *Recommended by Ann and Colin Hunt, Dr D J and Mrs S C Walker, Brian and Anna Marsden, Mike and Lynn Robinson, Alistair Stanier, the Didler and others*

BRIDGES SO3996   SY5 0ST

Bridges

Near Ratlinghope

Old beamed pub (former Horseshoe) recently bought by Three Tuns as their brewery tap and returned to its pre-1860 name; tables out by the little River Onny. *Recommended by Gavin Robinson, Dave Braisted*

BRIDGNORTH SO7293   WV16 4AX

George

Hollybush Road (A4373)

Refurbished family-run pub (was the Holyhead), airy modern interior with carpeted or polished wood floors, old beams, leather sofas and armchairs, some ornate high-backed cushioned benches, woodburner in rebuilt stone fireplace, open fire too, well kept real ales such as Brakspears, Marstons, Three Tuns and Wychwood, interesting wines, good value lunchtime food, more choice/expensive in evening, cheerful efficient staff, newspapers; piped music – live Sat; bedrooms. *Recommended by Chris and Angela Buckell*

BRIDGNORTH SO7193   WV16 4DS

Jewel of the Severn

High Street

Relatively new Wetherspoons, five well kept ales such as Woods Shropshire Lass, usual good value food (order and pre-pay at bar), relaxing modern décor, good friendly service; sports TV; children welcome, disabled facilities, open all day till late. *Recommended by Ann and Colin Hunt, Henry Pursehouse-Tranter, Dave Braisted, Alan and Eve Harding*

BRIDGNORTH SO7193   WV16 4QN

Kings Head

Whitburn Street

Well restored 17th-c timbered coaching inn with high-raftered back stable bar, food here from 5pm (all day weekends) or in all-day restaurant with separate menu, Hobsons, Wye Valley and several changing guests, log fires, beams and flagstones, pretty leaded windows; children and dogs welcome, courtyard picnic-sets. *Recommended by the Didler*

BRIDGNORTH SO7192   WV16 5DT

☆ **Railwaymans Arms**

Severn Valley Station, Hollybush Road (off A458 towards Stourbridge)

Bathams, Hobsons and other good value local ales kept well in chatty old-fashioned converted waiting-room at Severn Valley steam railway terminus, bustling on summer days, with coal fire, old station signs and train nameplates, superb mirror over fireplace, may be simple summer snacks, annual beer festival; children welcome, wheelchair access with help, tables out on platform – the train to Kidderminster (station bar there too) has an all-day bar and bookable Sun lunches, open all day weekends. *Recommended by Barbarrick, Dr Kevan Tucker, Ian and Helen Stafford, Alistair Stanier, the Didler, Pat and Tony Martin and others*

BRIDGNORTH SO7192   WV16 4AB
White Lion
West Castle Street

Fairly compact two-bar pub with smart flower hung exterior, seven well kept ales, Thatcher's cider, reasonably priced home-made lunchtime food (till 4pm weekends), comfortable carpeted lounge with open fire, some live music including folk club (first Tues of month); TV; children welcome, lawned garden with fenced play area and chickens, three bedrooms, open all day. *Recommended by Tony Hobden*

BROCKTON SO5793   TF13 6JR
☆ ## Feathers
B4378

Stylish restauranty country dining pub with good interesting food including lunchtime and early evening deals, home-baked bread, good friendly service even when busy, well kept changing ales such as Hobsons and Three Tuns, comfortable seats in attractively decorated beamed rooms and delightful conservatory; children allowed, has been closed Mon. *Recommended by Alan and Eve Harding, Dr D J and Mrs S C Walker*

BROMFIELD SO4877   SY8 2JR
☆ ## Clive
A49 2 miles NW of Ludlow

Sophisticated minimalist bar/restaurant taking its name from Clive of India who once lived here; emphasis mainly on imaginative modern food but they do serve Hobsons and Ludlow ales, several wines by the glass and various teas and coffees; dining room with light wood tables, door to sparsely furnished bar with metal chairs and glass-topped tables running down to sleek counter, step down to room with woodburner in huge fireplace, soaring beams and rafters, exposed stonework and well worn sofas, fresh flowers, daily papers; piped jazz; children welcome, tables under parasols on secluded terrace, fish pond, 15 stylish bedrooms, good breakfast, open all day. *Recommended by Mike and Mary Carter, Gerry and Rosemary Dobson, Alan and Eve Harding, Maurice and Gill McMahon, Rod Stoneman and others*

BURLTON SJ4526   SY4 5TB
☆ ## Burlton Inn
A528 Shrewsbury—Ellesmere, near B4397 junction

Attractively refurbished old pub with friendly helpful licensees and staff, wide choice of good food from imaginative menu, well kept Robinsons ales, sporting prints, log fires, comfortable snug, restaurant with garden dining room; children welcome, disabled facilities, pleasant terrace, comfortable well equipped bedrooms, good breakfast. *Recommended by John and Gina Ollier, Neville and Julia Lear*

BURWARTON SO6185   WV16 6QH
☆ ## Boyne Arms
B4364 Bridgnorth—Ludlow

Handsome Georgian coaching inn with enjoyable generous food (not Mon evening) including lunchtime/early evening set deals, Hobsons and other more or less local well kept ales, decent coffee, cheerful atmosphere, restaurant, separate bar with pool and other games; large garden with good timber adventure playground. *Recommended by Alan and Eve Harding*

CHURCH STRETTON SO4593   SY6 6BX
Bucks Head
High Street

Modernised old town pub with several good-sized areas including restaurant, four well kept Marstons ales, decent good value pubby food and vegetarian choices, friendly attentive staff, black beams and timbers, mixed dark wood tables and chairs; four bedrooms, open all day. *Recommended by Ann and Colin Hunt, Gerry and Rosemary Dobson, Pat and Tony Martin*

CLAVERLEY SO8095   WV5 7DG
Woodman
Corner B4176 and Danford Lane

Small 19th-c pub well run by brother and sister team, contemporary interior, good fairly priced bistro-style food using local produce (some from farm opposite) as well as fresh fish/shellfish, well kept Black Sheep and Enville, lots of wines by the glass, friendly service; garden, closed Sun evening. *Recommended by John Fessey*

CLEE HILL SO5975   SY8 3NB
Kremlin
Track up hill off A4117 Bewdley—Cleobury, by Victoria Inn

Shropshire's highest pub (former quarrymaster's house), enjoyable straightforward good value food including Sun roasts, friendly service, well kept ales such as Hobsons and Ludlow Gold, farm cider; splendid view from garden and terrace, play area, bedrooms, closed Mon till 4.30pm, otherwise open all day. *Recommended by Joe Green, Alan and Eve Harding*

CLEOBURY MORTIMER SO6775   DY14 8BS
Kings Arms
A4117 Bewdley—Ludlow

Refurbished 15th-c beamed inn, open-plan bar with good log fire, four well kept Hobsons ales, good value straightforward food, friendly staff; four well fitted bedrooms, open all day. *Recommended by Alan and Eve Harding*

CLUNTON SO3381   SY7 0HU
Crown
B4368

Cosy old country local, welcoming and friendly, with good choice of well kept changing ales and of generously served food at reasonable prices, log fire in small flagstoned bar, dining room, small games room. *Recommended by A N Bance*

COALBROOKDALE SJ6604   TF8 7DX
☆ ## Coalbrookdale Inn
Wellington Road, opposite Museum of Iron

Handsome dark brick 18th-c pub with half a dozen quickly changing ales from square counter in simple convivial tiled-floor bar, good sensibly priced food cooked to order here or in quieter dining room, farm ciders, country wines, good log fire, local pictures, piano, naughty beach murals in lavatories; long flight of steps to entrance; dogs welcome, a few tables outside, good bedrooms. *Recommended by the Didler*

COALPORT SJ6902   TF8 7HT
Shakespeare
High Street

Relaxing early 19th-c pub by pretty Severn gorge park, timbering, bare stone walls and tiled floors, well kept Hobsons and Ludlow, good value food from sandwiches through pub standards to mexican specialities; children welcome, picnic-sets in tiered garden with play area, handy for china museum, four bedrooms. *Recommended by Robert W Buckle*

CORFTON SO4985   SY7 9DF
☆ ## Sun
B4368 Much Wenlock—Craven Arms

Lived-in unchanging three-room country local, own good Corvedale ales (including an unfined beer) and guest, long-serving jolly landlord (if not busy in back brewery), decent well presented pubby food from baguettes up, lots of breweriana, basic quarry-tiled public bar with darts and pool, quieter carpeted lounge, dining room with covered well, tourist information; piped music; children welcome, dogs in bar, good wheelchair access throughout and disabled lavatories, tables on terrace and in large garden with good play area. *Recommended by Dr D J and Mrs S C Walker, MLR*

CRAVEN ARMS SO4382   SY7 9QJ

Craven Arms
Shrewsbury Road

Enjoyable low-priced food (not Mon) including carvery, bargain OAP midweek lunch, well kept Ludlow, Hobsons and Salopian; bar, lounge and restaurant. *Recommended by Alan and Eve Harding, Dr and Mrs A K Clarke, Joe Green*

DORRINGTON SJ4703   SY5 7ED

Bridge Inn
A49 N

Busy attractively refurbished streamside dining pub, well prepared food including good value set deals, Sun roasts, well kept Jennings Bitter, cheerful helpful staff, roomy bar/dining area with wood floor, conservatory restaurant; piped jazz, no dogs; children welcome, garden tables, open all day. *Recommended by Paul and Mary Walmsley, Alan and Eve Harding*

ELLESMERE SJ3934   SY12 0EG

☆ ## Black Lion
Scotland Street; back car park on A495

Good simple substantial food at bargain prices (pay at bar in advance), friendly helpful staff, two well kept Marstons-related ales, relaxed beamed bar with interesting décor and some unusual features such as the traditional wood-and-glass screen along its tiled entrance corridor, comfortable roomy dining room; piped music; bedrooms, handy car park, not far from canal wharf. *Recommended by Alan and Eve Harding, Tony Hobden, Dave Braisted*

GRINDLEY BROOK SJ5242   SY13 4QJ

Horse & Jockey
A41

Enjoyable good value food all day from varied menu, friendly helpful service, four well kept ales including Stonehouse and Three Tuns, teas and coffees; sports TV, pool; children welcome (big play area outside), handy for Sandstone Trail and Llangollen Canal, open all day. *Recommended by Alan and Eve Harding, Tony Hobden, Kedren Elliott*

GRINSHILL SJ5223   SY4 3BL

☆ ## Inn at Grinshill
Off A49 N of Shrewsbury

Civilised early Georgian country inn with comfortable 19th-c log-fire bar, Greene King and a local guest such as Rowton, spacious modern restaurant with view into open kitchen, enjoyable range of food from sandwiches up, cafetière coffee; piped music, TV; children and dogs welcome, back garden with plenty of tables and chairs, bedrooms, closed Sun evening, Mon. *Recommended by Martin Stafford, Steve Whalley, Dr Kevan Tucker, Stuart King, J S Burn, Paul Sayers and others*

HIGHLEY SO7483   WV16 6NU

Ship
Severnside

Refurbished 18th-c inn in lovely riverside location, good choice of food, Sun carvery, real ales including one brewed for the pub; children welcome, tables on raised front deck, handy for Severn Way walks (and Severn Valley Railway), fishing rights, bedrooms. *Recommended by John Coatsworth*

HINDFORD SJ3333   SY11 4NL

Jack Mytton
Village and pub signed from A495

Pleasant rustic bar with log fire, four changing ales including favourites such as Sharps Doom Bar, character landlord, food from bar snacks up, airy raftered dining room; children and dogs welcome, picnic-sets in attractive canalside garden, good-sized courtyard with summer bar and carved bear (pub named after eccentric squire who rode a bear), moorings. *Recommended by C A Bryson, Roger and Anne Newbury*

IRONBRIDGE SJ6603 TF8 7NH
 Malthouse
The Wharfage (bottom road alongside Severn)

Converted 18th-c malthouse wonderfully located in historic gorge, spacious bar with iron pillars supporting heavy pine beams, lounge/dining area, up to three well kept changing ales, good reasonably priced food all day including tapas, live music Fri, Sat; children and dogs welcome, terrace tables, 12 bedrooms including separate cottage, open all day. *Recommended by Ross Balaam, Dr Kevan Tucker, Gerry and Rosemary Dobson, Berwyn Owen*

IRONBRIDGE SJ6703 TF8 7AL
Tontine
Tontine Hill

Friendly 18th-c hotel overlooking the Iron Bridge, carpeted bar with pubby furniture and some old photographs, two woodburners, three changing ales such as Enville, Slaters and Stonehouse, good choice of food from sandwiches up, bargain Sun carvery, restaurant; no dogs; children welcome, pavement seats, 12 bedrooms, open all day. *Recommended by George Atkinson*

LEEBOTWOOD SO4798 SY6 6ND
☆ **Pound**
A49 Church Stretton—Shrewsbury

Ancient thatched cruck-framed building – thought to be oldest in village and dating from 1458; bar rooms are stylishly modern with minimalist fixtures and wooden furnishings, Fullers and changing guest such as Salopian Shropshire Gold, decent wines by glass, good bar food including deals (may be slow at busy times), friendly service; piped music; seats on flagstoned terrace; disabled parking spaces, open all day. *Recommended by MDN, Donald Thompson, Alan and Eve Harding, Christopher Vallely, Tracey and Stephen Groves*

LEINTWARDINE SO4175 SY7 0LX
☆ **Jolly Frog**
Toddings; A4113 out towards Ludlow

Restauranty pub/bistro with welcoming cheerful atmosphere, imaginative cooking without being fussy or pretentious with emphasis on good fresh fish, cheaper set menu lunchtime/early evening, also pizza oven and home-baked bread, good wine list and coffees, well kept Ludlow Gold, mix of table (high chairs for small children), log fire; glorious surrounding countryside, good views from tables on decking. *Recommended by Alan and Eve Harding, Roger White*

LLANFAIR WATERDINE SO2376 LD7 1TU
Waterdine
Signed from B4355; turn left after bridge

Spotless old inn nicely set near good stretch of Offa's Dyke path, emphasis on good if not cheap food (you must book) including inventive recipes in rambling series of heavy-beamed rooms with cosy alcoves, woodburner and some flagstones, small back conservatory looking down to River Teme (the Wales border); picnic-sets in lovely garden, good bedrooms. *Recommended by Peter and Sheila Longland*

LOPPINGTON SJ4729 SY4 5SR
Dickin Arms
B4397

Cheerful two-bar country local, comfortably plush banquettes, open fire, shallow steps to neat back dining room with good value generous food including landlady's speciality curries, lunchtime OAP deals, well kept Bass and an interesting guests such as Gertie Sweet and Wem Hanby, good service; pool; play area, pretty village. *Recommended by Alan and Eve Harding, Tim Williams*

LUDLOW SO5174
SY8 1PJ

Charlton Arms
Ludford Bridge

Refurbished former coaching inn in great spot overlooking River Teme and the town, bar, lounge and restaurant, good food, cheerful efficient service, well kept ales including local Ludlow; pleasant waterside garden and terrace, ten bedrooms (may be traffic noise), open all day. *Recommended by Joe Green, George Atkinson, Roy Payne*

LUDLOW SO5174
SY8 1RU

Queens
Lower Galdeford

Family-run pub with good food concentrating heavily on fresh local produce, well kept beer, long bar, pine tables in dining area, good friendly service, nice pub dog. *Recommended by Joe Green, Mr and Mrs A Curry, Roy Payne, N Pitt*

LUDLOW SO5174
SY8 1AP

Rose & Crown
Off Church Street, behind Buttercross

Small unpretentious pub with 13th-c origins, enjoyable bargain food all day, ales such as Bass, Greene King Abbot and Hobsons, clean comfortably lived-in L-shaped bar with hop-strung beams and open brick fireplace, separate dining area; approached through archway with a few courtyard seats at front, more on terrace behind, pretty spot, bedrooms. *Recommended by Dave Braisted, Phil Bryant*

LUDLOW SO7452
SY8 1LS

Squirrel
Foldgate Lane; off Sheet Road off A49

Popular modern pub with cheerful staff, wide choice of good value generous food from light dishes up, three Marstons-related ales, proper dining room; terrace tables, play area, next to Travelodge. *Recommended by Alan and Eve Harding, J S Hurst*

LUDLOW SO5174
SY8 1PQ

Wheatsheaf
Lower Broad Street

Traditional 17th-c beamed pub spectacularly built into medieval town gate, good value generous pubby food, Sun carvery, efficient cheerful staff, well kept Marstons and related ales; attractive comfortable bedrooms. *Recommended by Alan and Eve Harding, Joe Green, Roy Payne*

MAESBURY MARSH SJ3125
SY10 8JB

☆ Navigation
By bridge over the canal

Warehouse conversion in great location on restored stretch of Montgomery Canal, three well kept changing ales and farm cider in character bar area with beams, stripped brickwork and choir stalls complete with misericords, sofas by roaring fire, good food from pubby things to more enterprising dishes, early-bird deals (6-7 weekday evenings), friendly helpful service; children and dogs welcome, waterside terrace, closed Sun evening to Tues lunchtime. *Recommended by Pete Yearsley, Nigel Hemsted, Tony Hobden, Stephen Thomas*

MARTON SJ2903
SY21 8JX

Lowfield
B4386 Chirbury—Westbury

Comfortably rebuilt in traditional style, well kept ales such as Montys, Salopian and Woods, enjoyable fresh food including sandwiches, friendly efficient staff, relaxed atmosphere, woodburner; peaceful country views from teak terrace tables and garden picnic-sets, three bedrooms. *Recommended by Alan and Eve Harding*

MARTON SJ2802   SY21 8JP

☆ Sun
B4386 NE of Chirbury

Well cared-for village pub with welcoming efficient service, father and son team doing good bar food and more adventurous dishes in contemporary restaurant, good Sun lunch, well kept Marstons and Hobsons, nice choice of wines, friendly pub dogs; closed Sun evening to Tues lunchtime. *Recommended by Pete Yearsley, Peter and Sheila Longland*

MUCH WENLOCK SO6299   TF13 6AQ
Gaskell Arms
High Street (A458)

17th-c coaching inn with comfortable old-fashioned lounge divided by brass-canopied log fire, enjoyable straightforward bar food at fair prices, friendly attentive service, three well kept ales such as Stonehouse, Woods and Wye Valley, brasses and prints, civilised beamed restaurant, locals' public bar; subdued piped music; no dogs; well behaved children allowed, disabled facilities, roomy neat back garden with terrace, 14 bedrooms, open all day. *Recommended by Ann and Colin Hunt, Dr and Mrs A K Clarke, N R White*

MUCH WENLOCK SO6299   TF13 6EN
Raven
Barrow Street

Small friendly family-run hotel (former 17th-c coaching inn), bar with dining room off, good well priced food here and in more upmarket restaurant, may have set lunch deal, two ales including one brewed for them by Woods, interesting 1894 Olympic Games memorabilia; no dogs; children welcome, bedrooms around courtyard and in forge annexe, open all day. *Recommended by Pete Yearsley, Alan and Eve Harding*

MUCH WENLOCK SO6299   TF13 6AA

☆ Talbot
High Street (A458)

Friendly unspoilt medieval inn, several cosy traditional areas, low ceilings, red tapestry button-back wall banquettes, local pictures and cottagey plates on walls, art deco-style lamps, gleaming brasses, two real ales, several wines and whiskies, enjoyable fair-priced bar food and more elaborate evening choices including good value set menu, cheerful prompt service; piped music, TV; seats in courtyard; children welcome, characterful bedrooms, open all day till 2am. *Recommended by Ann and Colin Hunt, David and Lin Short, Andrew and Mary Ransom, Alan and Eve Harding, Anthony Bradbury, Mark, Amanda, Luke and Jake Sheard and others*

MUNSLOW SO5287   SY7 9ET

☆ Crown
B4368 Much Wenlock—Craven Arms

Former court house with imposing exterior and pretty back façade showing evidence of its Tudor origins; lots of nooks and crannies, split-level lounge bar with old-fashioned mix of furnishings on broad flagstones, old bottles, country pictures, bread oven by log fire, more seats in traditional snug with another fire, eating area with tables around central oven chimney, more beams and flagstones and stripped-stone walls, enjoyable imaginative food (local suppliers listed), ales such as Holdens, Ludlow, Salopian and Six Bells, local bottled farm cider, good wines, helpful efficient staff and friendly bustling atmosphere, Jenna the boxer may wander around; piped music; children welcome, level wheelchair access to bar only, bedrooms, closed Sun evening, Mon. *Recommended by Les and Sandra Brown, Ann and Colin Hunt, Gerry and Rosemary Dobson, Alan and Eve Harding, Maurice and Gill McMahon, Glenwys and Alan Lawrence and others*

> Post Office address codings confusingly give the impression that some pubs are in Shropshire, when they're really in Cheshire (which is where we list them).

☆ **Sun**

NORBURY SO3692   SY9 5DX

Off A488 or A489 NE of Bishop's Castle

Civilised dining inn in sleepy village beneath southern flank of Norbury Hill; tiled-floor bar with sofas and Victorian tables and chairs, cushioned stone wall seats, mysterious farming implements, woodburner, charming dining lounge with fresh flowers and candles, leather wing chairs and a chesterfield, dark oak dresser, log fire, good if not cheap food from sensibly short menu, friendly service, Wye Valley Bitter and usually a guest, decent wines; soft piped music; children welcome lunchtime/early evening, dogs in bar, pretty little rustic garden with pond, prime hill-walking country (not far from the Stiperstones), six bedrooms, good breakfast, closed weekday lunchtimes, Sun evening and Mon; up for sale as we went to press. *Recommended by Mike Scott, Anthony Barnes, Geraldine and James Fradgley*

☆ **Hundred House**

NORTON SJ7200   TF11 9EE

A442 Telford—Bridgnorth

Neatly kept pubby hotel bar with appealing gothic décor, Highgate and three guests, good wine choice, very good food in bar and two tucked-away dining areas including Sun set lunch deals, woodburners and working Coalbrookdale ranges in handsome old fireplaces, prompt pleasant service, spotless quirky ladies'; occasional piped music; lovely garden with herbs (seeds sold for charity), ten comfortable individual bedrooms (some with swings), open all day. *Recommended by Stuart Doughty, Brian and Ruth Young*

Fox

OSWESTRY SJ2929   SY11 2SU

Church Street/Cross Street

Ancient black and white timbered façade, little entrance bar down a step, attractive low-beamed and panelled main room, straightforward food including bargain midweek lunch menu, well kept Jennings and related ales, log fire. *Recommended by Alan and Eve Harding*

☆ **Bottle & Glass**

PICKLESCOTT SO4399   SY6 6NR

Off A49 N of Church Stretton

Remote 16th-c rambling country pub with lots of character, quarry-tiled bar and lounge/dining areas, candles on tables, low beams, oak panelling and log fires, enjoyable food from sandwiches and pubby things up, well kept ales such as Hobsons, Shropshire and Three Tuns, nice wines; dogs welcome in bar, picnic-sets out in raised front area, open all day Sun. *Recommended by Bob Broadhurst, Mike Tucker, Dr and Mrs James Harris, Dr Nigel Bowles, A N Bance*

☆ **Queens Head**

QUEENS HEAD SJ3326   SY11 4EB

Just off A5 SE of Oswestry, towards Nesscliffe

Emphasis on wide choice of generous good value food all day from speciality sandwiches and other snacks to lots of fish and steaks, well kept Theakstons and two guest beers, decent wines by the glass, pleasant helpful staff, two well refurbished dining areas with hot coal fires, nice roomy conservatory overlooking restored section of Montgomery Canal; picnic-sets with parasols in suntrap waterside garden, country walks, open all day. *Recommended by Lionel Townsend, Bruce and Sharon Eden, Tony Hobden, Ken Marshall*

Talbot

RUYTON XI TOWNS SJ3922   SY4 1LA

Church Street

Black and white pub reopened in 2010 after long closure, refurbished interior with bar and separate eating areas, well spaced tables, open fires, enjoyable fresh food from lunchtime sandwiches up, four local ales, good friendly service. *Recommended by Bruce and Sharon Eden, Sarah Farrington*

SHIFNAL SJ74508   TF11 8BH
White Hart
High Street

Half a dozen or more interesting changing ales in chatty 17th-c timbered pub, quaint and old-fashioned with separate bar and lounge, enjoyable home-made lunchtime food (not Sun), good choice of wines by the glass, welcoming staff; couple of steep steps at front door, open all day. *Recommended by the Didler*

SHREWSBURY SJ4912   SY1 1NF
Admiral Benbow
Swan Hill

Great choice of mainly local ales, bottled belgian beers, also real ciders and perry; no children; open all day weekends. *Recommended by the Didler*

SHREWSBURY SO4912   SY1 1NF
Coach & Horses
Swan Hill/Cross Hill

Friendly old-fashioned Victorian local, panelled throughout, with main bar, cosy little side room and back dining room, enjoyable fresh food including daily roast and some imaginative dishes, Salopian Shropshire Gold, Wye Valley and three guest ales, real cider, relaxed atmosphere, prompt helpful service even when busy, interesting Guinness prints, quiz night first Mon of month; piped music – live on Sun; children allowed in dining room, dogs in bar, disabled facilities, smokers' roof terrace, open all day. *Recommended by Tony and Wendy Hobden, Joe Green, the Didler, Alan and Eve Harding*

SHREWSBURY SJ4912   SY1 1PP
Kings Head
Mardol

Ancient jettied timbered pub with opened-up low-beamed interior, brass, bric-a-brac and pictures of old Shrewsbury, interesting medieval painting uncovered on chimney breast, enjoyable bargain food, one or two well kept changing ales, friendly landlord; piped radio, darts; open all day. *Recommended by Ann and Colin Hunt, Alan and Eve Harding*

SHREWSBURY SJ4912   SY1 1UY
Lion
Follow City Centre signposts across the English Bridge

Grand largely 18th-c coaching inn (some parts dating from the 16th c) with cosy oak-panelled bar and sedate series of high-ceilinged rooms opening off, good value food, tea, coffee and cakes, real ales, civilised service, restaurant; children welcome, 50 bedrooms, open all day. *Recommended by C A Bryson*

SHREWSBURY SJ4912   SY1 1UG
Loggerheads
Church Street

Chatty old-fashioned local under new management, panelled back room with flagstones, scrubbed-top tables, high-backed settles and coal fire, three other rooms with lots of prints, flagstones and bare boards, quaint linking corridor and hatch service of five Marstons-related ales, short choice of bargain pub food, friendly prompt service; open all day. *Recommended by Alan and Eve Harding, Joe Green, the Didler*

SHREWSBURY SO4812   SY3 8JR
Old Bucks Head
Frankwell

Quietly placed old inn with traditional bar and restaurant, cheerful staff, enjoyable pubby food including bargain deals, Salopian Darwins Origin and a couple of other well kept ales; flower-decked raised terrace and nice secluded little garden, ten good value bedrooms, open all day Sat. *Recommended by Alan and Eve Harding, Ian Phillips*

SHREWSBURY SO4912   SY1 1SZ
Old Post Office
Off Milk Street almost opposite Wheatsheaf, near St Julian's Craft Centre

Friendly half-timbered split-level town pub, enjoyable good value pubby food including deals in bar and restaurant, quick friendly service, well kept Marstons-related ales, open fires; piped and live music, comedy club last Sun of month; tables in heated courtyard, six bedrooms. *Recommended by Alan and Eve Harding*

SHREWSBURY SJ4912   SY1 1PW
Salopian Bar
Smithfield Road

Comfortable modern refurbishment, seven well kept ales including Dark Star, Stonehouse and Oakham, belgian beers and real ciders, cheap baguettes and pies, friendly staff; sports TV; closed Mon otherwise open all day. *Recommended by Alan and Eve Harding*

☆ SHREWSBURY SJ4912   SY1 1UR
Three Fishes
Fish Street

Well run timbered and heavily beamed 16th-c pub in quiet cobbled street, small tables around three sides of central bar, flagstones, old pictures, five changing beers from mainstream and smaller breweries like Stonehouse, good value wines, fairly priced food including blackboard specials ordered from separate servery, good friendly service even if busy, no mobiles; open all day Fri/Sat. *Recommended by Mark Sykes, George Atkinson, Pam Adsley, the Didler, Alan and Eve Harding*

SHREWSBURY SJ4912   SY1 1ST
Wheatsheaf
High Street

Comfortable open-plan beamed lounge, enjoyable low-priced home-made food, eight well kept Marstons-related ales, several wines by the glass, cheerful efficient staff; open all day. *Recommended by Alan and Eve Harding*

☆ STIPERSTONES SJ3600   SY5 0LZ
Stiperstones Inn
Village signed off A488 S of Minsterley

Cosy traditional pub useful for a drink after walking – some stunning hikes on Long Mynd or up dramatic quartzite ridge of the Stiperstones; small modernised lounge with comfortable leatherette wall banquettes and lots of brassware on ply-panelled walls, plainer public bar with TV, games machine and darts, Hobsons and Three Tuns, bar food usefully served all day, friendly service; piped music; children and dogs welcome, two good value bedrooms, open all day (till 2am Fri, Sat). *Recommended by DM, Dr and Mrs A K Clarke, Martin Smith, MLR*

TELFORD SJ6910   TF2 6EA
Crown
Market Street, Oakengates (off A442, handy for M54 junction 5)

Bright 19th-c local (list of licensees to 1835), Hobsons BB and many changing guests, May and Oct beer festivals with up to 60 ales, draught continentals and lots of foreign bottled beers, a real cider or perry, helpful knowledgeable staff, no food (can bring your own), bustling bare-boards front bar with woodburner, small sky-lit side room, quarry-tiled back room; live music Thurs, mid-Sept folk festival, comedy nights; suntrap courtyard, handy for station, open all day. *Recommended by the Didler*

WELLINGTON SJ6511   TF1 2DL
Cock
Holyhead Road (B5061 – former A5)

Former 18th-c coaching inn popular for its friendly real ale bar, Hobsons and six well kept quickly changing beers usually from small breweries, separate belgian beer bar, real cider, knowledgeable staff, big fireplace; closed lunchtime Mon-Weds, open all day Thurs-Sat. *Recommended by D Weston, Nick Jenkins, the Didler*

WHITTINGTON SJ3231   SY11 4DF
White Lion
Castle Street

Sizeable nicely refurbished pub just below castle, good value food, cheerful attentive young staff, two well kept ales, good wines by the glass, light wood tables in front bar, smaller area with leather sofas, dining room and conservatory beyond; plenty of tables in good outdoor space. *Recommended by Alan and Eve Harding*

YORTON SJ5023   SY4 3EP
Railway
Station Road

Same family for over 70 years, friendly and chatty mother and daughter, unchanging atmosphere, plain tiled bar with hot coal fire, old settles and a modicum of railway memorabilia, big back lounge (not always open) with fishing trophies, well kept Salopian, Woods and guests, farm ciders, may be sandwiches on request, darts and dominoes; seats out in yard. *Recommended by the Didler*

ALSO WORTH A VISIT IN STAFFORDSHIRE

Besides the region's top pubs, we recommend the following. Do tell us what you think of them: **feedback@goodguides.com**

ABBOTS BROMLEY SK0824   WS15 3BP
☆ ## Goats Head
Market Place

Well run beamed and timbered village pub with friendly local atmosphere, Black Sheep, Marstons, Timothy Taylors and a guest (May beer festival), lots of wines by the glass, good home-made food (not Sun evening) served by attentive staff, opened-up cream-painted interior, unpretentious but comfortable, with coal fire in big inglenook, oak floors and furnishings that take in the odd traditional settle; juke box and TV; children and dogs welcome, teak furniture on sheltered lawn looking up to church tower, bedrooms, open all day. *Recommended by Richard and Jean Green, DC, David Austin, David J Austin and others*

ALSTONEFIELD SK1355   DE6 2FX
☆ ## George
Village signed from A515 Ashbourne—Buxton

Unchanging stone-built pub with friendly landlady, straightforward bar with low beams, old Peak District photographs and pictures, warming coal fire, Burtons, Marstons and a guest from copper-topped counter, a dozen wines by the glass, woodburner in neatened-up dining room, enjoyable food from shortish menu; children welcome, dogs in bar, you can sit out by the village green or in the big sheltered back stableyard, open all day weekends (till 9.30pm Sun). *Recommended by Richard and Jean Green, Paul J Robinshaw, Bernard Stradling, the Didler, David and Sue Atkinson and others*

AMINGTON SK2304   B79 0ED
Pretty Pigs
Shuttington Road

Popular old inn based on former small manor house, cheap ales such as Bass and Greene King, good value food including carvery (restaurant up a couple of steps); tables outside. *Recommended by John and Helen Rushton, Tony Schoonderwoerd*

ANSLOW SK2125   DE13 9QD
Bell
Main Road

Friendly flagstoned bar with settles and log fire, Marstons ales, good enterprising food from set menu (choose two or three courses), helpful cheerful service, reasonably priced wine list, restaurant; children and dogs welcome in bar, garden with heated terrace, open all day weekends, closed Mon. *Recommended by Paul Humphreys*

BARTON-UNDER-NEEDWOOD SK1818   DE13 8AA
Shoulder of Mutton
Main Street

Village pub with low beams and panelling, pleasant staff, well kept Bass and guests, good range of bar meals and snacks, open fire, pool in public bar, live music Fri; seats out at front and on terrace, four bedrooms, open all day. *Recommended by Simon Le Fort, B M Eldridge*

BARTON-UNDER-NEEDWOOD SK2018   DE13 8DZ
Waterfront
Barton Marina, Barton Turns

Huge pub, new but cleverly done to look long-established, part of marina complex; wide choice of enjoyable quickly served food including pubby favourites (light dishes all day), six or more real ales including good value house beers brewed for them by Blythe, good friendly service, thriving atmosphere; children welcome until early evening, open all day. *Recommended by David M Smith, John and Helen Rushton, Sian Gillham, B M Eldridge*

BRANSTON SK2221   DE14 3EP
Riverside
Riverside Drive

Good-sized pub in lovely spot by River Trent, enjoyable fairly priced pubby food, good choice of wines by the glass, Greene King ales, friendly efficient service; lots of tables in big waterside garden, 20 bedrooms. *Recommended by Phil Pickstock*

BURSLEM SJ8649   ST6 3AA
Leopard
Market Place

Traditional old city-centre pub, three rooms including a snug, enjoyable home-made food, half a dozen good local ales, well priced wines. *Recommended by Susan and Nigel Brookes, Dave Webster, Sue Holland*

BURTON UPON TRENT SK2523   DE14 1SY
☆ ## Burton Bridge Inn
Bridge Street (A50)

Genuinely friendly down-to-earth local with own good Burton Bridge ales from its brewery across the old-fashioned brick yard; simple little front area leading into adjacent bar with pews, plain walls hung with notices, awards and brewery memorabilia, 20 malt whiskies and lots of country wines, small beamed and oak-panelled lounge with simple furniture and flame-effect fire, panelled upstairs dining room, simple but hearty bar food (lunchtimes only, not Sun); no credit cards; children welcome, dogs in bar, skittle alley, open all day Fri, Sat. *Recommended by the Didler, Barbarrick, Edward Leetham, P Dawn, Andy and Claire Barker, Joe Deuter and others*

BURTON UPON TRENT SK2423   DE14 1EG
☆ ## Coopers Tavern
Cross Street

Old-fashioned no-frills backstreet local, now tied to Joules but was tap for Bass brewery across the road and still has some glorious ephemera including mirrors and glazed adverts; homely and warm with coal fire, straightforward front parlour with pleasant jumble of furniture, back bar doubling as tap room, up to half a dozen guest ales including Bass, ciders and perries, friendly landlady, pork pies only but you can bring your own food (or take beer to next-door curry house); children and dogs welcome, small back garden, open all day Fri-Sun, closed Mon and Tues lunchtimes. *Recommended by the Didler, Barbarrick, Edward Leetham, Andy Dolan*

BURTON UPON TRENT SK2424   DE14 1RU
Derby Inn
Derby Road

The long-serving landlord has finally retired at this well worn idiosyncratic local, but it continues in good hands and no changes foreseen; well kept Greene King Abbot, Marstons Pedigree and two guests, cosy panelled lounge with collection of Burton beer festival glasses, lots of steam railway memorabilia in long narrow bar; outside lavatories, sports TV; well behaved children and dogs welcome, seats out in backyard, open all day Fri, Sat. *Recommended by the Didler*

BURTON UPON TRENT SK2522   DE15 9AE
Elms
Stapenhill Road (A444)

Well kept Bass, Tower and changing guests in small character bar with wall benches, larger lounge, friendly staff; open all day weekends. *Recommended by the Didler*

BURTON UPON TRENT SK2423   DE14 2EG
Old Cottage Tavern
Rangemoor Street/Byrkley Street

Burton Old Cottage and guest ales, good value food (not Sun evening, Mon), two bars, snug and compact back restaurant, games room with skittle alley upstairs; bedrooms, open all day. *Recommended by the Didler*

BUTTERTON SK0756   ST13 7SP
Black Lion
Off B5053

Nicely placed traditional 18th-c low-beamed stone-built inn, logs blazing in inner room's kitchen range, good-humoured efficient service, enjoyable food from filled rolls up, several well kept ales, reasonable prices, traditional games and pool room; piped music; children in eating areas, terrace tables, tidy bedrooms, closed Mon and Tues lunchtimes. *Recommended by the Didler, Phill Robinson*

CHORLEY SK0711   WS13 8DD
Malt Shovel
Off A51 N of Lichfield via Farewell

Friendly village pub popular for its good choice of reasonably priced food from snacks up, real ales, open fires. *Recommended by John and Helen Rushton*

CODSALL SJ8603   WV8 1BY
Codsall Station
Chapel Lane/Station Road

Simply restored vintage waiting room and ticket office of working station, comfortable and welcoming, with Holdens beers including one brewed for them, basic good value generous food (not Sun, Mon), lots of railway memorabilia, conservatory; terrace, open all day Fri-Sun. *Recommended by the Didler, Mrs Margo Finlay, Jörg Kasprowski*

CONSALL SK0049   ST9 0AJ
☆ # Black Lion
Consall Forge, OS Sheet 118 map ref 000491; best approach from Nature Park, off A522, using car park 0.5 miles past Nature Centre

Traditional take-us-as-you-find-us local tucked away in rustic old-fashioned canalside settlement by a restored steam railway station, generous helpings of enjoyable unpretentious food made by landlord (may be only sandwiches mid-week), wide range of well kept ales, good coal fire; piped music, can get very busy weekend lunchtimes; good walking area. *Recommended by S J and C C Davidson, the Didler, Clive and Fran Dutson, P Dawn, Edward Leetham*

☆ ## Cat
ENVILLE SO8286   DY7 5HA

A458 W of Stourbridge (Bridgnorth Road)

Ancient beamed pub on Staffordshire Way, two appealingly old-fashioned log-fire rooms on one side of servery, plush banquettes on the other, well kept Enville ales and interesting guests, well priced generous bar food including sandwiches and mix-and-match range of sausage, mash and gravies, efficient service, restaurant; children in family room and main lounge, dogs in bar, pretty courtyard sheltered by massive estate wall, closed Sun evening, Mon. *Recommended by the Didler, Guy Vowles, Pat and Tony Martin*

Travellers Rest/Knights Table
FLASH SK0267   SK17 0SN

A53 Buxton—Leek

Isolated main-road pub and one of the highest in Britain, clean and friendly, with good reasonably priced traditional food including nice home-made cakes, well kept ales, beams, bare stone walls and open fires, medieval knights' theme, live music Sat, Weds quiz; children welcome, great Peak District views from the back terrace, open all day (till 1.30am Sat). *Recommended by Manthos and Dorothy Pandeli, Kevin Upton*

Swan
FORTON SJ7521   TF10 8BY

A519 Newport—Eccleshall

Former estate manager's house; large open room with mirrors and small wooden bar, separate section with library and sofas, restaurant opening into modern conservatory, enjoyable reasonably priced food from sandwiches up including carvery (weekday lunchtimes, all day Sun), three or four ales including Marstons, good friendly service; piped music, no dogs; children welcome, shop selling wine and local produce, handy for Shropshire Union Canal walks, ten bedrooms (four in converted barn), open all day. *Recommended by Henry Pursehouse-Tranter, Alan and Eve Harding*

☆ ## White Swan
FRADLEY SK1414   DE13 7DN

Fradley Junction

Perfect canalside location at Trent & Mersey and Coventry junction, bargain food from cobs to Sun carvery, well kept Black Sheep, Greene King Abbot, Marstons Pedigree and a guest like Hydes, cheery traditional public bar with woodburner, quieter plusher lounge and lower vaulted back bar (where children allowed), cribbage, dominoes; waterside tables, monthly classic car/motorbike meetings, open all day. *Recommended by David M Smith, Paul J Robinshaw, B M Eldridge*

Spread Eagle
GAILEY SJ9010   ST19 5PN

A5/A449

Spacious Marstons roadhouse, variety of separate areas including relaxing sofas and family part with toys, good value usual food including carvery, efficient helpful service; good disabled access and facilities, big terrace, lawn with play area. *Recommended by Henry Pursehouse-Tranter, JCW*

Boat
GNOSALL SJ8220   ST20 0DA

Gnosall Heath, by Shropshire Union Canal Bridge 34

Small canalside pub under friendly hard-working family, first-floor bar with curved window seat overlooking barges, good generous pub food including deals, popular Sun lunch, homely local atmosphere, open fire; children welcome, tables out by canal, moorings. *Recommended by Charles and Pauline Stride*

GNOSALL SJ8120 — ST20 0EQ
Navigation
Newport Road

Relaxed two-bar pub with dining conservatory and terrace overlooking Shropshire Union Canal, good friendly service, popular reasonably priced traditional food and specials, well kept Banks's ales, good value wines. *Recommended by the Head family, Susan and Nigel Brookes*

HANLEY SJ8847 — ST1 3EA
Coachmakers Arms
Lichfield Street

Chatty traditional town local reopened after brief closure, but still under threat of demolition; four small rooms and drinking corridor, half a dozen or more good changing ales, farm cider, darts, cards and dominoes, original seating and local tilework, open fire; children welcome, open all day. *Recommended by the Didler, Dave Webster, Sue Holland*

HAUGHTON SJ8620 — ST18 9EX
Bell
A518 Stafford—Newport

Good value popular pub food (not Sun evening, Mon), well kept Banks's, Marstons, Timothy Taylors and a guest, good friendly service even when busy; open all day Fri-Sun. *Recommended by John and Helen Rushton*

HIGH OFFLEY SJ7725 — ST20 0NG
Anchor
Off A519 Eccleshall—Newport; towards High Lea, by Shropshire Union Canal Bridge 42; Peggs Lane

Real boaters' pub on Shropshire Union Canal, little changed in the century or more this family have run it, two small simple front rooms, Marstons Pedigree and Wadworths 6X in jugs from cellar, Weston's farm cider, may be lunchtime toasties, owners' sitting room behind bar, occasional weekend sing-alongs; no children inside; outbuilding with small shop and semi-open lavatories, lovely garden with great hanging baskets and notable topiary anchor, caravan/campsite, closed Mon-Thurs in winter. *Recommended by the Didler*

HIMLEY SO8990 — DY3 4DA
☆ # Crooked House
Signed down rather grim lane from B4176 Gornalwood—Himley, OS Sheet 139 map reference 896908

Extraordinary sight, building thrown wildly out of kilter (mining subsidence), slopes so weird things look as if they roll up not down them; otherwise a basic well worn low-priced pub with Marstons-related ales, farm cider, cheery staff, enjoyable straightforward food (all day in summer) including vegetables from own allotment, some local antiques in a level more modern extension, conservatory; children in eating areas, big outside terrace, open all day weekends and in summer. *Recommended by Dave Braisted, the Didler*

HOAR CROSS SK1323 — DE13 8RB
☆ # Meynell Ingram Arms
Abbots Bromley Road, off A515 Yoxall—Sudbury

Good interesting food (not Sun evening) from sandwiches to restaurant meals in comfortably extended country dining pub, friendly staff, well kept Timothy Taylors Landlord and Wells & Youngs Bombardier, several neat little rooms rambling around central counter, log fire, some beams and brasses, hunting pictures and bespectacled fox's head, dining room with coal-effect fire; children and dogs welcome, tables on front grass and in courtyard behind, open all day. *Recommended by Susan and Nigel Brookes, S J and C C Davidson, Clifford Blakemore, Andy Dolan*

HOPWAS SK1704 ☆ Tame Otter
B78 3AT

Hints Road (A51 Tamworth—Lichfield)

Welcoming 19th-c Vintage Inn by Birmingham & Fazeley Canal (moorings), refurbished beamed interior on different levels, cosy corners, three fires, nice mixed furnishings, old photographs and canalia, enjoyable fairly priced food all day, good service, well kept Adnams, Everards and Marstons, decent choice of wines; large garden with plenty of seating. *Recommended by David Green, Colin Gooch, Glenwys and Alan Lawrence*

HULME END SK1059 Manifold Inn
SK17 0EX

B5054 Warslow—Hartington

Light and airy 18th-c country dining pub near river, enjoyable traditional home-made food in generous helpings, reasonable prices, ales such as Marstons Pedigree, Thwaites Wainwright and Whim Hartington, pleasant staff, log fire in bar, some stripped stone, restaurant and conservatory; children welcome, dogs in certain areas, disabled facilities, tables outside, ten bedrooms off secluded back courtyard, campsite, open all day weekends. *Recommended by Malcolm and Pauline Pellatt*

KIDSGROVE SJ8354 ☆ Blue Bell
ST7 1EG

Hardings Wood; off A50 NW edge of town

Simple friendly pub (looks more like a house) with half a dozen thoughtfully chosen and constantly changing ales from smaller breweries, around 30 bottled continental beers, up to three draught farm ciders and a perry, filled rolls weekends only; four small, carpeted rooms, unfussy and straightforward, with blue upholstered benches, basic pub furniture, gas-effect coal fire; may be piped music, no credit cards; dogs and well behaved children welcome, tables in front and on little back lawn, open all day Sun, closed Mon and weekday lunchtimes. *Recommended by Mike Proctor, the Didler, Dave Webster, Sue Holland*

KINVER SO8483 Vine
DY7 6LJ

Dunsley Road

By Staffordshire & Worcestershire Canal, enjoyable low-priced bar food, five well kept changing ales such as Enville, Kinver and Sadlers; big garden (plastic glasses here). *Recommended by Alan and Eve Harding*

KINVER SO8582 Whittington Inn
DY7 6NY

A449 between Kidderminster and Wall Heath, by Staffordshire & Worcestershire Canal

Striking half-timbered house dating from the 14th c, genuine Dick Whittington connection and a priest hole upstairs, interesting old-fashioned bar, roaring fire, lots of panelling, little nooks and corners, low doorways, passages and wall paintings, conservatory, well kept Banks's, Marstons Pedigree and a guest, good value food all day, attentive staff; attractive garden with fountain. *Recommended by Ian Shorthouse*

LEEK SJ9856 Den Engel
ST13 5HG

Stanley Street

Relaxed belgian-style bar in high-ceilinged former bank, over 100 belgian beers including lots on tap, three dozen genevers, three or four changing real ales, enjoyable food in upstairs restaurant; piped classical music, can get packed at weekends; dogs welcome, tables on back terrace, closed lunchtimes, open all day weekends. *Recommended by S J and C C Davidson, the Didler*

You can send reports directly to us at **feedback@goodguides.com**

LEEK SJ9856   ST13 5DS

☆ Wilkes Head
St Edward Street

Convivial three-room local dating from the 18th c (still has back coaching stables), owned by Whim with their ales and interesting guests, good choice of whiskies, farm cider, friendly chatty landlord, welcoming regulars and dogs, filled rolls, pub games, gas fire, lots of pump clips; juke box in back room, Mon music night; children allowed in one room (but not really a family pub), fair disabled access, tables outside, open all day except Mon lunchtime. *Recommended by the Didler*

LICHFIELD SK1109   WS13 6JJ
Acorn
Tamworth Street

Comfortable spacious Wetherspoons, sofas near entrance, cosy drinking nooks opposite bar, dining area at back, usual food and good choice of well kept ales; TVs; children welcome, open all day from 8am (till 1am Fri, Sat). *Recommended by George Atkinson*

LICHFIELD SK0705   WS14 0BU
☆ Boat
3.8 miles from M6 toll junction T6; head E on A5, turn right at first roundabout into B4155, then left on to A461 Walsall Road; leaving pub, keep straight on to rejoin A5 at Muckley Corner roundabout

Efficiently run dining pub, handy break for a meal off M6 toll; most emphasis on food with huge floor-to-ceiling menu boards, views into kitchen and dishes ranging from lunchtime sandwiches through light snacks to interesting main choices, cheery café atmosphere, bright plastic flooring, striking photoprints, leather club chairs and sofas around coffee tables and potted palms, more conventional and comfortable dining areas with sturdy modern pine furniture on carpet and views of disused canal, three well kept changing ales, ten wines by the glass, friendly service; piped music; children welcome, good wheelchair access, seats on raised decking, open all day Sun (food all day then, too). *Recommended by S P Watkin, P A Taylor, David Green, John and Helen Rushton, Gary Law, Keith and Sandra Ross and others*

LICHFIELD SK1109   WS13 6PW
Kings Head
Bird Street

Beams, stripped wood and old prints, bargain home-made food from sandwiches up, well kept Marstons and guests, good friendly service, coachyard conservatory, some live music; children welcome. *Recommended by George Atkinson, Steven Massey*

LICHFIELD SK1109   WS13 6QD
☆ Queens Head
Queen Street

Handsome Victorian building with cheerful, friendly atmosphere, single long room done like an old-fashioned alehouse with mix of comfortable aged furniture on bare boards, big sash windows, some stripped brick, Lichfield and other pictures, Bathams, Marstons, Timothy Taylors and three changing guests, very good value bar food including all-day cheese platter, helpful staff; no credit cards, sports TV, darts and board games; small garden, open all day (till 11.30pm Fri, Sat). *Recommended by John Branston, the Didler, Alan and Eve Harding, Andy and Claire Barker*

LITTLE BRIDGEFORD SJ8727   ST18 9QA
Mill
Worston Lane; near M6 junction 14; turn right off A5013 at Little Bridgeford

Useful sensibly priced dining pub in attractive 1814 watermill, enjoyable food, ales such as Greene King and Marstons, good friendly service, conservatory; children welcome, attractive grounds with adventure playground and nature trail (lakes, islands, etc); open all day. *Recommended by Alan and Eve Harding, Clare Elsby*

MILWICH SJ9732　　　　　　　　　　　　　　　　　　　ST18 0EG
Green Man
B5027 Uttoxeter Road

Friendly old country local with some interesting good value food (all day Sun, not Mon, Tues), well kept ales such as Backyard, Holdens and Townhouse, Thatcher's cider, small restaurant, darts, dominoes and monthly quiz; seats in back garden, open all day Fri-Sun, closed lunchtime Mon-Weds. *Recommended by Susan and Nigel Brookes*

MILWICH SJ9533　　　　　　　　　　　　　　　　　　　ST15 8RU
Red Lion
Dayhills; B5027 towards Stone

Unpretentious bar at end of working farmhouse, old settles, tiled floor, inglenook log or coal fire, Bass, Worthington and a guest tapped from the cask, friendly welcome, darts, dominoes and cribbage; lavatories in converted cowshed; open all day Sun. *Recommended by the Didler*

ONECOTE SK0455　　　　　　　　　　　　　　　　　　　ST13 7RU
Jervis Arms
B5053

Busy country pub, black-beamed main bar with inglenook woodburner, well kept Titanic, Wadworths 6X and three or four changing guests, good value food, separate dining and family rooms; attractive streamside garden, open all day Sun. *Recommended by the Didler, B M Eldridge*

PENKRIDGE SJ9214　　　　　　　　　　　　　　　　　　　ST19 5AL
Littleton Arms
St Michael's Square/A449 – M6 detour between junctions 12 and 13

Busy M&B dining pub/hotel (former coaching inn) with contemporary layout, varied choice of enjoyable good value food including lunchtime deals, several wines by the glass, ales such as Salopian, Wells & Youngs and Wye Valley, friendly young staff; piped music; children welcome, ten bedrooms, open all day. *Recommended by Stuart Paulley, Nigel Espley, Alan and Eve Harding*

☆　**PENKRIDGE** SJ9214　　　　　　　　　　　　　　　　　　　ST19 5DJ
Star
Market Place

Attractive old brick-built pub, well kept and priced Marstons-related ales, good helpings of bargain food served by efficient cheery staff, open-plan interior with lots of low black beams, stripped brick and button-back red plush, open fires; no credit cards, piped music, sports TV, darts; a few tables out at front, open all day. *Recommended by Alan and Eve Harding, Jeremy King*

RANTON SJ8422　　　　　　　　　　　　　　　　　　　ST18 9JZ
Hand & Cleaver
Butt Lane, Ranton Green

Tastefully extended country pub freshened up under new licensees, home-made fairly traditional food, Hook Norton, Marstons Pedigree and a guest, open fires and woodburners, lots of exposed beams and timber, piano, darts, restaurant; children and dogs welcome, closed Mon. *Recommended by anon*

ROLLESTON ON DOVE SK23427　　　　　　　　　　　　　　　　　　　DE13 9BE
Spread Eagle
Church Road

Old Vintage Inn family dining pub by Alder Brook, enjoyable sensibly priced standard food all day, great choice of wines by the glass, Bass and Marstons Pedigree, three linked areas and separate dining room, beams and two-way log fire; disabled facilities, attractive shrubby garden, open all day. *Recommended by Phil Pickstock*

RUGELEY SK0220   ST17 0XS
Wolseley Arms
Wolseley Bridge, A51/A513 NW

Modernised Vintage Inn with cosy farmhouse-style interior, wide choice of food all day
including lunchtime set deals, changing ales such as Bass, Marstons and Timothy Taylors,
friendly helpful staff, log fire; children welcome, disabled access, handy for Shugborough
Hall and Cannock Chase, open all day. *Recommended by Henry Pursehouse-Tranter, Sian Gillham*

SHEEN SK1160   SK17 0ET
Staffordshire Knot
Off B5054 at Hulme End

Welcoming traditional 17th-c stone-built village pub, nice mix of old furniture on
flagstones or red and black tiles, stag's head and hunting prints, two log fires in hefty
stone fireplaces, interesting well presented food cooked by landlady including deals, well
kept ales such as Hartington and Marstons Pedigree, good value wine list, friendly helpful
staff; closed Mon. *Recommended by Phil Clasper, Elaine Wintle*

STAFFORD SJ9222   ST16 2HL
Picture House
Bridge Street/Lichfield Street

Art deco cinema converted by Wetherspoons keeping ornate ceiling plasterwork and
stained-glass name sign, bar on stage with up to five competitively priced ales, farm cider,
seating in stalls, circle and upper circle, popular bargain food all day (order and pay in
advance at bar), lively atmosphere, film posters, Peter Cushing mannequin in preserved
ticket box; good disabled facilities, spacious terrace overlooking the river, open all day.
Recommended by Dave Braisted, Alan and Eve Harding

STAFFORD SJ9126   ST16 1GZ
Shire Horse
1 mile from M6 junction 14 via A34 – junction A34/A513

New Chef & Brewer built to look old, small secluded areas and open fires, bric-a-brac,
welcoming staff and good atmosphere, wide choice of enjoyable all-day food including
lunchtime set deals (Mon-Thurs), three changing ales; parking fee refunded against
food/drink; children welcome, disabled facilities, outside tables by road, bedrooms in
next-door Premier Inn, open all day. *Recommended by Alan and Eve Harding, Henry Pursehouse-
Tranter, Christine and Neil Townend*

STOWE SK0027   ST18 0LF
Cock
Off A518 Stafford—Uttoxeter

Nicely laid out bistro-style conversion of old village pub (calls itself Bistro le Coq),
competently cooked french food including good value lunchtime/early evening set menus,
some reasonably priced wines, small bar area serving real ale, friendly efficient service;
well behaved children welcome, closed Mon lunchtime. *Recommended by Susan and
Nigel Brookes, Leslie and Barbara Owen*

TAMWORTH SK2004   B79 7PA
Bolebridge
Bolebridge Street

Comfortable Wetherspoons, well kept beers and wines by the glass and their usual food,
friendly service; games machines; small terrace. *Recommended by Colin Gooch*

Post Office address codings confusingly give the impression that some pubs are in
Staffordshire, when they're really in Cheshire or Derbyshire (which is where we list them).

TAMWORTH SK2004   B79 7QQ
Moat House
Lichfield Street

Impressive Tudor former manor house, much refurbished inside while keeping beams and panelling, friendly staff, wide food choice; children welcome, play area in big garden overlooking the river. *Recommended by Colin Gooch*

TRYSULL SO8594   WV5 7JB
Bell
Bell Road

Extended 19th-c village local with cosy bar, inglenook lounge and large dining area, well kept and priced Holdens, Bathams and a guest, popular good value food from cobs up including meal deals, friendly service; front terrace, open all day Fri-Sun. *Recommended by the Didler, John and Helen Rushton, Dave Braisted, Andy Dolan*

WESTON SJ9727   ST18 0HT
Saracens Head
Stafford Road

Simple pub doing enjoyable home-made food including bargain set lunch, friendly attentive staff, well kept Greene King IPA, Marstons Pedigree and guests such as Cottage and Lymestone, decent wine, large conservatory; unobtrusive piped music; not far from Trent & Mersey Canal. *Recommended by Michael Edwards, Alan and Eve Harding*

WETTON SK1055   DE6 2AF
☆ Olde Royal Oak
Village signed off Hulme End—Alstonefield road, between B5054 and A515

Old stone-built pub in lovely NT countryside – a popular stop for walkers; traditional bar with white ceiling boards above black beams, small dining chairs around rustic tables, oak corner cupboard, open fire in stone fireplace, more modern-feeling area leading to carpeted sun lounge overlooking small garden, three changing ales, 30 malt whiskies, reasonably priced pubby food, darts and shove-ha'penny; piped music, TV; children and dogs welcome, self-catering cottage and paddock for caravans/tents, closed Mon, Tues. *Recommended by Rob and Chris Warner, A J Liles, Paul J Robinshaw, the Didler, Helene Grygar, Reg Fowle, Helen Rickwood and others*

ALSO WORTH A VISIT IN WARWICKSHIRE & WEST MIDLANDS

Besides the region's top pubs, we recommend the following. Do tell us what you think of them: **feedback@goodguides.com**

ALCESTER SP0957   B49 5QX
Holly Bush
Henley Street (continuation of High Street towards B4089; not much nearby parking)

Eight changing ales are the main draw to this unpretentious 17th-c pub; smallish rooms with simple furniture on bare boards or flagstones, stripped masonry and dark board panelling, some antique prints, open fires; recent reader concerns over food and service; children and dogs welcome, good disabled access, pretty little garden with seats on sheltered side terrace, open all day. *Recommended by Michael and Sheila Hawkins, Rob and Catherine Dunster, MLR*

ALLESLEY SP3082 CV5 9FQ
White Lion
Just off A45 near Browns Lane Jaguar; right on Hawkes Mill Lane; on junction with Wall Hill Road

Well run cottage-fronted Vintage Inn with softly lit separate areas, good food and service, reasonable prices, well kept ales such as Bass and Marstons Pedigree, good choice of wines, beams and open fires; upstairs lavatories; children welcome, tables in small front garden, open all day. *Recommended by Mrs Jean Lewis*

ARDENS GRAFTON SP1153 B50 4LG
☆ Golden Cross
Off A46 or B439 W of Stratford, OS Sheet 150 map reference 114538; Wixford Road

18th-c stone-built open-plan dining pub, attractive and welcoming, with wide choice of good generous affordable food from sandwiches to game, set lunch deals too, pleasant welcoming service, well kept Wells & Youngs and guests such as Courage, Purity and St Austell, decent wines, comfortable light wood furniture on flagstones, log fire, nice décor and good lighting; piped music; wheelchair access, attractive garden with big heated umbrellas on terrace, nice views. *Recommended by Martin and Pauline Jennings, Stanley and Annie Matthews*

ARMSCOTE SP2444 CV37 8DD
☆ Fox & Goose
Off A3400 Stratford—Shipston

Nicely modernised former blacksmith's forge, small flagstoned bar with open fire, woodburner in larger dining area, three changing ales, good choice of enjoyable food including set deals, competent friendly staff; piped music, TV; children and dogs welcome, seats on deck overlooking lawn, four brightly painted bedrooms named after Cluedo characters, open all day. *Recommended by Anthony and Pam Stamer, Eithne Dandy, Dennis and Doreen Haward*

ASTON CANTLOW SP1360 B95 6HY
☆ Kings Head
Village signed off A3400 NW of Stratford

Wisteria-covered Tudor pub with low-beamed bar on right, old settles on flagstones and log fire in big inglenook, chatty quarry-tiled main room with attractive window seats and big country oak tables, Greene King, M&B and local guests, farm cider, wines by the glass from a good list, enjoyable bar food (not Sun evening) from sandwiches through to elaborate restaurant-style choices; piped music; children welcome, dogs in bar, seats in lovely garden with big chestnut tree and pretty summer hanging baskets, open all day weekends, till 8.30pm Sun (7.30pm in winter). *Recommended by Peter Sampson, John and Caroline Shaw, Anthony and Pam Stamer, Martin and Pauline Jennings, D W Stokes*

AVON DASSETT SP4049 CV47 2AS
Avon
Off B4100 Banbury—Warwick

Double-fronted mellow-stone pub with pleasant décor and relaxing atmosphere, chatty friendly staff, enjoyable food (all day Sun till 8pm) from pub staples to more imaginative dishes including good value set lunch, good choice of well kept changing ales and wines by the glass, live music Fri; children, dogs and muddy walkers welcome – the bar's flagstones cope well, tables out in front, small side garden, attractive village by country park, open all day weekends. *Recommended by Anthony and Marie Lewis, Guy Vowles, Clive and Fran Dutson*

BARNT GREEN SP0074 B45 8PZ
☆ Barnt Green Inn
Kendal End Road

Large civilised Elizabethan dining pub with friendly young staff, good choice of food from shared mezze through wood-fired pizzas to interesting main dishes, weekday fixed-price menu too, real ales such as Black Sheep and Greene King Old Speckled Hen, log fire, relaxed atmosphere, comfortable contemporary décor, clubby seating in panelled front bar, large brasserie area; can get very busy; tables outside, handy for Lickey Hills walks, open all day. *Recommended by anon*

BARSTON SP2078   B92 0JU
☆ Bulls Head
From M42 junction 5, A4141 towards Warwick, first left, then signed down Barston Lane

Unassuming and unspoilt partly Tudor village pub, friendly landlord and efficient service, well kept Adnams, Hook Norton and two guests, enjoyable traditional food from sandwiches to good fresh fish and Sun lunch, log fires, comfortable lounge with pictures and plates, oak-beamed bar with some Buddy Holly memorabilia, separate dining room; children and dogs allowed, good-sized secluded garden alongside, hay barn, open all day Fri-Sun. *Recommended by Martin Smith, Clive and Fran Dutson, Don Bryan*

BARSTON SP1978   B92 0JP
Malt Shovel
Barston Lane

Attractive village dining pub, light and airy, with some really good modern cooking (interesting fish dishes), three well kept changing ales, nice wines including two champagnes by the glass, helpful young staff, stylish country-modern décor, converted barn restaurant; teak furniture on pergola-covered terrace, long garden with picnic-sets. *Recommended by Anthony and Pam Stamer, Susan and John Douglas*

BINLEY WOODS SP3977   CV3 2AY
Roseycombe
Rugby Road

Warm and friendly 1930s pub with wide choice of bargain home-made food, Bass and Theakstons, Weds quiz night, some live music; children welcome, big garden. *Recommended by Alan Johnson*

BIRMINGHAM SP0788   B6 4UP
☆ Bartons Arms
High Street, Aston (A34)

Magnificent Edwardian landmark, a trouble-free oasis in rather a daunting area, impressive linked richly decorated rooms from the palatial to the snug, original tilework murals, stained glass and mahogany, decorative fireplaces, sweeping stairs to handsome upstairs rooms, several well kept ales including Oakham from ornate island bar with snob screens in one section, interesting imported bottled beers and frequent mini-beer festivals, nice choice of well priced thai food (not Mon), good young staff; open all day. *Recommended by Steve Jennings, the Didler*

BIRMINGHAM SP0686   B2 5RE
Briar Rose
Bennetts Hill

Civilised open-plan Wetherspoons with deep pink décor, well kept changing guest beers, their usual food offers from breakfast on, friendly staff, separate back family dining room; lavatories downstairs, can get busy; reasonably priced bedrooms, open all day. *Recommended by the Didler, Adrian Johnson*

BIRMINGHAM SP0786   B3 2HB
Old Contemptibles
Edmund Street

Spacious Edwardian pub with lofty ceiling and lots of woodwork, decent choice of real ales (customers vote for guest beers), enjoyable well priced food including good range of sausages, friendly efficient young staff; upstairs lavatories; handy central location, popular lunchtime with office workers. *Recommended by Jack Matthew, the Didler, Tim Green, Andy Dolan*

BIRMINGHAM SP0686   B1 1RQ
Pennyblacks
Mailbox shopping mall, Wharfside Street

Good atmosphere and service in a well run spacious pub with mix of contemporary and old furnishings on wood or slate floors, appealing up-to-date décor, enjoyable food, up to seven real ales such as Church End, Hook Norton, Slaters and St Austell (third of a pint glasses available); DJ Fri, Sat night, Mon quiz; good spot by the canal. *Recommended by Steve and Liz Tilley*

BIRMINGHAM SP0586   B1 2NP
Prince of Wales
Cambridge Street

Traditional pub surviving behind the repertory theatre and symphony hall amid the concrete newcomers, L-shaped bar with friendly mix of customers, half a dozen or more well kept beers such as Everards, Timothy Taylors and Wells & Youngs, bargain straightforward lunchtime food including good baguettes, fast friendly service; may be piped music; popular with Grand Union Canal users in summer. *Recommended by Chris Evans*

BIRMINGHAM SP0687   B3 2NR
Pub du Vin
Church Street

Their second pub venture (first in Brighton), arched slate-floor cellar bar with island servery, walk-in humidor/whisky room, unusual artwork, comfortable seating, well kept Purity, Kinver and Two Towers, simple food; sports TV; another bar and 66 good bedrooms in hotel upstairs, open all day, closed Sun. *Recommended by the Didler*

BIRMINGHAM SP0686   B2 5SN
☆ Wellington
Bennetts Hill

Old-fashioned high-ceilinged pub with superb range of changing beers (listed on TV screens – order by number), most from small breweries and always one from Black Country Ales, also farm ciders, experienced landlord and friendly staff, can get very busy; no food, but plates and cutlery if you bring your own; tables out behind, open all day. *Recommended by Jack Matthew, the Didler, LM, Jeremy King*

BLOXWICH SJ9902   WS3 2EZ
☆ Turf
Wolverhampton Road, off A34 just S of A4124

Utterly uncontrived and unchanging terraced pub in side street and run by the same family for nearly 140 years; entrance hall like a 1930s home, public bar through door on right (reminiscent of a waiting room) with wooden slatted wall benches and three small tables on fine tiled floor, William Morris curtains and wallpaper and simple fireplace, more comfortable old smoking room and tiny back parlour, friendly landladies and chatty locals, Oakham, Otter, RCH and a couple of guests, no food; no-frills lavatories outside at end of simple garden; best to check opening hours before setting out. *Recommended by Dr and Mrs A K Clarke, the Didler*

BRIERLEY HILL SO9286   DY5 2TN
☆ Vine
B4172 between A461 and (nearer) A4100; straight after the turn into Delph Road

Popular Black Country pub offering a true taste of the West Midlands; down-to-earth welcome and friendly chatty locals in meandering series of rooms, each different in character, traditional front bar with wall benches and simple leatherette-topped oak stools, comfortable extended snug with solidly built red plush seats, tartan-decorated back bar with brass chandeliers, well kept and priced Bathams from brewery next door, a couple of simple very cheap lunchtime dishes; no credit cards, big-screen TV, games machine; children and dogs welcome, tables in backyard, open all day. *Recommended by the Didler, Barbarrick, P Dawn, Theo, Anne and Jane Gaskin, Ian and Joan Blackwell, Theocsbrian and others*

CHERINGTON SP2836   CV36 5HS
Cherington Arms
Off A3400

Welcoming 17th-c stone-built pub, well kept Hook Norton ales including a house beer, decent wines, food from baguettes up, nice beamed bar with log fire, lots of old photographs, separate dining room, live music every other Mon; children and dogs welcome, tables on terrace and in big garden bordering the River Stour, good nearby walks. *Recommended by David Gunn, John and Sharon Hancock*

CHURCH LAWFORD SP4576   CV23 9EF
Old Smithy
Green Lane

Much-extended thatched and beamed 16th-c dining pub, L-shaped lounge on various levels, good range of popular food cooked to order from separate servery, well kept ales such as Everards and Thwaites, efficient service, conservatory; no dogs; children welcome, terrace tables. *Recommended by George Atkinson*

CHURCHOVER SP5180   CV23 0EP
Haywaggon
Handy for M6 junction 1, off A426; The Green

Good italian food from neapolitan landlord as well as pubbier staples (must book Sun lunch), well kept Purity UBU, good coffee, relaxed atmosphere and friendly staff, two snug eating areas, lots of beams, standing timbers, brasses, nooks and crannies; may be piped music; tables outside with play area, on edge of quiet village, beautiful views over Swift Valley, closed Mon. *Recommended by Rob and Catherine Dunster, JJW, CMW*

CLAVERDON SP2064   CV35 8PE
☆ ## Red Lion
Station Road; B4095 towards Warwick

Beamed Tudor dining pub doing enjoyable food (all day Sun) from pub favourites up, friendly attentive service, decent wines and well kept Purity Mad Goose, log fires, linked rooms including back dining area with country views over sheltered heated deck and gardens; open all day. *Recommended by Clive and Fran Dutson, Nick Stewart*

COVENTRY SP3279   CV1 3BA
Old Windmill
Spon Street

Timber-framed 15th-c pub with lots of tiny rooms, exposed beams in uneven ceilings, carved oak seats on flagstones, inglenook woodburner, half a dozen real ales, often farm cider, pubby lunchtime bar food (Tues evening curry); popular with students and busy at weekends, games machines and juke box, darts, no credit cards; open all day, closed Mon lunchtime. *Recommended by the Didler*

COVENTRY SP3379   CV1 4AH
Town Wall
Bond Street, among car parks behind Belgrade Theatre

Busy Victorian city-centre local with five real ales including Adnams, farm cider, nice hot drinks' choice, good generous lunchtime doorstep sandwiches, filled rolls and cheap hot dishes, unspoilt basic front bar and tiny snug, engraved windows, bigger back lounge with actor/playwright photographs and pictures of old Coventry, open fires; big-screen sports TV; open all day. *Recommended by Clive and Fran Dutson, Roger and Donna Huggins, Alan Johnson*

COVENTRY SP3378   CV1 5DL
☆ ## Whitefriars
Gosford Street

Pair of well preserved medieval townhouses, three old-fashioned rooms on both floors, lots of ancient beams, timbers and furniture, flagstones, cobbles and coal fire, up to nine well kept changing ales (more during beer festivals), daily papers, bar lunches; some live music, no children; smokers' shelter on good-sized terrace behind, open all day. *Recommended by Alan Johnson*

DUDLEY SO9487   DY1 4LW
Park
George Street/Chapel Street

Tap for adjacent Holdens brewery, their beers kept well, decent simple lunchtime food, low prices, friendly service, conservatory, small games room with pool; sports TV; open all day. *Recommended by the Didler*

DUNCHURCH SP4871   CV22 6NJ
Dun Cow
A mile from M45 junction 1: A45/A426

Handsomely beamed Vintage Inn with massive log fires and other traditional features, friendly efficient staff, popular reasonably priced food all day including specials and deals, good range of wines by the glass, well kept Bass, Everards Tiger and Wadworths 6X from a small counter; piped music; children welcome, tables in attractive former coachyard and on sheltered side lawn, bedrooms in adjacent Innkeepers Lodge, open all day. *Recommended by P M Newsome, George Atkinson*

EARLSWOOD SP1174   B94 6AQ
Red Lion
Lady Lane (past the Lakes)

Imposing twin-gabled black and white Georgian pub, good value traditional food all day (busy weekends) including good Sun roast, friendly service, several small but high-ceilinged rooms each with its own character, sturdy tables and chairs, some wall settles, back room with open fire, chandeliers and bigger tables; disabled access. *Recommended by Martin Smith, Joan and Tony Walker*

EASENHALL SP4679   CV23 0JA
☆ ## Golden Lion
Main Street

Spotless bar in 16th-c part of busy comfortable hotel, low beams, dark panelling, settles and inglenook log fire, well kept changing beers, enjoyable food including Sun carvery, friendly attentive service; piped music; children welcome, disabled access, tables out at side and on spacious lawn, 20 well equipped bedrooms, decent breakfast, attractive village, open all day. *Recommended by John Wooll, Rob and Catherine Dunster, June Holland*

EATHORPE SP3968   CV33 9DQ
☆ ## Plough
Village signed just off B4455 NW of Leamington Spa; The Fosse

Good value generous pub food cooked by landlord, speedy jolly service under hands-on landlady, good wine choice and coffee, Shepherd Neame Spitfire and Wychwood Hobgoblin, beams, flagstones, step up to long neat dining room, simple back bar with leather sofa by open fire; piped music; garden picnic-sets. *Recommended by Dennis and Doreen Haward*

EDGE HILL SP3747   OX15 6DJ
☆ ## Castle
Off A422

Curious crenellated octagonal tower built 1749 as gothic folly (marks where Charles I raised his standard at start of the Battle of Edge Hill); lots of interest in museum-like interior, eight-walled lounge bar decorated with maps, swords, pistols, photographs of re-enactments and a collection of Civil War memorabilia, arched doorways, open fire, decent bar food including good sandwiches, Hook Norton ales, 25 malt whiskies, friendly helpful service; piped music, TV; children and dogs welcome, seats on terrace and in attractive big garden with outstanding views (once leaves have fallen), beautiful Compton Wynyates nearby, four bedrooms, open all day. *Recommended by Susan and John Douglas, Pam and John Smith, Jocasta Blockley, Phil and Sally Gorton*

FARNBOROUGH SP4349   OX17 1DZ
☆ Inn at Farnborough
Off A423 N of Banbury

Upmarket dining pub with wide choice of good food from pubby things to pricier more restauranty dishes, good value fixed-price menu too, Hook Norton ales, good choice of wines by the glass, attentive service, modern minimalist décor blending attractively with flagstones and mullioned windows, open fire in bar; children welcome, garden picnic-sets. *Recommended by Anthony and Marie Lewis, Alison Squance, George Atkinson*

FIVE WAYS SP2270   CV35 7JD
☆ Case is Altered
Follow Rowington signs at junction roundabout off A4177/A4141 N of Warwick, then right into Case Lane

Convivial unspoilt old cottage, licensed for over three centuries, with four changing ales served by friendly landlady using rare type of handpump mounted on casks behind counter (three usually from smaller local breweries), no food, simple small main bar with fine old poster of Lucas Blackwell & Arkwright Brewery (now flats), clock with hours spelling out Thornleys Ale – another defunct brewery, and just a few sturdy old-fashioned tables and couple of stout leather-covered settles facing each other over spotless tiles, modest little back room with old bar billiards table protected by ancient leather cover (it takes pre-decimal sixpences); full disabled access, stone table on little brick courtyard. *Recommended by the Didler, Phil and Sally Gorton*

GREAT WOLFORD SP2434   CV36 5NQ
☆ Fox & Hounds
Village signed on right on A3400, 3 miles S of Shipston-on-Stour

Delightful unspoilt 16th-c inn with helpful friendly staff, inglenook log fire with bread oven, low hop-strung beams, appealing collection of old furniture including tall pews on flagstones, motley assortment of antique hunting prints, vintage photographs and so forth, Hook Norton, Purity and a guest from old-fashioned tap room, much enjoyed local food (not Sun evening and two weeks in Jan), home-baked bread; children and dogs welcome, terrace with solid wooden furniture and a well, three bedrooms, open all day Sun, closed Mon. *Recommended by Chris Glasson, Michael Doswell, M Mossman, Clive and Fran Dutson, Jill Hurley, Mrs Ann Revell and others*

HALESOWEN SO9683   B63 3UG
Hawne Tavern
Attwood Street

Banks's, Bathams and Bobs plus six interesting guests from side-street local's rough-cut central servery, bar with cushioned pews, darts, pool and juke box in games area, lounge with leatherette-backed wall banquettes, good value baguettes (not Sat lunchtime, Sun), friendly staff; small terrace, closed till 4.30pm weekdays, open all day weekends. *Recommended by the Didler*

HALFORD SP2645   CV36 5BN
☆ Halford Bridge
Fosse Way (A429)

Cotswold-stone inn with solid modern furniture in roomy civilised lounge bar, inglenook woodburner, tasty food (not Sun evening) from good lunchtime sandwiches and pubby favourites up, well kept Hook Norton and a guest, good choice of wines by the glass, friendly helpful staff, restaurant; piped music; attractive inner courtyard with modern sculpture/water feature, 11 bedrooms, open all day. *Recommended by Peter and Jean Hoare, John and Sharon Hancock, Michael Dandy*

HARBURY SP3959 — CV47 2ST
Great Western
Deppers Bridge; 4 miles N of M40 junction 12; B4451

Roomy spotless pub under temporary licensees as we went to press – the model train still clatters round overhead, though; enjoyable traditional food, well kept Black Country and a guest ale; terrace tables, good value bedrooms, closed Sun evening. *Recommended by Joan and Tony Walker, Susan and John Douglas, Simon Le Fort, Ross Balaam*

☆ HATTON SP2367 — CV35 7HA
Falcon
Birmingham Road, Haseley (A4177, not far from M40 junction 15)

Smartly refurbished dining pub with relaxing rooms around island bar, lots of stripped brickwork and low beams, tiled and oak-planked floors, good moderately priced food (not Sun evening) from pub favourites up, including Sun roasts, good choice of wines by the glass, well kept Marstons-related ales, friendly service, barn-style back restaurant; children welcome, disabled facilities, garden (dogs allowed here) with new heated terrace, eight bedrooms in converted barn, open all day. *Recommended by Paul Goldman, Andy Dolan*

HAWKESBURY SP3684 — CV6 6DF
Greyhound
Sutton Stop, off Black Horse Road/Grange Road; junction of Coventry and North Oxford canals

Cosy canalside pub with plenty of character, well kept Marstons Pedigree, John Smiths, Theakstons Mild and three guests, Aspall's cider, enjoyable traditional food including pies, friendly helpful staff, coal-fired stove, unusual tiny snug; children and dogs welcome, tables on attractive waterside terrace, nice spot (if you ignore the pylons), open all day. *Recommended by Spencer Davies*

☆ HENLEY-IN-ARDEN SP1566 — B95 5AT
Bluebell
High Street (A3400, M40 junction 16)

Impressive timber-framed dining pub with fine coach entrance, emphasis on imaginative food (not Sun evening) from sandwiches to restaurant-style dishes (not particularly cheap), rambling old-beamed and flagstoned interior with contemporary furnishings creating a stylish but relaxed atmosphere, big fireplace, well kept ales such as Weatheroak, 20 wines by the glass, good coffee and afternoon teas, friendly, helpful, neat staff, daily papers; may be piped music; children welcome if eating, dogs allowed, tables on back decking, closed Mon lunchtime, otherwise open all day. *Recommended by Martin Smith, R T and J C Moggridge, John and Sharon Hancock, George Atkinson*

☆ ILMINGTON SP2143 — CV36 4LT
Howard Arms
Village signed with Wimpstone off A3400 S of Stratford

Attractive golden-stone inn by the village green, several rooms with nice mix of furniture ranging from hardwood pews through old church chairs and wheelbacks to leather dining chairs around all sorts of tables, worn flagstones, bare boards and rugs, a good few prints, shelves of books, candles, small basic bar with Hook Norton, Wye Valley and a guest ale, quite a few wines by the glass from a thoughtful list, well liked interesting food in bar and restaurant; piped music; children welcome, dogs in bar, some tables on york-stone terrace, picnic-sets under parasols in garden with fruit trees, walks on nearby hills, bedrooms, open all day. *Recommended by Mike and Mary Carter, George and Linda Ozols, Karen Eliot, Clive and Fran Dutson, Liz Bell and others*

Ring the bull is an ancient pub game – you try to lob a ring on a piece of string over a hook (occasionally a bull's horn) on a wall or the ceiling.

KENILWORTH SP2872   CV8 1NB
Clarendon Arms
Castle Hill

Busy pub opposite castle, good value generous food in several rooms off long bare-boards bustling bar, largish peaceful upstairs dining room, good friendly staff, several real ales including locals such as Purity; daytime car park fee deducted from bill; metal tables on small raised terrace, open all day weekends. *Recommended by Alun Jones, John and Sharon Hancock, Alan Johnson*

KENILWORTH SP2872   CV8 1LY
Virgin & Castle
High Street

Maze of intimate rooms off inner servery, small snugs by entrance corridor, flagstones, heavy beams, lots of woodwork including booth seating, coal fire, well kept Everards and guests, reasonably priced bar food from sandwiches up, friendly service, games bar upstairs, restaurant; children in eating areas, disabled facilities, tables in sheltered garden, open all day. *Recommended by Nigel and Sue Foster, the Didler, Roger and Donna Huggins*

KNOWLE SP1876   B93 0EB
Black Boy
Off A4177 about 1.5 miles S

Much-extended open-plan canalside pub, isolated but popular, with wide choice of good food, well kept ales, reasonable prices, attentive staff; fruit machine; outside seating. *Recommended by Anthony and Pam Stamer, Martin Smith*

KNOWLE SP1875   B93 0EE
Herons Nest
A4110 (Warwick Road) about a mile S

Popular beamed Vintage Inn dining pub, updated but keeping character, sensibly priced traditional food all day (service can be slow), plenty of good value wines by the glass, three real ales, open fires, interesting décor, some flagstones and high-backed settles, big dining room overlooking Grand Union Canal; lots of tables out by the water, moorings, Innkeepers Lodge bedrooms, open all day. *Recommended by Martin Smith*

☆ LAPWORTH SP1871   B94 6JU
Boot
Old Warwick Road (B4439, by Warwickshire Canal)

Popular upmarket dining pub near Stratford Canal, good contemporary brasserie menu from panini and interesting light dishes up, efficient friendly service by smart young staff, upscale wines (big glasses), Wadworths 6X, cosy fires, charming raftered upstairs dining room; piped music; children and good-natured dogs welcome, beautifully done waterside garden, pleasant walks, open all day. *Recommended by Mike and Mary Carter, Leslie and Barbara Owen, Martin Smith*

LAPWORTH SP1970   B94 6NA
Navigation
Old Warwick Road (B4439 SE)

Two-bar beamed and flagstoned local by the Grand Union Canal, warm open fire and some bright canalware, modern back dining room, wide range of generous food from sandwiches and pizzas up, a couple of well kept ales; children welcome, hatch service to waterside terrace, open all day. *Recommended by Martin Smith, Gerry and Rosemary Dobson, Clive and Fran Dutson*

LIGHTHORNE SP3455   CV35 0AU
Antelope
Old School Lane, Bishops Hill; a mile SW of B4100 N of Banbury

Attractive 17th-c stone-built pub recently reopened under new management, pretty village setting, two neatly kept comfortable bars (one old, one newer), separate dining area; little waterfall in banked garden. *Recommended by anon*

LITTLE COMPTON SP2530   GL56 0RT
☆ **Red Lion**
Off A44 Moreton-in-Marsh—Chipping Norton

Low-beamed 16th-c Cotswold-stone inn smartened up under current licensees, enjoyable good value food cooked by landlady from pubby things up, Donnington ales, good choice of wines by the glass, snug alcoves, inglenook woodburner; darts and pool in public bar; well behaved children and dogs welcome, pretty garden with aunt sally, two nice bedrooms. *Recommended by P and J Shapley, Mr and Mrs William Hargraves, Michael Dandy, Barry and Anne*

LONG ITCHINGTON SP4165   CV47 8LD
Blue Lias
Stockton Road, off A423

Pretty flower-decked pub by the Grand Union Canal, spic and span, with well kept Adnams, Greene King, Wychwood and a local guest, pubby food, snug booth seating in eating area, friendly staff; children welcome, disabled facilities, plenty of tables in waterside grounds (dogs allowed here), marquee for functions, may open all day if busy. *Recommended by Adrian Johnson*

LONG ITCHINGTON SP4165   CV47 9PH
☆ **Buck & Bell**
The Green

Brick-built country dining pub with impressive interior, light linked rooms on different levels including galleried area up spiral staircase, slate floors and stripped brick, woodburners, good up-to-date food, well kept ales including Church End, Hook Norton and Wychwood Hobgoblin, ample wine choice, attentive personable staff; piped music; children and dogs welcome, picnic-sets in front, open all day. *Recommended by Martin Smith, Rob and Catherine Dunster, George Atkinson, Dr Kevan Tucker, Terry Buckland and others*

LONG ITCHINGTON SP4164   CV47 9QZ
Two Boats
A423 N of Southam, by Grand Union Canal

Lively canal views from waterfront terrace and alcove window seats in the long cheery picture-filled main room, generous well priced usual food, well kept ales such as Adnams Broadside; piped music; moorings, open all day. *Recommended by Ross Balaam*

LOWER BRAILES SP3139   OX15 5HN
☆ **George**
B4035 Shipston—Banbury

Handsome old stone-built inn under new licensees (previously at the George in Swerford), roomy flagstoned front bar with inglenook log fire and dark oak tables, beamed and panelled back bar, good food cooked by chef/landlord from bar snacks and pub favourites to imaginative restaurant-style dishes, well kept Hook Norton ales, country-style flagstoned restaurant, some live music; children and dogs welcome, aunt sally in sizeable neatly kept sheltered garden with terrace and covered area, lovely village with interesting church, good walks, four comfortable bedrooms, open from 9am and all day weekends. *Recommended by JHBS, Richard Eden*

LOWER GORNAL SO9291   DY3 2AE
Black Bear
Deepdale Lane

Simple split-level local based on former 18th-c farmhouse, Kinver ales and microbrewery guests, good choice of whiskies, friendly staff, coal fire; open all day weekends. *Recommended by the Didler*

LOWER GORNAL SO9191   DY3 2PE
Fountain
Temple Street

Lively two-room local with helpful friendly landlord and staff, nine changing ales (beer festivals), two farm ciders, country wines and imported beers, enjoyable inexpensive food all day (not Sun evening), back dining area, pigs-and-pen skittles; piped music; open all day. *Recommended by the Didler, Geoff Bennett*

LOWER GORNAL SO9291   DY3 2NU
Old Bulls Head
Redhall Road

Busy Victorian local with own Black Country ales from back microbrewery and two guest beers, well filled cobs, open fire, games room, some live music; open all day weekends, from 4pm weekdays. *Recommended by the Didler*

LYE SO9284   DY9 7DG
Windsor Castle
Stourbridge Road

Contemporary minimalist décor and furnishings, nine good value Sadlers ales brewed here (tours available), guest beers too, friendly helpful staff, good range of enjoyable cheap food including some imaginative dishes often using their beer (snacks all day, no evening meals Sun), bright lighting and lively acoustics, some brewing memorabilia; open all day. *Recommended by Dr Kevan Tucker, Pat and Tony Martin, the Didler*

MERIDEN SP2482   CV7 7NN
Bulls Head
Main Road

All-day M&B dining pub in former coaching inn, modernised interior with log fires, beams, bare boards and flagstones, lots of nooks and crannies, popular food from generous sandwiches up, three well kept ales such as Black Sheep, Timothy Taylors Landlord and Wadworths 6X, good choice of wines by the glass, efficient friendly service; disabled facilities, courtyard, 13 Innkeepers Lodge bedrooms, open all day. *Recommended by Val and Alan Green*

MONKS KIRBY SP4682   CV23 0QY
☆ Bell
Just off B4027 W of Pailton

Popular pub run by hospitable long-serving spanish landlord, dark beams, timber dividers, flagstones and cobbles, wide choice of good spanish food including starters doubling as tapas and notable zarzuela fish stew, fine range of spanish wines and of brandies and malt whiskies, relaxed informal service, two well kept Greene King ales, appropriate piped music; children and dogs welcome, streamside back terrace with country view, closed Mon. *Recommended by Jill and Julian Tasker, Susan and John Douglas*

NETHERTON SO9488   DY2 9PY
☆ Old Swan
Halesowen Road (A459 just S of centre)

Victorian tavern full of traditional character and known locally as Ma Pardoe's after a former long-serving landlady; wonderfully unspoilt front bar with big swan centrepiece in patterned enamel ceiling, engraved mirrors, traditional furnishings and old-fashioned cylinder stove, other rooms including cosy back snug and more modern lounge, own-brewed Olde Swan ales, wholesome bar food (not Sun evening), upstairs restaurant; dogs allowed in bar, open all day (Sun break 4-7pm). *Recommended by the Didler, Pat and Tony Martin, Dave Braisted*

NUNEATON SP3790   CV11 4PL
Attleborough Arms
Highfield Road, Attleborough

Large fairly recently rebuilt pub, attractively open, modern and comfortable, with wide choice of enjoyable low-priced food, good range of beers and wines, helpful attentive service; good disabled access. *Recommended by David Green, Ian and Joan Blackwell*

OFFCHURCH SP3665   CV33 9AQ
 ## Stag
N off Welsh Road, off A425 at Radford Semele

Refurbished 16th-c thatched village pub under enthusiastic licensees, good well presented imaginative food (fairly priced for the quality), home-baked bread, friendly efficient young staff, well kept ales such as Purity and Warwickshire, good wine choice, low beams, oak floors and log fires, two dining areas; garden with unusual black furniture on terrace, open all day. *Recommended by John Smart, Joan and Tony Walker, Dick Withington, Peter and Janet Astbury, Clive and Fran Dutson, Ken and Barbara Turner*

OLD HILL SO9686   B64 6RG
Waterfall
Waterfall Lane

Friendly unpretentious two-room local, well kept Bathams, Holdens and guests, low-priced plain home-made food, tankards and jugs hanging from boarded ceiling; piped music; children welcome, back garden with play area, open all day Fri-Sun. *Recommended by Dave Braisted, the Didler*

OLDBURY SO9989   B69 3AD
Waggon & Horses
Church Street, near Savacentre

Copper ceiling, original etched windows, open fire and Black Country memorabilia in busy town pub with Enville and two or three guest ales, wide choice of good value lunchtime food (not weekends) from sandwiches up including vegetarian, decent wines, friendly efficient service even if busy, ornate Victorian tiles in corridor to the lively comfortable back lounge with tie collection, side room with high-backed settles and big old tables, bookable upstairs bistro Weds-Fri nights; open all day. *Recommended by the Didler*

OXHILL SP3149   CV35 0QU
 ## Peacock
Off A422 Stratford—Banbury

Popular pleasantly upgraded stone-built country pub, good varied food including two-course deals (Mon-Sat lunchtime, Mon-Thurs evenings), friendly young staff, well kept Timothy Taylors and changing guests such as Wye Valley (May, Aug beer festivals), good selection of wines by the glass, cosy character bar, half-panelled bare-boards dining room; light piped music; children welcome, dogs in bar, nice back garden, pretty village, open all day. *Recommended by K H Frostick, Clive and Fran Dutson, Roger Braithwaite, David and Catharine Boston, Mr and Mrs J L Connington, Roger M Hancock and others*

PRINCETHORPE SP4070   CV23 9PR
Three Horseshoes
High Town; junction A423/B4453

Friendly old beamed village pub under newish licensee, Marstons EPA, Pedigree and Wells & Youngs Bombardier, enjoyable traditional food, decorative plates, pictures, comfortable settles and chairs, two restaurant areas; TV projector; big garden with terrace and play area, five bedrooms, open all day Fri-Sun. *Recommended by Alan Johnson*

Half pints: by law, a pub should not charge more for half a pint than half the price of a full pint, unless it shows that half-pint price on its price list.

PRIORS MARSTON SP4857   CV47 7RW
Holly Bush
Off A361 S of Daventry; Holly Bush Lane

Clean and smart with beams, flagstones and lots of stripped stone in rambling linked rooms, log fire and woodburners, above-average well presented food, real ales, good young staff; children welcome, sheltered garden, ten bedrooms. *Recommended by Dennis and Doreen Haward, Alan Johnson*

RUGBY SP5075   CV21 3AN
Merchants
Little Church Street

Busy open-plan pub with eight quickly changing ales, real ciders and lots of continental bottled beers (regular beer/cider festivals), lots of breweriana, live music Tues; big-screen sports TV; open all day, till 1am Fri, Sat. *Recommended by Karen Handley*

SALFORD PRIORS SP0751   WR11 8UU
Bell
Evesham Road (B439)

Welcoming smartly refurbished roadside pub, comfortable chairs and sofas in bar, separate dining room, changing choice of home-made food including good value set menus, special diets catered for and local suppliers listed, ales such as Sharps Doom Bar and Wye Valley, real cider and decent wines, friendly service; outside eating and drinking areas, self-catering apartment, open all day. *Recommended by Caroline and Michael Abbey, Martin and Pauline Jennings*

SEDGLEY SO9293   DY3 1JE
☆ # Beacon
Bilston Street; A463, off A4123 Wolverhampton—Dudley

Plain old brick pub with own highly thought of Sarah Hughes ales from traditional Victorian tower brewery behind; cheery locals in simple quarry-tiled drinking corridor, little snug on left with wall settles, imposing green-tiled marble fireplace and glazed serving hatch, old-fashioned furnishings like velvet and net curtains, mahogany tables, turkey carpeting and small landscape prints, sparse tap room on right with blackened range, dark-panelled lounge with sturdy red leather wall settles and big dramatic sea prints, plant-filled conservatory (no seats), little food apart from cobs; no credit cards; children allowed in some parts including garden with play area. *Recommended by the Didler, Dr and Mrs A K Clarke, Geoff Bennett*

SEDGLEY SO9194   DY3 1RH
Mount Pleasant
High Street

Busy mock-Tudor pub near town centre, comfortable friendly front bar with fire, cosy split-level back lounge, Enville and seven changing guest beers; opens 6pm. *Recommended by the Didler*

SHIPSTON-ON-STOUR SP2540   CV36 4BT
☆ # Black Horse
Station Road (off A3400)

Ancient thatched pub under capable family management, popular and cheerful, with good honest english cooking (not Sun evening), Greene King IPA and Wadworths 6X, low-beamed bars off central entrance passage, good inglenook log fire, darts, dominoes and cribbage, small dining room; children welcome if eating, dogs in bar, enclosed back garden, three bedrooms, open all day Fri-Sun, closed Mon. *Recommended by JHBS*

Real ale to us means beer which has matured naturally in its cask –
not pressurised or filtered.

SHIPSTON-ON-STOUR SP2540   CV36 4AJ
George
High Street

Splendid early Georgian façade, bistro-style inside with several linked areas including one with deep leather armchairs and log fire, enjoyable mildly upmarket blackboard food, good friendly service, ales such as Greene King, Hook Norton and St Austell from central marble-topped counter, good choice of wines, newspapers; a few seats out on pavement, smokers' area in courtyard, 16 well modernised bedrooms, open all day. *Recommended by Michael Dandy*

SHIPSTON-ON-STOUR SP2540   CV36 4AP
 ## Horseshoe
Church Street

Pretty 17th-c timbered coaching inn, friendly and relaxed, with open-plan carpeted bar, big fireplace, recently refurbished restaurant, ales such as Brakspears, Copper Dragon, Purity and Sharps Doom Bar, Hogan's Warwickshire Wobbler cider, enjoyable reasonably priced food (not Sun evening), pub games including aunt sally, live folk music (second Tues of month); free wi-fi; children and dogs welcome, sunny back terrace with heated smokers' shelter, open all day. *Recommended by David Gunn, Michael Dandy, JHBS*

SHUSTOKE SP2290   B46 2LB
 ## Griffin
Church End, a mile E of village; 5 miles from M6 junction 4; A446 towards Tamworth, then right on to B4114 straight through Coleshill

Unpretentious country local with ten real ales including own Griffin (brewed in next-door barn), farm cider and country wines, may be winter mulled wine, standard lunchtime bar food (not Sun), cheery low-beamed L-shaped bar with log fires in two stone fireplaces (one a big inglenook), fairly simple décor, cushioned café seats, elm-topped sewing trestles and a nice old-fashioned settle, beer mats on ceiling, conservatory (children allowed here); no credit cards, games machine; dogs welcome, old-fashioned seats on back grass with distant views of Birmingham, large terrace, play area. *Recommended by Clive and Fran Dutson, M S and M Imhoff, Dr D J and Mrs S C Walker*

STRATFORD-UPON-AVON SP2054   CV37 6BA
Dirty Duck
Waterside

Bustling 16th-c Greene King Wayside Inn near Memorial Theatre, their ales and good choice of wines, well presented fairly priced food all day from sandwiches up, helpful staff, lots of signed RSC photographs, open fire, modern conservatory restaurant (best to book at weekends); children allowed in dining area, attractive small terrace looking over riverside public gardens which tend to act as a summer overflow. *Recommended by Bob and Angela Brooks, Michael Dandy, Peter Dandy, Paul Humphreys*

STRATFORD-UPON-AVON SP2054   CV37 6AB
Encore
Bridge Street

Well refurbished town-centre dining pub in rambling old building with steps between various modernised areas, wood and stone floors, mix of mostly contemporary furniture, log fire, upstairs restaurant with great river views, good choice of food including fixed-price menu, Purity and Timothy Taylors, plenty of wines by the glass, nice coffee, pleasant helpful staff; open all day. *Recommended by Eithne Dandy, Peter Dandy, Dennis Jones, Val and Alan Green, Michael Dandy and others*

STRATFORD-UPON-AVON SP2054   CV37 6AU
☆ ## Garrick
High Street

Bustling ancient pub with heavy beams and timbers, odd-shaped rooms and simple furnishings on bare boards, good-natured efficient staff, enjoyable food all day from sandwiches and light dishes up, well kept Greene King ales, decent wines by the glass, small air-conditioned back restaurant; piped music, TV, games machine; children welcome. *Recommended by Chris and Jeanne Downing, Richard Endacott, Bob and Angela Brooks, Rob and Catherine Dunster, Michael Dandy, Eithne Dandy and others*

STRATFORD-UPON-AVON SP1955   CV37 6LE
Old Thatch
Rother Street/Greenhill Street

Cosy welcoming pub on corner of market square, well kept ales such as Wye Valley and Purity, nice wines, popular fairly priced food, log fire, rustic décor, slate or wood floors, country-kitchen furniture, old pillar box in one corner; covered tables outside.
Recommended by Val and Alan Green, George Atkinson

STRATFORD-UPON-AVON SP2055   CV37 7LT
Swans Nest
Corner of Banbury Road, by bridge

Called the Bear and part of the hotel sharing an entrance with brasserie; seven ales including one brewed for them from striking pewter-topped counter, lots of wines by the glass, enjoyable good value food from fresh sandwiches up, friendly competent staff, eclectic mix of furniture on light wood-strip floor, original panelling, good river view; discreet sports TV; tables outside. *Recommended by JHBS, Val and Alan Green*

STRATFORD-UPON-AVON SP1954   CV37 6HB
Windmill
Church Street

Ancient pub (with town's oldest licence) beyond the attractive Guild Chapel, very low beams, panelling, mainly stone floors, big fireplace (gas fire), enjoyable good value pub food (till 8pm) including Sun roasts, friendly efficient staff, Flowers Original, Greene King IPA and Purity; piped music, sports TV, games machines; courtyard tables, open all day. *Recommended by Michael Dandy, George Atkinson*

☆ TANWORTH-IN-ARDEN SP1170   B94 5AL
Bell
The Green

Smartly comfortable contemporary bar-style décor, good food from light lunchtime dishes to full meals, good choice of wines by the glass, well kept Greene King IPA and Timothy Taylors Landlord, friendly staff; children in eating areas, outlook on pretty village's green and lovely 14th-c church, back terrace with alloy planters, nine stylish modern bedrooms – good base for walks, also has a post office. *Recommended by Martin Smith*

TIPTON SO9792   DY4 7NH
Rising Sun
Horseley Road (B4517, off A461)

Friendly Victorian pub with great choice of well kept ales, farm ciders, enjoyable home-made lunchtime food, back lounge with coal fires, alcoves and original bare boards and tiles; tables outside, open all day. *Recommended by the Didler*

TREDINGTON SP2543   CV36 4NS
White Lion
A3400

Comfortably modernised stone-built pub, welcoming helpful landlord, enjoyable food from short blackboard menu, ales such as Bass and Greene King IPA, low beams, rugs on quarry tiles, log fire. *Recommended by K H Frostick, Clive and Fran Dutson*

With the iPhone Good Pub Guide App, you can use the iPhone's camera to send us pictures of pubs you visit – outside or inside.

UPPER BRAILES SP3039 · OX15 5AX
Gate
B4035 Shipston-on-Stour—Banbury

Attractively old-fashioned low-beamed village pub, welcoming landlord, wife cooks enjoyable well priced country food including good fresh fish and Sun roasts, well kept Hook Norton and guests, coal fire, sizeable half-panelled carpeted bar, smaller lounge; piped music in restaurant; dogs and well behaved children welcome, tables in extensive back garden with play area, aunt sally, pretty hillside spot, lovely walks, closed Sun evening, Mon lunchtime. *Recommended by Clive and Fran Dutson, K H Frostick*

UPPER GORNAL SO9292 · DY3 1UX
☆ Britannia
Kent Street (A459)

Popular old-fashioned 19th-c local with friendly chatty atmosphere, particularly well kept Bathams Best and Mild (bargain prices), tiled floors, coal fires in front bar and time-trapped little back room with its wonderful handpumps, some bar snacks including good local pork pies; sports TV; nice flower-filled backyard, open all day. *Recommended by the Didler*

UPPER GORNAL SO9292 · DY3 1UL
Jolly Crispin
Clarence Street (A459)

Friendly well run 18th-c local, Titanic Crispy Nail and eight interesting quickly changing guests, real ciders (cider/perry festivals), compact front bar, wall seats and mixed tables/chairs on tiled floor, beer bottle collection in larger back room, fresh baps, open fires; no children; dogs welcome, beer garden, open all day Fri-Sun, closed lunchtime Mon-Thurs. *Recommended by the Didler*

WARMINGTON SP4147 · OX17 1BX
☆ Plough
Just off B4100 N of Banbury

Attractive old stone-built pub, unspoilt and well cared for by friendly landlord, low heavy beams, log fire in big fireplace, nice chairs and an ancient settle, Victorian prints, books to read, five well kept real ales, varied choice of good value home-made food (not Mon), extended dining room; tables on back terrace, delightful village with interesting church. *Recommended by Roger and Kathy Elkin*

WARWICK SP2864 · CV34 4SH
☆ Rose & Crown
Market Place

Up-to-date uncluttered refurbishment, bustling and friendly, with big leather sofas and low tables by open fire, dining area with large modern photographs, good choice of sensibly priced interesting food all day, well kept Purity and Fullers London Pride, plenty of fancy keg dispensers, good wines and coffee, cheerful efficient service, newspapers; piped music; tables out under parasols, comfortable good-sized bedrooms, open all day from 8am for breakfast. *Recommended by Michael Dandy, Dick Vardy, Nigel and Sue Foster, Revd R P Tickle, Alan Johnson*

WARWICK SP2967 · CV34 5YN
☆ Saxon Mill
Guy's Cliffe, A429 just N

Well run M&B dining pub in charmingly set converted mill, beams and log fire, smart contemporary chairs and tables on polished boards and flagstones, cosy corners with leather armchairs and big rugs, mill race and turning wheel behind glass, friendly attentive service, enjoyable good value food in bar and (best to book) upstairs family restaurant, good choice of wines by the glass, local beer; piped music; tables out on terraces by broad willow-flanked river, more over bridge, delightful views across to ruins of Guy's Cliffe House, open all day. *Recommended by Adrian Johnson, Peter and Janet Astbury, M G Hart*

WARWICK SP2864   CV34 4AB
☆ **Zetland Arms**
Church Street

Cosy town pub with good sensibly priced traditional food (not weekend evenings) including nice sandwiches and set-menu deals, friendly quick service even when busy, Adnams, Black Sheep and Marstons, decent wines, small panelled front bar with toby jug collection, comfortable larger L-shaped back eating area with small conservatory, pictures of old Warwick; sports TV; children welcome, sheltered garden, bedrooms sharing bathroom. *Recommended by Dennis Jones, Alan Johnson*

WHICHFORD SP3134   CV36 5PE
Norman Knight
Ascott Road, opposite village green

Sympathetically extended beamed and flagstoned pub, well kept Patriot ales from own microbrewery and changing guests, real ciders and perry, enjoyable food (not Sun evening), friendly helpful service, some live music; children and dogs welcome, tables out by attractive village green, aunt sally, small back campsite, classic car/bike meetings third Thurs of month in summer, closed Sun evening, Mon in winter. *Recommended by Clive and Fran Dutson, P and J Shapley*

WOLVERHAMPTON SO9094   WV4 5JN
Barley Mow
Off A449, Vicarage Road into Penwood Lane

Friendly little 17th-c local tucked away in rural setting beyond housing estate, tasty well priced traditional food, good choice of beer. *Recommended by Christopher Vallely*

WOLVERHAMPTON SO9298   WV10 0DG
☆ **Great Western**
Corn Hill/Sun Street, behind railway station

Cheerful pub hidden away by a cobbled lane down from the main line station to GWR low-level one; Bathams, Holdens and guest beers all in top condition, real cider, bargain home-made food (not Sun – bar nibbles then), helpful friendly staff, traditional front bar, other rooms including neat dining conservatory, interesting railway memorabilia, open fires; Sky TV; yard with barbecues, open all day (may be Sun afternoon break). *Recommended by the Didler, Andy Lickfold, Barbarrick, P Dawn and others*

WOLVERHAMPTON SO8698   WV6 8BN
Mermaid
Bridgnorth Road (A454 W)

Comfortable 18th-c roadside Vintage Inn, good choice of food from enjoyable sandwiches up, two changing real ales, good service; children welcome, handy for NT Wightwick Manor, open all day. *Recommended by Martin and Pauline Jennings*

If a pub tries to make you leave a credit card behind the bar, be on your guard. The credit card firms and banks that issue them condemn this practice. After all, the publican who asks you to do this is in effect saying: 'I don't trust you'. Have you any more reason to trust his staff? If your card is used fraudulently while you have let it be kept out of your sight, the card company could say you've been negligent yourself – and refuse to make good your losses. So say that they can 'swipe' your card instead, but must hand it back to you. Please let us know if a pub does try to keep your card.

ALSO WORTH A VISIT IN WORCESTERSHIRE

Besides the region's top pubs, we recommend the following. Do tell us
what you think of them: **feedback@goodguides.com**

ABBERLEY SO7567   WR6 6BN
Manor Arms
Netherton Lane

Good value comfortable country inn nicely tucked away in a quiet village backwater
opposite a fine Norman church, façade emblazoned with coats of arms, warm welcome,
quick friendly service, six ales including Wye Valley HPA, enjoyable food from baguettes
up, lunchtime bargains, two bars and restaurant, interesting toby jug collection; ten
bedrooms. *Recommended by Brian and Jacky Wilson, Chris Evans*

BERROW GREEN SO7458   WR6 6PL
☆ Admiral Rodney
B4197, off A44 W of Worcester

Light and roomy high-beamed dining pub, big stripped kitchen tables and two
woodburners, good generous pubby food including weekend fish (should book Fri, Sat
evenings), friendly fast service, well kept Wye Valley and two guests at sensible prices,
good choice of wines by the glass, charming end restaurant in rebuilt barn, folk music
third Weds of month; surcharge on some credit cards; well behaved children and dogs
welcome, disabled facilities, tables outside with pretty view and heated covered terrace,
good walks, three good bedrooms, closed Mon lunchtime, open all day weekends.
Recommended by Eric Thomas Yarwood, Denys Gueroult

BIRLINGHAM SO9343   WR10 3AQ
☆ Swan
*Church Street; off A4104 S of Pershore, via B4080 Eckington Road, turn off at sign to
Birlingham with integral 'The Swan Inn' brown sign (not the 'Birlingham (village
only)' road), then left*

Pretty timbered and thatched cottage in quiet village location, beamed quarry-tiled bar
with old-fashioned copper-topped tables, woodburner in big stone fireplace, snug inner
carpeted part by smallish counter, chatty relaxed local atmosphere, comfortable back
dining extension, ales such as Slaters, Three Tuns and Wye Valley, Cheddar Valley cider,
simple popular food served with a smile; children and dogs welcome, back garden divided
by shrubs with variety of seats and tables under parasols, small front smokers' shelter.
Recommended by Chris Evans, Theocsbrian, Dave Braisted and others

BIRTSMORTON SO7936   WR13 6AP
☆ Farmers Arms
Birts Street, off B4208 W

Timbered village local, pubbily straightforward, with friendly staff and chatty regulars
(cribbage and darts teams), well kept Hook Norton and two changing guests, simple
cheap bar food, gently old-fashioned room on right with low dark beams and some
standing timbers, spindleback chairs and flowery-panelled cushioned settles on big
flagstones, large inglenook, lower-beamed room on left (even cosier); children and dogs
welcome, seats and swings on lovely big lawn with views over Malvern Hills, plenty of
surrounding walks. *Recommended by R T and J C Moggridge, Caroline and Michael Abbey,
Eric Thomas Yarwood, Reg Fowle, Helen Rickwood, the Didler*

BOURNHEATH SO9473   B61 9JE
Nailers Arms
4 miles from M5 junction 4; Doctors Hill

Contemporary open-plan lounge and restaurant, good choice of reasonably priced food
including carvery, ales such as Greene King and Wye Valley, busy more traditional back

bar with log fire; children welcome, seats outside, open all day. *Recommended by Ian Shorthouse*

BREDON SO9236   GL20 7LA

☆ # Fox & Hounds

4.5 miles from M5 junction 9; A438 to Northway, left at B4079, in Bredon follow sign to church

Cottagey 16th-c thatched pub with open-plan carpeted bar, low beams, stone pillars and stripped timbers, central woodburner, traditional furnishings including upholstered settles, a variety of wheelback, tub and kitchen chairs around handsome mahogany and cast-iron-frame tables, elegant wall lamps, smaller side bar, friendly staff, Banks's Bitter, Greene King Old Speckled Hen and a guest like Butcombe, several wines by the glass, wide choice of food; piped music; children welcome, dogs in bar, outside picnic-sets (some under cover), handy M5 break. *Recommended by R J Herd, Dr J Benbow, Dave and Jackie Kenward, Andy and Claire Barker*

BROAD HEATH SO6765   WR15 8QS

Fox

B4204

Comfortable 16th-c black and white timbered pub, Joseph Herbert Smith ales (brewed next door) and guests, real cider and perry, pubby food, open fire, games room, Aug bank holiday beer festival, some live music; nice garden with country views, open all day weekends. *Recommended by the Didler*

BROAD HEATH SO6665   WR15 8QX

Tally Ho!

Bell Lane

Elevated 14th-c inn with wonderful panoramic views (seven counties on a clear day), well kept Wye Valley, good choice of food in bar and restaurant including Sun carvery, friendly staff; darts, pool, juke box, fruit machine; children welcome, garden with play area, bedrooms in new extension, open all day (till 1am Fri, Sat). *Recommended by David Heath*

BROADWAS-ON-TEME SO7555   WR6 5NE

Royal Oak

A44

Red-brick roadside pub with relaxed lounge bar and dining area, unusual lofty-raftered medieval-style dining hall, and separate public bar with pool, well kept Jennings and Marstons ales, decent wines by the glass, food (all day weekends) from generous lunchtime sandwiches up including OAP weekday deals and Sun carvery, good service; children welcome, terrace picnic-sets, open all day weekends. *Recommended by Jane and Alan Bush, Nicola Oatway, Jonathan Niccol*

BROADWAY SP0937   WR12 7AA

Swan

The Green (B4362)

Sizeable reworked M&B dining pub with several linked areas, imaginative décor, good sensibly priced food, three well kept changing ales, polite friendly young staff; café-style tables on small front terrace looking over road to the village green. *Recommended by Michael Dandy, Richard Tilbrook, Steve and Julie Buckingham*

CALLOW END SO8349   WR2 4TE

Old Bush

Upton Road

Attractive local with good range of Marstons-related ales, decent wines, good value standard bar food from sandwiches up, attentive friendly staff, cosy small areas around central bar, traditional pleasantly worn furnishings, restaurant; children and dogs welcome, garden with play area. *Recommended by Dave and Jenny Hughes, Chris Glasson, Martin and Pauline Jennings*

CAUNSALL SO8480
DY11 5YL
Anchor
Off A449

Traditional unchanging two-room pub (in same family since 1927), friendly atmosphere, well kept Enville, Hobsons, Wye Valley and three guests, good filled cobs, efficient service; tables outside, near canal. *Recommended by the Didler*

CHADDESLEY CORBETT SO8973
DY10 4SD
Swan
Off A448 Bromsgrove—Kidderminster

Basic unsmart old local, lively and friendly, with good value generous food (not Sun-Weds evenings), well kept Bathams Bitter and Mild, roaring woodburner; piped and some live music; children welcome, good-sized garden with play area, open all day Fri-Sun. *Recommended by Dave Braisted, Ian Shorthouse, the Didler, Alan and Eve Harding*

CHADDESLEY CORBETT SO8973
DY10 4SA
Talbot
Off A448 Bromsgrove—Kidderminster

Comfortably refurbished and neatly kept late medieval timbered pub in a quiet village street, friendly staff, Marstons-related ales, enjoyable generous food; comfortable outside area, attractive village and church. *Recommended by Alan and Eve Harding, Andy*

CHILDSWICKHAM SP0738
WR12 7HP
☆ # Childswickham Inn
Off A44 NW of Broadway

Good restauranty dining pub with big rugs on boards or terracotta tiles, contemporary artwork on part-timbered walls, woodburner, good food from pubby things to more pricey brasserie food, friendly attentive staff, locals' lounge bar with leather sofas and armchairs (dogs allowed here), good choice of wines, beers such as Brakspears, Hook Norton and Greene King; piped music, TV; children welcome, disabled facilities, garden with decked area, barbecue, closed Sun evening, Mon. *Recommended by Michael Dandy, Chris Glasson, Dr A J and Mrs Tompsett*

CLENT SO9279
DY9 9PU
Fountain
Adams Hill/Odnall Lane; off A491 at Holy Cross/Clent exit roundabout, via Violet Lane, then right at T junction

---

Restauranty pub, often packed to overflowing, with decent choice of food (not Sun evening) from lunchtime sandwiches to elaborate main courses, uniformed staff, may be some standing room at bar for drinkers (Burton Bridge and Marstons ales) but three knocked-together room areas set for dining, teak chairs and pedestal tables, comfortable cushioned brocaded walls seats on carpeting, framed local photographs on ragged pink walls; piped music; children welcome till 8pm, skittle alley, tables out on decking, open all day (till 9pm Sun). *Recommended by David and Sally Cullen, Dr Kevan Tucker, Gill and Keith Croxton*

CROPTHORNE SO9944
WR10 3NE
New Inn
Main Road (B4084 former A44 Evesham—Pershore)

Comfortable stylishly renovated roadside pub, good well presented home-made food (all day weekends) from chef/landlord using local produce, friendly prompt service, well kept ales such as Black Sheep and Wadworths 6X, inglenook log fire, skittle alley; piped music; children welcome, picnic-sets out in front, large garden, open all day weekends. *Recommended by Trevor and Sheila Sharman*

> If we know a pub has an outdoor play area for children, we mention it.

CUTNALL GREEN SO8868   WR9 0PJ
Chequers
Kidderminster Road

Comfortable and stylish beamed country dining pub with enjoyable food from pubby lunchtime snacks and sandwiches to some imaginative dishes, good wine choice, well kept if pricey beer; can get very busy in evenings; dogs welcome in bar. *Recommended by Eric Thomas Yarwood, Chris Smith*

DEFFORD SO9042   WR8 9BW
☆ ## Monkey House
A4104, after passing Oak pub on right, it's the last of a small group of cottages

Tiny black and white cider house, a wonderful time warp and in the same family for 150 years; drinks limited to Weston's Medium or Special Dry cider and a perry tapped from barrels into pottery mugs and served from a hatch, no food; children welcome, garden with hens and cockerels wandering in from adjacent caravans and sheds, also Mandy the pony and Marie and Jana the rottweilers, small spartan outbuilding with a couple of plain tables, settle and open fire; open Fri and Sun lunchtimes, Weds, Thurs and Sat evenings. *Recommended by the Didler*

DRAYTON SO9075   DY9 0BW
Robin Hood
Off B4188

Recently refurbished early 19th-c dining pub, inglenook log fire, low beams and lovely stained glass in large lounge, good food from comprehensive sensibly priced menu, well kept ales such as Enville, Holdens and Wye Valley, Thatcher's cider; can get very busy at weekends; terrace and garden tables, play area, attractive surroundings and good walks, open all day. *Recommended by Eric Thomas Yarwood*

DROITWICH SO9063   WR9 8ED
Hop Pole
Friar Street

Heavy-beamed 16th-c local with friendly staff, well kept ales such as Malvern Hills and Wye Valley, bargain home-made lunchtime food including popular Sun roasts, dominoes, darts, pool table, live music (first Sun of month); partly canopied back garden, open all day. *Recommended by Dave Braisted*

EGDON SO9053   WR7 4QS
Nightingale
A4538

Roadside Vintage Inn with extensive choice of sensibly priced popular food, well kept ales such as Bass and Marstons Pedigree, decent wines, good attentive service, beams and inglenook log fire; disabled facilities, garden tables, open all day. *Recommended by Eric Thomas Yarwood*

EVESHAM SP0344   WR11 6DA
Evesham Hotel
Coopers Lane

Idiosyncratic hotel's busy bar with amazing range of malt whiskies and spirits, good if quirky wine list, no real ales, interesting menu including good value lunchtime buffet (no tips or service charge), redecorated elegant dining room, remarkable lavatories; children welcome, indoor swimming pool, 40 bedrooms. *Recommended by Edward Pearce, Denys Gueroult, Steve Whalley*

Post Office address codings confusingly give the impression that some pubs are in Worcestershire, when they're really in Gloucestershire, Herefordshire, Shropshire, or Warwickshire (which is where we list them).

FLYFORD FLAVELL SO9754 WR7 4BS
Boot
Off A422 Worcester—Alcester; Radford Road

Decent range of home-made food from lunchtime sandwiches and set deals to specials, ales such as Black Sheep, Greene King and Fullers London Pride, log fire in ancient heavily beamed and timbered back core, modern conservatory, little old-world beamed front bar with small inglenook; piped music; children welcome, terrace tables, popular with walkers, five bedrooms, open all day Sun. *Recommended by Martin and Pauline Jennings*

GUARLFORD SO8245 WR13 6NY
 ## Plough & Harrow
B4211 E of village

Smart civilised country dining pub with contemporary feel despite low beams in bar, modern prints on ragged pink walls, scatter cushions on grey-upholstered wall benches, comfortable and airy two-level bare-boards restaurant (a step or two down past an inner sanctum of red sofas), good food using some home-grown vegetables, Wadworths, fair choice of wines by the glass, neat, attentive staff, daily papers; children welcome, hedged back garden with picnic-sets under parasols, a couple of loungers and comfortable swing seat, closed Sun evening, Mon. *Recommended by J E Shackleton, Chris Flynn, Wendy Jones, John Redfern, JCW, Tim and Joan Wright*

HANLEY SWAN SO8142 WR8 0EA
Swan
B4209 Malvern—Upton

Contemporary rustic décor and furnishings blending well with old low beams, bare boards and log fire, extended back part set for dining, enjoyable food including good steaks and Sun carvery, friendly helpful service, well kept St Austell Tribute, Shepherd Neame Spitfire and Wells & Youngs Bombardier, good wines by the glass, lively atmosphere; piped and some live music; children welcome, disabled facilities, good-sized side lawn with play area, nice spot facing the green and big duck pond, five comfortable bedrooms (one over kitchen can be noisy), open all day weekends. *Recommended by Sara Fulton, Roger Baker, Reg Fowle, Helen Rickwood, David and Gill Carrington, P Dawn, Chris Clark, Sue*

HARVINGTON SO8774 DY10 4LN
Dog
A450

Three rooms pleasantly arranged around bar, popular good value food (two-for-one deals), fast friendly service, Marstons-related ales; close to Harvington House. *Recommended by Martin and Pauline Jennings*

KEMPSEY SO8649 WR5 3QB
Huntsman
Signed off A38 in Kempsey itself

Out-of-the-way 18th-c pub, plain and simply furnished, with well kept Bathams, Greene King and Wye Valley, inexpensive home-made food, restaurant, skittle alley with bar; dogs and children welcome, garden. *Recommended by the Didler*

KEMPSEY SO8548 WR5 3NA
☆ ## Walter de Cantelupe
3.7 miles from M5 junction 7: A44 towards Worcester, left on to A4440, then left on A38 at roundabout; Main Road

Traditional carpeted bar with inglenook and pleasant mix of well worn furniture, ales such as Blue Bear, Cannon Royall and Timothy Taylors Landlord, summer farm cider and locally pressed apple juice, enjoyable food (till 10pm Fri, Sat), table skittles; piped music, sports TV; children in dining area till 8.15pm, dogs in bar and bedrooms, pretty suntrap walled garden, closed Mon. *Recommended by R T and J C Moggridge, Roger and Donna Huggins, G Wordsworth, David and Katharine Cooke, Martin and Pauline Jennings, M G Hart and others*

KIDDERMINSTER SO8376   DY10 1QX
☆ **King & Castle**
Railway Station, Comberton Hill

Bustling and neatly re-created Edwardian refreshment room suiting its setting in Severn
Valley Railway terminus, steam trains outside and railway memorabilia and photographs
inside, simple furnishings, Bathams, very good value Wyre Piddle and guests, reasonably
priced straightforward food in adjacent dining room (9am-3pm), cheerful staff coping
well on busy bank holidays and railway gala days; little museum close by, open all day.
*Recommended by Eric Thomas Yarwood, Andy Lickfold, Joe Green, P Dawn, Ian Shorthouse, George
Atkinson and others*

KIDDERMINSTER SO7583   DY11 6TL
Watermill
Park Lane

Marstons pub with their ales kept well and a good choice of food including two-for-one
deals, friendly helpful service; can get crowded; children welcome, disabled facilities,
seats out by canal, waterwheel, play area, open all day. *Recommended by Eric Thomas Yarwood*

LONG BANK SO7674   DY12 2QP
Running Horse
A456 W of Bewdley

Large Chef & Brewer family dining pub, enjoyable food and well kept changing ales,
friendly staff, beams and log fires, pleasant busy atmosphere; disabled facilities, large
garden and terrace, big fenced play area. *Recommended by Lucy Hill*

MALVERN SO7746   WR14 4QS
Foley Arms
Worcester Road

Substantial Georgian hotel taken over by Wetherspoons, usual good value; splendid views
from sunny terrace and back bedrooms, open all day from 7am. *Recommended by S Holder*

MALVERN SO7746   WR14 4RG
Red Lion
St Ann's Road

Enjoyable food (all day weekends) from substantial sandwiches up, also adjacent thai
restaurant, well kept Marstons-related ales, cheerful prompt service, airy modern décor,
stripped pine, bare boards, flagstones and pastel colours; piped music; attractive partly
covered front terrace, well placed for walks. *Recommended by N R White, Alan and Eve Harding*

NEWBRIDGE GREEN SO8439   WR8 0QP
Drum & Monkey
B4211, off A4104 just W of Upton upon Severn

Popular, beamed and timbered pub with enjoyable food and well kept ales such as Wye
Valley, friendly staff; dogs welcome. *Recommended by Howard Hill-Lines*

OMBERSLEY SO8463   WR9 0EW
☆ **Crown & Sandys**
A4133

Big popular open-plan inn with wide choice of good food from lunchtime sandwiches to
imaginative specials, early evening discount (not Sun), several wines by the glass
including champagne, real ales, good friendly uniformed staff, airy modern décor mixing
with 17th-c beams and inglenook, various dining areas including conservatory; piped
music; children welcome, terrace with fountain, sizeable garden, seven bedrooms.
Recommended by Lesley Rackley, Eric Thomas Yarwood

PENSAX SO7368 WR6 6AE

☆ **Bell**

B4202 Abberley—Clows Top, Snead Common part of village

Mock-Tudor roadside pub with down-to-earth atmosphere, friendly landlord, good choice of real ales (festival last weekend in Jun), also cider and perry, tasty bar food (not Sun evening), L-shaped main bar with traditional décor, cushioned pews and pubby tables on bare boards, hops, woodburner, dining room with french windows opening on to decking; children welcome, dogs in bar, garden looking out over countryside, open all day on summer weekends, closed Mon. *Recommended by Gordon Tong, the Didler, Alistair Stanier*

PEOPLETON SO9350 WR10 2EE

Crown

Village and pub signed off A44 at Allens Hill

Refurbished cosy village pub, beamed bar with big inglenook fireplace, well laid out dining area, good generous food (must book) from sandwiches up including set deals, Fullers and Hook Norton ales, good wines by the glass, friendly prompt service; flower-filled back garden. *Recommended by Anne McCarthy, Sam Ward, Martin and Pauline Jennings, CES*

PERSHORE SO9545 WR10 1AJ

☆ **Brandy Cask**

Bridge Street

Plain high-ceilinged bow-windowed bar, own good ales from courtyard brewery and guests (Aug beer festival), quick friendly helpful service, coal fire, reasonably priced food from sandwiches to steaks, quaintly decorated dining room; well behaved children allowed, terrace, vine arbour and koi pond in the long attractive garden down to the river (watch the kids). *Recommended by Guy Vowles, the Didler, Michael Dandy*

PERSHORE SO9545 WR10 1AJ

Star

Bridge Street

Traditional old town pub with a fire in the snug timbered bar, good choice of food including bargains, two real ales, friendly attentive service. big restaurant; riverside garden with view of weir and lock, seven bedrooms. *Recommended by Alan and Eve Harding*

RASHWOOD SO9165 WR9 0BS

Robin Hood

A38, 0.5 miles SW of M5 junction 5

Bustling 19th-c Vintage Inn dining pub, good choice of enjoyable reasonably priced food including set-lunch deal, cheerful attentive service, Brains Rev James and a couple of guests, plenty of wines by the glass, log fire; piped music; no dogs inside; children welcome, seats on small front terrace, picnic-sets in pleasant back garden, open all day. *Recommended by Alan and Eve Harding, Mrs J P Cleall*

SHATTERFORD SO7981 DY12 1RN

☆ **Bellmans Cross**

Bridgnorth Road (A442)

Welcoming french-mood dining pub with good well presented interesting food from sandwiches up including a good Sun lunch, smart tasteful restaurant with kitchen view, french chefs and bar staff, pleasant deft service, neat timber-effect bar with Bass, Greene King Old Speckled Hen and a guest beer, good choice of wines by the glass including champagne, teas and coffees; picnic-sets outside, handy for Severn Woods walks, open all day weekends. *Recommended by Richard Clarke*

Virtually all pubs in the *Good Pub Guide* sell wine by the glass. We mention wines if they are a cut above the average.

STOKE WHARF SO9468   B60 4LB
Navigation
Hanbury Road (B4091), by Worcester & Birmingham Canal

Friendly and comfortable, popular for its good choice of reasonably priced food and well kept changing ales. *Recommended by Dave Braisted, Ian Shorthouse*

STOKE WORKS SO9365   B60 4BH
Bowling Green
A mile from M5 junction 5, via Stoke Lane; handy for Worcester & Birmingham Canal

Friendly comfortable pub, bargain traditional food, Banks's and Marstons EPA, polished fireplace; big garden with neat bowling green. *Recommended by Dave Braisted*

UPHAMPTON SO8464   WR9 0JW
Fruiterers Arms
Off A449 N of Ombersley

Homely country local (looks like a private house), good value Cannon Royall ales (brewed at back of pub) and guests, farm cider, simple rustic Jacobean panelled bar and lounge with comfortable armchairs, beamery, log fire, lots of photographs and memorabilia, filled rolls (Fri-Sun), pool room; garden, some seats out in front. *Recommended by Dave Braisted, the Didler*

UPTON UPON SEVERN SO8540   WR8 0HJ
White Lion
High Street

Family-run hotel's pleasant relaxed bar, well kept Greene King and other ales, friendly helpful staff, comfortable bucket chairs, sofas and old prints, good food in bar and brasserie; covered courtyard, 13 bedrooms. *Recommended by Theocsbrian*

WEST MALVERN SO7645   WR14 4BQ
☆ ## Brewers Arms
The Dingle

Attractive and friendly little two-bar beamed country local a down steep path, Malvern Hills, Marstons, Wye Valley and up to five guests (Oct beer festival), good value food including bargain OAP weekday lunches, neat airy dining room; walkers and dogs welcome, glorious view from small garden, smokers' folly. *Recommended by David and Gill Carrington, Jason Caulkin*

WILLERSEY SP1039   WR12 7PJ
New Inn
Main Street

Friendly and attractive old stone-built local in lovely village, generous good value pub food all day from sandwiches up, prompt service, well kept Donnington ales, ancient flagstones, darts and raised end area in traditional main bar with woodburner, pool in separate public bar, skittle alley; piped music, TV; tables outside, good local walks, open all day. *Recommended by Michael Dandy, Giles and Annie Francis*

WORCESTER SO8456   WR3 7HT
Alma
Droitwich Road (A38)

Good value hearty food including OAP deals, well kept ales such as Batemans and St Austell. *Recommended by Chris Evans*

WORCESTER SO8352   WR2 4XA
Maple Leaf
Canada Way, Lower Wick

Generous home-made food at bargain prices, well kept Banks's, friendly staff, spotless. *Recommended by Chris Evans*

WORCESTER SO8455   WR1 1JL

☆ **Marwood**

The Tything (A38); some nearby parking

Easy to miss this old building; quirky and civilised with a long narrow series of small
linked areas, simple cushioned benches and mixed dining chairs, stripped or cast-iron-
framed tables, dark flagstones, broad old floorboards, the odd chandelier, a few italian
deco posters, open fires, neater upstairs room looking across to the Law Courts, well kept
Greene King, Malvern Hills and a guest, enjoyable fair value seasonal bar food (not Sun
evening), friendly service; piped music; children (in bar till 7.30pm) and dogs welcome,
rattan seats and tables in sheltered flagstoned backyard, open all day (midnight Sat).
*Recommended by Dr and Mrs James Harris, Dave Braisted, R T and J C Moggridge, Peter Smith and
Judith Brown*

WORCESTER SO8555   WR1 2HN

Plough

Fish Street

Traditional corner pub with two simple rooms off the entrance lobby, six interesting
changing ales, farm cider, short choice of good value straightforward food including OAP
lunches, reasonable prices, open fire; outside lavatories; small back terrace, open all day.
Recommended by P Dawn, Edward Leetham

WORCESTER SO8455   WR1 1DN

Postal Order

Foregate Street

Popular Wetherspoons with good range of well kept beer, Weston's cider and their usual
food at reasonable prices. *Recommended by the Didler, P Dawn*

WORCESTER SO8554   WR1 2DP

Swan With Two Nicks

New Street/Friar Street

Rambling town pub dating from the 16th c, plenty of character in bare-boards low-
ceilinged front rooms, four or five well kept ales such as Banks's and Hobsons, simple
lunchtime food; other areas including one for live music; open all day (not Sun
lunchtime). *Recommended by Tracey and Stephen Groves*

A very few pubs try to make you leave a credit card at the bar, as a sort of deposit if you
order food. They are not entitled to do this. The credit card firms and banks that issue
them warn you not to let your card out of your sight. If someone behind the counter
used your card fraudulently, the card company or bank could in theory hold you liable,
because of your negligence in letting a stranger hang on to your card. Suggest
instead that if they feel the need for security, they 'swipe' your card and
give it back to you. And do name and shame the pub to us.

The North West

Cheshire

Cumbria

Greater Manchester

Lancashire

Merseyside

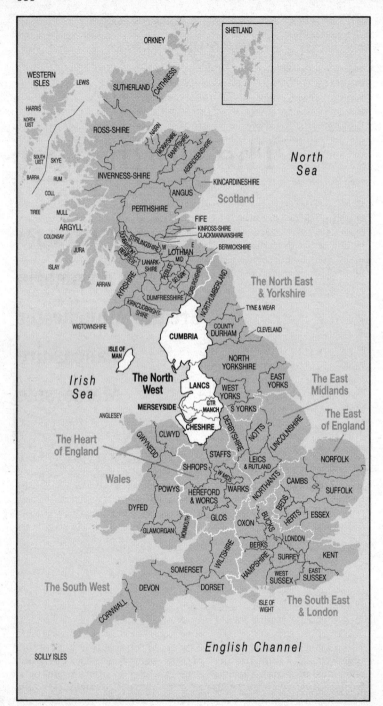

ORKNEY

SHETLAND

WESTERN
ISLES

LEWIS

HARRIS

NORTH
UIST

SOUTH
UIST

SKYE

BARRA

RUM

COLL

TIREE

MULL

ARGYLL

COLONSAY

JURA

ISLAY

ARRAN

SUTHERLAND

CAITHNESS

ROSS-SHIRE

NAIRN

MORAYSHIRE

BANFFSHIRE

ABERDEENSHIRE

INVERNESS-SHIRE

KINCARDINESHIRE

ANGUS

PERTHSHIRE

FIFE

KINROSS-SHIRE

CLACKMANNANSHIRE

STIRLINGSHIRE

DUNBARTON

RENFREW

W

LOTHAN

E

MID

BERWICKSHIRE

LANARK-
SHIRE

PEEBLES

SELKIRK

ROXBURGHSHIRE

AYRSHIRE

DUMFRIESSHIRE

KIRKCUDBRIGHT-
SHIRE

WIGTOWNSHIRE

*North
Sea*

Scotland

The North East
& Yorkshire

NORTHUMBERLAND

TYNE & WEAR

CUMBRIA

COUNTY
DURHAM

CLEVELAND

ISLE OF
MAN

NORTH
YORKSHIRE

*Irish
Sea*

**The North
West**

LANCS

WEST
YORKS

EAST
YORKS

MERSEYSIDE

GTR
MANCH

S YORKS

**The East
Midlands**

ANGLESEY

CHESHIRE

DERBYSHIRE

NOTTS

LINCOLNSHIRE

**The East
of England**

CLWYD

GWYNEDD

STAFFS

LEICS
& RUTLAND

NORFOLK

**The Heart
of England**

SHROPS

W MIDS

Wales

POWYS

HEREFORD
& WORCS

WARKS

NORTHANTS

CAMBS

SUFFOLK

DYFED

BEDS

HERTS

ESSEX

GLAMORGAN

MONMOUTH

GLOS

OXON

BUCKS

LONDON

WILTSHIRE

BERKS

SURREY

KENT

HAMPSHIRE

WEST
SUSSEX

EAST
SUSSEX

The South West

SOMERSET

DEVON

DORSET

ISLE OF
WIGHT

**The South East
& London**

CORNWALL

SCILLY ISLES

English Channel

EDITORS' FAVOURITES
THE NORTH WEST

This region's top pub for 2012 is the Masons Arms at Cartmel Fell in **Cumbria** (full of character, smashing food, friendly staff and special setting). Other great pubs in this county are the Hare & Hounds at Bowland Bridge (new to us this year and should do really well), Blacksmiths Arms at Broughton Mills (charming country pub, consistently good food, friendly welcome), George & Dragon at Clifton (inventive food using their estate produce), Highland Drove in Great Salkeld (popular, fair value food and cheerful welcome), Watermill at Ings (own brews plus 11 guests, reliable pubby food, lots of atmosphere), Strickland Arms in Levens (a much-loved all-rounder), Black Swan in Ravenstonedale (pubby bar in friendly, family-run hotel; super walks), Queens Head at Troutbeck (civilised relaxed atmosphere, seven real ales, imaginative food, nice bedrooms), Derby Arms at Witherslack (new to us and under the same ownership as the Strickland Arms; should do really well), and the Gate at Yanwath (**Cumbria Dining Pub of the Year**, first-class food and a friendly landlord). Other pubs worth visiting include the White Hart at Bouth, Bitter End in Cockermouth, Black Bull in Coniston, Punch Bowl at Crosthwaite, Bower House in Eskdale Green, Dog & Gun at Keswick, Sun in Kirkby Lonsdale, Plough at Lupton, and Herdwick at Penruddock.

Cheshire pubs are on jolly good form. Of note are the Egerton Arms in Astbury (welcoming with good value food), the Bhurtpore in Aston (impressive range of drinks and genuine atmosphere), Pheasant at Burwardsley (enjoyable all-rounder), Albion in Chester (utterly unique), Old Harkers Arms in Chester (lively town pub), Fox & Barrel at Cotebrook (stylish with terrific food and **Cheshire Dining Pub of the Year**), Hanging Gate at Langley (snug and unchanging) and Sutton Hall at Macclesfield (great dining in a stunning building). A really tremendous batch of new entries in this county includes the Egerton Arms at Chelford (something for everyone), Swan at Kettleshulme (charming cottage with great fish menu), Davenport Arms at Marton (maintaining the best of the traditional without being stuck in the past), Plough & Flail at Mobberley (comfortable dining pub) and the Yew Tree at Spurstow (top-notch all-rounder with entertaining décor). Other pubs doing well include the White Lion in Barthomley, Farmers Arms at Huxley and the Ship in Wincle.

Two new top pubs in **Lancashire** this year are the Waddington Arms in Waddington (a jolly good all-rounder) and the Freemasons Arms at Wiswell, a contender for County Dining Pub (top-notch restaurant). But the **Lancashire Dining Pub of the Year** is the Eagle & Child in Bispham Green (effortlessly good all-rounder). Good food is also to be had at the Three Fishes in Great Mitton, Clog & Billycock at Pleasington and Highwayman at Nether Burrow (all in the same ownership and featuring good local produce). The ancient Inn at Whitewell offers luxury on all fronts. For interesting beer, try the Church Inn at Uppermill (own-brew beers and lively atmosphere) and the Philharmonic Dining Rooms in

Liverpool (splendid old building). Other pubs worth a visit include the Duke of York in Grindleton, Britons Protection and Marble Arch in Manchester, Wheatsheaf in Raby, Spread Eagle at Sawley, and the Station Buffet in Stalybridge.

ALDFORD Cheshire   SJ4259   Map 7

Grosvenor Arms ★ ⑪ ♀ ◧

B5130 Chester—Wrexham; CH3 6HJ

Spacious place with buoyantly chatty atmosphere, impressive range of drinks, well balanced sensibly imaginative menu, good service; lovely big terrace and gardens

Although part of a small chain, this substantial building still retains plenty of individuality, and friendly staff engender a welcoming atmosphere. Spacious cream-painted areas are sectioned by big knocked-through arches with a variety of wood, quarry tile, flagstone and black and white tiled floor finishes – some richly coloured turkey rugs look well against these natural materials. Good solid pieces of traditional furniture, plenty of interesting pictures and attractive lighting keep it all intimate enough. A big panelled library room has tall bookshelves lining one wall, and a handsomely boarded floor; good selection of board games. Lovely on summer evenings, the airy terracotta-floored conservatory has lots of gigantic low-hanging flowering baskets and chunky pale wood garden furniture. This opens out to a large elegant suntrap terrace, and a neat lawn with picnic-sets, young trees and a characterful old tractor. Attentive staff dispense a very wide array of drinks from a fine-looking bar counter, including 20 wines by the glass, an impressive range of over 80 whiskies, distinctive soft drinks such as peach and elderflower cordial and Willington Fruit Farm pressed apple juice, as well as five real ales including Brunning & Price Original (brewed for them by Phoenix) and Deuchars IPA and guests such as Moorhouses Pride of Pendle and Red Willow Headless; more reports please.

Food here is very good. The well balanced changing menu includes something to please most tastes. As well as sandwiches, there might be chicken, mushroom and tarragon risotto, moroccan spiced lamb with sweet potato and chickpea salad with honey-roasted plum and yoghurt dressing, aubergine, spinach and lentil lasagne with feta and pepper salad, pork and chorizo meatballs with pasta and tomato sauce, battered haddock and chips, and roast duck breast with root vegetable casserole and bacon and puy lentils. *Benchmark main dish: shoulder of lamb with red wine and thyme gravy £16.75. Two-course evening meal £18.95.*

Brunning & Price ~ Manager Tracey Owen ~ Real ale ~ Bar food (12-9.30(9 Sun)) ~ (01244) 620228 ~ Children welcome ~ Dogs allowed in bar ~ Open 11.30-11; 12-10.30 Sun
Recommended by Clive Watkin, Phil and Gill Wass, John Andrew

> Stars after the name of a pub show exceptional character and appeal. They don't mean extra comfort. And they are nothing to do with food quality, for which there's a separate knife-and-fork symbol. Even quite a basic pub can win stars, if it's individual enough.

AMBLESIDE Cumbria   NY3704   Map 9

 **Golden Rule**

Smithy Brow; follow Kirkstone Pass signpost from A591 on N side of town; LA22 9AS

Simple town local with a cosy, relaxed atmosphere, and real ales

This is very much an honest, unchanging Lakeland local where all are welcomed. The bar area has built-in wall seats around cast-iron-framed tables (one with a local map set into its top), horsebrasses on the black beams, assorted pictures on the walls, a welcoming winter fire and a relaxed atmosphere. Robinsons Crusoe, Cumbria Way, Dark Mild, Dizzy Blonde, Double Hop and Hartleys XB on handpump. A brass measuring rule hangs above the bar (hence the pub's name). There's also a back room with TV (not much used), a left-hand room with darts and a games machine, and a further room, down a couple of steps on the right, with lots of seating. The backyard has benches and a covered heated area, and the window boxes are especially colourful. There's no car park.

There might be scotch eggs and pies but they tend to run out fast, so don't assume you'll be able to get something to eat.

Robinsons ~ Tenant John Lockley ~ Real ale ~ No credit cards ~ (015394) 32257 ~ Children welcome away from bar and must leave by 9pm ~ Dogs welcome ~ Open 11am-midnight

Recommended by David and Sue Atkinson, Dr and Mrs A K Clarke, Chris Johnson, John Prescott

 ASTBURY Cheshire   SJ8461   Map 7

Egerton Arms £ 🛏

Village signposted off A34 S of Congleton; CW12 4RQ

Cheery village pub with straightforward bar food, large garden, and nice bedrooms

With its long-standing staff and friendly caring landlord, this partly 16th-c farmhouse has a particularly welcoming atmosphere. Rambling around the bar, its pubby cream-painted rooms are decorated with the odd piece of armour and shelves of books. In summer, dried flowers replace the fire in the big fireplace. Mementoes of the Sandow Brothers who performed as 'the World's Strongest Youths' are particularly interesting as one of them was the landlady's father; piped music, TV. Four Robinsons ales are on handpump, in addition to Pimms (served hot in winter), a dozen wines by the glass and a range of malt whiskies. Well placed tables outside enjoy pleasant views of the church, and a play area has a wooden fort. Despite the large car park you might struggle for a place Sunday lunchtime; handy for Little Moreton Hall (National Trust).

As well as sandwiches, bar food might include mango and brie parcels, tempura prawns with lemon and lime mayonnaise, mini vegetable samosas with pear chutney, battered cod, chilli, grilled salmon with tarragon butter, macaroni cheese with roasted red peppers, and meatballs in bolognese sauce with pasta; good value lunchtime OAP specials. *Benchmark main dish: braised steak in ale £9.00. Two-course evening meal £14.00.*

Robinsons ~ Tenants Alan and Grace Smith ~ Real ale ~ Bar food (11.30-2, 6-9; 12-8 Sun) ~ Restaurant ~ (01260) 273946 ~ Children welcome ~ Open 11.30-11(10.30 Sun) ~ Bedrooms: £50S/£70B

Recommended by David Rutter, Joan and Tony Walker, John Branston, Brian and Janet Ainscough, Christopher Mobbs, Brian and Anna Marsden, Mike Proctor

ASTON Cheshire   SJ6146   Map 7

Bhurtpore ★ ♀ ◧ £

Off A530 SW of Nantwich; in village follow Wrenbury signpost; CW5 8DQ

Fantastic range of drinks (especially real ales) and tasty curries in a warm-hearted pub with some unusual artefacts; big garden

Tables in the comfortable public bar at this well cared for place are reserved for drinkers and, with the terrific range of drinks here, including 11 real ales, they are put to good use. They usually run through over 1,000 superbly kept real ales a year, sourced from an enterprising range of national brewers such as Acorn, Copper Dragon, Monty, Phoenix, Salopian, Slater, Titanic and Wincle. They also stock dozens of unusual bottled beers and fruit beers, a great many bottled ciders and perries, over 100 different whiskies, carefully selected soft drinks and a good wine list; summer beer festival. The pub is named to commemorate the siege of Bhurtpore (a town in India) during which local landowner Sir Stapleton Cotton (later Viscount Combermere) was commander in chief. The connection with India also explains some of the exotic artefacts in the carpeted lounge bar – look out especially for the sunglasses-wearing turbaned statue behind the counter; also good local period photographs and some attractive furniture; board games, pool, TV and games machine. Cheery staff usually cope superbly with the busy weekends.

The enjoyably varied menu includes sandwiches, toasted panini, smoked haddock pancake with cheese and leek sauce, sausage ring with sweet potato mash, battered haddock, chips and mushy peas, grilled duck breast on red cabbage with plum sauce, steak, kidney and ale pie, grilled goats cheese salad, and a range of curries. *Benchmark main dish: chicken and spinach balti £9.50. Two-course evening meal £16.00.*

Free house ~ Licensee Simon George ~ Real ale ~ Bar food (12-2, 7-9; 12-9.30 Sat (9 Sun)) ~ Restaurant ~ (01270) 780917 ~ Children welcome till 8.30pm ~ Dogs allowed in bar ~ Open 12-2.30, 6.30-11.30; 12-(11 Sun) midnight Fri and Sat

Recommended by Dr D J and Mrs S C Walker, the Didler, Mr and Mrs P R Thomas, Tony Hobden, Brian and Anna Marsden, Mike Proctor, Dave Webster, Sue Holland, Gill and Keith Croxton, Dennis Jones, Joe Hoyles

BASHALL EAVES Lancashire   SD6943   Map 7

Red Pump ◧

NW of Clitheroe, off B6478 or B6243; BB7 3DA

Cosy bar, good food in more contemporary dining rooms and regional beers in a beautifully placed country inn; bedrooms

This rewarding 18th-c pub is in lovely country where the River Hodder carves a course beneath Longridge Fell just south of the moors of the Forest of Bowland. There are splendid views from the terraced gardens and bedrooms, and residents can fish in the nearby river. As well as two pleasantly up-to-date dining rooms, there's a traditional, cosy central bar with bookshelves, cushioned settles and a log fire; board games. The choice of regional ales on handpump includes beers from Black Sheep and Moorhouses with a couple of guests from brewers such as Tirril; 11 wines by the glass and a good range of malt whiskies.

Using locally sourced meat, game from local shoots, and herbs from their own garden, robust country food might include smoked goats cheese tart and seared pigeon breast, ox cheek pie, linguine salsa verde, and blackcurrant sponge with liquorice ice-cream; good value Sunday lunch and perhaps a good value two-course weekday lunchtime menu. *Benchmark main dish: rabbit casserole £13.95. Two-course evening meal £18.00.*

Free house ~ Licensees Jonathan and Martina Myerscough ~ Real ale ~ Bar food (12-2, 6-9(7 Sun)) ~ Restaurant ~ (01254) 826227 ~ Open 12-2(3 Sat), 6-11; 12-9 Sun; closed Mon (except bank holidays), Tues in winter, two weeks in Jan ~ Bedrooms: £65S/£95B
Recommended by Steve Whalley, Margaret Dickinson, John and Eleanor Holdsworth

BASSENTHWAITE Cumbria   NY2332   Map 9
Sun
Off A591 N of Keswick; CA12 4QP

Bustling old pub with good views, real ales, and changing bar food

A new sun terrace with café screens and parasols has been added to this white-rendered slate house and there are fine views of the fells and Skiddaw. Inside, the rambling bar has been refurbished but there are still low 17th-c black oak beams, two good stone fireplaces with big winter log fires and built-in wall seats and plush stools around heavy wooden tables – these are on a first come first served basis, but you can reserve a table in the new cosy dining room. Jennings Bitter, Cumberland Ale, Golden Host, Sneck Lifter and a guest on handpump and several wines by the glass. The pub is handy for osprey viewing at Dodd Wood and the village is charming.

Well liked food includes sandwiches, creamy garlic mushrooms, chicken liver, Guinness and stilton pâté with a plum and apple chutney, battered cod and chips, lasagne, liver and bacon, pork steak in a brandy, peppercorn sauce, seafood pasta, and chicken breast stuffed with cumberland sausage and wrapped in bacon. *Benchmark main dish: steak in ale pie £9.15. Two-course evening meal £16.00.*

Jennings (Marstons) ~ Lease Mike and Susan Arnold ~ Real ale ~ Bar food (6-8.45 weekdays; 12-2, 6-8.45 weekends) ~ (017687) 76439 ~ Children welcome if dining with adults but must leave by 9pm ~ Dogs welcome ~ Open 4-11(11.30 Fri); 12-11 Sat and Sun; closed weekday lunchtimes
Recommended by Adrian Johnson, Tina and David Woods-Taylor, G Jennings, Geoff and Linda Payne, Howard Bowen, Andy and Alice Jordan

BASSENTHWAITE LAKE Cumbria   NY1930   Map 9
Pheasant ★ ⊕ ♀ ⇌
Follow Pheasant Inn sign at N end of dual carriageway stretch of A66 by Bassenthwaite Lake; CA13 9YE

Charming, old-fashioned bar in smart hotel with enjoyable bar food, and a fine range of drinks; comfortable bedrooms

Civilised and rather smart, this is a very well run hotel – so of course most customers are here to stay overnight in the comfortable bedrooms and to enjoy the particularly good food. But it's the surprisingly pubby and old-fashioned bar that many of our readers enjoy dropping into for a quiet pint or informal lunch. There are mellow polished walls, cushioned oak settles, rush-seat chairs and library seats, hunting prints and photographs, and Bass, Coniston Bluebird and Cumberland Corby Ale on handpump served by friendly, knowledgeable staff; also, 14 good wines by the glass, over 60 malt whiskies and several gins and vodkas. There's a front bistro, a formal back restaurant overlooking the garden and several comfortable lounges with log fires, beautiful flower arrangements, fine parquet flooring, antiques and plants. There are seats in the garden, attractive woodland surroundings and plenty of walks in all directions.

Interesting if not particularly cheap, the lunchtime bar food (sharing the same menu as the bistro which also serves evening food) includes sandwiches, potted shrimps with toasted crumpets, twice-baked cheese soufflé with mustard cress and pistachio vinaigrette, smoked haddock and chive risotto with a poached egg, fish and chips, fricassée of lemon and garlic chicken with lyonnaise potatoes, stout-braised beef, and daily specials. *Benchmark main dish: braised beef £14.00. Two-course evening meal £20.00.*

Free house ~ Licensee Matthew Wylie ~ Real ale ~ Bar food (12-2, 6-9) ~ Restaurant ~ (017687) 76234 ~ Children over 8 only ~ Dogs welcome ~ Open 11-2.30, 5-11; 12-2.30, 6-10.30 Sun ~ Bedrooms: £85B/£160B

Recommended by Adrian Johnson, Noel Grundy, Sylvia and Tony Birbeck, Henry Midwinter, Pat and Stewart Gordon, J F M and M West, Howard Bowen, Jane and Alan Bush

BICKLEY MOSS Cheshire   SJ5550 Map 7

Cholmondeley Arms ♀

Cholmondeley; A49 5.5 miles N of Whitchurch; the owners would like us to list them under Cholmondeley village, but as this is rarely located on maps we have mentioned the nearest village which appears more often; SY14 8HN

Imaginatively converted high-ceilinged schoolhouse with decent range of real ale and wines, well presented food, and a sizeable garden

By the time this edition is published there will have been some changes and refurbishment here. It's a clever schoolhouse conversion (handily placed for Cholmondeley Castle Gardens), is thoroughly good fun and makes a memorable setting for a meal or a drink. The cross-shaped lofty bar, high gothic windows, huge old radiators and old school desks on a gantry above the bar are all testament to its former identity. Well used chairs in all shapes and forms – some upholstered, some bentwood, some with ladderbacks and some with wheelbacks – are set in groups round an equally eclectic mix of tables, all on comfy carpets. There's a stag's head over one of the side arches, an open fire and lots of Victorian portraits and military pictures on colourwashed walls; piped music and board games. Salopian Shropshire Gold and Weetwood Eastgate, and a couple of guests from brewers such as Brakspears and Slaters, are served from a pine-clad bar, alongside around ten interesting and reasonably priced wines by the glass (listed on a blackboard), and a growing selection of whiskies. There are seats outside on the sizeable lawn and more in front overlooking the quiet road.

Readers very much enjoy the food here. As well as sandwiches there might be rabbit and ham hock terrine, oxtail and horseradish croquette, steak and kidney pie, chilli, roast cod loin with saffron sabayon and chorizo mash, moroccan goat stew with roast red pepper and herb couscous, and pork belly stuffed with pear and hazelnuts. *Benchmark main dish: steak and kidney pie £9.95. Two-course evening meal £16.90.*

Free house ~ Licensee Paul Dimelow ~ Real ale ~ Bar food (12-9.30) ~ (01829) 720300 ~ Children welcome ~ Dogs welcome ~ Open 11-11(10.30 Sun) ~ Bedrooms: £55B/£80B

Recommended by J S Burn, Alan and Eve Harding, R L Borthwick, P J and R D Greaves

 BISPHAM GREEN Lancashire   SD4813   Map 7

 **Eagle & Child**

Maltkiln Lane (Parbold—Croston road, off B5246); L40 3SG

LANCASHIRE DINING PUB OF THE YEAR

Successful all-rounder with antiques in stylishly simple interior, great food, interesting range of beers, appealing rustic garden

Hitting the nail on the head with unfussy effortless charm, this country pub is largely open-plan and discerningly furnished with a lovely mix of small old oak chairs, an attractive oak coffer, several handsomely carved antique oak settles (the finest apparently made partly from a 16th-c wedding bed-head), old hunting prints and engravings, and low hop-draped beams. There are red walls and coir matting up a step and oriental rugs on ancient flagstones in front of the fine old stone fireplace and counter; the pub's dogs are called Betty and Doris. Friendly young staff serve Thwaites Original alongside five guests from brewers such as Coniston, Phoenix, Prospect, Slaters and Southport, as well as Saxon farm cider, decent wines and around 25 malt whiskies. They hold a popular beer festival over the first May bank holiday weekend. The spacious gently rustic garden has a well tended but unconventional bowling green, and beyond this, a wild area that is home to crested newts and moorhens. Selling interesting wines and pottery, the shop housed in the handsome side barn includes a proper butcher and a deli.

There's quite an emphasis on the well cooked food (you need to book). As well as a good choice of wraps and ciabattas, there might be black pudding, potato and bacon salad, moules marinière, game salad, sausage and mash, thai-style vegetable curry, crayfish and lemon risotto, seared bass with saffron and vanilla tiger prawns, chicken breast with green peppercorn and brandy cream sauce, and braised oxtail with red wine sauce. *Benchmark main dish: steak and ale pie £10.00. Two-course evening meal £19.00.*

Free house ~ Licensee David Anderson ~ Real ale ~ Bar food (12-2, 5.30-8.30(9 Fri, Sat); 12-8.30 Sun) ~ (01257) 462297 ~ Children welcome away from bar ~ Dogs welcome ~ Open 12-3, 5.30-11; 12-11 Sat; 12-10.30 Sun

Recommended by Peter Heaton, Mike Tucker, Adrian and Dawn Collinge, Dr Clive Elphick, Yvonne and Mike Meadley, John and Helen Rushton, Ann and Tony Bennett-Hughes, Maurice and Gill McMahon, Jack Clark, Ed and Anna Fraser

 BOWLAND BRIDGE Cumbria   SD4189   Map 9

Hare & Hounds

Signed from A5074; LA11 6NN

17th-c inn in quiet spot with a friendly, cheerful landlady, real ales, popular food, and fine views; comfortable bedrooms

Now in the capable and friendly hands of the former management of the Strickland Arms at Levens, this attractive 17th-c coaching inn is getting high praise from our readers. There's a little bar with a log fire, daily papers to read and high chairs by the wooden counter where they serve Hare of the Dog (brewed especially for them by Tirril) and guests from Kirkby Lonsdale and Ulverston on handpump, a farm cider from half a mile away, and around a dozen wines by the glass. Leading off here are other rooms appealingly furnished with a happy mix of interesting dining chairs around all sorts of tables on the black slate or old pine-boarded floors, lots of prints on painted or stripped-stone walls, a candlelit moroccan-style lantern in a fireplace with neatly stacked logs to one side, and a relaxed atmosphere; piped music and board games. The bedrooms are comfortable and the breakfasts are first class. There are teak tables and chairs under parasols on the front terrace, with more seats in the spacious side garden and fine valley views. The inn is by the bridge itself in a quiet hamlet in the Winster Valley and Lake Windermere is just ten minutes away.

Using seasonal local produce, the very good food at lunchtime includes sandwiches, chicken liver pâté with date and orange chutney, home-made burger topped with a garlic field mushroom and cheese, and beer-battered haddock, with evening choices such as a smoked salmon parcel with crab and lemon mayonnaise, a seasonal vegetarian risotto, chicken stuffed with goats cheese, wrapped in bacon with a sweet chilli and tomato sauce, and lamb cutlets with a red wine, rosemary and mint jus. *Benchmark main dish: steak in ale pie £11.25. Two-course evening meal £17.20.*

Free house ~ Licensee Kerry Parsons ~ Real ale ~ Bar food (12-9(8.30 Sun); 12-2, 6-9 in winter) ~ (015395) 68333 ~ Children welcome ~ Dogs welcome ~ Live music during May bank holiday beer festival ~ Open 12-11(10.30 Sun) ~ Bedrooms: /£75B

Recommended by V and E A Bolton, Michael Doswell

 BROUGHTON MILLS Cumbria   SD2190   Map 9

 Blacksmiths Arms 🍴
Off A593 N of Broughton-in-Furness; LA20 6AX

Friendly little pub with imaginative food, local beers and open fires; fine surrounding walks

Going from strength to strength, this is a bustling pub run by warmly friendly licensees. It's tucked away in a little hamlet in peaceful countryside – just the place to relax after a day on the fells. There are four little bars that are simply but attractively decorated with straightforward chairs and tables on ancient slate floors and warm log fires. Barngates Cracker Ale, Dent Golden Fleece and Hawkshead Bitter on handpump, nine wines by the glass and summer farm cider; darts, cards and cribbage. The hanging baskets and tubs of flowers in front of the building are pretty in summer.

You must book a table in advance to enjoy the consistently good food which at lunchtime includes nibbles and sandwiches, ham hock and pigeon terrine with a fried egg, pineapple chutney and an apple, crackling and pea shoot salad, beer-battered hake with home-made chips, cumberland sausage with black pudding and an oxtail and red wine gravy, and creamy cheese, broccoli and sun-dried tomato tartlet with a pesto-dressed salad; evening extras such as chargrilled lime and coriander chicken with a carrot, beetroot and chickpea salad, and honey and lemon roasted duck breast with confit leg pie and madeira jus. *Benchmark main dish: slow-roasted lamb shoulder in mint and honey £13.55. Two-course evening meal £18.35.*

Free house ~ Licensees Mike and Sophie Lane ~ Real ale ~ Bar food (12-2, 6-9; not Mon) ~ Restaurant ~ (01229) 716824 ~ Children welcome ~ Dogs welcome ~ Open 12-11(5-11 Mon); 12-10.30 Sun; 12-2.30, 5-11 Tues-Fri in winter; closed Mon lunchtime

Recommended by Veronica Gwynn, Tina and David Woods-Taylor, John Luckes, E Ling, Michael Butler, the Didler, JES, Rosemary and Mike Fielder

 BUNBURY Cheshire   SJ5658 Map 7

Dysart Arms

Bowes Gate Road; village signposted off A51 NW of Nantwich; and from A49 S of Tarporley – coming this way, coming in on northernmost village access road, bear left in village centre; CW6 9PH

Civilised chatty dining pub attractively filled with good furniture in thoughtfully laid-out rooms; very enjoyable food, lovely garden with pretty views

Although very much opened up, the rooms at this comfortable country pub still retain a cottagey feel and an easy-going sociable atmosphere. Neatly kept, they ramble gently around the pleasantly lit central bar. Cream walls keep it all light, clean and airy, with deep venetian red ceilings adding cosiness, and each room (some with good winter fires) is nicely furnished with an appealing variety of well spaced sturdy wooden tables and chairs, a couple of tall filled bookcases and just the right amount of carefully chosen bric-a-brac, properly lit pictures and plants. Flooring ranges from red and black tiles, to stripped boards and some carpet. Service is efficient and friendly. Phoenix Brunning & Price Original, Weetwood and two or three guests from brewers such as Copper Dragon, Phoenix and Wooden Hand are on handpump alongside a good selection of 17 wines by the glass from a list of about 70, and just over 20 malts. Sturdy wooden tables on the terrace and picnic-sets on the lawn in the neatly kept slightly elevated garden are lovely in summer, with views of the splendid church at the end of this pretty village, and the distant Peckforton Hills beyond.

From a changing menu, food is tasty, just imaginative enough, attractively presented and fairly priced. As well as sandwiches, there might be fried scallops with carrot and cumin purée and crisp parma ham, crab linguine with ginger, red chilli and coriander, moroccan spiced lamb rump with apricot and date salad and chickpea cakes, coq au vin, home-made burger, and fried venison rump with venison faggot and juniper jus. *Benchmark main dish: battered haddock and chips £11.95. Two-course evening meal £18.60.*

Brunning & Price ~ Manager Greg Williams ~ Real ale ~ Bar food (12-9.30(9 Sun)) ~ Restaurant ~ (01829) 260183 ~ Children welcome ~ Dogs allowed in bar ~ Open 11.30-11; 12-10.30 Sun

Recommended by John Cook, Peter Webb, Gerry and Rosemary Dobson, Clive Watkin, Sian Davies, Dr and Mrs Michael Smith, Dave Webster, Sue Holland, Mark Delap

BURLEYDAM Cheshire   SJ6042 Map 7

Combermere Arms

A525 Whitchurch—Audlem; SY13 4AT

Roomy and attractive beamed pub successfully mixing a good drinking side with imaginative all-day food; rear and front garden

Décor and furnishings at this spreading pub take in a bric-a-brac-style mix of wooden chairs at dark wood tables, rugs on wood (some old and some new oak) or stone floors, frame-to-frame prints on cream walls, deep red ceilings, panelling and open fires. Friendly staff extend an equally nice welcome to drinkers and diners, with both aspects of the business seeming to do well here. Alongside Greene King Speckled Hen, Phoenix Brunning & Price Original and Weetwood Cheshire Cat, three or four guests might be from brewers such as Adnams, Acorn and Copper Dragon. They also stock around 100 whiskies and a dozen wines by the glass from an extensive list; a few board games. Outside there are good solid wood tables in a pretty, well tended garden; more reports please.

As well as interesting sandwiches and ploughman's, the enjoyable daily-changing menu might include ham hock and apricot terrine, sticky chilli and sesame seed chicken with noodle salad, cauliflower, chickpea and almond tagine with apricot and date couscous, steak, mushroom and ale pie, steamed hake fillet with crushed lemon and dill potato cake, and roast duck breast with sherry leeks, caramelised apple pastry and calvados gravy. *Benchmark main dish: steak burger £10.95. Two-course evening meal £18.00.*

Brunning & Price ~ Manager Lisa Hares ~ Real ale ~ Bar food (12-9.30; 12-10 Thurs-Sat; 12-9 Sun) ~ (01948) 871223 ~ Children welcome ~ Dogs allowed in bar ~ Open 12-11(10.30 Sun)
Recommended by R T and J C Moggridge

BURWARDSLEY Cheshire   SJ5256   Map 7

Pheasant ★ ⑪ ⚲

Higher Burwardsley; signposted from Tattenhall (which itself is signposted off A41 S of Chester) and from Harthill (reached by turning off A534 Nantwich—Holt at the Copper Mine); follow pub's signpost on up hill from Post Office; OS Sheet 117 map reference 523566; CH3 9PF

Fantastic views, local beer and good range of enjoyable food at this roomily fresh conversion of an old heavily beamed inn; open all day

This 17th-c sandstone and half-timbered pub is a terrific all-rounder (great food, beer and a lovely place to stay), benefiting too from its idyllic elevated position. It enjoys stunning views right across the Cheshire plains from nice hardwood furniture on the terrace – on a clear day their telescope sees as far as the pier head and cathedrals in Liverpool. Divided into separate areas and almost circling the bar, the beamed interior (great views from here too), quite airy and modern feeling in parts, has wooden floors, well spaced furniture, including comfy leather armchairs and some nice old chairs. They like to say that the see-through fireplace houses the largest log fire in the county. Local Weetwood Best and Cheshire Cat and Eastgate are served alongside a guest such as Mallard Spittin' Feathers, as well as local farm cider and apple juice; quiet piped music, daily newspapers. This is a great stop if you are walking the scenic Sandstone Trail along the Peckforton Hills.

Besides sandwiches (served until 6pm), the changing menu might include king prawns with lemon grass, chilli, coriander and samphire, seared scallops with caper, radish and chorizo salad and cannellini bean purée, home-made steak burger, mushroom and goats cheese feuilletée, thai green chicken curry, roast duck breast with braised gem lettuce and mushrooms, steak and mushroom pie, and well hung rib-eye steak. *Benchmark main dish: beer-battered haddock £12.50. Two-course evening meal £19.50.*

Free house ~ Licensee Andrew Nelson ~ Real ale ~ Bar food (12-3, 6-9.30 Mon, 12-9.30 Tues-Thurs, 12-10 Fri, Sat; 12-8.30 Sun) ~ (01829) 770434 ~ Children welcome ~ Dogs welcome ~ Open 12-11(10.30 Sun) ~ Bedrooms: £70B/£90B
Recommended by Val Carter, Maurice and Gill McMahon, Gerry and Rosemary Dobson, Pat and Graham Williamson, Bruce and Sharon Eden, Dave Webster, Sue Holland, Jonny Kershaw

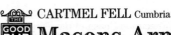 CARTMEL FELL Cumbria   SD4189 Map 9

Masons Arms
NORTH WEST PUB OF THE YEAR

Strawberry Bank, a few miles S of Windermere between A592 and A5074; perhaps the simplest way of finding the pub is to go uphill W from Bowland Bridge (which is signposted off A5074) towards Newby Bridge and keep right then left at the staggered crossroads – it's then on your right, below Gummer's How; OS Sheet 97 map reference 413895; LA11 6NW

Stunning views, beamed bar with plenty of character, good food and real ales plus many foreign bottled beers; self-catering cottages and flats

Rustic benches and tables on the heated terrace here take in the stunning views down over the Winster Valley to the woods below Whitbarrow Scar; it really is an idyllic spot. The pub itself is a favourite with many of our readers and the main bar has plenty of character, with low black beams in the bowed ceiling, and country chairs and plain wooden tables on polished flagstones. A small lounge has oak tables and settles to match its fine Jacobean panelling, there's a plain little room beyond the serving counter with pictures and a fire in an open range, a family room with an old-parlourish atmosphere and an upstairs dining room; piped music, board games and TV. Cumbrian Dickie Doodle, Hawkshead Bitter and Windermere Pale, Thwaites Wainwright and Winster Valley Old School on handpump, quite a few foreign bottled beers, 13 wines by the glass and a dozen malt whiskies; service is friendly and prompt. The stylish and comfortable self-catering cottages and apartments also have fine views.

As well as offering light breakfasts and afternoon snacks, the choice of excellent food might include interesting lunchtime sandwiches, wraps, melts and toasted ciabattas, sticky ribs, black pudding stack with home-made brown sauce, a trio of sausages (wild boar and apple, venison and cranberry, duck and chilli) with red wine and roast onion gravy, steak burger topped with cheese and cajun-spiced onion rings with thin fries and chilli jam, vegetarian shepherd's pie, and specials like chicken breast wrapped in smoked bacon on asparagus and spinach with a creamy white wine sauce, and cheese-topped fish pie. *Benchmark main dish: slow-cooked lamb in rich braising gravy with dauphinoise potatoes £16.95. Two-course evening meal £19.00.*

Individual Inns ~ Managers John and Diane Taylor ~ Real ale ~ Bar food (12-2.30, 6-9 (some afternoon snacks, too); all day weekends; light breakfasts 10am-midday) ~ Restaurant ~ (015395) 68486 ~ Children welcome ~ Dogs allowed in bar ~ Open 11.30-11; 12-10.30 Sun

Recommended by D M Heath, Tina and David Woods-Taylor, Nick Lawless, Brian Dawes, Bill Adie, G Jennings, Alison Ball, Ian Walton, Pat and Stewart Gordon, Mike Gorton, Andy and Jill Kassube, John and Hilary Penny, M G Hames, Mr and Mrs P R Thomas, Val Leonard

 CHELFORD Cheshire   SJ8175 Map 7

Egerton Arms
A537 Macclesfield—Knutsford; SK11 9BB

Well organised and welcoming, with something for everyone including food all day

This former Chef & Brewer is really flourishing since its liberation. It's quite a big place, but nicely broken up, with an appealingly varied mix of tables and chairs, including some attractive wicker dining chairs, carved settles and a wooden porter's chair by a grandfather clock. The long bar serves well kept ales from handpump such as Copper Dragon Golden Pippin, Red River Headless Dog, Tatton Best and Wells & Youngs Bombardier, and the staff are cheerful and helpful, making for a good relaxed atmosphere in the rambling dark-beamed bar. At one end a few steps take you down into a super little raftered games area, with tempting very squashy sofas and antique farm-animal prints on stripped-brick walls, as well as pool, darts, games machines and sports TV; piped music. An outside deck has canopied picnic-sets, with more on the grass by a toddlers' play area. There's a warm welcome for both dogs and children.

Ⅱ Besides sandwiches, good value cream teas and a bargain moules frites night on Wednesdays, enjoyable quickly served food here includes brandy and herb pâté, ploughman's, scampi, sweet potato, chickpea and aubergine saag, cod and chips, a good pie of the day such as steak and kidney, pizzas, burgers, grills, and a popular Sunday lunch. *Benchmark main dish: liver, bacon and sausages in gravy £8.95. Two-course evening meal £15.00.*

Free house ~ Licensees Jeremy and Anne Hague ~ Real ale ~ Bar food (12-9) ~ (01625) 861366 ~ Children welcome ~ Dogs allowed in bar ~ Open 12-11(10.30 Sun)
Recommended by Roger and Anne Newbury, John Wooll, Dr D J and Mrs S C Walker

CHESTER Cheshire   SJ4066 Map 7

Albion ★ ◖ £
Albion Street; CH1 1RQ

Strongly traditional pub with comfortable Edwardian décor and captivating World War I memorabilia; pubby food and good drinks

The homely interior of this peaceful Victorian pub is entirely dedicated to the Great War of 1914-18; most unusually it's also the officially listed site of four war memorials to soldiers from the Cheshire Regiment. It's been run by the same friendly sincere licensees for over 40 years and there's something inimitably genuine about its lovely old-fashioned atmosphere. Throughout its tranquil rooms you'll find an absorbing collection of World War I memorabilia, from big engravings of men leaving for war, and similarly moving prints of wounded veterans, to flags, advertisements and so on. The post-Edwardian décor is appealingly muted, with dark floral William Morris wallpaper (designed on the first day of World War I), a cast-iron fireplace, appropriate lamps, leatherette and hoop-backed chairs and cast-iron-framed tables. You might even be lucky enough to hear the vintage 1928 Steck pianola being played; there's an attractive side dining room too. Service is friendly, though groups of race-goers are discouraged (opening times may be limited during meets), and they don't like people rushing in just before closing time. A good range of drinks includes Adnams and a couple of guests from brewers such as Hook Norton and Titanic on handpump, new world wines, fresh orange juice, organic bottled cider and fruit juice, over 25 malt whiskies and a good selection of rums and gins. Dog owners can request a water bowl and cold sausage for their pets. Bedrooms are small but comfortable and furnished in keeping with the pub's style (free parking for residents and a bottle of house wine if dining).

Ⅱ Even the trench rations are in period, and served in such generous helpings that they don't offer starters: boiled gammon and pease pudding with parsley sauce, corned beef hash with picked red cabbage, liver, bacon and onions with cider sauce, haggis, tatties and vegetables, and filled staffordshire oatcakes. *Benchmark main dish: lambs liver and bacon in red cider gravy £9.00.*

Punch ~ Lease Michael Edward Mercer ~ Real ale ~ Bar food (12-13.50(2.20 Sat), 5-7.50(8.20 Sat); not Sun evening) ~ Restaurant ~ No credit cards ~ (01244) 340345 ~ Dogs allowed in bar ~ Open 12-3(3.30 Sat), 5(6 Sat)-11; closed Sun evening ~ Bedrooms: £70B/£85B

Recommended by Mrs M Smith, Alan and Eve Harding, Martin and Sue Radcliffe, Philip and Jan Medcalf, Roger and Anne Newbury, Keith Sale, Dennis Jones, Kim Mackay, Mary Mackay, the Didler, J S Burn, Barry Collett, Maurice and Gill McMahon, Joe Green, Mike and Eleanor Anderson, Paul Humphreys

 CHESTER Cheshire   SJ4166   Map 7

Mill  £
Milton Street; CH1 3NF

Big hotel with a huge range of real ales, good value food and cheery service in sizeable bar

We've included this modern hotel for its impressive range of a dozen real ales. Cornmill (brewed for them by Phoenix), Mill Premium (brewed for them by Coach House), Copper Dragon Golden Pippin and Weetwood Best are kept alongside guests from brewers such as Marstons, RCH and Whim; also a dozen wines by the glass, two farm ciders and 20 malt whiskies. Converted from an old mill, the building straddles either side of the Shropshire Union Canal, with a glassed-in bridge connecting its two halves. The very neatly kept bar has stripped light wood flooring throughout, marble-topped tables, some exposed brickwork and supporting pillars, and local photographs and cigarette cards framed on cream-papered walls. One comfortable area is reminiscent of a bar on a cruise liner. Service here is very friendly and you'll find a real mix of customers; quiet piped music and unobtrusively placed big-screen sports TV. Readers say the bedrooms are comfortable and make a handy base for exploring the city.

Very reasonably priced pubby food includes sandwiches, ciabattas, garlic bread and enjoyable hot dishes such as curry and rice, scampi, fish and chips, and their popular steak and ale pie. *Benchmark main dish: steak and ale pie £6.50. Two-course evening meal £8.75.*

Free house ~ Licensees Gary and Gordon Vickers ~ Real ale ~ Bar food (11.30-11; 12-10 Sun) ~ Restaurant ~ (01244) 350035 ~ Children welcome ~ Open 10am-midnight ~ Bedrooms: £73B/£95B

Recommended by Dennis Jones, Joe Green, Dave Webster, Sue Holland

CHESTER Cheshire   SJ4166   Map 7

Old Harkers Arms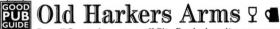
Russell Street, down steps off City Road where it crosses canal – under Mike Melody antiques; CH3 5AL

Well run spacious canalside building with lively atmosphere, great range of drinks (including lots of changing real ales), and good tasty food

The Shropshire Union Canal flows just feet away from the tall windows of this high-ceilinged early Victorian warehouse. Huge brick pillars cleverly divide the big airy interior into user-friendly spaces, and cheery staff spread a happy bustle. Mixed dark wood furniture is well grouped on stripped-wood floors, walls are covered with frame-to-frame old prints, and the usual Brunning & Price wall of bookshelves is to be found above a leather banquette at one end. Attractive lamps add cosiness, and the bar counter is apparently constructed from salvaged doors; selection of board games. You'll find a very wide range of drinks taking in around nine real ales on handpump including Phoenix Brunning & Price, Flowers Original and Weetwood Cheshire Cat, and half a dozen regularly changing guests from brewers such as Phoenix, Salopian and Titanic, more than 100 malt whiskies, 50 well described wines (with around half of them by the glass), eight or so farmhouse ciders and local apple juice.

As well as a good range of interesting sandwiches, nicely presented carefully sourced bar food – a good balance of homely dishes and more imaginative ones – might include ploughman's, mushroom and cheshire blue on walnut and raisin toast, crispy duck salad with spiced plum dressing, smoked fish and cider pie, beef, ale and stilton pudding, cauliflower, chickpea, sweet potato and apricot tagine with apricot couscous, battered haddock, and rump steak with tarragon butter. *Benchmark main dish: steak burger £10.95. Two-course evening meal £17.60.*

Brunning & Price ~ Manager Paul Jeffery ~ Real ale ~ Bar food (12-9.30) ~ (01244) 344525 ~ Dogs welcome ~ Open 11.30-11; 12-10.30 Sun

Recommended by Bruce and Sharon Eden, Dennis Jones, Charles and Pauline Stride, Simon J Barber, Clive Watkin, the Didler, Joe Green, Roger and Anne Newbury, Dave Webster, Sue Holland, Dr Kevan Tucker, Paul Humphreys

CLIFTON Cumbria   NY5326 Map 9

George & Dragon 🍴 ♟ ⇋

A6; near M6 junction 40; CA10 2ER

18th-c former coaching inn with attractive bars and sizeable restaurant, local ales, well chosen wines, imaginative food, and seats outside; smart bedrooms

Cyclists, walkers with their dogs and families are all made welcome in this carefully restored 18th-c coaching inn. There's a relaxed reception room with leather chairs around a low table in front of an open fire, bright rugs on flagstones, a table in a private nook to one side of the reception desk (just right for a group of six) and a comfortable bed for Porter, the patterdale terrier. Through some wrought-iron gates is the main bar area with more cheerful rugs on flagstones, assorted wooden farmhouse chairs and tables, grey panelling topped with yellow-painted walls, photographs of the Lowther Estate and of the family with hunting dogs, various sheep and fell pictures and some high bar stools by the panelled bar counter. Hawkshead Bitter, Lancaster Amber and a guest such as Cumberland Corby Blonde on handpump and 15 wines by the glass from a well chosen list. A further room with another open fire is similarly furnished. The sizeable restaurant to the left of the entrance is made up of four open-plan rooms: plenty of old pews and church chairs around tables set for dining, a woodburning stove, and a contemporary open kitchen. Outside, there are tables on the decoratively paved front entrance, with more in a high-walled enclosed courtyard, and a herb garden.

Using rare-breed meat, vegetables and fruit and roe and red deer – all from the Lowther Estate of which this pub is part – the inventive food might include lunchtime sandwiches, popular twice-baked cheese soufflé, wild rabbit hash with a fried duck egg, wild mushroom and wild garlic risotto, shorthorn beefburger with triple-cooked potatoes, beer-battered fish of the day, parmesan-crusted chicken with marinated tomato and basil aioli, and specials such as wild boar carpaccio with pear and truffle oil, and wild trout with baby fennel, almonds and hollandaise. *Benchmark main dish: venison medallions with a wild mushroom cream and mash £19.95. Two-course evening meal £19.95.*

Free house ~ Licensee Paul McKinnon ~ Real ale ~ Bar food (12-2.30, 6-9) ~ Restaurant ~ (01768) 865381 ~ Children welcome ~ Dogs allowed in bar and bedrooms ~ Open 11-midnight ~ Bedrooms: £70S/£90S

Recommended by Michael Doswell, Mr and Mrs Ian King, Richard J Holloway, V and E A Bolton, David Heath, Rosemary and Mike Fielder

 COCKERMOUTH Cumbria NY1230 Map 9

 **1761**

Market Place; CA13 9NH

Civilised and welcoming retreat with good drinks and interesting snacks – good value

Behind the shop-front windows of the handsome old building, this friendly place is laid out well for a comfortable chat, or a companionable game – they have lots of board games, and dominoes, cribbage, shove-ha'penny and bar skittles. Good value wines by the glass and foreign beers such as Erdinger and Liefmans Cuvée Brut join well kept Thwaites Bitter and a couple of guests from local breweries such as Barngates, Dent, Loweswater and Hesket Newmarket on handpump. There are two woodburning stoves (one in the back family room, which has some attractive ancient stripped brick), and the young owners are enthusiastic and welcoming. With slate flagstones by the bar counter on the left, bare boards on the right, and the polychrome tiles of a former corridor floor dividing the two, there are comfortably cushioned window seats, a couple of high-backed wing settles and other pleasing furnishings including some high tables. Big Lakeland landscape photographs show well against the colour scheme of pastel pinkish-beige and dark red; unobtrusive piped music. The back courtyard, below lawn and flowers sloping up to the church, has a couple of teak tables. Dogs must be kept on a lead.

Enjoyable light snacks at attractive prices might include watermelon with feta, potato wedges with various dips, garlic or chilli prawns, and local cheeses or smoked meats. *Benchmark main dish: tapas-style dishes £3.00.*

Free house ~ Licensee Nicola and Phil Sloan ~ Real ale ~ Bar food (available during serving times) ~ (01900) 829282 ~ Children welcome ~ Dogs allowed in bar ~ Open 3-11(11.30 Fri and Sat); closed lunchtimes

Recommended by Pam and John Smith

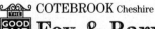 **COTEBROOK** Cheshire SJ5765 Map 7

Fox & Barrel

A49 NE of Tarporley; CW6 9DZ

CHESHIRE DINING PUB OF THE YEAR

Pretty white cottage with stylishly airy décor and an enterprising menu

Much enjoyed by readers, this warmly welcoming place is run with attention to detail and attracts both drinkers and diners alike. The tiled bar is dominated by a big log fireplace and has stools along its counter. A bigger uncluttered dining area has attractive rugs and an eclectic mix of period tables on polished oak floorboards, with extensive wall panelling hung with framed old prints. Outside is plentiful seating on a terrace and in the garden, which contains old fruit trees and a tractor. Real ales include Caledonian Deuchars IPA, Weetwood Eastgate and a couple of guests such as Morlands Original and Weetwood Cheshire Cat; good array of wines, with 20 by the glass.

As well as sandwiches and ploughman's, the changing menu might include roast tomato soup with pesto, venison faggot with celeriac mash and shallot sauce, scallop, pork belly and black pudding salad with caper dressing, seared salmon with chorizo, mussel and smoked haddock stew, chickpea and aubergine moussaka, mushroom and black truffle gnocchi with madeira butter sauce, cottage pie, and battered haddock and chips. *Benchmark main dish: beer-battered haddock £12.45. Two-course evening meal £19.30.*

Free house ~ Licensee Gary Kidd ~ Real ale ~ Bar food (12-9.30(9 Sun)) ~ (01829) 760529 ~ Children welcome but no pushchairs ~ Dogs allowed in bar ~ Open 12-11(10.30 Sun)

Recommended by Bruce and Sharon Eden, Lionel Townsend, Hilary Forrest, David A Hammond, Andy and Jill Kassube

EATON Cheshire   SJ8765   Map 7

Plough

A536 Congleton—Macclesfield; CW12 2NH

Neat and cosy village pub with up to four interesting beers, bar food, views from big attractive garden; good bedrooms

Friendly and welcoming, this tidy red-brick 17th-c pub has a fairly traditional feel. The carefully converted bar has plenty of beams and exposed brickwork, a couple of snug little alcoves, comfortable armchairs and cushioned wooden wall seats on red patterned carpets, long red curtains, leaded windows and a big stone fireplace. Service is attentive and readers have been given highchairs and a little table with crayons and paper for children. Beers include Flowers Original and Hydes Bitter (very reasonably priced) and a couple of guests from local Congleton and Macclesfield, and a decent wine list offers ten by the glass; piped music and occasional TV. Moved here piece by piece from its original home in Wales, the heavily raftered barn at the back makes a striking restaurant. Being not far from the fringes of the Peak District, you get good views of its nearby hills from the big tree-filled garden which has picnic-sets on the lawn and a covered decked terrace with outdoor heaters. The appealingly designed bedrooms are in a converted stable block.

It's advisable to book if you are eating. Food includes lunchtime sandwiches, as well as prawns in garlic butter, steak and kidney pudding, thai green curry, aubergine bake, well hung aberdeen angus steaks, and some interesting daily specials and unusual meats such as springbok and kangaroo; three-course Sunday lunch. *Benchmark main dish: fish and chips £11.00. Two-course evening meal £16.50.*

Free house ~ Licensee Mujdat Karatas ~ Real ale ~ Bar food (12-2.30, 6-9.30; 12-9.30 (8 Sun) Fri, Sat) ~ Restaurant ~ (01260) 280207 ~ Children welcome ~ Dogs allowed in bedrooms ~ Open 11am-midnight(1am Sat, 11 Sun) ~ Bedrooms: £60B/£75B

Recommended by Rob and Catherine Dunster, Mike Proctor

ELTERWATER Cumbria NY3204 Map 9

Britannia
Off B5343; LA22 9HP

Extremely popular inn surrounded by wonderful walks and scenery; up to six real ales and well liked food; bedrooms

As this very busy pub is so well placed in the heart of the Lake District, close to Langdale and the central lakes and with tracks over the fells to Grasmere and Easedale Tarn – it's a welcome haven for hungry and thirsty walkers. The atmosphere is old-fashioned and the little front bar has beams and a couple of window seats that look across to Elterwater itself through the trees. The small back bar is traditionally furnished: thick slate walls, winter coal fires, oak benches, settles, windsor chairs and a big old rocking chair. Coniston Bluebird, Thwaites Wainwright and guests such as Coniston Oatmeal Stout, Dent Aviator and Hesket Newmarket Catbells Pale Ale on handpump, and quite a few malt whiskies. The lounge is comfortable and there's a hall and dining room. Plenty of seats outside, and summer morris and step garland dancers.

Under the new licensee, the generous helpings of popular food (you must book in advance or you might be disappointed) include filled rolls, pâté with port sauce, burgers with cheese and red onion marmalade, cumberland sausage with mash and onion gravy, mushroom stroganoff, steak and mushroom in ale pie, and beer-battered fresh haddock with tartare sauce. *Benchmark main dish: lamb henry (in mint and honey) £12.50. Two-course evening meal £17.50.*

Free house ~ Licensee Andrew Parker ~ Real ale ~ Bar food (12-5.30, 6.30-9) ~ Restaurant ~ (015394) 37210 ~ Children welcome ~ Dogs allowed in bar and bedrooms ~ Open 10am-11pm ~ Bedrooms: £60S/£90S

Recommended by David and Sue Atkinson, Tina and David Woods-Taylor, Mr and Mrs J Hilton, Alison Ball, Ian Walton, G Jennings, Mrs Pam Mattinson, J Woodgate, John and Helen Rushton, Michael Doswell, Ewan and Moira McCall, Julia and Richard Tredgett, Richard Scrase, Mr and Mrs Richard Osborne, Steve and Sue Griffiths

 **GREAT MITTON** Lancashire SD7139 Map 7

Three Fishes 🍴 ♀ ◀
Mitton Road (B6246, off A59 NW of Whalley); BB7 9PQ

Stylish modern revamp, tremendous attention to detail, excellent regional food with a contemporary twist, interesting drinks

Despite its size, this imaginatively converted and well laid-out pub has plenty of intimate corners; the areas closest to the bar are elegantly traditional with a couple of big stone fireplaces, rugs on polished floors and upholstered stools. Then there's a series of individually furnished and painted rooms with exposed stone walls, careful spotlighting and wooden slatted blinds, ending with another impressive fireplace. Staff are young and friendly and there's a good chatty atmosphere. The long bar counter (with elaborate floral displays) serves Bowland Hen Harrier, Lancaster Bomber and Wainwright, a dozen wines by the glass and unusual soft drinks such as locally made sarsaparilla and dandelion and burdock. Overlooking the Ribble Valley, the garden and terrace have tables and perhaps their own summer menu. You write your name on a blackboard when you arrive and they find you when a table becomes free – the system works surprisingly well.

¶¶ Food products are carefully sourced from small local suppliers, many of whom are pictured in black and white photographs on the walls, and located on a map on the back of the menu – the beef particularly is exclusive to here. As well as imaginative lunchtime sandwiches, there might be dishes such as beech and juniper smoked salmon, baked whitebait, smoked pig's jowl, good lancashire hotpot, curd cheese and onion pie, slow-cooked saddleback pork with garlic mash and gravy, and scampi and crispy squid with chips. You may need to order side dishes with some main courses; limited afternoon snack menu. *Benchmark main dish: fish pie £10.75. Two-course evening meal £16.50.*

Free house ~ Licensee Andy Morris ~ Real ale ~ Bar food (12-8.30(9 Fri, Sat); 12-8 Sun) ~ (01254) 826888 ~ Children welcome ~ Dogs welcome ~ Open 12-11(10.30 Sun)

Recommended by Steve Whalley, Maurice and Gill McMahon, Hilary Forrest, Dr Kevan Tucker, John and Sylvia Harrop, Ed and Anna Fraser

 GREAT SALKELD Cumbria NY5536 Map 10

Highland Drove  £
B6412, off A686 NE of Penrith; CA11 9NA

Bustling place with a cheerful mix of customers, good food in several dining areas, fair choice of drinks, and fine views from the upstairs verandah; bedrooms

Our readers enjoy this well run, neatly kept pub very much and feel it's a smashing all-rounder. The chatty main bar has sandstone flooring, stone walls, cushioned wheelback chairs around a mix of tables and an open fire in a raised stone fireplace. The downstairs eating area has more cushioned dining chairs around wooden tables on the pale wooden floorboards, stone walls and ceiling joists and a two-way fire in a raised stone fireplace that separates this room from the coffee lounge with its comfortable leather chairs and sofas. There's also an upstairs restaurant. Best to book to be sure of a table. Theakstons Black Bull and a couple of guests such as Brains Milkwood and John Smiths on handpump, several wines by the glass and 30 malt whiskies. Piped music, juke box, darts, pool and dominoes. The lovely views over the Eden Valley and the Pennines are best enjoyed from seats on the upstairs verandah. There are more seats on the back terrace.

¶¶ As well as lunchtime baguettes (not Sunday), the well presented food might include black pudding and apple fritter on sweet potato and parsnip purée with wholegrain mustard sauce, smoked salmon parcel filled with prawn and dill mousse, a sharing charcuterie or fishy plate, herby pancakes stuffed with vegetables in a creamy white wine sauce, tray-baked steak in ale pie, chicken and oyster mushroom fricassée in puffy pastry with a baby onion and tarragon cream sauce, and slow-roasted pork belly on cheddar and chive mash with an apple, honey and mustard sauce. The Value Award is for the more pubby dishes. *Benchmark main dish: fillet of Nile perch in a red thai curry sauce with lemon grass and coconut rice £13.95. Two-course evening meal £17.50.*

Free house ~ Licensees Donald and Paul Newton ~ Real ale ~ Bar food (not Mon lunchtime) ~ Restaurant ~ (01768) 898349 ~ Children welcome ~ Dogs allowed in bar ~ Open 12-3, 6-11; 12-midnight Sat; closed Mon lunchtime ~ Bedrooms: £42.50S/£75S

Recommended by Richard J Holloway, Dr Kevan Tucker, Chris and Jo Parsons, Maurice and Gill McMahon, Dave Braisted, Richard and Stephanie Foskett, Rosemary and Mike Fielder, John and Hazel Hayward

INGS Cumbria   SD4498   Map 9

Watermill

Just off A591 E of Windermere; LA8 9PY

Busy, cleverly converted pub with fantastic range of real ales including own brews, and well liked food; bedrooms

With a genuinely friendly welcome, good hearty food, their own-brewed ales and comfortable bedrooms (some are bigger than others), it's not surprising that this well run inn is so popular; it's best to book a table in advance if you wish to eat. The building has plenty of character and is cleverly converted from a wood mill and joiner's shop and the bars have a lively atmosphere, a happy mix of chairs, padded benches and solid oak tables, bar counters made from old church wood, open fires, and interesting photographs and amusing cartoons by a local artist. The spacious lounge bar, in much the same traditional style as the other rooms, has rocking chairs and a big open fire. As well as their own brewed Watermill A Bit'er Ruff and Wruff Night, Collie Wobbles, Dogth Vadar and Isle of Dogs, they keep up to 11 other beers on handpump: Blackbeck Belle, Coniston Bluebird, Cumbrian Legendary Grasmoor Dark Ale, Hawkshead Bitter, Keswick Thirst Ascent, Kirkby Lonsdale Tiffin Gold, Theakstons Old Peculier and Ulverston Another Fine Mess. Also, scrumpy cider, a huge choice of foreign bottled beers and 40 malt whiskies; darts and board games. Seats in the gardens and lots to do nearby. Dogs may get free biscuits and water.

Using their own reared beef, the highly thought-of pubby food includes lunchtime sandwiches and baked french bread pizzas, chicken, ham hock and leek terrine, mushroom or beef stroganoff, cottage pie, venison sausage with mash and onion gravy, gammon with a free-range egg and pineapple, beer-battered fresh haddock, and lamb casserole. *Benchmark main dish: beef in ale pie £10.50. Two-course evening meal £15.00.*

Own brew ~ Licensee Brian Coulthwaite ~ Real ale ~ Bar food (12-9) ~ (01539) 821309 ~ Children welcome ~ Dogs allowed in bar and bedrooms ~ Storytelling first Tues evening of month ~ Open 11.30-11(10.30 Sun) ~ Bedrooms: £43S/£79S

Recommended by Margaret and Jeff Graham, John Clancy, Mr and Mrs Maurice Thompson, Martin Smith, Steve Whalley, A N Bance, Alison Ball, Ian Walton, Mike Gorton, Mr and Mrs Ian King, John and Helen Rushton, Chris Johnson, DC, Maurice and Gill McMahon, the Didler, Mike and Sue Loseby, Joe Green, V and E A Bolton, Jane Speed, Paul Hartley, Rosemary and Mike Fielder, Andy and Jill Kassube, Adam Brownhill, Colin Woodward

 KETTLESHULME Cheshire   SJ9879   Map 7

Swan

B5470 Macclesfield—Chapel-en-le-Frith, a mile W of Whaley Bridge; SK23 7QU

Charming 16th-c cottagey pub with enjoyable food (especially fish), good beer, and an attractive garden

This pretty white wisteria-clad cottage under its heavy stone roof lives up to its promise inside: snug rooms, latticed windows, very low dark beams hung with big copper jugs and kettles, timbered walls, antique coaching and other prints and maps, ancient oak settles on the turkey carpet, log fires. They have well kept Marstons on handpump with a couple of guest beers such as Bass and Tatton Hoppy Birthday; service is polite and efficient. The front terrace has teak tables, a second two-level terrace has further tables and steamer benches under cocktail parasols, and there's a sizeable streamside garden.

 The chef/landlord knows the Fleetwood fishing skippers well enough to order his supplies by email before the boats dock, and the fish is so popular here that it's wise to book. There's plenty of choice beyond that, including a fine Sunday lunch and good value bar snacks from sandwiches up. There might be langoustines in garlic butter, oysters, peppered lamb kidneys with green peppercorn and brandy cream, warm smoked duck with cranberry, greek rabbit stew, hot thai chicken, seafood risotto, roast hake with brown shrimps in spiced butter, mushroom risotto, veal T-bone steak, and well hung rib-eye with beef gravy. *Benchmark main dish: fish and chips £11.50. Two-course evening meal £26.70.*

Free house ~ Licensee Robert Cloughley ~ Real ale ~ Bar food (12-2, 6.30-8.30 Tues; 12-9 Weds-Sat; 12-4 Sun; not Mon) ~ (01663) 732943 ~ Children welcome ~ Dogs welcome ~ Open 5-11 Mon; 12-3, 5-11 Tues; 12-11 Weds-Sat; 12-8.30 Sun; closed Mon lunchtime
Recommended by David Heath, Phil and Helen Holt

LACH DENNIS Cheshire
SJ7072   Map 7

Duke of Portland 🍴 ♟ 🍺
Holmes Chapel Road (B5082, off A556 SE of Northwich); CW9 7SY

Good food in stylish upscale dining pub which nurtures the beer side

The carefully prepared food tends to be the main draw at this civilised pub, but you are equally welcome to sink into one of their comfortable leather sofas to enjoy a relaxing drink. The bar area is decorated in calm beige, grey and creams, with square leather pouffes opposite sofas, chunky low tables on neutral carpets and nicely framed prints above its panelled dado. Friendly young staff behind its handsomely carved counter serve five ales from handpump, including Brakspear Oxford Gold, Jennings Cocker Hoop, Marstons Pedigree, Ringwood Best and a guest such as Jennings Cumberland. The interesting changing choice of about ten wines by the glass is fairly priced; daily papers. The main dining room, with its lofty ceiling, sturdy balustrades and big pictures, gives quite a sense of occasion, but keeps a fairly relaxed feel – perhaps because of the friendly mixture of styles in the comfortable dining chairs on its floorboards; piped music. Outside, a neat terrace has picnic-sets among modernist planters and lovely countryside views. This is the sister to the Belle Epoque in Knutsford.

They take great care over sourcing really good ingredients from named local suppliers, and take pride in their meats and cheeses; even the chips come in for admiration and are cooked in beef dripping, and bread is home-baked. Dishes might include mushroom and chive pancake, curried cauliflower risotto cakes, olive, lemon and parsley polenta cake with goats cheese fritter and basil pesto, lemon and thyme roasted chicken breast and wings with tapenade and mayonnaise, steak burger, and lamb rump with baby greek salad and dauphinoise potatoes. *Benchmark main dish: beef & Guinness pie £11.95. Two-course evening meal £18.20.*

Marstons ~ Lease Matthew Mooney ~ Real ale ~ Bar food (12-2.30, 5.30-9.30; 12-9.30 Fri, Sat; 12-8 Sun) ~ Restaurant ~ (01606) 46264 ~ Children welcome ~ Dogs allowed in bar ~ Sausage and jazz last Thurs of month ~ Open 12-3, 5-11; 12-11 Sat; 12-10.30 Sun
Recommended by Paul and Margaret Baker, Dr and Mrs A K Clarke, Ran, Ian Mayland

---

Tipping is not normal for bar meals, and not usually expected.

THE NORTH WEST'S TOP PUBS | 835

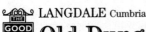

LANGDALE Cumbria   NY2806 Map 9

Old Dungeon Ghyll ◀ £

B5343; LA22 9JY

Straightforward place in a lovely position with real ales and fine walks; bedrooms

Even on sodden, chilly days there's always a boisterous atmosphere and plenty of fell walkers and climbers in this straightforward local; the fell setting is pretty dramatic. The whole feel of the place is basic but cosy and there's no need to remove boots or muddy trousers – you can sit on seats in old cattle stalls by the big warming fire and enjoy the fine choice of up to eight real ales on handpump: Dent Porter, Jennings Cumberland, Theakston Old Peculier, Yates Best Bitter and IPA and changing guests. Also, around 20 malt whiskies and Weston's Old Rosie cider; darts. It may get lively on a Saturday night (there's a popular National Trust campsite opposite).

Decent helpings of traditional food include lunchtime sandwiches, soup with home-made bread, a changing pâté, cumberland sausage with apple sauce and onion gravy, a pie of the day, vegetable goulash, beer-battered fish, and half a roasted chicken. *Benchmark main dish: chilli con carne £9.50. Two-course evening meal £14.75.*

Free house ~ Licensee Neil Walmsley ~ Real ale ~ Bar food (12-2, 6-9) ~ Restaurant ~ (015394) 37272 ~ Children welcome ~ Dogs allowed in bar and bedrooms ~ Open 11-11(10.30 Sun) ~ Bedrooms: £51/£102(£112S)

Recommended by Tim Maddison, Mike Gorton, John and Helen Rushton, the Didler, Mr and Mrs Maurice Thompson

LANGLEY Cheshire   SJ9569 Map 7

Hanging Gate ♀

Meg Lane, Higher Sutton; follow Langley signpost from A54 beside Fourways Motel, and that road passes the pub; from Macclesfield, heading S from centre on A523 turn left into Byrons Lane at Langley, Wincle signpost; in Sutton (0.5 miles after going under canal bridge, ie before Langley) fork right at Church House Inn, following Wildboarclough signpost, then 2 miles later turning sharp right at steep hairpin bend; OS Sheet 118 map reference 952696; SK11 0NG

Remotely set old place with fires in traditional cosy rooms, lovely views from airy extension and terrace

Unchanging over the years and well worth a detour, this low-beamed old drovers' pub (first licensed in 1621 but built earlier) is tucked on to the side of a hill high up in the Peak District. Its terrace, traditional pubby little rooms and airy dining room command panoramic views over a patchwork of valley pastures to distant moors and the tall Sutton Common transmitter. Still in their original layout, the three cosy little low-beamed rooms are simply furnished. The tiny little snug bar, at its pubbiest at lunchtime, has a welcoming log fire in a big brick fireplace, just one single table, plain chairs and cushioned wall seats, a few old pub pictures and seasonal photographs on its creamy walls. Beers are served in here and include well kept Hydes Original, Jekylls Gold and Over A Barrel and a guest such as Greene King Old Speckled Hen on handpump; also quite a few malt whiskies and ten wines by the glass. The second room, with just a section of bar counter in the corner, has five tables, and there's a third appealing little oak-beamed blue room; piped music, board games, dominoes, books. It does get busy so it's best to book at weekends. Walkers are made to feel welcome with tap water and there's a dog bowl outside.

🍴 As well as good sandwiches and ploughman's made with home-baked bread, tasty enjoyable bar food might include black pudding, home-made burger with stilton, ham, pâté and cheese platter, rabbit, ham and leek pie, lamb hotpot, vegetable burger, fish and chips, roast wild boar with plums, and well hung rib-eye steak. *Benchmark main dish: steak and ale pie £14.00. Two-course evening meal £20.00.*

Hydes ~ Tenants Ian and Luda Rottenbury ~ Real ale ~ Bar food (12-2, 6-9; 12-4, 6-8 Sun) ~ Restaurant ~ (01260) 252238 ~ Children welcome ~ Dogs welcome ~ Open 11-3, 5.30-11; 11-11 Sat; 10am-10pm Sun

Recommended by the Didler, Mr & Mrs N Hall, Dr John and Mrs Shirley Minns, Bob Broadhurst, N R White

 LEVENS Cumbria SD4987 Map 9

Strickland Arms ♀ ◀

4 miles from M6 junction 36, via A590; just off A590, by Sizergh Castle gates; LA8 8DZ

Friendly, open-plan pub with much enjoyed food, local ales, and a fine setting; seats outside

This extremely popular dining pub, owned by the National Trust, is in a fine spot by the entrance to Sizergh Castle. It's largely open-plan with a light and airy feel, and the bar on the right has oriental rugs on the flagstones, a log fire, Thwaites Lancaster Bomber and Wainwright and guests like Cumbrian Legendary Loweswater Pale Ale, Hesket Newmarket Scafell Blonde and Tirril Old Faithful on handpump, several malt whiskies and nine wines by the glass. On the left are polished boards and another log fire, and throughout there's a nice mix of sturdy country furniture, candles on tables, hunting scenes and other old prints on the walls, heavy fabric for the curtains and some staffordshire china ornaments; it's best to book ahead if you want to eat downstairs but there is a further dining room upstairs. Piped music and board games. The flagstoned front terrace has plenty of seats. The castle, a lovely partly medieval house with beautiful gardens, is open in the afternoon (not Friday or Saturday) from April to October. They have disabled access and facilities.

🍴 Using Estate beef and other local produce, the high-quality food includes filled baguettes, smoked salmon and dill mousse, home-potted morecambe bay shrimps, chicken casserole with smoked paprika, cranberry, mushroom and blue cheese tart, steak, button mushroom and red wine pie, lamb hotpot with pickled red cabbage, and specials such as king prawns in sweet chilli sauce, and partridge stuffed with apricot and pork, wrapped in bacon with a hazelnut and rosemary sauce; they also offer a very good value two-course weekday lunch menu. *Benchmark main dish: beer-battered fish and chips £11.50. Two-course evening meal £17.70.*

Free house ~ Licensee Martin Ainscough ~ Real ale ~ Bar food (12-2(2.30 Sat), 6-9; all day Sun and bank holidays) ~ (015395) 61010 ~ Children welcome ~ Dogs welcome ~ Open 11.30-11; 12-10.30 Sun; 11.30-3, 5.30-11 weekdays in winter

Recommended by Margaret and Jeff Graham, Michael Doswell, Pat and Stewart Gordon, Michael Butler, John and Sylvia Harrop, Mike Gorton, Maurice and Gill McMahon, V and E A Bolton, Mrs M B Gregg, David A Hammond, Dr and Mrs R G J Telfer, Malcolm and Pauline Pellatt, Dr Kevan Tucker, Mr and Mrs Maurice Thompson, Jack Clark, David and Sue Atkinson, Mr and Mrs P R Thomas, David Hartley

LITTLE LANGDALE Cumbria   NY3103   Map 9

Three Shires 🍺 🛏

From A593 3 miles W of Ambleside take small road signposted The Langdales, Wrynose Pass; then bear left at first fork; LA22 9NZ

Friendly inn with valley views from seats on the terrace, enjoyable food and several local real ales; comfortable bedrooms

This year there have been some smart new changes to this well managed, popular inn – run by the same friendly family for 29 years. The front restaurant has been refurbished and now has chunky leather dining chairs around solid tables on the new wooden flooring, fresh flowers, and wine bottle prints on the dark red walls. The new snug leads off here, with country-kitchen chairs and tables on slate floor tiles, blue wall banquettes and the same dark red walls; there's now much more room for walkers at lunchtime. The comfortably extended back bar still has a mix of green Lakeland stone and homely red patterned wallpaper (which works rather well), stripped timbers and a beam-and-joist stripped ceiling, antique oak carved settles, country-kitchen chairs and stools on its big dark slate flagstones, and Lakeland photographs. Barngates Cat Nap, Coniston Old Man, Hawkshead Bitter, Jennings Cumberland, and Whitehaven Ennerdale Blonde on handpump, over 50 malt whiskies and a decent wine list; darts and board games. There are lovely views from seats on the terrace over the valley to the partly wooded hills below and more seats on a neat lawn behind the car park, backed by a small oak wood. The award-winning summer hanging baskets are very pretty. The three shires are the historical counties of Cumberland, Westmorland and Lancashire, which meet at the top of the nearby Wrynose Pass.

Enjoyable food includes lunchtime sandwiches, mixed game and white pudding terrine with home-made chutney, cumberland sausages, beef in ale pie, leek, mushroom and smoked parmesan risotto, pork loin steak with herb mash, crispy pork belly and a lemon and sage cream sauce, organic salmon and garlic king prawns on wilted chard and sunblush tomatoes, and venison loin steak with a swede fondant, wild mushrooms and bordelaise sauce. *Benchmark main dish: slow-braised lamb shank £14.95. Two-course evening meal £18.45.*

Free house ~ Licensee Ian Stephenson ~ Real ale ~ Bar food (12-2, 6-9) ~ Restaurant ~ (015394) 37215 ~ Children welcome ~ Dogs allowed in bar ~ Open 11-10.30(11 Fri and Sat); 12-10.30 Sun ~ Bedrooms: /£100B

Recommended by Tina and David Woods-Taylor, Mr and Mrs Maurice Thompson, Val Carter, John and Helen Rushton, Barry Collett, Ewan and Moira McCall, Ann Balmforth

LIVERPOOL Merseyside   SJ3589   Map 7

Philharmonic Dining Rooms ★ 🍺 £

36 Hope Street; corner of Hardman Street; L1 9BX

Beautifully preserved Victorian pub with superb period interior, ten real ales, and sensibly priced food

One reader told to us that 'superlatives cannot overrate' this spectacularly ornate Victorian former club that positively drips with period details. Its centrepiece is a mosaic-faced serving counter, from which heavily carved and polished mahogany partitions radiate under the intricately plasterworked high ceiling. The echoing main hall boasts stained glass depicting Boer War heroes Baden-Powell and Lord Roberts, rich panelling, a huge mosaic floor, and copper panels of musicians in an alcove above the fireplace. More stained glass in one of the little lounges declares 'Music is the universal language of mankind' and backs this up with illustrations of musical instruments. Two side rooms are called Brahms and Liszt, and there are two plushly comfortable sitting rooms. However, this is no museum piece and it can be very busy with ten handpumps as testament to a high turnover. As well as Cains Finest Bitter and Jennings Cumberland, up to eight changing guest ales might be from brewers such as Adnams, Caledonian Deuchars, Kelham Island and Sharps, and several malt whiskies; quiz machine, fruit machine and piped music. Don't miss the original 1890s Adamant gents' lavatory (all pink marble and mosaics); ladies are allowed a look if they ask first.

Reasonably priced food (available in the bar or in the table-service grand lounge dining room) includes pork and sage terrine, calamari, sandwiches, a range of recommended pies (including steak in ale), chicken and chorizo salad, sausage and mash, and rump steak. *Benchmark main dish: fish and chips £7.95. Two-course evening meal £12.20.*

Mitchells & Butlers ~ Manager Emma Mason ~ Real ale ~ Bar food (11-10) ~ Restaurant ~ (0151) 707 2837 ~ Children welcome until 7pm ~ Open 11am-midnight

Recommended by Ben Williams, Tony and Wendy Hobden, Eric Larkham, Rob and Catherine Dunster, Andy Lickfold, the Didler, Edward Mirzoeff, David Crook, Andrew Bosi, Ed and Anna Fraser

LONGRIDGE Lancashire   SD6038   Map 7

Derby Arms ♀

Chipping Road, Thornley; 1.5 miles N of Longridge on back road to Chipping; PR3 2NB

Welcoming, traditional country pub with hunting and fishing paraphernalia (and menu to match), and very decent wine list

This convivial old stone-built country pub has been run by the same charming family for nearly thirty years. Among hunting and fishing bric-a-brac in the main bar, old photographs commemorate notable catches and there's some nicely mounted bait above the comfortable red plush seats, together with a stuffed pheasant that seems to be flying in through the wall. To the right a smaller room has sporting trophies and mementoes, and a regimental tie collection; piped music and darts. The gents' has dozens of riddles on the wall – you can buy a sheet of them in the bar and the money goes to charity. Along with a particularly good range of wines, including several by the glass and half bottles, you'll find Black Sheep and a guest such as Moorhouses Pride of Pendle on handpump. A few tables out in front, and another two behind the car park, have fine views across to the Forest of Bowland, and there's a boules piste. The licensees put on lots of themed evenings – such as jazz, flamenco, cabaret, and game dinners.

They do lots of seasonal game here – maybe pheasant, hare, rabbit, partridge, woodcock, rabbit and mallard, as well as fresh fish and seafood. Other enjoyable food might include sandwiches, ploughman's, steak and kidney pudding, well hung steak, and home-baked fruit pies. *Benchmark main dish: roast duck £14.95. Two-course evening meal £15.00.*

Punch ~ Lease Will and Carole Walne ~ Real ale ~ Bar food (12-2.15, 6-9.30; 12-9.30 Sat, Sun) ~ Restaurant ~ (01772) 782623 ~ Children welcome ~ Open 12-3.30, 6-12; 12-12 Sat, Sun

Recommended by Margaret Dickinson, Maurice and Gill McMahon, Andy and Jill Kassube, Ed and Anna Fraser

LOWESWATER Cumbria   NY1421   Map 9

Kirkstile Inn 🍺 🛏

From B5289 follow signs to Loweswater Lake; OS Sheet 89 map reference 140210; CA13 0RU

Popular inn in lovely spot with busy bar, own-brewed beers and tasty bar food; bedrooms

As this country inn is between Loweswater and Crummock Water and has stunning views of the surrounding peaks and soaring fells, it's nearly always pretty packed out; you must book in advance to be sure of a table. The bustling main bar is low-beamed and carpeted with a friendly atmosphere, comfortably cushioned small settles and pews, partly stripped-stone walls, and a roaring log fire; there's a slate shove-ha'penny board. As well as their own-brewed Cumbrian Legendary Loweswater Gold, Grasmoor Dark Ale and Melbreak Bitter, they keep a guest like Yates Bitter on handpump; several wines by the glass. The fine view can be enjoyed from picnic-sets on the lawn, from the very attractive covered verandah in front of the building and from the bow windows in one of the rooms off the bar. There are marvellous surrounding walks of all levels, and maybe red squirrels in the garden.

 Well liked food includes lunchtime sandwiches and wraps, haggis and black pudding balls with whisky and onion marmalade, chicken, leek and chorizo pudding with brandy and black pepper sauce, meaty or spinach, ricotta, feta and roast vegetable lasagne, steak in ale pie, and moroccan-style salmon with a spicy tomato sauce. *Benchmark main dish: slow-cooked lamb shoulder £13.50. Two-course evening meal £15.75.*

Own brew ~ Licensee Roger Humphreys ~ Real ale ~ Bar food (12-2, 6-9) ~ Restaurant ~ (01900) 85219 ~ Children welcome ~ Dogs allowed in bar and bedrooms ~ Open 11-11 ~ Bedrooms: £62.50B/£97B

Recommended by JDM, KM, Roger and Kathy Elkin, Sylvia and Tony Birbeck, Val Carter, Geoff and Linda Payne, Simon Watkins, Alison Ball, Ian Walton, Chris Clark, Comus and Sarah Elliott, Maurice and Gill McMahon, the Didler, Mike and Sue Loseby, Adrian Johnson, John Wooll, Peter Smith and Judith Brown, Richard and Tanya Smith

---

LYTHAM Lancashire   SD3627   Map 7

Taps 🍺 £

A584 S of Blackpool; Henry Street – in centre, one street in from West Beach; FY8 5LE

Thriving seaside pub with down-to-earth atmosphere, spirited landlord, eight real ales, and straightforward lunchtime snacks; open all day

The Taps Best served here is brewed exclusively for this bustling town pub by Titanic and is served alongside Greene King IPA and an impressive choice of six ever-changing guests – you can see them lined up in the view-in cellar; also country wines and a farm cider. With a good mix of customers, the Victorian-style bare-boarded bar has a sociable unassuming feel, plenty of stained-glass decoration in the windows, depictions of fish and gulls reflecting the pub's proximity to the beach (it's a couple of minutes' walk away), captain's chairs in bays around the sides, open fires, and a coal-effect gas fire between two built-in bookcases at one end. The landlord is a rugby fan and displays his expanding collection of rugby memorabilia, old photographs and portraits of rugby stars on the walls; TV, shove-ha'penny, dominoes, quiz machine and fruit machine. There are a few seats and a heated canopied area outside. Parking is difficult near the pub so it's probably best to park at the West Beach car park on the seafront (free on Sunday) and walk.

A handful of cheap bar snacks includes sandwiches, soup, hot roast sandwich, filled baked potatoes, burgers, chilli and curry. *Benchmark main dish: soup and roast sandwich £4.95.*

Greene King ~ Manager Ian Rigg ~ Real ale ~ Bar food (12-2, not Sun) ~ No credit cards ~ (01253) 736226 ~ Children welcome till 7.30pm ~ Dogs welcome ~ Open 11-11(midnight Fri, Sat)

Recommended by G Jennings, Steve Whalley, the Didler

MACCLESFIELD Cheshire   SJ9271 Map 7

Sutton Hall ♈ ◀

Leaving Macclesfield southwards on A523, turn left into Byrons Lane signposted Langley, Wincle, then just before canal viaduct fork right into Bullocks Lane; OS Sheet 118 map reference 925715; SK11 0HE

Historic building set in attractive grounds; fine range of drinks and good food

You can't help but have the feeling of a special occasion at this rather splendid 16th-c manor house. The original hall that forms the heart of the building is beautifully impressive, particularly in its entrance space. Quite a series of delightful bar and dining areas, some divided by tall oak timbers have plenty of character with antique squared oak panelling, warmly coloured rugs on broad flagstones, boarded and tiled floors, frame-to-frame pictures and a raised open fire – all very Brunning & Price. Kind efficient staff serve five real ales including Flowers Original, Phoenix Brunning & Price Original, Wincle Lord Lucan and three guests from brewers such as Adnams, Storm and Titanic, plus several wines by the glass. The atmosphere has just enough formality, with bubbly staff and an enjoyable mix of customers from dog walkers up keeping it nicely relaxed. Pleasant gardens have good solid wood tables on terraces surrounded by a tree-sheltered lawn.

Bar food includes imaginative sandwiches, interestingly turned-out pub staples like ploughman's and beer-battered haddock, and more imaginative dishes such as salt fish pâté with baby capers and crisp poached egg, pigeon breast with madeira braised cabbage, roast pork belly with celeriac and pear gratin and mustard gravy, hake fillet poached in cockle broth with saffron potatoes, roast beetroot risotto with goats cheese and watercress, and rump steak with watercress and horseradish butter. *Benchmark main dish: beer-battered cod and chips £11.95. Two-course evening meal £21.00.*

Brunning & Price ~ Manager Syd Foster ~ Real ale ~ Bar food (12-10(9.30 Sun)) ~ (01260) 253211 ~ Children welcome ~ Dogs allowed in bar ~ Open 11.30-11; 12-10.30 Sun

Recommended by Bruce and Sharon Eden, Michael Butler, Maurice and Gill McMahon, Andy and Claire Barker, Dave Webster, Sue Holland, Brian and Anna Marsden

It's very helpful if you let us know up-to-date food prices when you report on pubs.

MARTON Cheshire   SJ8568   Map 7

Davenport Arms ◀

A34 N of Congleton; SK11 9HF

Handsome former 18th-c farmhouse with welcoming bar, comfortable restaurant, good food and drink, and good-sized sheltered garden

Two linked front bar rooms, with a third leading off on the left, have a good traditional feel, with their woodburning stove, ticking clock, comfortably cushioned wall settles, wing armchairs and other hand-picked furnishings on the patterned carpet, old prints on the cream walls, and colourful jugs hanging from sturdy beams. You can eat anywhere here (or just have a drink or coffee), and there are more formal dining areas behind, pleasantly light and airy; piped music. They have well kept Courage Directors, Theakstons Black Bull and a couple of guests such as Wentworth Hunt the Shunt and Wincle Waller on handpump, and staff are friendly and helpful. Outside is a terrace with metal garden furniture, a fairy-lit arbour, and a timber shelter, with well spaced picnic-sets and a set of swings in the garden beyond, and a substantial separate play area. For many years they have held one of Cheshire's major gooseberry shows here, on the first Saturday in August, and the 14th-c timbered church is well worth a look. They take caravans here but you must book.

Bar food includes filled baguettes, chicken caesar salad, parmesan breaded chicken, curry of the day, pork tenderloin wrapped in parma ham with black pudding bread and butter pudding with calvados cream sauce, mushroom ratatouille with melted brie, salmon fillet with salsa of cucumber, tomato and red onion, and steak in ale pie. *Benchmark main dish: fish and chips £12.50. Two-course evening meal £15.00.*

Free house ~ Licensees Ron Dalton and Sara Griffith ~ Real ale ~ Bar food (12-2.30, 6-9; 12-9 Sat; 12-8 Sun; not Mon) ~ Restaurant ~ (01260) 224269 ~ Children welcome ~ Dogs allowed in bar ~ Open 12-3, 6-11; 12-11 Fri-Sun; closed Mon lunchtime except bank holidays
Recommended by John Wooll, Pam and John Smith

MOBBERLEY Cheshire   SJ8179   Map 7

Plough & Flail ♀

Off B5085 Knutsford—Alderley Edge; at E end of village turn into Moss Lane, then left into Paddock Hill Lane (look out for small green signs to pub); WA16 7DB

Extensive family country dining pub, comfortable and well run, with enjoyable food, and plenty of outside tables

Such a spacious place comes as something of a surprise, as it's tucked away down narrow lanes. It's well laid out, with chunky cushioned dining chairs around sturdy stripped tables in the softly lit main area around the bar, which has low rustic beams, flagstones, and feels nicely up-to-date with its plain cream walls and bare panelled dado. Near the entrance, a handsomely floored side area has low sofas with scatter cushions, and sports TV. At the far end is a smaller second dining room, comfortable, light and airy, and a further conservatory dining room. They have a good choice of wines by the glass, and two guest beers such as Courage and Storm Bosley Cloud on handpump; attentive cheerful service, well reproduced nostalgic piped music. There are lots of teak tables out on heated flagstoned terraces at each end of the pub, with picnic-sets on neat lawns around the car park, and a robust play area.

🍴 Besides pubby favourites such as burgers and steaks, good more unusual but still pleasantly unpretentious food runs from light dishes such as fried pigeon breast with black pudding and pancetta on a croûton to massive sustenance for Cheshire horsemen such as a slow-cooked lamb shoulder plus a chop in mint jelly with red wine jus. *Benchmark main dish: battered haddock with marrowfat peas £12.75. Two-course evening meal £19.00.*

Deckers Hospitality Group ~ Manager Jose Lourenco ~ Real ale ~ Bar food (12-2.30, 6-9.30(10 Fri, Sat); 12-8 Sun) ~ (01565) 873537 ~ Children welcome ~ Open 12-11 (10.30 Sun)
Recommended by W K Wood, Helen Cobb

🏠 MOBBERLEY Cheshire   SJ7879 Map 7

GOOD PUB GUIDE **Roebuck** 🍴 ♀
Mill Lane; down hill from sharp bend on B5085 at E edge of 30mph limit; WA16 7HX

Stylishly simple country interior, warm welcome and very helpful service, good food, good wine list, courtyard and garden

Old tiled and boarded floors at this discerningly laid out airy place carry a comfortable mix of country furnishings, from cushioned long wood pews (rescued from a welsh chapel) to scrubbed pine farmhouse tables and a mix of old chairs. The wine list (well over a dozen by the glass) is short but well chosen and very reasonably priced, and beers are Black Sheep, Tetleys, Timothy Taylors Landlord and a guest from local Storm; piped music. Outside you'll find picnic sets on a cobbled courtyard, metal café furniture on a wooden deck, and picnic-sets in an enclosed well manicured beer garden.

🍴 Food is thoughtfully prepared and features traditional dishes with an appealing twist. As well as a short snack menu (they call it british tapas) and upmarket sandwiches (not evenings), dishes might include pigeon and roast shallot puff pastry pie with watercress and spinach purée, crab cakes with grilled chilli marinated prawns with tomato and coriander salsa, battered fish with mushy peas, provençale style fish stew with saffron potatoes and crisp air-dried ham, roast chicken breast with pea mousse, chorizo purée and mushroom tart, and ewe cheese and onion tart with rocket leaves, artichoke hearts, almonds and scorched cherry tomatoes. *Benchmark main dish: fish and chips £10.95. Two-course evening meal £18.60.*

Free house ~ Licensee Melissa Kanaris ~ Real ale ~ Bar food (12-2.30, 5-9, Sat 12-9.30; 12-8 Sun) ~ (01565) 873322 ~ Children welcome ~ Open 12-11(10.30 Sun)
Recommended by Neil and Karen Dignan, Mrs P J Carroll, Dr and Mrs A K Clarke, P J and R D Greaves, Hilary Forrest, John and Helen Rushton, Peter Webb

---

🏠 MUNGRISDALE Cumbria   NY3630 Map 10

GOOD PUB GUIDE **Mill Inn**
Off A66 Penrith—Keswick, 1 mile W of A5091 Ullswater turn-off; CA11 0XR

Bustling pub in fine setting with marvellous surrounding walks, real ales, home-cooked bar food and seats in garden; bedrooms

With the Glenderamakin river flowing below and the Blencathra Fell above, this 17th-c Lakeland inn is in a striking spot; there are lots of surrounding walks. The neatly kept bar has a wooden counter with an old millstone built into it, traditional dark wooden furnishings, hunting pictures on the walls, an open log fire in the stone fireplace and Robinsons Cumbria Way, Dizzy Blonde, Hartleys XB and a guest beer on handpump; there's a separate dining room and an upstairs residents' lounge. Darts, winter pool, bar billiards and dominoes. There are seats in the garden.

🍴 Tasty bar food includes lunchtime sandwiches, chicken liver pâté, italian-style prawns, cumberland sausages with onion gravy, a changing vegetarian dish, steak in ale pie, haddock mornay, and duck breast with honey and port. *Benchmark main dish: slow-cooked lamb shoulder £12.95. Two-course evening meal £14.95.*

Robinsons ~ Tenant Andrew Teasdale ~ Real ale ~ Bar food (12-2, 6-9; all day weekends) ~ Restaurant ~ (017687) 79632 ~ Children welcome ~ Dogs allowed in bar and bedrooms ~ Open 10am-1am(midnight Sun) ~ Bedrooms: £47.50S/£75S

Recommended by Noel Grundy, Dave Braisted, Geoff and Linda Payne, Comus and Sarah Elliott, James Morrell, J Buckby, John and Angie Millar

 NEAR SAWREY Cumbria — SD3795 Map 9

 # Tower Bank Arms 🍺

B5285 towards the Windermere ferry; LA22 0LF

Backing on to Beatrix Potter's farm, with well kept real ales, tasty bar food, and a friendly welcome; nice bedrooms

Our readers very much enjoy their visits to this friendly, well run inn, and staying overnight has come in for particularly warm praise this year; smashing breakfasts, too. The low-beamed main bar has plenty of rustic charm, seats on the rough slate floor, game and fowl pictures, a grandfather clock, a log fire and fresh flowers; there's also a separate restaurant. The three real ales on handpump and two tapped from the cask come from breweries like Barngates, Cumbrian Legendary, Hawkshead, Ulverston and Yates; several wines by the glass and a good choice of soft drinks; board games. There are pleasant views of the wooded Claife Heights from seats in the garden. It does get pretty crowded during the school holidays – especially in the summer. Many illustrations in the Beatrix Potter books can be traced back to their origins in this village – including the pub, which features in *The Tale of Jemima Puddleduck.*

🍴 Using locally sourced produce, the generous helpings of well liked food include lunchtime sandwiches, moules marinière, cumberland sausage with a rich onion gravy, vegetable wellington, beer-battered haddock, chicken breast stuffed with mozzarella, cherry tomatoes and basil, wrapped in air-dried ham with a tomato sauce, and slow-braised lamb shoulder with a mint and rosemary jus. *Benchmark main dish: beef in ale stew £11.50. Two-course evening meal £16.75.*

Free house ~ Licensee Anthony Hutton ~ Real ale ~ Bar food (12-2, 6-9(8 Sun, winter Mon-Thurs and bank holidays) ~ Restaurant ~ (015394) 36334 ~ Children welcome ~ Dogs allowed in bar and bedrooms ~ Open 11.30-11; 12-10.30 Sun; 11.30-2.30, 5.30-10.30 (11 weekends) weekdays in winter ~ Bedrooms: /£90S

Recommended by Michael Doswell, Adrian Johnson, Margaret Dickinson, Jayne Inman, Dave Braisted, David and Ruth Hollands

---

The price we give for a two-course evening meal in the featured top pub entries is the mean (average of cheapest and most expensive) price of a starter and a main course – no drinks.

 **NETHER ALDERLEY** Cheshire   SJ8576 Map 7

Wizard
Bradford Lane; SK10 4UE

Bustling dining pub on National Trust land with interesting food, real ales, a friendly welcome and relaxed atmosphere

Of course, most customers come to this well run dining pub to enjoy the particularly good food – but you will be made just as welcome if it's only a pint or a cup of coffee that you want. It's just a few minutes from Alderley Edge, a dramatic red sandstone escarpment with fine views and woodland walks, and there are seats and tables in the pub's sizeable back garden that are just right for a relaxing lunch afterwards. Inside, the various rooms are connected by open doorways and cleverly done up in a mix of modern rustic and traditional styles: beams and open fires, a happy mix of antique dining chairs (some prettily cushioned) and settles around all sorts of tables, rugs on pale wooden floorboards, prints and paintings on contemporary paintwork and items ranging from a grandfather clock to staffordshire dogs and modern lampshades; lovely fresh flowers and plants dotted about. Thwaites Wainwright and a guest from Storm on handpump, and several wines by the glass served by helpful, friendly staff.

Using locally sourced produce, the highly thought-of food includes spiced smoked haddock and shallot pie, beetroot cured smoked salmon with lime jelly and horseradish cream, ploughman's, fish plate, smoked eel, rocket and pea risotto, sausage, cheese mash and onion gravy, crispy pork belly with puy lentils and black pudding, seared chicken breast with chorizo, moroccan couscous salad and orange and cinnamon dressing, roast squash with chillies and pine nuts and tagliatelle with crème fraîche, lamb steak with mint butter, and steaks. *Benchmark main dish: steak and ale pie £12.50. Two-course evening meal £21.00.*

Free house ~ Licensee Dominic Gottelier ~ Real ale ~ Bar food (12-2, 7-9; 12-10 Sat, 12-7 Sun) ~ (01625) 584000 ~ Children welcome ~ Dogs welcome ~ Open 12-2, 5.30-11; 12-11 Sat; 12-10 Sun
Recommended by Richard Gibbs

NETHER BURROW Lancashire   SD6175 Map 7

Highwayman
A683 S of Kirkby Lonsdale; LA6 2RJ

Substantial and skilfully refurbished old stone house with country interior serving carefully sourced food; lovely gardens

Black and white wall prints and placemats show the characterful local farmers and producers (a map on the menu even locates these 'regional food heroes') that supply ingredients to this friendly and inviting pub. Although large, the stylishly simple flagstoned 17th-c interior is nicely divided into intimate corners, with a couple of big log fires and informal wooden furnishings. French windows open to a big terrace and lovely gardens. Local Thwaites Original and Lancaster Bomber and Wainwright are served on handpump, alongside good wines by the glass, just over a dozen whiskies and a particularly good range of soft drinks. They don't take bookings at the weekend (except for groups of six or more), but write your name on a blackboard when you arrive, and they'll find you when a table is free. Service is busy, welcoming and efficient.

🍴 As well as bar nibbles, imaginative sandwiches, ploughman's and some traditional lancastrian dishes, the menu might include ploughman's, scotch quail eggs with chicken and mushroom watercress mayonnaise and pickled white cabbage, warm salad of wood pigeon and black pudding and local bacon with cumberland sauce, scampi, twice-baked chestnut mushroom soufflé with mushroom crisp and mushroom cappuccino, battered haddock, devilled chicken breast, shepherd's pie, and well hung rump steak; they do just snacks in the afternoon; Sunday roasts. *Benchmark main dish: lancashire hotpot £10.50. Two-course evening meal £16.50.*

Thwaites ~ Lease Andy Morris and Craig Bancroft ~ Real ale ~ Bar food (12-8.30(9 Fri, Sat; 8 Sun)) ~ (01254) 826888 ~ Children welcome ~ Dogs allowed in bar ~ Open 12-11 (10.30 Sun)

Recommended by Noel Thomas, Liz Bell, Paul and Penny Dawson, Maurice and Gill McMahon, Karen Eliot, Brian and Janet Ainscough

PEOVER HEATH Cheshire   SJ7973   Map 7

Dog 🍺

Off A50 N of Holmes Chapel at the Whipping Stocks, keep on past Parkgate into Wellbank Lane; OS Sheet 118 map reference 794735; note that this village is called Peover Heath on the OS map and shown under that name on many road maps, but the pub is often listed under Over Peover instead; WA16 8UP

Homely pub with interesting range of beers and generously served food; bedrooms

What makes this unpretentious pub special is that it has a genuine local atmosphere, with its areas set aside for a drink, regular clientele, games room and very friendly welcome. Gently old fashioned and comfortably cottagey, the neatly kept bar has tied-back floral curtains at little windows, a curved cushioned banquette built into a bay window and mostly traditional dark wheelbacks arranged on a patterned carpet. A coal fire, copper pieces and pot plants add to the homely feel. The games room has darts, pool, a games machine, dominoes, board games and TV; piped music. Hydes (very good value at £2.30 a pint) and two beers from Weetwood are on handpump. They also have a good range of malt whiskies and wines by the glass. Friendly efficient staff cope well when it's busy. There are picnic-sets beneath colourful hanging baskets on the peaceful lane, and more out in a pretty back garden. It's a pleasant walk from here to the Jodrell Bank Centre and Arboretum.

🍴 As well as sandwiches, bar food might include fried squid and king prawns in garlic butter with coriander and watercress salad, confit of duck terrine with plum chutney and toasted brioche, steak and ale pie, braised lamb shank on roast garlic mash with rosemary pan gravy, fish pie, grilled tuna steak with soy, ginger and chilli sauce, and baby stuffed aubergine with tomato and basil sauce. *Benchmark main dish: cod and chips with mushy peas £12.50. Two-course evening meal £17.60.*

Free house ~ Licensee Steven Wrigley ~ Real ale ~ Bar food (12-2.30, 6-9; 12-8.30 Sun) ~ Restaurant ~ (01625) 861421 ~ Children welcome ~ Dogs allowed in bar ~ Open 11.30-3, 4.30-11.30; 11.30-midnight Sat; 12-11.30 Sun ~ Bedrooms: £60B/£80B

Recommended by John Cook, Sylvia and Tony Birbeck, S Bloomfield, Gerry and Rosemary Dobson, Brian and Janet Ainscough, Brian and Anna Marsden

---

We include some hotels with a good bar that offers facilities comparable to those of a pub.

PLEASINGTON Lancashire SD6528 Map 7

Clog & Billycock

Village signposted off A677 Preston New Road on W edge of Blackburn;
Billinge End Road; BB2 6QB

Carefully sourced local food in appealingly modernised stone-built village pub

Rumour has it that the name of this skilfully refurbished and extended village pub comes from the preferred attire of a former landlord. Light and airy with flagstoned floors and pale grey walls, in places it has the feel of an upmarket barn conversion. A cosier room has high-backed settles and a fireplace at the end. The whole pub is packed with light wooden tables, and although you may find them all full on arrival, such is the size of the place that you probably won't have to wait long in the little bar area for one to come free. The sheer volume of satisfied customers ensures a good, chatty atmosphere and service is polite and helpful. Drinks include well kept Thwaites Bomber and Original and Wainwright and a good choice of wines. There are some tables outside, beside a small garden.

Dishes here tend to be traditionally british, and the menu identifies many of their suppliers, some of whom can also be seen in photographs on the walls. Particularly good food includes well filled sandwiches, twice-baked cheese soufflé, cauliflower fritters with curried mayonnaise, fish pie, slow-cooked pork belly with garlic mash, cheese and onion pie, lancashire hotpot, and well hung steak. There's a snack menu during the afternoon. *Benchmark main dish: fish pie £10.75. Two-course evening meal £16.50.*

Thwaites ~ Lease Andy Morris and Craig Bancroft ~ Real ale ~ Bar food (12-9 (8.30 Sun)) ~ (01254) 201163 ~ Children welcome ~ Dogs allowed in bar ~ Open 12-11(10.30 Sun)
Recommended by RJH, Karen Eliot, Steve Whalley, W K Wood, Alex Blyth, Ed and Anna Fraser

PLUMLEY Cheshire SJ7075 Map 7

Smoker

2.5 miles from M6 junction 19: A556 towards Northwich and Chester;
WA16 0TY

Spotless comfortable lounges and a breakfast menu; handy for M6

Tucked in among the military prints you'll find a rather delightful Edwardian print of a hunt meeting outside this neatly kept 400-year-old thatched coaching inn. It shows how little it has changed over the years. Popular with an older set, its three connecting rooms have dark panelling, open fires in impressive period fireplaces, deep sofas, other comfortable seats and settles, and a sweet collection of copper kettles; piped music. Particularly kind staff serve five Robinsons beers from handpumps and they've a good choice of wines and whiskies. The sizeable garden has roses, flower beds and a children's play area.

Breakfast is served till midday, followed by sandwiches, potted shrimps, tempura king prawns, black pudding fritter with crispy pancetta and poached egg, fishcakes with lemon mayonnaise, red thai chicken curry, lamb marinated with mint and herbs, fried lambs liver with fried onions and crispy pancetta, and fried salmon and scallops with chilli and ginger. *Benchmark main dish: steak braised in red wine with mushrooms £10.95. Two-course evening meal £18.00.*

Robinsons ~ Tenants John and Diana Bailey ~ Real ale ~ Bar food (10-2.15, 6-9.15; 10-9

Sun) ~ Restaurant ~ (01565) 722338 ~ Children welcome away from bar ~ Open 10-3,
6-11; 10am-10.30pm Sun

Recommended by Peter Webb, John and Helen Rushton, David and Sue Atkinson, Clive Watkin,
Gordon and Margaret Ormondroyd, Lesley and Peter Barrett, Andy Dolan

 RAVENSTONEDALE Cumbria   NY7203   Map 10

Black Swan

Just off A685 SW of Kirkby Stephen; CA17 4NG

Bustling hotel with thriving bar, several real ales, enjoyable food, and
good surrounding walks; bedrooms

This smart, family-run Victorian hotel is a fine place for a break when
crossing from North Yorkshire to Cumbria – though you may want to
stay overnight in the comfortable bedrooms; it's in a charming peaceful
village and surrounded by lots of good walks (the inn has leaflets
describing the walks and their lengths). There's a friendly atmosphere
and plenty of original period features and the thriving U-shaped bar has
stripped-stone walls, plush bar stools by the bar counter, a comfortable
green button-back banquette, various dining chairs and little plush stools
around a mix of tables, and fresh flowers. Black Sheep Ale and Bitter,
John Smiths, and three changing guests from Hesket Newmarket or Tirril
on handpump, eight wines by the glass, 25 malt whiskies and a good
choice of fruit juices and pressés; piped music, TV, darts, board games,
and newspapers and magazines to read. Service is genuinely friendly and
helpful. There are picnic-sets in the tree-sheltered streamside garden over
the road; they also run the village store with outside café seating.

Using seasonal, local produce, the highly thought-of food might include
sandwiches, various nibbles, terrine of smoked trout, mackerel and salmon
with horseradish and home-made bread, black pudding in a creamy pepper sauce
with sautéed apple and crispy bacon, beer-battered fresh haddock, tasty chicken or
vegetable curry, slow-cooked beef in Guinness, and specials like scallops with a
butternut squash purée and crispy pancetta, and lamb cutlets on a mushroom and
potato rösti with parsnip crisps and madeira syrup. *Benchmark main dish: slow-*
roasted pork belly £12.95. Two-course evening meal £16.75.

Free house ~ Licensees Louise and Alan Dinnes ~ Real ale ~ Bar food (12-2, 6-9 but
some sort of food all day) ~ Restaurant ~ (015396) 23204 ~ Children welcome ~ Dogs
allowed in bar and bedrooms ~ Live music monthly (phone to check) ~ Open 8am-
midnight(1am Sat) ~ Bedrooms: £50B/£75B

Recommended by Noel Thomas, David Heath, Liz Bell, Lesley and Peter Barrett, Dr Kevan Tucker,
Andy and Jill Kassube, C Cooper

 SANDBACH Cheshire   SJ7560   Map 7

Old Hall

1.2 miles from M6 junction 17: A534 into town, then right into High Street;
CW11 1AL

Stunning mid-17th-c hall house with wonderful original features, plenty
of drinking and dining space, interesting décor, six real ales, imaginative
food, and seats outside

Opened just as we went to press, this is a magnificent Grade I listed
manor house with wonderful timbering and fine carved gable-ends.
Brunning & Price spent two years restoring the abandoned building which

English Heritage had on their 'buildings at risk' register as category A. There are many lovely original features – particularly in the room to the left of the entrance hall which is much as it has been for centuries with a Jacobean fireplace, oak panelling and priest's hole. This leads into the Oak Room with standing timbers creating two dining rooms – heavy beams, oak flooring and reclaimed panelling. Other rooms in the original building have more hefty beams and oak boards and there are three open fires and a woodburning stove; the cosy snugs are carpeted. The newly built Garden Room is big and bright with reclaimed quarry tiling and exposed A-frame oak timbering and opens onto the suntrap back terrace with teak tables and chairs among flowering tubs. Throughout, the walls are covered with countless interesting prints, there's a happy mix of antique dining chairs and tables of all sizes, and plenty of rugs, bookcases and plants. From the handsome bar counter they serve a beer named for them from Phoenix, Beartown Kodiak Gold, Storm Silk of Amnesia, Thornbridge Kipling, Three Tuns XXX, and Wincle Sir Philip on handpump, 15 good wines by the glass and 40 malt whiskies. There are picnic-sets in front of the building by rose bushes and clipped box hedging.

🍴 Enjoyable food includes sandwiches, avocado, crème fraîche and chilli panna cotta with black olive tapenade, potted salmon, smoked mackerel and trout with pickled vegetables, pork sausages with red wine and onion gravy, sweet potato, red pepper and dolcelatte filo pie with spinach and fennel salad, malaysian chicken curry, fish pie, and rose veal with sage, spinach and lemon tagliatelle. *Benchmark main dish: braised lamb shoulder with crushed potatoes and tarragon £16.95. Two-course evening meal £17.75.*

Brunning & Price ~ Manager Chris Button ~ Real ale ~ Bar food (12-10(9.30 Sun) ~ (01270) 758170 ~ Children welcome ~ Dogs allowed in bar ~ Open 11.30-11; 12-10.30 Sun
Recommended by Richard Gibbs

SPURSTOW Cheshire   SJ5657   Map 7

Yew Tree ★ 🍴 ♀ 🍺

Off A49 S of Tarporley; follow Bunbury 1, Haughton 2 signpost into Long Lane; CW6 9RD

Great place, a top-notch all-rounder with a good deal of individuality and plenty of bounce

Giant bees swarming on the bar ceiling sum up the thriving bustle of this cheerful pub, and other witty decorative touches include panels of most unexpected wallpaper – hugely magnified hunting print, or tartans in variety. It's all been kept nicely simple, though, with terracotta tiles or bare boards, uncluttered pale grey or off-white paintwork, and a log fire in the raised fireplace. The island bar has well kept and sensibly priced ales such as Acorn Blonde, Adnams, Merlins Gold, Moorhouses Black Cat and Stonehouse Station on handpump, a beer of the month (on our visit Gorlovka, a mind-blasting bottle-conditioned Imperial Stout from Barnsley), a local cider, and a good range of wines by the glass from an interesting bin ends list of about 50. The informal service is quick even when they are busy. A more dining-oriented area spreads off, sharing the same feeling of relaxed bonhomie (our favourite table there was the one snugged into a stable-stall-style alcove of stripped wood). A terrace outside has teak tables, with more on the grass beside it.

🍴 A quickly changing menu might include duck and pistachio terrine, crab tian with lemon and chervil mayonnaise, seared bass fillet with saffron mash, asparagus and dill sabayon and duck breast with dauphinoise potatoes, oyster mushroom and pepper sauce; they also do sausage and mash, fish and chips or a vegetarian dish, with a pint or a glass of wine, for £10. *Benchmark main dish: fish pie £11.95. Two-course evening meal £19.00.*

Free house ~ Licensees Jon and Lindsay Cox ~ Real ale ~ Bar food (12-2.30, 6-9.30 (10 Fri); 12-10 Sat; 12-8 Sun) ~ (01829) 260274 ~ Well behaved children welcome ~ Dogs allowed in bar ~ Open 12-11(10.30 Sun)

Recommended by Alun Jones

 STAVELEY Cumbria   SD4797   Map 9

Eagle & Child

Kendal Road; just off A591 Windermere—Kendal; LA8 9LP

Welcoming inn with warming log fires, a good range of local beers and enjoyable food; bedrooms

With comfortable bedrooms and hearty breakfasts, this little inn is just right as a base for those exploring the area; there are plenty of surrounding walks (the pub is on the Dales Way). There's a welcoming fire under an impressive mantelbeam, a friendly, bustling atmosphere, and a roughly L-shaped flagstoned main area with plenty of separate parts to sit in, furnished with pews, banquettes, bow window seats and high-backed dining chairs around polished dark tables. Also, police truncheons and walking sticks, some nice photographs and interesting prints, a few farm tools, a delft shelf of bric-a-brac and another log fire. The five real ales on handpump come from breweries such as Caledonian Deuchars IPA, Coniston Bluebird, Cumbrian Legendary Grasmoor Dark Ale, Hawkshead Bitter and Yates Bitter on handpump, several wines by the glass, 30 malt whiskies and farm cider; piped music and board games. An upstairs barn-theme dining room (with its own bar for functions and so forth) doubles as a breakfast room. There are picnic-sets under cocktail parasols in a sheltered garden by the River Kent, with more on a good-sized back terrace and a second garden behind.

Fair value, generous helpings of tasty food include sandwiches, chicken and port pâté, Guinness pancakes filled with bacon and cheese, vegetarian shepherd's pie, local cumberland sausages with red wine and caramelised onion gravy, steak in ale pie, chicken wrapped in smoked bacon with barbecue sauce and a cheese topping, and changing fresh fish dishes. *Benchmark main dish: cumberland hotpot £9.95. Two-course evening meal £16.95.*

Free house ~ Licensees Richard and Denise Coleman ~ Real ale ~ Bar food (12-2.30, 6-9) ~ Restaurant ~ (01539) 821320 ~ Children welcome ~ Dogs allowed in bar ~ Open 12-2.30, 6-9 ~ Bedrooms: £50S/£70S

Recommended by Chris Evans, Bob Broadhurst, Dennis Jones, Ann and Tony Bennett-Hughes, the Didler, Joe Green, Dr Kevan Tucker, John and Helen Rushton, Steve and Sue Griffiths

 TALKIN Cumbria   NY5457   Map 10

Blacksmiths Arms ♀ 🛏

Village signposted from B6413 S of Brampton; CA8 1LE

Neatly kept and welcoming with tasty bar food, several real ales, and good surrounding walks; bedrooms

Run by genuinely friendly licensees, this former blacksmith's has plenty of walks from the door or just a short drive away; it's a quiet and comfortable place to stay. There are several neatly kept, traditionally furnished rooms and the warm lounge on the right has a log fire, upholstered banquettes and wheelback chairs around dark wooden tables on the patterned red carpeting, and country prints and other pictures on the walls. The restaurant is to the left, there's a long lounge opposite the bar, and another room up a couple of steps at the back. Cumberland Corby Ale, Geltsdale Brampton Bitter and Cold Fell and Yates Bitter on handpump, 20 wines by the glass and 30 malt whiskies; piped music, darts and board games. There are a couple of picnic-sets outside the front door with more in the back garden.

Reliable, pubby food includes lunchtime sandwiches, creamy garlic mushrooms, vegetable curry, lasagne, sweet and sour chicken, beer-battered haddock, beef stroganoff, and specials like black pudding topped with wholegrain mustard, bacon and cheese sauce, liver, bacon and onion casserole, and duck breast in a port and plum sauce. *Benchmark main dish: steak and kidney pie £8.25. Two-course evening meal £16.50.*

Free house ~ Licensees Donald and Anne Jackson ~ Real ale ~ Bar food (12-2, 6-9) ~ Restaurant ~ (016977) 3452 ~ Children welcome ~ Open 12-3, 6-11 ~ Bedrooms: £50S/£70S

Recommended by Dr and Mrs Leach, Maurice and Gill McMahon, Dr Peter D Smart, David and Katharine Cooke

TARPORLEY Cheshire   SJ5562   Map 7

Rising Sun £
High Street; village signposted off A51 Nantwich—Chester; CW6 0DX

Friendly, bustling and quaint, with pubby food

Run by the same family for over 25 years, this brick-fronted old place is charmingly friendly and down-to-earth. The low-ceilinged characterful interior is prettily furnished with eye-catching old seats and tables, including creaky 19th-c mahogany and oak settles and features an attractively blacked iron kitchen range. Sporting and other old-fashioned prints decorate the walls. Accommodating staff serve Robinsons Dizzy Blonde, Unicorn and a seasonal ale from handpumps. There are one or two seats and a TV for sporting events in a tiny side bar; piped music. More reports please.

A good range of reasonably priced bar food includes dim sum, smoked fish platter, spicy chicken wings, lots of pies, poached chicken breast with leek and stilton sauce, fruity beef curry, spinach pancake, rack of lamb, and a good range of steaks. *Benchmark main dish: fish and chips £7.10. Two-course evening meal £13.50.*

Robinsons ~ Tenant Alec Robertson ~ Real ale ~ Bar food (12-2, 7-9; 12-9 Sat, Sun) ~ Restaurant (evening) ~ (01829) 732423 ~ Children welcome away from public bar ~ Open 11.30-3, 5.30-11; 11.30-11 Sat; 12-10.30 Sun

Recommended by the Didler, Alistair Stanier, P J and R D Greaves, Don Bryan

---

Real ale to us means beer that has matured naturally in its cask – not pressurised or filtered. We name all real ales stocked. We usually name ales preserved under a light blanket of carbon dioxide too, though purists – pointing out that this stops the natural yeasts developing – would disagree (most people, including us, can't tell the difference!).

THRELKELD Cumbria   NY3225   Map 9

Horse & Farrier ◀ £

A66 Penrith—Keswick; CA12 4SQ

Well run 17th-c fell-foot dining pub with good food and drinks; bedrooms

Even if you are a bedraggled walker or cyclist, you can be sure of a warm welcome in this attractive 17th-c inn. The neat, mainly carpeted bar has sturdy farmhouse and other nice tables, seats from comfortably padded ones to pubby chairs and from stools to bigger housekeeper's chairs and wall settles, country pictures on its white walls, one or two stripped beams and some flagstones; several open fires. Jennings Bitter, Cocker Hoop, Cumberland and Sneck Lifter on handpump and several wines by the glass; friendly, efficient service. The partly stripped-stone restaurant is smart and more formal, with quite close-set tables. There are a few picnic-sets outside. If you plan to stay, the rooms in the inn itself are the best bet. The views towards Helvellyn range are stunning and there are walks straight from the door. Good disabled access and facilities.

Good value bar food (which is what our Value Award is for) includes lunchtime sandwiches, a curry of the day, steak and kidney pie, mediterranean vegetable lasagne, and gammon with fresh pineapple with more elaborate (and pricey) restaurant choices such as chicken breast stuffed with gruyère and wrapped in bacon on fennel risotto and a mushroom, garlic and creamy white wine sauce, and slow-roasted belly pork on grain mustard mash and an apple, sage and spring onion sauce; they also offer breakfasts to non-residents and afternoon tea. *Benchmark main dish: slow-braised lamb shoulder £14.35. Two-course evening meal £19.00.*

Jennings (Marstons) ~ Lease Ian Court ~ Real ale ~ Bar food (12-9) ~ Restaurant ~ (017687) 79688 ~ Children welcome ~ Dogs allowed in bar and bedrooms ~ Open 7.30am-midnight ~ Bedrooms: £50B/£80B

Recommended by Tina and David Woods-Taylor, Geoff and Linda Payne, Dominic McGonigal, Maurice and Gill McMahon, James Morrell, Phil Bryant, Adele Summers, Alan Black

TIRRIL Cumbria   NY5026   Map 10

Queens Head

B5320, not far from M6 junction 40; CA10 2JF

18th-c Lakeland pub with several bars, real ales, speciality pies, and seats outside; bedrooms

The oldest parts of the main bar in this busy old inn have low beams, black panelling, original flagstones and floorboards, and there are nice little tables and chairs on either side of the inglenook fireplace (always lit in winter). Another bar to the right of the door has pews and chairs around sizeable tables on the wooden floor and candles in the fireplace, and the back locals' bar has heavy beams and a pool table; there are two dining rooms as well. Robinsons Dizzy Blonde, Hatters, Old Stockport and Unicorn on handpump and several wines by the glass. At the front of the building are some picnic-sets, with modern chairs and tables under covering on the back terrace. They also run the village shop. The pub is very close to a number of interesting places, such as Dalemain House at Dacre, and is just 2.5 miles from Ullswater.

As well as lunchtime sandwiches and popular pies made by their sister company, the Pie Mill, the bar food might include chicken liver pâté with cumberland sauce, creamy garlic mushrooms and crispy bacon, a curry of the day, roasted mediterranean vegetable lasagne, local cumberland sausage, salmon fillet with parsley butter, and chicken breast with a mushroom, fresh tarragon, white wine and cream sauce. *Benchmark main dish: home-made pies £8.95.*

Robinsons ~ Tenants Margaret and Jim Hodge ~ Bar food (12-2.30, 5.30-8.30) ~ Restaurant ~ (01768) 863219 ~ Children welcome ~ Dogs allowed in bar and bedrooms ~ Open 12-11; 12-10.30 Sun ~ Bedrooms: /£70B

Recommended by Richard Gibbs

TORVER Cumbria   SD2894   Map 10

Church House 🍴 ♀

A593/A5084 S of Coniston; LA21 8AZ

Rambling coaching inn with bustling bar, interesting food, five real ales, and seats in a neat garden with fine views; bedrooms

Just a short walk from Coniston Lake and in the shadow of Coniston Old Man, this rambling 14th-c coaching house has seats in a big garden with splendid hill views. Inside, the bar has a pubby atmosphere, heavy beams, built-in wall seats and stools around plain tables on the slate flooring, a fine log fire in a sizeable stone fireplace, bits and pieces of Lakeland bric-a-brac and a bar made from polished wooden barrels. Barngates Tag Lag, Copper Dragon Golden Pippin, Cumbrian Legendary Loweswater Gold, Hawkshead Lakeland Gold, and a guest beer on handpump, several wines by the glass and quite a few malt whiskies; friendly staff. There's also a comfortable lounge and a separate yellow-walled dining room; the jack russell terrier, Molly, loves catching beer mats. As well as bedrooms, they have hard standing for six caravans.

Using local produce, the changing food might include sandwiches, chicken liver parfait with red onion marmalade, seared scallops and crispy pork belly with a celeriac and apple purée, red wine and star anise dressing and spring onion oil, lentil, mushroom and aubergine lasagne, steamed steak and kidney in ale pudding, beer-battered haddock, and a proper cassoulet. *Benchmark main dish: cumbrian hotpot £13.75. Two-course evening meal £19.30.*

Enterprise ~ Lease Mike and Mandy Beaty ~ Real ale ~ Bar food (12-3, 6-9) ~ Restaurant ~ (015394) 41282 ~ Children welcome ~ Dogs allowed in bar and bedrooms ~ Open 12-12 ~ Bedrooms: £45S/£70S

Recommended by Dennis Jones, John and Hilary Penny, JCW, Jon Quirk

---

TROUTBECK Cumbria   NY4103   Map 9

Queens Head 🍴 ♀ 🍺 🛏

A592 N of Windermere; LA23 1PW

Civilised inn with several rambling rooms, interesting food, quite a few real ales, and friendly staff; comfortable bedrooms

Right at the heart of Lakeland, this is a gently upmarket and extended old coaching inn with a lot of character. It's a fine place to stay, they keep seven real ales and the food is extremely good. The big rambling, original U-shaped bar has a very nice mix of old cushioned settles and mate's chairs around some sizeable tables, beams and flagstones and a log fire in the raised stone fireplace with horse harness and so forth on either side of it; there's also a coal fire, some trumpets, cornets and saxophones on one wall with country pictures on others, stuffed pheasants in a big glass case, and a stag's head with a tie around his neck. A massive Elizabethan four-poster bed is the basis of the finely carved counter where they serve Robinsons Cumbrian Way, Dizzy Blonde, Double Hop, Hannibals Nectar, Hartleys XB, Old Tom and Unicorn on handpump and eight wines by the glass. Other dining rooms are decorated similarly to the main bar, with oak beams and stone walls, settles along big tables, and one has an open fire; piped music. Seats outside have a fine view over the Troutbeck Valley to Applethwaite Moors. The highly thought-of bedrooms are in the inn itself or in the carefully transformed barn opposite.

Imaginative – if not particularly cheap – food includes nibbles, filled baguettes (up until 6pm), a trio of pork (pressed and potted ham hock with apple and calvados purée, roasted confit of honeyed belly pork and szechuan-style pork parcel with satay sauce), home-made black pudding with sautéed scallops, a drizzle of mustard sauce and topped with crispy streaky smoked bacon, moules thai-style or marinière, sausages of the day with crispy onion rings and home-made gravy, venison and Guinness cottage pie with a red berry compote, and bobotie (a delicious south african dish). *Benchmark main dish: creamy fish pie with tempura green beans and home-made tartare sauce £13.95. Two-course evening meal £21.45.*

Robinsons ~ Lease Ian and Anette Dutton ~ Real ale ~ Bar food (12-9(10 Fri and Sat) ~ Restaurant ~ (015394) 32174 ~ Children welcome ~ Dogs allowed in bar ~ Open 10am-midnight ~ Bedrooms: /£120B

Recommended by Peter and Josie Fawcett, Martin Smith, Hugh Roberts, Adrian Johnson, Lesley and Peter Barrett

TUNSTALL Lancashire   SD6073   Map 7

Lunesdale Arms ⦿ ♀

A683 S of Kirkby Lonsdale; LA6 2QN

Civilised pub with emphasis on good imaginative food; separate area with traditional games

The light and airy opened-up interior of this bustling dining pub has bare boards and a lively acoustic that gives it a cheery buzz. A white-walled area has a good mix of stripped dining tables and blue sofas facing each other across a low table (with daily papers) by a woodburning stove in a solid stone fireplace. Another area has pews and armchairs (some of the big unframed oil paintings are for sale) and to one end, an airy games section with pool, table football, board games and TV. A snugger little flagstoned back part has another woodburning stove. Black Sheep and a couple of local guests from brewers such as Brysons are on handpump alongside a farm cider; table football. The church in this Lune Valley village has Brontë associations.

Real care goes into the food here which is prepared using locally sourced ingredients and home-grown herbs and vegetables. They make their own bread and have their own blend of coffee. The seasonally changing menu might include shallot tart with goats cheese, mezze to share, tiger prawn and smoked salmon salad with dill and chervil dressing, steak and kidney pie, pork loin chop on crushed carrot and celeriac with sausage stuffing, battered haddock, ginger sponge with poached rhubarb and orange crème brûlée. *Benchmark main dish: burger and chips £11.00. Two-course evening meal £15.50.*

Free house ~ Licensee Emma Gillibrand ~ Real ale ~ Bar food (12-2(2.30 Sat, Sun, bank holidays), 6-9) ~ (01524) 274203 ~ Children welcome ~ Dogs welcome ~ Pianist some Thurs evenings ~ Open 11-3.30, 6-midnight; closed Mon except bank holidays
Recommended by Mr and Mrs D Mackenzie, Malcolm and Pauline Pellatt, Dr Kevan Tucker

ULVERSTON Cumbria   SD3177   Map 7

Bay Horse ♀ ⇌

Canal Foot signposted off A590 and then you wend your way past the huge Glaxo factory; LA12 9EL

Civilised waterside hotel with lunchtime bar food, three real ales and a fine choice of wines; smart bedrooms

Lunchtime is when this civilised hotel – on the water's edge of the Leven Estuary – is at its most informal. The bar has a relaxed atmosphere despite its smart furnishings: attractive wooden armchairs, some pale green plush built-in wall banquettes, glossy hardwood traditional tables, blue plates on a delft shelf, a huge stone horse's head, and black beams and props with lots of horsebrasses. Magazines are dotted about, there's an open fire in the handsomely marbled grey slate fireplace and decently reproduced piped music; board games. Jennings Cross Buttocks, Cumberland and Golden Host on handpump, 16 by the glass (including champagne and prosecco) from a carefully chosen and interesting wine list and several malt whiskies. The conservatory restaurant has fine views over Morecambe Bay (as do the bedrooms) and there are some seats out on the terrace.

Good lunchtime bar food includes interesting sandwiches, chicken liver pâté with cranberry and ginger purée, chilli prawns on a sweet and sour sauce, pasta with leeks, basil and asparagus in a light cream sauce, lambs liver with black and white puddings on a madeira sauce, poached smoked haddock on a mushroom and onion pâté and a wine and herb sauce, smoked pork cutlet on an apple and stilton cream, and steak and kidney pie. *Benchmark main dish: home-made corned beef £18.00. Two-course evening meal £25.00.*

Free house ~ Licensee Robert Lyons ~ Real ale ~ Bar food (12-3(2 Mon, 4 weekends); one evening restaurant sitting 7.30-8pm; no bar food evenings) ~ Restaurant ~ (01229) 583972 ~ Children welcome but must be over 9 in bedrooms or in evening ~ Dogs allowed in bar and bedrooms ~ Open 11-11; 12-10.30 Sun ~ Bedrooms: $80B/$120B
Recommended by John and Sylvia Harrop, Henry Midwinter, V and E A Bolton, Peter Salmon

UPPERMILL Lancashire   SD0006   Map 7

Church Inn ◀ £

From the main street (A607), look out for the sign for Saddleworth Church, and turn off up this steep narrow lane – keep on up! OL3 6LW

Lively good value community pub with big range of own-brew beers, lots of pets, and good food; children very welcome

The burgeoning menagerie of animals at this enjoyably quirky pub, high up on the moors, and with fine views down the valley includes rabbits, chickens, dogs, ducks, geese, alpacas, horses, 14 peacocks in the next-door field and some cats resident in an adjacent barn. The big unspoilt L-shaped main bar has high beams and some stripped stone, settles, pews, a good individual mix of chairs, and lots of attractive prints and staffordshire and other china on a high delft shelf, jugs, brasses and so forth; TV (only when there's sport on) and unobtrusive piped music; the conservatory opens on to a terrace. The horse-collar on the wall is worn by the winner of their annual gurning (face-pulling) championship which is held during the lively traditional Rush Cart Festival, which is usually over the August bank holiday. Local bellringers arrive on Wednesdays to practise with a set of handbells that are kept here, while anyone is invited to join the morris dancers who meet here on Thursdays. When the spring water levels aren't high enough for brewing, they bring in guest beers such as Black Sheep and Hydes Jekylls Gold. At other times, you might find up to 11 of their own-brew Saddleworth beers, starting at just £1.70 a pint. Some of the seasonal ones (look out for Ruebens, Ayrtons, Robyns and Indya) are named after the licensee's children, only appearing around their birthdays; dark lager on tap, too. Children and dogs are made to feel very welcome.

Very reasonably priced bar food includes soup, sandwiches, steak and ale pie, jumbo cod, a range of pies, and mixed grill. *Benchmark main dish: cod and chips £9.75. Two-course evening meal £11.80.*

Own brew ~ Licensee Christine Taylor ~ Real ale ~ Bar food (12-2.30, 5.30-9; 12-9 Sat, Sun and bank holidays) ~ Restaurant ~ (01457) 820902 ~ Children welcome ~ Dogs allowed in bar ~ Open 12-12(1am Sat)
Recommended by Ben Williams, the Didler, John Fiander, Roger and Lesley Everett, Bob Broadhurst

WADDINGTON Lancashire   SD7243   Map 7

Lower Buck £
Edisford Road; BB7 3HU

Hospitable village pub with reasonably priced, tasty food; five real ales

Readers enjoy the gently relaxing atmosphere at this pretty 18th-c village pub which is handily placed for walks in the Ribble Valley. It's split into several little neatly kept cream-painted bars and dining rooms, each with a warming coal fire and good solid wood furnishings on new wood floors. Staff and other customers are chatty and welcoming; darts and pool; two dining rooms. The friendly landlord keeps a range of five ales, usually Bowland Hen Harrier, Moorhouses Premier and guests such as Bowland Sky Dancer, over a dozen malts and several wines by the glass. There are picnic-sets out on cobbles at the front and in the sunny back garden.

Using meat reared at a farm in nearby Longridge and vegetables grown in Longridge too, the reasonably priced tasty food includes lunchtime sandwiches and ploughman's, duck breast terrine, potted morecambe bay shrimps, lancashire cheese and onion pie, lancashire hotpot, fish and chips, and grilled chicken breast marinated in garlic, lemon and herbs with garlic mayonnaise. *Benchmark main dish: steak and mushroom pie £10.25. Two-course evening meal £15.90.*

Free house ~ Licensee Andrew Warburton ~ Real ale ~ Bar food (12-2.30, 6-9; 12-9 Sat, Sun and bank holidays) ~ (01200) 423342 ~ Children welcome ~ Dogs welcome ~ Open 11(12 Sun)-11(midnight Sat)
Recommended by Roger and Donna Huggins, Lucien Perring, Ed and Anna Fraser

A few pubs try to make you leave a credit card at the bar, as a sort of deposit if you order food. This is a bad practice, and the banks and credit card firms warn you not to hand over your card like this.

WADDINGTON Lancashire

SD7243 Map 7

Waddington Arms ★ ♀ ◗ ⇌

Clitheroe Road (B6478 N of Clitheroe); BB7 3HP

Classic *Guide* pub, good all round, with plenty of character, cheerful landlord, good value bedrooms – and open all day

This lovely place has four linked rooms, the one on the left is snuggest in winter, with its blazing woodburning stove in a monumental fireplace putting real warmth into the ancient flagstones. There's plenty to look at in the various low-beamed rooms, from antique prints through an interesting series of vintage motor-racing posters to the contemporary Laurie Williamson prints over on the right – and some intriguing wallpaper (an enlarged 19th-c sporting print here, leather-bound books there). The furniture too gives the feeling that it's all been carefully chosen and thought through, with some fine antique oak settles as well as chunky stripped-pine tables. They have a good choice of wines by the glass, an ale Moorhouses brew for them (The Waddy), and other well kept ales on handpump such as Goose Eye and Grays Best; the helpful and welcoming landlord ensures a friendly easy-going atmosphere. Wicker chairs on a sunny flagstoned front terrace look across to this attractive village's church (it's just on the edge of the Forest of Bowland, too), and there are more tables on a two-level back terrace, with picnic-sets on a neat tree-sheltered lawn.

Besides generous sandwiches, enjoyable country cooking here includes light dishes such as nourishing soups, duck confit or black pudding and poached egg, as well as robust main courses like sausage and mash, steak and ale pie, fried bass with spring vegetables, hotpot, and steaks. *Benchmark main dish: lancashire hotpot £10.95. Two-course evening meal £16.50.*

Free house ~ Real ale ~ Bar food (12-2, 7-9.30; 12-9.30 Sat, Sun) ~ (01200) 423262 ~ Children welcome ~ Dogs allowed in bar ~ Open 11-12 ~ Bedrooms: /£65B
Recommended by Philip and Helen Temperley, Steve Whalley

WHEATLEY LANE Lancashire

SD8338 Map 7

Sparrowhawk

Wheatley Lane Road; towards E end of village road which runs N of and parallel to A6068; one way of reaching it is to follow Fence, Newchurch 1¾ signpost, then turn off at Barrowford ¾ signpost; BB12 9QG

Comfortably civilised pub, with well prepared food and five real ales

Smart young waitresses work their way through the attractively laid out areas of this imposing black and white pub. The interior has quite a 1930s feel with its quirky domed stained-glass skylight, parquet flooring, oak panelling, leather tub chairs and red floor tiles; daily papers. The cushioned leatherette bar counter (cheerful with fresh flowers) serves Bass, Greene King IPA, Thwaites Original, a couple of guests such as Bank Top Flat Cap and Pavillion on handpump, draught Fransizkaner wheat beer and good wines by the glass. TV, piped music and board games. Heavy wood tables out on a spacious and attractive front terrace with pretty flower beds and a water feature have good views to the moors beyond Nelson and Colne.

Good fresh bar food includes sandwiches, ploughman's, smoked haddock tart with poached egg, salmon fishcake with grilled king prawn and tomato and coriander salsa, steak, ale and mushroom pie, steak burger, crab linguine, duck pasty with apple and currant chutney, baked rump of lamb with minted pea pudding and braised lentils, and pork fillet wrapped in prosciutto with brandy soaked prunes and truffle mash. *Benchmark main dish: fish and chips £11.95. Two-course evening meal £20.00.*

Mitchells & Butlers ~ Lease Neil Morley ~ Real ale ~ Bar food (12-2.30, 5-9; 12-9.30 Sat; 12-8 Sun) ~ (01282) 603034 ~ Children welcome ~ Dogs allowed in bar ~ Open 12-11(midnight Sat, 10.30 Sun)

Recommended by Dr Kevan Tucker, Roger and Donna Huggins, Steve Whalley, Ann and Tony Bennett-Hughes

WHITEWELL Lancashire   SD6546 Map 7

Inn at Whitewell ★ ♀ ⇔
Most easily reached by B6246 from Whalley; road through Dunsop Bridge from B6478 is also good; BB7 3AT

Elegant manor house hotel with smartly pubby atmosphere, good bar food, and luxury bedrooms

This ancient upmarket inn is a stylish place to stay, dine or just enjoy a drink. Handsome old wood furnishings, including antique settles, oak gateleg tables and sonorous clocks, are set off beautifully against powder blue walls that are neatly hung with big attractive prints. The pubby main bar has roaring log fires in attractive stone fireplaces and heavy curtains on sturdy wooden rails; one area has a selection of newspapers and magazines, local maps and guide books; there's a piano for anyone who wants to play and even an art gallery; board games. Early evening sees a cheerful bustle which later settles to a more tranquil and relaxing atmosphere. Drinks include a good wine list of around 230 wines with 16 by the glass (there is a good wine shop in the reception area), organic ginger beer, lemonade and fruit juices and up to five real ales on handpump that might be from Bowland, Copper Dragon, Moorhouses and Timothy Taylor. Staff are courteous and friendly. The building is nicely positioned in a super setting deep among the hills and moors that rise to the high points of the Forest of Bowland and has delightful views from the riverside bar and adjacent terrace. They own several miles of trout, salmon and sea-trout fishing on the Hodder, and can arrange shooting and make up a picnic hamper.

Besides lunchtime sandwiches, well presented bar food might include spicy fried squid, duck terrine with poached pear and apple jelly, fish and chips, roast chicken breast with sage and onion stuffing and smoked bacon and onion jus, cheese and onion pie, and grilled salmon fillet with basil and olive mash and ratatouille; they also have a separate dining room menu. *Benchmark main dish: fish pie £10.72. Two-course evening meal £21.00.*

Free house ~ Licensee Charles Bowman ~ Real ale ~ Bar food (12-2, 7.30-9.30) ~ Restaurant ~ (01200) 448222 ~ Children welcome ~ Dogs allowed in bar and bedrooms ~ Open 11-midnight ~ Bedrooms: £85B/£115B

Recommended by Noel Thomas, Steve Whalley, Mark Sowery, Dr Clive Elphick, Yvonne and Mike Meadley, Roger and Donna Huggins, David Heath, John Taylor

---

Children – if the details at the end of a featured top pub don't mention them, you should assume that the pub doesn't allow them inside.

WINSTER Cumbria   SD4193 Map 9

Brown Horse

A5074 S of Windermere; LA23 3NR

Welcoming bar, smart restaurant, a friendly, informal atmosphere, first-class food, own-brewed real ales, good wines, and seats outside; comfortable bedrooms

This charming inn now has its own microbrewery up and running, Winster Valley, which produces Best and Old School, and they keep guests such as Kirkby Lonsdale Tiffin Gold and Lytham Lowther on handpump; also, a dozen wines by the glass, ten malt whiskies and raspberry lemonade and elderflower pressé. There's a chatty, bustling atmosphere in the bar which has beams and some half-panelling, stools and a mix of wooden chairs around pubby tables (each with a light candle), a woodburning stove in a little stone fireplace, and high bar chairs by the counter. The restaurant has a relaxed, informal atmosphere, high-backed leather dining chairs around attractive light and dark wood tables, more candles and fresh flowers. Piped music, TV, darts and board games. There's a front terrace with solid tables and chairs, and a side garden with views of the Winster Valley. Our readers enjoy staying here very much.

Using their own Estate-reared and own-grown produce, the excellent food might include sandwiches, home tea-smoked mackerel with horseradish cream, home-smoked salmon and prawn fishcake with a soft poached egg and watercress mayonnaise, tomato and olive tagliatelle, pheasant and apricot sausages with red wine jus, trout from Ullswater with almond beurre blanc, corn-fed chicken with bacon and a light poultry cream, and 21-day-hung rib-eye steak with dripping-cooked chips and a creamed peppercorn reduction; they offer a good value two- and three-course set lunch menu. *Benchmark main dish: pheasant breast with bacon, black pudding and cranberry sauce £14.95. Two-course evening meal £20.25.*

Free house ~ Licensees Karen and Steve Edmondson ~ Real ale ~ Bar food (12-2, 6-9) ~ Restaurant ~ (015394) 43443 ~ Children welcome ~ Dogs allowed in bar ~ Open 11-11 ~ Bedrooms: £65S/£97S

Recommended by Tina and David Woods-Taylor, Peter Webb, Walter and Susan Rinaldi-Butcher, Henry Midwinter, Michael Doswell, Alison Ball, Ian Walton, Malcolm and Pauline Pellatt, Brian and Janet Ainscough, Jane and Alan Bush, Peter Smith and Judith Brown

WISWELL Lancashire   SD7437 Map 7

Freemasons Arms ★

Village signposted off A671 and A59 NE of Whalley; pub on Vicarage Fold, a gravelled pedestrian passage between Pendleton Road and Old Back Lane in village centre (don't expect to park very close); BB7 9DF

Top-drawer dining pub, a place for a special treat

Best thought-of as a good civilised restaurant, this does have the look and comfortably informal feel of an upmarket pub – not to mention the thoroughly pubby plus point of its well kept local ales on handpump, such as Bank Top Golden Legacy, Moorhouses Pride of Pendle and Tirril Nameless, as well as the racks of well chosen wine bottles behind its tempting bar counter (there's an excellent choice by the glass). Three rooms open together, with lots of mainly sporting antique prints on the cream or pastel walls, rugs on polished flagstones, carved oak settles and an attractive variety of chairs around handsome stripped or salvaged candlelit tables (all beautifully laid), and open fires, with a woodburning stove on the right. There are more rooms upstairs, including a comfortable one that's popular for pre-meal drinks, or their good coffee afterwards. Service by neatly uniformed young staff is meticulous and courteous. Teak seats for the candlelit tables under an extendable awning on the quiet flagstoned front terrace have not only infra-red heaters, but also plaid rugs to wrap around you.

Besides lunchtime sandwiches (try the dry-aged sirloin), dishes we or readers have particularly enjoyed here include beef bourguignon, pork belly rissoles, bream done with shrimps from Morecambe Bay, and an outstanding banana soufflé with toffee ice-cream; best value is the two- or three-course lunch, with around three choices for each course. *Benchmark main dish: tandoori monkfish with pork nuggets and scratchings and sweet potato £21.95. Two-course evening meal £33.60.*

Free house ~ Licensee Steven Smith ~ Real ale ~ Bar food (12-2.30, 5.30-9(6-9.30 Fri, Sat); 12-7.30 Sun; not Mon) ~ (01254) 822218 ~ Dogs allowed in bar ~ Open 12-2.30, 5.30-midnight; 12-midnight Sat; 12-11 Sun; closed first two weeks in Jan

Recommended by Margaret Dickinson, Nick White, Steve Whalley, W K Wood

WITHERSLACK Cumbria   SD4482   Map 10

Derby Arms 🍴 🍺 🛏

Just off A590; LA11 6RH

Bustling country inn with six real ales, good wines, excellent food and a friendly welcome; reasonably priced bedrooms

Handy for Levens Hall with its topiary garden and for Sizergh Castle (NT), this stylish country inn is a fine place for an interesting meal, a drink and a chat (they keep up to half a dozen real ales) or to stay overnight in the comfortable bedrooms. The main bar has lots of sporting prints on pale grey walls, elegant old dining chairs and tables on large rugs over floorboards, some hops over the bar counter, and an open fire. A larger room to the right is similarly furnished (with the addition of some cushioned pews), and has lots of political cartoons and local castle prints, a cumbrian scene over another open fire and alcoves in the back wall full of nice Bristol blue glass, ornate plates and staffordshire dogs and figurines; the large windows do lighten up the rooms, helped by evening candles in brass candlesticks. There are two further rooms – one with dark red walls, a red velvet sofa, more sporting prints and a handsome mirror over the fireplace. Barngates Cat Nap, Hawkshead Bitter, Lytham Blonde, Thwaites Lancaster Bomber and Wainwright, and a beer named for the pub brewed for them by Cumbrian Legendary and several wines by the glass. The atmosphere is friendly and relaxed, and the staff are helpful and courteous. They have plans for the garden.

Very good food includes sandwiches (the sandwich and soup deal is smashing value), duck and chicken liver pâté with home-made fruit chutney, grilled black pudding on a crispy pancetta and goats cheese salad with a grain mustard dressing, butternut squash and sage risotto, steak in ale pie, organic beefburger on a toasted muffin with cream lancashire cheese, a bacon skewer, onion rings and their own tomato relish, and a trio of sausages with red onion marmalade and cider gravy. *Benchmark main dish: beer-battered fish and chips £12.65. Two-course evening meal £17.45.*

Free house ~ Licensee Sue Luxton ~ Real ale ~ Bar food (12-2(2.30 Sat), 6-9; 12-8.30 Sun) ~ Restaurant ~ (015395) 52207 ~ Children welcome ~ Dogs welcome ~ Open 12-3, 5.30-11; 12-12 Fri and Sat; 12-10.30 Sun ~ Bedrooms: /£65S

Recommended by Sarah Priday, Jack Clark, Michael Doswell

YANWATH Cumbria   NY5128 Map 9

Gate Inn ⊕ �️

2.25 miles from M6 junction 40; A66 towards Brough, then right on A6, right on B5320, then follow village signpost; CA10 2LF

CUMBRIA DINING PUB OF THE YEAR

Emphasis on imaginative food but with local beers and thoughtful wines, a pubby atmosphere and warm welcome from the helpful staff

Handy for Ullswater and a civilised break from the M6, this is an immaculately kept 17th-c dining pub, much loved by our readers. There's a cosy bar of charming antiquity with country pine and dark wood furniture, lots of brasses on the beams, church candles on all the tables and a good log fire in the attractive stone inglenook. Friendly, courteous staff serve real ales on handpump from breweries such as Cumbrian Legendary, Hesket Newmarket and Tirril, and they keep around a dozen good wines by the glass, quite a few malt whiskies and maybe Weston's cider. Two restaurant areas have oak floors, panelled oak walls and heavy beams; piped music. There are seats on the terrace and in the garden. They have a self-catering cottage to let.

Using top quality local produce, free-range and organic where possible, the excellent food at lunchtime includes sandwiches, seafood ceviche, a platter of smoked meats, fish, cheese and home-baked bread with chutney and pickles, squash, rosemary and pine nut risotto, and venison burger with plum chutney, with evening choices such as steamed mussels with creamed leeks and scrumpy cider, braised belly of saddleback pork stuffed with apricots and spinach forcemeat with a sweet potato purée and coriander and lemon couscous, and wild bass fillet with sunblush tomato and black olive potatoes. *Benchmark main dish: herdwick mutton loin with home-made black pudding and a berry sauce £18.95. Two-course evening meal £22.00.*

Free house ~ Licensee Matt Edwards ~ Real ale ~ Bar food (12-2.30, 6-9) ~ Restaurant ~ (01768) 862386 ~ Children welcome ~ Dogs allowed in bar ~ Open 12-11
Recommended by Richard J Holloway, John and Eleanor Holdsworth, Chris and Jo Parsons, Mr and Mrs Maurice Thompson, Michael Doswell, J S Burn, Neil and Karen Dignan, Maurice and Gill McMahon, V and E A Bolton, Terry Davis, Michael and Maggie Betton, Gordon and Margaret Ormondroyd, Rosemary and Mike Fielder, Dave Snowden, Andy Orton, Pat and Stewart Gordon, Dr and Mrs T E Hothersall

---

ALSO WORTH A VISIT IN CHESHIRE

Besides the region's top pubs, we recommend the following. Do tell us what you think of them: **feedback@goodguides.com**

ALPRAHAM SJ5759   CW6 9JA
Travellers Rest
A51 Nantwich—Chester

Unspoilt four-room country local in same friendly family for three generations, well kept Tetleys, Weetwood and a guest, low prices, leatherette, wicker and Formica, some flock wallpaper, fine old brewery mirrors, darts and dominoes, back bowling green; no machines, piped music or food (apart from crisps/nuts), closed weekday lunchtimes.
Recommended by the Didler, Dave Webster, Sue Holland

ANDERTON SJ6475   CW9 6AG
Stanley Arms
Just NW of Northwich; Old Road

Busy friendly local by Trent & Mersey Canal overlooking amazing restored Anderton boat lift, wide choice of good value, well presented pubby food from sandwiches up, well kept ales including Greene King, John Smiths and Tetleys, nice family dining area; tables on decked terrace, play area, overnight mooring. *Recommended by Tom and Jill Jones, Ben Williams*

BARTHOMLEY SJ7752   CW2 5PG
☆ ## White Lion
M6 junction 16, B5078 N towards Alsager, then Barthomley signed on left

Charming 17th-c thatched tavern with wide mix of customers, good value straightforward tasty food (lunchtime only), five real ales, friendly timeless main bar with latticed windows, heavy low beams, moulded black panelling, prints on walls and blazing open fire, steps up to room with another fire, more panelling and a high-backed winged settle; children allowed away from bar, dogs welcome, seats out on cobbles overlooking attractive village and the early 15th-c red sandstone church, open all day. *Recommended by the Didler, Mr and Mrs P R Thomas, Edward Mirzoeff, Dr and Mrs A K Clarke, Edward Leetham, Dave Webster, Sue Holland and others*

BARTON SJ4454   SY14 7HU
☆ ## Cock o' Barton
Barton Road (A534 E of Farndon)

Stylish and witty contemporary décor and furnishings in spreading bright and open skylit bar, good enterprising up-to-date food, good choice of wines by the glass, Moorhouses Pride of Pendle and Stonehouse Station, plenty of neat courteous staff; unobtrusive piped music; tables in sunken heated inner courtyard with artful canopies and modern water feature, picnic-sets on back lawn, open all day, closed Mon. *Recommended by Jonny Kershaw, Tony Husband, Bradley Beazley*

BICKERTON SJ5254   SY14 8BE
Bickerton Poacher
A534 E of junction with A41

Rambling 17th-c poacher-themed pub, linked beamed rooms with open fires, glass-covered well, copper-mining memorabilia and talkative parrot, good choice of enjoyable reasonably priced food including carvery (Sat evening, Sun), cheerful attentive staff, up to four well kept ales including Wells & Youngs Bombardier, selection of wines, skittle alley; sheltered partly covered courtyard, play area, bedrooms, adjoining campsite. *Recommended by Alan and Eve Harding, Edward Leetham*

BOLLINGTON SJ9377   SK10 5JT
Vale
Adlington Road

Friendly refurbished 19th-c village pub under same ownership as nearby Bollington Brewery, several of their ales and local guests, good range of well priced food including some imaginative dishes, young efficient staff; nice outside area behind looking over cricket pitch, near Middlewood Way and Macclesfield Canal, open all day weekends. *Recommended by Andy and Jill Kassube, Brian and Anna Marsden, the Didler, Ludo McGurk, Malcolm and Pauline Pelliatt*

CHESTER SJ4065   CH1 1RU
☆ ## Bear & Billet
Lower Bridge Street

Handsome 17th-c timbered Okells pub with four changing guest ales, belgian and american imports and a nice range of wines by the glass, reasonably priced home-made pubby food, interesting features and some attractive furnishings in friendly and comfortable open-plan bar with fire, sitting and dining rooms upstairs; sports TVs; pleasant courtyard, open all day. *Recommended by the Didler, Paul Humphreys*

CHESTER SJ4065
CH1 1RU
Brewery Tap
Lower Bridge Street

Tap for Spitting Feathers Brewery in interesting Jacobean building with 18th-c brick façade, steps up to hall-like bar serving their well kept ales plus guests (mainly local) and real cider, good home-made food all day using local suppliers. *Recommended by Edward Leetham, Rosalyn Thomas, Dave Webster, Sue Holland, Anton*

CHESTER SJ4066
CH1 2HQ
Coach House
Northgate Street

Refurbished 19th-c coaching inn by town hall and cathedral, comfortable lounge with central bar, Shepherd Neame, Spitting Feathers and Thwaites, decent choice of food from semi-open kitchen including good fish and chips, prompt friendly service; nine bedrooms. *Recommended by Gerry and Rosemary Dobson, Eileen McCarthy*

CHESTER SJ4066
CH1 1LQ
Olde Boot
Eastgate Row N

Good value in lovely 17th-c Rows building, heavy beams, dark woodwork, oak flooring, flagstones, some exposed Tudor wattle and daub, old kitchen range in lounge beyond, old-fashioned settles and oak panelling in upper area popular with families, standard food, bargain Sam Smiths OB kept well, good cheerful service, bustling atmosphere; piped music. *Recommended by Tom and Jill Jones, Eric Larkham, the Didler, George Atkinson, Joe Green*

CHESTER SJ4066
CH1 4EZ
Telfords Warehouse
Tower Wharf, behind Northgate Street near railway

Well kept interesting ales in large converted canal building, generous fresh up-to-date food including good sandwich menu, efficient staff, bare brick and boards, high-pitched ceiling, big wall of windows overlooking water, massive iron winding gear in bar, some old enamel signs, steps to heavy-beamed area with sofas, artwork and restaurant; late-night live music, bouncers on door; tables out by water, open all day. *Recommended by the Didler, Andy and Jill Kassube*

CHESTER SJ4166
CH1 3ND
Union Vaults
Francis Street/Egerton Street

Friendly old-fashioned street-corner local, well kept Caledonian Deuchars IPA and two changing guests, three separate dining areas, old local photographs, back games room; piped music, sports TV; good outside seating for smokers, open all day. *Recommended by the Didler, Dave Webster, Sue Holland*

CHRISTLETON SJ4465
CH3 6AE
Cheshire Cat
Whitchurch Road

Large canalside Vintage Inn in restored early 19th-c building, popular good value food all day including weekday lunch deal, well kept ales such as Black Sheep, Cains and Purity, attentive cheerful service; garden, 14 bedrooms, open all day. *Recommended by Alan and Eve Harding*

CHRISTLETON SJ4565
CH3 7PT
Plough
Plough Lane

Popular 18th-c country local with three linked areas, ales such as Caledonian Deuchars IPA and Theakstons, enjoyable home-made local food (not Sun), friendly staff; garden with play area, nice setting. *Recommended by the Didler, Alan Hardy*

CHURCH LAWTON SJ8255
Red Bull
Congleton Road S (A34), by Trent & Mersey Canal

ST7 3AJ

Welcoming three-room pub by Trent & Mersey Canal, good value home-made food, well kept Robinsons and guest ales, beams and open fire, old photographs of canal barges, upstairs lounge and eating area; no credit cards; outside grassy area by the lock, walkers welcome (on Cheshire Ring path). *Recommended by Peter and Vivienne Shilston*

COMBERBACH SJ6477
 ## Spinner & Bergamot
Warrington Road

CW9 6AY

Comfortable 18th-c beamed village pub (named after two racehorses) with two-room carpeted lounge, good home-made bar and restaurant food (12-7.30 Sun) including fresh fish, well kept Robinsons ales, good wines, log fires, hunting prints, toby jugs and brasses, daily papers, pitched-ceiling timber dining extension, simple tiled-floor public bar; unobtrusive piped music, service pleasant but can be slow; dogs welcome, picnic-sets on sloping lawn, lots of flowers, small verandah, bowling green, open all day. *Recommended by Mark Sowery, Simon J Barber, Dr and Mrs D Scott, Mike Moss and others*

CONGLETON SJ8663
Beartown Tap
Willow Street (A54)

CW12 1RL

Friendly tap for small nearby Beartown Brewery, their interesting beers well priced and perhaps a guest microbrew, farm cider, bottled belgian beers, bare boards in down-to-earth bar and two light airy rooms off, no food, games or music; upstairs lavatories; open all day Fri-Sun. *Recommended by the Didler*

CONGLETON SJ8659
Horseshoe
Fence Lane, Newbold Astbury, between A34 and A527 S

CW12 3NL

Former farmhouse in peaceful countryside, three small carpeted rooms with decorative plates, copper and brass and other knick-knacks (some on delft shelves), mix of seating including plush banquettes and iron-base tables, well kept Robinsons, enjoyable good value pub food, friendly staff and locals, log fire; children welcome, rustic garden furniture, play area with tractor, good walks. *Recommended by Dr D J and Mrs S C Walker*

DISLEY SJ9784
Rams Head
A6

SK12 2AE

Large M&B dining pub doing enjoyable food all day including fixed-price menu and children's meals, well kept Bass, Timothy Taylors Landlord and Thwaites Lancaster Bomber, good choice of wines by the glass, prompt friendly service, unusual gothic-arched interior, lots of different areas, some with open fires; big enclosed garden behind, open all day. *Recommended by Murtagh David, Gerry and Rosemary Dobson*

FADDILEY SJ5852
☆ Thatch
A534 Wrexham—Nantwich

CW5 8JE

Attractive, thatched, low-beamed and timbered dining pub carefully extended from medieval core, open fires, raised room to right of bar, back barn-style dining room (children allowed here), friendly helpful service, relaxing atmosphere, ales including Greene King Old Speckled Hen, Timothy Taylors Landlord and Wells & Youngs Bombardier, enjoyable food including children's helpings; soft piped music, silent games machine; charming country garden, landlords listed on outside plaque, open all day. *Recommended by R L Borthwick*

FIVECROSSES SJ5276   WA6 6SL
Travellers Rest
B5152 Frodsham—Kingsley

Well run and focus on food since 2011 refurbishment (booking advised), well kept beers; superb views across Weaver Valley. *Recommended by Linda Carter*

FRODSHAM SJ5277   WA6 6BS
Bulls Head
Bellemonte Road, Overton – off B5152 at Parish Church sign; M56 junction 12 not far

Cheerful relaxed local with good choice of well kept ales, enjoyable food including good specials and popular Sun lunch, attentive service, sensible prices, darts and dominoes. *Recommended by Sue and Alex Crooks, Linda Carter*

FRODSHAM SJ5177   WA6 6PN
Helter Skelter
Church Street

Well kept Weetwood BB and seven changing guests from long counter on right, imported beers too, good selection of wines, freshly made imaginative food from sandwiches up in bar and upstairs restaurant, friendly efficient service, airy and comfortable, with tall stools, leaning-post seating, window tables and raised back area, real fire; open all day. *Recommended by Stephen H Johnston, Darren and Clare Jones*

FRODSHAM SJ5177   WA6 6UL
Netherton Hall
A56 towards Helsby

Large converted town-edge farmhouse with emphasis on good food, competent service, real ales and good choice of wines by the glass; nice setting. *Recommended by Gill and Keith Croxton*

FULLERS MOOR SJ4954   CH3 9JH
Sandstone
A534

Refurbished dining pub, light and airy, with wide choice of enjoyable good value fresh food from sandwiches and lunchtime snacks up, well kept local ales, friendly staff, modern décor, woodburner, dining conservatory, Tues quiz; children welcome, spacious garden with lovely views, handy for Sandstone Trail, open all day weekends. *Recommended by R L Borthwick, John and Susan Hacking*

GAWSWORTH SJ8869   SK11 9RJ
☆ # Harrington Arms
Church Lane

Rustic 17th-c farm pub, well run and now doing food, Robinsons Hatters Mild, Unicorn and a guest ale, two small gently updated rooms (children allowed in one), bare boards and panelling, fine carved oak bar counter; sunny benches on small front cobbled terrace. *Recommended by the Didler*

GRAPPENHALL SJ6386   WA4 3EP
☆ # Parr Arms
Near M6 junction 20 – A50 towards Warrington, left after 1.5 miles; Church Lane

Charming solidly traditional black-beamed pub in picture-postcard setting with picnic-sets out on cobbles by the church, more tables on canopied back deck, well kept Robinsons ales, friendly personal service, decent food from sandwiches up, daily papers, central bar serving lounge and smaller public bar (both comfortable), open fire; open all day Fri-Sun. *Recommended by Andy West*

HENBURY SJ8873
SK10 3LH

Cock
Chelford Road

Well kept Robinsons ales, short choice of enjoyable fairly simple food, friendly staff.
Recommended by Ben Williams

HUXLEY SJ5061
CH3 9BG

☆ ## Farmers Arms
Off A51 SE of Chester

Long low white building with bar and separate restaurant, small cosy rooms with bric-a-brac and open fires, good food (not Sun evening) including speciality steaks and lunchtime/early evening set deals, good choice of beers, over 90 wines (own wine shop), friendly staff and locals, nice relaxed atmosphere; children welcome, attractive garden area with gazebo, hanging baskets and wisteria, open all day weekends, closed Mon lunchtime. *Recommended by Ann and Tony Bennett-Hughes, Simon Ely*

LANGLEY SJ9471
SK11 0NE

☆ ## Leather's Smithy
Off A523 S of Macclesfield, OS Sheet 118 map reference 952715

Isolated stone-built pub up in fine walking country next to reservoir, four well kept ales including Black Sheep and Wells & Youngs Bombardier, lots of whiskies, enjoyable food from sandwiches and bloomers up, good welcoming service, beams and log fire, flagstoned bar, carpeted dining areas, interesting local prints and photographs; unobtrusive piped music, no dogs; picnic-sets in garden behind and on grass opposite, open all day weekends. *Recommended by Malcolm and Pauline Pellatt*

LITTLE BOLLINGTON SJ7387
WA14 4TJ

Swan With Two Nicks
2 miles from M56 junction 7 – A56 towards Lymm, then first right at Stamford Arms into Park Lane; use A556 to get back on to M56 westbound

Extended village pub full of beams, brass, copper and bric-a-brac, some antique settles, log fire, welcoming helpful service, good choice of enjoyable food from filling baguettes up including popular Sun lunch (best to book), several good local ales including one brewed for the pub, decent wines and coffee; children and dogs welcome, tables outside, attractive hamlet by Dunham Massey (NT) deer park, walks by Bridgewater Canal, open all day. *Recommended by Peter Webb*

LITTLE BUDWORTH SJ5965
CW6 9BY

Red Lion
Vicarage Lane

Traditional beamed local in unspoilt spot, hospitable licensees serving well kept Robinsons and good helpings of sensibly priced pub food, long bar with ladder-back chairs and stools around dark wood tables, patterned carpets, nice fire; a couple of picnic-sets out in front, more seats in garden, country walks. *Recommended by Roger and Anne Newbury, John Andrew*

LOWER PEOVER SJ7474
WA16 9PZ

☆ ## Bells of Peover
Just off B5081; The Cobbles

Lovely old refurbished building in a charming spot, panelling, beams, open fires and antiques, three well kept Robinsons ales, good food from sandwiches up, dining room; piped music, children till 8pm, disabled facilities, terrace tables, big side lawn with trees, rose pergolas and little stream, on quiet cobbled lane with fine black and white 14th-c church, open all day. *Recommended by Mrs P J Carroll, Donna Somerset*

We say if we know a pub allows dogs

LYMM SJ7087   WA13 0SW
Barn Owl
Agden Wharf, Warrington Lane (just off B5159 E)

Comfortably extended building in picturesque setting by Bridgewater Canal, good value fresh food all day including OAP bargains, Marstons and guest beers, decent wines by the glass, friendly atmosphere, pleasant service even when busy; disabled facilities, may be canal trips, moorings, open all day. *Recommended by Ben Williams*

LYMM SJ6886   WA13 0AP
Church Green
Higher Lane

Chef/landlord doing good seasonal food (some of it quite pricey) in refurbished bar and restaurant, Caledonian Deuchars IPA and Greene King Old Speckled Hen; piped music; children welcome, disabled facilities, heated side terrace, open all day. *Recommended by W K Wood*

MACCLESFIELD SJ9272   SK11 7JW
Railway View
Byrons Lane (off A523)

Pair of 1700 knocked-through cottages under new owners, attractive snug corners, up to eight well kept changing ales (cheaper Mon evening), good value food, friendly service, remarkably shaped gents'; back terrace overlooking railway, open all day weekends. *Recommended by the Didler*

MACCLESFIELD SJ9173   SK11 6LH
Waters Green Tavern
Waters Green, opposite station

Seven quickly changing and interesting largely northern ales in roomy L-shaped open-plan local, good value home-made lunchtime food (not Sun), friendly staff and locals, back pool room. *Recommended by the Didler, David Crook*

MARBURY SJ5645   SY13 4LS
Swan
NNE of Whitchurch; OS Sheet 117 map reference 562457

Reopened under new management; good range of food from traditional things up, three real ales including Caledonian Deuchars IPA and local Woodlands, roomy partly panelled lounge with upholstered banquettes and copper-canopied log fire, cottagey dining room with another inglenook; piped and occasional live music; children and dogs welcome, picnic-sets in big back garden with vegetable patch, attractive village with lakeside church, not far from the Llangollen Canal (Bridges 23/24). *Recommended by anon*

MIDDLEWICH SJ7066   CW10 9DN
Big Lock
Webbs Lane

Sizeable 19th-c canalside pub on two floors, good value food including deals, mainstream ales; tables out by the water, good for boat watching. *Recommended by Ben Williams*

NANTWICH SJ6452   CW5 5ED
 ## Black Lion
Welsh Row

Old black and white building smartened up but keeping beams, timbered brickwork and an open fire, good food from short but interesting menu, three Weetwood ales and three regularly changing guests, upstairs rooms with old wooden tables and sumptuous leather sofas on undulating floors; open all day. *Recommended by Edward Leetham, Dave Webster, Sue Holland*

NANTWICH SJ6551   CW5 7EA
Globe
Audlem Road

Full range of well kept Woodlands ales and a guest, ten wines by the glass, regularly changing good value food all day using local produce, lunchtime deals, friendly helpful staff, comfortable open-plan layout keeping distinct areas, local artwork, newspapers and magazines, occasional live music; garden tables. *Recommended by David Webster*

NANTWICH SJ6552   CW5 5RP
Vine
Hospital Street

Dates from the 17th c, sympathetically modernised and stretching far back with old prints, books and dimly lit quiet corners, well kept Hydes and a guest, friendly staff and locals, lunchtime sandwiches, baguettes, wraps, baked potatoes and simple hot dishes, raised seating areas; unobtrusive piped music and TV; children welcome, small outside area behind, open all day. *Recommended by Charles and Pauline Stride, Edward Leetham*

NESTON SJ2976   CH64 0TB
☆ ## Harp
Quayside, SW of Little Neston; keep on along track at end of Marshlands Road

Tucked-away two-room country local, well kept Holts and up to five interesting guests, some good malt whiskies, good value unfussy home-made lunchtime food (not weekends), woodburner in pretty fireplace, pale quarry tiles and simple furnishings, hatch servery in one room; children allowed in lounge, dogs welcome, garden behind, picnic-sets up on front grassy bank facing Dee marshes and Wales, glorious sunsets with wild calls of wading birds, open all day. *Recommended by Roger and Anne Newbury, Maurice and Gill McMahon, Andy and Jill Kassube, Don Bryan, MLR*

OLLERTON SJ7776   WA16 8RH
☆ ## Dun Cow
Chelford Road; outskirts of Knutsford towards Macclesfield

Attractive well run Robinsons country pub, emphasis on good food but room for drinkers too, modern décor, cosy alcoves, two fine log fires, dominoes; children welcome, good disabled access, seats in nice outside area, open all day Sat, closed Sun evening and Mon. *Recommended by David Heath, P J and R D Greaves, Andrew Jackson*

PARKGATE SJ2778   CH64 6RN
Boathouse
Village signed off A540

Popular black and white timbered pub with attractively refurbished linked rooms, good food including fresh fish, cheerful attentive staff, well kept changing ales including local Brimstage, good choice of wines by the glass, big conservatory with great views to Wales over silted Dee estuary (RSPB reserve). *Recommended by Maurice and Gill McMahon, Pat and Tony Hinkins, Clive Watkin*

PLUMLEY SJ7275   WA16 9RX
Golden Pheasant
Plumley Moor Lane (off A556 by The Smoker)

Civilised well extended pub, locally sourced food including Sun carvery, Lees ales, comfortable lounge areas, roomy restaurant and conservatory, friendly efficient staff; children welcome, spacious gardens including play area and bowling green, bedrooms. *Recommended by Malcolm and Pauline Pellatt*

Post Office address codings give the impression that some pubs are in Cheshire, when they're really in Derbyshire or in Greater Manchester (which is where we list them).

PRESTBURY SJ8976   SK10 4DG

☆ **Legh Arms**

A538, village centre

Smart beamed hotel with divided up bar and lounge areas, Robinsons ales, decent wines, bar food (all day weekends) and more elaborate restaurant choices, soft furnishings, ladder-back chairs around solid dark tables, brocaded bucket seats, stylish french prints and italian engravings, staffordshire dogs on mantelpiece, cosy panelled back part with comfy narrow offshoot, coal fire, daily papers; piped music; children and dogs welcome, seats on heated terrace, bedrooms, open all day. *Recommended by Pam and John Smith*

SHOCKLACH SJ4349   SY14 7BL

☆ **Bull**

Off B5069 W of Malpas

Welcoming and comfortable, with exhilarating mix of some contemporary furnishings and artwork with much more traditional features, beams, open fire and mixed furniture on stone and wood floors, nice range of interesting fresh food from changing menu, good choice of wines and of well kept local ales (summer beer festival), friendly informal service, conservatory; teak tables under cocktail parasols on back terrace, garden; open all day at least Fri-Sun, closed Mon. *Recommended by Alun Jones*

STOAK SJ4273   CH2 4HW

Bunbury Arms

Little Stanney Lane; a mile from M53 junction 10, A5117 W then first left

Big but cosy beamed lounge with antique furniture, pictures and books, small snug, wide choice of enjoyable food (all day Sun) from sandwiches to interesting specials including fresh fish, good changing ales, extensive wine list, jovial landlord and friendly staff, open fires, board games; can get busy; garden tables (some motorway noise), short walk for Shrophire Union Canal users from Bridge 136 or 138, handy for Cheshire Oaks shopping outlet, open all day. *Recommended by Jack Spratt, Janet McClure*

SWETTENHAM SJ7967   CW12 2LF

☆ **Swettenham Arms**

Off A54 Congleton—Holmes Chapel or A535 Chelford—Holmes Chapel

Attractive gently upmarket country pub in pretty setting by a lavender plot and the scenic Quinta arboretum, good popular food from sandwiches and pubby things to more imaginative dishes in an immaculate line of individually furnished rooms, early evening deals too, several well kept ales such as Moorhouses and Sharps Doom Bar, good wine choice, friendly service, log fires, some live jazz; children welcome, picnic-sets on quiet side lawn, open all day weekends. *Recommended by Malcolm and Pauline Pellatt, Brian and Anna Marsden*

WARMINGHAM SJ7161   CW11 3QN

Bears Paw

School Lane

Attractive 19th-c inn with well liked food served in bar or restaurant, good choice of local ales and of wines by the glass, quick friendly service; good spot by the river and ancient church in a picturesque village, seats in front garden, 17 good bedrooms. *Recommended by Rachel Hine, Andrew Williams, William and Ann Reid*

WILLINGTON SJ5367   CW6 0NH

☆ **Boot**

Boothsdale, off A54 at Kelsall

Attractive hillside dining pub in a row of converted cottages, views over Cheshire plain to Wales, popular food from pub staples to daily specials (they may ask to keep a credit card while you run a tab), Greene King and local Weetwood ales, decent wines, 30 malt whiskies, friendly staff, small opened-up unpretentiously furnished room areas, lots of original features, woodburner, extension with french windows overlooking garden, pub cats, dog and donkey; well behaved children welcome (no pushchairs), picnic-sets in front on raised suntrap terrace, open all day. *Recommended by Roger and Anne Newbury, Brian and Anna Marsden, Grahame and Myra Williams*

☆ WINCLE SJ9665   SK11 0QE
Ship
Village signposted off A54 Congleton—Buxton

16th-c stone-built country pub under friendly new licensees, bare-boards bar leading to carpeted dining room, old stables area with flagstones, beams, woodburner and open fire, good fresh food from daily-changing varied menu, up to five Lees ales, 11 wines by the glass, good attentive service; children and dogs welcome, tables in small well kept side garden, good Dane Valley walks. *Recommended by Malc Newton, Al M*

WRENBURY SJ5947   CW5 8HG
Dusty Miller
Cholmondeley Road; village signed from A530 Nantwich—Whitchurch

New landlord for well converted corn mill with fine canal views from gravel terrace and series of tall glazed arches in bar, spacious modern feel with comfortable mix of seats, oak settle and refectory table in quarry-tiled part by counter, old lift hoist under rafters, Robinsons beers tapped from the cask, bar food has been liked, restaurant; piped music; children and dogs welcome, open all day. *Recommended by Mike Proctor*

ALSO WORTH A VISIT IN CUMBRIA

Besides the region's top pubs, we recommend the following. Do tell us what you think of them: **feedback@goodguides.com**

☆ AMBLESIDE NY4008   LA22 9LQ
Kirkstone Pass Inn
A592 N of Troutbeck

Lakeland's highest pub, in grand scenery, hiker-friendly décor of flagstones, stripped stone and dark beams and furniture, lots of old photographs and bric-a-brac, open fires, good value food all day from 9.30am, changing ales such as Hesket Newmarket Kirkstone Pass and Tirril Old Faithful, hot drinks, daily papers, games and books; soft piped music, they may try to keep your credit card while you eat; well behaved children and dogs welcome, tables outside with incredible views to Windermere, camping field next door, three bedrooms, open all day. *Recommended by Robin Constable*

☆ AMBLESIDE NY3703   LA22 0EP
Wateredge Inn
Borrans Road

Lovely spot with sizeable garden running down to edge of Windermere (own moorings), lots of tables here, same splendid view through big windows in much-modernised bar (originally two 17th-c cottages), prompt cheerful staff, ales from Barngates, Theakstons, Tirril and local Watermill, several wines by the glass, wide choice of enjoyable food till 8.30pm, cosy beamed area down steps with fireside sofa; piped music, can get very busy; children welcome, dogs in bar, 22 comfortable bedrooms, open all day. *Recommended by Hugh Roberts, Margaret and Jeff Graham, Mr and Mrs D J Nash, Ian and Deborah Carrington, Margaret Dickinson*

☆ APPLEBY NY6819   CA16 6UN
Royal Oak
B6542/Bongate

Attractive old beamed and timbered coaching inn, popular bar food (all day Sun), well kept ales such as Black Sheep, Hawkshead and Jennings, friendly efficient young staff, log fire in panelled bar, armchair lounge with carved settle, traditional snug, nicely refurbished dining room; piped music; children and dogs welcome, terrace tables, good-sized bedrooms, nice breakfast, open all day. *Recommended by Maurice and Gill McMahon, Ivan and Margaret Scott, Claes Mauroy*

☆ **ARMATHWAITE** NY5046   CA4 9PB
Dukes Head
Off A6 S of Carlisle; right at T junction

Genuine friendly welcome for all at this traditional family-run Eden Valley inn; comfortable properly old-fashioned lounge with settles and little armchairs around oak and mahogany tables, antique hunting and other prints, brass and copper powder-flasks above open fire, ales such as Black Sheep and Jennings, Weston's cider, may be home-made lemonade and ginger beer, enjoyable bar food including daily specials, public bar with table skittles and TV; children and dogs welcome, seats on heated area outside, more on back lawn, boules, bedrooms, open all day. *Recommended by Roger and Anne Newbury, Alan Thwaite, Dr A M Rankin, Helen Cradock, A J Barker, Archibald Rankin*

☆ **ARMATHWAITE** NY5045   CA4 9PY
Fox & Pheasant
E of village, over bridge

Friendly licensees and locals in attractive spotless coaching inn, lovely River Eden views, well kept Robinsons ales, decent wines by the glass, sensibly short choice of good fresh reasonably priced food, inglenook log fire in main beamed and flagstoned bar, another in second bar, charming small dining room; picnic-sets outside, comfortable bedrooms. *Recommended by Brad Oud*

ASKHAM NY5123   CA10 2PF
Punch Bowl
4.5 miles from M6 junction 40

Attractive 18th-c village inn reopened under new management, spacious beamed main bar, locals' bar, snug lounge and dining room, open fires, traditional food including early-bird deals (not at Sun lunchtime), ales such as Adnams, Cumberland, Hawkshead, Copper Dragon and Greene King; picnic-sets out in front, on edge of green opposite Askham Hall, bedrooms being refurbished. *Recommended by anon*

ASKHAM NY5123   CA10 2PF
Queens Head
Lower Green; off A6 or B5320 S of Penrith

Traditional 17th-c beamed pub under new enthusiastic local licensees, enjoyable good value home-made food all day, well kept beers, open fires; tables out at front and in pleasant garden, four bedrooms. *Recommended by Colin and Sue Wilkinson, Rosemary and Mike Fielder*

BAMPTON NY5118   CA10 2RQ
Mardale
Village signposted off A6 in Shap; in Bampton turn left over bridge by Post Office

Pretty village pub under newish management, several opened-up rooms decorated in contemporary style, chunky modern country tables and chairs on big flagstones, a few rugs, one or two big Lakeland prints and some rustic bygones, log fire and woodburner, four local ales including one brewed for the pub, fairly traditional food; well behaved children and dogs welcome, good walks from the door, four bedrooms, open all day. *Recommended by Pam and John Smith, David and Katharine Cooke*

☆ **BEETHAM** SD4979   LA7 7AL
Wheatsheaf
Village (and inn) signed off A6 S of Milnthorpe

Striking 17th-c coaching inn with handsome timbered cornerpiece, opened-up front lounge bar, lots of exposed beams and joists, main bar (behind on right) with open fire, two upstairs weekend dining rooms, good often interesting food, three changing regional ales and several wines by the glass, friendly accommodating staff; soft piped music; children welcome, pretty 14th-c church opposite, quiet village with surrounding walks, bedrooms, open all day. *Recommended by Dennis Jones, Noel Grundy, William and Ann Reid, Stephen Funnell, Simon Le Fort, Francesca Salvini*

BOOT NY1701   CA19 1TG
☆ Boot Inn
aka Burnmoor; signed just off the Wrynose/Hardknott Pass road

Comfortable beamed pub with ever-burning fire, Black Sheep, Jennings and a guest ale (June beer festival), decent wines and malt whiskies, good friendly staff, realistically priced home-made local food from sandwiches up, restaurant and dining conservatory; games room with pool and TV; children and dogs welcome, sheltered front lawn with play area, lovely surroundings and walks, nine bedrooms, open all day. *Recommended by Adrian Johnson, Mr and Mrs D J Nash, Mike and Eleanor Anderson, Ludo McGurk*

BOOT NY1701   CA19 1TG
☆ Brook House
Handy for Eskdale railway terminus

Good views and walks, friendly family service, wide choice of good sensibly priced country cooking including some interesting dishes and unusual sandwiches, great whisky selection, well kept ales such as Barngates, Cumbrian and Hesket Newmarket, decent wines, Weston's farm cider, log fires, relaxed and comfortable raftered bar with woodburner and stuffed animals, smaller plush snug, peaceful separate restaurant; tables on flagstoned terrace, seven good value bedrooms, good breakfast (for nearby campers too), mountain weather reports, excellent drying room, open all day. *Recommended by John and Sylvia Harrop, Alison Ball, Ian Walton, Neil Whitehead, Victoria Anderson, the Didler, Kay and Alistair Butler, Pam and John Smith and others*

BOOT NY1901   CA19 1TH
Woolpack
Bleabeck, mid-way between Boot and Hardknott Pass

Last pub before the notorious Hardknott Pass; refurbished and welcoming, main walkers' bar with big woodburner, snug and restaurant, enjoyable home-made locally sourced food all day, up to eight well kept ales including Woolpackers (still brewed for the pub by previous landlord), Thatcher's cider, good choice of malts, June beer festival; children and dogs welcome, mountain-view garden, play area, seven bedrooms. *Recommended by Alan Hill, Neil Whitehead, Victoria Anderson, Mike and Eleanor Anderson*

BOUTH SD3285   LA12 8JB
☆ White Hart
Village signed off A590 near Haverthwaite

Cheerful bustling old inn with Lakeland feel, six changing ales, 25 malt whiskies, popular generously served food (all day Sun) using local beef and lamb, good friendly service, sloping ceilings and floors, old local photographs, farm tools, stuffed animals, collection of long-stemmed clay pipes, two woodburners; piped music; children welcome and dogs (not at mealtimes), seats outside, fine surrounding walks, five comfortable bedrooms, open all day. *Recommended by Dennis Jones, Alison Ball, Ian Walton, Peter Smith and Judith Brown, Lucien Perring*

BOWNESS-ON-WINDERMERE SD4096   LA23 3BY
Albert
Queens Square

Refurbished Robinsons inn keeping traditional feel, their ales and guests kept well, good choice of food all day; children welcome, terrace tables, six comfortable bedrooms. *Recommended by John and Helen Rushton, Dr E Scarth and Miss A Pocock*

BOWNESS-ON-WINDERMERE SD4096   LA23 3DH

☆ ## Hole in t' Wall

Lowside

Bustling unchanging pub – the town's oldest and packed in high season; split-level rooms, beams, stripped stone and flagstones, country knick-knacks and old pictures, fine log fire under vast slate mantelpiece, upper room with attractive plasterwork, Robinsons ales, decent traditional food (not Sun evening), friendly staff; piped music; children welcome, sheltered picnic-sets in small flagstoned and heated front courtyard, open all day.
Recommended by Dennis Jones, Dr Kevan Tucker, John and Helen Rushton, Kurt Woods

BRAITHWAITE NY2323   CA12 5SY

Royal Oak

B5292 at top of village

Bustling local atmosphere, four well kept Jennings ales, reasonable choice of food including children's helpings, prompt helpful service, well worn-in flagstoned bar; piped music, Sky TV; dogs welcome except mealtimes, open all day. *Recommended by Mr and Mrs D J Nash, John and Angie Millar*

BRIGSTEER SD4889   LA8 8AN

☆ ## Wheatsheaf

Off Brigsteer Brow

Attractive relaxed dining pub with good well priced food from interesting sandwiches (nice breads baked here) to local trout, steaks and game, stylishly simple contemporary décor, cheerful attentive staff, real ale such as Langdale, good choice of wines by the glass, sofas and dining tables in entrance bar, further two-room dining area; well reproduced nostalgic piped music; picnic-sets on pretty little terrace across the quiet lane, attractive village, bedrooms. *Recommended by anon*

BROUGHTON-IN-FURNESS SD2187   LA20 6HY

Manor Arms

The Square

Fine choice of interesting well priced changing ales in this open-plan drinkers' pub a quiet sloping square, flagstones and nice bow-window seat in well worn front bar, coal fire in big stone fireplace, chiming clocks, old photographs, limited food (rolls and soup), two pool tables; stairs down to lavatories; children allowed, bedrooms, open all day.
Recommended by David and Sue Smith

BUTTERMERE NY1716   CA13 9XA

Fish

B5289 SE of Buttermere

Spacious, light and airy former coaching inn on NT property between Buttermere and Crummock Water, fine views, Jennings ales and guests, wide range of good value food, friendly helpful staff; suntrap terrace attracting greedy sparrows and finches, popular with walkers and anglers, bedrooms. *Recommended by the Didler, John Wooll*

CARLETON NY5329   CA11 8TP

☆ ## Cross Keys

A686, off A66 roundabout at Penrith

Under same management as Highland Drove at Great Salkeld; modernised beamed main bar with straightforward furniture on light boards, pictures on bare stone walls, steps down to small area and up again to airy vaulted-ceiling restaurant with doors to verandah, well liked food including steaks and grills, Theakstons Black Bull, Tirril 1823 and a guest, good choice of wines by the glass, two further rooms with games machine, pool, juke box and TV; piped music; children and dogs welcome, fell views from garden, open all day weekends. *Recommended by Phil Bryant, Richard J Holloway, Michael Doswell, Rosemary and Mike Fielder and others*

CARLISLE NY4056
CA3 8RF
Kings Head
Pedestrianised Fisher Street

Heavy beams, lots of old local prints, drawings and black and white photographs, friendly bustling atmosphere, generous bargain pub lunches, good range of mainly cumbrian beers including Yates, raised dining area; piped music, TV; interesting historical plaque outside, partly covered courtyard, open all day. *Recommended by Eric Larkham, Derek and Sylvia Stephenson, the Didler, Robert Turnham, Barbarrick, Meg and Colin Hamilton and others*

CARTMEL SD3778
LA11 6QB
 ## Kings Arms
The Square

This previously well liked pub has recently reopened after refurbishment – news please. *Recommended by anon*

CARTMEL SD3778
LA11 6QB
Royal Oak
The Square

Low-beamed flagstoned local with cosy nooks and big log fire, ornaments and brasses, enjoyable good value bar food including specials, well kept Coniston Bluebird, Timothy Taylors Landlord and two changing local guests (Aug beer festival), decent wines, welcoming helpful staff; piped music and sports TV, autographed sporting memorabilia in gents'; dogs welcome, nice big riverside garden with summer bar, four bedrooms, open all day. *Recommended by Ben Williams, Phil Hollowood, Adrian Johnson*

CASTERTON SD6379
LA6 2RX
 ## Pheasant
A683

Traditional 18th-c inn with neat beamed rooms, straightforward pubby furniture, coal-effect gas fire, Dent, Greene King and Theakstons, several malt whiskies, restaurant, board games; piped music; children welcome, seats under cocktail parasols by road, more in pleasant garden, near church with pre-Raphaelite stained glass and paintings, bedrooms. *Recommended by Pat and Stewart Gordon, Mr and Mrs Ian King*

CHAPEL STILE NY3205
LA22 9JH
Wainwrights
B5343

White-rendered former farmhouse, up to eight real ales, plenty of wines by the glass, enjoyable quickly served food from pubby things up including sandwiches and baguettes, roomy new-feeling bar welcoming walkers and dogs, slate floor and fire, other spreading carpeted areas with beams, some half-panelling, cushioned settles and mix of dining chairs around wooden tables, old kitchen range; piped music, TV and games machines; children welcome, terrace picnic-sets, fine views, open all day in summer. *Recommended by John Woodward, John and Helen Rushton, Michael Doswell, Ewan and Moira McCall, Mr and Mrs Maurice Thompson*

COCKERMOUTH NY1230
CA13 9PJ
 ## Bitter End
Kirkgate, by cinema

Liked for its eight own-brewed ales and lots of bottled beers in three interesting bars – each with a different atmosphere from quietly chatty to sporty (décor reflecting this with unusual pictures of old Cockermouth to up-to-date sporting memorabilia), also framed beer mats, various bottles, jugs and books, log fire, good choice of traditional food; piped music; no dogs; children welcome, public car park round the back, open all day Sat in summer. *Recommended by Adrian Johnson, Geoff and Linda Payne, Pat and Stewart Gordon, the Didler, Helen, J Chilver and others*

CONISTON SD3097   LA21 8DU

 ## Black Bull
Yewdale Road (A593)

Own-brewed Coniston beers remain a draw to this bustling old inn; back area (liked by walkers and their dogs) with slate flagstones, carpeted front part more comfortable with open fire and Donald Campbell memorabilia, bar food served all day, residents' lounge with 'big toe' of Old Man of Coniston (large piece of stone in the wall), restaurant; children welcome, plenty of seats in former coachyard, bedrooms, open all day from 8am (parking not easy at peak times). *Recommended by Mr and Mrs D J Nash, Michael Butler, Mike Gorton, Rob and Catherine Dunster*

CONISTON SD3098   LA21 8HQ

Sun
Signed left off A593 at the bridge

16th-c inn in terrific setting below dramatic fells, interesting Donald Campbell and other Lakeland photographs in extended old-fashioned bar with beams, flagstones, log-fire range, cask seats and old settles, well kept Black Sheep, Coniston Bluebird, Copper Dragon, Hawkshead and four local guests, several wines by the glass, wide choice of food all day, big conservatory restaurant off carpeted lounge, more seating in large refurbished upstairs room with suspended rowing boat; well behaved children and dogs welcome, great views from front terrace, big tree-sheltered garden, eight comfortable bedrooms, hearty breakfast, open all day. *Recommended by Luke Bosman, Mr and Mrs J Hilton, E Ling, Brian Fairey, Mike Gorton*

CROOK SD4695   LA8 8LA

 ## Sun
B5284 Kendal—Bowness

Good bustling atmosphere in low-beamed bar with two dining areas off, good generous traditional food (all day weekends), reasonable prices, prompt cheerful service, Fullers London Pride and John Smiths, good value wines, roaring log fire. *Recommended by G Jennings, Martin Smith, Hugh Roberts*

CROSTHWAITE SD4491   LA8 8HR

Punch Bowl
Village signed off A5074 SE of Windermere

Civilised, stylish and well run dining pub, raftered and hop-hung public bar, stools by the slate-topped counter, eye-catching rugs on slate floor, Barngates, Ulverston and a guest, lots of wines by the glass including champagne, a dozen malt whiskies, two linked carpeted and beamed rooms with country pine furnishings, attractive prints, dresser with china and glass, log fire and woodburner, light and airy oak-floored restaurant, good if pricey food, friendly helpful staff; children welcome, dogs in bar, seats on stepped hillside terrace overlooking lovely Lyth Valley, nine well equipped bedrooms, open all day. *Recommended by D M Heath, Michael Harrison, David Thornton, Bill Adie, G Jennings, Rob and Catherine Dunster and others*

DACRE NY4526   CA11 0HL

Horse & Farrier
Between A66 and A592 SW of Penrith

Pleasant 18th-c village pub with well priced home-made food (not Sun evening) from sandwiches up, well kept Jennings, unsmart front room with big old-fashioned range and nice beam-and-plank ceiling, more modern dining extension down steps on the left, darts and dominoes; children and dogs welcome, post office, pretty village, closed Mon lunchtime. *Recommended by Brian Abbott, Noel Grundy, Natalie Wittering, Comus and Sarah Elliott*

We can always use photos of pubs on our website – do email one to us:
feedback@thegoodpubguide.co.uk

DEAN NY0725 CA14 4TJ
Royal Yew
Just off A5086 S of Cockermouth

Busy modernised village local in a nice spot, good range of enjoyable food from sandwiches up, well kept ales such as Bitter End and Jennings, good choice of wines by the glass, cheerful service. *Recommended by Richard and Tanya Smith*

DENT SD7086 LA10 5QL
George & Dragon
Main Street

Two-bar corner pub owned by Dent with seven of their well kept beers (including a real lager) and Weston's cider, some dark panelling, partitioned tables and open fire, food from light meals up, prompt friendly service, comfortable back restaurant, games room with pool; sports TV; children, walkers and dogs welcome, ten bedrooms, lovely village, open all day. *Recommended by Brian and Anna Marsden, Dr Kevan Tucker, J C Burgis*

DOCKRAY NY3921 CA11 0JY
Royal
A5091, off A66 or A592 W of Penrith

Former coaching inn with bright open-plan bar including walkers' part with stripped settles on flagstones, Black Sheep, Jennings and a guest, good food here from sandwiches up or in more formal restaurant, good friendly service; piped music; children welcome, dogs in bar, picnic-sets in large peaceful garden, great setting, ten comfortable bedrooms, open all day. *Recommended by James Morrell, Comus and Sarah Elliott*

ESKDALE GREEN NY1200 CA19 1TD
☆ Bower House
0.5 miles W of Eskdale Green

Civilised old-fashioned stone-built inn extended around a beamed and alcoved core, good fires, well kept local ales, good choice of interesting food in bar and biggish restaurant including home-made black pudding, friendly relaxed atmosphere; nicely tended sheltered garden by cricket field, charming spot with great walks, bedrooms, open all day. *Recommended by Tina and David Woods-Taylor, Paul J Robinshaw*

FAUGH NY5054 CA8 9EG
String of Horses
S of village, on left as you go down hill

Welcoming 17th-c coaching inn with cosy communicating beamed rooms, log fires, panelling and some interesting carved furniture, tasty well prepared food, Theakstons Bitter and another ale, restaurant; children welcome, sheltered terrace, comfortable bedrooms, good breakfast. *Recommended by Les and Sandra Brown*

FOXFIELD SD2085 LA20 6BX
☆ Prince of Wales
Opposite station

Cheery bare-boards pub with half a dozen good changing ales including bargain beers brewed here and at their associated Tigertops Brewery, bottled imports, farm cider, enjoyable home-made food including lots of unusual pasties, hot coal fire, bar billiards and other pub games, daily papers and beer-related reading matter; children very welcome, games for them too, reasonably priced bedrooms, open all day Fri-Sun, from mid-afternoon weekdays. *Recommended by the Didler, Clifford Walker*

GOSFORTH NY0703 CA20 1AZ
Gosforth Hall
Off A595 and unclassified road to Wasdale

Jacobean building with interesting history, beamed carpeted bar (popular with locals) with fine plaster coat-of-arms above woodburner, lounge/reception area with huge fireplace, ales such as Hawkshead, Keswick and Yates, enjoyable food including good range of pies, restaurant; TV; back garden with boules, nine bedrooms, self-catering lodge. *Recommended by Mr and Mrs Maurice Thompson, Pam and John Smith*

GREAT CORBY NY4854   CA4 8LR
Queen
Centre of village

Friendly extended pub with well kept local ales including Cumberland Corby brewed in the village, enjoyable locally sourced food from a short menu, spacious beamed bar with two log fires, airy mediterranean-themed lounge with own terrace, two dining rooms (one upstairs); children welcome, tables out at front overlooking green. *Recommended by Marylou*

GREYSTOKE NY4430   CA11 0TP
Boot & Shoe
By village green, off B5288

Cosy two-bar pub by the green in pretty 'Tarzan' village; low ceilings, exposed brickwork and dark wood, good generous reasonably priced food including popular theme nights, well kept Black Sheep and local microbrews, bustling friendly atmosphere; sports TV; on national cycle route, bedrooms. *Recommended by Phil Bryant, Maurice and Gill McMahon, D A Warren*

HALE SD5078   LA7 7BH
Kings Arms
A6 S of Beetham

Traditional place doing good generous pubby food (all day weekends) including good Sun roasts, friendly landlord and attentive uniformed staff, real ales, plenty of brass, china and hunting prints, two open fires, restaurant section. *Recommended by Mr and Mrs Ian King*

HAWKSHEAD NY3501   LA22 0NG
☆ Drunken Duck
Barngates; the hamlet is signposted from B5286 Hawkshead—Ambleside, opposite the Outgate Inn; or it may be quicker to take the first right from B5286, after the wooded caravan site; OS Sheet 90 map reference 350013

Civilised inn with more informal feel during the day when popular with walkers – get there early for a seat; small smart bar with beams and oak boards, stools by slate-topped counter, leather club chairs, photographs, coaching and hunting pictures, own good Barngates ales, continental draught beers, 17 wines by the glass from fine list, good bar food from sandwiches up, more elaborate and pricey evening choice, three restaurant areas; children welcome, dogs in bar, tables and benches out on grass with spectacular fell views, profusion of spring and summer bulbs, good bedrooms, open all day. *Recommended by Chris Johnson, Brian Dawes, David and Sue Atkinson, Janet and Peter Race, Mike and Sue Loseby, Marianne and Peter Stevens and others*

HESKET NEWMARKET NY3438   CA7 8JG
☆ Old Crown
Village signed off B5299 in Caldbeck

Straightforward cooperative-owned local in an attractive village, good own-brewed Hesket Newmarket beers (can book tours – £10 including meal); small friendly bar with bric-a-brac, mountaineering kit and pictures, log fire, dining room and garden room, simple bar food; pool, juke box and board games; children and dogs welcome, closed Mon-Thurs lunchtimes (open Weds and Thurs lunchtimes in school holidays). *Recommended by Maurice and Gill McMahon, John and Anne Mackinnon, Howard Bowen*

HIGH NEWTON SD4082   LA11 6JH
Crown
Just off A590 Lindale—Newby Bridge, towards Cartmel Fell

Refurbished 18th-c coaching inn, enjoyable food from well filled sandwiches to good value Sun lunch, changing ales and decent wines by the glass, beamed and flagstoned bar with log fire in stone fireplace, restaurant, trad jazz first Mon of month; children and dogs welcome, beer garden, seven bedrooms, open all day weekends. *Recommended by Michele Pearson*

KENDAL SD5192 LA9 4TN
Globe
Market Place

Compact town pub with carpeted beamed split-level bar, good new landlord and friendly staff, well kept Thwaites, enjoyable locally sourced food including Sun roasts, separate dining room upstairs. *Recommended by John and Helen Rushton*

KESWICK NY2623 CA12 5BT
☆ Dog & Gun
Lake Road; off top end of Market Square

Unpretentious town pub liked by locals and their dogs, homely bar with low beams and timbers, partly slate, part wood, part carpeted flooring, fine collection of striking mountain photographs, brass and brewery artefacts, half a dozen ales, all-day pubby food including popular goulash, log fires; children welcome if eating before 9pm, open all day. *Recommended by John Luckes, Bill Adie, Chris and Jo Parsons, Geoff and Linda Payne, J Buckby, Brendon Skinner and others*

KIRKBY LONSDALE SD6178 LA6 2BD
Orange Tree
Fairbank

Family-run inn acting as tap for Kirkby Lonsdale brewery, well kept guest beers too and good choice of wines, beams, sporting pictures, old range, enjoyable food in back dining room including a lunchtime bargain special; pool, darts, piped music; children and dogs welcome, comfortable bedrooms (some next door). *Recommended by David Baldwin, the Didler, Andy and Jill Kassube*

KIRKBY LONSDALE SD6278 LA6 2AH
Snooty Fox
Main Street (B6254)

Rambling partly panelled 17th-c coaching inn, beams, country furniture, two open fires, dining annexe, four real ales, generous good quality traditional food, reasonable prices, cheerful attentive young staff; piped music, sports TV and machines; children and dogs welcome, garden tables, bedrooms, open all day. *Recommended by JCW*

KIRKBY LONSDALE SD6178 LA6 2AU
☆ Sun
Market Street (B6254)

Friendly 17th-c inn striking a good balance between pub and restaurant; unusual-looking building with upper floors supported by three sturdy pillars above the pavement, attractive rambling beamed bar with flagstones and stripped-oak boards, pews, armchairs and cosy window seats, big landscapes and country pictures on cream walls, two log fires, comfortable back lounge and modern dining room, good contemporary food (booking advised), well kept Kirkby Lonsdale, Timothy Taylors and Thwaites, good service; piped music; children and dogs welcome, bedrooms, open all day from 9am, closed Mon till 3pm. *Recommended by Chris and Meredith Owen, G and P Vago, Stu Mac, Michael Doswell, Malcolm and Pauline Pellatt, John and Eileen Mennear and others*

KIRKBY STEPHEN NY7808 CA17 4QN
Kings Arms
A685 corner of High Street and Market Square

Former 17th-c posting inn with oak-panelled bar, well kept ales from Copper Dragon, Dent, Greene King and Kirkby Lonsdale, range of malt whiskies, decent food, restaurant; popular with walkers, tables in walled garden, nine bedrooms. *Recommended by Clive Gibson*

LANGDALE NY2906   LA22 9JU
Stickle Barn
By car park for Stickle Ghyll

Lovely views from this roomy and busy walkers'/climbers' bar (boots welcome), three or four changing ales such as Barngates, decent good value food including packed lunches, quick friendly service, mountaineering photographs; piped music (live on Sat), TV, games machines; big terrace with inner verandah, bunkhouse, open all day. *Recommended by Chris Johnson, Jane and Alan Bush*

LEVENS SD4885   LA8 8PN
Hare & Hounds
Off A590

Welcoming smartened-up village pub handy for Sizergh Castle, well kept ales including Black Sheep, friendly efficient service, good home-made pub food, partly panelled low-beamed lounge bar, front tap room with coal fire, pool room down steps, restaurant; children welcome, good views from terrace. *Recommended by Mr and Mrs Richard Osborne*

LORTON NY1526   CA13 9UW
☆ ## Wheatsheaf
B5289 Buttermere—Cockermouth

Friendly local atmosphere in neatly furnished bar with two log fires, affable hard-working landlord, Jennings and regular changing guests, several good value wines, good home-made food (all day Sun) from sandwiches to fresh fish (Thurs, Fri evening), smallish restaurant; children welcome, dogs on leads, tables out behind, campsite, open all day weekends, closed Mon lunchtime and weekday lunchtimes in winter. *Recommended by Sylvia and Tony Birbeck, Edward Mirzoeff, Geoff and Linda Payne, Pat and Stewart Gordon, Julian Cox*

LUPTON SO5581   LA6 1PJ
☆ ## Plough
A65, near M6 junction 36

Large refurbished slate-roofed pub with lots of spreading open-plan bar rooms, rugs on wood floors, beams and grey walls throughout, stools by granite-topped counter, ales such as Hawkshead, Jennings, Kirkby Lonsdale and Wychwood Hobgoblin, good interesting modern food, area to the left with logs stacked by open stone fireplace, some nice oval tables and rush-seated chairs, hunting prints and *Punch* cartoons, two further areas with station clock above woodburner, dark wood tables and leather sofa, fresh flowers and daily papers, large carpeted dining room, friendly chatty staff; picnic-sets to one side behind white picket fence, more in back garden. *Recommended by Margaret Dickinson, Dr Kevan Tucker, Christopher Mobbs, David Heath, Pat and Graham Williamson and others*

MELMERBY NY6137   CA10 1HF
Shepherds
A686 Penrith—Alston

Friendly split-level country pub with comfortable heavy-beamed dining room off flagstoned bar, spacious end room with woodburner, hearty helpings of tasty food served promptly, well kept local ales, good wine and whisky choice, games area with darts and pool; children welcome, terrace tables. *Recommended by Kevin and Rose Lemin*

NENTHEAD NY7843   CA9 3PF
Miners Arms
A689

Friendly early 18th-c village pub, good freshly made food from pub standards and wood-fired pizzas to interesting specials, reasonable prices, well kept changing ales, stripped-stone lounge, partly panelled flagstoned public bar, view from big dining conservatory; pool, TV; children welcome, picnic-sets out in front, two bedrooms, Sept leek show, handy for Pennine Way and cycle path, open all day. *Recommended by Mr and Mrs Maurice Thompson, Averell Kingston*

NETHER WASDALE NY1204   CA20 1ET
☆ # Strands
SW of Wast Water

Lovely spot below the remote high fells around Wast Water, brews its own Strands ales (lots of varieties), popular good value food, good-sized well cared-for high-beamed main bar with woodburner and relaxed friendly atmosphere, smaller public bar with pool, separate dining room, pleasant staff; piped music may obtrude; children and dogs welcome, neat garden with terrace and belvedere, 14 bedrooms, open all day. *Recommended by Mr and Mrs Maurice Thompson, Pam and John Smith, Ludo McGurk*

PENRITH NY5130   CA11 7XD
Lowther Arms
Queen Street

Comfortable and welcoming local in handsome 17th-c building, long bar with beams, bare boards and flagstones, log fire and mix of traditional furniture in various alcoves and recesses, reasonably priced food, several real ales, friendly service. *Recommended by Rosemary and Mike Fielder*

PENRUDDOCK NY4227   CA11 0QU
☆ # Herdwick
Off A66 Penrith—Keswick

Attractively cottagey and sympathetically renovated 18th-c inn, warm welcoming atmosphere, well kept Jennings, Marstons and summer guests from unusual curved bar, decent wines, friendly efficient service, enjoyable sensibly priced food from lunchtime sandwiches up, good open fire, stripped stone and white paintwork, nice dining room with upper gallery, games room with pool and darts; children in eating areas, five good value bedrooms. *Recommended by S D and J L Cooke, Comus and Sarah Elliott, Maurice and Gill McMahon, Phil Bryant, Dr and Mrs S G Barber, Mr and Mrs Maurice Thompson*

ROSTHWAITE NY2514   CA12 5XB
Scafell
B5289 S of Keswick

Hotel's big plain slate-floored back bar useful for walkers, weather forecast board, four well kept ales such as Black Sheep and Theakstons, blazing log fire, enjoyable food from sandwiches up, afternoon teas, also, an appealing cocktail bar/sun lounge and dining room, friendly helpful staff; piped music, pool; children and dogs welcome, tables out overlooking beck, bedrooms. *Recommended by Sylvia and Tony Birbeck, Simon Watkins, Lawrence R Cotter, Mr and Mrs Maurice Thompson*

RYDAL NY3606   LA22 9LR
Glen Rothay Hotel
A591 Ambleside—Grasmere

Attractive small 17th-c hotel with enjoyable pubby food from sandwiches up in back bar, well kept changing local ales, helpful friendly staff, banquettes and stools, lots of badger pictures, fireside armchairs in beamed lounge bar, restaurant; walkers and dogs welcome, tables in pretty garden, boats for residents on nearby Rydal Water, eight comfortable bedrooms. *Recommended by Andy and Jill Kassube, Mr and Mrs Maurice Thompson*

SANDFORD NY7316   CA16 6NR
☆ # Sandford Arms
Village and pub signposted just off A66 W of Brough

Neat former 18th-c farmhouse in peaceful village, enjoyable food (all day weekends Apr-Oct) from chef/landlord, L-shaped carpeted main bar with stripped beams and stonework, collection of Royal Doulton character jugs and some Dickens ware, ales from Black Sheep, Lancaster and Tirril, comfortable raised and balustraded eating area, more formal dining room and second flagstoned bar, log fire; piped music; children and dogs welcome, seats in front garden and covered courtyard, bedrooms, closed Tues. *Recommended by C J Beresford-Jones, M and GR*

☆ **Bridge Inn**

SANTON BRIDGE NY1101   CA19 1UX

Off A595 at Holmrook or Gosforth

Charming riverside spot with fell views, beamed and timbered bar bustling with locals, log fire, some booths around stripped-pine tables, Jennings and guest ales, enjoyable traditional food including Sun carvery, family dining room, italian-style bistro, friendly helpful staff, small reception hall with log fire and daily papers; piped music, games machine; dogs welcome in bar, seats outside by quiet road, plenty of walks, 16 bedrooms, open all day. *Recommended by Susan and Nigel Brookes*

☆ **Eagles Head**

SATTERTHWAITE SD3392   LA12 8LN

S edge of village

Pretty and prettily placed on the edge of beautiful Grizedale Forest, low black beams, comfortable traditional furnishings, big log fire, lots of local photographs and maps, welcoming and obliging landlord, good fairly priced generous pubby food (not Mon) including notable filled rolls, wider evening choice, well kept local ales including Barngates and one brewed for the pub; children welcome, picnic-sets in attractive tree-shaded courtyard garden with pergola, comfortable bedrooms, open all day on summer weekends, closed Mon and Tues lunchtimes. *Recommended by Roger and Kathy Elkin*

☆ **Newfield Inn**

SEATHWAITE SD2295   LA20 6ED

Duddon Valley, near Ulpha (ie not Seathwaite in Borrowdale)

Genuinely friendly 16th-c cottage despite weekend and holiday popularity; local atmosphere in slate-floored bar, wooden tables and chairs, interesting pictures, Jennings and quickly changing guests, straightforward food all day, comfortable side room, games room; no credit cards; children and dogs welcome, tables in nice garden with hill views, play area, good walks, self-catering flats, open all day. *Recommended by John Luckes, E Ling, Alan Hill*

Dalesman

SEDBERGH SD6592   LA10 5BN

Main Street

Three linked modernised rooms, good freshly made seasonal food from sandwiches up, well kept ales including Tetleys and one brewed for the pub, stripped stone and beams, central woodburner; piped music; children welcome, picnic-sets out in front, bedrooms, open all day. *Recommended by John and Helen Rushton*

☆ **Red Lion**

SEDBERGH SD6592   LA10 5BZ

Finkle Street (A683)

Cheerful beamed local, down to earth and comfortable, with good value generous food (meat from next-door butcher), well kept Jennings, good coal fire; sports TV, can get very busy at weekends, no dogs. *Recommended by John and Helen Rushton*

☆ **Greyhound**

SHAP NY5614   CA10 3PW

A6, S end, handy for M6 junction 39

Good value former coaching inn, quickly served enjoyable food in open-plan bar with sofas and armchairs as well as dining tables, more choice in two restaurants, several well kept ales such as Dent, Keswick and Timothy Taylors Landlord, good house wines, daily papers, cheerful bustle and friendly helpful young staff; TV, unobtrusive piped music; dogs welcome, picnic-sets under canopy on flagstoned back terrace, ten comfortable bedrooms, good breakfast, open all day. *Recommended by John Wymer, Andy West, Christine and Neil Townend*

STONETHWAITE NY2513   CA12 5XG

☆ **Langstrath**

Off B5289 S of Derwent Water

Neat, simple bar (pubbiest at lunchtime) with welcoming fire in the big stone fireplace, traditional furniture, several walking cartoons and attractive Lakeland mountain photographs, Black Sheep and Jennings ales, 25 malt whiskies, decent bar food including some interesting dishes, residents' lounge in small left room (original 16th-c cottage), restaurant with fine views; piped music; children over 7 welcome, picnic-sets under big sycamore, fine surrounding walks – in heart of Borrowdale and en route for Cumbrian Way and Coast to Coast Walk, bedrooms, closed Mon, plus Tues and Weds in winter and part of Dec and Jan, otherwise open all day. *Recommended by Simon Watkins, Alison Ball, Ian Walton, Peter Smith and Judith Brown, Mr and Mrs Maurice Thompson*

TROUTBECK NY4103   LA23 1PL

Mortal Man

A592 N of Windermere; Upper Road

Refurbished beamed and partly panelled bar with cosy room off, log fires, Black Sheep, Coniston, Timothy Taylors Landlord and a beer brewed for them by Hawkshead, several wines by the glass, generally well liked food in bar and picture-window restaurant, young willing staff; children and dogs welcome, great views from sunny garden, lovely village, bedrooms, open all day. *Recommended by Dave Traynor, Ian and Rose Lock, Mr and Mrs Richard Osborne*

TROUTBECK NY4028   CA11 0SG

Sportsman

B5288, just off A66 – the 'other' Troutbeck, near Penrith

Small welcoming bar and large dining area with great views, enjoyable standard food, well kept Jennings ales and an interesting guest, good wine choice; children welcome, pretty back terrace overlooking valley, open all day. *Recommended by E Clark*

TROUTBECK NY4103   LA23 1HH

Sun

A591 N of Windermere

Well refurbished hotel with enjoyable reasonably priced food including lunchtime sandwiches, Hawkshead and Jennings ales; 12 bedrooms, open all day Fri-Sun, from 3pm Mon-Thurs (all day in school holidays). *Recommended by V and E A Bolton*

TROUTBECK NY3827   CA11 0SJ

Troutbeck Inn

A5091/A66

Refurbished old railway hotel with bar, lounge and restaurant, good food, real ales, efficient friendly service; children and dogs welcome, seven bedrooms, self-catering cottages in former stables. *Recommended by E Clark*

ULDALE NY2436   CA7 1HA

Snooty Fox

Village signed off B5299 W of Caldbeck

Comfortable well run two-bar village inn with good-quality food using local ingredients, well kept changing ales, friendly attentive staff; bedrooms. *Recommended by Dr Nigel Bowles*

ULVERSTON SD2878   LA12 7BA

☆ **Farmers Arms**

Market Place

Convivial attractively modernised town pub, front bar with comfortable sofas, contemporary wicker chairs, original fireplace, daily newspapers, quickly changing real ales, a dozen wines by the glass, interesting fairly priced food, second bar leading to big raftered dining area (children here only); unobtrusive piped music; seats on attractive heated front terrace, lots of colourful tubs and hanging baskets, Thurs market day (pub busy then), three cottages to rent, open all day from 9am. *Recommended by Chris Clark*

WHITEHAVEN NX9718   CA28 7LL
Vagabond
Marlborough Street

Old-fashioned town-centre pub with bare boards and oak settles, lots of american memorabilia – Jack Kerouac posters, car number plates etc, good basic low-priced food, well kept Jennings, friendly helpful staff. *Recommended by Susan and Nigel Brookes*

ALSO WORTH A VISIT IN
GREATER MANCHESTER, LANCASHIRE
& MERSEYSIDE

Besides the region's top pubs, we recommend the following. Do tell us what you think of them: **feedback@goodguides.com**

ALTRINCHAM SJ7689   WA14 5NT
Railway Inn
153 Manchester Road (A56), Broadheath

Early Victorian with lounge, bar, games room (darts and dominoes), snug and dining room, church pews, well kept bargain Holts Bitter and Mild, friendly landlady and chatty locals; back terrace, open all day (Sun 3-7pm). *Recommended by the Didler*

APPLEY BRIDGE SD5210   WN6 9DY
Dicconson Arms
B5375 (Appley Lane North)/A5209, handy for M6 junction 27

Well run and civilised, with good nicely presented food (all day Sun), friendly attentive service, two well kept ales in uncluttered bar area with clubby chairs, dining room beyond, pine floors, woodburner; some seats outside. *Recommended by Jeremy King, Mr and Mrs I Templeton, Norma and Noel Thomas*

AUGHTON SD3905   L39 6SA
Stanley Arms
St Michael Road

Spacious and spotless cottagey pub behind medieval church, wide choice of changing ales, reasonably priced home-made food from sandwiches to daily specials, helpful service; picnic-sets in garden with smokers' shelter, open all day. *Recommended by Peter Hacker*

BARLEY SD8240   BB12 9JX
Pendle
Barley Lane

Friendly 1930s pub in shadow of Pendle Hill, three cosy rooms, two open fires, simple substantial pub food (all day weekends), well kept local ales, conservatory; garden, lovely village and good walking country, bedrooms, open all day. *Recommended by Len Beattie, Dr Kevan Tucker*

Post Office address codings confusingly give the impression that some pubs are in Lancashire when they're really in Cumbria or Yorkshire (which is where we list them).

BARNSTON SJ2783   CH61 1BW
☆ **Fox & Hounds**
3 miles from M53 junction 3: A552 towards Woodchurch, then left on A551

Spotless well run pub with cheerful welcome, six real ales including Theakstons, 60 malt whiskies, good value traditional lunchtime food, roomy carpeted bay-windowed lounge with built-in banquettes and plush-cushioned captain's chairs around solid tables, old local prints and collection of police and other headgear, charming old quarry-tiled corner with antique range, copper kettles, built-in pine kitchen cupboards, enamel food bins and earthenware, small locals' bar (worth a look for its highly traditional layout and collection of horsebrasses and metal ashtrays), snug where children allowed; dogs welcome in bar, picnic-sets under cocktail parasols and colourful hanging baskets in back yard, open all day. *Recommended by Tony Nolan, John and Helen Rushton, Maurice and Gill McMahon, Clive Watkin*

BARROW SD7337   BB7 9AQ
☆ **Eagle**
Village signed off A59; Clitheroe Road (A671 N of Whalley)

Stylish dining pub with modern light leather chairs, sofas and big low tables in bar, brasserie-style dining room with busy open kitchen and cabinet displaying their 35-day dry-aged steaks, good food (all day Sun) including sandwiches, excellent home-made sausages and imaginative main choices, five real ales, good wines, young uniformed staff, back area with chandeliers and big mirrors, clubby panelled piano bar; children welcome, tables outside overlooking big car park, open all day. *Recommended by John and Eleanor Holdsworth, Steve Whalley, Mr and Mrs John Taylor*

BAY HORSE SD4952   LA2 0HR
☆ **Bay Horse**
1.2 miles from M6 junction 33: A6 southwards, then off on left

Civilised redecorated country dining pub – a useful motorway stop; cosily pubby bar with good log fire, cushioned wall banquettes, fresh flowers, Black Sheep and Hawkshead, 15 wines by the glass, smarter restaurant with cosy corners, another log fire and carefully presented innovative food; children welcome, tables in garden, bedrooms, closed Mon. *Recommended by Adrian Johnson, Karen Eliot, Dave Braisted, David and Katharine Cooke, Dr Kevan Tucker, Mr and Mrs J E Fisher and others*

BEBINGTON SJ3385   CH62 1BQ
Travellers Rest
B5151, not far from M53 junction 4; New Ferry Road, Higher Bebington

Friendly semi-rural pub with several areas around central bar, good value food all day from lunchtime sandwiches and snacks to more substantial evening meals (till 7pm), up to eight well kept real ales including some from small breweries, efficient staff, alcoves, beams, brasses etc; no children; open all day. *Recommended by MLR*

BELMONT SD6715   BL7 8AB
☆ **Black Dog**
Church Street (A675)

Nicely set Holts pub with their usual good value food (all day Fri-Sun, not Tues evening), bargain beers, friendly prompt staff, cheery small-roomed traditional core, coal fires, picture-window extension; children welcome, seats outside with moorland views above village, attractive part-covered smokers' area, good walks, decent well priced bedrooms (breakfast from 9am), open all day. *Recommended by Peter Heaton, Simon Le Fort, Yvonne and Mike Meadley, the Didler, Norma and Noel Thomas and others*

BIRKENHEAD SJ3389   CH41 5DQ
Gallaghers
Chester Street

Friendly 19th-c place uniquely combining barbershop at back with traditional pub at front, local real ales including a house beer appropriately named Half Cut, interesting books, ship pictures and military memorabilia. *Recommended by Colin Ebbrell*

BIRKENHEAD SJ3289   CH41 6JN
Stork
Price Street

Welcoming early Victorian pub with tiled façade, four well restored civilised rooms around island bar, polished mosaic floor, old photographs, several well kept changing ales, bargain basic food weekday lunchtime and early evening; open all day. *Recommended by the Didler*

BLACKO SD8641   BB9 6LS
Rising Sun
A682 towards Gisburn

Welcoming traditional village pub with good Moorhouses ales, enjoyable well priced pubby food, tiled entry, open fires in three rooms off main bar; tables out on front terrace, open all day weekends. *Recommended by Dr Kevan Tucker*

☆ BLACKSTONE EDGE SD9617   OL15 0LG
White House
A58 Ripponden—Littleborough, just W of B6138

Beautifully placed moorland dining pub with remote views, emphasis on good value hearty food from sandwiches up (all day Sun), prompt service, well kept Theakstons Best and changing regional guests, belgian bottled beers, cheerful atmosphere, carpeted main bar with hot fire, other areas off, most tables used for food; children welcome. *Recommended by Gordon and Margaret Ormondroyd, Clive Flynn*

BOLTON SD7112   BL1 7AN
Brewery Tap
Belmont Road

Simply refurbished tap for Bank Top (their first pub), well kept guest ales too, no food. *Recommended by Ben Williams*

BOLTON SD7109   BL1 2JU
Howcroft
Pool Street

Friendly local serving as tap for good Bank Top ales, guests including Timothy Taylors Landlord, enjoyable good value pubby lunches, screened-off rooms around central servery with fine glass and woodwork, cosy snug, open fires, conservatory, pub games; crown bowling green, open all day. *Recommended by the Didler*

BOLTON SD6809   BL1 5AG
Victoria
Markland Hill

Extensively refurbished and extended inn known locally as Fannys, decent food, beer and wine; open all day. *Recommended by W K Wood*

BOLTON SD6913   BL1 7BT
Wilton Arms
Belmont Road, Horrocks Fold

Friendly low-beamed roadside pub, consistently good well priced fresh food, well kept ales such as Bank Top Flat Cap and Coniston Bluebird, open fires; garden overlooking valley, Pennine walks, open all day. *Recommended by W K Wood, Rob and Gill Wood*

BOLTON BY BOWLAND SD7849   BB7 4NW
Coach & Horses
Main Street

Refurbished stone-built beamed pub/restaurant with bar and two dining areas, good interesting food from open sandwiches up at reasonable prices, bargain Weds evening set menu, changing ales such as Bowland, Copper Dragon and Moorhouses, good choice of wines, friendly helpful staff, log fires; children welcome, tables out at back, lovely streamside village with interesting church, bedrooms. *Recommended by Neil and Jacqui Victor-Corrie, Mary Hill*

☆ **Plough at Eaves**

BROUGHTON SD4838   PR4 0BJ

A6 N through Broughton, first left into Station Lane under a mile after traffic lights, then left after 1.5 miles

Pleasantly unpretentious old country tavern with two beamed homely bars, Thwaites ales, straightforward food (all day Sun), lattice windows and traditional furnishings, old guns over woodburner in one room, Royal Doulton figurines above log fire in dining bar with conservatory; quiet piped music, games machine; children welcome, front terrace and spacious side/back garden, well equipped play area, open all day weekends (till 1am Sat), closed Mon (except bank holidays). *Recommended by Dr and Mrs A K Clarke*

Bridge

BURNLEY SD8432   BB11 1UH

Bank Parade

Open-plan town-centre pub with well kept Hydes Original, several other changing ales (hundreds each year), continental beers on tap and many dozen by the bottle, farm ciders, bargain lunchtime food, friendly atmosphere and good young staff, simple chairs and tables on left, small snug and leather sofas on right; open all day (till 1am Fri, Sat), closed Mon, Tues. *Recommended by Dr Kevan Tucker*

Trackside

BURY SD8313   BL9 0EY

East Lancashire Railway Station, Bolton Street

Welcoming busy station bar by East Lancashire steam railway, bright, airy and clean with eight changing ales, bottled imports, farm cider and great range of whiskies, enjoyable home-made food (not Mon, Tues), fine display of beer labels on ceiling; children welcome till 7.30, platform tables, open all day. *Recommended by the Didler, Don Bryan, Ben Williams*

Longlands

CARNFORTH SD5173   LA6 1JH

Tewitfield, about 2 miles N; A6070, off A6

Bustling family-run village inn with good local beer range, friendly helpful staff, good interesting food in bar and restaurant (worth booking), live music Mon; bedrooms, self-catering cottages. *Recommended by Tony and Maggie Harwood, Becky Mason*

Church Inn

CHEADLE HULME SJ8785   SK8 7EG

Ravenoak Road (A5149 SE)

Bustling friendly local, smart and genuinely old, with good fresh mediterranean-influenced food (all day Sun) in restaurant and (ordered from small hatch) in bar, pleasant waitresses, four well kept Robinsons, coal fire; open all day. *Recommended by Stuart Paulley, Andy and Jill Kassube*

☆ **Dog & Partridge**

CHIPPING SD6141   PR3 2TH

Hesketh Lane; crossroads Chipping—Longridge with Inglewhite—Clitheroe

Comfortable old-fashioned and much altered 16th-c dining pub in grand countryside, enjoyable food (all day Sun) served by friendly staff, Tetleys ales, beams, exposed stone walls and good log fire, small armchairs around close-set tables in main lounge, smart casual dress for evening restaurant; children welcome, open all day Sun, closed Mon. *Recommended by anon*

CHORLEY SD5817   PR6 9HA
Yew Tree
Dill Hall Brow, Heath Charnock – out past Limbrick towards the reservoirs

Attractive tucked-away restauranty pub with good food from open kitchen (all day Sun – best to book at weekends), lunchtime sandwiches too, helpful friendly staff; children welcome, picnic-sets out on decked area, closed Mon. *Recommended by Simon Stott*

CHORLTON CUM HARDY SJ8193   M21 9HS
Horse & Jockey
Chorlton Green

Refurbished low-beamed pub with mock-Tudor façade, own-brewed Bootleg ales and guests, knowledgeable chatty staff, all-day bar food, more restauranty things in high-ceilinged evening/weekend dining room (part of former Victorian brewery), good mix of customers from mothers with prams to the local history society; dogs allowed in tap room, picnic-sets on front terrace looking across to green, open all day. *Recommended by Pete Yearsley, Malcolm and Pauline Pelliatt*

CONDER GREEN SD4655   LA2 0BD
Thurnham Mill Hotel
Signed off A588 just S

Converted early 19th-c stone-built mill, comfortable beamed and flagstoned bar with good reasonably priced food, Everards and other ales, lots of whiskies, friendly helpful staff, log fires, restaurant overlooking Lancaster Canal lock; children welcome, tables out on terrace, fenced play area, 15 comfortable bedrooms, good breakfast, open all day. *Recommended by Margaret Dickinson*

CROSBY SJ3100   L23 7XY
Crows Nest
Victoria Road, Great Crosby

Unspoilt character roadside local with cosy bar, snug and Victorian-style lounge, all neatly looked after by welcoming landlady, well kept Cains, Theakstons and guests; tables outside, open all day. *Recommended by the Didler, Brian Conrad*

DENSHAW SD9710   OL3 5SN
Printers Arms
Oldham Road

Above Oldham in shadow of Saddlesworth Moor, modernised interior with small log-fire bar and three other rooms, popular competitively priced food including OAP midweek deals, a beer brewed for them by Bazens and Timothy Taylors Golden Best, several wines by the glass, friendly efficient young staff. *Recommended by Michael Butler, Stuart Paulley*

☆ DENSHAW SD9711   OL3 5UN
Rams Head
2 miles from M62 junction 2; A672 towards Oldham, pub N of village

Sweeping moorland views from inviting dining pub with four thick-walled traditional little rooms, tasty food (all day Sun) including seasonal game and plenty of seafood, well kept Black Sheep and Timothy Taylors, good attentive service, beam-and-plank ceilings, panelling, oak settles and built-in benches, log fires, tea room and adjacent delicatessen selling locally sourced meat and other produce; soft piped music; children welcome (not Sat evening), open all day Sun, closed Mon (except bank holidays). *Recommended by Gordon and Margaret Ormondroyd, Dr Kevan Tucker, Gill and Malcolm Stott, Clive Flynn, Brian and Anna Marsden and others*

Please tell us if any pub deserves to be included or upgraded to a featured top pub – and why: **feedback@goodguides.com**, or (no stamp needed) The Good Pub Guide, FREEPOST TN1569, Wadhurst, E Sussex TN5 7BR.

DENTON SJ9395   M34 3FF

Lowes Arms
Hyde Road (A57)

For now no longer brewing their own LAB ales but serving good local Hornbeam and Phoenix, jovial landlord and helpful friendly staff, wide choice of good bargain food including offers, bar with games, restaurant; tables outside, smoking shelter, open all day weekends. *Recommended by Dennis Jones, Stuart Paulley and others*

DOWNHAM SD7844   BB7 4BJ

☆ ## Assheton Arms
Off A59 NE of Clitheroe, via Chatburn

Neatly kept 18th-c pub in lovely village location with Pendle Hill view, cosy low-beamed L-shaped bar with pews, big oak tables and massive stone fireplace, good range of food (all day Sun) including seafood menu, quick service, lots of wines by the glass, two real ales; piped music; children and dogs welcome, picnic-sets outside, open all day weekends. *Recommended by C A Bryson*

DUNHAM TOWN SJ7288   WA14 5RP

Rope & Anchor
Paddock Lane, Dunham Massey

Popular recently refurbished dining pub, good food, first-rate service, well kept Holts, garden room for families. *Recommended by Hilary Forrest, David Heath, David M Smith*

ECCLES SJ7798   M30 0LS

Albert Edward
Church Street

Popular cheery local with main bar and three other rooms, flagstones and old tiles, fire, old local photographs, bargain Sam Smiths; small back terrace, open all day. *Recommended by the Didler*

ECCLES SJ7598   M30 7HD

Grapes
Liverpool Road, Peel Green; A57 0.5 miles from M63 junction 2

Handsome brawny Edwardian local with superb etched glass, wall tiling and mosaic floor, lots of mahogany, eye-catching staircase, well kept bargain Holts and maybe a guest beer, good service, fairly quiet roomy lounge areas (children welcome till 7pm), pool in classic billiards room, vault with Manchester darts, drinking corridor; tables outside, open all day. *Recommended by the Didler*

ECCLES SJ7798   M30 0BP

Lamb
Regent Street (A57)

Full-blooded Edwardian three-room local, splendid etched windows, fine woodwork and furnishings, extravagantly tiled stairway, trophies in display case, bargain Holts and lunchtime sandwiches, full-size snooker table in original billiards room, friendly atmosphere with many older regulars; open all day. *Recommended by the Didler*

ECCLES SJ7798   M30 0EN

Royal Oak
Barton Lane

Large old-fashioned Edwardian corner pub, several busy rooms off corridor, handsome tilework, mosaic floors and fittings, well kept cheap Holts, good licensees, pool; children allowed daytime in back lounge (may be organ sing-alongs), open all day from 9.30am. *Recommended by the Didler*

ECCLES SJ7698   M30 0QN
Stanley Arms
Eliza Ann Street/Liverpool Road (A57), Patricroft

Unspoilt mid-Victorian corner local with bargain Holts, popular front bar, hatch serving lobby and corridor to small back rooms, one with cast-iron range, lunchtime cobs, friendly licensees; open all day. *Recommended by the Didler*

EUXTON SD5318   PR7 6EG
Travellers Rest
Dawbers Lane (A581 W)

Refurbished old dining pub (most here to eat) with good varied range of popular food including daily specials, well organised staff, real ales; dogs welcome in part of back bar, nice side garden. *Recommended by Margaret Dickinson, Sandie and Andrew Geddes*

FENCE SD8338   BB12 9QG
Old Sparrow Hawk
Wheatley Lane Road

Big rambling black and white timbered pub, good selection of real ales, enjoyable popular food, good service. *Recommended by Guy Vowles, Ken and Lynda Taylor, Dr Kevan Tucker*

FRECKLETON SD4328   PR4 1HA
Ship
Towards Naze Lane industrial estate, then right into Bunker Street

Old pub with roomy main bar, big windows overlooking water meadows, good choice of enjoyable generous well priced pubby food (all day weekends), attentive service, half a dozen well kept ales, games area with TV, upstairs restaurant; children allowed, disabled facilities, tables out behind, open all day. *Recommended by E A Eaves*

GARSTANG SD4945   PR3 1PA
☆ Th'Owd Tithebarn
Off Church Street

Large barn with flagstoned terrace overlooking Lancaster Canal marina, Victorian country life theme with long refectory table, old kitchen range, masses of farm tools, stuffed animals and birds, flagstones and high rafters, generous simple food all day from filled baguettes up, Black Sheep and York ales, good value wine by the glass, quieter parlour welcoming children; piped music; open all day summer. *Recommended by Dr Kevan Tucker, Francesca Salvini*

GOOSNARGH SD5636   PR3 2AU
☆ Stags Head
Whittingham Lane (B5269)

Lots of separate mainly old-world areas rambling around central servery, plenty of nice features including proper old-fashioned radiators, open fires too, good value interesting home-made food from local produce (even their own pork scratchings), children's helpings, good service, well kept changing ales, popular restaurant; piped and some live music; dogs welcome, tables out in pleasant pergola and on lawn, closed Tues otherwise open all day. *Recommended by Margaret Dickinson, Denise L Painter*

GREAT HARWOOD SD7332   BB6 7BA
Royal
Station Road

Substantial Victorian pub with good changing range of beers from small breweries, tap for nearby Red Rose brewery, good soft drinks choice (own sarsaparilla), great selection of bottled beers, enjoyable wholesome food, simple traditional fittings, friendly atmosphere, pub games including pool and darts; big-screen TV, live music Fri; partly covered terrace, three bedrooms, closed lunchtime Mon-Thurs, open all day Fri-Sun. *Recommended by the Didler*

GRINDLETON SD7545   BB7 4QR
☆ **Duke of York**
Off A59 NE of Clitheroe, either via Chatburn, or off A671 in W Bradford; Brow Top

Welcoming chef/landlord and neat helpful staff in comfortable and civilised dining pub, good imaginative well presented food including set deals, good wines, Black Sheep Best and Thwaites Original, various areas including one with open fire, views over Ribble Valley to Pendle Hill; tables on raised decking and in garden behind, closed Mon.
Recommended by John and Sylvia Harrop, Michael Ellis, Peter and Josie Fawcett, Steve Whalley

HAWKSHAW SD7515   BL8 4JS
Red Lion
Ramsbottom Road

Refurbished pub/hotel now owned by Lees, their ales, enjoyable good value food; children welcome, bedrooms, quiet spot by River Irwell. *Recommended by Ben Williams, Norma and Noel Thomas, John and Sylvia Harrop*

HESKIN GREEN SD5315   PR7 5NP
☆ **Farmers Arms**
Wood Lane (B5250, N of M6 junction 27)

Popular family-run country pub, good choice of well priced home-made food in two-level dining area, cheerful helpful staff, Black Sheep, Jennings, Prospect and Timothy Taylors Landlord, heavy black beams, sparkling brasses, china and stuffed animals, darts in public bar; piped and some live music, Sky TV, Thurs quiz; picnic-sets in big colourful garden, play area, more tables front and side, good value bedrooms, open all day weekends. *Recommended by Margaret Dickinson, Norma and Noel Thomas*

HEST BANK SD4766   LA2 6DN
☆ **Hest Bank Inn**
Hest Bank Lane; off A6 just N of Lancaster

Good choice of enjoyable food in picturesque three-bar coaching inn, nice setting close to Morecambe Bay, well kept ales, decent wines, friendly helpful young staff, separate restaurant area with pleasant conservatory; children welcome, plenty of tables out by Lancaster Canal, open all day. *Recommended by Tony and Maggie Harwood*

HURST GREEN SD6837   BB7 9QJ
☆ **Shireburn Arms**
Whalley Road (B6243 Clitheroe—Goosnargh)

Quiet comfortable 17th-c hotel with peaceful Ribble Valley views from big light and airy restaurant and lovely neatly kept garden with attractive terrace and wendy house, friendly helpful staff, decent reasonably priced food from sandwiches and snacks (9-5) through pubby favourites to restaurant dishes, Bowland Hen Harrier and Theakstons Best, daily papers, armchairs, sofas and log fire in beamed lounge bar with linked dining area; faint piped music; pretty Tolkien walk from here, comfortable bedrooms.
Recommended by anon

HYDE SJ9495   SK14 2BJ
Cheshire Ring
Manchester Road (A57, between M67 junctions 2 and 3)

Welcoming pub tied to Beartown brewery, their good value ales kept well, guest beers and imports on tap, farm ciders and perries, good house wines, nice home-made pies and curries; piped and some live music; open all day weekends, from 4pm Mon and Tues, 1pm Weds-Fri. *Recommended by Dennis Jones, the Didler and others*

Cribbage is a card game where you use a block of wood with holes for matchsticks or special pins to score with; regulars in cribbage pubs are usually happy to teach strangers how to play.

HYDE SJ9493 SK14 5EZ
Joshua Bradley
Stockport Road, Gee Cross

Former mansion handsomely converted to pub/restaurant keeping panelling, moulded ceilings and imposing fireplaces, good range of well priced pubby food, three well kept Hydes ales and a guest, friendly efficient staff; heated terrace, play area. *Recommended by Dennis Jones*

HYDE SJ9595 SK14 2NN
Sportsman
Mottram Road

Bright cheerful Victorian local, Pennine ales and lots of changing guests (frequent beer festivals), welcoming licensees, bargain bar food, upstairs cuban restaurant, bare boards and open fires, pub games, full-size snooker table upstairs; children and dogs welcome. *Recommended by Dennis Jones, the Didler and others*

IRBY SJ2586 CH49 3NT
Irby Mill
Mill Lane, off Greasby Road

Converted miller's cottage (original windmill demolished 1898) doing well under present management, eight well kept ales, good choice of wines by the glass, popular reasonably priced food all day (till 6pm Sun) from generous sandwiches up, friendly service, two low-beamed traditional flagstoned rooms and comfortable carpeted lounge, log fire, interesting old photographs and history; tables on terraces and side grass, open all day. *Recommended by David Duff, Tony Tollitt, Clive Watkin and others*

LANCASTER SD4761 LA1 1PP
☆
Borough
Dalton Square

Popular city-centre pub, stylishly civilised, with chandeliers, dark leather sofas and armchairs, antique tables and lamps, chunky candles, high stools and elbow tables, good variety of ales including locals such as Bowland, Hawkshead, Lancaster and Thwaites, lots of bottled beers, big dining room with central tables and booths along one side, enjoyable all-day food with emphasis on local suppliers, good value two course lunch (not Sun), snacks from deli counter, jams and local produce for sale; comedy last Sun of month, poker Mon night; children welcome, dogs in bar, lovely tree-sheltered garden. *Recommended by Karen Eliot, Mike Horgan, Di Wright, Colin Woodward*

LANCASTER SD4761 LA1 1SU
☆ ## Water Witch
Parking in Aldcliffe Road behind Royal Lancaster Infirmary, off A6

Attractive conversion of 18th-c canalside barge-horse stabling, flagstones, stripped stone, rafters and pitch-pine panelling, seven well kept ales (third-of-a-pint glasses available) from mirrored bar, enjoyable food all day including specials, prompt pleasant service, upstairs restaurant; children in eating areas, tables outside. *Recommended by Brian and Anna Marsden*

LEIGH SJ6599 WN7 4DB
Waterside
Twist Lane

Civilised pub in tall converted 19th-c warehouses by Bridgewater Canal, handy for indoor and outdoor markets, wide choice of enjoyable bargain food all day including OAP and other deals, Greene King ales, good friendly service, chatty lunchtime atmosphere; live music or disco Thurs-Sat; children welcome, disabled access and facilities, plenty of waterside tables, ducks and swans, open all day. *Recommended by Ben Williams*

LITTLE ECCLESTON SD4240   PR3 0YP

 Cartford

Cartford Lane, off A586 Garstang—Blackpool, by toll bridge

Prettily placed 17th-c coaching inn on river banks, unusual four-level layout combining traditional and contemporary elements, oak beams, light wood floors, log fire, changing real ales and speciality bottled beers, Weston's cider, food generally well liked, french owners and friendly young staff, restaurant; TV; children welcome, tables in garden looking out over River Wyre (crossed by toll bridge), the Trough of Bowland and Beacon Fell, bedrooms, open all day, closed Mon lunchtime. *Recommended by Nik Maguire, Phil and Helen Holt, P M Dodd*

LIVERPOOL SJ3489   L1 8DQ

 Baltic Fleet

Wapping, near Albert Dock

Unusual bow-fronted pub, easy convivial local atmosphere, wide range of interesting beers including own good Wapping brews, several wines by the glass, enjoyable straightforward well priced food (not Sat lunchtime) including traditional scouse, weekend breakfasts, bare boards, big arched windows, simple mix of furnishings, nautical paraphernalia, newspapers, upstairs lounge; piped music, TV; children welcome in eating areas, dogs in bar, back terrace, open all day. *Recommended by Tony and Wendy Hobden, Eric Larkham, Rob and Catherine Dunster, the Didler, Peter Smith and Judith Brown, Andy and Jill Kassube and others*

LIVERPOOL SJ3589   L7 7EB

Belvedere

Sugnall Street

Unspoilt Victorian pub with friendly chatty bar, original fittings including etched glass, coal fires, four changing ales, good pizzas, darts and other games; open all day. *Recommended by the Didler*

LIVERPOOL SJ3588   L8 5XJ

 Brewery Tap

Cains Brewery, Stanhope Street

Victorian pub with full Cains range at reasonable prices, guest beers, friendly efficient staff, good value food weekday lunchtimes, nicely understated clean décor, wooden floors, plush raised side snug, interesting old prints and breweriana, handsome bar, gas fire, daily papers; sports TV, no dogs; children till 8pm, disabled access, brewery tours, open all day. *Recommended by Eric Larkham, the Didler, Claes Mauroy*

LIVERPOOL SJ3589   L1 9BB

Cracke

Rice Street

Friendly unsmart local popular with students, Liverpool Organic, Thwaites, and several guests, farm cider, sandwiches till 6pm, small unspoilt bar with bare boards and bench seats, snug and bigger back room with unusual Beatles diorama, lots of posters for local events; juke box, sports TV; picnic-sets in sizeable back garden, open all day. *Recommended by the Didler*

LIVERPOOL SJ3589   L1 2SP

Dispensary

Renshaw Street

Small busy central pub with up to ten well kept ales including Cains and other local brews, bottled imports, no food, polished panelling, wonderful etched windows, bare boards, comfortable raised back bar with coal fire, Victorian medical artefacts; piped music, silent TVs; open all day. *Recommended by Tony and Wendy Hobden, Eric Larkham, Maurice and Gill McMahon, the Didler, Andy and Jill Kassube and others*

892 | THE NORTH WEST

LIVERPOOL SJ3490   L1 1HF
☆ **Doctor Duncan**
St Johns Lane

Friendly Victorian pub with several rooms including impressive back area with pillared
and vaulted tiled ceiling, full Cains range and guest beers well kept, belgian beers on tap,
enjoyable good value food, pleasant helpful service, daily papers; may be piped music, can
get lively in evenings and busy weekends; family room, open all day. *Recommended by
Eric Larkham, the Didler, Claes Mauroy*

LIVERPOOL SJ3590   L1 9BH
Everyman Bistro
Hope Street, below Everyman Theatre

Busy low-ceilinged clattery basement, spotless with long wooden tables on tiled floor, four
well kept ales, side room with good reasonably priced home-made food, friendly service;
closed Sun, otherwise open all day. *Recommended by the Didler*

LIVERPOOL SJ3589   L1 9AS
Fly in the Loaf
Hardman Street

Former bakery with smart gleaming bar serving Okells and up to seven ales from smaller
brewers, foreign beers too, simple low-priced home-made food (not Mon), friendly
service, long room with panelling, some raised sections, even a pulpit; piped music, sports
TV, upstairs lavatories, open all day, till midnight weekends. *Recommended by Eric Larkham,
Rachel Platonov, Nigel Schaay, the Didler, Jeremy King, Claes Mauroy*

LIVERPOOL SJ3490   L1 1HW
Globe
Cases Street, opposite station

Chatty traditional little local in busy shopping area (can get packed), friendly staff, good
selection of well kept ales, lunchtime filled cobs, sloping floor, quieter cosy back room,
prints of old Liverpool; 60s piped music; open all day. *Recommended by the Didler*

LIVERPOOL SJ3490   L2 2AW
Hole In Ye Wall
Off Dale Street

Well restored 18th-c pub, thriving local atmosphere in high-beamed panelled bar, seven
changing ales (fed by gravity from upstairs – no cellar as pub is on Quaker burial site),
sandwiches and basic food till 5pm, free chip butties Sun when there's a traditional sing-
along, friendly staff, plenty of woodwork, stained glass, old Liverpool photographs, coal-
effect gas fire in unusual brass-canopied fireplace; no dogs; children allowed till 5pm,
open all day. *Recommended by the Didler, Claes Mauroy*

LIVERPOOL SJ3490   L2 2BP
Lion
Moorfields, off Tithebarn Street

Beautifully preserved ornate Victorian tavern, great changing beer choice, over 80 malt
whiskies, friendly landlord interested in pub's history, good value lunchtime food
including splendid cheese and pie specialities, sparkling etched glass and serving
hatches in central bar, unusual wallpaper and matching curtains, big mirrors, panelling
and tilework, two small back lounges one with fine glass dome, coal fire; silent fruit
machine; open all day. *Recommended by the Didler, Andy and Jill Kassube, Claes Mauroy*

LIVERPOOL SJ3489   L1 5AG
Monro
Duke Street

Stylish gastropub, popular comfortable and well run, with good choice of interesting food
including vegetarian menu, early evening deals (not Sun), well kept Marstons and guests

from small bar, fast friendly service; courtyard tables, open all day till late. *Recommended by the Didler, Peter Smith and Judith Brown*

LIVERPOOL SJ3589   L8 7LY
Peter Kavanaghs
Egerton Street, off Catherine Street

Shuttered Victorian pub with interesting décor in several small rooms including old-world murals, stained glass and lots of bric-a-brac (bicycle hanging from ceiling), piano, wooden settles and real fires, well kept Cains, Greene King, Wychwood and guests, friendly licensees happy to show you around including cellars, popular with locals and students; open all day. *Recommended by Eric Larkham, the Didler, Claes Mauroy*

LIVERPOOL SJ3490   L1 1EB
Richmond
Williamson Street

Popular small corner pub in pedestrianised area, nice old interior and fittings including original Bass mirror, Bass, Black Sheep Cains, Caledonian Deuchars IPA, Timothy Taylors Landlord and changing guests, over 50 malts; sports TV; tables out in front, open all day from 10am. *Recommended by the Didler*

LIVERPOOL SJ3589   L1 2SX
Roscoe Head
Roscoe Street

Unassuming old local with cosy bar, snug and two other spotless unspoilt little rooms, friendly long-serving landlady, well kept Jennings, Tetleys and four guests, inexpensive home-made lunches (not weekends), interesting memorabilia, traditional games including cribbage, quiz Tues and Thurs; open all day till midnight. *Recommended by Eric Larkham, the Didler, Sean Brophy, Andy and Jill Kassube, Claes Mauroy*

LIVERPOOL SJ3490   L2 2JH
Ship & Mitre
Dale Street

Friendly local with fine art deco exterior and ship-like interior, popular with university people, up to 12 changing unusual ales (many beer festivals), over 70 bottled continental beers, farm ciders, good value basic food (all day Fri-Sun), upstairs function room with original 1930s décor; well behaved children till 7pm, dogs welcome, open all day. *Recommended by Eric Larkham, the Didler, Andy and Jill Kassube*

LIVERPOOL SJ3589   L1 4DQ
Swan
Wood Street

Neon sign for this busy unsmart three-floor pub, bare boards and dim lighting, up to eight beers including good value Hydes, bottled belgian beers, Weston's cider, good value cobs and weekday lunches, friendly staff; loud juke box draws younger crowd, silent fruit machine; open all day (till 2am Thurs-Sat). *Recommended by the Didler, Jeremy King*

LIVERPOOL SJ3490   L2 2EZ
 ## Thomas Rigbys
Dale Street

Spacious beamed and panelled Victorian pub with mosaic flooring, old tiles and etched glass, Okells and five changing guests, lots of bottled imports, impressively long bar, steps up to main area, table service from attentive staff, reasonably priced hearty home-made food (such as scouse) all day till 7pm; disabled access, seats in big courtyard, open all day. *Recommended by the Didler, Frank Blanchard, Matt Haycox, David Crook and others*

There are report forms at the back of the book.

LIVERPOOL SJ3197   L22 8QR
Volunteer
East Street

Classic friendly old local with superb etched glass and wood panelling, busy bar,
comfortable lounge (table service here), well kept Black Sheep, Tetley and guests,
newspapers; open all day. *Recommended by the Didler*

LIVERPOOL SJ3490   L2 6PT
White Star
Rainford Gardens, off Matthew Street

Lively traditional local dating to the 18th c, cosy bar, lots of woodwork, boxing
photographs, White Star shipping line and Beatles memorabilia (they used to rehearse in
back room), well kept ales including Bass, Bowland and Caledonian Deuchars IPA, basic
lunchtime food, friendly staff; sports TVs; open all day. *Recommended by the Didler, Andy and
Jill Kassube, Claes Mauroy*

LONGRIDGE SD6137   PR3 2YJ
Corporation Arms
Lower Road (B6243)

Comfortably refurbished 18th-c pub next to reservoir, wide range of largely traditional
food all day, small helpings available, three or four well kept changing ales such as
Bowland and Brysons, lots of malt whiskies, good atmosphere in three small linked rooms
and restaurant; good bed and breakfast, open all day. *Recommended by Andy and
Jill Kassube, Ron Neville*

☆ LYDGATE SD9704   OL4 4JJ
White Hart
*Stockport Road; Lydgate not marked on some maps and not the one near Todmorden;
take A669 Oldham—Saddleworth, right at brow of hill to A6050 after almost 2.5 miles*

Smart up-to-date dining pub overlooking Pennine moors, mix of locals in bar or simpler
end rooms and diners in elegant brasserie with smartly dressed staff, high quality (not
cheap) food, Lees, Timothy Taylors and a guest beer, 16 wines by the glass, old beams and
exposed stonework contrasting with deep red or purple walls and modern artwork, open
fires, newspapers; TV in lounge; children welcome, dogs in bar, picnic-sets on back lawn
making most of position, bedrooms, open all day. *Recommended by Brian and Anna Marsden,
P J and R D Greaves, David and Cathrine Whiting, Gill and Malcolm Stott, Ed and Anna Fraser*

LYDIATE SD3604   L31 4HD
Scotch Piper
Southport Road; A4157

Medieval thatched pub, well worn-in, with heavy low beams, flagstones, thick stone walls
and dogs sprawled in front of roaring fires, Banks's and a guest from tiny counter in main
room, corridor to middle room with darts and back snug, no food; bikers' night Weds,
outside lavatories; big garden, open all day weekends. *Recommended by the Didler,
Mike Leadbetter*

MANCHESTER SJ8498   M4 4BR
Angel
Angel Street, off Rochdale Road

Good value home-made food from pub standards to more upscale dishes, eight well kept
changing ales including Bobs, bottled beers, farm cider and perry, bare boards bar with
piano, smaller upstairs restaurant with log fire, and paintings by local artist; children and
dogs welcome, back beer garden, open all day, closed Sun. *Recommended by
Chris Johnson, the Didler*

MANCHESTER SJ8398   M2 6HQ
Ape & Apple
John Dalton Street

Big no-frills open-plan pub, well kept bargain Holts, hearty bar food (Weds curry night), comfortable seats in bare-boards bar with lots of old prints and posters, armchairs in upstairs lounge, friendly atmosphere; piped music, TV area, games machines, Thurs quiz; beer garden, bedrooms, open all day, closes 9pm Sun. *Recommended by the Didler, Dr and Mrs A K Clarke*

MANCHESTER SJ8498   M4 5JN
Bar Fringe
Swan Street

Long bare-boards bar specialising in continental beers, also five changing ales from small local breweries and farm cider, friendly staff, basic snacks till 4pm (no food at weekends), daily papers, shelves of empty beer bottles, cartoons, posters, motorcycle hung above door, rock juke box; no children or dogs; tables out behind, open all day, till late Sat, Sun. *Recommended by Jeremy King, Chris Johnson, the Didler*

☆ MANCHESTER SJ8397   M1 5LE
Britons Protection
Great Bridgewater Street, corner of Lower Mosley Street

Lively unpretentious city pub with five well kept ales, 235 malt whiskies and cheap lunchtime snacks including range of pies, unspoilt little rooms including two cosy inner lounges with hatch service, attractive brass, solidly comfortable furnishings, tiled murals of 1819 Peterloo Massacre (took place nearby), massive bar counter with heated footrails, coal-effect gas fire, may have storytelling, silent film shows and acoustic music; gets very busy lunchtime and weekends; tables in back garden, open all day. *Recommended by Simon Greenwood, Dr and Mrs A K Clarke, Jeremy King, the Didler, Dennis Jones and others*

MANCHESTER SJ8498   M4 1LE
Castle
Oldham Street, about 200 yards from Piccadilly, on right

Refurbished 17th-c pub well run by former *Coronation Street* actor, simple traditional front bar, small snug, full Robinsons range from fine bank of handpumps, games in back room, nice tilework outside, live music; open all day. *Recommended by the Didler*

MANCHESTER SJ8497   M1 4GX
Circus
Portland Street

Traditional little bare-boards local with particularly well kept Tetleys from minute corridor bar (or may be table service), friendly landlord and staff, walls covered with photos of regulars and local celebrities, football memorabilia, leatherette banquettes in panelled back room; often looks closed but normally open all day (you may have to knock), can get very busy. *Recommended by the Didler, Mike and Eleanor Anderson*

MANCHESTER SJ8398   M2 4BQ
City Arms
Kennedy Street, off St Peters Square

Well kept Tetleys and five quickly changing guests, belgian bottled beers, occasional beer festivals, busy for bargain bar lunches, quick friendly service, coal fires, bare boards and banquettes, prints, panelling and masses of pump clips, handsome tiled façade and corridor; piped music, TV, games machine; wheelchair access but steps down to back lounge, open all day. *Recommended by the Didler, Dennis Jones, Dean Johnson, Jamie Price*

With the iPhone Good Pub Guide App, you can use the iPhone's camera to
send us pictures of pubs you visit – outside or inside.

MANCHESTER SD8104   M45 6TB
Coach & Horses
Old Bury Road, Whitefield; A665 near Besses o' the Barn Station

Thriving early 19th-c Holts pub with traditional bar and lounge, their well kept ales at bargain prices, table service, darts and cards; open all day. *Recommended by the Didler*

MANCHESTER SJ8298   M5 4PF
Crescent
Crescent (A6) – opposite Salford University

Three areas off central servery with eight changing ales (regular beer festivals), many continental bottled beers and real cider, friendly licensees and young staff, buoyant local atmosphere (popular with university), low-priced home-made food including good breakfast and Weds curry night, bare boards and open fire, plenty of character, pool room, juke box; small enclosed terrace, open all day. *Recommended by Ben Williams, the Didler*

☆ MANCHESTER SJ8397   M3 4LZ
Dukes 92
Castle Street, below the bottom end of Deansgate

Imaginatively converted spacious stable block by Rochdale Canal, bare whitewashed walls, old and modern furnishings including comfortable chaises-longues and deep armchairs, spiral staircase to stylish gallery bar with canal views, well kept Moorhouses ales, decent wines and wide choice of spirits from handsome granite-topped counter, pubby food including excellent range of over three dozen cheeses and pâtés, pizzas only mid-afternoon onwards, grill menu in restaurant; piped music; children welcome till 8.30pm, waterside tables on big terrace, open all day. *Recommended by Jeremy King, Andy and Jill Kassube, Tracey and Stephen Groves*

MANCHESTER SJ8399   M3 1EU
Dutton
Park Street, Strangeways

Welcoming old-fashioned corner local near prison, three unusually shaped cosy rooms, Hydes from central servery, lots of bric-a-brac; open all day. *Recommended by the Didler*

MANCHESTER SJ8398   M3 5FP
Egerton Arms
Gore Street, Salford; A6 by station

Well cared-for character local with chandeliers, art nouveau lamps, attractive prints and dark varnished tables, well kept low-priced Holts and guests, friendly service, small room with pool and TV; piped music, silent fruit machines; open all day. *Recommended by the Didler*

MANCHESTER SJ8491   M20 6RQ
Fletcher Moss
William Street

Popular traditional local with well kept Hydes (always a mild) and interesting guests, friendly knowledgeable staff, lunchtime pies, small comfortable rooms, modern conservatory; outside seating area with smokers' shelter, open all day. *Recommended by Craig Stott*

MANCHESTER SJ8497   M1 4QX
Grey Horse
Portland Street, near Piccadilly

Small traditional one-bar Hydes local, their Bitter and Mild kept well, some unusual malt whiskies, friendly licensees, panelled servery with colourful gantry, lots of prints, photographs and plates; piped 60s/70s music, small TV, net curtains; can bring good sandwiches from next door, open all day. *Recommended by the Didler*

MANCHESTER SJ8498
Hare & Hounds
M4 4AA
Shudehill, behind Arndale

Old-fashioned 18th-c local with long narrow bar linking front snug and comfortable back lounge, notable tilework, panelling and stained glass, cheap Holts beer, friendly staff; piped music, TV; open all day. *Recommended by Jeremy King, the Didler, Douglas Wren*

MANCHESTER SJ8398
Kings Arms
M3 6AN
Bloom Street, Salford

Plain tables, bare boards and flagstones contrasting with opulent maroon/purple décor and stained glass, Bazens and changing guests, no food; juke box, music, poetry or theatre nights upstairs, knitting in snug Mon evening; children welcome till 7pm, open all day, closed Sun. *Recommended by the Didler*

MANCHESTER SJ8397
Knott Fringe
M3 4LY
Deansgate

Friendly modern glass-fronted café-bar under railway arch by Castlefield heritage site; Marble organic ales and guests, lots of continental imports, good value all-day food with emphasis on greek dishes, upstairs smokers' balcony overlooking Rochdale Canal; open all day. *Recommended by Chris Johnson, the Didler, Dr and Mrs A K Clarke, Andy and Jill Kassube*

MANCHESTER SJ8497
Lass o' Gowrie
M1 7DB
36 Charles Street; off Oxford Street at BBC

Unspoilt tiled Victorian sidestreet local, welcoming big-windowed long bar with cosy room off, stripped brickwork, nine well kept ales including Greene King, Wadworths and a good house beer (Betty's Bitter) brewed by Outstanding, bargain food (good home-made pies), friendly service; terrace overlooking river, open all day. *Recommended by the Didler*

MANCHESTER SJ8499
☆ ## Marble Arch
M4 4HY
Rochdale Road (A664), Ancoats; corner of Gould Street, just E of Victoria Station

Cheery own-brew pub with fine Victorian interior, magnificently restored lightly barrel-vaulted high ceiling, extensive marble and tiling, look out for sloping mosaic floor and frieze advertising various spirits, rustic furniture, their own five beers plus guests (brewery visible from windows in back dining room – tours by arrangement), sandwiches and simple bar food; piped music, juke box and Laurel and Hardy Preservation Society meetings third Weds of month showing old films; children welcome, small garden, open all day (till midnight Fri, Sat). *Recommended by Chris Johnson, the Didler, Andy and Jill Kassube, Ben Williams, Pat and Tony Martin*

MANCHESTER SJ8398
Mark Addy
M3 5EJ
Stanley Street, off New Bailey Street, Salford

Unusual converted waiting rooms for boat passengers, barrel-vaulted red sandstone bays with wide glassed-in brick arches, cast-iron pillars and flagstones, views over river, enjoyable food including signature cheese and pâté board, four real ales, lots of wines by the glass, brisk friendly service; piped music, sports TV facing bar; flower-filled waterside courtyard. *Recommended by Dennis Jones*

MANCHESTER SJ8492
Metropolitan
M20 2WS
Lapwing Lane, Didsbury

Large gabled dining pub (former railway hotel) with good imaginative food, well kept Caledonian Deuchars IPA, Timothy Taylors Landlord and Wells & Youngs Bombardier, extensive wine list, efficient service, numerous airy rooms, impressive period décor, open fires; tables out on decking. *Recommended by Malcolm and Pauline Pellatt*

MANCHESTER SJ8298   M3 6DB
New Oxford
Bexley Square, Salford

Up to 16 well kept ales including Mallinsons and Moorhouses (regular beer festivals), good range of imported beers, farm cider, friendly staff, light and airy café-style feel in small front bar and back room, coal fire, good value basic food till 6pm; nice terrace, open all day. *Recommended by Ben Williams, the Didler*

MANCHESTER SJ8397   M1 4BH
Paramount
Oxford Street

Well run Wetherspoons with their usual good value, particularly friendly service, beer festivals. *Recommended by Ben Williams*

☆ MANCHESTER SJ8397   M1 5JQ
Peveril of the Peak
Great Bridgewater Street

Vivid art nouveau external tilework, three sturdily furnished bare-boards rooms, interesting pictures, lots of mahogany, mirrors and stained or frosted glass, log fire, very welcoming family service, changing mainstream ales from central servery, cheap basic lunchtime food (not Sun), busy lunchtime but friendly and homely evenings; TV; children welcome, pavement tables, closed weekend lunchtimes, open all day Fri. *Recommended by the Didler*

☆ MANCHESTER SJ8397   M1 5JG
Rain Bar
Great Bridgewater Street

Bare boards and lots of woodwork in former umbrella works, well kept Lees ales, plenty of wines by the glass, generous good value pubby food all day, friendly efficient staff, relaxed atmosphere, nooks and corners, coal fire in small snug, large upstairs bar/function room; Weds quiz, piped music may be loud, can be busy with young crowd in evenings; good back terrace overlooking spruced-up Rochdale Canal, handy for Bridgwater Hall, open all day. *Recommended by Jeremy King, the Didler, Dr and Mrs A K Clarke*

MANCHESTER SJ8398   M2 1HN
Sams Chop House
Back Pool Fold, Chapel Walks

Small pleasant dining pub, offshoot from Mr Thomas Chop House, with thriving atmosphere, huge helpings of good plain english food, well kept beers, good wine choice, formal waiters, original Victorian décor, live music Mon night. *Recommended by Ian Leadbetter*

☆ MANCHESTER SJ8398   M3 1SW
Sinclairs
Cathedral Gates, off Exchange Square

Charming low-beamed and timbered 18th-c Sam Smiths pub (rebuilt here in redevelopment), all-day food including fresh oysters, no real ale (keg beers), brisk friendly service, bustling atmosphere, quieter upstairs bar with snugs and Jacobean fireplace; tables out in Shambles Square (plastic glasses), open all day. *Recommended by Ben Williams, the Didler*

MANCHESTER SJ8498   M4 5JZ
Smithfield
Swan Street

Clean bright refurbishment by welcoming new owners, one long room with eight interesting ales including Phoenix and a house beer brewed by Facers, plenty of bottled beers too, enjoyable food; good value bedrooms in nearby building, open all day. *Recommended by Chris Johnson, the Didler*

MANCHESTER SJ8284
M4 1PW
Unicorn
Church Street

Friendly and relaxed four-room pub, well kept Bass and Copper Dragon from island bar, oak panelling, lovely snug; open all day, Sun till 7pm. *Recommended by the Didler*

MARPLE SJ9389
SK6 7EJ
Hare & Hounds
Dooley Lane (A627 W)

Popular dining pub above River Goyt, modern layout and décor, some imaginative food including good mezze, well kept Hydes ales from stainless servery, good service; sports TV, no dogs; well behaved children welcome, open all day. *Recommended by Dennis Jones*

MARPLE SJ9588
SK6 7AY
Ring o' Bells
Church Lane; by Macclesfield Canal, Bridge 2

Popular old-fashioned local with newish licensees, canal and other local memorabilia in four linked rooms, well kept Robinsons ales, decent food at reasonable prices, darts and quiz nights; canalside garden, own narrowboat, open all day. *Recommended by David Hoult, Dennis Jones*

MARPLE BRIDGE SJ9889
SK6 5LW
Hare & Hounds
Mill Brow: from end of Town Street in centre turn left up Hollins Lane and keep on uphill

Comfortable and civilised stone-built country pub in lovely spot, smallish and can get crowded, good interesting local food (not Mon, Tues) from short menu, well kept Robinsons, log fires; garden behind. *Recommended by David Hoult, Gary Wilkinson*

MELLOR SJ9888
SK6 5PP
☆ ## Devonshire Arms
This is the Mellor near Marple, S of Manchester; heading out of Marple on the A626 towards Glossop, Mellor is the next road after the B6102, signposted off on the right at Marple Bridge; Longhurst Lane

Cheerful, unpretentious and cosy, front bar with old leather-seated settles and open fire, two small back rooms with Victorian fireplaces, well kept Robinsons ales, reliable pubby food; children welcome, garden with waterfall tumbling into fish pond crossed by japanese bridge, large pergola, play area on small tree-sheltered lawn; new licensee took over in spring 2011. *Recommended by David Hoult*

MELLOR SD6530
BB2 7JR
☆ ## Millstone
The Mellor near Blackburn; Mellor Lane

Restauranty stone-built village dining pub, smart and well run, panelled bar with comfortable lounge one side, modern dining extension the other, good food from all-day bar meals to enterprising cooking and popular substantial Sun lunch, obliging friendly staff, well kept Thwaites, good choice of wines by the glass, big log fire, mementoes of former landlord and England cricketer Big Jim Smith; good bedrooms and breakfast, open all day. *Recommended by Andy and Jill Kassube, P M Dodd*

Though we don't usually mention it in the text, most pubs now provide coffee or tea – so it's always worth asking.

MORECAMBE SD4264   LA4 4BZ
Midland Grand Plaza
Marine Road W

Classic art deco hotel in splendid seafront position, comfortable if unorthodox contemporary furnishings in spacious seaview Rotunda Bar, rather pricey but enjoyable food from interesting lancashire tapas to restaurant meals, good service; children welcome, 44 bedrooms, open all day. *Recommended by Mr and Mrs John Taylor, Peter and Eleanor Kenyon*

MORECAMBE SD4364   LA4 5BZ
Palatine
The Crescent

Comfortable seafront pub, enjoyable reasonably priced wholesome food, four Lancaster ales and guests, friendly helpful staff, leather armchairs and some high tables with stools, upstairs sea-view dining lounge. *Recommended by Pat and Tony Martin, Rev Mike Peatman*

NEWTON SD6950   BB7 3DY
Parkers Arms
B6478 7 miles N of Clitheroe

Friendly welcome from chatty landlord, good locally sourced food (suppliers listed) from lunchtime sandwiches up, you can eat in bar or restaurant, four real ales including Bowland, good range of wines, nice coffee and afternoon tea, log fires; children welcome, garden with lovely views, four bedrooms, pretty spot. *Recommended by R L Borthwick, Steve Whalley*

PRESTON SD5329   PR1 2EJ
Black Horse
Friargate

Friendly unspoilt pub in pedestrianised street, good Robinsons ales, inexpensive lunchtime food, unusual ornate curved and mosaic-tiled Victorian main bar, panelling, stained glass and old local photographs, two quiet cosy snugs, mirrored back area, upstairs 1920s-style bar, good juke box; no children, open all day from 10.30am, closed Sun evening. *Recommended by the Didler, Barbarrick*

☆ RABY SJ3179   CH63 4JH
Wheatsheaf
Raby Mere Road, The Green; from A540 heading S from Heswall, turn left into Upper Raby Road, village about a mile further

Up to nine real ales in pretty thatched black and white pub, simply furnished rambling rooms with homely feel, cosy central bar and nice snug formed by antique settles around fine old fireplace, small coal fire in more spacious room, reasonably priced bar food (not Sun or Mon evenings), à la carte menu in large restaurant (Tues-Sat evenings) in former cowshed leading to conservatory (piped music); children welcome, dogs in bar, picnic-sets on terrace and in pleasant back garden, open all day. *Recommended by MLR, Clive Watkin, Maurice and Gill McMahon, Roger and Anne Newbury*

RADCLIFFE SD7608   M26 3WY
Sparking Clog
Radcliffe Moor Road

Bright and clean with welcoming friendly staff, wide choice of good value enjoyable food, three Marstons ales. *Recommended by Ben Williams*

RAINFORD SD4898   WA11 7QT
Bottle & Glass
St Helens Road

Spacious but cosy Chef & Brewer popular with families, generous tasty food all day, reasonable prices, good friendly staff; tables outside. *Recommended by Adrian and Dawn Collinge*

RAMSBOTTOM SD8017   BL0 0HH
☆ **Fishermans Retreat**
Twine Valley Park/Fishery signed off A56 N of Bury at Shuttleworth; Bye Road

Remote yet busy pub/restaurant, generous food all day using produce from surrounding
estate and trout lakes (they can arrange fishing), also have own land where they raise
cattle, mountain-lodge-feel bar with beams and bare-stone walls, four well kept ales, over
500 malt whiskies (some sold in shop), good wine list, small dining room, helpful friendly
staff; children welcome, a few picnic-sets with lovely valley views, closed Mon, otherwise
open all day. *Recommended by John and Helen Rushton, Brian and Anna Marsden, David Schofield,
Simon Bessell, Stuart and Sarah Barrie*

RIBCHESTER SD6535   PR3 3ZP
Ribchester Arms
B6245

Enjoyable generous food from bar snacks to imaginative specials and Sun roasts,
welcoming staff, comfortable bar and two pleasant dining rooms; children welcome,
bedrooms, tables outside with plenty of space. *Recommended by Hilary Forrest*

RILEY GREEN SD6225   PR5 0SL
☆ **Royal Oak**
A675/A6061

Cosy low-beamed three-room former coaching inn, good generous home cooking including
notable steaks and game, four well kept Thwaites ales from long back bar, friendly
efficient service, ancient stripped stone, open fires, seats from high-backed settles to red
plush armchairs on carpet, lots of nooks and crannies, soft lighting, impressive
woodwork, fresh flowers, interesting model steam engines and plenty of bric-a-brac, two
comfortable dining rooms; can get packed at weekends; tables outside, short walk from
Leeds & Liverpool Canal, footpath to Hoghton Tower, open all day Sun. *Recommended by
Eric Ruff, Yvonne and Mike Meadley, Margaret Dickinson, Norma and Noel Thomas, Mrs Cooper*

RIMINGTON SD8045   BB7 4DS
Black Bull
Rimington Lane

French-themed inn/restaurant, small red-walled bar with mixed furniture and open fire,
large smart dining room, top-notch french country cooking, attentive service, two well
kept ales including one brewed for them, good choice of wines by the glass, decent coffee,
back function room; good local walks, five bedrooms. *Recommended by Yvonne and
Mike Meadley, Peter and Liz Smalley, Margaret Dickinson, Dr Kevan Tucker, John and Eleanor Holdsworth*

ROCHDALE SD8913   OL12 0NU
Baum
Toad Lane

Old-fashioned charm, great choice of changing ales, lots of bottled beers, food from tapas
and good sandwiches to home-made casseroles etc, bare boards, old advertisements,
conservatory; garden tables, handy for Co-op Museum (reopening in 2012 after
refurbishment), open all day. *Recommended by Ken and Lynda Taylor, Henry Paulinski*

SAWLEY SD7746   BB7 4NH
☆ **Spread Eagle**
Village signed just off A59 NE of Clitheroe

Well run carefully updated dining pub by River Ribble and near substantial 12th-c abbey
ruins; low ceilings and cosy sectioning, cottagey windows, pleasing mix of nice old and
quirky modern furniture, open fire, more formal dining areas, Theakstons, Thwaites,
Timothy Taylors and a guest ale, good food (all day Sun till 7.30pm) from sandwiches up,
afternoon teas, friendly helpful service; piped music; children welcome, handy for Forest
of Bowland walks, open all day. *Recommended by R L Borthwick, Steve Whalley, Dr Kevan Tucker,
Brian and Anna Marsden and others*

☆ **SLAIDBURN** SD7152   BB7 3EP
Hark to Bounty
B6478 N of Clitheroe

Attractive old stone-built pub with homely linked rooms, some gentle refurbishment, wide choice of enjoyable fresh food from sandwiches and light dishes up, friendly hard-working young staff, four real ales, decent wines and whiskies, comfortable chairs by open fire, games room one end, restaurant the other; pleasant back garden, charming Forest of Bowland village, good walks, nine bedrooms, open all day. *Recommended by Yvonne and Mike Meadley, Michael Lamm, Norma and Noel Thomas*

SOUTHPORT SD3316   PR9 0QE
Guest House
Union Street

Old-fashioned no-frills town pub with three rambling rooms, friendly atmosphere, up to ten well kept ales, simple lunchtime food; pleasant garden. *Recommended by David Martin, David Rainey*

SOUTHPORT SD3317   PR8 1RH
Sir Henry Segrave
Lord Street

Well placed comfortable Wetherspoons, good choice of food all day, well kept cheap beer, efficient service even when busy; open from 7am till late. *Recommended by George Atkinson, Ben Williams*

☆ **STALYBRIDGE** SJ9598   SK15 1RF
Station Buffet
The Station, Rassbottom Street

Eight quickly changing ales, foreign bottled beers and farm cider in classic Victorian station buffet bar, cheap basic meals (including all day breakfast and pots of tea), cheerful and bustling with period advertisements, station photographs and other railway memorabilia on wood panelled and red walls, newspapers and magazines, cards and board games, newish conservatory, an extension into what was ladies' waiting room and part of station-master's quarters featuring original ornate ceilings and Victorian-style wallpaper; no credit cards; children till 8pm, dogs welcome, picnic-sets on sunny Platform One by the Manchester to Huddersfield line, open all day. *Recommended by Dennis Jones, the Didler, Chris Flynn, Wendy Jones, John Fiander and others*

STALYBRIDGE SJ9896   SK15 2SU
Waggon & Horses
Mottram Road

Popular family-run pub/restaurant with good choice of enjoyable generously served food, Robinsons ales, wines by the glass, Thurs quiz; children welcome. *Recommended by JCW*

STALYBRIDGE SJ9698   SK15 2AG
White House
Water Street

Traditionally refurbished beamed Hydes pub, their ales and guests kept well, friendly welcoming staff. *Recommended by Daniel Davies*

STANDISH SD5711   WN1 2XF
Crown
Not far from M6 junction 27; Platt Lane

Refurbished traditional country pub with comfortable panelled bar, impressive range of ales kept in top condition by enthusiastic landlord (regular festivals), several bottled continental beers, enjoyable food all day including grills priced and chosen by weight from chiller, good value fixed-price menu, airy dining extension and pleasant conservatory; children allowed away from bar, comfortable clean bedrooms. *Recommended by Andy Witcomb, Bill Worthington*

STOCKPORT SJ8990   SK1 2LX

☆ ## Arden Arms
Millgate Street/Corporation Street, opposite pay & display car park

Cheerful Victorian pub in handsome dark brick building, several well preserved high-ceilinged rooms off island bar (one tiny old-fashioned snug accessed through servery), good reasonably priced daytime food, half a dozen well kept Robinsons ales, friendly efficient service, tiling and panelling, two coal fires; piped pop music may obtrude; tables in sheltered courtyard with much-used smokers' shelter, open all day. *Recommended by Dennis Jones, the Didler, Mr and Mrs Butler and others*

STOCKPORT SJ8989   SK2 6NU

Blossoms
Buxton Road (A6)

Bustling main-road Victorian local, Robinsons ales including Old Tom from bar-top cask, nice home-made pies weekday lunchtimes, three rooms off corridor including attractive back lounge with handsome fireplace, pool room; open all day weekends. *Recommended by the Didler*

STOCKPORT SJ8990   SK4 1AR

Crown
Heaton Lane, Heaton Norris

Partly open-plan Victorian pub popular for its 16 well kept changing ales, also bottled beers and real cider, three cosy lounge areas off bar, spotless stylish décor, wholesome bargain lunches, darts; frequent live music; tables in cobbled courtyard, huge viaduct above. *Recommended by Chris Morris, Dennis Jones, the Didler*

STOCKPORT SJ8991   SK4 1TY

Navigation
Manchester Road (B6167, former A626)

Friendly pub refurbished under new licensees, well kept Beartown ales and a guest, farm ciders, good pies; open all day. *Recommended by the Didler, Simon Bessell*

STOCKPORT SJ8890   SK4 2NA

Nursery
Green Lane, Heaton Norris; off A6

Popular 1930s pub on narrow cobbled lane (E end of N part of Green Lane), enjoyable straightforward lunchtime food from kitchen servery on right, friendly efficient service, well kept Hydes, big bays of banquettes in panelled stained-glass front lounge, brocaded wall banquettes in back one; children welcome if eating, immaculate bowling green behind, open all day weekends. *Recommended by the Didler*

STOCKPORT SJ8990   SK1 1JT

Queens Head
Little Underbank (can be reached by steps from St Petersgate)

Splendid Victorian restoration, long and narrow, with charming separate snug and back dining area, rare brass cordials fountain, double bank of spirits taps and old spirit lamps, old posters and adverts, reasonably priced lunchtime snacks, bargain Sam Smiths, daily papers, good friendly bustle, bench seating and bare boards; famous tiny gents' upstairs; open all day, till 7pm Sun. *Recommended by the Didler*

STOCKPORT SJ8990   SK1 2BZ

Railway
Avenue Street (just off M63 junction 13, via A560)

Bright and airy L-shaped bar with up to 15 real ales (always a mild), lots of foreign beers, farm cider, no food, friendly staff, old Stockport and railway photographs, bar billiards, tables out behind; open all day. *Recommended by Dennis Jones, the Didler*

☆ STOCKPORT SJ8990   SK1 3AY
Red Bull
Middle Hillgate

Steps up to friendly well run local, impressive beamed and flagstoned bar with dark panelling, substantial settles and seats, open fires, lots of pictures, mirrors and brassware, traditional island servery with well kept Robinsons ales, good value home-cooked bar lunches (not Sun); has expanded into adjoining building, open all day except Sun afternoon. *Recommended by the Didler*

STOCKPORT SJ8990   SK1 1RY
Swan With Two Necks
Princes Street

Traditional welcoming local with comfortable panelled bar, back lounge with skylighting and drinking corridor, bargain pub lunches from sandwiches up, teas with home-made scones, Robinsons ales; open all day (till 6pm Sun). *Recommended by the Didler, M J Winterton*

STRINES SJ9686   SK6 7GE
Sportsmans Arms
B6101 Marple—New Mills

Pleasant well kept roadside local with panoramic Goyt Valley view from picture-window lounge bar, good ever-changing ale range, enjoyable well priced home-made food including specials board, small separate bar; children welcome, tables out on side decking, heated smokers' shelter, open all day weekends. *Recommended by David Hoult, Frank Blanchard*

TODMORDEN SD9125   OL14 8JF
Staff of Life
A646

Revitalised roadside pub in steep wooded valley, five ales including Timothy Taylors and Moorhouses, traditional food using local ingredients, bargain lunch (Mon-Fri), beams, flagstones and exposed stonework, woodburner; children welcome if eating, dogs in bar, two new bedrooms. *Recommended by Geoff Boswell*

TYLDESLEY SD6902   M29 8DG
Mort Arms
Elliott Street

Bargain Holts ales in two-room 1930s pub, etched glass and polished panelling, comfortable lounge with old local photographs, friendly staff and regulars, darts and dominoes; nice back terrace, open all day. *Recommended by the Didler*

WEST KIRBY SJ2186   CH48 4EE
White Lion
Grange Road (A540)

Interesting 17th-c sandstone building, friendly proper pub with several small beamed areas on different levels, four well kept ales including a couple of local brews, good value simple bar lunches, coal stove; no children even in attractive secluded back garden up steep stone steps, open all day. *Recommended by Clive Watkin, Calvin Morton, MLR*

☆ WHALLEY SD7336   BB7 9SN
Swan
King Street

Good value food, well kept ales such as Timothy Taylors Landlord and Bowland Hunters Moon and Hen Harrier, decent choice of wines by the glass and quick friendly service in large cheery bar with colourful blinds and some modern artwork, quieter room off with leather sofas and armchairs; unobtrusive piped music, games machine, Weds quiz night; disabled access, picnic-sets on back terrace and grass strip by car park, bedrooms, open all day. *Recommended by Yvonne and Mike Meadley*

WHEELTON SD6021   PR6 8HD

☆ **Dressers Arms**

Briers Brow; off A674, 2.1 miles from M61 junction 8

Traditional pub in converted cottage, eight real ales including own brew, several malt whiskies, pubby food (all day weekends), snug low-beamed rooms with simple furnishings on patterned carpets, handsome woodburner, newspapers and magazines, restaurant; piped music, juke box, pool, games machine, TV; children welcome (not in bar after 9.30pm), dogs allowed in bar, picnic-sets under large umbrella on heated front terrace, open all day till 12.30am (1am Sat). *Recommended by Yvonne and Mike Meadley, Peter Heaton, Maurice and Gill McMahon, Ben Williams, Norma and Noel Thomas and others*

WHEELTON SD5921   PR6 8LS

Top Lock

Copthurst Lane

Picturesque spot on Leeds & Liverpool Canal, friendly hard-working staff, canal-related décor, nine well kept ales (beer festivals), enjoyable inexpensive food all day including curries, prompt friendly service, upstairs dining room, good value food; picnic-sets outside. *Recommended by Peter Heaton, Brian and Anna Marsden*

WOODFORD SJ8882   SK7 1PS

Davenport Arms

A5102 Wilmslow—Poynton

Good down-to-earth country local, well kept Robinsons ales, decent pub food, snug rooms and open fires; children allowed, tables on front terrace and in nice back garden. *Recommended by Andrew Todd*

WORSLEY SD7500   M28 2ED

Barton Arms

Stablefold; just off Barton Road (B5211, handy for M60 junction 13)

Bright clean Ember Inn, popular and friendly, with good value food, Black Sheep, Timothy Taylors Landlord and a guest; children welcome in dining areas, open all day. *Recommended by Ben Williams*

WORSLEY SD7201   M28 1ES

Woodside

Ellenbrook Road, just off A580

Vintage Inn with several eating areas around central bar, good choice of enjoyable food all day, well kept Thwaites and guests, decent wines by the glass, open fires; children welcome. *Recommended by Gerry and Rosemary Dobson*

WORSTON SD7642   BB7 1QA

Calfs Head

Village signed off A59 NW of Clitheroe

Large old stone-built coaching inn, very busy with mostly older people eating wide choice of moderately priced food including popular Sun carvery in bar and spacious conservatory looking towards Pendle Hill, well kept ales such as Black Sheep and Jennings, friendly attentive service, snug with coal fire; lovely big garden with summerhouse and stream, 11 comfortable bedrooms, open all day. *Recommended by E A Eaves*

WRAY SD6067   LA2 8QN

☆ **Inn at Wray**

2 miles E of Hornby off A683 Kirkby Lonsdale—Lancaster

Family-run dining pub, snug sitting room with soft leather sofas and easy chairs, further rooms with oriental rugs on polished boards or flagstones, open fires and woodburner, larger end room with cabinet of home-made preserves, two elegant upstairs carpeted dining rooms with comfortably upholstered chairs around smart tables, food from sandwiches to restaurant-style meals, Thwaites and Tirril ales; piped music; children welcome, dogs in bar, bedrooms, open all day weekends, closed Mon. *Recommended by Chris and Meredith Owen, Dr Kevan Tucker, Maurice and Gill McMahon*

WRIGHTINGTON SD5011   WN6 9QB
Rigbye Arms
3 miles from M6 junction 27; off A5209 via Robin Hood Lane and left into High Moor Lane

17th-c inn in attractive moorland setting, welcoming and relaxed, with good value generous food (all day Sun) including some interesting specials, friendly prompt service even when busy, well kept Tetleys and guests, several carpeted rooms, open fires; garden, bowling green, regular car club meetings, open all day Sun. *Recommended by Margaret Dickinson, Yvonne and Mike Meadley, Jack Clark*

YEALAND CONYERS SD5074   LA5 9SJ
New Inn
3 miles from M6 junction 35; village signed off A6

Ivy-covered 17th-c village pub under new management, traditionally furnished cosy beamed bar, log fire, Robinsons ales and a guest, good choice of malt whiskies, two communicating dining rooms, pubby food; piped radio; children welcome, dogs in bar, picnic-sets on sheltered lawn, smokers' shelter, usefully positioned for walks through Leighton Moss RSPB reserve and up Warton Crag, open all day. *Recommended by Don Bryan*

'Children welcome' means the pub says it lets children inside without any special restriction. If it allows them in, but to restricted areas such as an eating area or family room, we specify this. Places with separate restaurants often let children use them, and hotels usually let them into public areas such as lounges. Some pubs impose an evening time limit – let us know if you find one earlier than 9pm.

The North East & Yorkshire

Cleveland

County Durham

Northumberland

Tyne & Wear

Yorkshire

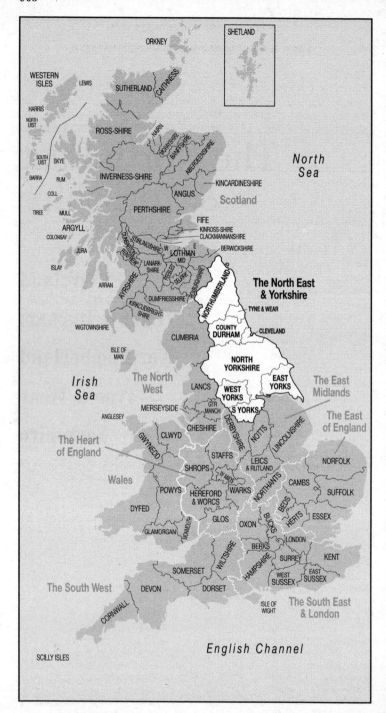

SHETLAND

ORKNEY

WESTERN
ISLES
LEWIS

HARRIS

NORTH
UIST

SOUTH
UIST

BARRA

SKYE

RUM

COLL

TIREE

MULL

ARGYLL

COLONSAY

JURA

ISLAY

ARRAN

SUTHERLAND

CAITHNESS

ROSS-SHIRE

NAIRN

INVERNESS-SHIRE

MORAYSHIRE

BANFFSHIRE

ABERDEENSHIRE

KINCARDINESHIRE

ANGUS

PERTHSHIRE

Scotland

FIFE

KINROSS-SHIRE
CLACKMANNANSHIRE

STIRLINGSHIRE

DUNBARTONSHIRE

W.
LOTHIAN
E.
MID

BERWICKSHIRE

RENFREW

LANARK-
SHIRE

PEEBLES

SELKIRK

ROXBURGHSHIRE

AYRSHIRE

DUMFRIESSHIRE

KIRKCUDBRIGHT-
SHIRE

WIGTOWNSHIRE

*North
Sea*

**The North East
& Yorkshire**

NORTHUMBERLAND

TYNE & WEAR

COUNTY
DURHAM

CLEVELAND

CUMBRIA

**NORTH
YORKSHIRE**

ISLE OF
MAN

*Irish
Sea*

*The North
West*

LANCS

**WEST
YORKS**

**EAST
YORKS**

S YORKS

*The East
Midlands*

MERSEYSIDE

GTR
MANCH

ANGLESEY

CHESHIRE

DERBYSHIRE

NOTTS

LINCOLNSHIRE

*The East
of England*

CLWYD

GWYNEDD

STAFFS

LEICS
& RUTLAND

NORFOLK

*The Heart
of England*

SHROPS

S W MIDS

WARKS

NORTHANTS

CAMBS

SUFFOLK

POWYS

HEREFORD
& WORCS

BEDS

HERTS

ESSEX

Wales

DYFED

GLOS

OXON

BUCKS

MONMOUTH

GLAMORGAN

WILTSHIRE

BERKS

LONDON

SURREY

KENT

The South West

SOMERSET

HAMPSHIRE

WEST
SUSSEX

EAST
SUSSEX

DEVON

DORSET

ISLE OF
WIGHT

*The South East
& London*

CORNWALL

SCILLY ISLES

English Channel

EDITORS' FAVOURITES
THE NORTH EAST & YORKSHIRE

This region's top pub for 2012 is the Crown at Roecliffe in **Yorkshire** (our **North East & Yorkshire Pub of the Year**: a smashing all-rounder, warm welcome from friendly family owners, fine choice of drinks and excellent food – it's also our **Yorkshire Dining Pub of the Year**). Other special pubs in this county are the Bay Horse in Burythorpe (highly enjoyable dining pub, good mix of customers), Fauconberg Arms at Coxwold (hospitable family, interesting food, huge breakfasts, pretty bedrooms), Blue Lion at East Witton (civilised dining pub with proper bar, imaginative food), Tempest Arms at Elslack (well run and bustling, generous helpings of well liked food), Horseshoe in Levisham (two jovial landlord brothers – one cooks the particularly good food – friendly atmosphere, nice bedrooms), Sandpiper in Leyburn (locals' bar, dogs welcome, delicious landlord-cooked food), Old Bridge at Ripponden (charming old pub, popular lunchtime salad carvery), and Pack Horse in Widdop (honest, traditional inn, hearty breakfasts). Also worth a visit are the Fleece in Addingham, Game Cock at Austwick, Birch Hall in Beck Hole, Carpenters Arms at Felixkirk, General Tarleton in Ferrensby, Grantley Arms in Grantley, Angel at Hetton, Blacksmiths Arms at Lastingham, Black Sheep Brewery in Masham, Dog & Gun at Oxenhope, Laurel in Robin Hood's Bay, Anvil in Sawdon and the Fat Cat in Sheffield.

Pubs that are doing well in the **North East** include the Rat at Anick (cosy all rounder), Barrasford Arms at Barrasford (delicious food, super staff and **Northumberland Dining Pub of the Year**), Feathers at Hedley on the Hill (well cooked traditional food), Rose & Crown at Romaldkirk (another terrific all-rounder) and Olde Ship at Seahouses (unchanging and stuffed with seafaring memorabilia). Other pubs worth a visit include the Red Lion in Alnmouth, Bacchus and Crown Posada which are both in Newcastle upon Tyne, Ship at Newton-by-the-Sea and the Travellers Rest at Slaley.

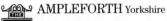 AMPLEFORTH Yorkshire   SE5878   Map 10

White Swan
Off A170 W of Helmsley; East End; YO62 4DA

Quite a choice of seating areas in this attractive pub, attentive service, enjoyable food and real ales; seats on back terrace

As this first-class pub is close to Ampleforth College and Abbey, many of the customers are visitors and parents – but there's a warm welcome for all. It's a civilised place with a beamed lounge, cream-coloured décor, sporting prints, quite a mix of tables and chairs on the slate flooring and a double-sided woodburning stove. The more conventional beamed front bar, liked by locals, has a blazing log fire, red patterned wall seating and plenty of stools, some standing timbers and a comfortable end seating area with big soft red cushions; piped music, pool table, darts and dominoes. Black Sheep Best and Theakstons Best on handpump, good wines by the glass and ten malt whiskies. The restaurant area is more formal with plush furnishings and crisp, white linen-covered tables. There are seats and tables on the large, attractive back terrace overlooking the valley.

🍽 Good, popular food includes lunchtime sandwiches, mushroom, cream and brandy linguine, a burger with melted mozzarella and bacon, gammon and egg, and steak in ale pie, with evening choices like smoked, fresh and marinated seafood salad, slow-roasted pork ribs in a barbecue sauce, salmon with a prawn and chive sauce, and half a gressingham duckling with orange sauce. *Benchmark main dish: deep-fried haddock with mushy peas £13.30. Two-course evening meal £19.50.*

Free house ~ Licensees Mr and Mrs R Thompson ~ Real ale ~ Bar food (12-2, 6-9) ~ Restaurant ~ (01439) 788239 ~ Children welcome ~ Open 12-3, 6-11.15; midday-1am(11.15 Sun) Sat

Recommended by John and Eleanor Holdsworth, Walter and Susan Rinaldi-Butcher, Janet and Peter Race, Margaret Dickinson, Dr and Mrs R G J Telfer, Ed and Anna Fraser

ANICK Northumberland
NY9565 Map 10

Rat 🍽 🍺

Village signposted NE of A69/A695 Hexham junction; NE46 4LN

Views over North Tyne Valley from terrace and garden, refurbished bar and lounge, lots of interesting knick-knacks, half a dozen mainly local real ales and interesting bar food

All seems to be going very well at this relaxed country pub, with plenty of care and thought being put in by the hard-working and enthusiastic licensees – so much so that we've given them a new Food Award this year. The traditional bar is snug and welcoming with a coal fire in the blackened kitchen range, lots of cottagey knick-knacks from antique floral chamber-pots hanging from the beams to china and glassware on a delft shelf, and little curtained windows that allow in a soft and gentle light. A conservatory has pleasant valley views and the garden is quite charming with its dovecote, statues, pretty flower beds and North Tyne Valley views from seats on the terrace; piped music, daily papers and magazines. Half a dozen changing beers on handpump are from mostly local brewers such as Allendale, Bass, Cumberland, Geltsdale, High House Farm and Wylam. They also keep ten wines (including champagne) by the glass, a local gin and farm cider. Parking is limited, but you can park around the village green.

🍽 Using carefully sourced local meat, game and seasonal local and own-grown vegetables and fruit, the good, interesting bar food, all cooked from scratch, includes sandwiches, terrine of local game, charcuterie, fried coley with creamed samphire, lemon and capers, sausage, leek and potato cake, confit duck leg with dauphinoise potato, butternut and local cheese risotto, and popular roast rib of beef with béarnaise sauce (for two people). *Benchmark main dish: braised local beef in ale £10.95. Two-course evening meal £18.30.*

Free house ~ Licensees Phil Mason and Karen Errington ~ Real ale ~ Bar food (12-2 (3 Sun), 6-9; not Sun evening, or Mon in winter except bank holidays; sandwiches only Mon 12-6 in summer) ~ Restaurant ~ (01434) 602814 ~ Open 12-3, 6-11 Mon; 12-11 Tues-Sat (10.30 Sun)

Recommended by GNI, Eric Larkham, Pat and Stewart Gordon, Chris Clark, W K Wood, Denis Newton, Comus and Sarah Elliott

AYCLIFFE County Durham   NZ2822 Map 10

County

The Green, Aycliffe village; just off A1(M) junction 59, by A167; DL5 6LX

Friendly, well run pub with four real ales, good wines and popular, interesting food; bedrooms

More or less open-plan throughout, this popular pub is cheerily decorated with blue, green and yellow paintwork, some bright red carpeting, local art and careful lighting. The wood-floored bar has attractive solid pine dining chairs and cushioned settles around a mix of pine tables, and some high bar chairs by the counter from which genuinely friendly staff serve a beer named for the pub from Yard of Ale, three guests such as Black Sheep and Harviestoun Bitter & Twisted on handpump and several wines by the glass. The carpeted lounge has a woodburning stove in a brick fireplace with candles in brass candlesticks on either side, a second fireplace with nightlights, similar furniture to the bar and painted ceiling joists. The wood-floored restaurant is minimalist with high-backed black leather dining chairs and dark window blinds. Metal tables and chairs in front overlook the pretty village green.

Good, interesting bar food includes sandwiches, ploughman's, ham hock terrine with pineapple chutney and fried quail egg, salmon fishcake with sautéed samphire and spinach cream sauce, battered cod, garlic king prawns, haunch of venison with grilled celeriac and sweet chilli and chocolate sauce, pumpkin tortellini with sage butter, parmesan and asparagus, and well hung steak with peppercorn sauce. *Benchmark main dish: steak and ale pie £9.95. Two-course evening meal £20.00.*

Free house ~ Licensee Colette Farrell ~ Real ale ~ Bar food (12-2, 5.30-9; 12-9 Sun) ~ Restaurant ~ (01325) 312273 ~ Children welcome ~ Open 11.30-3, 5-midnight; 11.30-midnight Sun ~ Bedrooms: £49S/£69S(£89B)
Recommended by Alan Thwaite, S Bloomfield, MJVK, Dave and Jenny Hughes

 BARRASFORD Northumberland   NY9173 Map 10

Barrasford Arms

Village signposted off A6079 N of Hexham; NE48 4AA

NORTHUMBERLAND DINING PUB OF THE YEAR

Friendly proper pub with good country cooking, real ales, a bustling bar, and plenty of nearby walks; bedrooms

On really good form at the moment, this bustling sandstone inn is a terrific all-rounder with great food and super staff. The traditional bar plays a big part, with its genuinely local atmosphere, good log fire, old local photographs, country bric-a-brac from horsebrasses to antlers and three interesting guests such as Caledonian Deuchars IPA, Hadrian & Border Gladiator and Wylam Gold Tankard on handpump; also good value wines by the glass. Two nice dining rooms; one is carefully decorated in greys and creams, dominated by a great stone chimneybreast hung with guns and copper pans, and has wheelback chairs around half a dozen neat tables. The second, perhaps rather more restrained, has more comfortably upholstered dining chairs; piped music, darts and TV. They have well equipped bunkhouse accommodation as well as 11 proper bedrooms. The pub is on the edge of a small North Tyne village quite close to Hadrian's Wall and looks across lovely valleys to the impressive medieval Haughton Castle (not open to the public).

🍴 Cooked by the landlord and his team using carefully sourced local meats, game and fish, the enjoyable food might include twice-baked cheddar soufflé, spinach, roast pepper and ricotta pie with bean cassoulet, brioche-crumbed fillet of plaice with chunky tomato salad and garlic mayonnaise, roast chicken with cider and honey sauce, and roast loin of deer with boulangère potatoes. *Benchmark main dish: rib-eye steak with peppercorn sauce £16.00. Two-course evening meal £19.65.*

Free house ~ Licensee Tony Binks ~ Real ale ~ Bar food ~ Restaurant ~ (01434) 681237 ~ Children welcome ~ Open 12-2.30, 6-midnight; 12-midnight Sat; 12-11.30 Sun; closed Mon lunchtime ~ Bedrooms: £65B/£85B

Recommended by Bruce and Sharon Eden, W K Wood, Michael Doswell, M A Borthwick

BLAKEY RIDGE Yorkshire SE6799 Map 10

Lion 🍺 🛏

From A171 Guisborough—Whitby follow Castleton, Hutton le Hole signposts; from A170 Kirkby Moorside—Pickering follow Keldholm, Hutton le Hole, Castleton signposts; OS Sheet 100 map reference 679996; YO62 7LQ

Extended pub in fine scenery and open all day; bedrooms

Despite this extended old pub being so remote – it's at the highest point of the North York Moors National Park – there's always a good crowd of customers. The views are stunning and there are also lots of surrounding hikes; the Coast to Coast Footpath is nearby. The beamed and rambling bars have warm open fires, a few big high-backed rustic settles around cast-iron-framed tables, lots of small dining chairs, a nice leather sofa, and stone walls hung with some old engravings and photographs of the pub under snow (it can easily get cut off in winter; eight days in the record so far). There are up to seven real ales on handpump: Black Sheep Best, Copper Dragon Golden Pippin, Greene King Old Speckled Hen, Theakstons Best, Old Peculier and XB, and Thwaites Wainwright; piped music and games machine. If you are thinking of staying, you must book well in advance. This is a regular stop-off for coach parties.

🍴 Usefully served all day, the generous helpings of traditional bar food include lunchtime sandwiches, pâté and toast, giant yorkshire pudding with gravy, home-cooked ham and egg, beef curry, haddock in batter, half a chicken, stilton and vegetable crumble, and specials like pork fillet with a watercress and ginger cream sauce, salmon with seafood sauce, and beef wellington. *Benchmark main dish: steak and mushroom pie £10.95. Two-course evening meal £18.25.*

Free house ~ Licensee Barry Crossland ~ Real ale ~ Bar food (12-10) ~ Restaurant ~ (01751) 417320 ~ Children welcome ~ Dogs allowed in bar ~ Open 10am-11pm(midnight Sat) ~ Bedrooms: £22(£43.50B)/£76B

Recommended by Dr J Barrie Jones, WAH

Bedroom prices normally include full english breakfast, VAT and any inclusive service charge that we know of. Prices before the '/' are for single rooms, after the '/' for two people in a double or twin (B includes a private bath, S a private shower). If there is no '/', the prices are only for twin or double rooms (as far as we know there are no singles). If there is no B or S, as far as we know no rooms have private facilities.

BLANCHLAND County Durham   NY9650 Map 10

Lord Crewe Arms

B6306 S of Hexham; DH8 9SP

Ancient, historic building with some unusual features, real ales, straightforward bar food and a more elaborate restaurant menu; bedrooms

The pubbiest part of this comfortable high moorland hotel is the ancient-feeling bar that is housed in an unusual long and narrow, stone barrel-vaulted crypt. In here, plush stools on ancient flagstones are lined along a narrow drinks' shelf attached to the curving wall (which is up to eight feet thick in some places) down one side of the room, with a similar row opposite along the counter. They serve Black Sheep Best, Hadrian & Border Tyneside Blonde, Wylam and a guest on handpump and several wines by the glass; flatscreen TV, darts. The Hilyard Room has a massive 13th-c fireplace once used as a hiding place by the Jacobite Tom Forster (part of the family who had owned the building before it was sold in 1704 to the formidable Lord Crewe, Bishop of Durham). Upstairs, the Derwent Room has low beams, old settles and sepia photographs on its walls and the restaurant overlooks a lovely walled garden that was formerly the cloisters.

Pubby bar food includes sandwiches, fish and chips, steak mince burger, seared lambs liver, bacon and gravy, gammon and chips, and mixed fish grill. *Benchmark main dish: mixed fish grill £13.95. Two-course evening meal £20.00.*

Free house ~ Licensee Mat Thomson ~ Real ale ~ Bar food (12-9) ~ Restaurant ~ (01434) 675251 ~ Children welcome ~ Dogs allowed in bar and bedrooms ~ Open 11-11; 12-10.30 Sun ~ Bedrooms: £60B/£90B

Recommended by Dr A McCormick, Comus and Sarah Elliott, M and J White, Claes Mauroy

BOROUGHBRIDGE Yorkshire   SE3966 Map 7

Black Bull ♀ £

St James Square; B6265, just off A1(M); YO51 9AR

Bustling town pub with real ales, several wines by the glass and traditional bar food; bedrooms

A good break from the busy A1, this is an attractive old town pub on the edge of the market square. It's said to date from the 13th c and has been looking after travellers between England and Scotland for centuries. There are lots of separate drinking and eating areas where plenty of cheerful locals drop in regularly for a pint and a chat, and the main bar area has a big stone fireplace and comfortable seats and is served through an old-fashioned hatch; there's also a cosy snug with traditional wall settles, a tap room, lounge bar and restaurant. John Smiths, Timothy Taylors Best and Theakstons XB on handpump, nine wines by the glass and 17 malt whiskies; dominoes. The two borzoi dogs are called Spot and Sadie and the two cats Kia and Mershka. The hanging baskets are lovely.

Fair value bar food includes sandwiches, chicken liver pâté, pork and chive sausages with onion gravy, a pie of the day, vegetable lasagne, beef curry and chicken pasta in a spicy tomato sauce, with more restauranty choices like pork tenderloin in a pink peppercorn and calvados sauce, chargrilled tuna loin, and venison steak with smoked bacon and blue cheese with a berry glaze. *Benchmark main dish: pie of the day £8.90. Two-course evening meal £17.50.*

Free house ~ Licensees Anthony and Jillian Burgess ~ Real ale ~ Bar food (12-2(2.30 Sun), 6-9(9.30 Fri and Sat) ~ Restaurant ~ (01423) 322413 ~ Children welcome ~ Dogs welcome ~ Folk music Sun lunchtime ~ Open 11(12 Sun)-11(midnight Fri and Sat) ~ Bedrooms: £45S/£68S

Recommended by Bob Broadhurst, the Didler, Ian and Nita Cooper, Mike and Lynn Robinson, C J Beresford-Jones

 BRADFIELD Yorkshire   SK2290   Map 7

Strines Inn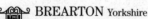

From A57 heading E of junction with A6013 (Ladybower Reservoir) take first left turn (signposted with Bradfield) then bear left; with a map can also be reached more circuitously from Strines signpost on A616 at head of Underbank Reservoir, W of Stocksbridge; S6 6JE

Surrounded by fine scenery with quite a mix of customers and traditional beer and bar food; bedrooms

Walkers and their well behaved dogs are made very welcome in this traditional old pub – which is just as well as it's surrounded by superb scenery on the edge of the High Peak National Park and there are fine walks and views all around. The main bar has black beams liberally decked with copper kettles and so forth, quite a menagerie of stuffed animals, homely red-plush-cushioned traditional wooden wall benches and small chairs, and a coal fire in the rather grand stone fireplace. Two other rooms to the right and left are similarly furnished. Bradfield Farmers Blonde, Jennings Cocker Hoop, and Marstons Pedigree on handpump and several wines by the glass; piped music. There are plenty of picnic-sets outside, and peacocks, geese and chickens. The bedrooms have four-poster beds and a dining table as the good breakfasts are served in your room – the front room overlooks the reservoir.

As well as seasonal game and daily fish dishes, the reasonably priced food includes sandwiches, game pâté, chilli con carne in a giant yorkshire pudding, a pie of the day, broccoli and cream cheese bake, liver and onions, and a huge mixed grill. *Benchmark main dish: steak in ale pie £9.25. Two-course evening meal £14.00.*

Free house ~ Licensee Bruce Howarth ~ Real ale ~ Bar food (12-2.30, 5.30-8.30 winter weekdays; all day in summer and on winter weekends) ~ (0114) 285 1247 ~ Children welcome ~ Dogs welcome ~ Open 10.30am-11pm; 10.30-3, 5.30-11 weekdays in winter ~ Bedrooms: £60B/£80B

Recommended by the Didler, Brian and Anna Marsden, Malcolm and Barbara Southwell, Gordon and Margaret Ormondroyd

BREARTON Yorkshire   SE3260   Map 7

Malt Shovel 🍴 🍷

Village signposted off A61 N of Harrogate; HG3 3BX

Friendly, family-run dining pub with imaginative food and good choice of drinks in heavily beamed rooms; airy conservatory

The Bleiker family and their staff could not be more welcoming to all their customers – our readers enjoy their visits here very much. It's mainly a dining pub with excellent food but they do keep Black Sheep Best and Timothy Taylors Landlord and a very good wine list with 14 by the glass. The heavily beamed rooms have a warm, friendly atmosphere and radiate from the attractive linenfold oak bar counter, with painted walls and light blue skirting, an attractive mix of wooden dining chairs around tables on wood or slate floors, and some partitioning that separates several candlelit dining areas. The conservatory is light and airy with lemon trees and a piano (which is used for Sunday jazz); they also hold occasional live opera evenings. There are seats in the parasoled garden. The family are also associated with Bleiker's Smokehouse near Harrogate.

The family rear their own pigs and use top-quality local produce for the imaginative, restaurant-style food: chicken and game liver pâté with home-made toasted bread, oxtail and kidney pudding, free-range chicken marinated in lemon and home-grown thyme on spinach and rösti with beetroot crisps, their speciality smoked platter, slow-cooked pork belly and crackling with black pudding mash and cider gravy, skate wing with black butter and capers, and slices of fillet steak on a sizzling platter with oyster and mint sauce and chilli; they also have a lunchtime and early evening two- and three-course set menu. *Benchmark main dish: smoked haddock with free-range egg, wild mushroom risotto and hollandaise £12.95. Two-course evening meal £20.90.*

Free house ~ Licensee Jurg Bleiker ~ Real ale ~ Bar food (12-2(3 Sat, 4 Sun), 5.30-9.30; not Sun evening, Mon or Tues) ~ Restaurant ~ (01423) 862929 ~ Children welcome ~ Jazz pianist Sun, occasional opera evenings with dinner ~ Open 12-3, 5.30-11; 12-5 Sun; closed Sun evening, all day Mon and Tues
Recommended by Peter Hacker, Michael Butler, Emma Parr

BROUGHTON Yorkshire SD9450 Map 7

Bull

A59; BD23 3AE

Handsome, carefully refurbished inn making good use of pale oak and contemporary paintwork, good choice of drinks and enjoyable food

This handsome stone inn is a welcoming place whatever the season. In summer you can eat at the solid benches and tables on the terrace and look over the grounds of Broughton Hall, and in winter there are open log fires; you can walk through the Hall Estate's 3,000 acres of rolling countryside and parkland at any time of year. They've sensibly kept the various carefully furnished rooms separate: lots of pale oak, handsome flagstones, exposed stone walls, built-in wall seats and a mix of dining chairs around polished tables, contemporary paintwork hung with photographs of local suppliers and open log fires. Copper Dragon Scotts 1816, Dark Horse Hetton Pale Ale, and Thwaites Original on handpump, several malt whiskies and a dozen wines (including champagne) by the glass; if you are dining, they will let you bring your own wine for a £10 corkage fee per bottle.

Interesting food using carefully sourced local produce includes sandwiches, nibbles with home-made bread, rabbit faggots with courgette purée and tomato relish, local seafood platter, a pie with braised veal tails, ham shank, smoked pig's jowl, button mushrooms, yellow split peas and broccoli, chargrilled minced rump steak with dripping chips and mustard mayonnaise on a toasted muffin, and seasonal sea trout with asparagus and wild garlic mash. *Benchmark main dish: fish pie £10.75. Two-course evening meal £17.50.*

Free house ~ Licensee Leanne Richardson ~ Real ale ~ Bar food (all day) ~ (01756) 792065 ~ Children welcome ~ Dogs allowed in bar ~ Open 12-11(10.30 Sun)
Recommended by Steve Whalley, John and Eleanor Holdsworth, Karen Eliot, Stu Mac, Keith Moss, Claire Hall, G Jennings, Hilary Forrest, Margaret and Jeff Graham, Ed and Anna Fraser

BURYTHORPE Yorkshire   SE7964   Map 7

Bay Horse  ♀ £

Off A64 8.5 miles NE of York ring road, via Kirkham and Westow; 5 miles S of Malton, by Welham Road; YO17 9LJ

Friendly, civilised dining pub with contemporary décor in stylish rooms, real ales, good wines and highly enjoyable food

As well as a good mix of both locals and visitors (and there's a welcome for all from the genuinely friendly staff), this well run dining pub has a lovely atmosphere and excellent food, and is surrounded by plenty of fine walks. The linked rooms are cosy, candlelit and civilised with up-to-date paintwork, stripped floorboards, a mix of chunky pine tables and elegant high-backed black or wooden dining chairs, and shelves of books. The end dining room has several attractive and amusing farmyard animal paintings, the main bar has a couple of nice old carved antique pews with interesting cushions and some ancient hunting prints, and there's a tiny end room with a sofa and open log fire and yet another red-walled room with rugs on flagstones. Tetleys, Theakstons Black Bull and Timothy Taylors Landlord on handpump and 11 good wines by the glass. On the outside terrace are some good contemporary tables and seats under parasols. The nearby Burythorpe House hotel, a former gentleman's residence, is under the same ownership.

First-rate food includes sandwiches, lunchtime choices such as garlic mushrooms on eggy bread, fish and chips with mushy peas, ham and egg and a good burger with bacon, cheese and guacamole, and evening dishes like smoked salmon rose with lemon and baby capers, risotto verde with parmesan, stir-fried beef with noodles, thai chicken curry and grilled swordfish steak with chilli and lime. The Value Award is for fair-priced lunchtime dishes. *Benchmark main dish: gressingham duck breast with raspberry sauce £14.75. Two-course evening meal £16.50.*

Free house ~ Licensee Dawn Pickering ~ Real ale ~ Bar food (12-2.30(4 Sun), 6.30-9.30 (9 Sun); not Mon) ~ Restaurant ~ (01653) 658302 ~ Children welcome ~ Dogs allowed in bar ~ Open 12-3, 6-11.30; 12-11.30 Sun; closed Mon
Recommended by Christopher Turner, Pat and Graham Williamson, C A Hall, Ed and Anna Fraser

CARTERWAY HEADS County Durham   NZ0452   Map 10

Manor House Inn ◖

A68 just N of B6278, near Derwent Reservoir; DH8 9LX

Handy after a walk with a simple bar and more comfortable lounge, bar food and five real ales; bedrooms

Homely and old-fashioned, this simple slate-roofed stone inn is a useful place if you've been walking around the nearby Derwent Valley and Reservoir. The straightforward locals' bar has an original boarded ceiling, pine tables, chairs and stools, old oak pews and a mahogany counter. The comfortable lounge bar (warmed by a woodburning stove) and restaurant both have picture windows that make the most of the lovely setting. Copper Dragon Golden Pippin, Greene King Old Speckled Hen and Ruddles County, Timothy Taylors Landlord and a guest beer from a brewer such as Concertina are on handpump alongside 70 malt whiskies; TV, darts, board games and piped music. There are rustic tables in the garden.

🍴 Usefully served all day, bar food includes sandwiches and wraps, sausage and mash, fish pie, pasta of the day, and daily specials such as baked vegetable pancake with cheese sauce, fried scallops with sweet chilli sauce, confit duck leg with sweet chilli noodles, peppered venison loin with red wine jus, and roast trout with chorizo. *Benchmark main dish: fish and chips £9.95. Two-course evening meal £16.60.*

Free house ~ Licensees Neil and Emma Oxley ~ Real ale ~ Bar food (12-9) ~ Restaurant ~ (01207) 255268 ~ Children welcome ~ Dogs allowed in bar and bedrooms ~ Open 11-11; 12-10.30 Sun ~ Bedrooms: £45B/£65B

Recommended by Stuart and Sarah Barrie, Eric Larkham, Michael Doswell, Comus and Sarah Elliott, Mr and Mrs M Hargrave, GSB, Henry Paulinski

CONSTABLE BURTON Yorkshire   SE1690   Map 10

Wyvill Arms 🍴 � ◖ ⇔

A684 E of Leyburn; DL8 5LH

Well run, friendly dining pub with interesting food, a dozen wines by the glass, real ales and efficient helpful service; comfortable bedrooms

The friendly Stevens family have now run this 18th-c former farmhouse for over a decade, and this year they've added more comfortable bedrooms, which our readers enjoy very much. There's a small bar area with a mix of seating, a finely worked plaster ceiling with the Wyvill family's coat of arms and an elaborate stone fireplace with a warm winter fire. The second bar has a lower ceiling with fans, leather seating, old oak tables, various alcoves and a model train on a railway track running around the room; the reception area includes a huge leather sofa which can seat up to eight people, another carved stone fireplace and an old leaded church stained-glass window partition. Both rooms are hung with pictures of local scenes. John Smiths and Theakstons Best on handpump, a dozen wines by the glass and some rare malt whiskies; board games. There are several large wooden benches under large white parasols for outdoor dining and picnic-sets by the well. Constable Burton Gardens are opposite and worth a visit.

🍴 Using home-grown herbs and vegetables and game from the estate across the road, the highly thought-of food includes lunchtime sandwiches, ham, pork, chicken and cheese terrine with pear and apple chutney, wild mushroom risotto, parmesan pork with a tomato and herb sauce, breaded chicken suprême stuffed with mozzarella and smoked bacon on creamed leeks with stilton sauce, sea bream with potted prawns and shrimps with a lemon butter sauce, and venison on roast vegetable purée with a cranberry and cassis jus. *Benchmark main dish: fillet steak black jack (mixed herbs and spices and a red wine and smoked bacon sauce) £23.45. Two-course evening meal £20.93.*

Free house ~ Licensee Nigel Stevens ~ Real ale ~ Bar food (12-2, 5.30-9) ~ Restaurant ~ (01677) 450581 ~ Children welcome ~ Dogs allowed in bar and bedrooms ~ Open 11-3, 5.30-11; 12-3, 5.30-10.30 Sun; closed Mon (except bank holidays) ~ Bedrooms: £60B/£75B

Recommended by John and Eleanor Holdsworth, Noel Thomas, Janet and Peter Race, Walter and Susan Rinaldi-Butcher, Ed and Anna Fraser

---

The price we give for a two-course evening meal in the featured top pub entries is the mean (average of cheapest and most expensive) price of a starter and a main course – no drinks.

COXWOLD Yorkshire   SE5377 Map 7

Fauconberg Arms 🍴 ♀ ⇌

Off A170 Thirsk—Helmsley, via Kilburn or Wass; easily found off A19, too;
YO61 4AD

**Friendly family-run inn with enjoyable generous food, a good range of
drinks, and seats in the back garden; comfortable bedrooms**

The extremely friendly and hospitable Rheinberg family always make
their customers feel glad they came for a drink, a meal or an
overnight stay in this nicely updated 17th-c inn; the breakfasts are
especially good. The heavily beamed and flagstoned bar has log fires in
both linked areas – one in an unusual arched fireplace in a broad low
inglenook – muted contemporary colours, some attractive oak chairs by
local craftsmen alongside more usual pub furnishings, nicely chosen old
local photographs and other pictures, and copper implements and china.
Hambleton Bitter, Theakstons Best and Wold Top Gold on handpump, a
thoughtful choice of wines by the glass and 28 malt whiskies. The pub
dogs, Peggy, Bramble and Phoebe, welcome other four-legged friends, if
well behaved. The candlelit dining room is quietly elegant with a gently
upmarket yet relaxed atmosphere. The garden behind the inn has seats
and tables on the terrace and views across the fields to Byland Abbey;
picnic-sets and teak benches out on the front cobbles look along this
charming village's broad tree-lined verges, bright with flower tubs. This
year, they've opened a shop selling home-baked bread, their own cheese
and other groceries.

🍴 Cooked by the landlord and his daughters using seasonal local produce and
game, the excellent food includes lunchtime sandwiches, a daily-changing
terrine or pâté, black pudding with crispy, dry-cured bacon on a cucumber and red
onion salad, fresh whitby cod in beer batter, ham and eggs, home-made burgers,
vegetable pancakes, corn-fed chicken, prawns and mushrooms in a pernod-laced
creamy sauce, daily fresh fish dishes, and pork medallions flamed in madeira with
walnuts, figs and ginger. *Benchmark main dish: beer-battered fish and chips £9.75.
Two-course evening meal £19.00.*

Free house ~ Licensee Simon Rheinberg ~ Real ale ~ Bar food (12-2, 6-9(10 Sat); 12-8
Sun) ~ Restaurant ~ (01347) 868214 ~ Children welcome ~ Dogs welcome ~ Open 11-3,
6-midnight; 11-midnight Sat ~ Bedrooms: £75B/£95S
*Recommended by Brian and Jacky Wilson, Alan McDougall, Pete Coxon, Tony and Glenys Dyer,
Peter Hacker, Michael Doswell, Janet and Peter Race*

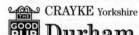

CRAYKE Yorkshire   SE5670 Map 7

Durham Ox 🍴 ♀ ⇌

Off B1363 at Brandsby, towards Easingwold; West Way; YO61 4TE

**Friendly, well run inn, interesting décor in old-fashioned, relaxing
rooms, fine drinks and smashing food; lovely views and comfortable
bedrooms**

A new Burns Bar with a woodburning stove, exposed brickwork and
large french windows that open on to a balcony area has been
created in this particularly well run inn – a favourite with quite a few of
our readers. The old-fashioned lounge bar has an enormous inglenook
fireplace, pictures and photographs on the dark red walls, interesting
satirical carvings in the panelling (Victorian copies of medieval pew

ends), polished copper and brass, and venerable tables, antique seats and settles on the flagstones. In the bottom bar is a framed illustrated account of the local history (some of it gruesome) dating back to the 12th c, and a large framed print of the original famous Durham Ox which weighed 171 stone. Black Sheep Best and Timothy Taylors Landlord on handpump, 15 wines by the glass and ten malt whiskies; piped music. There are seats in the courtyard garden, and fantastic views over the Vale of York on three sides; on the fourth side there's a charming view up the hill to the medieval church – the tale is that this is the hill up which the Grand Old Duke of York marched his men. The comfortable bedrooms are in converted farm buildings and the breakfasts are good.

Using the best seasonal, local produce and making their own bread and petits fours, the good, flavoursome food includes sandwiches, ham hock terrine with pineapple and piccalilli dressing, baked queen scallops with garlic, butter and cheese, butternut squash and sage risotto, beefburger with cheese, bacon and onion rings, sticky pork ribs with home-made spicy beans, pollack with a fricassée of clams and peas, and confit duck leg with cassoulet of toulouse sausage and pork belly. *Benchmark main dish: rib-eye steak £19.95. Two-course evening meal £20.95.*

Free house ~ Licensee Michael Ibbotson ~ Real ale ~ Bar food (12-2.30(3 Sun), 6-9.30 (8.30 Sun) ~ Restaurant ~ (01347) 821506 ~ Children welcome but must be well behaved ~ Dogs allowed in bedrooms ~ Open 11-11 ~ Bedrooms: /£100B

Recommended by Comus and Sarah Elliott, Karen Eliot, Christopher Turner, Pete Coxon, Michael Doswell, Tony and Wendy Hobden, Jeff and Wendy Williams, Peter and Anne Hollindale, Ed and Anna Fraser

CROPTON Yorkshire   SE7588 Map 10

New Inn ◗

Village signposted off A170 W of Pickering; YO18 8HH

Genuinely warm welcome in a modernised village pub with own-brew beers, traditional furnishings and brewery tours; bedrooms

By the time this edition is published, this comfortable, modernised village inn will be heading towards its 17th annual beer festival. Of course, it's their own-brewed beers that customers are here to enjoy and of the six on handpump at any one time, they might offer Blackout, Endeavour, Monkmans Slaughter, North Peaks Vicious, Two Pints and Yorkshire Warrior. They also keep a dozen malt whiskies and seven wines by the glass. The traditional village bar has wood panelling, plush seating, lots of brass and a small fire. A local artist has designed historical posters all around the downstairs conservatory that doubles as a visitor centre during busy times. The elegant restaurant has locally made furniture and paintings by local artists. Piped music, TV, games machine, darts, pool and a juke box. There's a neat terrace, a garden with a pond and a brewery shop. Brewery tours are available most days at £4.95 per person.

Generous helpings of bar food includes lunchtime sandwiches and filled ciabatta rolls, terrines, fishcakes, steak in ale pie, beer-battered cod, a trio of local sausages, and slow-braised leg of lamb with rosemary and redcurrant jus. *Benchmark main dish: steak in stout pie £9.75. Two-course evening meal £18.00.*

Own brew ~ Licensee Philip Lee ~ Real ale ~ Bar food (12-2(2.30 Sun), 6-9(8.30 Sun) ~ Restaurant ~ (01751) 417330 ~ Children welcome ~ Dogs allowed in bar and bedrooms ~ Folk festival four times a year ~ Open 11(11.30 Sun)-11(midnight Sat) ~ Bedrooms: £60B/£85B

Recommended by Tony and Wendy Hobden, Mike and Mary Strigenz, Mo and David Trudgill

DOWNHOLME Yorkshire   SE1197 Map 10

Bolton Arms

Village signposted just off A6108 Leyburn—Richmond; DL11 6AE

Enjoyable food in unusual village's cosy country pub, lovely views; bedrooms

This little stone-built pub is one of the last pubs in Britain to be owned by the state – the Ministry of Defence owns the place and it's surrounded by MoD land (a largely unspoilt swathe of Swaledale); the red-walled, simple and attractive back conservatory dining room enjoys the fine views. Down a few steps, the friendly and softly lit black-beamed and carpeted bar has two smallish linked areas off the servery where they keep Black Sheep Best and Theakstons Best on handpump, eight wines by the glass at fair prices, ten malt whiskies and interesting cordials. There are comfortable plush wall banquettes, a log fire in one neat fireplace, quite a lot of gleaming brass, a few small country pictures and drinks, advertisements on pinkish rough-plastered walls. Service is friendly and efficient; piped music and dominoes. The neat garden, on the same level as the dining room (and up steps from the front), shares the same view; there are also some lower picnic-sets and benches, and quoits. The two bedrooms, sharing a bathroom, are good value.

Cooked by the landlord, the popular bar food includes sandwiches, tasty caesar salad with smoked chicken and hot crispy bacon, spinach and ricotta pancakes, steak and mushroom pie, chicken in a creamy mushroom sauce, fresh seafood pasta, lambs liver and bacon, gammon and egg, and crispy duck with an orange, ginger and honey sauce; they also offer a two- and three-course early-bird menu Monday-Thursday evenings 6-7pm and takeaway fish and chips. *Benchmark main dish: lamb kleftiko (slow-baked and marinated) £14.50. Two-course evening meal £19.00.*

Free house ~ Licensees Steve and Nicola Ross ~ Real ale ~ Bar food (not Tues lunchtime) ~ Restaurant ~ (01748) 823716 ~ Children welcome ~ Open 10.30-3, 6-midnight; closed Tues lunchtime ~ Bedrooms: £45S/£60S
Recommended by John and Sylvia Harrop, Dr D Jeary, Ed and Anna Fraser

DURHAM County Durham   NZ2742 Map 10

Victoria ◀

Hallgarth Street (A177, near Dunelm House); DH1 3AS

Unchanging and neatly kept Victorian pub with royal memorabilia, cheerful locals, and well kept regional ales; bedrooms

The unspoilt layout of this welcoming 19th-c local consists of three little rooms leading off a central bar. Their typical Victorian décor takes in mahogany, etched and cut glass and mirrors, colourful William Morris wallpaper over a high panelled dado, some maroon plush seats in little booths, leatherette wall seats and long narrow drinkers' tables. There are also some handsome iron and tile fireplaces for the coal fires, photographs and articles showing a very proper pride in the pub, lots of period prints and engravings of Queen Victoria, and staffordshire figurines of her and the Prince Consort. It's been in the same friendly family for 36 years and attracts a good mix of locals and students. Big Lamp Bitter and Wylam Gold Tankard and up to three usually local guests from brewers such as Durham and York are on handpump, they've over 40 irish whiskies and cheap house wines; dominoes.

Bar food is limited to toasties. *Benchmark main dish: toasties £1.70.*

Free house ~ Licensee Michael Webster ~ Real ale ~ Bar food ~ (0191) 386 5269 ~ Children welcome ~ Dogs welcome ~ Open 11.45-3, 6-11; 12-2, 7-10.30 Sun ~ Bedrooms: £49B/£68B

Recommended by Comus and Sarah Elliott, Eric Larkham, the Didler, Phil and Sally Gorton, Dr and Mrs P Truelove, Peter Smith and Judith Brown, Peter F Marshall

EAST WITTON Yorkshire SE1486 Map 10

Blue Lion ⊗ ♀ ⇌
A6108 Leyburn—Ripon; DL8 4SN

Civilised dining pub with interesting rooms, daily papers, real ales, delicious food, and courteous service; comfortable bedrooms

Although most customers are here to enjoy the excellent food or to stay overnight in the individually decorated bedrooms, this civilised but informal dining pub does have a proper small bar where drinkers and their dogs mingle quite happily with those waiting to eat. This big squarish room has high-backed antique settles and old windsor chairs on the turkey rugs and flagstones, ham-hooks in the high ceiling decorated with dried wheat, teazles and so forth, a delft shelf filled with appropriate bric-a-brac, several prints, sporting caricatures and other pictures, a log fire and daily papers. Black Sheep Best and Golden Sheep and Theakstons Best on handpump, and an impressive wine list with quite a few (plus champagne) by the glass; courteous, attentive service. Picnic-sets on the gravel outside look beyond the stone houses on the far side of the village green to Witton Fell, and there's a big, pretty back garden.

Excellent and interesting – if not cheap – food might include sandwiches, slow-braised pig's cheek with red wine sauce, black pudding and apple and parsnip purée, duck and orange parfait with sage and onion toast and piccalilli, home-made tagliatelle with pancetta, wild mushrooms, cream and truffle oil, poached fillet of smoked haddock on new potatoes topped with a poached egg, leek and mushroom sauce and gruyère, a trio of free-range herb-fed chicken (breast, thigh and drumstick) each with their own garnish, and chargrilled rib-eye steak with caramelised onion butter and duck fat potatoes. *Benchmark main dish: slow-braised beef with red wine and thyme risotto £16.95. Two-course evening meal £24.45.*

Free house ~ Licensee Paul Klein ~ Real ale ~ Bar food ~ Restaurant ~ (01969) 624273 ~ Children welcome ~ Dogs allowed in bar and bedrooms ~ Open 11-11 ~ Bedrooms: £67.50S/£94S(£109B)

Recommended by Jon Clarke, David and Sue Atkinson, Mike and Shelley Woodroffe, Brian and Janet Ainscough, Pat and Stewart Gordon, the Didler, Michael Butler, Susan and Neil McLean, Dr Kevan Tucker, Janet and Peter Race, Hunter and Christine Wright, Comus and Sarah Elliott

ELSLACK Yorkshire SD9249 Map 7

Tempest Arms ⊗ ♀ ◗ ⇌
Just off A56 Earby—Skipton; BD23 3AY

Friendly inn with three log fires in stylish rooms, six real ales, good wines and extremely popular food; bedrooms

Even when this 18th-c stone dining inn is at its busiest – which it often deservedly is – the licensees and their staff remain willing and friendly. There's a wide mix of customers coming and going from families to diners and walkers with their dogs, but everyone feels welcomed and relaxed. It's stylish but understated with plenty of character in the bar and surrounding dining areas: cushioned armchairs, built-in wall seats with comfortable cushions, stools and lots of tables and three log fires – one greets you at the entrance and divides the bar and restaurant. There's quite a bit of exposed stonework, amusing prints on the cream walls, half a dozen real ales such as Dark Horse Hetton Pale Ale, Theakstons Best, Thwaites Lancaster Bomber, Timothy Taylors Golden Best and Landlord, and a beer named for the pub on handpump, 16 wines by the glass and 25 malt whiskies. There are tables outside largely screened from the road by a raised bank. The comfortable bedrooms are in a newish purpose-built extension.

Highly enjoyable and generously served, the food includes lunchtime sandwiches, tapas-style nibbles, stir-fried baby squid with asian greens and noodles, beer-battered corned beef and black pudding fritters with curry sauce, onion and cheese pie with asparagus sauce, toad in the hole, fish pie, liver and bacon with onion and madeira gravy, and chicken breast filled with mushroom mousse on rösti potato with creamy mushroom sauce. *Benchmark main dish: slow-cooked lamb shank in a redcurrant and mint gravy £12.50. Two-course evening meal £17.25.*

Free house ~ Licensees Martin and Veronica Clarkson ~ Real ale ~ Bar food (12-2.30, 6-9(9.30 Fri and Sat); 12-7.30 Sun) ~ Restaurant ~ (01282) 842450 ~ Children welcome ~ Dogs allowed in bar and bedrooms ~ Open 11-11; 12-10.30 Sun ~ Bedrooms: £62.50B/£79.95B

Recommended by Brian and Janet Ainscough, John and Eleanor Holdsworth, Ian Malone, Pat and Tony Martin, Michael Butler, Christopher Mobbs, Janet and Peter Race, Chris Brewster, Tony and Maggie Harwood, Mrs Edna M Jones, Gordon and Margaret Ormondroyd, David and Ruth Shillitoe, Jeremy King

GRETA BRIDGE County Durham   NZ0813 Map 10

Morritt Arms 🍴 🍷 🛏

Hotel signposted off A66 W of Scotch Corner; DL12 9SE

Country house hotel with nice bar, extraordinary mural, interesting food, and attractive garden with play area; bedrooms

The walls of the Dickens bar at this striking 17th-c former coaching inn were painted in 1946 by J T Y Gilroy (better known for his Guinness advertisements) with a remarkable mural depicting a series of larger-than-life Dickensian characters. Although part of a thriving and busy hotel with weddings and the like sometimes taking place, this friendly bar right at its heart does maintain a proper pubby atmosphere. Big windsor chairs and sturdy oak settles cluster around traditional cast-iron-framed tables, large windows look out on the extensive lawn and there are warm open fires. Friendly knowledgeable staff serve Thwaites Major Morritt (brewed for the pub) and Timothy Taylors Landlord from handpumps, alongside 19 wines by the glass from an extensive list; piped music. The attractively laid-out garden has some seating and teak tables in a pretty side area looking along to the graceful old bridge by the stately gates to Rokeby Park; there's also a play area for children.

Good tasty food includes sandwiches, fried lambs liver with garlic mash and thyme gravy, battered cod, lasagne, vegetable ratatouille in a filo basket, pork and leek sausages, grilled pork loin steak with creamy mushroom sauce, and chicken caesar salad. *Benchmark main dish: home-made burger £9.50. Two-course evening meal £14.00.*

Free house ~ Licensees Peter Phillips and Barbara Johnson ~ Real ale ~ Bar food (12-3, 6-9) ~ Restaurant ~ (01833) 627232 ~ Children welcome ~ Dogs allowed in bar and bedrooms ~ Open 11-11; 12-10.30 Sun ~ Bedrooms: £85S(£90B)/£110B

Recommended by Maurice Ricketts, Comus and Sarah Elliott, Jerry Brown, Barry Collett, Dr and Mrs R G J Telfer

GRINTON Yorkshire   SE0498   Map 10

Bridge Inn ◖ ⇖

B6270 W of Richmond; DL11 6HH

Bustling pub with traditional, comfortable bars, log fires, several real ales and malt whiskies, and tasty bar food; neat bedrooms

This former coaching inn, in a pretty Swaledale village, is popular with walkers and their dogs – which is appropriate since there are plenty of good, surrounding walks. There are bow-window seats and a pair of stripped traditional settles among more usual pub seats, all well cushioned, a good log fire, Jennings Cumberland and Cocker Hoop and guests such as Brakspears Oxford Gold and Ringwood Best on handpump, several wines by the glass and 25 malt whiskies. On the right, a few steps take you down into a room with darts, a well lit pool table and ring the bull. On the left, past leather armchairs and a sofa by a second log fire (and a glass chess set) is an extensive two-part dining room. The décor is in mint-green and shades of brown, with a modicum of fishing memorabilia. The bedrooms are neat and simple, and breakfasts are good. There are picnic-sets outside and the inn is right opposite a lovely church known as the Cathedral of the Dales.

Using local produce where possible, the well liked food includes sandwiches, black pudding with bacon, onion and mushrooms in a creamy mustard sauce on a herb croûton, leek, wild mushroom and parmesan risotto, steak in ale pie, free-range chicken filled with cheese, wrapped in bacon with a cranberry and wine sauce, moroccan lamb casserole, and salmon steak with a gruyère and parsley crust on vegetable stew. *Benchmark main dish: fish and chips £9.25. Two-course evening meal £16.00.*

Jennings (Marstons) ~ Lease Andrew Atkin ~ Real ale ~ Bar food (all day) ~ Restaurant ~ (01748) 884224 ~ Children welcome ~ Dogs allowed in bar and bedrooms ~ Open 12-midnight(1am Sat) ~ Bedrooms: £50B/£80B

Recommended by David Thornton, JJW, CMW, Sandie and Andrew Geddes

HALIFAX Yorkshire   SE1027   Map 7

Shibden Mill ⑪ ♀ ◖

Off A58 into Kell Lane at Stump Cross Inn, near A6036 junction; keep on, pub signposted from Kell Lane on left; HX3 7UL

Tucked-away 300-year-old mill with cosy rambling bar, five real ales and inventive bar food; comfortable bedrooms

This 17th-c restored mill comes as a nice surprise – tucked away as it is at the bottom of a peaceful wooded valley. There's a good, bustling atmosphere and a happy mix of both locals and visitors who are here to enjoy the first-class food and well equipped, individually decorated bedrooms. The rambling, friendly bar has cosy side areas with banquettes heaped with cushions and rugs, there are well spaced nice old tables and chairs, and the candles in elegant iron holders give a feeling of real intimacy; also, old hunting prints, country landscapes and so forth, and a couple of big log fires. Little Valley Hebdens Wheat and Withens IPA, Moorhouses Premier Bitter, and a couple of guest beers on handpump, and 16 wines by the glass from a wide list. There's also an upstairs restaurant; piped music and TV. Outside on the attractive heated terrace, there are plenty of seats and tables, and the building is prettily floodlit at night.

Highly thought-of and interesting, the food might include sandwiches, potted ham hock and foie gras with piccalilli, slow-cooked rabbit with confit onions and a coddled duck egg, beetroot and red wine risotto with apple and blue cheese salad, beer-battered haddock with dripping chips, chorizo-stuffed free-range pork belly with smoked paprika cream, and braised wild bass with crispy potato and cauliflower, pickled fennel, cumin and a hazelnut and peppercorn sauce. *Benchmark main dish: confit duck leg £16.95. Two-course evening meal £22.20.*

Free house ~ Licensee Glen Pearson ~ Real ale ~ Bar food (12-2, 6-9.30; 12-7.30 Sun) ~ Restaurant ~ (01422) 365840 ~ Children welcome ~ Dogs allowed in bar and bedrooms ~ Open 12-2.30, 5.30-11; 12-11(10.30 Sun) Sat ~ Bedrooms: £81B/£100B

Recommended by Michael Butler, Ian Malone, Peter Burton, Derek and Sylvia Stephenson

HALTWHISTLE Northumberland NY7166 Map 10

Milecastle Inn £

Military Road; B6318 NE – OS Sheet 86 map reference 715660; NE49 9NN

Close to Hadrian's Wall and some wild scenery, with cosy little rooms warmed by winter log fires; fine views and a walled garden

This useful place is just 500 metres from Hadrian's Wall and some of its most celebrated sites. It's open all day in summer when it makes a perfect stop for liquid refreshments, and in winter you can have a pleasant warm-up by the two log fires. The snug little rooms of the beamed bar are decorated with brasses, horsey and local landscape prints and attractive fresh flowers; at lunchtime, the small comfortable restaurant is used as an overflow. Big Lamp Prince Bishop and a couple of guests are on handpump and they stock several malt whiskies. There are tables and benches in the pleasantly sheltered big walled garden, with a dovecote and rather stunning views; two self-catering cottages and a large car park.

Straightforward bar food includes sandwiches, potato skins with garlic dip, game pâté, prawn cocktail, battered haddock, scampi, lasagne, vegetable curry, venison in red wine and Guinness, various pies and steaks. *Benchmark main dish: wild boar and duckling pie £9.75. Two-course evening meal £14.50.*

Free house ~ Licensees Clare and Kevin Hind ~ Real ale ~ Bar food (12-8.45(8.30 Sun); 12-2.30, 6-8.30 in winter) ~ (01434) 321372 ~ Children welcome ~ Dogs welcome ~ Open 12-10.30(11 Sat); 12-3, 6-10 in winter

Recommended by Bruce and Sharon Eden, Sheena W Makin, Maurice and Gill McMahon, Mr and Mrs John Taylor, Clive Watkin, Jean and Douglas Troup

---

If a service charge is mentioned prominently on a menu or accommodation terms, you must pay it if service was satisfactory. If service is really bad, you are legally entitled to refuse to pay some or all of the service charge as compensation for not getting the service you might reasonably have expected.

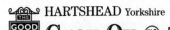 HARTSHEAD Yorkshire   SE1822   Map 7

Gray Ox 🍴 🍷

3.5 miles from M62 junction 25; A644 towards Dewsbury, left on to A62, next left on to B6119, then first left on to Fall Lane; left into Hartshead Lane; pub on right; WF15 8AL

Attractive dining pub with cosy beamed bars, inventive cooking, real ales, several wines by the glass, and fine views

At its most pubby at lunchtime, this is an attractive stone-built dining pub that's handy for the M62. The main bar has beams and flagstones, bentwood chairs, leather stools around stripped-pine tables and a roaring log fire. Comfortable carpeted dining areas with bold paintwork and leather dining chairs around polished tables lead off; the hunting-theme wallpaper is interesting and unusual. Jennings Cumberland, Cocker Hoop, Sneck Lifter and a changing guest on handpump, 14 wines by the glass and two champagnes; piped music. There are picnic-sets outside, and fine views through the latticed pub windows across the Calder Valley to the distant outskirts of Huddersfield – the lights are pretty at night.

 Using local, seasonal produce, the good, modern food at lunchtime includes sandwiches, hot smoked salmon and dill risotto topped with a poached egg, beer-battered haddock and spicy lamb with coriander and coconut milk, with more pricey evening dishes like duck liver and foie gras parfait with apricot chutney, pork fillet wrapped in smoked pancetta, blue cheese croquettes, fennel and apple salad and cider cream sauce, and goan fish curry with king prawns and cashew nuts; they also offer a good value two- and three-course set menu (Monday-Friday lunchtimes and from 6-7pm). *Benchmark main dish: special fish pie £9.95. Two-course evening meal £20.20.*

Banks's (Marstons) ~ Lease Bernadette McCarron ~ Real ale ~ Bar food (12-2, 6-9 (9.30 Sat); 12-7 Sun) ~ (01274) 872845 ~ Children welcome ~ Open 12-3, 6-midnight; 12-midnight Sat; 12-11 Sun

Recommended by Dr Kevan Tucker, DC, Gordon and Margaret Ormondroyd, Carl Rahn Griffith, Tim and Sue Halstead, Sam and Christine Kilburn, Jeremy King

HAYDON BRIDGE Northumberland   NY8364   Map 10

General Havelock

A69 Corbridge—Haltwhistle; NE47 6ER

Bustling, chatty riverside dining pub with local beers and interesting food

The attractively lit L-shaped bar at this homely terrace house is imaginatively decorated in shades of green. It's at its best in the back part with a stripped-pine chest of drawers topped with bric-a-brac, colourful cushions on long pine benches and a sturdy stripped settle, interestingly shaped mahogany-topped tables and good wildlife photographs. They serve Allendale Curlew's Return and a local guest such as Geltsdale Cold Fell or Houston Killellan on handpump, ten wines by the glass and a choice of apple juices; board games and boules. Both the stripped-stone barn dining room and the terrace enjoy fine South Tyne river views and it's just a short, pretty stroll downstream from Haydon Bridge itself.

Cooked by the landlord (who makes his own bread and ice-cream) using local produce, the well liked bar food includes lunchtime baguettes, cullen skink, ham hock terrine with warm pease pudding and mustard sauce, sautéed scallops on black pudding and cauliflower purée, chicken caesar salad, pork belly stuffed with prunes on asparagus, calves liver with pancetta and chive gravy, and fish of the day. *Benchmark main dish: duck breast on apple mash with gravy £14.00. Two-course evening meal £20.00.*

Free house ~ Licensees Gary and Joanna Thompson ~ Real ale ~ Bar food (not Sun evening) ~ Restaurant ~ (01434) 684376 ~ Children welcome ~ Dogs allowed in bar ~ Open 12-3, 7-midnight; 12-5, 7.30-10.30 Sun; closed Mon

Recommended by Bruce and Sharon Eden, Comus and Sarah Elliott, James Thompson, Mrs L Wells, Andy and Jill Kassube, Helen and Brian Edgeley, Alan Sutton

---

HEATH Yorkshire   SE3520 Map 7

Kings Arms ◧ £

Village signposted from A655 Wakefield—Normanton – or, more directly, turn off to the left opposite the Horse & Groom; WF1 5SL

Old-fashioned gaslit pub in interesting location with dark-panelled original bar, up to 11 real ales and well liked bar food; seats outside

Now owned by Ossett and with a new landlady, this remains an old-fashioned pub – still making the most of the village green setting opposite. The original bar has gas lighting which adds a lot to the atmosphere, a fire burning in the old black range (with a long row of smoothing irons on the mantelpiece), plain elm stools, oak settles built into the walls, and dark panelling. A more comfortable extension has carefully preserved the original style, down to good wood-pegged oak panelling (two embossed with royal arms) and a high shelf of plates; there are also two other small flagstoned rooms and a conservatory that opens on to the garden. Ossett Silver King, Yorkshire Blonde and a beer named for the pub from Ossett, as well as Fullers London Pride and five guest beers on handpump. There are some sunny benches facing the green (which is surrounded by 19th-c stone merchants' houses), picnic-sets on a side lawn and a nice walled garden.

Bar food now includes sandwiches, thai salmon fishcakes, a poached duck egg with asparagus and bacon soldiers, pea and home-grown mint risotto, chicken with bacon, cheese and barbecue sauce, giant battered haddock, and lambs liver with crispy parma ham. *Benchmark main dish: beef in ale pie £9.95. Two-course evening meal £14.95.*

Ossett ~ Manager Angela Cromack ~ Real ale ~ Bar food (12-2, 6-9; 12-9 Fri and Sat; 12-5 Sun; not Sun evening) ~ Restaurant ~ (01924) 377527 ~ Children allowed away from main lounge ~ Dogs allowed in bar ~ Open 12-11(midnight Sat); may open 12-3, 5-11 weekdays in winter

Recommended by the Didler, Pat and Tony Martin

HEDLEY ON THE HILL Northumberland   NZ0759 Map 10

Feathers ❢ ♀ ◧

Village signposted from New Ridley, which is signposted from B6309 N of Consett; OS Sheet 88 map reference 078592; NE43 7SW

Imaginative food, interesting beers from small breweries, and friendly welcome in quaint tavern

Although most tables at this thoughtfully run hilltop tavern are laid for dining, its three neat beamed bars do still at least look properly pubby with their open fires, stripped stonework, solid furniture, including settles, and old black and white photographs of local places and farm and country workers. Friendly knowledgable staff serve four ales from a different local brewer each time a barrel is changed; maybe Jarrow, Mordue Workie Ticket, Wylam Gold Tankard and a guest such as Orkney Red MacGregor from handpumps, as well as farm ciders, 28 wines by the glass, 34 malt whiskies and several bourbons. They hold a beer and food festival at Easter with over two dozen real ales, a barrel race on Easter Monday and other traditional events; darts and dominoes. Picnic-sets in front are a nice place to sit and watch the world drift by.

Leaning towards traditional british cooking and using home-butchered game from local shoots, beef from rare breeds and home-baked bread (and listing their carefully chosen suppliers on the daily-changing menu), the imaginative food might include ploughman's, lobster and crayfish cocktail, charcuterie, roe deer merguez sausages with couscous and harissa, battered haddock and chips, mushroom risotto, pigeon pie, lamb shank with dauphinoise potatoes and braised red cabbage, and saddle of rabbit stuffed with black pudding with cream cider sauce. *Benchmark main dish: pot-roast beef £12.00. Two-course evening meal £19.80.*

Free house ~ Licensees Rhian Cradock and Helen Greer ~ Real ale ~ Bar food (12-2(2.30 Sun), 6-8.30 not Mon or first two weeks in Jan) ~ (01661) 843607 ~ Children welcome ~ Folk music first Sun of month ~ Open 12-11(10.30 Sun); closed Mon lunchtime except bank holidays

Recommended by David and Cathrine Whiting, Eric Larkham, James Thompson, Mike and Lynn Robinson, John Coatsworth, Lawrence Pearse, Andy and Jill Kassube, Peter and Eleanor Kenyon, Graham Oddey, Dr and Mrs P Truelove, GSB, Comus and Sarah Elliott

LEDSHAM Yorkshire 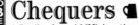 SE4529 Map 7

Chequers

1.5 miles from A1(M) junction 42: follow Leeds signs, then Ledsham signposted; Claypit Lane; LS25 5LP

Friendly village pub, handy for the A1, with hands-on landlord, log fires in several beamed rooms, real ales and interesting food; pretty back terrace

Although many customers come to this well-run 16th-c stone inn to enjoy the interesting food, the friendly hands-on landlord also keeps five real ales on handpump. There are several small, individually decorated rooms with low beams, lots of cosy alcoves, toby jugs and all sorts of knick-knacks on the walls and ceilings, and log fires. From the old-fashioned little central panelled-in servery, they offer beers from breweries such as Brown Cow, John Smith, Theakston and Timothy Taylor; good, attentive service. A sheltered two-level terrace behind the house has tables among roses and the hanging baskets and flowers are very pretty. RSPB Fairburn Ings reserve is close by. This is a lovely village and the pub is handy for the A1.

As well as some pubby choices like sandwiches, corned-beef hash, pork, leek and apple sausages and gammon with a duck egg and sweetcorn rösti, the more pricey, restaurant-style food might include a tian of smoked fish with a honey and mustard dressing, king scallops with pea purée, crispy pancetta and truffle oil, butternut squash and pine nut risotto, halibut fillet with potted shrimps and parsley butter, and venison loin with black pudding, smoked bacon and red cabbage; side dishes are extra. *Benchmark main dish: steak in mushroom pie £10.85. Two-course evening meal £23.45.*

Free house ~ Licensee Chris Wraith ~ Real ale ~ Bar food (12-9 Mon-Sat; not Sun) ~
Restaurant ~ (01977) 683135 ~ Well behaved children allowed ~ Dogs allowed in bar ~
Open 11-11; closed Sun

*Recommended by Christine Vallely, MJVK, Neil Whitehead, Victoria Anderson, Pat and
Stewart Gordon, Sam and Christine Kilburn, Terry and Nickie Williams, Andy and Jill Kassube,
the Didler, GSB, Jeff and Wendy Williams, Grahame Brooks, Gerard Dyson, Paul Cooper*

LEVISHAM Yorkshire   SE8390 Map 10

Horseshoe 🍴 🛏

Off A169 N of Pickering; YO18 7NL

**Friendly village pub run by two brothers; neat rooms, real ales, very
good food, and seats on the village green; bedrooms**

Our readers very much enjoy their visits to this friendly, traditional
pub, well run by two jovial brothers; they also have warm praise for
the smart, comfortable bedrooms – some of which have fine views. The
bars have beams, smart blue banquettes, wheelback and captain's chairs
around a variety of tables on the polished wooden floors, vibrant
landscapes by a local artist on the walls, and a log fire in the stone
fireplace; an adjoining snug has a woodburning stove, comfortable
leather sofas and old photographs of the pub and the village. Black Sheep
and a guest such as Cropton Endeavour Ale or Yorkshire Moors Bitter on
handpump, home-made elderflower cordial, 20 malt whiskies and a farm
cider; board games and piped music. There are seats on the attractive
green, more in the back garden, and fine surrounding walks.

🍴 Using their own chicken and goose eggs and cooked by one of the landlords, the
particularly good, attractively presented food includes sandwiches, grilled
black pudding with sautéed potatoes and apple sauce, wild mushroom risotto,
whitby haddock with home-made chips, duck breast on sweet potato mash with a
red wine and port sauce, and specials such as seafood platter, and venison suet
pudding with sloe gin gravy. *Benchmark main dish: pork belly with thyme mash and
cider gravy £11.95. Two-course evening meal £17.75.*

Free house ~ Licensees Toby and Charles Wood ~ Real ale ~ Bar food (12-2, 6-8.30) ~
(01751) 460240 ~ Children welcome but bedrooms not ideal for them ~ Dogs welcome ~
Open 11-11 ~ Bedrooms: £40/£80S

*Recommended by Ann and Tony Bennett-Hughes, Andy Lickfold, Nick Dalby, P G Wooler,
Michael Goodden, Ed and Anna Fraser*

LEYBURN Yorkshire   SE1190 Map 10

Sandpiper 🍴 ♟ 🛏

Just off Market Place; DL8 5AT

**Emphasis on appealing food though cosy bar for drinkers in 17th-c
cottage, real ales, and amazing choice of whiskies; bedrooms**

This is a first-class pub with a warm welcome for all – and several
readers were delighted that their dogs were allowed to sit in front of
the fire in the snug; this cosy room is liked by locals for a drink and a chat,
which keeps the atmosphere relaxed and informal. Another little bar has a
couple of black beams in the low ceiling, wooden or cushioned built-in
wall seats around a few tables, and the back room up three steps has
attractive Dales photographs; get here early to be sure of a seat. Down by
the nice linenfold panelled bar counter, there are stuffed sandpipers, more

photographs and a woodburning stove in the stone fireplace; to the left is the attractive restaurant, with fresh flowers and dark wooden tables and chairs on floorboards. Black Sheep Golden and a beer from Copper Dragon or Daleside on handpump, up to 100 malt whiskies and a decent wine list with several by the glass; piped music. In good weather, you can enjoy a drink on the front terrace among the lovely hanging baskets and flowering climbers. The boutique-style bedrooms are comfortable.

Cooked by the landlord, who also makes his own bread and ice-creams, the excellent, imaginative food might include lunchtime sandwiches and specials like smoked haddock and potato omelette, beer-battered fish and chips, and a rib burger with thin fries, as well as pigeon, blood orange and walnut salad, ham hock and chicken terrine with home-made piccalilli, double-baked vintage cheese soufflé, moroccan-style chicken with lemon and coriander couscous, and fish, crayfish and fennel pasta. *Benchmark main dish: pressed local lamb with creamed leeks and garlic £15.75. Two-course evening meal £21.80.*

Free house ~ Licensee Jonathan Harrison ~ Real ale ~ Bar food (12-2.30, 6.30-9(9.30 Fri and Sat); not Mon or winter Tues) ~ Restaurant ~ (01969) 622206 ~ Children welcome ~ Dogs allowed in bar and bedrooms ~ Open 11.30-3, 6.30-11(10.30 Sun); closed Mon and some winter Tues ~ Bedrooms: £75S(£80B)/£85S(£90B)

Recommended by Gordon Briggs, Pat and Graham Williamson, Sandie and Andrew Geddes, John and Eleanor Holdsworth

LONG PRESTON Yorkshire   SD8358   Map 7

Maypole ◗ ⇦
A65 Settle—Skipton; BD23 4PH

A good base for walkers with friendly staff, a bustling atmosphere, well liked pubby food, and a fair choice of real ales

This comfortably traditional village pub usefully offers food all day and makes a good base for walking in the Dales; the bedrooms are quiet and clean. Mr and Mrs Palmer have been at the helm here for over 25 years and there's a list of landlords dating back to 1695 on the butter-coloured walls of the bar. This carpeted two-room bar also has good solid pub furnishings – red leather wall seats, heavy carved wall settles and plush red-topped bar stools around cast-iron-framed pub tables with unusual inset leather tops on the red patterned carpet, and plenty of local photographs. There's a separate dining room. Moorhouses Premier Bitter, Timothy Taylors Landlord and a couple of guests like Goose Eye Barm Pot Bitter and Moorhouses Pendle Witches Brew on handpump, ten wines by the glass, Weston's cider and a dozen malt whiskies. The left-hand tap room has darts, dominoes, and TV for important sporting events. On a back terrace, there are a couple of picnic-sets under an ornamental cherry tree, with more tables under umbrellas on another terrace (which has outdoor heaters).

Tasty bar food includes sandwiches, chicken liver pâté with plum chutney, cheese and spinach or meaty lasagne, various salads, ham and eggs, battered haddock with mushy peas, sausages with mash and onion gravy, braised lamb shank with mint, and daily specials. *Benchmark main dish: steak in ale pie £9.95. Two-course evening meal £15.50.*

Enterprise ~ Lease Robert Palmer ~ Real ale ~ Bar food (12-9(9.30 Fri and Sat)) ~ Restaurant ~ (01729) 840219 ~ Children welcome ~ Dogs allowed in bar and bedrooms ~ Quiz first Weds night of month; live mike evening quarterly ~ Open 12-11(12.30 Sat) ~ Bedrooms: £42S/£75B

Recommended by Mrs Judith Kirkham, Dudley and Moira Cockroft, Clive Flynn, Gerard Dyson, Dr Ann Henderson

LOW CATTON Yorkshire   SE7053 Map 7

Gold Cup

Village signposted with High Catton off A166 in Stamford Bridge or A1079 at Kexby Bridge; YO41 1EA

Friendly, pleasant pub with attractive bars, real ales, decent food, seats in garden, and ponies in paddock

At weekends, this spacious white-rendered house usefully serves food all day and is just the place to head for after a walk. It's run by a helpful and informative landlord and the beamed bars have a country feel with coach lights on the rustic-looking walls, smart tables and chairs on the stripped wooden floors, an open fire at one end opposite the woodburning stove, and quite a few pictures. The restaurant has solid wooden pews and tables (said to be made from a single oak tree) and pleasant views of the surrounding fields. Theakstons Best and maybe a guest beer on handpump; piped music and pool. The garden has a grassed area for children and the back paddock houses Candy the horse and Polly the shetland pony. They have fishing rights on the adjoining River Derwent.

As well as lunchtime sandwiches (not Sunday), the reasonably priced food using some home-grown produce includes creamed stilton mushrooms, chicken liver pâté with onion marmalade, three-egg omelette, beer-battered cod, spicy cajun chicken with a mint and yoghurt dip, salmon and prawn pie, and venison steak in red wine gravy. *Benchmark main dish: braised lamb shank in port and redcurrant gravy £13.50. Two-course evening meal £15.50.*

Free house ~ Licensees Pat and Ray Hales ~ Real ale ~ Bar food (12-2.30, 6-9; all day weekends; not Mon lunchtime) ~ Restaurant ~ (01759) 371354 ~ Children welcome ~ Dogs allowed in bar ~ Open 12-2.30, 6-11; 12-11(10.30 Sun) Sat; closed Mon lunchtime

Recommended by Pat and Graham Williamson, Gerard Dyson, Pete Coxon, Peter and Anne Hollindale

LUND Yorkshire   SE9748 Map 8

Wellington

Off B1248 SW of Driffield; YO25 9TE

Busy, smart pub with plenty of space in several rooms, real ales, helpfully noted wine list, and interesting changing food

Smart and neatly kept, this bustling village pub is run by friendly people. The cosy Farmers Bar has a good mix of both drinkers and diners, beams, a quirky fireplace, well polished wooden banquettes and square tables and gold-framed pictures and corner lamps on the walls. Off to one side is a plainer, no less smart, flagstoned room with a wine theme. At the other end of the bar, a york-stoned walkway leads to a room with a display of the village's Britain in Bloom awards. There's also a restaurant and a bistro dining area with another open log fire. The main bar in the evening is a haven for drinkers only: Black Sheep Ruddy Ram, John Smiths, Timothy Taylors Landlord and a guest like York Yorkshire Terrier on handpump, a good wine list with a helpfully labelled choice by the glass and 25 malt whiskies. Piped music, board games and TV. There are some benches in a small, pretty back courtyard.

🍴 Good, interesting food includes sandwiches, pressed ham hock terrine with a quail's egg and pineapple piccalilli, pigeon, apple and raspberry salad with raspberry gin dressing, aubergine, chickpea and green olive tagine with toasted almond couscous, chicken breast with gnocchi carbonara, sautéed leeks and truffle oil, grilled wild bass fillets with crab and samphire risotto and crab bisque, and loin of venison, haunch cobbler, fondant potato and braised red cabbage. *Benchmark main dish: beef and mushroom suet pudding £16.10. Two-course evening meal £23.30.*

Free house ~ Licensees Russell Jeffery and Sarah Jeffery ~ Real ale ~ Bar food (not Sun evening or Mon lunchtime) ~ Restaurant (Tues-Sat evenings) ~ (01377) 217294 ~ Children welcome ~ Open 12-3, 6.30-midnight; 12-midnight Sun; closed Mon lunch
Recommended by Roger and Ann King, Adrian Johnson, Pat and Stewart Gordon, Gerard Dyson

MOULTON Yorkshire   NZ2303 Map 10

Black Bull 🍴 ⛾

Just E of A1, 1 mile E of Scotch Corner; DL10 6QJ

Character bar in civilised dining pub, interesting lunchtime bar food (more elaborate restaurant menu, strong on fish), and smart dining areas (one is a Pullman dining car)

Decidedly civilised, this is strictly a dining pub but it does have a bar with a lot of proper character. There's a huge winter log fire, an antique panelled oak settle and an old elm housekeeper's chair, built-in red cushioned black settles and pews around cast-iron tables, silver-plated turkish coffee pots and copper cooking utensils hanging from black beams, and fresh flowers. There's also a Fish Bar (first come, first served as no bookings are taken), an airy conservatory with a massive grapevine and antique train company signs on the walls, a traditional restaurant with nooks and crannies leading off it, and the elegant *Brighton Belle* dining car. Eight wines by the glass (including champagne) and 50 malt whiskies. There are some seats outside in the central court. The pub is handy for the A1.

🍴 At lunchtime, the very good bar food includes sandwiches, chicken and ham terrine with onion jam, smoked haddock and spring onion risotto with a soft poached egg, cheddar and spinach soufflé, local sausages with mustard mash and crispy onions, minute steak with crispy onion rings and chips, and seafood mixed grill with sauce antiboise (tomatoes, olives, coriander, cress, shallots and garlic). *Benchmark main dish: dover sole with black butter £28.50. Two-course evening meal £24.50.*

Free house ~ Licensee Mr Barker ~ Bar food (12-2.30(2 Sat), 6-9.30(10 Fri and Sat); 12-4 Sun; not Sun evening) ~ Restaurant (evening) ~ (01325) 377289 ~ Children over 12 welcome ~ Open 12-2.30(2 Sat, 4 Sun), 6-11; closed Sun evening
Recommended by GNI, Pat and Stewart Gordon, Chris Flynn, Wendy Jones, Derek Thomas

'Children welcome' means the pub says it lets children inside without any special restriction. If it allows them in, but to restricted areas such as an eating area or family room, we specify this. Some pubs may impose an evening time limit. We do not mention limits after 9pm as we assume children are home by then.

NUNNINGTON Yorkshire

SE6679 Map 7

Royal Oak

Church Street; at back of village, which is signposted from A170 and B1257; YO62 5US

Friendly staff and good food in reliable, neat pub, lots to look at in beamed bar, winter open fires, and real ales

Standards are as high as ever at this well run and attractive little pub. The neatly kept bar has high black beams strung with earthenware flagons, copper jugs and lots of antique keys, one of the walls is stripped back to the bare stone to display a fine collection of antique farm tools, and there are open fires; also, carefully chosen furniture such as kitchen and country dining chairs and a long pew around the sturdy tables on the turkey carpet. The dining area is linked to the bar by a double-sided wood-burning stove. Black Sheep Ale and Wold Top Wolds Way on handpump, ten wines by the glass and several malt whiskies; piped music. There are seats on the terrace. Nunnington Hall (National Trust) is a ten-minute walk away.

Using game from the local estate and other local produce, the enjoyable food includes sandwiches, smoked salmon mousseline with cucumber and dill pickle, black pudding with parmentier potatoes, quail's egg and roasted garlic toast, mixed wild mushroom stroganoff, pork medallions in a cider, cream and apple sauce, chicken breast stuffed with stilton and wrapped in Italian ham, and specials like roast cod with garlic king prawns and pheasant or rabbit casserole. *Benchmark main dish: steak pie £11.50. Two-course evening meal £18.90.*

Free house ~ Licensee Anita Hilton ~ Real ale ~ Bar food (not Mon – except bank holiday lunchtimes) ~ Restaurant ~ (01439) 748271 ~ Children welcome ~ Dogs welcome ~ Open 11.45(12 weekends)-2.30, 6.30(7 Sun)-11; closed Mon (except bank holiday lunchtimes)

Recommended by Neil Whitehead, Victoria Anderson, Nick Dalby, John and Eleanor Holdsworth, Michael Butler, Gerard Dyson

OLDSTEAD Yorkshire

SE5380 Map 7

Black Swan

Main Street; YO61 4BL

16th-c restaurant-with-rooms in remote countryside with first-class food, real ales, several wines by the glass and friendly staff; comfortable bedrooms

Of course, much emphasis is placed on the excellent food in this 16th-c restaurant-with-rooms but they do have a proper bar with real ales and you can be sure of a friendly welcome. This bar has beams and flagstones, furniture by 'Mousey' Thompson, window seats with soft cushions and pretty valley views, an open log fire, Black Sheep Best and Copper Dragon Best on handpump, 13 wines by the glass and several malt whiskies; courteous, attentive staff. The back dining rooms are comfortable and attractive. At the front of the building are some picnic-sets under parasols beneath the cherry trees. The well equipped ground floor bedrooms have their own terrace and breakfasts are highly thought of. There are plenty of fine surrounding walks in the glorious National Park countryside. Please note that the bedroom price includes dinner for two.

🍴 At lunchtime, the imaginative, beautifully presented food includes sandwiches, ham hock ballottine with cider jelly and apples, beer-battered haddock with pea purée, home-made sausages with mash and buttered greens, and a french-style rib of beef stew, with more pricey evening choices such as hand-dived king scallops with sweetcorn, chorizo and tortilla chips, confit and cured wild sea trout niçoise, slow-braised belly and soy-glazed pig's cheek with a pork and vegetable spring roll and pak choi, and gressingham duck breast with duck confit potatoes, braised chicory, french onion purée and sherry vinegar jus; they also offer a two- and three-course set lunch menu. *Two-course evening meal £33.00.*

Free house ~ Licensee Tom Banks ~ Real ale ~ Bar food (12-2(2.30 Sun), 6-9; not Mon-Weds lunchtimes) ~ Restaurant ~ (01347) 868387 ~ Children welcome but must be over 10 in bedrooms ~ Open 12-3, 6-10.30(11 Sat); closed Mon-Weds lunchtimes; two weeks in Jan ~ Bedrooms: /£210S
Recommended by Jill and Julian Tasker, Dr Ian S Morley, John and Verna Aspinall

PICKERING Yorkshire　　　　　　　　　　　　　SE7984　Map 10

White Swan 🍴 ♀ 🛏

Market Place, just off A170; YO18 7AA

Relaxed little bar in civilised coaching inn with several smart lounges, an attractive restaurant, real ales, an excellent wine list and first-class food; lovely bedrooms

At the heart of this smart and civilised old coaching inn is a small bar with a friendly welcome. The atmosphere is relaxed and there are sofas and a few tables, wood panelling, a log fire, Black Sheep Best and Copper Dragon Golden Pippin on handpump, 14 wines by the glass from an extensive list that includes fine old St Emilions and pudding wines, and 20 malt whiskies. Opposite, a bare-boards room with a few more tables has another fire in a handsome art nouveau iron fireplace, a big bow window and pear prints on its plum-coloured walls. The restaurant has flagstones, yet another open fire, comfortable settles and gothic screens, and the residents' lounge is in a converted beamed barn. The old coach entry to the car park is very narrow. Luxurious bedrooms and delicious breakfasts.

🍴 Excellent food at lunchtime might include sandwiches, venison carpaccio with redcurrant jelly, green vegetable risotto with white truffle oil, and whitby fish and chips, with evening choices like potted crab and celeriac remoulade, free-range chicken with parmentier potatoes, wild mushrooms, crisp ham and bread sauce, and grilled sea bream with aioli, skinny chips and watercress salad. *Benchmark main dish: slow-cooked gloucester old spot belly pork with crackling, mustard mash and apple sauce £17.50. Two-course evening meal £24.90.*

Free house ~ Licensees Marion and Victor Buchanan ~ Real ale ~ Bar food ~ Restaurant ~ (01751) 472288 ~ Children welcome ~ Dogs allowed in bar and bedrooms ~ Open 10am-11pm; 11am-10.30pm Sun ~ Bedrooms: £115B/£150B
Recommended by Marian and Andrew Ruston, Janet and Peter Race, Peter Burton

---

Bedroom prices normally include full english breakfast, VAT and any inclusive service charge that we know of. Prices before the '/' are for single rooms, after the '/' are for two people in a double or twin (B includes a private bath, S a private shower). If there is no '/', the prices are only for twin or double rooms (as far as we know there are no singles).

RIPLEY Yorkshire
SE2860 Map 7

Boars Head ♀ ◖ ⇐
Off A61 Harrogate—Ripon; HG3 3AY

Smart coaching inn with friendly bar/bistro, several real ales, an excellent wine list, good food and helpful service; comfortable bedrooms

The bar in this welcoming old coaching inn has been refurbished this year and the restaurant is now more of a brasserie. This bar/bistro now has a nice mix of dining chairs around various wooden tables, warm yellow walls hung with golf clubs, cricket bats and jolly little drawings of cricketers or huntsmen, a boar's head (part of the family coat of arms), an interesting religious carving, and Black Sheep Best, Daleside Pride of England, Hambleton White Boar and Theakston Best on handpump; also, 20 wines by the glass and several malt whiskies. Some of the furnishings in the hotel came from the attic of next-door Ripley Castle, where the Ingilbys have lived for over 650 years. A pleasant little garden has plenty of tables.

Using their own kitchen garden produce (within Ripley Castle), the food includes lunchtime open sandwiches, morecambe bay potted shrimps, wild mushroom stroganoff, sausages of the day with spring onion mash and onion gravy, an open pie of beef, mushrooms and Guinness, braised lamb shank with glazed root vegetables, kilnsey trout with lemon and caper butter, and Estate venison with rösti and jus. *Benchmark main dish: honey-roast belly pork with black pudding mash and glazed apples £14.95. Two-course evening meal £20.45.*

Free house ~ Licensee Sir Thomas Ingilby ~ Real ale ~ Bar food (12-2, 6.30-9.30; 12-9 Sun) ~ Restaurant ~ (01423) 771888 ~ Children welcome ~ Dogs allowed in bedrooms ~ Open 11-11; 12-10.30 Sun; 11-3, 5-11 weekdays in winter ~ Bedrooms: £105B/£125B

Recommended by Adrian and Dawn Collinge, Jeremy King, the Didler, Susan and Nigel Brookes, Janet and Peter Race, Pete Coxon

RIPPONDEN Yorkshire
SE0419 Map 7

Old Bridge ♀ ◖
From A58, best approach is Elland Road (opposite the Golden Lion), park opposite the church in pub's car park and walk back over ancient hump-back bridge; HX6 4DF

Pleasant old pub by medieval bridge with relaxed communicating rooms, half a dozen real ales, quite a few wines by the glass, lots of whiskies, and well liked food

This is a charming 14th-c pub by a beautiful medieval pack-horse bridge over the little River Ryburn, and there are seats in the garden overlooking the water. Inside, the three communicating rooms, each on a slightly different level, all have a relaxed, friendly atmosphere. Oak settles are built into the window recesses of the thick stone walls, and there are antique oak tables, rush-seated chairs, a few well chosen pictures and prints, and a big woodburning stove. The fine range of real ales on handpump might include Timothy Taylors Best, Dark Mild, Golden Best and Landlord and a couple of guests such as Empire Royal Scot and York First Light; also, quite a few foreign bottled beers, a dozen wines by the glass and 30 malt whiskies. If you have trouble finding the pub (there is no traditional pub sign outside), just head for the church.

On weekday lunchtimes, bar food only includes sandwiches and soup or the popular help-yourself salad carvery (rare roast beef, virginia ham, home-made scotch eggs and so forth); at weekends and in the evening (not Sunday evening), there might potted salmon and shrimps with lemon and capers, steak in ale pie, mediterranean vegetable and goats cheese wraps, crispy belly pork with pak choi and oriental sauce, and corn-fed chicken with tomato, red pepper and butter bean stew. *Benchmark main dish: smoked haddock and spinach pancakes £9.25. Two-course evening meal £17.25.*

Free house ~ Licensees Tim and Lindsay Eaton Walker ~ Real ale ~ Bar food (12-2(2.30 Sat), 6.30-9.30; not Sun evening) ~ (01422) 822595 ~ Children allowed until 8pm but must be seated away from bar ~ Open 12-3, 5.30-11; 12-11(10.30 Sun) Fri and Sat

Recommended by Roger and Anne Newbury, Tony Hill

ROECLIFFE Yorkshire   SE3765 Map 7

Crown 🍴 🍷 🍺 🛏

NORTH EAST & YORKSHIRE PUB OF THE YEAR
Off A168 just W of Boroughbridge; handy for A1(M) junction 48; YO51 9LY
YORKSHIRE DINING PUB OF THE YEAR

Smartly updated and attractively placed pub with a civilised bar, excellent enterprising food and a fine choice of drinks; lovely bedrooms

Going from strength to strength under the hard-working and friendly Mainey family, this well run place is extremely popular with our readers. Of course, much emphasis is placed on the top-class food but they do keep Black Sheep Ale, Ilkley Mary Jane, Theakstons Best and Timothy Taylors Landlord on handpump, 20 wines by the glass and home-made lemonade. The bar has a contemporary colour scheme of dark reds and near-whites with attractive prints carefully grouped and lit; one area has chunky pine tables on flagstones and another part, with a log fire, has dark tables on plaid carpet. For meals, you have a choice between a small candlelit olive-green bistro with nice tables, a longcase clock and one or two paintings and a more formal restaurant; at weekends, it's wise to book ahead. The country-style bedrooms are highly thought-of. The pub faces the village green.

They make their own goats cheese, bread, jams and chutneys, home-smoke their fish and use only small local suppliers and game from local estates for the first-class, imaginative food which might include lunchtime sandwiches, delicious whitby crab soup, smoked salmon terrine with ricotta and dill with a spiced cucumber and lemon salad, a proper steak and mushroom pie, pink trout fillets with a king prawn, basil and roast red pepper piperade, leek and lemon grass risotto with spiced cauliflower fritters, free-range chicken with a wild mushroom and tarragon mousse, and 24-day-hung rib-eye steak with pepper sauce and aioli. *Benchmark main dish: fish pie £12.95. Two-course evening meal £23.00.*

Free house ~ Licensee Karl Mainey ~ Real ale ~ Bar food (12-2.30, 6-9.30; 12-7 Sun) ~ Restaurant ~ (01423) 322300 ~ Children welcome ~ Dogs allowed in bar ~ Open 12-4, 5-11; 12-10 Sun ~ Bedrooms: £82B/£97B

Recommended by Les and Sandra Brown, Michael and Maggie Betton, Michael Doswell, Hunter and Christine Wright, Peter Hacker

---

All *Guide* inspections are anonymous. Anyone claiming to be a *Good Pub Guide* inspector is a fraud. Please let us know.

ROMALDKIRK County Durham   NY9922 Map 10

Rose & Crown ★ 🍴 ♉ 🛏

Just off B6277; DL12 9EB

A civilised base for the area, with accomplished cooking, attentive service, and a fine choice of drinks; lovely bedrooms

Firmly rooted in quite a special league, this handsome 18th-c country coaching inn is run with keen attention to detail, resulting in a charming environment, fabulous service, superbly cooked food (you do need to book) and a first-class place to stay. The cosily traditional beamed bar has lots of brass and copper, old-fashioned seats facing a warming log fire, a Jacobean oak settle, a grandfather clock, and gin traps, old farm tools and black and white pictures of Romaldkirk on the walls. Allendale, Black Sheep and Theakstons are on handpump alongside 14 wines by the glass, organic fruit juices and pressed vegetable juices. The smart brasserie-style Crown Room (bar food is served in here, too) has large cartoons of french waiters, big old wine bottles and high-backed dining chairs. The hall has farm tools, wine maps and other interesting prints, along with a photograph (taken by a customer) of the Hale Bopp comet over the interesting old village church. There's also an oak-panelled restaurant. Pleasantly positioned tables outside look out over the village green with its original stocks and water pump. The extraordinary Bowes Museum and High Force waterfall are close by and the owners can provide their own in-house guide to days out in the area, and a *Walking in Teesdale* book.

🍴 As well as making their own ice-creams, jams, chutneys and marmalade, using only seasonal local produce (they list their suppliers on the menu) and eggs from their own hens (whose names are on a board in the brasserie), the imaginative bar food might include baked smoked salmon soufflé with tomato fondue and chive cream, linguine with butternut and pumpkin seed pesto, fish and chips with mushy peas, steak, kidney and mushroom pie, bass fillets with pea and prawn risotto, pancetta and chive cream, and fried pigeon with carrot and parsnip rösti and mushrooms. *Benchmark main dish: steak, kidney, mushroom and ale pie £13.95. Two-course evening meal £22.65.*

Free house ~ Licensees Christopher and Alison Davy ~ Real ale ~ Bar food (12-1.45, 6.30-9.30) ~ Restaurant ~ (01833) 650213 ~ Children welcome, must be over 6 in restaurant ~ Dogs allowed in bar and bedrooms ~ Open 11(12 Sun)-11 ~ Bedrooms: £95B/£135S(£170B)

Recommended by Roxanne Chamberlain, John Coatsworth, Mike and Sue Loseby, Lesley and Peter Barrett, Richard Cole, Peter and Josie Fawcett

SANDHUTTON Yorkshire   SE3882 Map 10

Kings Arms 🍺

A167, 1 mile N of A61 Thirsk—Ripon; YO7 4RW

Good chef/landlord in cheerful and appealing pub with friendly service, good food and beer, and comfortable furnishings; bedrooms

A cosy new dining extension has been added to this interestingly furnished village pub and they now have a shop selling their own ready meals as well as cheese, chutneys and local produce. The bustling bar has an unusual circular woodburner in one corner, a high central table with four equally high stools, high-backed brown leather-seated dining chairs around light pine tables, a couple of cushioned wicker armchairs, some attractive modern bar stools, and photographs of the pub in years gone by; a shelf has odd knick-knacks such as fish jaws and a bubble-gum machine, there are various pub games, and a TV. Black Sheep Best, Hambleton Stud and White Boar and John Smiths on handpump, several wines by the glass and efficient, friendly service. The two connecting dining rooms have similar furnishings to the bar (though there's also a nice big table with smart high-backed dining chairs), arty flower photographs on the cream walls and a shelf above the small woodburning stove with more knick-knacks and some candles.

Cooked by the landlord using local produce, the good, interesting bar food includes lunchtime choices such as sandwiches, chilli con carne, generous beer-battered cod and chips and game or cottage pie, as well as queenie scallops with sautéed black pudding and pea purée, chicken liver pâté with plum chutney, wild mushroom tagliatelle with parmesan crisps, pork chops with caramelised stuffed apple and proper gravy, monkfish with a compote of peppers with caramelised olives and rocket pesto, and rack of lamb with spinach, feta and pomegranate seeds. *Benchmark main dish: salmon, cod and prawn fishcake with sweet chilli dressing £10.50. Two-course evening meal £20.25.*

Free house ~ Licensees Raymond and Alexander Boynton ~ Real ale ~ Bar food (12-2.30, 5.30-9; 12-5 Sun; not Sun evening) ~ Restaurant ~ (01845) 587887 ~ Children welcome ~ Open 11-11 ~ Bedrooms: £45S/£70S
Recommended by Michael Doswell, John and Eleanor Holdsworth, Mike and Lynn Robinson

SAWLEY Yorkshire   SE2467 Map 7

Sawley Arms ♀
Village signposted off B6265 W of Ripon; HG4 3EQ

Old-fashioned dining pub with good restauranty food, decent house wines and comfortable furnishings in small rooms; pretty garden

Ultra-civilised in a decorous sort of way, this is a spotlessly kept dining pub with cheerful, friendly staff and good restaurant-style food – though locals do pop in for a chat and a drink (mainly in the evening). The small turkey-carpeted rooms have log fires and comfortable furniture ranging from small soft-cushioned armed dining chairs and sofas, to the wing armchairs down a couple of steps in a side snug; maybe daily papers and magazines to read, and quiet piped music. There's also a conservatory; good house wines. In fine weather you can sit in the pretty garden where the flowering tubs and baskets are lovely; they have two stone cottages in the grounds for rent. Fountains Abbey (the most extensive of the great monastic remains – floodlit on late summer Friday and Saturday evenings, with a choir on the Saturday) is not far away.

As well as selling home-made chutneys, relishes, pickles and biscuits, there's a 'take and bake' menu, too. In-house, the highly thought-of food includes lunchtime sandwiches, duck liver and orange pâté with port jelly, toasted brie with candied walnut and pear salad, their famous pies (steak, vegetarian, chicken and game), pork and apricot cassoulet, plaice mornay with duchesse potatoes, and rump of local lamb with bubble and squeak mash and red wine and rosemary gravy. *Benchmark main dish: various pies £10.95. Two-course evening meal £19.45.*

Free house ~ Licensee Mrs June Hawes ~ Bar food ~ Restaurant ~ (01765) 620642 ~ Well behaved children in conservatory but phone beforehand ~ Open 11.30-3, 6-11; closed Mon evenings in winter ~ Bedrooms: £50B/£85B
Recommended by Janet and Peter Race, Alan Thwaite, Ian and Nita Cooper, R J Cowley

SEAHOUSES Northumberland   NU2232   Map 10

Olde Ship ★
Just off B1340, towards harbour; NE68 7RD

Lots of atmosphere and maritime memorabilia in bustling little hotel; views across harbour to Farne Islands; bedrooms

This unchanging homely little hotel has been run by the same friendly family for over 100 years. Popular with locals, the snugly old-fashioned bar is packed with a rich assemblage of nautical bits and pieces. Even the floor is scrubbed ship's decking. Besides lots of other shiny brass fittings, ship's instruments and equipment, and a knotted anchor made by local fishermen, there are sea pictures and model ships, including fine ones of the North Sunderland Lifeboat, and Seahouses' lifeboat the *Grace Darling*. There's also a model of the *Forfarshire*, the paddle steamer that local heroine Grace Darling went to rescue in 1838 (you can read more of the story in the pub), and even the ship's nameboard. If it's working, an anemometer takes wind speed readings from the top of the chimney. It's all gently lit by stained-glass sea picture windows, lantern lights and a winter open fire. Simple furnishings include built in leatherette pews round one end, and stools and cast-iron tables. Black Sheep Best, Courage Directors, Greene King Old Speckled Hen and Ruddles and Hadrian & Border Farne Island Pale are on handpump and they've a good wine list and quite a few malt whiskies; piped music and TV. The battlemented side terrace (you'll find fishing memorabilia out here, too) and one window in the sun lounge look out across the harbour to the Farne Islands, and if you find yourself here as dusk falls, the light of the Longstones lighthouse shining across the fading evening sky is a charming sight. It's not really suitable for children, though there is a little family room, and along with walkers, they are welcome on the terrace. You can book boat trips to the Farne Islands Bird Sanctuary at the harbour, and there are bracing coastal walks, particularly to Bamburgh, Grace Darling's birthplace.

A short choice of reasonably priced bar food includes sandwiches, ploughman's, mushroom and cashew nut pâté, scampi, gammon and egg, steak and ale pie, crab salad, and chicken and mushroom casserole. *Benchmark main dish: fish chowder £11.50. Two-course evening meal £15.60.*

Free house ~ Licensees Judith Glen and David Swan ~ Real ale ~ Bar food (no evening food mid-Dec to mid-Jan) ~ Restaurant ~ (01665) 720200 ~ Children in louge and dining room and must be over 10 if staying ~ Open 11(12 Sun)-11 ~ Bedrooms: £59S/£130B

Recommended by Emma Harris, George Cowie, Frances Gosnell, John and Angie Millar, Andy and Jill Kassube, Mike and Sue Loseby, Comus and Sarah Elliott, the Didler, Dave and Shirley Shaw, P Dawn, Lawrence Pearse, Simon Watkins, J F M and M West, Pat and Graham Williamson, Colin and Louise English, Graham Oddey, Andrew Todd, D Crook

 STANNERSBURN Northumberland   NY7286   Map 10

Pheasant £
Kielder Water road signposted off B6320 in Bellingham; NE48 1DD

Friendly village local close to Kielder Water with quite a mix of customers, and homely bar food; streamside garden; bedrooms

The comfortable low-beamed lounge at this warmly traditional inn has ranks of old local photographs on stripped stone and panelling, dark wood pubby tables and chairs on red patterned carpets and upholstered stools ranged along the counter. A separate public bar is simpler and opens into a further cosy seating area with beams and panelling; piped music. The friendly licensees and courteous staff serve Black Isle Red Kite, Timothy Taylors Landlord and Wylam Rocket on handpump and 40 malt whiskies. The pub is in a restful valley amid quiet forests, not far from Kielder Water, with picnic-sets in its streamside garden and a pony paddock behind. More reports please.

Good bar food includes farmhouse pâté, sweet marinated herring, ploughman's, steak and kidney or game and mushroom pie, dressed crab, cream cheese and broccoli bake, and roast lamb with rosemary and redcurrant sauce. *Benchmark main dish: roast lamb £10.95. Two-course evening meal £15.00.*

Free house ~ Licensees Walter and Robin Kershaw ~ Real ale ~ Bar food (12-2.30, 6(6.30 in winter)-8.30) ~ Restaurant ~ (01434) 240382 ~ Children welcome ~ Dogs allowed in bedrooms ~ Open 12-3, 6(6.30 Sun)-12; closed Mon and Tues Nov-Mar ~ Bedrooms: £55S/£90S

Recommended by Dave Braisted, Claes Mauroy

 THORNTON WATLASS Yorkshire   SE2385   Map 10

 **Buck** 🍺 🛏
Village signposted off B6268 Bedale—Masham; HG4 4AH

Honest village pub with five real ales, traditional bars, well liked food, and popular Sunday jazz

Very much the heart of the local community – but with a warm welcome for visitors as well – this friendly village pub has now been run by the long-serving licensees for 25 years. The pleasantly traditional bar on the right has upholstered old-fashioned wall settles on the carpet, a fine mahogany bar counter, a high shelf packed with ancient bottles, several mounted fox masks and brushes, and a brick fireplace. The Long Room (which overlooks the cricket green) has large prints of old Thornton Watlass cricket teams, signed bats, cricket balls and so forth. Barngates Mothbag, Black Sheep Best, Theakstons Best and Black Bull and Walls Gun Dog Bitter on handpump, a few wines by the glass and over 40 interesting malt whiskies; darts and board games. The sheltered garden has an equipped children's play area and summer barbecues, and they have their own cricket team; quoits.

Popular bar food, using local produce, includes sandwiches, chicken liver parfait with red onion marmalade, rarebit with home-made pear chutney, a choice of omelette, lasagne, beer-battered fish and chips, spinach and ricotta pasta, and specials like potato pancake with smoked salmon and chive crème fraîche, and a mild chicken curry with almonds, sultanas and banana cream. *Benchmark main dish: steak in ale pie £9.95. Two-course evening meal £17.95.*

Free house ~ Licensees Michael and Margaret Fox ~ Real ale ~ Bar food (12-2(3 Sun), 6.30-9.15(9 Sun) ~ Restaurant ~ (01677) 422461 ~ Children welcome ~ Dogs allowed in bedrooms ~ Trad jazz Sun lunchtimes ~ Open 11-11(midnight Sat) ~ Bedrooms: £55(£65S)/£80(£90B)

Recommended by Stuart and Sarah Barrie, Richard Gibbs

Most pubs with any outside space now have some kind of smokers' shelter. There are regulations about these – for instance, they have to be substantially open to the outside air. The best have heating and lighting and are really quite comfortable.

WARK Northumberland   NY8676 Map 10

Battlesteads

B6320 N of Hexham; NE48 3LS

Good local ales, fair value interesting food, and a relaxed atmosphere; comfortable bedrooms

An enjoyable all-rounder, this popular stone hotel still manages to convey a relaxed unhurried atmosphere. The nicely restored carpeted bar has a woodburning stove with a traditional oak surround, low beams, comfortable seats including some comfy deep leather sofas and easy chairs, and old *Punch* country life cartoons on the terracotta walls above its dark dado. Four good changing local ales such as Black Sheep Best, Durham Magus and a couple of guests from brewers such as Hadrian & Border and Wylam are on handpumps on the heavily carved dark oak bar counter. This leads through to the restaurant and spacious conservatory; good coffee, cheerful service, piped music and TV. There are tables on a terrace in the walled garden. Disabled access to some of the ground-floor bedrooms and they are licensed to hold civil marriages.

Using home-grown vegetables and other local produce, the good value bar food includes lunchtime sandwiches, ham hock terrine with pickle, potted shrimp and crab, venison carpaccio with hot and sour beetroot, cajun spiced chicken with sweet chilli sauce, cod and chips with mushy peas, mushroom and halloumi stack, and rib-eye steak with peppercorn sauce. *Benchmark main dish: home-made venison burger £8.75. Two-course evening meal £18.80.*

Free house ~ Licensees Richard and Dee Slade ~ Real ale ~ Bar food (12-3, 6.30-9) ~ Restaurant ~ (01434) 230209 ~ Children welcome ~ Dogs allowed in bar ~ Open 11-11 ~ Bedrooms: £60S/£105B

Recommended by David Heath, S D and J L Cooke, David and Christine Merritt, Kay and Mark Denison, Helen and Brian Edgeley, Bruce and Sharon Eden, Kevin Appleby, Michael Doswell

WASS Yorkshire   SE5579 Map 7

Wombwell Arms

Back road W of Ampleforth; or follow brown tourist-attraction sign for Byland Abbey off A170 Thirsk—Helmsley; YO61 4BE

Consistently enjoyable village pub with friendly atmosphere, good mix of locals and visitors, interesting bar food and real ales; bedrooms

Handy for Byland Abbey, this bustling pub is in a pretty village below the Hambleton Hills. The two bars are neatly kept with plenty of simple character, pine farmhouse chairs and tables, some exposed stone walls, and log fires; the walls of the Poacher's Bar are hung with brewery memorabilia. From the panelled bar counter, the friendly staff serve Theakstons Best, Timothy Taylors Landlord and York Yorkshire Terrier on handpump, nine wines by the glass (quite a few from Mrs Walker's South Africa) and several malt whiskies; darts. The two restaurants are incorporated into a 17th-c former granary and there are seats outside.

Using the best local produce, the well thought-of food includes sandwiches, pigeon with mushroom sauce bruschetta, smoked salmon and scrambled eggs, pork and apple sausages, beer-battered haddock, vegetarian open lasagne, bobotie (a south african fruity mince curry), chicken with a creamy leek, bacon and stilton sauce, and specials like mini smoked trout cakes with lemon and caper sauce, and beef stroganoff. *Benchmark main dish: steak pie £11.15. Two-course evening meal £19.00.*

Free house ~ Licensees Ian and Eunice Walker ~ Real ale ~ Bar food (12-2(2.30 Sat), 6.30-9(9.30 Fri and Sat); 12-7.30 Sun) ~ Restaurant ~ (01347) 868280 ~ Children welcome ~ Dogs allowed in bar ~ Folk music second Thurs of month ~ Open 12-3, 6-11; 12-11 Sat; 12-10.30 Sun ~ Bedrooms: £55S/£75S

Recommended by Janet and Peter Race, Val Carter, Edward Leetham, WW, Margaret Dickinson, Mr and Mrs D G Hallows, Michael Doswell

WATH IN NIDDERDALE Yorkshire   SE1467   Map 7

Sportsmans Arms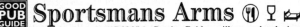

Nidderdale road off B6265 in Pateley Bridge; village and pub signposted over hump-back bridge on right after a couple of miles; HG3 5PP

Beautifully placed restaurant-with-rooms plus welcoming bar, real ales and super choice of other drinks, and imaginative food; comfortable bedrooms

As well as being a special place to stay in lovely, comfortable bedrooms, this civilised restaurant-with-rooms has now been run by the charming Mr Carter for well over 30 years – and the atmosphere is friendly and relaxed. Of course, much emphasis is placed on the exceptional food but there is a welcoming bar with an open fire and Black Sheep Best and Timothy Taylors Best on handpump – and locals do still pop in for a pint and a chat. There's a very sensible and extensive wine list with 20 by the glass (including champagne), over 40 malt whiskies, several russian vodkas and Thatcher's cider; maybe quiet piped music. Benches and tables outside and seats in the pretty garden; croquet. As well as their own fishing on the River Nidd, this is an ideal spot for walkers, hikers and ornithologists, and there are plenty of country houses, gardens and cities to explore.

Using butchers who breed their own animals, trout from the next village, game shot under a mile away and fish and shellfish delivered six times a week, the first-class food might include lunchtime sandwiches, king scallops with minted pea purée and grilled pancetta, home-cured gravadlax with crème fraîche and their own quail eggs, chicken stuffed with wensleydale cheese and ham with a tarragon and mushroom sauce, best end of nidderdale lamb with creamed cabbage, roasted garlic and cherry vine tomatoes, gressingham duck with cherries, oranges and preserved lemons, and venison on aubergine chutney with home-made plum jam. *Benchmark main dish: line-caught bass with roast asparagus and béarnaise sauce £13.50. Two-course evening meal £22.00.*

Free house ~ Licensee Ray Carter ~ Real ale ~ Bar food ~ Restaurant ~ (01423) 711306 ~ Children welcome ~ Dogs allowed in bar ~ Open 12-2.30, 6.30-11 ~ Bedrooms: £70B/£120B

Recommended by Janet and Peter Race, Jill and Julian Tasker, Stephen Woad, Keith Moss, Malcolm and Pauline Pellatt, David and Jenny Reed, Derek Thomas, Bruce and Sharon Eden, R and S Bentley

WELDON BRIDGE Northumberland   NZ1398 Map 10

Anglers Arms 🛏

B6344, just off A697; village signposted with Rothbury off A1 N of Morpeth; NE65 8AX

Large helpings of food in appealing bar or converted railway dining car, real ales, and a friendly welcome; fishing on River Coquet; bedrooms

Although emphasis at this sizeable but warmly welcoming place is on the comfortable bedrooms and enjoyable food, the whole thing is nicely rounded out by a traditional turkey-carpeted bar tucked into its heart. This bustling bar is divided into two parts: cream walls on the right and oak panelling and some shiny black beams hung with copper pans on the left, with four constantly changing real ales from brewers such as Adnams, Courage, Greene King and Timothy Taylor on handpump, and around 30 malt whiskies and decent wines. There's also a grandfather clock and sofa by the coal fire, staffordshire cats and other antique ornaments on its mantelpiece, old fishing and other country prints, a profusion of fishing memorabilia and some taxidermy. Some of the tables are lower than you'd expect for eating, but their chairs have short legs to match – different and rather engaging; piped music. The restaurant is in a former railway dining car with crisp white linen and a red carpet. There are tables in the attractive garden which has a good play area that includes an assault course. The pub is beside a bridge over the River Coquet and they have rights to fishing along a mile of the riverbank.

Generously served bar food includes sandwiches, chicken liver pâté, ploughman's, goats cheese and pea risotto, pork belly with apple compote and black pudding, cod and chips, and king prawns with peppers in garlic sauce. *Benchmark main dish: cod and chips £10.95. Two-course evening meal £15.00.*

Enterprise ~ Lease John Young ~ Real ale ~ Bar food (12-9.30) ~ Restaurant ~ (01665) 570271 ~ Dogs allowed in bedrooms ~ Open 11-11; 12-10.30 Sun ~ Bedrooms: £49.50S/£90S

Recommended by Jenny and Peter Lowater, Dennis Jones, Ann and Tony Bennett-Hughes, Colin McKerrow, Dr Peter D Smart, Jean and Douglas Troup

WIDDOP Yorkshire   SD9531 Map 7

Pack Horse 🛏 £

The Ridge; from A646 on W side of Hebden Bridge, turn off at Heptonstall signpost (as it's a sharp turn, coming out of Hebden Bridge road signs direct you around a turning circle), then follow Slack and Widdop signposts; can also be reached from Nelson and Colne, on high, pretty road; OS Sheet 103 map reference 952317; HX7 7AT

Friendly pub high up on the moors and liked by walkers for generous, tasty food, five real ales and lots of malt whiskies; bedrooms

Our readers very much enjoy their visits to this isolated, traditional inn, and if staying overnight, the breakfasts are particularly good. The bar has welcoming winter fires, window seats cut into the partly panelled stripped-stone walls that take in the moorland view, sturdy furnishings and horsey mementoes. Black Sheep Best, Copper Dragon Golden Pippin, Thwaites Bitter and a changing guest on handpump, around 130 single malt whiskies and some irish ones as well, and ten wines by the glass. The friendly golden retrievers are called Padge and Purdey and the alsatian, Holly. There are seats outside and pretty summer hanging baskets. As well as the comfortable bedrooms, they also offer a smart self-catering apartment.

🍴 Honest food at sensible prices includes sandwiches, pâté, garlic mushrooms, large burgers, black pudding and bacon on mash, pheasant and mushroom pie, lasagne, vegetable bake, gammon and eggs, and daily specials. *Benchmark main dish: rack of lamb £13.00. Two-course evening meal £15.00.*

Free house ~ Licensee Andrew Hollinrake ~ Real ale ~ Bar food (all day Sun; not Mon or weekday lunchtimes Oct-Easter) ~ (01422) 842803 ~ Children in eating area of bar until 8pm ~ Dogs allowed in bar ~ Open 12-3, 7-11; 12-11 Sun; closed Mon and weekday lunchtimes Oct-Easter ~ Bedrooms: £43S/£48S(£69B)

Recommended by Ian and Nita Cooper, Simon Le Fort, Geoff Boswell, Martin Smith

ALSO WORTH A VISIT IN THE NORTH EAST

Besides the region's top pubs, we recommend the following. Do tell us what you think of them: **feedback@goodguides.com**

ALLENDALE NY8355   NE47 9BD
Kings Head
Market Place (B6295)

Refurbished early 18th-c former coaching inn, popular with locals, with four real ales, good selection of wines and soft drinks, decent food served by friendly staff, glowing coal fire, newspapers; children welcome, bedrooms, open all day. *Recommended by JJW, CMW, John Coatsworth, Brett Jones, Comus and Sarah Elliott*

ALNMOUTH NU2511   NE66 2RA
Hope & Anchor
Northumberland Street

Old pub with cheery bar and long beamed dining room, well kept Hadrian & Border Farne Island Pale and Northumberland Sheepdog, hearty home-made food, china and brass, local art for sale; children and dogs welcome, quietly appealing coastal village, attractive beaches and good coastal walks, seven bedrooms, open all day. *Recommended by John Beeken*

☆ **ALNMOUTH** NU2410   NE66 2RJ
Red Lion
Northumberland Street

Welcoming 18th-c coaching inn, relaxed and unpretentious, with good choice of traditional food from good crab sandwiches to popular reasonably priced Sun lunch, cheerful efficient staff, well kept ales such as Black Sheep, Hadrian & Border, Northumberland and Wylam, mainly New World wines by the glass, attractive bistro-style dining room, log fire in cosy panelled locals' bar; dogs welcome, neat garden by alley with raised deck looking over Aln estuary, comfortable bedrooms, open all day (till 8pm Sun). *Recommended by Comus and Sarah Elliott, Celia Minoughan, Michael Doswell, Ann and Tony Bennett-Hughes, John Beeken and others*

ALNMOUTH NU2410   NE66 2RA
Sun
Northumberland Street

Comfortable banquettes in long low-beamed bar with open fire and woodburner at either end, carpet or bare-boards, decorations made from driftwood, friendly chatty staff, good value food including interesting sandwiches, Black Sheep and Mordue, good coffee, small contemporary dining area; piped music; attractive seaside village. *Recommended by Colin and Louise English*

ALNWICK NU1813   NE66 1PN
Blackmores
Bondgate Without

Smart contemporary pub/boutique hotel in Victorian stone building, well kept Black Sheep and Caledonian Deuchars IPA in lively front bar, several wines by the glass, consistently good food all day from snacky things up in bar, bistro or upstairs restaurant, attentive service; pleasant street-side raised terrace, 13 bedrooms. *Recommended by Jenny and Peter Lowater, Comus and Sarah Elliott, Michael Doswell, Richard and Stephanie Foskett, Rosemary and Mike Fielder and others*

ALNWICK NU1813   NE66 1UY
John Bull
Howick Street

Popular chatty drinkers' pub, essentially front room of early 19th-c terraced house, four changing ales, real cider, bottled belgian beers and over 100 malt whiskies; closed weekday lunchtime. *Recommended by the Didler*

AMBLE NU2604   NE65 0LD
Wellwood Arms
High Street

Recently refurbished dining pub with pleasant welcoming staff, enjoyable food from traditional things up including set menu choices, well selected wines, separate nicely laid-out restaurant area with own bar. *Recommended by Dr Peter D Smart*

BACKWORTH NZ3072   NE27 0FG
Pavilion
Hotspur North

Brightly modern Fitzgeralds pub (opened 2008), good food and service, four ales including Black Sheep and Consett; children welcome, disabled facilities, terrace tables, open all day. *Recommended by the Dutchman*

BAMBURGH NU1834   NE69 7BW
Castle
Front Street

Clean comfortably old-fashioned pub with friendly landlord and staff, well kept ales such as Black Sheep and Mordue, decent house wines, winter mulled wine, standard modestly priced food all day including good kippers from Craster, recently expanded dining area to cope with summer visitors, open fires; big courtyard, garden. *Recommended by Lawrence Pearse, Comus and Sarah Elliott*

BAMBURGH NU1734   NE69 7BS
Mizen Head
Lucker Road

Refurbished hotel with light airy bar, open fire, enjoyable locally sourced food, ales such as Black Sheep, good house wines, friendly staff; children and dogs welcome, nice bedrooms. *Recommended by Penny and Peter Keevil, Comus and Sarah Elliott*

☆ BAMBURGH NU1834   NE69 7BP
Victoria
Front Street

Substantial Victorian hotel with sofas, squashy leather chairs and high stools in mildly contemporary partly divided bar, chunky tables and chairs in dining room, good food all day from sandwiches up, two real ales from Black Sheep and/or Mordue, good wines by the glass, young children's playroom; lovely setting, comfortable bedrooms, open all day. *Recommended by Colin and Louise English*

BARDON MILL NY7566
NE47 7AN
Twice Brewed
Military Road (B6318 NE of Hexham)

Large busy inn well placed for fell-walkers and major Wall sites, six ales including local microbrews and two for the pub by Yates, 50 rums, 20 malts, reasonably priced wines, good value hearty pub food from baguettes up, quick friendly staff, local photographs and art for sale; quiet piped music, no dogs; children welcome, picnic-sets in back garden, 14 bedrooms, open all day. *Recommended by Dave Braisted, Pete Coxon, Peter Dearing*

BARNINGHAM NZ0810
DL11 7DW
Milbank Arms
On main road into village from Newsham

Cosy little one-room village local, simple and unspoilt with welcoming landlord (in same family for 70 years), no bar counter or kitchen, drinks brought from the cellar. *Recommended by C Elliott*

BEADNELL NU2229
NE67 5AY
Beadnell Towers
The Wynding, off B1340

Large slightly old-fashioned pub/hotel with unusual mix of furnishings, good food including local game and fish, well kept ales such as Hadrian & Border Farne Island, reasonably priced wines by the glass, nice coffee, pleasant obliging service; can get more touristy in summer; seats outside, bedrooms. *Recommended by DHV, Comus and Sarah Elliott, Michael Doswell*

BEADNELL NU2229
NE67 5AX
Craster Arms
The Wynding

Popular pubby food and blackboard specials including local fish, well kept Black Sheep and Mordue, good choice of wines by the glass, friendly efficient staff, roomy neatly kept old building with modern fittings, red banquettes, patterned carpets, stripped-brick and stone walls, pictures for sale, nice local atmosphere; children welcome, enclosed gardens, open all day. *Recommended by DHV, Michael Doswell*

BEAMISH NZ2154
DH9 0YB
Beamish Hall
NE of Stanley, off A6076

Converted stone-built stables in courtyard at back of hotel, popular and family friendly (can get crowded), five or six good beers from own microbrewery, decent choice of food all day, uniformed staff; plenty of seats outside. *Recommended by Peter Smith and Judith Brown, GSB, Mr and Mrs Maurice Thompson, Rob Weeks*

BEAMISH NZ2153
DH9 0QH
☆ # Beamish Mary
Off A693 signed No Place and Cooperative Villas, S of museum

Friendly down-to-earth former pit village inn under new management, eight well kept mainly local ales (May beer festival), farm cider, good home-made pubby food at bargain prices, coal fires, two bars with 1960s-feel mix of furnishings, bric-a-brac, 1920s/30s memorabilia and Aga with pots and pans, regular live music in converted stables; sports TV; children allowed until evening, updated bedrooms. *Recommended by Peter Smith and Judith Brown*

BELSAY NZ1277
NE20 0DN
Highlander
A696 S of village

Roomy country dining pub with enjoyable food from lunchtime baguettes up, good friendly service, Black Sheep and Caledonian Deuchars IPA, comfortable raised side area with nice plain wood tables and high-backed banquettes, plenty of nooks and corners for character, good log fires, plainer locals' bar; unobtrusive piped music; open all day. *Recommended by Guy and Caroline Howard*

BERWICK-UPON-TWEED NT9952   TD15 1ES
Barrels
Bridge Street

Small friendly pub with interesting collection of pop memorabilia and other bric-a-brac, eccentric furniture including dentist's chair in bare-boards bar, red banquettes in back room, five well kept changing ales, foreign bottled beers, live music (Fri) and DJs (Sat) in basement bar, good quality piped music; open all day, may be closed weekday lunchtimes in winter. *Recommended by Dave and Shirley Shaw*

 BERWICK-UPON-TWEED NT9952   TD15 1AB
Foxtons
Hide Hill

More chatty and comfortable two-level wine bar than pub, with wide choice of good imaginative food at reasonable prices, prompt friendly service, good range of wines, whiskies and coffees, real ales such as Caledonian, a local cider, lively side bistro; busy, so worth booking evenings, open all day, closed Sun. *Recommended by John and Sylvia Harrop, M Mossman*

BERWICK-UPON-TWEED NT9952   TD15 1BG
Leaping Salmon
Golden Square

Wetherspoons in late 18th-c former school, very reasonably priced beer and usual food choices; modern conservatory extension. *Recommended by Ian Phillips*

BIRTLEY NZ2856   DH3 1RE
Mill House
Blackfell, via A1231 slip road off southbound A1

Extensively refurbished dining pub with enjoyable food all day including bargain two-course lunches, oyster bar and tapas too, compact bar area, changing real ale, nice wines by the glass, dining room with olde-barn décor, alcoved eating areas and conservatory, friendly staff. *Recommended by Dave and Jenny Hughes, Deb Dawson*

BISHOPTON NZ3621   TS21 1HE
Talbot
The Green

Busy village dining pub with wide choice of good food from light dishes up, good value set lunch too, modern bar with smart dining areas either side, three real ales and several wines by the glass, friendly efficient uniformed staff. *Recommended by Ed and Anna Fraser*

BLYTH NZ2779   NE24 4HF
Three Horseshoes
Just off A189, W of town

Isolated and much-extended building (dates from 1780) perched above dual carriageway, various rooms off central bar (some with view to coast), front conservatory, good value food (all day Fri-Sun) from sandwiches up, wide choice of well kept ales, efficient friendly service from uniformed staff; children welcome, outside play area, tree house, open all day. *Recommended by GSB*

BOULMER NU2614   NE66 3BP
Fishing Boat
Beach View

Worth knowing for its position, with conservatory dining room and decking overlooking sea; light and airy inside with interesting nautical memorabilia, good value food, real ales such as Black Sheep and Tetleys; dogs welcome. *Recommended by John Beeken, Richard Pearson*

CARLBURY NZ2115   DL2 3SJ
Carlbury Arms
Just off A67 just E of Piercebridge

Welcoming dining pub locally popular for good choice of reasonably priced food, well kept Black Sheep and Jennings Cumberland, good wine choice, pine tables on wood floors.
Recommended by Pat and Stewart Gordon

CASTLE EDEN NZ4237   TS27 4SD
Castle Eden Inn
B1281 S of Peterlee

Refurbished dining pub with enjoyable fairly priced local food, ales such as Black Sheep, Caledonian Deuchars IPA and Timothy Taylors Landlord. *Recommended by Andy Maher, JHBS*

CATTON NY8257   NE47 9QS
 ## Crown
B6295

Cosy 19th-c pub under new management (same owners as the Rat at Anick), four or five well kept changing local ales, maybe a farm cider, very good locally sourced food from daily changing menu, stripped stone, big log fire, warm friendly atmosphere, dining extension; children welcome, no dogs at food times, pretty beer garden, lovely walks, open all day except Mon afternoon. *Recommended by Michael Doswell, Comus and Sarah Elliott, S Jackson, B Thompson, Philip Huddleston*

CORBRIDGE NY9964   NE45 5LA
☆ ## Angel
Main Street

Imposing white coaching inn at end of broad street facing handsome bridge over Tyne; sizeable modernised main bar, plain light wood chairs and tables, just a few prints on pastel walls, big-screen TV, carpeted lounge bar also with modern feel, strongly patterned wallpaper, tall metal-framed café-bar seats and leather bucket chairs, up to six real ales, a dozen wines by the glass, 30 malt whiskies, Weston's cider, well liked bar food; separate lounge with oak panelling, big stone fireplace, sofa and button-back wing armchairs, daily papers, smart raftered restaurant with stripped masonry and local art; piped music; children welcome, seats in front on cobbles below wall sundial, bedrooms, open all day.
Recommended by Eric Larkham, Michael Doswell, Mike and Lynn Robinson, Andy and Jill Kassube, Pete Coxon, Clive Watkin and others

CORBRIDGE NY9864   NE45 5AT
☆ ## Black Bull
Middle Street

Rambling linked old rooms, reasonably priced food all day from sandwiches and light lunches up, good friendly service, Black Sheep and Greene King ales, good attractively priced wine choice, roaring fire, neat comfortable seating including traditional settles on flagstones in softly lit low-ceilinged core; open all day. *Recommended by Comus and Sarah Elliott*

CORBRIDGE NY9863   NE45 5AY
Dyvels
Station Road

Refurbished traditional stone inn, friendly and well run, with good value pub food from duck egg sandwiches up, well kept ales such as Black Sheep, Mordue and Shepherd Neame, decent wines by the glass; children welcome, picnic-sets on side terrace and lawn, three bedrooms, open all day. *Recommended by Andy and Jill Kassube, Comus and Sarah Elliott*

We include some hotels with a good bar that offers facilities comparable to those of a pub.

CORBRIDGE NY9868   NE45 5QB
☆ **Errington Arms**
About 3 miles N of town; B6318, on A68 roundabout

18th-c stone-built roadside pub by Hadrian's Wall, good mix of diners and walkers, beamed bars with pine panelling, stone and burgundy walls, mix of chairs around pine tables on strip-wood flooring, log fire and woodburner, well liked home-made food, Jennings and Wylam ales, friendly staff; piped music; children welcome, tables out in front, closed Sun evening, Mon. *Recommended by David and Sue Smith, Comus and Sarah Elliott, David and Katharine Cooke, Andy and Jill Kassube*

COTHERSTONE NZ0119   DL12 9PF
☆ **Fox & Hounds**
B6277

18th-c inn with simple beamed bar, log fire, various alcoves and recesses, local photographs and country pictures, Black Sheep and a guest, malt whiskies from smaller distilleries, generous food using local ingredients, efficient friendly service, restaurant, african grey parrot called Reva; children welcome if eating, seats on terrace, quoits, bedrooms, pretty spot overlooking village green, good nearby walks. *Recommended by GNI, Guy Morgan, Chris and Jo Parsons, Ian Herdman, SGN Bennett, Jerry Brown and others*

CRAMLINGTON NZ2373   NE23 8AU
☆ **Snowy Owl**
Just off A1/A19 junction via A1068; Blagdon Lane

Large Vintage Inn, relaxed and comfortable, with reasonable prices, good choice of well-liked food all day including popular Sun lunch, friendly efficient young staff, beers such as Black Sheep, Jennings Cumberland and Timothy Taylors Landlord, nice wines, beams, flagstones, stripped stone and terracotta paintwork, soft lighting and an interesting mix of furnishings and decorations, daily papers; may be piped music; disabled access, bedrooms in adjoining Innkeepers Lodge, open all day. *Recommended by Guy and Caroline Howard, Dr Peter D Smart, Comus and Sarah Elliott*

CRASTER NU2519   NE66 3TR
☆ **Jolly Fisherman**
Off B1339, NE of Alnwick

Simple local in great spot, long a favourite for its lovely sea and coast views from picture window and grass behind, and for its good value crab sandwiches, crab soup and locally smoked seafood; this makes up for the take-us-as-you-find-us style, which can verge on scruffiness (not to everyone's taste); ales such as Black Sheep or Mordue, good cider, local art for sale, games area with pool; children and dogs welcome, smokehouse opposite, open all day in summer. *Recommended by Penny and Peter Keevil, Christine and Malcolm Ingram, John and Sylvia Harrop, the Didler, Ann and Tony Bennett-Hughes and others*

DARLINGTON NZ2814   DL3 7RG
No Twenty 2
Coniscliffe Road

Long bistro-feel Victorian pub with high ceiling, bare boards and exposed brickwork, up to 22 beers on handpump including own Village ales (brewed by Hambleton), draught continentals, decent lunchtime food in compact panelled back room, good friendly service; open all day, closed Sun. *Recommended by Mark Brittain, Julian Pigg, Peter Abbott*

DIPTONMILL NY9261   NE46 1YA
☆ **Dipton Mill Inn**
S of Hexham; off B6306 at Slaley

Small two-roomed pub tucked away in little hamlet, five good own-brewed Hexhamshire beers, Weston's cider, lots of wines by the glass, 20 malt whiskies, neatly kept snug bar, dark ply panelling, low ceilings, red furnishings, two open fires, good homely food and prompt friendly service; no credit cards; children welcome, seats in sunken crazy-paved terrace by restored mill stream or in attractively planted garden with aviary, nice walk

through woods along little valley; Hexham racecourse nearby, closed Sun evening.
Recommended by Eric Larkham, the Didler, Lawrence Pearse, GSB, Claes Mauroy and others

DURHAM NZ2642   DH1 4EG
Colpitts
Colpitts Terrace/Hawthorn Terrace

Comfortable two-bar traditional backstreet pub, friendly landlady and locals, cheap well kept Sam Smiths, open fires and original Victorian fittings, back pool room; seats in yard, open all day. *Recommended by the Didler, Phil and Sally Gorton, Mr and Mrs Maurice Thompson*

DURHAM NZ2742   DH1 3AW
Court
Court Lane

Comfortable town pub with good hearty home-made food all day from sandwiches to steaks and late-evening bargains, real ales such as Bass, Marstons Pedigree and Mordue, friendly helpful staff, extensive stripped-brick eating area, no mobile phones; bustling in term-time with students and teachers, piped music; seats outside, open all day.
Recommended by Eric Larkham, Mike and Lynn Robinson, P and D Carpenter

☆ DURHAM NZ2742   DH1 3HN

Dun Cow
Old Elvet

Unchanging backstreet pub in pretty 16th-c black-and-white timbered cottage, cheerful licensees, tiny chatty front bar with wall benches, corridor to long narrow back lounge with banquettes, machines etc (can be packed with students), particularly well kept Camerons and other ales such as Black Sheep and Caledonian Deuchars IPA, good value basic lunchtime snacks, decent coffee; piped music; children welcome, open all day except Sun in winter. *Recommended by Eric Larkham, the Didler, Phil and Sally Gorton*

DURHAM NZ2642   DH1 4PS
Old Elm Tree
Crossgate

Comfortable friendly pub on steep hill across from castle, two-room main bar and small lounge, four well kept local ales (occasional beer festivals), reasonably priced home-made food, open fires, folk and quiz nights; dogs welcome, small back terrace.
Recommended by Phil and Sally Gorton, Mr and Mrs Maurice Thompson

DURHAM NZ2742   DH1 3NU
Shakespeare
Saddler Street

Unchanging pub with signed actor photographs in busy basic front bar, charming panelled snug and neatly refurbished back room, well kept Caledonian Deuchars IPA, Fullers London Pride and two guests, simple cheap bar snacks, friendly staff, pub and board games; children (till 6pm) and dogs welcome, convenient for castle, cathedral and river, open all day. *Recommended by the Didler, Eric Larkham*

DURHAM NZ2742   DH1 3AG
Swan & Three Cygnets
Elvet Bridge

Refurbished Victorian pub in good bridge-end spot high above river, city views from big windows and picnic-sets out on terrace, bargain lunchtime food and Sam Smiths OB, helpful personable young staff; open all day. *Recommended by the Didler, Phil and Sally Gorton, Peter Smith and Judith Brown*

Half pints: by law, a pub should not charge more for half a pint than half the price of a full pint, unless it shows that half-pint price on its price list.

EGLINGHAM NU1019   NE66 2TX
Tankerville Arms
B6346 Alnwick—Wooler

Traditional pub with contemporary touches, cosy friendly atmosphere, beams, bare boards, some stripped stone, banquettes, warm fires, well kept local ales like Hadrian & Border and Wylam, nice wines, good imaginative food from changing menu, raftered split-level restaurant; children welcome, nice views from garden, three bedrooms, attractive village. *Recommended by Comus and Sarah Elliott, John and Sylvia Harrop*

ELWICK NZ4532   TS27 3EF
McOrville
0.25 miles off A19 W of Hartlepool

Open-plan dining pub with good blackboard food, Black Sheep and a changing ale, carved panelling, slippers provided for walkers. *Recommended by JHBS*

ELWICK NZ4533   TS27 3EF
Spotted Cow
0.25 miles off A19 W of Hartlepool

18th-c two-bar pub facing village green, three real ales, good food (not Sun evening), lounge and dining room, Weds quiz night. *Recommended by JHBS*

EMBLETON NU2322   NE66 3UY
Greys
Stanley Terrace, off W T Stead Road, turn at the Blue Bell

Carpeted main front bar with pubby furniture, more lived-in part with old photographs and cuttings, cottagey back dining room, open fires, well priced home-made food from sandwiches and pizzas to good specials including local fish, four well kept changing local ales, afternoon teas; small walled back garden, raised decking with village views. *Recommended by Andy and Jill Kassube, Michael Doswell*

FALSTONE NY7287   NE48 1AA
Blackcock
E of Yarrow and Kielder Water

Cosy, clean and friendly 17th-c inn, homely bar with beams and open fires, well kept ales such as Camerons, High House Farm and their own cheap Blackcock, bottled beers, Webster's cider, 50 malt whiskies, lunchtime bar food, evening restaurant with good vegetarian choice, pool room; quiet juke box; children allowed, dogs very welcome (own menu), garden with covered smokers' area, six bedrooms, handy for Kielder Water, open all day weekends, closed winter weekday lunchtimes (all day Weds). *Recommended by Alan Sutton*

FRAMWELLGATE MOOR NZ2644   DH1 5EE
Tap & Spile
Front Street; B6532 just N of Durham

Thriving two-bar pub with fine range of well kept changing local ales, farm ciders, good friendly staff, warm and comfortable atmosphere, pub and board games; children welcome. *Recommended by Jeff Brunton*

GATESHEAD NZ2559   NE9 6JA
Aletaster
Durham Road (A167), Low Fell

Great range of real ales and friendly helpful staff, traditional pub, Newcastle United memorabilia; TV. *Recommended by Mike Gerrard*

Every entry includes a postcode for use in Sat Nav devices.

GATESHEAD NZ2563
NE8 2AN
Central
Half Moon Lane

Large multi-room pub recently renovated by the Head of Steam chain, good choice of changing ales, lots of bottled beers, real ciders, low-priced food including themed evenings, roof terrace, live music; open all day (till 1am Fri, Sat). *Recommended by Eric Larkham, Peter Smith and Judith Brown*

 ### GREAT WHITTINGTON NZ0070
NE19 2HP
Queens Head
Village signed off A68 and B6018 N of Corbridge

Handsome golden-stone pub with dark leather chairs around sturdy tables, one or two good pictures on stripped-stone or grey/green walls, soft lighting, Caledonian Deuchars IPA, Hadrian & Border and Jennings, several malt whiskies, nice hunting mural above old fireplace in long narrow bar, much emphasis on popular food (not Sun evening) in tartan-carpeted dining areas with modern furnishings, friendly efficient staff; piped music; children and dogs welcome, picnic-sets under parasols on little front lawn, open all day Fri-Sun. *Recommended by GSB, Michael Doswell, Graham Oddey, John Prescott*

HART NZ4634
TS27 3AW
White Hart
Just off A179 W of Hartlepool; Front Street

Interesting nautical-theme pub with old ship's figurehead outside, fires in both bars, food from landlady-chef, two changing real ales; open all day (closed Mon afternoon). *Recommended by JHBS*

HARTLEPOOL NZ5132
TS24 7ED
Rat Race
Hartlepool Station

Former station newsagents, one small room (no bar), four well kept changing ales, real cider and perry, you can bring your own food, newspapers; open all day Sat till 8pm, closed Sun and four hours either side of home football matches. *Recommended by Arthur Pickering, JHBS*

HAWTHORN NZ4145
SR7 8SD
Stapylton Arms
Off B1432 S of A19 Murton exit

Chatty carpeted bar with old local photographs, enjoyable food from sandwiches to steaks and Sun roasts, one well kept changing ale, friendly service; dogs welcome, nice wooded walk to sea (joins Durham Coastal Path). *Recommended by JHBS*

HIGH HESLEDEN NZ4538
TS27 4QD
Ship
Off A19 via B1281

Half a dozen good value changing ales from the region, log fire, sailing ship models including a big one hanging with lanterns from boarded ceiling, landlady cooks enjoyable bar food and some interesting restaurant dishes; yacht and shipping views from car park, six bedrooms in new block, closed Mon. *Recommended by JHBS*

HOLY ISLAND NU1241
TD15 2RX
Crown & Anchor
Causeway passable only at low tide, check times: (01289) 330733

Comfortably unpretentious pub/restaurant, enjoyable food from shortish menu including good fish and chips, Wells & Youngs Bombardier and Caledonian Deuchars IPA, welcoming helpful staff, compact bar, roomy modern back dining room; dogs welcome, enclosed garden with picnic-sets, bedrooms. *Recommended by Mr and Mrs D J Nash, Dr A McCormick, Jean and Douglas Troup*

HURWORTH-ON-TEES NZ2814   DL2 2AQ
Bay Horse
Church Row

Welcoming dining pub with top-notch imaginative food, quite pricey but they offer a fixed-price lunch menu, children's choices too, three real ales, smiling efficient young staff, sizeable bar with good open fire, restaurant; seats on back terrace and in well tended walled garden beyond, charming village by River Tees. *Recommended by Peter Thompson, Michael Doswell, Jill and Julian Tasker*

LANGDON BECK NY8531   DL12 0XP
Langdon Beck Hotel
B6277 Middleton—Alston

Isolated unpretentious inn with two cosy bars and spacious lounge, well placed for walks and Pennine Way, Black Sheep, Jarrow and a guest ale (late May beer festival), good choice of enjoyable generous food including good local teesdale beef and lamb, decent coffee, helpful friendly staff; garden with wonderful fell views, bedrooms, open all day, closed Mon winter. *Recommended by Roxanne Chamberlain, Mr and Mrs Maurice Thompson, M and J White, John H Smith*

LEAMSIDE NZ3147   DH4 6QQ
Three Horseshoes
Pit House Lane

Popular welcoming pub with enjoyable food all day including bargain two-course lunch, five changing ales, good wine and whisky choice, bright airy dining room. *Recommended by David Hughes, Tim Skelton*

LESBURY NU2311   NE66 3PP
☆ ## Coach
B1339

Welcoming attractively refurbished stone pub at heart of pretty village, Black Sheep and Mordue, generous helpings of well liked food all day (till 7pm Sun), good service, pubby tables and stools in tartan-carpeted low-beamed bar, small left-hand area with sofas and armchairs, compact dining room with high-backed cane and leather dining chairs around light wood tables, yet another seating area with woodburner; piped music, TV; no small children after 7.30pm, rustic furniture under parasols on neat terrace, tubs and hanging baskets, handy for Alnwick Castle Gardens, open all day, but closed Sun evening Oct-March. *Recommended by Michael Doswell, P A Rowe, Dr Peter D Smart, Comus and Sarah Elliott and others*

LONGHORSLEY NZ1597   NE65 8XF
Linden Tree
N of Longhorsley on A697

Former granary behind country house conference hotel in extensive grounds; comfortable bar and light conservatory restaurant, enjoyable food, Greene King ales, good wines by the glass, efficient uniformed staff; children welcome, terrace tables, bedrooms in main hotel, golf course, open all day from 9.30am. *Recommended by Comus and Sarah Elliott*

LONGHORSLEY NZ1494   NE65 8SY
Shoulder of Mutton
East Road; A697 N of Morpeth

Comfortable bar and restaurant, welcoming landlady, good choice of generous home-made food including some imaginative dishes, Courage Directors, Caledonian Deuchars IPA and Everards Tiger, good selection of other drinks, Tues quiz night; piped music; children welcome, tables outside. *Recommended by JJW, CMW, Robert Wivell*

Ring the bull is an ancient pub game – you try to lob a ring on a piece of string over a hook (occasionally a bull's horn) on a wall or the ceiling.

MIDDLESTONE NZ2531   DL14 8AB
Ship
Low Road

Half a dozen well kept interesting ales including local ones, welcoming licensees and bustling friendly atmosphere, standard good value pub food, oak boards and nice fire, May beer festival and lots of other events including Thurs quiz, darts; piped music; good view from roof terrace, closed till 4pm Mon-Thurs, otherwise open all day. *Recommended by Mr and Mrs Maurice Thompson, Andrew Quinn*

MILFIELD NT9333   NE71 6JD
Red Lion
Main Road (A697 Wooler—Cornhill)

Welcoming 17th-c former coaching inn with good sensibly priced food (may be local game) from chef/landlord, well kept Black Sheep and Wylam, organic wine, good service; pretty garden by car park at back. *Recommended by Comus and Sarah Elliott, Michael Doswell, M Mossman*

NETHERTON NT9807   NE65 7HD
Star
Off B6341 at Thropton, or A697 via Whittingham

Simple unchanging village local under charming long-serving landlady (licence has been in her family since 1917), welcoming regulars, Camerons Strongarm tapped from cellar casks and served from hatch in small entrance lobby, large high-ceilinged room with wall benches, many original features; no food, music, children or dogs; closed lunchtime, open from 7pm, closed Mon, Thurs. *Recommended by Eric Larkham, the Didler*

NEW YORK NZ3269   NE29 8DZ
☆ # Shiremoor Farm
Middle Engine Lane; at W end of New York A191 bypass turn S into Norham Road, then first right (pub signed)

Incredibly busy dining pub – the transformation of derelict agricultural buildings with several well divided spacious areas, beams and joists (the conical rafters of former gin-gan in one part), broad flagstones, several kelims, a mix of interesting and comfortable furniture, farm tools, shields and swords, country pictures, wide range of customers of all ages, bar quieter and more civilised, Mordue and Timothy Taylors, good wines by the glass, enjoyable popular food all day, efficient service even when busy; picnic-sets on heated terrace. *Recommended by Lawrence Pearse, Sheena W Makin, Mike and Lynn Robinson, GSB*

NEWBURN NZ1665   NE15 8ND
☆ # Keelman
Grange Road: follow Riverside Country Park brown signs off A6085

Converted 19th-c pumping station, eight well kept/priced Big Lamp beers from on-site brewery, relaxed atmosphere and good mix of customers, high-ceilinged airy bar with lofty arched windows and well spaced tables and chairs, upper gallery with more seats, modern all-glass conservatory dining area, straightforward food; piped music; children welcome, plenty of tables on spacious terraces among flower tubs and baskets, good play area, bedrooms, open all day. *Recommended by David and Sue Smith, Stuart and Sarah Barrie, Eric Larkham, GSB, Joe Green*

NEWCASTLE UPON TYNE NZ2464   NE1 6BX
☆ # Bacchus
High Bridge E, between Pilgrim Street and Grey Street

Smart, spacious and comfortable with ocean liner look, ship and shipbuilding photographs, good lunchtime food from sandwiches and panini through pubby things to some interesting specials, Sun roasts, keen prices, great choice of well kept changing ales, plenty of bottled imports, farm cider, decent coffee, relaxed civilised atmosphere (but busy on match days), pleasant staff; disabled facilities, handy for Theatre Royal, open all day. *Recommended by Eric Larkham, Michael Doswell, Peter Smith and Judith Brown, Henry Paulinski, Derek Wason and others*

NEWCASTLE UPON TYNE NZ2464   NE1 4AG
Bodega
Westgate Road

Majestic Edwardian drinking hall next to Tyne Theatre, Big Lamp Prince Bishop, Durham Magus and six interesting guests, farm cider, friendly service, colourful walls and ceiling, bare boards, snug front cubicles, spacious back area with two magnificent stained-glass cupolas; piped music, machines, big-screen TV, very busy on Newcastle United match days; open all day. *Recommended by Eric Larkham, Jeremy King*

NEWCASTLE UPON TYNE NZ2563   NE1 1RQ
☆ Bridge Hotel
Castle Square, next to high-level bridge

Big cheery well divided high-ceilinged bar around servery with replica slatted snob screens, well kept changing ales, farm cider, friendly staff, bargain generous lunchtime food (not Sat), Sun afternoon teas, magnificent fireplace, great river and bridge views from raised back area; sports TV, piped music, games machines, live music upstairs including long-standing Mon folk club; flagstoned back terrace overlooking part of old town wall, open all day. *Recommended by Eric Larkham, James Thompson, Andy Lickfold, the Didler, Graham Oddey and others*

NEWCASTLE UPON TYNE NZ2464   NE1 5HL
Centurion
Central Station, Neville Street

Glorious high-ceilinged Victorian décor with tilework and columns in former first-class waiting room, well restored with comfortable leather seats giving club-like feel, Black Sheep and local ales such as Allendale and Jarrow, farm cider, friendly staff; piped music, unobtrusive sports TV; useful deli next door. *Recommended by Mike and Eleanor Anderson, Eric Larkham, Mike and Lynn Robinson, Tony and Wendy Hobden*

NEWCASTLE UPON TYNE NZ2664   NE1 2PQ
☆ Cluny
Lime Street

Trendy bar/café in interesting 19th-c mill/warehouse, striking setting below Metro bridge, good value home-made food all day from massive sandwiches up, cheerful staff, up to eight well kept ales including Banks's and Big Lamp, exotic beers and rums, sofas in comfortable raised area with daily papers and local art magazines, back gallery with artwork from studios in same complex; piped music, good live music nightly; children welcome till 7pm, picnic-sets out on green, open all day. *Recommended by Alex and Claire Pearse, Eric Larkham, James Thompson, Mike and Lynn Robinson*

NEWCASTLE UPON TYNE NZ2563   NE1 3JE
☆ Crown Posada
The Side; off Dean Street, between and below the two high central bridges (A6125 and A6127)

Popular unchanging city-centre pub with grand architecture, long narrow room with elaborate coffered ceiling, stained glass in counter screens, line of gilt mirrors each with tulip lamp on curly brass mount (matching the great ceiling candelabra), long built-in green leather wall seat flanked by narrow tables, fat low-level heating pipes, old working record player in wooden cabinet, six well kept ales, lunchtime sandwiches, helpful staff and good mix of regular customers (packed at peak times); piped music; only a stroll to castle, open all day, but closed Sun lunchtime. *Recommended by Mike and Eleanor Anderson, Eric Larkham, James Thompson, Myke and Nicky Crombleholme, the Didler, P Dawn and others*

NEWCASTLE UPON TYNE NZ2664   NE6 1LD
Cumberland Arms
Byker Buildings

Friendly unspoilt traditional local, seven particularly well kept mainly local ales (straight from the cask if you wish) including a house beer from Wylam, eight farm ciders, beer/cider festivals, good value pubby food all day, obliging staff; live music or other events most nights (regular ukulele band), tables out overlooking Ouseburn Valley, four bedrooms, closed Mon lunchtime otherwise open all day. *Recommended by Eric Larkham, Mike and Lynn Robinson, the Didler*

NEWCASTLE UPON TYNE NZ2470   NE3 5EH
Falcons Nest
Rotary Way, Gosforth – handy for racecourse

Roomy Vintage Inn with comfortably olde-worlde linked rooms, good value food, pleasant staff, good choice of wines by the glass, well kept Black Sheep and Timothy Taylors Landlord; open all day, bedrooms in adjacent Innkeepers Lodge. *Recommended by Dr Peter D Smart*

NEWCASTLE UPON TYNE NZ2664   NE6 1AP
Free Trade
St Lawrence Road, off Walker Road (A186)

Splendidly basic proper pub with outstanding views up river from big windows, terrace tables and seats on grass, real ales such as High House, Jarrow and Mordue, good sandwiches, warmly friendly atmosphere, real fire, original Formica tables; steps down to back room and lavatories; open all day. *Recommended by Eric Larkham*

NEWCASTLE UPON TYNE NZ2464   NE1 5SE
Newcastle Arms
St Andrew's Street

Open-plan drinkers' pub on fringe of Chinatown, Caledonian Deuchars IPA and five quickly changing guests including a porter or stout, farm ciders and perries, beer festivals, friendly staff, interesting old local photographs; piped music, big-screen sports TV, can get very busy especially on match days; open all day. *Recommended by Eric Larkham, Mr and Mrs Maurice Thompson, Ab Hamed*

NEWTON NZ0364   NE43 7UL
Duke of Wellington
Off A69 E of Corbridge

Extensively refurbished old stone inn in attractive farming hamlet, good interesting well presented food, real ales, large open L-shaped bar/dining area, comfortable mix of modern and traditional furnishings, sofas and armchairs in one corner, woodburner, daily papers, darts; dogs welcome in bar area, back terrace, seven bedrooms. *Recommended by Mourveen Scott, W K Wood, Graham Oddey*

NEWTON ON THE MOOR NU1705   NE65 9JY
☆ Cook & Barker Arms
Village signed from A1 Alnwick—Felton

Nicely traditional stone-built country inn, beamed bar with stripped-stone and partly panelled walls, broad-seated settles around oak-topped tables, horsebrasses, coal fires, Black Sheep, Timothy Taylors and a guest beer, extensive wine list, popular food using own-farm meat (early-bird deal midweek evenings), friendly helpful staff, separate restaurant with french windows opening on to terrace; piped music, TV; children welcome, comfortable bedrooms, open all day. *Recommended by J A Snell, Bruce and Sharon Eden, John and Angie Millar, P A Rowe, Jenny and Peter Lowater, John and Sylvia Harrop and others*

NEWTON-BY-THE-SEA NU2424   NE66 3EL
☆ Ship
Village signed off B1339 N of Alnwick

In charming square of fishermen's cottages by green sloping to sandy beach, plainly furnished but cosy bare-boards bar, nautical charts on dark pink walls, simple room on left with beams, hop bines, bright modern pictures on stripped-stone walls and woodburner in stone fireplace, own-brewed ales, real cider and tasty bar food (good crab sandwiches), live folk, blues and jazz; no credit cards, can get very busy; children and dogs welcome, seats among flowering pots on edge of square and picnic-sets on green, no nearby parking (unless disabled), open all day in summer, phone for winter hours (01665) 576262. *Recommended by Penny and Peter Keevil, James Thompson, Andy and Jill Kassube, Mike and Sue Loseby, Comus and Sarah Elliott, the Didler and others*

NORTH SHIELDS NZ3568   NE30 1NH
Magnesia Bank
Camden Street

Lively well run pub in former bank, Caledonian Deuchars IPA, Durham Magus, Theakstons Old Peculier and guests, good value pubby food, friendly staff, bare boards, cherry walls and green button-back banquettes, regular live music; children welcome, open all day. *Recommended by Michael Doswell*

PONTELAND NZ1771   NE20 9BT
Badger
Street Houses; A696 SE, by garden centre

Vintage Inn with relaxing rooms and alcoves, old furnishings and olde-worlde décor, good log fire, five well kept beers such as Black Sheep, Leeds and Timothy Taylors, decent range of wines by the glass, standard food all day, prompt friendly service; piped music; children welcome. *Recommended by Dr Peter D Smart*

PONTELAND NZ1773   NE20 9UH
Blackbird
North Road

Imposing recently refurbished old pub opposite church, stylish open-plan interior with mix of furniture including striped tub chairs and button-backed banquettes, unframed prints, skilful lighting, good imaginative food attracting attention, nice lunchtime sandwiches too, including rare roast beef. *Recommended by Michael Doswell, Peter and Eleanor Kenyon*

RENNINGTON NU2118   NE66 3RS
☆ ## Horseshoes
B1340

Comfortable family-run flagstoned pub with nice local feel (may be horses in car park), well kept ales such as Hadrian & Border and John Smiths, good value generous food including two-course lunch deals, good local fish and meat, decent wines by the glass, friendly efficient unrushed service, simple neat bar with woodburner, spotless compact restaurant; children welcome, tables outside, attractive quiet village near coast, closed Mon. *Recommended by Guy and Caroline Howard, Mike and Lynn Robinson, Dr Peter D Smart*

RENNINGTON NU2118   NE66 3RX
☆ ## Masons Arms
Stamford Cott; B1340 N

Comfortably carpeted beamed bar with neat pubby furniture, well kept ales such as Black Sheep, Hadrian & Border, High House Farm and Northumberland, good malt whisky range, enjoyable straightforward food, smiling relaxed service, brassware, flintlock pistols etc, woodburner between bar and family room; tables on lavender-edged roadside terrace, more picnic-sets behind, comfortable bedrooms in former stables block. *Recommended by George Cowie, Frances Gosnell, Michael Butler, the Dutchman, Ann and Tony Bennett-Hughes, John Beeken*

ROOKHOPE NY9342   DL13 2BG
Rookhope Inn
Off A689 W of Stanhope

Friendly old inn on coast-to-coast bike route, real ales such as Black Sheep and Timothy Taylors Landlord, enjoyable home-made food from fresh sandwiches to good Sun roasts, black beams and open fires, small dining room; sports TV; seats outside, spectacular views, five bedrooms. *Recommended by Andy and Jill Kassube, Claes Mauroy*

SEATON NZ3950   SR7 0LP

Seaton Lane Inn
Seaton Lane

Contemporary roadside bar/restaurant/hotel, popular with locals, good choice of enjoyable food (all day) from sandwiches and pub favourites up including two-course set menu, well kept Mordue, Theakstons and Wells & Youngs, lounge and restaurant on split levels, attentive staff; 18 bedrooms. *Recommended by Mr and Mrs Maurice Thompson, Barry Moses, Mike and Lynn Robinson*

SEDGEFIELD NZ3528   TS21 3AT

Dun Cow
Front Street

Popular refurbished village inn with low-beamed bar, back tap room and dining room, above-average food including good Sun roast, cheerful efficient staff, well kept ales such as Black Sheep and Camerons; children welcome, reasonably priced comfortable bedrooms, good breakfast. *Recommended by John and Sylvia Harrop, Andy Cole*

SHINCLIFFE NZ2940   DH1 2NU

 ## Seven Stars
High Street N (A177 S of Durham)

Comfortable old-fashioned 18th-c village inn, varied choice of good food from pub favourites to gently upmarket dishes, good value set menus, four well kept ales including Black Sheep, coal fire and plenty of atmosphere in lounge bar, candlelit panelled dining room, caring service from licensees; children in eating areas, dogs in bar, some picnic-sets outside, eight bedrooms, open all day. *Recommended by Bruce and Sharon Eden, Richard and Stephanie Foskett, Tim Tomlinson*

SLALEY NY9658   NE46 1TT

 ## Travellers Rest
B6306 S of Hexham (and N of village)

Attractive and busy stone-built country pub, spaciously opened up, with farmhouse-style décor, beams, flagstones and polished wood floors, huge fireplace, comfortable high-backed settles forming discrete areas, friendly uniformed staff, popular fairly standard food (not Sun evening) in bar and appealingly up-to-date dining room, good children's menu, basic sandwiches, friendly staff, real ales such as Allendale, Black Sheep and Wylam, limited wines by the glass; dogs welcome, tables outside with well equipped adventure play area on grass behind, three good value bedrooms, open all day. *Recommended by Mr and Mrs Maurice Thompson, GSB*

SOUTH SHIELDS NZ3666   NE33 4PG

Maltings
Claypath Road

Former dairy now home to Jarrow brewery, their full range and guest ales from upstairs bar (showpiece staircase); open all day, no food Fri-Sun evenings. *Recommended by Eric Larkham*

SOUTH SHIELDS NZ3767   NE33 2LD

Sand Dancer
Sea Road

Great location on beach, with views from raised terrace, decent well priced food including fresh fish and lobster tank, rustic décor, friendly staff and good atmosphere. *Recommended by John Coatsworth*

STAMFORDHAM NZ0772   NE18 0PB

Bay Horse
Off B6309

Refurbished beamed and stone-built pub at end of green in attractive village, good fresh food from new owners (both chefs) with emphasis on local produce, well kept ales, bareboards bar area with woodburner, restaurant; bedrooms. *Recommended by Michael Doswell*

STANNINGTON NZ2179   NE61 6EL

☆ **Ridley Arms**

Village signed off A1 S of Morpeth

Attractive extended 18th-c stone pub with several linked rooms, each with slightly different mood and style, proper front bar with stools along counter, Black Sheep, Caledonian, Derwent and Jarrow, beamed dining areas with comfortable bucket armchairs around dark tables on bare boards or carpet, cartoons and portraits on cream, panelled or stripped-stone walls, bar food (not Sun evening) from sandwiches up (mixed reports lately); piped music, fruit machine; children welcome, good disabled access, front picnic-sets by road, more on back terrace, open all day. *Recommended by Michael Doswell, Dr Peter D Smart, Eric Larkham, GSB, Comus and Sarah Elliott and others*

WARDEN NY9166   NE46 4SQ

Boatside

0.5 miles N of A69

Cheerful attractively modernised old stone-built pub with enjoyable pubby food, well kept ales and good friendly service; children and muddy walkers welcome, small neat enclosed garden, attractive spot by Tyne bridge, bedrooms in adjoining cottages. *Recommended by Angela*

WARENFORD NU1429   NE70 7HY

White Swan

Off A1 S of Belford

Simply decorated friendly bar with changing ales such as Adnams and Black Sheep, steps down to cosy restaurant with good imaginative food including prettily presented puddings, good value set lunch, efficient helpful service, warm fires; dogs welcome. *Recommended by Mr J V Nelson, Mr and Mrs J P Syner, Michael Doswell*

WARKWORTH NU2406   NE65 0UL

Hermitage

Castle Street

Rambling local (former coaching inn) doing tasty home-made food (all day Mon-Sat) such as rabbit pie, Jennings ales, friendly staff, quaint décor with old range for heating, small upstairs restaurant; piped music; children welcome, benches out in front, attractive setting, five bedrooms. *Recommended by Ann and Tony Bennett-Hughes*

WARKWORTH NU2406   NE65 0UR

Masons Arms

Dial Place

Welcoming village pub in shadow of castle, enjoyable food including daily specials and Sun carvery, local beers, friendly staff, Tues quiz night; dogs and children welcome, disabled facilities, back flagstoned courtyard, appealing village not far from sea, open all day. *Recommended by Guy and Caroline Howard, Clive Flynn*

WEST BOLDON NZ3460   NE36 0PZ

Red Lion

Redcar Terrace

Bow-widowed and flower-decked family-run pub, hop-strung beamed bar with open fire, ales such as Mordue Workie Ticket from ornate wood counter, separate snug and conservatory dining room, good choice of well priced pubby food; seats out on back decking, open all day. *Recommended by Roger and Donna Huggins*

If we know a pub has an outdoor play area for children, we mention it.

WHITLEY BAY NZ3473   NE26 1UE
Briar Dene
The Links

Smart brightly decorated two-room pub, fine sea-view spot, with up to eight interesting changing ales, good value pubby food from sandwiches up, friendly efficient staff; children welcome, seats outside, open all day. *Recommended by Eric Larkham, Dr Peter D Smart, Henry Paulinski, Guy and Caroline Howard*

WIDDRINGTON NZ2596   NE61 5DY
Widdrington Inn
Off A1068 S of Amble

Open-plan busy family pub, comfortably carpeted and popular for good value fresh food all day, good friendly staff, beers including John Smiths, reasonably priced wines by the glass; open all day. *Recommended by Jean and Douglas Troup*

WOLVISTON NZ4525   TS22 5JX
Ship
High Street

Gabled red-brick Victorian pub in centre of bypassed village, open-plan multi-level carpeted bar, bargain food, changing real ales from northern breweries, quiz nights; garden. *Recommended by JHBS*

WOOLER NT9928   NE71 6AD
Tankerville Arms
A697 N

Pleasant hotel bar in modernised early 17th-c coaching inn, relaxed and friendly, with reasonably priced food including local meat and fish, ales such as Hadrian & Border, good wines by the glass, small restaurant and larger airy one overlooking nice garden, big log fire; disabled facilities, 16 bedrooms, good local walks. *Recommended by Comus and Sarah Elliott, Dr Peter D Smart*

WYLAM NZ1164   NE41 8HR
☆ ## Boathouse
Station Road, handy for Newcastle—Carlisle rail line; across Tyne from village (and Stephenson's birthplace)

Thriving convivial pub with splendid ale range including local Wylam, keen prices, good choice of malt whiskies, bargain weekend lunches, polite helpful young staff, open stove in bright low-beamed bar, dining room; children and dogs welcome, seats outside, close to station and river, open all day. *Recommended by Mr and Mrs Maurice Thompson, Eric Larkham, the Didler*

ALSO WORTH A VISIT IN YORKSHIRE

Besides the region's top pubs, we recommend the following. Do tell us what you think of them: **feedback@goodguides.com**

ABERFORD SE4337   LS25 3AA
Swan
Best to use A642 junction to leave A1; Main Street N

Busy dining pub (may have to wait for a table), vast choice of good generous food from sandwiches to bargain carvery, lots of black timber, prints, pistols, cutlasses and stuffed animals, well kept Black Sheep and Tetleys, generous glasses of wine, good friendly uniformed service, upstairs evening restaurant; children welcome, tables outside. *Recommended by Pete Coxon, Ed and Anna Fraser*

ADDINGHAM SE0749   LS29 0LY
☆ **Fleece**
Main Street

Comfortable two-level pub, nice farmhouse-style eating area with good value home-made food from hearty sandwiches (home-baked bread) to interesting blackboard choices using good local ingredients (some from own back allotment), popular all-day Sun roasts, friendly service, well kept Yorkshire ales, good choice of wines by the glass, low ceilings, flagstones and log fire, plain tap room with darts and dominoes, quiz nights Tues, trad jazz Weds; very busy weekends (worth booking then); children and dogs welcome, lots of picnic-sets on front terrace, open all day. *Recommended by Gordon and Margaret Ormondroyd, Jeremy King, John and Sylvia Harrop, Tina and David Woods-Taylor, Peter and Judy Frost and others*

ALDBOROUGH SE4166   YO51 9ER
Ship
Off B6265 just S of Boroughbridge, close to A1

Attractive 14th-c beamed village dining pub, enjoyable food and good service, Greene King, John Smiths and Theakstons, some old-fashioned seats around cast-iron-framed tables, lots of copper and brass, inglenook fire, restaurant; a few picnic-sets outside, handy for Roman remains and museum, bedrooms, open all day Sun, closed Mon lunchtime. *Recommended by Susan Davey, NS Orr*

APPLETON-LE-MOORS SE7388   YO62 6TF
☆ **Moors**
N of A170, just under 1.5 miles E of Kirkby Moorside

Traditional stone-built village pub, beamed bar with built-in high-backed settle next to old kitchen fireplace, plenty of other seating, some sparse decorations (a few copper pans, earthenware mugs, country ironwork), Black Sheep and Timothy Taylors, tasty bar food (all day Sun), darts; piped music; children and dogs welcome, tables in lovely walled garden with quiet country views, walks to Rosedale Abbey or Hartoft End, paths to Hutton-le-Hole, Cropton and Sinnington, bedrooms, open all day. *Recommended by Greta and Christopher Wells, Ann and Tony Bennett-Hughes, Ed and Anna Fraser*

APPLETREEWICK SE0560   BD23 6DA
☆ **Craven Arms**
Off B6160 Burnsall—Bolton Abbey

Character creeper-covered 17th-c beamed pub, comfortably down-to-earth settles and rugs on flagstones, oak panelling, fire in old range, good friendly service, up to eight well kept ales, good choice of wines by the glass, home-made food from baguettes up, small dining room and splendid thatched and raftered barn extension with gallery; children, dogs and boots welcome (plenty of surrounding walks), nice country views from front picnic-sets, more seats in back garden, open all day Weds-Sun. *Recommended by WW, John and Eleanor Holdsworth, Dr Kevan Tucker*

APPLETREEWICK SE0560   BD23 6DA
New Inn
W end of main village

Unpretentious warmly welcoming country local with lovely views, six well kept ales including Black Sheep and Daleside, good choice of continental bottled beers, generous tasty home cooking, distinctive décor, interesting old local photographs; children and dogs welcome, three garden areas, good walking, five bedrooms and nearby camping, open all day. *Recommended by Dr Kevan Tucker, John and Helen Rushton*

Tipping is not normal for bar meals, and not usually expected.

ARTHINGTON SE2644   LS21 1NL
Wharfedale
A659 E of Otley (Arthington Lane)

Good value food from sandwiches and pub staples to popular Sun lunch, four ales including Black Sheep and Copper Dragon, several wines by the glass, efficient friendly service, spacious open-plan bar, lots of dark wood and some intimate alcoves, separate restaurant in long, beamed room; disabled facilities, big garden with terrace, three bedrooms, open all day. *Recommended by Richard Meek, Jeremy King*

ASENBY SE3975   YO7 3QL
☆ Crab & Lobster
Dishforth Road; village signed off A168 – handy for A1

Most emphasis on civilised hotel and restaurant side, but has rambling L-shaped bar with Copper Dragon and Theakstons, interesting jumble of seats from antique high-backed settles through sofas to rather theatrical corner seats, mix of tables too and a jungle of bric-a-brac, especially good (not cheap) food in smart main restaurant and dining pavilion (big tropical plants), live jazz Sun lunchtime; well behaved children allowed, seats on mediterranean-style terrace, opulent bedrooms in surrounding house with seven acres of gardens and 180-metre golf hole, open all day till midnight. *Recommended by Janet and Peter Race, Jon Clarke, Comus and Sarah Elliott, Dr D Jeary, Dr and Mrs R G J Telfer and others*

ASKRIGG SD9491   DL8 3HQ
☆ Kings Arms
Signed from A684 Leyburn—Sedbergh in Bainbridge

Great log fire in former coaching inn's flagstoned high-ceilinged main bar, traditional furnishings and décor, well kept ales such as Black Sheep, John Smiths and Theakstons, decent wines by the glass, good choice of malts, enjoyable food from sandwiches up, friendly staff, restaurant with inglenook, barrel-vaulted former beer cellar; piped music; children and dogs welcome, pleasant courtyard, bedrooms run separately as part of Holiday Property Bond complex behind, open all day weekends. *Recommended by Eric Ruff, Gordon and Margaret Ormondroyd*

ASKWITH SD1648   LS21 2JQ
Black Horse
Off A65

Biggish stone-built open-plan family pub in lovely spot (superb Wharfedale views from dining conservatory and good terrace), well kept Timothy Taylors Landlord, wide choice of enjoyable home-made food including Sun carvery, good service, woodburner; children welcome. *Recommended by Gordon and Margaret Ormondroyd, Robert Wivell*

AUSTWICK SD7668   LA2 8BB
☆ Game Cock
Just off A65 Settle—Kirkby Lonsdale

Quaint civilised place in a pretty spot below Three Peaks, good log fire in old-fashioned beamed bare-boards back bar, cheerful efficient staff and friendly locals, good choice of well kept ales, winter mulled wine, nice coffee, most space devoted to the food side, with good fairly priced choice from french chef/landlord including evening special offers, pizzas and children's meals as well, two dining rooms and modern front conservatory-type extension; walkers and dogs welcome, tables out in front with play area, three neat bedrooms, open all day Sun. *Recommended by Michael Lamm, Peter Fryer, David Heath, Martin Smith, John and Verna Aspinall*

AYSGARTH SE0088   DL8 3AD
George & Dragon
Just off A684

Welcoming 17th-c posting inn with emphasis on good varied food from sandwiches up, two big dining areas, small beamed and panelled bar with log fire, well kept Black Sheep Bitter, Theakstons Best and a beer brewed for the pub, good choice of wines by the glass;

may be piped music; children welcome, nice paved garden, lovely scenery and walks, handy for Aysgarth Falls, seven bedrooms, open all day. *Recommended by Mr and Mrs Maurice Thompson, Keith Moss*

BAILDON SE1538 BD17 6AB
Junction
Baildon Road

Wedge-shaped traditional local with three linked rooms, friendly atmosphere, well kept Dark Star and changing microbrews, home-made weekday lunchtime food, live music and sing-alongs Sun evening, pool; open all day. *Recommended by the Didler, Andy Barker*

BARKISLAND SE0419 HX4 0DJ
Fleece
B6113 towards Ripponden

18th-c beamed moorland pub smartened up under new landlord, two rooms laid out for the enjoyable reasonably priced food including a set menu, good service, well kept Black Sheep, stripped stone, woodburner and open fire, mezzanine, brightly painted children's room with games; Pennine views from first-floor terrace and garden, bedrooms, handy for M62. *Recommended by Gordon and Margaret Ormondroyd*

BARMBY ON THE MARSH SE6828 DN14 7HT
Kings Head
High Street

Early 19th-c refurbished and extended beamed village pub, enjoyable locally sourced home-made food with some interesting choices, four ales including Black Sheep, good service, large restaurant, deli; children welcome, disabled facilities, open all day weekends, closed Mon and Tues lunchtimes. *Recommended by Ross Gibbins, Michael Butler*

☆ BECK HOLE NZ8202 YO22 5LE
Birch Hall
Off A169 SW of Whitby, from top of Sleights Moor

Tiny pub-cum-village-shop in stunning surroundings, two unchanging rooms (shop sells postcards, sweets and ice-creams), simple furnishings – built-in cushioned wall seats, wooden tables (one with 136 pennies embedded in the top), flagstones or composition flooring, unusual items like french breakfast cereal boxes, tube of toothpaste priced 1/3d and model train running around head-height shelf; Durham, Wentworth and a guest, bar snacks including local pies and cakes (lovely beer cake), exceptionally friendly service, dominoes and quoits; no credit cards; children in small family room, dogs welcome, old painting of river valley outside and benches, steps up to steeply terraced side garden, self-catering cottage, good walks – one along disused railway, open all day in summer, closed Mon evening in winter, all day Tues Nov-Mar. *Recommended by Comus and Sarah Elliott, the Didler, Kevin Thomas, Nina Randall, Matt and Vikki Wharton*

BEDALE SE2688 DL8 1ED
Old Black Swan
Market Place

Attractive façade, welcoming efficient staff, good choice of generously served straightforward food, well kept ales including Theakstons Old Peculier, log fire, darts, pool; sports TV; children welcome, disabled facilities, small back terrace, Tues market, open all day. *Recommended by Janet and Peter Race, Mike Horgan, Di Wright*

BEVERLEY TA0339 HU17 8BH
Dog & Duck
Ladygate

Cheerful popular two-bar local handy for playhouse and Sat market, good home-made lunchtime food using local produce from sandwiches to bargain Sun lunch, OAP deals too, well kept Caledonian Deuchars IPA, Copper Dragon, John Smiths and guests, good value wines, several malts, helpful friendly staff, coal fires; piped music, TV for racing, games machine; cheap basic courtyard bedrooms up iron stairs. *Recommended by the Didler, Mike and Lynn Robinson*

BEVERLEY TA0339
White Horse
Hengate, off North Bar

HU17 8BN

Carefully preserved Victorian interior with basic little rooms huddled around central bar, brown leatherette seats (high-backed settles in one little snug) and plain chairs and benches on bare boards, antique cartoons and sentimental engravings, gaslit chandelier, open fires, games room, upstairs family room, bargain Sam Smiths and guest beers, basic food; children till 7pm, open all day. *Recommended by the Didler, Huw Jones*

BEVERLEY TA0239
Woolpack
Westwood Road, W of centre

HU17 8EN

Small welcoming pub with no pretensions in a pair of 19th-c cottages, sound traditional food and well kept ales such as Jennings, cosy snug, real fires, simple furnishings, brasses, teapots, prints and maps; no nearby parking; open all day weekends, closed lunchtimes Mon and Tues. *Recommended by Pat and Graham Williamson*

BILBROUGH SE5346
Three Hares
Off A64 York—Tadcaster

YO23 3PH

Smart neatly kept village dining pub with enjoyable good value food all day, Sun roasts, well kept real ale, good choice of wines by the glass, leather sofas and log fire. *Recommended by Marlene and Jim Godfrey*

BIRSTALL SE2126
Black Bull
Kirkgate, off A652; head down hill towards church

WF17 9HE

Medieval stone-built pub opposite part-Saxon church, dark panelling and low beams in a long row of five small linked rooms, traditional décor complete with stag's head, low-priced home-made food including bargain OAP menu, John Smiths, upstairs former courtroom (now a function room, but they may give you a guided tour); children welcome. *Recommended by Michael Butler, John and Eleanor Holdsworth*

BLUBBERHOUSES SE1755
Hopper Lane
A65 Skipton—Harrogate

LS21 2NZ

Fully refurbished Inns of Yorkshire pub/hotel, enjoyable reasonably priced food; garden, bedrooms. *Recommended by John and Eleanor Holdsworth*

BOLSTERSTONE SK2796
Castle Inn
Off A616

S36 3ZB

Stone-built local in small hilltop conservation-area village, spectacular surroundings by Ewden Valley at edge of Peak District National Park, great views from picnic-sets outside; open-plan but with distinct areas including tap room and restaurant, well kept Black Sheep, Caledonian Deuchars IPA and Marstons Pedigree, enjoyable good value basic food, unofficial HQ of award-winning male voice choir. *Recommended by Michael Butler*

BRADFIELD SK2692
Old Horns
High Bradfield

S6 6LG

Friendly old stone-built pub with comfortable divided L-shaped bar, lots of pictures, good value generous home-made pub food, efficient service, real ales including Thwaites and continental beers on tap; children welcome, picnic-sets and play area outside, hill village with stunning views, interesting church, good walks. *Recommended by Roger and Pauline Pearce*

BRADFORD SE1528   BD12 0HP
Chapel House
Chapel House Buildings, Low Moor

Busy stone-built beamed pub in pretty setting opposite church, plenty of atmosphere in L-shaped bare-boards bar, open fires, well kept Greene King, traditional food, helpful friendly staff, restaurant; open all day. *Recommended by Clive Flynn*

BRADFORD SE1533   BD7 1JE
Fighting Cock
Preston Street (off B6145)

Busy bare-boards alehouse by industrial estate, great choice of well kept changing ales, foreign draught and bottled beers, farm ciders, lively atmosphere, all-day doorstep sandwiches and good simple lunchtime hot dishes (not Sun), may be free bread and dripping on the bar, low prices, coal fires; open all day. *Recommended by the Didler, Barbarrick*

BRADFORD SE1533   BD1 3AA
New Beehive
Westgate

Robustly old-fashioned Edwardian inn with several rooms including good pool room, wide range of changing ales, gas lighting, candles and coal fires, friendly atmosphere and welcoming staff; basement music nights; nice back courtyard, bedrooms, open all day (till 2am Fri, Sat). *Recommended by the Didler*

BRAMHAM SE4242   LS23 6QA
Swan
Just off A1 2 miles N of A64

Civilised and unspoilt three-room country local with engaging long-serving landlady, good mix of customers, well kept Black Sheep, Hambleton and Leeds Pale. *Recommended by Les and Sandra Brown*

BURN SE5928   YO8 8LJ
☆ ## Wheatsheaf
Main Road (A19 Selby—Doncaster)

Welcoming busy mock-Tudor roadside pub, comfortable seats and tables in partly divided open-plan bar with masses to look at – gleaming copper kettles, black dagging shears, polished buffalo horns, cases of model vans and lorries, decorative mugs above one bow-window seat, open log fire with drying rack above, John Smiths, Timothy Taylors and guests, 20 malt whiskies, good value straightforward food (not Sun-Weds evenings), roasts only on Sun; pool table, games machine, TV and may be unobtrusive piped music; children and dogs welcome, picnic-sets on heated terrace in small back garden, open all day till midnight. *Recommended by Rob and Catherine Dunster, Terry and Nickie Williams, Lawrence R Cotter, Barbarrick, Lesley and Peter Barrett, Bob and Tanya Ekers*

BURNSALL SE0361   BD23 6BU
Red Lion
B6160 S of Grassington

Family-run 16th-c inn in lovely spot by the River Wharfe, looking across village green to Burnsall Fell, tables out on front cobbles and on big back terrace; attractively panelled, sturdily furnished front dining rooms with log fire, good imaginative food (all day weekends), well kept ales such as Copper Dragon and Timothy Taylors, nice wines, efficient friendly service, conservatory; children welcome, comfortable bedrooms (dogs allowed in some and in bar), fishing permits available, open all day. *Recommended by Robert Wivell, John and Helen Rushton, Michael Butler*

By law, pubs must show a price list of their drinks. Let us know if you are inconvenienced by any breach of this law.

BURTON LEONARD SE3263   HG3 3SG
☆ **Hare & Hounds**
Off A61 Ripon—Harrogate, handy for A1(M) exit 48

Civilised and welcoming country dining pub, good popular food from sandwiches up
including Sun roasts, well kept ales such as Black Sheep and Timothy Taylors from long
counter, good coffee, large carpeted main area divided by log fire, traditional furnishings,
bright little side room; children in eating areas, pretty back garden. *Recommended by*
James and Melanie Blades, Peter Hacker, Phil and Gill Wass

CALDER GROVE SE3017   WF4 3DL
British Oak
A639 towards Denby Dale from M1 junction 39

Popular for good value quickly served food (all day), well kept ales such as Marstons and
Tetleys, regular quiz and karaoke nights; children welcome, garden with good play area,
heated smokers' shelter, less than a mile from the M1. *Recommended by Dave Braisted*

CARLTON NZ5004   TS9 7DJ
Blackwell Ox
Just off A172 SW of Stokesley

Three linked rooms off big central bar, thai landlady and helpful friendly staff, standard
pub and good thai food including weekday lunchtime deals, lots of dark wood, blazing log
fire; children welcome, garden with play area, bedrooms, picturesque village location,
handy for Coast to Coast and Cleveland Way walkers. *Recommended by WW, Graham Denison*

CARLTON HUSTHWAITE SE4976   YO7 2BW
Carlton Bore
Butt Lane

Cosy modernised beamed dining pub, good food from traditional favourites to interesting
restaurant dishes including seasonal game, everything home-made from bread to ice-
cream, good value set lunch (Mon-Sat), well kept ales including local Hambleton, nice
wines, capable cheerful service, country tables and chairs with colourful cushions, lots of
odds and ends including four stuffed boars' heads; garden picnic-sets. *Recommended by*
Peter Thompson, Michael Doswell, Ed and Anna Fraser

CARTHORPE SE3083   DL8 2LG
☆ **Fox & Hounds**
Village signed from A1 N of Ripon, via B6285

Welcoming neatly kept dining pub with emphasis on good well presented food, attractive
high-raftered restaurant with lots of farm and smithy tools, Black Sheep and Worthington
in L-shaped bar with two log fires, plush seating, plates on stripped beams and evocative
Victorian photographs of Whitby, some theatrical memorabilia in corridors; piped
classical music; children welcome, handy for the A1, closed Mon and first week in Jan.
Recommended by P A Rowe, Jon Clarke, Peter and Eleanor Kenyon, Walter and Susan Rinaldi-Butcher,
Janet and Peter Race

CHAPEL HADDLESEY SE5826   YO8 8QQ
Jug
Quite handy for M62 junction 34; off A19 towards Selby

Small three-room village local with enjoyable reasonably priced home-made food from
traditional things up, children's meals and weekday early-bird deal (5-7pm), four
changing ales, carpets and comfortable banquettes, restaurant; TV; garden with play
equipment, open all day weekends. *Recommended by Matthew Teft*

CHAPEL LE DALE SD7477   LA6 3AR
☆ **Hill Inn**
B5655 Ingleton—Hawes, 3 miles N of Ingleton

Former farmhouse with fantastic views to Ingleborough and Whernside, a haven for weary walkers (wonderful remote surrounding walks); relaxed, chatty atmosphere, beams, log fires, straightforward furniture on stripped wooden floors, nice pictures, bare-stone recesses, Black Sheep, Dent and Theakstons, enjoyable bar food, separate dining room and well worn-in sun lounge; children welcome, dogs in bar, bedrooms, open all day Sat, closed Mon except bank holidays. *Recommended by Brian and Anna Marsden*

CLIFTON SE1622   HD6 4HJ
☆ **Black Horse**
Westgate/Coalpit Lane; signed off Brighouse Road from M62 junction 25

Friendly 17th-c inn/restaurant, pleasant décor, front dining rooms with good generous food from lunchtime snacks up, can be pricey but good value set meals, efficient uniformed service, back bar area with beam-and-plank ceiling and open fire, well kept Timothy Taylors Landlord and a house beer brewed by Brass Monkey, decent wines; nice courtyard area, 21 comfortable bedrooms, pleasant village, open all day. *Recommended by Michael Butler, John and Eleanor Holdsworth, Tim and Sue Halstead*

COLEY SE1226   HX3 7SD
Brown Horse
Lane Ends, Denholme Gate Road (A644 Brighouse—Keighley, a mile N of Hipperholme)

Attractive and comfortable with open fires in three bustling rooms, popular good value traditional food (restaurant booking advised evenings/weekends), Greene King, Timothy Taylors and Tetleys, decent house wines, good service, lots of bric-a-brac on ceilings and walls, small back conservatory overlooking garden; open all day. *Recommended by John and Eleanor Holdsworth, Clive Flynn*

COLTON SE5444   LS24 8EP
☆ **Old Sun**
Off A64 York—Tadcaster

Some accomplished and inventive cooking at this 18th-c beamed dining pub, also traditional pub dishes and set deals (food till 7pm Sun, not Mon lunchtime), good wine list with ten by the glass, well kept Black Sheep and Cropton ales, competent service, several linked low-ceilinged rooms (tables a little close in some), log fires, cookery demonstrations, deli; children welcome, front terrace and decking, new bedrooms in separate building. *Recommended by David and Sue Smith, Tim and Sue Halstead, Ian Prince*

CONEYTHORPE SE3958   HG5 0RY
☆ **Tiger**
E of Knaresborough

Pretty dining pub on the green of a charming village, friendly efficient staff, enjoyable wholesome home-made food sensibly priced including Sun carvery, well kept local ales, straightforward open-plan décor in linked areas around bar and adjoining dining room. *Recommended by WW, Pat and Graham Williamson, Les and Sandra Brown, Peter Hardisty, Ed and Anna Fraser*

CRAY SD9479   BD23 5JB
☆ **White Lion**
B6160 N of Kettlewell

Highest Wharfedale pub in lovely countryside and popular with walkers; welcoming licensees, simple bar with open fire and flagstones, enjoyable well priced food including filled yorkshire puddings and good local trout, Copper Dragon, John Smiths and Timothy Taylors Landlord, back room, original bull 'ook game; children and dogs welcome, picnic-sets above quiet steep lane or you can sit on flat limestone slabs in the shallow stream opposite, bedrooms. *Recommended by Walter and Susan Rinaldi-Butcher, the Didler, Michael Lamm, David M Potts, Lawrence Pearse, Dr Kevan Tucker and others*

DACRE BANKS SE1961   HG3 4EN
☆ **Royal Oak**
B6451 S of Pateley Bridge

Popular solidly comfortable 18th-c pub with Nidderdale views, traditional food done very
well, attentive friendly staff, well kept Boddingtons, Rudgate and Theakstons, good wine
choice, beams and panelling, log-fire dining room, games room with darts, dominoes and
pool; TV, piped music; children in eating areas, terrace tables, informal back garden,
three character bedrooms, good breakfast. *Recommended by Robert Wivell, Angus and
Carol Johnson*

DEWSBURY SE2622   WF12 7SW
Huntsman
Walker Cottages, Chidswell Lane, Shaw Cross – pub signed

Cosy low-beamed converted cottages alongside urban-fringe farm, lots of agricultural
bric-a-brac, blazing log fire, small front extension, long-serving landlord and friendly
locals, well kept Chidswell (brewed for them), Timothy Taylors Landlord and guests,
decent home-made food (not lunchtimes Sun, Mon or evenings except Thurs, Fri).
Recommended by Michael Butler, the Didler

DEWSBURY SE2420   WF12 9BD
Leggers
Robinsons Boat Yard, Savile Town Wharf, Mill Street E (SE of B6409)

Good value basic hayloft conversion by Calder & Hebble Navigation marina, low-beamed
upstairs bar, well kept Everards Tiger and five guests, bottled belgian beers, farm cider
and perry, straightforward food, real fire, friendly staff, daily papers, brewery and pub
memorabilia, pool; picnic-sets outside, boat trips, open all day. *Recommended by Eric Ruff,
the Didler*

DEWSBURY SE2321   WF13 2RP
Shepherds Boy
Huddersfield Road, Ravensthorpe

Four-room pub with interesting ales and good range of foreign lagers, bottled beers and
wines, bargain generous basic lunchtime food; open all day. *Recommended by the Didler*

DEWSBURY SE2421   WF13 1HF
☆ **West Riding Licensed Refreshment Rooms**
Station, Wellington Road

Convivial three-room early Victorian station bar, eight well kept changing ales such as
Acorn, Anglo Dutch, Fernandes and Timothy Taylors, foreign bottled beers and farm
ciders, bargain generous lunchtime food on scrubbed tables, popular pie night Tues, curry
night Weds and steak night Thurs, good weekend breakfast too, friendly staff, daily
papers, coal fire, lots of steam memorabilia including paintings by local artists,
impressive juke box, jazz nights; children in two end rooms, disabled access, open all day.
Recommended by Andy Lickfold, Andy and Jill Kassube, the Didler, Joe Green

DONCASTER SE5702   DN1 3AH
Corner Pin
St Sepulchre Gate West, Cleveland Street

Plushly refurbished beamed lounge with old local pub prints, welsh dresser and china,
John Smiths and interesting guests kept well (beer festivals), good value traditional food
from fine hot sandwiches to Sun roasts, friendly landlady, cheery bar with darts, games
machine and TV; open all day. *Recommended by the Didler*

DONCASTER SK6299   DN4 7PB
Hare & Tortoise
Parrots Corner, Bawtry Road, Bessacarr (A638)

Popular Vintage Inn all-day dining pub, their standard well priced food, Adnams

Broadside, Black Sheep and Everards Tiger, friendly attentive young staff, several small rooms off central bar, log fire; piped music. *Recommended by Stephen Woad, Kay and Alistair Butler and others*

DONCASTER SE5703
DN1 1SF
Plough
West Laith Gate, by Frenchgate shopping centre

Small old-fashioned local with friendly long-serving licensees and chatty regulars, Acorn Barnsley Bitter, Bass and guests, bustling front room with darts, dominoes and sports TV, old town maps, quieter back lounge; tiny central courtyard, open all day (Sun afternoon break). *Recommended by Tim Mountain, the Didler*

DONCASTER SE5703
DN1 1SF
Tut 'n' Shive
West Laith Gate

Well kept ales such as Black Sheep, Batemans, Brewsters and Greene King, farm cider, bargain food all day, small raised carpeted area, eccentric décor (even old doors pressed into service as wall/ceiling coverings), flagstones lots of pump clips, dim lighting; good juke box, pinball, games machines, big-screen sports TV, music nights; open all day. *Recommended by the Didler*

DORE SK3081
S17 3AB
Dore Moor Inn
A625 Sheffield—Castleton

Extended well cared for Vintage Inn (built 1816) on edge of the Peak District, extensive choice of reasonably priced tasty food, good range of wines by the glass, ales such as Black Sheep, Marstons Pedigree and Timothy Taylors Landlord, pleasant young staff, comfortably appointed with superb central log fires; tables outside, views over Sheffield. *Recommended by Jo Rees, Margaret and Jeff Graham*

EASINGWOLD SE5270
YO61 3AD
☆ George
Market Place

Neat, bright and airy, market town hotel (former 18th-c coaching inn), quiet corners even when busy, helpful cheerful service, well kept Black Sheep, Moorhouses and a guest, enjoyable food in bar and restaurant, beams, horsebrasses and warm log fires, slightly old-fashioned feel and popular with older customers; pleasant bedrooms, good breakfast. *Recommended by Pete Coxon, Ian and Helen Stafford, Tony and Wendy Hobden, Michael Butler, Janet and Peter Race, Ed and Anna Fraser*

EAST WITTON SE1487
DL8 4SQ
☆ Cover Bridge Inn
A6108 out towards Middleham

Cosy 16th-c flagstoned country local with friendly accommodating landlord and staff, good choice of well kept Yorkshire ales, enjoyable generous pub food, sensible prices, small restaurant, roaring fires; children and dogs welcome, riverside garden, three bedrooms, open all day. *Recommended by Mr and Mrs Maurice Thompson, the Didler, Simon Le Fort, Jon Forster, Ed and Anna Fraser*

EGTON NZ8006
YO21 1TZ
Wheatsheaf
Village centre

Village pub of real character, interesting paintings and prints in simple main bar, good choice of enjoyable well presented food, charming service, Black Sheep, Timothy Taylors Landlord and a guest, several wines by the glass, restaurant; bedrooms, open all day weekends, closed Mon. *Recommended by Peter Dearing*

EGTON BRIDGE NZ8005   YO21 1XE

☆ **Horseshoe**

Village signed off A171 W of Whitby

Attractively placed 18th-c inn with open fire, high-backed built-in winged settles, wall seats and spindleback chairs, a big stuffed trout (caught nearby in 1913), Black Sheep, John Smiths and three guests, good home-made bar food, friendly service; piped music; children welcome, dogs in bar, seats on quiet terrace in attractive mature garden, redecorated bedrooms, open all day weekends. *Recommended by Pat and Stewart Gordon, Chris and Jeanne Downing, Peter Burton, Matt and Vikki Wharton*

EGTON BRIDGE NZ8005   YO21 1UX

☆ **Postgate**

Village signed off A171 W of Whitby

Moorland village pub doing good imaginative fairly priced food, friendly staff, well kept Black Sheep and a guest, traditional quarry-tiled panelled bar with beams, panelled dado and coal fire in an antique range, elegant restaurant; children and dogs welcome, garden picnic-sets, three nice bedrooms. *Recommended by Dr and Mrs R G J Telfer*

ELLERBY NZ7914   TS13 5LP

Ellerby Hotel

Just off A174 Whitby Road; Ryeland Lane

Small friendly well looked after hotel with good pub atmosphere, enjoyable nicely presented traditional food from lunchtime sandwiches up, well kept ales including Theakstons, log fire, restaurant; comfortable reasonably priced bedrooms, good breakfast. *Recommended by C A Hall*

FADMOOR SE6789   YO62 7HY

☆ **Plough**

Village signed off A170 in or just W of Kirkbymoorside

This village-green dining pub was closed and for sale as we went to press. *Recommended by John Hume, Marlene and Jim Godfrey, Stanley and Annie Matthews, Stephen Woad, Pat and Stewart Gordon*

FELIXKIRK SE4684   YO7 2DP

☆ **Carpenters Arms**

Village signed off A170 E of Thirsk

Dining pub now under same ownership as the good Durham Ox at Crayke; refurbished opened-up interior with beams and stone-floors, deep-red walls, log fires and woodburner, good food including early evening deal (not Sat) in bar and restaurant, extensive wine list with good choice by the glass, Black Sheep and Timothy Taylors Landlord, bright attentive service, some live acoustic music Weds; terrace and garden, open all day weekends. *Recommended by Robert Wivell, Ed and Anna Fraser*

FERRENSBY SE3660   HG5 0PZ

☆ **General Tarleton**

A655 N of Knaresborough

Smart civilised atmosphere and more restaurant-with-rooms than pub, excellent modern cooking including good value early evening set deal, good attentive service (framed pictures of staff on walls), Black Sheep and Timothy Taylors, nice wines by the glass from good list, beamed bar area divided up by brick pillars, dark brown leather dining chairs around wooden tables, more formal restaurant with exposed stonework; children welcome, covered courtyard and pleasant tree-lined garden, white-painted or plain wood furniture under blue parasols, comfortable contemporary bedrooms, good breakfast. *Recommended by Jon Clarke, G Jennings, David Thornton, Janet and Peter Race, Richard and Mary Bailey, Pat and Graham Williamson and others*

FINGHALL SE1889   DL8 5ND
☆ **Queens Head**
Off A684 E of Leyburn

Welcoming comfortable dining pub, log fires either end of tidy low-beamed bar, settles
making stalls around big tables, Black Sheep, Greene King, John Smiths and Theakstons,
wide choice of good food from traditional things up, extended back Wensleydale-view
dining room; children and dogs welcome, disabled facilities, back garden with decking
sharing same view, three bedrooms. *Recommended by Karen Sharman, Ed and Anna Fraser*

FIXBY SE1119   HD2 2EA
Nags Head
New Hey Road, by M62 junction 24 south side, past Hilton

Fairly large chain dining pub, attractive outside and comfortable in, four well kept ales,
decent well priced food including carvery, good friendly service, linked areas with wood
and slate floors; garden tables, bedrooms in adjoining Premier Inn. *Recommended by
John and Eleanor Holdsworth, Gordon and Margaret Ormondroyd*

FLAXTON SE6762   YO60 7RJ
Blacksmiths Arms
Off A64

Small welcoming traditional pub on attractive village green, enjoyable home-made food,
well kept Black Sheep, Timothy Taylors, Theakstons and York, good friendly service,
carpeted L-shaped bar and restaurant, open fire; seats out at front and behind, three
bedrooms, closed Sun evening, Mon, lunchtimes Tues-Sat. *Recommended by David and
Ruth Hollands, Roger and Anne Newbury*

FLOCKTON SE2314   WF4 4DW
Sun
Off A642 Wakefield—Huddersfield at Blacksmiths Arms

Nicely refurbished old beamed pub with open fires in bar and dining area, enjoyable
reasonably priced food from shortish menu, real ales, prompt efficient service; children
welcome, garden tables with lovely views, open all day. *Recommended by Michael Butler,
John and Eleanor Holdsworth*

GIGGLESWICK SD8164   BD24 0BE
☆ **Black Horse**
Church Street

Very hospitable father and son landlords in prettily set 17th-c village pub, spotless cosy
bar with horsey bric-a-brac and gleaming brasses, coal-effect fire, reasonably priced
hearty food, well kept Timothy Taylors, Tetleys and guests, intimate dining room, good
service, piano (often played); no dogs; children till 9pm, heated back terrace, smokers'
shelter, three good value comfortable bedrooms, good breakfast, open all day weekends.
Recommended by the Didler, Dudley and Moira Cockroft, Tony and Maggie Harwood, Trevor Spalding

GIGGLESWICK SD8164   BD24 0EB
Craven Arms
Just off A65, opposite station

Modern refurbishment and interesting well presented food including meat from
licensee's organic farm (good vegetarian options too), moderate prices, well kept ales
such as Black Sheep, Copper Dragon and Tetleys, attentive friendly service, restaurant;
suntrap garden, seven bedrooms, closed Mon. *Recommended by Peter and Liz Smalley, John and
Susan Miln, Tony and Maggie Harwood*

GIGGLESWICK SD8164   BD24 0BA
Harts Head
Belle Hill

Cheerful bustling village inn, well kept ales such as Black Sheep, public bar (dogs welcome) with dominoes, good choice of enjoyable reasonably priced food in restaurant, folk music night first Fri of month; Sky TV; outside smokers' area, bedrooms. *Recommended by Tony and Maggie Harwood*

GILLAMOOR SE6890   YO62 7HX

☆ **Royal Oak**
Off A170 in Kirkbymoorside

Stone-built 18th-c dining pub with interesting food at fair prices, friendly staff, ales such as Black Sheep and Copper Dragon, reasonably priced wines, roomy bar with heavy dark beams, log fires in two tall stone fireplaces (one with old kitchen range), overspill dining room (dogs allowed here); children welcome, eight comfortable modern bedrooms, good breakfast, attractive village handy for Barnsdale Moor walks. *Recommended by Stanley and Annie Matthews, WAH, C A Hall, Ed and Anna Fraser*

GILLING EAST SE6176   YO62 4JH

☆ **Fairfax Arms**
Main Street (B1363)

Attractive refurbished stone-built country inn under same management as the good White Swan at Ampleforth, enjoyable traditional food with some upmarket twists, well kept Black Sheep and Tetleys, good wine choice, friendly staff, beams and log fires, restaurant; piped music; children welcome, dogs outside only, disabled access, streamside front lawn, pleasant village with castle and miniature steam railway, 11 bedrooms, good breakfast, open all day weekends. *Recommended by WW, Michael Butler*

GOLCAR SE0815   HD7 4JR
Golcar Lily
Slades Road, Bolster Moor

Unusual building (former Co-op and manager's house) with fine Colne Valley views, small carpeted bar area with comfortable pink wall seats and stools, swagged curtains, good value food here and in big restaurant leading off (special diets catered for), Tetleys and two guests from brick-faced bar, decent wines; Sun quiz night; open all day weekends. *Recommended by John and Eleanor Holdsworth*

GRANTLEY SE2369   HG4 3PJ

☆ **Grantley Arms**
Off B6265 W of Ripon

Attractive, popular and well run 17th-c stone-built dining pub in quiet Dales village, beams and big open fire, good freshly made food from traditional things to enterprising well presented restaurant dishes, set menus available too, attentive friendly service, good wines and well kept beers, linen-clothed tables in carpeted restaurant, quiz supper (last Sun of month); soft piped music; terrace with lovely country views. *Recommended by Janet and Peter Race, John and Eleanor Holdsworth, Grahame Brooks, Ed and Anna Fraser*

GRASSINGTON SE0064   BD23 5AD

☆ **Devonshire**
The Square

Small handsome reliably run hotel, good window seats and tables outside overlooking sloping village square, decent food from sandwiches up, three real ales, interesting pictures and ornaments, beams and open fires, pleasant family room, big restaurant; comfortable bedrooms, open all day Sun. *Recommended by Janet and Peter Race, Dr Kevan Tucker, B and M Kendall*

GRASSINGTON SE0064   BD23 5AA
Foresters Arms
Main Street

Comfortable opened-up old coaching inn with friendly bustling atmosphere, good generous well priced food, good choice of ales including Black Sheep and Timothy Taylors, cheerful efficient service, log fires, dining room off on right, pool and sports TV on left, popular Mon quiz; children welcome, outside tables, 14 affordable bedrooms, good walking country, open all day. *Recommended by Linda Carter, Dudley and Moira Cockroft, the Didler, Michael Lamm, Dr Kevan Tucker, B and M Kendall*

GREAT HABTON SE7576 — YO17 6TU

☆ **Grapes**

Corner of Habton Lane and Kirby Misperton Lane

Homely and cosy traditionally refurbished beamed dining pub in small village, good cooking including fresh local fish and game, home-baked bread, Marstons-related ales, open fire, friendly hard-working young couple; piped music, small public bar with darts and TV; a few roadside picnic-sets (water for dogs – nice walks), open all day Sun, closed Tues lunchtime and Mon. *Recommended by Chris Paxton*

GREAT OUSEBURN SE4461 — YO26 9RF

Crown

Off B6265 SE of Boroughbridge

Nicely refurbished and welcoming, enjoyable food from pubby to more restauranty dishes, good choice of well kept ales, back dining extension; garden with terrace tables, open all day weekends, closed Mon lunchtime, Tues. *Recommended by Alison and Pete, David Brown, Ed and Anna Fraser*

GREWELTHORPE SE2376 — HG4 3BS

Crown

Back road NW of Ripon

Comfortable two-room Dales bar, decent good value food, Marstons-related ales, log fires, separate back dining room; picnic-sets out in front, pleasant small village, good walks nearby including Hackfall Wood. *Recommended by Janet and Peter Race*

GUISELEY SE1941 — LS20 8AH

Coopers

Otley Road

Light and modern Market Town Taverns café-bar with good food from lunchtime sandwiches through pastas and pies to evening paella and steaks, eight real ales including Black Sheep and Timothy Taylors Landlord, jazz and blues nights in upstairs function/dining room, open all day. *Recommended by the Didler*

HALIFAX SE1026 — HX3 7AY

Stump Cross Inn

Kell Lane, Stump Cross

Smart dining pub, airy and modern, with enjoyable reasonably priced food, pleasant helpful staff, well kept Copper Dragon Golden Pippin, good coffee; attractive terrace. *Recommended by Pat and Tony Martin*

HALIFAX SE0924 — HX1 2LX

Three Pigeons

Sun Fold, South Parade; off Church Street

Carefully restored, four-room 1930s pub (Grade II listed), art deco fittings, ceiling painting in octagonal main area, original flooring, panelling and tiled fireplaces with log fires, up to six well kept Ossett ales and local guests, friendly chatty staff; tables outside, handy for Eureka! Museum and Shay Stadium, open all day Fri-Sun, from 3pm other days. *Recommended by Pat and Tony Martin*

HARDROW SD8691 — DL8 3LZ

☆ **Green Dragon**

Village signed off A684

Friendly traditional Dales pub dating from the 13th c and full of character; stripped stone, antique settles on flagstones, lots of bric-a-brac, low-beamed snug with log fire in old iron range, another in big main bar, four well kept ales including one brewed for them by Yorkshire Dales, enjoyable generous food, small neat restaurant, annual brass band competition; children and dogs welcome, bedrooms, next to Hardraw Force – England's highest single-drop waterfall. *Recommended by Mr and Mrs Maurice Thompson, Peter Salmon, Steve Short, Claes Mauroy*

HAROME SE6482 YO62 5JE
☆ **Star**
High Street; village signed S of A170, E of Helmsley

Restaurant-with-rooms (need to book for both well in advance) in pretty 14th-c thatched building, but bar does have informal feel, bowed beam-and-plank ceiling, plenty of bric-a-brac, interesting furniture including 'Mousey' Thompson pieces, log fire, well polished tiled kitchen range, daily papers, Black Sheep and Wold Top, 18 wines by the glass, home-made fruit liqueurs, snacks served in cocktail bar, popular coffee loft in the eaves, inventive ambitious modern cooking (not cheap); piped music; children welcome, seats on sheltered front terrace, more in garden, stylish bedrooms and suites, Pheasant Hotel nearby under same ownership as is Corner Shop opposite and Pern's delicatessen in Helmsley, open all day Sun, closed Mon lunchtime. *Recommended by Noel Thomas, Christine Vallely, David Thornton, Pat and Stewart Gordon, Walter and Susan Rinaldi-Butcher and others*

HARROGATE SE3155 HG1 1BJ
Coach & Horses
West Park

Very friendly bustling pub with speciality pies and other enjoyable reasonably priced food, several good Yorkshire ales, obliging service, nice interior with booth seating; open all day. *Recommended by D W Stokes, Eric Larkham, the Didler, Pete Coxon, Adrian Johnson, Tim and Sue Halstead and others*

HARROGATE SE3157 HG1 4DH
Gardeners Arms
Bilton Lane (off A59 either in Bilton itself or on outskirts towards Harrogate – via Bilton Hall Drive)

Stone-built 17th-c house converted into friendly down-to-earth local, tiny bar and three small rooms, flagstone floors, panelling, old prints, big fire in stone fireplace, very cheap Sam Smiths OBB, decent bar lunches (not Tues), dominoes; children welcome, surrounding streamside garden with play area, lovely peaceful setting near Nidd Gorge. *Recommended by the Didler, Alan and Shirley Sawden*

HARROGATE SE2955 HG1 2RS
☆ **Hales**
Crescent Road

Classic Victorian décor in gas-lit 18th-c welcoming local close to Pump Rooms, leather seats in alcoves, stuffed birds, comfortable saloon and tiny snug, seven real ales including Daleside, simple good value lunchtime food including Sun roast; can get lively on weekend evenings. *Recommended by Eric Larkham, Greta and Christopher Wells, Michael Butler, David and Ruth Shillitoe*

HARROGATE SE2955 HG1 2SZ
☆ **Old Bell**
Royal Parade

Thriving Market Town Taverns pub with eight mainly Yorkshire beers from a handsome counter, lots of bottled continental beers, impressive choice of wines by the glass, friendly helpful staff, lunchtime snacks including sandwiches (interesting choice of breads), more elaborate evening meals upstairs, newspapers, panelling, old sweet shop ads and breweriana, no music or machines; no children; open all day. *Recommended by Eric Larkham, the Didler, Tod and Dawn Hannula, Roger and Donna Huggins*

HARTHILL SK4980   S26 7YH
Beehive
Union Street

Two-bar village pub opposite attractive church, chef/landlord doing a wide range of
enjoyable generous food including proper pies and Sun lunch, friendly service, three or
four well kept ales including Timothy Taylors Landlord, good choice of wines, malts and
soft drinks, fresh flowers, games room with pool; piped music can be loud; children
welcome till 9pm if eating, picnic-sets in attractive garden, walks nearby, closed Mon.
Recommended by JJW, CMW, Rebecca Walker, Derek and Sylvia Stephenson and others

HEADINGLEY SE2736   LS6 2UE
Arcadia
Arndale Centre

Bustling small bank conversion, good choice of changing Yorkshire ales kept well, lots of
continental bottled beers, knowledgeable staff, bar food; a Market Town Tavern, open all
day. *Recommended by Peter Smith and Judith Brown, Daniel Lezcano*

HEBDEN BRIDGE SD9827   HX7 6LU
Stubbings Wharf
1 mile W

Warm and friendly pub in good spot by Rochdale Canal with adjacent moorings, enjoyable
food (all day weekends) from sandwiches to good value Sun lunch, wide range of ales
including local microbrews, usually three real ciders; open all day; dogs welcome.
Recommended by Dave Sumpter, Jon Moody, Andy and Jill Kassube

HEBDEN BRIDGE SD9927   HX7 8EX
☆ White Lion
Bridge Gate

Solid stone-built inn with welcoming comfortable bar and country-style-furnished bare-
boards back area with coal fire, reasonably priced generous home-cooked food all day
(just lunchtime Sun), fish specialities, well kept Timothy Taylors Landlord and a guest
beer, good friendly service; disabled facilities, attractive secluded riverside garden, ten
comfortable bedrooms. *Recommended by Martin Smith, Ian and Nita Cooper*

HELMSLEY SE6183   YO62 5BH
Feathers
Market Place

Substantial stone inn with sensibly priced generous all-day bar food from sandwiches up,
popular Sun lunch, well kept Black Sheep and Tetleys, good friendly service, several
rooms with comfortable seats, oak and walnut tables, flagstones or tartan carpet, nice
prints, huge inglenook log fire, heavy medieval beams, panelled corridors; children in
eating area, tables in attractive back garden, clean comfortable bedrooms, open all day.
Recommended by Philip and Jan Medcalf, Ben and Ruth Levy

HEPWORTH SE1606   HD9 1TE
Butchers Arms
Off A616 SE of Holmfirth; Towngate

Refurbished dark-beamed country dining pub with very good enterprising food (not cheap
and emphasis on local ingredients) from Le Manoir-trained chef/owner, efficient pleasant
service, Black Sheep and Timothy Taylors, traditional flagstone/bare-boards interior
enhanced with contemporary décor, large log fire; outside decked seating area, open all
day. *Recommended by David and Cathrine Whiting, John Holt, Oliver Richardson*

HETTON SD9658   BD23 6LT
☆ Angel
Off B6265 Skipton—Grassington

Busy dining pub with three neatly kept timbered and panelled rooms mainly set for the good imaginative food (all day Sun), friendly helpful staff, main bar with farmhouse range in stone fireplace, well kept Black Sheep, Dark Horse and a guest, 20 wines by the glass, lots of nooks and alcoves, country-kitchen and smart dining chairs, plush seats, all sorts of tables, Ronald Searle wine-snob cartoons, older engravings and photographs, log fires; children welcome, smart furniture on two covered terraces, nice bedrooms, closed Jan. *Recommended by Margaret and Jeff Graham, Ian Malone, James Stretton, Karen Eliot, Bruce and Sharon Eden, WAH and others*

HIGH BENTHAM SD6769   LA2 7HE
Coach House
Main Street

Centrally placed 17th-c coaching inn, low beams, alcoves, nooks and crannies, enjoyable good value food including OAP lunch deal, Robinsons ales; bedrooms. *Recommended by Karen Eliot*

HOLMFIRTH SD1408   HD9 2DN
Nook
Victoria Square/South Lane

Tucked-away basic 18th-c stone pub brewing its own good ales alongside Timothy Taylors and other guests, home-made pubby food all day and adjoining tapas bar, low beams, flagstones and big open fire, some live music; heated streamside terrace, open all day. *Recommended by the Didler*

HOLYWELL GREEN SE0919   HX4 9BS
Rock
Broad Carr Lane; handy for M62 junction 24

Smart comfortable hotel/restaurant rather than pub, very popular for its good food (all day Sun) including well priced set menu, friendly efficient service, small bar area serving Timothy Taylors Landlord, Churchill-themed restaurant; children welcome, 27 bedrooms, good breakfast. *Recommended by Gordon and Margaret Ormondroyd and others*

HORBURY SE2918   WF4 6LP
Boons
Queen Street

Lively, chatty and comfortably unpretentious flagstoned local, Clarks, John Smiths, Timothy Taylors Landlord and up to four quickly changing guests, no food, Rugby League memorabilia, warm fire, back tap room with pool; TV, no children; courtyard tables, open all day Fri-Sun. *Recommended by Michael Butler, the Didler*

HORBURY SE2917   WF4 5AR
Bulls Head
Southfield Lane

Large well divided pub deservedly popular for food, smart attentive staff, Black Sheep and Tetleys, lots of wines by the glass, panelling and wood floors, relaxing linked rooms including library, snug and more formal restaurant; front picnic-sets. *Recommended by Michael Butler*

HORSEHOUSE SE0481   DL8 4TS
Thwaite Arms
Coverdale Road, Middleham—Kettlewell

Early 19th-c former farm building in wonderful village setting near beautiful little church, lots of paths to nearby villages and moors, great drive along Coverdale; bargain simple home-cooked food including fine Sun roast (only a few tables in pretty homely dining room, so worth booking), well kept Theakstons Best, farm cider, genial landlord, good coal fire in cosy snug, bigger plainer locals' bar; children welcome, fell views from charming garden, two bedrooms. *Recommended by Susan and Neil McLean*

☆ **HOVINGHAM** SE6675   YO62 4LA
Worsley Arms
High Street

Smart inn in pretty village handy for Castle Howard, good food in friendly and welcoming
back bar and separate restaurant (different menu), Hambleton ales, several malts, good
wines and coffee, friendly attentive staff, lots of Yorkshire cricketer photographs
especially from 1930/40s; attractive gardens with tables by stream, 19 pleasant bedrooms,
some in cottages across the green. *Recommended by Michael Butler, George Atkinson*

☆ **HUBBERHOLME** SD9278   BD23 5JE
George
Dubbs Lane

Small beautifully placed ancient Dales inn with River Wharfe fishing rights, heavy beams,
flagstones and stripped stone, quick simple enjoyable food, three well kept ales including
Black Sheep and Copper Dragon, good log fire, perpetual candle on bar; no dogs, outside
lavatories; children allowed in dining area, terrace, seven comfortable bedrooms, closed
Mon. *Recommended by David and Sue Atkinson, Dr Kevan Tucker, Peter Dearing*

HUDDERSFIELD SE1416   HD1 4BP
Grove
Spring Grove Street

Lots of exotic bottled beers, well kept Timothy Taylors, Thornbridge and 16 interesting
changing guest ales at sensible prices, 120 malt whiskies and 60 vodkas, no food but
choice of snacks from dried crickets to biltong, traditional irish music Thurs evening, art
gallery; children and dogs welcome, back terrace, open all day. *Recommended by the Didler,
Andy and Jill Kassube*

☆ **HUDDERSFIELD** SE1416   HD1 1JF
Head of Steam
St Georges Square

Railway memorabilia, model trains, cars, buses and planes for sale, friendly staff, long bar
with up to eight changing ales, lots of bottled beers, farm ciders and perry, fruit wines,
black leather easy chairs and sofas, hot coal fire, good value enjoyable back buffet, some
live jazz and blues nights; unobtrusive piped music, can be very busy; open all day.
*Recommended by Andy Lickfold, Chris Flynn, Wendy Jones, the Didler, David Hoult, Peter Smith and
Judith Brown, Ian and Helen Stafford and others*

HUDDERSFIELD SE1520   HD2 1PX
High Park
Bradley Road, Bradley

Neatly kept modern dining pub, attractively done and keeping plenty of room for drinking
and chatting, Greene King ales, wide choice of good value pub food including OAP and
other deals, quick friendly service; children welcome, disabled facilities, outside seating,
open all day. *Recommended by Gordon and Margaret Ormondroyd*

HUDDERSFIELD SE1416   HD1 1JF
Kings Head
Station, St Georges Square

Handsome Victorian station building housing friendly well run pub, large open-plan room
with original tiled floor, two smaller rooms off, Dark Star, Pictish, Timothy Taylors
Landlord and six guests, good sandwiches and cobs, live afternoon/evening music (Sun,
Thurs), Jimi Hendrix pub sign; disabled access via Platform 1, open all day. *Recommended
by Andy Lickfold, Chris Flynn, Wendy Jones, the Didler*

We say if we know a pub has piped music.

HUDDERSFIELD SE1119   HD2 2EA
Nags Head
New Hey Road, Ainley Top; handy for M62 junction 24, by A643

Comfortably refurbished and quite busy, good choice of enjoyable food at fair prices including OAP deals, well kept Courage Directors and three other beers, friendly chatty staff; open all day. *Recommended by Gordon and Margaret Ormondroyd*

HUDDERSFIELD SE1416   HD1 3EB
Rat & Ratchet
Chapel Hill

Flagstoned local with Fullers, Fernandes, Ossett and lots of guest beers, farm ciders, cheap lunchtime food (not Sun-Tues), friendly staff, more comfortable seating up steps, brewery memorabilia and music posters; open all day. *Recommended by the Didler*

HUDDERSFIELD SE1417   HD1 5AY
Sportsman
St Johns Road

Same owners as the West Riding Licensed Refreshment Rooms at Dewsbury, Timothy Taylors and six changing guests, regular beer festivals, good value lunchtime bar snacks, comfortable lounge and two cosy side rooms; handy for the station, open all day.
Recommended by Andy and Jill Kassube, the Didler

HUDDERSFIELD SE1415   HD1 3PJ
Star
Albert Street, Lockwood

Unpretentious friendly local with up to 12 competitively priced changing ales, such as Empire, Mallinsons and Pictish, particularly well kept by enthusiastic landlady, continental beers, farm cider, beer festivals in back marquee (food then), bric-a-brac and customers' paintings, open fire; closed Mon, and lunchtimes Tues-Thurs, open all day weekends. *Recommended by the Didler, Andy and Jill Kassube*

HULL TA0929   HU1 3TG
Hop & Vine
Albion Street

Small pub with three real ales, bottled belgian beers, farm ciders and perries, friendly licensees, good sandwiches and bargain basic specials all day, cellar bar; closed Sun, Mon. *Recommended by the Didler*

 HULL TA1028   HU1 1JG
☆ Olde White Harte
Passage off Silver Street

Ancient pub with Civil War history, carved heavy beams, attractive stained glass, two big inglenooks with frieze of delft tiles, Caledonian Deuchars IPA, Theakstons Old Peculier and guests from copper-topped counter, 80 or so malt whiskies, bargain pubby food; children welcome in upstairs restaurant, dogs in bar, heated courtyard, open all day.
Recommended by the Didler

HULL TA0929   HU2 0PA
Whalebone
Wincolmlee

Friendly local brewing its own ales, also Copper Dragon, Timothy Taylors Landlord and a guest, two real ciders and perry, bar food, old-fashioned décor; open all day. *Recommended by the Didler*

HUTTON-LE-HOLE SE7089   YO62 6UA
Crown
The Green

Spotless pub overlooking pretty village green with wandering sheep in classic coach-trip country, generous unfussy food (all day Sun) from sandwiches up, Black Sheep and Theakstons, cheerful efficient service, opened-up bar with varnished woodwork and whisky-water jugs, dining area; children and dogs welcome, near Folk Museum, handy for Farndale walks. *Recommended by Dr and Mrs R G J Telfer*

ILKLEY SE1048   LS29 0BE
Riverside
Nesfield Road

Friendly family run hotel in a good position by River Wharfe, cosy with nice open fire, well kept Copper Dragon, Ilkley, Tetleys and Timothy Taylors Landlord, good home-cooking all day (till early evening in winter); handy for start of Dales Way, 13 bedrooms, open from 10am. *Recommended by the Didler*

KEIGHLEY SE0941   BD20 5LY
Airedale Heifer
Bradford Road, Sandbeds (B6265 towards Bingley)

Stone-built pub with spreading series of rooms, enjoyable reasonably priced food, well kept ales including Timothy Taylors Landlord, friendly staff, open fire; children welcome, tables out in front and behind, open all day. *Recommended by Trevor and Sylvia Millum*

KEIGHLEY SE0641   BD21 5HX
Boltmakers Arms
East Parade

Small open-plan split-level characterful local, friendly and bustling, with full Timothy Taylors range and a guest kept well, keen prices, limited food, nice brewing pictures, coal fire; sports TV; short walk from Worth Valley Railway, open all day. *Recommended by Bruce Bird, the Didler, Neil Whitehead, Victoria Anderson, Allan Wolf*

KEIGHLEY SE0541   BD21 2LQ
Brown Cow
Cross Leeds Street

Extensively refurbished local, popular and friendly, with good licensee keeping Timothy Taylors ales and guests in top condition; open from 4pm Mon-Sat, all day Sun. *Recommended by Bruce Bird, the Didler*

KEIGHLEY SE0641   BD21 5JE
Cricketers Arms
Coney Lane

Moorhouses and five guests, farm cider, good value bottled beers, downstairs bar open Fri, Sat for live music; sports TV; open all day. *Recommended by the Didler*

KETTLESING SE2257   HG3 2LB
☆ # Queens Head
Village signposted off A59 W of Harrogate

Welcoming stone pub with good value food popular with older diners; L-shaped carpeted main bar with lots of close-set cushioned dining chairs and tables, open fires, little heraldic shields on walls, 19th-c song sheet covers and lithographs of Queen Victoria, delft shelf of blue and white china, smaller bar on left with built-in red banquettes and cricketing prints, life-size portrait of Elizabeth I in lobby, Black Sheep, Roosters and Theakstons ales, good service; piped radio; children welcome, seats in neatly kept suntrap back garden, benches in front by the lane, seven bedrooms, open all day Sun. *Recommended by Peter Hacker, Margaret and Peter Staples, Adrian and Dawn Collinge, Simon Le Fort, B and M Kendall, Michael Butler and others*

KETTLEWELL SD9672
BD23 5QX

Blue Bell
Middle Lane

Roomy knocked-through 17th-c coaching inn, Copper Dragon ales kept well, home-made food all day using local ingredients, low beams and snug simple furnishings, old country photographs, woodburner, restaurant, newspapers; TV, free wi-fi, Sun quiz; children welcome, shaded picnic-sets on cobbles facing a River Wharfe bridge, six annexe bedrooms. *Recommended by D W Stokes, John and Helen Rushton*

KETTLEWELL SD9672
BD23 5QZ

☆ Racehorses
B6160 N of Skipton

Comfortable, civilised and friendly two-bar pub with dining area, generous good value food from substantial lunchtime rolls through pub favourites to local game, popular early evening bargains Sun-Thurs, well kept Timothy Taylors and Tetleys, good log fire; children welcome, dogs in bars, front and back terrace seating, well placed for Wharfedale walks, parking can be difficult, 13 good bedrooms, open all day. *Recommended by Bruce and Sharon Eden, Lois Dyer, John and Helen Rushton, B and M Kendall*

KIRKBY FLEETHAM SE2894
DL7 0SH

☆ Black Horse
Lumley Lane

Nicely refurbished old village pub with some contemporary touches but keeping a pubby atmosphere, good food including reasonably priced Sun lunch, well kept Black Sheep, John Smiths, Theakstons and a guest, good choice of wines by the glass, restaurant, darts; children welcome, tables in garden, quoits, three good bedrooms. *Recommended by Richard Cole, Bill Adie, Jane Taylor and David Dutton, Michael Doswell, John and Eleanor Holdsworth*

KIRKBY MALHAM SD8960
BD23 4BS

Victoria
Village centre

Understated Victorian décor in small simple rooms, good pub food including cheap Sun carvery, well kept ales such as Timothy Taylors and Tetleys, good wine choice, friendly staff, nice log fire, separate restaurant (not always in use); children welcome, lovely village with interesting church, good value bedrooms. *Recommended by John Withnell, Meg and Colin Hamilton*

KIRKBYMOORSIDE SE6986
YO62 6AA

George & Dragon
Market Place

17th-c coaching inn, front bar with beams, panelling, tubs seats around wooden tables on carpet or stripped wood, log fire, Copper Dragon, Greene King and a guest, several malt whiskies, bar food including early-bird menu, afternoon teas, also a snug, bistro and more formal restaurant; piped music; children welcome, seats and heaters on front and back terraces, bedrooms, Weds market day, open all day. *Recommended by Margaret Dickinson, Ed and Anna Fraser*

KNARESBOROUGH SE3556
HG5 8AL

☆ Blind Jacks
Market Place

Simply done multi-floor tavern in 18th-c building (pub since 1990s), old-fashioned traditional character with low beams, bare brick and floorboards, cast-iron-framed tables, pews and stools, brewery mirrors, etc, nine well kept ales including own Village Brewer (made by Hambleton), seven continental draught beers, friendly helpful staff, limited food (cheese and pâté), two small downstairs rooms, quieter upstairs; well behaved children allowed away from bar, dogs welcome, open all day Fri-Sun, closed Mon-Thurs till 4pm; shop next door sells all sorts of rare bottled beers. *Recommended by the Didler, Tim and Ann Newell, B and M Kendall, Adrian Johnson*

LANGTHWAITE NY0002   DL11 6EN

☆ **Charles Bathurst**

Arkengarthdale, a mile N towards Tan Hill

Busy country inn (worth checking no corporate events/weddings on your visit) with a
strong emphasis on dining and bedrooms, but pubby feel in long bar; scrubbed pine
tables and country chairs on stripped floors, snug alcoves, open fire, some bar stools by
counter, Black Sheep, Theakstons and Timothy Taylors, several wines by the glass from
list with helpful notes, popular often interesting food, dining room with views of Scar
House, Robert 'the Mouseman' Thompson furniture, several other dining areas; piped
music, TV, pool, darts and other games; children welcome, lovely walks from door and
views over village and Arkengarthdale, smart bedrooms (best not above dining room),
open all day. *Recommended by Pat and Stewart Gordon, John and Sylvia Harrop, Bruce and
Sharon Eden*

LASTINGHAM SE7290   YO62 6TL

☆ **Blacksmiths Arms**

Off A170 W of Pickering

Popular old-fashioned beamed pub opposite beautiful Saxon church in an attractive
village, log fire in open range, traditional furnishings, Theakstons and other regional ales,
several wines by the glass, good food including impressive seafood platter, friendly
prompt service, darts, board games; piped music – live music second Sun of month;
children and walkers welcome, seats in back garden, nice bedrooms, open all day in
summer. *Recommended by Brian Brooks, Dr and Mrs R G J Telfer, Michael Butler, Ed and Anna Fraser,
W M Hogg*

LEALHOLM NZ7607   YO21 2AJ

Board

Off A171 W of Whitby

In a wonderful moorland village spot by wide pool of River Esk, old-fashioned stripped-
stone bars, big log fire, welcoming licensees and chatty friendly staff, four changing ales,
real ciders, over 60 malts, bar snacks (own pickled eggs) and good seasonal food in
restaurant including home-reared meats; some live music, darts; children, dogs and
muddy boots welcome, secluded riverside garden with decking, five bedrooms, self-
catering cottage, open all day Sat, may be closed weekday lunchtimes in winter.
Recommended by Liz Partridge, Mike and Mary Strigenz, Mo and David Trudgill

LEEDS SE3033   LS10 1JQ

Adelphi

Hunslet Road

Refurbished but keeping handsome mahogany screens, panelling, tiling, cut and etched
glass and impressive stairway, Leeds, Timothy Taylors Landlord and guests, foreign
draught beers, decent all-day food including fixed-price weekday menu, friendly service,
upstairs room, live music, comedy nights and other events. *Recommended by the Didler,
Paul Bromley*

LEEDS SE3033   LS1 5DL

Brewery Tap

New Station Street

Tied to Leeds Brewery, their ales and guests kept well, good value food, neat, friendly,
efficient staff; piped music; open all day. *Recommended by Bruce Bird, the Didler, Peter Smith and
Judith Brown*

LEEDS SE2932   LS11 5WD

Cross Keys

Water Lane

Designer bar with flagstone floors, stripped brick, original tiling, metal and timbers, good
choice of Yorkshire ales and imported bottled beers, friendly knowledgeable staff,
enjoyable good value interesting food, good Sun roasts, upstairs room; children welcome,

tables under big parasols in sheltered courtyard, barbecues, open all day. *Recommended by Stu Mac, the Didler*

LEEDS SE3131   LS10 2QB
Garden Gate
Whitfield Place, Hunslet

Impressive early Edwardian pub (Grade II* listed) now owned by Leeds Brewery, their well kept ales served from a rare curved ceramic counter, a wealth of other period features in rooms off central drinking corridor including intricate glass and woodwork, art nouveau tiling, moulded ceilings and mosaic floors, hearty pub food (not Tues evening); tables out in front, open all day weekends. *Recommended by the Didler*

LEEDS SE2932   LS11 5PL
☆ Grove
Back Row, Holbeck

Unspoilt 1930s-feel local overshadowed by towering office blocks, friendly long-serving landlord, tables and stools in main bar with marble floor, panelling and original fireplace, large back room (some live musicin in here) and snug off drinking corridor, good choice of well kept ales including Caledonian Deuchars IPA, Weston's cider, good live acoustic music; open all day. *Recommended by Barrie Pepper, the Didler*

LEEDS SE2932   LS11 5QN
Midnight Bell
Water Lane

Friendly tap for Leeds Brewery, their full range and guests, enjoyable home-made food, flagstones and light contemporary décor; waterside tables outside. *Recommended by the Didler, Tim and Sue Halstead*

LEEDS SE2236   LS2 7DJ
Palace
Kirkgate

Pleasantly uncityfied, with stripped boards and polished panelling, unusual lighting from electric candelabra to mock street-lamps, lots of old prints, friendly helpful staff, good value lunchtime food till 7pm from sandwiches up including popular Sun roasts in dining area, fine changing choice of ales, may be bargain wine offers; games end with pool, TV, piped music; tables out in front and in small heated back courtyard, open all day. *Recommended by the Didler, Joe Green*

LEEDS SE3033   LS2 7NU
Templar
Templar Street

Tiled pub with fine panelling, stained glass and some unusual booths, well kept Tetleys and guest beers, popular with older locals; open all day. *Recommended by the Didler*

LEEDS SE3033   LS1 3DL
☆ Victoria
Great George Street

Opulent early Victorian pub with grand, cut and etched mirrors, impressive globe lamps extending from majestic bar, carved beams, leather-seat booths with working snob-screens, smaller rooms off, changing ales such as Cottage, Leeds, Timothy Taylors and Tetleys, friendly efficient service even when busy, reasonably priced food 12-6pm from sandwiches and light dishes up in separate room with serving hatch; open all day. *Recommended by the Didler, Andy Lickfold*

Virtually all pubs in the *Good Pub Guide* sell wine by the glass. We mention wines if they are a cut above the average.

LEEDS SE3033   LS1 6HB
☆ **Whitelocks**
Turks Head Yard, off Briggate

Classic Victorian pub (unspoilt but some signs of wear) with long narrow old-fashioned
bar, tiled counter, grand mirrors, mahogany and glass screens, heavy copper-topped
tables and green leather, well kept Caledonian Deuchars IPA, John Smiths, Theakstons
Best and Old Peculier and fine range of guests, good generous all-day food (not Sun
evening), friendly hard-working young staff; crowded at lunchtime; children in restaurant
and top bar, tables in narrow courtyard, open all day. *Recommended by Eric Ruff, Greta and
Christopher Wells, Dr Kevan Tucker, Bruce Bird, the Didler, Michael Butler and others*

LEYBURN SE1190   DL8 5AS
Black Swan
Market Place

Attractive old creeper-clad hotel with chatty locals in the cheerful open-plan bar,
entertaining landlord, good service, decent range of food including popular Sun carvery,
well kept Black Sheep and other ales, good wines by the glass; no credit cards; children
and dogs welcome, good disabled access, tables on cobbled terrace, seven bedrooms,
open all day. *Recommended by Andy Lickfold, the Didler, Ed and Anna Fraser*

LEYBURN SE1190   DL8 5BW
Bolton Arms
Market Place

Substantial stone-built inn at top of the market place, varied choice of well priced home-
made food including good Sun carvery, ales such as Black Sheep, good mix of customers;
bedrooms. *Recommended by R C Vincent, Mr and Mrs Ian King*

LEYBURN SE1190   DL8 5AS
Golden Lion
Market Place

Comfortable panelled and bay-windowed hotel bar, two light and airy rooms with log-
effect gas fire in eating area, varied good value generous food, well kept Black Sheep,
decent coffee, friendly efficient service, paintings for sale, evening restaurant; very busy
on Fri market day; dogs allowed, tables out in front, good value bedrooms, open all day.
Recommended by Gordon Briggs, Ed and Anna Fraser

LINTHWAITE SE1014   HD7 5SG
☆ **Sair**
Lane Top, Hoyle Ing, off A62

Old-fashioned four-room pub brewing its own good value Linfit beers, pews and chairs on
rough flagstones or wood floors, log-burning ranges, dominoes, cribbage and shove-
ha'penny, vintage rock juke box; no food or credit cards; dogs welcome, children till 8pm,
plenty of tables out in front with fine Colne Valley views, restored Huddersfield Narrow
Canal nearby, open all day weekends, from 5pm weekdays. *Recommended by John Fiander,
the Didler*

LINTON IN CRAVEN SD9962   BD23 5HJ
☆ **Fountaine**
Off B6265 Skipton—Grassington

Neatly kept pub in a charming village (parking not easy at peak times), beams in low
ceilings, log fires (one in beautifully carved heavy wooden fireplace), attractive built-in
cushioned wall benches and stools, plenty of prints, tasty well priced bar food, a beer
named for the pub plus Dark Horse, John Smiths, Tetleys and guests; piped music, darts;
children welcome, dogs in bar, teak benches and tables under parasols on terrace, pretty
hanging baskets, fine surrounding walks, open all day. *Recommended by Lynda and
Trevor Smith, Margaret and Peter Staples, Dr Phil Putwain, Jeremy King, Peter Salmon and others*

LITTON SD9074
BD23 5QJ

Queens Arms
Off B6160 N of Grassington

Beautifully placed Dales pub, main bar with coal fire, rough stone walls, beam-and-plank ceiling, stools around cast-iron-framed tables on stone floor, dining room with old photographs, own-brewed Litton ales and guests, hearty food; children and dogs welcome, two-level garden, plenty of good surrounding walks, bedrooms, camping, open all day weekends, closed Mon. *Recommended by Claes Mauroy*

LOCKTON SE8488
YO18 7NQ

☆ Fox & Rabbit
A169 N of Pickering

Attractive neatly kept roadside pub with a warm inviting atmosphere, good choice of generous well presented food (sandwiches too), quick cheerful service, well kept Black Sheep and Cropton ales, decent coffee, beams, panelling and some exposed stonework, plush banquettes, fresh flowers, brasses, hunting prints and old local photographs, big log fire, busy locals' bar with pool, good views from comfortable restaurant; tables outside and in sun lounge, nice spot on moors' edge, bedrooms. *Recommended by Pamela Thorne, A and N Hooper, George Atkinson*

LOW BRADFIELD SK2691
S6 6HW

☆ Plough
New Road

Popular pub with very good value home-made food (not Mon or Tues evenings), well kept and priced local Bradfield and guest beers, cheery efficient service, spotless inside with big inglenook log fire, restaurant; children welcome, picnic-sets in attractive garden, lovely scenery and local walks. *Recommended by Peter F Marshall*

LOW BRADLEY SE0048
BD20 9DE

Slaters Arms
Crag Lane, off A629 S of Skipton

Well kept ales such as Black Sheep, Timothy Taylors and Wells & Youngs, belgian beers, good sensibly priced food, real fires. *Recommended by John and Eleanor Holdsworth*

LOW ROW SD9898
DL11 6PF

☆ Punch Bowl
B6270 Reeth—Muker

Under same ownership as Charles Bathurst at Langthwaite, fresh, light and almost scandinavian in style, with friendly helpful staff, interesting food (menu on huge mirror), popular Sun carvery (best to book), several good wines by the glass, well kept Black Sheep, log fire, leather armchairs, sturdy tables and chairs; no dogs inside; children welcome, great Swaledale views from terrace, 11 comfortable bedrooms, good breakfast, open all day in summer. *Recommended by Bruce and Sharon Eden, Robin M Corlett, Walter and Susan Rinaldi-Butcher*

MALHAM SD9062
BD23 4DA

Buck
Off A65 NW of Skipton

Superbly set creeper-clad stone inn popular with walkers, enjoyable traditional food, six ales including Timothy Taylors Landlord and Theakstons Old Peculier, log fire in panelled lounge, big basic hikers' bar, dining room; children and dogs welcome, picnic-sets in small heated yard, picture-book village, many good walks from the door, 12 clean bedrooms. *Recommended by Chris and Jeanne Downing*

MALHAM SD9062   BD23 4DB
Lister Arms
Off A65 NW of Skipton

Friendly creeper-covered stone-built inn tied to Thwaites, their ales kept well, lots of bottled imports, good value enjoyable food including lunchtime sandwiches, roaring fire; pool and games machines; children and dogs welcome, seats out overlooking a small green, more in back garden, lovely spot by river, good walking country, comfortable clean bedrooms, open all day. *Recommended by Chris and Jeanne Downing, Barry Collett, Peter Salmon*

MANFIELD NZ2213   DL2 2RF
Crown
Vicars Lane

Traditional unpretentious village local, friendly and welcoming, with eight interesting regularly changing ales, enjoyable simple home-made food, two bars and games room with pool; dogs welcome (pub dog is called Leah), garden, good walks nearby. *Recommended by Mr and Mrs Maurice Thompson, Julian Pigg, Brian Jones, D G Collinson*

MARSDEN SE0612   HD7 6EZ
New Inn
Manchester Road

Brightly modernised well run 18th-c coaching inn, open-plan interior with stripped-wood floors, fresh flowers on bar, open fires, good choice of enjoyable evening food from regularly changing menu (all day weekends), well kept ales, friendly attentive service, restaurant; children and dogs welcome, tables in garden, attractive countryside nearby, six bedrooms (named after famous local characters), closed till 5pm weekdays, open all day weekends. *Recommended by Gill and Malcolm Stott*

☆ MARSDEN SE0411   HD7 6BR
Riverhead Brewery Tap
Peel Street, next to Co-op; just off A62 Huddersfield—Oldham

Owned by Ossett with up to ten well kept ales including Riverhead range (microbrewey visible from bar), good value food from sandwiches to interesting specials in airy upstairs beamed dining room with stripped tables and open kitchen; unobtrusive piped music; dogs welcome, wheelchair access, riverside tables, open all day. *Recommended by Gill and Malcolm Stott*

MARTON CUM GRAFTON SE4263   YO51 9QY
Olde Punch Bowl
Signed off A1 3 miles N of A59

Clean welcoming old pub under newish management, half a dozen well kept ales, good reasonably priced food (not Mon, Tues lunchtimes) from interesting snacks up, good friendly service, roomy heavy-beamed open-plan bar, real fires, restaurant; children and dogs have been welcome, disabled facilities, picnic-sets in pleasant garden, open all day Fri-Sun. *Recommended by Allan Westbury, Gordon and Margaret Ormondroyd*

MASHAM SE2281   HG4 4YD
Black Bull in Paradise
Theakstons Visitor Centre, off Church Street; signed from market place

Converted outhouse of some character attached to Theakstons Visitor Centre; high-vaulted roof and galleried area, thick stone walls hung with portraits of the Theakston family and old photographs of the brewery and Masham itself, traditional furnishings on flagstones, winter open fire and full range of Theakstons ales from six handpumps; restricted hours, brewery tours. *Recommended by Adrian and Dawn Collinge, Hunter and Christine Wright*

We say if we know a pub allows dogs

MASHAM SE2281   HG4 4EN

☆ **Black Sheep Brewery**
Wellgarth, Crosshills

Unusual décor in this big warehouse room alongside brewery, more bistro than pub with a lively atmosphere and good mix of customers, well kept Black Sheep range and several wines by the glass, enjoyable reasonably priced food, friendly staff, tables with cheery patterned cloths and brightly cushioned green café chairs, pubbier tables by bar, lots of bare wood, some rough stonework, green-painted steel girders and pillars, free-standing partitions and big plants, glass wall with view into the brewing exhibition centre; piped music; children welcome, picnic-sets out on grass, brewery tours and shop, open all day Thurs-Sat, till 4.30pm Mon-Weds and Sun. *Recommended by Janet and Peter Race, WW, John and Eleanor Holdsworth, Ian and Helen Stafford and others*

MASHAM SE2381   HG4 4HR

Bruce Arms
Morton Row

Friendly local by the side of the market square, Black Sheep and Theakstons, authentic inexpensive indian food (evenings), pubby furniture on patterned carpet, some exposed stonework, hunting prints; TV, free juke box, karaoke; garden picnic-sets, nice Dales views. *Recommended by Mike and Jayne Bastin*

MASHAM SE2280   HG4 4EF

Kings Head
Market Place

Handsome 18th-c stone inn (Chef & Brewer), two modernised linked bars with stone fireplaces, well kept Black Sheep and Theakstons, good wine choice, enjoyable standard food served by friendly helpful staff, part-panelled restaurant; piped music, TV; children welcome, tables out at front and in sunny courtyard behind, 27 bedrooms, open all day. *Recommended by Peter and Anne Hollindale, Mike and Jayne Bastin, Janet and Peter Race, Ed and Anna Fraser*

MASHAM SE2281   HG4 4EN

White Bear
Wellgarth, Crosshills; signed off A6108 opposite turn into town

Comfortable stone-built beamed pub, small public bar with full range of Theakstons ales kept well, larger lounge with coal fire, food from sandwiches up (not Sun evening), decent wines by the glass, pleasant efficient staff, restaurant extension; piped music; children and dogs welcome, terrace tables, 14 bedrooms, open all day. *Recommended by Adrian and Dawn Collinge, the Didler, Dennis Jones, Ed and Anna Fraser*

MENSTON SE1744   LS29 6EB

Fox
Bradford Road (A65/A6038)

Contemporary M&B dining pub in a former coaching inn, good choice of enjoyable fairly priced food, friendly staff, Black Sheep, Timothy Taylors Landlord and a guest such as Adnams, big fireplace, flagstones and polished boards in one part; piped music; two terraces looking beyond car park to cricket field. *Recommended by D M Jack, John and Eleanor Holdsworth*

MIDDLEHAM SE1287   DL8 4NP

Black Swan
Market Place

Popular old inn by the castle, heavy-beamed bar with built-in high-backed settles, big stone fireplace, well kept ales including Theakstons and Black Sheep, bistro-style food, small restaurant; piped music, TV; children welcome, dogs in bar, tables on cobbles outside and in back garden, good walking country, eight bedrooms (can be noisy), good breakfast, open all day. *Recommended by Simon Le Fort, Michael Butler*

MIDDLEHAM SE1287   DL8 4PE
☆ **White Swan**
Market Place

Extended coaching inn opposite cobbled market town square, beamed and flagstoned
entrance bar with built-in window pew and pubby furniture, open woodburner, well kept
Theakstons ales, several wines by the glass and malt whiskies, enjoyable bistro-style food,
friendly efficient staff, modern spacious dining room, large fireplace and small area with
contemporary leather seats and sofa, more dining space in back room; piped music;
children welcome, comfortable bedrooms. *Recommended by Dennis Jones, Ed and Anna Fraser*

MIDHOPESTONES SK2399   S36 4GW
Mustard Pot
Mortimer Road, S off A616

Cosy and friendly characterful 17th-c country local, three small rooms, flagstones,
stripped stone and pine, assorted chairs, tables and settles, two log fires, Black Sheep
and Timothy Taylors Landlord, enjoyable home-made food all day including Sun carvery,
weekend restaurant; piped music; no dogs; children welcome, seats out front and back,
three bedrooms, open all day, closed Mon. *Recommended by Carl Rahn Griffith*

MILLINGTON SE8351   YO42 1TX
Gait
Main Street

Friendly 16th-c beamed village pub, good straightforward food, happy staff, five well kept
ales including York, nice mix of old and newer furnishings, large map of Yorkshire on
ceiling, big inglenook log fire; children welcome, garden picnic-sets, appealing village in
good Wolds walking country, closed Mon-Thurs lunchtimes, open all day Sun. *Recommended
by Christopher Turner, Roger and Anne Newbury*

MIRFIELD SE2017   WF14 8EE
Hare & Hounds
Liley Lane (B6118 2 miles S)

Popular smartly done Vintage Inn, open-plan interior with several distinct areas, good
choice of reasonably priced food all day, well kept Black Sheep and Leeds, cheerful
helpful staff; tables outside with good Pennine views. *Recommended by Gordon and
Margaret Ormondroyd, Michael Butler*

MIRFIELD SE2019   WF14 9JJ
Yorkshire Puddin'
Dunbottle Lane

Modernised and extended with emphasis on low-priced food including bargain OAP menu
and Sun carvery, real ales; Tues quiz; children welcome, terrace picnic-sets, open all day.
Recommended by John and Eleanor Holdsworth

MUKER SD9097   DL11 6QG
☆ **Farmers Arms**
B6270 W of Reeth

New owners for this small unpretentious walkers' pub in a beautiful valley village, warm
fire, friendly staff and locals, well kept Black Sheep, John Smiths and Theakstons, wines,
teas and coffees, enjoyable straightforward good value food including lunchtime
sandwiches, simple modern pine furniture, flagstones and panelling, darts and dominoes;
children and dogs welcome, hill views from terrace tables, stream across the road, open
all day. *Recommended by Lawrence Pearse, the Didler, Arthur Pickering*

MYTHOLMROYD SD9922   HX7 5TA
Hinchcliffe Arms
Off B6138 S at Cragg Vale

Spotless old stone-built pub with enjoyable food including a good value set menu, well kept real ales, friendly staff, open fires; attractive setting near village church on road that leads only to a reservoir, popular with walkers. *Recommended by Mr and Mrs P R Thomas*

NEWLAY SE2346   LS13 1EQ
Abbey
Bridge 221, Leeds & Liverpool Canal

Six or so well kept ales, enjoyable generously served food including deals, friendly cat called Smudge. *Recommended by Alan and Shirley Sawden*

NEWTON UNDER ROSEBERRY NZ5613   TS9 6QR
Kings Head
The Green, off A173

Nicely converted 17th-c cottage row in an attractive village below Roseberry Topping (known locally as the Cleveland Matterhorn), emphasis on a wide choice of enjoyable well priced food in large restaurant area, good service, real ales including Theakstons; disabled facilities, terrace with water feature, eight bedrooms, good breakfast.
Recommended by
Ed and Anna Fraser

NEWTON-ON-OUSE SE5160   YO30 2BN
Blacksmiths Arms
Cherry Tree Avenue, S off Moor Lane

Attractive welcoming village pub, comfortable interior with big fireplace, lots of pump clips and other bits and pieces, well kept Jennings and Ringwood, wide-ranging menu.
Recommended by Roger and Lesley Everett

NORLAND SE0521   HX6 3RP
Moorcock
Moor Bottom Lane

Simply refurbished L-shaped bar and beamed restaurant, wide choice of enjoyable generous food including good value Sun lunch, children's helpings too, Timothy Taylors and Thwaites, friendly hard-working staff. *Recommended by Pat and Tony Martin*

NORTHALLERTON SE3794   DL6 1DP
Tithe Bar
Friarage Street

Market Town Tavern with half a dozen good, mainly Yorkshire ales changing quickly, plenty of continental beers, friendly staff, tasty food lunchtime and early evening, three traditional bar areas with tables and chairs, settle and armchairs, bare boards and brewery posters, upstairs evening brasserie; open all day. *Recommended by Mr and Mrs Maurice Thompson, Adrian Johnson, Tony and Wendy Hobden, Ed and Anna Fraser*

NORWOOD GREEN SE1326   HX3 8QG
☆ ## Old White Beare
Signed off A641 in Wyke, or off A58 Halifax—Leeds just W of Wyke; Village Street

Nicely renovated and extended old pub named after ship whose timbers it incorporates, well kept Copper Dragon and Timothy Taylors, traditional good value home-made food all day including sandwiches and set deals, friendly service, bar with steps up to dining area, small character snug, imposing galleried flagstoned barn restaurant; children and dogs welcome, front terrace, back garden, Calderdale Way and Brontë Way pass the door, open all day. *Recommended by John and Eleanor Holdsworth, Gordon and Margaret Ormondroyd, Clive Flynn*

OAKWORTH SE0138   BD22 0RX
Grouse
Harehills, Oldfield; 2 miles towards Colne

Comfortable old Timothy Taylors pub, well altered and extended, their ales kept well, enjoyable food all day from baguettes up including weekday set deal (12-5pm), friendly staff; undisturbed hamlet in fine moorland surroundings, picnic-sets on terrace with good Pennine views. *Recommended by John and Eleanor Holdsworth*

☆ OSMOTHERLEY SE4597   DL6 3AA
Golden Lion
The Green, West End; off A19 N of Thirsk

Busy attractive old stone pub with friendly welcome, Timothy Taylors and three guests, around 50 malt whiskies, roomy beamed bar on left with old pews and a few decorations, similarly unpretentious well worn-in eating area on right, weekend dining room, well liked pubby food and good service; piped music; children welcome, dogs in bar, seats in covered courtyard, benches out front looking across the village green, 44-mile Lyke Wake walk starts here and Coast to Coast walk nearby, bedrooms, closed Mon and Tues lunchtimes, otherwise open all day. *Recommended by Brian Brooks, John and Eleanor Holdsworth, J F M and M West, Marlene and Jim Godfrey, Ed and Anna Fraser, Mrs J P Cleall*

☆ OSSETT SE2719   WF5 8ND
Brewers Pride
Low Mill Road/Healey Lane (long cul-de-sac by railway sidings, off B6128)

Friendly basic local with Bob's Brewing Comany's White Lion (brewed at back of pub), Rudgate Ruby Mild and several guests such as Ossett, cosy front rooms and flagstoned bar, open fires, brewery memorabilia, good well priced food (not Sun), new dining extension, small games room, live music first Sun of month; well behaved children welcome, big back garden, near Calder & Hebble Canal, open all day. *Recommended by Michael Butler, the Didler*

OSSETT SE2719   WF5 8JS
Tap
The Green

Basic décor with flagstones and open fire, pleasant relaxed atmosphere, Ossett ales and guests (usually Fullers London Pride), decent wines by the glass, friendly service and locals, photos of other Ossett pubs; open all day Thurs-Sun. *Recommended by the Didler, Michael Butler*

OTLEY SE2045   LS29 6BE
Chevin
West Chevin Road, off A660

Well maintained pub largely rebuilt after a fire, young enthusiastic staff, good home-made food including some inventive choices, Greene King Old Speckled Hen and Timothy Taylors Landlord; children welcome, garden with splendid Wharfedale views, open all day. *Recommended by D W Stokes*

OTLEY SE1945   LS21 3DT
Fleece
Westgate (A659)

Stone-built pub reopened after major refurbishment, full range of Wharfebank ales and three changing guests, good choice of enjoyable food; open all day. *Recommended by the Didler*

OTLEY SE2045   LS21 1AD
Junction
Bondgate (A660)

Welcoming family-run beamed pub, single smallish bar with tiled floor, wall benches and fire, 11 well kept ales (cheaper Mon) including Caledonian Deuchars IPA, Timothy Taylors Landlord, Tetleys and Theakstons, a real cider, over 60 malts, no food but you can bring your own (good bakery nearby), live music Tues and eclectic DJ night Sun; children (till 9pm) and dogs welcome, covered smokers' area at back, open all day. *Recommended by Paul Rowe, the Didler*

OVERTON SE2516
WF4 4RF
Black Swan
Off A642 Wakefield—Huddersfield; Green Lane

Traditional local, two cosy knocked-together low-beamed rooms full of brasses and bric-a-brac, well kept John Smiths, popular Thurs quiz night. *Recommended by Michael Butler*

OXENHOPE SE0434
BD22 9SN
☆ ## Dog & Gun
Off B6141 towards Denholme

Beautifully placed roomy 17th-c moorland pub, smartly extended and comfortable, with good varied food from sandwiches to lots of fish and Sun roasts (worth booking then), thriving atmosphere, cheerful landlord and attentive staff, full Timothy Taylors range kept well, good choice of malts, beamery, copper, brasses, plates and jugs, big log fire each end, padded settles and stools, glass-covered well in one dining area, wonderful views; five bedrooms in adjoining hotel. *Recommended by Pat and Tony Martin, Gordon and Margaret Ormondroyd and others*

PICKHILL SE3483
YO7 4JG
☆ ## Nags Head
Masham turn-off from A1, and village signed off B6267 in Ainderby Quernhow

Well run dining pub with friendly landlord and staff, tables all laid for eating, but tap room (lots of ties, jugs, coach horns and ale-yards) serves Black Sheep, Theakstons and a guest ale, smarter lounge bar with green plush banquettes on matching carpet, pictures for sale, open fire, library-themed restaurant with good popular food (all day weekends); TV, piped music; well behaved children till 7.30pm (after that in dining room), seats on front verandah, boules and quoits pitch, nine-hole putting green, comfortable bedrooms, handy for an A1 break, open all day. *Recommended by Jon Clarke, Ian Malone, Don Mitchell, J F M and M West and others*

POOL SE2546
LS21 2PS
Hunters
A658 towards Harrogate

Split-level country pub with well kept Tetleys, Theakstons and lots of changing microsbrews (tasting-notes on board), farm cider, helpful staff, simple lunchtime food from sandwiches to good Sun roasts, balcony for warm weather, open fires, pool, dominoes, table skittles; open all day. *Recommended by the Didler*

POOL SE2445
LS21 1LH
White Hart
Just off A658 S of Harrogate, A659 E of Otley

Light and airy M&B dining pub (bigger inside than it looks), well liked italian-based food all day including sharing plates, pizzas and more restauranty dishes, fixed-price menu too, friendly young staff, good choice of wines by the glass, Greene King and Timothy Taylors, stylishly simple bistro eating areas, armchairs and sofas on bar's flagstones and bare boards; plenty of tables outside. *Recommended by Gordon and Margaret Ormondroyd, John and Eleanor Holdsworth, Michael Butler, Robert Turnham, Jeremy King and others*

POTTO NZ4703
DL6 3HQ
Dog & Gun
Cooper Lane

Tucked-away modern bar/restaurant/hotel, clean contemporary décor, enjoyable food (not Sun evening) from shortish menu including some interesting choices, well kept Captain Cook ales (brewed at sister pub, the White Swan at Stokesley) and guests, friendly attentive staff; tables under parasols on front decking, five bedrooms, open all day. *Recommended by David and Sue Smith*

RAMSGILL SE1171   HG3 5RL
☆ **Yorke Arms**
Nidderdale

Upmarket 18th-c hotel (not a pub), small smart bar with some heavy Jacobean furniture
and log fires, Black Sheep Best, a fine wine list, good choice of spirits and fresh juices,
Michelin-starred restaurant; piped music, no under-12s; seats outside (snack menu),
comfortable bedrooms, good quiet moorland and reservoir walks. *Recommended by*
Robert Wivell

REDMIRE SE0491   DL8 4EA
Bolton Arms
Hargill Lane

Nicely refurbished village pub under friendly new licensees, good food, well kept Black
Sheep, Wensleydale and a guest, comfortable carpeted bar, attractive dining room;
disabled facilities, small garden, handy for Wensleydale Railway and Bolton Castle, good
walks, three courtyard bedrooms. *Recommended by Michael Tack, David Field*

RIBBLEHEAD SD7678   LA6 3AS
Station Inn
B6255 Ingleton—Hawes

Great spot up on the moors by Ribblehead Viaduct (Settle–Carlisle trains), friendly
licensees doing varied food from snacks up, log fire, real ales, low-priced wine and coffee,
simple public bar with darts and pool, dining room with viaduct mural (the bar has
relevant photographs, some you can buy); piped music, TV; children welcome, muddy
boots in bar, picnic-sets outside, five bedrooms (some sharing bath), bunkhouse, open all
day. *Recommended by Ann and Tony Bennett-Hughes, R C Vincent*

RIPON SE3171   HG4 1LQ
☆ **One-Eyed Rat**
Allhallowgate

Friendly little bare-boards pub with numerous well kept real ales (occasional festivals),
farm cider, lots of bottled beers and country wines, long narrow bar with warming fire,
cigarette cards, framed beer mats, bank notes and old pictures, no food but may have free
black pudding, pool; children welcome, pleasant outside area, open all day Sat, closed
weekday lunchtimes. *Recommended by Alan Thwaite, Nick and Alison Dowson, Tim and Ann Newell*

RIPON SE3170   HG4 1QW
Water Rat
Bondgate Green, off B6265

Small pub on two levels, prettily set by a footbridge over River Skell, with good choice of
well kept ales such as Adnams and York, several wines by the glass, reliable
straightforward food including sandwiches, friendly service, conservatory; charming view
of cathedral, ducks and weir from the riverside terrace. *Recommended by Janet and Peter Race,*
Chris and Jeanne Downing

RISHWORTH SE0316   HX6 4QU
☆ **Old Bore**
Oldham Road (A672)

Comfortable and quirkily stylish country dining pub, good interesting seasonal food, all
home-made including breads and ice-cream, not cheap but some deals, good choice of
wines by the glass, Timothy Taylors and guests, friendly helpful staff, beams and standing
timbers, plenty of bric-a-brac and old prints, mixed furnishings, woodburners; outside
picnic-sets, closes 8pm Sun evening. *Recommended by Andy and Jill Kassube, Pat and Tony Martin,*
Gordon and Margaret Ormondroyd

If you know a pub's ever open all day, please tell us.

RISHWORTH SE0216   HX6 4RH
Turnpike
Opposite Booth Wood Reservoir, near M62 junction 22

Restored 19th-c country inn well placed for motorway, spacious modern interior keeping original features, friendly efficient staff, good choice of enjoyable food all day (till 7pm Sun) including good value set menu (Mon-Thurs) and popular Sun lunch; children welcome, fine view of reservoir and surrounding moorland, six bedrooms, open all day. *Recommended by Gordon and Margaret Ormondroyd*

ROBIN HOOD'S BAY NZ9504   YO22 4SJ
Bay Hotel
The Dock, Bay Town

Friendly old village inn at end of the 191-mile Coast to Coast walk, fine sea views from cosy picture-window upstairs bar (Wainwright bar downstairs open too, if busy), ales such as Caledonian Deuchars IPA, Courage Directors, John Smiths and Theakstons, good value home-made food in bar and separate dining area, young staff coping well, log fires; piped music; lots of tables outside, cosy bedrooms, steep road down and no parking at bottom. open all day. *Recommended by the Didler, Chris and Jeanne Downing, George Atkinson*

ROBIN HOOD'S BAY NZ9505   YO22 4SE
☆ Laurel
Bay Bank; village signed off A171 S of Whitby

Charming welcoming little pub at the heart of an especially pretty unspoilt fishing village, beamed neatly kept main bar with old local photographs, Victorian prints and brasses, and lager bottles from all over the world, warm open fire, Adnams and Theakstons, you can buy sandwiches from the Old Bakery Tearooms and eat them in the pub, darts and board games; piped music; children in snug bar only, dogs welcome, pretty hanging baskets and window boxes, self-contained apartment for two, open all day (from 2pm Mon-Thurs in winter). *Recommended by Eric Ruff, the Didler*

SALTBURN-BY-THE-SEA NZ6621   TS12 1HF
Ship
A174 towards Whitby

Beautiful setting among beached fishing boats, sea views from nautical-style black-beamed bars and a big dining lounge, wide range of inexpensive generous food including fresh fish, Tetleys and good choice of wines by the glass, friendly helpful service, restaurant, family room; busy at holiday times; tables outside, open all day in summer. *Recommended by Julie Halliday*

SANCTON SE9039   YO43 4QP
Star
King Street (A1034 S of Market Weighton)

Neatly modernised and recently extended village dining pub, competently cooked food (local produce including own vegetables), extensive wine list, well kept ales such as Black Sheep, good friendly service; lovely surrounding countryside, open all day Sun, closed Mon. *Recommended by Marlene and Jim Godfrey, Jonathan Laverack, Eileen and David Webster*

SAWDON TA9484   YO13 9DY
☆ Anvil
Main Street

Pretty high-raftered former smithy with good locally sourced food from chef/landlord, well kept Black Sheep and guests, good range of wines, friendly attentive staff and immaculate housekeeping, feature smith's hearth and woodburner, lower-ceilinged second bar leading through to small neat dining room; two self-catering cottages, closed Mon, Tues. *Recommended by Keith and Margaret Kettell, Peter Burton, Steve Crosley, Matthew James*

SCARBOROUGH TA0488

YO11 1QW

Leeds Arms
St Marys Street

Proper traditional pub, interesting and friendly, with lots of fishing and RNLI memorabilia, well kept ales, great atmosphere, no food or music. *Recommended by Alan Burns*

SCAWTON SE5483

YO7 2HG

☆ # Hare
Off A170 Thirsk—Helmsley

Attractive popular dining pub in a quiet spot, good carefully cooked well presented food including plenty of fish and a good vegetarian choice, enthusiastic hospitable landlord and friendly staff, good wines by the glass, three well kept ales including Black Sheep and Timothy Taylors, stripped-pine tables, heavy beams and some flagstones, old-fashioned range and woodburner, William Morris wallpaper, appealing prints and old books; children welcome, wrought-iron garden furniture, open all day in summer, closed Mon. *Recommended by Brian and Pat Wardrobe, John and Verna Aspinall, Ed and Anna Fraser, Ben and Ruth Levy*

SETTLE SD8163

BD24 0HB

☆ # Golden Lion
B6480 (main road through town), off A65 bypass

Warm friendly old-fashioned atmosphere in a market-town inn with grand staircase sweeping down into baronial-style high-beamed hall bar, lovely log fire, comfortably worn settles, plush seats, brass, prints and plates on dark panelling, enjoyable good value food (all day weekends) including interesting specials, well kept Thwaites, decent wines by the glass, good-humoured helpful staff, splendid dining room; public bar with darts, pool, games machines and TV; children in eating area, 12 good-sized comfortable bedrooms, hearty breakfast, open all day. *Recommended by Neil and Anita Christopher, Peter Salmon, Clive Flynn, Tony and Maggie Harwood*

SHEFFIELD SK3487

S3 7QL

Bath
Victoria Street, off Glossop Road

Two small colourfully restored bare-boards rooms with friendly staff, well kept Abbeydale, Acorn, Tetleys and guests from a central servery, lunchtime bar food (not Sat), nice woodwork, tiles and glass, live jazz/blues Sun (usually), irish music Mon; open all day, closed Sun lunchtime. *Recommended by the Didler*

SHEFFIELD SK3687

S3 8SA

☆ # Fat Cat
23 Alma Street

Deservedly busy town local with good own-brewed ales and changing guests, draught and bottled belgian beers, Weston's cider and country wines, low-priced mainly vegetarian bar food (not Sun evening), friendly staff, two small downstairs rooms with coal fires, simple wooden tables and cushioned seats, brewery-related prints, jugs, bottles and advertising mirrors, upstairs room with sports TV; children welcome away from main bar, dogs allowed, picnic-sets in fairylit back courtyard, brewery visitor centre (you can book tours on 0114 249 4804), open all day. *Recommended by Marian and Andrew Ruston, John and Sharon Hancock, DC, the Didler, Ian and Helen Stafford, Mike and Eleanor Anderson and others*

SHEFFIELD SK3687

S3 8AT

Gardeners Rest
Neepsend Lane

Welcoming beer-enthusiast landlord serving his own good Sheffield ales from a light wood counter, also several changing guests tapped from the cask, farm cider and continental beers, no food, old brewery memorabilia, changing local artwork, daily papers, games including bar billiards, live music, popular Sun quiz; children welcome (till 9pm) and well behaved dogs, disabled facilities, back conservatory and tables out overlooking River Don, open all day Thurs-Sun, from 3pm other days. *Recommended by Simon Wigglesworth-Baker, the Didler*

SHEFFIELD SK3588   S3 8GG
Harlequin
Nursery Street

Welcoming open-plan corner pub owned by nearby Brew Company, their well kept ales and a great selection of changing guests, also bottled imports and real ciders/perries, straightforward cheap lunchtime food including Sun roasts, beer festivals, regular live music, Weds quiz; dogs welcome, children till 7pm, outside seating, open all day. *Recommended by the Didler, Peter Monk*

SHEFFIELD SK3687   S6 2UB
☆ Hillsborough
Langsett Road/Wood Street; by Primrose View tram stop

Chatty and friendly pub in a hotel, eight beers including own microbrews and quickly changing guests, good wine and soft drinks' choice, generous good value food including Sun roasts, daily papers, open fire, bare-boards bar, lounge, views to ski slope from attractive back conservatory and terrace tables; silent TV; children and dogs welcome, six good value bedrooms, covered parking, open all day. *Recommended by JJW, CMW, the Didler*

SHEFFIELD SK4086   S3 8RY
☆ Kelham Island Tavern
Kelham Island

Busy backstreet local with up to 12 competitively priced ales including a mild and stout/porter, real ciders, knowledgeable helpful staff, traditional pubby furnishings, some nice artwork on yellow walls, perhaps Puss Cat the ginger pub cat, cheap well liked bar food (not Sun), live folk music Sun evening; children and dogs welcome, plenty of seats and tables in unusual flower-filled back courtyard with woodburner for chilly evenings, award-winning front window boxes, open all day. *Recommended by Simon Wigglesworth-Baker, the Didler, Tony Hobden, Matthew Lidbury*

SHEFFIELD SK3290   S6 2GA
☆ New Barrack
601 Penistone Road, Hillsborough

Lively and friendly pub with 11 changing ales, lots of bottled belgian beers and 28 malt whiskies, tasty good value bar food (Fri, Sat light suppers till midnight), comfortable front lounge with log fire and upholstered seats on old pine floors, tap room with another fire, back room for small functions, daily papers, regular events including a chess club, live weekend music and comedy nights; TV; children till 9pm, dogs welcome, award-winning small walled garden, difficult local parking, open all day. *Recommended by JJW, CMW, the Didler, Matthew Lidbury*

SHEFFIELD SK3186   S10 3GD
Ranmoor
Fulwood Road

Comfortable open-plan Victorian local with good value home cooking (not Sun, Mon), Abbeydale and guest ales, piano (often played); pleasant garden, open all day. *Recommended by the Didler*

SHEFFIELD SK3389   S6 2LN
Rawson Spring
Langsett Road

Popular airy Wetherspoons in former swimming baths, their usual value, well kept changing ales, impressive décor with unusual skylights. *Recommended by the Didler*

SHEFFIELD SK3185   S10 3QA
Rising Sun
Fulwood Road

Friendly drinkers' pub with up to 14 ales including full Abbeydale range (many more during summer beer festival), bottled beers, decent food, large lounge with games and reference books; dogs welcome, nice back garden, open all day. *Recommended by the Didler, Mr and Mrs Alesbrook*

SHEFFIELD SK3687   S1 2BS
Rutland Arms
Brown Street/Arundel Lane

Comfortable one-room corner pub with handsome façade, Jennings Cumberland and a great range of changing guests, real cider, food all day till 8pm (not Sun); tables in compact garden, handy for the Crucible and station, bedrooms. *Recommended by the Didler*

SHEFFIELD SK3585   S2 3AA
Sheaf View
Gleadless Road, Heeley Bottom

Wide range of local and other changing ales, farm cider, spotless unusually shaped bar, pleasant staff; very busy on match days; disabled facilities, tables outside, open all day weekends, closed Mon lunchtime. *Recommended by the Didler*

SHEFFIELD SK3586   S1 2BP
Sheffield Tap
Station, Platform 1B

Busy station bar in restored Victorian refreshment room, popular for its huge choice of world beers on tap and in bottles, also five Thornbridge ales and half a dozen guests, knowledgeable helpful staff may offer tasters, snacky food, tiled interior with vaulted roof; open all day. *Recommended by Ian and Helen Stafford, the Didler, Mike and Eleanor Anderson, Adam Gordon, Terry Barlow and others*

SHEFFIELD SK3487   S3 7HG
University Arms
Brook Hill

Former university staff club, comfortable and relaxed, with well kept Thornbridge and changing guests, decent food (not Sat evening), unspoilt interior with old woodwork and alcove seating, back conservatory and small garden, some live music; open all day, closed Sun. *Recommended by the Didler*

SHEFFIELD SK3687   S3 7EQ
☆ ## Wellington
Henry Street; Shalesmoor tram stop right outside

Unpretentious relaxed pub with up to ten changing beers including own bargain Little Ale Cart brews, bottled imports, real cider, coal fire in lounge, photographs of old Sheffield, daily papers and pub games, friendly staff; tables out behind, open all day with afternoon break on Sun. *Recommended by the Didler*

SHELLEY SE2112   HD8 8LR
☆ ## Three Acres
Roydhouse (not signed); from B6116 towards Skelmanthorpe, turn left in Shelley (signposted Flockton, Elmley, Elmley Moor), go up lane for 2 miles towards radio mast

Civilised former coaching inn with all emphasis now on hotel and dining side; roomy lounge with leather chesterfields, old prints and so forth, tankards hanging from main beam, Copper Dragon, 40 malt whiskies and up to 17 wines by the glass from serious (not cheap) list, several formal dining rooms, wide choice of often interesting expensive food from lunchtime sandwiches up, good service; conferences, weddings and events; children welcome, fine moorland setting and lovely views, smart well equipped bedrooms. *Recommended by Andy and Jill Kassube, Gordon and Margaret Ormondroyd*

SHEPLEY SE1809   HD8 8AP
☆ **Farmers Boy**
Junction of A629 and A635, from village centre by Black Bull

Good if pricey food (some from own smokery) in comfortably modern barn restaurant at the back, friendly efficient service, welcoming cottage-conversion beamed bar, well kept ales such as Black Sheep, Copper Dragon and Tetleys; terrace, open all day. *Recommended by David and Cathrine Whiting, Stu Mac, Matthew Lidbury*

SHIPLEY SE1437   BD18 3JN
Fannys Ale House
Saltaire Road

Cosy and friendly bare-boards alehouse on two floors, gas lighting, log fire and woodburner, brewery memorabilia, up to ten well kept ales including Timothy Taylors and Theakstons, bottled beers and farm ciders, new back extension; can be crowded on weekend evenings; dogs welcome, open all day, closed Mon lunchtime. *Recommended by James Stretton, the Didler, Neil Whitehead, Victoria Anderson, David Bishop, C Cooper*

SINNINGTON SE7485   YO62 6SQ
☆ **Fox & Hounds**
Off A170 W of Pickering

Popular neat 18th-c coaching inn, carpeted beamed bar with woodburner, various pictures and old artefacts, comfortable seats, good imaginative food, particularly friendly and helpful staff, well kept Black Sheep and Copper Dragon, several wines by the glass, a few rare whiskies, lounge and smart separate evening restaurant; piped music; children and dogs welcome, picnic-sets in front, more in garden, pretty village, comfortable bedrooms. *Recommended by Marian and Andrew Ruston, Pat and Stewart Gordon, M S Catling, Leslie and Barbara Owen, Martin Clerk and others*

SKIPTON SD9851   BD23 1JE
☆ **Narrow Boat**
Victoria Street; pub signed down alley off Coach Street

Lively extended pub down cobbled alley, eight real ales, draught and bottled continental beers, farm cider and perry, church pews, dining chairs and stools around wooden tables, old brewery posters, mirrors decorated with beer advertisements, upstairs gallery area with interesting canal mural, decent reasonably priced bar food (not Sun evening), folk club Mon evening; children allowed if eating, dogs welcome, picnic-sets under front colonnade; Leeds & Liverpool Canal nearby, open all day. *Recommended by Dennis Jones, the Didler, Steve Nye*

SKIPTON SD9851   BD23 1HY
Woolly Sheep
Sheep Street

Big bustling pub with full Timothy Taylors range, prompt friendly enthusiastic service, two beamed bars off flagstoned passage, exposed brickwork, stone fireplace, lots of sheep prints and bric-a-brac, daily papers, attractive and comfortable raised lunchtime dining area, good value food (plenty for children); unobtrusive piped music; spacious pretty garden, six good value bedrooms, good breakfast. *Recommended by Stuart Paulley*

SLEDMERE SE9364   YO25 3XQ
☆ **Triton**
B1252/B1253 junction, NW of Great Driffield

Handsome old inn by Sledmere House, open-plan bar with old-fashioned atmosphere, dark wooden furniture on red patterned carpet, 15 clocks ranging from a grandfather to a cuckoo, lots of willow pattern plates, all manner of paintings and pictures, open fire, John Smiths, Timothy Taylors, Tetleys and a guest, 50 different gins, honest bar food (only take bookings in separate restaurant); children welcome till 8pm, bedrooms, open all day Sun till 9pm, closed Mon lunchtime in winter. *Recommended by WW, Gerard Dyson, Pete Coxon, Ed and Anna Fraser*

SNAINTON TA9182 YO13 9PL
Coachman
Pickering Road W (A170)

More restaurant-with-rooms but also a small bar serving Wold Top ales, good well presented food in smart white-tableclothed dining room, friendly service, comfortable lounge with squashy sofas; well tended gardens, smokers' shelter at front, three bedrooms, good breakfast. *Recommended by Ian Malone, Peter Burton*

SNAITH SE6422 DN14 9JS
Brewers Arms
Pontefract Road

Converted mill brewing its own good range of distinctive beers, fairly priced home-made food from shortish menu, friendly staff, open-plan bar and conservatory-style dining area, old well, open fireplace; children welcome in eating areas. *Recommended by Ross Gibbins, John and Eleanor Holdsworth, Pat and Stewart Gordon*

SNAPE SE2684 DL8 2TB
☆ ## Castle Arms
Off B6268 Masham—Bedale

Neat homely pub in pretty village, flagstoned bar with open fire, horsebrasses on beams, straightforward pubby furniture, Banks's, Jennings and Marstons, well liked bar food, dining room (also flagstoned) with another fire and plenty of dark tables and chairs; children and dogs welcome, picnic-sets out at front and in courtyard, fine walks in the Yorkshire Dales and on North York Moors, bedrooms. *Recommended by Tim and Sue Halstead*

SOUTH DALTON SE9645 HU17 7PN
☆ ## Pipe & Glass
West End; brown sign to pub off B1248 NW of Beverley

Charmingly tucked-away village dining pub with very good inventive food (not Sun evening) cooked by young landlord; small bar area with beams, traditional pubby furniture, old prints, bow windows and log fire, Black Sheep and guests, several wines by the glass, 50 malt whiskies, contemporary area beyond with leather chesterfields leading to a stylish restaurant overlooking Dalton Park, serious cookbooks on shelves and framed big-name restaurant menus, attentive staff, piped music; children welcome, seats and tables on quiet lawn with picnic-sets on front terrace, ancient yew tree, luxury bedroom suites, open all day, closed Mon (except bank holidays) and two weeks in Jan. *Recommended by G Jennings, Richard Cole, Robert Wivell*

SOWERBY BRIDGE HX6 3AB
Jubilee Refreshment Rooms
Sowerby Bridge Station

Refurbished station building run by two railway-enthusiast brothers, up to five real ales, bottled continental beers, simple food including breakfast and good home-made cakes, railway memorabilia, old enamel signs, art deco ceiling lamps and feature jeweller's clock; open all day from 9.30am (12 Sun). *Recommended by Pat and Tony Martin*

SOWERBY BRIDGE SE0623 HX6 2BD
Shepherds Rest
On A58 Halifax to Sowerby Bridge

Friendly two-room Ossett pub, their full range and guests, no food; suntrap terrace, open all day Fri-Sun, from 3pm other days. *Recommended by Pat and Tony Martin*

SOWERBY BRIDGE SE0523 HX6 2QG
Works
Hollins Mill Lane, off A58

Big airy two-room bare-boards pub in converted joinery workshop, seating from pews to comfortable sofas, eight real ales and a couple of ciders, good bargain home-made food from pies and casseroles to vegetarian choices, Weds curry night, Sun brunch (10-3pm), poetry readings and live music in backyard (covered in poor weather), comedy night in upstairs room; children and dogs welcome, disabled facilities, open all day. *Recommended by Pat and Tony Martin*

STAMFORD BRIDGE SE7055   YO41 1AX

 ## Three Cups
A166 W of town

Clean and spacious Vintage Inn family dining pub in cosy, timbered, country style, enjoyable good value food all day from regularly changing menu, plenty of wines by the glass, real ales, friendly helpful staff, two blazing fires, glass-topped well; children welcome, disabled access, play area behind, bedrooms. *Recommended by Pat and Graham Williamson*

STANBURY SE0037   BD22 0HW
Old Silent
Hob Lane

Neatly rebuilt moorland dining pub near Ponden Reservoir, friendly atmosphere, good reasonably priced fresh food including specials, real ales such as Timothy Taylors, attentive helpful service, character linked rooms with beams, flagstones, mullioned windows and open fires, games room, restaurant and conservatory; children welcome, bedrooms. *Recommended by John and Eleanor Holdsworth*

STILLINGTON SE5867   YO61 1JU
☆ ## Bay Tree
Main Street; leave York on outer ring road (A1237) to Scarborough, first exit on left signposted B1363 to Helmsley

Cottagey pub in pretty village's main street, contemporary bar areas with civilised chatty atmosphere, comfortable cushioned wall seats and leather/bamboo tub chairs around mix of tables, church candles and lanterns, fresh flowers, basketwork and attractive prints on cream or brick walls, central gas-effect coal fire, good bistro-style food including sandwiches, Copper Dragon, fair-priced wines, friendly helpful staff, steps up to cosy dining area, larger conservatory-style back restaurant; piped music; seats in garden and picnic-sets at front under parasols, closed Mon. *Recommended by anon*

STOKESLEY NZ5208   TS9 5BL
☆ ## White Swan
West End

Good Captain Cook ales brewed in attractive flower-clad pub, L-shaped bar with three relaxing seating areas, log fire, lots of brass on elegant dark panelling, lovely bar counter carving, assorted memorabilia and unusual clock, good lunchtime ploughman's (Weds-Sat), live music, beer festivals; no children; open all day. *Recommended by the Didler*

SUTTON UPON DERWENT SE7047   YO41 4BN
☆ ## St Vincent Arms
Main Street (B1228 SE of York)

Enjoyable consistently cheerful pub with Fullers and up to seven guests, 14 wines by the glass, good popular bar food (more elaborate evening meals), bustling parlour-style front bar with panelling, traditional high-backed settles, windsor chairs, cushioned bow-window seat and gas-effect coal fire, another lounge and separate dining room open off here; children welcome, dogs in bar, garden tables, handy for Yorkshire Air Museum. *Recommended by G Dobson, Stanley and Annie Matthews, David and Ruth Hollands, Kay and Alistair Butler, Pat and Tony Martin, Roger and Anne Newbury and others*

SUTTON-UNDER-WHITESTONECLIFFE SE4983   YO7 2PR
Whitestonecliffe Inn
A170 E of Thirsk

Well located beamed roadside pub with wide choice of good value food from sandwiches up in bar and restaurant, ales such as Black Sheep, John Smiths and Tetleys in good condition, interesting 17th-c stone bar, log fire, friendly staff, pool room; children welcome, six self-catering cottages. *Recommended by Michael Butler, Stanley and Annie Matthews*

TAN HILL NY8906   DL11 6ED
Tan Hill Inn
Arkengarthdale Road Reeth—Brough, at junction Keld/West Stonesdale Road

Basic old pub in wonderful bleak setting on Pennine Way – Britain's highest, full of bric-a-brac and interesting photographs, simple sturdy furniture, flagstones, ever-burning big log fire (with prized stone side seats), chatty atmosphere, five real ales including one for the pub by Dent, good cheap pubby food, family room, live music weekends, Swaledale sheep show here last Thurs in May; can get overcrowded, often snowbound; children, dogs and even the pub's ducks welcome, seven bedrooms, bunkrooms and camping, open all day; still for sale as we went to press but operating as usual. *Recommended by Claes Mauroy*

TERRINGTON SE6770   YO60 6PP
☆ # Bay Horse
W of Malton

Friendly landlord at 17th-c pub with cosy log-fire lounge bar, own Storyteller ales and a guest like Wylam, several wines by the glass, over 30 whiskies, shortish choice of good value home-made pub food including good set Sun lunch (best to book), refurbished dining area, conservatory with old farm tools, traditional games in public bar; children and dogs welcome, garden tables, unspoilt village, may be closed lunchtimes Mon-Weds in winter, open all day Thurs-Sun. *Recommended by Christopher Turner, Pat and Tony Martin*

THIRSK SE4282   YO7 1LL
Golden Fleece
Market Place

Comfortable bustling old coaching inn with enjoyable generous bar food, local real ales, friendly competent service, restaurant, view across market place from bay windows; 23 bedrooms, good breakfast. *Recommended by Janet and Peter Race*

THORNTON SE0933   BD13 3QL
☆ # Ring o' Bells
Hill Top Road, off B6145 W of Bradford

19th-c moortop dining pub very popular for its reliably good food including early evening deals, themed and gourmet evenings too, well kept ales from Black Sheep, Courage and Saltaire, panelled bar/dining area with photographs of old Thornton, elegant more modern restaurant with paintings from local artist, pleasant conservatory lounge; no dogs; children welcome, wide views towards Shipley and Bingley. *Recommended by Stanley and Annie Matthews, Keith Moss*

THORNTON SE0832   BD13 3SJ
White Horse
Well Heads

Deceptively large country pub popular for its wide choice of good value generous food and five well kept Timothy Taylors ales, pleasant helpful staff, four separate areas, two with log fires; upstairs lavatories (disabled ones on ground level), also disabled space in car park. *Recommended by Andrew Bosi, Pat and Tony Martin*

THORNTON IN LONSDALE SD6873   LA6 3PB
Marton Arms
Off A65 just NW of Ingleton

Good choice of beers such as Black Sheep, Coniston Bluebird and Sharps Doom Bar, 280 whiskies, friendly helpful staff, standard food, beamed bar with stripped-pine tables and chairs, pews and built-in seats in airy main part, flagstoned public bar with darts and piped music, log fires; picnic-sets on front terrace and at back, great walking country, 13th-c church opposite, comfortable bedrooms, good breakfast. *Recommended by Ian Herdman, Mike and Shelley Woodroffe, David Heath*

☆ THORNTON-LE-CLAY SE6865   YO60 7TG
White Swan
Off A64 York—Malton; Low Street

Comfortable and welcoming early 19th-c family-run dining pub, good generous fairly traditional food including daily roasts and children's meals, John Smiths and a guest, decent wines, reasonable prices, beams and brasses, board games and toys; disabled access, neat grounds with terrace tables, duck pond, herb and vegetable gardens, orchard, two summerhouses, donkey paddock, attractive countryside near Castle Howard, closed all day Mon. *Recommended by Paul Tutill, Matthew Tritton- Hughes, Michael Page, Harry Gordon-Finlayson, Mr and Mrs R W Haste, Mr and Mrs R J Oliver*

THRESHFIELD SD9863   BD23 5HB
Old Hall Inn
B6160/B6265 just outside Grassington

Popular place with three old-world linked rooms including smart candlelit dining room, well kept John Smiths, Timothy Taylors and Theakstons, helpful friendly staff, enjoyable food, nice coffee, log fires, high beam-and-plank ceiling, cushioned wall pews, tall well blacked kitchen range; children in eating area, neat garden. *Recommended by John and Eleanor Holdsworth, Bruce and Sharon Eden, Greta and Christopher Wells*

THUNDER BRIDGE SE1811   HD8 0PX
Woodman
Off A629 Huddersfield—Sheffield

Stone-built village pub with two roomy spotless bars, low beams and heavy wooden tables, smart fresh décor, good welcoming service, popular reasonably priced food, well kept Timothy Taylors and Tetleys, upstairs restaurant; tables outside, 12 good bedrooms in adjoining cottages. *Recommended by John and Eleanor Holdsworth, Matthew Lidbury, Gordon and Margaret Ormondroyd*

TICKTON TA0742   HU17 9SH
New Inn
Just off A1035 NE of Beverley

Friendly, efficiently run country pub and restaurant, good up-to-date well presented food all day (including sandwiches) using local produce in modern simply decorated dining area (closed Sun evening, Mon), traditional log-fire locals' bar (closed Mon lunchtime) with well kept Black Sheep and Tetleys, Sun quiz night; farm shop in car park. *Recommended by Marlene and Jim Godfrey*

TIMBLE SE1852   LS21 2NN
Timble
Off Otley—Blubberhouses moors road

Well restored 18th-c stone-built village inn, popular food from pub favourites up (not Sun evening, Mon, Tues – booking advised), real ales; good bedrooms. *Recommended by John and Eleanor Holdsworth*

TOCKWITH SE4652   YO26 7PY
Spotted Ox
Westfield Road, off B1224

Welcoming traditional beamed village local, three areas off central bar, well kept ales, including Tetleys, carefully served the old-fashioned way, good choice of enjoyable sensibly priced home-made food, attentive staff, relaxed atmosphere, interesting local history; open all day Fri-Sun. *Recommended by Les and Sandra Brown*

TONG SE2230 BD4 0RR
Greyhound
Tong Lane

Traditional stone-built, low-beamed and flagstoned local by the village cricket field, distinctive areas including small dining room, enjoyable good value local food, Black Sheep, Greene King Abbot and Tetleys, many wines by the glass, good service; tables outside. *Recommended by Michael Butler, Frank Dowsland*

TOPCLIFFE SE4076 YO7 3RW
Angel
Off A1, take A168 to Thirsk, after 3 miles follow signs for Topcliffe; Long Street

Big bustling place with well kept Camerons ales, enjoyable pubby food, separately themed areas including softly lit stripped-stone faux-irish bar, also billiards room and two dining rooms; piped music, no credit cards; tables outside, bedrooms. *Recommended by William and Ann Reid, Ed and Anna Fraser*

TOTLEY SK3080 S17 3AZ
Cricket
Signed from A621; Penny Lane

Tucked-away stone-built pub opposite rustic cricket field, much focus on dining but still a friendly local atmosphere, pews, mixed chairs and pine tables on bare boards and flagstones, good-quality blackboard food (all day weekends) from sandwiches and pubby staples to some interesting imaginative cooking, friendly service, Thornbridge ales, log fires, good Peak District views, local artwork for sale; children and dogs welcome, tables outside, open all day. *Recommended by W K Wood, Matthew Lidbury*

WAKEFIELD SE3320 WF1 1DL
Bull & Fairhouse
George Street

Welcoming chatty 19th-c pub (was O'Donoghues), well kept Bobs White Lion, Great Heck Golden Bull and four other changing ales (beer festivals), bare-boards bar with comfortable rooms off, open fire, no food, live music weekends, quiz Thurs; children welcome till 8pm, dogs on leads, open all day Sat, Sun, from 5pm other days. *Recommended by the Didler*

WAKEFIELD SE3320 WF1 1UA
Fernandes Brewery Tap
Avison Yard, Kirkgate

Owned by Ossett but still brewing Fernandes ales in the cellar, interesting guest beers, bottled imports, farm ciders, newish ground-floor bar with flagstones, bare brick and panelling, original raftered top-floor bar with unusual breweriana; closed Mon-Thurs lunchtime, open all day Fri-Sun with some lunchtime food. *Recommended by the Didler*

WAKEFIELD SE3220 WF1 1EL
Harrys Bar
Westgate

Cheery, well run one-room local, Bobs, Leeds, Ossett and guests, free buffet early Fri evening, stripped-brick walls, open fire; small back garden, open all day Sun, closed lunchtime other days. *Recommended by the Didler*

WALTON SE4447 LS23 7DQ
Fox & Hounds
Hall Park Road, off back road Wetherby—Tadcaster

Popular dining pub with enjoyable food from good sandwiches up (should book Sun lunch), well kept John Smiths and a guest such as Black Sheep or Caledonian Deuchars IPA, good friendly service, thriving atmosphere. *Recommended by Greta and Christopher Wells, Pat and Graham Williamson, Les and Sandra Brown*

WEST TANFIELD SE2678   HG4 5JJ
Bruce Arms
Main Street (A6108 N of Ripon)

Comfortable and welcoming under new licensees, good affordable freshly made food, well kept Black Sheep and Copper Dragon, friendly service, flagstones and log fires; two bedrooms, good breakfast, closed Sun evening, Mon. *Recommended by Philip Silvester, Guy, I M Harbinger, Helen Tilford*

WEST TANFIELD SE2678   HG4 5JQ
Bull
Church Street (A6108 N of Ripon)

Open-plan with slightly raised dining area to the left and flagstoned bar on right, popular blackboard food (all day Sat, not Sun evening) from lunchtime sandwiches up, well kept Theakstons and guests, decent wines, brisk pleasant service; piped music; children allowed away from bar, tables on terraces in attractive garden sloping steeply to River Ure and its old bridge, five bedrooms, open all day weekends, closed Tues. *Recommended by Earl and Chris Pick, Dennis Jones, Tim and Sue Halstead*

WESTOW SE7565   YO60 7NE
Blacksmiths Inn
Off A64 York—Malton; Main Street

18th-c inn doing well under current friendly landlord; attractive beamed bar, woodburner in big inglenook, good choice of beers and well liked pub food, darts and dominoes, restaurant; picnic-sets on side terrace, separate bedroom block. *Recommended by Christopher Turner*

WHITBY NZ9011   YO22 4DE
☆ ## Duke of York
Church Street, Harbour East Side

Busy pub in fine harbourside position, handy for famous 199 steps leading up to abbey; comfortable beamed lounge bar with fishing memorabilia, Black Sheep, Caledonian and three guests, decent wines and several malt whiskies, straightforward bar food all day; piped music, TV, games machine; children welcome, bedrooms overlooking water, no nearby parking. *Recommended by the Didler, Roger and Ann King, Pete Coxon, Adrian Johnson*

WHITBY NZ8911   YO21 1DH
Station Inn
New Quay Road

Friendly three-room bare-boards drinkers' pub, wide range of well kept changing ales, farm cider, good wines by the glass, traditional games; piped music – live music Weds; open all day. *Recommended by the Didler, Tony and Wendy Hobden*

WHIXLEY SE4457   YO26 8AG
Anchor
New Road, E of village (first left turn heading N from Green Hamerton on B6265)

Family-friendly pub with traditional generous food including bargain lunchtime carvery particularly popular with OAPs, friendly young staff, John Smiths and Tetleys, straightforward main eating extension, original core with some character and coal fire in the small lounge. *Recommended by Mrs Joy Griffiths, Pete Coxon*

WIGHILL SE4746   LS24 8BQ
White Swan
Main Street

Updated village pub with enjoyable food from local suppliers including Yorkshire tapas and seasonal game, pub favourites too, ales such as Black Sheep, Timothy Taylors Landlord and a house brew from Moorhouses, pub shop; quiz (first Sun of month); tables outside. *Recommended by anon*

YORK SE5951   YO1 6LN
Ackhorne
St Martins Lane, Micklegate

Proper unspoilt pub under new management, friendly and welcoming, with good choice of changing ales and ciders, simple food, beams, bare boards, panelling, stained glass, leather wall seats, old range and open fire, Civil War prints, bottles and jugs, carpeted snug, traditional games; suntrap back terrace, smokers' shelter, open all day. *Recommended by the Didler, Pete Coxon*

YORK SE5952   YO30 7BH
Bay Horse
Marygate

Large mock-Tudor pub with comfortably refurbished open-plan interior, six well kept changing ales (beer festivals), tea/coffee, fresh food from sandwiches up; piped music, TV; seats out in front, four bedrooms. *Recommended by the Didler*

YORK SE6051   YO1 7PR
☆ Black Swan
Peaseholme Green (inner ring road)

Striking timbered and jettied Tudor building, compact panelled front bar, crooked-floored central hall with fine period staircase, black-beamed back bar with vast inglenook, good choice of real ales, decent wines, good value pubby food from sandwiches up; piped music; children welcome, useful car park, bedrooms, open all day. *Recommended by the Didler, Pete Coxon*

YORK SE6051   YO1 9TF
☆ Blue Bell
Fossgate

Delightfully old-fashioned little Edwardian pub, very friendly and chatty, with well kept Black Sheep, Roosters, Timothy Taylors Landlord and three guests, a mild always available too, good value lunchtime sandwiches (not Sun), daily papers, tiny tiled-floor front bar with roaring fire, panelled ceiling, stained glass, bar pots and decanters, corridor to small back room, hatch service, lamps and candles, pub games; soft piped music; no children; dogs welcome, open all day. *Recommended by Eric Ruff, Eric Larkham, Greta and Christopher Wells, the Didler, Pete Coxon and others*

YORK SE5951   YO1 6JX
☆ Brigantes
Micklegate

Comfortably traditional Market Town Taverns bar/bistro, eight well kept mainly Yorkshire ales, good range of bottled beers, good wines and coffee, enjoyable unpretentious brasserie food all day including snacks and sandwiches, friendly helpful staff, simple pleasant décor, upstairs dining room; open all day. *Recommended by Brian and Janet Ainscough, Eric Larkham, the Didler, Pete Coxon and others*

YORK SE6051   YO1 6DU
Golden Ball
Cromwell Road/Bishophill

Unspoilt and buoyant 1950s local feel in this friendly and well preserved four-room Edwardian corner pub, enjoyable straightforward weekday lunchtime food, six well kept changing ales, Sept beer festival, bar billiards, cards and dominoes; TV, can be lively evenings, live music Thurs; lovely small walled garden, open all day Fri-Sun. *Recommended by the Didler, Richard Marvell*

By law, pubs must show a price list of their drinks. Let us know if you are inconvenienced by any breach of this law.

YORK SE6052   YO1 7LG
Golden Slipper
Goodramgate

Dating from the 15th c with an unpretentious bar and three comfortably old-fashioned
small rooms, one lined with books, cheerful efficient staff, good cheap plain lunchtime
food from sandwiches up including an OAP special, John Smiths and up to three other
beers; TV; tables in back courtyard. *Recommended by Pete Coxon, Eric Larkham*

YORK SE6052   YO1 7HP
Guy Fawkes
High Petergate

Friendly pub in splendid spot next to the Minster, dark panelled interior with small bar to
the left and two sizeable rooms to right, good real ale choice, decent food including
bargain Sun lunch; bedrooms. *Recommended by Dr Kevan Tucker, Eric Larkham, Dave Webster,
Sue Holland, the Didler*

YORK SE6052   YO1 7EH
Lamb & Lion
High Petergate

Sparse furnishings and low lighting including candles giving a spartan Georgian feel,
friendly helpful service, four well kept ales including Black Sheep and one brewed for the
pub locally, enjoyable simple bar food plus a more elaborate evening set menu (Tues-Sat),
no food Sun evening, compact rooms off dark corridors; steep steps up to small attractive
garden below city wall and looking up to the Minster, 12 bedrooms, open all day.
Recommended by Eric Larkham, Richard Marvell

YORK SE6051   YO1 8BN
☆ Last Drop
Colliergate

Basic traditional York Brewery pub, their own beers and one or two well kept guests,
samples offered by friendly knowledgeable young staff, decent wines and country wines,
nice fresh good value food (12-4pm) including sandwiches and shared platters, big
windows, bare boards, barrel tables and comfortable seats (some up a few steps); no
children, can get very busy at lunchtime, may ask to keep a credit card while you eat,
attic lavatories; tables out behind, open all day. *Recommended by Dennis Jones, Rob and
Catherine Dunster, Eric Larkham, the Didler, Derek and Sylvia Stephenson and others*

YORK SE6051   YO1 8AA
Lendal Cellars
Lendal

Split-level ale house in broad-vaulted 17th-c cellars, stripped brickwork, stone floor,
linked rooms and alcoves, good choice of changing ales and wines by the glass, foreign
bottled beers, farm cider, decent coffee, enjoyable generous pub food all day, friendly
helpful staff; piped music; no dogs; children allowed if eating, open all day. *Recommended by
Edward Pearce, Jeremy King, the Didler*

YORK SE5951   YO1 6HU
☆ Maltings
Tanners Moat/Wellington Row, below Lendal Bridge

Lively friendly city pub by the river, cheerful landlord, well kept Black Sheep and half a
dozen quickly changing interesting guests, several continental beers, 13 ciders, country
wines, generous standard bar food (not evenings), old doors for bar front and ceiling, fine
collection of railway signs and amusing notices, old chocolate dispensing machine,
cigarette and tobacco advertisements, cough and chest remedies and even a lavatory pan
in one corner, day's papers framed in gents'; games machine, no credit cards, difficult
nearby parking; children allowed mealtimes only, dogs welcome, handy for Rail Museum
and station, open all day. *Recommended by Dennis Jones, Eric Larkham, Andy Lickfold, Tim and
Ann Newell, Andy and Jill Kassube, the Didler and others*

YORK SE5952   YO30 7BH
Minster Inn
Marygate

Multi-roomed Edwardian local, bric-a-brac and dark old settles, fires and woodburners, corridor to distinctive back room, friendly staff, well kept changing Marstons-related ales, sandwiches, table games; children welcome, tables out behind. *Recommended by Dr Kevan Tucker, Eric Larkham, the Didler*

YORK SE6052   YO1 7LF
Old White Swan
Goodramgate

Bustling spacious pub with Victorian, Georgian and Tudor-themed bars, popular lunchtime food including nine types of sausage, Black Sheep and several other well kept ales, good whisky choice, central glass-covered courtyard good for families; piped and frequent live music, big-screen sports TV, games machines, Mon quiz; open all day. *Recommended by Jeremy King, Derek and Sylvia Stephenson, Pete Coxon*

YORK SE6051   YO1 9PT
Phoenix
George Street

Friendly, well restored little pub next to the city walls, proper front public bar and comfortable back horseshoe-shaped lounge, fresh flowers and candles, four well kept Yorkshire ales, good wines, simple food, popular live jazz Sun evening; beer garden, handy for Barbican, open all day. *Recommended by Rick Howell, Stewart Morris, David Gamston, Pat and Tony Martin, Jon Fulton*

YORK SE6051   YO1 8AN
Punch Bowl
Stonegate

Bustling old black and white fronted pub, friendly helpful service, wide range of generous bargain food all day, small panelled rooms off corridor, TV in beamed one on left of food servery, well kept ales such as Black Sheep Leeds, John Smiths and Thornbridge, good wine choice; piped music, games machines, regular quiz nights; open all day. *Recommended by Jeremy King, Edna Jones, Eric Larkham, Mrs Edna M Jones, Pete Coxon*

YORK SE6151   YO10 3WP
Rook & Gaskill
Lawrence Street

Traditional Castle Rock pub with up to a dozen ales including guests like York, enjoyable food (not Sun), dark wood tables, banquettes, chairs and high stools, conservatory; open all day. *Recommended by Eric Larkham, the Didler, Pete Coxon*

YORK SE6052   YO1 7LS
Snickleway
Goodramgate

Interesting little open-plan pub behind big shop-front window, lots of antiques, copper and brass, cosy fires, five well kept ales such as Brains Rev James, John Smiths and Timothy Taylors Landlord, some lunchtime food including good doorstep sandwiches, prompt friendly service. *Recommended by T Gott, Gerard Dyson, D Walkden*

YORK SE6051   YO23 1JH
Swan
Bishopgate Street, Clementhorpe

Unspoilt 1930s pub (Grade II listed), hatch service to lobby for two small rooms off main bar, several changing ales and ciders, friendly knowledgeable staff may offer tasters; busy with young people at weekends; small pleasant walled garden, near city walls, closed weekday lunchtimes, open all day weekends. *Recommended by the Didler, James Hibbins*

YORK SE6052   YO31 7PB
☆ Tap & Spile
Monkgate

Friendly open-plan late-Victorian pub with Roosters and other mainly northern ales, farm cider, decent choice of wines by the glass including country ones, bookshelves, games in raised back area, cheap straightforward lunchtime bar food (not Mon); children in eating area, garden and heated terrace, closed Mon lunchtimes otherwise open all day.
Recommended by the Didler, Eric Larkham, Pete Coxon

YORK SE6052   YO1 7EN
☆ Three Legged Mare
High Petergate

Bustling light and airy modern café-bar with York Brewery's full range and guests kept well (12 handpumps), plenty of belgian beers, quick friendly young staff, interesting sandwiches and some basic lunchtime hot food, low prices, back conservatory; no children; disabled facilities (other lavatories down spiral stairs), back garden with replica gallows after which pub is named, open all day till midnight (11pm Sun).
Recommended by Eric Larkham, Richard Marvell, Pete Coxon, Barry Webber

YORK SE5951   YO1 6JT
☆ York Brewery Tap
Toft Green, Micklegate

Members only for York Brewery's upstairs lounge (annual fee £3 unless you live in Yorkshire or go on brewery tour), their own full cask range in top condition, also bottled beers, nice clubby atmosphere with friendly staff happy to talk about the beers, lots of breweriana and view of brewing plant, comfortable sofas and armchairs, magazines and daily papers, brewery shop; no food; children allowed, open all day except Sun evening.
Recommended by the Didler, Pete Coxon, Ian and Nita Cooper, Eric Larkham

YORK SE6052   YO1 8AS
Yorkshire Terrier
Stonegate

York Brewery shop: behind this, a smallish well worn-in bar with their full beer range and guests, tasting trays of four one-third pints, interesting bottled beers, winter mulled wine, dining room upstairs (where the lavatories are – there's a stair lift) allowing children, limited range of food including bargain 'curry and pint' Weds evening, small conservatory; handy for the Minster, open all day. *Recommended by Eric Larkham, Andy Lickfold, the Didler, Pete Coxon, Derek and Sylvia Stephenson and others*

A very few pubs try to make you leave a credit card at the bar, as a sort of deposit if you order food. They are not entitled to do this. The credit card firms and banks that issue them warn you not to let your card out of your sight. If someone behind the counter used your card fraudulently, the card company or bank could in theory hold you liable, because of your negligence in letting a stranger hang on to your card. Suggest instead that if they feel the need for security, they 'swipe' your card and give it back to you. And do name and shame the pub to us.

Scotland

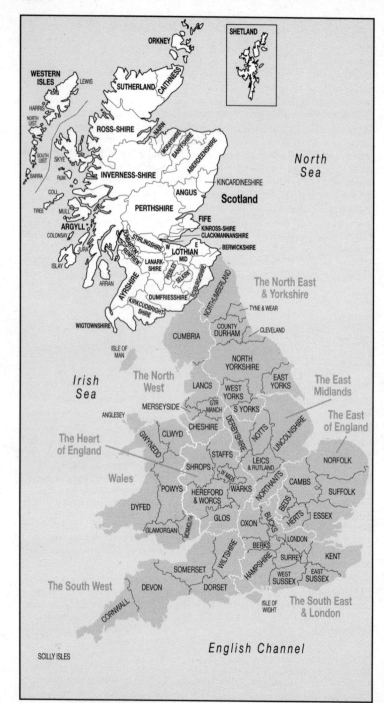

EDITORS' FAVOURITES
SCOTLAND

Scotland's top pub for 2012 is the Applecross Inn at Applecross (tranquil and remote but with a lively bar, excellent fish and seafood, and charming landlady). Other special pubs are the Café Royal in Edinburgh (amazing opulent interior, a buzzy atmosphere and well liked food), Bon Accord in Glasgow (incredibly cheap food and ten interesting ales), Border at Kirk Yetholm (walkers love it, interesting food, good service and well liked bedrooms), Burts Hotel in Melrose (enjoyable small-town hotel with long-serving owners, inventive food, several real ales), Tigh an Eilean Hotel at Shieldaig (stunning setting, bright contemporary bar, local beers and delicious fish and seafood – it's our **Scotland Dining Pub of the Year**), and Stein Inn at Stein (Skye's oldest pub, wonderful sunsets, simple fresh food and lots of malt whiskies). Other good pubs include the George at Inveraray (Argyll), Wheatsheaf at Swinton (Berwickshire), Ship in Elie (Fife), Port Charlotte Hotel at Port Charlotte (Scottish Islands, Islay), Selkirk Arms in Kirkcudbright (Kirkcudbrightshire) and Anderson at Fortrose (Ross-shire).

APPLECROSS   NG7144   Map 11

Applecross Inn ★ 🛏
SCOTLAND PUB OF THE YEAR
Off A896 S of Shieldaig; IV54 8LR

Wonderfully remote pub on famously scenic route on west coast; particularly friendly welcome, real ales, and good seafood; bedrooms

The exhilarating west coast drive to get here over the Beallach na Ba Pass, the pass of the cattle, is one of the highest in Britain and not to be tried in bad weather. The pub itself is splendidly remote and tables in the nice shoreside garden enjoy magnificent views across to the Cuillin Hills on Skye. The no-nonsense, welcoming bar (extremely busy in high season with a good mix of locals and visitors) has a woodburning stove, exposed stone walls and upholstered pine furnishings on the stone floor; Isle of Skye Red Cuillin and Young Pretender on handpump and over 50 malt whiskies; pool (winter only), TV, and board games; some disabled facilities. The alternative route here, along the single-track lane winding round the coast from just south of Shieldaig, has equally glorious sea loch and then sea views nearly all the way.

It's the excellent local fish and seafood that stands out: prawns or squat lobsters in chilli and mango, fresh battered haddock, dressed crab salad, king scallops with crispy bacon and garlic, and a seafood platter. They also offer sandwiches, local haggis in Drambuie and cream, chicken green thai curry, gammon and eggs, and sirloin steak with caramelised onions and mushrooms. *Benchmark main dish: local prawns in garlic and lemon £17.50. Two-course evening meal £16.50.*

Free house ~ Licensee Judith Fish ~ Real ale ~ Bar food (12-9) ~ (01520) 744262 ~ Children welcome until 8.30pm ~ Dogs allowed in bar and bedrooms ~ Occasional live traditional music ~ Open 11am-11.30pm(11.45 Sat); 12-11.30 Sun ~ Bedrooms: £80B/£120B

Recommended by Sylvia and Tony Birbeck, Michael and Maggie Betton, Barry Collett, Dave and Shirley Shaw, Mr and Mrs M Stratton, the Dutchman, Kate Vogelsang, Malcolm Cox

EDINBURGH

NT2574 Map 11

Abbotsford £

Rose Street; E end, beside South St David Street; EH2 2PR

Bustling, friendly city pub with period features, changing beers, and bar and restaurant food

At lunchtime you'll usually find an eclectic mix of business people and locals in this handsome Edwardian pub – it's long been an old favourite of city folk. There's a green and gold plaster-moulded high ceiling and, perched at its centre on a sea of red flooring, a hefty highly polished island bar ornately carved from dark spanish mahogany. Stools around the bar, and long wooden tables and leatherette benches running the lengths of the dark wooden high-panelled walls, keep it feeling pubby. Up to six changing scottish real ales are served from a set of air pressure tall founts and might include Cairngorm Sheepshaggers Gold, Fyne Highlander, Orkney Dark Island, Stewarts Pentland IPA and a couple of guests; around 50 malt whiskies. The smarter upstairs restaurant, with its white tablecloths, black walls and high ornate white ceilings, looks impressive.

 Bar food includes cullen skink, linguine with roast mediterranean vegetables in a tomato sauce, haggis, neeps and tatties, battered haddock, steak pie, and sirloin steak; the restaurant menu is much wider and more elaborate. *Benchmark main dish: fish and chips £8.95. Two-course evening meal £17.40.*

Stewart ~ Licensee Daniel Jackson ~ Real ale ~ Bar food (all day) ~ Restaurant (12-3, 5-10; all day Fri and Sat) ~ (0131) 225 5276 ~ Children over 5 in restaurant only ~ Open 11am-11pm(midnight Sat); 12.30-11 Sun

Recommended by Simon Daws, Roger and Donna Huggins, Comus and Sarah Elliott, Joe Green, the Didler, Trystan Williams, Jeremy King

EDINBURGH

NT2574 Map 11

Bow Bar ★ ◖

West Bow; EH1 2HH

Eight splendidly kept beers – and lots of malts – in a well run and friendly alehouse

This cheerfully traditional alehouse remains unchanging and full of character. The neatly kept rectangular bar has an impressive carved mahogany gantry, and from the tall 1920s founts on the bar counter, knowledgeable staff dispense eight well kept real ales such as Caledonian Deuchars IPA, Stewarts Edinburgh No 3 Premium Scotch Ale, Timothy Taylors Landlord and guests like Fyne Hurricane Jack, Highland Orkney Best, Hornbeam Black Coral Stout, Tempest Re-Wired, and Tryst Raj IPA. Also on offer are some 200 malts, including five 'malts of the moment', a good choice of rums, 25 international bottled beers and quite a few gins. The walls are covered with a fine collection of enamel advertising signs and handsome antique brewery mirrors, and there are sturdy leatherette wall seats and café-style bar seats around heavy narrow tables on the wooden floor; free wi-fi access.

 Lunchtime snacks are limited to tasty pies. *Benchmark main dish: steak pie and gravy £2.00.*

Free house ~ Licensee Helen McLoughlin ~ Real ale ~ Bar food (12-2; not Sun) ~ (0131) 226 7667 ~ Dogs allowed in bar ~ Open 12-12; 12.30-11 Sun

Recommended by Simon Daws, Roger and Donna Huggins, Barbarrick, Joe Green, Andy and Jill Kassube, the Didler, Jeremy King, Claes Mauroy

EDINBURGH　　　　　　　　　　　　　　　　　NT2574　Map 11

Café Royal

West Register Street; EH2 2AA

Stunning listed interior, bustling atmosphere, and rewarding food

You might be better visiting this lovely pub after the lunchtime crush when you can appreciate the dazzling, opulent Victorian interior better – and find a free table. It was built with no expense spared – with state-of-the art plumbing and gas fittings that were probably the pride and joy of its owner, Robert Hume, who was a local plumber. The floors and stairway are laid with marble, chandeliers hang from the magnificent plasterwork ceilings, and the substantial island bar is graced by a carefully re-created gantry. The high-ceilinged viennese café-style rooms have a particularly impressive series of highly detailed Doulton tilework portraits of historical innovators Watt, Faraday, Stephenson, Caxton, Benjamin Franklin and Robert Peel (forget police – his importance here is as the introducer of calico printing), and the stained glass in the restaurant is well worth a look. Caledonian Deuchars IPA and guests such as Cairngorm Black Gold and Kelburn Dark Moor and Misty Law on handpump, a decent choice of wines by the glass, and 20 malt whiskies. Piped music and TV (when the rugby is on).

 As well as popular mussels done several ways (and served by a half or whole kilo) and oysters (by the half-dozen or dozen), the well liked food might include cullen skink, chicken and heather honey pâté, beer-battered fish and chips, mediterranean vegetable bake, rump steak burger, and fish stew. *Benchmark main dish: fresh mussels and oysters £8.15. Two-course evening meal £17.00.*

Punch ~ Manager Christine Annan ~ Real ale ~ Bar food (11(12.30 Sun)-10) ~ Restaurant ~ (0131) 556 1884 ~ Open 11am(midday Sun)-1am

Recommended by Simon Daws, Peter Dandy, Roger and Donna Huggins, Michael Butler, Barry Collett, Dr Kevan Tucker, Joe Green, E McCall, T McLean, D Irving, the Didler, Dr and Mrs A K Clarke, Comus and Sarah Elliott, Barbarrick, Richard Tingle, Christine and Neil Townend, Claes Mauroy

EDINBURGH　　　　　　　　　　　　　　　　　NT2574　Map 11

Guildford Arms  £

West Register Street; EH2 2AA

Busy and friendly, with spectacular Victorian décor, and a marvellous range of real ales

Purpose-built in 1902 and with an elaborate façade, this is always reliable for well kept and unusual ales. The interior is opulently excessive with ornate painted plasterwork, dark mahogany fittings, heavy swagged velvet curtains at the huge arched windows and a busy patterned carpet. Served by knowledgeable, efficient staff, the fine range of ten quickly changing beers might include Caledonian Deuchars IPA, Fyne Avalanche, Harviestoun Bitter & Twisted and Orkney Dark Island, with guests like Atlas (Orkney) Golden Amber, Blue Monkey BG Sips, Dancing Duck Gold, Isle of Skye Black Cuillin, Spire Dark Side of the Moon, and a beer from Stewarts on handpump; there are regular beer festivals. Also, a good range of wines by the glass and two dozen or so malt whiskies; board games, TV, a silent fruit machine, piped music. The snug little upstairs gallery restaurant, with strongly contrasting modern décor, gives a fine dress-circle view of the main bar (notice the lovely old mirror decorated with two tigers on the way up).

🍴 Tasty food includes lunchtime open sandwiches, haggis, neeps and tatties, sausages of the day, pasta in a tomato, mushroom and courgette sauce, breaded haddock, chicken suprême stuffed with black pudding with a whisky glaze, and venison casserole. *Benchmark main dish: aberdeen angus beef in ale pie £9.90. Two-course evening meal £16.70.*

Stewart ~ Lease Steve Jackson ~ Real ale ~ Bar food (12-10) ~ Restaurant (12(12.30 Sun)-2.30, 6-9.30(10 Fri and Sat)) ~ (0131) 556 4312 ~ Children in upstairs restaurant only, must be dining with an adult ~ Live music during Festival ~ Open 11-11(12 Fri and Sat); 12.30-11 Sun

Recommended by Simon Daws, Roger and Donna Huggins, Janet and Peter Race, Dr Kevan Tucker, Barbarrick, Joe Green, E McCall, T McLean, D Irving, the Didler, Mrs Margo Finlay, Jörg Kasprowski, Richard Tingle, Jeremy King, Claes Mauroy

EDINBURGH

NT2574 Map 11

Kays Bar ♠ £

Jamaica Street West; off India Street; EH3 6HF

Cosy, enjoyably chatty backstreet pub with an excellent choice of well kept beers

Many of our readers feel that no visit to Edinburgh is complete without a visit to this warmly welcoming and great fun pub. The interior is decked out with various casks and vats, old wine and spirits merchant notices, gas-type lamps, well worn red plush wall banquettes and stools around cast-iron tables, and red pillars supporting a red ceiling. A quiet panelled back room (a bit like a library) leads off, with a narrow plank-panelled pitched ceiling and a collection of books ranging from dictionaries to ancient steam-train books for boys; lovely warming coal fire in winter. The seven real ales include Caledonian Deuchars IPA and Theakstons Best, plus guests like Atlas (Orkney) Tempest, Cairngorm Trade Winds, Houston Texas, Summer Wine Apache and Timothy Taylors Landlord on handpump; they also stock more than 70 malt whiskies between eight and 50 years old, and ten blended whiskies. TV and board games. In days past, the pub was owned by John Kay, a whisky and wine merchant; wine barrels were hoisted up to the first floor and dispensed through pipes attached to nipples (still visible around the light rose).

🍴 Very good value lunchtime food includes sandwiches, herring salad, haggis and neeps, mince and tatties, steak pie, chilli con carne, and beef or chicken curry. *Benchmark main dish: haggis, neeps and tatties £4.10.*

Free house ~ Licensee David Mackenzie ~ Real ale ~ Bar food (12(12.30 Sun)-2.30) ~ (0131) 225 1858 ~ Dogs welcome ~ Open 11am-midnight(1am Sat); 12.30-11 Sun

Recommended by Roger and Donna Huggins, David and Sue Atkinson, Barbarrick, the Didler, Peter F Marshall

---

Real ale may be served from handpumps, electric pumps (not just the on-off switches used for keg beer) or – common in Scotland – tall taps called founts (pronounced 'fonts') where a separate pump pushes the beer up under air pressure.

GAIRLOCH   NG8075   Map 11

Old Inn ♀ ◖

Just off A832/B8021; IV21 2BD

Quietly positioned old inn with local fish and seafood; good beers

The setting of this 18th-c inn is delightful as it's at the bottom of Flowerdale Glen, tucked comfortably away from the modern waterside road. One of the main draws are their own-brewed beers like Blind Piper, Erradale, Flowerdale and Slattadale – in addition to ales from An Teallach, Cairngorm and Orkney (and Atlas) breweries. Quite a few fairly priced wines by the glass and around 20 malt whiskies, too. The relaxed public bar is popular with chatty locals and is quite traditional, with paintings and murals on exposed stone walls and stools lined up along the counter; board games, TV, fruit machine and juke box. There are picnic-sets prettily placed by the trees lining the stream that flows past under the old stone bridge. Credit (but not debit) cards incur a surcharge of £1.75.

They have their own smokery and bake their own bread, and as well as fresh local fish (scallops, mussels, haddock, crab and lobster) and game (pheasant and venison), the tasty food includes sandwiches, cullen skink, lamb, steak or wild mushroom burgers, pizzas, vegetable tajine, and specials like smoked mackerel pâté and chicken breast on warm potato and black pudding salad with a cheese and whisky sauce. *Benchmark main dish: beer-battered fish and chips £9.25. Two-course evening meal £15.75.*

Free house ~ Licensees Alastair and Ute Pearson ~ Real ale ~ Bar food (12-3, 5-9) ~ Restaurant ~ (01445) 712006 ~ Children welcome ~ Dogs allowed in bar and bedrooms ~ Live music Fri evening ~ Open 11am(midday Sun)-11.45pm ~ Bedrooms: £57B/£99B

Recommended by Sylvia and Tony Birbeck

GLASGOW   NS5965   Map 11

Babbity Bowster ⊕ ♀

Blackfriars Street; G1 1PE

A Glasgow institution: friendly, comfortable and sometimes lively mix of traditional and modern, with almost a continental feel; good food

This 18th-c town house is quite a Glasgow institution and has something of the feel of a continental café-bar. A big ceramic of a kilted dancer and piper in the bar illustrates the mildly cheeky 18th-c lowland wedding pipe tune ('Bab at the Bowster') from which the pub takes its name – the friendly landlord or his staff will be happy to explain further. The simply decorated light interior has fine tall windows, well lit photographs and big pen-and-wash drawings of the city, its people and musicians, dark grey stools and wall seats around dark grey tables on the stripped wooden boards, and a peat fire. The bar opens on to a pleasant terrace with tables under cocktail parasols, trellised vines and shrubs; they may have barbecues out here in summer. Caledonian Deuchars IPA, Kelburn Misty Law and a guest such as Harviestoun Bitter & Twisted on air pressure tall fount, and a remarkably sound collection of wines and malt whiskies; good tea and coffee, too. On Saturday evenings, they have live traditional scottish music, while at other times you may find games of boules in progress outside. Note the bedroom price is for the room only.

Enjoyable food at fair prices from a short bar menu includes sandwiches, cullen skink, mussels in a creamy curry sauce, mushroom and spinach lasagne, toulouse sausage with onion gravy, breaded chicken escalope with sage butter, and specials like hare in a rich red wine and mushroom sauce with pancetta on tagliatelle. The airy upstairs restaurant has more elaborate choices. *Benchmark main dish: haggis, neeps and tatties £6.65. Two-course evening meal £15.75.*

Free house ~ Licensee Fraser Laurie ~ Real ale ~ Bar food (12-10) ~ Restaurant ~ (0141) 552 5055 ~ Children welcome if eating ~ Live traditional music on Sat ~ Open 11am(12.30 Sun)-midnight ~ Bedrooms: £45S/£60S

Recommended by Dr and Mrs A K Clarke, Andy and Jill Kassube, Barry Collett

GLASGOW
NS5765 Map 11

Bon Accord ⬤ £
North Street; G3 7DA

Fabulous choice of drinks, with an impressive range of whiskies, ten real ales, a good welcome, and bargain food

Serving over 1,000 different real ales a year and incredibly cheap food, this is a well run pub with a warm welcome for all – even when packed out. The friendly landlord keeps ten daily changing beers sourced from breweries around Britain, with Caledonian Deuchars IPA and Marstons Pedigree as house beers and eight guests served from swan-necked handpumps. They also have continental bottled beers, a farm cider, 240 malt whiskies and lots of gins, vodkas and rums. The bars are neatly kept with a mix of chairs and tables, a leather sofa and plenty of bar stools on polished bare boards or carpeting, and there are terracotta walls, pot plants and a happy mix of customers; TV, fruit machine, piped music and board games. There are circular picnic-sets on a small terrace with modern tables and chairs out in front.

As well as their incredible value two-course special, the other very reasonably priced food includes sandwiches, macaroni cheese, all-day breakfast, beefburgers with cheese and bacon or chilli, cajun chicken, gammon and egg, and steaks. *Benchmark main dish: battered fresh haddock and chips £6.35. Two-course evening meal £9.00.*

Free house ~ Licensee Paul McDonagh ~ Real ale ~ Bar food (12(12.30 Sun)-8) ~ (0141) 248 4427 ~ Children welcome until 8pm ~ Quiz night Weds, live band Sat ~ Open 11am-midnight; 12.30-11 Sun

Recommended by Barry Collett, John Martin

HOUSTON
NS4066 Map 11

Fox & Hounds ♀ ⬤
South Street at junction with Main Street (B789, off B790 at Langbank signpost E of Bridge of Weir); PA6 7EN

Village pub with award-winning beers from own brewery, and tasty food

The own-brewed beers in this family-run pub continue to draw praise from their many customers. From the Houston Brewery, the five constantly changing ales might include Blonde Bombshell, Killellan Bitter, Peters Well, Texas or Warlock Stout – you can look through a window in the bar to the little brewery where they are produced. They also keep 12 wines by the glass and more than 100 malt whiskies. The clean, plush, hunting-theme lounge has beams, comfortable seats by a fire and polished brass and copper; piped music. Popular with a younger crowd, the lively downstairs bar has a large-screen TV, pool, juke box and fruit machines. At the back is a covered and heated area with decking.

Served upstairs (downstairs they only do substantial sandwiches), the food includes arbroath smokie pâté, steamed west coast mussels, wild mushroom risotto, steak and mushroom in ale pie, sesame-coated chicken goujons, hot seafood platter, and well hung steaks. *Benchmark main dish: beer-battered haddock £10.00. Two-course evening meal £16.00.*

Own brew ~ Licensee Jonathan Wengel ~ Real ale ~ Bar food (12-10(9 Sun)) ~ Restaurant ~ (01505) 612448 ~ Children in lounge till 8pm and restaurant till 10pm ~ Dogs allowed in bar ~ Open 11am-midnight(12.30 Fri and Sat); 12.30-midnight Sun
Recommended by Richard J Holloway, Dr and Mrs A K Clarke, Andy and Jill Kassube, David Hoult

INNERLEITHEN   NT3336 Map 9

Traquair Arms 🛏

B709, just off A72 Peebles—Galashiels; follow signs for Traquair House; EH44 6PD

Attractively modernised inn, popular locally, with a friendly welcome and nice food

Very much the heart of a pretty Borders village, this is a modernised inn with a good mix of locals and visitors. It's one of only three places where you can taste draught Traquair ale, which is produced using original oak vessels in the 18th-c brewhouse at nearby Traquair House. They also keep Caledonian Deuchars IPA and Timothy Taylors Landlord on handpump, and 40 malt whiskies; piped music and TV. The main bar has a warm open fire and there's a relaxed light and airy bistro-style restaurant with high chairs, and another log fire. The garden at the back has picnic-sets and a big tree on a neatly kept lawn.

Quite a choice of bar food might include sandwiches and filled ciabattas, cullen skink, vegetarian lasagne, chicken and haggis with whisky sauce, pork chops with black pudding and apple mash topped with a poached egg, battered haddock with home-made tartare sauce, and steak in ale pie. *Benchmark main dish: steak in ale pie £9.50. Two-course evening meal £14.00.*

Free house ~ Licensee Dave Rogers ~ Real ale ~ Bar food (12-2.30, 5-9; 12-9 weekends) ~ Restaurant ~ (01896) 830229 ~ Children welcome ~ Dogs allowed in bar and bedrooms ~ Open 11(12 Sun)-11 ~ Bedrooms: £50S/£80B
Recommended by Joe Green, the Didler

ISLE OF WHITHORN   NX4736 Map 9

Steam Packet ♀ 🛏

Harbour Row; DG8 8LL

Waterside views from this friendly family-run inn with five real ales and tasty pubby food; bedrooms

Big picture windows at this modernised inn have fine views out over a busy throng of yachts and fishing boats in the harbour, and then beyond to calmer waters; several bedrooms look over the water, too. It's a welcoming, family-run place and the comfortable low-ceilinged bar is split into two: on the right, plush button-back banquettes and boat pictures, and on the left, green leatherette stools around cast-iron-framed tables on big stone tiles, and a woodburning stove in the bare stone wall. Bar food can be served in the lower beamed dining room, which has excellent colour wildlife photographs, rugs on its wooden floor and a solid fuel stove, and there's also a small eating area off the lounge bar, as well as a conservatory. Timothy Taylors Landlord and guest beers such as Atlas (Orkney) Three Sisters, Fyne Ales Jarl, Kelburn Dark Moor and Sulwath The Grace on handpump, quite a few malt whiskies and a good wine list; TV and pool. There are white tables and chairs in the garden. This is an enchanting spot near the end of the Machars peninsula at the most southerly point of Scotland and you can walk from here up to the remains of St Ninian's kirk, on a headland behind the village.

🍴 Quite a choice of bar food might include lunchtime sandwiches, mussels in wine, cream and tomatoes, stir-fried chicken, steak pie, gammon and egg, burgers with cheese and bacon, and specials like cumberland sausage with red wine gravy and local turbot with a herby cream sauce; they also offer good value two-course options (best to phone). *Benchmark main dish: beer-battered haddock and chips £9.95. Two-course evening meal £17.00.*

Free house ~ Licensee Alastair Scoular ~ Real ale ~ Bar food (12-2, 6.30-9) ~ Restaurant ~ (01988) 500334 ~ Children welcome but not in bar ~ Dogs allowed in bar and bedrooms ~ Open 11(12 Sun)-11; 11-3, 6-11 Mon-Thurs in winter ~ Bedrooms: /£40B

Recommended by the Didler, Dr A McCormick, Norma and Noel Thomas, John and Angie Millar, John and Sylvia Harrop

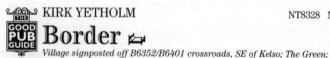

KIRK YETHOLM   NT8328 Map 10

Border 🛏

Village signposted off B6352/B6401 crossroads, SE of Kelso; The Green; TD5 8PQ

Welcoming, comfortable hotel with good interesting food, several real ales, attentive staff – and a renowned objective for walkers

This hospitable inn in the Cheviot Hills is a welcoming sight for walkers, placed as it is at the very northern end of the 256-mile Pennine Way National Trail. The cheerfully unpretentious bar has beams and flagstones, a log fire, a signed photograph of Wainwright and other souvenirs of the Pennine Way, and appropriate Borders scenery etchings and murals; snug side rooms lead off. A beer named for the pub from Broughton, Cairngorm Trade Winds and a changing guest on handpump, a farm cider, several malt whiskies and gins, and decent wines by the glass. There's also a roomy dining room, a comfortable lounge with a second log fire and a neat conservatory; TV, board games and children's games and books. A sheltered back terrace has picnic-sets and a play area, and the colourful window boxes and floral tubs are very pretty. The bedrooms are comfortable. The author of the classic guide to the Pennine Way, Alfred Wainwright, was keen to reward anyone who walked the entire length of the trail with a free drink. He left some money here to cover the cost, but it has long since run out, and the pub now generously foots the bill. There's a water bowl for dogs.

🍴 Using local fish and shellfish, seasonal game and other carefully sourced ingredients, the good, enjoyable food includes lunchtime sandwiches, potted brown shrimps with home-made bread, black pudding topped with a poached free-range egg, crispy bacon and honey and mustard dressing, tagliatelle with spinach, blue cheese and creamy garlic sauce, wild boar and apple sausages with onion gravy, chicken with haggis and whisky sauce, wild salmon (when available), and saddle of venison with red wine and redcurrant jus. *Benchmark main dish: slow-cooked marinated lamb shoulder £13.95. Two-course evening meal £16.70.*

Free house ~ Licensees Philip and Margaret Blackburn ~ Real ale ~ Bar food (12-2, 6-9(8.30 in winter)) ~ Restaurant ~ (01573) 420237 ~ Children welcome away from public bar ~ Dogs allowed in bar and bedrooms ~ Open 11.30-11(midnight Sat); may close earlier in Feb and Mar if quiet in winter ~ Bedrooms: £45B/£90B

Recommended by C A Hall, the Didler, M Mossman

MELROSE
NT5433   Map 9

Burts Hotel ⊕ ⇐
B6374, Market Square; TD6 9PL

Comfortably civilised town-centre hotel with interesting food and lots of malt whiskies

Our readers are very fond of this civilised hotel run by the same friendly, hands-on family for almost 40 years. Pleasantly informal and inviting, the bar has cushioned pews and wall seats and windsor armchairs around pubby tables, scottish prints on the walls, Caledonian Deuchars IPA, Timothy Taylors Landlord and a guest like Scottish Borders Game Bird on handpump, several wines by the glass from a good wine list, a farm cider and around 80 malt whiskies; staff are particularly helpful and polite. The comfortable lounge has plenty of sofas and armchairs; piped music. The bedrooms are neatly kept and the breakfasts very good. In summer you can sit out in the well tended garden and the abbey ruins are within strolling distance.

 As well as lunchtime sandwiches (not Sunday), the good food includes crab salad with gazpacho dressing, ham hock and apricot terrine with piccalilli, home-made burger with tomato chutney, steak in ale pie, vegetarian moussaka, lamb rump with rosemary jus and wild garlic dauphinoise, and salmon fillet topped with prawn mousse with a chive cream. *Benchmark main dish: battered haddock and chips £10.95. Two-course evening meal £17.25.*

Free house ~ Licensees Graham and Nick Henderson ~ Real ale ~ Bar food (12-2, 6-9.30) ~ Restaurant ~ (01896) 822285 ~ Children welcome but must be over 10 in restaurant ~ Dogs allowed in bar and bedrooms ~ Open 11-2.30, 5(6 Sun)-11; closed 2-9 Jan ~ Bedrooms: £72B/£133B

Recommended by Tom and Rosemary Hall, Pat and Stewart Gordon, Comus and Sarah Elliott, John and Sylvia Harrop

PITLOCHRY
NN9459   Map 11

Moulin ◀
Kirkmichael Road, Moulin; A924 NE of Pitlochry centre; PH16 5EH

Attractive 17th-c inn with own-brewed beers and a nicely pubby bar; comfortable bedrooms

Consistently well run and highly enjoyable, this is a bustling pub with four own-brew beers, brewed in the little stables across the street, on handpump: Ale of Atholl, Braveheart, Light and the stronger Old Remedial. They also keep around 40 malt whiskies and a good choice of wines by the glass and carafe. Although much extended over the years, the lively bar, in the oldest part of the building, still seems an entity in itself, nicely pubby and with plenty of character. Above the fireplace in the smaller room is an interesting painting of the village before the road was built (Moulin used to be a bustling market town, far busier than upstart Pitlochry), while the bigger carpeted area has a good few tables and cushioned banquettes in little booths divided by stained-glass country scenes, another big fireplace, some exposed stonework, fresh flowers, antique golf clubs, and local and sporting prints around the walls; bar billiards and board games; there's also a restaurant. On a gravelled area and surrounded by tubs of flowers, picnic-sets outside look across to the village kirk and there are excellent walks nearby.

Well liked bar food using local fish and game includes lunchtime sandwiches, venison terrine with beetroot and orange chutney, stuffed peppers, haggis, neeps and tatties, seafood pancake, chicken in a creamy mustard sauce, beer-battered haddock and chips, and game casserole; the restaurant is more pricey. *Benchmark main dish: steak in ale pie £9.50. Two-course evening meal £16.80.*

Own brew ~ Licensee Heather Reeves ~ Real ale ~ Bar food (12-9.30) ~ Restaurant ~ (01796) 472196 ~ Children welcome ~ Dogs allowed in bar ~ Open 11(12 Sun)-11(11.30 Sat) ~ Bedrooms: £57B/£72B

Recommended by S G N Bennett, Pat and Stewart Gordon, Barry Collett, Claes Mauroy

PLOCKTON

NG8033   Map 11

Plockton Hotel ★ ⊗ ⇌

Village signposted from A87 near Kyle of Lochalsh; IV52 8TN

Lovely views from this family-run loch-side hotel with very good food and real ales; bedrooms

Now run by the younger generation, this family-owned hotel is in the centre of a lovely National Trust for Scotland village and part of a long, low terrace of stone-built houses. The comfortably furnished lounge bar has window seats looking out to the boats on the water, as well as antiqued dark red leather seating around neat Regency-style tables on a tartan carpet, three model ships set into the woodwork and partly panelled stone walls. The separate public bar has pool, board games, TV, a games machine and piped music. Cairngorm Trade Winds and the local Plockton Bay on handpump, 25 malt whiskies and several wines by the glass. Most of the comfortable bedrooms (it's worth booking well ahead) are in the adjacent building – one has a balcony and woodburning stove and half of them have extraordinary views over the loch; good breakfasts. Tables in the front garden look out past the village's trademark palm trees and colourfully flowering shrub-lined shore, across the sheltered anchorage to the rugged mountainous surrounds of Loch Carron; a stream runs down the hill into a pond in the attractive back garden. There's a hotel nearby called the Plockton Inn, so don't get the two confused.

Especially strong on fresh local seafood, the enjoyable food includes lunchtime sandwiches, whisky pâté with home-made chutney, langoustines, moules marinière, monkfish and pepper brochette, salmon fillet topped with spring onion and chilli, a daily vegetarian dish, beer-battered haddock, venison casserole, and seafood platter. *Benchmark main dish: seared local hand-dived scallops £16.95. Two-course evening meal £17.25.*

Free house ~ Licensee Alan Pearson ~ Real ale ~ Bar food (12-2.15, 6-9) ~ Restaurant ~ (01599) 544274 ~ Children welcome ~ Local musicians Weds evening ~ Open 11am-midnight(11.30 Sat); 12.30-11 Sun ~ Bedrooms: £55B/£130B

Recommended by Joan and Tony Walker, Cedric Robertshaw, M J Winterton, T Harrison, Les and Sandra Brown

SHIELDAIG NG8153 Map 11

Tigh an Eilean Hotel 🍴 ⇦

Village signposted just off A896 Lochcarron—Gairloch; IV54 8XN

SCOTLAND DINING PUB OF THE YEAR

Separate, contemporary bar of stunningly set hotel with exceptional views, real ales, and delicious food; tranquil bedrooms

The setting of this friendly hotel easily stands out as one of the best of our top pubs in Scotland – it looks over the forested Shieldaig Island to Loch Torridon and then out to the sea beyond. It's a bright and attractive place and the bar, separate from the hotel, is on two storeys with an open staircase, dining on the first floor and a decked balcony with a magnificent loch and village view. It's gently contemporary and nicely relaxed with timbered floors, timber-boarded walls, shiny bolts through exposed timber roof beams, and an open kitchen. Isle of Skye Black Cuillin and Blaven on handpump and up to a dozen wines by the glass; board games, pool, TV, darts, wi-fi and piped music. Tables outside in a sheltered little courtyard are well placed to enjoy the gorgeous position – if you are lucky, you might spot the sea eagles (as well as seals and other bird life). Next door, the bedrooms are comfortable and peaceful.

Using delicious, sustainably sourced seafood from the village fishermen and other local produce, the food might include sandwiches, herring roes on toast, linguine with surf clams, coq au vin, salmon (hot or cold smoked) from the village smokehouse, hand-made pizzas from their own woodburning oven, crab cakes with home-made lemon mayonnaise, bangers and mash with onion and red wine gravy, and steak frites. *Benchmark main dish: seafood stew £15.50. Two-course evening meal £16.75.*

Free house ~ Licensee Cathryn Field ~ Real ale ~ Bar food (12-9; 12-2.30, 6-9 in winter) ~ Restaurant ~ (01520) 755251 ~ Children welcome ~ Dogs welcome ~ Traditional live folk music some weekends and holidays ~ Open 11-11 ~ Bedrooms: £70B/£140B
Recommended by Mr and Mrs M Stratton, the Dutchman, T Harrison

STEIN NG2656 Map 11

Stein Inn ⇦

End of B886 N of Dunvegan in Waternish, off A850 Dunvegan—Portree; OS Sheet 23 map reference 263564; IV55 8GA

Lovely setting on northern corner of Skye, welcoming 18th-c inn with good, simple food, and lots of whiskies; a rewarding place to stay

This is Skye's oldest inn and stands just above a sheltered inlet on the island's west side with views out to the Hebrides; the sunsets are glorious. The unpretentious original public bar has great character, with its sturdy country furnishings, flagstones, beam-and-plank ceiling, partly panelled stripped-stone walls and coal fire in a grate between the two rooms. There's a games area with pool table, darts, board games, dominoes and cribbage, and maybe piped music. Caledonian Deuchars IPA and a couple of local guests such as Isle of Skye Red Cuillin and Orkney Golden Amber on handpump, 11 wines by the glass and over 125 malt whiskies. Good service from smartly uniformed staff. There's a lively children's inside play area and showers for yachtsmen. All the bedrooms have sea views and breakfasts are good – it's well worth pre-ordering the tasty smoked kippers if you stay.

Using local fish and highland meat, the short choice of good, simple and very sensibly priced food includes lunchtime sandwiches (the haggis toastie and the seasonal crab are extremely popular), hot smoked salmon platter and breaded haddock, with evening choices such as steak in ale pie, pork chop with walnut and blue cheese butter, duck breast with a creamy cider sauce, venison pie, and a fresh fish dish of the day. *Benchmark main dish: battered haddock and chips £10.25. Two-course evening meal £15.50.*

Free house ~ Licensees Angus and Teresa Mcghie ~ Real ale ~ Bar food (12(12.30)-4, 6-9.30(10 Sun)) ~ (01470) 592362 ~ Children welcome until 10pm ~ Dogs allowed in bar and bedrooms ~ Open 11am-midnight (12-11 Mon-Sat in winter); 12.30-11 Sun ~ Bedrooms: $42S/$72S($106B)

Recommended by Sylvia and Tony Birbeck, Ian and Barbara Rankin, Joan and Tony Walker, C A Bryson, T Harrison, Claes Mauroy, Phil Bryant

WEEM
NN8449 Map 11

Ailean Chraggan ⑪ ♀
B846; PH15 2LD

Changing range of well sourced creative food in homely, family-run hotel

There are lovely views from the two flower-filled terraces in front of this family-run hotel to the mountains beyond the Tay, and up to Ben Lawers – the highest peak in this part of Scotland; the owners can arrange fishing nearby. The simple bar has plenty of chatty locals, a couple of beers from the local Inveralmond Brewery on handpump, over 100 malt whiskies and a very good wine list. There's also an adjoining neatly old-fashioned dining room. Winter darts and board games; homely bedrooms and good breakfasts.

As well as lunchtime sandwiches, the changing menu, served in either the comfortably carpeted modern lounge or the dining room, might include moules marinière, local venison, pheasant and pistachio terrine with chutney, gnocchi with roast mediterranean vegetables topped with goats cheese, gressingham duck breast with red onion marmalade, and monkfish skewers with broad bean risotto and a shrimp velouté. *Benchmark main dish: venison haunch with a rich jus and red cabbage £14.95. Two-course evening meal £19.90.*

Free house ~ Licensee Alastair Gillespie ~ Real ale ~ Bar food ~ Restaurant ~ (01887) 820346 ~ Children welcome ~ Dogs allowed in bar and bedrooms ~ Open 11-11; closed 25 and 26 Dec, 1 and 2 Jan ~ Bedrooms: $57.50B/$105B

Recommended by Sylvia and Tony Birbeck, Kevin and Rose Lemin, Les and Sandra Brown

---

'Children welcome' means the pub says it lets children inside without any special restriction. If it allows them in, but to restricted areas such as an eating area or family room, we specify this. Places with separate restaurants often let children use them, and hotels usually let them into public areas such as lounges. Some pubs impose an evening time limit – let us know if you find one earlier than 9pm.

ALSO WORTH A VISIT IN SCOTLAND

Besides the region's top pubs, we recommend the following. Do tell us
what you think of them: **feedback@goodguides.com**

ABERDEENSHIRE

ABERDEEN NJ9406   AB11 5BQ
Archibald Simpson
Castle Street

Good bank-conversion Wetherspoons, well kept beers at low prices, good value food.
Recommended by Mike and Lynn Robinson

ABERDEEN NJ9305   AB11 6BA
Grill
Union Street

Old-fashioned traditional local with enormous range of whiskies, well kept Caledonian
80/- and guest beers, polished dark panelling, basic snacks; open all day. *Recommended by
Joe Green, the Didler, Mike and Lynn Robinson*

ABERDEEN NJ9406   AB11 5BB
Old Blackfriars
Castle Street

Welcoming and cosy ancient building on two levels, several well kept mainly scottish
beers, enjoyable interesting food, good service, plenty of character. *Recommended by
Mike and Lynn Robinson, David Hills*

ABERDEEN NJ9406   AB10 1HF
☆ **Prince of Wales**
St Nicholas Lane

Eight changing ales from individual and convivial old tavern's very long bar counter,
bargain hearty food, flagstones, pews and screened booths, smarter lounge; children
welcome lunchtime in eating area, open all day from 10am. *Recommended by Joe Green,
the Didler, Mike and Lynn Robinson, Christine and Neil Townend*

ABOYNE NO5298   AB34 5EL
☆ **Boat**
Charlestown Road (B968, just off A93)

Friendly country inn with fine views across River Dee, partly carpeted bar with model
train chugging its way around just below ceiling height, scottish pictures, brasses and
woodburner in stone fireplace, games in public-bar end, spiral stairs up to roomy
additional dining area, three ales such as Belhaven, Deeside and Inveralmond, some 30
malts, tasty bar food from sandwiches up, more elaborate seasonal evening menu; piped
music, games machine; children welcome, dogs in bar, six comfortable well equipped
bedrooms, open all day. *Recommended by Graham Keithley, J F M and M West, Christine and
Neil Townend*

CRATHIE NO2293   AB35 5XN
Inver
A93 Balmoral—Braemar

Friendly chatty family-run 18th-c inn by River Dee, comfortable bar areas with log fires,
some stripped stone and good solid furnishings including leather sofas, enjoyable fresh
home-made food cooked by landlord, decent wines by the glass, lots of whiskies, may be a
real ale in summer, restaurant; comfortable bedrooms. *Recommended by J F M and M West*

ANGUS

ARBROATH NO6440   DD11 1HR
Corn Exchange
Market Place

Well run Wetherspoons with good staff and their usual good value pricing. *Recommended by Mike and Lynn Robinson*

BRECHIN NO6060   DD9 6DZ
Caledonian
Southesk Street

White-painted stone building in quiet terrace near Caledonian steam railway terminus; large bar and smaller dining/function room, good value standard bar food, Inveralmond, Houston and guest ales (including english ones), good choice of bottled beers, friendly service, live folk music last Fri of month. *Recommended by GSB*

BROUGHTY FERRY NO4630   DD5 2AD
☆ # Fishermans Tavern
Fort Street; turning off shore road

Once a row of fishermen's cottages, this friendly unchanging pub is just steps from the beach, six changing real ales (May beer festival) and a good range of malt whiskies, secluded lounge area with coal fire, small carpeted snug with basket-weave wall panels, back bar with another fire and popular with diners for the reasonably priced pubby food, fiddle music Thurs night from 10pm, Mon quiz night; TV, fruit machine; children and dogs welcome, disabled facilities, tables on front pavement, more in secluded walled garden, bedrooms, open all day (till 1am Thurs-Sat). *Recommended by Joe Green*

MEMUS NO4259   DD8 3TY
Drovers
N of Sheilhill

Quaint, nicely updated bar and cosy lounge, real ales and good choice of whiskies, good food, two-room restaurant divided by woodburner, large dining conservatory; children welcome, charming garden with peaceful country views, adventure play area, open all day. *Recommended by Mike and Lynn Robinson*

BRIDGE OF ORCHY NN2939   PA36 4AB
☆ # Bridge of Orchy Hotel
A82 Tyndrum—Glencoe

Spectacular spot on West Highland Way, very welcoming with good fairly priced food in bar and restaurant, good choice of well kept ales, house wines and malt whiskies, interesting mountain photographs; lovely bedrooms, good value bunkhouse. *Recommended by Michael and Maggie Betton*

CONNEL NM9034   PA37 1PJ
Oyster
A85, W of Connel Bridge

18th-c pub opposite former ferry slipway, lovely view across the water (especially at sunset), decent-sized bar with friendly Highland atmosphere, log fire in stone fireplace, enjoyable food including good local seafood, keg beers but good range of wines and malts, attentive service; sports TV, pool and darts; modern hotel part next door with separate restaurant. *Recommended by D and K, Richard J Holloway*

GLENCOE NN1058   PH49 4HX
☆ # Clachaig
Old Glencoe Road, behind NTS Visitor Centre

In scenic grandeur of Glencoe and loved by hikers and climbers; log-fire Boots Bar with half a dozen changing scottish ales and 180 malt whiskies, pine-panelled slate-floored snug, lounge (children allowed here) with mix of dining chairs and leather sofas, photographs signed by famous climbers, tasty bar food; piped music, live bands most Sat evenings, TV, games machine, pool; dogs welcome, bedrooms and self-catering, open all day. *Recommended by D and K, Stanley and Annie Matthews*

 INVERARAY NN0908   PA32 8TT

George
Main Street East

Very popular Georgian hotel (packed during holiday times) at hub of this appealing small town; bustling pubby bar with exposed joists, bare stone walls, old tiles and big flagstones, antique settles, carved wooden benches and cushioned stone slabs along the walls, four log fires, two local beers, 100 malt whiskies, food in the bar and smarter restaurant, live entertainment Fri, Sat; children and dogs welcome, well laid-out terraces with plenty of seats, comfortable bedrooms (up grand staircase), Inveraray Castle and walks close by, open all day till 1am. *Recommended by Mr and Mrs Richard Osborne, Andy and Jill Kassube, Kay and Alistair Butler, Cedric Robertshaw*

LOCH ECK NS1491   PA23 8SG

Coylet
South end – A815

Attractive 17th-c inn above the loch, between Benmore and Whistlefield, good reasonably priced local food in cosy bar with fire or pleasant restaurant, helpful staff, well kept ales and good range of malt whiskies, friendly atmosphere; quite handy for Younger Botanic Gardens, boat hire available, bedrooms (spiral stair could be awkward for some). *Recommended by John*

SYMINGTON NS3831   KA1 5QB

Wheatsheaf
Just off A77 Ayr—Kilmarnock; Main Street

Former 17th-c posting inn in a quiet pretty village, charming and cosy, two dining rooms with wide choice of consistently good food served all day (must book weekends), quick friendly service, racehorse décor, log fire; keg beers; children welcome, attractively set tables outside, open all day. *Recommended by Christine and Malcolm Ingram, Deryn Mitchell, M Rowley*

BANFFSHIRE

ABERLOUR NJ2642   AB38 9LS

Dowans Hotel
Signed off A95

Good choice of wine and over 150 whiskies, nice food in bar, friendly staff; 16 bedrooms. *Recommended by Pat and Stewart Gordon*

BERWICKSHIRE

AUCHENCROW NT8560   TD14 5LS

Craw
B6438 NE of Duns; pub signed off A1

Attractive little 18th-c pub in row of cream-washed slate-roofed cottages, welcoming courteous landlord, good well presented food including fresh fish/seafood, changing ales from smaller brewers, good wines by the glass, beams decorated with hundreds of beer mats, pictures on panelled walls, woodburner, more formal back restaurant; children welcome, tables on decking behind and out on village green, three bedrooms, open all day weekends. *Recommended by Marlene and Jim Godfrey, Robbie Pennington, GSB*

LAUDER NT5347   TD2 6SR

Black Bull
Market Place

Comfortable 17th-c inn with cosy rustic-feel bar, lots of fishing cartoons and country scenes on panelled walls, ales such as Caledonian Deuchars IPA and Timothy Taylors

Landlord, food from good sandwiches up, efficient service; children welcome, bedrooms, open all day. *Recommended by the Dutchman*

SWINTON NT8347   TD11 3JJ

☆ **Wheatsheaf**

A6112 N of Coldstream

Civilised upmarket restaurant and most customers here for the imaginative elaborate food (not cheap); main lounge area with attractive long oak settle, comfortable armchairs and sporting prints, pubbier furnishings in small lower-ceilinged part, 40 malt whiskies and a dozen wines by the glass, further lounge area with fishing theme and front conservatory; piped music, TV; no children under 6 after 7pm, pretty village surrounded by rolling countryside not far from the River Tweed, bedrooms, open all day. *Recommended by Christine and Malcolm Ingram, Ian and Helen Stafford, Mike and Hilary Doupe, Ian Phillips*

CAITHNESS

HALKIRK ND1359   KW12 6XY

Ulbster Arms

Bridge Street

Comfortable bar with good range of well priced traditional food and carvery, several local ales, decent wine and whisky choice, friendly attentive staff, lots of angling pictures; good disabled access. *Recommended by M J Winterton*

DUMFRIESSHIRE

DUMFRIES NX9776   DG1 2AH

☆ **Cavens Arms**

Buccleuch Street

Good home-made food all day (not Mon) from pubby standards to imaginative dishes using prime ingredients, up to eight well kept interesting ales, Aspall's and Stowford Press cider, fine choice of malts, friendly landlord and good helpful staff, civilised front part with lots of wood, drinkers' area at back with bar stools, banquettes and traditional cast-iron tables, newly added lounge areas; can get very busy, discreet TV, no under-14s or dogs; disabled facilities, small terrace at back, open all day. *Recommended by Deirdre Holding, Joe Green, the Didler, Dr J Barrie Jones*

KINGHOLM QUAY NX9773   DG1 4SU

☆ **Swan**

B726 just S of Dumfries

Small refurbished dining pub in a quiet spot overlooking old fishing jetty on the River Nith, above-average pub food, Timothy Taylors Landlord, good friendly service; piped music; children welcome, delightful garden, good walks and handy for Caerlaverock nature reserve, open all day Thurs-Sun. *Recommended by John and Sylvia Harrop, Lucien Perring*

MOFFAT NT0805   DG10 9ET

Buccleuch Arms

High Street

Friendly rather old-fashioned Georgian coaching inn with roomy carpeted bar and lounge areas, open fire, good food using local produce (suppliers listed), informal upstairs restaurant, interesting wines by the glass, good choice of malts and bottled beers, cocktails; keg beer, soft piped music, Sky TV; dogs welcome, garden, 16 bedrooms, open all day. *Recommended by Joe Green, Gordon and Margaret Ormondroyd*

DUNBARTONSHIRE

ARROCHAR NN2903   G83 7AX

Village Inn

A814, just off A83 W of Loch Lomond

Friendly, cosy and interesting with well kept ales such as Caledonian and Fyne, enjoyable home-made hearty food in simple all-day dining area (can get booked up) with heavy beams, bare boards, some panelling and big open fire, steps down to unpretentious bar, several dozen malts, good coffee, fine sea and hill views; piped music, juke box, can be loud on busy summer Sats; children welcome in eating areas till 8pm, tables out on deck and lawn, comfortable bedrooms including spacious ones in former back barn, good breakfast, open all day. *Recommended by Andy and Jill Kassube, Andy Sharpe, David Hoult*

LUSS NS3498 — G83 8PD
Inverbeg Inn
A82, about 3 miles N

Large refurbished open-plan inn across the road from Loch Lomond with tables overlooking it, decent choice of enjoyable food all day including local fish in lounge and restaurant, well kept real ales, good range of whiskies, friendly attentive staff; children welcome, private jetty with boat trips, bedrooms including eight in water's-edge lodge – great views. *Recommended by Andy and Jill Kassube, JJW, CMW*

EAST LOTHIAN

DIRLETON NT3183 — EH39 5EP
Castle
Manse Road opposite village green

Refurbished 19th-c coaching inn in pretty village overlooking the green and castle, good bistro food all day with an emphasis on fish (should book), two local beers; terrace and garden, five bedrooms. *Recommended by Christine and Malcolm Ingram, Marlene and Jim Godfrey*

GULLANE NT4882 — EH31 2AF
 ## Old Clubhouse
East Links Road

Two spotless bars with Victorian pictures and cartoons, stuffed birds, pre-war sheet music and other memorabilia, open fires, good choice of enjoyable well priced food, four ales including Belhaven and Caledonian, nice house wines, fast friendly service, views over golf links to Lammermuirs; children welcome, open all day. *Recommended by Comus and Sarah Elliott, GSB*

HADDINGTON NT5173 — EH41 3JD
Victoria
Court Street

Popular pub/restaurant with good imaginative local food cooked by chef/landlord at fair prices, good range of real ales, friendly competent service. *Recommended by Dr and Mrs R G J Telfer*

FIFE

ABERDOUR NT1985 — KY3 0TR
Cedar
Shore Road

Two-bar pub with friendly young staff, decent food from tapas to traditional things, Caledonian Deuchars IPA and a guest like Black Sheep, some interesting whiskies, restaurant; piped music, TV, machines; short pretty walk to the shore, comfortable bedrooms, good breakfast. *Recommended by Ian Herdman*

ELIE NO4999 — KY9 1DT
☆ ## Ship
The Toft, off A917 (High Street) towards harbour

Pleasant seaside inn, very much part of the community, and in good position for enjoying a drink overlooking the sandy bay and on towards the stone pier and old granary; unspoilt beamed nautical-feel bar with old prints and maps on partly panelled walls, coal fires, Caledonian Deuchars IPA, a few malt whiskies, decent bar food, simple carpeted back room with board games (children welcome here); dogs allowed in bar, comfortable bedrooms in next-door guesthouse, open all day (till 1am Fri, Sat). *Recommended by Dave Braisted*

FREUCHIE NO2806   KY15 7EY
Lomond Hills
High Street

Family-run hotel with good food and well kept ales including Cairngorm Wildcat, pleasant lounge bar; good bedrooms, indoor swimming pool and gym for residents, handy for Falkirk Palace (NTS). *Recommended by Ian Herdman*

INVERNESS-SHIRE

AVIEMORE NH8612   PH22 1PE
Cairngorm
Grampian Road (A9)

Large flagstoned bar in traditional hotel, lively and friendly, with prompt helpful service, good value bar food using local produce, Cairngorm Gold and Stag, good choice of other drinks, informal dining lounge/conservatory; sports TV; children welcome, comfortable bedrooms. *Recommended by Joe Green, Christine and Neil Townend*

FORT WILLIAM NN1274   PH33 6TE
Ben Nevis Inn
N off A82: Achintee

Roomy, well converted, raftered stone barn in stunning spot by path up to Ben Nevis, good mainly straightforward food (lots of walkers so best to book), an ale such as Isle of Skye, prompt cheery service, bare-boards dining area with steps up to bar, live music; seats out at front and back, bunkhouse below, open all day Apr-Oct, otherwise closed Mon-Weds. *Recommended by Phil Bryant, Michael and Maggie Betton, John Fiander*

GLEN SHIEL NH0711   IV63 7YW
☆ ## Cluanie Inn
A87 Invergarry—Kyle of Lochalsh, on Loch Cluanie

Welcoming inn in lovely isolated setting by Loch Cluanie, stunning views, friendly table service for drinks including well kept Isle of Skye, fine malt range, big helpings of enjoyable food including good local venison in three knocked-together rooms with dining chairs around polished tables, overspill into restaurant, warm log fire, chatty parrots in lobby (watch your fingers); children and dogs welcome, big comfortable pine-furnished modern bedrooms, bunkhouse, great breakfasts including for non-residents. *Recommended by Sylvia and Tony Birbeck, Michael and Maggie Betton, Claes Mauroy*

GLENUIG NM6576   PH38 4NG
Glenuig Inn
A861 SW of Lochailort, off A830 Fort William—Mallaig

Friendly refurbished bar on a picturesque bay, enjoyable locally sourced food, well kept ales and a scottish cider on tap, lots of bottled beers and a good range of whiskies; bedrooms in adjoining block, also bunkhouse popular with walkers and divers. *Recommended by Ian and Tina Humphrey*

WHITE BRIDGE NH4815   IV2 6UN
White Bridge
B862 SW of village

White-painted 19th-c hotel set in the foothills of the Monadhliath Mountains, good home-made food from sandwiches up, ales from Cairngorm and Isle of Skye, 50 malts, friendly staff, two bars (one with woodburner), restaurant; 12 bedrooms, open all day in summer, all day on winter weekends. *Recommended by Pat and Stewart Gordon*

KINCARDINESHIRE

FETTERCAIRN NO6573   AB30 1XX
Ramsay Arms
Burnside Road

Hotel with enjoyable food in tartan-carpeted bar and smart oak-panelled restaurant, friendly service, well kept beer, several malts including local Fettercairn; children welcome, garden tables, attractive village (liked by Queen Victoria who stayed at the hotel), 12 bedrooms. *Recommended by Mike and Lynn Robinson*

KINROSS-SHIRE

WESTER BALGEDIE NO1604   KY13 9HE
Balgedie Toll
Corner of A911 and A919

Traditional place with oak beams and several small rooms, sensibly priced scottish food including smokies and local venison, Belhaven beers, good wine and whisky choice; good disabled access. *Recommended by M J Winterton*

KIRKCUDBRIGHTSHIRE

GATEHOUSE OF FLEET NX6056   DG7 2HU
☆ ### Masonic Arms
Ann Street; off B727

Spacious dining pub with comfortable two-room pubby bar, Caledonian and a guest beer, good choice of malts, traditional seating, pictures on timbered walls, blue and white plates on delft shelf, attractive conservatory with cane bucket chairs on terracotta tiles, contemporary restaurant, ambitious food; piped music – live folk music Thurs night, games machine, pool; no children in bar after 9pm, dogs allowed, picnic-sets under parasols in neatly kept sheltered garden, more seats in front, appealing small town between the Solway Firth and Galloway Forest Park, open all day weekends, closed middle two weeks of Nov. *Recommended by GSB, M J Winterton, Richard J Holloway, Joe Green*

HAUGH OF URR NX8066   DG7 3YA
☆ ### Laurie Arms
B794 N of Dalbeattie; Main Street

Neatly kept and attractively decorated 19th-c pub, a few tables in log-fire bar with steps up to similar area, decent food from bar snacks to steaks, good changing real ales, decent wines by the glass, welcoming attentive service, restaurant, games room with darts, pool and juke box, splendid Bamforth comic postcards in the gents'; tables out at front and on sheltered terrace behind, open all day weekends. *Recommended by Joe Green, Terry Davis*

KIRKCUDBRIGHT NX6850   DG6 4JG
☆ ### Selkirk Arms
High Street

Comfortable well run 18th-c hotel in a pleasant spot by mouth of the River Dee, simple locals' front bar (own street entrance), partitioned high-ceilinged lounge with upholstered armchairs, wall banquettes and paintings for sale, two beers specially brewed for them, food ranging from pub standards to some interesting dishes in bistro and restaurant, good helpful service; piped music, TV; welcomes children (not in bar) and dogs, smart wooden furniture under blue parasols in neat garden with 15th-c font, 17 bedrooms, open all day. *Recommended by Sheila Topham, Chris Clark, the Didler*

NEWTON STEWART NX4165   DG8 6DB
Galloway Arms
Victoria Street

Family-run hotel with good range of enjoyable food, modern lounge with exposed brick, leather chairs, banquettes and assorted tables on wooden floor, well kept Caledonian Deuchars IPA, Belhaven 60/- and 70/- from cask-fronted bar, 125 or so whiskies, second transport-theme bar with sports TVs, restaurant; dogs welcome, garden, good value bedrooms. *Recommended by M Rowley*

All *Guide* inspections are anonymous. Anyone claiming to be a *Good Pub Guide* inspector is a fraud. Please let us know.

LANARKSHIRE

GLASGOW NS5865   G41 3DJ
Church on the Hill
Algie Street

Converted church with modern open interior on different levels, well kept beers, good choice of tasty well priced food; sports TVs, DJs some evenings. *Recommended by Jeremy King*

GLASGOW NS5965   G1 2DH
☆ ### Counting House
St Vincent Place/George Square

Impressive Wetherspoons bank conversion, imposing interior rising into lofty richly decorated coffered ceiling culminating in a great central dome, big windows, decorative glasswork, wall-safes, several areas with solidly comfortable seating, smaller rooms (once managers' offices) around perimeter, one like a well stocked library, a few themed with pictures and prints of historical characters, half a dozen ales from far and wide, bottled beers, 35 malt whiskies, wide choice of usual good value food all day; children welcome if eating, open 9am-midnight. *Recommended by Dr and Mrs A K Clarke*

GLASGOW NS5965   G2 8BG
Sloans
Argyle Arcade

Restored Grade A listed building over three floors, many original features including a fine mahogany staircase, etched glass, ornate woodwork and moulded ceilings, good choice of food from sandwiches up in ground-floor bar/bistro and upstairs restaurant, events in impressive barrel-vaulted parquet-floored ballroom; children welcome, tables in courtyard. *Recommended by Andy and Jill Kassube*

GLASGOW NS5865   G2 4NG
State
Holland Street

High-ceilinged bar with marble pillars, lots of carved wood including handsome oak island servery, half a dozen or so well kept changing ales, bargain basic lunchtime food from sandwiches up, good atmosphere, friendly staff, armchairs among other comfortable seats, coal-effect gas fire in big wooden fireplace, old prints and theatrical posters; piped music, silent sports TVs, games machine, weekend live music. *Recommended by Ian Barker*

GLASGOW NS5666   G11 6PR
Three Judges
Dumbarton Road, opposite Byres Road

Traditional corner bar with nine quickly changing real ales from small breweries far and wide (they get through several hundred a year), pump clips on walls, friendly staff and locals, live jazz Sun afternoons, no food; dogs welcome, open all day. *Recommended by Andy and Jill Kassube*

MIDLOTHIAN

DALKEITH NR3264   EH22 4TR
Sun
A7 S

Refurbished dining pub/boutique hotel, good-quality local food including some unusual choices and nice puddings, early-bird deals Mon-Thurs, changing real ales; courtyard garden, five individually styled bedrooms, good generous breakfast. *Recommended by Andy and Jill Kassube, David McKinlay*

EDINBURGH NT2471   EH10 4QU
☆ ### Canny Man's
Morningside Road; aka Volunteer Arms

Utterly individual and distinctive, saloon, lounge and snug with fascinating bric-a-brac, ceiling papered with sheet music, huge range of appetising smorgasbord, very efficient friendly service, lots of whiskies, good wines, well kept ales such as Caledonian and Timothy Taylors Landlord, cheap children's drinks, no credit cards, mobile phones or backpackers; courtyard tables. *Recommended by Mr and Mrs Richard Osborne, Barbarrick*

EDINBURGH NT2573   EH1 2NT
Deacon Brodies
Lawnmarket

Entertainingly commemorating the notorious highwayman town councillor who was eventually hanged on the scaffold he'd designed; ornately high-ceilinged city bar, Belhaven and Caledonian from long counter, good whisky selection, upstairs waitress-service dining lounge; piped music, TV; pavement seating. *Recommended by Jeremy King*

EDINBURGH NT2574   EH2 2PF
Dome
George Street

Opulent italianate former bank, huge main bar with a magnificent dome, elaborate plasterwork and stained glass, well kept Caledonian Deuchars IPA from central servery, food from sandwiches up, friendly efficient service, smart dining area and smaller quieter art deco Frasers bar (not always open) with atmospheric period feel; complex includes hotel bedrooms. *Recommended by Richard Tingle*

EDINBURGH NT2573   EH1 1BX
☆ Halfway House
Fleshmarket Close (steps between Cockburn Street and Market Street, opposite Waverley Station)

Tiny one-room pub off steep steps, part carpeted, part tiled, with a few small tables and high-backed settles, lots of prints (some golf and railway themes), four scottish ales such as Kelburn and Strathhaven (third of a pint glasses available), good range of malt whiskies, short choice of decent cheap food all day; 60s/70s juke box, TV turned up for racing; dogs and children welcome. *Recommended by Joe Green, Jeremy King*

EDINBURGH NT2573   EH1 2PB
Jolly Judge
James Court, by 495 Lawnmarket

Small comfortable basement of 16th-c tenement with traditional fruit-and-flower-painted wooden ceiling, welcoming relaxed atmosphere, Belhaven and McEwans ales, good range of malts, lunchtime bar meals (children allowed then) and afternoon snacks, nice log fire; open all day, closed Sun lunchtime. *Recommended by Peter and Giff Bennett, Jon Cumming*

EDINBURGH NT2676   EH6 6QU
Kings Wark
The Shore, Leith

Named to commemorate a visit by George IV, one of several pubs on Leith's restored waterfront; plenty of atmosphere in stripped-stone bare-boards interior, good selection of well kept ales and nice food; open all day. *Recommended by Peter F Marshall*

EDINBURGH NT2473   EH2 4JB
Oxford
Young Street

No-frills pub with two built-in wall settles and friendly locals in tiny bustling bar, steps up to quieter back room with dominoes, lino floor, well kept Caledonian Deuchars IPA and Belhaven 80/- and a good whisky range, cheap filled cobs; links with scottish writers and artists. *Recommended by Peter F Marshall, Joe Green*

It's very helpful if you let us know up-to-date food prices when you report on pubs.

EDINBURGH NT2574 EH2 2JP
Standing Order
George Street

Grand Wetherspoons bank conversion in three elegant Georgian houses, imposing columns, enormous main room with elaborate colourful ceiling, lots of tables, smaller side booths, other rooms including two with floor-to-ceiling bookshelves, comfortable clubby seats, Adam fireplace and portraits, real ales including some interesting ones from long counter; sports TV, weekend live music, gets very busy particularly on a Sat night; disabled facilities, open all day till 1am. *Recommended by Roger and Donna Huggins, Richard Tingle*

EDINBURGH NT2574 EH5 3BZ
☆ ## Starbank
Laverockbank Road, off Starbank Road, just off A901 Granton—Leith

New landlady for this cheerful pub in a fine spot with terrific views over the Firth of Forth, long light and airy bare-boards bar, some leather bench seats, up to eight well kept ales, good choice of malt whiskies, reasonably priced food in conservatory restaurant; piped music, sports TV; children welcome till 9pm if dining, dogs on leads, sheltered back terrace, parking on adjacent hilly street, open all day. *Recommended by Jeremy King, David Goodenough, Brian Banks, Richard Tingle*

EDINBURGH NT2573 EH1 2JU
White Hart
Grassmarket

One of Edinburgh's oldest pubs and popular with tourists, small, basic and relaxed with efficient friendly young staff, enjoyable good value food all day, ales such as Belhaven 80/- and a decent whisky choice, various coffees; piped music – live music weekday nights and Sun afternoon, Sky TV; pavement tables popular with smokers, open all day. *Recommended by Richard Tingle*

RATHO NT1470 EH28 8RA
Bridge
Baird Road

Extended 18th-c pub with enjoyable food all day from a varied menu using local produce including some of their own, daily specials too, good selection of scottish ales such as Fyne and Stewart, friendly staff; children very welcome, garden by Union Canal with wandering ducks, trips on own canal boats, bedrooms. *Recommended by Andy and Jill Kassube*

PERTHSHIRE

BLAIR ATHOLL NN8765 PH18 5SG
☆ ## Atholl Arms
B8079

Sizeable hotel's cosy stable-themed Bothy Bar in a lovely setting near the castle, four local Moulin ales, good well priced food all day from sandwiches to interesting dishes, local meat and wild salmon, helpful friendly staff, open fire; 31 good value bedrooms. *Recommended by Jules Akel, Joe Green, Comus and Sarah Elliott*

BRIG O' TURK NN5306 FK17 8HT
☆ ## Byre
A821 Callander—Trossachs, just outside village

Beautifully placed byre conversion under newish owners, popular fairly priced food including local trout and some imaginative dishes (best to book), friendly staff, flagstoned log-fire bar, roomier high-raftered restaurant area; tables out on extensive decking, good walks, open all day, closed Jan. *Recommended by Mr and Mrs P Morris, Gordon and Margaret Ormondroyd*

DUNKELD NO0242

PH8 0AQ

Taybank
Tay Terrace

Traditional pub with view over River Tay and Georgian bridge, bare boards and big open fire, good value home-made food including stovies, well kept Atlas and Timothy Taylors, regular scottish music including open sessions and workshops (instruments provided). *Recommended by Jules Akel, Christine and Neil Townend*

DUNNING NO0114

PH2 0RR

Kirkstyle
B9141, off A9 S of Perth; Kirkstyle Square

Unpretentious olde-worlde streamside pub with chatty landlady and regulars, log fire in snug bar, good real ale and whisky choice, enjoyable generous home-made food including interesting dishes (book in season), good service, charming flagstoned and stripped-stone back restaurant; closed Mon lunchtime Oct-May. *Recommended by Jules Akel*

KENMORE NN7745

PH15 2NU

☆ # Kenmore Hotel
A827 W of Aberfeldy

Civilised small hotel dating from the 16th c in pretty Loch Tay village, comfortable traditional front lounge with warm log fire and poem pencilled by Burns himself on the chimney breast, dozens of malts helpfully arranged alphabetically, polite uniformed staff, restaurant; back bar and terrace overlooking River Tay with some enjoyable food from lunchtime soup and sandwiches up, Inveralmond Ossian, decent wines by the glass; pool and winter darts, juke box, TV, fruit machine, and entertainment Weds, Sun; children and dogs welcome, good bedrooms, open all day. *Recommended by Comus and Sarah Elliott, Pat and Stewart Gordon*

KILMAHOG NN6008

FK17 8HD

☆ # Lade
A84 just NW of Callander, by A821 junction

Lively place with a strong scottish theme – traditional weekend music, real ale shop with over 130 bottled beers from regional microbreweries and their own-brew WayLade ales; plenty of character in several cosy beamed areas with red walls, panelling and stripped stone, Highland prints and works by local artists, 40 malt whiskies, pubby bar food, more ambitious dishes in big-windowed restaurant; piped music; children welcome, dogs in bar, terrace tables, pleasant garden with three fish ponds and bird-feeding station, open all day (till 1am Fri, Sat). *Recommended by Michael A Butler*

LOCH TUMMEL NN8160

PH16 5RP

☆ # Loch Tummel Inn
B8019 4 miles E of Tummel Bridge

Beautifully placed traditional lochside inn renovated over the last couple of years by present owners, great views over water to Schiehallion, cosy bar area with woodburner, good fresh seasonal food, Inveralmond ales, converted hayloft restaurant; children and dogs welcome, lots of walks and wildlife, six bedrooms, open all day, but closed early Jan to early Feb, and Mon, Tues in Feb and Mar. *Recommended by Comus and Sarah Elliott*

MEIKLEOUR NO1539

PH2 6EB

☆ # Meikleour Hotel
A984 W of Coupar Angus

Early 19th-c creeper-covered inn, well run and a good base for rural Perthshire; main lounge bar is basically two rooms (one carpeted, the other with stone floor), comfortable seating, some angling equipment and fishing/shooting pictures, oil-burning fires, Inveralmond ales including one brewed for them, tasty food from lunchtime snacks to local fish and game, attentive friendly service, elegant panelled restaurant; piped music; children welcome, seats on small colonnaded verandah, picnic-sets on sloping lawn with distant Highland view, spectacular nearby beech hedge planted over 250 years ago, comfortable bedrooms, good breakfast, open all day weekends. *Recommended by Les and Sandra Brown, Sandy Butcher, Christine and Neil Townend*

☆ **Killiecrankie Hotel**

PITLOCHRY NN9163   PH16 5LG

Killiecrankie, off A9 N

Comfortable and splendidly placed country hotel smartened up under current owner, attractive panelled bar, airy and relaxed conservatory, good nicely varied and reasonably priced food here and in restaurant, friendly efficient service, well kept ales, good choice of wines; children in eating areas, extensive peaceful grounds and dramatic views, bedrooms. *Recommended by Joan and Tony Walker*

ROSS-SHIRE

☆ **Badachro Inn**

BADACHRO NG7873   IV21 2AA

2.5 miles S of Gairloch village turn off A832 on to B8056, then after another 3.25 miles turn right in Badachro to the quay and inn

Superbly positioned hotel by Loch Gairloch with terrific views from decking down to water's edge, popular (especially in summer) with happy mix of sailing visitors (free moorings) and chatty locals, welcoming bar with interesting photographs and collages, An Teallach, Caledonian and Crofters, over 50 malt whiskies and good changing wine list, quieter eating area with big log fire, dining conservatory overlooking the bay, good food including locally smoked fish and seafood; piped music; children and dogs welcome, bedrooms, open all day. *Recommended by Sylvia and Tony Birbeck, Pat and Stewart Gordon*

☆ **Anderson**

FORTROSE NH7256   IV10 8TD

Union Street, off A832

Friendly enthusiastic american licensees at this seaside hotel with one of the largest collections of belgian beers in the UK, 200 malt whiskies, quite a few wines and three real ales, good food in homely bar and light airy dining room with open fire, puzzle-type games; piped music, games machine, juke box; children welcome, dogs allowed in bar (resident dog and cat), chickens in garden, bedrooms, closed lunchtimes except Sun. *Recommended by Iain and Nancy Taylor, Charles and Pauline Stride*

Myrtle Bank

GAIRLOCH NG8076   IV21 2BS

Low Road, off B8021

Small modern hotel on the shores of Loch Gairloch with lovely views over to Skye, great choice of good sensibly priced scottish food including venison and fresh fish, Belhaven beers, numerous whiskies, lounge and public bars, two dining areas, conservatory; good disabled access, 12 bedrooms. *Recommended by M J Winterton*

Kintail Lodge

SHIEL BRIDGE NG9319   IV40 8HL

A87

Lots of varnished wood in large plain bar adjoining hotel, convivial bustle in season, lots of malt whiskies, Isle of Skye Black Cuillin, particularly good food from same kitchen as attractive conservatory restaurant with magnificent view down Loch Duich to Skye, local game, wild salmon and own smokings, also children's helpings, friendly efficient service, traditional music Thurs night; 12 good value bedrooms, bunkhouse, good breakfast. *Recommended by Ian and Helen Stafford*

Morefield Motel

ULLAPOOL NH1294   IV26 2TQ

A835 N edge of town

Modern family-run place, clean and bright, with cheerful L-shaped lounge bar, good food including local fish and seafood, well kept changing ales such as Cairngorm, Isle of Skye and Orkney, decent wines, plenty of malt whiskies, large conservatory; piped music, pool and darts; children welcome, terrace tables, bedrooms, open all day. *Recommended by Stanley and Annie Matthews*

ROXBURGHSHIRE

ANCRUM NT6224
TD8 6XH
Cross Keys
Off A68 Jedburgh—Edinburgh

Pleasant village green setting, friendly landlord, well kept Broughton and guests, small panelled locals' bar with sewing-machine tables and open fire, linked lounge/dining areas (one with original overhead tracks for carrying beer to the cellar), enjoyable home-made food; garden, open all day weekends. *Recommended by the Didler, Robbie Pennington*

KELSO NT7234
TD5 7JH
Cobbles
Bowmont Street

Small comfortably refurbished 19th-c dining pub just off the main square, friendly and well run with a good range of food from pub standards to more enterprising dishes, local Tempest ales, decent wines and malts from end bar, wall banquettes and panelling, welcoming fire, overspill dining room upstairs, folk music evenings Fri till late; children welcome, disabled facilities. *Recommended by Robbie Pennington*

ST BOSWELLS NT5930
TD6 0EW
Buccleuch Arms
A68 just S of Newtown St Boswells

Civilised sandstone hotel with calm unchanging feel, good popular food served by prompt friendly staff, real ale, Georgian-style plush bar with light oak panelling, restaurant; children welcome, tables in attractive garden behind, bedrooms. *Recommended by Adele Summers, Alan Black*

STIRLINGSHIRE

KIPPEN NS6594
FK8 3DN
☆ ## Cross Keys
Main Street; village signposted off A811 W of Stirling

Homely and welcoming 18th-c inn, timelessly stylish bar with attractive dark panelling and subdued lighting, straightforward lounge with good fire, another in attractive family dining room, Harviestoun Bitter & Twisted and a guest such as Caledonian Deuchars IPA, several malts and wines by the glass, well liked bar food (all day weekends) from lunchtime sandwiches up; piped music; children (till 9pm) and dogs welcome, garden tables, good views towards the Trossachs, bedrooms, open all day weekends (till 1am Sat), closed Mon. *Recommended by Neil and Anita Christopher, Dr and Mrs A K Clarke, Lucien Perring, Justin and Emma King*

THORNHILL NS6699
FK8 3PJ
☆ ## Lion & Unicorn
A873

Back pubby-feel bar with exposed stone walls, bare boards and stools lining the counter, carpeted front rooms set for dining, one with log fire in a massive 17th-c fireplace, enjoyable home-made food, a couple of changing ales and quite a few malt whiskies, games room with pool, fruit machine and TV; children welcome till 9pm, dogs in public bar, picnic-sets in back garden, four bedrooms, open all day (till 1am Fri, Sat). *Recommended by Dr and Mrs A K Clarke, R and S Bentley*

Places with gardens or terraces usually let children sit there – we note in the text the very few exceptions that don't.

SUTHERLAND

LAIRG NC5224 IV27 4AB

☆ Crask Inn

A836 13 miles N towards Altnaharra

Remote homely inn on a single-track road through peaceful moorland, good simple food cooked by landlady including their own lamb (the friendly hard-working licensees keep sheep on this working croft), comfortably basic bar with large peat stove to dry the sheepdogs (other dogs welcome), Black Isle organic bottled beers, interesting books, piano, pleasant separate dining room, no piped music; three or four bedrooms (lights out when generator goes off), simple nearby bunkhouse. *Recommended by Jules Akel, Les and Sandra Brown*

WEST LOTHIAN

LINLITHGOW NS0077 EH49 7ED

☆ Four Marys

High Street; 2 miles from M9 junction 3 (and little further from junction 4) – town signposted

Evocative 16th-c place – named after Mary, Queen of Scots' four ladies-in-waiting – and filled with mementos of the ill-fated queen including pictures and written records, pieces of bed curtain and clothing, even a facsimile of her death-mask; neatly kept L-shaped bar with mahogany dining chairs around stripped period and antique tables, attractive old corner cupboards, elaborate Victorian dresser serving as bar gantry, mainly stripped-stone walls with some remarkable masonry in the inner area, up to eight real ales (May, Oct beer festivals), good range of malt whiskies, fair value food including good cullen skink, cheery landlord and courteous staff; piped music; children in dining area until 9.30pm, heated outdoor smoking area, difficult parking, open all day (till 1am Fri, Sat). *Recommended by Richard J Holloway, Peter F Marshall*

QUEENSFERRY NT1378 EH30 9TA

Hawes

Newhalls Road

Vintage Inn renovation featured famously in *Kidnapped*, a great spot for tourists with fine views of the Forth bridges (one rail bridge support in the car park); wide choice of enjoyable food all day including a good value set menu (Mon-Sat till 5pm), roomy separate dining areas, friendly efficient staff, wide range of wines by the glass, three well kept ales including Caledonian Deuchars IPA; children welcome, tables on back lawn with play area, 14 bedrooms. *Recommended by the Dutchman*

WIGTOWNSHIRE

BARGRENNAN NX3576 DG8 6RN

House O'Hill

E off A1714

Refurbished under welcoming newish owners and in a lovely position near Glen Trool and Merrick mountain, enjoyable reasonably priced food, real ales, some live music; two bedrooms and holiday cottage. *Recommended by Dr A McCormick*

BLADNOCH NX4254 DG8 9AB

Bladnoch Inn

Corner of A714 and B7005

Cheerful bar, neat and bright, with eating area, enjoyable well prepared pubby food from sandwiches up, friendly obliging service, restaurant; keg beer, piped radio; children and dogs welcome, picturesque riverside setting across from the Bladnoch distillery (tours), good value bedrooms. *Recommended by Mr and Mrs P G Mitchell, John and Sylvia Harrop*

Real ale to us means beer which has matured naturally in its cask –
not pressurised or filtered.

PORT LOGAN NX0940   DG9 9NG

Port Logan Inn
Laigh Street

Lovely sea-view spot in a pretty fishing harbour, family-run and welcoming, well kept ales such as Caledonian Deuchars IPA or Sulwath Criffel, lots of malt whiskies, enjoyable food including local fish and game, log fire, old local photographs and electronic equipment; handy for Logan Botanic Garden, bedrooms. *Recommended by V and E A Bolton*

SCOTTISH ISLANDS

COLONSAY

SCALASAIG NR3893   PA61 7YP
Colonsay
W on B8086

Stylish 18th-c hotel, a haven for ramblers and birders, with log fires, interesting old islander pictures, pastel walls and polished painted boards, bar with sofas and board games, enjoyable food from soup and toasties to fresh seafood, game and venison, good local Colonsay ale, lots of malt whiskies, informal restaurant; children and dogs welcome, pleasant views from gardens, comfortable bedrooms. *Recommended by David Hoult*

ISLAY

BOWMORE NR3159   PA43 7LB
Lochside Hotel
Shore Street

Neatly modernised hotel under new family ownership, well kept Islay ales along with some mainstream beers, amazing collection of Islay malts (over 300 including some real rarities) and 50 other whiskies, enjoyable food (booking advised) making use of local seafood and lamb, good friendly service, two bars, bright conservatory-style back restaurant with lovely Loch Indaal views, traditional music Sat night; children (till 8pm), dogs in public bar, lochside terrace, ten bedrooms, open all day (till 1am Fri, Sat).
Recommended by Richard J Holloway, David Hoult

PORT CHARLOTTE NR2558   PA48 7TU
Port Charlotte Hotel
Main Sreet

Most beautiful of Islay's Georgian villages and in a lovely position with sweeping views over Loch Indaal, exceptional collection of about 140 Islay malts including rare ones, Black Sheep and Islay ales, decent wines by the glass, good food using local meat and seafood, civilised bare-boards pubby bar with padded wall seats and modern art, comfortable back bar, separate restaurant and roomy conservatory, traditional live music weekly; children welcome (not in bar after 10pm), garden tables, near sandy beach, bedrooms, open all day till 1am. *Recommended by Richard J Holloway, David Hoult*

PORTNAHAVEN NN1652   PA47 7SJ
An Tighe Seinnse
Queen Street

Friendly little end-of-terrace harbourside pub tucked away in a remote attractive fishing village, cosy bar with room off, open fire, good food including local seafood, Belhaven 80/- and bottled Islay ales, good choice of malts, can get crowded. *Recommended by David Hoult, Tom and Rosemary Hall*

JURA

CRAIGHOUSE NR5266   PA60 7XU
Jura Hotel
A846

Doing well under newish young couple; superb setting with view over the Small Isles to the mainland; garden down to water's edge, bedrooms, most with sea view. *Recommended by David Hoult*

MULL

DERVAIG NM4251   PA75 6QW
☆ **Bellachroy**
B8073

Island's oldest inn refurbished by friendly licensees, enjoyable pub and restaurant food including local seafood and plenty of other fresh produce, generous helpings, good choice of beers, whiskies and wine, traditional bar, informal dining area and lounge used more by residents; children and dogs welcome, covered outside area, nice spot in sleepy lochside village, six comfortable bedrooms, open all year. *Recommended by Mr and Mrs Richard Osborne, Barry Collett, Mr and Mrs M Stratton, Chris Clark*

ORKNEY

ST MARY'S HY4700   KW17 2RU
Commodore
A961

Well kept Orkney beers, enjoyable food in popular restaurant; on-site chalets. *Recommended by John Winstanley*

SKYE

CARBOST NG3731   IV47 8SR
☆ **Old Inn**
B8009

Unpretentious simply furnished bare-boards bar in idyllic peaceful spot close to Talisker distillery, friendly staff, traditional home-made food including local seafood, cream teas too, perhaps a real ale such as Isle of Skye, peat fire, darts, pool, cribbage and dominoes; TV, piped scottish music; children welcome, terrace with fine Loch Harport and Cuillin views (bar's at the back, though), sea-view bedrooms in annexe (breakfast for non-residents if you book the night before), bunkhouse, moorings and showers for yachtsmen, open all day, closed mid-winter afternoons. *Recommended by Sylvia and Tony Birbeck, Ian and Deborah Carrington, Bren and Val Speed, Phil Bryant*

ISLE ORNSAY NG7012   IV43 8QR
☆ **Eilean Iarmain**
Off A851 Broadford—Armadale

Small traditional bar at smart determinedly old-fashioned hotel in a beautiful location, friendly locals and staff, bar food most of the day from same kitchen as charming sea-view restaurant, an Isle of Skye real ale, good choice of vatted (blended) malt whiskies including its own Te Bheag, banquettes, open fire; piped gaelic music; children welcome, outside tables with spectacular views, very comfortable bedrooms. *Recommended by Kate Vogelsang*

SLIGACHAN NG4930   IV47 8SW
☆ **Sligachan Hotel**
A87 Broadford—Portree, junction with A863

Climbers' haunt in summer-opening mountain hotel, huge modern pine-clad main bar, spaciously open to ceiling rafters, with geometrically laid out dark tables and chairs on neat carpeting, splendid range of 300 malt whiskies, own-brew Cuillin beers and guests, more sedate lounge with leather bucket chairs and coal fire, hearty food from short menu, more elaborate meals in restaurant, little museum charting history of island; piped scottish music – live music some nights; children and dogs welcome, seats in garden with big play area, self-catering and campsite with caravan hook-ups, open 8am-midnight (11-11 Sun), closed Nov-Mar. *Recommended by Ian and Deborah Carrington, C A Bryson, Phil Bryant*

Wales

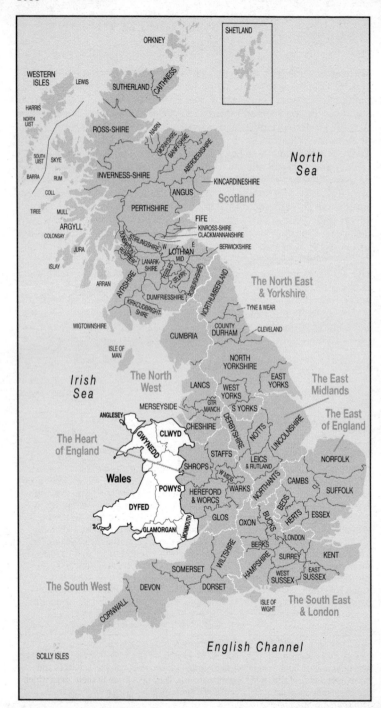

EDITORS' FAVOURITES
WALES

Wales has some truly lovely pubs and we've picked out the Olde Bulls Head at Beaumaris (a terrific all-rounder with everything from traditional bar to smart restaurant) as our **Wales Pub of the Year**. Other pubs that stand out for special mention are the Bear at Crickhowell (lovely place to stay), Plough & Harrow at Monknash (good range of real ales), Griffin at Felinfach (charmingly accomplished and **Wales Dining Pub of the Year**), and the Pant-yr-Ochain at Gresford, Corn Mill at Llangollen and Glasfryn at Mold (all relaxing Brunning & Price pubs). Three great new entries this year are the Old Point House at Angle (idyllically situated and unspoilt old seafarers' place), Riverside at Pennal (fresh refurbishment with brasserie-style food) and White Eagle at Rhoscolyn (lively with great sea views). Two other pubs of real individuality also deserve a mention: the Tafarn Sinc at Rosebush (historical re-creation of an old station halt) and the Pen-y-Gwryd at Llanberis (a deeply characterful mountaineers' haunt). Other pubs doing well and worth a visit include the Golden Groves at Burton Green (Clwyd), Druidstone Hotel at Broad Haven, Cresselly Arms at Cresswell Quay, Dyffryn Arms at Cwm Gwaun (all in Dyfed), Bell at Caerleon, Goose & Cuckoo at Rhyd-y-Meirch, Anchor at Tintern (all in Gwent), Bear at Cowbridge, Bush at St Hilary (both in South Glamorgan) and King Arthur at Reynoldston (West Glamorgan).

ANGLE   SM8703 Map 6

Old Point House £
Signed off B4320 in village, along long rough waterside track; SA71 5AS

Simple welcoming seafarers' haunt with fresh fish and waterside tables

This ruggedly built 15th-c white-painted building sits on the Pembrokeshire Coastal Path in an idyllic spot overlooking a sheltered anchorage. The approach to the pub is on an unmade road around Angle Bay, which gets cut-off about four times a year for a couple of hours by spring tides. Some of its snug little windows and picnic sets on the big gravelled terrace give charming views over the water. Run by a friendly landlord and his staff, it's been known in the area as the 'Lifeboatman's local' since the neighbouring lifeboat station opened in 1868, and has plenty of seafaring character with all its photographs and charts. Until the 1980s the tiny spartan snug bar was the only public room. It has a small length of bar on one corner: Felinfoel Double Dragon, cheap soft drinks and a concrete floor, two simple wood settles and a warming fire in a lovely old fireplace. There's also a lounge bar and a dining room; outside lavatories; readers tell us there's a good beach nearby.

They serve lots of fresh fish here, including prawn cocktail and a pint of prawns, their famous fish chowder and whatever the daily catch brings in. They also offer a more pubby menu with lunchtime sandwiches, fish pie, sausages and mash, half a rack of ribs, and vegetable risotto. They take pride in their chips which are made from local potatoes. *Benchmark main dish: haddock and chips £8.00. Two-course evening meal £15.00.*

Free house ~ Licensee Robert Noble ~ Real ale ~ (01646) 641205 ~ Children welcome ~
Dogs allowed in bar and bedrooms ~ Open 12-10(11 Sat); 12-3, 6-10; closed Tues winter;
closed two weeks in Nov ~ Bedrooms: £43/£95B

Recommended by Louise Mallard

BEAUMARIS
SH6076 Map 6

Olde Bulls Head 🍴 🍷 🛏
WALES PUB OF THE YEAR
Castle Street; LL58 8AP

**Interesting historic pub with brasserie food, around 20 wines by the
glass, and well equipped bedrooms**

The various areas at this relaxed inn cover quite a range of styles –
there's a simple but cosy bar, a popular brasserie and a smart upstairs
restaurant. It was built in 1472 and well known visitors have included
Samuel Johnson and Charles Dickens, both of whom would find much of
it familiar today. The low-beamed bar is nicely rambling, with plenty of
interesting reminders of the town's past: a rare 17th-c brass water clock,
a bloodthirsty crew of cutlasses and even an oak ducking stool tucked
among the snug alcoves. There are lots of copper and china jugs,
comfortable low-seated settles, leather-cushioned window seats, and a
good log fire. Kindly staff serve Bass, Hancocks and a guest such as
Conwy Welsh Pride on handpump. Quite a contrast, the busy brasserie
behind is lively and stylishly modern, with a wine list that includes
around 20 by the glass; the exceptionally good restaurant list runs to
120 bottles. The entrance to the pretty courtyard is closed by huge
simple-hinged door that's an astonishing 11 feet wide and 13 feet high.
Named after characters in Dickens's novels, the bedrooms are very well
equipped; some are traditional, and others more contemporary in style,
and there are also bedrooms in the Townhouse, an adjacent property with
disabled access.

🍴 Soup and sandwiches are served in the bar. The much-enjoyed brasserie menu
includes cured salmon sushi, goats cheese, mushroom and red onion filo tart,
hotpot of smoked haddock, smoked trout, tomatoes, cream and parmesan, pork and
chorizo meatballs with spaghetti, grilled cod with basil pesto, fish and chips, chilli
bean and quorn pie with mushy peas, and grilled rib-eye steak with herb butter.
Benchmark main dish: slow-cooked lamb £13.95. Two-course evening meal £18.50.

Free house ~ Licensee David Robertson ~ Real ale ~ Bar food (12-2(3 Sun), 6-9) ~
Restaurant ~ (01248) 810329 ~ Children welcome in China Bar only till 9pm ~ Open
11-11(10.30 Sun) ~ Bedrooms: £80B/£100B

*Recommended by Lucie Merrick, Peter and Josie Fawcett, Mike and Mary Carter, Bruce and
Sharon Eden, N R White, Martin Smith*

CAPEL CURIG
SH7257 Map 6

Bryn Tyrch 🛏
A5 E; LL24 0EL

**Perfectly placed for the mountains of Snowdonia, welcoming licensees,
pleasant bedrooms, and interesting food**

Large picture windows that run the length of one wall in the walkers'
bar at this friendly family owned inn in the heart of Snowdonia
National Park take in terrific views of the surrounding countryside

including the peaks of the Carneddau, Tryfan and Glyders in close range. This bar has large, communal tables, natural stone walls and Great Orme Cambria and Orme on handpump alongside a guest such as Theakstons, and they've quite a few malt whiskies, including some local ones; board games. A second relaxed bar has big menu blackboards, leather sofas round low tables, an eclectic mix of pine tables (some rescued from a local church) on its bare boards, and a coal fire. There are tables on a steep little garden at the side, and on a terrace off the breakfast room, and picnic-sets across the road on a floodlit patch of grass by a stream running down to a couple of lakes. Some of the country-style bedrooms have views.

Bar food includes lunchtime sandwiches, fried scallops with squash purée, chorizo and pancetta, twice-baked leek and shropshire blue soufflé with parsnip crayfish and pea risotto with chorizo, lamb burger with sweetcorn relish, roast butternut and sweet pepper risotto, smoked haddock and salmon fishcakes, herb-crusted bass with stir-fried vegetables, cod and chips, and braised lamb with rosemary jus. *Benchmark main dish: lamb shank £16.50. Two-course evening meal £24.40.*

Free house ~ Licensees Rachel and Neil Roberts ~ Real ale ~ Bar food (12-3(during holidays); 6-9) ~ (01690) 720223 ~ Children welcome ~ Dogs allowed in bar ~ Open 4.30-11pm(opens midday during holidays); 12-11 Sat, Sun ~ Bedrooms: £49.50B/£79.50B
Recommended by Mike and Eleanor Anderson, N R White, Paul Humphreys, Doug Kennedy

COLWYN BAY   SH8478   Map 6

Pen-y-Bryn 🍴 ♀ 🍺

B5113 Llanwrst Road, on southern outskirts; when you see the pub, turn off into Wentworth Avenue for its car park; LL29 6DD

Modern pub in great position overlooking the bay, reliable food all day, good range of drinks, obliging staff

Welcoming and well cared-for, the light and airy open-plan interior at this single-storey pub has big windows looking far across the bay and to the Great Orme. Extending around the three long sides of the bar counter, the seating and well spaced tables, oriental rugs on pale stripped boards, shelves of books, welcoming coal fires, a profusion of pictures, big pot plants, careful lighting and dark green school radiators are all typical of the pubs in this small, well-received chain. Friendly interested young staff serve Phoenix Brunning & Price, Purple Moose Snowdonia ale and three or four changing guests from brewers such as Cairngorm, Copper Dragon and Great Orme on handpump, well chosen good value wines including 20 by the glass, and more than 60 malts; board games and piped music. There are sturdy tables and chairs on a side terrace and on a lower one by a lawn with picnic-sets.

Served all day, reliable much-liked food from their changing menu could typically include substantial sandwiches, ploughman's with welsh cheeses, charcuterie for two, home-cured duck breast with pickled beetroot and orange dressing, spicy potted crab, smoked haddock kedgeree with boiled egg, crispy pork belly, apple and roast chorizo salad, grilled thai chicken with coconut rice, goats cheese and mushroom lasagne, and rump steak with watercress and horseradish butter. *Benchmark main dish: braised shoulder of lamb £16.75. Two-course evening meal £19.20.*

Brunning & Price ~ Managers Andrew Grant and Graham Price ~ Real ale ~ Bar food (12-9.30(9 Sun)) ~ (01492) 533360 ~ Children welcome ~ Open 11.30-11(10.30 Sun)

Recommended by Mike and Mary Carter, Mr and Mrs Ian King, Frank Blanchard, Bruce and Sharon Eden

CRICKHOWELL

SO2118 Map 6

Bear ★ ♀ ⇌

Brecon Road; A40; NP8 1BW

Civilised, interesting inn with splendid, old-fashioned bar area warmed by a log fire, good and sensibly priced food, comfortable bedrooms

This well established and rather fine old inn is a particularly appealing place to stay. Older bedrooms have antiques while some of the refurbished ones are in a country style, some with jacuzzis and four-poster beds, and breakfast is excellent. Reception rooms, hosted by patient yet efficient staff, have a thoroughly convivial atmosphere and are comfortably furnished. The heavily beamed lounge has fresh flowers on tables, lots of little plush-seated bentwood armchairs and handsome cushioned antique settles, and a window seat looking down on the market square. Up by the great roaring log fire, a big sofa and leather easy chairs are on rugs on oak parquet flooring. Other good antiques include a fine oak dresser filled with pewter mugs and brassware, a longcase clock and interesting prints. Brains Rev James, Rhymney Bitter Wadworths IPA and a guest such as Wickwar Severn Bore are on handpump, as well as 40 malt whiskies, vintage and late-bottled ports, unusual wines (with several by the glass); disabled lavatories. There's a small garden.

Enjoyable bar food from a changing menu (with sandwiches and baguettes) might include crayfish tail and scallop salad with thyme dressing, shredded duck with chilli sauce and parmesan shavings, salmon fishcake with wholegrain mustard, braised welsh lamb shank, liver and bacon with onions and mash, roast chicken breast with mushroom, black peppercorn and marsala cream, and local steaks; booking is advised. *Benchmark main dish: fish and chips £11.50. Two-course evening meal £23.00.*

Free house ~ Licensee Judy Hindmarsh ~ Real ale ~ Bar food ~ Restaurant ~ (01873) 810408 ~ Children welcome ~ Dogs allowed in bar and bedrooms ~ Open 11-3, 6-11; 12-3, 7-10.30 Sun ~ Bedrooms: £75S(£86B)/£92S(£102B)

Recommended by Tom and Ruth Rees, B and M Kendall, Bob and Angela Brooks, Guy Vowles, Maurice and Gill McMahon, Simon and Mandy King, Barry and Anne, Ken and Barbara Turner, Michael Mellers, Tony and Maggie Harwood, Anthony Barnes, Terry Davis, Dr and Mrs C W Thomas, Taff Thomas, LM

EAST ABERTHAW

ST0366 Map 6

Blue Anchor ◖ £

B4265; CF62 3DD

Ancient thatched pub with five real ales

A charming warren of little rooms and cosy corners is contained within this character-laden 600-year-old tavern. The building has massive walls, low-beamed rooms and tiny doorways, with open fires everywhere, including one in an inglenook with antique oak seats built into its stripped stonework. Other seats and tables are worked into a series of chatty little alcoves, and the more open front bar still has an ancient lime-ash floor. Brains Bitter, Theakstons Old Peculier, Wadworths 6X and Wye

Valley HPA are on handpump, alongside a changing guest, perhaps from Tomos Watkins; games machine. Rustic seats shelter peacefully among tubs and troughs of flowers outside, with stone tables on a newer terrace. The pub can get very full in the evenings and on summer weekends, and it's used as a base by a couple of local motorbike clubs. A path from here leads to the shingly flats of the estuary.

Good value bar food includes baguettes, smoked haddock fishcakes with mustard tarragon sauce, breaded goats cheese with roast squash and pesto and rocket salad, ploughman's, pork and leek sausages, fried hake fillet with marinated courgette, avocado and lime salad, rib-eye steak, and daily specials such as thai green curry, and chicken breast with madeira cream. *Benchmark main dish: faggots with mash and mushy peas £8.75. Two-course evening meal £14.00.*

Free house ~ Licensee Jeremy Coleman ~ Real ale ~ Bar food (not Sun evening) ~ Restaurant ~ (01446) 750329 ~ Children welcome ~ Dogs allowed in bar ~ Open 11-11; 12-10.30 Sun

Recommended by H L Dennis, Roger Fox

FELINFACH

SO0933   Map 6

Griffin

A470 NE of Brecon; LD3 0UB

WALES DINING PUB OF THE YEAR

A classy dining pub for enjoying good, unpretentious cooking featuring lots of home-grown vegetables; upbeat rustic décor, nice bedrooms

Readers say 'charming', 'fabulous', 'difficult to fault', and 'one of the best pubs in the *Guide*' about this tremendously accomplished dining pub that pays close attention to getting every aspect of its business just right, and looks after its guests extremely well. They stock a terrific range of drinks, serve great carefully sourced food, care about the children and dogs that visit them and set a relaxed atmosphere. The back bar is quite pubby in an up-to-date way: three leather sofas sit around a low table on pitted quarry tiles, by a high slate hearth with a log fire, and behind them mixed stripped seats around scrubbed kitchen tables on bare boards, and a bright blue-and-ochre colour scheme, with some modern prints. The acoustics are pretty lively, due to so much bare flooring and uncurtained windows; maybe piped radio. The two smallish front dining rooms that link through to the back bar are attractive: on the left, mixed dining chairs around mainly stripped tables on flagstones, and white-painted rough stone walls, with a cream-coloured Aga in a big stripped-stone embrasure; on the right, similar furniture on bare boards, big modern prints on terracotta walls and smart dark curtains. Efficient staff serve a fine array of drinks, including a thoughtful choice of wines (with 20 by the glass and carafe), welsh spirits, cocktails, an award-winning local bottled cider, locally sourced apple juice, non-alcoholic cocktails made with produce from their garden, unusual continental and local bottled beers, sherries and beers from Breconshire, Montys, Otley and Tomos Watkins, on handpump. Good wheelchair access, and outside tables. This is a lovely place to stay, with nothing missed. Bedrooms are comfortable and tastefully decorated, and the hearty breakfasts nicely informal: you make your own toast and help yourself to home-made marmalade and jam. Children can play with the landlady's dog and visit the chickens in the henhouse and dogs may sit with owners at certain tables while dining.

🍴 Using carefully sourced ingredients and organic produce from the pub's own kitchen garden (from which the surplus is often for sale), not cheap but consistently good food from the lunch and evening menus might include ploughman's, mozzarella with boar saucisson, broccoli and almonds, braised cuttlefish with roast chorizo and rice, shepherd's pie, roast pork belly with squash, mushrooms, wild garlic and thyme butter, roast hake in paprika with poached egg, capers and spinach, tomato, olive and cheese tart, rabbit with spinach and ricotta ravioli and grain mustard cream, and braised shin of beef with cep risotto, asparagus and wet garlic. They also do a more reasonably priced set-course menu. *Benchmark main dish: pork loin with garlic pomme purée, black pudding, pancetta and shallots £18.00. Two-course evening meal £28.00.*

Free house ~ Licensees Charles and Edmund Inkin and Julie Bell ~ Real ale ~ Bar food (12-2(2.30 Fri-Sun), 6-9(9.30 Fri, Sat)) ~ Restaurant ~ (01874) 620111 ~ Children welcome ~ Dogs allowed in bar and bedrooms ~ Acoustic session lunchtimes first and third Sun of month ~ Open 11.30-11(10.30 Sun); closed four days in early Jan ~ Bedrooms: £105B/£120B

Recommended by K Hunt, M Smith, Mike and Mary Carter, David and Cathrine Whiting, David Heath, Mrs P Bishop, Kate Vogelsang, Suzi Clay, MLR, Bernard Stradling

GRESFORD   SJ3453   Map 6

Pant-yr-Ochain 🍴 ♼ ◪

Off A483 on N edge of Wrexham: at roundabout take A5156 (A534) towards Nantwich, then first left towards the Flash; LL12 8TY

Thoughtfully run, gently refined dining pub with rooms, good food all day, very wide range of drinks, pretty lakeside garden

Doing exceedingly well at the moment, this 16th-c former country house is a particularly fine example of the pubs in the Brunning & Price chain. Its light and airy rooms are stylishly decorated, with a wide range of interesting prints and bric-a-brac, and a good mix of individually chosen country furnishings, including comfortable seats for relaxing as well as more upright ones for eating, and there's a recently rebuilt conservatory as well as a good open fire; one area is set out as a library, with floor-to-ceiling bookshelves. Their terrific range of drinks includes Flowers Original, Snowdonia Gold, Phoenix Brunning & Price Original and a couple of guests from brewers such as Butty Bach, Slaters, Wincle and Wye Valley, a good range of decent wines (strong on up-front new world ones), with 15 by the glass, and around 100 malt whiskies. Disabled access is good. The particularly charming garden has solid wooden furniture overlooking a pretty lake visited by waterfowl, mature trees and shrubs, lovely herbaceous borders and thriving box-edged herb beds.

🍴 Thoughtfully prepared food from a well balanced daily changing menu, using free-range eggs and chicken, includes sandwiches and ploughman's, with changing dishes such as moroccan lamb skewer with aubergine pickle and flat bread, fig, roquefort and chestnut tart with red wine dressing, spiced tempura mackerel fillet with mango chutney, crab linguine with ginger, red chilli and coriander, hazelnut gnocchi with mushroom sauce, wilted spinach and fried duck egg, beef, mushroom and ale casserole with herb dumplings, and seared duck breast with beetroot and potato rösti and red wine sauce. *Benchmark main dish: battered fish and chips £11.95. Two-course evening meal £18.20.*

Brunning & Price ~ Licensee James Meakin ~ Real ale ~ Bar food (12-9.30(9 Sun)) ~ (01978) 853525 ~ Well behaved children welcome ~ Dogs allowed in bar ~ Open 11.30-11; 12-10.30 Sun

LLANBERIS

SH6655 Map 6

Pen-y-Gwryd 🍺

Nant Gwynant; at junction of A498 and A4086, ie across mountains from Llanberis – OS Sheet 115 map reference 660558; LL55 4NT

Run by the same family since 1947, an illustrious favourite with the mountain fraternity, with a slightly eccentric but cheerily simple atmosphere

With its mountaineering fraternity, scheduled suppers and simple interior, this isolated inn reminds us just a little of an alpine refuge. Mentioned in the Everest Museum in Darjeeling, this long-established climbers' haunt, high in the mountains of Snowdonia, was used as a training base for the 1953 Everest team. Their fading signatures can still be made out, scrawled on the ceiling, and among the memorabilia is the rope that connected Hilary and Tensing on top of the mountain. One snug little room in the homely slate-floored log cabin bar has built-in wall benches and sturdy country chairs. From here you can look out on the surrounding mountain landscape, including to precipitous Moel Siabod beyond the lake opposite. A smaller room has a worthy collection of illustrious boots from famous climbs, and a cosy panelled smoke room has more fascinating climbing mementoes and equipment; darts, pool, board games and table tennis. Purple Moose Glaslyn and Madogs are on handpump and they've several malts. Staying in the comfortable but basic bedrooms can be quite an experience, and the excellent, traditional breakfast is served between 8.30 and 9am (they may serve earlier); dogs £2 a night. The inn has its own chapel (built for the millennium and dedicated by the Archbishop of Wales), sauna and outdoor natural pool, and the garden overlooks a lake.

The short choice of simple, good-value but carefully sourced home-made lunchtime bar food (you order through a hatch) includes filled rolls, ploughman's and quiche of the day. The three- or four-course hearty fixed-price meal in the evening restaurant is signalled by a gong at 7.30pm – if you're late, you'll miss it; maybe sweet potato and coconut soup followed by welsh cutlet of lamb with herby crust and shallots glazed in port. *Benchmark main dish: roast lamb £8.50.*

Free house ~ Licensee Jane Pullee ~ Real ale ~ Bar food (12-2, evening meal at 7.30pm) ~ Restaurant (evening) ~ (01286) 870211 ~ Children welcome ~ Dogs welcome ~ Open 11-11; closed all Nov-Dec, and midweek Jan-Feb ~ Bedrooms: £40/£80(£96B)

Please keep sending us reports. We rely on readers for news of new discoveries, and particularly for news of changes – however slight – at the fully described pubs:
feedback@goodguides.com, or (no stamp needed)
The Good Pub Guide, FREEPOST TN1569, Wadhurst, E Sussex TN5 7BR.

LLANELIAN-YN-RHOS

SH8676 Map 6

White Lion

Signed off A5830 (shown as B5383 on some maps) and B5381, S of Colwyn Bay; LL29 8YA

Pretty pub with friendly staff, pleasantly traditional bar, and roomy dining area

You'll find the welcoming landlord behind the bar at this cosy looking village inn, with his friendly wife and staff helping out elsewhere. It comprises two distinct parts, each with its own cheery personality, linked by a broad flight of steps. Up at the top is a neat and very spacious dining area, while down at the other end is a traditional old bar, with antique high-backed settles angling snugly around a big fireplace, and flagstones by the counter where they serve Marstons Burton and Pedigree, a guest such as Brakespear and a good wine list; on the left, another dining area has jugs hanging from the beams and teapots above the window. Prompt service; piped music. There are tables in an attractive courtyard (also used for parking) next to the church.

Tasty food includes sandwiches, pâté, steak and kidney pie, fish stew, macaroni cheese and daily specials such as grilled pork chop with caramelised apple and cider sauce, salmon and smoked haddock fishcakes, and fried duck with rich berry sauce. *Benchmark main dish: roast beef £9.95. Two-course evening meal £17.00.*

Free house ~ Licensee Simon Cole ~ Real ale ~ Bar food (12-2, 6-9; 12-2.30, 6-8.30 Sun) ~ Restaurant ~ (01492) 515807 ~ Children welcome ~ Live jazz Tues evening, bluegrass Weds evening ~ Open 12-3.30, 6-11(midnight Sat); 12-4, 6-10.30 Sun; closed Mon except bank holidays

Recommended by Michael and Jenny Back, Noel Grundy

LLANFERRES

SJ1860 Map 6

Druid

A494 Mold—Ruthin; CH7 5SN

Warmly welcoming traditional inn with beams, log fire, well-liked food, and wonderful views

Originally a farmhouse, this extended 17th-c whitewashed inn in the Alyn Valley has glorious views across to the Clwydian Range; you can enjoy the setting from tables outside at the front and from the broad bay window in the civilised, smallish plush lounge. The hills are also in sight from the bigger beamed back bar, with its two handsome antique oak settles, pleasant mix of more modern furnishings, quarry-tiled area by the log fire, and three-legged cat, Chu. Marstons Burton, Ringwood Boondoggle and a guest such as Wychwood Hobgoblin are on handpump alongside an array of up to 30 malt whiskies. A games room has darts and pool, along with board games; piped music, TV. There are superb nearby hill walks along the Offa's Dyke Path and up to the summit of Moel Famau.

Bar food (which you can eat in the bar or restaurant) might include several soups, filled baps, steak and ale pie, baked trout with lemon, mediterranean-style lamb shank, mushrooms stuffed with stilton, and sirloin steak with mushroom sauce. *Benchmark main dish: steak, ale and mushroom pie £10.45. Two-course evening meal £16.20.*

Union Pub Company ~ Lease James Dolan ~ Real ale ~ Bar food (12-3, 6-9; 12-9 Fri-Sun and bank holidays) ~ Restaurant ~ (01352) 810225 ~ Children welcome ~ Dogs allowed in bar and bedrooms ~ Open 12-3, 5.30-11; 12-11 Sat-Sun ~ Bedrooms: £48S/£70S

Recommended by Maurice and Gill McMahon, Roger and Diana Morgan, Ian Phillips, Christine and Neil Townend, Mrs Margo Finlay, Jörg Kasprowski, David Jackman

LLANFRYNACH   SO0725   Map 6

White Swan ♀

Village signposted from B4558, off A40 E of Brecon – take second turn to village, which is also signed to pub; LD3 7BZ

Comfortably upmarket country dining pub with a pretty terrace

There's a nice contrast here between the pubby bar and rather smart dining rooms at this isolated old place in the heart of the Brecon Beacons. The original part of the beamed bar has stripped stone and flagstones, with sturdy oak tables and nice carver chairs in a polished country-kitchen style, a woodburning stove, and leather sofas and armchairs in groups around low tables. On handpump are Brains Bitter, Breconshire Brecon County and Rhymney Bitter; good wines and coffees; piped music. The greater part of the building consists of the apricot-walled high-ceilinged extension which is light and airy, with bare boards and smartly upholstered harlequin sets of chairs around each table. The charming secluded back terrace has stone and wood tables is attractively divided into sections by low privet hedges and wisteria. From here, there are plenty of undemanding saunters along the towpath of the Monmouthshire and Brecon Canal or more energetic hikes up the main Brecon Beacons' summits; more reports please.

The good food is very much the centre of attention, with changing lunch menus and à la carte evening fare. As well as ploughman's, and baguettes and salads, dishes might include trio of bruschetta, crumbed confit duck leg around a boiled egg with pickled vegetables and cumberland dressing, crab spring roll with fennel and orange salad, venison drizzled with chocolate oil with poached pear, beetroot mash and parsnip ice-cream, chicken breast in serrano ham with spring vegetable risotto and cheese and asparagus scone, smoked butternut and roast vegetable risotto with roast mushrooms and butternut ice-cream, and steaks. *Benchmark main dish: welsh lamb three ways with spinach and leek mash, welsh cake with minted cucumber sorbet and jus £17.95. Two-course evening meal £23.80.*

Free house ~ Licensee Richard Griffiths ~ Real ale ~ Bar food ~ Restaurant ~ (01874) 665276 ~ Children welcome ~ Open 11.30-3, 6.30-11.30(midnight Sat); closed Mon, Tues and first two weeks in Jan

Recommended by David and Cathrine Whiting, David Heath, Taff Thomas

LLANGOLLEN   SJ2142   Map 6

Corn Mill ⑪ ♀ ◖

Dee Lane, very narrow lane off Castle Street (A539) just S of bridge; nearby parking can be tricky, may be best to use public park on Parade Street/East Street and walk; LL20 8PN

Excellent on all counts, with personable young staff, super food all day, good beers, and a fascinating riverside building

Dramatically positioned right on the rocky rushing River Dee, this enjoyable all-rounder is housed in a restored mill. Quite a bit of the working machinery remains – most obviously the great waterwheel, (sometimes turning) and the interior has been interestingly refitted with pale pine flooring on stout beams, a striking open stairway with gleaming timber and tensioned steel rails, and mainly stripped-stone walls. A bustling chatty atmosphere greets you, with quick service from plenty of pleasant young staff, good-sized dining tables, big rugs, thoughtfully chosen pictures (many to do with water) and lots of pot plants. One of the two serving bars, away from the water, has a much more local feel, with pews on dark slate flagstones, daily papers, and regulars on the bar stools. As well as Phoenix Brunning & Price, they have a great range of drinks, with four guests from brewers such as Caledonian Deuchars and Woodland, around 50 sensibly priced malt whiskies and a decent wine choice. A long narrow deck along one side of the building juts out over the water, with views from its teak tables and chairs across the river to the steam trains puffing away at the nearby station, and you may see a horse-drawn barge on the Llangollen Canal.

The pub can get busy, so do book if you're planning to eat. Good food from a daily changing menu includes sandwiches, ploughman's, crab linguine with red chilli and coriander, gnocchi with roast butternut and salsa verde, steak, mushroom and ale pie, fried bass fillet with sautéed bacon, roast pork belly with dauphinoise potatoes and grain mustard sauce, marinated chicken breast with saffron, pea and broad bean risotto and watercress sauce, and rump steak with horseradish butter. *Benchmark main dish: fish and chips £11.95. Two-course evening meal £17.60.*

Brunning & Price ~ Manager Andrew Barker ~ Real ale ~ Bar food (12-9.30(9 Sun)) ~ (01978) 869555 ~ Children welcome ~ Open 12-11(10.30 Sun)

Recommended by Brian Brooks, Bruce and Sharon Eden, Tony Hobden, Clive Watkin, Dennis Jones, Alastair Stevenson, N R White, Martin Smith

MAENTWROG
SH6640   Map 6

Grapes
A496; village signed from A470; LL41 4HN

Lively inn with good mix of customers, pleasant garden views; accommodation

In the heart of the Snowdonia National Park, this rambling old inn has three bars, each furnished with stripped pitch-pine pews, settles, and pillars and carvings, mostly salvaged from chapels; elsewhere are soft furnishings. Warming woodburning stoves are on the go in winter, with one in the great hearth of the restaurant. Four beers on handpump are all from Evan Evans – Best, Cwrw, Warrior, and they bring in a seasonal guest; piped music, TV, darts; disabled lavatories. From the good-sized conservatory you can see trains on the Ffestiniog Railway puffing through the wood, beyond the pleasant back terrace and walled garden.

Bar food might include prawn cocktail, welsh rarebit on rosemary focaccia, scampi and chips, chicken and mushroom pie, curry of the day, tenderloin of pork with creamy cider sauce, pesto risotto, and duck breast with orange and ginger sauce. *Benchmark main dish: pork belly and ribs £9.95. Two-course evening meal £19.70.*

Evan Evans ~ Manager Simon Williams ~ Real ale ~ Bar food (12-2.30, 6-9(8.30 Sun)) ~ Restaurant ~ (01766) 590208 ~ Children welcome ~ Dogs allowed in bar ~ Open 12-11(midnight Sat) ~ Bedrooms: £50B/£85B

Recommended by Christopher Viner

MOLD   SJ2465   Map 6

Glasfryn ⑪ ♀ ◖

N of the centre on Raikes Lane (parallel to the A5119), just past the well signposted Theatr Clwyd; CH7 6LR

Open-plan bistro-style pub with inventive, upmarket food available all day, nice décor, wide drinks' choice

This is a lively place run with verve by the enthusiastic and friendly licensee and staff. Decorated in this fine chain's usual successful style, its open-plan interior is cleverly laid out to create plenty of nice quiet corners. It has a mix of informal attractive country furnishings, turkey-style rugs on bare boards, deep red (some high) ceilings, a warming fire and plenty of homely close-hung pictures. Besides 20 wines by the glass, local apple juice, farm cider and around 70 whiskies, they've nine beers on handpump, with Facers Flintshire, Phoenix Brunning & Price Original and Purple Moose Snowdonia, alongside swiftly changing guests from brewers such as Greene King and Hobsons; board games. On warm days, the large terrace in front of the pub makes an idyllic place to sit out by the wooden tables – you get sweeping views of the Clwydian Hills. Theatr Clwyd is just across the road.

From a daily changing menu, the full choice of good, well prepared food might include sandwiches, ploughman's, ham and pea croquettes, potted salt beef, fish pie, steak and kidney pudding, salmon fillet with hot samphire and lemon butter sauce, monkfish tikka masala with vegetable bhajis, roast five spice pork belly with pak choi, and rump steak with horseradish butter. *Benchmark main dish: smoked haddock and salmon fishcakes £9.95. Two-course evening meal £18.00.*

Brunning & Price ~ Manager Graham Arathoon ~ Real ale ~ Bar food (12-9.30(9 Sun)) ~ (01352) 750500 ~ Children welcome ~ Dogs allowed in bar ~ Open 11.30-11; 12-10.30 Sun

Recommended by Brian Brooks, Bruce and Sharon Eden, Clive Watkin, Steve Whalley, Chris Flynn, Wendy Jones, C A Bryson, Andy and Jill Kassube, David Jackman

MONKNASH   SS9170   Map 6

Plough & Harrow ◖ £

Signposted Marcross, Broughton off B4265 St Brides Major—Llantwit Major – turn left at end of Water Street; OS Sheet 170 map reference 920706; CF71 7QQ

Old building full of history and character, with a good choice of real ales

Dating back to the early 12th c, this ancient-feeling and idyllic looking country pub was once part of a monastic grange. Built with massively thick stone walls, the dimly lit unspoilt main bar used to be the scriptures room and mortuary. The heavily black-beamed ceiling has ancient ham hooks, an intriguing arched doorway to the back, and a comfortably informal mix of furnishings that includes three fine stripped-pine settles on the broad flagstones. There's a log fire in a huge fireplace with a side bread oven large enough to feed a village. The room on the left has lots of Wick Rugby Club memorabilia (it's their club room); daily papers, piped music and darts. It can get crowded at weekends, when it's popular with families. Six real ales, with up to eight at the weekend on handpump or tapped from the cask, include Everards Hancocks HB and Wye Valley HPA alongside changing guests from brewers such as Bass, Newmans, Otley, St Austell and Wickwar, and they hold beer festivals in June and

September. They also have a good range of local farm cider and welsh and malt whiskies; helpful service from knowledgeable staff. There are picnic-sets in the front garden which has a boules pitch, and they hold barbecues out here in summer. Dogs are welcome in the bar – but not while food is being served.

🍴 Bar food includes sandwiches, tempura king prawns with chilli mayonnaise, smoked salmon with caper salad, beef and ale casserole, chicken curry, faggots and mushy peas, salmon and coriander fishcakes, goats cheese and mediterranean tartlet, lava bread with bacon and sauté potatoes, and roast pork belly with mustard mash and sweet cider sauce. *Benchmark main dish: salmon and coriander cakes £7.95. Two-course evening meal £13.10.*

Free house ~ Licensee Paula Jones ~ Real ale ~ Bar food (12-2.30(5 Sat, Sun), 6-9; not Sun evening) ~ Restaurant ~ (01656) 890209 ~ Children welcome ~ Live music Sat evening ~ Open 12-11

Recommended by James Morris, Taff Thomas, R T and J C Moggridge, Kevin Thomas, Nina Randall

NEWPORT
SN0539   Map 6

Golden Lion 🛏
East Street (A487); SA42 0SY

Nicely redone, friendly local, with tasty food, pleasant staff, and well appointed bedrooms

The genuinely pubby bar rubs along nicely with the stylish restaurant and hotel side of this pleasant country inn. There's a welcoming local atmosphere in its cosy series of beamed rooms, some with distinctive old settles, and three changing beers from brewers such as Hook Norton, Sharps and St Austell on handpump; pool, darts, juke box, TV and games machine. The stylish dining room has elegant blond wood oak furniture, whitewashed walls and potted plants. There are tables outside at the front and in a side garden; good disabled access and facilities. The bedrooms are very comfortable.

🍴 Enjoyable, carefully presented food includes lunchtime sandwiches, ploughman's and burgers, thai chicken curry, italian bean casserole, steak and ale pie, cod and chips, chicken breast with spicy jerk sauce, and steaks. *Benchmark main dish: fried hake with sauce of the day £13.95. Two-course evening meal £18.70.*

Free house ~ Licensee Daron Paish ~ Real ale ~ Bar food (12-2.30, 6.30-9) ~ Restaurant ~ (01239) 820321 ~ Children welcome ~ Dogs allowed in bar and bedrooms ~ Open midday-2am ~ Bedrooms: £70B/£90B

Recommended by R T and J C Moggridge, Angela Crum Ewing, M E and F J Thomasson

OLD RADNOR
SO2459   Map 6

Harp 🍽 🛏
Village signposted off A44 Kington—New Radnor in Walton; LD8 2RH

Delightfully placed with cottagey bar and tasty food; comfortable bedrooms

This charmingly evocative stone-built inn is in a glorious hilltop position at the end of a lane in a tiny village. Loved equally by locals and tourists, the warmly welcoming public bar has high-backed settles, an antique reader's chair and other elderly chairs around a log fire; board games, cribbage. The snug slate-floored lounge has a handsome curved antique settle, a log fire in a fine inglenook, and lots of local books and guides for residents; a dining area is off to the right. They have two changing real ales from brewers such as Hobsons and Wye Valley, five farm ciders and perries, local apple juice and several malt whiskies, and they hold a beer and cider festival in June; friendly, helpful service. Tables out on the grassy area beneath a sycamore tree have fabulous views across to the high massif of Radnor Forest. The impressive village church is worth a look for its interesting early organ case (Britain's oldest), fine rood screen and ancient font.

Featuring produce from the publicans' own garden and other carefully sourced seasonal ingredients, including lamb from the local butcher's flock, the well liked food typically includes evening dishes such as leek and nettle soup, grilled plaice fillets with warm salad of summer vegetables and couscous, and shoulder of welsh lamb and aromatic spices, baked aubergine, tomato and spelt tabbouleh. They serve fish and chips Saturday lunchtime and a roast Sunday lunchtime. *Benchmark main dish: welsh black rump steak £16.00. Two-course evening meal £18.70.*

Free house ~ Licensees Chris Ireland and Angela Lyne ~ Real ale ~ Bar food (12-2.30 Sat, Sun; 6.30-9; not Sun evening) ~ (01544) 350655 ~ Children welcome ~ Dogs allowed in bar and bedrooms ~ Open 6-11; 12-3, 6-11 Sat; 12-3, 6-10.30 Sun; closed weekday lunchtimes, all day Mon (except bank holidays when 12-3, 6-11) ~ Bedrooms: £45B/£75B
Recommended by Chris Wall, Mr and Mrs J Mandeville, John Taylor, Marcus Thorpe

OVERTON BRIDGE   SJ3542   Map 6
Cross Foxes 🍴 ♉
A539 W of Overton, near Erbistock; LL13 0DR

Terrific river views from well run 18th-c coaching inn with good food and extensive drinks' range

Good oak chairs and tables on a raised terrace and one light and airy dining room with a curved wall of great big sash windows at this beautifully placed Brunning & Price pub have really lovely views over the River Dee sweeping past below; picnic-sets down on a lawn are even closer to the water. The ancient low-beamed bar, with its red tiled floor, dark timbers, a warm fire in the big inglenook and built-in old pews, is more traditional than you'd usually expect from this small chain, though the characteristic turkey rugs and frame-to-frame pictures are present, as they are in the dining areas; newspapers. Friendly competent staff serve Brakspear, Jennings Cumberland and a couple of guests from brewers such as Ringwood and Wychwood from handpumps, a farm cider, 50 malts, an excellent range of armagnacs and a changing choice of around 27 wines by the glass.

As well as sandwiches, carefully prepared bar food from a tempting menu might include ploughman's, pressed ham hock and mushroom terrine, home-smoked trout with new potato, red onion and caper salad and mustard dressing, coq au vin with tarragon mash, crab, clam and mussel linguine, pork and sage sausages with champ mash, fried tiger prawn salad with roast peppers and courgettes and orange and chilli dressing, and rump steak with watercress and horseradish butter. *Benchmark main dish: honey-roast ham, egg and chips £9.95. Two-course evening meal £17.80.*

Brunning & Price ~ Manager Ian Pritchard-Jones ~ Real ale ~ Bar food (12-9.30(9 Sun)) ~ (01978) 780380 ~ Children welcome ~ Dogs allowed in bar ~ Open 12-11(10.30 Sun)
Recommended by S P Watkin, P A Taylor, T M Griffiths, Brian and Anna Marsden, Dave Webster,

Sue Holland, Bruce and Sharon Eden, Peter and Josie Fawcett

PANTYGELLI

SO3017 Map 6

Crown ♀ ◖

Old Hereford Road N of Abergavenny; off A40 by war memorial via Pen y Pound, passing leisure centre; Pantygelli also signposted from A465; NP7 7HR

Prettily placed country pub, attractive inside and out, with good food and drinks

The licensee couple here take great pride in the running of this friendly country free house which is in a quiet spot between the Sugarloaf and Skirrid Mountains. The neat and efficient staff take their cue from the friendly hands-on owners, giving a warmly welcoming atmosphere. The dark flagstoned bar, with sturdy timber props and beams, has a piano at the back, darts opposite, a log fire in the stone fireplace, and – from its slate-roofed counter – well kept Bass, Rhymney Best, Wye Valley HPA and a guest such as Otley Boss on handpump, Stowford Press farm cider, good wines by the glass, and good coffees. On the left are four smallish, linked, carpeted dining rooms, the front pair separated by a massive stone chimneybreast; thoughtfully chosen individual furnishings and lots of attractive prints by local artists make it all thoroughly civilised; piped music. Comfortable wrought-iron and wicker chairs on the flower-filled front terrace look up from this lush valley to the lower slopes of the Black Mountains; a smaller back terrace is surrounded by lavender.

Bar food includes baguettes and pubby standards, with additional daily specials such as fried scallops with grilled aubergine and chorizo, crab and celeriac rémoulade with parmesan tuile, duck breast with blackcurrant and rosemary sauce, braised local beef with horseradish mash, pea purée and wild rocket, vegetable and coconut curry, and bass on red wine puy lentils with slow-roasted tomatoes. *Benchmark main dish: cold welsh black beef with bubble and squeak £9.75. Two-course evening meal £16.20.*

Free house ~ Licensees Steve and Cherrie Chadwick ~ Real ale ~ Bar food (12-2, 7-9; not Sun evening) ~ Restaurant ~ (01873) 853314 ~ Children welcome ~ Dogs allowed in bar ~ Open 12-2.30(3 weekends), 6-11(10.30 Sun); closed Mon lunchtime

Recommended by Trevor Swindells, Carol Phillips

PENNAL

SH6900 Map 6

Riverside

A493; opposite church; SY20 9DW

Fresh refurbishment with tasty food and local beers

Bought not long ago by its enthusiastic licensees, this 16th-c building has been neatly refurbished with fresh green and white walls, slate flooring tiles, a woodburning stove, modern light wood dining furniture and some funky fabrics. High-backed stools are lined up along the stone-fronted counter where they serve three changing beers such as Conwy Welsh Pride, Purple Moose Madog and Salopian Golden Greene and around a dozen wines by the glass; piped music, TV, and garden.

Tasty brasserie-style bar food includes goats cheese and red onion tart, fried scallops with pea purée and crispy pancetta, cured meat platter, steak burger, chicken caesar salad, duck breast with port, redcurrant and tarragon sauce, fish stew, fillet of salmon with hollandaise, and fillet steak with mushroom and brandy sauce. *Benchmark main dish: fried fillets of bass with king prawns and orange, thyme and ginger sauce £14.95. Two-course evening meal £18.70.*

Free house ~ Licensees Glyn and Corina Davies ~ Real ale ~ Bar food (12-2.30, 6-9.30) ~ Restaurant ~ (01654) 791285 ~ Children welcome ~ Dogs allowed in bar ~ Open 11-11(12.30 Sat, 10.30 Sun); closed two weeks in Jan
Recommended by Mike and Mary Carter

RAGLAN   SO3609   Map 6

Clytha Arms 🍽 🍺 🛏
Clytha, off Abergavenny road – former A40, now declassified; NP7 9BW

Beautifully placed in parkland, a relaxing spot for enjoying good food and beer; comfortable bedrooms

Run by charming licensees, this civilised white house is the sort of relaxed place where everyone feels welcome, from locals who've walked here for a pint, to diners in the contemporary linen-set restaurant. With long heated verandahs and diamond-paned windows, it's comfortable, light and airy, with scrubbed wood floors, pine settles, big faux fur cushions on the window seats, a good mix of old country furniture and a couple of warming fires. An impressive choice of drinks includes well kept Felinfoel Best, Rhymney Bitter, Wye Valley and four swiftly changing guests, an extensive wine list with about a dozen or so by the glass, over 20 malt whiskies, about three farm ciders and maybe their own perry. They have occasional cider and beer festivals; darts, shove-ha'penny, boules, bar billiards, draughts, large-screen TV for rugby matches, and board games. The pub has its own english setter and collie. Don't miss the murals in the lavatories. The bedrooms are comfortable, with good welsh breakfasts, and this is a nice setting on the edge of Clytha Park.

🍽 As well as a tapas menu (part welsh, part spanish) and sandwiches, the enjoyable menu includes seared scallops with provençale vegetables, pork and mushroom faggots, beer-battered oysters with coconut and chilli sauce, salmon in filo pastry, malay fruit curry, stuffed loin of lamb with sweetbreads and wild garlic, boar and duck cassoulet, and grilled plaice with orange and chilli butter. *Benchmark main dish: home-made faggots £9.95. Two-course evening meal £24.00.*

Free house ~ Licensees Andrew and Beverley Canning ~ Real ale ~ Bar food (12.30-2.15(2.30 Sun), 7-9.30; not Sun evening) ~ Restaurant ~ (01873) 840206 ~ Children welcome ~ Dogs allowed in bar and bedrooms ~ Open 12-3.30, 6-11; 12-11.30 Fri-Sun; closed Mon lunchtime ~ Bedrooms: £65B/£90B
Recommended by Dr A Y Drummond, Richard Cole, Peter Dearing, Guy Vowles, the Didler

RHOSCOLYN   SH2675   Map 6

White Eagle 🍺
Off B4545 South of Holyhead; LL65 2NJ

Modern reconstruction with friendly welcome and half a dozen real ales

Rebuilt almost from scratch on the site of an old pub, this immaculately kept modern-feeling place is spacious enough to deal with the crowds that gather here despite its remote setting. Its airy rooms are relaxed and friendly with staff coping well under pressure. Cobblers Ale (brewed for the pub by Thornbridge), Marstons Best and Pedigree, Weetwood Eastgate and a guest such as Great Orme Celtica are served

from a smart new oak counter with rows of shiny glasses hung above.
There are terrific views of the sea from decking and picnic-sets in the
good-sized garden, and a lane runs from here down to the beach.

🍴 Quickly served generous bar food includes sandwiches, prawn cocktail, pork
liver pâté, warm chive scone with ham hock and leek and cheese sauce,
gammon steak, bass with salsa verde and roast cherry tomatoes, chicken breast with
sweet corn and spring onion risotto, burgers, sweet potato, spinach and puy lentil
curry, and smoked chicken caesar salad. *Benchmark main dish: haddock, chips and
peas £12.00. Two-course evening meal £18.40.*

Free house ~ Licensees John and Alex Timpson ~ Real ale ~ Bar food (12-2.30, 6-9; 12-9
Sat, Sun) ~ (01407) 860267 ~ Children welcome ~ Dogs allowed in bar ~ Open 12-11
(10.30 Sun); 12-3, 6-11 weekdays in winter except during school holidays

*Recommended by Margaret and Trefor Howorth, Michael Drury, Brian and Anna Marsden,
Bruce and Sharon Eden, Mrs Cooper, Martyn Sibley, Paul Humphreys, N R White*

ROSEBUSH

SN0729   Map 6

Tafarn Sinc

B4329 Haverfordwest—Cardigan; SA66 7QU

Unique 19th-c curio, a slice of social and industrial history

Laden with idiosyncratic character, this firmly run place must be one of
the most eccentric pub buildings in all of Wales. A maroon-painted
corrugated iron shed, it was built in 1876 as a basic hotel on a long-
defunct railway serving quarries beneath the Preseli Hills. The halt itself
has been more or less re-created, even down to life-size dummy
passengers waiting out on the platform; the sizeable garden is
periodically enlivened by the sounds of steam trains chuffing through –
actually broadcast from a replica signal box. Inside is really interesting,
almost a museum of local history, with sawdust on the floor, hams,
washing and goodness knows what else hung from the ceiling, and an
appealingly buoyant atmosphere, and you will hear Welsh spoken here.
The bar has plank panelling, an informal mix of old chairs and pews, a
woodburner, and Cwrw Tafarn Sinc (brewed locally for the pub),
Worthington and a guest such as Evan Evans Warrior on handpump;
piped music, darts, games machine, board games and TV.

🍴 Basic food includes gammon steak with pineapple, vegetable lasagne, lamb
burgers, and steaks; no starters. *Benchmark main dish: faggots and mushy
peas £10.50.*

Free house ~ Licensee Hafwen Davies ~ Real ale ~ Bar food (12-2, 6-9) ~ Restaurant ~
(01437) 532214 ~ Children welcome ~ Open 12-midnight(1am Sat, 11pm Sun); closed
Mon except bank and summer holidays

*Recommended by Ann and Tony Bennett-Hughes, John Hancock, John and Enid Morris, the Didler,
R T and J C Moggridge, Simon Watkins, Paul Goldman, Pete Flower*

Stars after the name of a pub show exceptional quality. One star means most people
(after reading the report to see just why the star has been won) would think a
special trip worth while. Two stars mean that the pub is really outstanding –
for its particular qualities it could hardly be bettered.

SKENFRITH Wales   SO4520   Map 6

Bell 🍴 ♈ 🛏

Just off B4521, NE of Abergavenny and N of Monmouth; NP7 8UH

Elegant but relaxed, generally much praised for classy food and excellent accommodation

Everything at this smart, beautifully located country inn is run with intelligent thought and care, with the lovingly prepared and presented food and charming bedrooms at the core of the business. It's the little details, like the set of walks leaflets from the pub and their immaculate kitchen garden that make all the difference. For a special occasion, head for the big bare-boards dining area at the back. It's neat, light and airy, with dark country-kitchen and rush-seat dining chairs, church candles and flowers on dark tables, canary walls, a cream ceiling and brocaded curtains on sturdy big-ring rails. The flagstoned bar on the left has a rather similar décor, with old local and school photographs, a couple of pews plus tables and café chairs. From an attractive bleached oak bar counter, a couple of beers, usually from Kingstone and Wye Valley are on handpump, plus bottled local cider. They have good wines by the glass and half bottle, and a good range of brandies. The lounge bar on the right, opening into the dining area, has a nice Jacobean-style carved settle and a housekeeper's chair by a log fire in the big fireplace. There are good solid round picnic-sets as well as the usual rectangular ones out on the terrace, with steps up to a sloping lawn. Disabled access is good. The pub is handy for the Three Castles area of the Marches and is within sight of the massive ruins of Skenfrith Castle.

🍴 Food here is prepared using named local suppliers of carefully chosen fresh ingredients, vegetables, soft fruit and herbs from their organic kitchen garden (you are welcome to look around), and at some point in the life of this edition of the *Guide*, pork from their own-reared saddleback pigs. As well as lunchtime sandwiches, the changing menus might include ham hock terrine, warm pigeon salad, scallops with spring vegetables and pancetta crisps, dressed crab with lovage vichyssoise, avocado ice-cream and crab biscuit, posh fish fingers, warm panna cotta of spring vegetables, poached brill fillet with fennel, cabbage, braised celery, citrus risotto and orange dressing, and poached sirloin steak. *Benchmark main dish: rib-eye steak £18.00. Two-course evening meal £26.00.*

Free house ~ Licensees William and Janet Hutchings ~ Real ale ~ Bar food (12-2.30, 7-9.30(9 Sun)) ~ Restaurant ~ (01600) 750235 ~ Children over 8 welcome in evening ~ Dogs allowed in bar and bedrooms ~ Open 11-11; 12-10 Sun; closed Tues Nov-March, and last week in Jan and first week in Feb ~ Bedrooms: £75B/£110B

Recommended by Dr and Mrs Michael Smith, Maurice and Gill McMahon, John Wooll, R and S Bentley, Mr and Mrs P R Thomas

TRESAITH Wales   SN2751   Map 6

Ship ★ 🛏

Off A487 E of Cardigan; bear right in village and keep on down – pub's car park fills quickly; SA43 2JL

Charming pub in splendid setting overlooking broad sandy surfing beach with enjoyable food, nice terrace, and seaview bedrooms

Perched up above the coastal road, this spacious pub has terrific views, not just of the beach but also of cliffs on either side – one with a high waterfall – and some say they've spotted dolphins and seals out in the vast expanse of the sea. Teak tables and chairs under a glass canopy on heated front decking and unusual picnic-sets on a two-level terrace make the most of this, and picture windows open the views to the front dining area, too. Behind here is a winter log fire, with some chunky pine tables, tub armchairs and sofas in the carpeted part on the right, and large attractive local photographs. They have three Brains beers on handpump, and a good choice of wines by the glass and other drinks; the young staff are friendly, cheerful and efficient. Two back rooms, possibly a quieter escape in summer, are appealing, especially the one on the right with its striking blue and red décor, bright flooring tiles, old-fashioned range stove, and snug alcove with a shelf of board games; piped music. There are good coast walks from this steep little village.

Popular for its fresh fish and hot seafood platter, the menu here might include whitebait, sardines grilled with garlic and tomato, creamy cockles and bacon, calamari, antipasti, honey-glazed king prawns, bream roasted with chilli and lime, battered hake with mushy peas and chips, coconut chilli chicken, mushroom and stilton bake, vegan salad, and rib-eye steak. *Benchmark main dish: bass roasted with lemon and thyme £14.95. Two-course evening meal £20.00.*

Brains ~ Manager Carl O'Shaughnessy ~ Real ale ~ Bar food (8am-11am, midday-3pm, 5pm-9pm; 12-9 in summer) ~ Restaurant ~ (01239) 811816 ~ Children welcome ~ Open 11-11(10.30 Sun) ~ Bedrooms: /£59.95B

Recommended by Julia Morris, Rob McGeehan, Mrs H J Pinfield, Roger Jones, Mr and Mrs A Burton

---

TY'N-Y-GROES Wales   SH7773 Map 6

Groes

B5106 N of village; LL32 8TN

Lots of antiques, local beer, and lovely garden at this beamed northern Snowdonia hotel

The characterfully timeless interior of this gracious old inn is kept spotless. Past the hot stove in the entrance area, its rambling, low-beamed and thick-walled rooms are nicely decorated with antique settles and an old sofa, old clocks, portraits, hats and tins hanging from the walls, and fresh flowers. A fine antique fireback is built into one wall, perhaps originally from the formidable fireplace in the back bar, which houses a collection of stone cats as well as cheerful winter log fires. You might find a harpist playing here on certain days. From the family's own Great Orme brewery, a couple of miles away, come Great Orme and Groes Ale (brewed for the pub), and several bottled Great Orme beers too, also 15 wines by the glass; piped music. There are several options for dining, including an airy conservatory and a smart white linen dining restaurant. The idyllic back garden has flower-filled hayracks and lovely verdant views, and there are more seats on a narrow flower-decked roadside terrace. Well equipped bedroom suites (some have terraces or balconies) have gorgeous views. They also rent out a well appointed wooden cabin, and a cottage in the historic centre of Conwy. Dogs are allowed in some bedrooms and in certain areas of the bar.

Using local lamb, salmon and game, and herbs from the hotel garden, bar food includes sandwiches, crispy duck salad with cranberry marmalade dressing, garlic king prawns, caramelised red onion quiche, mushroom tagliatelle, chicken curry, sausage and mash, seafood pie, and fillet steak. *Benchmark main dish: lamb shank £12.50. Two-course evening meal £18.60.*

Free house ~ Licensee Dawn Humphreys ~ Real ale ~ Bar food ~ Restaurant ~

(01492) 650545 ~ Children welcome until 7.30pm if eating ~ Dogs allowed in bar and bedrooms ~ Open 12-3, 6.30-11 ~ Bedrooms: £85B/£105B

Recommended by Margaret and Jeff Graham, Mike and Mary Carter, Tony and Shirley Albert, Noel Grundy, W N F Boughey, Peter Holmes, Maurice and Gill McMahon, Mike and Jayne Bastin, Dr and Mrs P Truelove, N R White, Dave Webster, Sue Holland, Alun Jones

USK Wales   SO3700   Map 6
Nags Head ♀
The Square; NP15 1BH

Spotlessly kept by the same family for 44 years, traditional in style with hearty welcome, and good food and drinks

Pubs don't get more welcoming than this flower-swathed old place – Usk is a regular winner of Wales in Bloom. The beautifully kept traditional main bar is cheerily chatty and cosy, with lots of well polished tables and chairs packed under its beams (some with farming tools), lanterns or horsebrasses and harness attached, as well as leatherette wall benches, and various sets of sporting prints and local pictures – look out for the original deeds to the pub. Tucked away at the front is an intimate little corner with some african masks, while on the other side of the room a passageway leads to a new dining area converted from the old coffee bar; piped music. There may be prints for sale, and perhaps a group of sociable locals. They do ten wines by the glass, along with Brains Bread of Heaven, Rev James and Sharps Doom Bar on handpump. The church here is well worth a look. The pub has no parking and nearby street parking can be limited.

Huge helpings of reasonably priced popular food includes grilled sardines, frog's legs in hot provençale sauce, rabbit pie, steak pie, chicken in red wine, faggots, and vegetable pancake, with specials such as duck in Cointreau, half a guinea fowl in wine and fig sauce, pheasant in port, and poached salmon. You can book tables, some of which may be candlelit at night; nice, proper linen napkins. *Benchmark main dish: rabbit pie £10.00. Two-course evening meal £17.50.*

Free house ~ Licensee the Key family ~ Real ale ~ Bar food (11.30-2, 5.30-9.30(6-9 Sun)) ~ Restaurant ~ (01291) 672820 ~ Children welcome ~ Dogs welcome ~ Open 10-3, 5-11(5.30-10.30 Sun)

Recommended by Meg and Colin Hamilton, Eryl and Keith Dykes, John and Joan Nash, GSB, Harry Williams, Phil and Jane Hodson, Dr and Mrs C W Thomas, M E and F J Thomasson

ALSO WORTH A VISIT IN WALES

Besides the region's top pubs, we recommend the following. Do tell us what you think of them: **feedback@goodguides.com**

ANGLESEY
BEAUMARIS SH6076   LL58 8AB
Sailors Return
Church Street

Cheery partly divided open-plan pub with good honest food, friendly helpful staff, open fire. *Recommended by Paul Humphreys*

BEAUMARIS SH6076   LL58 8DA
White Lion
Castle Street

Improved 19th-c family-run hotel overlooking Castle Square, two bars, one with open fire, well kept ales including Marstons Pedigree, enjoyable locally sourced food, restaurant; tables out at front and in sheltered beer garden behind, nine bedrooms with castle or Menai Strait views. *Recommended by Philip Hollington*

DULAS SH4787   LL70 9EX
Pilot Boat
A5025 N of Moelfre

Three-room Robinsons pub, family friendly, with decent choice of promptly served food, their ales kept well, sensible prices, lots of bric-a-brac in bar; garden with play bus, handy for coast path. *Recommended by Brian and Anna Marsden*

☆ **RED WHARF BAY** SH5281   LL75 8RJ
Ship
Village signed off B5025 N of Pentraeth

Whitewashed old pub worth visiting for position right on Anglesey's east coast (get there early to bag a seat with fantastic views of miles of tidal sands); big old-fashioned rooms either side of bar counter, nautical bric-a-brac, long varnished wall pews, cast-iron-framed tables and open fires, Adnams, Tetleys and a guest, 50 malt whiskies and decent choice of wines, food can be good; if you run a tab they'll lock your card in a numbered box and hand you the key, piped Classic FM in lounge; children welcome, disabled access, open all day. *Recommended by Gordon and Margaret Ormondroyd, Mike and Mary Carter, Paul Goldman, Matthew Bradley, Martin Smith*

CLWYD

☆ **BURTON GREEN** SJ3558   LL12 0AS
Golden Groves
Llyndir Lane, off B5445 W of Rossett

Fresh modern revamp for timbered pub in lovely hidden-away setting, partly knocked-through rooms dating from the 13th c, figures carved in beams, open fires, good locally sourced food (all day) from light dishes and sharing plates up, friendly staff, Marstons ales, good wine choice, live acoustic music Sun lunchtime; large attractive streamside garden with modern wicker furniture, open all day. *Recommended by Mr and Mrs J Palmer*

CARROG SJ1143   LL21 9AT
Grouse
B5436, signed off A5 Llangollen—Corwen

Small unpretentious pub with superb views over River Dee and beyond from bay window and balcony, Lees ales, enjoyable food all day from sandwiches up, reasonable prices, friendly helpful staff, local pictures, pool in games room; piped music, narrow turn into car park; children welcome, wheelchair access (side door a bit narrow), tables in pretty walled garden (covered terrace for smokers), handy for Llangollen steam railway, bedrooms. *Recommended by Mr and Mrs M Stratton, Myke Crombleholme*

HANMER SJ4539   SY13 3DE
Hanmer Arms
Village and pub signed from A539

Relaxed country inn with good range of reasonably priced straightforward food including popular Sun lunch, friendly efficient staff, well kept ales such as Stonehouse, big family dining room upstairs; attractive garden with church as pleasant backdrop, good value bedrooms in former courtyard stable block, pretty village. *Recommended by Alan and Eve Harding*

There are report forms at the back of the book.

☆ **LLANARMON DYFFRYN CEIRIOG** SJ1532   LL20 7LD
Hand
B4500 from Chirk

Comfortable inn (former farmhouse) at heart of Upper Ceiriog valley and set against backdrop of the Berwyn Mountains; black-beamed, carpeted bar on left of broad-flagstoned entrance hall, inglenook log fire and mix of old chairs and settles, Weetwood and a guest beer, several malts and wines by the glass, well liked seasonal food in largely stripped-stone dining room with woodburner, residents' lounge, games room with pool and TV; children and dogs welcome, tables on crazy-paved front terrace, more in garden, attractive spacious bedrooms, good breakfast, open all day. *Recommended by John and Joan Nash, Lois Dyer, Clive Watkin, Noel Grundy*

☆ **LLANARMON DYFFRYN CEIRIOG** SJ1532   LL20 7LD
West Arms
End of B4500 W of Chirk

16th-c beamed and timbered inn in lovely surroundings, cosy atmosphere in picturesque upmarket lounge bar full of antique settles, sofas, even an elaborately carved confessional stall, good original bar food strong on local produce, friendly staff, good range of wines, malt whiskies and well kept ales, more sofas in old-fashioned entrance hall, comfortable back bar too, roaring log fires, good restaurant; children welcome, pretty lawn running down to River Ceiriog (fishing for residents), good walks, comfortable character bedrooms. *Recommended by Noel Grundy*

LLANELIDAN SJ1150   LL15 2PT
Leyland Arms
Signed off A494 S of Ruthin

Interesting old village pub in charming surroundings, cheerful landlord, well kept ales and enjoyable pub food, blazing fire; three bedrooms, open all day Sun till 6pm, closed Mon. *Recommended by Simon Stephens*

RUABON SJ3043   LL14 6DA
Bridge End
Bridge Street

Proper old-fashioned pub owned by McGivern, their ales and guests, decent wines, enthusiastic staff, basic home-made food, open fires, folk music Weds evening, Thurs quiz night; open all day weekends and from 5pm weekdays. *Recommended by Mrs Ginny Weston, Nick Jones*

DYFED

ABERAERON SN4562   SA46 0AU
Cadwgan Arms
Market Street

Small late 18th-c pub opposite harbour, basic with friendly regulars, well kept Brains and two changing guests, interesting old photographs, open fire; nice outside drinking area, open all day except Mon lunchtime. *Recommended by the Didler*

☆ **ABERAERON** SN4562   SA46 0BA
Harbourmaster
Harbour Lane

Stylish waterside dining pub/hotel overlooking attractive yacht-filled harbour, cleanly decorated bar with blue walls, leather sofas, a zinc-clad counter and stuffed albatross (reputed to have collided with ship belonging to chatty owner's great-grandfather), Purple Moose and a beer brewed for them, a dozen wines by the glass, good often interesting food (not cheap), efficient friendly service, minimalist dining room with modern light wood furniture, four-seater cwtch (or snug) in former porch; piped music, TV; children over five welcome if staying, good up-to-date bedrooms, self-catering cottage, open all day from 8am. *Recommended by Mike and Mary Carter, Mr and Mrs P R Thomas, the Didler, B and M Kendall and others*

ABERAERON SN4562   SA46 0AS
Monachty Arms
Market Street

Well run Brains pub next to inner harbour, comfortable front bar with woodburner, other areas including restaurant; nice beer garden with great views, open all day. *Recommended by the Didler*

ABERGORLECH SN5833   SA32 7SN
☆ # Black Lion
B4310

Friendly old coaching inn in fine rural position, traditionally furnished stripped-stone bar with flagstones, coal stove, oak furniture and high-backed black settles, copper pans on beams, old jugs on shelves, fresh flowers, local paintings, dining extension with french windows opening on to enclosed garden, one Rhymney ale and a guest, good varied choice of inexpensive food; piped music; children and dogs welcome, lovely views of Cothi valley from sloping riverside garden, self-catering cottage, open all day weekends, closed Mon. *Recommended by Mike and Eleanor Anderson, Peter and Carol Heaton*

BROAD HAVEN SM8614   SA62 3NE
☆ # Druidstone Hotel
N on coast road, bear left for about 1½ miles then follow sign left to Druidstone Haven

Cheerfully informal, the family's former country house in a grand spot above the sea, individualistic and relaxed, terrific views, inventive cooking with fresh often organic ingredients (best to book), helpful efficient service, folksy cellar bar with local ale tapped from the cask, country wines and other drinks, ceilidhs and folk events, friendly pub dogs (others welcome), all sorts of sporting activities from boules to sand-yachting; attractive high-walled garden, spacious homely bedrooms, even an eco-friendly chalet and an underground apartment built into the hill, closed Nov and Jan, restaurant closed Sun evening. *Recommended by Geoff and Linda Payne, John and Enid Morris, Simon Watkins, Mrs H J Pinfield and others*

CAIO SN6739   SA19 8RD
Brunant Arms
Off A482 Llanwrda—Lampeter

Unpretentious and interestingly furnished village pub, comfortable and friendly, with nice log fire, good choice of local ales, enjoyable regularly changing home-made food from baguettes up, stripped-stone public bar with games including pool; juke box, TV; children and dogs welcome, small Perspex-roofed verandah and lower terrace, has been open all day weekends. *Recommended by the Didler, John Crellin*

CAREW SN0403   SA70 8SL
☆ # Carew Inn
A4075 off A477

Stone-built pub with unpretentious panelled public bar, bentwood stools at counter, mixed tables and chairs on bare boards, neat eating area, dining rooms upstairs with colour photos of local scenes, sky-blue tongue-and-groove partitions and black leather chairs, well liked bar food, Brains and Worthington ales, open fires; piped music, darts and outdoor pool table; children welcome away from bar, dogs allowed, seats in front looking down to river (tidal watermill open for summer afternoon visits), back garden with play equipment and view of imposing Carew Castle ruins and remarkable 9th-c Celtic cross, summer barbecues, open all day. *Recommended by Norma and David Hardy, the Didler, C A Bryson*

CILGERRAN SN1942   SA43 2SL
Pendre Inn
Off A478 S of Cardigan; High Street

Friendly local with massive medieval stone walls and broad flagstones, enjoyable home-made pub food (more evening choice), great value Evan Evans and two changing guests, real cider; open all day. *Recommended by Ann and Tony Bennett-Hughes, the Didler*

CRESSWELL QUAY SN0506 SA68 0TE
☆ Cresselly Arms
Village signed from A4075

Simple unchanging alehouse overlooking tidal creek, plenty of local customers in two old-fashioned linked rooms, built-in wall benches, kitchen chairs and plain tables on red and black tiles, open fire in one room, Aga in the other with lots of pictorial china hanging from high beam-and-plank ceiling, a third more conventionally furnished red-carpeted room, Worthington and a winter guest ale served from glass jugs, no food apart from rolls on Sat; no children; seats outside making most of view, you can arrive by boat if tide is right, open all day weekends. *Recommended by Giles and Annie Francis, the Didler*

CWM GWAUN SN0333 SA65 9SE
☆ Dyffryn Arms
Cwm Gwaun and Pontfaen signed off B4313 E of Fishguard

Classic rural time warp, virtually the social centre for this lush green valley, very relaxed, basic and idiosyncratic, with much-loved veteran landlady (her farming family have run it since 1840, and she's been in charge for well over a third of that time); 1920s front parlour with plain deal furniture and draughts boards inlaid into tables, coal fire, well kept Bass served by jug through sliding hatch, low prices, World War I prints and posters, darts, duck eggs for sale; lovely outside view, open more or less all day (may close if no customers). *Recommended by Ann and Tony Bennett-Hughes, Giles and Annie Francis, the Didler*

DALE SM8105 SA62 3RB
Griffin
B4327, by sea on one-way system

Old waterside pub under friendly newish management, two cosy rooms, open woodburner, well kept local ales and enjoyable bar food, good estuary views – you can sit out on seawall. *Recommended by Geoff and Linda Payne, Ed Cole*

DINAS SN0139 SA42 0SE
Old Sailors
Pwllgwaelod; from A487 in Dinas Cross follow Bryn-Henllan signpost

Shack-like building in superb position, snugged down into the sand by isolated cove below Dinas Head with its bracing walks; specialising in fresh local seafood including crab and lobster, also good snacks, coffee and summer cream teas, well kept Felinfoel, decent wine, maritime bric-a-brac; children and dogs welcome, picnic-sets on grass overlooking beach, open 11-6ish and all day Fri, Sat Nov-Easter (all day Weds-Sat Easter-Oct). *Recommended by Ann and Tony Bennett-Hughes, V and E A Bolton*

FISHGUARD SM9537 SA65 9HJ
☆ Fishguard Arms
Main Street (A487)

Tiny unspoilt pub; front bar with changing jug-served ales from unusually high counter, chatty character landlord and friendly staff, open fire, rugby photographs, woodburner and traditional games in back room, no food; sports TV; smokers' area out at back, open all day, closed Weds evening. *Recommended by the Didler, Giles and Annie Francis*

FISHGUARD SM9637 SA65 9ND
Ship
Newport Road, Lower Town

Cheerful atmosphere and seafaring locals in ancient dim-lit red-painted pub near old harbour, friendly staff, well kept ales including Theakstons tapped from the cask, homely food from sandwiches and cawl up, coal fire, lots of boat pictures, model ships, photos of Richard Burton, piano; children welcome, toys provided. *Recommended by Giles and Annie Francis*

We include some hotels with a good bar that offers facilities comparable to those of a pub.

LAWRENNY SN0106   SA68 0PR
Lawrenny Arms
Signed from Broad Lane

In lovely position overlooking river with own landing stage, generous good value food all day, pleasant staff; tables outside. *Recommended by Mr and Mrs B Hobden*

LITTLE HAVEN SM8512   SA62 3UF
☆ Castle Inn
Grove Place

Welcoming pub well placed by green looking over sandy bay (lovely sunsets), popular food including pizzas and good local fish, Marstons ales, good choice of wines by the glass, tea and cafetière coffee, bare-boards bar and carpeted dining area with big oak tables, beams, some stripped stone, castle prints, pool in back area; children welcome, front picnic-sets, New Year's day charity swim, open all day. *Recommended by John Hancock, John and Fiona McIlwain, Bob Butterworth, Pete Flower*

LITTLE HAVEN SM8512   SA62 3UN
☆ St Brides Inn
St Brides Road

Just 20 metres from Pembrokeshire Coast Path; neat stripped-stone bar and linked carpeted dining area, log fire, interesting well in back corner grotto thought to be partly Roman, Banks's, Marstons and a guest, fairly priced bar food; piped music and TV; children welcome, dogs in bar, seats in sheltered suntrap terrace garden across road, two bedrooms, open all day summer. *Recommended by Geoff and Linda Payne, Jennie George, Pete Flower*

LITTLE HAVEN SM8512   SA62 3UL
☆ Swan
Point Road

Attractive seaside pub overlooking sandy bay, emphasis on enjoyable food from snacks and pubby dishes to more upscale expensive food, up-to-date bar with leather sofas and comfortable alcove seating on wood-laminate floor, nice views from window tables, fires at each end, Brains and guest ales, good but expensive wines, young staff, contemporary upstairs dining room. *Recommended by Geoff and Linda Payne, John and Enid Morris, Ann and Tony Bennett-Hughes*

LLANDDAROG SN5016   SA32 8NS
☆ Butchers Arms
On back road by church

Ancient heavily black-beamed local with three intimate eating areas off small central bar, welcoming with charming service, enjoyable generous home-made food at reasonable prices, Felinfoel ales tapped from the cask, good wines by the glass, conventional pub furniture, gleaming brass, candles in bottles, open woodburner in biggish fireplace; piped music; children welcome, tables outside, nice window boxes, closed Mon. *Recommended by Tom Evans, the Didler*

LLANDDAROG SN5016   SA32 8NT
White Hart
Off A48 E of Carmarthen, via B4310; aka Yr Hydd Gwyn

Ancient thatched pub with good own-brew beers using water from 300-foot borehole, comfortable lived-in beamed rooms with lots of engaging bric-a-brac and antiques including a suit of armour, 17th-c carved settles by huge log fire, interestingly furnished high-raftered dining room, generous if not cheap food, Zac the macaw and Bendy the galah; piped music, cash and debit cards only, no dogs inside; children welcome, disabled access (ramps provided), picnic-sets on front terrace and in back garden, play area, small farmyard (eggs for sale at the bar), closed Weds. *Recommended by Mr and Mrs P R Thomas, Glenys and John Roberts, Chris and Angela Buckell, KT*

LLANDEILO SN6222   SA19 6EN
White Horse
Rhosmaen Street

Friendly well run 16th-c local, several linked bare-boards rooms, fine range of Evan Evans ales, nice chatty mix of customers, woodburner in stone fireplace; piped and occasional live music, games machine, TV; tables outside front and back, open all day. *Recommended by the Didler*

LLANDOVERY SN7634   SA20 0AA
Red Lion
Market Square

One basic welcoming room with no bar, changing ales tapped from cask, jovial character landlord; restricted opening – may be just Fri evening and Sat. *Recommended by the Didler*

LLANGADOG SN7028   SA19 9AA
Red Lion
Church Street

Striking stone-built coaching inn with a warm welcome, good straightforward food and well kept local ales; comfortable bedrooms. *Recommended by Taff Thomas*

NEWPORT SN0539   SA42 0TA
☆ # Royal Oak
West Street (A487)

Bustling and well run sizeable pub with friendly helpful landlady and staff, good generous food including lunchtime light dishes, local lamb and lots of authentic curries, Tues OAP lunch, Greene King and guest beers, children welcome in lounge with eating areas, separate stone and slate bar with pool and games, upstairs dining room; some tables outside, easy walk to beach and coast path. *Recommended by Stephen Healey*

PENRHIWLLAN SN3641   SA44 5NG
☆ # Daffodil
A475 Newcastle Emlyn—Lampeter

Smart contemporary open-plan dining pub with comfortable welcoming bar (though most there to eat), scatter-cushion sofas and leather tub chairs on pale limestone floor, woodburner, bar chairs by granite-panelled counter serving well kept Evan Evans and Greene King, two lower-ceilinged end rooms with big oriental rugs, steps down to two airy dining rooms, one with picture windows by open kitchen, good varied menu including interesting evening specials (lots of fresh fish), helpful friendly staff; piped music; children welcome, nicely furnished decked area with valley views. *Recommended by Ruth Green*

PONTRHYDFENDIGAID SN7366   SY25 6BE
☆ # Black Lion
Off B4343 Tregaron—Devils Bridge

Relaxed country inn, only open in evenings, with emphasis on food; smallish main bar set for the sensibly modest choice of well liked meals, Felinfoel beer and decent wines, helpful service, dark beams and floorboards, lots of stripped stone, woodburner and big pot-irons in vast fireplace, copper, brass and so forth on mantelpiece, tiled back room with pool; unobtrusive piped music; children and dogs welcome, picnic-sets out in front, back courtyard and informal tree-shaded garden, bedrooms in separate block, good walking country and not far from Strata Florida Abbey, open 5pm-midnight. *Recommended by Ralph Wilmot*

PORTHGAIN SM8132   SA62 5BN
☆ # Sloop
Off A487 St Davids—Fishguard

Especially popular at holiday times, this well run tavern is snuggled down in cove wedged tightly between headlands on Pembrokeshire Coast Path – fine walks in either direction; plank-ceilinged bar with lots of lobster pots and fishing nets, ship's clocks and lanterns and even some relics from local wrecks, decent-sized eating area with simple furnishings and freezer for children's ice-creams, well liked bar food from sandwiches to seasonal fish (own fishing business), Brains, Felinfoel and Green King, separate games room with juke box, seats on heated terrace overlooking harbour, self-catering cottage in village, open all day from 9.30 for breakfast, till 1am Fri, Sat. *Recommended by Giles and Annie Francis, John Hancock, Simon Watkins, John and Enid Morris, R T and J C Moggridge, David Hoult and others*

STACKPOLE SR9896 SA71 5DF
☆ ## Stackpole Inn
Village signed off B4319 S of Pembroke

L-shaped dining pub on four levels, neat light oak furnishings, ash beams and low ceilings, locally sourced food including fish specials board, Brains and a guest beer, good choice of wines by the glass, friendly staff; piped music, pool; children welcome, dogs in bar, attractive colourful gardens, good woodland and coastal walks in the Stackpole Estate, seaside-themed bedrooms, open all day Sat, closed Sun evening Oct-Mar. *Recommended by Simon Daws, Richard Cole, Julia Morris, Fergus Dowding, Geoff and Linda Payne, John and Enid Morris and others*

WOLF'S CASTLE SM9526 SA62 5LS
Wolfe
A40 Haverfordwest—Fishguard

Good fresh home-made food from varied menu including OAP deals, friendly service, two beers from Brains and nine wines by the glass, comfortable brasserie dining lounge with woodburner, garden room and conservatory, TV and darts in bar (dogs allowed here); piped music; children welcome, picnic-sets in landscaped garden, three bedrooms, open all day in summer. *Recommended by David and Anne Day*

GLAMORGAN

BISHOPSTON SS5789 SA3 3EJ
Joiners Arms
Bishopston Road, just off B4436 SW of Swansea

Thriving local brewing its own good value Swansea ales, usually three of these along with well kept guests, reasonably priced straightforward food, friendly staff, unpretentious quarry-tiled bar with massive solid fuel stove, comfortable lounge; TV for rugby; children welcome, open all day (from 2pm Mon). *Recommended by Marcus Burtonshaw*

CARDIFF ST1776 CF11 9LL
☆ ## Cayo Arms
Cathedral Road

Helpful young staff, well kept Marstons and Tomos Watkins, enjoyable good value standard food all day from ciabattas up including Sun lunch, daily papers, pubby front bar with comfortable side area in Edwardian style, more modern back dining area; piped music, big-screen TV in one part, very busy at weekends; tables out in front, more in yard behind (with parking), good value bedrooms, open all day. *Recommended by Andy and Jill Kassube, the Didler*

CARDIFF ST1776 CF1 9HW
Mochyn Du
Sophia Closed; aka Y Mochyn Du

Enjoyable home-made food, well kept Brains and Vale of Glamorgan, good welcoming atmosphere, interesting décor; terrace tables, open all day. *Recommended by Andy and Jill Kassube, the Didler*

COWBRIDGE SS9974   CF71 7AF

☆ **Bear**

High Street, with car park behind off North Street; signed off A48

Busy well run Georgian coaching inn in smart village, well kept Bass, Hancocks HB and two guests, decent house wines, enjoyable usual food from good sandwiches up, friendly young uniformed staff, three attractively furnished bars with flagstones, bare boards or carpet, some stripped stone and panelling, big hot open fires, barrel-vaulted cellar restaurant; children welcome, dogs in one bar, comfortable quiet bedrooms. *Recommended by Dennis Jenkin, GSB*

GWAELOD-Y-GARTH ST1183   CF15 9HH

Gwaelod y Garth Inn

Main Road

Popular for its enjoyable home-made food, good friendly service, Wye Valley and regional guests from pine-clad bar, log fires, recently refurbished upstairs restaurant; table skittles, pool, digital juke box; children and dogs welcome, fine valley views, on Taff-Ely Ridgeway path, three bedrooms, open all day. *Recommended by Mrs H J Pinfield*

KENFIG SS8081   CF33 4PR

☆ **Prince of Wales**

2.2 miles from M4 junction 37; A4229 towards Porthcawl, then right when dual carriageway narrows on bend, signed Maudlam and Kenfig

Ancient local with plenty of individuality by historic sand dunes, cheerful welcoming landlord, well kept Bass and Worthington tapped from cask and usually two guests, good choice of malts, decent wines, enjoyable generous straightforward food at low prices, chatty panelled room off main bar, log fires, stripped stone, lots of wreck pictures, traditional games, small upstairs dining room for summer and busy weekends (best to book); big-screen TV for special sports events; children and (in non-carpet areas) dogs welcome, handy for nature reserve (orchids in June). *Recommended by John and Joan Nash, the Didler, Kevin Thomas, Nina Randall*

LLANCARFAN ST0570   CF62 3AD

Fox & Hounds

Signed off A4226; can also be reached from A48 from Bonvilston or B4265 via Llancadle

Good carefully cooked food using local ingredients including fresh fish, welsh black beef and farmhouse cheeses in neat comfortably modernised village pub, friendly open-plan bar rambling through arches, coal fire, Brains Bitter and Rev James kept well, good wine choice, traditional settles and plush banquettes, candlelit bistro with woodburners, simple end family room; unobtrusive piped music; children welcome, tables out behind, pretty streamside setting by interesting church, eight comfortable bedrooms, good breakfast, open all day weekends. *Recommended by Fergus Dowding, Bill and Jackie Parfitt, Guy Masdin*

OGMORE SS8876   CF32 0QP

☆ **Pelican**

Ogmore Road (B4524)

Nice spot above ruined castle, attractive rambling revamp with plenty of beamery and bare boards, welcoming open fire, enjoyable food in generous helpings, good real ale choice, cheerful service; may try to keep your credit card while you eat; dogs allowed in lounge (flagstoned floor), tables on side terrace, rather grand smokers' hut, lovely views and quite handy for beaches, open all day. *Recommended by Glenys and John Roberts, Chris Smith, Kevin Thomas, Nina Randall, Sue Humphreys*

PENTYRCH ST1081   CF15 9QF

Kings Arms

Church Road

16th-c village pub with snug flagstoned bar, lounge and restaurant, good often interesting food (not Mon or lunchtimes Tues, Weds, Thurs) from chef/landlord, Brains ales; children welcome, tables outside, open all day Fri, Sat, closed Sun evening and lunchtimes Mon and Tues. *Recommended by Lisa Jarman*

PONTYPRIDD ST0790   CF37 4DA
Bunch of Grapes
Off A4054; Ynysangharad Road

Refurbished early 19th-c pub backing on to remnants of Glamorganshire Canal, well kept Otley ales and plenty of guests, good food in bar and restaurant, deli. *Recommended by Taff Thomas*

REYNOLDSTON SS4889   SA3 1AD
☆ **King Arthur**
Higher Green, off A4118

Cheerful pub/hotel with timbered main bar and hall, back family summer dining area (games room with pool in winter), good fairly priced food with emphasis on fish, friendly helpful staff coping well when busy, Breconshire, Felinfoel and Tomos Watkins, country-house bric-a-brac, log fire; lively local atmosphere in evenings, piped music; tables out on green, play area, open all day, bedrooms. *Recommended by Steff Rees, Matt and Vikki Wharton, Mel Lawrence*

ST FAGANS ST1277   CF5 6DU
Plymouth Arms
Crofft-y-genau Road

Stately Victorian pub, now a rambling Vintage Inn with log fires, panelling and local prints in bustling linked areas, good all-day food including fixed-price and children's menus, Brains, St Austell Tribute and Timothy Taylors Landlord, decent wines by the glass; lots of tables on extensive back lawn, water bowls outside for dogs, handy for Museum of Welsh Life. *Recommended by Richard and Stephanie Foskett*

ST HILARY ST0173   CF71 7DP
☆ **Bush**
Off A48 E of Cowbridge

Cosy 16th-c thatched and beamed pub restored by new owners after devastating fire; flagstoned main bar with inglenook, snug, bare-boards lounge, good mix of old furniture, Bass, Green King Abbot, Hancocks HB and a guest, Weston's Old Rosie cider, good choice of wines by the glass, hearty country food including range of home-made pies, gluten-free choices too, carpeted restaurant with open ceiling; children welcome, dogs in bar, some benches out at front, garden behind, open all day Fri-Sun. *Recommended by Tony Cheeseman*

GWENT

ABERGAVENNY SO2914   NP7 5EN
Angel
Cross Street, by Town Hall

Comfortable old coaching inn with good friendly staff and thriving local atmosphere, lovely bevelled glass behind servery, some big sofas, enjoyable varied food in bar and popular restaurant; pretty courtyard. *Recommended by Eryl and Keith Dykes*

ABERGAVENNY SO3111   NP7 9AA
☆ **Hardwick**
Hardwick; B4598 SE, off A40 at A465/A4042 exit – coming from E on A40, go right round the exit system, as B4598 is final road out

Smart heavy-beamed dining pub with talented chef/landlord cooking noteworthy (if not cheap) food using fresh local produce – booking advised; three linked dining rooms with nice mix of furniture and some interesting artwork, huge fireplace in one room, a glassed-off wine store in another, new bar area with open pitched roof and centrepiece chandelier, sofas, pews and captain's chairs, Rhymney and a guest, local bottled ciders and good interesting wines by the glass, friendly helpful staff; piped music; children welcome, disabled facilities, courtyard tables, eight bedrooms in new block, open all day, closed second week in Jan. *Recommended by Maurice and Gill McMahon, M E and F J Thomasson*

ABERGAVENNY SO2914
Hen & Chickens
NP7 5EG

Flannel Street

Popular traditional local with wholesome cheap lunchtime food (not Sun), friendly efficient staff, well kept Brains and a guest from bar unusually set against street windows, mugs of tea and coffee, interesting side areas with some nice stripped masonry, pews and wonky tables on wood or tiled floors, darts, cards and dominoes, Sun jazz; TV, very busy on market day, they may ask to keep a credit card if you're running a tab; summer pavement tables. *Recommended by the Didler, Chris Flynn, Wendy Jones, John Wooll, Anthony Barnes, Reg Fowle, Helen Rickwood*

CAERLEON ST3490
☆ ### Bell
NP18 1QQ

Bulmore Road; off M4 junction 24 via B4237 and B4236

Nicely furnished linked beamed areas, good food including some interesting welsh dishes, well kept ales such as Bath and Vale of Glamorgan, farm cider, daily papers, big open fireplace, good Weds folk night, jazz Sun evening; unobtrusive piped music; children welcome, pretty back terrace with koi tank, open all day. *Recommended by Andy and Jill Kassube, Dr and Mrs R E S Tanner*

GROSMONT SO4024
Angel
NP7 8EP

On corner of B4347 and Poorscript Lane

Friendly 17th-c local owned by village co-operative, rustic interior with simple wooden furniture, Fullers, Tomos Watkins and Wye Valley ales, real ciders, decent good value straightforward bar food (not Sun or Mon), pool room with darts, live music (instruments provided); no lavatories – public ones close by; a couple of garden tables and boules behind, seats out by ancient market cross on attractive steep single street in sight of castle, open all day Sat, closed Mon lunchtime. *Recommended by GSB, R T and J C Moggridge, Guy Vowles, Reg Fowle, Helen Rickwood, the Didler*

LLANDENNY SO4103
☆ ### Raglan Arms
NP15 1DL

Centre of village

Well run dining pub with good interesting fresh food, home-baked bread, good selection of wines, Wye Valley Butty Bach, friendly welcoming young staff, big pine tables and a couple of leather sofas in linked dining rooms leading through to conservatory, log fire in flagstoned bar's handsome stone fireplace, pastel paintwork giving slight scandinavian feel, relaxed informal atmosphere; children welcome, garden tables, closed Mon. *Recommended by Reg Fowle, Helen Rickwood, LM*

LLANGYBI ST3797
White Hart
NP15 1NP

On main road

Friendly village dining pub in delightful 12th-c monastery building, part of Jane Seymour's dowry, pubby bar with roaring log fire, steps up to pleasant light restaurant, good if not cheap food, several well kept mainly welsh ales. *Recommended by Dr and Mrs C W Thomas*

LLANOVER SO2907
☆ ### Goose & Cuckoo
NP7 9ER

Upper Llanover signed up track off A4042 S of Abergavenny; after 0.5 miles take first left

Unchanging simple pub much loved by walkers (Monmouthshire and Brecon Canal towpath nearby, or over hilltops towards Blorenge and Blaenavon); essentially one small room with rustic furniture and woodburner, Newmans, Rhymney and a couple of guests, over 80 malt whiskies, wholesome Aga-cooked bar food, friendly landlady, small picture-window extension making most of valley view, daily papers, darts and board games; no credit cards; children and dogs welcome, rather ad hoc picnic-sets on gravel below, they keep sheep, goats, geese and chickens, may have honey for sale, bedrooms, open all day weekends, closed Mon. *Recommended by Howard Deacon, Guy Vowles, Anthony Barnes, LM, Reg Fowle, Helen Rickwood, the Didler*

LLANTHONY SO2827   NP7 7NN
☆ **Priory Hotel**
aka Abbey Hotel, Llanthony Priory; off A465, back Road Llanvihangel Crucorney—Hay

Magical setting for plain bar in dim-lit vaulted flagstoned crypt of graceful ruined Norman abbey, lovely in summer, with lawns around and the peaceful border hills beyond; well kept ales such as Brains, Felinfoel and Newmans, summer farm cider, good coffee, simple lunchtime bar food (queue can be long on fine summer days, but number system then works well), evening restaurant, occasional live music; no dogs or children; great walks, four bedrooms in restored parts of abbey walls, open all day Sat and summer Sun, closed winter Mon-Thurs, Sun evening. *Recommended by the Didler, MLR, Reg Fowle, Helen Rickwood*

MONMOUTH SO5012   NP25 3DY
Kings Head
Agincourt Square

Wetherspoons in former substantial coaching inn, plenty of seating with extensive central family area, usual value-minded food and drink, quick friendly service, lots of books; TVs and games machines. *Recommended by RS, ES*

MONMOUTH SO5012   NP25 3EQ
Robin Hood
Monnow Street

Ancient pub with low-beamed panelled bar, popular hearty food from sandwiches up, well kept ales including Bass and Greene King, friendly service, restaurant; children welcome, tables and play area outside. *Recommended by George Atkinson, B M Eldridge*

NEWPORT ST3188   NP20 1GA
Olde Murenger House
High Street

Fine 16th-c building with ancient dark woodwork, bargain Sam Smiths; open all day. *Recommended by the Didler*

PANDY SO3322   NP7 8DR
Old Pandy
A465 Abergavenny—Hereford

Welcoming old slate-built family pub with emphasis on good reasonably priced bar food including good value Sun lunch, attentive service, well kept Wye Valley ales, comfortable modern settles, 3D Brecon Beacons maps; no dogs; adjacent walkers' bunkhouse. *Recommended by M G Hart, Reg Fowle, Helen Rickwood*

PENALLT SO5209   NP25 4SE
Inn at Penallt
Village signed off B4293; at crossroads in village turn left

Refurbished 17th-c stone pub (was the Bush), good home-made bar and restaurant food with emphasis on local produce, also local ales and cider, well priced wine list, courteous efficient service, airy slate-floored bar with woodburner, restaurant and small back conservatory; children and dogs welcome, big garden with terrace and play area, Wye Valley views, four bedrooms, closed Mon, Tues lunchtime, and Weds and Thurs lunchtimes in winter. *Recommended by LM, Leo and Susan Horton, Geoff and Linda Payne*

RAGLAN SO4107   NP15 2DY
Beaufort Arms
High Street

Pub/hotel (former 16th-c coaching inn) with two character beamed bars, one with big stone fireplace and comfortable seats on slate floor, well kept Brains and Fullers London Pride, good range of locally sourced food including set-price Sun lunch in light airy brasserie, attentive friendly staff; piped music; children welcome, terrace tables, 17 good bedrooms. *Recommended by Andy and Jill Kassube, Reg Fowle, Helen Rickwood, Eryl and Keith Dykes, B M Eldridge, Chris Flynn, Wendy Jones*

SHIRENEWTON ST4894   NP16 6BU
Huntsman
B4235 outside village

Cheerful welcoming landlord, wide choice of enjoyable food including smaller lunchtime helpings from evening menu, special diets catered for, good courteous service even at busy times, Brains Rev James and Fullers London Pride, nice wines by the glass, comfortably carpeted bar and dining room; children and well behaved dogs welcome, picnic-sets outside with lovely hill views, nine bedrooms. *Recommended by Dennis Jenkin*

ST ARVANS ST5196   NP16 6EJ
Piercefield
A466 N of Chepstow Racecourse

Modern décor and setting in roomy comfortable country-style dining pub, good choice of enjoyable food including set deals, Brains ales, friendly efficient staff; handy for walkers and Chepstow races. *Recommended by Mike and Mary Carter, Tony and Gill Powell, Reg Fowle, Helen Rickwood*

TINTERN SO5300   NP16 6TE
☆ ## Anchor
Off A466 at brown Abbey sign

Prime spot by the abbey, friendly landlord and staff, wide choice of nicely presented good value food (separate café and restaurant), well kept Wye Valley and a guest, Weston's Old Rosie cider, great medieval stone mill in heavy-beamed main bar, flagstones and stripped stone, children and dogs welcome, extensive lawn with sturdy play area and further grounds, River Wye just behind, open all day. *Recommended by Geoff Dawe, K and B Barker, Ian and Rose Lock*

TINTERN SO5200   NP16 6SG
Moon & Sixpence
A466 Chepstow—Monmouth

Stripped stone, beams, open fires and woodburners, two dining areas, another room with sofas, natural spring feeding indoor goldfish pool, well kept Wye Valley ales and two ciders from back bar, pubby food including good value Sun roasts, friendly staff; piped music, sports TV; children welcome, terrace with views along River Wye to abbey, good walks, open all day. *Recommended by B M Eldridge*

TRELLECK SO5005   NP25 4PA
Lion
B4293 6 miles S of Monmouth

Open-plan bar with one or two low black beams, comfortably worn-in mix of furnishings, two log fires, several changing real ales such as Potbelly and Wye Valley, wide range of good inexpensive food including hungarian and thai specialities, Fri evening fish and chips, even basket meals, cribbage, dominoes, shove-ha'penny and table skittles; piped music, TV; children and dogs welcome, picnic-sets and aviary out on grass, side courtyard overlooking church, bedrooms in separate cottage, closed Sun evening, open all day summer Sats. *Recommended by R T and J C Moggridge, B M Eldridge*

TRELLECK GRANGE SO5001
Fountain
Minor road Tintern—Llanishen, SE of village

NP16 6QW

Traditional country pub under friendly new licensees (from the Cherry Tree in Tintern – now closed), enjoyable food from pub favourites to game specials, three well kept welsh ales, local cider and perry, roomy low-beamed flagstoned interior with log fire; small walled garden, peaceful spot on back road, open all day, closed Mon. *Recommended by LM*

USK SO3700
Cross Keys
Bridge Street

NP15 1BG

Small two-bar stone pub dating from the 14th c, wide choice of popular good value food from snacks to restaurant dishes, two well kept ales, good service and friendly atmosphere, nice log fire in handsome fireplace, oak beams, interesting Last Supper tapestry, lots of brass, copper and old photographs, wall plaques marking past flood levels; sports TV; back terrace, disabled access, comfortable bedrooms, good breakfast, open all day. *Recommended by Phil and Jane Hodson, Robert Turnham*

GWYNEDD

ABERDOVEY SN6196
☆ Penhelig Arms
Opposite Penhelig Station

LL35 0LT

Friendly family-run waterside hotel, bare-boards bar with bright red built-in banquettes and stools, some panelling, open fire in stone fireplace, Brains, Rev James and a guest, two dozen malt whiskies, 18 wines by the glass, enjoyable food (all day weekends) including local fish in bar and restaurant, efficient service; children and dogs welcome, comfortable bedrooms some with balconies overlooking estuary (ones nearest road can be noisy), open all day from 8am. *Recommended by Mike and Mary Carter, Dr Kevan Tucker, David Glynne-Jones, S J and C C Davidson, John Burgess and others*

CAERNARFON SH4762
Black Buoy
Northgate Street

LL55 1RW

Busy traditional pub by castle walls, renamed losing its historical connection (properly Black Boy, from King Charles II's nickname in its Kings Head days), but attractively renovated, with cheery fire, beams from ships wrecked here in the 16th c, bare floors and thick walls, lots of welsh chat, enjoyable food all day from baguettes and doorstep sandwiches to interesting fish and vegetarian dishes, well kept ales such as Brains, Conwy and Purple Moose, good friendly service, character lounge bar, restaurant, public bar with TV; a few pavement picnic-sets, bedrooms. *Recommended by Hugh Tattersall, Peter and Anne Hollindale*

CAPEL CURIG SH7357
Tyn y Coed
A5, SE of village

LL24 0EE

Friendly pub across road from River Llugwy, enjoyable good value home-made food using local produce, ales such as Flowers IPA, Purple Moose and Wadworths kept well, pool room; pleasant terrace, bedrooms. *Recommended by Rita and Keith Pollard, Peter Harper*

LLANDUDNO SH7782
Kings Head
Old Road, behind tram station

LL30 2NB

Rambling place much extended around 16th-c flagstoned core, wide range of popular generous food, well kept Greene King and two guests, good range of wines by the glass, friendly efficient staff, huge log fire, brightly open-plan but with interesting corners and comfortable traditional furnishings, old local tramway photographs, back dining room up a few steps, summer live music events; children welcome, seats on front terrace overlooking quaint Victorian cable tramway's station, open all day. *Recommended by N R White*

LLANDUDNO JUNCTION SH8180   LL31 9JP
☆ **Queens Head**
Glanwydden; heading towards Llandudno on B5115 from Colwyn Bay, turn left into
Llanrhos Road at roundabout as you enter the Penrhyn Bay speed limit; Glanwydden
is signed as the first left turn

Comfortable modern dining pub with good well presented bar food and efficient friendly
service, spacious lounge partly divided by wall of broad arches, brown plush wall
banquettes and windsor chairs around neat black tables, small public bar with well kept
Adnams and guests, decent wines; unobtrusive piped music; children welcome, seats
outside, you can rent the pretty stone cottage next door, open all day weekends (food all
day then too). *Recommended by Dave Johnson, Mike and Mary Carter, Paul Humphreys*

PENMAENPOOL SH6918   LL40 1YD
George III
just off A493, near Dolgellau

Attractive inn worth knowing for lovely views over Mawddach estuary from civilised partly
panelled upstairs bar opening into cosy inglenook lounge; beamed and flagstoned
downstairs bar for peak times, usual bar food, a real ale such as Black Sheep, restaurant;
dogs and children welcome, sheltered terrace, good bedrooms including some in
converted station (line now a walkway), open all day. *Recommended by Tony and Jill Radnor,*
Mr and Mrs M Stratton, Norma and Noel Thomas

PORTH DINLLAEN SH2741   LL53 6DB
☆ **Ty Coch**
Beach car park signed from Morfa Nefyn, then 15 minutes' walk

Idyllic location right on beach with great view along coast to mountains, far from roads
and only reached on foot; bar crammed with nautical paraphernalia, pewter, old miners'
and railway lamps, RNLI memorabilia and so forth, simple furnishings and coal fire, a
couple of real ales (served in plastic as worried about glass on beach), short lunchtime
bar menu; children and dogs welcome, open all day, till 4pm Sun, only open 12-4pm Oct-
Easter. *Recommended by Mike and Eleanor Anderson, Tim Maddison, Richard, Anne and Kate Ansell*

RHOSNEIGR SH3173   LL64 5QE
Y Morfa
Ffordd Maelog

Welcoming pub in quiet village, good competently cooked food (fish the main attraction)
in lounge or upstairs restaurant, bar with TV; disabled facilities. *Recommended by*
Bernadette and Tony Hackett

TREFRIW SH7863   LL27 0JH
Old Ship
B5106

Particularly well kept Marstons-related beers and local guests such as Conwy, good selection
of wines, friendly staff, varied choice of enjoyable fresh food from baguettes up including
good fish and chips, log fire, cheerful local atmosphere, restaurant with inglenook; children
welcome. *Recommended by Martin Cawley, Jan Bertenshaw, Miles Dobson, Doug Kerr*

POWYS

BERRIEW SJ1800   SY21 8PQ
Lion
B4390; village signed off A483 Welshpool—Newtown

Black and white beamed 17th-c coaching inn in attractive riverside village (with lively
sculpture gallery), friendly welcome from mother and daughter team, old-fashioned
inglenook public bar and partly stripped-stone lounge, food here or in restaurant from
sandwiches up, helpful cheerful service, well kept Banks's and Jennings, decent house
wines, dominoes; quiet piped music; children welcome, dogs in bar, seven bedrooms, open
all day Fri and Sat. *Recommended by David Glynne-Jones, Patrick and Daphne Darley, Reg Fowle,*
Helen Rickwood

CARNO SN9696   SY17 5LL
Aleppo Merchant
A470 Newtown—Machynlleth

Good choice of reasonably priced pub food from sandwiches up (open for breakfast, too), helpful friendly staff, Boddingtons and Six Bells, plushly modernised stripped-stone bar, peaceful lounge on right with open fire, restaurant (well behaved children allowed here), back extension with big-screen TV in games room; piped music; disabled access, steps up to tables in back garden, bedrooms, nice countryside, open all day. *Recommended by Michael and Jenny Back*

CRICKHOWELL SO2118   NP8 1AR
Bridge End
Bridge Street

Friendly 16th-c coaching inn by many-arched bridge over the Usk, popular with locals, ales such as Brains Rev James and Hancocks HB, enjoyable food from good value lunchtime baguettes to well liked Sun roasts, good service, lots of knick-knacks and fishing photographs, small restaurant; beer garden across road overlooking river, three bedrooms. *Recommended by Barry and Anne, Tony and Maggie Harwood, MLR*

CRICKHOWELL SO2118   NP8 1AR
Bridge End
Bridge Street

Enjoyable food including good Sun lunch, well kept Hancocks HB and Wychwood Hobgoblin; a few riverside picnic-sets across road, bedrooms in adjacent cottage. *Recommended by Barry and Anne, Tony and Maggie Harwood, MLR*

CRICKHOWELL SO2118   NP8 1BE
Dragon
High Street

Refurbished old inn (more hotel/restaurant than pub but with small bar), good varied choice of enjoyable well presented food from reasonably priced bar meals up including speciality tapas, prompt friendly service, Brains Rev James, log fire; 15 comfortable bedrooms. *Recommended by Guy Vowles, Eryl and Keith Dykes, C A Bryson*

CRICKHOWELL SO1919   NP8 1LP
☆ # Nantyffin Cider Mill
A40/A479 NW

Much emphasis on food (booking advised) in this former 16th-c drovers' inn, open-plan grey-stone bar with woodburner in broad fireplace, solid comfortable wooden tables and chairs, ales such as Brains, Felinfoel and Rhymney, farm cider, quite a choice of wines and maybe home-made elderflower cordial, attractive high-raftered restaurant with old cider press; children welcome, dogs in bar, disabled access using ramp, seats outside making most of rural River Usk views, closed Mon (except bank holidays) and Sun evening Oct-March. *Recommended by Mike and Mary Carter, Guy Vowles, Michael Mellers, B and M Kendall and others*

DERWENLAS SN7299   SY20 8TN
☆ # Black Lion
A487 just S of Machynlleth

Cosy 16th-c country pub, good range of enjoyable well priced food including nice children's menu, friendly staff coping well at busy times, Wye Valley Butty Bach and a guest, decent wines, heavy black beams, thick walls and black timbering, attractive pictures, brasses and lion models, tartan carpet over big slate flagstones, good log fire; piped music; garden up behind with play area and steps up into woods, limited parking, bedrooms. *Recommended by Dr Kevan Tucker, B and M Kendall, John Evans*

GLADESTRY SO2355   HR5 3NR
Royal Oak
B4594

Village pub on Offa's Dyke Path with friendly licensees, simple stripped-stone slate-floor walkers' bar, beams hung with tankards and lanterns, piano, darts, carpeted lounge, open fires, two Golden Valley ales, basic bar food; no credit cards; children welcome, dogs in bar (and in bedrooms by arrangement), sheltered back garden, camping, open all day (may close if quiet but will reopen if you ring the bell). *Recommended by Dr Kevan Tucker, Reg Fowle, Helen Rickwood*

GLANGRWYNEY SO2416   NP8 1EH
Bell
A40 Crickhowell—Abergavenny

Friendly old beamed pub comfortably updated by two brothers, three or four well kept changing ales, enjoyable generous food mostly using local produce, live jazz and folk; children welcome, four bedrooms. *Recommended by David Hassall*

GLASBURY SO1839   HR3 5NR
Harp
B4350 towards Hay, just N of A438

Welcoming, relaxed and homely with good value pubby food cooked by landlady including proper pies, log-fire lounge with eating areas, airy bar, real ales, picture windows over wooded garden sloping to River Wye; terrace tables, campsite and canoeing, river-view bedrooms. *Recommended by MLR, Reg Fowle, Helen Rickwood*

HAY-ON-WYE SO2242   HR3 5DF
☆ ## Blue Boar
Castle Street/Oxford Road

Medieval bar in character pub, cosy corners, dark panelling, pews and country chairs, open fire in Edwardian fireplace, four ales including a house beer from Hydes, organic bottled cider and several wines by the glass, enjoyable food (from breakfast on) in quite different long open café dining room, bright light décor, local artwork for sale and another open fire, good friendly service; piped music or Radio 4; children and dogs welcome, tables in tree-shaded garden, open all day from 9am. *Recommended by Michael Butler, Mike and Eleanor Anderson, Andy Lickfold, Sue Demont, Tim Barrow, R T and J C Moggridge*

HAY-ON-WYE SO2342   HR3 5AG
☆ ## Kilverts
Bell Bank/Bear Street

High-beamed bar in friendly hotel (some refurbishment), six well kept ales such as Breconshire, Hobsons and Wye Valley, a couple of ciders, several wines by the glass, good food including nice steak and kidney pudding; well behaved children welcome till 8pm if eating, dogs allowed but not in restaurant or on lawn, front flagstoned courtyard, pretty back garden with terrace and fountain, refurbished bedrooms, good breakfast, open all day. *Recommended by Bob and Angela Brooks, Dr Kevan Tucker, Andy Lickfold, John and Bryony Coles*

HAY-ON-WYE SO2342   HR3 5AD
☆ ## Old Black Lion
Lion Street

Comfortable low-beamed bar with old pine tables and original fireplace, mostly laid out for dining, bar and restaurant food available throughout, Wye Valley (labelled as Old Black Lion) and a guest such as Brains Rev James, efficient service; no dogs; children over 5 allowed if eating, sheltered back terrace, bedrooms (some above bar), open all day. *Recommended by Guy Vowles, Dr Kevan Tucker, Mike and Eleanor Anderson, Sue Demont, Tim Barrow, Pete Coxon, Reg Fowle, Helen Rickwood*

☆ **Three Tuns**
HAY-ON-WYE SO2242   HR3 5DB
Broad Street

Good affordable food (not Sun evening) including lovely home-baked bread in big pub
with low black beams, inglenook woodburners, lighter sofa area, ancient stairs to raftered
restaurant, well kept ales including Three Tuns and Wye Valley, good wine choice; no
dogs; children welcome, disabled facilities, sheltered courtyard, open all day weekends,
closed Mon, Tues. *Recommended by Guy Vowles, Howard Deacon, C A Bryson*

Hundred House Inn
HUNDRED HOUSE SO1154   LD1 5RY
A481 NE Builth Wells

Two-room roadside country pub with welcoming landlord, one or more well kept ales, low-
priced food including lunchtime winter specials, woodburner in public bar; garden
picnic-sets. *Recommended by MLR*

Horse & Jockey
KNIGHTON SO2872   LD7 1AE
Wylcwm Place

Several cosy areas, one with log fire, enjoyable good value food from traditional up in bar
and adjoining restaurant, cheerful service, real ales such as Stonehouse and Three Tuns,
pool; tables in pleasant medieval courtyard, handy for Offa's Dyke. *Recommended by Alan and
Eve Harding*

Llanerch
LLANDRINDOD WELLS SO0561   LD1 6BG
High Street/Waterloo Road; pub signed from station

Cheerful rambling 16th-c inn, enjoyable reasonably priced usual food, well kept ales,
cider and perry, good friendly service, old-fashioned main bar with big inglenook log fire
and more up-to-date lounges off, games room with pool; piped music, sports TV; children
and dogs welcome, pleasant terrace and garden with play area, 12 bedrooms, open all
day. *Recommended by N R White*

Blue Bell
LLANGURIG SN9079   SY18 6SG
A44 opposite church

Friendly old-fashioned country inn with well kept beer and good value pubby food in
comfortable flagstoned bar, games room with darts, dominoes and pool, small dining
room; piped music, no dogs; children welcome, nine inexpensive simple bedrooms, open
all day. *Recommended by C A Bryson*

Crown & Anchor
LLANIDLOES SN9584   SY18 6EF
Long Bridge Street

Friendly unspoilt town-centre pub known locally as Rubys after landlady who has run it
for 46 years, well kept Brains Rev James and Worthington Bitter, chatty locals' bar,
lounge, snug, and two other rooms, one with pool and games machine separated by
central hallway; open all day. *Recommended by the Didler*

Radnor Arms
LLOWES SO1941   HR3 5JA
A438 Brecon—Hereford

Attractive country pub under welcoming newish licensee, simple down-to-earth food
including good home-made pizzas, traditional beamed bar with stripped stone and log
fire, two small dining rooms; tables in garden looking out over fields towards the Wye.
Recommended by Simon Daws

MALLWYD SH8612   SY20 9HJ
Brigands
On A470

Sizeable former 15th-c coaching inn, friendly welcoming uniformed staff, wide choice of good reasonably priced food all day, well kept ales such as Purple Moose and Titanic, Gwynt y Ddraig cider, good selection of wines; children and dogs welcome, extensive lawns with play area, lovely views, fishing on River Dovey, bedrooms, good breakfast. *Recommended by Bob and Tanya Ekers, Paul and Sonia Broadgate*

MIDDLETOWN SJ3012   SY21 8EL
Breidden
A458 Welshpool—Shrewsbury

Friendly family-run pub with well kept ales such as Adnams, Bass and Shepherd Neame, varied choice of food from well prepared pubby things to chinese, japanese and thai dishes, takeaway service; children welcome, decent-sized garden with play area. *Recommended by Keith and Ann Arnold, Melvin Spear*

PAINSCASTLE SO1646   LD2 3JL
☆ ## Roast Ox
Off A470 Brecon—Builth Wells, or from A438 at Clyro

Well restored pub with beams, flagstones, stripped stone, appropriate simple furnishings and some rustic bric-a-brac, well kept ales such as Hook Norton tapped from the cask, good range of farm ciders, decent roasts as well as other enjoyable hearty food including good lunchtime baps, friendly quick service; dogs welcome, picnic-sets outside, attractive hill country, ten simple comfortable bedrooms. *Recommended by Guy Vowles, Geoffrey Hughes, MLR, Reg Fowle, Helen Rickwood*

PENCELLI SO0925   LD3 7LX
Royal Oak
B4558 SE of Brecon

Unpretentious and friendly with two small bars, low beams, assorted pine furniture on polished flagstones, autographed sporting memorabilia, log fires, well kept Brains Rev James and guest such as Breconshire Red Dragon, small blackboard choice of good home-made food (standard times in summer, Thurs-Sat evening and weekend lunchtimes in winter), simple modern candlelit dining room; children welcome, terraces backing on to Monmouth & Brecon Canal, nearby moorings, lovely canalside walks and handy for Taff Trail, closed Mon-Weds out of season. *Recommended by Tony and Maggie Harwood, Brian and Anna Marsden*

PEN-Y-CAE SN8313   SA9 1YY
Ancient Briton
Brecon Road

Friendly opened-up roadside pub, half a dozen well kept ales from far and wide, a local cider, reasonably priced food (service may be slow); outside seats and play area, campsite, handy for Dan-yr-Ogof caves and Carig-y-Nos country park, open all day. *Recommended by MLR*

PRESTEIGNE SO3164   LD8 2BE
Radnorshire Arms
High Street (B4355 N of centre)

Fine Elizabethan timbered hotel full of rambling individuality and historical charm; relaxed bar, venerable dark oak panelling, latticed windows, elegantly moulded black oak beams, polished copper pans and measures, a handful of armchairs, lovely dining room, friendly efficient staff, enjoyable honest food including good well priced Sun roasts, a couple of ales such as Hancocks HB and Sharps Doom Bar, local cider; piped music; children welcome, garden area with marquee, bedrooms. *Recommended by George Atkinson, James Miller*

RHAYADER SN9668   LD6 5AR

 ☆ **Triangle**

Cwmdauddwr; B4518 by bridge over Wye, SW of centre

Interesting mainly 16th-c pub, small and spotless with nice chatty atmosphere and welcoming helpful service, shortish choice of good value home-made pubby food (best to book evenings), well kept Brains Rev James, Greene King Abbot and Hancocks HB, small selection of reasonably priced wines, separate dining area with nice view over park to Wye, darts and quiz nights; three tables on small front terrace. *Recommended by Nigel and Sue Foster*

TALYBONT-ON-USK SO1122   LD3 7YX

☆ **Star**

B4558

Old-fashioned canalside inn unashamedly stronger on character than creature comforts, fine choice of changing ales from all over the country served by enthusiastic landlord, real ciders too, fair-priced standard bar food, good mix of customers including walkers with dogs, several plainly furnished pubby rooms, open fires (one in splendid stone fireplace), games room with pool, fruit machine, TV and juke box, live music last Fri, quiz Tues in winter; children welcome, picnic sets in sizeable tree-ringed garden with path leading to river, lovely village surrounded by Brecon Beacons National Park, bedrooms, open all day summer. *Recommended by the Didler, D Crook, Mrs P Bishop, Taff Thomas, Brian and Anna Marsden*

TALYBONT-ON-USK SO1122   LD3 7JD

White Hart

B4558, before bridge travelling NE

Comfortable stone-built coaching inn, big relaxed bar divided by working fireplace from beamed dining area, good hearty home-made food including vegetarian options and all-day Sun roast, half a dozen well kept changing ales, Thatcher's cider, Brecon gin and Penderyn whisky, welcoming knowledgeable landlord; on Taff Trail, some tables out by Monmouth & Brecon Canal, bunkhouse. *Recommended by the Didler, Taff Thomas, Oliver Bowler*

Post Office address codings confusingly give the impression that some pubs are in Gwent or Powys, Wales when they're really in Gloucestershire or Shropshire (which is where we list them).

A LITTLE FURTHER AFIELD

The stars beside pubs indicate those which we and readers judge to match the quality of top pubs in the rest of the *Guide*.

CHANNEL ISLANDS

GUERNSEY

KING'S MILLS   GY5 7JT
☆ **Fleur du Jardin**
King's Mills Road

Lovely country hotel in attractive walled garden, relaxing low-beamed flagstoned bar with good log fire, old prints and subdued lighting, unusually good food strong on local produce and seafood, friendly helpful service, several real ales such as Adnams Broadside and Jersey Liberation, good choice of wines by the glass, local cider, restaurant; piped music; children and dogs welcome, plenty of tables on back terrace, clean comfortable bedrooms, open all day. *Recommended by N R White, Mr and Mrs John Clifford*

JERSEY

ST AUBIN   JE3 8AB
☆ **Old Court House Inn**
Harbour Boulevard

Pubby low-beamed downstairs bar with open fire, other rambling areas including smarter bar partly built from schooner's gig, food from pubby snacks to lots of good fresh fish, well kept Jersey Special, nice wines by the glass, handsome upstairs restaurant, glorious views across harbour to St Helier, board games; piped music, TV; children welcome, comfortable bedrooms, open all day. *Recommended by Michael Dandy, Col and Mrs Patrick Kaye, David Hoult, Martin Smith*

ST BRELADE   JE3 8AW
Old Smugglers
Ouaisne Bay; OS map reference 595476

Happily unpretentious black-beamed pub, four well kept real ales, farm cider, enjoyable reasonably priced pubby food, friendly service, log fires, traditional built-in settles, darts, cribbage and dominoes, restaurant; TV; children and dogs welcome, sun porch with interesting coast views, just above Ouaisne beach, open all day. *Recommended by S J and C C Davidson, Martin Smith*

ST HELIER   JE2 3NJ
☆ **Lamplighter**
Mulcaster Street

Small pub with up to nine well kept ales including Liberation, local cider, over 40 malt whiskies, bargain simple food such as crab sandwiches, heavy timbers, rough panelling and scrubbed pine tables; sports TV, can get very busy early evening; interesting façade (with only Union Flag visible during Nazi occupation), open all day. *Recommended by David Hoult, Joan and Michel Hooper-Immins*

NORTHERN IRELAND

BELFAST
☆ Crown
Great Victoria Street, opposite Europa Hotel

Restored ornate 19th-c National Trust gin palace well worth sampling, lively and bustling, with pillared entrance, opulent tiles outside and in, elaborately coloured windows, dark brown curlicued ceiling, handsome mirrors, gleaming intricately carved woodwork, ten snug booths with little doors and bells for aproned waiter service, gas lighting, mosaic tiled floor, three well kept ales including Whitewater from imposing granite-top counter with colourful tiled facing, food upstairs from good irish stew to local oysters; can be incredibly noisy, very wide range of customers; open all day. *Recommended by Andy and Jill Kassube, Jeremy King, Paul Humphreys, Dr and Mrs A K Clarke, G Jennings*

BELFAST   BT2 7BA
Robinsons
Great Victoria Street

Fine Victorian saloon bar with original tiled floor, etched glass, ornate pillars supporting intricate moulded ceiling, green leather banquettes and spindleback bar stools, collection of *Titanic* relics in display cabinets, good Guinness, reasonably priced pubby bar food till 5pm, upstairs bistro, a nightclub above that and a contemporary bar in the basement, also back Fibber Magees bar with big stone fireplace, masses of bric-a-brac and traditional live music. *Recommended by Ian and Joan Blackwell*

REPUBLIC OF IRELAND

DUBLIN
O'Neills
Suffolk Street

Spreading early Victorian pub, welcoming and popular with all ages, lots of dark panelling and cubby-holes off big lively bar, more rooms upstairs, good food and service, well served Guinness, live music; main tourist information centre in converted church opposite. *Recommended by Nigel and Jean Eames*

PUBS SERVING FOOD ALL DAY

We list here all the top pubs that have told us they plan to serve food all day, even if it's only one day of the week. The individual entries for the pubs themselves show the actual details.

THE SOUTH WEST
Cornwall

Crafthole, Finnygook
Lanlivery, Crown
Morwenstow, Bush

Devon

Avonwick, Turtley Corn Mill
Postbridge, Warren House
Sidbury, Hare & Hounds
Sidford, Blue Ball

Dorset

Tarrant Monkton, Langton Arms
Worth Matravers, Square & Compass

Somerset

Hinton St George, Lord Poulett Arms
Stanton Wick, Carpenters Arms

Wiltshire

Bradford-on-Avon, Castle
Brinkworth, Three Crowns

THE SOUTH EAST & LONDON
Berkshire

Sonning, Bull
White Waltham, Beehive

Buckinghamshire

Coleshill, Harte & Magpies
Forty Green, Royal Standard of England
Grove, Grove Lock
Wooburn Common, Chequers

Hampshire

Bransgore, Three Tuns
Southsea, Wine Vaults

Isle of Wight

Arreton, White Lion
Shorwell, Crown

Kent

Brookland, Woolpack
Langton Green, Hare
Penshurst, Bottle House
Sevenoaks, White Hart
Stalisfield Green, Plough
Stowting, Tiger

Oxfordshire

Kingham, Plough
Oxford, Bear, Turf Tavern
Stanton St John, Talk House

Surrey

Blindley Heath, Red Barn
Elstead, Mill at Elstead
Horsell, Red Lion
Milford, Refectory

Sussex

Alfriston, George
Charlton, Fox Goes Free
East Chiltington, Jolly Sportsman
Horsham, Black Jug
Ringmer, Cock

London
Central London:
    Bountiful Cow, Old Bank of England,
    Olde Mitre, Seven Stars
Outer London:
    Bishop Out of Residence, Old Orchard
South London:
    Telegraph

EAST OF ENGLAND
Cambridgeshire

Pampisford, Chequers
Stilton, Bell

Essex

Fyfield, Queens Head
South Hanningfield, Old Windmill

Hertfordshire

Ashwell, Three Tuns
Batford, Gibraltar Castle

Norfolk

Larling, Angel
Stiffkey, Red Lion
Stow Bardolph, Hare Arms
Swanton Morley, Darbys
Woodbastwick, Fur & Feather

Suffolk

Chelmondiston, Butt & Oyster
Snape, Plough & Sail
Stoke-by-Nayland, Crown
Waldringfield, Maybush

EAST MIDLANDS
Derbyshire

Alderwasley, Bear
Beeley, Devonshire Arms
Chelmorton, Church Inn
Fenny Bentley, Coach & Horses
Hathersage, Plough
Hayfield, Lantern Pike
Hope, Cheshire Cheese
Litton, Red Lion

Leicestershire

Coleorton, George
Swithland, Griffin
Woodhouse Eaves, Wheatsheaf

Lincolnshire

Kirkby la Thorpe, Queens Head
Stamford, George of Stamford

Northamptonshire

Oundle, Ship
Wadenhoe, Kings Head

Rutland

Lyddington, Marquess of Exeter

THE HEART OF ENGLAND
Gloucestershire

Brimpsfield, Golden Heart
Coates, Tunnel House
Didmarton, Kings Arms
Ford, Plough

Guiting Power, Hollow Bottom
Nailsworth, Weighbridge
Sheepscombe, Butchers Arms

Shropshire

Chetwynd Aston, Fox
Shrewsbury, Armoury

Staffordshire

Salt, Holly Bush
Wrinehill, Hand & Trumpet

Warwickshire

Barford, Granville
Hunningham, Red Lion
Long Compton, Red Lion
Welford-on-Avon, Bell

West Midlands

Birmingham, Old Joint Stock

Worcestershire

Ombersley, Kings Arms

THE NORTH WEST
Cheshire

Aldford, Grosvenor Arms
Astbury, Egerton Arms
Aston, Bhurtpore
Bickley Moss, Cholmondeley Arms
Bunbury, Dysart Arms
Burleydam, Combermere Arms
Burwardsley, Pheasant
Chester, Mill, Old Harkers Arms
Cotebrook, Fox & Barrel
Eaton, Plough
Lach Dennis, Duke of Portland
Macclesfield, Sutton Hall
Marton, Davenport Arms
Mobberley, Roebuck
Peover Heath, Dog
Plumley, Smoker
Tarporley, Rising Sun

Cumbria

Cartmel Fell, Masons Arms
Elterwater, Britannia
Ings, Watermill
Levens, Strickland Arms
Ravenstonedale, Black Swan
Threlkeld, Horse & Farrier

Lancashire

Bashall Eaves, Red Pump
Bispham Green, Eagle & Child
Great Mitton, Three Fishes
Longridge, Derby Arms
Nether Burrow, Highwayman
Pleasington, Clog & Billycock
Uppermill, Church Inn
Waddington, Lower Buck
Wheatley Lane, Sparrowhawk

Merseyside

Liverpool, Philharmonic Dining Rooms

THE NORTH EAST & YORKSHIRE
County Durham

Aycliffe, County
Blanchland, Lord Crewe Arms
Carterway Heads, Manor House Inn
Greta Bridge, Morritt Arms

Northumberland

Weldon Bridge, Anglers Arms

Yorkshire

Blakey Ridge, Lion

Bradfield, Strines Inn
Broughton, Bull
Elslack, Tempest Arms
Grinton, Bridge Inn
Halifax, Shibden Mill
Hartshead, Gray Ox
Ledsham, Chequers
Long Preston, Maypole
Widdop, Pack Horse

SCOTLAND

Applecross, Applecross Inn
Edinburgh: Abbotsford, Café Royal
Gairloch, Old Inn
Glasgow: Babbity Bowster, Bon Accord
Houston, Fox & Hounds
Innerleithen, Traquair Arms
Pitlochry, Moulin
Shieldaig, Tigh an Eilean Hotel

WALES

Colwyn Bay, Pen-y-Bryn
Gresford, Pant-yr-Ochain
Llanferres, Druid
Llangollen, Corn Mill
Rhoscolyn, White Eagle
Tresaith, Ship

PUBS NEAR MOTORWAY JUNCTIONS

The number at the start of each line is the number of the junction. Detailed directions are given in the entry for each pub. To help you find the pubs quickly before you're past the junction, we give the name of the chapter where you'll find the text.

M1
9: Redbourn, Cricketers (East of England) 3.2 miles
16: Nether Heyford, Olde Sun (East Midlands) 1.8 miles
18: Crick, Red Lion (East Midlands) 1 mile

M3
1: Sunbury, Flower Pot (South East & London) 1.6 miles
3: West End, Inn at West End (South East & London) 2.4 miles
5: North Warnborough, Mill House (South East & London) 1 mile; Hook, Hogget (South East & London) 1.1 miles
7: North Waltham, Fox (South East & London) 3 miles
9: Easton, Chestnut Horse (South East & London) 3.6 miles

M4
9: Bray, Crown (South East & London) 1.75 miles; Bray, Hinds Head (South East & London) 1.75 miles
13: Winterbourne, Winterbourne Arms (South East & London) 3.7 miles
14: East Garston, Queens Arms (South East & London) 3.5 miles
17: Norton, Vine Tree (South West) 4 miles

M5
4: Holy Cross, Bell & Cross (Heart of England) 4 miles
19: Clapton-in-Gordano, Black Horse (South West) 4 miles
26: Clayhidon, Merry Harriers (South West) 3.1 miles
30: Woodbury Salterton, Diggers Rest (South West) 3.5 miles

M6
17: Sandbach, Old Hall (North West) 1.2 miles
19: Plumley, Smoker (North West) 2.5 miles
36: Levens, Strickland Arms (North West) 4 miles

40: Yanwath, Gate Inn (North West) 2.25 miles; Tirril, Queens Head (North West) 3.5 miles

M11
8: Birchanger, Three Willows (East of England) 0.8 miles
9: Hinxton, Red Lion (East of England) 2 miles
10: Pampisford, Chequers (East of England) 2.6 miles; Thriplow, Green Man (East of England) 3 miles

M20
11: Stowting, Tiger (South East & London) 3.7 miles

M25
13: Laleham, Three Horseshoes (South East & London) 5 miles
16: Denham, Swan (South East & London) 0.75 miles
18: Chenies, Red Lion (South East & London) 2 miles; Flaunden, Bricklayers Arms (East of England) 4 miles
21A: Potters Crouch, Holly Bush (East of England) 2.3 miles

M40
2: Hedgerley, White Horse (South East & London) 2.4 miles; Forty Green, Royal Standard of England (South East & London) 3.5 miles
12: Gaydon, Malt Shovel (Heart of England) 0.9 miles
15: Barford, Granville (Heart of England) 1.7 miles

M42
6: Hampton in Arden, White Lion (Heart of England) 1.25 miles

M50
1: Baughton, Jockey (Heart of England) 4 miles

M62
25: Hartshead, Gray Ox (North East and Yorkshire) 3.5 miles

Maps

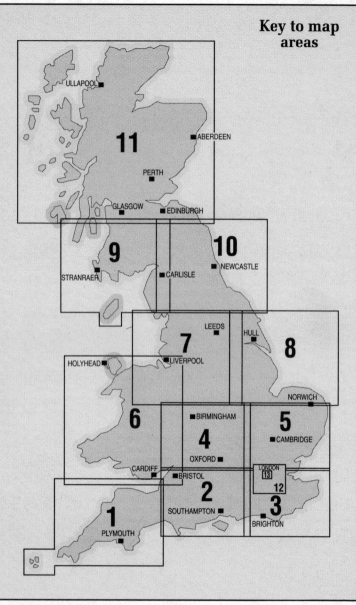

Key to map areas

ULLAPOOL ■

ABERDEEN ■

11

PERTH ■

GLASGOW ■ ■ EDINBURGH

9 **10**

STRANRAER ■ CARLISLE ■ ■ NEWCASTLE

LEEDS ■ ■ HULL

7 **8**

HOLYHEAD ■ LIVERPOOL ■

6

■ BIRMINGHAM

4 **5**

OXFORD ■ ■ CAMBRIDGE

CARDIFF ■ ■ BRISTOL LONDON ⊡ 13

2 **12**

SOUTHAMPTON ■ **3**

1 BRIGHTON ■

PLYMOUTH ■

Reference to sectional maps

▰▰▰	Motorway	● **Totnes**	Guide entry
▰▰▰	Major road	⊡ **Lynton**	Guide entry with accommodation
– – –	County boundary	■ BODMIN	Place name to assist location

The South West	Map 1
Southern England	Map 2
The South East	Map 3
Central & Western England	Map 4
Central England & East Anglia	Map 5
Wales	Map 6
The North West	Map 7
Eastern England	Map 8
The North West & Scotland	Map 9
The North East & Scotland	Map 10
Scotland	Map 11
Greater London	Map 12
Central London	Map 13

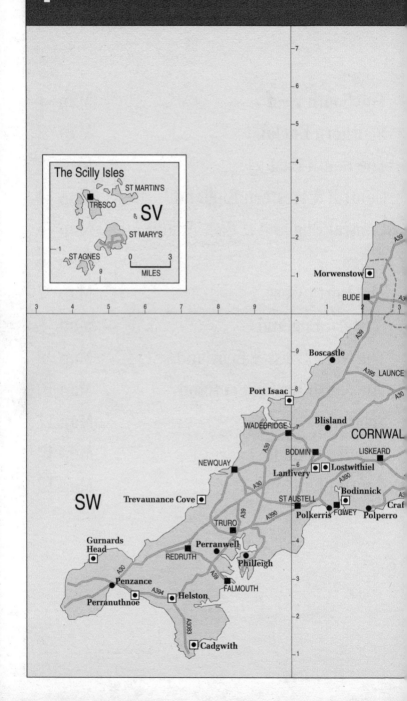

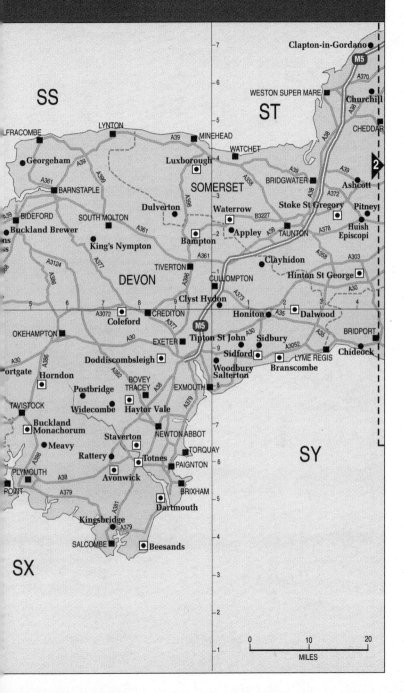

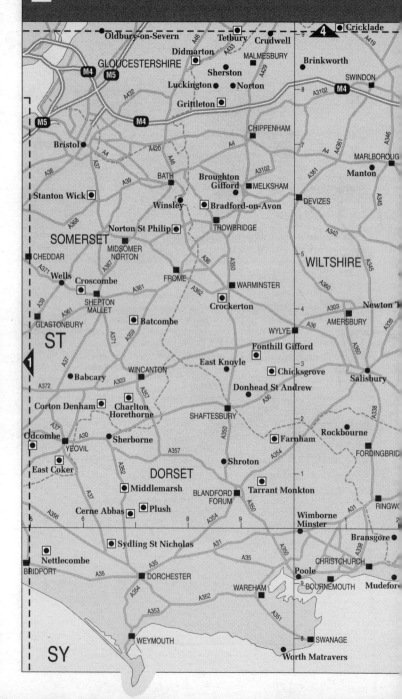

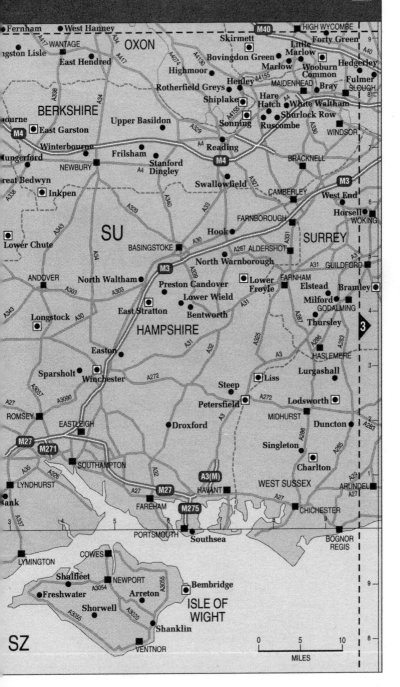

2

Fernham • West Hanney
M40
HIGH WYCOMBE
WANTAGE
OXON
Skirmett
Little
Forty Green
ngston Lisle
Bovingdon Green
Marlow
East Hendred
Highmoor
Marlow
Wooburn
Hedgerley
Rotherfield Greys
Henley
Common
Fulmer
Shiplake
MAIDENHEAD
Bray
SLOUGH
BERKSHIRE
Hare
White Waltham
ourne •East Garston
Upper Basildon
Hatch
Sherlock Row
M4
Sonning
Ruscombe
WINDSOR
Winterbourne
Reading
ungerford
Frilsham
M4
NEWBURY
Stanford
BRACKNELL
reat Bedwyn
Dingley
M3
Inkpen
Swallowfield
CAMBERLEY
West End
FARNBOROUGH
Horsell
Lower Chute
SU
Hook
WOKING
BASINGSTOKE
SURREY
ALDERSHOT
ANDOVER
North Warnborough
GUILDFORD
M3
FARNHAM
North Waltham
Lower
Elstead
Bramley
Preston Candover
Froyle
Milford
East Stratton
Lower Wield
GODALMING
Longstock
Bentworth
Thursley
A343
HAMPSHIRE
HASLEMERE
Easton
Lurgashall
Sparsholt
Winchester
Liss
Lodsworth
Steep
ROMSEY
Petersfield
MIDHURST
Duncton
EASTLEIGH
Droxford
M27
M271
Singleton
SOUTHAMPTON
Charlton
LYNDHURST
A3(M)
WEST SUSSEX
ank
HAVANT
ARUNDEL
FAREHAM
M275
CHICHESTER
PORTSMOUTH
BOGNOR
Southsea
REGIS
COWES
LYMINGTON
Shalfleet
NEWPORT
Bembridge
Freshwater
Arreton
ISLE OF
Shorwell
WIGHT
SZ
Shanklin
0   5   10
VENTNOR
MILES

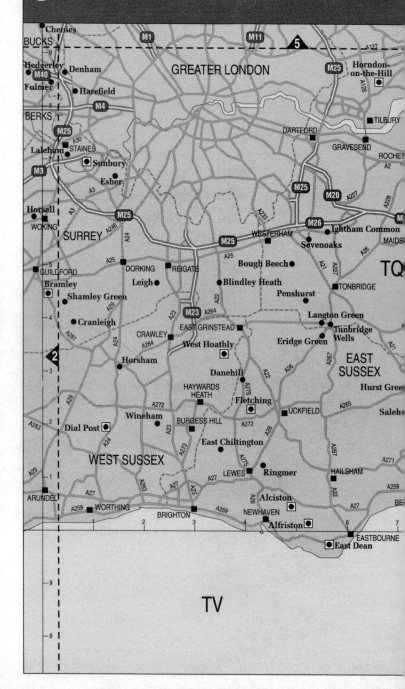

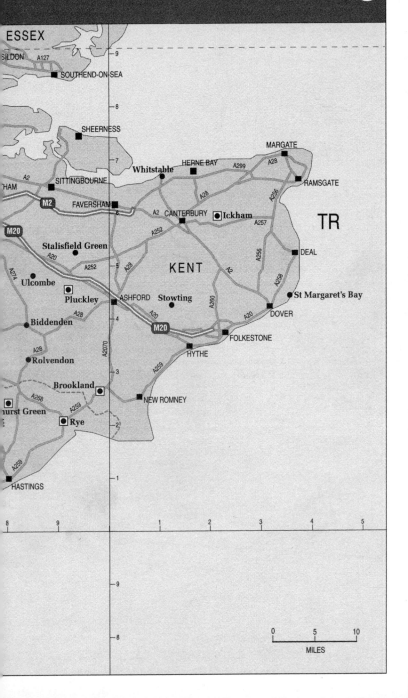

ESSEX

BASILDON A127

SOUTHEND-ON-SEA

SHEERNESS

MARGATE

HERNE BAY A299 A28

Whitstable SITTINGBOURNE RAMSGATE

HAM A2

M2 FAVERSHAM A2 CANTERBURY Ickham A256

A257 TR

M20

Stalisfield Green

A20 A252 DEAL

Ulcombe KENT A256

A274

Pluckley A28 A258 St Margaret's Bay

Biddenden ASHFORD Stowting

A28 A260 DOVER

A20

Rolvendon M20

A2070 FOLKESTONE

Brookland HYTHE

A268 A259

hurst Green A259 NEW ROMNEY

Rye

A259

HASTINGS

8 9 1 2 3 4 5

9

8 0 5 10

MILES

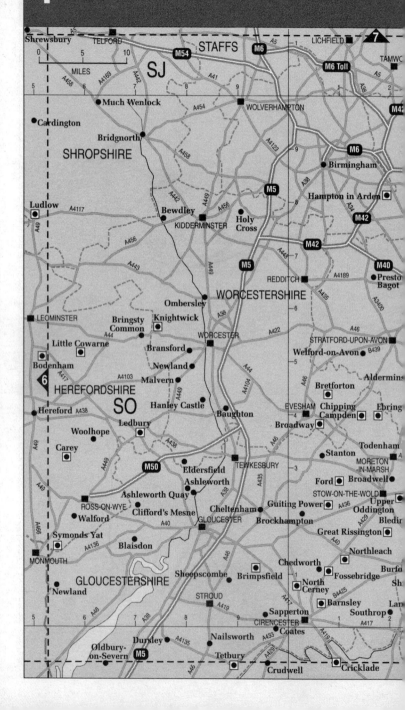

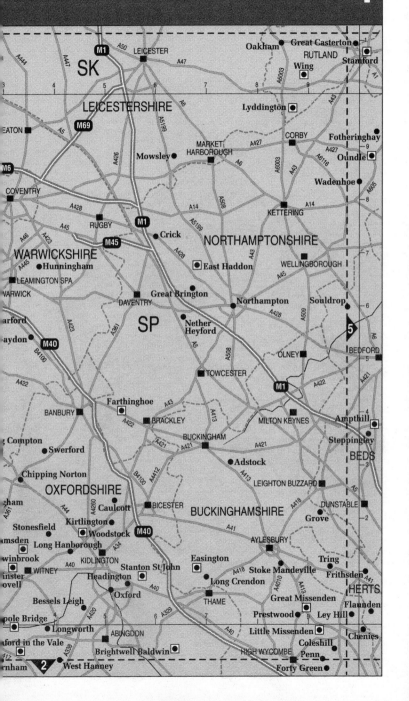

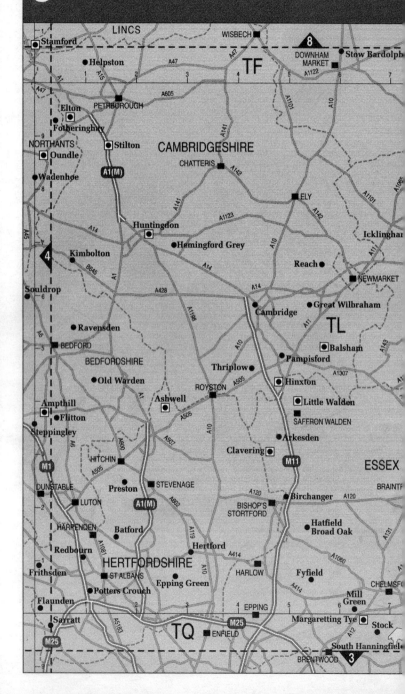

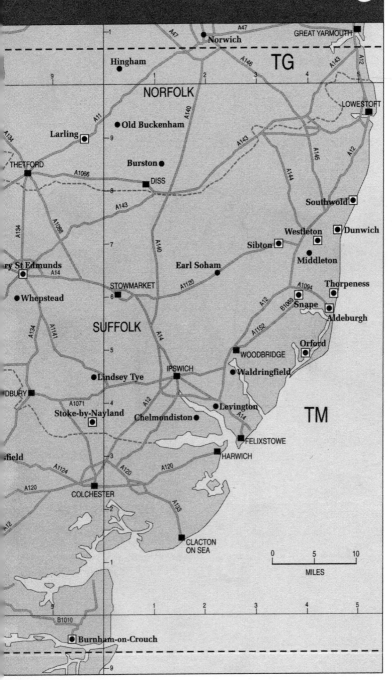

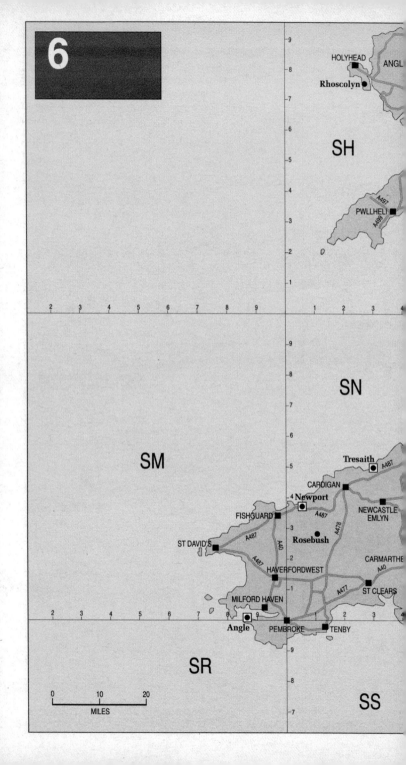

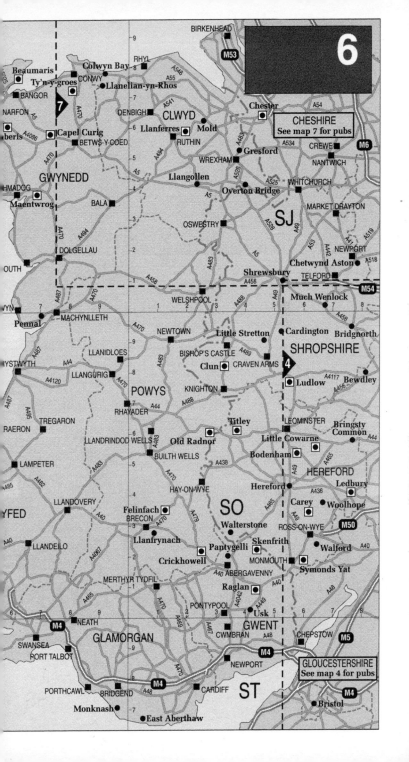

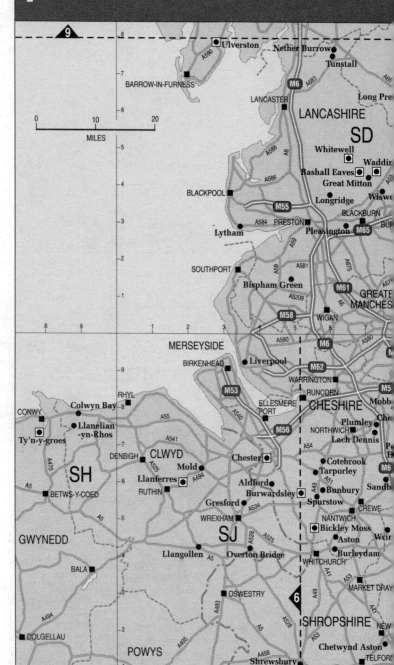

7

9

Ulverston   Nether Burrow

Tunstall

A590

BARROW-IN-FURNESS

M6   A683

LANCASTER

Long Pre

A65

LANCASHIRE

SD

0   10   20

MILES

Whitewell

Waddir

Bashall Eaves

A59

Great Mitton

A588

A6

A586

BLACKPOOL

Longridge   Wiswe

M55

BLACKBURN

A584   PRESTON

Pleasington   M65   BUI

Lytham

A59

SOUTHPORT

A581

A675

A671

Bispham Green

M61

A5209

GREATE

MANCHES

M58

WIGAN   5   6

A580   M6   A580

MERSEYSIDE

BIRKENHEAD   Liverpool

M62

RHYL

WARRINGTON   M5

M53

RUNCORN

CONWY   Colwyn Bay

ELLESMERE PORT

CHESHIRE   Mobb

Llanelian -yn-Rhos

M56

Plumley   Che

Ty'n-y-groes

A55

NORTHWICH

A541

Lach Dennis

SH

A540

A54

DENBIGH   CLWYD   Chester

Cotebrook   P H

A525

Mold

Tarporley

A470

Llanferres

A494

Aldford   Bunbury   M6

BETWS-Y-COED

RUTHIN

Burwardsley   Spurstow   Sandb

A5

Gresford

A49

A51

CREWE

GWYNEDD

A534

WREXHAM

NANTWICH

SJ

Bickley Moss   Wrir

A528   A525

Aston

BALA

Llangollen   A5   Overton Bridge

Burleydam

WHITCHURCH

A494

OSWESTRY

6

A41   A53

MARKET DRAY

A483

A49

A5

A525

SHROPSHIRE   NEW

A53   A7

A495

POWYS

A458

Chetwynd Aston

DOLGELLAU

Shrewsbury

TELFOR

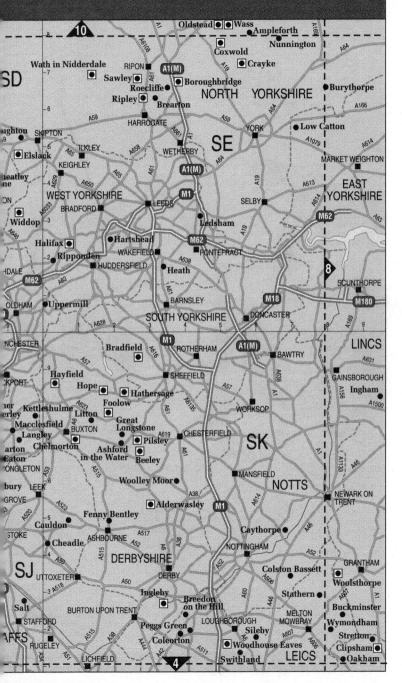

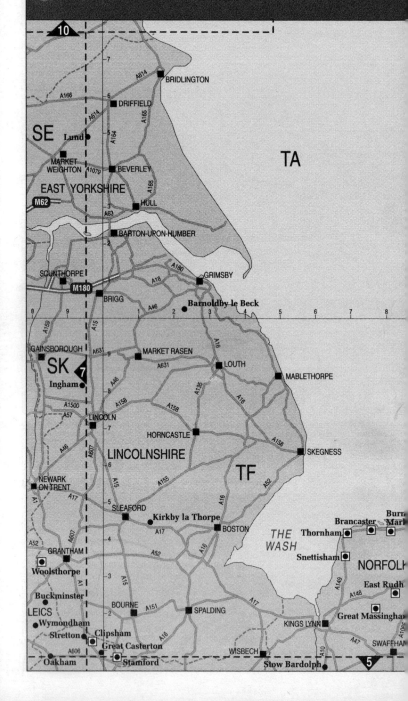

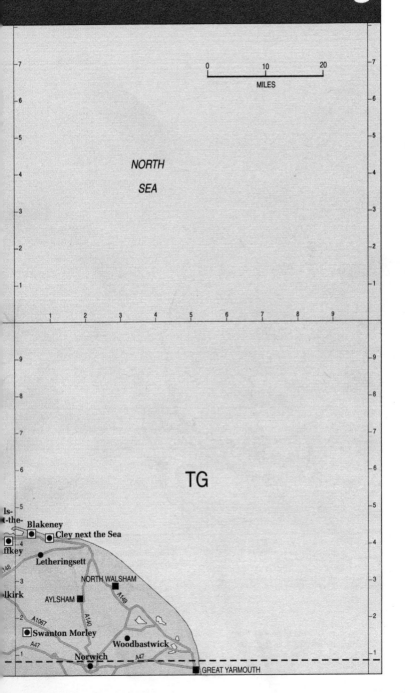

0   10   20
MILES

7

6

5

4   *NORTH*

3   *SEA*

2

1

1   2   3   4   5   6   7   8   9

9

8

7

6   TG

5

ls-
-the-
ffkey
Blakeney
Cley next the Sea

Letheringsett

lkirk
NORTH WALSHAM
AYLSHAM

Swanton Morley

Woodbastwick

Norwich

GREAT YARMOUTH

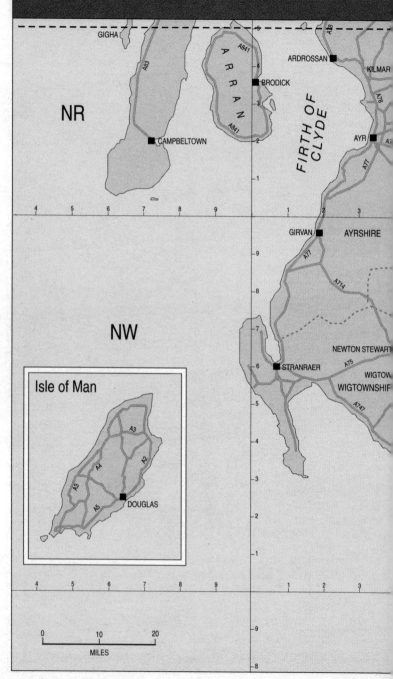

GIGHA

ARRAN

A841

BRODICK

A841

NR

CAMPBELTOWN

ARDROSSAN

KILMAR

A78

FIRTH OF CLYDE

AYR

A77

A63

GIRVAN

AYRSHIRE

A77

A714

NW

NEWTON STEWART

STRANRAER

A75

WIGTOW

WIGTOWNSHIF

A747

Isle of Man

A3

A4

A2

A3

A5

DOUGLAS

0   10   20

MILES

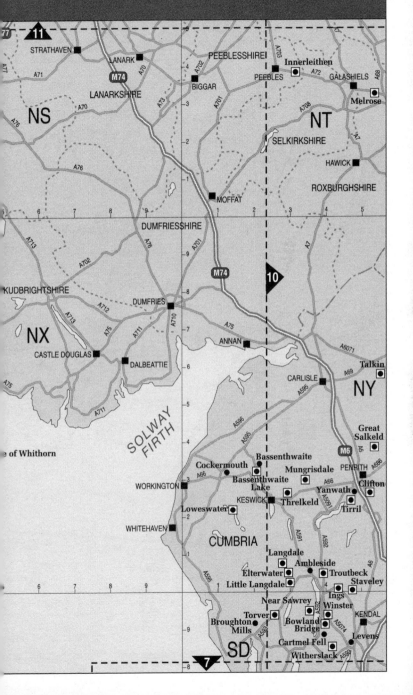

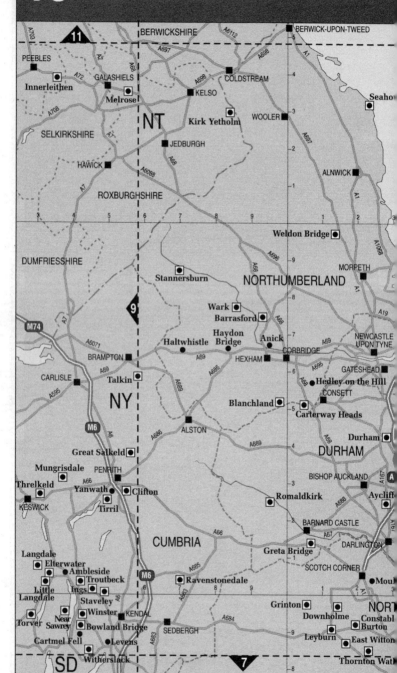

NU

NORTH

SEA

OUTH SHIELDS

SUNDERLAND

NZ

A19

■ HARTLEPOOL

■ MIDDLESBROUGH A174

A171

■ WHITBY

A172

A171

ORKSHIRE
SE

Blakey Ridge
◉

Cropton ◉

◉ Levisham

■ SCARBOROUGH

dhutton

■ THIRSK

A170

Pickering ◉

A170

A169

A165

dstead ◉ ◉ Wass

● Ampleforth

A169

8

0   10   20
MILES

5

4

3

2

1

4   5   6   7   8   9   1   2   3   4

9

8

7

6

5

4

3

2

1

4   5   6   7   8   9   A171   1   2   3   4

9

8

TA

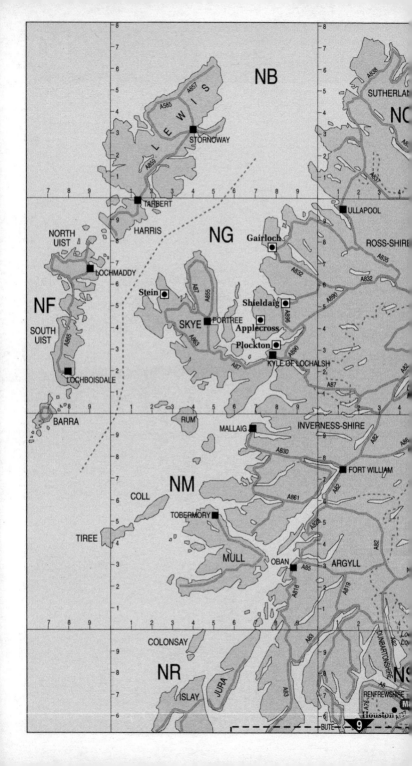

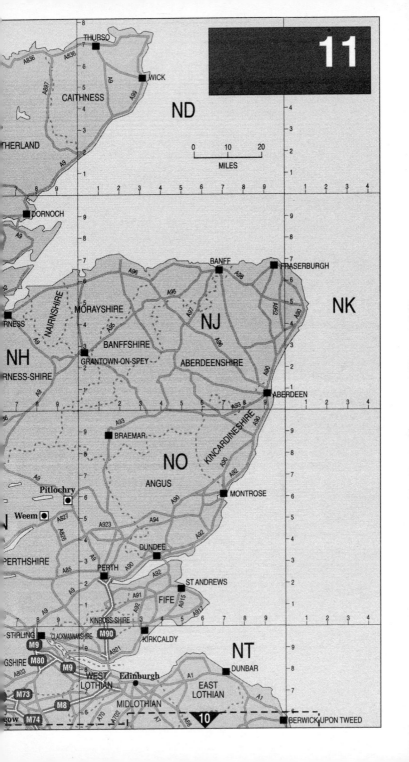

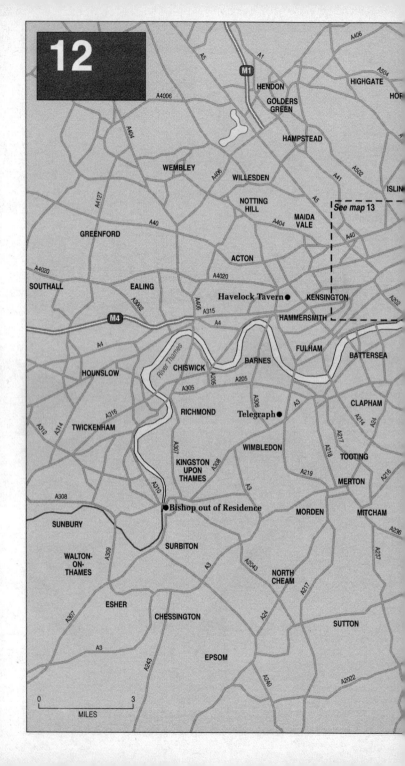

12

See map 13

A5
M1
A4006
HENDON
GOLDERS GREEN
HIGHGATE
A406
A504
HOF
A
HAMPSTEAD
A41
A502
ISLIN
A4
WEMBLEY
A406
WILLESDEN
A404
A5
GREENFORD
A40
NOTTING HILL
MAIDA VALE
A4020
A40
A4127
SOUTHALL
EALING
A4020
ACTON
A40
A4006
KENSINGTON
A202
Havelock Tavern ●
A315
HAMMERSMITH
M4
A3002
A4
A4
River Thames
CHISWICK
A315
FULHAM
BATTERSEA
A305
A205
BARNES
A205
HOUNSLOW
RICHMOND
A306
Telegraph ●
CLAPHAM
A214
A24
A316
TWICKENHAM
A312
A314
A307
A338
WIMBLEDON
A217
A218
TOOTING
A216
KINGSTON UPON THAMES
A3
A219
MERTON
A310
A308
● Bishop out of Residence
MORDEN
MITCHAM
A236
SUNBURY
A309
SURBITON
A3
A2043
NORTH CHEAM
A217
A237
WALTON-ON-THAMES
A307
ESHER
CHESSINGTON
A24
SUTTON
A3
A243
EPSOM
A240
A2022

0 ————— 3
MILES

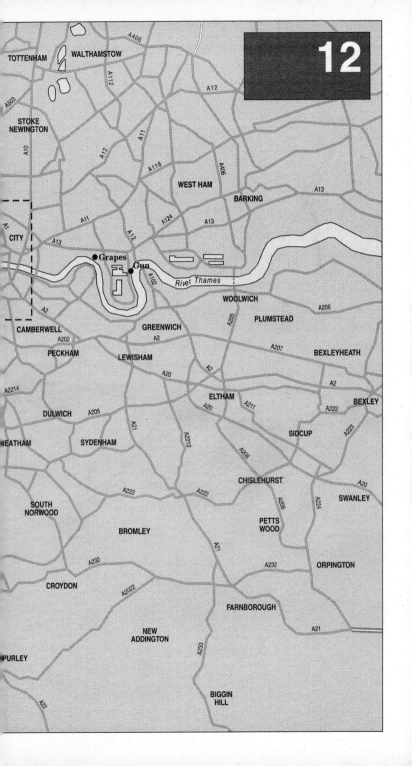

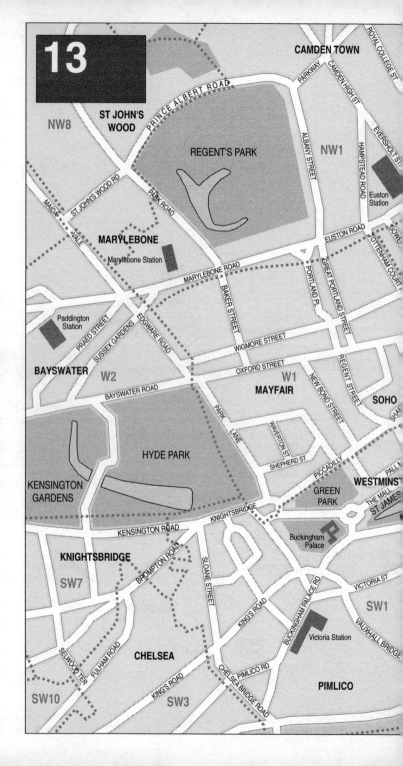

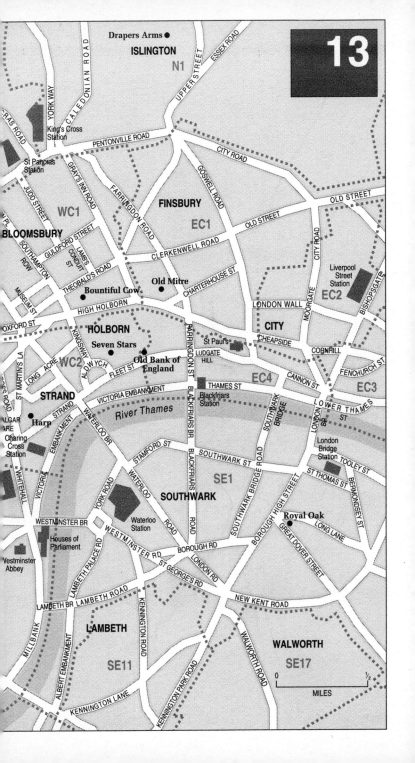

Report Forms

We need to know about pubs in this edition, pubs worthy of inclusion and ones that should not be included. Sometimes pubs are dropped simply because very few readers have written to us about them. You can use the cut-out forms on the following pages, email us at **feedback@goodguides.com** or write to us and we'll gladly send you more forms:

The Good Pub Guide
FREEPOST TN1569
WADHURST
East Sussex TN5 7BR

Though we try to answer all letters, please understand if there's a delay (particularly in summer, our busiest period). We'll assume we can print your name or initials as a recommender unless you tell us otherwise.

FULL ENTRY OR OTHER GOOD PUBS?

Please try to gauge whether a pub should be a top pub with a full entry or whether it should be in the Also Worth a Visit section (and tick the relevant box). Full entries need qualities that would make it worth other readers' while to travel some distance to them. If a pub is an entirely new recommendation, the Also Worth a Visit section may be the best place for it to start its career in the *Guide* – to encourage other readers to report on it.

The more detail you can put into your description of a pub, the better. Any information on how good the landlord or landlady is, what it looks like inside, what you like about the atmosphere and character, the quality and type of food, whether the real ale is well kept and which real ales are available, whether bedrooms are available, and how big/attractive the garden is. Other things that help (if possible) include prices for food and bedrooms, food service and opening hours, and if children or dogs are welcome.

If the food or accommodation are outstanding, tick the **FOOD AWARD** or the **STAY AWARD** box.

If you're in a position to gauge a pub's suitability or otherwise for **disabled people**, do please tell us about that.

If you can, give the full address or directions for any pub not yet in the *Guide* – best of all please give us its post code. If we can't find a pub's post code, we don't include it in the *Guide*.

I have been to the following pubs in *The Good Pub Guide 2012* in the last few months, found them as described, and confirm that they deserve continued inclusion:

Continued overleaf
PLEASE GIVE YOUR NAME AND ADDRESS ON THE BACK OF THIS FORM

Pubs visited continued...

Your own name and address *(block capitals please)*

Postcode

Please return to
The Good Pub Guide,
FREEPOST TN1569,
WADHURST,
East Sussex
TN5 7BR

IF YOU PREFER, YOU CAN SEND US REPORTS
BY EMAIL:
feedback@goodguides.com

I have been to the following pubs in *The Good Pub Guide 2012* in the last few months, found them as described, and confirm that they deserve continued inclusion:

Continued overleaf
PLEASE GIVE YOUR NAME AND ADDRESS ON THE BACK OF THIS FORM

Pubs visited continued...

Your own name and address *(block capitals please)*

Postcode

Please return to
The Good Pub Guide,
FREEPOST TN1569,
WADHURST,
East Sussex
TN5 7BR

IF YOU PREFER, YOU CAN SEND US REPORTS
BY EMAIL:
feedback@goodguides.com

REPORT ON   (PUB'S NAME)

Pub's address

☐ **YES** TOP PUB   ☐ **YES** WORTH A VISIT   ☐ **NO** DON'T INCLUDE
Please tick one of these boxes to show your verdict, and give reasons and descriptive
comments, prices etc

☐ DESERVES **FOOD award**   ☐ DESERVES **PLACE-TO-STAY award**   2012:1

PLEASE GIVE YOUR NAME AND ADDRESS ON THE BACK OF THIS FORM

REPORT ON   (PUB'S NAME)

Pub's address

☐ **YES** TOP PUB   ☐ **YES** WORTH A VISIT   ☐ **NO** DON'T INCLUDE
Please tick one of these boxes to show your verdict, and give reasons and descriptive
comments, prices etc

☐ DESERVES **FOOD award**   ☐ DESERVES **PLACE-TO-STAY award**   2012:2

PLEASE GIVE YOUR NAME AND ADDRESS ON THE BACK OF THIS FORM

Your own name and address *(block capitals please)*
In returning this form I confirm my agreement that the information I provide may be used by
The Random House Group Ltd, its assignees and/or licensees in any media or medium whatsoever.

DO NOT USE THIS SIDE OF THE PAGE FOR WRITING ABOUT PUBS

✂ ....

Your own name and address *(block capitals please)*
In returning this form I confirm my agreement that the information I provide may be used by
The Random House Group Ltd, its assignees and/or licensees in any media or medium whatsoever.

DO NOT USE THIS SIDE OF THE PAGE FOR WRITING ABOUT PUBS

IF YOU PREFER, YOU CAN SEND US REPORTS BY EMAIL:
feedback@goodguides.com

REPORT ON (PUB'S NAME)

Pub's address

☐ **YES** TOP PUB ☐ **YES** WORTH A VISIT ☐ **NO** DON'T INCLUDE

Please tick one of these boxes to show your verdict, and give reasons and descriptive comments, prices etc

☐ DESERVES **FOOD award** ☐ DESERVES **PLACE-TO-STAY award** 2012:3

PLEASE GIVE YOUR NAME AND ADDRESS ON THE BACK OF THIS FORM

✂ -

REPORT ON (PUB'S NAME)

Pub's address

☐ **YES** TOP PUB ☐ **YES** WORTH A VISIT ☐ **NO** DON'T INCLUDE

Please tick one of these boxes to show your verdict, and give reasons and descriptive comments, prices etc

☐ DESERVES **FOOD award** ☐ DESERVES **PLACE-TO-STAY award** 2012:4

PLEASE GIVE YOUR NAME AND ADDRESS ON THE BACK OF THIS FORM

Your own name and address *(block capitals please)*

In returning this form I confirm my agreement that the information I provide may be used by
The Random House Group Ltd, its assignees and/or licensees in any media or medium whatsoever.

DO NOT USE THIS SIDE OF THE PAGE FOR WRITING ABOUT PUBS

✂ ....

Your own name and address *(block capitals please)*

In returning this form I confirm my agreement that the information I provide may be used by
The Random House Group Ltd, its assignees and/or licensees in any media or medium whatsoever.

DO NOT USE THIS SIDE OF THE PAGE FOR WRITING ABOUT PUBS

IF YOU PREFER, YOU CAN SEND US REPORTS BY EMAIL:
feedback@goodguides.com

REPORT ON (PUB'S NAME)

Pub's address

☐ **YES** TOP PUB ☐ **YES** WORTH A VISIT ☐ **NO** DON'T INCLUDE
Please tick one of these boxes to show your verdict, and give reasons and descriptive
comments, prices etc

☐ DESERVES **FOOD** award ☐ DESERVES **PLACE-TO-STAY** award 2012:5

PLEASE GIVE YOUR NAME AND ADDRESS ON THE BACK OF THIS FORM

✂ --

REPORT ON (PUB'S NAME)

Pub's address

☐ **YES** TOP PUB ☐ **YES** WORTH A VISIT ☐ **NO** DON'T INCLUDE
Please tick one of these boxes to show your verdict, and give reasons and descriptive
comments, prices etc

☐ DESERVES **FOOD** award ☐ DESERVES **PLACE-TO-STAY** award 2012:6

PLEASE GIVE YOUR NAME AND ADDRESS ON THE BACK OF THIS FORM

Your own name and address *(block capitals please)*

In returning this form I confirm my agreement that the information I provide may be used by
The Random House Group Ltd, its assignees and/or licensees in any media or medium whatsoever.

DO NOT USE THIS SIDE OF THE PAGE FOR WRITING ABOUT PUBS

Your own name and address *(block capitals please)*

In returning this form I confirm my agreement that the information I provide may be used by
The Random House Group Ltd, its assignees and/or licensees in any media or medium whatsoever.

DO NOT USE THIS SIDE OF THE PAGE FOR WRITING ABOUT PUBS

IF YOU PREFER, YOU CAN SEND US REPORTS BY EMAIL:
feedback@goodguides.com

REPORT ON   (PUB'S NAME)

Pub's address

☐ **YES** TOP PUB   ☐ **YES** WORTH A VISIT   ☐ **NO** DON'T INCLUDE
Please tick one of these boxes to show your verdict, and give reasons and descriptive
comments, prices etc

☐ DESERVES **FOOD award**   ☐ DESERVES **PLACE-TO-STAY award**   2012:7

PLEASE GIVE YOUR NAME AND ADDRESS ON THE BACK OF THIS FORM

--✂

REPORT ON   (PUB'S NAME)

Pub's address

☐ **YES** TOP PUB   ☐ **YES** WORTH A VISIT   ☐ **NO** DON'T INCLUDE
Please tick one of these boxes to show your verdict, and give reasons and descriptive
comments, prices etc

☐ DESERVES **FOOD award**   ☐ DESERVES **PLACE-TO-STAY award**   2012:8

PLEASE GIVE YOUR NAME AND ADDRESS ON THE BACK OF THIS FORM

Your own name and address *(block capitals please)*
In returning this form I confirm my agreement that the information I provide may be used by
The Random House Group Ltd, its assignees and/or licensees in any media or medium whatsoever.

DO NOT USE THIS SIDE OF THE PAGE FOR WRITING ABOUT PUBS

✂ ....

Your own name and address *(block capitals please)*
In returning this form I confirm my agreement that the information I provide may be used by
The Random House Group Ltd, its assignees and/or licensees in any media or medium whatsoever.

DO NOT USE THIS SIDE OF THE PAGE FOR WRITING ABOUT PUBS

IF YOU PREFER, YOU CAN SEND US REPORTS BY EMAIL:
feedback@goodguides.com

REPORT ON (PUB'S NAME)

Pub's address

☐ **YES** TOP PUB ☐ **YES** WORTH A VISIT ☐ **NO** DON'T INCLUDE

Please tick one of these boxes to show your verdict, and give reasons and descriptive comments, prices etc

☐ DESERVES **FOOD award** ☐ DESERVES **PLACE-TO-STAY award** 2012:9

PLEASE GIVE YOUR NAME AND ADDRESS ON THE BACK OF THIS FORM

✂ ··

REPORT ON (PUB'S NAME)

Pub's address

☐ **YES** TOP PUB ☐ **YES** WORTH A VISIT ☐ **NO** DON'T INCLUDE

Please tick one of these boxes to show your verdict, and give reasons and descriptive comments, prices etc

☐ DESERVES **FOOD award** ☐ DESERVES **PLACE-TO-STAY award** 2012:10

PLEASE GIVE YOUR NAME AND ADDRESS ON THE BACK OF THIS FORM

Your own name and address *(block capitals please)*

In returning this form I confirm my agreement that the information I provide may be used by
The Random House Group Ltd, its assignees and/or licensees in any media or medium whatsoever.

DO NOT USE THIS SIDE OF THE PAGE FOR WRITING ABOUT PUBS

✂ ···

Your own name and address *(block capitals please)*

In returning this form I confirm my agreement that the information I provide may be used by
The Random House Group Ltd, its assignees and/or licensees in any media or medium whatsoever.

DO NOT USE THIS SIDE OF THE PAGE FOR WRITING ABOUT PUBS

IF YOU PREFER, YOU CAN SEND US REPORTS BY EMAIL:

feedback@goodguides.com

REPORT ON (PUB'S NAME)

....

Pub's address

☐ **YES** TOP PUB   ☐ **YES** WORTH A VISIT   ☐ **NO** DON'T INCLUDE

Please tick one of these boxes to show your verdict, and give reasons and descriptive comments, prices etc

☐ DESERVES **FOOD** award   ☐ DESERVES **PLACE-TO-STAY** award   2012:11

PLEASE GIVE YOUR NAME AND ADDRESS ON THE BACK OF THIS FORM

....✂

REPORT ON (PUB'S NAME)

....

Pub's address

☐ **YES** TOP PUB   ☐ **YES** WORTH A VISIT   ☐ **NO** DON'T INCLUDE

Please tick one of these boxes to show your verdict, and give reasons and descriptive comments, prices etc

☐ DESERVES **FOOD** award   ☐ DESERVES **PLACE-TO-STAY** award   2012:12

PLEASE GIVE YOUR NAME AND ADDRESS ON THE BACK OF THIS FORM

Your own name and address *(block capitals please)*

In returning this form I confirm my agreement that the information I provide may be used by
The Random House Group Ltd, its assignees and/or licensees in any media or medium whatsoever.

DO NOT USE THIS SIDE OF THE PAGE FOR WRITING ABOUT PUBS

Your own name and address *(block capitals please)*

In returning this form I confirm my agreement that the information I provide may be used by
The Random House Group Ltd, its assignees and/or licensees in any media or medium whatsoever.

DO NOT USE THIS SIDE OF THE PAGE FOR WRITING ABOUT PUBS

IF YOU PREFER, YOU CAN SEND US REPORTS BY EMAIL:
feedback@goodguides.com

REPORT ON (PUB'S NAME)

Pub's address

☐ **YES** TOP PUB ☐ **YES** WORTH A VISIT ☐ **NO** DON'T INCLUDE
Please tick one of these boxes to show your verdict, and give reasons and descriptive
comments, prices etc

☐ DESERVES **FOOD award** ☐ DESERVES **PLACE-TO-STAY award** 2012:13

PLEASE GIVE YOUR NAME AND ADDRESS ON THE BACK OF THIS FORM

REPORT ON (PUB'S NAME)

Pub's address

☐ **YES** TOP PUB ☐ **YES** WORTH A VISIT ☐ **NO** DON'T INCLUDE
Please tick one of these boxes to show your verdict, and give reasons and descriptive
comments, prices etc

☐ DESERVES **FOOD award** ☐ DESERVES **PLACE-TO-STAY award** 2012:14

PLEASE GIVE YOUR NAME AND ADDRESS ON THE BACK OF THIS FORM

Your own name and address *(block capitals please)*

In returning this form I confirm my agreement that the information I provide may be used by
The Random House Group Ltd, its assignees and/or licensees in any media or medium whatsoever.

DO NOT USE THIS SIDE OF THE PAGE FOR WRITING ABOUT PUBS

✂ ....

Your own name and address *(block capitals please)*

In returning this form I confirm my agreement that the information I provide may be used by
The Random House Group Ltd, its assignees and/or licensees in any media or medium whatsoever.

DO NOT USE THIS SIDE OF THE PAGE FOR WRITING ABOUT PUBS

IF YOU PREFER, YOU CAN SEND US REPORTS BY EMAIL:
feedback@goodguides.com

REPORT ON (PUB'S NAME)

Pub's address

☐ **YES** TOP PUB ☐ **YES** WORTH A VISIT ☐ **NO** DON'T INCLUDE
Please tick one of these boxes to show your verdict, and give reasons and descriptive comments, prices etc

☐ DESERVES **FOOD** award ☐ DESERVES **PLACE-TO-STAY** award 2012:15

PLEASE GIVE YOUR NAME AND ADDRESS ON THE BACK OF THIS FORM

✂ ....

REPORT ON (PUB'S NAME)

Pub's address

☐ **YES** TOP PUB ☐ **YES** WORTH A VISIT ☐ **NO** DON'T INCLUDE
Please tick one of these boxes to show your verdict, and give reasons and descriptive comments, prices etc

☐ DESERVES **FOOD** award ☐ DESERVES **PLACE-TO-STAY** award 2012:16

PLEASE GIVE YOUR NAME AND ADDRESS ON THE BACK OF THIS FORM

Your own name and address *(block capitals please)*

In returning this form I confirm my agreement that the information I provide may be used by
The Random House Group Ltd, its assignees and/or licensees in any media or medium whatsoever.

DO NOT USE THIS SIDE OF THE PAGE FOR WRITING ABOUT PUBS

By returning this form, you consent to the collection, recording and use of the information you submit, by The Random House Group
Ltd. Any personal details which you provide from which we can identify you are held and processed in accordance with the
Data Protection Act 1998 and will not be passed on to any third parties. The Random House Group Ltd may wish to send
you further information on their associated products. Please tick box if you do not wish to receive any such information.

✂ ....

Your own name and address *(block capitals please)*

In returning this form I confirm my agreement that the information I provide may be used by
The Random House Group Ltd, its assignees and/or licensees in any media or medium whatsoever.

DO NOT USE THIS SIDE OF THE PAGE FOR WRITING ABOUT PUBS

By returning this form, you consent to the collection, recording and use of the information you submit, by The Random House Group
Ltd. Any personal details which you provide from which we can identify you are held and processed in accordance with the
Data Protection Act 1998 and will not be passed on to any third parties. The Random House Group Ltd may wish to send
you further information on their associated products. Please tick box if you do not wish to receive any such information.

IF YOU PREFER, YOU CAN SEND US REPORTS BY EMAIL:
feedback@goodguides.com

INDEX OF ADVERTISERS

Adnams 8
Anglesea Arms 30
The Avon 17
Biddenden Vineyards 13
Black Sheep Brewery 12
The Blue Lion 27
cottages4you 22
The Cricketers 11
The Crown Inn 16
Exeter Red Coat Guided Tours 12
The Hoop 26
Individual Inns 6
Jennings 14
The King's Arms 18
The Live & Let Live 17
Mill Green Brewery 26
The Pheasant 31
The Phoenix Tavern 25
The Potting Shed 23
The Queen's Head 2
realale.com 9
The Red Cow 26
The Royal Borough of Windsor & Maidenhead 29, 300
The Saracen's Head 30
Theakston 1
Tourism South East 28, 254
Visit Derby 27
Visit Essex 10, 514
Visit Portsmouth 24, 285
Visit Worcestershire 32, 710
Within Warwickshire 20, 716